Fodors 97

Mexico

"When it comes to information on regional history, what to see and do, and shopping, these guides are exhaustive."

—*USAir Magazine*

"Usable, sophisticated restaurant coverage, with an emphasis on good value."

—Andy Birsh, *Gourmet Magazine* columnist

"Valuable because of their comprehensiveness."

—*Minneapolis Star-Tribune*

"Fodor's always delivers high quality...thoughtfully presented...thorough."

—*Houston Post*

"An excellent choice for those who want everything under one cover."

—*Washington Post*

Fodor's Travel Publications, Inc.
New York • Toronto • London • Sydney • Auckland
http://www.fodors.com/

P9-ECW-124

Fodor's Mexico

Editor: Edie Jarolim

Contributors: Patricia Alisau, Rob Andrews, Trudy Balch, Robert Blake, Judy Blumenberg, Audra Epstein, Richard Harris, Chris Humphrey, Wendy Luft, Gloria McDarrah, Bevin McLaughlin, Maribeth Mellin, Mary Ellen Schultz, M. T. Schwartzman, Susana Sedgwick, Pancho Shiell, Dinah Spritzer.

Creative Director: Fabrizio La Rocca

Cartographer: David Lindroth

Cover Photograph: Peter Guttman

Text Design: Between the Covers

Copyright

Copyright © 1996 by Fodor's Travel Publications, Inc.

Fodor's is a registered trademark of Fodor's Travel Publications, Inc.

All rights reserved under International and Pan-American Copyright Conventions. Published in the United States by Fodor's Travel Publications, Inc., a subsidiary of Random House, Inc., New York, and simultaneously in Canada by Random House of Canada Limited, Toronto. Distributed by Random House, Inc., New York.

No maps, illustrations, or other portions of this book may be reproduced in any form without written permission from the publishers.

ISBN 0–679–03249–5

Special Sales

Fodor's Travel Publications are available at special discounts for bulk purchases for sales promotions or premiums. Special editions, including personalized covers, excerpts of existing guides, and corporate imprints, can be created in large quantities for special needs. For more information, contact your local bookseller or write to Special Markets, Fodor's Travel Publications, 201 East 50th Street, New York, NY 10022. Inquiries from Canada should be directed to your local Canadian bookseller or sent to Random House of Canada Ltd., Marketing Dept., 1265 Aerowood Drive, Mississauga, Ontario L4W 1B9. Inquiries from the United Kingdom should be sent to Fodor's Travel Publications, 20 Vauxhall Bridge Road, London, England SW1 2SA.

PRINTED IN THE UNITED STATES OF AMERICA

10 9 8 7 6 5 4 3 2 1

CONTENTS

Maps

ON THE ROAD WITH FODOR'S

WE'RE ALWAYS THRILLED to get letters from readers, especially one like this:

It took us an hour to decide what book to buy and we now know we picked the best one. Your book was wonderful, easy to follow, very accurate, and good on pointing out eating places, informal as well as formal. When we saw other people using your book, we would look at each other and smile.

Our editors and writers are deeply committed to making every Fodor's guide "the best one"— not only accurate but always charming, brimming with sound recommendations and solid ideas, right on the mark in describing restaurants and hotels, and full of fascinating facts that make you view what you've traveled to see in a rich new light.

About Our Writers

Our success in achieving our goals—and in helping to make your trip the best of all possible vacations—is a credit to the hard work of our extraordinary writers and editors.

A psychologist-turned-journalist and archaeology buff, **Patricia Alisau** updated the Oaxaca, Chiapas and Tabasco, Veracruz and Northeastern Mexico, and Mexico City chapters of this book. She was so drawn to the surrealism of Mexico City— "Where in the U.S. can you find pyramids?" she asks—that she moved to the capital some 20 years ago. She spends much of her time in the colorful markets, where fresh fruit is piled high next to stacks of dried batwings, an ancient cure for a faithless lover. She was restaurant and night-club columnist for the *News*, Mexico's English-language daily, worked as a photo stringer for AP during the Nicaragua Revolution, and has written for Mexico's *Vogue* magazine.

Guadalajara updater **Trudy Balch** has been a Tapatía (as residents of the city are called) *in absentia* since the early 1990s, when a stint as a newspaper reporter there sent her scouring for local stories. Now based in New York City, she writes about travel and business in Mexico and other Latin American countries and spends her spare time searching for good birria and mariachi music.

Richard Harris, who updated the Campeche and Mérida and the State of Yucatán section of the Yucatán Peninsula chapter, left a law practice in 1981 to study Pre-Columbian Indian ruins. He is the author of two books on the archaeology and ecology of the Yucatán Peninsula. As president of PEN New Mexico, the only English-Spanish bilingual chapter of the writers'-rights group PEN International, he spends much of his time in Mexico as an advocate for imprisoned or threatened Latin American writers.

Chris Humphrey combed the Heartland for us this year while taking part in Generation Dos Equis (XX), as *Newsweek* dubbed the growing group of twentysomethings seeking fame and fortune (well, mostly fortune) south of the border. He's back in the states after working as an editor/correspondent for the Mexico City *News,* a highly-regarded source of English-language information for much of the country, and subsequently for its new competitor, *The Times.*

When she was fresh out of college, our Acapulco and Pacific Coast Resorts correspondent **Wendy Luft** jumped at the chance to take a job with the Mexican tourist office—for a year or two at most, she figured. Some 25 years later, she and her Mexican husband and their adolescent sons, inveterate travelers all, traverse the country together from their home base in Mexico City. As a writer, editor, and public relations representative, Wendy has written and collaborated on many travel books and articles about her adopted country.

Gloria McDarrah, this year's Cancún, Isla Mujeres, and Cozumel correspondent, reports that her interest in the Yucatán dates back to a fourth-grade geography class, when she completed a (rather tipsy) model of a Maya pyramid. She has been to Mexico many times since to check out the originals. She is the author of a number of travel guides and has worked as a senior guidebook editor.

Maribeth Mellin, our long-time Baja California and Yucatán updater, covers Mexico for *San Diego Magazine.* She writes in an office filled with photos and artifacts from Mexico's two isolated peninsulas, including a snapshot of the 140-pound marlin she caught in the Sea of Cortés. She refused to marry her husband (who'd been traveling to Baja for over 20 years) until he rambled through her beloved Yucatán with her in a rented VW bug. She finally said "yes" enroute to Chichén Itzá while humming the Mexican ballad "Amor," which became their wedding song.

It was the quixotic silver jewelry that her aunt brought back from Mazatlán that hooked **Kate Rice,** who wrote the introduction to this book, on Mexico. During a summer spent in the country in a vain attempt to improve her Spanish, she fell hard for its art and cuisine—especially the mangoes dipped in hot sauce sold on the street corners of Guadalajara. It's been a family affair all along: Her brothers lead mule rides into remote reaches of Baja California's Sierra San Francisco and traced the paths of the Maya along the rivers of Chiapas. For the past few years, Kate has been covering Mexico for publications including *Tour & Travel News* and *Business Traveler International.*

Susana Sedgwick, who updated the Sonora and Copper Canyon chapters, grew up with the sounds of Sonora echoing just across the wash and over the fence of where she lived with her family in Nogales, Arizona. It wasn't long before the land of fiesta and siesta drew her ever deeper into Mexico's regional history, mysteries, and cultural traditions, which she continues to explore. She's an elected member of the Explorer's Club in New York and a fellow of the Royal Geographical Society in London.

Editor **Edie Jarolim** first got a taste for Mexico in the late 1970s, when she attempted (unsuccessfully) to visit every Maya ruin in the Yucatán on a two week vacation. Her frequent return forays—she wrote the Copper Canyon chapter of this book and often covers the resorts for *Bride's* magazine—have been made easier by a recent move to neighboring Arizona. She knows the Spanish conquistadors were a cruel bunch, but can't help but admire the good sense of a group who set out to vanquish Veracruz and Acapulco instead of, say, Saskatchewan.

New This Year

This year we've reformatted our guides to make them easier to use. Each chapter of *Mexico '97* begins with brand-new recommended itineraries to help you decide what to see in the time you have; a section called When to Tour points out the optimal time of day, day of the week, and season for your journey. You may also notice our fresh graphics, new in 1996. More readable and more helpful than ever? We think so—and we hope you do, too.

We've rearranged the chapters a bit this year to make it easier for you to find the places you want to explore (*see* How to Use This Book, *below*). We also beefed up the shopping sections throughout, the better to help you indulge in one of Mexico's great pastimes. And we've greatly expanded our coverage of the state of Veracruz, home to great seafood, outdoor cafés, and little-visited archaeological sites—in short, one of the country's hidden tourist treasures.

Also check out Fodor's Web site (http://www.fodors.com/), where you'll find travel information on major destinations around the world and an ever-changing array of travel-savvy interactive features.

How to Use This Book

Organization

Up front is the **Gold Guide.** Its first section, **Important Contacts A to Z,** gives addresses and telephone numbers of organizations and companies that offer destination-related services and detailed information and publications. **Smart Travel Tips A to Z,** the Gold Guide's second section, gives specific information on how to accomplish what you need to in Mexico as well as tips on savvy traveling. Both sections are in alphabetical order by topic.

Chapter 1 introduces you to the entire country of Mexico, giving you a capsule overview of the chapters and of the country's favorite pleasures and pastimes. The remaining chapters of the book are arranged geographically: We take you first to Mexico City, the capital and main transportation hub, and then move from the northwest (Baja California) to the southeast (the Yucatán Peninsula), heading roughly north to south along the two coasts.

Each city chapter begins with an Exploring section, which is subdivided by neighborhood; each subsection recommends a walking or driving tour and lists sights in alphabetical order. Each regional chapter is divided by geographical area; within each area, towns are covered in logical geographical order, and attractive stretches of road and minor points of interest between them are indicated by the designation *En Route*. Throughout, Off the Beaten Path sights appear after the places from which they are most easily accessible. And within town sections, all restaurants and lodgings are grouped together.

To help you decide what to visit in the time you have, all chapters begin with recommended itineraries; you can mix and match those from several chapters to create a complete vacation. The A to Z section that ends all chapters covers getting there, getting around, and helpful contacts and resources.

Icons and Symbols

★ Our special recommendations
✕ Restaurant
🏠 Lodging establishment
✕🏠 Lodging establishment whose restaurant warrants a detour
🕭 Rubber duckie (good for kids)
☞ Sends you to another section of the guide for more info
✉ Address
☎ Telephone number
FAX Fax number
☉ Opening and closing times
💴 Admission prices (those we give apply only to adults; substantially reduced fees are almost always available for children, students, and senior citizens)

Numbers in white and black circles—② and ❷, for example—that appear on the maps, in the margins, and within the tours correspond to one another.

Dining and Lodging

The restaurants and lodgings we list are the cream of the crop in each price range. Price charts appear in the Pleasures and Pastimes section that follows each chapter introduction.

Hotel Facilities

We always list the facilities that are available—but we don't specify whether they cost extra: When pricing accommodations, always ask what's included.

Assume that hotels operate on the **European Plan** (EP, with no meals) unless we note that they use the **Full American Plan** (FAP, with all meals), the **Modified American Plan** (MAP, with breakfast and dinner daily), the **Continental Plan** (CP, with a Continental breakfast daily), or are **all-inclusive** (all meals and most activities).

Restaurant Reservations and Dress Codes

In the big cities and the more touristed areas of Mexico, reservations are always a good idea. In the remote regions, unless otherwise indicated, a reservation would surprise most proprietors, though it is likely to be politely accepted. Throughout the book, we indicate only when reservations are essential or when they are not accepted. Unless otherwise noted, the restaurants listed are open daily for lunch and dinner. We mention dress only when men are required to wear a jacket or a jacket and tie. Look for an overview of local habits under Dining in Smart Travel Tips A to Z and in the Pleasures and Pastimes section that follows each chapter introduction.

Credit Cards

The following abbreviations are used: **AE,** American Express; **DC,** Diners Club; **MC,** MasterCard; and **V,** Visa.

Don't Forget to Write

You can use this book in the confidence that all prices and opening times are based on information supplied to us at press time; Fodor's cannot accept responsibility for any errors. Time inevitably brings changes, so always confirm information when it matters—especially if you're making a detour to visit a specific place. In addition, when making reservations be sure to mention if you have a disability or are traveling with children, if you prefer a private bath or a certain type of bed, or if you have specific dietary needs or any other concerns.

Were the restaurants we recommended as described? Did our hotel picks exceed your expectations? Did you find a museum we recommended a waste of time? If you have complaints, we'll look into them and revise our entries when the facts warrant it. If you've discovered a special place that we haven't included, we'll pass the information along to our correspondents and have them check it out. So send your feedback, positive *and* negative, to the Mexico Editor at 201 East 50th Street, New York, New York 10022—and have a wonderful trip!

Karen Cure

Karen Cure
Editorial Director

Mexico

Tijuana
Ensenada
Mexicali
CA.
ARIZONA
Tucson
NEW MEXICO
Nogales
Ciudad Juárez
BAJA
Golfo
Nuevo Casas Grandes
de
Hermosillo
Chihuahua
Guaymas
CALIFORNIA
Ciudad Obregón
California
SIERRA
Los Mochis
Gómez Palacio
Torreón
La Paz
Culiacán
MADRE
San José del Cabo
Durango
Cabo San Lucas
Mazatlán
Fresnillo
OCCIDENTAL
Túxpan
Zacatecas
Tepic
San Luis Potosí
Puerto Vallarta
León
Guadalajara
Guanajuato
Colima
Morelia
Me
Manzanillo
Pátzcuaro
SIERRA
Tol
M
Ixtapa/
Zihuatanejo
Acapulco

PACIFIC OCEAN

N

0   200 miles
0   300 km

CALIFORNIA

Mexicali ★

ARIZONA

NEW MEXICO

BAJA
CALIFORNIA

Golfo

de

Hermosillo ★

SONORA

CHIHUAHUA

Chihuahua ★

Ri...

COAHUILA

BAJA
CALIFORNIA
SUR

California

SINALOA

La Paz ★

Culiacán ★

DURANGO

Se...
★

Durango ★

ZACATECAS

Zacatecas
★

Tepic
★
NAYARIT

AGUASCALIENTES
★
Aguascalientes

Sa...
Pot...
★

Guanajuato
★
GUANAJUATO

Guadalajara ★

JALISCO

Colima ★
COLIMA

Morelia ★

MICHOACAN

ME...
Tol...

MC...

GUERRERO

PACIFIC OCEAN

N

0   200 miles

0   300 km

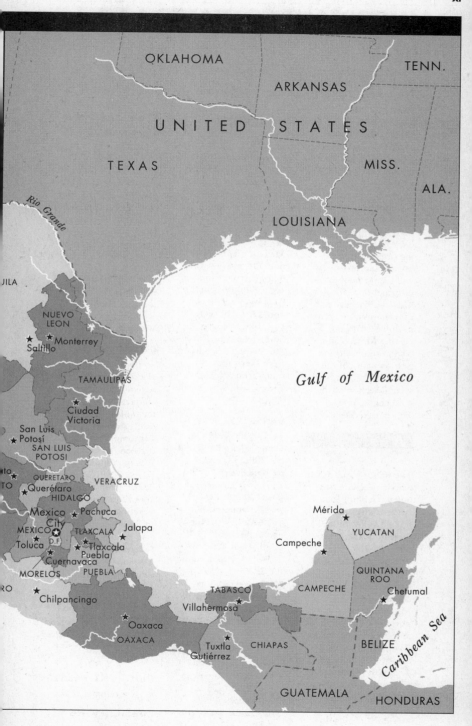

THE GOLD GUIDE / IMPORTANT CONTACTS

IMPORTANT CONTACTS A TO Z

An Alphabetical Listing of Publications, Organizations, & Companies That Will Help You Before, During, & After Your Trip

No single travel resource can give you every detail about every topic that might interest or concern you at the various stages of your journey—when you're planning your trip, while you're on the road, and after you get back home. The following organizations, books, and brochures will supplement the information in Fodor's *Mexico '97*. For related information, including both basic tips on visiting Mexico and background information on many of the topics below, study the second section of the gold pages, Smart Travel Tips A to Z.

A
AIR TRAVEL

The major gateways to Mexico include **Acapulco** (General Juan Alvarez airport, ☎ 011–52–748/40887), **Cancún** (Cancún airport, ☎ 011–52–981/42239), **Cozumel** (Cozumel airport, ☎ 011–52–987/20485), **Guadalajara** (Don Miguel Hidalgo airport, ☎ 011–52–36/89–00–24), **Ixtapa** (Ixtapa/Zihuatanejo airport, ☎ 011–52–473/42070), **Mazatlán** (General Rafael Buena airport, ☎ 011–52–678/24–87–42), **Mérida** (Licenciado Manuel Crescencio Rejon airport, ☎ 011–52–99/24–87–42),

Mexico City (Benito Juàrez airport, ☎ 011–52–5/571–3600), **Puerto Vallarta** (☎ 011–52–322/21298), and **San José** (Los Cabos airport, ☎ 011–52–684/30341) in Los Cabos.

FLYING TIME

Mexico City is 4½ hours from New York, 4 hours from Chicago, and 3½ hours from Los Angeles. Cancún is 3½ hours from New York and from Chicago, 4½ hours from Los Angeles. Acapulco is 6 hours from New York, 4 hours from Chicago, and 3½ hours from Los Angeles.

CARRIERS

To MEXICO CITY➤ Contact **Aero California** (☎ 800/237–6225), **Aeromexico** (☎ 800/237–6639), **America West** (☎ 800/235–9292), **American** (☎ 800/433–7300), **Continental** (☎ 800/525–0280), **Delta** (☎ 800/241–4141), **Mexicana** (☎ 800/531–7921), **Northwest** (☎ 800/447–4747), **United** (☎ 800/538–2929), and **USAir** (☎ 800/428–4322).

To CANCÚN➤ Contact **Aeromexico** (☎ 800/237–6639), **American** (☎ 800/433–7300), **Continental** (☎ 800/525–0280), **Mexicana** (☎ 800/531–7921), **Northwest** (☎ 800/447–4747), and **United** (☎ 800/538–2929).

FROM THE U.K.

British Airways has a direct flight from the United Kingdom to Mexico City. Other airlines flying to Mexico, with brief stops en route, include **Air France** (via Paris), **American** (via Dallas or Miami), **Continental** (via Houston), **Delta** (via Atlanta), **Iberia** (via Madrid), **KLM** (via Amsterdam), **Lufthansa** (via Frankfurt), and **United** (via Chicago or Washington–Dulles).

COMPLAINTS

To register complaints about charter and scheduled airlines, contact the U.S. Department of Transportation's **Aviation Consumer Protection Division** (⊠ C-75, Washington, DC 20590, ☎ 202/366–2220). Complaints about lost baggage or ticketing problems and safety concerns may also be logged with the **Federal Aviation Administration (FAA) Consumer Hotline** (☎ 800/322–7873).

CONSOLIDATORS

For services that will help you find the lowest airfares, *see* Discounts, *below*.

DISCOUNT PASSES

☞ Discounts, *below*.

PUBLICATIONS

For general information about charter carriers, ask for the Department of Transportation's free brochure **"Plane Talk: Public Charter Flights"** (✉ Aviation Consumer Protection Division, C-75, Washington, DC 20590, ☎ 202/366–2220). The Department of Transportation also publishes a 58-page booklet, **"Fly Rights,"** available from the Consumer Information Center (✉ Supt. of Documents, Dept. 133B, Pueblo, CO 81009; $1.75).

For other tips and hints, consult the Consumers Union's monthly **"Consumer Reports Travel Letter"** (✉ Box 53629, Boulder, CO 80322, ☎ 800/234–1970; $39 1st year) and the newsletter **"Travel Smart"** (✉ 40 Beechdale Rd., Dobbs Ferry, NY 10522, ☎ 800/327–3633; $37 per year).

Some worthwhile publications on the subject are **The Official Frequent Flyer Guidebook,** by Randy Petersen (✉ Airpress, 4715-C Town Center Dr., Colorado Springs, CO 80916, ☎ 719/597–8899 or 800/487–8893; $14.99 plus $3 shipping); **Airfare Secrets Exposed,** by Sharon Tyler and Matthew Wunder (✉ Studio 4 Productions, Box 280400, Northridge, CA 91328, ☎ 818/700–2522 or 800/408–7369; $16.95 plus $2.50 shipping); **202 Tips Even the Best Business Travelers May Not Know,** by Christopher McGinnis (✉ Irwin Professional Publishing, 1333 Burr Ridge Pkwy., Burr Ridge, IL 60521, ☎ 800/634–3966; $11 plus $3.25 shipping); and **Travel Rights,**

by Charles Leocha (✉ World Leisure Corporation, 177 Paris St., Boston, MA 02128, ☎ 800/444–2524; $7.95 plus $3.95 shipping).

For information on how to avoid jet lag, there are two publications: **Jet Lag, A Pocket Guide to Modern Treatment** (✉ MedEd Publishers, 1421 W. 3rd Ave., Columbus, OH 43212, ☎ 800/875–8489; $5.95) and **How to Beat Jet Lag** (✉ Henry Holt, 115 W. 18th St., New York, NY 10011, ☎ 800/288–2131; $14.95).

Travelers who experience motion sickness or ear problems in flight should get the brochures **"Ears, Altitude, and Airplane Travel"** and **"What You Can Do for Dizziness & Motion Sickness"** from the American Academy of Otolaryngology (✉ 1 Prince St., Alexandria, VA 22314, ☎ 703/836–4444, FAX 703/683–5100, TTY 703/519–1585).

WITHIN MEXICO

Mexicana and Aeromexico provide the bulk of air service within Mexico, and regional airlines have filled in most of the gaps. **Aerocaribe** (reserve through Mexicana) serves the Yucatán and the Southeast; **Aeromar** (reserve through Mexicana or Aeromexico) serves central Mexico; **Aerolitoral** (reserve through Aeromexico or Mexicana) serves northeastern Mexico, and **Aeroponiente** (reserve through Aeromexico) serves southwestern Mexico. **Aviacsa** (☎ 961/2–80–81 in Chia-

pas; ☎ 5/559–1955 in Mexico City) flies between Mexico City and Tuxtla Guttiérez; and **AeroCalifornia** (☎ 800/237–6225) serves Colima, Guadalajara, Loreto, Los Mochis, Puebla, Tepic, Tijuana, and several other gateways.

B
BETTER BUSINESS BUREAU

For local contacts in the hometown of a tour operator you may be considering, consult the **Council of Better Business Bureaus** (✉ 4200 Wilson Blvd., Suite 800, Arlington, VA 22203, ☎ 703/276–0100, FAX 703/525–8277).

BUS TRAVEL

Gateway cities such as El Paso, Del Rio, Laredo, McAllen, Brownsville, and San Antonio, Texas, and Tijuana are served by several small private bus lines as well as by **Greyhound Lines** (☎ 800/231–2222). If you'll be leaving Mexico by bus, you can buy tickets for the U.S. leg of your trip from the Greyhound representative in Mexico City (✉ Paseo de la Reforma 27, ☎ 5/535–42–00 or 5/535–26–81).

WITHIN MEXICO

In Mexico City, the best first-class bus lines include **ADO** (☎ 5/542–7192 or 5/542–7193), serving Yucatán, Cancún, Villahermosa, and Veracruz from the Eastern Bus Terminal (known by its Spanish acronym, TAPO), and Matamoros, Oaxaca, Guadalajara, San Luis

Potosí, and Tampico from the Northern Bus Terminal (*Terminal Central Autobuses del Norte*) (☎ 5/587–6688); **Cristóbal Colón** (☎ 5/576–9926), which goes to Chiapas, Oaxaca, and the Guatemala border from the Eastern Bus Terminal; **ETN** (☎ 5/273–0251), which goes to Acapulco, Mazatlán, and Morelia from the Western Bus Terminal (*Terminal Central Poniente*); and **Transportes del Norte** (☎ 5/587–5377), which goes up to the U.S. border from the Northern Bus Terminal.

C

CAR INSURANCE

Experienced and reliable sources for Mexican car insurance are **Sanborn's Mexican Insurance** (✉ 2009 South 10th St., McAllen TX 78505, ☎ 210/686–0711) and **Instant Mexico Auto Insurance** (✉ 223 Via de San Ysidro, San Ysidro, CA 92173, ☎ 619/428–3583).

CAR RENTAL

The major car-rental companies represented in Mexico are **Avis** (☎ 800/331–1084; in Canada, 800/879–2847), **Budget** (☎ 800/527–0700; in the U.K., 0800/181181), **Hertz** (☎ 800/654–3001; in Canada, 800/263–0600; in the U.K., 0345/555888), and **National InterRent** (sometimes known as Europcar InterRent outside North America; ☎ 800/227–3876; in the U.K., 01345/222–525). In Mexico, rental prices vary by location, type of car, and travel season. Rates in Mexico City begin at $29 a day or $165 a week for an economy car with unlimited mileage. This does not include tax, which in Mexico is 15%.

RENTAL WHOLESALERS

Contact **Auto Europe** (☎ 207/828–2525 or 800/223–5555).

CHILDREN & TRAVEL

FLYING

Look into **"Flying with Baby"** (✉ Third Street Press, Box 261250, Littleton, CO 80163, ☎ 303/595–5959; $4.95 includes shipping), cowritten by a flight attendant. **"Kids and Teens in Flight,"** free from the U.S. Department of Transportation's Aviation Consumer Protection Division (✉ C-75, Washington, DC 20590, ☎ 202/366–2220), offers tips on children flying alone. Every two years the February issue of *Family Travel Times* (☞ Know-How, *below*) details children's services on three dozen airlines. **"Flying Alone, Handy Advice for Kids Traveling Solo"** is available free from the American Automobile Association (AAA) (✉ Flying Alone, Mail Stop 800, 1000 AAA Dr., Heathrow, FL 32746; send stamped, self-addressed, legal-size envelope).

GAMES

Milton Bradley has games to help keep little (and not so little) children from fidgeting while in planes, trains, and automobiles. Try packing the Travel Battleship sea-battle game ($7); Travel Connect Four, a vertical strategy game ($8); the Travel Yahtzee dice game ($6), the Travel Trouble dice and board game ($7), and the Travel Guess Who mystery game ($8). Parker Brothers has travel versions of Clue!, Sorry, and Monopoly.

KNOW-HOW

Family Travel Times, published quarterly by Travel with Your Children (✉ TWYCH, 40 5th Ave., New York, NY 10011, ☎ 212/477–5524; $40 per year), covers destinations, types of vacations, and modes of travel.

The *Family Travel Guides* catalog (✉ Carousel Press, Box 6061, Albany, CA 94706, ☎ 510/527–5849; $1 postage) lists about 200 books and articles on traveling with children. Also check *Take Your Baby and Go! A Guide for Traveling with Babies, Toddlers and Young Children,* by Sheri Andrews, Judy Bordeaux, and Vivian Vasquez (✉ Bear Creek Publications, 2507 Minor Ave. E, Seattle, WA 98102, ☎ 206/322–7604 or 800/326–6566; $5.95 plus $1.50 shipping).

TOUR OPERATORS

Contact **Rascals in Paradise** (✉ 650 5th St., Suite 505, San Francisco, CA 94107, ☎ 415/978–9800 or 800/872–7225).

If you're outdoorsy, look into the family adventure tours, ranches, and lodges of **American Wilderness Experience** (✉ Box 1486, Boulder, CO 80306, ☎ 303/444–2622 or 800/444–0099). Other family-oriented programs are run by the **American Museum of Natural History** (✉ 79th St. and Central Park West, New York, NY 10024, ☎ 212/769–5700 or 800/462–8687).

CRUISING

Among the many cruise lines that ply Mexican waters are **Commodore** (☎ 800/529–3000), **Cunard** (☎ 800/221–4770), **Holland America** (☎ 800/426–0327), **Carnival** (☎ 800/327–9501; reservations should be made through a travel agent), **Costa** (☎ 800/462–6782), **Dolphin/Majesty** (☎ 800/222–1003), **Fantasy/Celebrity** (☎ 800/423–2100), **Holland America** (☎ 800/426–0327), **Norwegian** (☎ 800/327–7030), **Princess** (☎ 800/421–0522), **Regency** (☎ 212/972–4499 or 800/388–5500), and **Royal Caribbean** (☎ 305/539–6000 or 800/327–6700).

Usually, the best deals on cruise bookings can be found by consulting a cruise-only travel agency. Contact the **National Association of Cruise Only Travel Agencies (NACOA)** (✉ 3191 Coral Way, Suite 622, Miami, FL 33145, ☎ 305/446–7732 or 305/446–9732) for a listing of such agencies in your area.

SPECIAL-INTEREST CRUISES

For whale watching and educational cruises,

contact the **Oceanic Society Expeditions** (✉ Fort Mason Center, Bldg. E, San Francisco, CA 94123, ☎ 415/441–1106 or 800/326–7491), **Classical Cruises** (✉ 8132 E. 70th St., New York, NY 10021, ☎ 800/367–6766, FAX 212/249–6896), or the **Smithsonian Institution**'s Study Tours and Seminars (✉ 1100 Jefferson Dr. SW, Room 3045, Washington, DC 20560, ☎ 202/357–4700).

CUSTOMS

U.S. CITIZENS

The **U.S. Customs Service** (✉ Box 7407, Washington, DC 20044, ☎ 202/927–6724) can answer questions on duty-free limits and publishes a helpful brochure, "Know Before You Go." For information on registering foreign-made articles, call 202/927–0540.

COMPLAINTS➤ Note the inspector's badge number and write to the commissioner's office (✉ 1301 Constitution Ave. NW, Washington, DC 20229).

CANADIANS

Contact **Revenue Canada** (✉ 2265 St. Laurent Blvd. S, Ottawa, Ontario K1G 4K3, ☎ 613/993–0534) for a copy of the free brochure **"I Declare/Je Déclare"** and for details on duty-free limits. For recorded information (within Canada only), call 800/461–9999.

U.K. CITIZENS

HM Customs and Excise (✉ Dorset House, Stamford St., London SE1 9NG, ☎ 0171/202–4227) can answer

questions about U.K. customs regulations and publishes a free pamphlet, **"A Guide for Travellers,"** detailing standard procedures and import rules.

D

DISABILITIES & ACCESSIBILITY

COMPLAINTS

To register complaints under the provisions of the Americans with Disabilities Act, contact the U.S. Department of Justice's **Disability Rights Section** (✉ Box 66738, Washington, DC 20035, ☎ 202/514–0301 or 800/514–0301, FAX 202/307–1198, TTY 202/514–0383 or 800/514–0383). For airline-related problems, contact the U.S. Department of Transportation's **Aviation Consumer Protection Division** (☞ Air Travel, *above*). For complaints about surface transportation, contact the Department of Transportation's **Civil Rights Office** (☎ 202/366–4648).

ORGANIZATIONS

TRAVELERS WITH HEARING IMPAIRMENTS➤ The **American Academy of Otolaryngology** (✉ 1 Prince St., Alexandria, VA 22314, ☎ 703/836–4444, FAX 703/683–5100, TTY 703/519–1585) publishes a brochure, "Travel Tips for Hearing Impaired People."

TRAVELERS WITH MOBILITY PROBLEMS➤ Contact the **Information Center for Individuals with Disabilities** (✉ Box 256, Boston, MA 02117, ☎ 617/450–9888; in MA, 800/462–5015; TTY 617/424–6855); **Mobil-**

ity International USA (✉ Box 10767, Eugene, OR 97440, ☎ and TTY 503/343–1284, FAX 503/343–6812), the U.S. branch of a Belgium-based organization (☞ below) with affiliates in 30 countries; MossRehab Hospital Travel Information Service (☎ 215/456–9600, TTY 215/456–9602), a telephone information resource for travelers with physical disabilities; the Society for the Advancement of Travel for the Handicapped (☎ 347 5th Ave., Suite 610, New York, NY 10016, ☎ 212/447–7284, FAX 212/725–8253; membership $45); and Travelin' Talk (✉ Box 3534, Clarksville, TN 37043, ☎ 615/552–6670, FAX 615/552–1182) which provides local contacts worldwide for travelers with disabilities.

TRAVELERS WITH VISION IMPAIRMENTS➤ Contact the American Council of the Blind (✉ 1155 15th St. NW, Suite 720, Washington, DC 20005, ☎ 202/467–5081, FAX 202/467–5085) for a list of travelers' resources or the American Foundation for the Blind (✉ 11 Penn Plaza, Suite 300, New York, NY 10001, ☎ 212/502–7600 or 800/232–5463, TTY 212/502–7662), which provides general advice and publishes "Access to Art" ($19.95), a directory of museums that accommodate travelers with vision impairments.

IN THE U.K.

Contact the Royal Association for Disability and Rehabilitation (✉ RADAR, 12 City Forum, 250 City Rd.,

London EC1V 8AF, ☎ 0171/250–3222) or Mobility International (✉ rue de Manchester 25, B-1080 Brussels, Belgium, ☎ 00–322–410–6297, FAX 00–322–410–6874), an international travel-information clearing-house for people with disabilities.

PUBLICATIONS

Several publications for travelers with disabilities are available from the Consumer Information Center (✉ Box 100, Pueblo, CO 81009, ☎ 719/948–3334). Call or write for its free catalog of current titles. The Society for the Advancement of Travel for the Handicapped (☞ Organizations, above) publishes the quarterly magazine "Access to Travel" ($13 for 1-year subscription).

The 500-page Travelin' Talk Directory (✉ Box 3534, Clarksville, TN 37043, ☎ 615/552–6670, FAX 615/552–1182; $35) lists people and organizations who help travelers with disabilities. For travel agents worldwide, consult the Directory of Travel Agencies for the Disabled (✉ Twin Peaks Press, Box 129, Vancouver, WA 98666, ☎ 360/694–2462 or 800/637–2256, FAX 360/696–3210; $19.95 plus $3 shipping).

TRAVEL AGENCIES & TOUR OPERATORS

The Americans with Disabilities Act requires that all travel firms serve the needs of all travelers. That said, you should note that some agencies and operators specialize in making

travel arrangements for individuals and groups with disabilities, among them Access Adventures (✉ 206 Chestnut Ridge Rd., Rochester, NY 14624, ☎ 716/889–9096), run by a former physical-rehab counselor; and CareVacations (✉ 5019 49th Ave., Suite 102, Leduc, Alberta T9E 6T5, ☎ 403/986–8332; in Canada, 800/648–1116), which has group tours and is especially helpful for cruises.

TRAVELERS WITH MOBILITY PROBLEMS➤ Contact Accessible Journeys (✉ 35 W. Sellers Ave., Ridley Park, PA 19078, ☎ 610/521–0339 or 800/846–4537, FAX 610/521–6959), a registered nursing service that arranges vacations; Hinsdale Travel Service (✉ 201 E. Ogden Ave., Suite 100, Hinsdale, IL 60521, ☎ 708/325–1335 or 800/303–5521), a travel agency that benefits from the advice of wheelchair traveler Janice Perkins; and Wheelchair Journeys (✉ 16979 Redmond Way, Redmond, WA 98052, ☎ 206/885–2210 or 800/313–4751), which can handle arrangements worldwide.

TRAVELERS WITH DEVELOPMENTAL DISABILITIES➤ Contact the nonprofit New Directions (✉ 5276 Hollister Ave., Suite 207, Santa Barbara, CA 93111, ☎ 805/967–2841).

TRAVEL GEAR

The Magellan's catalog (☎ 800/962–4943, FAX 805/568–5406), includes a range of products designed for travelers with disabilities.

DISCOUNTS & DEALS

AIRFARES

For the lowest airfares to Mexico, call 800/FLY–4–LESS. Also try 800/FLY–ASAP.

CLUBS

Contact **Entertainment Travel Editions** (✉ Box 1068, Trumbull, CT 06611, ☎ 800/445–4137; $28–$53, depending on destination), **Great American Traveler** (✉ Box 27965, Salt Lake City, UT 84127, ☎ 800/548–2812; $49.95 per year), **Moment's Notice Discount Travel Club** (✉ 163 Amsterdam Ave., Suite 137, New York, NY 10023, ☎ 212/486–0500; $25 per year, single or family), **Privilege Card** (✉ 3391 Peachtree Rd. NE, Suite 110, Atlanta, GA 30326, ☎ 404/262–0222 or 800/236–9732; $74.95 per year), **Travelers Advantage** (✉ CUC Travel Service, 49 Music Sq. W, Nashville, TN 37203, ☎ 800/548–1116 or 800/648–4037; $49 per year, single or family), or **Worldwide Discount Travel Club** (✉ 1674 Meridian Ave., Miami Beach, FL 33139, ☎ 305/534–2082; $50 per year for family, $40 single).

STUDENTS

Members of Hostelling International–American Youth Hostels (☞ Students, *below*) are eligible for discounts on car rentals, admissions to attractions, and other selected travel expenses.

PUBLICATIONS

Consult *The Frugal Globetrotter*, by Bruce Northam (✉ Fulcrum Publishing, 350 Indiana St., Suite 350, Golden, CO 80401, ☎ 800/992–2908; $15.95). For publications that tell how to find the lowest prices on plane tickets, *see* Air Travel, *above*.

G
GAY & LESBIAN TRAVEL

ORGANIZATIONS

The **International Gay Travel Association** (✉ Box 4974, Key West, FL 33041, ☎ 800/448–8550, FAX 305/296–6633), a consortium of more than 1,000 travel companies, can supply names of gay-friendly travel agents, tour operators, and accommodations.

PUBLICATIONS

The premier international travel magazine for gays and lesbians is *Our World* (✉ 1104 N. Nova Rd., Suite 251, Daytona Beach, FL 32117, ☎ 904/441–5367, FAX 904/441–5604; $35 for 10 issues). The 16-page monthly *"Out & About"* (☎ 212/645–6922 or 800/929–2268, FAX 800/929–2215; $49 for 10 issues and quarterly calendar) covers gay-friendly resorts, hotels, cruise lines, and airlines.

TOUR OPERATORS

Cruises and resort vacations for gays are handled by **R.S.V.P. Travel Productions** (✉ 2800 University Ave. SE, Minneapolis, MN 55414, ☎ 612/379–4697 or 800/328–7787). **Olivia** (✉ 4400 Market St., Oakland, CA 94608, ☎ 510/655–0364 or 800/631–6277) specializes in such bookings for lesbians. For mixed gay and lesbian travel, contact **Atlantis Events** (✉ 9060 Santa Monica Blvd., Suite 310, West Hollywood, CA 90069, ☎ 310/281–5450 or 800/628–5268) or **Toto Tours** (✉ 1326 W. Albion St., Suite 3W, Chicago, IL 60626, ☎ 312/274–8686 or 800/565–1241), which offer group tours to worldwide destinations.

TRAVEL AGENCIES

The largest agencies serving gay travelers are **Advance Travel** (✉ 10700 Northwest Fwy., Suite 160, Houston, TX 77092, ☎ 713/682–2002 or 800/695–0880), **Islanders/Kennedy Travel** (✉ 183 W. 10th St., New York, NY 10014, ☎ 212/242–3222 or 800/988–1181), **Now Voyager** (✉ 4406 18th St., San Francisco, CA 94114, ☎ 415/626–1169 or 800/255–6951), and **Yellowbrick Road** (✉ 1500 W. Balmoral Ave., Chicago, IL 60640, ☎ 312/561–1800 or 800/642–2488). **Skylink Women's Travel** (✉ 3577 Moorland Ave., Santa Rosa, CA 95407, ☎ 707/588–9961 or 800/225–5759) serves lesbian travelers.

H
HEALTH ISSUES

FINDING A DOCTOR

For its members, the **International Association for Medical Assistance to Travellers** (✉ IAMAT, 417 Center St., Lewis-

THE GOLD GUIDE / IMPORTANT CONTACTS

ton, NY 14092, ☎ 716/754–4883; 40 Regal Rd., Guelph, Ontario N1K 1B5, ☎ 519/836–0102; 1287 St. Clair Ave., Toronto, Ontario M6E 1B8, ☎ 416/652–0137; 57 Voirets, 1212 Grand-Lancy, Geneva, Switzerland, no phone; membership free) publishes a worldwide directory of English-speaking physicians meeting IAMAT standards.

MEDICAL ASSISTANCE COMPANIES

The following companies are concerned primarily with emergency medical assistance, although they may provide some insurance as part of their coverage. For a list of full-service travel insurance companies, *see* Insurance, *below.*

Contact **International SOS Assistance** (✉ Box 11568, Philadelphia, PA 19116, ☎ 215/244–1500 or 800/523–8930; Box 466, Pl. Bonaventure, Montréal, Québec H5A 1C1, ☎ 514/874–7674 or 800/363–0263; 7 Old Lodge Pl., St. Margarets, Twickenham TW1 1RQ, England, ☎ 0181/744–0033), **Medex Assistance Corporation** (✉ Box 10623, Baltimore, MD 21285, ☎ 410/453–6300 or 800/573–2029), **Traveler's Emergency Network** (✉ 3100 Tower Blvd., Suite 3100A, Durham, NC 27702, ☎ 919/490–6065 or 800/275–4836, FAX 919/493–8262), **TravMed** (✉ Box 5375, Baltimore, MD 24094, ☎ 800/732–5309), or **Worldwide Assistance Services** (✉ 1133 15th St. NW, Suite 400,

Washington, DC 20005, ☎ 202/331–1609 or 800/821–2828, FAX 202/828–5896).

PUBLICATIONS

The Safe Travel Book, by Peter Savage (✉ Lexington Books, Simon & Schuster Order Dept., 200 Old Tappan Rd., Old Tappan, NJ 07675, ☎ 800/223–2336, FAX 800/445–6991; $12.95 plus $2.50 shipping), and *Traveler's Medical Resource,* by William W. Forgey (✉ ICS Books, Box 10767, Merrillville, IN 46410, ☎ 219/769–0585 or 800/541–7323, FAX 219/769–6085; $19.95 plus $3 shipping), are authoritative.

WARNINGS

The hot line of the **National Centers for Disease Control** (✉ CDC, National Center for Infectious Diseases, Division of Quarantine, Traveler's Health Section, 1600 Clifton Rd., M/S E-03, Atlanta, GA 30333, ☎ 404/332–4559, FAX 404/332–4565) provides information on health risks abroad and vaccination requirements and recommendations. You can call for an automated menu of recorded information or use the fax-back service to request printed matter.

I

INSURANCE

IN CANADA

Contact **Mutual of Omaha** (✉ Travel Division, 500 University Ave., Toronto, Ontario M5G 1V8, ☎ 800/268–8825 or 416/598–4321).

IN THE U.S.

Travel insurance covering baggage, health, and trip cancellation or interruptions is available from **Access America** (✉ Box 90315, Richmond, VA 23286, ☎ 804/285–3300 or 800/284–8300), **Carefree Travel Insurance** (✉ Box 9366, 100 Garden City Plaza, Garden City, NY 11530, ☎ 516/294–0220 or 800/323–3149), **Near Travel Services** (✉ Box 1339, Calumet City, IL 60409, ☎ 708/868–6700 or 800/654–6700), **Tele-Trip** (✉ Mutual of Omaha Plaza, Box 31716, Omaha, NE 68131, ☎ 800/228–9792), **Travel Guard International** (✉ 1145 Clark St., Stevens Point, WI 54481, ☎ 715/345–0505 or 800/826–1300), **Travel Insured International** (✉ Box 280568, East Hartford, CT 06128, ☎ 203/528–7663 or 800/243–3174), and **Wallach & Company** (✉ 107 W. Federal St., Box 480, Middleburg, VA 22117, ☎ 703/687–3166 or 800/237–6615).

IN THE U.K.

The **Association of British Insurers** (✉ 51 Gresham St., London EC2V 7HQ, ☎ 0171/600–3333) gives advice by phone and publishes the free pamphlet **"Holiday Insurance,"** which sets out typical policy provisions and costs.

L

LANGUAGE
INSTITUTES

Recommended places to learn Spanish and live with a Mexican family include **Cetlalic** (✉ Aptdo. 1-201 Cuernavaca, Morelos, CP 62001 ☎ 73/13–35–79), with an emphasis on social justice as well as language acquisition; the **Spanish Language Institute Center for Latin American Studies** (✉ Apdo. Postal 2–3, Cuernavaca, Morelos 62191, ☎ 73/17–52–94 or 73/11–00–63; in the U.S., contact Language Link Inc., Box 3006, Peoria, IL 61612, ☎ 800/552–2051); **El Instituto de Estudios para Estranjeros de la Universidad de Guadalajara** (✉ Apdo. 1 Giuillón 2130, Guadalajra, Jalisco 44000, ☎ 3/353–21–50 or 3/363–60–24); **Instituto Falcón** (✉ Mora 158, Guanajuato, Guanajuato 36000, ☎ FAX 473/2–36–94); **Instituto Allende** (✉ Ancha de San Antonio No. 20, San Miguel de Allende, Guanajuato 37700, ☎ 465/2–01–90, FAX 465/2–45–38), also an art school; **Centro de Idiomas de la Universidad Autónoma Benito Juárez** (✉ Burgoa, at Armenta y López, Oaxaca, Oaxaca 68000, ☎ 951/659–22, FAX 951/91–95–1), which offers classes in Mixtec and Zapotec as well as in Spanish; and **Instituto Jovel, A.C.** (✉ Apdo. Postal 62, Ma. Adelina Flores 21, San Cristóbal de las Casas, Chiapas 29200, ☎ FAX 967/8–40–69). **AmeriSpan Unlimited** (✉ Box 40513, Philadelphia, PA 19106, ☎ 800/879–6640, FAX 215/986–4524) can arrange for language study and homestay in a number of Mexican cities.

LODGING

For information on hotel consolidators, see Discounts, above.

APARTMENT & VILLA RENTAL

Among the companies to contact are **At Home Abroad** (✉ 405 E. 56th St., Suite 6H, New York, NY 10022, ☎ 212/421–9165, FAX 212/752–1591), **Europa-Let** (✉ 92 N. Main St., Ashland, OR 97520, ☎ 541/482–5806 or 800/462–4486, FAX 541/482–0660), **Property Rentals International** (✉ 1008 Mansfield Crossing Rd., Richmond, VA 23236, ☎ 804/378–6054 or 800/220–3332, FAX 804/379–2073), **Rental Directories International** (✉ 2044 Rittenhouse Sq., Philadelphia, PA 19103, ☎ 215/985–4001, FAX 215/985–0323), **Rent-a-Home International** (✉ 7200 34th Ave. NW, Seattle, WA 98117, ☎ 206/789–9377 or 800/488–7368, FAX 206/789–9379, hmaria@aol. com), **Vacation Home Rentals Worldwide** (✉ 235 Kensington Ave., Norwood, NJ 07648, ☎ 201/767–9393 or 800/633–3284, FAX 201/767–5510), **Villas and Apartments Abroad** (✉ 420 Madison Ave., Suite 1003, New York, NY 10017, ☎ 212/759–1025 or 800/433–3020, FAX 212/755–8316), and **Villas International** (✉ 605 Market St., Suite 510, San Francisco, CA 94105, ☎ 415/281–0910 or 800/221–2260, FAX 415/281–0919). Members of the travel club

Hideaways International (✉ 767 Islington St., Portsmouth, NH 03801, ☎ 603/430–4433 or 800/843–4433, FAX 603/430–4444, info@hideaways.com; $99 per year) receive two annual guides plus quarterly newsletters and arrange rentals among themselves.

HOME EXCHANGE

Some of the principal clearinghouses are **HomeLink International/Vacation Exchange Club** (✉ Box 650, Key West, FL 33041, ☎ 305/294–1448 or 800/638–3841, FAX 305/294–1148; $70 per year), which sends members three annual directories, with a listing in one, plus updates; and **Intervac International** (✉ Box 590504, San Francisco, CA 94159, ☎ 415/435–3497, FAX 415/435–7440; $65 per year), which publishes four annual directories.

HOTELS

International hotel chains with Mexican properties include **Best Western** (☎ 800/528–1234), **Club Med** (☎ 800/CLUB MED), **Hyatt International** (☎ 800/228–9000), **Marriott** (☎ 800/228–9290), **Posadas de México** (Fiesta Americana and Fiesta Inn hotels, ☎ 800/FIESTA–1); **Holiday Inn** (☎ 800/HOLIDAY), **Omni** (800/THE–OMNI), **Princess** (☎ 800/442–8418, or in NY 800/223–1818), **Quality Inn** (Hoteles Calinda, ☎ 800/228–5151), **Radisson** (☎ 800/333–3333), **Sheraton** (☎ 800/325–3535), **Presidente** (☎ 800/447–6147), and **Westin**

Regina Hotels (☎ 800/228–3000). **Grupo Sol's Meliá Hotels** (☎ 800/336–3542) are part of a reliable Spanish-owned chain. Good Mexican-owned chains include **Krystal** (☎ 800/231–9860) and **Camino Real** (☎ 800/722–6466).

If you arrive in Mexico City without a reservation, the **Mexican Hotel and Motel Association** operates a booth at the airport that will assist you (☎ 5/571–3268 or 5/571–3262).

M
MAIL

American Express card- or traveler's-check holders can have mail sent to them at the local American Express office. For a list of the offices worldwide, write for the *Traveler's Companion* from **American Express** (✉ Box 678, Canal Street Station, New York, NY 10013). Another option for receiving mail is the Mexican postal service's *lista de correos* (poste restante) service. For specifics, *see* Mail *in* Smart Travel Tips A to Z, *below.*

MONEY MATTERS

ATMS

For specific foreign **Cirrus** locations, call 800/424–7787; for foreign **Plus** locations, consult the Plus directory at your local bank.

CURRENCY EXCHANGE

If your bank doesn't exchange currency, contact **Thomas Cook Currency Services** (☎ 800/287–7362 for locations). **Ruesch**

International (☎ 800/424–2923 for locations) can also provide you with foreign bank-notes before you leave home and publishes a number of useful brochures, including a "Foreign Currency Guide" and "Foreign Exchange Tips." All major airports have 24-hour currency exchange booths.

WIRING FUNDS

Funds can be wired via **MoneyGram**ˢᴹ (for locations and information in the U.S. and Canada, ☎ 800/926–9400) or **Western Union** (for agent locations or to send money using MasterCard or Visa, ☎ 800/325–6000; in Canada, 800/321–2923; in the U.K., 0800/833833; or visit the Western Union office at the nearest major post office).

P
PACKING

For strategies on packing light, get a copy of *The Packing Book,* by Judith Gilford (✉ Ten Speed Press, Box 7123, Berkeley, CA 94707, ☎ 510/559–1600 or 800/841–2665, ℻ 510/524–4588; $7.95).

PASSPORTS & VISAS

IN THE U.S.

For fees, documentation requirements, and other information, call the State Department's **Office of Passport Services** information line (☎ 202/647–0518).

CANADIANS

For fees, documentation requirements, and other information, call the

Ministry of Foreign Affairs and International Trade's **Passport Office** (☎ 819/994–3500 or 800/567–6868).

U.K. CITIZENS

For fees, documentation requirements, and to request an emergency passport, call the **London Passport Office** (☎ 0990/210410).

PHOTO HELP

The **Kodak Information Center** (☎ 800/242–2424) answers consumer questions about film and photography. The *Kodak Guide to Shooting Great Travel Pictures* (available in bookstores; or contact Fodor's Travel Publications, ☎ 800/533–6478; $16.50) explains how to take expert travel photographs.

S
SAFETY

"Trouble-Free Travel," from the AAA, is a booklet of tips for protecting yourself and your belongings when away from home. Send a stamped, self-addressed, legal-size envelope to Flying Alone (✉ Mail Stop 75, 1000 AAA Dr., Heathrow, FL 32746).

SENIOR CITIZENS

EDUCATIONAL TRAVEL

The nonprofit **Elderhostel** (✉ 75 Federal St., 3rd Floor, Boston, MA 02110, ☎ 617/426–7788), for people 60 and older, has offered inexpensive study programs since 1975. Courses cover everything from marine science to Greek mythology and cowboy poetry.

Fees for programs in the United States and Canada, which usually last one week, run about $300, not including transportation. Costs for two- to three-week international trips—including room, board, and transportation from the United States—range from $1,800 to $4,500.

For people 50 and over and their children and grandchildren, **Interhostel** (✉ University of New Hampshire, 6 Garrison Ave., Durham, NH 03824, ☎ 603/862–1147 or 800/733–9753) runs 10-day summer programs that feature lectures, field trips, and sightseeing. Most last two weeks and cost $2,125–$3,100, including airfare.

ORGANIZATIONS

Contact the **American Association of Retired Persons** (✉ AARP, 601 E St. NW, Washington, DC 20049, ☎ 202/434–2277; annual dues $8 per person or couple). Its Purchase Privilege Program secures discounts for members on lodging, car rentals, and sightseeing.

Additional sources for discounts on lodgings, car rentals, and other travel expenses, as well as helpful magazines and newsletters, are the **National Council of Senior Citizens** (✉ 1331 F St. NW, Washington, DC 20004, ☎ 202/347–8800; annual membership $12) and Sears's **Mature Outlook** (✉ Box 10448, Des Moines, IA 50306, ☎ 800/336–6330; annual membership $9.95).

PUBLICATIONS

The 50+ Traveler's Guidebook: Where to Go, Where to Stay, What to Do, by Anita Williams and Merrimac Dillon (✉ St. Martin's Press, 175 5th Ave., New York, NY 10010, ☎ 212/674–5151 or 800/288–2131; $13.95), offers many useful tips. **"The Mature Traveler"** (✉ Box 50400, Reno, NV 89513, ☎ 702/786–7419; $29.95), a monthly newsletter, covers all sorts of travel deals.

SPORTS

TENNIS AND GOLF

For tennis and golf tournament information, contact the **Federación Mexicana de Tenis** (✉ Miguel Angel de Quevedo 953, Colonia El Rosedal, Coyoacán, Mexico D.F. 04330, ☎ 5/689–9733) and the **Federación Mexicana de Golf** (✉ Av. Lomas de Sotelo 1112, Despacho 103, Col. Lomas de Sotelo, Mexico, D.F. 11200, ☎ 5/395–8642), respectively.

STUDENTS

HOSTELING

In the United States, contact **Hostelling International–American Youth Hostels** (✉ 733 15th St. NW, Suite 840, Washington, DC 20005, ☎ 202/783–6161 or 800/444–6111 for reservations at selected hostels, FAX 202/783–6171); in Canada, **Hostelling International–Canada** (✉ 205 Catherine St., Suite 400, Ottawa, Ontario K2P 1C3, ☎ 613/237–7884); and in the United Kingdom,

the **Youth Hostel Association of England and Wales** (✉ Trevelyan House, 8 St. Stephen's Hill, St. Albans, Hertfordshire AL1 2DY, ☎ 01727/855215 or 01727/845047). Membership (in the U.S., $25; in Canada, C$26.75; in the U.K., £9.30) gives you access to 5,000 hostels in 77 countries that charge $5–$30 per person per night.

I.D. CARDS

To be eligible for discounts on transportation and admissions, get either the **International Student Identity Card,** if you're a bona fide student, or the **GO 25: International Youth Travel Card,** if you're not a student but under age 26. Each includes basic travel-accident and illness coverage, plus a toll-free travel hot line. In the United States, either card costs $18; apply through the Council on International Educational Exchange (☞ Organizations, *below*). In Canada, cards are available for $15 each ($16 by mail) from Travel Cuts (☞ Organizations, *below*), and in the United Kingdom for £5 each at student unions and student travel companies.

ORGANIZATIONS

A major contact is the **Council on International Educational Exchange** (✉ mail orders only: CIEE, 205 E. 42nd St., 16th Floor, New York, NY 10017, ☎ 212/661–1450, info@ciee. org), with walk-in locations in Boston (✉ 729 Boylston St., 02116, ☎ 617/266–

THE GOLD GUIDE / IMPORTANT CONTACTS

1926), Miami (✉ 9100 S. Dadeland Blvd., 33156, ☎ 305/670–9261), Los Angeles (✉ 10904 Lindbrook Dr., 90024, ☎ 310/208–3551), 43 other college towns in the U.S., and in the United Kingdom (✉ 28A Poland St., London W1V 3DB, ☎ 0171/437–7767). Twice per year, it publishes *Student Travels* magazine. The CIEE's Council Travel Service offers domestic air passes for bargain travel within the United States and is the exclusive U.S. agent for several student discount cards.

The **Educational Travel Centre** (✉ 438 N. Frances St., Madison, WI 53703, ☎ 608/256–5551 or 800/747–5551, FAX 608/256–2042) offers rail passes and low-cost airline tickets, mostly for flights that depart from Chicago.

In Canada, also contact **Travel Cuts** (✉ 187 College St., Toronto, Ontario M5T 1P7, ☎ 416/979–2406 or 800/667–2887).

PUBLICATIONS

Check out the *Berkeley Guide to Mexico* (available in bookstores; or contact Fodor's Travel Publications, ☎ 800/533–6478; $17.50).

T

TELEPHONE MATTERS

The country code for Mexico is 52. **AT&T** USA Direct may be accessed from within Mexico by dialing 95–800/462–4240 from any private or hotel

phone, or any public phone marked "LADA-TEL." From the same phones, dial 95–800/674–7000 for **MCI** WorldPhone, or 95–800/877–8000 for **Sprint.**

TOUR OPERATORS

Among the companies that sell tours and packages to Mexico, the following are nationally known, have a proven reputation, and offer plenty of options.

GROUP TOURS

SUPER-DELUXE➤ **Abercrombie & Kent** (✉ 1520 Kensington Rd., Oak Brook, IL 60521-2141, ☎ 708/954–2944 or 800/323–7308, FAX 708/954–3324) and **Travcoa** (✉ Box 2630, 2350 S.E. Bristol St., Newport Beach, CA 92660, ☎ 714/476–2800 or 800/992–2003, FAX 714/476–2538).

ALL DESTINATIONS➤ **Armadillo Tours International** (✉ 4301 Westbank Dr., Bldg. B360, Austin, TX 78746, ☎ 512/328–7800 or 800/284–5678), **Gadabout Tours** (✉ 700 E. Tahquitz Canyon Way, Palm Springs, CA 92262, ☎ 619/325–5556 or 800/952–5068), and **Go with Jo** (✉ 910 Dixieland Rd., Harlingen, TX 78552, ☎ 210/423–1446 or 800/999–1446, FAX 210/421–5787). **Mexico Travel Advisors,** based in Chicago, Illinois, sells packages only through travel agents.

COPPER CANYON➤ **American Wilderness Experience** (✉ Box 1486, Boulder, CO 80306, ☎ 303/444–2622 or 800/444–

3833, FAX 303/444–3999), **Armadillo Tours International** (☞ All Destinations, *above*), **Brendan Tours** (✉ 15137 Califa St., Van Nuys, CA 91411, ☎ 818/785–9696 or 800/421–8446, FAX 818/902–9876), **Brennan Tours** (✉ 1402 3rd Ave., No. 717, Seattle, WA 98101, ☎ 206/622–9155 or 800/237–7249), **Frontier Tour and Travel** (✉ 1923 N. Carson St., Carson City, NV 89706, ☎ 702/882–2100 or 800/647–0800), **Gadabout Tours** (☞ All Destinations, *above*), **Globus/Cosmos** (✉ 5301 S. Federal Circle, Littleton, CO 80123, ☎ 303/797–2800 or 800/221–0900), **Maupintour** (✉ Box 807, Lawrence, KS 66047, ☎ 913/843–1211 or 800/255–4266, FAX 913/843–8351), **Mayflower Tours** (✉ Box 490, 1225 Warren Ave., Downers Grove, IL 60515, ☎ 708/960–3793 or 800/323–7604), **Mexico Travel Advisors** (☞ All Destinations, *above*), **Questers** (✉ 381 Park Ave. S, New York, NY 10016, ☎ 212/251–0444 or 800/468–8668, FAX 212/251–0890), **Remarkable Journeys** (✉ Box 31855, Houston, TX 77231-1855, ☎ 713/721–2517 or 800/856–1993), **Smithsonian Study Tours and Seminars** (✉ 1100 Jefferson Dr. SW, Room 3045, MRC 702, Washington, DC 20560, ☎ 202/357–4700, FAX 202/633–9250), and **Tauck Tours** (✉ Box 5027, 276 Post Rd. W, Westport, CT 06881, ☎ 203/226–6911 or

800/468–2825,
FAX 203/221–6828).

PACKAGES

Independent vacation packages are available from major tour operators and airlines. Contact **Aeromexico Vacation Planners** (☎ 800/245–8585), **American Airlines Fly AAway Vacations** (☎ 800/321–2121), **Certified Vacations** (⊠ Box 1525, Fort Lauderdale, FL 33302, ☎ 954/522–1440 or 800/233–7260), **Club Med** (⊠ 40 W. 57th St., New York, NY 10019, ☎ 800/258–2633), **Continental Vacations** (☎ 800/634–5555), **Delta Dream Vacations** (☎ 800/872–7786), **United Vacations** (☎ 800/328–6877), and **USAir Vacations** (☎ 800/455–0123). **Gogo Tours,** based in Ramsey, New Jersey, sells Mexico packages only through travel agents.

Regional operators specialize in putting together Mexico packages for travelers from their local area. Arrangements may include charter or scheduled air. Contact **Apple Vacations** (⊠ 25 N.W. Point Blvd., Elk Grove Village, IL 60007, ☎ 708/640–1150 or 800/365–2775), **Friendly Holidays** (⊠ 1983 Marcus Ave., Lake Success, NY 11042, ☎ 800/344–5687), **GWV International** (⊠ 300 1st Ave., Needham, MA 02194-2721, ☎ 617/449–5450 or 800/225–5498), and **Travel Impressions** (⊠ 465 Smith St., Farmingdale, NY 11735, ☎ 516/845–

8000 or 800/284–0044, FAX 516/845–8095).

FROM THE U.K.

Companies with packages to Mexico include **Bales Tours** (⊠ Bales House, Junction Rd., Dorking, Surrey RH4 3HB, ☎ 01306/876–881 or 01306/885–991, FAX 01306/740–048), **British Airways Holidays** (⊠ Astral Towers, Betts Way, London Rd., Crawley, West Sussex RH10 2XA, ☎ 01293/723–121, FAX 01293/722–624), **Journey Latin America** (⊠ 14–16 Devonshire Rd., Chiswick, London W4 2HD, ☎ 0181/747–8315, FAX 0181/742–1312), and **Kuoni Travel** (⊠ Kuoni House, Dorking, Surrey RH5 4AZ, ☎ 01306/742–222, FAX 01306/744-222).

For a custom-designed holiday contact **Steamond Travel** (⊠ 23 Eccleston St., London SW1 9LX, ☎ 0171/286–4449, FAX 0171/730–3024) or **Trailfinders** (⊠ 42–50 Earls Court Rd., London W8 6FT, ☎ 0171/937–5400, FAX 0171/938–3305).

THEME TRIPS

ADVENTURE➤ Adventure travel in Mexico can mean hiking through the Copper Canyon, volcano climbing outside Mexico City, or river rafting on the Río Usumancita (known as the Mayan River of Ruins) and on the Río Antigua near Veracruz. Baja adventures may include sea kayaking, whale watching, scuba diving, and natural-history crusies. Contact **Adventure Center**

(⊠ 1311 63rd St., No. 200, Emeryville, CA 94608, ☎ 510/654–1879 or 800/227–8747, FAX 510/654–4200), **American Wilderness Experience** (☞ Copper Canyon, *above*), **Baja Expeditions** (⊠ 2625 Garnet Ave., San Diego, CA 92109, ☎ 619/581–3311 or 800/843–6967, FAX 619/581–6542), **Himalayan Travel** (⊠ 112 Prospect St., Stamford, CT 06901, ☎ 203/359–3711 or 800/225–2380, FAX 203/359–3669), **Mountain Travel-Sobek** (⊠ 6420 Fairmount Ave., El Cerrito, CA 94530, ☎ 510/527–8100 or 800/227–2384, FAX 510/525–7710, Info@MTSobek.com, http://www.MTSobek.com), **OARS** (⊠ Box 67, Angels Camp, CA 95222, ☎ 209/736–4677 or 800/346–6277, FAX 209/736–2902, reservations@oars.com, http://www.oars.com), **Remarkable Journeys** (☞ Copper Canyon, *above*), and **Trek America** (⊠ Box 189, Rockaway, NJ 07866, ☎ 201/983–1144 or 800/221–0596, FAX 201/983–8551).

ART AND ARCHAEOLOGY➤ A nonprofit educational organization, the **Archaeological Conservancy** (⊠ 5301 Central Ave. NE, No. 1218, Albuquerque, NM 87108-1517, ☎ 505/266–1540) leads archaeological tours to all of the major Mexican ruins. **Smithsonian Study Tours and Seminars** (☞ Copper Canyon, *above*) explore the culture and ruins of Mexico's native peoples. **Recursos de Santa Fe** (⊠ 826 Camino de

Monte Rey, Santa Fe, NM 87505, ☎ 505/982–9301, FAX 505/989–8608, rescursos@aol.com) gears its excursions to a group's interests but is especially strong on Mexico's ancient artifacts. Commercial tour operators that focus on archaeological ruins include **Armadillo Tours International** (☞ All Destinations, *above*), **Far Horizons Archaeological & Cultural Trips** (✉ Box 91900, Albuquerque, NM 87199-1900, ☎ 505/343–9400 or 800/552–4575, FAX 505/343–8076), **Maya-Carib Travel** (✉ 7 Davenport Ave., No. 3F, New Rochelle, NY 10805, ☎ 914/354–9824 or 800/223–4084, FAX 914/235–2221), **M.I.L.A.** (✉ 100 S. Greenleaf Ave., Gurnee, IL 60031-3378, ☎ 847/249–2111 or 800/367–7378, FAX 847/249–2772, milalatin@aol.com, http://www.a2z.com/mila), and **Sanborn's Viva Tours** (✉ 2015 S. 10th St., Box 519, McAllen, TX 78505-0519, ☎ 210/682–9872 or 800/395–8482, FAX 210/682–0016).

BICYCLING➤ For mountain biking in the Baja region or road-biking tours through the Yucatán try **Backroads** (✉ 1516 5th St., Berkeley, CA 94710-1740, ☎ 510/527–1555 or 800/462–2848, FAX 510/527–1444, goactive@Backroads.com).

FISHING➤ For boat charters and vacation packages throughout Mexico, contact **Anglers Travel** (✉ 3100 Mill St., No. 206, Reno, NV

89502, ☎ 702/324–0580 or 800/624–8429, FAX 702/324–0583), **Cutting Loose Expeditions** (✉ Box 447, Winter Park, FL 32790-0447, ☎ 407/629–4700 or 800/533–4746), **Fishing International** (✉ Box 2132, Santa Rosa, CA 95405, ☎ 800/950–4242), **Mexico Sportsman** (✉ 202 Milam Bldg., San Antonio, TX 78205, ☎ 210/212–4566 or 800/633–3085, FAX 210/212–4568), and **Rod and Reel Adventures** (✉ 3507 Tully Rd., No. B6, Modesto, CA 95356-1052, ☎ 209/524–7775 or 800/356–6982, FAX 209/524–1220).

GOLF➤ **Stine's Golftrips** (✉ Box 2314, Winter Haven, FL 33883-2314, ☎ 941/324–1300 or 800/428–1940, FAX 941/325–0384, golftrip@cris.com) sells resort-based golf packages that include confirmed tee times and golfing fees and lessons.

NATURAL HISTORY➤ **Earthwatch** (✉ Box 403, 680 Mount Auburn St., Watertown, MA 02272, ☎ 617/926–8200 or 800/776–0188, FAX 617/926–8532, info@earthwatch.org, http://www.earthwatch.org) recruits volunteers to serve in its EarthCorps as short-term assistants to scientists on research expeditions. **Forum Travel International** (✉ 91 Gregory La., No. 21, Pleasant Hill, CA 94523, ☎ 510/671–2900, FAX 510/671–2993) operates wildlife and bird-watching programs in some of Mexico's less visited natural habitats. The **National Audubon Society** (✉ 700 Broad-

way, New York, NY 10003, ☎ 212/979–3066) charters vessels for its natural-history-theme cruises in the Sea of Cortez. **Natural Habitat Adventures** (✉ 2945 Center Green Ct., Boulder, CO 80301, ☎ 303/449–3711 or 800/543–8917, FAX 303/449–3712), **Ocean Voyages** (✉ 1709 Bridgeway, Sausalito, CA 94965, ☎ 415/332–4681, FAX 415/332–7460), **Oceanic Society Expeditions** (✉ Fort Mason Center, Bldg. E, San Francisco, CA 94123-1394, ☎ 415/441–1106 or 800/326–7491, FAX 415/474–3395), and **Pacific Sea-Fari Tours** (✉ 2803 Emerson St., San Diego, CA 92106, ☎ 619/226–8224) run whale-watching expeditions in the Sea of Cortez.

RIVER RAFTING➤ **Far Flung Adventures** (✉ Box 377, Terlingua, TX 79852, ☎ 915/371–2489 or 800/359–4138, FAX 915/371–2325) takes rafters down Rio Usumacinta and Rio Antigua.

SCUBA DIVING➤ Packages are available to Cozumel, Cabo San Lucas, and La Paz. Among the leading dive packagers are **Go Diving** (✉ 5610 Rowland Rd. No. 100, Minnetonka, MN 55343, ☎ 612/931–9101 or 800/328–5285, FAX 612/931–0209), **Rothschild Consultants** (✉ 900 West End Ave., No. 1B, New York, NY 10025-3525, ☎ 212/662–4858 or 800/359–0747, FAX 212/749–6172, rothdive@ix.netcom.com, http://www.empg.com/rothschild), and **Tropical**

Adventures (⊠ 111 2nd Ave. N, Seattle, WA 98109, ☎ 206/441–3483 or 800/247–3483, FAX 206/441–5431).

SPAS➤ **Spa-Finders** (⊠ 91 5th Ave., No. 301, New York, NY 10003-3039, ☎ 212/924–6800 or 800/255–7727) represents several spas in Mexico.

TRAIN TOURS➤ Contact **Mexico by Train** (⊠ Box 2782, Laredo, TX 78044-2782, FAX 210/725–3659 or 800/321–1699) for rail and hotel packages.

VILLA RENTALS➤ Contact **Villas International** (⊠ 605 Market St., San Francisco, CA 94105, ☎ 415/281–0910 or 800/221–2260, FAX 415/281–0919).

WALKING➤ For walking tours of the Baja region try **Backroads** (☞ Bicycling, *above*). To roam the colonial cities of northern Mexico, contact **Butterfield & Robinson** (⊠ 70 Bond St., Toronto, Ontario, Canada M5B 1X3, ☎ 416/864–1354 or 800/678–1147, FAX 416/864–0541, info@butterfield.com). For the Yucatán region contact **Country Walkers** (⊠ Box 180, Waterbury, VT 05676-0180, ☎ 802/244–1387 or 800/464–9255, FAX 802/244–5661).

YACHT CHARTERS➤ **The Moorings** (⊠ 19345 U.S. Hwy. 19 N, 4th floor, Clearwater, FL 34624-3193, ☎ 813/530–5424 or 800/535–7289, FAX 813/530–9474).

ORGANIZATIONS

The **National Tour Association** (⊠ NTA, 546 E. Main St., Lexington, KY 40508, ☎ 606/226–4444 or 800/755–8687) and the **United States Tour Operators Association** (⊠ USTOA, 211 E. 51st St., Suite 12B, New York, NY 10022, ☎ 212/750–7371) can provide lists of members and information on booking tours.

PUBLICATIONS

Contact the USTOA (☞ Organizations, *above*) for its **"Smart Traveler's Planning Kit."** Pamphlets in the kit include the "Worldwide Tour and Vacation Package Finder," "How to Select a Tour or Vacation Package," and information on the organization's consumer protection plan. Also get a copy of the Better Business Bureau's **"Tips on Travel Packages"** (⊠ Publication 24-195, 4200 Wilson Blvd., Arlington, VA 22203; $2).

TRAIN TRAVEL

In general, rail travel in Mexico is slower than and not as comfortable as bus travel, which is recommended for most journeys; the slight savings in price are not worth the extra hassle. The exception is the spectacular train ride through the Copper Canyon (☞ Chapter 5). **Ferrocarriles Nacionales de México** (Mexican National Railways, ☎ 5/547–6593) has information on trains throughout Mexico.

From the United States, you can get information on trains and rail-hotel packages by calling **Mexico by Train** (☎ and FAX 210/725–3659 or 800/321–1699). See also Train Tours *under* Tour Operators, *below*.

On the U.S. side, **Amtrak** (☎ 800/USA–RAIL) will get you only as far as San Antonio; **Greyhound** (☎ 800/231–2222) offers bus service from there to Nuevo Laredo, where you can change for the coach to Monterrey.

TRAVEL GEAR

For travel apparel, appliances, personal-care items, and other travel necessities, get a free catalog from **Magellan's** (☎ 800/962–4943, FAX 805/568–5406), **Orvis Travel** (☎ 800/541–3541, FAX 703/343–7053), or **TravelSmith** (☎ 800/950–1600, FAX 415/455–0554).

TRAVEL AGENCIES

For names of reputable agencies in your area, contact the **American Society of Travel Agents** (⊠ ASTA, 1101 King St., Suite 200, Alexandria, VA 22314, ☎ 703/739–2782), the **Association of Canadian Travel Agents** (⊠ Suite 201, 1729 Bank St., Ottawa, Ontario K1V 7Z5, ☎ 613/521–0474, FAX 613/521–0805) or the **Association of British Travel Agents** (⊠ 55-57 Newman St., London W1P 4AH, ☎ 0171/637–2444, FAX 0171/637–0713).

U

U.S. GOVERNMENT TRAVEL BRIEFINGS

The U.S. Department of State's American Citizens Services office (⊠ Room 4811, Wash-

THE GOLD GUIDE / IMPORTANT CONTACTS

ington, DC 20520; enclose SASE) issues **Consular Information Sheets** on all foreign countries. These cover issues such as crime, security, political climate, and health risks as well as listing embassy locations, entry requirements, currency regulations, and providing other useful information. (Travel warnings that counsel travelers to avoid a country entirely are issued in extreme cases.) For the latest information, stop in at any U.S. passport office, consulate, or embassy; call the interactive hot line (☎ 202/647–5225, FAX 202/647–3000); or, with your PC's modem, tap into the department's computer bulletin board (☎ 202/647–9225).

V

VISITOR INFORMATION

For a current calendar of events, train schedules and fares, brochures, and other general information about travel in Mexico, contact the nearest **Mexican Government Tourism Office (MGTO).** If you're planning to drive into Mexico, contact the **Mexico Surface Tourism Office for U.S. and Canada** (✉ 2707 N. Loop W,

Suite 440, Houston, TX 77008, ☎ 713/880–8772, FAX 713/880–0286).

IN THE U.S.

If there is no MGTO near you, call 800/446–3942.

New York: ✉ 405 Park Ave., Suite 1401, New York, NY 10022, ☎ 212/421–6655 or 212/838–2949, FAX 212/753–2874.

Washington, D.C.: ✉ 1911 Pennsylvania Ave. NW, Washington, DC 20006, ☎ 202/728–1750, FAX 202/728–1758.

Coral Gables: ✉ 128 Aragon Ave., Coral Gables, FL 33134, ☎ 305/443–9160, FAX 305/443–1186.

Chicago: ✉ 70 E. Lake St., Suite 1413, Chicago, IL 60601, ☎ 312/565–2786, FAX 312/606-9012.

Houston: ✉ 2707 N. Loop W, Suite 450, Houston, TX 77008, ☎ 713/880–5153, FAX 713/880–1833.

Los Angeles: ✉ 10100 Santa Monica Blvd., Suite 224, Los Angeles, CA 90067, ☎ 310/203–8191, FAX 310/203–8316.

IN CANADA

Montréal: ✉ 1 Place Ville Marie, Suite 1526, Montréal, Québec H3B 2B5, ☎ 514/871–1052, FAX 514/871–3825

Toronto: ✉ 2 Bloor St. W, Suite 1801, Toronto, Ontario M4W 3E2, ☎ 416/925–0704, FAX 416/925–6061.

Vancouver: ✉ 1610–999 W. Hastings St., Vancouver, British Columbia V6C 2W2, ☎ 604/669–2845, FAX 604/669–3498.

FROM THE U.K.

MGTO (✉ 60 Trafalgar Sq., London WC2N 5DS, ☎ 0171/734–1058, FAX 0171/930–9202).

W

WEATHER

For current conditions and forecasts, plus the local time and helpful travel tips, call the **Weather Channel Connection** (☎ 900/932–8437; 95¢ per minute) from a Touch-Tone phone.

The *International Traveler's Weather Guide* (✉ Weather Press, Box 660606, Sacramento, CA 95866, ☎ 916/974–0201 or 800/972–0201; $10.95 includes shipping), written by two meteorologists, provides month-by-month information on temperature, humidity, and precipitation in more than 175 cities worldwide.

SMART TRAVEL TIPS A TO Z

Basic Information on Traveling in Mexico & Savvy Tips to Make Your Trip a Breeze

The more you travel, the more you know about how to make trips run like clockwork. To help make your travels hassle-free, Fodor's editors have rounded up dozens of tips from our contributors and from travel experts all over the world, as well as basic information on visiting Mexico. For names of organizations to contact and publications that can give you more information, *see* Important Contacts A to Z, *above.*

A
ADDRESSES

The Mexican method of naming streets is exasperatingly arbitrary, so **be patient when searching for street addresses.** Streets in the centers of many colonial cities (those built by the Spaniards) are laid out in a grid surrounding the main square, or *zócalo,* and often change names on different sides of the square; other streets simply acquire a new name after a certain number of blocks. As in the United States, numbered streets are usually designated "north/south" (*norte/sur*) or "east/west" (*oriente/poniente*) on either side of a central avenue. Streets with proper names, however, can change mysteriously from Avenida Juárez, for example, to Calle Francisco Madero; one

has no way of knowing where one begins and the other ends. On the other hand, blocks are often labeled numerically, according to distance from a chosen starting point, as in "1a Calle de Pachuca," "2a Calle de Pachuca," etc.

Many Mexican addresses have "s/n" for *sin número* (no number) after the street name. This is common in small towns where there are fewer buildings on a block. Similarly, many hotels give their address as "Km 30 a Querétaro," which indicates that the property is on the main highway 30 kilometers from Querétaro.

As in Europe, addresses in Mexico are written with the street name first, followed by the street number. The five-digit zip code (*código postal*) precedes, rather than follows, the name of the city. "Apdo." (*apartado*) means "post office box number."

Veteran travelers to Mexico invariably make one observation about asking directions in the country: Rather than say that they do not know, Mexicans tend to offer guidance that may or may not be correct. This is not out of malice, but out of a desire to please. It is impossible to avoid this problem entirely, but one good strategy is, rather than asking "Is the so-

and-so this way?" (which often elicits a smiling affirmative, regardless of the truth of the matter), "Where is the so-and-so?"

AIR TRAVEL

If time is an issue, **always look for nonstop flights,** which require no change of plane. If possible, **avoid connecting flights,** which stop at least once and can involve a change of plane, even though the flight number remains the same; if the first leg is late, the second waits.

CUTTING COSTS

The Sunday travel section of most newspapers is a good place to look for deals.

MAJOR AIRLINES➤ The least-expensive airfares from the major airlines are priced for round-trip travel and are subject to restrictions. Usually, you must **book in advance and buy the ticket within 24 hours** to get cheaper fares, and you may have to **stay over a Saturday night.** The lowest fare is subject to availability, and only a small percentage of the plane's total seats is sold at that price. It's smart to **call a number of airlines, and when you are quoted a good price, book it on the spot**—the same fare may not be available on the same flight the next day. Airlines generally allow you to change your return date for a $25 to $50 fee. If you don't use your ticket, you can apply the cost toward the purchase of a new ticket, again for a small charge. However, most low-fare tickets are nonrefundable. To get the lowest airfare, **check different routings.** If your destination has more than one gateway, **compare prices to different airports.**

FROM THE U.K.➤ To save money on flights, **look into an APEX or Super-Pex ticket.** APEX tickets must be booked in advance and have certain restrictions. Super-PEX tickets can be purchased right at the airport.

CHARTER FLIGHTS➤ Charters usually have the lowest fares and most restrictions. Departures are infrequent and seldom on time, and you can lose all or most of your money if you cancel. (The closer to departure you cancel, the more you lose, although sometimes you can pay only a small fee if you supply a substitute passenger.) The flight may be canceled for any reason up to 10 days before departure (after that, only if it is physically impossible to operate). The charterer may also revise the itinerary or increase the price after you have bought the ticket, but only if the new arrangement constitutes a "major change" do you have the right to a refund. Before buying a charter ticket, **read the fine print** regarding the company's refund policies. Money for charter flights is usually paid into a bank es-

crow account, the name of which should be on the contract, and if you don't pay by credit card, **make your check payable to the carrier's escrow account** (unless you're dealing with a travel agent, in which case his or her check should be made payable to the escrow account). The U.S. Department of Transportation's Aviation Consumer Protection Division has jurisdiction over charters.

Charter operators may offer flights alone or with ground arrangements that constitute a charter package. Normally, you must book charters through a travel agent.

CONSOLIDATORS➤ Consolidators buy tickets for scheduled flights at reduced rates from the airlines, then sell them at prices below the lowest available from the airlines directly—usually without advance restrictions. Sometimes you can even get your money back if you need to return the ticket. Carefully read the fine print detailing penalties for changes and cancellations. If you doubt the reliability of a consolidator, **confirm your reservation with the airline.**

ALOFT

AIRLINE FOOD➤ If you hate airline food, **ask for special meals when booking.** These can be vegetarian, low-cholesterol, or kosher, for example; commonly prepared to order in smaller quantities than standard fare, they can be tastier.

SMOKING➤ Smoking is banned on all flights of less than six hours' duration within the United States and on all Canadian flights; the ban also applies to domestic segments of international flights aboard U.S. and foreign carriers. On U.S. carriers flying to Mexico and other destinations abroad, a seat in a no-smoking section must be provided for every passenger who requests one, and the section must be enlarged to accommodate such passengers as long as they have complied with the airline's deadline for check-in and seat assignment. If smoking bothers you, request a seat far from the smoking section. Delta has banned smoking system-wide, Northwest has banned it on flights to and from Mexico, and Aeromexico has recently designated all flights from Dallas, Atlanta, and Phoenix to Mexico as nonsmoking.

B

BUS TRAVEL

Getting to Mexico by bus is no longer for just the adventurous or budget-conscious. In the past, bus travelers were required to change to Mexican vehicles at the border, and vice versa. Now, however, in an effort to bring more American visitors and their tourist dollars to off-the-beaten-track markets and attractions, the Mexican government has removed this obstacle and a growing number of trans-border bus tours are available.

For travel within Mexico, buses run the gamut from comfortable air-conditioned coaches with bathrooms, televisions, and hostess service (*especial,* deluxe and first-class) to dilapidated "vintage" buses (second- and third-class) on which pigs and chickens travel and stops are made in the middle of nowhere. While a lower-class bus ride can be interesting if you are not in a hurry and want to see the sights and experience the local culture, these fares are only about 10% to 20% lower than those in the premium categories. Therefore, travelers planning a long-distance haul are well advised to **buy the first-class or especial tickets when traveling by bus within Mexico;** unlike tickets for the other classes, these can be reserved in advance.

The Mexican bus network is extensive, far more so than that of the railroads. Buses go where trains do not, service is more frequent, tickets can be purchased on the spot (except during holidays and on long weekends, when advance purchase is crucial), and first-class buses are faster and much more comfortable than trains. **Bring something to eat on all overnight bus rides** in case you don't like the restaurant where the bus stops, and **bring toilet tissue,** as rest rooms vary in cleanliness. Smoking is prohibited on a growing number of Mexican buses, though the rule is occasionally ignored.

In large cities, bus stations are a good distance from the center of town. Though there's a trend toward consolidation, some towns have different stations for each bus line. Bus service in Mexico City is well organized, operating out of four terminals (☞ Bus Travel *in* Important Contacts A to Z, *above*).

BUSINESS HOURS

BANKS

Banks are generally open weekdays 9 AM to 1:30 PM. In some larger cities, a few also open weekdays 4 to 6 PM, Saturday 10 AM to 1:30 PM and 4 to 6 PM, and Sunday 10 AM to 1:30 PM; however, the extended hours are often for deposits only. Banks will give you cash advances in pesos (for a fee) if you have a major credit card.

GOVERNMENT OFFICES

Government offices are usually open 8 AM to 3 PM; along with banks and most private offices, they are closed on national holidays.

MUSEUMS

Along with theaters and most archaeological zones, museums close on Monday, with few exceptions.

STORES

Hours are generally weekdays and Saturday from 9 or 10 AM to 7 or 8 PM; in resort areas, shops may also be open on Sunday. Business hours are 9 AM to 7 PM, with a two-hour lunch break (siesta) from about 2 to 4 PM.

C

CAMERAS, CAMCORDERS, & COMPUTERS

LAPTOPS

Before you depart, **check your portable computer's battery;** at security you may be asked to turn on the computer to prove that it is what it appears to be. At the airport, you may prefer to **request a manual inspection,** although security X-rays do not harm hard-disk or floppy-disk storage. Also, **register your foreign-made laptop with U.S. Customs.** You do not need to register your laptop with local customs upon arrival as long as it is used (i.e. not in its original packaging, ready to be resold) and as long as its value is under $3,000. For more information about restrictions, call the nearest Mexican consulate. You may want to **find out about repair facilities at your destination** in case of problems.

PHOTOGRAPHY

If your camera is new or if you haven't used it for a while, **shoot and develop a few rolls of film** before you leave. Always **store film in a cool, dry place**—never in your car's glove compartment or on the shelf under the rear window.

Select the right film for your purpose—**use print film if you plan to frame or display your pictures,** but **use slide film if you hope to publish your shots.** Also, **consider black-and-white film** for different and dramatic images. For best results, **use a custom lab** for processing; use a one-hour lab only if time is a factor.

The chances of your film growing cloudy increase with each pass through an X-ray machine. To protect against this, carry it in a clear plastic bag and **ask for hand inspection at security.** Such requests are virtually always honored at U.S. airports and are usually accommodated abroad. Don't depend on a lead-lined bag to protect film in checked luggage—the airline may increase the radiation to see what's inside.

Keep a skylight or haze filter on your camera at all times to protect the expensive (and delicate) lens glass from scratches. Better yet, **use an 81B warming filter,** which—unlike skylight or haze filters—really works in overcast conditions and will pump up those sunrises and sunsets.

VIDEO

Before your trip, **test your camcorder, invest in a skylight filter to protect the lens, and charge the batteries.** (Airport security personnel may ask you to turn on the camcorder to prove that it's what it appears to be.)

Videotape is not damaged by X-rays, but it may be harmed by the magnetic field of a walk-through metal detector, so **ask that videotapes be hand-checked.** Prerecorded videotape sold in Mexico is based on the PAL standard, which will not play back in the United States. Blank tapes bought in Mexico can be used for camcorder taping, but they are pricey. Some U.S. audiovisual shops convert foreign tapes to U.S. standards; contact an electronics dealer to find the nearest.

CAR RENTAL

When considering this option, consider that you may be sharing the road with some less-than-ideal drivers (sometimes acquiring a driver's license in Mexico is more a question of paying someone off than of having tested skill). In addition, the highway system is very uneven: In some regions, modern, well-paved superhighways prevail; in others, particularly the mountains, potholes, untethered livestock, and dangerous, unrailed curves are the rule.

CUTTING COSTS

To get the best deal, **book through a travel agent who is willing to shop around.** Ask your agent to **look for fly-drive packages,** which also save you money, and **ask if local taxes are included** in the rental or fly-drive price. These can be as high as 20% in some destinations. Don't forget to find out about required deposits, cancellation penalties, drop-off charges, and the cost of any required insurance coverage.

Also **ask your travel agent about a company's customer-service record.** How has it responded to late plane arrivals and vehicle mishaps? Are there often lines at the rental counter, and—if you're traveling during a holiday period—does a confirmed reservation guarantee you a car?

INSURANCE

When driving a rented car, you are generally responsible for any damage to or loss of the rental vehicle, as well as any property damage or personal injury that you cause. Before you rent, **see what coverage you already have** under the terms of your personal auto insurance policy and credit cards.

If you do not have auto insurance or an umbrella insurance policy that covers damage to third parties, purchasing CDW or LDW is highly recommended.

When you drive in Mexico, it is necessary at all times to **carry proof of Mexican auto liability insurance,** which is usually provided by car-rental agencies and included in the cost of the rental. If you don't have proof of insurance and happen to injure someone—whether it's your fault or not—you stand the risk of being jailed.

LICENSE REQUIREMENTS

In Mexico your own driver's license is acceptable. An International Driver's Permit is a good idea; it's available from the American or Canadian automobile associations, or, in the United Kingdom, from the AA or RAC.

SURCHARGES

Before you pick up a car in one city and leave

it in another, **ask about drop-off charges or one-way service fees,** which can be substantial. Note, too, that some rental agencies charge extra if you return the car before the time specified on your contract. To avoid a hefty refueling fee, **fill the tank just before you turn in the car**—but be aware that gas stations near the rental outlet may overcharge.

CHILDREN & TRAVEL

All children, including infants, must have proof of citizenship for travel to Mexico. Children traveling with a single parent must also have a notarized letter from the other parent stating that the child has his or her permission to leave their home country. In addition, parents must now fill out a tourist card for each child traveling with them.

When traveling with children, **plan ahead** and **involve your youngsters** as you outline your trip. When packing, **include a supply of things to keep them busy** en route (☞ Children & Travel *in* Important Contacts A to Z). On sightseeing days, try to **schedule activities of special interest to your children,** like a trip to a zoo or a playground. If you **plan your itinerary around seasonal festivals,** you'll never lack for things to do. In addition, **check local newspapers for special events** mounted by public libraries, museums, and parks.

BABY-SITTING

For recommended local sitters, **check with your hotel desk.**

DRIVING

If you are renting a car, don't forget to **arrange for a car seat when you reserve.** Sometimes they're free.

FLYING

Always **ask about discounted children's fares.** On international flights, infants under 2 not occupying a seat generally travel free or for 10% of the accompanying adult's fare; the fare for children ages 2–11 is usually half to two-thirds of the adult fare. On domestic flights, children under 2 not occupying a seat travel free, and older children are charged at the lowest applicable adult rate.

BAGGAGE➤ In general, the adult baggage allowance applies to children paying half or more of the adult fare. If you are traveling with an infant, **ask about carry-on allowances** before departure. In general, for infants charged 10% of the adult fare you are allowed one carry-on bag and a collapsible stroller; you may be limited to less if the flight is full.

FACILITIES➤ When making your reservation, **request children's meals or freestanding bassinets** if you need them; the latter are available only to those seated at the bulkhead, where there's enough legroom. If you don't need a bassinet, **think twice before requesting bulkhead seats**—the

only storage space for in-flight necessities is in inconveniently distant overhead bins.

SAFETY SEATS➤ According to the FAA, it's a good idea to **use safety seats aloft** for children weighing less than 40 pounds. Airline policies vary. U.S. carriers allow FAA-approved models but usually require that you buy a ticket, even if your child would otherwise ride free, since the seats must be strapped into regular seats. Foreign carriers may not allow infant seats, may charge a child rather than an infant fare for their use, or may require you to hold your baby during takeoff and landing—defeating the seat's purpose.

LODGING

Most hotels allow children under a certain age to stay in their parents' room at no extra charge; others charge them as extra adults. Be sure to **ask about the cutoff age.**

CRUISES

Cruises that call at ports on the Caribbean coast and Mexican Riviera are available from Miami, Tampa, and Los Angeles. For more information, *see* Important Contacts A to Z, *above.* Some ships also call in Mexico as part of a Panama Canal transit. To get the best deal on a cruise, **consult a cruise-only travel agency.**

CUSTOMS & DUTIES

IN MEXICO

Upon entering Mexico, you will be given a

baggage declaration form and asked to itemize what you're bringing into the country. You are allowed to bring in 2 liters of spirits or wine for personal use; 400 cigarettes, 50 cigars, or 250 grams of tobacco; a reasonable amount of perfume for personal use; one movie camera and one regular camera and 12 rolls of film for each; and gift items not to exceed a total of $300. You are not allowed to bring meat, vegetables, plants, fruit, or flowers into the country.

IN THE U.S.

You may bring home $400 worth of foreign goods duty-free if you've been out of the country for at least 48 hours and haven't already used the $400 allowance, or any part of it, in the past 30 days.

Travelers 21 or older may bring back 1 liter of alcohol duty-free, provided the beverage laws of the state through which they reenter the United States allow it. In addition, regardless of their age, they are allowed 100 non-Cuban cigars and 200 cigarettes. Antiques and works of art more than 100 years old are duty-free.

Duty-free, travelers may mail packages valued at up to $200 to themselves and up to $100 to others, with a limit of one parcel per addressee per day (and no alcohol or tobacco products or perfume valued at more than $5); on the outside, the package should be labeled as being either for personal use or an unsolicited gift, and a list of its contents and their retail value should be attached. Mailed items do not affect your duty-free allowance on your return.

IN CANADA

If you've been out of Canada for at least seven days, you may bring in C$500 worth of goods duty-free. If you've been away for fewer than seven days but for more than 48 hours, the duty-free allowance drops to C$200; if your trip lasts between 24 and 48 hours, the allowance is C$50. You cannot pool allowances with family members. Goods claimed under the C$500 exemption may follow you by mail; those claimed under the lesser exemptions must accompany you.

Alcohol and tobacco products may be included in the seven-day and 48-hour exemptions but not in the 24-hour exemption. If you meet the age requirements of the province or territory through which you reenter Canada, you may bring in, duty-free, 1.14 liters (40 imperial ounces) of wine or liquor *or* 24 12-ounce cans or bottles of beer or ale. If you are 16 or older, you may bring in, duty-free, 200 cigarettes, 50 cigars or cigarillos, and 400 tobacco sticks or 400 grams of manufactured tobacco. Alcohol and tobacco must accompany you on your return.

An unlimited number of gifts with a value of up to C$60 each may be mailed to Canada duty-free. These do not affect your duty-free allowance on your return. Label the package "Unsolicited Gift— Value Under $60." Alcohol and tobacco are excluded.

IN THE U.K.

From countries outside the EU, including Mexico, you may import, duty-free, 200 cigarettes, 100 cigarillos, 50 cigars, or 250 grams of tobacco; 1 liter of spirits or 2 liters of fortified or sparkling wine or liqueurs; 2 liters of still table wine; 60 milliliters of perfume; 250 milliliters of toilet water; plus £136 worth of other goods, including gifts and souvenirs.

D

DINING

Mexican restaurants run the gamut from humble hole-in-the-wall shacks, street stands, *taquerías,* and American-style fast-food joints to internationally acclaimed gourmet restaurants. Prices, naturally, follow suit. To save money, **look for the fixed-menu lunch known as** *comida corrida or menú del día,* which is served between 1 and 4 PM almost everywhere in Mexico.

Lunch is the big meal; dinner is rarely served before 8 PM. There is no government rating of restaurants, but you'll know which ones cater to tourists simply by looking at the clientele and the menu (bilingual menus usually mean slightly higher prices than at nontourist restaurants). Credit cards—especially MasterCard and Visa—are increasingly accepted.

DISABILITIES & ACCESSIBILITY

When discussing accessibility with an operator or reservationist, **ask hard questions.** Are there any stairs, inside *or* out? Are there grab bars next to the toilet *and* in the shower/tub? How wide is the doorway to the room? To the bathroom? For the most extensive facilities, meeting the latest legal specifications, **opt for newer accommodations,** which more often have been designed with access in mind. Older properties or ships must usually be retrofitted and may offer more limited facilities as a result. Be sure to **discuss your needs before booking.**

DISCOUNTS & DEALS

You shouldn't have to pay for a discount. In fact, you may already be eligible for all kinds of savings. Here are some time-honored strategies for getting the best deal.

DIAL FOR DOLLARS

To save money, **look into "1-800" discount reservations services,** which often have lower rates. These services use their buying power to get a better price on hotels, airline tickets, and sometimes even car rentals. When booking a room, always **call the hotel's local toll-free number** (if one is available) rather than the central reservations

number—you'll often get a better price. Ask the reservationist about special packages or corporate rates, which are usually available even if you're not traveling on business.

GET A GUARANTEE

When shopping for the best deal on hotels and car rentals, **look for guaranteed exchange rates,** which protect you against a falling dollar. With your rate locked in, you won't pay more even if the price goes up in the local currency.

JOIN A CLUB?

Discount clubs can be a legitimate source of savings, but you must use the participating hotels and visit the participating attractions in order to realize any benefits. Remember, too, that you have to pay a fee to join, so **determine if you'll save enough to warrant your membership fee.** Before booking with a club, **make sure the hotel or other supplier isn't offering a better deal.**

LOOK IN YOUR WALLET

When you **use your credit card to make travel purchases,** you may get free travel-accident insurance, collision damage insurance, medical or legal assistance, depending on the card and bank that issued it. Visa and MasterCard provide one or more of these services, so **get a copy of your card's travel benefits.** If you are a member of the AAA or an oil-company-sponsored road-assistance plan, always **ask hotel or car-**

rental reservationists for auto-club discounts. Some clubs offer additional discounts on tours, cruises, or admission to attractions. And don't forget that auto-club membership entitles you to free maps and trip-planning services.

SENIORS CITIZENS & STUDENTS

As a senior-citizen traveler, you may be eligible for special rates, but you should mention your senior-citizen status up front. If you're a student or under 26 you can also get discounts, especially if you have an official ID card (☞ Senior-Citizen Discounts *and* Students on the Road, *below*).

DRIVING

There are two absolutely essential things to remember about driving in Mexico. First and foremost is to **carry Mexican auto insurance,** which can be purchased near border crossings on either the U.S. or Mexican side. If you injure anyone in an accident, you could well be jailed—whether it was your fault or not—unless you have insurance. Guilty until proven innocent is part of the country's Code Napoléon. **Purchase enough Mexican automobile insurance at the border to cover your estimated trip.** It's sold by the day, and if your trip is shorter than your original estimate, some companies may issue a pro-rated refund for the unused time upon application after you exit the country.

The second item is that **if you enter Mexico with**

a car, you must leave with it. In recent years, the high rate of U.S. vehicles being sold illegally in Mexico has caused the Mexican government to enact stringent regulations for bringing a car into the country—at great inconvenience to motoring American tourists. In order to drive into the country, you must cross the border with the following documents: Title or registration for your vehicle; a birth certificate or passport; a credit card (AE, DC, MC, or V); a valid driver's license with a photo. The title holder, driver, and credit card owner must be one and the same—that is, if your spouse's name is on the title of the car and yours isn't, you cannot be the one to bring the car into the country. For financed cars, leased cars, rental cars, or company cars, a notarized letter of permission from the bank, lien holder, rental agency, or company is required.

When you submit your paperwork at the border and pay a $12 charge on your credit card, you will receive a tourist visa, a car permit, and a sticker to put on your vehicle, all valid for six months. Be sure to turn in the permit and the sticker at the border prior to their expiration date; otherwise you could incur high fines.

One alternative to going through this hassle when you cross is to **have your paperwork done in advance** at a branch of Sanborn's Mexican Insurance; look in the Yellow Pages for an office in almost every town on the U.S.–Mexico border. You'll still have to go through some of the procedures at the border, but all your paperwork will be in order and Sanborn's express window will ensure that you get through relatively quickly. For this service Sanborn's charges $10 to those who buy insurance through the company, $25 to those who don't. The fact that you drove in with a car is stamped on your tourist card, which you must give to immigration authorities at departure. If an emergency arises and you must fly home, there are complicated customs procedures to face.

For day trips and local sightseeing, engaging a car and driver (who often acts as a guide) for a day can be a hassle-free, more economical way to travel than renting a car and driving yourself. Hotel desks will know which taxi companies to call, and you can negotiate a price with the driver.

ROAD AND TRAFFIC CONDITIONS

There are several well-kept toll roads in Mexico—primarily of the two-lane variety—covering mostly the last stretches of major highways (*carreteras*) leading to the capital. (*Cuota* means toll road; *libre* means no toll, and such roads are usually not as smooth.) Some excellent new roads have recently opened, making car travel safer and faster. These include highways connecting Acapulco and Mexico City; Oaxaca and Mexico City; Cancún and Mérida; Nogales and Mazatlán; León and Aguascalientes; Guadalajara and Tepic; Puebla, Tehuacán, and Oaxaca; and Nuevo Laredo and Monterrey. However, tolls as high as 40¢ per mile can make using these thoroughfares prohibitively expensive. Approaches to most of the large cities are also in good condition, and the government-sponsored Northern Border Program is cleaning up some of the ubiquitous potholes.

In rural areas, roads are quite poor: **Use caution, especially during the rainy season,** when rock slides are a problem. Driving in Mexico's central highlands may also necessitate adjustments to your carburetor. Generally, driving times are longer than for comparable distances in the United States. *Topes* (road cops, or bumps) are also common; it's best to slow down when approaching a village.

Driving at night is not recommended and should be avoided especially in remote and rural areas because of free-roaming livestock, the difficulty of getting assistance, and the risk of banditry. The last can occur anywhere, though the coast road between Manzanillo and Playa Azul is reported to be particularly risky at present. Common sense goes a long way: If you have a long distance to cover, **start early and fill up on gas;** don't let your tank get below half-full. Allow extra time for unforeseen occurrences as well as for the trucks that seem to be everywhere. By day, **be alert to animals,** especially cattle and dogs. (The number of dead dogs lying beside—and in the middle of—Mexican highways is appalling.)

Traffic can be horrendous in the cities, particularly in Mexico City. As you would in metropolitan areas anywhere, **avoid rush hour** (7–9 AM and 5–7 PM) and lunchtime (1–3 PM). Signage is not always adequate in Mexico, so if you are not sure where you are going, **travel with a companion and a good map.** Always lock your car, and never leave valuable items in the body of the car (the trunk will suffice for daytime outings).

The Mexican Tourism Ministry distributes free road maps from its tourism offices outside the country. *Guía Roji* and PEMEX (the government petroleum monopoly) publish current city, regional, and national road maps, which are available in bookstores; gas stations generally do not carry maps.

RULES AND SAFETY REGULATIONS

Illegally parked cars are either towed or their license plates removed, which requires a trip to the traffic police headquarters for payment of a fine. When in doubt, **park in a lot instead of**

on the street; your car will probably be safer there, anyway.

If an oncoming vehicle flicks its lights at you in daytime, slow down: It could mean trouble ahead. When approaching a narrow bridge, the first vehicle to flash its lights has right of way. One-way streets are common. One-way traffic is indicated by an arrow; two-way, by a two-pointed arrow. A circle with a diagonal line superimposed on the letter *E* (for *estacionamiento*) means "no parking." Other road signs follow the now widespread system of international symbols, a copy of which will usually be provided when you rent a car in Mexico.

In Mexico City, watch out for *"Hoy no Circula"* notices. Because of pollution, all cars in the city are prohibited from driving one day a week. Posted signs show certain letters or numbers paired with each day of the week, indicating that vehicles with those letters or numbers in their license plates are not allowed to drive on the corresponding day. Foreigners are not exempt.

SPEED LIMITS➤ Mileage and speed limits are given in kilometers: 100 kph and 80 kph (62 and 50 mph, respectively) are the most common maximums. A few of the newer toll roads allow 110 kph (68.4 mph). In cities and small towns, **observe the posted speed limits,** which can be as low as 20 kph (12 mph).

NATIONAL ROAD EMERGENCY SERVICES➤ To help motorists on major highways, the Mexican Tourism Ministry operates a fleet of more than 275 pickup trucks, known as the *Angeles Verdes,* or Green Angels. The bilingual drivers provide mechanical help, first aid, radio-telephone communication, basic supplies and small parts, towing, tourist information, and protection. Services are free, and spare parts, fuel, and lubricants are provided at cost. Tips are always appreciated (figure $5 to $10 for big jobs, $1 to $2 for minor repairs).

The Green Angels patrol fixed sections of the major highways twice daily from 8 AM to 8 PM (later on holiday weekends). If you break down, pull off the road as far as possible, lift the hood of your car, hail a passing vehicle, and ask the driver to notify the patrol. Most bus and truck drivers will be quite helpful. To reach the local Green Angels, call their toll-free hot line at ☎ 91/800/903–0092. In Mexico City, the number is ☎ 5/250–8221.

If you witness an accident, do not stop to help but instead locate the nearest official.

FUEL AVAILABILITY AND COSTS

PEMEX franchises all the gas stations in Mexico. Stations are located at most road junctions, cities, and towns but generally do not accept U.S. credit cards or dollars. Fuel prices are the same at all stations (except near the U.S. border, where they are a bit lower) and run slightly higher than in the United States. Unleaded gas—called Magna Sin—is now available nationwide, but it's still a good idea to fill up whenever you can. Fuel quality is generally lower than that in the United States and Europe. Vehicles with fuel-injected engines are likely to have problems after extended driving.

At the gas stations, keep a close eye on the attendants, and if possible, avoid the rest rooms: They're generally filthy.

G

GAY & LESBIAN TRAVEL

Same-sex couples keep a low profile in Mexico, and two people of the same gender can often have a hard time getting a *cama matrimonial* (double bed), especially in smaller hotels. This could be attributed to the influence of the Catholic Church—Mexico is a devoutly Catholic country and the Church has historically exerted a powerful influence on both Mexican politics and the mores and attitudes of the Mexican people. However, the same rule that applies all over the world holds in Mexico as well: Alternative lifestyles (whether they be homosexuality or any other bending of conventional roles) are more easily accepted in metropolitan centers such as Acapulco, Guadalajara, and Mexico City.

H

HEALTH CONCERNS

AIR POLLUTION

The air pollution in Mexico City can pose a health risk. The sheer number of people in the capital, thermal inversions, and the inability to process sewage have all contributed to the high levels of lead, carbon monoxide, and other pollutants in the atmosphere in Mexico City. Though the long-term effects are not known, children, the elderly, and those with respiratory problems are advised to avoid jogging, participating in outdoor sports, and being outdoors more than necessary.

SHOTS AND MEDICATIONS

According to the Centers for Disease Control and Prevention (CDC), there is a limited risk of malaria and dengue fever in certain rural areas of Mexico. Travelers in most urban or easily accessible areas need not worry. However, if you plan to visit remote regions or stay for more than six weeks, **check with the CDC's International Travelers Hotline.** In areas with malaria and dengue, which are both carried by mosquitoes, take mosquito nets, wear clothing that covers the body, apply repellent containing DEET, and use a spray against flying insects in living and sleeping areas. The hot line recommends chloroquine (analen) as an antimalarial agent; no vaccine exists against dengue.

The major health risk in Mexico is posed by the contamination of drinking water, fresh fruit, and vegetables by fecal matter, which causes the intestinal ailment known as traveler's diarrhea. To prevent it, **watch what you eat and drink.** Stay away from uncooked food and unpasteurized milk and milk products, and **drink only bottled water or water that has been boiled** for at least 20 minutes. When ordering cold drinks at untouristed establishments, skip the ice: *sin hielo.* (You can usually identify ice made commercially from purified water by its uniform shape and the hole in the center.) Hotels with water purification systems will post signs to that effect in the rooms. *Tacos al pastor*—thin pork slices grilled on a spit and garnished with the usual cilantro, onions, and chile—are delicious but dangerous. Be wary of Mexican hamburgers, because you can never be certain what meat they are made with (horsemeat is very common).

If these measures fail, try paregoric, a good antidiarrheal agent that dulls or eliminates abdominal cramps, which requires a doctor's prescription in Mexico; or in mild cases, Pepto-Bismol or Imodium (loperamide), which can be purchased over the counter. Get plenty of purified water or tea—chamomile is a good folk remedy for diarrhea. In severe cases, rehydrate yourself with a salt-sugar solution (½ tsp. salt and 4 Tbsp. sugar per quart/liter of water).

SUN BURN

Caution is advised when venturing out in the Mexican sun. Sunbathers lulled by a slightly overcast sky or the sea breezes can be burned badly in just 20 minutes. To avoid overexposure, **use strong sunscreens and avoid the peak sun hours** of noon to 2 PM.

DIVERS' ALERT

Scuba divers take note: **Do not fly within 24 hours of scuba diving.**

I

INSURANCE

Travel insurance can protect your monetary investment, replace your luggage and its contents, or provide for medical coverage should you fall ill during your trip. Most tour operators, travel agents, and insurance agents sell specialized health-and-accident, flight, trip-cancellation, and luggage insurance as well as comprehensive policies with some or all of these coverages. Comprehensive policies may also reimburse you for delays due to weather—an important consideration if you're traveling during the winter months. Some health-insurance policies do not cover preexisting conditions, but waivers may be available in specific cases. Coverage is sold by the companies listed in Important Contacts A to Z; these companies act as the

policy's administrators. The actual insurance is usually underwritten by a well-known name, such as the Travelers or Continental Insurance.

Before you make any purchase, **review your existing health and homeowner's policies** to find out whether they cover expenses incurred while traveling.

BAGGAGE

Airline liability for baggage is limited to $1,250 per person on domestic flights. On international flights, it amounts to $9.07 per pound or $20 per kilogram for checked baggage (roughly $640 per 70-pound bag) and $400 per passenger for unchecked baggage. Insurance for losses exceeding the terms of your airline ticket can be bought directly from the airline at check-in for about $10 per $1,000 of coverage; note that it excludes a rather extensive list of items, shown on your airline ticket.

COMPREHENSIVE

Comprehensive insurance policies include all the coverages described above plus some that may not be available in more specific policies. If you have purchased an expensive vacation, especially one that involves travel abroad, comprehensive insurance is a must; **look for policies that include trip delay insurance,** which will protect you in the event that weather problems cause you to miss your flight, tour, or cruise. A few insurers will also sell you a waiver for preexisting

medical conditions. Some of the companies that offer both these features are Access America, Carefree Travel, Travel Insured International, and TravelGuard (☞ Important Contacts A to Z).

FLIGHT

You should **think twice before buying flight insurance.** Often purchased as a last-minute impulse at the airport, it pays a lump sum when a plane crashes, either to a beneficiary if the insured dies or sometimes to a surviving passenger who loses his or her eyesight or a limb. Supplementing the airlines' coverage described in the limits-of-liability paragraphs on your ticket, it's expensive and basically unnecessary. Charging an airline ticket to a major credit card often automatically provides you with coverage that may also extend to travel by bus, train, and ship.

HEALTH

Medicare generally does not cover health care costs outside the United States; nor do many privately issued policies. If your own health insurance policy does not cover you outside the United States, **consider buying supplemental medical coverage.** It can reimburse you for $1,000–$150,000 worth of medical and/or dental expenses incurred as a result of an accident or illness during a trip. These policies also may include a personal-accident, or death-and-dismemberment, provision, which pays a lump sum ranging from $15,000 to $500,000 to your beneficiaries if you die or to you if you lose one or more limbs or your eyesight, and a medical-assistance provision, which may either reimburse you for the cost of referrals, evacuation, or repatriation and other services, or automatically enroll you as a member of a particular medical-assistance company. (☞ Health Issues *in* Important Contacts A to Z.)

U.K. TRAVELERS

You can buy an annual travel insurance policy valid for most vacations during the year in which it's purchased. If you are pregnant or have a preexisting medical condition make sure you're covered before buying such a policy.

TRIP

Without insurance, you will lose all or most of your money if you cancel your trip regardless of the reason. Especially if your airline ticket, cruise, or package tour is nonrefundable and cannot be changed, it's essential that you **buy trip-cancellation-and-interruption insurance.** When considering how much coverage you need, look for a policy that will cover the cost of your trip plus the nondiscounted price of a one-way airline ticket should you need to return home early. Read the fine print carefully, especially sections that define "family member" and

"preexisting medical conditions." Also **consider default or bankruptcy insurance,** which protects you against a supplier's failure to deliver. Be aware, however, that if you buy such a policy from a travel agency, tour operator, airline, or cruise line, it may not cover default by the firm in question.

L

LANGUAGE

Spanish is the official language of Mexico, although Indian languages are spoken by approximately 20% of the population, many of whom speak no Spanish at all. Basic English is widely understood by most people employed in tourism, less so in the less developed areas. At the very least, shopkeepers will know the numbers for bargaining purposes.

As in most other foreign countries, knowing the mother tongue has a way of opening doors, so **learn some Spanish words and phrases.** Mexicans are not scornful of visitors' mispronunciations and grammatical errors; on the contrary, they welcome even the most halting attempts to use their language.

The Spanish most Americans learn in high school is based on Castilian Spanish, which is different from Latin American Spanish. Not only are there differences in pronunciation and grammar but also in vocabulary: Words or phrases that

are harmless or everyday in one country can take on offensive meanings in another. Unless you are lucky enough to be briefed on these nuances by a native coach, the only way to learn is by trial and error.

LANGUAGE PROGRAMS

Attending a language institute is an ideal way not only to learn Mexican Spanish but also to acquaint yourself with the customs and the people of the country. For total immersion, most language schools offer boarding with a Mexican family, but your choice of lodgings and of length of stay is generally flexible (☞ Language Institutes *in* Important Contacts A to Z, *above*).

LODGING

The price and quality of accommodations in Mexico vary about as much as the country's restaurants, from superluxurious, international-class hotels and all-inclusive resorts to modest budget properties, seedy places with shared bathrooms, *casas de huéspedes* (guest houses), youth hostels, and *cabañas* (beach huts). You may find appealing bargains while you're on the road, but if your comfort level is high, **look for an English-speaking staff, guaranteed dollar rates, and toll-free reservation numbers in the United States.**

Hotel rates are subject to the 10% value-added tax, and service charges and meals are generally not included. The Mexican government categorizes hotels, based on qualitative evaluations, into *gran turismo* (superdeluxe hotels, of which there are only about 50 nationwide); five-star down to one-star; and economy class. Keep in mind that many hotels that might otherwise be rated higher have opted for a lower category to avoid higher interest rates on loans and financing.

High- versus low-season rates can vary significantly (*see* When to Go, *below*). Hotels in this guide have air-conditioning and private bathrooms with showers, unless stated otherwise, but bathtubs are not common in inexpensive hotels and properties in smaller towns.

Mexican hotels—particularly those owned or managed by the international chains—are always being expanded. In older properties, travelers may often have to choose between newer annexes with modern amenities and rooms in the original buildings with possibly fewer amenities and—equally possible, but not certain—greater charm.

It's essential to **reserve in advance** if you are traveling during high season or holiday periods. Overbooking is a common practice in some parts of Mexico, such as Cancún. Travelers to remote areas will encounter little difficulty in obtaining rooms on a "walk-in" basis.

One last note of advice: If you are particularly sensitive to noise, you should **call ahead to learn if your hotel of choice is located on a busy street.** Many of the most engaging accommodations in Mexico are on downtown intersections that experience heavy automobile and pedestrian traffic. And large hotels are known to feature lobby bars with live music in the middle of an open-air atrium leading directly to rooms. When you book, **request a room far from the bar.**

APARTMENT & VILLA RENTAL

If you want a home base that's roomy enough for a family and comes with cooking facilities, **consider taking a furnished rental.** This can also save you money, but not always—some rentals are luxury properties (economical only when your party is large). Home-exchange directories list rentals—often second homes owned by prospective house swappers—and some services search for a house or apartment for you (even a castle if that's your fancy) and handle the paperwork. Some send an illustrated catalog; others send photographs only of specific properties, sometimes at a charge; up-front registration fees may apply.

HOME EXCHANGE

If you would like to find a house, an apartment, or some other type of vacation property to exchange for your own while on holiday, **become a member of a home-exchange organization,** which will send you its updated listings of available exchanges for a year and will include your own listing in at least one of them. Arrangements for the actual exchange are made by the two parties involved, not by the organization.

M
MAIL

The Mexican postal system is notoriously slow and unreliable; **never send packages** or expect to receive them, as they may be stolen (for emergencies, use a courier service or the new express-mail service, with insurance). There are post offices (*oficinas de correos*) even in the smallest villages, and numerous branches in the larger cities. Always **use airmail for overseas correspondence;** it will take anywhere from 10 days to two weeks or more, where surface mail might take three weeks to arrive. Service within Mexico can be equally slow. It costs NP$2 to send a postcard or letter weighing under 20 grams to the United States, Canada, or Great Britain.

RECEIVING MAIL

To receive mail in Mexico, you can have it sent to your hotel or use *poste restante* at the post office. In the latter case, include the words "a/c Lista de Correos" (general delivery), followed by the city, state, postal code, and country. A list of names for whom mail has been received is posted and updated daily by the post office. American Express card members can have mail sent to them at the local American Express office. For a list of locations, ask for a copy of *Traveler's Companion* at any American Express office; or write to American Express (✉ Box 678, Canal Street Station, New York, NY 10013).

MEDICAL ASSISTANCE

No one plans to get sick while traveling, but it happens, so **consider signing up with a medical assistance company.** These outfits provide referrals, emergency evacuation or repatriation, 24-hour telephone hot lines for medical consultation, cash for emergencies, and other personal and legal assistance. They also dispatch medical personnel and arrange for the relay of medical records.

MONEY & EXPENSES

As of January 1, 1993, the unit of currency in Mexico became the *nuevo peso,* or new peso, which is subdivided into 100 centavos. At press time, the peso was still recovering from the devaluation enacted by the Zedillo administration. While exchange rates were as favorable as one U.S. dollar to NP$7.50, one Canadian dollar to NP$5.5, and a pound sterling to 11.4, the market and prices are likely to continue to adjust.

You might still encounter some of the old currency in rural areas, where not all the public phones and vending machines have been converted, but for the most part the transition has been complete. The new paper currency differs in design and, in some cases, size, from the old and comes in denominations of 10, 20, 50, 100, 200, and 500. The new 10-, 20-, 50-, and 100-peso bills are equal to the old 10,000, 20,000, 50,000 and 100,000 notes, respectively. Newly introduced were the 2-, 5-, 10-, and 20-peso coins. The 1,000-, 500-, 200-, 100-, and 50-peso coins were replaced by the smaller, newly designed 1-peso and 50-, 20-, 10-, and 5-centavo coins. "Nuevos Pesos" appears on all new bills printed before 1996, at which point the marking was dropped. Travelers should **examine coins carefully before paying and when receiving change.** Note: NP$ generally precedes prices in new pesos. To avoid fraud, it's wise to make sure that "NP" is clearly marked on all credit-card receipts.

Dollars are widely accepted in many parts of Mexico, particularly near the border and in Cancún and Cozumel. Many tourist shops and market vendors, as well as virtually all hotel service personnel, take them, too.

Traveler's checks and all major U.S. credit cards (except Discover) are accepted in most tourist areas of Mexico. The large hotels, restaurants, and department stores accept cards readily. Some of the smaller restaurants and shops, however, will only take cash. Credit cards are generally not accepted in small towns and villages, except in tourist-oriented hotels. When shopping, you can usually get much better prices if you **bargain with dollars.**

ATMS

CASH ADVANCES➤ Cirrus, Plus, and many other networks that connect automated teller machines operate internationally. Chances are that you can **use your bank card, MasterCard, or Visa at ATMs** to withdraw money from an account or get a cash advance. Before leaving home, **check on frequency limits** for withdrawals and cash advances. Also **ask whether your card's PIN must be reprogrammed** for use in Mexico. Four-digit numbers are commonly used overseas. Note that Discover is not accepted in Mexico.

TRANSACTION FEES➤ On credit-card cash advances you are charged interest from the day you receive the money, whether from a teller or an ATM. Although fees charged for ATM transactions may be higher abroad than at home, Cirrus and Plus exchange rates are excellent, because they are based on wholesale rates offered only by major banks.

COSTS

Mexico has a reputation for being inexpensive, particularly compared with other North American vacation spots such as the Caribbean; the devaluation of the peso, started in late 1994, has made this particularly true, though prices of the large chain hotels, calculated in dollars, have not gone down, and some restaurant owners and merchants have raised their prices to compensate for the devaluation. In general, costs will vary with the when, where, and how of your travel in Mexico. "When" is discussed in When to Go, *below*. As to "how," tourists seeking a destination as much as possible like home, who travel only by air or package tour, stay at international hotel chain properties, eat at restaurants catering to tourists, and shop at fixed-price tourist-oriented malls may not find Mexico such a bargain. Anyone who wants a closer look at the country and is not wedded to standardized creature comforts can spend as little as $35 a day on room, board, and local transportation. Speaking Spanish is also helpful in bargaining situations and when asking for dining recommendations. As a rule, the less English is spoken in a region, the cheaper things will be.

Cancún, Puerto Vallarta, Mexico City, Acapulco, Ixtapa, southern Baja California, and to a lesser extent Mazatlán, Manzanillo, and Huatulco are the most expensive places to visit in Mexico. Taxis are supposed to charge fixed rates to and from the airport and between hotels and beaches or downtown, but be sure to **agree upon a price before hiring a cab.** Water sports can cost as much as they do in the Caribbean islands. All the beach towns, however, offer budget accommodations, and the smaller, less accessible ones are often more moderately priced, examples being the Gulf coast and northern Yucatán, parts of Quintana Roo, Puerto Escondido and the smaller Oaxacan coastal towns as well as those of Chiapas.

Average costs in the major cities vary, although less than in the past because of the increase in business travelers. A stay in one of Mexico City's top hotels can cost more than $200 (as much or more than at the coastal resorts), but meal prices have gone down with the devaluation of the peso; you can get away with a tab of $45 for two at what was once an expensive restaurant.

Probably the best value for your travel dollar is found in the smaller inland towns, such as San Cristóbal de las Casas, Mérida, Morelia, Guanajuato, and Oaxaca, where tourism is less developed. Although Oaxaca lodging can run more than $150 a night, simple colonial-style hotels with adequate accommodations for under $40 can be found these days, and tasty, filling meals are rarely more than $15.

EXCHANGING CURRENCY

For the most favorable rates, **change money at banks.** You won't do as well at exchange booths in airports or rail and bus stations, which charge large commissions. Sometimes you'll find, however, that hotels offer only slightly less favorable exchange rates, which are compensated for by the convenience of not having to negotiate complicated bank procedures. To avoid lines at airport exchange booths, **get a small amount of the local currency before you leave home.**

TAXES

AIRPORT➤ An airport departure tax of U.S. $12 or the peso equivalent must be paid at the airport for international flights from Mexico, and there is a domestic air departure tax of around U.S. $6. Traveler's checks and credit cards are not accepted.

VAT➤ Mexico has a value-added tax of 10% called I.V.A. (*impuesto de valor agregado*), which is occasionally (and illegally) waived for cash purchases. Other taxes and charges apply for phone calls, dining, and lodging.

TRAVELER'S CHECKS

Whether or not to buy traveler's checks depends on where you are headed; **take cash to rural areas and small towns, traveler's checks to cities.** The most widely recognized checks are issued by American Express, Citicorp, Thomas Cook, and Visa. These are sold by major commercial banks for 1%–3% of the checks' face value—it pays to

shop around. Both American Express and Thomas Cook issue checks that can be countersigned and used by either you or your traveling companion. So you won't be left with excess foreign currency, **buy a few checks in small denominations** to cash toward the end of your trip. Before leaving home, **contact your issuer for information on where to cash your checks** without a incurring a transaction fee. Record the numbers of all your checks, and keep this listing in a separate place, crossing off the numbers of checks you have cashed.

WIRING MONEY

For a fee of 3%–10%, depending on the amount of the transaction, you can have money sent to you from home through Money-Gram℠ or Western Union (☞ Money Matters *in* Important Contacts A to Z). The transferred funds and the service fee can be charged to a Master-Card or Visa account.

P
PACKING FOR MEXICO

Pack light: Though baggage carts are available now at airports, luggage restrictions on international flights are tight, and you'll want to save space for purchases. Mexico is filled with bargains on textiles, leather goods, arts and crafts, and silver jewelry.

What clothing you bring depends on your destination. For the resorts, bring lightweight sports clothes, bathing suits, and cover-ups for the beach. Bathing suits and immodest clothing are inappropriate for shopping and sightseeing, both in cities and beach resorts. Mexico City is a bit more formal than the resorts and, because of its high elevation, cooler. Men will want to bring lightweight suits or slacks and blazers for fancier restaurants; and women should pack tailored dresses. Many restaurants require jacket and tie. Jeans are acceptable for shopping and sightseeing, but shorts are frowned upon for men and women. You'll need a lightweight topcoat for winter and an all-weather coat and umbrella in case of sudden summer rainstorms.

Resorts, such as Cancún and Acapulco, are both casual and elegant; you'll see high-style designer sportswear, tie-dyed T-shirts, cotton slacks and walking shorts, and plenty of colorful sundresses. The sun can be fierce; **bring a sun hat (or buy one locally) and sunscreen for the beach and for sightseeing.** You'll need a sweater or jacket to cope with hotel and restaurant air-conditioning, which can be glacial. Few restaurants require a jacket and tie.

Bring an extra pair of eyeglasses or contact lenses in your carry-on luggage, and if you have a health problem, **pack enough medication** to last the trip or have your doctor write you a prescription using the drug's generic name, because brand names vary from country to country (you'll then need a duplicate prescription from a local doctor). It's important that you **don't put prescription drugs or valuables in luggage to be checked,** for it could go astray. To avoid problems with customs officials, carry medications in the original packaging. Also, don't forget the addresses of offices that handle refunds of lost traveler's checks.

TRAVEL GEAR

Travel catalogs specialize in useful items that can **save space when packing** and make life on the road more convenient. Compact alarm clocks, travel irons, travel wallets, and personal-care kits are among the most common items you'll find. They also carry dual-voltage appliances, currency converters and foreign-language phrase books. Some catalogs even carry miniature coffeemakers and water purifiers.

ELECTRICITY

Electrical converters are not necessary because Mexico operates on the 60-cycle, 120-volt system; however, many Mexican outlets have not been updated to accommodate three-prong and polarized plugs (those with one larger prong), so you may need an adapter. Hotels sometimes have 110-volt outlets for low-wattage appliances marked "For Shavers Only" near the sink; don't use them for high-wattage appliances like blow-dryers.

LUGGAGE

Airline baggage allowances depend on the airline, the route, and the class of your ticket; ask in advance. In general, on domestic flights and on international flights between the United States and foreign destinations, you are entitled to check two bags. A third piece may be brought on board, but it must fit easily under the seat in front of you or in the overhead compartment. In the United States, the FAA gives airlines broad latitude regarding carry-on allowances, and they tend to tailor them to different aircraft and operational conditions. Charges for excess, oversize, or overweight pieces vary.

If you are flying between two foreign destinations, note that baggage allowances may be determined not by piece but by weight—generally 88 pounds (40 kilograms) in first class, 66 pounds (30 kilograms) in business class, and 44 pounds (20 kilograms) in economy. If your flight between two cities abroad *connects* with your transatlantic or transpacific flight, the piece method still applies.

SAFEGUARDING YOUR LUGGAGE➤ Before leaving home, **itemize your bags' contents** and their worth, and label them with your name, address, and phone number. (If you use your home address, cover it so that potential thieves can't see it readily.) Inside each bag, **pack a copy of your itinerary.** At check-in, **make sure that each bag is correctly tagged** with the destination airport's three-letter code. If your bags arrive damaged—or fail to arrive at all—file a written report with the airline before leaving the airport.

PASSPORTS & VISAS

If you don't already have one, **get a passport.** It is advisable that you **leave one photocopy of your passport's data page** with someone at home and keep another with you, separated from your passport, while traveling. If you lose your passport, promptly call the nearest embassy or consulate and the local police; having the data page information can speed replacement.

IN THE U.S.

For short stays, any proof of citizenship is sufficient for entry into Mexico. Minors also need parental permission. All U.S. citizens, even infants, need a valid passport or a certified birth certificate, notarized affidavit of citizenship, or voter's registration card, plus a photo I.D. to enter Mexico for stays of more than 180 days. Application forms for both first-time and renewal passports are available at any of the 13 U.S. Passport Agency offices and at some post offices and courthouses. Passports are usually mailed within four weeks; allow five weeks or more in spring and summer.

CANADIANS

You need only a valid passport to enter Mexico for stays of up to six months. Passport application forms are available at 28 regional passport offices, as well as post offices and travel agencies. Whether for a first or a renewal passport, you must apply in person. Children under 16 may be included on a parent's passport but must have their own to travel alone. Passports are valid for five years and are usually mailed within two to three weeks of application.

U.K. CITIZENS

Citizens of the United Kingdom need only a valid passport to enter Mexico for stays of up to three months. Applications for new and renewal passports are available from main post offices and at the passport offices in Belfast, Glasgow, Liverpool, London, Newport, and Peterborough. You may apply in person at all passport offices, or by mail to all except the London office. Children under 16 may travel on an accompanying parent's passport. All passports are valid for 10 years. Allow a month for processing.

PERSONAL SECURITY & COMFORT

Many Americans are aware of Mexico's reputation for corruption. The patronage system is a well-entrenched part of Mexican politics and industry, and workers in the public sector—

notably policemen and customs officials—are notoriously underpaid. Everyone has heard, at least secondhand, a horror story about highway assaults, pickpocketing, bribes, or foreigners (not to mention the Mexicans themselves) languishing in Mexican jails.

Just as you would anywhere, **use common sense.** Wear a money belt; put valuables in hotel safes; avoid driving on untraveled streets and roads at night; and carry your own baggage whenever possible. Reporting a crime to the police is often a frustrating experience unless you speak excellent Spanish and have a great deal of patience.

Women traveling alone are likely to be subjected to *piropos* (catcalls). To avoid this, try not to wear tight clothes or enter street bars or cantinas alone. Your best strategy is always to try and ignore the offender and go on about your business. If the situation seems to be getting out of hand, do not hesitate to ask someone for help. *Piropos* are one thing, but outright harassment of women is not considered acceptable behavior. If you express outrage, you should find no shortage of willing defenders.

S

SENIOR-CITIZEN DISCOUNTS

To qualify for age-related discounts, **mention your senior-citizen status up front**

when booking hotel reservations, not when checking out, and before you're seated in restaurants, not when paying the bill. Note that discounts may be limited to certain menus, days, or hours. When renting a car, **ask about promotional car-rental discounts**—they can net even lower costs than your senior-citizen discount.

SHOPPING

At least three varieties of outlets sell Mexican crafts: indoor and outdoor municipal markets, shops run by Fonart (a government agency to promote Mexican crafts), and tourist boutiques in towns, shopping malls, and hotels. If you **buy in the municipal shops or markets** you can avoid the VAT, and you'll be able to pay in pesos or dollars. You'll have to have patience and a good eye here: Bargains are to be had, but quality may be inconsistent. Fonart shops are a good reference for quality and price (the latter are fixed). Boutiques usually accept credit cards if not dollars; although they are overpriced, they are also convenient. (You may be asked to pay up to 10% more on credit card purchases; savvy shoppers with cash have greater bargaining clout.) The 10% tax (I.V.A.) is charged on most purchases but is often disregarded by eager or desperate vendors.

It is not always true that the closer you are to the source of an

article, the better the selection and price are likely to be. Mexico City, Oaxaca, and San Miguel de Allende have some of the best selections of crafts from around the country, and if you know where to go, you will find bargains. Prices are usually higher at beach resorts.

Bargaining is widely accepted in the markets, but you should understand that not all vendors will start out with outrageous prices. If you feel the price quoted is too high, start off by offering no more than half the asking price and then slowly go up, usually to about 70% of the original price. Always shop around. In major shopping areas like San Miguel, shops will wrap and send purchases back to the United States via a package delivery company. In some areas you will be able to have items such as huaraches (leather sandals), clothing, and blankets tailor-made. If you buy woolens or wood items, it's wise to freeze or microwave them when you return to destroy possible insect infestation. Keep in mind that buying items made from tortoiseshell and black coral contributes to ecological destruction. Furthermore, such items are not allowed into the United States.

STUDENTS ON THE ROAD

To save money, **look into deals available through student-oriented travel agencies.** To qualify, you'll need to have a bona fide student ID card. Members of international student groups are also eligible (☞ Students *in* Important Contacts A to Z).

T
TAXIS

Government-certified taxis have a license with a photo of the driver and a taxi number prominently displayed, as well as a meter. More often than not, however, the meter is "broken." In this case, be sure to agree on a fare before setting off. Tipping is not necessary unless the driver helps you with our bags, in which case a few pesos are appropriate.

AT THE AIRPORT

From the airport, **take a government-subsidized cab;** the driver will accept the taxi vouchers sold at stands inside or just outside the airport, which in theory ensure that your fare is established beforehand. However, in practice you may be overcharged, so prepare yourself by locating the taxi originating and destination zones on a map and make sure your ticket is properly zoned; if you only need a ticket from zone three to zone four, don't pay for a ticket from zone one. Even then, the rates for non-government-subsidized cabs routinely exceed the official taxi rate.

IN CITIES AND BEACH RESORTS

In Mexican cities, **take a taxi rather than public transportation,** which, though inexpensive, is frequently slow and sometimes patrolled by pickpockets. Always **establish the fare beforehand,** and **always count your change.** In most of the beach resorts, there are inexpensive fixed-route fares, but if you don't ask, or your Spanish isn't great, you may get taken. In the cities, and especially the capital, meters do not always run, and if they do, their rates have usually been updated by a chart posted somewhere in the cab. For distances more than several kilometers, negotiate a rate in advance; many drivers will start by asking how much you want to pay to get a sense of how street-smart you are. In all cases, if you are unsure of what a fare should be, ask your hotel's front desk personnel or bell captain.

Taxis are available on the street, at taxi stands (*sitios*), and by phone. Street taxis—usually green Volkswagen Beetles—are subsidized cabs and are always the cheapest; sedans standing in front of hotels will charge far more. Never leave luggage unattended in a taxi.

In addition to private taxis, many cities operate a bargain-price collective taxi service using VW minibuses (called *combis*) and sedans, both downtown and at the airports. The service is called *colectivo* or, in Mexico City, *pesero.* Peseros run along fixed routes, and you hail them on the street and tell the driver where you are going. The fare—which you pay before you get out—is based on distance traveled. (For information on taxis in Mexico City, *see* Chapter 2.)

TELEPHONES

Thanks to the privatization of Telefónos de México in 1991, Mexico's phone service, long exasperatingly inefficient, is gradually being overhauled. In the meantime, the variety of public phones that exist in the country can be confusing at best. You'll see traditional black, square phones with push buttons or dials; although they have a coin slot on top, you may make local calls on them for free. Then there are the new blue or ivory push-button phones with digital screens. Some phones in rural areas have coin slots that accept only old peso coins; the large, 1,000-peso coins allow for ample local conversations. Other new phones have both a coin slot and an unmarked slot; the latter are for LADATEL (Spanish acronym for "long-distance direct dialing") cards, handy magnetic-strip debit cards that can be purchased at tourist offices as well as at newsstands and stores with a LADATEL logo. They come in denominations of up to NP$50 and can be used for both local and long-distance calls. Still other phones have two unmarked slots, one for a LADATEL card and the other for a credit card. These are primarily for Mexican bank cards, but some accept U.S. Visa or MasterCard, though *not* U.S. telephone credit cards. U.S. calling cards can be used from LADATEL phones with the appropriate access code (see Phone Matters in Important Contacts A to Z, above).

So far, there is still no touch-tone (digital) circuitry in operation in Mexico. Although some hotel, office, and residence phones have a "tone/pulse" switch, if you think you'll need to access an automated phone system or voice mail in the United States, it's a good idea to take along a touch-tone simulator (you can buy them for about $17 at most electronic stores). Nor are multi-line phones that automatically bounce incoming calls to the next available line common in Mexico; this is why there are often many telephone numbers listed for a single place. With the increased installation of new phone and fax lines in major Mexican cities, many phone numbers are in the process of being changed; a recording may offer the new number, so it's useful to learn the Spanish words for numbers 1 through 9.

LONG-DISTANCE

The long-distance services of AT&T, MCI, and Sprint make calling home relatively convenient, but in many hotels you may find it impossible to dial the access number. The hotel operator may also refuse to make the connection. Instead, the hotel will charge you a premium rate—as much as 400% more than a

calling card—for calls placed from your hotel room. To avoid such price gouging, travel with more than one company's long-distance calling card—a hotel may block Sprint but not MCI. If the hotel operator claims that you cannot use any phone card, ask to be connected to an international operator, who will help you to access your phone card. You can also dial the international operator yourself. If none of this works, try calling your phone company collect in the United States. If collect calls are also blocked, call from a pay phone in the hotel lobby. Before you go, **find out the local access codes** for your destinations.

TIPPING

When tipping in Mexico, remember that the minimum wage is the equivalent of $6 a day and that the vast majority of workers in the tourist industry live barely above the poverty line. However, there are Mexicans who think in dollars and know, for example, that in the United States porters are tipped about $1 a bag; many of them expect the peso equivalent from foreigners but are happy to accept NP$1 from Mexicans. They will complain either verbally or with a facial expression if they feel they deserve more—you and your conscience must decide. Following are some general guidelines, in pesos.

Porters and bellboys at airports and at moder-

ate and inexpensive hotels: NP$4 per bag

Porters at expensive hotels: NP$7 per bag

Maids: NP$3 per night (all hotels)

Waiters: 10%–15% of the bill, depending on service (make sure a 10%–15% service charge has not already been added to the bill, although this practice is not common in Mexico)

Taxi drivers: Tipping necessary only if the driver helps with your bags—NP$3–NP$7 should be sufficient, depending on the extent of the help.

Gas station attendants: 50 centavos

Parking attendants and theater ushers: NP$2–NP$3; some theaters have set rates.

TOUR OPERATORS

A package or tour to Mexico can make your vacation less expensive and more hassle-free. Firms that sell tours and packages reserve airline seats, hotel rooms, and rental cars in bulk and pass some of the savings on to you. In addition, the best operators have local representatives available to help you at your destination.

A GOOD DEAL?

The more your package or tour includes, the better you can predict the ultimate cost of your vacation. Make sure you know exactly what is covered, and **beware of hidden costs.** Are taxes, tips, and service charges included? Transfers and baggage handling? Entertainment and excursions? These can add up.

Most packages and tours are rated deluxe, first-class superior, first class, tourist, or budget. The key difference is usually accommodations. Remember, tourist class in the United States might be a comfortable chain hotel, but in Mexico you might share a bath and do without hot water. If the package or tour you are considering is priced lower than in your wildest dreams, **be skeptical.** Also, **make sure your travel agent knows the accommodations** and other services. Ask about the hotel's location, room size, beds, and whether it has a pool, room service, or programs for children, if you care about these. Has your agent been there in person or sent others you can contact?

BUYER BEWARE

Each year a number of consumers are stranded or lose their money when operators—even very large ones with excellent reputations—go out of business. To avoid becoming one of them, take the time to **check out the operator**—find out how long the company has been in business and ask several agents about its reputation. Next, **don't book unless the firm has a consumer-protection program.** Members of the USTOA and the NTA are required to set aside funds for the sole purpose of covering your payments and travel arrangements in case of default. Nonmember operators may instead carry insurance; look for the details in the

operator's brochure—and for the name of an underwriter with a solid reputation. Note: When it comes to tour operators, **don't trust escrow accounts.** Although there are laws governing those of charter-flight operators, no governmental body prevents tour operators from raiding the till.

Next, **contact your local Better Business Bureau and the attorney general's offices** in both your own state and the operator's; have any complaints been filed? Finally, **pay with a major credit card.** Then you can cancel payment, provided that you can document your complaint. Always **consider trip-cancellation insurance** (☞ Insurance, *above*).

BIG VS. SMALL➤ Operators that handle several hundred thousand travelers per year can use their purchasing power to give you a good price. Their high volume may also indicate financial stability. But some small companies provide more personalized service; because they tend to specialize, they may also be more knowledgeable about a given area.

USING AN AGENT

Travel agents are excellent resources. In fact, large operators accept bookings made only through travel agents. But it's good to **collect brochures from several agencies** because some agents' suggestions may be skewed by promotional relationships with tour and package firms that reward them for volume sales. If you

have a special interest, **find an agent with expertise in that area;** ASTA can provide leads in the United States. (Don't rely solely on your agent, though; agents may be unaware of small-niche operators, and some special-interest travel companies only sell direct.)

SINGLE TRAVELERS

Prices are usually quoted per person, based on two sharing a room. If traveling solo, you may be required to pay the full double-occupancy rate. Some operators eliminate this surcharge if you agree to be matched up with a roommate of the same sex, even if one is not found by departure time.

TRAIN TRAVEL

In recent years, train schedules and first-class service from the U.S.–Mexico border have been cut significantly, in part because of the introduction of good trans-border bus transport (☞ Bus Travel, *above*). Although Ferrocarriles Nacionales de México (☞ Train Travel *in* Important Contacts A to Z, *above*) began upgrading service in 1987 with air-conditioning and dining, club, and sleeping cars, the effort lost its steam. The Mexican government officially announced in 1994 that it was slowly moving out of the luxury rail business and would be looking to privatize this segment of the industry over the next several years. As first-class bus service proliferates throughout the country, first-class rail cars and schedules are being cut, often with little or no advance notice.

Primera especial (special first-class) tickets on overnight trains entitle passengers to reserved, spacious seats. *Primera regular* (regular first-class) service, also available on many trains, gets you the same seat, but no place reservation. Second-class tickets are not available from U.S. agents, but first-class seats are not expensive and, in terms of comfort, are well worth the few extra pesos.

Sleeping accommodations consist of *camarines* (private rooms with bath and a single lower berth), *alcobas* (same as *camarines,* but with an upper and a lower berth), and couchettes, also called *camarotes*.

Train tickets must be purchased at least one day in advance, from Mexico City's Buenavista Station, local stations, or local Mexican travel agents, who will, of course, charge you extra. You can also reserve first-class tickets and rail-hotel packages in advance (10 to 15 days is recommended) from the United States

by calling Mexico by Train (☞ Train Travel *in* Important Contacts A to Z, *above*).

W
WHEN TO GO

Mexico is sufficiently large and geographically diverse that you can find a place to visit any time of the year. October through May are generally the driest months; during the peak of the rainy season (June–September), it may rain for a few hours every day. But the sun often shines for the rest of the day, and the reduced off-season rates may well compensate for the reduced tanning time.

From December through February, the Mexican resorts—where the vast majority of tourists go—are the most crowded and therefore the most expensive. To avoid the masses, the highest prices, and the worst rains, **consider visiting Mexico during October, April, or May.** Hotel rates at the beach resorts can be cut by as much as 30% in the shoulder season, 50% in the off-season.

Mexicans travel during traditional holiday periods—Christmas

through New Year's, Semana Santa (Holy Week, the week before Easter), and school vacations in the summertime—as well as over extended national holiday weekends, called *puentes* (bridges). Festivals play a big role in Mexican national life. If you plan to travel during a major national event, reserve both lodgings and transportation well in advance (see Festivals and Seasonal Events *in* Chapter 1).

CLIMATE

The variations in Mexico's climate are not surprising considering the size of the country. The coasts and low-lying sections of the interior are often very hot if not actually tropical, with temperatures ranging from 24°C to 31°C (75°F to 88°F) in winter and well above 32°C (90°F) in summer. A more temperate area ranging from 16°C to 21°C (60°F to 70°F) is found at altitudes of 1,220–1,830 meters (4,000–6,000 feet). In general, the high central plateau on which Mexico City, Guadalajara, and many of the country's colonial cities are located is springlike year-round.

Climate in Mexico

ACAPULCO

Jan.	88F	31C	May	90F	32C	Sept.	90F	32C
	72	22		77	25		77	25
Feb.	88F	31C	June	90F	32C	Oct.	90F	32C
	72	22		77	25		77	25
Mar.	88F	31C	July	91F	33C	Nov.	90F	32C
	72	22		77	25		75	24
Apr.	88F	31C	Aug.	91F	33C	Dec.	88F	31C
	72	22		77	25		73	23

COZUMEL

Jan.	82F	28C	May	89F	32C	Sept.	89F	32C
	68	20		73	23		75	24
Feb.	84F	29C	June	89F	32C	Oct.	87F	31C
	68	20		75	24		73	23
Mar.	86F	30C	July	89F	32C	Nov.	84F	29C
	69	21		75	24		71	22
Apr.	89F	32C	Aug.	91F	33C	Dec.	84F	29C
	71	22		75	24		68	20

ENSENADA

Jan.	64F	18C	May	70F	21C	Sept.	77F	25C
	45	7		54	12		61	16
Feb.	66F	19C	June	72F	22C	Oct.	73F	23C
	46	8		57	14		55	13
Mar.	66F	19C	July	75F	24C	Nov.	72F	22C
	46	8		61	16		48	9
Apr.	68F	20C	Aug.	75F	24C	Dec.	66F	19C
	52	11		63	17		46	8

GUADALAJARA

Jan.	75F	24C	May	88F	31C	Sept.	79F	26C
	45	7		57	14		59	15
Feb.	77F	25C	June	84F	29C	Oct.	79F	26C
	46	8		61	16		59	15
Mar.	82F	28C	July	79F	26C	Nov.	77F	25C
	48	9		59	15		48	9
Apr.	86F	30C	Aug.	79F	26C	Dec.	75F	24C
	54	12		59	15		46	8

LA PAZ

Jan.	72F	22C	May	88F	31C	Sept.	92F	33C
	57	14		64	18		76	24
Feb.	74F	23C	June	92F	33C	Oct.	89F	32C
	56	13		69	21		71	22
Mar.	80F	27C	July	95F	35C	Nov.	81F	27C
	56	13		75	24		66	19
Apr.	83F	28C	Aug.	93F	34C	Dec.	74F	23C
	60	16		76	24		59	15

MEXICO CITY

Jan.	70F	21C	May	79F	26C	Sept.	72F	22C
	41	5		52	11		52	11
Feb.	73F	23C	June	77F	25C	Oct.	72F	22C
	45	7		54	12		52	11
Mar.	79F	26C	July	73F	23C	Nov.	72F	22C
	48	9		52	11		52	11
Apr.	81F	27C	Aug.	73F	23C	Dec.	70F	21C
	50	10		52	11		43	6

MONTERREY

Jan.	68F	20C	May	88F	31C	Sept.	88F	31C
	48	9		68	20		70	21
Feb.	73F	23F	June	91F	33C	Oct.	81F	27C
	52	11		72	22		63	17
Mar.	79F	26C	July	91F	34C	Nov.	75F	24C
	55	13		72	22		55	13
Apr.	86F	30C	Aug.	93F	34C	Dec.	70F	21C
	64	18		72	22		50	10

PUERTO VALLARTA

Jan.	84F	29C	May	91F	33C	Sept.	93F	34C
	63	17		68	20		73	23
Feb.	86F	30C	June	93F	34C	Oct.	93F	34C
	61	16		73	23		73	23
Mar.	86F	30C	July	95F	35C	Nov.	91F	33C
	63	17		73	23		68	20
Apr.	88F	31C	Aug.	95F	35C	Dec.	86F	30C
	64	18		73	23		64	18

SAN MIGUEL DE ALLENDE

Jan.	79F	26C	May	91F	33C	Sept.	82F	28C
	48	9		61	16		61	16
Feb.	82F	28C	June	91F	31C	Oct.	82F	28C
	52	11		63	17		61	16
Mar.	88F	31C	July	84F	29C	Nov.	81F	27C
	55	13		61	16		52	11
Apr.	90F	32C	Aug.	84F	29C	Dec.	77F	25C
	59	15		61	16		48	9

1 Destination: Mexico

MEXICO: WHERE PAST AND PRESENT MEET

MEXICO IS LIKE *mole,* the complex and uniquely Mexican sauce whose myriad variations appeal to many tastes at once.

It is a nation so diverse that most Americans have only a vague inkling of what it's about. It's a place of ethereal cloud forests and regions so barren they were the setting for *Dune,* the science fiction film about a desert planet; of chill mountain heights and tropical jungles filled with shrill monkeys and a verdant growth of mango, papaya, and avocado. Its dimensions can be mind-boggling: Sections of the Copper Canyon are half again as deep as the Grand Canyon in Arizona.

It is a land of powerful muralists whose works chronicle the struggles of its people, while at the same time its musicians and dancers celebrate their survival.

Worlds collide in Mexico. It can be a bastion of Spanish formality or enclave of California casualness, with businesspeople dressed in flip-flops and shorts, their cellular telephones poking out of their shirt pockets.

It is a vacation mecca of computer-designed resorts—sites chosen for their perfect confluence of white beach and crystal sea, where hotels have sprouted shoulder-to-shoulder for high-glitz destinations of sand, sun, and fun.

Yet much of it remains unchanged since the days of the conquistadors. In Chiapas, Maya Indians still work their fields with little more than machetes, smiling with benign amusement at the mountains of gear that adventure-travel outfitters use for rafting the rivers that have served as Maya highways for a millennium.

A past that is still very much a part of the present is central to Mexico's allure. In Mexico City's Zócalo—as the main square of any Mexican town or city is called—the pre-Hispanic Templo Mayor sits in the corner created by the juxtaposition of the 16th-century Cathedral and the 17th-century National Palace. Nearby, the ruins of an-

other Aztec temple have been incorporated into a subway stop.

Some contrasts verge on the comic. Even as Jack Nicklaus declares an ocean-front hole in one of his new courses in Cabo San Lucas his favorite, drivers on the new four-lane highway nearby must beware of the area's greatest traffic hazard in the cool desert night: cows drawn to the pavement, which retains the warmth of the sun hours after sunset. Fences remain a relatively new concept in Cabo, but cows are beginning to sprout Day-Glo collars.

And halfway up the Baja Peninsula from Los Cabos, where bulldozers and construction crews are busily erecting condos for golfers, 1,000-year-old polychrome paintings of men and women, sea turtles, and whales lie hidden in the Sierra San Francisco, mountainous terrain so rough that only adventure travelers willing to travel by burro can see them.

Passengers on private trains crossing Mexico's Copper Canyon in cruise ship–style luxury wander through tiny gems of colonial villages and watch the dances of the Tarahumara, indigenous people who live in caves or stone huts, just one step removed from hunter-gatherers.

An air-conditioned bus ride from the beaches of ultramodern Cancún stand Maya temples, built with such cunning that on spring and autumn equinoxes the sun's shadows make it appear as though a giant serpent were descending a pyramid's steps, melding with a carved serpent's head at the base. Tent cities of vendors hawking T-shirts and other souvenirs have sprouted outside some temples; yet others remain entwined in the vines of the jungles that surround them, looking much as they did when another era of tourists sought them out a century ago.

In the Pacific resort of Mazatlán, the old city center is a mix of Spanish and French-style buildings carefully restored, while a string of modern, beachfront hotels lines the water's edge. Beyond the city limits lie the Sierra Madres and the mountain villages where the veins of gold that first attracted the fortune-seeking, empire-building conquistadors are still mined.

Cities such as Querétaro, San Miguel de Allende, and Morelia were also of major importance in the days of colonial Mexico—at one point, a third of the world's silver came from the mines of Guanajuato. Their architecture—European baroque facades and French doors opening onto wrought-iron balconies—has the feel of a Parisian neighborhood suddenly relocated to the American West.

The colorful colonial capital of Oaxaca is itself a babe compared to the Zapotec pyramids outside the city dating as far back as 500 BC. Villagers living in the ring of settlements that surround Oaxaca like moons still practice crafts honed and perfected by their ancestors centuries before the arrival of the first Europeans.

Mexico, in short, is a land that has blended the legacies and traditions of both conqueror and vanquished and made them so uniquely Mexican that it is hard to see where one ends and the other begins.

T IS A BLEND so distinct that visitors can quite literally taste the difference in seemingly familiar foods. A simple cup of American hot chocolate is pale and insipid next to Mexican hot chocolate, a virile, lusty drink sweetened by honey or sugar, thickened with cornmeal, and spiced with pumpkins and peppers to make a powerful cup of substance.

Certainly, much of Mexico is familiar to many Americans—16 million visit annually. With the advent of the wide-bodied jet and cheap charters, resorts such as Acapulco and Puerto Vallarta, once getaways for movie stars and the super-rich, opened to the masses. More recently, isolated enclaves like Cabo San Lucas, whose private airstrips kept it accessible only to fanatic and idiosyncratic fishermen and their celebrity cronies, opened international airports. The result: a desert-by-the-sea golf mecca.

But for all that Mexico is America's next-door neighbor, it can also seem remote. Only recently has Mexico's Ministry of Tourism sought to deal with the red tape that made it almost impossible for Americans to drive across the border. And to simplify border crossing regulations for mo-

torists, tourism officials had to deal with border crossing guards demanding bribes before agreeing to institute some of the new procedures.

An airline system centered on Mexico City can make domestic travel complicated—often the way to get from one resort to another is only via Mexico City. And despite repeated efforts to privatize and improve Ferrocarriles Nacionales de Mexico (FNM), the federal rail system, Mexican trains make Amtrak look like the Concorde.

Communication with home can be tough, too—even in major resorts. Anyone who has actually tried to use Mexican phones can do nothing but marvel at the popularity of Telmex, the Mexican phone company, on the stock market. Cellular phones abound because they are faster to get and often more reliable.

Still, privatization has greatly improved the quality of the nation's buses. Brazilian-built Mercedes motorcoaches and American imports have replaced smoke-belching recycled inter-city buses used in the past on tours. Moreover, with the new, deluxe service between many cities—plush reclining seats, hostesses dispensing drinks and snacks, and current movies playing overhead—Mexican bus travel has entered what was once the exclusive realm of the airlines.

And more than 7,000 miles of new roads were built under the Salinas administration. They link major tourist centers such as the megaresort of Cancún with the colonial city of Mérida, which has been a major center in the Yucatán since the days the Maya flourished. The Green Angels, a highway patrol whose mechanics aid motorists in distress, patrol these roads.

Indeed, tying it all together is the great common denominator of Mexico: It is a land of great courtesy. That could be one reason that tourist crime is relatively low. Mexico's vacation destinations are as safe as—if not safer than—major U.S. destinations. A fundamentally Mexican security springs from the innate graciousness of a friendly and hospitable people.

—*Kate Rice*

WHAT'S WHERE

Mexico City

Two volcanoes and a pyramid complex flank Mexico's capital, once the center of Aztec civilization and now the country's cosmopolitan business, art, and culinary hub. From the Alameda, a leafy center of activity since Aztec times, to the Zona Rosa, a chic shopping neighborhood, and the marvelous Chaputltepec Park, with its many museums, gardens, and walking paths, Mexico City offers endless options to urban adventurers. Day trips might include colonial Puebla, where mole sauce and Talavera tiles originated, the floating gardens of Xochimilco, the massive Aztec ruins of Teotihuacán, or the graceful city of Cuernavaca.

Baja California

Separated from mainland Mexico by the Gulf of California, Baja has a 2,000-mile-long coast that stretches from Tijuana to Los Cabos. The earliest of south-of-the-border retreats for the rich, reclusive, or rebellious against Prohibition, Baja still hosts isolated fishing enclaves and raucous watering holes; nature lovers come to watch the whales migrate in winter.

Sonora

Rancheros continue to ride the range in Mexican cowboy country, but beef has been upstaged by beaches in this northwestern state's economy. Along with relatively unspoiled (and inexpensive) coastal towns such as Kino Bay and Guaymas, Sonora's lures include colonial Alamos, an immaculate former silver mining center, and a sprinkling of Spanish missions.

The Copper Canyon: From Los Mochis to Chihuahua City

The Copper Canyon is actually a series of gorges, some of them deeper than the United States' Grand Canyon; they are home to the Tarahumara Indians, renowned for their running ability. A train trip through this magnificent, largely uncharted region usually begins or ends in Chihuahua, a lively midsize city with a museum devoted to Pancho Villa.

Pacific Coast Resorts

Hollywood introduced us to two of the Mexican Riviera's most popular towns: Liz Taylor and Richard Burton's sleepy, steamy Puerta Vallarta in *Night of the Iguana* and the sparkling Manzanillo coast that served as the backdrop to Bo Derek in *10*. These days both places are prime cruise ship destinations, as is Mazatlán, a bustling port that attracts sportsfishing enthusiasts and surfers. Ixtapa/Zihuatenejo is a twofer attraction, a laid-back fishing village adjoined by a glitzy resort.

Guadalajara

The colonial architecture that dates to Guadalajara's heyday as a silver lode for the Spanish is among the lures of Mexico's second-largest city; Guadalajara also introduced the world to mariachis and tequila. Some of the best arts and crafts in the country can be found at Tlaquepaque, on the outskirts of town, and Tonalá, about 10 minutes away.

The Heartland of Mexico

Rich with the history of Mexico's revolution, the heartland is a treasure of colonial towns—Zacatecas, Guanajuato, Querétaro, Morelia, and Pátzcuaro—whose residents now lead quiet, largely traditional lives. Even in San Miguel de Allende, an American art colony and home to a well-known language institute, women wash their clothes and gossip at the local *lavandería* as they have for hundreds of years.

Acapulco

If Acapulco no longer tops the glitterati top-ten list, it remains both a sentimental favorite and a party-hearty resort town, boasting some of the glitziest discos this side of the Pacific. The cobblestoned streets of nearby Taxco, the silver city, are lined with master jewelers.

Oaxaca

The geographic, ethnic, and culinary diversity of Oaxaca has made the state a favorite of Mexico aficionados. Descendents of the Mixtec and Zapotec Indians, who built the Monte Albán and Mitla complexes near Oaxaca City, compose the majority of residents; their handicrafts and festivals are extremely colorful. Although less exotic, the state's coastal developments of Puerto Escondido and Bahías de Huatulco are beloved by surfers and beach bums.

Chiapas and Tabasco

Much in the news in recent years because of the rebellion of its indigenous people, the state of Chiapas has always been an off-the-beaten-path destination, a gateway to Guatemala best known for the colonial town of San Cristóbal and for the jungle-covered ruins of Palenque, considered by many to be the most interesting in Mexico.

Northeastern Mexico and Veracruz

Many winter Texans get their first taste of Mexico in the northeastern border towns of Nueva Laredo, Reynosa, and Matamoros; those who venture farther down to Monterrey are rewarded with the far more sophisticated dining and shopping of the country's third-largest city. The little-explored pyramids of El Tajín and the raffish charm of Veracruz, the first European city established on the North American mainland, are among the many reasons to continue south.

The Yucatán Peninsula

Mexico's most visited region, the Yucatán has something for everyone: the high-profile sparkle of Cancún; the spectacular snorkeling of Cozumel; the laid-back beachcombing of Isla Mujeres; the fascinating Spanish-Maya mix of Mérida; and the evocative Maya ruins of Tulum, Chichén Itzá, and Uxmal. The region is an ecotourist's dream, too, from the huge Sian Ka'an Biosphere Reserve on the Caribbean Coast to Río Lagartos National Park on the Gulf of Mexico, migration ground for thousands of flamingos and other birds.

PLEASURES AND PASTIMES

Beaches

Beaches are the reason most tourists visit Mexico. Generally speaking, the Pacific is rougher and the waters less clear than the Caribbean; consequently there is better snorkeling and scuba diving at the latter. Cancún, Cozumel, and Isla Mujeres, as well as what has come to be called the Cancún–Tulum Corridor, are among the best and most popular beach destinations on the Caribbean coast. Beaches on the Gulf of Mexico are often covered with tar. The Acapulco waters, though much improved by a recent clean-up effort, are still somewhat polluted, but there is no problem at the other Pacific resorts. All beach resorts offer a variety of water sports, including waterskiing, windsurfing, parasailing, and if the water is clear enough, snorkeling and scuba diving. Surfers favor Puerto Escondido, near Huatulco, and Santa Cruz, near San Blas.

Bullfighting

Of all the imports to Mexico of the Spanish conquest, bullfighting was perhaps the most sympathetic to the character of the native peoples, who took up the stylized, ceremonial contest between man and beast with enthusiasm and skill. The sport was refined and popularized over the centuries, until every major city and most small towns had a bullring or some semblance of an arena. As in Spain, the last few decades have seen some decline of the popularity of the sport in Mexico, where it has been superseded by such modern games as soccer and has been the object of negative publicity by animal-rights activists. It remains a strong part of the Latin American culture, however, and can be thrilling to watch when performed by a skilled toreador. Ask at your hotel about arenas and schedules; most fights are held on Sunday afternoon, and the most prestigious toreadores perform during the high-profile fall season.

Charreada

This Mexican rodeo is a colorful event involving elegant flourishes and maneuvers, handsome costumes, mariachi music, and much fanfare. There are charreadas most Sunday mornings at Mexico City's Rancho del Charro; inquire at your hotel or at a travel agency.

Dining

Mexico's food, like its art, is as diverse and abundant as its geography. Distinct regional specialties typify each of the republic's 32 states and even the different provinces within the states. Fresh ingredients are bountiful, recipes are passed down through generations, and preparation requires much patience and loving care. (Mexican gastronomes are dismayed by foreigners' glaring misconceptions of Mexican food as essentially tacos, enchiladas, and burritos; they are bewildered by Tex-Mex and appalled by Taco Bell.)

The staples of rice, beans, and tortillas on which the poor subsist form the basis for creative variations of sophisticated national dishes but are by no means the only ingredients commonly used. As Mexican cooking continues to develop an international reputation and popularity, more people are recognizing its versatility.

Seafood is abundant, not just on the coasts but also in the lake regions around Guadalajara and in the state of Michoacán. Ceviche—raw fish and shellfish (*mariscos*) marinated in lime juice and topped with cilantro (coriander), onion, and chili—is almost a national dish, though it originated in Acapulco. It is worth trying, but make sure it's fresh. Shrimp, lobster, and oysters can be huge and succulent; bear in mind the folk adage about eating oysters only in months with names that contain the letter *r*, and be sure to avoid raw shellfish in any area where cholera or water pollution may be a risk. Other popular seafood includes *huachinango* (red snapper), abalone, crab, and swordfish.

Mexicans consume lots of beef, pork, and barbecued lamb (*barbacoa*), with a variety of sauces. Chicken and other poultry tend to be dry and stringy, but when drenched in sauces or disguised in enchiladas, tacos, or burritos, they are quite palatable. *Mole,* a complex, spicy sauce with more than 100 ingredients, including many kinds of chiles and even a bit of chocolate, is one of Mexico's proudest culinary inventions. It is usually served over chicken or lamb. Regional variations are described in the appropriate chapters.

Maize was sacred to the Indians, who invented innumerable ways of preparing cornmeal, from the faithful tortilla to the *tamale* (cornmeal wrapped in banana leaves or corn husks), tostada (lightly fried, open tortilla heaped with meat, lettuce, etc.), and simple taco (a tortilla briefly heated, filled, and wrapped into a slim cylinder; one variation on this is called *flauta,* or flute). *Atole* (a sweet, corn-based drink similar in consistency to hot chocolate) is a favorite breakfast or before-bed treat.

Fresh fruits and vegetables are another Mexican pleasure. Jicama, papaya, mamey, avocado, mango, guayaba, peanuts, squash, and tomatoes are just some of the produce native to Mexico. (All fresh produce should be washed in purified water, however, because bacteria exist in Mexico to which foreigners may not have been exposed.)

Other Mexican specialties less common abroad are any number of local *antojitos* or *botanas* (appetizers), *chilaquiles* (a rich breakfast dish made with eggs and tortilla strips scrambled with chile, tomatoes, onions, cream, and cheese), and *chiles en nogada* (a large poblano chili stuffed with pork, raisins, onion, olives, and almonds and topped with a creamy walnut sauce and pomegranate seeds). Soups are hearty—particularly the corn-and-pork-based *pozole, sopa azteca* (avocado and tortilla in a broth) and *sopa de flor de calabaza* (squash-flower soup).

But this barely touches on the plenitude and diversity of Mexican cuisine, which also encompasses an astonishing assortment of breads, sweets, beers, wines (which are fast improving), and cactus-based liquors. Freshly squeezed fruit juices and fruit shakes (*licuados*) are safe to drink—if ordered in a restaurant with hygienic practices—and taste heavenly. Coffee varies from standard American-style and Nescafé to espresso and *café de jarra,* which is laced with chocolate and served in a coarse clay mug. Imported liquor is very expensive; middle-class Mexicans stick with the local rum and tequila.

Horseback Riding

Horseback riding is a sport the Mexicans love. The dry ranchlands of northern Mexico have countless stables and dude ranches, as do San Miguel de Allende and Querétaro in the heartland. Horses can be rented by the hour at most beaches, and horseback expeditions can be arranged to the Copper Canyon in Chihuahua and the forest near San Cristóbal, Chiapas.

Hot Springs

Mexico is renowned for its *balnearios* (mineral bath springs), which today are surrounded by a cluster of spa resorts and hacienda-type hotels. Most of the spas are concentrated in the center of the country, in the states of Aguascalientes, Guanajuato, México, Morelos, Puebla, and Querétaro.

Hunting, Fishing, and Bird-Watching

The best area for these activities is Baja California and the Sea of Cortés. Deep-sea fishing off the northern Pacific and near Cozumel are also renowned. For calendar and permit information for both hunting and fishing, contact your local Mexican consulate.

Jai Alai

Bet on a good time—and also on the winners—if you watch this fast-paced Basque sport, a bit like handball but played with a large scoop called a *fronton*. Tijuana and Mexico City have the largest stadiums, but you'll find smaller arenas in other cities around the country.

Ruins

Amateur archaeologists will find heaven in Mexico, where some of the greatest ancient civilizations—among them, the Aztecs, the Olmecs, and the Maya—left their mark. Pick your period and your preference, whether for well-excavated sites or overgrown, out-of-the-way ruins barely touched by a scholar's shovel. The Yucatán is, hands down, the greatest source of ancient treasure, with such heavy hitters as Chichén Itzá and Uxmal, but you're unlikely to find any region in the country that doesn't have some interesting vestige of Mexico's pre-Columbian past. A visit to Mexico City's archaelogical museum, arguably the best in the world, could ignite the imagination of even those who thought they had no interest in antiquity, and help others focus on the places they'd most like to explore further.

Shopping

Mexico is one of the best countries in the world to purchase *artesanías* (handicrafts), and many items are exempt from duty. The work is varied, original, colorful, and inexpensive, and it supports millions of families who are carrying on ancient traditions. Though cheap, shoddy merchandise masquerading as "native handicraft" is increasingly common, careful shoppers who take their time can come away with real works of art.

Mexican craftspeople excel in ceramics, weaving and textiles, silver, gold, and semiprecious stone jewelry, leather, woodwork, and lacquerware; each region has its specialty.

CERAMICS➤ Blue majolica (Talavera-style) tiles and other ceramic ware are at their best in Puebla. Oaxaca state is known for the burnished black pots hand-produced by its craftspeople. Inventive masks and figurines come from Michoacán, Jalisco, Taxco, Valle de Bravo, Tlaquepaque, and Chiapas.

JEWELRY➤ Silver is best bought in Taxco, San Miguel de Allende, and Oaxaca; be sure purchases are stamped "925," which means 92.5% pure silver. Gold filigree is sold in Oaxaca and Guanajuato. Oaxaca and Chiapas are also known for their amber, but beware, because much of what is sold as amber is in fact glass or plastic. (Good rules of thumb: Don't buy amber off the street, and if it seems like a great bargain, it's probably fake.) For semiprecious stones, try the jewelers of Puebla and Querétaro. Coral jewelry is sold in the Yucatán and other coastal areas, but buying it is discouraged, because of the massive ecological damage caused by coral harvesting.

LEATHER➤ The Yucatán, Chiapas, Oaxaca, and Jalisco are key destinations.

METALWORK➤ Look for copper in Santa Clara del Cobre in Michoacán, tin in San Miguel de Allende.

WEAVINGS AND TEXTILES➤ Options are many and varied: shawls (*rebozos*) and blankets around Oaxaca, Guadalajara, Jalapa, and Pátzcuaro; *huipiles* (heavily embroidered tunics worn by Indian women) and other embroidered clothing in Oaxaca state, the Yucatán, and Michoacán; masterfully woven rugs, some colored with natural dyes, in Oaxaca; hammocks and baskets in Oaxaca and the Yucatán; lace in the colonial cities of the heartland area; *guayaberas* (comfortable, embroidered tunic-style shirts, now usually mass-produced) along the Gulf coast; and reed mats in Oaxaca and Valle de Bravo. The Mezquital region east of Querétaro can also be rewarding, as can shopping for Huichol Indian yarn paintings and embroidery near Puerta Vallarta.

WOODWORK➤ Best bets include masks (Guerrero, Mexico City), *alebrijes* (painted wooden animals, Oaxaca), furniture (Guadalajara, Michoacán, San Miguel de Allende, and Cuernavaca), lacquerware (Uruapan and Michoacán, as well as Chiapa de Corzo in Chiapas and Olinalá in Guerrero), and guitars (Paracho, Michoacán).

Soccer

As in Europe, this is Mexico's national sport (known as *futból*). It is played almost year-round at the *Estadio Azteca* in Mexico City as well as in other large cities.

Tennis and Golf

Most major resorts have lighted tennis courts, and there is an abundance of 18-hole golf courses, many designed by such noteworthies as Percy Clifford, Joe Finger, and Robert Trent Jones. At private golf and tennis clubs, you must be accompanied by a member to gain admission. Hotels that do not have their own facilities will often secure you access to ones in the vicinity.

FODOR'S CHOICE

Archaeological Sites

★ **Chichén Itzá.** The best known Maya ruin, Chichén Itzá was the most important city in the Yucatán from the 11th to 13th centuries. Its eclectic architecture is evidence of a complex intermingling of ancient cultures.

★ **Palenque.** Nestled in a rainforest in Chiapas, these Maya ruins have a magical quality, perhaps because of their intimacy. The most magificent royal tomb in the Maya empire was uncovered here.

★ **Teotihuacan.** Predating the Aztecs and believed by them to be the birthplace of the gods, this pyramid complex outside Mexico City was one of the largest cities in the ancient world.

★ **Tulum.** The spectacular backdrop of the Caribbean and proximity to Cancún explain why Tulum is the most visited archaeological site in the Yucatán.

★ **Uxmal.** Arguably the most beautiful of Mexico's ruins, Uxmal represents Maya style at its purest, including ornate stone friezes, intricate cornices, and soaring arches.

Beaches

★ **Playa de Amor, Cabo San Lucas.** From this secluded cove at the very tip of Baja California you can see the Sea of Cortés on one side, the Pacific Ocean on the other.

★ **Yelapa, near Puerta Vallarta.** Walk from the beach of this small fishing village, accessible only by boat, to stunning waterfalls in the jungle.

★ **Bara Vieja, near Acapulco.** Those tired of being hassled by vendors in Acapulco often retreat to Bara Vieja, a magnificent beach about 16 miles to the east.

★ **Zicatela, Oaxaca Coast.** A long stretch of cream-colored sand, Zacatela is one of the top 10 surfing beaches in the world.

★ **Playa Norte and Playa Cocoteros, Isla Mujeres.** These adjoining beaches on sleepy Isla are ideal for watersports and palapa lounging alike.

Special Moments

★ **The divers at La Quebrada, Acapulco.** It's heart-stopping to see these swimmers take the plunge off 130-foot-high cliffs—after praying at a small cliffside chapel.

★ **Whale-watching at Scammon's and San Ignacio lagoons, Baja.** Go out on a boat for the best views of the great gray mammals, who pass here en route from Alaska each winter.

★ **Los voladores, Papantla.** A precursor of bungee jumping, this ancient ceremony involves five "flyers" who hurl themselves from a tiny platform set atop a 100-foot pole.

★ **A *calesa* (horse-drawn carriage) ride through Mérida.** Discover Old World graciousness by trotting slowly through the wide streets and French-style neighborhoods of Yucatán's capital.

★ **Overlooking the Copper Canyon from Divisadero.** Whether you just get off the train briefly or stop overnight, you'll be astounded by the vista of the grand abyss.

Museums

★ **Museum of Contemporary Art, Monterrey.** The best of postmodern Latin American art is gathered at this gallery, where a chic coffeehouse attracts the city's intellectuals.

★ **Museo Nacional de Antropología, Mexico City.** There are 100,000 square feet of displays at the greatest museum in the country, which hosts archaeological treasures from all of Mesoamerica.

★**Museo de Frida Kahlo, Mexico City.** The characterful former home of the now-fashionable Kahlo is filled with her disturbing, surrealistic paintings and those of friends such as Klee and Duchamp.

★**Na-Bolom, San Cristobal de las Casas.** Franz and Gertrude Blom lived in a lovely garden-filled setting; their former residence contains displays reflecting their extensive archaeological, ethnological, and ecological interests.

★**La Venta Museum Park, Villahermosa.** Giant Olmec heads placed along a jungle pathway are among the most fascinating exhibits of the pre-Hispanic jaguar cult on which this park complex focuses.

Shopping

★**Tlaquepaque, outside Guadalajara.** Crafts-seekers throng to this village where some of the most talented glass-blowers, potters, and jewelers in Mexico gather.

★**Saturday market, Oaxaca.** At the largest Indian market in Mexico you'll find a wealth of colorful wares, including native *huipiles* (embroidered blouses), handcarved wooden animals, and black regional pottery.

★**Zona Rosa, Mexico City.** Antiques, crafts, and the latest fashions are abundant in this tony neighborhood, chockful of galleries, boutiques, and cafés.

★**Casa de Artesania and San Jolobil, San Cristóbal de Las Casas.** Some of Mexico's most striking Indian weavings, hand-embroidered blouses and tunics, multicolored *fajas* (sashes), and beribboned hats may be found in these two outlets.

★**El Centro (downtown), Puerto Vallarta.** Few Mexican cities have a collection of native crafts, among them clothing and household goods, as representative as that of Puerta Vallarta.

Restaurants

★**Coyuca 22, Acapulco.** Some diners book a year in advance to ensure a table at this Continental restaurant for high season; it's one of the most expensive dining rooms in town, and one of the most beautiful. **$$$$**

★**El Centenario, Mexico City.** The setting, in a restored 17th-century mansion, is superb, and the menu is enticing, featuring inventive versions of authentic pre-Hispanic dishes. **$$$$**

★**La Belle Epoque, Mérida.** Middle Eastern, French, and Yucatecan specialties star in the former ballroom of an elegant mansion, overlooking a pretty urban park. **$$$$**

★**Nuu-luu, Oaxaca.** Excellent Oaxacan cooking is the draw at this open-air restaurant, which lives up to its Mixtec name, "picturesque place." **$$**

★**Rincón Maya, Cozumel.** This friendly downtown restaurant, decorated with folk art, serves good versions of traditional Maya fare. **$$**

Hotels

★**La Casa Que Canta, Zihuatanejo.** Perched on a cliff overlooking Zihuatanejo Bay, this thatch-roof complex features individualized suites with handcrafted furnishings. **$$$$**

★**Las Brisas, Acapulco.** Jeeps transport guests around this secluded hillside haven, set on 110 acres that offer every imaginable activity and amenity. **$$$$**

★**Quinta Real, Guadalajara.** Classical Mexican architecture and Spanish-style furnishings distinguish this luxury hotel in a quiet residential neighborhood. **$$$$**

★**Chan Kah, Palenque.** A resident monkey is among the charms of this jungle retreat near the Maya ruins; accommodations are in comfortable bungalows. **$$$**

★**La Mansión del Bosque, San Miguel de Allende.** This renovated hacienda across the street from a park rents moderately priced rooms on a short- or long-term basis. **$$**

After Hours

★**Fantasy and Extravaganzza discos, Acapulco.** Two standouts in a city where Saturday-night fever still rages, Fantasy is Acapulco's most exclusive disco, while Extravaganzza boasts the best light-and-sound show as well as a drop-dead view of Acapulco Bay.

★**Plaza de los Mariachis, Guadalajara.** A personal serenade is expensive, but the price of a beer will let you listen in on the heart-rending songs in the city where they originated.

⭐ **Gran Café Portal, Veracruz.** People-watch into the wee hours over a cup of *café con leche* at this classic coffeehouse, renowned all over Mexico.

⭐ **Zona Rosa, Mexico City.** Niza and Florencia streets in the capital's Pink Zone are lined with lively nightclubs, bars, and discos that don't get hopping until after midnight.

⭐ **Carlos 'n' Charlie's, Cancún.** For raucous, crawl-out-of-the-rafters action, it's hard to beat this link in the ubiquitous Anderson chain.

NEW AND NOTEWORTHY

The big news this year continues to be the **devaluation of the peso** that began at the end of 1994. On the one hand, this signals increased purchasing power for travelers (though prices of chain hotels, generally calculated in dollars, remain stable); on the other, it means that projects in progress before the devaluation—including many tourist developments—have been put on hold until the dust from the economic bombshell clears.

To add to its economic woes, Mexico was subjected to a series of **natural disasters** in late 1995—a series of storms on the Caribbean Coast (the worst since Hurricane Hugo hit in 1988) and earthquakes on the Pacific Coast. By the time you read this, however, most of the damage incurred by these events should have been repaired.

At the same time, new types of tourism ventures continue to be developed. The opening of the first of several planned environmentally friendly jungle lodges in the Xpujil area of the state of **Campeche** (see the Yucatán Peninsula chapter) has made possible extended visits to the ruins at Bécan, Xpujil, Hormiguero, Río Bec, and Calakmul, all of which are undergoing continued restoration. In the state of **Veracruz,** the new Ruta de Cortés (Route of Cortés) allows visitors to follow the conquistador's footsteps. The tour starts at the beaches in the port of Veracruz, where the Spaniards first landed on what is now Mexican soil, and continues through the ruins, colonial cities, and battle sites that mark the conquistador's path to Mexico City. The states of Tlaxcala, Puebla, and Mexico play a smaller part in this route.

More recent events in Mexican history are explored in the new Museo de Historia Mexicana in the city of **Monterrey.** Part of the city's ongoing expansion of its cultural attractions, this state-of-the-art interactive museum offers the liveliest exhibits on the Mexican Revolution in the country.

FESTIVALS AND SEASONAL EVENTS

Mexico has a full calendar of national holidays, saints' days, and special events; below are some of the most important or unusual ones. For further information and dates, contact the Mexican Government Tourism Office (☞ Important Contacts A to Z) or the Mexico Ministry of Tourism's information hot line at 800/44–MEXICO.

WINTER

The month of January is full of long, regional festivals. Notable are the celebrations of the **Fiesta de la Inmaculada Concepción** (Feast of the Immaculate Conception), which transforms the city of Morelia into a sea of lights and flowers for much of the month; and a series of folkloric dances held in Chiapa de Corzo, Chiapas, and culminating in the **Feast of San Sebastian,** held there the third week in January.

JAN. 1➤ **New Year's Day** is a major celebration throughout the country. Agricultural and livestock fairs are held in the provinces; in Oaxaca, women display traditional *tehuana* costumes.

JAN. 6➤ **Feast of Epiphany** is the day the Three Kings bring gifts to Mexican children and the day the founding of Mérida is celebrated.

JAN. 17➤ **Feast of San Antonio Abad** honors animals all over Mexico. Household pets and

livestock alike are decked out with flowers and ribbons and taken to a nearby church for a blessing.

FEB. 2➤ **Día de la Candelaria,** or Candlemas Day, means fiestas, parades, bullfights, and lantern-decorated streets. Festivities include a running of the bulls through the streets of Tlacotalpan, Veracruz.

FEB.–MAR.➤ **Carnaval** is celebrated throughout Mexico but most notably in Mazatlán and Veracruz, where there are parades with floats and bands.

SPRING

MAR. 21➤ **Benito Juárez's Birthday,** a national holiday, is most popular in Guelatao, Oaxaca, where Juárez, the beloved 19th-century president of Mexico and champion of the people, was born. This is also the day that Fiesta de la Primavera, held in Cuernavaca near Mexico City, marks the beginning of spring with carnivals and agricultural fairs.

MAR.–APR.➤ **Semana Santa** (Holy Week) is observed throughout the country with special passion plays during this week leading up to Easter Sunday.

APR.–MAY➤ **San Marcos National Fair,** held in Aguascalientes, is one of the country's best fairs. It features lively casino gambling, Indian *ma-*

tachnes (dances performed by grotesque figures), mariachi bands, and bullfights. Also during this time, the **Feria de la Primavera** (Spring Fair) in Cuernavaca celebrates the local flower industry with flower shows and open-air concerts, and the 10-day **Festival de las Artes** (Arts Festival) brings music, theater, and dance troupes from all over Latin America to San Luis Potosí.

MAY 1➤ **Labor Day** is a day for workers to parade through the streets.

MAY 5➤ **Cinco de Mayo** marks the anniversary of the French defeat by Mexican troops in Puebla in 1862 with great fanfare throughout the country.

MAY 15➤ **Feast of San Isidro Labrador** is noted nationwide by the blessing of new seeds and animals. In Cuernavaca, a parade of oxen wreathed in flowers is followed by street parties and feasting.

SUMMER

JUNE 1➤ **Navy Day** is commemorated in all Mexican seaports and is especially colorful in Acapulco, Mazatlán, and Veracruz. The **Feast of Corpus Christi** is celebrated in different ways. In Mexico City, children are dressed in native costumes and taken to the cathedral on the *zócalo* (main square) for a blessing. In Papantla, Veracruz, the Dance of the Flying Bird-men, a pre-Hispanic ritual to the sun, is held throughout the day.

JUNE 24➤ **Saint John the Baptist Day,** a popular national holiday, sees many Mexicans observing a tradition of tossing a "blessing" of water on most anyone within reach.

EARLY JULY➤ The **Feria Nacional** (National Fair) in Durango runs from the Day of Our Lady of Refuge (July 4) to the anniversary of the founding of Durango in 1563 (July 22). The celebration, which has the feel of an old-time agricultural fair, has taken on national renown for its carnival rides, livestock shows, and music.

JULY 16➤ **Our Lady of Mt. Carmel Day** is celebrated with fairs, bullfights, fireworks, sporting competitions, even a major fishing tournament.

JULY 24–31➤ **Guelaguetza Dance Festival,** a Oaxacan affair, dates back to pre-Columbian times.

LATE JULY➤ **Feast of Santiago,** a national holiday, features *charreadas,* Mexican-style rodeos.

AUG.➤ The **Festival de San Agustin** brings a month of music, dance, and fireworks to Puebla. On August 26 (Saint Augustine's feast day) it is customary to prepare the famous *chiles en nogada* (☞ Dining, *above*).

AUG. 15➤ **Feast of the Assumption of the Blessed Virgin Mary** is celebrated

nationwide with religious processions. In Huamantla, Tlaxcala, the festivities include a running of the bulls down flower-strewn streets.

AUG. 25➤ **San Luis Potosí Patron Saint Fiesta** is the day the town honors its patron, San Luis Rey, with traditional dance, music, and foods.

AUTUMN

SEPT. 15–16➤ **Independence Day** is marked throughout Mexico with fireworks and parties that outblast those on New Year's Eve. The biggest celebrations take place in Mexico City.

SEPT. 29➤ **San Miguel Day** honors St. Michael, the patron saint of all towns with San Miguel in their names—especially San Miguel de Allende—with bullfights, folk dances, concerts, and fireworks.

OCT.➤ **October Festivals** mean a month of cultural and sporting events in Guadalajara.

OCT. 4➤ **Feast of St. Francis of Assisi** is a day for processions dedicated to St. Francis in various parts of the country.

OCT. 12➤ **Columbus Day** is a national holiday in Mexico.

OCT.–NOV.➤ **International Cervantes Festival,** in Guanajuato, is a top cultural event that attracts dancers, singers, and actors from a number of different countries.

NOV. 1–3➤ **All Souls' Day,** or **Day of the Dead,** the Mexican version of Halloween, commemorates the departed in a merry way, with candy skulls sold on street corners and picnickers spreading blankets in cemeteries.

NOV. 20➤ **Anniversary of the Mexican Revolution** is a national holiday.

NOV.–DEC.➤ **National Silver Fair,** an annual Taxco event, is an occasion for even more silver selling than usual, the crowning of a Silver Queen, jewelry and silver exhibitions, and various cultural events.

DEC. 12➤ **Feast Day of the Virgin of Guadalupe** is the day on which Mexico's patron saint is feted with processions and native folk dances, particularly at her shrine in Mexico City.

DEC. 23➤ **Feast of the Radishes,** a pre-Christmas tradition in Oaxaca, is one of the most colorful in Mexico: Farmers carve prize radishes into amusing shapes and display them in the city's main plaza, while celebrants devour fritterlike *buñuelos* and smash their ceramic plates in the streets.

DEC. 16–25➤ **The Posadas** and **Christmas** are candlelight processions that lead to Christmas parties and to piñatas (suspended paper animals or figurines) that are broken open to yield gifts. Mexico City is brightly decorated, but don't expect any snow.

2 Mexico City

Two volcanoes and a pyramid complex flank Mexico's capital, once the center of Aztec civilization and now the country's cosmopolitan business, art, and culinary hub. From the Alameda, a leafy center of activity since Aztec times, to the Zona Rosa, a chic shopping neighborhood, Mexico City offers endless options to urban adventurers. Day trips might include colonial Puebla, where mole sauce and Talavera tiles originated, or the floating gardens of Xochimilco.

MEXICO CITY is a city of superlatives: It is both the oldest (670 years) and the highest (2,240 meters, or 7,349 feet) city on the North American continent, and with nearly 24 million inhabitants, it is the most populous city in the world. It is Mexico's cultural, political, and financial core—on the verge of the 21st century but clinging to its deeply entrenched Aztec heritage.

By Frank
"Pancho" Shiell

Updated by
Patricia Alisau

As the gargantuan pyramids of Teotihuácan attest, the area around Mexico City was occupied from early times by a great civilization, whose name is as yet unknown (they were precursors of the Toltecs). The founding of the Aztec capital nearby did not occur until more than 500 years after Teotihuácan was abandoned. As the annals have it, the nomadic Aztecs were searching for a promised land in which to settle. Their prophesies said they would recognize the spot when they encountered an eagle, perched on a prickly-pear cactus, holding a snake in his beak. In 1325, the disputed date given for the founding of the city of Tenochtitlán, the Aztecs discovered this eagle in the valley of Mexico. They built Tenochtitlán on what was then an island in shallow Lake Texcoco and connected it to lakeshore satellite towns (now neighborhoods) by a network of *calzadas* (canals and causeways, now freeways). Even then it was the largest city in the Western Hemisphere and, according to historians, one of the three largest cities on earth. When he first laid eyes on the city in the 16th century, Spanish conquistador Hernán Cortés was dazzled by the glistening metropolis, which reminded him and his men of Venice.

A combination of factors made the conquest possible. The superstitious Aztec emperor Moctezuma II believed the white, bearded Cortés on horseback to be the mighty plumed serpent-god Quetzalcoatl, who, according to a tragically ironic prophesy, was supposed to arrive from the east in the year 1519 to rule the land. Moctezuma therefore welcomed the foreigner with gifts of gold and palatial accommodations.

But in return, Cortés initiated the bloody massacre of Tenochtitlán, which lasted almost two years. Joining forces with him was a massive army of Indian "allies," gathered from other settlements like Cholula and Tlaxcala, who were fed up with the Aztec empire's domination and taxation. With the strength of their numbers and the European tactical advantages of brigantines built to cross the lake; imported horses, firearms, and armor; and, inadvertently, smallpox and the common cold, Cortés succeeded in devastating Tenochtitlán. Only two centuries after it was founded, the young Aztec capital lay in ruins, about half of its population dead from battle, starvation, and contagious European diseases to which they had no immunity.

Cortés began building the capital of what he patriotically dubbed New Spain, the Spanish empire's colony that would spread north to cover what is now the United States southwest and south to Panama. Because he had difficulty pronouncing the word Tenochtitlán, he named the city Mexica (Meh-*she*-ka), which was the real name of the Aztecs (the Spaniards were the ones who had originally dubbed the Mexica Indians "Aztecs"). At the site of the demolished Aztec ceremonial center—now the 10-acre Zócalo—he started building a church (the precursor of the gigantic Metropolitan Cathedral), mansions, and government buildings. He utilized the slave labor—and artistry—of the vanquished native Mexicans. On top of the ruins of their city, and using rubble from it, they were forced to build what became the most European-style city in North America; but instead of having the random layout of contemporary medieval European cities, it followed the sophisticated grid pattern of the Aztecs. The Spaniards also drained and filled in Lake Texcoco, preferring wheels and horses (which they introduced to Mexico) over canals and canoes for transport. (The filled-in lake bed turned out to be a soggy support for the immense buildings that have been slowly sinking into it ever since they were built.) For much of the construction material they quarried local volcanic porous stone called *tezontle,* which is the color of dried blood and forms the thick walls of many historic downtown buildings.

During the colonial period, the city grew, and the Franciscans converted the Aztecs to Christianity. In 1571 the Spaniards established the Inquisition in New Spain and burned heretics at its palace headquarters, which still stands in Plaza de Santo Domingo.

More than 200 years later, Mexicans rose up against Spain. The historic downtown street 16 de Septiembre commemorates the "declaration" of the War of Independence. On that date in 1810, Father Miguel Hidalgo rang a church bell and cried out his history-making *grito* (shout): "Viva Ferdinand VII [king of Spain at the time]! Death to bad government!" Some historians conclude that Hidalgo's cry to arms in the name of the Spanish monarch was just a facade to start an independence movement, which Hidalgo successfully accomplished. That "liberty bell," which now hangs above the main entrance to the National Palace, is rung on the eve of every September 16 by the president of the republic, who then shouts a revised version of the patriot's cry: "Viva Mexico! Viva Mexico! Viva Mexico!"

Today, travelers flying into or out of Mexico City get an aerial view of the still-remaining portion of Lake Texcoco on the eastern outskirts of the city; at night the vast expanse of city lights abruptly ends at a black void that appears to be an ocean. In-flight views also provide a panorama of the vast, flat 1,482-square-kilometer (572-square-mile) Valley of Mexico, the Meseta de Anáhuac, completely surrounded by mountains—including, on its south side, two supposedly extinct and usually snowcapped volcanoes, Popocatepetl and Iztaccihuatl, both well over 17,000 feet high. The volcanoes are separated by the 2½-mile-high Cortés Pass, from where the arriving conquistador, after a nine-month trek from Veracruz, gazed down for his first astonishing glimpse of Tenochtitlán.

Unfortunately, the single most widely known fact about Mexico City is that its air is polluted. Many foreigners envision the city as being wrapped in black smog every day; they picture gray skies and streets packed with vehicles. But in reality, although the capital does have a serious pollution problem, it also has some of the clearest, bluest skies anywhere. At 7,349 feet, it often has mild daytime weather perfect for sightseeing and cool evenings comfortable for sleeping. Mornings can be glorious—chilly, but bright with the promise of the warming sun.

Smog is not the only thing Mexico City has in common with Los Angeles: The city lies on a fault similar to the San Andreas in California. In 1957 a major earthquake took a tragic toll, and scars are still visible from the devastating 1985 earthquake (8.1 on the Richter scale); the government reported 7,000 deaths, but according to vox populi, the death toll reached 50,000.

Growing nonstop, Mexico City covers about a 1,000-square-kilometer (386-square-mile) area of the valley. The city limits are surrounded on three sides by the state of Mexico and bordered on the south by the state of Morelos. Advertising campaigns and tour packages usually tout Mexico's paradisiacal beach resorts and ancient ruins, but cosmopolitan, historic Mexico City is an important destination in itself—more foreign and fascinating than many major capitals on faraway continents.

Pleasures and Pastimes

Dining

Mexico City has been a culinary capital ever since the time of Moctezuma. Chronicles tell of the daily banquet extravaganzas prepared for the slender Aztec emperor by his palace chefs. More than 300 different kinds of dishes were served for every meal, comprising vast assortments of meat and fowl seasoned in dozens of ways; limitless fruit, vegetables, and herbs; freshwater fish; and fresh seafood that was rushed to Tenochtitlán from both seacoasts by sprinting relay runners.

Until the 15th century, Europeans had never seen indigenous Mexican edibles such as corn, chilies of all varieties, tomatoes, potatoes, pumpkin, squash, avocado, turkey, cacao (chocolate), and vanilla. In turn, the colonization brought European gastronomic influence and ingredients—wheat, onion, garlic, olives, citrus fruit, cattle, sheep, goats, chickens, pigs (and lard for frying)—and ended up broadening the already complex pre-Hispanic cuisine into one of the most multifaceted and exquisite in the world: traditional Mexican.

Today's cosmopolitan Mexico City, with some 15,000 restaurants, is a gastronomic melting pot. Here you can find establishments ranging from simple family-style eateries to five-star world-class restaurants. In addition, there are fine international restaurants specializing in cuisines of practically every foreign culture. Among them, the most prevalent are Spanish and haute-cuisine French—France also invaded Mexico and influenced its eating traditions.

In the past decade a renaissance of Mexican cooking has brought about a new wave known as *cocina mexicana moderna* (modern Mexican cuisine), which is featured in many Mexico City restaurants. Emphasis is on the back-to-basics, delicate tastes of traditional regional dishes served in smaller portions with refined aesthetic presentation. Also significant in this modern trend is the revival of ancient indigenous cuisine—foods, especially fish, that were baked, grilled, or steamed in leaves.

Lodging

As might be expected of a megalopolis, Mexico City has 25,000 hotel rooms—enough to accommodate every taste and budget. You can lodge in the quaint or the colonial, the smoked-glass-and-steel high rise pampering the business traveler or in an elegant replica of an Italianate palace. Wherever you decide to unpack your bags, you'll be soaking up the atmosphere of something truly Mexican in all its amazing facets.

Museums

Mexico City is the cultural as well as political capital of the country, as evidenced by its museums—some of the finest in Latin America. In buildings often notable for their architecture, you can see the sweeping murals of famous native sons like Rivera, Orozco, and O'Gorman; the gripping surrealism of Frida Kahlo; stunning pre-Hispanic ceremonial pieces, and outstanding collections of religious art.

Nightlife and the Arts

Mexico City is the cultural capital of Latin America and, with the exception of Río de Janiero, has the liveliest nightlife of the region. There's something for every taste, from classical opera to symphony concerts, from a deservedly renowned folklore ballet to a lively square where mariachi (street musicians) play, and from discos to offbeat places where salsa and *danzon* (Cuban dance music) are headliners.

Shopping

Native crafts and specialties from all regions of Mexico—some already big export items abroad—are available in the capital, as are designer clothes. You'll also find modern art by some of the best young painters on the contemporary art circuit today, many of whom are already making a name for themselves in the United States, but you might come across some undiscovered talent, too. You can really pick up quality goods at big savings if you buy here instead of at overseas outlets of Mexican goods.

Sports and the Outdoors

Latin sports like jai alai and the *fiesta brava* (bullfighting)—both brought to Mexico by the Spanish conquerers—have enjoyed popularity for more than four centuries in the capital, which attracts the best athletes the country has to offer in these fields. The racetrack at the swank *hipódromo* offers live thoroughbred races daily. (These are getting harder to find in the country, as horses are being swapped for Foreign Book off-track betting operations, which feature instead reception of major U.S. derbies via satellite.) Tennis, golf, jogging—even rowing a boat in a park—are other sporting options for visitors.

EXPLORING

Most of Mexico City is aligned around two major intersecting thoroughfares: Paseo de la Reforma and Avenida Insurgentes. Administratively, the city is divided into 16 *delegaciones* (districts) and about 400 *colonias* (neighborhoods), each with street names fitting a given theme, such as river, philosopher, doctor, or revolutionary hero. The same street can change names as it goes through different colonias, making it a bit more difficult to find an address. Hence, most street addresses include the colonia they are in, and, unless you're going to an obvious place, it is very important to tell your taxi driver the name of the colonia.

The principal sights of Mexico City are organized into three areas. You need a full day to cover each thoroughly, though each can be done at breakneck speed in four or five hours. The first two areas—Alameda Central and the Zócalo, and Chapultepec Park and the Zona Rosa—can be covered on foot; exploring Coyoacán and San Angel in southern Mexico City will require a taxi ride or two.

Great Itineraries

You can spend a month in Mexico City and hardly touch the tip of the iceberg of its sights and attractions. But for stays shorter than this, here are some highlights.

IF YOU HAVE 3 DAYS

Start with the Zócalo with its exotic ruins, museums, and public buildings; then stroll to the Palace of Fine Arts and surroundings (don't forget a stop at the Casa de Azulejos for a Mexican lunch), and end the day at the Alameda Park area. Day 2, head for the Museum of Anthropology in the morning and the Zona Rosa in the afternoon, when it starts to come alive; visit the Insurgentes Market for some fun shopping or any other of the stores on our list. Day 3, go to Chapultepec Park to stroll the green pathways past the rowing lake and visit the Chapultepec Castle, the Museum of Modern Art, Rufino Tamayo,

Mexico City Orientation *(Boxes Refer to Detail Maps)*

Chapultepec Park and Zona Rosa

Alameda Central and Zócalo

Coyoacán and San Angel

and, of course, the zoo to see the pandas. Visit downtown's Plaza Garibaldi on your last night in town for a rousing mariachi send-off.

IF YOU HAVE 5 DAYS

Follow the itinerary of the first three days (☞ *above*); on Day 4 spend your time in San Angel (start with the Bazar Sábado if you are lucky enough to hit this area on a Saturday) and Coyoacán with its lovely casa-museums, especially those devoted to Frida Kahlo and Leon Trotsky. On Day 5 take an excursion to the Basílica of the Virgin of Guadalupe, Latin America's holiest shrine, and the pyramids of Teotihuacán, the holy site of a culture that reached its zenith before the arrival of the Spanish conquistadors. Climb at least one pyramid, visit the museum, and head back to Mexico City.

IF YOU HAVE 10 DAYS

Follow the five-day option and add a visit to the resort town of Cuernavaca, about an hour's drive from Mexico City; spend the day browsing in its museums and pretty main square, and then stay overnight at one of the converted mansions here. On Day 7 head back to Mexico City by Highway 95 and stop in Xochimilco, where you can ride through the floating gardens on a gondolalike boat and view an outstanding private collection of works by Diego Rivera and Frida Kahlo at the Dolores Olmedo Patino Museum. On Day 8 go to see the ancient Toltec ruins at Tula and then drive to the village of Tepozotlán, which has a beautiful Jesuit church. The next day, head to Puebla for a couple hours' tour, including the main square and the fine Amparo Museum, and then continue on for a short distance to the small town of Cholula, once a sacred ceremonial site. Climb to the top of the church built over a pyramid, and return to Puebla to overnight. Before returning to Mexico City on this last day, drive to Cacaxtla to see some of the best-preserved Mesoamerican murals in Mexico and stop in Cacaxtla en route.

Alameda Central and the Zócalo

This area is historical in focus: The Zócalo, its surrounding Centro Histórico and Alameda Park were the heart of both the Aztec and Spanish cities. Many of the streets in downtown Mexico City have been converted into pedestrian-only thoroughfares, adding to the ease of strolling here.

A Good Walk

Numbers in the text correspond to numbers in the margin and on the Alameda Central and the Zócalo map.

An excellent departure point for any tour of the city's center is the **Zócalo** ①, the heart and soul of old downtown. On the north side of this huge square you'll see the **Catedral Metropolitana** ② and, adjacent to it, the comparatively small 18th-century **Sagrario Chapel,** even more tilted than the cathedral. The **Templo Mayor** ③, temple ruins from the Aztec capital, are northeast of the cathedral on Calle Seminario. If you're interested in modern art, walk south about half a block from the Templo Mayor to the end of Seminario; then detour two blocks east to Calle Academia, where the **Museo José Luis Cuevas** ④ is located. Take Academia two blocks west to return to the Zócalo. The first building you'll see on your left is the massive **Palacio Nacional** ⑤, covering two city blocks. Walk south past the palacio to the corner, cross the street, and turn right to reach the part of the Zócalo occupied by the **Ayuntamiento** ⑥; then recross the street and walk across the open square in a northwest direction to Calle 5 de Mayo, where the **Monte de Piedad** building ⑦ stands.

Leaving the Zócalo, go five blocks west and then one block north to Calle Tacuba; here, at the colonial Plaza Manuel Tolsá, you'll see the **Museo Nacional de Arte** ⑧. From Calle Tacuba, head two short blocks south to Calle Madero, one of the city's most architecturally varied streets. On the south side of Madero, between Bolivar and Gante, is the **Palacio de Iturbide** ⑨. Continue along on the south side of Madero; less than a block west of the palacio you'll come to the colonial **La Iglesia de San Francisco** ⑩. An eye-catching blue facade just across the street will attract your attention to the **Casa de los Azulejos** ⑪, on the north side of Calle Madero at the corner of Callejón de la Condesa. In stark contrast to the church and the house is the 20th-century **Torre Latinoamericana** ⑫, less than half a block west on the Eje Central Lázaro Cárdenas, a wide four-lane avenue. Two other noteworthy buildings are on the same avenue to the north: the beautiful **Palacio de Bellas Artes** ⑬, whose one long side skirts Lázaro Cárdenas, though its entrance is actually on Juárez; and the **Dirección General de Correos** ⑭.

Continue north past the post office to Calle Tacuba and cross Lázaro Cárdenas; here Calle Tacuba turns into Avenida Hidalgo. One block to the west, you'll come to the **Museo Franz Mayer** ⑮, and across Avenida Hidalgo from the museum is the north side of the leafy **Alameda Central** ⑯. Avenida Juárez composes the southern border of the park; on this street you'll notice **Fonart,** a government-owned handicrafts store (☞ Shopping, *below*). To reach the **Museo Mural Diego Rivera** ⑰, take Juárez west to Calle Balderes (about 3½ blocks from Fonart); turn right and walk a short block to Calle Colon.

TIMING

The Zócalo area will be the quietest on Sunday, when the bureaucrats have their day of rest. However, Alameda Park will be jumping with children and their parents enjoying a Sunday outing. The park will be particularly festive during Christmas, when dozens of "Santas" will appear with plastic reindeer to take wish lists from long lines of children. The traditional Mexican Christmas kicks in on January 5, the eve of the Day of the Three Kings, and the Three Wise Men of biblical lore replace the Santas in the Alameda. Gorgeous Christmas paintings in lights deck the entire Zócalo from end to end and stream up Calle Madero past the Alameda Park to Paseo de la Reforma beyond the museums in Chapultepec Park.

During the daytime, the downtown area is filled with people and vibrant with activity. As in any other big city, travelers should be alert to pickpockets, especially on crowded buses and subways, and should avoid dark, deserted streets at night.

The streets in the walking tour are fairly close to one another and can be covered in half a day. The National Palace, Templo Mayor and its museum, and Franz Mayer Museum are worth an hour each of your time; you can do the Palace of Fine Arts in a half hour.

Sights to See

Numbers in the margin correspond to points of interest on the Alameda Central and the Zócalo map.

⑯ **Alameda Central** (Alameda Park). This park has been one of the capital's oases of greenery and a center for activities since Aztec times, when the Indians held their *tianguis* (market) on the site. In the early days of the Viceroyalty, it was where victims of the Inquisition were burned at the stake. National leaders, from 18th-century viceroys to Emperor Maximilian and President Díaz, clearly envisioned the park as a symbol of civic pride and prosperity: Over the centuries, it has been endowed with fountains, railings, a Moorish kiosk imported from Paris, and ash, willow, and poplar trees. Its most conspicuous man-made structure is the white marble semicircular **Hemiciclo a Benito Juárez** (monument to Juárez) on the Avenida Juárez side of the park. It is a fine place for strolling (and resting) and listening to live music on Sundays and holidays.

⑥ Ayuntamiento (City Hall). Mexico's city hall comprises twin buildings on the south side of the Zócalo. The one on the west is decorated with colonial tiles of arms of Cortés and other conquistadores; it was originally built in 1532, destroyed by fire in 1692, and rebuilt in 1722. In 1935, the Distrito Federal needed more office space; to maintain architectural symmetry in the Zócalo, the "matching" structure across the street (20 de Noviembre) was built.

⑪ Casa de los Azulejos (House of Tiles). Built as the palace of the counts of the Valle de Orizaba, an aristocratic family from early Spanish rule, this 17th-century masterpiece acquired its name from the tilework installed by a later descendant, a ne'er-do-well scion who married a rich woman. In addition to its well-preserved white, blue, and yellow tiles, the facade also features iron grillwork balconies and gray stonework. One of the prettiest Baroque structures in the country, it is currently occupied by Sanborns, a chain store–restaurant. Reopened in March 1995 following refurbishing, it has an interior more dazzling than ever, with two floors of dining instead of one. A Moorish patio, a monumental staircase, and a mural by Orozco are worth seeing, and this is a good place to stop for breakfast, lunch, or dinner. ⊠ *Calle Madero 4,* ☎ *5/512–9820.* ⊙ *Daily 7 AM–1 PM.*

❷ Catedral Metropolitana (Metropolitan Cathedral). Construction on this oldest and largest cathedral in Latin America began in 1573 on the north side of the Zócalo and continued intermittently throughout the next three centuries. The result is a medley of Baroque and neoclassical touches. Inside are four identical domes, their airiness made earthbound by rows of supportive columns. There are five altars and 14 chapels, mostly in the fussy, Churrigueresque style, an extremely decorative form of Spanish Baroque from the mid-17th century. Like most other Mexican churches, the cathedral is all but overshadowed by the innumerable paintings, altarpieces, and statues—in graphic color—of Christ and the saints. Over the centuries, this cathedral has sunk noticeably into the spongy subsoil. Its lopsidedness is evident when it is viewed from across the square, but engineering projects to stabilize the structure are always being undertaken.

⑭ Dirección General de Correos (General Post Office). Mexico City's main post-office building is a lovely example of neo-Renaissance architecture. Constructed of white sandstone in 1908, it epitomizes the grand imitations of European architecture common in Mexico during the Porfiriato, or dictatorship of Porfirio Díaz (1876–1910). On the upper floor, the **Museo de la Filatelia** exhibits the postal history of Mexico. ⊠ *Calle Tacuba and Eje Central Lázaro Cardenas, museum* ☎ *5/564–3133 or 5/510–2999.* ☞ *Free.* ⊙ *Museum weekdays 9–7, post office Mon.–Sat. 8 AM–midnight, Sun. 8–4.*

⑩ La Iglesia de San Francisco. Built on the site of Mexico's first convent (1524), this church supposedly was also the site of Moctezuma's zoo in Aztec times. The present 18th-century French Gothic church is one of the newest buildings on the street. The beautiful ceiling paintings have been restored. ⊠ *Calles Madero and 16 de Septiembre.* ⊙ *Daily 9–5.*

❼ Monte de Piedad (Mountain of Pity). Now housing the National Pawn Shop—which sells jewelry, antiques, and other goods not reclaimed by their owners—this structure was built to help the poor in the late 18th

23

Alameda Central and the Zócalo

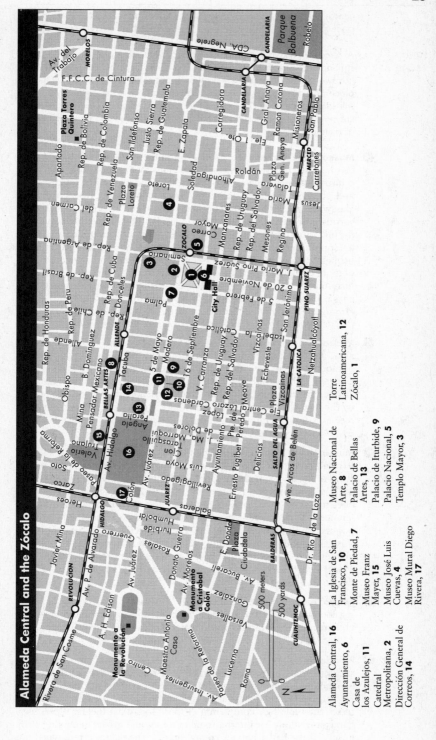

Alameda Central, **16**
Ayuntamiento, **6**
Casa de
los Azulejos, **11**
Catedral
Metropolitana, **2**
Dirección General de
Correos, **14**

La Iglesia de San
Francisco, **10**
Monte de Piedad, **7**
Museo Franz
Mayer, **15**
Museo José Luis
Cuevas, **4**
Museo Mural Diego
Rivera, **17**

Museo Nacional de
Arte, **8**
Palacio de Bellas
Artes, **13**
Palacio de Iturbide, **9**
Palacio Nacional, **5**
Templo Mayor, **3**

Torre
Latinoamericana, **12**
Zócalo, **1**

century. It's on the far northwest corner of the Zócalo, on what was once the site of an Aztec palace. ☉ *Mon.–Sat. about 10–7.*

At Cinco de Mayo 10 is one of Mexico City's most venerable and atmospheric cantinas, **Bar la Opera** (☎ 5/512–8959). The bar-restaurant has two claims to fame: Pancho Villa supposedly rode his horse into the place and demanded service by shooting a hole in the ceiling (you can still see it), and it was one of the first cantinas to allow women (though they were confined to a back room). Stop in for a drink, lunch, dinner, or a snack.

⑮ Museo Franz Mayer. Opened in 1986 in the 16th-century Hospital de San Juan de Dios, this museum has exhibits that include 16th- and 17th-century antiques, such as wooden chests inlaid with ivory, tortoiseshell, and ebony; tapestries, paintings, and lacquerware; Rococo clocks, glassware, and architectural ornamentation; and an unusually large assortment of Talavera ceramics and tiles. Wall plaques explain in detail the history of the production of tiles (*azulejos*), a technique carried from Mesopotamia and Egypt to the Persians, Arabs, and Spaniards, who brought it to Mexico. The museum also has an impressive collection of more than 700 different editions of the book *Don Quixote.* The old hospital building is faithfully restored, with pieces of the original frescoes peeking through; classical music plays in the background. ⊠ *Av. Hidalgo 45 at Plaza Santa Veracruz,* ☎ *5/518–2267.* ☞ *$1.25.* ☉ *Tues.–Sun. 10–5. Call ahead for English-speaking guide.*

④ Museo José Luis Cuevas. One of the newest museums in the downtown area, installed in a refurbished ex-convent, offers a superb collection of modern art, as well as works by Mexico's enfant terrible, José Luis Cuevas, who is ranked as one of the country's best contemporary artists. The sensational Sala Picasso contains more than 30 original works by the Spanish master. Up-and-coming Latin American artists may be seen at rotating temporary exhibits. ⊠ *Academia 13,* ☎ *5/542–8959.* ☞ *Small fee.* ☉ *Tues.–Sun. 10–6.*

⑰ Museo Mural Diego Rivera. The museum was built to display Diego Rivera's controversial mural *Sunday Afternoon Dream in the Alameda Park,* originally painted on a lobby wall of the Hotel Del Prado in 1947–48. The controversy was due to the Marxist Rivera's inscription, "God does not exist," which the artist later replaced with the bland "Conference of San Juan de Letrán" to placate Mexico's dominant Catholic population. Following the hotel's destruction in the 1985 earthquake, this gentle and poetic mural, which survived undamaged, was moved in its entirety across the street to the museum built to house it. ⊠ *Museo Mural Diego Rivera at Calles Balderas and Colón,* ☎ *5/510–2329.* ☞ *$2.* ☉ *Tues.–Sun. 10–6.*

⑧ Museo Nacional de Arte (National Art Museum). This neoclassical building contains a superb collection of religious and contemporary artwork, both on permanent display and in temporary exhibitions. ⊠ *Calle Tacuba 8,* ☎ *5/521–7320.* ☞ *$1.25.* ☉ *Tues.–Sun. 10–5.*

★ ⑬ Palacio de Bellas Artes (Fine Arts Palace). Construction on this colossal white-marble opera house was begun in 1904 by Porfirio Díaz, who wanted to add yet another ornamental building to his accomplishments. He was ousted during the same revolution that he bred and never got to see the building's completion (1934). Today the theater serves as a handsome venue for international and national artists, including such groups as the Ballet Folklórico de México. The palace is renowned for its architecture, by the Italian Adamo Boari, who also designed the post office; it includes an art nouveau facade trimmed in pre-Hispanic motifs. Inside are a Tiffany stained-glass curtain (depicting the two volcanoes outside Mexico City) and paintings by several celebrated Mexican artists, including Rufino Tamayo and Mexico's trio of muralists: Rivera, Orozco, and Siqueiros. It was here that Rivera reconstructed his mural *Man at the Crossroads,* which was commissioned for and then torn down from Rockefeller Center in New York City because of its political message (epitomized by the face of Lenin). Temporary art exhibits are also held at the palace museum. ⊠ *Eje Central Lázero Cardenas and Av. Juárez,* ☎ *5/709–3111.* ◪ *$1.25.* ◷ *Tues.–Sun. 10:30–6:30.*

OFF THE BEATEN PATH	**Tlatelolco –** At Avenida Reforma's northern end, about 2 kilometers (1 mile) north of the Palacio de Bellas Artes, the area known as Tlatelolco (Tla-tel-*ohl*-coh) was the domain of Cuauhtémoc—the last Aztec emperor before the conquest—and the sister city of Tenochtitlán. In modern times its name makes residents shudder, because it was here that several hundred protesting students were massacred by the Mexican army in 1968. The 1985 earthquake destroyed several high-rise apartments in Tlatelolco, killing hundreds.

The center of Tlatelolco is the **Plaza de las Tres Culturas,** so named because Mexico's three cultural eras—pre-Hispanic, colonial, and modern—are represented on the plaza in the form of the small ruins of a pre-Hispanic **ceremonial center** (visible from the roadway); the **Iglesia de Santiago Tlatelolco** (1609) and **Colegio de la Santa Cruz de Tlatelolco** (1535–36); and the ultracontemporary **Ministry of Foreign Affairs** (1970). The church contains the baptismal font of Juan Diego, the Indian to whom the Virgin of Guadalupe appeared in 1531. The Colegio (college), founded by the Franciscans after the conquest, was once attended by the sons of the Aztec nobility. ⊠ *Plaza is bounded on north by Manuel González, on west by Av. San Juan de Letrán Norte, and on east by Paseo de la Reforma, between Glorieta de Peralvillo and Glorieta Cuitláhuac.*

❾ Palacio de Iturbide (Emperor Iturbide's Palace). Built in 1780, this handsome Baroque structure—note the imposing door and its carved-stone trimmings—became the residence of Iturbide in 1822. One of the heroes of the independence movement, the misguided Iturbide proclaimed himself emperor of a country that had thrown off the imperial yoke of the Hapsburgs only a year before; his own empire, needless to say, was short-lived. Now his home is owned by Banamex (Banco Nacional de México) and sponors major cultural exhibitions in the atrium. ⊠ *Calle Madero 17,* ☎ *5/518–2187.* ◪ *Free.* ◷ *Inner atrium weekdays 9–6 and weekends during exhibitions.*

★ **❺ Palacio Nacional** (National Palace). This grand government building was initiated by Cortés on the site of Moctezuma's home and remodeled by the viceroys; its current form dates from 1693, although a third floor was added in 1926. Now the seat of government, it has always served as a public-function site. In fact, during colonial times, the first bullfight in New Spain took place in the inner courtyard.

Diego Rivera's sweeping, epic murals on the second floor of the main courtyard have the power to mesmerize. For more than 16 years (1929–45), he and his assistants mounted the scaffolds day and night, perfecting techniques adapted from Renaissance Italian frescoes. The result, nearly 1,200 square feet of vividly painted wall space, is grandiosely entitled *Epic of the Mexican People in Their Struggle for Freedom and Independence.* The larger-than-life paintings represent two millennia of Mexican history, as seen through the artist's vivid imagination. The innocence of pre-Hispanic times is portrayed by idyllic, almost sugary scenes of Tenochtitlán. Only a few vignettes—a lascivious woman baring her leg in the marketplace, a man offering a human arm for sale, and the carnage of warriors—acknowledge other aspects of ancient life. As you walk around the floor, you'll pass images depicting the savagery of the conquest and the hypocrisy of the Spanish priests, the noble independence movement, and the bloody revolution. Marx appears amid scenes of class struggles, toiling workers, industrialization (which Rivera idealized), the decadence of the bourgeoisie, and nuclear holocaust. The murals are among Rivera's finest works. They are also the most accessible and probably the most visited of the artist's paintings. The palace also houses two minor museums—dealing with 19th-century president Benito Juárez and the Mexican Congress—and the liberty bell rung by Padre Hidalgo to proclaim independence in 1810 hangs high on the central facade. It chimes every eve of September 16, while from the balcony below, the president repeats *el grito*, the historic shout of independence. *East side of Zócalo.* 🎫 *Free.* ☉ *Daily 9–5; closed holidays.*

❸ **Templo Mayor** (Great Temple). The excavated ruins of the ancient hub of the Aztec empire was unearthed accidentally in 1978 by telephone repairmen and has since been turned into a vast and historically significant archaeological site and museum. At this temple, dedicated to the Aztec cult of death, captives from rival tribes—as many as 10,000 at a time—were sacrificed to the bloodthirsty god of war, Huitzilopochtli. Seven rows of leering stone skulls adorn one side of the structure.

The adjacent **Museo del Templo Mayor** contains 3,000 pieces unearthed from the site and from other ruins in central Mexico; they include ceramic warriors, stone carvings and knives, skulls of sacrificial victims, a rare gold ingot, models and scale reproductions, and a room on the destruction of Tenochtitlán by the Spaniards. The centerpiece is an 8-ton disk discovered at the Templo Mayor; it depicts the myth of the moon goddess Coyolxauhqui, who was decapitated and dismembered by her brother Huitzilopochtli for trying to persuade her 400 other brothers to murder their mother. ✉ *Guatemala and Argentina.* ☎ *5/542–4784, 5/542–4785, or 5/542–4786.* 🎫 *$2.25.* ☉ *Tues.–Sun. 9–5. Call to schedule English-language tours.*

⓬ **Torre Latinoamericana** (Latin American Tower). Once touted as the tallest building in the capital before the Hotel de Mexico was built in the 1980s, this 47-story skyscraper was completed in 1956, and on clear days the observation deck and restaurant on the top floors afford fine views of the city. ✉ *Calle Madero and Eje Central Lázaro Cárdenas.* 🎫 *$1.25.* ☉ *Observation deck daily 10 AM–11 PM.*

❶ **Zócalo** (formal name: **Plaza de la Constitución**). Mexico City's historical plaza was built by the Spaniards, using Indian slave labor. This enormous paved square, the largest in the Western Hemisphere, occupies the site of the ceremonial center of Tenochtitlán, the capital of the Aztec empire, which once comprised 78 buildings. Throughout the 16th, 17th, and 18th centuries, the Spaniards and their descendants constructed elaborate churches and convents, elegant mansions, and stately public edifices, many of which have long since been converted to other uses. There is an air of Old Europe to this section of the city, which, in its entirety (the Centro Histórico), is a national monument that has been undergoing a major refurbishing; at press time, much had already been accomplished and even more was under way. Imposing buildings are constructed with the ubiquitous blood-red volcanic *tezontle* stone and the quarry stones that the Spaniards recycled from the rubble of the Aztec temples they razed. Throngs of small shops, eateries, cantinas, street vendors, and women dressed in native Indian dress contribute to an inimitably Mexican flavor, even an exuberance.

Zócalo means "pedestal" or "base": In the mid-19th century an independence monument was envisioned for the square, but it was never built. The term stuck, however, and now the word *zócalo* is applied to the main plazas of most Mexican cities. Mexico City's Zócalo (because it's the original, it is always capitalized) is used for government rallies, protest marches and sit-ins, and festive events. It is also the focal point for Independence Day celebrations on the eve of September 16 and is spectacularly festooned during the Christmas–New Year holiday season. Flag-raising and -lowering ceremonies take place here in the early morning and late afternoon. ⊠ *Bounded by 16 de Septiembre to south, 5 de Mayo to north, Piño Suarez to east, and Monte de Piedad to west.*

Chapultepec Park and Zona Rosa

The Paseo de la Reforma, modeled after the Champs-Elysées in Paris, was built by Emperor Maximilian in 1865 to connect the Palacio Nacional (☞ Alameda Central and the Zócalo, *above*) with his residence, the Castillo de Chapultepec. At the northern end of Reforma are Tlatelolco (☞ Alameda Central and the Zócalo, *above*), the Lagunilla Market, and Plaza Garibaldi, where the mariachis gather; to the south, Reforma wends its leisurely way west into the wealthy neighborhoods of Lomas de Chapultepec, where most of the houses and estates are behind stone walls.

Two areas along Reforma of particular interest are the Zona Rosa (Pink Zone) and Chapultepec Park. Start your exploration of these sections at the junction of Reforma, Avenida Juárez, and Bucareli, just west of the Alameda Central. Along the stretch of Reforma west of this intersection are a number of statues erected at the request of Porfirio Díaz to honor illustrious men, including Simón Bolívar, Columbus, Pasteur, and Cuauhtémoc. The best known, the Monumento a la Independencia (or Angel Monument), marks the western edge of the Zona Rosa.

For years, the Zona Rosa has been a favorite part of the city for tourists and locals because of the plethora of restaurants, cafés, art and antiques galleries, hotels, discos, and shops (many of which are detailed in the Dining, Nightlife, and Shopping sections, *below*). With the mushrooming of fast-food places and some tacky bars and stores, the Zona—as it is affectionately called—has lost some of its former gloss but nonetheless still draws the faithful. Most of the buildings in the Zona Rosa are two or three stories high; they were originally private homes built in the 1920s for the wealthy. All the streets are wistfully named after European cities; some, such as Genova, are garden-lined pedestrian malls accented with contemporary bronze statuary.

To enjoy the Pink Zone, just walk the lengths of Hamburgo and Londres and some of the side streets, especially Copenhague—a veritable restaurant row. The large handicrafts market on Londres is officially Mercado Insurgentes, though most people call it either Mercado Zona Rosa or Mercado Londres. Just opposite the market's Londres entrance is Plaza del Angel, a small shopping mall that has a *minitianguis* (native market) on weekends. Contrasting with the mercado is the sleek Plaza La Rosa shopping mall.

Four blocks southwest of the Zona Rosa, at Avenida Chapultepec, you'll come to the main entrance to Bosques de Chapultepec, or Chapultepec Park.

TIMING

You can easily spend an hour each at the museums (☞ Sights to See, *below*), with the exception of the National Museum of Anthropology, which is gigantic compared to its sister cultural centers. You can have a quick go-through in two hours, but to really appreciate the fine exhibits anywhere from a half-day to two full days would be more appropriate. Tuesday to Saturday are good days to visit the museums and stroll around the park. On Sunday and Mexican holidays the park and museums are packed with families with lots of small children because the entrance to the museums is free.

Sights to See

Numbers in the margin correspond to points of interest on the Chapultepec Park and Zona Rosa map.

❷ Bosque de Chapultepec (Chapultepec Park). This 1,600-acre green space, divided into three sections, draws families on weekend outings, cyclists, joggers, and museum goers. It is one of the oldest parts of Mexico City, having been inhabited by the Mexica (Aztec) tribe as early as the 13th century. The Mexica poet-king Nezahualcoyotl had his palace here and ordered construction of the aqueduct that brought water to Tenochtitlán. Ahuehuete trees (Moctezuma cypress) still stand from that era, when the woods were used as hunting preserves.

At the park's principal entrance, one block west of the Chapultepec metro station, you'll see the **Monumento a los Niños Héroes** (Monument to the Boy Heroes), consisting of six marble columns adorned with eaglets. In the monument are supposedly buried the six young cadets who wrapped themselves in the Mexican flag and then jumped to their deaths from the ramparts during the U.S. invasion of 1847. (That war may not take up much space in American textbooks, but to the Mexicans it is still a troubling symbol of their neighbor's aggressive dominance: The war cost Mexico almost half of its national territory—the present states of Texas, California, Arizona, New Mexico, and Nevada.)

Uphill from the entrance is the ☞ **Castillo de Chapultepec** and its National History Museum. Heading downhill again after leaving the Castillo, you'll go past the much smaller ☞ **Museo del Caracol.** North of the Castillo on the south side of Paseo de la Reforma is the ☞ **Museo de Arte Moderno;** almost directly across Paseo de La Reforma on its south side and west of Calle Gandhi, the **Museo Rufino Tamayo** may be found. Just west of the Museo Rufino Tamayo on the same side of Reforma is the ☞ **Museo Nacional de Antropologia.** Cross Reforma again and you'll come to the entrance to the ☞ **Zoologico.**

Other sights in the first section of Chapultepec Park include three small boating lakes; the Casa del Lago, a cultural center; and a botanical garden. **Los Pinos,** the residential palace of the president of Mexico, is located along a small highway called Avenida Constituyentes, which cuts through the park. This is heavily guarded and cannot be visited.

The less crowded second and third sections of Chapultepec Park contain a fancy restaurant; ☞ **Chapultapec Magico;** ☞ **El Papolate;** the national cemetery; and the **Lienzo Charro,** or Mexican rodeo.

★ **❸ Castillo de Chapultepec.** Located on Cerro del Chapulín (Grasshopper Hill), the Castillo (Castle) has borne witness to the turbulence and grandeur of all Mexican history. In its earliest permutations, it was a Mexica palace, where the Indians made one of their last stands against the Spaniards; later it was a Spanish hermitage, gunpowder plant, and

Chapultepec Park and Zona Rosa

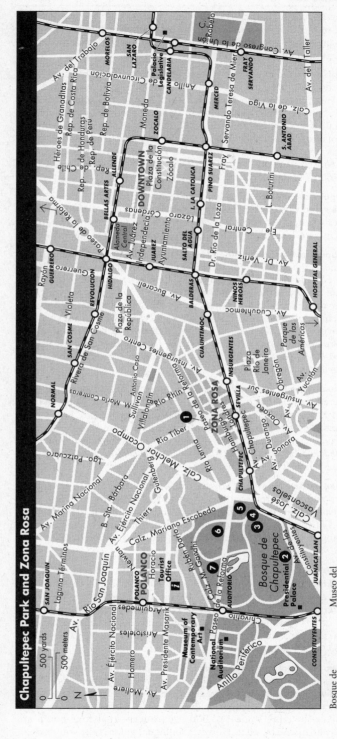

Bosque de
Chapultepec, **2**
Castillo de
Chapultepec, **3**
Monumento a la
Independencia
(El Angel), **1**
Museo de Arte
Moderno, **5**

Museo del
Caracol, **4**
Museo Nacional de
Antropología, **7**
Museo Rufino
Tamayo, **6**

military college. Emperor Maximilian used the castle (parts of which date from 1783) as his residence, and his example was followed by various presidents from 1872 to 1940, when Lázaro Cárdenas decreed that it be turned into the **National History Museum.**

Displays on the museum's ground floor cover Mexican history from the conquest to the revolution; the bathroom, bedroom, tea salon, and gardens were used by Maximilian and his wife, Carlotta, during the 19th century. The ground floor also contains works by 20th-century muralists O'Gorman, Orozco, and Siqueiros, while the upper floor is devoted to temporary exhibits, Díaz's malachite vases, and religious art. A free, but unreliable, shuttle bus runs between this museum and the Museo Caracol (☞ *below*). ⊠ *Section 1 of Chapultepec Park,* ☎ *5/286–0700.* ☜ *$2.* ☉ *Tues.–Sun. 9–5.*

☾ **Chapultepec Mágico.** This children's amusement park offers various games and rides, including a *montaña rusa* ("Russian mountain," or roller coaster). ⊠ *Section 2 of Chapultepec Park,* ☎ *5/515–0535.* ☜ *Under $2; includes 30 free rides or games.* ☉ *Tues.–Sun. 9–4:15.*

☾ **El Papalote, Museo del Niño** (The Butterfly, Children's Museum). Five theme sections compose this excellent interactive museum: *Our World*; *The Human Body*; the pun-intended *Con-Sciencia,* with exhibits relating to both consciousness and science; *Communication,* which focuses on topics ranging from language to computers; and *Expression,* which includes art, music, theater, and literature. There are also temporary exhibits, workshops, an IMAX theater, store, and restaurant. ⊠ *Av. Constituyentes 268, Section 2 of Chapultepec Park,* ☎ *5/224–1260.* ☜ *$3 adults, $2.20 children.* ☉ *Daily 9–1 and 2–6 plus Thurs. 7 PM–11 PM.*

❶ **Monumento a la Independencia.** A Corinthian column topped by a gold-covered angel is the city's most beautiful monument, built to celebrate the 100th anniversary of Mexico's War of Independence. Beneath the pedestal lie the remains of the principal heroes of the independence movement; an eternal flame burns in their honor. ⊠ *Traffic circle between Calle Río Tiber, Paseo de la Reforma, and Calle Florencia, 1 block west of U.S. embassy.*

❺ **Museo de Arte Moderno** (Museum of Modern Art). Two rooms are devoted to plastic arts from the 1930s to the 1960s; a third focuses on the past 20 years; and a fourth room and annex house temporary exhibits of contemporary Mexican painting, lithography, sculpture, and photography. ⊠ *Reforma and Gandhi, Section 1 of Chapultepec Park,* ☎ *5/553–6233.* ☜ *$3.* ☉ *Tues.–Sun. 10–6.*

❹ **Museo del Caracol.** Officially, it's the **Galería de la Lucha del Pueblo Mexicano por su Libertad,** but most people refer to it by the more fanciful name "Museum of the Snail," because of its spiral shape. The gallery concentrates on the 400 years from the Viceroyalty to the Constitution of 1917, using dioramas and light-and-sound displays that children can appreciate. ⊠ *Section 1 of Chapultepec Park,* ☎ *5/553–6285.* ☜ *$1.25.* ☉ *Tues.–Sun. 9–5.*

★ ❼ **Museo Nacional de Antropología** (National Museum of Anthropology). This is the greatest museum in the country—and arguably one of the finest archaeological museums anywhere. Even its architectural design (by Pedro Ramírez Vázquez) is distinguished. The collection is so extensive—covering some 100,000 square feet—that four hours are barely adequate to see it. However, bilingual guides take you through the highlights in two-hour tours. English guidebooks are available in the bookshop.

Begin in the Orientation Room, which traces the course of Mexican prehistory and the pre-Hispanic cultures of Mesoamerica. The 12 rooms on the ground floor include preclassical cultures, Teotihuacán, the Toltecs, Oaxaca, the Maya, and the north and west of Mexico. The so-called Aztec calendar stone and profusely feathered Aztec headdresses, reconstructed Maya temples, and reproductions of the Maya paintings from the ruins of Bonampak are just some of the highlights. Statuary, jewelry, weapons, clay figurines, and pottery evoke the brilliant, quirky, and frequently bloodthirsty civilizations that peopled Middle America during Europe's Dark Ages. The nine rooms on the upper floor contain faithful ethnographic displays of current indigenous peoples, using maps, photographs, household objects, folk art, clothing, and religious articles. ⊠ *Section 1 of Chapultepec Park,* ☎ *5/553–1902.* ⊡ *$2.50.* ۞ *Tues.–Sat. 9–7, Sun. and holidays 10–6.*

❻ Museo Rufino Tamayo. Within its modernistic trappings, this sleek museum contains the private collection of the noted Mexican muralist as well as many of his own paintings. Tamayo's unerring eye for great art is evidenced by paintings and sculptures by such contemporary masters as Picasso, Miró, Warhol, and Henry Moore. ⊠ *Av. Reforma west of Gandhi, Section 1 of Chapultepec Park,* ☎ *5/286–6519.* ⊡ *$1.25.* ۞ *Tues.–Sun. 10–6.*

<table>
<tr><td>NEED A
BREAK?</td><td>There is no restaurant in the park, only a rather dreary snack bar in the Anthropological Museum. It's worth taking a five-minute taxi ride just north of the museum to Colonia Polanco, which is quickly upstaging the Zona Rosa as the chic place for shopping and dining. The outdoor tables at Sanborcito's, also known as Restaurante Polanco, are usually filled by the residents of this well-heeled, tranquil neighborhood. It has a brunch. ⊠ Julio Verne and Emilio Castelar, overlooking park with statue of Lincoln.</td></tr>
</table>

☺ Ripley's Museo de lo Increíble (Museum of the Incredible). Fun for children of all ages, it has 14 exhibit rooms chockablock with believe-it-or-not items. ⊠ *Londres 4 (east of Zona Rosa),* ☎ *5/546–3784 or 5/546–76700.* ⊡ *$3 adults, $2.50 children.* ۞ *Weekdays 11–7, weekends 10–7.*

☺ Zoológica. In the early 16th century, Mexico City's zoo housed a small private collection of animals belonging to Moctezuma II; it became quasi-public when he allowed favored subjects to visit it. The current zoo opened on this site in the 1920s and features the usual suspects as well as some superstar pandas; a gift from China, the original pair produced the world's first baby born in captivity (much to competitive China's chagrin). The zoo is surrounded by a miniature train depot, botanical gardens, and lakes where you can go rowing. You'll see the entrance on Reforma, across the street from the Museum of Anthropology. ⊠ *Section 1 of Chapultepec Park, no phone.* ⊡ *Free.* ۞ *Tues.–Sun. 9–4:15.*

Coyoacán and San Angel

Originally separate colonial towns, Coyoacán and San Angel were both absorbed by the ever-growing capital, yet they retain their original pueblo charm and tranquillity.

Coyoacán means "Place of the Coyotes"—according to local legend, a coyote used to bring chickens to a friar who had saved the coyote from being strangled by a snake. Coyoacán was founded by Toltecs in the 10th century and later settled by the Aztecs, or Mexica. Bernal Díaz Castillo, a Spanish chronicler, wrote that there were 6,000 houses at the time of the conquest. Cortés set up headquarters in Coyoacán during his siege of Tenochtitlán and at one point considered making it his capital. He changed his mind for political reasons, but many of the Spanish buildings left from the two-year period it took to build Mexico City still stand.

Today, Coyoacán still exudes its charm as an old pueblo. The neighborhood has had many illustrious residents from Mexico's rich and intellectual elite, including Miguel de la Madrid, president of Mexico from 1982 to 1988; Orozco, the muralist; Gabriel Figueroa, cinematographer for Luis Buñuel and John Huston; the film star Dolores del Río; El Indio Fernández, a film director; and writers Carlos Monsiváis, Elena Poniatowska, and Jorge Ibargüengoitia. While superficially it resembles San Angel, Coyoacán has a more animated street life. Most of the houses and other buildings honor the traditions of colonial Mexican architecture, and the neighborhood is very well kept. The generations upon generations of families living here have guarded their treasure well.

San Angel is a little colonial enclave of cobblestoned streets, gardens drenched in bougainvillea, stone walls, and pastel houses. It became an enclave of wealthy Spaniards during the Viceroyalty period, around the time of the construction of the Ex-Convento del Carmen (☞ *below*). Drawn to the area because of its rivers, pleasant climate, and rural ambience, the elite class proceeded to build haciendas and mansions that, for many, were country homes. Like neighboring Coyoacán, San Angel was known only as a suburb of Mexico City until the goverment decided to incorporate it into the capital.

A Good Tour
Numbers in the text correspond to numbers in the margin and on the Coyoacán and San Angel map.

To explore the southern part of the city—which until 50 years ago comprised separate pueblos—take a taxi or *pesero* (minibus) down Avenida Insurgentes and get off at Avendia La Paz. (The longest avenue in the city, at 34 kilometers, or 21 miles, Insurgentes did not exist as such before the 1920s.) On the east side of Insurgentes is the bizarre **Monumento al General Alvaro Obregón** ①. Cross Insurgentes on Avenida La Paz, and take the southern fork off Avenida La Paz (Calle Madero) until you come to the **Plaza San Jacinto** ②. You are now in San Angel. Stroll to the **Casa del Risco** ③ on the south side of the plaza and, if it's a Saturday, visit the **Bazar Sabado** (☞ Shopping, *below*) on the northern end. Return to Avenida Revolución and Plaza del Carmen, which lies at the corner of Calle Monasterio; inside is the colonial **Ex-Convento del Carmen** ④. Now take Avenida Revolución one long block north to the **Museo Alvar y Carmen T. de Carrillo Gil** ⑤.

The next part of the tour is set in Coyoacán, which extends east of Avenida Insurgentes about 1 kilometer (less than a mile) from San Angel. Consider taking a taxi to the Plaza de Santa Catarina on Avenida Francisco Sosa, about halfway into the center of Coyoacán, because the tour involves a lot of walking.

If you decide to hoof it, go south on Avenida Universidad past the **Viveros de Coyoacán**—an expansive, tree-filled park. A long block past the end of the Viveros, you'll come to Avenida Francisco Sosa. Head east on this major thoroughfare until you come to the pretty 16th-century **Iglesia de Santa Catarina,** which dominates the tiny **Plaza Santa Catarina**; the plaza also features a bust of Mexican historian Francisco Sosa, who lived here and wrote passionately about Coyoacán. Continue east along Avenida Francisco Sosa until you come to No. 202, the **Casa de Jesús Reyes Heroles**; the former home of the late minister of education is a fine example of 20th-century architecture on the colonial model (it's now used as a cultural center). If you keep going in the same direction, you'll pass **Casa de Diego de Ordaz** at the corner of Tres Cruces. This *mudéjar* (Spanish-Arabic) structure, adorned with inlaid mortar, was home to a former captain in Cortés's army.

Now you're standing at the entrance of the **Jardin Centenario** ⑥. The **Templo de San Juan Bautist** and the **Casa de Cortés** ⑦ sit in the small **Plaza Hidalgo** adjacent to and north of the Jardin. Walk two blocks southeast of Plaza Hidalgo on Calle Higuera to the corner of Calle Vallarta where the **Casa de la Malinche** ⑧ is. The house, darkened with age, faces an attractive park called **Plaza de la Conchita,** in the center of which lies an 18th-century church.

Return to Plaza Hidalgo and walk five blocks north on Calle Allende to the corner of Calle Londres and the **Museo de Frida Kahlo** ⑨. It's linked historically with the fortresslike **Museo de Leon Trotsky** ⑩; to reach it, go three blocks east on Londres and two long blocks north on Morelos to Calle Viena.

TIMING

You're likely to want to linger in these elegant and beautiful sections of town, especially in Coyoacán. The Frida Kahlo and Leon Trotsky museums give you an intense and intimate look at the lives of two famous people who were friends and lovers and who breathed their personalities into the places where they lived; you should spend at least an hour at each one. The other museums are much smaller and merit less time. The weekends are the liveliest at the Plaza Hidalgo and its neighboring Jardin Centenario, where the street life explodes into a fiesta.

Sights to See

❼ **Casa de Cortés.** The place where the Aztec emperor Cuauhtémoc was held prisoner by the conquistador Cortés is reputed to have been rebuilt in the 18th century from the stones of his original house by one of Cortés's descendants; the municipal government now has offices here. Dominating the little square on which it sits, this was almost the city's first city hall, but Cortés decided to rebuild Tenochtitlán instead. The two-story, salmon-color structure is gorgeous, with its wide arches and tiled patio. ✉ *Plaza Hidalgo off Av. Hidalgo and Av. Francisco Sosa.*

NEED A BREAK?

A few blocks from Plaza Hidalgo, **La Guadalupana** (✉ Av. Higuera between Caballocalco and San Francisco Figeroca) is a popular refurbished cantina from the 1920s with snacks (such as shrimp broth and *totopos con frijoles,* a crispy fried corn tortilla with beans). The place has a definite bohemian feeling and is packed with young professionals of both sexes. The quesadillas served in the little restaurants on Higuera have attained citywide fame.

❽ **Casa de la Malinche.** One of the most powerful symbols of the conquest is located in Coyoacán but, significantly perhaps, is not even marked. It's the somber-looking, fortresslike residence of Malinche, Cortés's Indian mistress and interpreter, whom the Spaniards called Doña María and the Indians called Malintzín. By enabling Cortés to communicate with the Nahuatl-speaking tribes he met en route to Tenochtitlán, Malinche was instrumental in aiding the conquest. Today she is a much-reviled Mexican symbol of a traitorous xenophile—hence the term *malinchista,* used to describe a Mexican who prefers things foreign. The legends say that Cortés's wife died in this house, poisoned by the conquistador. They also say he wrote his famous letter to Emperor Charles V here: Tired of his administrative duties, Cortés asked Charles for permission to start another exploratory expedition into south-

Coyoacán and San Angel

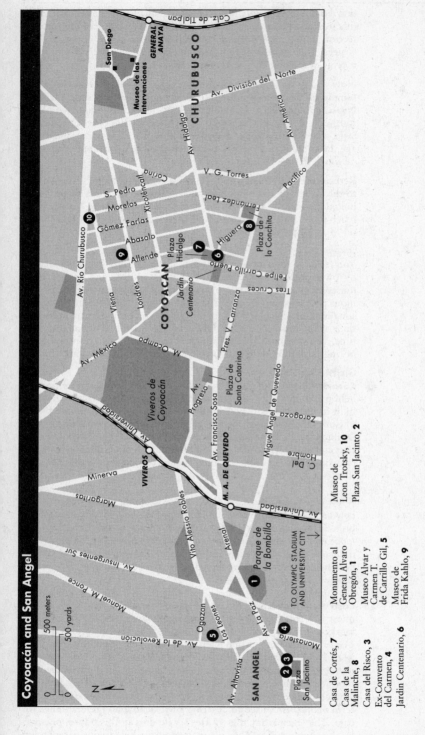

Casa de Cortés, **7**

Casa de la
Malinche, **8**

Casa del Risco, **3**

Ex-Convento
del Carmen, **4**

Jardin Centenario, **6**

Monumento al
General Alvaro
Obregón, **1**

Museo Alvar y
Carmen T.
de Carrillo Gil, **5**

Museo de
Frida Kahlo, **9**

Museo de
Leon Trotsky, **10**

Plaza San Jacinto, **2**

ern Mexico and Central America. The trip almost cost him his life and the command of New Spain. ⊠ *2 blocks east of Plaza Hidalgo on Calle Higuera at Vallarta.*

❸ Casa del Risco. If you visit this 1681 mansion, you'll see one of the prettiest houses facing the Plaza de San Jacinto. A huge free-form sculpture—exploding with colorful porcelain, tiles, shells, and mosaics— covers the entire eastern wall of its patio. Although it's not ranked among the city's top museums, the **Museo de la Casa del Risco** houses a splendid collection of 14th- to 18th-century European and colonial Mexican paintings as well as period furnishings. ⊠ *Plaza de San Jacinto 5 and 15,* ☎ *5/616–2711.* ☒ *Free.* ☉ *Tues.–Sun. 10–5.*

❹ Ex-Convento del Carmen (Carmelite Convent and Church). Erected by Carmelite friars with the help of an Indian chieftain between 1615 and 1628, this cloister with its tile-covered domes, fountains, and gardens is one of the most interesting examples of colonial religious architecture in this part of the city. The church still operates, but the convent is now the **Museo Regional del Carmen,** with a fine collection of 18th-century religious paintings, icons, and mummified corpses. Two exhibit salons were added recently. ⊠ *Av. Revolución 4 at Monasterio 10,* ☎ *5/616– 2816 or 5/616–1177.* ☒ *$2, Sun. free.* ☉ *Tues.–Sun. 10–5.*

❻ Jardín Centenario. Small fairs, amateur musical performances, poetry readings, and palm readings are frequent occurrences in this large park surrounded by outdoor cafés. At the far end of the Jardín you'll see **Templo San Juan Bautista,** one of the first churches to be built in New Spain. It was completed in 1582, and its door is decorated with a Baroque arch. ⊠ *Between Calles Centenario, Hidalgo, and Caballo Calco.*

❶ Monumento al General Alvaro Obregón. This somber gray granite monument marks the spot where the national hero Obregón was gunned down in a restaurant in 1928. Its main attraction used to be none other than Obregón's hand and forearm, which he lost in a 1915 battle and were eerily preserved in formaldehyde. However, they've been removed for burial. ⊠ *Parque de la Bombilla, east of Av. La Paz at Av. Insurgentes.*

❺ Museo Alvar y Carmen T. de Carrillo Gil. This private collection contains early murals by Orozco, Rivera, and Siqueiros; works by modern artists from Europe such as Klee and Picasso; and temporary expositions of young Mexican artists. ⊠ *Av. Revolución 1608 at Desierto de los Leones,* ☎ *5/550–3983.* ☒ *$1.* ☉ *Tues.–Sun. 10–6.*

★ **❾ Museo de Frida Kahlo.** The house where the painter Frida Kahlo was born—and lived with Diego Rivera almost continuously from 1929 until her death in 1954—is fascinating. Kahlo has become quite a cult figure in recent years, not only because of her paintings—mostly self-portraits in the surrealist tradition—but also because of her bohemian lifestyle and flamboyant individualism. As a child Kahlo was crippled by polio, and several years later she was impaled on a tramway rail. She had countless operations, including the amputation of a leg; was addicted to painkillers; had affairs with Leon Trotsky and several women; and married Rivera twice. Kahlo's astounding vitality and originality are reflected in this house, from the giant papier-mâché skeletons outside and the painted tin retablos on the staircase to the gloriously decorated kitchen and the bric-a-brac in her bedroom. Even if you know nothing about Kahlo, a visit to the museum—also filled with letters, diaries, clothes, and paintings by Kahlo and other great moderns, including Klee and Duchamp—will leave you with a strong, visceral impression of this early feminist artist. ⊠ *Londres 127,* ☎ *5/554–5999.* 🎟 *$1.25.* ⊘ *Tues.–Sun. 10–6.*

⑩ Museo de Leon Trotsky. Resembling an anonymous and forbidding fortress, with turrets for armed guards, this is where Leon Trotsky lived and was murdered. It is difficult to believe that it's the final resting place for the ashes of one of the most important figures of the Russian Revolution, but that only adds to the allure of the house, which is owned by Trotsky's grandson.

This is a modest, austere dwelling—anyone taller than five feet must stoop to pass through doorways to Trotsky's bedroom (with bullet holes in the walls from the first assassination attempt, in which the muralist Siqueiros was implicated), his wife's study, the dining room, and the study where Ramón Mercader finally drove an ice ax into Trotsky's head. (On his desk, cluttered with writing paraphernalia and an article he was revising in Russian, the calendar is open to that fateful day of August 20, 1940.) The volunteers will tell you how Trotsky's teeth left a permanent scar on Mercader's hand; how he clung to life for 26 hours; what his last words were; and how his death was sponsored by the United States. Not all of the volunteers, however, speak English. ⊠ *Viena 45,* ☎ *5/658–8732.* 🎟 *$1.25.* ⊘ *Tues.–Sun. 10–5.*

� Reino Aventura. This 100-acre theme park on the southern edge of the city comprises six "villages": Mexican, French, Swiss, Polynesian, American, and Children's World. Shows include performances by trained dolphins. ⊠ *Southwest of Coyoacán on Carretera Picacho a Ajusco, Km 1.5.* 🎟 *About $8; includes entrance and all rides.* ⊘ *Fri.–Sun. 10–6:30.*

★ ② Plaza San Jacinto. This cozy plaza with a grisly history is the center of San Angel. In 1847 about 50 Irish soldiers of St. Patrick's Battalion—who had sided with the Mexicans in the Mexican-American War—had their foreheads branded here with the letter *D* (for deserters) and were then hanged by the Americans. These men had been enticed to swim the Rio Grande and desert the ranks of U.S. General Zachary Taylor by pleas to the historic and religious ties between Spain and Ireland; as settlers in Mexican Texas, they felt their allegiance lay with Catholic Mexico, and they were among the bravest fighters in the war. They met their end when the American flag flew over Chapultepec Castle (☞ *above*) after the death of the *niños héroes.* A memorial plaque at No. 23 listing their names and expressing Mexico's gratitude for their help in the "unjust North American invasion" now stands in the plaza, where each September a ceremony is conducted in their honor. Off to one side of the plaza, the excellent handicrafts market, **Bazar Sábado,** is held on Saturday (☞ *Shopping, below*). ⊠ *Between Miramon, Cda. Santisima, Dr. Galvez, and Madero.*

DINING

Mexico City mealtime hours are 7–11 AM for breakfast (*desayuno*), 1–4 PM for lunch (*comida*), and 7 PM–midnight for dinner (*cena*). At deluxe restaurants, dress is generally formal (jacket and tie), and reservations are almost always required; see reviews for details. (Even if a deluxe restaurant doesn't *require* a jacket and tie, diners are likely to feel out-of-place if they're not well dressed.) For tourists on the run there are American-style coffee shops (VIPS, Denny's, Shirley's, and Sanborns) all over the city; some are open 24 hours.

Zona Rosa restaurants get filled pretty quickly on Saturday nights, especially the Saturday coinciding with the *quincena*, or payday, for nearly everyone in the city, which falls on the 1st and 15th of each month.

The following selection of recommended restaurants is organized by cuisine and price range.

CATEGORY	COST*
$$$$	over $40
$$$	$25–$40
$$	$15–$25
$	under $15

*per person, excluding drinks and service

French

$$$$ ✕ **Fouquet's de Paris.** Located in the Camino Real hotel, this is a branch of the renowned Parisian restaurant and an elegant haven of peace and tranquillity. The best pâtés in Mexico and tender, juicy lamb chops are part of the diverse and stylish menu. The desserts are in a class all their own. The sorbets, such as the delicately flavored passion fruit, are outstanding, and the cakes, mousses, and pastries are light and delicious. Monthlong gastronomic festivals are held here throughout the year, and each October or November, chefs from the original Fouquet's in Paris take over the kitchen. ✉ *Hotel Camino Real, Mariano Escobedo 700,* ☎ *5/203–2121. Reservations essential. Jacket required. AE, DC, MC, V. Closed Sun. No lunch Sat.*

$$$ ✕ **Champs Elysées.** On the corner of Amberes and Reforma, com-
★ manding an impressive view of the Independence (Angel) Monument, is one of the bastions of haute cuisine in Mexico City, and it has a fresh look after a remodeling in 1995. The variety of sauces served with both meat and fish dishes is impressive, with the hollandaise sauce over sea bass or red snapper probably taking top honors. Regulars find either the roast duck (carved at your table) or the pepper steak hard to resist. Of particular note is the generous cheese board. ✉ *Amberes 1, Zona Rosa,* ☎ *5/514–0450. AE, DC, MC, V. Closed Sun.*

$$ ✕ **La Petite France.** This restaurant in the Pasaje de Polanco has a very Mediterranean feel, with tables spilling out onto the street, hanging plants, and white wrought-iron furniture. The imaginative menu includes such specialties as fish soup with Pernod and roast lobster with basil, along with such typically Mediterranean dishes as stuffed mushrooms and *moules Provençales* (mussels Provençale). Fish dishes are popular, with *truite meunière* (trout, lightly fried and served with lemon), a giant prawn brochette, and deep-fried sea bass claiming most of the attention. Beautifully garnished and presented, the dishes catch the eye with a colorful, good selection of steamed vegetables. Soft piano music is played nightly from 9 to 11:30. ✉ *Av. Presidente Masaryk 360, Col. Polanco,* ☎ *5/280–8851 or 5/280–9335. AE, DC, MC, V. No dinner Sun.*

$ ✕ **El Buen Comer.** One of the more original Polanco eating spots, El Buen Comer (Eating Well) consists of not more than 20 tables in the covered garage of a private house. The entrance is discreet and can easily be missed, and the atmosphere inside is that of a large, private lunch party. The emphasis is on French cuisine from Lyon. House specialties include an endive salad with a cream-and-nut vinaigrette served with scallops. The fondues and pâtés are excellent. A favorite main course of the habitués is quiche Lorraine, and the quiche royale with shrimp is a must for seafood lovers. Whole steaks can be served to order with fine herbs, pepper, tartar, or shallots. Desserts include mango or chocolate mousse or raspberries smothered in cream. El Buen Comer makes a great stop after shopping in Polanco. ✉ *Edgar Allan Poe 50, Col.*

Mexico City Dining

Bellinghausen, **17**
Café de Tacuba, **26**
Champs Elysées, **15**
Cicero Centenario, **28**
El Arroyo, **20**
El Buen Comer, **4**
El Jug, **14**

El Parador de
Manolo, **3**
El Tajin, **32**
Estoril, **6**
Focolare, **16**
Fonda del
Recuerdo, **10**
Fonda Don Chón, **29**

Fonda El Refugio, **18**
Fouquet's de Paris, **9**
Hacienda de los
Morales, **1**
Hosteria de Santa
Domingo, **27**
Isadora, **2**
La Jolla, **12**

La Lanterna, **11**
La Petite France, **5**
Las Cazuelas, **19**
Las Fuentes, **13**
Les Célébrités, **8**
Lincoln, **23**
Los Girasoles, **24**

Los Irabien, **31**
Maxim's de Paris, **7**
Meson El Cid, **22**
Prendes, **25**
San Angel Inn, **30**
Suntory, **21**

Polanco, ☎ 5/281–1094 or 5/282–0325. *Reservations essential. AE, D, MC, V. Closed Sun. No dinner.*

International

$$$$ ✕ **Estoril.** Rosa Martin, who founded this highly successful restaurant
★ in an exquisitely furnished 1930s town house in fashionable Polanco, runs it with her daughter Diana. It boasts only the very best ingredients and serves French and Swiss cuisine with a Mexican flair. The *perejil frito* (fried parsley) is a popular starter. The main dishes offer some unusual taste combinations: giant prawns in Chablis or curry sauce, and sea bass in fresh coriander sauce. To finish, try either the delicious *tart Tatin* (an upside-down apple tart with caramel) or the homemade sorbets, especially the refreshing mint flavor. ⊠ *Alejandro Dumas 24, Col. Polanco,* ☎ 5/280–9828. *Jacket and tie. AE, DC, MC, V. Closed Sun.*

$$$$ ✕ **Hacienda de los Morales.** This Mexican institution, set in a former hacienda that dates back to the 16th century, is grandly colonial in style, with dark wood beams and huge terra-cotta expanses. The menu combines both international and Mexican cuisines, with some imaginative variations on both. The walnut soup, served either hot or cold, is a delicate and unusual specialty. Fish is seemingly unlimited, with a rainbow trout meunière (lightly sautéed in butter, served with lemon juice and parsley), sea bass *marinière* (in a white-wine sauce), and a mixed seafood gratin. The charcoal-broiled grain-fed chicken has a distinct flavor, and the paillard is always of the highest quality. The Hacienda de los Morales is regularly hired for functions, so don't be surprised if there's a lot of activity. ⊠ *Vázquez de Mella 525, Col. Chapultepec Morales,* ☎ 5/281–4554 or 5/281–4703. *AE, DC, MC, V.*

$$$$ ✕ **La Jolla.** This chic, intimate restaurant in the Marquis Reforma is the first in the country to specialize in Belgian cuisine. The menu, which also includes fine Mexican fare, is supervised by Dutch executive-chef Raul Reicharth, who has won many awards for his creative cookery. Some of the most popular entrées are succulent pheasant with pureed celery and warm endive salad, and steamed dorado (sea bass) with a bread-crumb crust. There are scrumptious tarts and mousses for dessert. La Jolla is especially romantic at night, with its candlelit tables, soft piano music, and splendid view of Paseo de la Reforma, the city's grand avenue. Well-heeled Mexican executives pack the place at breakfast. ⊠ *Paseo de la Reforma 465,* ☎ 5/211–3600. *Jacket and tie. AE, DC, MC, V. Closed weekends.*

$$$$ ✕ **Les Célébrités.** In addition to offering superb French fare, this ele-
★ gant restaurant also serves good Mexican cuisine. When the Nikko México hotel opened in 1987, chef Joël Robouchon, one of the creators of nouvelle cuisine in France, came to Mexico to set up this restaurant off the hotel lobby. With him came the ultimate in restaurant technology and a policy of using only the very finest ingredients. The menu, which changes every three months, features such one-of-a-kind entrées as medallions of lobster in guayaba sauce or smoked salmon with spinach crêpes; for dessert you might find pomegranate or prickly-pear sherbet. ⊠ *Nikko México, Campos Elíseos 204, Col. Polanco,* ☎ 5/280–1111. *Reservations essential. Jacket and tie. AE, DC, MC, V. Closed Sun. No lunch Sat.*

$$$$ ✕ **Maxim's de Paris.** This restaurant—which became famous under the tutelege of Yves Ferrer, one of the city's finest French chefs—serves classic Gallic cuisine spiced up with the best of Mexican ingredients. Among the offerings are tongue in a delicate vermouth sauce, duck à l'orange, and abalone dressed in zesty chipotle chilies. Some of the irresistible desserts whipped up by the pastry chef include mouthwatering Grand Marnier or hazelnut soufflés and extra-rich chocolate *turrón*

(Spanish nougat). Operated under the auspices of the original Maxim's in Paris, this spacious but intimate restaurant is Parisian art deco under a stained-glass ceiling; the wine cellar is nonpareil, and the service impeccable. ✉ *Hotel Presidente Inter-Continental México, Campos Elíseos 218, Col. Polanco,* ☎ *5/327–7700. Reservations essential. Jacket and tie. AE, DC, MC, V. Closed Sun. No lunch Sat.*

$$–$$$ ✕ **Bellinghausen.** This is one of the most pleasant lunch spots in the Zona Rosa. The partially covered hacienda-style courtyard at the back, set off by an ivy-laden wall, is a magnet midday for executives and tourists alike. A veritable army of waiters scurries back and forth serving such tried-and-true favorites as *sopa de hongos* (mushroom soup) and *filete chemita* (broiled steak with mashed potatoes). The *higaditos de pollo* (chicken livers) with a side order of sautéed spinach is another winner. Other specials include *cabrito* (baby goat), roast lamb, and Spanish paella; the fish and seafood are also superb. ✉ *Londres 95, Zona Rosa,* ☎ *5/525–8738 or 5/207–4978. Reservations advised. AE, DC, MC, V. Closed Sun.*

Italian

$$ ✕ **La Lanterna.** The Petterino family has run this two-story restaurant in the same building for more than 20 years. The downstairs has the rustic feel of a northern Italian trattoria, with the cramped seating adding to the intimacy. Upstairs is more spacious. All the pastas are made on the premises, and the Bolognese sauce, in particular, is a local favorite. Try the raw artichoke salad, *conejo al Salmi* (rabbit in a wine sauce), *filete al burro nero* (steak in black butter), and *saltimbocca à la Romana* (veal and ham in Marsala sauce). ✉ *Paseo de la Reforma 458, Col. Juárez,* ☎ *5/207–9969. Reservations not accepted. MC, V. Closed Sun.*

Japanese

$$$ ✕ **Suntory.** Suntory restaurants in Boston, Singapore, Paris, and São Paulo have led the name to become synonymous with the best in Japanese dining. As you enter this one, by way of three rocks in a bed of well-raked sand, you are transported into a small-town patio in a dense green garden. In this enchanted world you are not absolved of the difficulty of choice. Is it the teppanyaki room to watch your fresh meat or fish prepared with a variety of vegetables? Or perhaps the shabu-shabu room beckons with wafer-thin sashimi and a copper pot of steaming vegetable broth in which elegant slices of beef are cooked? If you are a raw-fish enthusiast, perhaps the sushi bar? Prices are high, especially for Mexico, but the ingredients are of the highest quality. ✉ *Torres Adalid 14, Col. del Valle,* ☎ *5/536–9432; Montes Urales 555, Lomas Chapultepec,* ☎ *5/202–4711. AE, DC, MC, V.*

Mexican

$$$$ ✕ **Cicero Centenario.** The talk of the town since its inauguration in 1993,
★ this thoroughly Mexican restaurant occupies a restored 17th-century mansion in the heart of the downtown historic center. Elegant colonial antiques are strikingly posed against folk art and pastel walls. The enticing menu includes excellent versions of authentic colonial dishes such as *pollo en pipián verde* (chicken in green-pumpkin-seed sauce) and *huachinango mixote* (red snapper steamed in a parchment bag). Try the *chicharrón* (crispy pork rind) or guacamole appetizer, but be sure to leave room for desserts such as cactus-fruit ice cream with tequila. An ebullient street-level cantina features drinks, *botanas* (appetizers), and old-time piano music. ✉ *República de Cuba 79,* ☎ *5/521–2934 or 5/521–7866. Reservations essential. AE, MC, V. Closed Sun.*

$$$ ✕ **San Angel Inn.** In the south of the city, this magnificent old hacienda
★ and ex-convent, with its elegant grounds and immaculately tended gardens, is both a joy to the eye and an inspiration to the palate. The dark
mahogany furniture, crisp white table linens, and beautiful blue-and-white Talavera place settings all combine to strike the right note of restrained opulence. Many dishes are to be recommended, especially the
crepas de huitlacoche (corn-fungus crepes) and the *sopa de tortilla* (tortilla soup). The *puntas de filete* (sirloin tips) are liberally laced with
chili, and the *huachinango* (red snapper) is offered in a variety of
ways. Desserts—from light and crunchy meringues to pastries bulging
with cream—can be rich to the point of decadence. ✉ *Calle Diego Rivera
50 at Altavista, Col. San Angel Inn,* ☏ *5/516–1527 or 5/516–1402.
Jacket required. AE, DC, MC, V.*

$$ ✕ **El Arroyo.** More than just a restaurant, this dining complex is a famous attraction in itself, complete with its own bullring. Located at
the south end of town near the beginning of the highway to Cuernavaca,
it was founded more than 50 years ago by the Arroyo family and is
now run by jovial Jesús ("Chucho") Arroyo. His loyal following includes celebrities, dignitaries, and bullfighters, along with local families, groups, and tourists: More than 2,600 people can dine
simultaneously in a labyrinth of 11 picturesque dining areas. Typical
Mexican specialties—roast baby lamb wrapped in maguey leaves,
chicken mole, a dozen types of tacos, and much more—are prepared
in open kitchens. There's mariachi music galore and the full gamut of
Mexican drinks, including pulque. The small bullring is the forum for
novilleros, or young bullfighters just beginning their careers, during
the season (from about April through October), as well as for special
banquets and lively fiestas. Breakfast starts at 8 AM and lunch is served
until 7 PM. ✉ *Insurgentes Sur 4003, Col. Tlalpan,* ☏ *5/573–4344. Reservations essential for groups. AE, DC, MC, V.*

$$ ✕ **El Tajín.** Named after a magnificent pre-Columbian pyramid in Veracruz, this restaurant is a good example of the innovative Mexican
cooking that is taking the metropolis by storm. Opened in 1993 by
Alicia De'Angeli, El Tajín adds zest and style to many well-known
dishes—and makes them low in fat to boot. For example, the tortillas
are served with *epazote* leaves, a Mexican herb; tostadas come with
delicate crumbles of goat cheese. Dazzling main dishes include softshell crab accented by sesame seeds and a tad of chipotle chili, while
the coconut ice cream with prickly-pear dessert celebrates the fruit
of the common roadside cactus. This lovely restaurant is hidden behind the functional facade of the Veracruz Cultural Center in Col.
Coyoacán; ancient Huastecan faces grinning from a splashing fountain add a bit of levity to the dining experience. ✉ *Miguel Angel de
Quevedo 687 in Coyoacán,* ☏ *5/659–4447 or 5/659–5759. AE, MC,
V. Closed Sun.–Wed.*

$$ ✕ **Focolare.** Among the prettiest eateries in the Zona Rosa, Focolare
serves fine Mexican regional fare on a covered patio with a fountain
in the middle and a blue-tile staircase leading to the second floor. This
is a great breakfast spot. The buffet caters to the Mexican taste (redhot chili first thing in the morning), but it also has less violent ways
to start the day. If you wanted to do a gastronomic tour of Mexico,
Focolare would be a good guide to the places that should be given priority. From Puerto Angel, for example, comes a delicious *calamares*
dish in a delicate tangerine sauce. There's a strong representation of
dishes from the Yucatán, such as *conchinita píbil* (pork baked in banana leaves), and several varieties of mole from Oaxaca. It's best to
come on a night other than Friday or Saturday, when the *Fiesta Mexicana* (including a buffet and live entertainment) attracts large tour groups
and incurs a hefty per person cover charge ($8 on Friday, $7 on Sat-

urday); you can see better versions of such shows elsewhere. On Sunday a healthy brunch is accompanied by a live band. ✉ *Hamburgo 87, Zona Rosa,* ☎ *5/207–8257. Dinner reservations essential Fri. and Sat. AE, DC, MC, V.*

$$ ✕ **Fonda del Recuerdo.** A popular family restaurant, the *fonda* (inn)
★ also has a solid reputation among tourists. Every day from 2 to 10, five different marimba groups from Veracruz provide music that creates a festive atmosphere. The place made its name with its fish and seafood platters from the Gulf state of Veracruz, and the house special is *huachinango à la Veracruzano* (a whole red snapper swimming in a succulent sauce made of tomato, chopped onion, olives, and mild spices). Sharing its fame is the *torito*, a drink made from tequila and exotic tropical fruit juices (be careful—it really packs a punch). The rest of the traditional Mexican menu features meat and *antojitos* (appetizers). Meat from the kitchen's own *parillas* (grills) is always first-rate. The portions here are huge, but if you have room for dessert, the *crepas de cajeta al tequila* (milk-caramel crepes with tequila) are worth trying. ✉ *Bahía de las Palmas 39, Col. Anzures,* ☎ *5/260–1290. AE, DC, MC, V.*

$$ ✕ **Fonda Don Chón.** This simple family-style restaurant, deep in downtown, is famed for its indigenous Mexican dishes. Fonda Don Chón is for the adventurous, although some pre-Hispanic delicacies, such as corn fungus, are featured at some of Mexico's most elegant restaurants. A knowledge of zoology, Spanish, and Nahuatl helps in deciphering the menu, which changes daily. A gamut of products from throughout the republic is prepared fresh every day, and no processed foods are used. *Escamoles de hormiga* (red-ant roe), 97% protein, is known as the "caviar of Mexico" for both its deliciousness and its costliness. Among the exotic entrées are armadillo in sesame mole sauce, iguana soup, and snake (boa or rattle) steak. More traditional specialties include *mixiote de carnero* (barbecued lamb in maguey leaves). The coconut cake dessert is excellent, and live music adds to the atmosphere. ✉ *Misionarios 213 near La Merced market, Col. Centro,* ☎ *5/522–2160. Reservations not accepted. AE, MC, V.*

$$ ✕ **Fonda El Refugio.** Since it opened in 1954, this Zona Rosa restaurant in a converted two-story town house has featured the best dishes from each major region of the country—for example, Guerrero, Michoacán, Sonora, and Veracruz. Atmosphere is casual but classy in the intimate colonial-decor dining rooms (the one downstairs is the prettiest). Along with the varied regular menu, there is a daily selection of featured appetizers and entrées; you might find a mole sauce made with pumpkin seeds or *albóndigas en chile chipotle* (meatballs in chipotle chile sauce). Try the refreshing *aguas* (fresh-fruit and seed juices) with your meal and the *café de olla* (cinnamon-flavored coffee sweetened with brown sugar) after dessert. ✉ *Liverpool 166, Zona Rosa,* ☎ *5/207–2732 or 5/525–8128. AE, DC, MC, V. Closed Sun. and holidays.*

$$ ✕ **Isadora.** Some of Mexico City's most inventive and exciting cooking takes place in this converted private house in Polanco. The three smallish dining rooms have a 1920s feel but are uncharacteristically ascetic—pale walls dabbed with modern-art squiggles. The management sponsors "cooking festivals," and every three months the kitchen produces dishes from a different country. The basic menu changes six times a year, and over that same period it will include three Mexican foodfests. What might be called the set menu features coarse duck pâté and excellent seafood pasta, with no holding back on the juicy prawns, shellfish, and squid. Ice creams, meringues, and chocolate cake for dessert benefit from the addition of the chef's delicate, pale green mint sauce.

✉ *Molière 50, Col. Polanco,* ☎ *5/280–1586. Jacket and tie. AE, DC, MC, V. Closed Sun.*

\$\$ ✗ **Lincoln.** With its portrait of the great statesman in the entrance and a large following of local politicians, Lincoln is reminiscent of a New England club—leather upholstery, discreet dining booths, and plenty of dark wood—but the menu is traditional Mexican, with an emphasis on fish. The range and choice are impressive. Soups include such delicacies as *sopa de almejas* (clam soup) and a thick crab soup. Among the main dishes, the *huachinango a la veracruzana* (red snapper Veracruz-style) is notable. The typical *albóndigas en chipotle* (meatballs in spicy chili sauce) is another favorite. ✉ *Revillagigedo 24, Col. Centro,* ☎ *5/510–1468. AE, DC, MC, V. No dinner Sun.*

\$\$ ✗ **Los Irabien.** This beautiful dining area filled with leafy plants and the owner's impressive art collection is a worthwhile stop for the gourmet and culture hound alike. Chef Arturo Fuentes turns out nouvelle cuisine à la Mexicaine along with traditional Mexican dishes. His *ensalada Irabien* triumphs as a mixture of smoked salmon, abalone, prawn, quail eggs, lettuce, and watercress. Two outstanding entrées include nopal cactus stuffed with fish fillet in garlic and fillet steak in strawberry sauce *à la pimienta.* Less exotic dishes, such as juicy porterhouse and rib-eye steaks, are also available, and lavish care in preparation and presentation is evident in all courses. Los Irabien is one of the city's breakfast spots par excellence. Where else could one be tempted by *huevos de codorniz huitzilopochtli* (quail eggs with tortilla on a bed of corn fungus in a squash-blossom sauce)? ✉ *Av. de la Paz 45, Col. San Angel,* ☎ *5/616–0014. Jacket and tie. AE, DC, MC, V. No dinner Sun.*

\$\$ ✗ **Prendes.** This downtown institution, first opened in 1892, has an air of history and legend—the president of Mexico comes here, as did his predecessors. Trotsky ate here with Ramón Mercader, who axed him to death two days later. The decor is minimal but is highlighted by the famous Prendes murals, which depict such celebrities as Gary Cooper and Walt Disney, who also dined here. Some traditional Mexican dishes remain on the menu, but the emphasis is now on delicate and decorative nouvelle Mexican cuisine. Oysters, ceviche, or a cream of maize soup are typical starters. The *filete chemita* (fillet of beef) and the fillet of fish meunière with nuts are two popular main courses. ✉ *16 de Septiembre 10, Col. Centro,* ☎ *5/512–7517. Reservations essential. Jacket and tie. AE, DC, MC, V. No dinner.*

\$\$ ✗ **Los Girasoles.** This downtown "in" spot, which has been staked out by the local yuppies and trendsetters, is owned by two prominent Mexico City society columnists who know how to get their names in print. Los Girasoles (Sunflowers) is located on a lovely old square in a restored three-story colonial home and features nouvelle Mexican cuisine—light and tasty and very innovative. Dishes gleaned from the best local cooking masters are offered. For example, the traditional Mexican bean soup is dressed up with a pinch of chili and noodles. Meat, fish, and seafood dishes are blended with exotic herbs and spices. The newest additions to the menu are pre-Hispanic delicacies such as ant roe (*escamoles*), chilied cactus worms (*gusanos de maguey*), and crispy fried grasshoppers (*chapulines*). The desserts pay homage to the fine fruits found in the country with such creations as *guanabana* and *zapote* mousse. One of the nicest places for dining is the covered terrace outdoors on the street level. ✉ *Plaza Manuel Tolsa on Calle Tacuba,* ☎ *5/510–0630 or 5/510–3281. AE, DC, MC, V.*

\$ ✗ **Café de Tacuba.** This typically Mexican restaurant is an essential breakfast, lunch, dinner, or snack stop for those exploring the city's downtown historic district. Since it opened in 1912, in a section of an old convent, it has charmed locals and visitors with its warm colonial decor and traditional Mexican fare. In the rear dining room, huge 18th-century oil paintings depict the historic invention of *mole poblano*, a complex sauce including a variety of chilies and chocolate, created by the nuns in the Santa Rosa Convent of Puebla. Of course, mole poblano is on the menu here, as are delicious tamales made fresh every morning—Oaxaca style with black mole and wrapped in banana leaf, or a fluffy Mexico City version. Enjoy pastries galore. ✉ *Tacuba 28, Col. Centro,* ☎ *5/518–4950. Reservations not accepted. MC, V.*

$ ✕ **Hosteria de Santo Domingo.** This dining institution near downtown's Plaza Santo Domingo has been serving *authentico* colonial dishes for more than a century in an atmospheric turn-of-the-century town house. Genteel waiters are schooled to provide good service and old-fashioned courtesy. Feast on tried-and-true favorites such as stuffed cactus paddles, thousand-flower soup, pot roast, and a stunning array of quesadillas filled with meat or the delicious pumpkin flower (*flor de calabaza*). Among what may be the best homemade Mexican desserts in town are the comforting flan, rice pudding (*arroz con leche*), and the rich milk-based *natilla* (another type of pudding). The place is open for breakfast and always full at lunch. ✉ *Belisario Dominguez 72, Col. Centro,* ☎ *5/510–1434 or 5/526–5276. AE, MC, V. No dinner Sun.*

$ ✕ **Las Cazuelas.** Traditional Mexican cooking at its best is on tap at
★ one of the most famous of the capital's fondas. The open-view kitchens are kept immaculately clean, and diners often take a peek at the bubbling mole and *pipián* sauces (the latter, a piquante sesame-flavored Yucatecan specialty) before being seated. The large dining area is brightened by hand-painted chairs from Michoacán and by the crisp green-and-white table linen. Ideal Mexican appetizers to share are *ranchero de carnitas* (pork morsels in red sauce). The tortilla soup, with its dash of *chili pasilla* and bits of cheese, makes another excellent starter. Main courses center on various moles or pipián sauces with pork or chicken. Finish with a *café de olla* (cinammon coffee in a clay mug) and a domestic brandy. ✉ *San Antonio 143 at Illinois, Col. Napoles,* ☎ *5/563–4118. Reservations not accepted. AE, MC, V.*

Spanish

$$ ✕ **El Parador de Manolo.** A period two-story house was remodeled into this Spanish restaurant in fashionable Polanco. The Bar Porrón on the ground floor serves a variety of Spanish tapas, including an excellent prawn mix in a spicy sauce. In the brasserie-style dining room upstairs, choose from a Spanish menu or from the list of the chef's recommendations. The specially cured Serrano ham is possibly the best in the city, while the *calamares fritos* (fried squid) or the *crepas de flor de calabaza al gratin* (squash-blossom crepes) make other fine starters. Fish dishes are the most appealing for a main course, although the chateaubriand Parador for two (in a black corn-fungus sauce) is truly original. Desserts cater to the Spanish sweet tooth and are less notable. Wines are on display downstairs, as are the fresh fish of the day. ✉ *Presidente Masaryk 443, Polanco,* ☎ *5/281–4918 or 5/281–1118. AE, MC, V. No dinner Sun.*

$$ ✕ **Meson El Cid.** The Meson (tavern), which exudes Old Spain atmosphere, was founded about 15 years ago by a real Spanish emigré. During the week, classic dishes like paella, spring lamb, suckling baby pig, and Cornish hens with truffles keep customers happy, but on Saturday night this place really comes into its own with a unique dining experience: a medieval banquet. The fun unfolds with a procession of costumed waiters carrying huge trays of steaming hot viands. A caged cat (the grandson of the first feline to play this role, the waiters will tell you) heads the parade as in olden days, when a king's food was tested for poisoning by letting a cat nose around in it first. (The cat

was always smart enough not to touch the stuff if it was tampered with.) Entertainment is provided by a student singing group dressed in Spanish medieval capes and hats. ⊠ *Humboldt 61, Col. Centro,* ☎ *5/521– 1940 or 5/521–1661. AE, DC, MC, V. No dinner Sun.*

Vegetarian

$ ✕ **El Jug.** For a respite from the madding crowd, head for this small, tidy retreat near the Pink Zone. You'll enjoy delicious vegetarian fare to the accompaniment of soothing New Age music. Heaping salads, homemade soups, and entrées such as chilies rellenos are accompanied by chunks of whole-grain bread. You can choose the filling daily *comida corrida* or order à la carte. After lunch, you might want to browse through the store on the premises and soak in the vibes of crystals, Vision Wands, incense holders, aromatherapy pillows, and the like. ⊠ *Puebla 326-A (entrance on Calle Cozumel), Col. Roma,* ☎ *5/553–3872. Reservations not accepted. No credit cards.* ☉ *Mon.–Sat. 11–6.*

$ ✕ **Las Fuentes.** About three blocks from the U.S. Embassy, Las Fuentes is run by Philipe Culbert, a life-long vegetarian who ascribes to the time-honored diet dictates of ancient Persia in balancing the nutrients of his menu. A sample meal might be tacos stuffed with carrots and potatoes accompanied by apple salad and followed by whole-grain cookies made with honey. This place gets packed for lunch, but service is efficient. Don't be put off by the sterile Formica tables; most of the suit-and-tie professionals come here for the food rather than the ambience. ⊠ *Rio Panuco 27 at Río Tiber, Col. Cuauhtemoc,* ☎ *5/525– 7095. Reservations not accepted. MC, V.*

LODGING

Though the city is huge and spread out, most hotels are located within the districts listed below, which are not far from one another. Chapultepec Park and the swank Polanco neighborhood are on the west side of the city. Paseo de la Reforma runs from Chapultepec, northeast through "midtown," and intersects with Avenida Juárez at the beginning of the downtown area. Juárez becomes Avenida Madero, which continues east to the downtown historic district and its very core, the Zócalo. The Zona Rosa, replete with boutiques, cafés, restaurants, and night spots, is just south of Reforma in the western midtown area. Huge numbers of business travelers tend to fill up deluxe hotels during the week; some major hotels discount their weekend rates. You can expect hotels in the $$$ and $$$$ categories to have purified water, air-conditioning, cable TV, radio, minibars, and extended (often 24-hour) room service. Note: Not yet ready for us to review when we went to press, the posh Marriot-owned Mandarin Hotel should be open in Polanco by the time you read this.

The following selection is organized by the major areas of the city and then by price.

CATEGORY	COST*
$$$$	over $160
$$$	$90–$160
$$	$40–$90
$	under $40

All prices are for a standard double room, excluding service charge and sales tax (10%). At press time, an extra 5% room tax was under consideration for Mexico City hotels.

Indian woman at market, Oaxaca, Mexico
Photo © 1985 Peter Guttman,
author of Fodor's *Nights to Imagine*

Fodor's is a registered trademark of Fodor's Travel Publications, Inc.

Airport

$$$ ☷ **The Continental Plaza Aeropuerto.** Formerly the Fiesta Americana, this deluxe hotel—with climate control, a satellite color TV, radio, minibar, and purified water in every room—is located over a short covered footbridge from the airport terminal, making it convenient for those who arrive late and have an early morning flight. For this convenience you pay a price. Discounted corporate rates are available. ⊠ *Benito Juárez International Airport, 15520,* ☎ *5/230–0505 or 800/88–CONTI,* ℻ *5/230–0134. 600 rooms and suites. Restaurant, bar, coffee shop, pool, sauna, health club, car rental, free parking. AE, DC, MC, V.*

Chapultepec Park and Polanco

$$$$ ☷ **Camino Real.** Super luxurious and immense—about the size of the
★ Pyramid of the Sun in Teotihuacán—this 8-acre city within a city hosts heads of state and celebrities as well as business and pleasure travelers. Impressive works of art embellishing the endless corridors and lounges include Rufino Tamayo's mural of *Man Confronting the Universe* and an imposing sculpture by Calder. The fifth-floor executive level features 100 extralarge guest rooms with special amenities. Fouquet's de Paris restaurant (☞ Dining, *above*) holds frequent culinary festivals, and the airy Azulejos features Mexican cuisine and special Sunday buffet brunches. The hotel finished a complete refurbishing of all its rooms and public areas in June 1996. A popular disco has been transformed into a nightclub featuring top Latin American artists who perform Thursday–Saturday starting at 11 PM; there's dancing after the show. ⊠ *Mariano Escobedo 700, 11590,* ☎ *5/203–2121 or 800/722–6466,* ℻ *5/250–6897 or 5/250–6723. 713 rooms and suites. 10 restaurants and bars, pool, 4 tennis courts, health club, nightclub, business services. AE, DC, MC, V.*

$$$$ ☷ **Casa Vieja.** This classically elegant and sumptuously decorated mansion in Polanco opened in 1994 as the most exclusive property in town. It's the dream-come-true of a local businessman who took his love of things Mexican and expressed it in his all-suites hotel. Tastefully selected folk art, handsomely hand-carved furniture, and gilded wall trimmings complement patios and splashing fountains. Mexican colors like canary yellow, mauve, and cobalt blue add a light-hearted touch to the suites, all of which are different (some have four-poster beds, for example); all come equipped with a full kitchen, fax machine, CD player, hot tub, and huge picture window overlooking an inside garden. The hotel's Mexican restaurant is named after the floor-to-ceiling *Tree of Life* sculpture that dominates it. Breakfast is complimentary, and room rates are lower the longer you stay. ⊠ *Eugenio Sue 45, Col. Polanco, 11560,* ☎ *5/282–0067,* ℻ *5/281–3780. 10 1- and 2-bedroom suites. Restaurant, bar, concierge, free parking. AE, MC, V.*

$$$$ ☷ **Presidente Inter-Continental México.** This 42-story hotel is—like its next-door neighbor, the Nikko—adjacent to Chapultepec Park and the posh Colonia Polanco. The dramatic five-story lobby is a hollow pyramid of balconies, with music presented daily at the lively lobby bar. The rooms are very spacious, and all have minibars and work areas. On clear days, those on the top two floors afford views of two snow-capped volcanoes, Popocatepetl and Iztaccihuatl. A $15 million remodeling completed in 1995 has freshened up all rooms and public areas and expanded the Executive Club area to eight floors. There are a number of smart stores and no fewer than six eateries on the premises, including a branch of Maxim's of Paris (☞ Dining, *above*) and a new restaurant, the Palm, a franchise of the venerable Washington, DC, eatery.

Mexico City Lodging

Park Villa Motel, **5**
Plaza Florencia, **9**
Presidente
Inter-Continental
México, **2**
Sevilla Palace, **18**

⊠ *Campos Elíseos 218, 11560,* ☎ *5/327–7700 or 800/327–0200,* FAX *5/327–7750. 659 rooms and suites. 5 restaurants, coffee shop, lobby lounge, gym, baby-sitting, parking. AE, DC, MC, V.*

$$$ 🏨 **Nikko México.** Part of the Japanese Nikko chain, this glistening, 42-floor high rise occupies a prime position: It's in Polanco and adjacent to Chapultepec Park, just a five-minute walk to the Anthropology Museum. The executive floor has better rooms and extra facilities. Three top restaurants excel in their gastronomic specialties: Les Célébrités (French), Teppan Grill (Japanese), and El Jardín (Mexican). The elegant, cozy Shelty's Pub is also a big hit with locals and in 1995 added a fancy high tea (weekdays 5–7). ⊠ *Campos Elíseos 204, 11560,* ☎ *5/280–1111 or 800/NIKKO–US,* FAX *5/280–9191. 771 rooms and suites. 3 restaurants, 2 bars, indoor pool, 3 tennis courts, health club, jogging, travel services. AE, DC, MC, V.*

$ ★ 🏨 **Park Villa Motel.** This two-story colonial hacienda, in a tranquil residential setting, is ideal for travelers with a car. Overlooking its pretty garden is the Restaurant Jardín del Corregidor, which serves authentic Spanish cuisine. If you are driving, you'll need to get directions to its secluded site near the southeast side of Chapultepec Park. The nearest subway stop is Juanacatlán. ⊠ *Gómez Pedraza 68 (enter at Constituyentes), 11850,* ☎ *5/515–5245,* FAX *5/515–4514. 45 rooms. Restaurant. No credit cards.*

Zona Rosa

$$$$ ★ 🏨 **Galería Plaza.** Part of the Westin Hotel deluxe chain, this ultramodern property is conveniently located on a quiet street in the elegant Zona Rosa, ideal for shopping, enjoying the nightlife, and dining out. Standard rooms are relatively small, but service and facilities are faultless. Rooms on the Executive Floor, where a special concierge desk provides personalized service and easy checkout, are larger. Other advantages include the 24-hour restaurant, which has a popular buffet breakfast; voice mail in all rooms; a rooftop heated pool with sun deck; and a secure underground parking lot. ⊠ *Hamburgo 195 at Varsovia, 06600,* ☎ *5/211–0014 or 800/228–3000,* FAX *5/207–5867. 450 rooms and suites. Restaurant, lobby lounge, 24-hr room service, concierge, valet parking. AE, DC, MC, V.*

$$$ 🏨 **Aristos.** This 15-story hotel is on the busy Paseo de la Reforma, on the edge of the Zona Rosa, in front of the U.S. Embassy, and near the Mexican Stock Exchange. The rooms are well supplied with all the amenities and are attractively decorated in shades of peach and mauve, with brass and wood accents. The business center has a bilingual staff and a message service. ⊠ *Paseo de la Reforma 276, 06600,* ☎ *5/211–0112,* FAX *5/525–6783. 360 rooms and suites. Restaurant, beauty salon, sauna, exercise room, travel services. AE, DC, MC, V.*

$$$ 🏨 **Calinda Geneve.** A Quality Inn, referred to locally as El Génova, this is an older but continually refurbished five-story hotel in the Zona Rosa. Traditional colonial-style carved wood chairs and tables furnish the pleasant lobby, and guest rooms are smallish but comfortable. The hotel's attraction as a gathering place has always been the Salón Jardín, a striking Belle Epoque gallery with a profusion of plants and a high stained-glass ceiling. It's a popular place for both guests and nonguests for meals and cocktails. The hotel's informal streetfront Café Jardín serves until 11 PM. ⊠ *Londres 130, 06600,* ☎ *5/211–0071 or 800/228–5151,* FAX *5/208–7422. 318 rooms. Restaurant, café, room service, coin laundry, travel services. AE, DC, MC, V.*

$$$ 🏨 **Century.** This zebra-stripe high rise stands out in the middle of the Zona Rosa. Rooms have round Roman-style marble baths, round beds, and semicircular private balconies. The rooftop Regine restau-

rant is romantic, and the street-level Petit Pois serves a good breakfast and luncheon buffet. All rooms have a private balcony. The large penthouse suites are superb. ✉ *Liverpool 152, 06600,* ☎ *5/726–9911,* 𝔽𝔸𝕏 *5/525–7475. 143 rooms. 2 restaurants, bar, pool, massage, sauna, baby-sitting, car rental, free parking. AE, DC, MC, V.*

$$$　🏨 **Krystal Rosa.** Part of the Mexican Krystal Hotel chain, this superbly run, recently remodeled high-rise hotel is centrally located in the heart of the Zona Rosa and has an excellent view of the city from the rooftop pool terrace. There is a chic lobby cocktail lounge; a bar with local entertainers; and a restaurant, Kama Kura, that serves superb Japanese cuisine. Three club floors feature VIP check-in and service, complimentary Continental buffet breakfast, and rooms with extra amenities. ✉ *Liverpool 155, 06600,* ☎ *5/228–9928 or 800/231–9860. 300 rooms and suites. 2 restaurants, 2 bars, pool, business services. AE, DC, MC, V.*

$$$　🏨 **Marco Polo.** Posh and right in the center of the Zona Rosa, this
★　　intimate yet ultramodern all-suite hotel offers the amenities and outstanding personalized service often associated with a small European property. All rooms feature climate control, color cable TV, FM radio, minibar, and kitchenette; some suites have hot tubs, too. Rooms on the top floor facing north have excellent views of Paseo de la Reforma (the four penthouse suites boast terraces), and the U.S. Embassy is close by. In the street-level El Bistro de Marco Polo, you can listen to sophisticated jazz at lunch, over cocktails, and at dinner. ✉ *Amberes 27, 06600,* ☎ *5/207–1893,* 𝔽𝔸𝕏 *5/533–3727. 60 rooms. Restaurant, bar, business services, valet parking. AE, DC, MC, V.*

$$　🏨 **Misión Park Plaza México.** A part of the Misión chain, this very comfortable hotel is well placed for shopping and sightseeing. All rooms are air-conditioned and have a color TV with a VCR and movies courtesy of the hotel. ✉ *Nápoles 62, 06600,* ☎ *5/533–0535,* 𝔽𝔸𝕏 *5/533–1589. 50 rooms. Coffee shop, lobby lounge. AE, MC, V.*

$$　🏨 **Plaza Florencia.** This is a modern hotel on a busy avenue that borders the Zona Rosa. Rooms are well furnished, cheerfully decorated, and soundproofed against the location's heavy traffic noise; the higher floors have views of the Angel monument. Some large family suites are available. All rooms have air-conditioning, heat, a color TV, and a phone. ✉ *Florencia 61, 06600,* ☎ *5/211–0064,* 𝔽𝔸𝕏 *5/511–1572. 130 rooms, 10 suites. Restaurant, bar, coffee shop. AE, DC, MC, V.*

Midtown and along the Reforma

$$$$　🏨 **Four Seasons Mexico City.** Inaugurated in 1994, this is one of the newest and—perhaps by definition—one of the most luxurious hotels in the capital. Surrounding a traditional courtyard with a fountain, the stately eight-story building was modeled after the 18th-century Iturbide Palace downtown. A spacious marble lobby is filled with huge bowls of fresh flowers and lovely European furnishings. Definitely geared to the business traveler, rooms have outlets for PCs; there's also a board room on the premises and a business center with computer and cellular phone rentals. Dining and drinking areas have original names: El Restaurant (for breakfast, lunch and dinner), El Bar, El Café, and El Lobby Bar. All Four Seasons amenities are featured. ✉ *Paseo de la Reforma 500, 06600,* ☎ *5/286–6020 or 800/332–3442,* 𝔽𝔸𝕏 *5/286–5588. 240 rooms and suites. 2 restaurants, bar, pool, exercise deck, health club, business services. AE, DC, MC, V.*

$$$$　🏨 **María Isabel Sheraton.** Don Antenor Patiño, the Bolivian "Tin King," inaugurated this Mexico City classic in 1969 and named it after his granddaughter, socialite Isabel Goldsmith. The entire hotel was remodeled in 1992, but the glistening brown marble and Art Deco details in the lobby and other public areas remain. All guest and public

rooms are impeccably maintained, but penthouse suites in the 22-story Tower Section are extraspacious and exceptionally luxurious. The location—across from the Angel and the Zona Rosa, with Sanborns next door and the U.S. Embassy a half block away—is prime. ✉ *Paseo de la Reforma 325, 06500,* ☎ *5/207–3933 or 800/325–3535,* FAX *5/207–0684. 751 rooms and suites. 3 restaurants, bar, room service, pool, massage, sauna, health club, concierge floor, business services, valet parking. AE, DC, MC, V.*

$$$$ 🖫 **Marquis Reforma.** Opened in 1991, this privately owned hotel is
★ not only plush but also within walking distance of the Zona Rosa. It has a striking pink stone and curved glass facade, and its seventh-floor suites afford picture-perfect views of Chapultepec Castle. The elegant lobby is done up in classic European style, with paintings, sculpture, and palatial furniture. Guest-room furniture and decor are Art Deco–inspired. The award-winning La Jolla Restaurant specializes in Belgian cuisine (☞ *Dining, above*). The fully staffed Corporate Center offers state-of-the-art computer services, and guest-room phones feature a second plug for computers with fax modem. The health club offers hard-to-find holistic, stress-busting massages. ✉ *Paseo de la Reforma 465, 06500,* ☎ *5/211–3600 or 800/525–4800,* FAX *5/211–5561. 209 rooms, including 84 suites. 2 restaurants, bar, health club, business services, valet parking. AE, DC, MC, V.*

$$$ 🖫 **Crowne Plaza Reforma 1.** Perched at the junction of Reforma, Juárez, and Bucareli—convenient to downtown, the Pink Zone, and the Stock Exchange—this flashy 22-story smoked-glass behemoth looks quite spectacular in its otherwise nondescript surroundings. Opened in September 1995, it touts the ultimate in high-tech amenities for the business traveler: stock market indicator; computers; secretarial, translation, messenger, and shipping services; cellular phones. All rooms have PC and fax-modem outlets, coffeemakers, and three telephone lines. Public areas include a coffee bar with 20 different java concoctions, an oyster-jazz bar, and a French restaurant. Other amenities include limousine rental, pharmacy, and boutiques. ✉ *Reforma 1, Col. Tabacalera, 06030,* ☎ *5/128–5000 or 800/227–6963,* FAX *5/128–5050. 500 rooms and suites. 2 restaurants, 2 bars, room service, beauty salon, shops, business services, travel services, car and limousine rental. AE, DC, MC, V.*

$$$ 🖫 **Fiesta Americana Reforma.** This immense hotel is well organized for business travelers and large groups. It has an ample selection of bars, restaurants, and entertainment, including a popular nightclub, the Barbarella. There is not much Mexican atmosphere, but you can get a good tan on the sun deck, work out in the gym, listen to live jazz in the lobby bar, or eat in one of the three restaurants. All rooms are equipped with minibars. ✉ *Paseo de la Reforma 80, 06600,* ☎ *5/705–1515 or 800/343–7821,* FAX *5/705–1313. 610 rooms. 3 restaurants, 2 bars, exercise room. AE, DC, MC, V.*

$$$ 🖫 **Sevilla Palace.** This is a glistening modern showplace with five panoramic elevators to its 23 floors, a covered rooftop pool with hot tub, health club, terraced rooftop lounge with a city view, restaurants, a top-floor supper club with entertainment, and convention halls with capacities of up to 1,000. It's well located near the Columbus traffic circle and attracts lots of tourists from Spain. ✉ *Paseo de la Reforma 105, 06030,* ☎ *5/566–8877 or 800/732–9488,* FAX *5/535–3842 or 5/703–1521. 414 rooms. 2 restaurants, 3 bars, pool, health club, nightclub, meeting rooms, valet parking. AE, DC, MC, V.*

$$ 🖫 **Imperial.** Opened in 1990, the Imperial occupies a stately turn-of-the-century European-style building right on the Reforma alongside the Columbus Monument. Quiet elegance and personal service are keynotes of this privately owned property. The hotel's Restaurant

Gaudí has an understated, tony atmosphere and serves fine Continental cuisine with some Spanish selections. All rooms have safes, minibars, cable TV, and air-conditioning. ✉ *Paseo de la Reforma 64, 06600,* ☎ *5/705–4011,* FAX *5/703–3122. 60 rooms, junior and master suites. Restaurant, bar, café, business services, meeting rooms, travel services. AE, DC, MC, V.*

$$ 🏨 **María Cristina.** Full of Old World charm, this Spanish colonial–style
★ gem is a Mexico City classic. Impeccably maintained since it was built in 1937 (it was last refurbished January 1995), the peach-color building surrounds a delightful garden courtyard, which is the setting for its El Retiro bar. Three tastefully decorated apartment-style master suites, complete with hot tubs, were added in the early '90s. All rooms have color cable TV, a minibar, and a safe. Located in a quiet residential setting near Sullivan Park, the hotel is just a block from the Paseo de la Reforma and close to the Zona Rosa. ✉ *Río Lerma 31, 06500,* ☎ *5/703–1787,* FAX *5/566–9194. 156 rooms and suites. Room service, beauty salon, travel services, valet parking. DC, MC, V.*

Downtown

$$ 🏨 **Gran Hotel Howard Johnson.** The name was changed, but locals still refer to this establishment by its original (and more appropriate) name: Gran Hotel de la Ciudad de México. Ensconced in what was formerly a 19th-century department store, this older, more traditional hotel has contemporary rooms with all the amenities. Its central location—adjacent to the Zócalo and near the Templo Mayor—makes it the choice of serious sightseers. And its distinctive Belle Epoque lobby is worth a visit in its own right, with a striking stained-glass Tiffany dome, chandeliers, gilded cages, and 19th-century wrought-iron elevators. The fourth-floor Mirador breakfast restaurant overlooks the Zócalo. The Del Centro restaurant-bar is run by Delmónicos, one of Mexico City's best. The hotel has been undergoing a long-term, gradual refurbishing; be sure to request a renovated room and one that does not look out onto a brick wall. ✉ *16 de Septiembre 82, 06000,* ☎ *5/510–4040 or 800/654–2000,* FAX *5/512–2085. 125 rooms. 2 restaurants, bar, concierge, travel services, parking (fee). AE, DC, MC, V.*

$$ 🏨 **Hotel de Cortés.** This delightful small hotel, operated by Best West-
★ ern, is housed in a colonial building (1780) that has been designated a national monument. A major renovation in 1990 gave luster and luxury to the colonial-decor rooms and added two lovely soundproofed suites overlooking Alameda Park across the busy street. A restaurant also views the park, and a friendly bar opens to the tree-shaded central courtyard and fountain, a lovely setting for tea or cocktails. The Franz Mayer Museum is just a block away, and it's an easy walk to Bellas Artes. Loyal guests make reservations many months in advance. ✉ *Av. Hidalgo 85, 06000,* ☎ *5/518–2181 or 800/334–7234,* FAX *5/512–1863. 29 rooms and suites. Restaurant, bar. AE, DC, MC, V.*

$$ 🏨 **Majestic.** The atmospheric, colonial-style Majestic, built in 1937, is a Best Western hotel and perfectly located for anyone interested in exploring the downtown historic district: It is right on the Zócalo at the corner of Madero. It's also perfect for viewing the Independence Day (September 16) celebrations, which draw hundreds of thousands of people to this square. In fact, many tourists book a room a year in advance of the festivities. Rooms have new king-size beds, remote-control color TVs, and minibars. The service is efficient and courteous. The seventh-floor dining room and terrace—which feature international and Mexican specialties—have marvelous panoramas of the entire Zócalo. The Sunday buffet (1–5 PM) features live Mexican music. Colorful hand-painted ceramic tiles and potted plants decorate the pub-

lic areas. ⊠ *Madero 73, 06000,* ☎ *5/521–8600 or 800/528–1234,*
📠 *5/512–6262. 85 rooms. Restaurant, air-conditioning, minibar. AE,*
DC, MC, V.

$ 🏨 **Catedral.** Located in the heart of the downtown historic district, this
★   older but recently refurbished hotel is a great bargain, offering many
     of the amenities of the more upscale hotels at less than half the price.
     Public areas sparkle with marble and glass. The guest rooms are done
     in a cheerful contemporary fashion and all offer color TVs (local chan-
     nels only) and phones. You can get one with a view of the namesake
     Catedral, but keep in mind that its bells chime every 15 minutes late
     into the night. Service is friendly, the hotel restaurant is excellent, and
     the El Retiro bar attracts a largely Mexican clientele to hear live Latin
     music. ⊠ *Donceles 95, 06000,* ☎ *5/512–8581,* 📠 *5/512–4344. 116*
     rooms. Bar, coffee shop, room service, nightclub, dry cleaning, laun-
     dry service, travel services. AE, MC, V.

NIGHTLIFE AND THE ARTS

Good places to check for current events are the Friday edition of *The
News,* a daily English-language newspaper, and *Tiempo Libre,* a weekly
magazine listing activities and events in Spanish. Both are available at
newsstands.

The Arts

Dance

The world-renowned **Ballet Folklórico de México,** directed by Amalia
Hernández, offers a stylized presentation of Mexican regional folk dances
and is one of the most popular shows in Mexico. Performances are given
on Sundays at 9:30 AM and at 8 PM at the beautiful Palacio de Bellas
Artes (Palace of Fine Arts), at Avenue Juárez and Eje Central Lazaro
Cardenas; it's a treat to see the Tiffany glass curtain lowered. On
Wednesday evenings at 8, the troupe performs at the excellent Museum
of Anthropology in Chapultapec Park. Call the Palace of Fine Arts box
office, ☎ 5/512–3633, or TicketMaster, ☎ 5/325–9000, for information
on prices and for reservations. Hotels and travel agencies can also
secure tickets.

Not to be confused with the above is the **Ballet Folklórico Nacional de
México,** directed and choreographed by Silvia Lozano. The company
performs authentic regional folk dances Sunday and Tuesday at the
Teatro de la Ciudad, also known as the Mexico City Opera House
(⊠ Donceles 36, ☎ 5/510–2942).

The **National Dance Theater,** a component of the National Auditorium
complex in Chapultepec Park (☎ 5/202–3502), and the **Dance Center** (⊠ Campos Elíseos 480, ☎ 5/520–2271) frequently sponsor mod-
ern-dance performances.

Music

The primary venue for classical music is the **Palace of Fine Arts** (⊠ Av.
Juárez and Eje Central Lázaro Cárdenas, ☎ 5/709–3111), which has
a main auditorium and the smaller Manuel Ponce concert hall. The
National Opera has two seasons at the Palace: January–March and
August–October. The National Symphony Orchestra stages classic
and modern pieces at the palace in the spring and fall.

The top concert hall, often touted as the best in Latin America, is **Ollin
Yolitzli** (⊠ Periférico Sur 1541, ☎ 5/606–7573), which hosts the
Mexico City Philharmonic several times a year. The State of Mexico
Symphony performs at **Nezahualcoyotl Hall** in University City

(☎ 5/622–7112). The **Teatro de la Ciudad** (✉ Donceles 36, ☎ 5/510–2942) is also a popular site for a number of musical programs, both classical and popular, year-round.

Theater

An amateur theater group called the **Theater Workshop** puts on plays in English at various times of the year at the Universidad de las Americas (University of the Americas), Puebla 223 (no tel.), within walking distance of the Zona Rosa; check *The News* for listings. Visitors with a grasp of Spanish will find a much wider choice of theatrical entertainment, including recent Broadway hits. Prices are reasonable compared with those for stage productions of similar caliber in the United States. Though Mexico City has no central theater district, most theaters are within a 15- to 30-minute taxi ride from the major hotels. The top theaters include **Hidalgo** (✉ Av. Hidalgo 23, ☎ 5/521–3859), **Insurgentes** (✉ Av. Insurgentes Sur 1587, ☎ 5/595–2117), and **Virginia Fabregas** (✉ Velasquez de Leon 29, ☎ 5/592–0577). Theater tickets are available through TicketMaster (☎ 5/325–9000).

Nightlife

Night is the key word to understanding the timing of going out in Mexico City. People generally have cocktails at 7 or 8 PM, take in dinner and a show at 10 or 11, head to the discos at midnight, and then find a spot for a nightcap somewhere around 3 AM. The easiest way for the non–Spanish-speaking visitor to do this is on a nightclub tour (☞ Guided Tours *in* Mexico City A to Z, *below*). However, those who set off on their own should have no trouble getting around. For starters, Niza and Florencia streets in the Zona Rosa are practically lined with nightclubs, bars, and discos that are especially lively on Friday and Saturday nights. The big hotels offer both bars and places to dance or be entertained, and they are frequented by locals. Outside of the Zona Rosa, Paseo de la Reforma and Insurgentes Sur have the greatest concentration of night spots. Remember that the capital's high altitude makes liquor extremely potent, even jolting. Imported booze is very expensive, so you may want to stick with what the Mexicans order: tequila, rum, and *cerveza* (beer).

Dancing

Dance emporiums in the capital run the gamut from cheek-to-cheek romantic to throbbing strobe lights and ear-splitting music. Most places have a cover charge, but it is rarely more than $10. **Lipstick** (✉ Hotel Aristos, Paseo de la Reforma 274, ☎ 5/211–0112) is a longtime favorite where the action begins nightly at around 10. **Antillanos** (✉ Francisco Pimentel 78, ☎ 5/592–0439), a short cab ride from the Zona Rosa, is *the* place to go for hot salsa music and dancing to well-known local bands. One of the capital's best-kept secrets is **Mamá Rumba** (✉ Medillín and Querétaro in Col. Roma, a 10-minute cab ride from the Pink Zone, ☎ 5/564–6920). A nondescript Cuban restaurant during the day, it turns on the hot salsa, danzón, cha-cha-cha, and conga beat Thursday, Friday and Saturday nights, when a lineup of Cuban bands take the stand. The habitués not only pack the tiny dance floor but take to the tables as well. Reservations for these nights are definitely encouraged by the management.

Dinner Shows

The splashiest shows are found in the big hotels and in Zona Rosa clubs. **La Bohemia** (✉ Camino Real Hotel, ☎ 5/203–2121) is the newest venue for well-known singers from Mexico and the rest of Latin America, including Armando Manzanero and Tania Libertad. Showtime is Thursday through Saturday starting at 11 PM; the dance music starts around 12:30 AM after the show. In the Fiesta Americana Reforma, **Barbarella** (⊠ Paseo de la Reforma 80, ☎ 5/705–1515) features top international entertainers Thursday through Saturday nights. **La Veranda** (⊠ María Isabel Sheraton, Paseo de la Reforma 325, ☎ 5/207–3933, ext. 3718) serves dinner while international-caliber stars perform; afterward the dance floor is open.

Hotel Bars

The lobby bars in the **María Isabel Sheraton** (⊠ Reforma 325, ☎ 5/207–3933), **Presidente Inter-Continental México** (⊠ Campos Elíseos 218, Polanco, ☎ 5/327–7700), **Camino Real** (⊠ Mariano Escobedo 700, ☎ 5/203–2121), and **Galería Plaza** (⊠ Hamburgo 195, Zona Rosa, ☎ 5/211–0014) are all good bets for a sophisticated crowd and lively music, usually until long after midnight.

Midnight and Later

Gitanerías (⊠ Oaxaca 15, Col. Roma, ☎ 5/208–9066) continues to be an authentic Spanish flamenco nightclub (*tablao*). Now, in addition to a fiery flamenco there is also disco dancing to flamenco and Latin rhythms. Only light supper and drinks are served, and the first show starts at 11:30 Thursday to Saturday only. There is a $6.50 cover.

The traditional last stop for nocturnal Mexicans is **Plaza Garibaldi** (⊠ east of Eje Central Lázaro Cárdenas, between República de Honduras and República de Perú), where exuberant mariachis gather to unwind after evening performances—by performing even more. The mariachis play in the square—well-to-do Mexicans usually park along the west side to enjoy some "drive-up" serenading—and inside the cantinas and clubs surrounding it; the better ones are **Guadalajara de Noche** (☎ 5/526–5521) and **Tenampa** (☎ 5/526–6176). Choose a cantina and order a tequila; the musicians will be around shortly to serenade you (tipping is essential). These places stay open Sunday through Thursday until 4 AM, and even later on Friday and Saturday. Note: The square was spruced up in 1993 to rid it of its seedy image, but things can still get a bit raucous late at night.

OUTDOOR ACTIVITIES AND SPORTS

Bullfights

The main season is the dry season, around November through March, when celebrated *matadores* appear at **Plaza México** (⊠ Calle A. Rodín and Holbein, Col. Nápoles, ☎ 5/563–3961), the world's largest bullring, which seats 40,000. Gray Line Tours offers bullfight tour packages (☞ Guided Tours *in* Mexico City A to Z, *below*); or tickets, which range from about $3 to $16, can be purchased at hotel travel desks. Try the bullring ticket booths on Saturday between 11 AM and 2 PM or Sunday between 11 AM and 3:30 PM for tickets as well. The ring is located next to the Cuidad de Deportes sports complex, and the show goes on at 4 PM.

Golf

All golf courses are private in Mexico City, but you can play if you are a guest of a member. Travelers staying at the Sheraton Maria Isabel and the Camino Real hotels can have the hotel arrange admittance to the Bella Vista Golf Club, located off the Querétaro Highway (☎ 5/360–3501). Green fees Tuesday through Friday are $38; weekends, $75.

Horse Racing

The season at the beautiful **Hipódromo de las Américas** (✉ Av. Industria Militar, Lomas de Sotelo, ☎ 5/557–4100) lasts from mid-January through December, when thoroughbreds run daily. Betting is pari-mutuel. The races are especially enjoyable to watch from the swank Derby or Jockey Club restaurant. Tickets cost about 1 peso (about 15¢) and can be purchased at the track, which is located in the northwest section of the city near the Querétaro Highway.

Jai Alai

You can watch and bet on men playing this lightning-fast Basque-style handball game at the remodeled **Frontón México** (✉ Plaza de la Re-publica 17, ☎ 5/566–9679) Tuesday through Sunday at 8 PM. Women's matches are played at **Frontón Metropolitano** (✉ Bahía de Todos los Santos 190) daily except Sundays, 4 PM–10 PM. Betting, which goes on while the games are being played, is a fascinating skill in itself; instructions on the betting sheets are in Spanish and English. Dress up if you attend a game; jacket and tie for men are customary.

Jogging

There are jogging tracks in Chapultepec Park and at the Villa Olímpica (Olympic Village). Another joggers' favorite is along the pastoral paths of the Coyoacán Nurseries by the Viveros Station of the No. 3 metro line. Early morning runners will probably see young novice bullfight-ers there going through their training maneuvers. Keep in mind, by the way, that air quality is often poor and this is the highest city in North America—2,240 meters (7,349 feet) above sea level—so take it easy until your heart and lungs become accustomed to the altitude.

Tennis

Tennis clubs are private in Mexico, so tennis buffs should consider stay-ing at one of the hotels (☞ Lodging, *above*) that have courts on site.

Water Sports

The best place for swimming is your hotel pool. The vast **Cuemanco** sports park (✉ Canal de Cuemanco, on the way to Xochimilco) has an artificial lake for canoeing. Rowers can also ply their sport in the lakes of Chapultepec Park. Rentals are nearby.

SHOPPING

The best, most concentrated shopping area is the **Zona Rosa,** a 29-square-block area bounded by Reforma on the north, Niza on the east, Avenida Chapultepec on the south, and Varsovia on the west. The neigh-borhood is chock-full of boutiques, jewelry stores, leather-goods shops, antiques stores, and art galleries, as well as dozens of great little restaurants and coffee shops. Day or night, the Zona Rosa is always lively.

Polanco, a choice residential neighborhood along the northeast perime-ter of Chapultepec Park, is blossoming with fine shops and boutiques, many of which are branches of Zona Rosa or downtown establishments. Many are located in malls like the huge ultramodern **Plaza Polanco** (✉ Jaime Balmes 11) and the **Plaza Mazaryk** (✉ Mazaryk and Ana-tole France).

There are hundreds of shops with more modest trappings and better prices spread out along the length of Avenida Insurgentes, as well as along Avenida Juárez and in the old downtown area.

Department Stores, Malls, and Shopping Arcades

The major department-store chains are **Liverpool** (✉ Av. Insurgentes Sur 1310, Mariano Escobedo 425, and in the Plaza Satélite and Perisur shopping centers), **Suburbia** (✉ Horacio 203, Sonora 180, Av. Insurgentes Sur 1235, and also in Plaza Satélite and Perisur), and **El Palacio de Hierro** (✉ Durango and Salamanca), which is noted for fashions by well-known designers at prices now on par with those found in the United States. The posh and pricey shopping mall **Perisur** is out on the southern edge of the city near where the Periférico Expressway meets Avenida Insurgentes. **Plaza Satélite** mall is in a northern suburb called Satellite on the Anillo Periférico. Department stores are generally open Mondays, Tuesdays, Thursdays, and Fridays from 10 AM to 7 PM, and on Wednesdays and Saturdays from 10 AM to 8 PM.

Sanborns is a mini department-store chain with 20 branches in Mexico City alone. Those most convenient for tourists are at Madero 4 (its original store in the House of Tiles, downtown); on the Reforma at La Fragua (one at the Angel monument and another four blocks west of the Diana Fountain); and in the Zona Rosa (one at the corner of Niza and Hamburgo and another at Londres 130 in the Hotel Calinda Geneve). They feature a good selection of quality ceramics and handicrafts (they can ship anywhere), and most have restaurants or coffee shops, a pharmacy, and periodical and book departments carrying English-language publications.

Plaza La Rosa, a sparkling modern shopping arcade (✉ between Amberes and Génova in Zona Rosa), houses 72 prestigious shops and boutiques. It spans the entire depth of the block from Londres to Hamburgo, with entrances on both streets.

Bazar del Centro (✉ downtown, at Isabel la Católica 30, just below Madero) is a restored late-17th-century noble mansion built around a garden courtyard that houses several chic boutiques, top-quality handicraft shops, and prestigious jewelers such as **Aplijsa** (☎ 5/521–1923 or 5/510–1800), known for its fine gold, silver, pearls, and gemstones. Other shops sell Taxco silver, Tonalá stoneware, and Mexican tequilas and liqueurs. This complex is elegant and also has a congenial bar.

Portales de los Mercaderes (Merchants' Arcade; extending along the entire west side of the Zócalo between Madero and 16 de Septiembre avenues) has attracted merchants since 1524. Today it is lined with jewelry shops, selling gold (sometimes by the gram) and authentic Taxco silver at prices lower than those in Taxco itself, where the overhead is higher. In the middle of the arcade is **Tardán** (✉ Plaza de la Constitución 17, ☎ 5/512–2459), an unusual shop specializing in fine quality and fashionable men's and women's hats of every imaginable type and style.

Markets

A Saturday "must" for shoppers and browsers is a visit to the **Bazar Sábado** (Saturday Bazaar) at Plaza San Jacinto in the southern San Angel district. It's been specializing in unique high-quality handicrafts at excellent prices for more than three decades. Outside, vendors sell embroidered clothing, leather goods, wooden masks, beads, *amates* (bark paintings), and trinkets. Inside the bazaar building, a renovated two-story colonial mansion, are the better-quality—and higher-priced—goods, including *alebrijes* (painted wooden animals from Oaxaca), glassware, pottery, jewelry, and papier-mâché flowers. There is an indoor restaurant as well. Market and restaurant are open 10–7.

On Sundays, more than 100 artists exhibit and sell their paintings and sculptures at the **Jardín del Arte** (Garden of Art) in Parque Sullivan, just northeast of the Reforma–Insurgentes intersection. Along the west side of the park, a colorful weekend mercado with scores of food stands is also worth a visit.

The **Mercado Insurgentes** (also called **Mercado Zona Rosa**) is an entire block deep, with entrances on both Londres and Liverpool (⊠ between Florencia and Amberes). This is a typical neighborhood public market with one big difference: Most of the stalls (222 of them) sell crafts. You can find all kinds of handmade items—including serapes and ponchos, baskets, pottery, silver, and onyx, as well as regional Mexican dresses and costumes.

Also in the Zona Rosa, the pink neocolonial Plaza del Angel (⊠ Londres 161) has a **Centro de Antigüedades** (antiques center) with several fine shops. On Saturday, together with other vendors, the antiques dealers set up a flea market in the arcades and patios. On Sunday, bibliophiles gather here to sell, peruse, and buy collectors' books and periodicals.

The Zócalo and Alameda Park areas have interesting markets for browsing and buying handicrafts and curios; polite bargaining is customary. The biggest is the **Centro Artesanal Buenavista** (⊠ Aldama 187, by Buenavista Train Station, about 1½ kilometers (1 mile) northwest of downtown). **La Lagunilla** market (⊠ Libertad, between República de Chile and Calle Allende) attracts antiques hunters who know how to determine authenticity, and also coin collectors. The best day is Sunday, when flea-market stands are set up outside, with everything from collectibles to interesting knickknacks to junk. This market is known affectionately as the Thieves' Market: Local lore says you can buy back on Sunday what was stolen from your home on Saturday. Within the colonial walls of **La Ciudadela** market (⊠ Balderas and Ayuntamiento, about 4 blocks south of Avenida Juárez) are 344 artisans' stalls selling a variety of good handicrafts from all over the country, at better prices than you can find at the rest of the markets.

Specialty Shops

Antiques
Antigues Coloniart (⊠ Estocolmo 367, Zona Rosa, ☎ 5/514–4799) has good-quality antique paintings, furniture, and sculpture. The store is open by appointment only.

Art
The **Juan Martín Gallery** (⊠ Dickens 33-B, Polanco, ☎ 5/280–0277) is an avant-garde studio. The store and gallery of the renowned **Sergio Bustamante** (⊠ Amberes 13, Zona Rosa, ☎ 5/525–5029; Campos Eliseos 204–6, Polanco, ☎ 5/282–2638) displays and sells the artist's wildly surrealistic sculptures and interior-design pieces. The **Oscar Roman Gallery** (⊠ Anatole France 26, Polanco, ☎ 5/ 281–4939) is packed with work by good Mexican painters with a contemporary edge. The **Nina Menocal de Rocha Gallery** (⊠ Zacatecas 93, Colonia Roma, ☎ 5/564–7209) specializes in up-and-coming Cuban painters.

Candy
Celaya (⊠ Cinco de Mayo 13, ☎ 5/521–1787), in the downtown historic section, is a decades-old haven for those with a sweet tooth. It

specializes in candied pineapple, papaya, guava, and other exotic fruit, almond-paste, candied walnut rolls, and *cajeta,* a typical Mexican dessert of thick caramelized milk.

Clothing

Acapulco Joe's (✉ Amberes 19, Zona Rosa, ☎ 5/533–4774; Mazaryk 318, Polanco, ☎ 5/581–3044) has great T-shirts, beachwear, and hip unisex sportsclothes. **Guess** (✉ Amberes 17, Zona Rosa, ☎ 5/207–2891) features chic denim sportswear for guys and gals.

Designer Items

Cartier (✉ Amberes 9, Zona Rosa, ☎ 5/207–6104; Masaryk 438, Polanco, ☎ 5/545–8064) sells genuine designer jewelry and clothes, under the auspices of the French Cartier. However, **Gucci** (✉ Hamburgo 136, Zona Rosa, ☎ 5/207–9997) has no connection with the European store of the same name; nevertheless, it has a fine selection of shoes, gloves, and handbags. **Ralph Lauren** (✉ Amberes 21, Zona Rosa, ☎ 5/514–1563) is the home of Polo sportswear made in Mexico under license and sold at Mexican prices.

Girasol (✉ Génova 39, Zona Rosa, ☎ 5/511–5589) offers hand-loomed fabrics and delightful contemporary-looking hand-embroidered clothing—gowns, dresses, jackets, and skirts—by Mexican designers.

Jewelry

The owner of **Los Castillo** (✉ Amberes 41, Zona Rosa, ☎ 5/511–8396) developed a unique method of melding silver, copper, and brass and is considered by many to be Taxco's top silversmith. Taxco silver of exceptional style is sold at **Arte en Plata** (✉ Londres 162, Zona Rosa, ☎ 5/511–1422), with many designs inspired by pre-Hispanic art. **Pelletier** (✉ Torcuato Caso 237, Polanco, ☎ 5/250–8600) sells fine jewelry and watches. **Tane** (✉ Amberes 70, Zona Rosa, ☎ 5/511–9429; Edgar Allan Poe 68, Polanco, ☎ 5/281–4775; and other locations) is a treasure trove of superb silver works—jewelry, flatware, candelabra, museum-quality reproductions of antique pieces, and bold new designs by young Mexican silversmiths. The **Mexican Opal Company** (✉ Hamburgo 203, Zona Rosa, ☎ 5/528–9263) is run by Japanese who sell set and loose opals as well as jewelry in silver and gold. It's open by appointment only.

Leather

For leather goods, you have more than a few choices in Mexico City. **Gaitán** (✉ Hamburgo 97, Zona Rosa, ☎ 5/203–9061) features an extensive array of leather coats, luggage, golf bags, and saddles. **Aries** (✉ Florencia 14, Zona Rosa, ☎ 5/533–2509; Santa Catarina 207, San Angel, ☎ 5/616–2248) is Mexico's finest purveyor of leather goods, with a superb selection of clothes, shoes, and accessories for both men and women; the prices are high. **Antil** (✉ Florencia 22, Zona Rosa, ☎ 5/525–1573) also specializes in high-quality leather goods.

Mexican Handicrafts

Browse for fine works of folk art, sculpture, and handicraft, from silver to ceramics, in the two-story gallery **Manos Mexicanas** (✉ Amberes 57, Zona Rosa, ☎ 5/514–7455). Handwoven wool rugs, tapestries, and fabrics with original and unusual designs can be found at **Tamacani** (✉ Varsovia 51, Zona Rosa, ☎ 5/207–3696). **Arte Popular en Miniatura,** with two new Zona Rosa locations (✉ Hamburgo 85, ☎ 5/525–8145; in the Plaza del Angel at Londres 161, ☎ 5/208–2222), are tiny shops filled with tiny things, from dollhouse furniture and lead soldiers to miniature Nativity scenes. **Flamma** (✉ Hamburgo 167, Zona Rosa,

☎ 5/511–8499 or 5/511–0266) is a town house that sells a beautiful array of handmade candles.

Under the auspices of the National Council for Culture and Arts, **Fonart** (National Fund for Promoting Handicrafts) operates four stores in Mexico City and others around the country. The most convenient locations are at Londres 136, 2nd floor, Zona Rosa (☎ 5/525–2026), and at Juárez 89 (☎ 5/521–0171), downtown just west of Alameda Park. Prices are fixed, and the diverse, top-quality folk art and hand-crafted furnishings from all over Mexico represent the best artisans. Major sales at near wholesale prices are held at the main store-ware-house (✉ Av. Patriotismo 691, Col. Mixcoac) all year round.

Museo de Artes Populares (Museum of Arts and Crafts) could well be a museum but is in fact a large store displaying and selling an array of folk art and handicrafts—pottery, ceramics, glassware, textiles, and more—from practically every region of the country. Housed in an early 18th-century convent (✉ across from Alameda Park and Juárez Monument, Juárez 44, ☎ 5/518–3058), it is open Monday-Saturday.

Feders (✉ factory at Bufon 25 in Colonia Nueva Anzures, ☎ 5/250–3241; booth at Bazar Sábado, Plaza San Jacinto 11, San Angel) has great hand-blown glass, Tiffany-style lamps, and artistic wrought iron.

SIDE TRIPS

North of Mexico City

Hugging the roads to the north of Mexico City are several of the coun-try's most celebrated pre-Columbian and colonial monuments. The Basílica de Guadalupe, a church dedicated to Mexico's patron saint, and the pyramids of Teotihuacán make an easy day tour, as does the combination of the ex-convent (now a magnificent museum of the vicere-gal period) at Tepotzotlán and the ruins at Tula, also to the north but in a slightly different direction.

La Villa de Guadalupe

"La Villa"—more formally known as La Villa de Guadalupe, the site of the two Basilicas of the Virgin of Guadalupe—is Mexico's holiest shrine. Its importance derives from the miracle that the devout believe transpired here on December 12, 1531, when an Indian named Juan Diego received from the Virgin a cloak permanently imprinted with her image so he could prove to the priests that he had indeed had a holy vision. On that date each year, millions of pilgrims arrive, many crawling on their knees for the last few hundred yards, and praying for cures and other divine favors. The **Antigua Basílica** (Old Basilica) dates from 1536, although various additions were made during the in-tervening centuries; the altar was executed by sculptor Manuel Tolsá. The basilica now houses a museum of ex-votos (hand-painted tin retablos) and popular religious art, painting, sculpture, and decorative and applied arts from the 15th to the 18th century.

Because the structure of the old church had weakened over the years and the building was no longer large enough, or safe enough, to ac-commodate all the worshipers, Pedro Ramírez Vázquez, the architect responsible for Mexico City's splendid National Museum of Anthro-pology, was commissioned to design a new shrine. In this case the ar-chitect's inspiration failed him, however: The **Nueva Basílica,** completed in 1976, is a grotesque and most unspiritual mass of steel, wood, resinous fibers, and polyethylene designs. It holds 10,000 people; the famous cloak is enshrined in its own altar and can be viewed from a moving sidewalk that passes below it.

Teotihuacán

Most tour buses to the ruins stop briefly in **San Agustín Acolmán** to see the outstanding Gothic church and ex-convent, now a museum. The original Augustinian church (1539) is noteworthy for its vaulted roof and pointed towers; the ornate cloister and Plateresque facade, set off with candelabralike columns, were added a century later by the monks.

Teotihuacán occupies a monumental place in early Mexican history that is easily matched by the physical grandeur and scale of the site itself. It was, most likely, settled around 100 BC and reached its zenith about four centuries later. At the time of its decline in the 8th century, it was one of the largest cities in the world, with possibly as many as 200,000 people. It was set on fire and destroyed around AD 750 and over the years was completely buried. Its history and even its original name were lost.

Centuries later, the Aztecs arrived in the Valley of Mexico. Because the memory of the grandeur of the city in this area survived the passage of time, these new settlers named the site Teotihuacán, which meant "place where the gods were born." It was here, the Aztecs believed, that the gods created the universe.

The major structures along the mile-long **Calzada de los Muertos** (Avenue of the Dead) are the **pyramids of the Sun and Moon; the Ciudadela** (Citadel) with its **Temple of Quetzalcóatl** (Plumed Serpent) and **Tlaloc** (the goggle-eyed Rain God); and the **palaces of Quetzalpápalotl** (Plumed Butterfly), **Caracoles Emplumados** (Plumed Conch Shells), and **Los Jaguares** (Jaguars).

Climbing one pyramid is probably enough for most people. The Pyramid of the Sun is the largest, standing 210 feet high, and affords a spectacular view of the entire area. Wear comfortable clothes (especially shoes) and bring sunscreen or a visored hat when you visit.

Many of the artifacts uncovered at Teotihuacán are on display at the Museum of Anthropology in Mexico City. The new on-site museum, opened in mid-1995 near the Pyramid of the Sun, contains fabulous pieces from the archaeological zone such as stone sculptures of Tlaloc, the goggle-eyed god of rain; black and green obsidian arrowheads; and simulated burial sites of exalted personages of the empire, their skeletons arranged as they were upon discovery. 💷 *$4.25, Sun. free.* ☼ *Archaeological site daily 8–5, on-site museum Tues.–Sun. 8–5.*

Seeing the ruins will take two to four hours, depending on how taken you are with the place (or when your tour bus leaves).

DINING AND LODGING

If you would like to overnight at the pyramids, there's a **Villa Arqueologica** hotel (☎ 595/60909 in Teotihuacán; ☎ 5/203–3086; in the U.S., 800/258–2633) across the road from the fenced-off site with 20 snug rooms and a huge garden and patio restaurant-bar surrounding a pool. This Club Med is the only hotel that has permission to be in the area.

Tepotzotlán

The **Jesuit church** and **school of San Francisco Javier** at Tepotzotlán rank among the masterpieces of Mexican Churrigueresque architecture. The unmitigated Baroque facade of the church (1682) is the first thing to catch the eye, but inside and out, every square inch has been worked over, like an overdressed Christmas tree. Note especially the gilded, bemirrored Chapel of the Virgin of Loreto.

Teotihuacán

0 — 400 meters
0 — 400 yards

N

Palace of the Jaguars
Pyramid of the Moon
Palace of the Plumed Butterfly
Palace of the Plumed Conch Shells
Plaza of Columns
Avenue of the Dead
Pyramid of the Sun
Viking Group
Rio San Juan
The Citadel
Museum
Temple of the Plumed Serpent and the Rain God

This village is also famous for its traditional Christmas *pastorela,* a charming and humorous morality play, which has been taking place for more than 30 years and tells the story of the birth of Jesus Christ. Staged every year from December 15 to 23 in the patio of the church at night, the cast includes a few professionals and loads of extras from the town who portray shepherds, angels and, of course, the Devil. Tickets are available through Ticketmaster (☎ 5/325–9000 in Mexico City or 5/876–0243 in Tepotzolán).

Tula

Tula, capital of the Toltecs (its original name was Tollán), was founded in about AD 1000 and abandoned two centuries later. Quetzalcoatl was born in Tula and became its priest-king; under his rule, the Toltecs reached the pinnacle of their civilization, with art, science, and philosophy flourishing. According to myth, Quetzalcoatl went into exile in Yucatán but vowed to return—on a date (1519) that unfortunately coincided with the arrival of Hernán Cortes, whom the Aztecs therefore welcomed. The 4.5-meter (15-foot) **warrior statues** (called *atlantes*), rather than the ruins themselves, give Tula its fame. These basalt figures tower over Pyramid B, their harsh geometric lines looking vaguely like totem poles. Crocodiles, jaguars, coyotes, and eagles are also depicted in the carvings and represent the various warrior orders of the Toltecs.

North of Mexico City A to Z

GETTING THERE

To reach La Villa de Guadalupe by car, take Paseo de la Reforma Norte until it forks into Calzada de Guadalupe, which leads directly to the shrine. Alternatively, you can take the No. 3 metro from downtown to the Basílica stop. Buses run every half hour from the Central de Autobuses del Norte to Teotihuacán, and the trip takes about one hour.

In addition, many tour companies offer combination visits to the two sights.

To get to Tepotzotlán from Mexico City, follow Periférico Norte. After 41 kilometers (25 miles), you'll come to the exit for Tepotzotlán. Tula is about 8 kilometers (5 miles) north of Tepotzotlán. Buses to Tula/Tepotzotlán leave Mexico City every 20 minutes.

VISITOR INFORMATION

There are no tourist offices in the area, but a good English-language guidebook to Teotihuacán is sold at the site.

South and Southwest of Mexico City

This excursion to the south and southwest of Mexico City begins in Xochimilco (So-chee-*meel*-co), famous for its floating gardens, where visitors can take rides in gondolalike boats and get a fleeting sense of pre-Hispanic Mexico City. Beyond Xochimilco, in the neighboring state of Morelos, lies Cuernavaca, a weekend retreat for wealthy *chilangos* (residents of Mexico City) and foreigners. From Cuernavaca we suggest a detour to the town of Tepoztlán, which features a 16th-century Dominican convent, a lively Sunday market, its own little pyramid, and lots of New Age devotees.

Xochimilco

When the first nomadic settlers arrived in the Valley of Mexico, they found an enormous lake. As the years went by and their population grew, the land was not sufficient to satisfy their agricultural needs. They solved the problem by devising a system of *chinampas* (floating gardens), rectangular structures something like barges, which they filled with reeds, branches, and mud. They planted them with willows, whose roots anchored the floating gardens to the lake bed, making a labyrinth of small islands and canals on which they carried the flowers and produce grown on the chinampas to market.

Today Xochimilco is the only place in Mexico where the gardens still exist. Go on a Saturday, when the *tianguis* (market) is most active, or on a Sunday. (Note that Xochimilco is a popular destination for families on Sundays.) On weekdays the place is practically deserted, so it loses much of its charm. Hire a *trajinera* (flower-painted launch); an arch over each launch spells out its name—usually a diminutive for a woman's name—in flowers. As you sail through the canals, you'll pass mariachis and women selling tacos from other launches.

Folks are also flocking to Xochimilco for its newest attraction, the **Museo Dolores Olmedo Patino,** which carries the largest private collection of works by the flamboyant Mexican muralist Diego Rivera; it was put together by Olmedo, his lifelong model, patron, and onetime mistress (although she denies it). The lavish display of works, housed in a magficently restored 18th-century hacienda, includes nearly 140 pieces from his cubist, post-cubist, and mural periods. The museum also has works by Rivera's legal wife, Frida Kahlo, and his common-law wife, Angelina Beloff; a bust of Rivera holds the ashes of his Russian lover, Marinka. ⊠ *Avenida México 5843,* ☎ *5/555–1016.* 🎟 *$2.* ☉ *Tues.–Sun. 10–6.*

Cuernavaca

The climate in Cuernavaca, just 85 kilometers (53 miles) from Mexico City, changes dramatically to lush semitropical as the altitude descends almost 2,500 feet. In fact, it was this balmy springlike temperature that first attracted the rich and famous to the resort—starting with Hernán Cortés, who built a summer palace here in the 16th century. The city is also known for its many Spanish-language schools, some spectacular hotels and restaurants, the beautiful Borda Gardens, and Diego Rivera murals in the Palacio de Cortés (Palace of Cortés). An overnight stay is recommended.

Cuernavaca is built on a series of small hills whose streets intertwine at a maddening pace. If you're not used to driving in San Francisco, say, it's better to take a cab to get around, especially on the weekends, when the number of cars swells to disproportionate numbers.

Most of the attractions are concentrated around the main plaza called **Plaza de la Constitución,** which is surrounded by handicraft shops, sidewalk cafés, and government buildings. The square itself is filled with sidewalk vendors from neighboring villages hawking local arts and crafts throughout the week. On weekends, one side of the square is taken over by stalls selling leather as well as silver and gold jewelry from other regions of the country. A smaller square called **Jardín Juárez** lies just across the street from the Plaza de la Constitución and has the charming tradition of putting on free band concerts every Sunday afternoon under the archways of the colonial kiosk. Either of these two squares is the perfect place for whiling away a pleasant afternoon after a visit to the tourist sights.

The major attractions include the **Palacio de Cortés** (Cortés's palace-cum-fortress), which now houses the **Museo de Cuauhnáhuac** (Museum of Cuauhnáhuac, the Indian name for Cuernavaca), which focuses on Mexican history before and after the conquest. On permanent exhibit is a collection of some of Diego Rivera's finest murals, which, like those of Mexico City's National Palace, dramatize the history and the horrors of the conquest, colonialism, and the revolution. The murals were donated to the museum by former U.S. Ambassador to Mexico Dwight Morrow. ✉ *Av. Juárez,* ☎ *73/12–81–71.* 🎫 *$2.* ⊙ *Tues.–Sun. 10–5.*

Three blocks west are the beautiful and spacious **Jardín Borda** (Borda Gardens), the most visited attraction in Cuernavaca. They were designed in the late 18th century by a member of the Borda family (rich miners of French extraction) for one of his relatives; Maximilian and Carlotta visited the gardens frequently. This is where Maximilian had a dalliance with the gardener's wife, La India Maria. She was immortalized in a portrait by a noted painter of the time, and in this century novelist Malcolm Lowry turned them into a sinister symbol in *Under the Volcano.*

Opposite the gardens is the **Catedral de la Asunción,** an architecturally eclectic structure begun in 1529 by Hernán Cortes and noteworthy for its 17th-century Japanese wall paintings. It's also famous for its mariachi Masses each Sunday morning. Diagonally opposite the cathedral is the **Palacio Municipal;** the paintings inside depict life in the city before the Spaniards.

Also near the main square is the **Robert Brady Museum,** a delightful restored colonial mansion housing an diverse collection of art and artifacts assembled by the late Brady, an artist, antiquarian, and decorator who hailed from Fort Dodge, Iowa. ✉ *Netzahuacóyotl 4,* ☎ *73/18–8554.* 🎫 *$2.* ⊙ *Tues.–Sun. 10–6.*

Twenty-three miles southwest of the city lie the small ruins of **Zochicalco,** which have a pyramid and ball court. Showing Maya, Toltec and Zapotec influences, the site was believed to have been inhabited five centuries before the arrival of Cortés.

DINING AND LODGING

If you've not been invited to one of the mansions of the wealthy weekenders set in the hills on the edge of town, not to worry: There are a number of spectacular hotels and restaurants with equally spectacular gardens—several of them housed in restored colonial mansions and even haciendas—where visitors can get a sampling of life behind the high stone walls. Indeed, many people come here just for a sumptuous, relaxed meal in a glorious garden setting. Many Cuernavaca hostelries began as restaurants and added on rooms to satisfy clients who felt too lazy to drive back to Mexico City after a heavy meal.

Among the most spectacular—and pricier—places, both for dining and lodging, is **Las Mañanitas** (⊠ Ricardo Linares 107, ☎ 73/14–14–66); near the center of town, it offers 23 exquisite suites as well as gardens inhabited by flamingos, peacocks, and cranes. About 15 minutes south of town, **Camino Real Sumiya** (⊠ Interior del Fracc. Sumiya, Col. Joe Parres, 62550, Juitepec, Moreles, ☎ 73/19–02–04), the romantic hideaway built by Woolworth heiress Barbara Hutton, was converted into a restaurant after she died. In 1993 new owners took over and turned it into a posh 163-room hotel. It's set amid formal Japanese gardens (including a rock garden for contemplation) and boasts an original Kabuki theater that was brought over from Kyoto. To get here, take the Civac exit on the Acapulco Highway.

Another lodging alternative is **Hacienda de Cortés** (⊠ Plaza Kennedy 90, 62250, Atlacomulco, Moreles, ☎ 73/15–88–44), in the nearby town of Atlacomulco. This 22-room hacienda dates to the 16th century and actually once belonged to *El Conquistador* himself.

Those who want a change from Mexican food can enjoy a good Italian meal on a colonial candlelit patio at **La Strada** (⊠ Salazar 3, ☎ 73/18–60–85), just around the corner from the Palace of Cortés. And one block west of the main plaza, **Vienes** (⊠ Lerdo de Tejada 302, ☎ 73/18–40–44) serves excellent Austrian and Hungarian dishes and irresistible pastries.

Tepoztlán

Some say Teopoztlán, surrounded by beautiful sandstone monoliths that throw off a russet glow at sunset, is a magical place—Mexico's answer to Sedona, Arizona. It attracts the esoteric, which means you can find practitioners of hatha yoga, meditation, crystal healing, herbal cures, astrology, and native sorcery, among others. This town of 13,000, with a village atmosphere and cobblestoned streets, is primarily known for its tiny **Tepozteco pyramid,** probably of Aztec origin, perched on top of a hill; hundreds of people come each weekend to climb it. Other attractions include the lively **Sunday market** filled with fruits, vegetables and handicrafts, and the **dances held during the pre-Lenten Carnival,** when celebrants don bright masks depicting birds, animals, and Christian figures. Anthropologists Robert Redfield and Oscar Lewis both did fieldwork here in the 1950s. The town's landmark is the multibuttressed **Templo y Ex-Convento de la Natividad de la Virgen María** (1559), its fine paneled doors adorned with Indian motifs.

Teopoztlán drew national attention to itself in September 1995, when townspeople stormed City Hall with sticks and stones and took government officials hostage to protest the proposed building of a mega–golf resort on their revered Tepozteco terrain. They eventually ousted the mayor and town police and were still up in arms at press time because the developers had not abandoned the project.

South and Southwest of Mexico City A to Z

GETTING THERE

To reach Xochimilco by car, take Periférico Sur to the extension of División del Norte; an alternate route is from Calzada de Tlalpán to Calzada México Xochimilco and then Calzada Guadalupe Ramírez. Xochimilco is 21 kilometers (13 miles) from the Zócalo in Mexico City; the trip should take between 45 minutes and 1 hour, depending on traffic. If Xochimilco is your final destination, you are probably best off taking a taxi. By public transportation, take metro line No. 2 to Taxqueña and then any bus marked Xochimilco.

To continue south by car, return to Periférico Sur, turn left (south) on Viaducto Tlalpán, and watch for signs to Cuernavaca in about a half hour. The *cuota,* or toll road (Rte. 95D), costs about US$7 but is much faster than the *carretera libre,* or free road (Rte. 95). On Route 95D, it will take you about 1½ hours to cover 85 kilometers (53 miles).

Tepoztlán is 26 kilometers (16 miles) east of Cuernavaca via Route 95D. Buses also run every 20 minutes.

VISITOR INFORMATION

The **Morelos State Tourist Office** in Cuernavaca is located in Colonia Las Palmas. ⊠ *Morelos Sur 802,* ☎ *73/14–38–60.* ⊙ *Weekdays 8–7.*

Southeast of Mexico City

Southeast of Mexico City lies Puebla, a well-preserved colonial city and once the center of the Spanish tile industry. Nearby Cholula is a sacred spot in ancient Mexico and home to an important pyramid and scores of churches. You can detour along the way to see the volcanoes, Popocatepetl (Poh-poh-kah-*teh*-petal) and Iztaccihuatl (Eez-tah-*see*-waddle). On your return to the capital, leave time—an entire day would be best—to visit the city of Tlaxcala, with its rare church and former convent, and an amazing archaeological site nearby.

The Volcanoes

As you leave Mexico City—if the smog is not too thick—the Popocatepetl and Iztaccihuatl will be visible to the south. "Popo," 5,455 meters (17,887 feet) high, last erupted in 1802, but rumblings and bubblings in late 1994 were sufficiently strong to cause nearby villages to be evacuated temporarily. It continued to burp and belch during 1995 and caused a bit of alarm when it sent forth large clouds of smoke in 1996, though seismologists found no cause for alarm. Climbing Popo or "Izta" is for serious mountaineers, but the Parque Nacional, a verdant pine forest, makes a good spot for a picnic.

The legend states that Popocate, an Aztec warrior, had been sent by the emperor—father of his beloved Iztaccihuatl—to bring back the head of a feared enemy in order to win Iztaccihuatl's hand. He returned triumphantly only to find that Iztaccihuatl had killed herself, believing him dead. The grief-stricken Popo laid out her body on a small knoll and lit an eternal torch that he watches over, kneeling. Each of the four peaks composing the volcano is named after different parts of her body—hence its nickname "The Sleeping Lady." (In addition, the silhouette of the volcano resembles the figure of a reclining woman.)

LODGING

At the 12,000-foot marker on Popo, there's a park shelter with spartan (cement slab beds) dormitory accommodations, for which you pay a few dollars a night; you must bring your own sleeping bag. You can drive here from the main highway, but this is the end of the road; if you want to go higher, you'll have to hoof it.

Cholula

The town fathers claim that Cholula has 365 church cupolas, one for every day in the year. Most of the 40 colonial churches in Cholula are in poor condition, but 6½ kilometers (4 miles) south of town, in **San Francisco Acatepec,** is one of the two most stunning and well-preserved churches in the country. Completely covered with Puebla tiles, it has been called the most ornate Poblano Rococo facade in Mexico. Equally unusual is the interior of the church in **Santa María Tonantzintla,** 3 kilometers (2 miles) toward Cholula. Its polychrome wood-and-stucco carvings—inset columns, altarpieces, and the main archway—are the epitome of Churrigueresque. Set off by ornate gold-leaf figures of vegetal forms, angels, and saints, the carvings were done by native craftsmen.

Closer to town, the **Great Pyramid** was the centerpiece of a Toltec and then Aztec religious center and consists of seven superimposed structures connected by tunnels and stairways. The Spaniards, as they often did, built a chapel to **Nuestra Señora de los Remedios** (Our Lady of the Remedies) on top of it. Behind the pyramid is a vast temple complex of 43 acres, once dedicated to Quetzalcoatl. ☞ *About $5.* ☉ *Daily 10–5.*

Puebla

Maize was first cultivated in the Tehuacán Valley; later, the region was a crossroads for many ancient Mesoamerican cultures, including the Olmecs and Totonacs. The town of Puebla is notable for its idiosyncratic Baroque structures, which are built of red brick, gray stone, white stucco, and the beautiful Talavera tiles produced from local clay. The Battle of May 5, 1862—resulting in a short-lived victory against French invaders—took place just north of town. The national holiday, Cinco de Mayo, is celebrated yearly on that date in its honor.

Puebla today retains a strong conservative religious element and was one of the cities chosen by Pope John Paul II to visit during his 1978 Mexican tour. Overrun with religious structures, this city probably has more ex-convents and monasteries, chapels, and churches per square mile than anywhere else in the country. Don't miss the **cathedral.** Onyx, marble, and gold adorn the high altar, designed by Mexico's most illustrious colonial architect, Manuel Tolsá. In addition, the **Iglesia de Santo Domingo** (Santo Domingo Church) is especially famous for its Rosary Chapel, where almost every centimeter of the walls, ceilings, and altar is covered with gilded carvings and sculptures. The **Amparo Museum,** filled with the private collection of pre-Hispanic and colonial art of Mexican banker and philanthropist Manuel Espinoza Yglesias, is one of the most beautiful in Mexico.

The colonial **Convento de Santa Rosa,** now a museum of native crafts, contains the intricately tiled kitchen where Puebla's renowned mole sauce was believed to have been invented by the nuns as a surprise for their demanding gourmet bishop. Puebla is also famous for *camote,* a popular candy made from sweet potatoes and fruit. **La Calle de las Dulces** (Sweets Street) is lined with shops competing to sell a wide variety of freshly made camote.

DINING AND LODGING

Puebla is noted for its cuisine, considered by some to be the best in the country; two of Mexico's most popular dishes were created here to celebrate special occasions. Already noted above, *mole* is a type of spicy sauce made with about 15 different ingredients; the best known mole includes bitter chocolate. Another Puebla specialty believed to have been initiated by the town's nuns is *chilies en nogada,* a green poblano chili filled with ground meats, fruits, and nuts, then covered with a sauce of chopped walnuts and cream, and topped with red pomegranate seeds; the colors represent the red, green, and white of the Mexican flag.

Las Bodegas del Molino, set in a 16th-century hacienda at the edge of town (✉ Molino de San José del Puente, ☎ 22/49–03–99), is truly remarkable, both for its setting and its cuisine. A traditional favorite is **Fonda Santa Clara** (✉ 307 Calle 3 Poniente, ☎ 22/42–26–59), just a few blocks from the zócalo.

Fine hotels in Puebla include the 83-room **Camino Real** (✉ 7 Poniente 105, ☎ 22/32–89–83), located in a converted 16th-century convent two blocks from the zócalo, and the 192-room **El Meson del Angel,** at the entrance to the city (✉ Hermanos Serdan 807, ☎ 22/24–30–00). The 47-room **Royalty** on the main square (☎ 22/42–47–40) is small, well maintained, and considerably less expensive.

Tlaxcala

Capital of the tiny state of the same name, Tlaxcala (Tlas-*ca*-la) will interest both archaeology buffs and church lovers. The **monastery complex of San Francisco** (1537–40), standing atop a hill one block from the handsome main square, was the first permanent Catholic edifice in the New World. The most unusual feature of the church is its wood ceiling beams, carved and gilded after the Moorish fashion. (Moorish, or *mudéjar,* architecture appeared in Mexico only during the very early years after the conquest, when Spain was still close enough in time to the Moorish occupation to be greatly influenced by Arabic architectural styles.) The austere convent, now a museum of history, displays 18th-century religious paintings and a small collection of pre-Columbian pieces. Near the convent is a beautiful outdoor chapel whose symmetrical rear arches show Moorish and Gothic traces.

The **Palacio de Gobierno** (Government Palace), which occupies the north side of the zócalo, was built in about 1550. Inside are vivid epic murals of Tlaxcala before the conquest, painted in the 1960s by local artist Desiderio Hernández Xochitiotzin.

About 1 kilometer (less than a mile) west of Tlaxcala is the large, ornate **Sanctuary of Ocotlán.** It dates from the 18th century and was built on the site where a miracle was believed to have been performed by the Virgin. (In 1541, during a severe drought, she answered the prayers of an Indian by causing water to flow from the ground.) Noteworthy sights here are the Churrigueresque white-plaster facade, which conjures up images of a wedding cake; the two Poblano (red-tile) towers; and, inside, the brilliantly painted and gilded Camarín de la Virgen (the Virgin's Dressing Room).

Cacaxtla

This archaeological site, accidentally discovered in 1975, contains a breathtaking series of frescoes, dating back to about AD 100, which depict scenes of a fierce battle between Maya and Central Mexican warriors. It's located some 22 kilometers (13 miles) southwest of Tlaxcala.

Southeast of Mexico City A to Z

GETTING THERE

From Mexico City, head east toward the airport and turn onto Calzada Zaragoza, the last wide boulevard before arriving at the airport; it becomes the Puebla Highway at the toll booth. Route 190D is the toll road straight to Puebla; Route 150 is the more scenic free road (the trip on the former takes about 1½ hours, on the latter approximately 3 hours). To go directly to Cholula, take the exit at San Martín Texmelucan and follow the signs. From Puebla, Cholula is 8 kilometers (5 miles) west. To stop at the volcanoes, take the free road 33 kilometers (20 miles) to Chalco. From there it is 4 kilometers (2½ miles) to the Amecameca-Chalco sign, from which you continue 22 kilometers (13½ miles) on Route 115 to Amecameca. You'll need to go to Puebla to get to Tlaxcala; from there, take Highway 119 north.

VISITOR INFORMATION
Puebla Tourist Office: *5 Oriente 3,* ☎ *22/46–12–85.* ⊙ *Mon.–Sat. 9:30–8:30, Sun. 9:30–2.*

West of Mexico City

A good excursion west of Mexico City would encompass a stop at Toluca, renowned for its Friday market, and a longer stay at Valle de Bravo, a lovely lakeside village popular with vacationing chilangos; it's often called Mexico's Switzerland because of its green, hilly setting. We suggest a brief stop en route at Desierto de los Leones, a forested national park whose centerpiece is an intriguing Carmelite monastery, and a detour from Toluca for a picnic at Nevado de Toluca Park.

Desierto de los Leones
There are several walking trails throughout the pine forest of this 5,000-acre national park. Its focal point is the ruined 17th-century **Carmelite ex-monastery**, strangely isolated amid an abundance of greenery. The park played a significant role during the War of Independence: At a spot called Las Cruces, the troops of Father Hidalgo trounced the Spaniards but resolved not to go on and attack Mexico City, an error that cost the insurgents 10 more years of fighting.

Toluca
The capital of the state of Mexico, Toluca is an industrial town. Once famous only for its Friday market, Toluca now has much more to offer. Indians still come in from the surrounding villages on Friday to sell their produce and handicrafts at the huge municipal market, but it's hard to find any indigenous goods among the radios and CDs from Asia and the denim jackets and jeans from the United States. For local crafts, your best bet is the **Casa de Artesanías** on Paseo Tolloca. Two sights that shouldn't be missed are the **Jardín Botánico Cosmovitral** (Cosmovitral Botanical Garden), located in a remodeled, turn-of-the-century Art Nouveau structure that once housed the public market, and the **Museo de Artes Populares** (Museum of Popular Arts) in the Centro Cultural (Cultural Center).

Nevado de Toluca Park
At 4,691 meters (15,390 feet), the Nevado de Toluca, a now-extinct volcano, is Mexico's fourth-largest mountain; on clear days its crater affords wonderful views of the valley. You can hire a guide at the entrance to go with your car to the top of the crater and lead you down to its sandy floor, which surrounds two lakes. There are also self-guided hiking trails throughout the park.

Valle de Bravo
Valle de Bravo is colonial, with white-stucco houses trimmed with wrought-iron balconies, red-tile roofs, and red-potted succulents cluttering the doorways. A hilly town that rises from the shores of Lake Avandaro and is surrounded by pines and mountains, Valle was founded in 1530 but has no historical monuments to speak of other than the town church, which has a famous figure of a rare black Christ. It does, however, offer plenty of diversions: boating, waterskiing, and swimming in the lake and its waterfalls, and the more sociable pleasures of the Sunday market, where exceptionally good pottery is the draw. Although Valle and its suburb of Avandaro are enclaves for artists and the wealthy, it attracts inhabitants who prefer a low profile.

LODGING
For a weekend stay, head for the posh **Avandaro Golf & Spa Resort** (⊠ Vega del Río s/n, Fracción Avandaro, Valle de Bravo, 52100; ☎ 800/525–4800 in the U.S.; 726/6–03–66 in Mexico, FAX 726/6–

01–22), a former country club. All 110 junior suites have romantic fireplaces. In addition to its 18-hole golf course, the resort also has one of the best high-tech spas in Mexico, equipped with hot tubs and offering massage, facial, body toning, and aerobic classes.

West of Mexico City A to Z

GETTING THERE

By car from Mexico City, follow Paseo de la Reforma all the way west. It eventually merges with the Carretera Libre at Toluca, and after 20 kilometers (12 miles), you'll see signs for the turnoff to the Desierto de los Leones; it's another 10 kilometers (6 miles) to the park. To go straight to Toluca, take the toll highway (expensive, but worth it); alternatively, buses depart Terminal Poniente every 20 minutes. To reach Nevado de Toluca Park, make a 44-kilometer (27-mile) detour south of Toluca on Route 130. There are two choices for getting to Valle de Bravo: the winding but scenic route, which you pick up 3 kilometers (2 miles) west of Zincantepec, or Route 15. The former takes twice as much time but is worth it if you have the leisure and enjoy unspoiled mountain scenery.

VISITOR INFORMATION

Mexico State Tourist Office: *Edificio Plaza Toluca, Av. 5 Lerdo de Tejada Pte. 101, Toluca,* ☎ *721/4–10–99.* ☼ *Weekdays 9–3 and 5–8.*

MEXICO CITY A TO Z

Arriving and Departing

By Bus

Greyhound (☎ 800/231–2222) buses make connections to major U.S. border cities, from which Mexican bus lines depart throughout the day. Reserved seating is available on first-class coaches, which are comfortable but not nearly as plush as the new intercity buses. If you plan stopovers en route, make sure in advance that your ticket is written up accordingly. In Mexico, platform announcements are in Spanish only.

Within Mexico, buses are becoming the most popular way to travel: You can board ultramodern, superdeluxe motorcoaches that show U.S. movies and serve soft drinks and coffee. ETN (Enlaces Terrestres Nacionales, ☎ 5/271–1262 or 5/273–0251) serves cities to the west and northwest, such as Guadalajara, Morelia, Querétaro, Guanajuato, and Toluca. ADO (☎ 5/8785–9659) buses depart southeast to such destinations as Puebla, Oaxaca, Veracruz, Mérida, and Cancún. Reserved-seat tickets can be purchased at Mexico City travel agencies.

Various other classes of intercity bus tickets can be purchased at **Mexicorama** (☎ 5/525–2050) in the Plaza del Angel arcade in Zona Rosa. Buses depart from four outlying stations (*terminales de autobuses*), where tickets can also be purchased: Central de Autobuses del Norte (going north), Cién Metros 4907; Central de Autobuses del Sur (going south), Taxqueña 1320; Central de Autobuses del Oriente, known as TAPO (going east), Ignacio Zaragoza 200; and Terminal de Autobuses del Poniente (going west), Río Tacubaya and Sur 122.

By Car

Major arteries into Mexico City include Highway 57 to the north, which starts at Laredo, Texas, and goes through Monterrey and Querétaro. Highway 95 comes in from Cuernavaca to the south, and Highway 190D from Puebla to the east. Highway 15 via Toluca and Valle de Bravo is the main western route.

By Plane

AIRPORTS AND AIRLINES

All roads (and flights) lead to Mexico City. **Mexicana** (☎ 5/325–0990) has scheduled service from Chicago, Denver, Los Angeles, Miami, New York, Newark, Philadelphia, Pittsburgh, San Antonio, San Francisco, and San Jose. It has direct or connecting service at 30 locations throughout the country. **Aeromexico** (☎ 5/228–9910) serves Mexico City daily from Houston, Los Angeles, Miami, New Orleans, New York, Ontario (California), Phoenix, San Diego, Tampa, San Antonio, Tucson, and Washington, DC (as well as Tijuana). Aeromexico and Mexicana offer special low joint fares with certain U.S. airlines for connections from throughout the United States to their gateway cities. Aeromexico serves some 35 cities within Mexico. **Aerolitoral,** a subsidiary of Aeromexico based in Monterrey, serves north-central cities as well as San Antonio and McAllen, Texas, via Monterrey from Mexico City. **Taesa** (☎ 5/227–0700), a fast-growing Mexican airline, has direct flights (but not nonstop) to Mexico City from Chicago and Oakland; directs and nonstops from Tijuana; and nonstops from New York (JFK) and Laredo, Texas.

U.S. carriers serving Mexico City include **American, America West, Continental, Delta, Trans World Airlines, and United. Air France** flies nonstop between Houston and Mexico City.

BETWEEN THE AIRPORT AND CENTER CITY

The new wing of Mexico City's *Aeropuerto Internacional Benito Juárez,* inaugurated in February 1994, is a high-tech, state-of-the-art elongation of the east end of the existing airport. It is occupied by American, Delta, and United airlines, as well as by all the major car-rental agencies; four banks and seven currency exchanges (*casas de cambio*); Cirrus and Plus ATMs that disburse pesos to Visa and MasterCard holders; places to rent cellular phones; and a food court, pharmacy, bookstore and pricey shops. A multilevel parking garage for 2,500 cars has also been added (short-term parking: about $1 per hour).

Porters and free carts are available in the baggage-retrieval areas. Banks and currency exchanges rotate their schedules to provide around-the-clock service. Though dollar bills (not coins!) are acceptable at the airport, for convenience—and especially if you prefer a rapid departure from the airport—bring $100 in pesos with you. The Mexico City Tourist Office and the Hotel Association both have stands in the arrival areas that can provide information and find visitors a room for the night, respectively.

If you're taking a taxi, be sure to purchase your ticket at one of the official airport taxi counters marked **Transportación Terrestre** (ground transportation), located in the baggage carousel areas as well as in the concourse area and curbside. (Avoid *pirata,* taxi drivers offering their services.) Government-controlled fares are based on which *colonia* (neighborhood) you are going to and are usually about $7 (per car, not per person) to most hotels. A 10% tip is customary for airport drivers because they help with baggage. All major car-rental agencies have booths at both arrival areas, but renting a car is not recommended unless you are heading out of town or know Mexico City *very* well.

By Train

The train system in Mexico is currently in a state of flux and badly in need of refurbishing. At press time, there was no nonstop train service from the U.S. border to Mexico City; bus service from Nuevo Laredo, across from Laredo, Texas, departed to Monterrey, where passengers could pick up the *Regiomontano* to Mexico City. We don't recommend train travel, but if you're determined to go by rail, you can get up-to-date information about schedules and prices in the U.S. from **Mexico by Train** (☎ FAX 210/725–3659 or 800/321–1699).

Getting Around

By Bus

The Mexico City bus system is used by millions of commuters daily because it's cheap and goes everywhere. Buses are packed during rush hours, so as in all big cities, you should be wary of pickpockets. One of the principal bus routes runs along Paseo de la Reforma, Avenida Juárez, and Calle Madero. This west–east route connects Chapultepec Park with the *Zócalo* (main plaza). A southbound bus also may be taken along Avenida Insurgentes Sur to San Angel and University City, or northbound along Avenida Insurgentes Norte to the Guadalupe Basilica. Mexico City Tourism offices provide free bus-route maps. The price was raised at the end of 1995 from 40 centavos to 1 peso—still a bargain, especially for foreigners.

By Car

Millions of intrepid drivers brave Mexico City's streets every day and survive, but for out-of-towners the experience can be frazzling. One-way streets are confusing, rush-hour traffic is nightmarish, and parking places can be hard to come by. Police tow trucks haul away illegally parked vehicles, and the owner is heavily fined. As in any large city, getting your car back here is a byzantine process. LOCATEL (☎ 5/658–1111) is an efficient 24-hour service for tracing vehicles that are towed, stolen, or lost (in case you forgot where you parked). There's a chance an operator on duty may speak English, but the service is primarily in Spanish. Visitors can hire a chauffeur for their cars through a hotel concierge or travel service such as American Express.

Also keep in mind that the *strictly enforced* law *Un Día Sin Auto* (One Day Without a Car) applies to all private vehicles, including your own. One of several efforts to reduce smog and traffic congestion, this law prohibits every privately owned vehicle (including out-of-state, foreign, and even rental cars) from being used on one designated weekday. During emergency smog-alert months, mainly December and January, cars are prohibited from circulating on two days of the week. Cars in violation are inevitably impounded by the police. Expect a hefty fine as well. The weekday is specified by the last number or letter of the license plate. To find out which is your day (or days) to be without a car, contact the Mexican Government Tourism Office nearest you, and by all means plan your schedule accordingly.

By Pesero

Originally six-passenger sedans, then vans, and now minibuses, *peseros* operate on a number of fixed routes and charge a flat rate (a peso once upon a time, hence the name). Peseros offer a good alternative to buses and taxis; however, be prepared for a jolting ride because many drivers like to turn their buses into bucking broncos. Likely routes for tourists are along the city's major west–east axis (Chapultepec Park–Reforma–Avenida Juárez–Zócalo) and north–south along Insurgentes, between the Guadalupe Basilica and San Angel–University City. Peseros pick up passengers at bus stops and outside almost all metro stations these days. Just stand on the curb, check the route sign on the oncoming pesero's windshield, and hold out your hand. Tell the driver where to stop, or press the button by the back door; if it's really crowded and you can't reach the back door in time, just bang on the ceiling and yell, "Baja," which means "Getting off" in Spanish. Base fares are 2 pesos, with the price going up the farther you travel. Exact change is appreciated by drivers.

By Subway

Transporting 5 million passengers daily, Mexico City's metro is one of the world's best, busiest, safest, and cheapest transportation systems—the fare is the same as for buses, 1 peso. The impeccably clean marble-and-onyx stations are brightly lit, and modern French-designed trains run quietly on rubber tires. Some stations, such as Insurgentes, are shopping centers. Even if you don't take a ride, visit the Zócalo station, which has large models of central Mexico City during three historic periods. The Bellas Artes station has replicas of archaeological treasures on exhibit, and inside the Pino Suárez station is a small Aztec pyramid, a surprise discovery during construction.

There are nine intersecting metro lines covering more than 160 kilometers (100 miles). It's a bit confusing: The number 8 had been previously assigned to a line whose construction was canceled because it would have destroyed unearthed Aztec ruins. Line 9 was subsequently built. Now number 8 (which completes the numerical sequence) designates the newest (ninth) line, which was approaching completion at press time. Segments of lines 1 and 2 cover most points of interest to tourists, including the Zona Rosa, Bellas Artes, and the Centro Histórico. At the southern edge of the city, the Taxqueña station (line 2) connects with the electric train (*tren eléctrico*) that continues south to Xochimilco. To the southeast, the new *Metro Ligero* from the Pantitlán station (lines 1, 5, and 9) heads east to Chalco in the state of Mexico. The various lines also serve all four bus stations, the Buenavista train station, and the airport; however, only light baggage is allowed on board during rush hours. User-friendly, color-coded maps are available free at metro-station information desks and Mexico City tourism offices, and color-keyed signs and maps are posted all around.

Trains run frequently (about a minute apart) and are least crowded at night and between 10 AM and 4 PM. To reduce discomfort during crowded rush hours, regulations require men to ride separate cars from women and children. Hours vary somewhat according to the line, but service is essentially from 5 or 6 AM to 12:30 AM on weekdays; 6 AM to 1:30 AM on Saturday; 7 AM to 12:30 AM on Sunday and holidays.

By Taxi

The Mexico City variety comes in several colors, types, and sizes. Unmarked *turismo* sedans with hooded meters are usually stationed outside major hotels and in tourist areas; however, they are uneconomical for short trips. Their drivers are almost always English-speaking guides and can be hired for sightseeing on a daily or hourly basis (always negotiate the price in advance). *Sitio* (stationed) taxis operate out of stands, take radio calls, and are authorized to charge a small premium. Among these, **Servi-Taxis** (☎ 5/516–6020) and **Radio-Taxis** (☎ 5/566–0077) offer 24-hour service. Taxis that cruise the streets range from sedans to Volkswagen Beetles—the latter with the front passenger seat removed for more legroom. (Some Beetles are green and called *ecologicos* because they use lead-free gas.) They are available either when the *libre* (free) light is on or when the windshield *libre* sign is displayed. Taxi drivers are authorized to charge 10% more at night, usually after 10. Taking a taxi in Mexico City is extremely inexpensive and tips are not expected unless you have luggage—then 10% is sufficient.

Mexico City Subways

El Rosario **6 7**
Politécnico **5**
Indios Verdes **3**
Martín Carrera **4 6**

Tezozomoc
Azcapotzalco
Ferrería
Vallejo
Lindavista
La Villa

Aquiles
Serdán
Camarones
Norte 45
Instituto
del Petróleo
Basílica
Potrero
Talismán

Refinería
Autobuses del
Norte
La Raza
Misterios
Bondojito

Panteones
Tacuba
Cuitláhuac
Valle Gómez
Consulado

Cuatro
Caminos **2**
Popotla
Tlatelolco
Eduardo
Molina
San Juan
de Aragón
Oceanía

San Joaquín
Colegio Militar
Guerrero
Canal del
Norte

Normal
Hidalgo
Garibaldi **8**
Morelos

Polanco
San Cosme
Revolución
Bellas Artes
Allende
Zócalo

Auditorio
Chapultepec
Insurgentes
Juárez
Balderas
San Juan
de Letran
Merced
San Lázaro
Moctezuma
Balbuena
Terminal Aérea

Sevilla
Cuauhtémoc
del Agua
Pino
Suárez
Candelaria
Hangares

Constituyentes
Niños
Héroes
Católica
Doctores
San
Antonio
Abad
Fray
Servando
Aeropuerto
Gómez
Farías
Pantitlán **1 5 9**

Juanacatlán
Hospital
General
Obrera
Zaragoza
Cd. Deportiva
Puebla
Metro Ligero

Tacubaya **9**
Patriotismo
Chilpancingo
Centro
Médico
Chabacano
La
Viga
Jamaica
Mixihuca
Velódromo

Observatorio **1**
Etiopía
Lázaro Cárdenas
Viaducto
Santa Anita **4**
Coyuya
TOWARD PUEBLA

San Pedro de
los Piños
Eugenia
Xola
Tezontle

San Antonio
División del
Norte
Villa de Cortés
Apatlaco

Mixcoac
Nativitas
Aculco

Zapata
Portales
Escuadron 201

Barranca del
Muerto **7**
Coyoacán
Ermita
Iztapalapa
Constitucion
de 1917 **8**

Viveros
Atlalilco
Cerro de la
Estrella
La Purisima

M.A. de Quevedo
General Anaya

Copilco
Tasqueña **2**
Metro Ligero

Universidad **3**
TO XOCHIMILCO

N

Contacts and Resources

Consulates and Embassies

The **U.S. Embassy** (✉ Paseo de la Reforma 305, ☎ 5/211–0042) is open weekdays 8:30–5:30 but is closed for American and Mexican holidays; however, there's always a duty officer to take calls on holidays and after closing hours. The embassy keeps a list of English-speaking local doctors on hand if you need to consult one. The **Canadian Embassy** (✉ Schiller 529, ☎ 5/254–3288) is open weekdays 9–4 and is closed for Canadian and Mexican holidays. The **British Embassy** (✉ Lerma 71, ☎ 5/207–2449) is open weekdays 9:30–1 and 4–7.

Emergencies

HOSPITAL

American British Cowdray Hospital (✉ Calle Sur 137–201, corner of Observatorio, Col. las Américas; ☎ 5/272–8500 for emergencies, 516–8077 for the switchboard).

POLICE

Dial **06** for police, Red Cross, ambulance, fire, or other emergency situations. If you are not able to reach an English-speaking operator, call the SECTUR hot line (☞ Visitor Information, *below*). For missing persons or cars, call LOCATEL (☎ 5/658–1111).

English-Language Bookstores and Publications

The best place for English-language and foreign-language newspapers and magazines is **Casa de la Prensa,** which has two locations in the Pink Zone (✉ Florencia 57 and Hamburgo 141). **Sanborns** (☞ Shopping, *above*) carries a limited number of U.S. newspapers but an ample supply of magazines, paperbacks, and guidebooks. The **American Book Store** at Calle Madero 25 has an even more extensive selection. Two daily English-language newspapers, *The News* and newcomer *The Mexico City Times,* are available at hotels and at newsstands in the tourist areas; they provide a summary of what is happening in Mexico and the rest of the world with cultural and entertainment listings and daily stock-market reports. Remember that most U.S. or foreign-published publications are about double the price you'd pay for them at home.

Guided Tours

Except for the Tren Turístico, the tours described below can be booked through the agents listed in the Travel Agencies section (☞ *below*).

ORIENTATION

The basic city tour ($27) lasts four hours and takes in the Zócalo, Palacio Nacional, Catedral Metropolitana, and Bosque de Chapultepec. A four-hour pyramid tour costs around $30 and covers the Basílica de Nuestra Señora de Guadalupe and the major ruins at Teotihuacán.

A wonderful way to see the downtown historic center is via the **Tren Turístico** (☎ 5/709–5589), which runs charming replicas of 1920s 20-passenger trolleys. The 30-minute narrated tour covers sights including the Zócalo, Colegio de San Idelfonso, Plaza de Santo Domingo, Plaza Manuel Tolsá (location of the Palacio de Minería and Museo Nacional de Arte), Plaza de la Santa Veracruz (Museo Franz Mayer), and the Palacio de Iturbide. The trolleys depart from and return to Pino Suárez 30 (three blocks south of the Zócalo at the corner of República de Salvador). You can get off at any stop you wish and board a subsequent trolley. Departures are every half hour from 10 AM to 5 PM, Tuesday–Sunday; English-language tours depart Tuesday and Sunday at 11 AM. The price is $3.

Cultural: The seven-hour tour ($55) is run on Sunday mornings only and includes a performance of the folkloric dances at the Palacio de Bellas Artes, a gondola ride in the canals of Xochimilco's floating gardens, and a visit to the modern campus of the National University.

Bullfights: Also on Sundays only are trips to the bullring with a guide who will explain the finer points of this spectacle. This four-hour afternoon tour ($41) can usually be combined with the Ballet Folklórico–Xochimilco trip.

Nightlife: These tours are among the most popular tours of Mexico City. The best are scheduled to last five hours and include transfers by private car rather than bus; dinner at an elegant restaurant (frequently Del Lago); a drink and a show at the Plaza Garibaldi, where mariachis play; and a nightcap at Gitanerías, which features Spanish flamenco performances. Nightlife tours begin at $78.

Travel Agencies

American Express (⊠ Paseo de la Reforma 234, ☎ 5/207–7132), **Mexico Travel Advisors** (**MTA**) (⊠ Génova 30, ☎ 5/525–7520), and **Gray Line** (⊠ Londres 166, ☎ 5/208–1163; night phone 8 PM–7 AM, 5/208–2833).

Visitor Information

The **Mexico City Tourist Office** (Departamento de Turismo del Distrito Federal, or DDF) maintains information booths at both the international and domestic arrivals areas at the airport, at the Buenavista train station, and inside the Fonart handicraft store at Avenida Juárez 89. In town visit the lobby of its main office at Amberes 54 at the corner of Londres in the Zona Rosa. This office also provides information by phone with its INFOTUR service (☎ 5/525–9380) from 9 AM to 9 PM daily. Operators are multilingual and have access to an extensive data bank. The **Secretariat of Tourism** (**SECTUR**) operates a 24-hour multilingual hot line that provides information on both Mexico City and the entire country (☎ 5/250–0123, 5/250–0493, 5/250–0027, 5/250–0589, 5/250–0151, 5/250–0292, or 5/250–0741). If the lines are busy, keep trying. You can also call toll-free from anywhere in Mexico other than Mexico City (☎ 91–800/9–03–92 or, from the U.S., 800/482–9832). These numbers reach SECTUR's Tourist Information Center at Presidente Masaryk 172 (in Polanco), open weekdays 8 AM–8 PM.

3 Baja California

Separated from mainland Mexico by the Sea of Cortés, the Baja California peninsula stretches 1,000 miles from Tijuana to Los Cabos. The desert landscape harbors isolated fishing retreats, Prohibition-era gambling palaces, state-of-the-art golf courses, and one of the busiest international borders in the world. Adventurers delight in kayaking with migrating gray whales, diving with hammerhead sharks, and hiking to hidden cave paintings.

By Maribeth
Mellin

BAJA (LOWER) CALIFORNIA is a moonscaped finger of land dipping southward from the international boundary that divides California and Mexico. Separated from the Mexican mainland by the 240-kilometer-wide (150-mile-wide) Sea of Cortés—also called the Gulf of California—Baja extends about 1,625 kilometers (1,000 miles) into the Pacific. Despite their names, both Baja California and the Gulf of California are part of Mexico.

Although only 21 kilometers (13 miles) across at one point and 193 kilometers (120 miles) at its widest, Baja features one of the most varied and beautiful terrains on the planet. The peninsula's two coasts are separated by soaring mountain ranges, with one peak more than 10,000 feet high. Countless bays and coves with pristine beaches indent both shores, and islands big and small—many inhabited only by sea lions—grace the 3,364 kilometers (2,000 miles) of coastline. There are stretches of desert as empty as the Sahara where only cacti thrive and, in contrast, there are cultivated farmlands and vineyards.

Varied, too, is the demographic makeup of Baja. The border strip of northern Baja is densely populated. Tijuana, Mexico's fourth-largest city, is home to nearly 2 million people, making it more populous than the rest of the entire peninsula. La Paz, with about 170,000 residents, is the only city of any size south of Ensenada. The two towns at Los Cabos (The Capes) have yet to reach city status.

Baja is divided politically into two states—Baja California (also referred to as Baja Norte, or North Baja) and Baja California Sur (South)—at the 25th parallel, about 710 kilometers (440 miles) south of the border. Near the tip of the peninsula, a monument marks the spot where the Tropic of Cancer crosses the Transpeninsular Highway (Mexico Highway 1).

Native Baja Californians will tell you in no uncertain terms that they live in the first California, discovered by pirates, missionaries, and explorers long before the California of the United States. To this day, most of Baja's visitors have that same sense of adventure and the unquenchable desire to discover nature's holdouts. As there are cult films and cult books, perhaps there are cult travel destinations. If so, Baja heads the list. Long before the rich and famous stumbled upon the resorts of mainland Mexico, they found Baja. Back in the days of Prohibition, when Hollywood was new, the movie crowd learned the joy of having an international border so near. John Steinbeck brought attention to La Paz when he made it a setting for his novella *The Pearl*. Erle Stanley Gardner put aside his typewriter in Baja to battle marlin off Los Cabos. Bing Crosby put up some of the money for the first resort hotel in San José del Cabo, when the only way to get there was aboard a yacht or private plane.

Pleasures and Pastimes

Dining

Baja's cuisine reflects its natural setting, highlighting food from the sea. Fresh fish, lobster, and shrimp are the dining draws here, along with abalone and quail. Throughout Baja, scores of restaurants and kitchens serve great Mexican seafood dishes, unadulterated for foreign tastes. Beef and pork are also excellent, both grilled and marinated. Imported steaks, quail, lamb, and duck are popular in the more expensive places. Mexicali, the capital of Baja, offers several good Chinese restaurants (the construction of the Imperial Canal in 1902 brought an influx of Chinese residents to the region). And although very few restaurants serve regional Mexican cuisine, plenty of spots throughout the peninsula combine U.S. and Mexican flavors in tacos, burritos, burgers, and pizza.

Two special dishes that originated in Baja have become standard fare in southern California. Lobster Puerto Nuevo–style (the shellfish grilled or boiled in oil and served with beans, rice, and tortillas) comes from the fishing settlement of the same name near Tijuana. Fish tacos (chunks of deep-fried fish wrapped with condiments in a corn tortilla) are said to have originated in the northern Baja town of San Felipe. Mexico's best domestic wines are nurtured in the vineyards and wineries in the Santo Tomás and Guadalupe valleys: Ensenada—and one of the country's most popular beers, Tecate—comes from the Baja Norte town of the same name.

Restaurants as a rule are low-key, except in Tijuana, Ensenada, and Los Cabos, where dining options range from *taquerías* (taco stands) to upscale Continental palaces. Dress is accordingly casual at nearly all Baja restaurants, and reservations are not required unless otherwise noted. Moderate prices prevail even in city restaurants—except in Los Cabos, where the tariffs as well as the selections reflect a distinct California influence. Some restaurants add a 15% service charge to the bill.

CATEGORY	COST*
$$$	over $20
$$	$10–$20
$	under $10

per person for a three-course meal, excluding drinks and service

Fishing

Sportfishing is one of Baja's greatest attractions. The fishing is best in the south, with large fishing fleets in Loreto, La Paz, and Los Cabos. Though the summer months bring the most fish, anglers are sure to catch something year-round. Fishing from Ensenada is best in the late summer and early fall.

Golf

Baja is becoming a great destination for golfers, with championship-level courses in Tijuana and nearby Rosarito Beach. Los Cabos is experiencing a particular golfing boom; several excellent courses have opened in the past few years.

Lodging

Lodgings throughout Baja are mostly low-key, except in Los Cabos, which has evolved into a world-class coastal destination. Until the 1980s, Los Cabos's hotels were mostly fishing lodges where diehard sportsmen took refuge. Today, Los Cabos draws golfers, too, and deluxe hotels front championship courses. Rates are much higher here than in the rest of Baja, where some great deals can found at small one-of-a-kind hostelries.

Reservations are a must on holiday weekends for most of Baja's coastal towns; some hotels require a minimum two-night stay for a confirmed reservation. A few of the out-of-the-way and budget-priced hotels do not accept credit cards; some of the more lavish places add a 10%–20% service charge to your bill. Most properties also raise their rates for the December–April high season. Rates here are based on high-season standards. Expect to pay 25% less during the off-season.

Several agencies in the United States book reservations at Baja hotels, condos, and time-share resorts, which may actually cost less than hotel rooms if you are traveling with a group of four or more (☞ Baja Norte A to Z, *below*, for details).

CATEGORY	COST*
$$$$	over $160
$$$	$90–$160
$$	$40–$90
$	under $40

*All prices are for a standard double room, excluding service charge and sales tax (10%).

Whale Watching

Gray whales migrate to the Pacific coast of Baja from January through March. Whale-watching expeditions are available in Ensenada, Guerrero Negro, Loreto, La Paz, and Los Cabos.

Exploring Baja California

The Baja California Peninsula is made up of two states: Baja California Norte, at the border with the United States, and Baja California Sur. We describe each of these regions in its own section below.

The northern half of the peninsula contains the largest cities and highest population. Tijuana, Tecate, and Mexicali—the peninsula's border cities—are U.S. suburbs in a sense. San Felipe, the northernmost town on the Sea of Cortés, is a popular weekend escape for travelers from Arizona and southern California. Similarly, Rosarito Beach and Ensenada, on Baja Norte's Pacific coast, are practically extensions of southern California's coast, offering an experience both familiar and foreign.

Baja California Sur is a more remote region, though strongly steeped in American influences. The most populated areas lie along the coast bordering the Sea of Cortés. The Pacific side is more popular with migrating gray whales, who travel by the thousands every winter from the Bering Strait to isolated coves and lagoons along this coast. For those few months, travelers come from all over the world to Guerrero Negro and a few bays and lagoons farther south. Loreto, on the Sea of Cortés, is beloved by sportfishing enthusiasts who find seclusion in this small, largely undiscovered town. La Paz, capital of Baja Sur, is the region's major port and a busy center of commerce and government. Los Cabos, made up of the two towns of Cabo San Lucas and San José del Cabo, has become one of the fastest-growing resort areas in Mexico. Despite all the development that has taken place there and its steep prices, however, it remains a mysteriously natural hideaway.

Great Itineraries

Baja aficionados will tell you that you haven't really explored the peninsula unless you've driven its entire length, stopping at small towns and secluded beaches along the way. Such a journey is a major undertaking, however, requiring at least 10 days of travel time. Those with more restricted time allotments can still see plenty of the peninsula's attractions by limiting their explorations to the region around their point of entry. A full week would allow a quick rush through the peninsula or a more leisurely exploration of Baja Norte or Baja Sur. If you have five days, you can see the most interesting towns and still be able to linger a bit. With three days you're best off staying within the immediate vicinity of your entry point.

IF YOU HAVE 3 DAYS

In Baja Norte a three-day stay would allow you to explore Tijuana, Rosarito Beach, and Ensenada. Start in Tijuana at the **Centro Cultural**; then visit **Mexitlán** and take a stroll down **Avenida Revolución.** Head south before nightfall to a hotel in **Rosarito Beach** or **Puerto Nuevo.** Tour **Ensenada** the next day, taking in the **Fish Market,** the **Riviera del Pacifico,** and the shops on **Avenida López Mateos.** Devote your third day to the coast and Rosarito Beach.

In Baja Sur, you're best off staying in **Los Cabos,** allowing time for golfing, sportfishing, and snorkeling at **Playa de Amor** or **Bahía Chileno.**

IF YOU HAVE 5 DAYS

You can do a thorough tour of Baja Norte, starting with a full day and overnight in Tijuana. From there head to the small town of **Tecate,** then on to **Mexicali** and **San Felipe.** Overnight in San Felipe; then spend Day 3 checking out the beaches before driving the backcountry to **Ensenada.** Devote Day 4 to exploring **La Bufadora** and downtown Ensenada; then head up the coast for a lobster feast at **Puerto Nuevo.** On Day 5 head back to Tijuana and the border.

In Baja Sur, start your tour in **Los Cabos,** spending the night there and starting out early the next day for **La Paz.** Spend Day 2 exploring downtown La Paz; don't miss the **Museum of Anthropology** and the main plaza. On Day 3, head up the coast to the small mission town of **Loreto.** Spend Days 4 and 5 making your way back to Los Cabos at a leisurely pace, stopping to explore the desert and coast along the way.

IF YOU HAVE 7 DAYS

It's possible to drive the entire peninsula in a week, especially if you arrange to begin your tour in the north and drop off your car in the south. Start in Tijuana on Day 1, touring the Centro Cultural, **Mexitlán** and **Avenida Revolución.** Head south before nightfall to a hotel in **Rosarito Beach** or **Puerto Nuevo.** On Day 2, move on to **Ensenada** for a brief tour of the city; then head south to Guerrero Negro. If you're traveling between January and March, arrange for a whale-watching tour for the next day and spend Nights 2 and 3 in Guerrero Negro. If not, overnight in Guerrero Negro and then move on for a full day's trip to **Mulege** on the Sea of Cortés. The drive between the two coasts, through stark desert scenery, is one of the most beautiful and desolate in Baja. Spend Night 3 or 4 in Mulege, allowing plenty of relaxation time after the long drive. Move on to **Loreto,** stopping off for a swim at **Bahía Concepción,** and spend the next night there. If you didn't stay in Guerrero Negro for whale-watching, spend an extra night in Loreto and arrange a boat tour of the Sea of Cortés. Devote Day 6 to the drive to **La Paz,** spending the evening strolling the waterfront malecón. On Day 7, continue on to **Los Cabos.**

When to Tour Baja

Baja's climate is one of extremes, thanks to its desert locale. Temperatures are less drastic in the northern regions; the climate in Tijuana, Ensenada, and Rosarito Beach is similar to that in southern California. Mexicali, on the other hand, gets extremely hot in the summer months. Baja Norte's resort cities are very crowded on holiday weekends, and advance reservations are a must. Tijuana's attractions are rarely overcrowded, and you should be able to tour them easily at any time of day.

Baja Sur's winters are mild, but not warm; Loreto, La Paz and Los Cabos can get downright chilly in the evening. Sportfishing aficionados prefer the summer months: Though the temperatures are high, the fish are abundant. Again, the towns only tend to be crowded on holiday weekends.

BAJA NORTE

The most densely populated area of the Baja California peninsula, Baja Norte begins at the U.S. border and extends 699 kilometers (437 miles) to the border with Baja California Sur. Tijuana, just 29 kilometers (18 miles) south of San Diego, is Baja's largest city; in fact, with a population nearing 2 million, it is the fourth largest city in Mexico. Tijuana's promoters like to call it "the most visited city in the world," and certainly the border crossing to Tijuana is the busiest in the United States.

By comparison, the state's capital, Mexicali, has a population of only 800,000 residents. Though it also sits on the U.S. border, Mexicali attracts few tourists. Tecate, located between Tijuana and Mexicali, is a typical village whose main claim to fame is the Tecate brewery, where one of Mexico's most popular beers originates. Those travelers who do pass through Tecate and Mexicali are usually enroute to San Felipe, the northernmost town on the Sea of Cortés.

On Baja's Pacific coast, travelers stream down the Transpeninsular Highway to Rosarito Beach and Ensenada. These beach communities are like Mexican suburbs of southern California, where English is spoken as freely as Spanish and the dollar is as readily accepted as the peso. Between Baja Norte's towns, the landscape is unlike any other, with cacti growing beside the sea, and stark mountains and plateaus rising against clear blue skies.

Highway 3 runs east from Ensenada to San Felipe through the foothills of the Sierra Pedro San Martir. The same highway runs north from Ensenada to Tecate through the Guadalupe Valley, where many of the area's vineyards and wineries are located. If you are traveling south, Ensenada is the last major city you'll see for hundreds of miles on Mexico Highway 1 or the Transpeninsular Highway. San Quintín, 184 kilometers (115 miles) south of Ensenada, is an agricultural community said to be the windiest spot in Baja. Sportfishing is particularly good here, and tourism is increasing. Farther south are turnoffs for a dirt road to San Felipe and a paved road to Bahía de los Angeles, a formerly remote bay beloved by fishermen and naturalists.

At the end of the northern section of Baja, 595 kilometers (372 miles) from Ensenada, stands a steel monument in the form of an eagle, 42 meters (138 feet) high. It marks the border between the states of Baja Norte and Baja Sur. The time changes from Pacific to Mountain as you cross the 28th parallel. Guerrero Negro, Baja Sur's northernmost town, with hotels and gas stations, is 2 kilometers (1½ miles) south.

Tijuana

29 km (18 mi) south of San Diego.

Tijuana is the only part of Mexico many people see, and it gives both a distorted and an accurate view of the country's many cultures. Before the city became a gigantic recreation center for southern Californians, it was a ranch populated by a few hundred Mexicans. In 1911, a group of Americans invaded the area and attempted to set up an independent republic; they were quickly driven out by Mexican soldiers. When Prohibition hit the United States in the 1920s and the Agua Caliente Racetrack and Casino opened (1929), Tijuana boomed. Americans seeking alcohol, gambling, and more fun than they could find back home flocked across the border, spending freely, which fueled the region's growth. Tijuana became the entry port for what some termed

Baja California (North)

CALIFORNIA

El Centro

Tecate

Tijuana

Mexicali

Yuma

ARIZONA

Rosarito Beach

Laguna Salada

San Luis Rio Colorado

Puerto Nuevo

Ensenada

SIERRA DE JUAREZ

National Park

Desierto de Altar

Santo Tomas

BAJA

Sonoyta

Colonet

SIERRA SAN PEDRO MARTIR

San Felipe

Bahía San Felipe

Puerto Peñasco

San Quintín

El Socorro

CALIFORNIA

El Rosario

Golfo de California

C. Lobos

Puerto Sta. Catarina

Cataviña

Isla Angel de la Guarda

Punta Prieta

Bahía de Los Angeles

Isla del Tiburón

Bahía de Sebastián Vizcaíno

Pta. San Gabriel

Isla Cedros

Parque Natural Ojo de Liebre

Guerrero Negro

El Arco

Scammon's Lagoon

Desierto de Vizcaíno

BAJA

San Ignacio

CALIFORNIA

PACIFIC OCEAN

N

Laguna de San Ignacio

SUR

KEY

Rail Lines

0   100 miles

0   150 km

a "sinful, steamy playground" frequented by Hollywood stars and the idle rich.

Then Prohibition was repealed, Mexico outlawed gambling, and Tijuana's fortunes dwindled. However, although the flow of travelers from the north slowed to a trickle for a while, Tijuana still captivated those in search of the sort of fun that was illegal or just frowned upon at home. The ever-growing numbers of servicemen stationed in San Diego kept Tijuana's sordid reputation alive, while southern Californians continued to cross the border to explore the foreign culture and landscape. Drivers headed into Baja's wilderness drove through downtown Tijuana, stopping along Avenida Revolución and its side streets for supplies and souvenirs.

When the toll highway to Ensenada was finished in 1967, travelers bypassed the city and tourism dropped again. But Tijuana began attracting residents from throughout Latin America. The city's population mushroomed from a mere 300,000 in 1970 to more than 2 million today. The city has spread into canyons and dry riverbeds, over hillsides, and onto ocean cliffs. As the government struggles to keep up with the growth and demand for services, thousands live without electricity, running water, and adequate housing in squatters' villages along the border.

City leaders, realizing that tourism creates jobs and bolsters Tijuana's fragile economy, are working hard to attract visitors. Avenida Revolución, the main street that was once lined with brothels and bars, now features shops and restaurants that cater to tourists. The city has an international airport; a fine cultural center that presents professional music, dance, and theater groups from throughout the world; and deluxe high-rise hotels. Park benches and shade trees on brick paths winding away from the traffic encourage visitors to linger. Still, although it's no longer considered just a bawdy border town, the city remains best known as a place for an intense, somewhat exotic, daylong adventure.

Tijuana's tourist attractions have remained much the same throughout the century. The impressive El Palacio Frontón (Jai Alai Palace), where betting is allowed, draws crowds of cheering fans to its fast-paced matches. Some of Mexico's greatest bullfighters appear at the oceanfront and downtown bullrings, and there are an extraordinary number of places in town that provide good food and drinks.

And then, of course, there's shopping. From the moment you cross the border, people will approach you or call out and insist that you look at their wares. If you drive, workers will run out from auto-body shops to place bids on new paint or upholstery for your car. All along Avenida Revolución and its side streets, shops sell everything from tequila to Tiffany lamps; serious shoppers can spend a full day searching and bargaining for their items of choice. If you intend to buy food in Mexico, get the U.S. customs list of articles that are illegal to bring back so that your purchases won't be confiscated.

Numbers in the margin correspond to points of interest on the Tijuana map.

❶ At the **San Ysidro Border Crossing,** locals and tourists jostle each other along the pedestrian walkway through the Viva Tijuana dining and shopping center and into the center of town. Artisans' stands line the walkway and adjoining streets, offering a quick overview of the wares to be found all over town.

❷ The best perspective on the city's cultural roots can be found at **Mexitlán,** a fascinating combination of museum and entertainment-shopping center. Designed by architect Pedro Ramírez Vásquez, the complex has scale models of all the major architectural and cultural landmarks throughout Mexico; restaurants and shops featuring authentic cuisine and folk art; and frequent performances by folkloric dancers and musical groups. ⊠ *Av. Ocampo between Calles 2 and 3,* ☎ *66/38–41–01.* ▦ *$1.50.* ⊙ *Tues.–Sun. 9–5.*

❸ Tijuana's main tourism zone has long been the raffish **Avenida Revolución,** lined with designer-clothing shops and restaurants, all catering to tourists. Shopkeepers call out from their doorways, offering low prices for an odd assortment of garish souvenirs. Many shopping arcades open onto Avenida Revolución; inside the front doors are mazes of small stands with low-priced pottery and other handicrafts.

❹ The Moorish-style **El Palacio Frontón** (Jai Alai Palace) is a magnificent building and an exciting place for watching and betting on fast-paced jai alai games. Next door, at a large branch of the Caliente Race Book, bettors can wager on horse races and sports events broadcast via satellite TV (☞ Outdoor Activities and Sports, *below*).

❺ Most of Baja's legendary wineries are located in the Ensenada region, but Tijuana now has a branch of the **L.A. Cetto Winery.** Visitors are invited to tour the bottling plant, sample the wines, and spend as long as they'd like in the gift and wine shop. ⊠ *Cañon Johnson 8151 at Av. Constitución,* ☎ *66/85–30–31.* ▦ *$1; $2 with wine tasting.* ⊙ *Tues.–Sun. 10–5.*

❻ **Mundo Divertido** is a popular family attraction in the Río zone. The amusement park includes a miniature golf course, batting cages, an exciting roller coaster, and a video-game parlor with more than 130 games. The park has a food court with hot dogs and burgers along with tacos and corn on the cob. Admission is free, and it costs just a few pesos to ride the rides. ✉ *Paseo de los Héroes at Calle Rodriguez, no tel.* ☉ *Weekdays 11–10, weekends 11–11.*

7 **Pueblo Amigo** contains enough distractions to be a destination unto itself. This entertainment center is built to resemble a colonial Mexican village, with stuccoed buildings painted soft yellow, blue, and rose and tree-lined pathways leading to a gazebo with a brick dome. The complex includes the fanciest hotel near downtown, several restaurants and clubs, a huge grocery store, and a large branch of the Caliente Race Book, where gambling on televised races and sporting events is legal. ✉ *Paseo Tijuana between Puente Mexico and Av. Independencia.*

8 The **Río Tijuana** area—as the section that runs along Avenida Paseo de los Héroes parallel to the dry Tia Juana River is called—is one of the city's main thoroughfares, with large statues of historical figures, including one of Abraham Lincoln, in the center of the *glorietas* (traffic circles). With its impressive Cultural Center, several shopping complexes, fine restaurants, and fashionable discos, this part of town rivals Avenida Revolución for the tourists' and locals' attention. ✉ *Between Blvd. Agua Caliente and border.*

9 The **Tijuana Cultural Center** was designed by architects Manuel Rosen and Pedro Ramírez Vásquez, who also created Mexico City's famous Museum of Anthropology. The center's exhibits of Mexican history are a good introduction for the thousands of visitors whose first taste of Mexico is at the border. The Omnimax Theater, with its curving 180-degree screen, features several different films on a rotating basis, often coinciding with temporary exhibits. Usually one English-language film is shown daily. Guest artists and musicians appear here regularly, and the exhibits on art and culture change frequently. The center's bookstore has an excellent selection of Mexican history, culture, and arts in both Spanish and English. ✉ *Paseo de los Héroes and Av. Independencia,* ☎ *66/84–11–11.* ✉ *Museum $1; museum and Omnimax Theater $3.50.* ☉ *Daily 9–9.*

10 **Plaza Río Tijuana,** the area's largest shopping complex, is enormous, with good restaurants, department stores, hundreds of shops, and a multiplex theater where at least one English-language film is usually shown. The plaza has become a central square of sorts, where holiday fiestas are held. The area has been landscaped with shade trees and flowers, and there are long, wide sidewalks leading from the shopping complex to the Cultural Center. ✉ *Paseo de los Héroes across from Cultural Center.*

11 **Playas Tijuana,** along the oceanfront, is a mix of modest and expensive residential neighborhoods, with a few restaurants and hotels. The long, isolated beaches are visited mostly by locals.

12 **Plaza de Toros Monumental,** the "Bullring by the Sea," sits at the northwest corner of the beach area, right by the border (☞ Outdoor Activities and Sports, *below*). The bullring is occasionally used for summer concerts as well.

Dining and Lodging

$$$ ✕ **Argentino de Tony.** Dark wood walls, padded booths, and wine bottle displays create the ambience of a private club where men and women in suits negotiate major deals while spearing chops and fillets from their mixed grills. It's hard to imagine that these power lunchers could get any work done in the office after the meal. Tony's specializes in heavy, filling dishes featuring imported beef—the smallest steak weighs in at 12 ounces, and even the lamb chops seem enormous.

⊠ *Pueblo Amigo center, Paseo Tijuana,* ☎ *66/82–81–11. MC, V. Closed Sun.*

$$$ ✕ **El Taurino.** Walk a few blocks west of Avenida Revolución and
★ you're in the true downtown Tijuana, where residents work, shop, and
eat. One of their favorite spots is this cozy steak house. The host greets
his guests in Spanish or English, recognizing regular patrons from
both sides of the border. Request a menu in English and zero in on the
beef selections, especially the New York steak, called *cabrería.* Shrimp
and lobster are also good choices, and all come with soup or salad. ⊠
Calle 6 No. 7531, ☎ *66/85–70–75. MC, V.*

$$ ✕ **El Faro de Mazatlán.** Fresh fish simply prepared is the hallmark of
one of Tijuana's best seafood restaurants. This is the place to try ce-
viche, abalone, squid, and lobster without spending a fortune. Meals
start with a savory soup and crusty rolls. The dining room, frequented
by professionals from nearby offices, is a peaceful spot for a long, leisurely
lunch. Appetizers and soup are included in the price of the meal.
⊠ *Blvd. Sanchez Taboada 9542,* ☎ *66/84–88–82. MC, V.*

$$ ✕ **La Fonda Roberto.** Roberto is by far the best restaurant in Tijuana
for traditional cuisine from the many culinary regions of Mexico. Try
the *chiles en nogada* (chilies stuffed with raisins and meat and topped
with cream and pomegranate seeds), meats with spicy achiote sauce,
and many varieties of mole. Portions are small, so order liberally and
share samples of many dishes. ⊠ *Siesta Motel, Old Ensenada Hwy.
(also called Calle 16 de Septiembre) near Blvd. Agua Caliente,* ☎ *66/
86–16–01. MC, V.*

$$ ✕ **La Leña.** The sparkling clean, white dining room in La Leña faces
an open kitchen where chefs grill unusual beef dishes, such as *Gao-
nera* (a tender fillet stuffed with cheese and guacamole). The owner
often visits with his guests, asking their opinion on the menu and offering samples of tripe—only for the strong of stomach. ⊠ *Blvd. Agua
Caliente 4560,* ☎ *66/86–47–52; Av. Revolución between Calles 4 and
5. AE, MC, V.*

$$ ✕ **La Taberna Española.** The mainstay of Plaza Fiesta's multiethnic cafés,
this Spanish tapas bar attracts a youthful, sophisticated crowd. The
tapa (appetizer) menu is printed only in Spanish, but with a bit of imag-
ination you should be able to select a representative sampling, such as
octopus in its own ink, a plate of spicy sausages, a wedge of Spanish
tortilla with potatoes and eggs, and a bowl of fava beans. Inside the
café, it's smoky, fragrant, and invariably crowded; sit at the outdoor
tables for a better view of the crowd waiting in line. ⊠ *Plaza Fiesta,
Paseo de los Héroes 10001,* ☎ *66/84–94–01. No credit cards.*

$$ ✕ **Tia Juana Tilly's.** Popular with both tourists and locals looking for
revelry and generous portions of Mexican specialties, this is one of the
few places where you can get *cochinita píbil* (a Yucatecan dish made
of roast pig, red onions, and bitter oranges) or the traditionally bitter
and savory chicken mole. Part of the same chain is Tilly's Fifth Ave.,
catercorner to the original on Avenida Revolución. ⊠ *Av. Revolución
at Calle 7,* ☎ *66/85–60–24. AE, MC, V.*

$ ✕ **Carnitas Uruapan.** At this large, noisy restaurant, patrons mingle
at long wood tables, toasting one another with chilled *cervezas* (beer).
The main attraction here is *carnitas* (marinated pork), sold by weight
and served with homemade tortillas, salsa, cilantro, guacamole, and
onions. ⊠ *Blvd. Díaz Ordaz 550,* ☎ *66/81–61–81; Paseo de los
Héroes at Av. Rodríguez, no tel. No credit cards.*

$ ✕ **La Especial.** Located at the foot of the stairs leading to an under-
★ ground shopping arcade, this restaurant attracts diners in search of home-
style Mexican cooking at low prices. The gruff, efficient waiters,
decked out in black slacks and vests, shuttle platters of carne asada,
enchiladas, and burritos, all with a distinctive flavor found nowhere

but in this busy, cavernous basement dining room. ⊠ *Av. Revolución 718,* ☎ *66/85–66–54. No credit cards.*

$ ✕ **Señor Frog's.** Heaping plates of barbecued chicken and ribs and buckets of ice-cold bottles of cerveza are the mainstay at this fun and festive formula eatery, one of many in the Carlos Anderson chain. The loud music and laughter make for a raucous atmosphere, and the food is consistently good. ⊠ *In Pueblo Amigo Center, Paseo Tijuana,* ☎ *66/82–49–58. AE, MC, V.*

$$$ 🏨 **Holiday Inn Pueblo Amigo.** The only thoroughly modern hotel in the center of Tijuana's tourist zone, the bright, white Holiday Inn has several sizes of rooms, from standard to presidential suites; all are elegantly decorated in green, beige, and peach, with cable TV, minibars, and direct-dial long-distance telephones. The indoor pool, sauna, and gym are especially popular with business travelers, who also have use of meeting facilities and a business center. The hotel's Café Alcazar is a favorite luncheon meeting spot for executives from the businesses in the Zona Río district. At press time, Holiday Inn was planning to open a second hotel on the grounds of the old Agua Caliente casino. ⊠ *Via Oriente 9211 at Pueblo Amigo, 22450,* ☎ *66/83–50–30 or 800/465–4329,* ℻ *66/83–50–32. 108 rooms and suites. Restaurant, indoor pool, beauty salon, sauna, exercise room. AE, MC, V.*

$$ 🏨 **Gran Hotel.** The two mirrored towers of the hotel are Tijuana's most
★ ostentatious landmarks, signs of prosperity and faith in the economic potential of this lucrative border town. The Gran Hotel often hosts receptions and parties for Tijuana's elite and is considered by many to be the city's most glamorous place for a drink or meal. The rooms on the club floors are particularly extravagant, with separate seating areas, king-size beds, and astounding views of Tijuana's sprawl. The hotel is inconveniently located for those without a car, but golfers can take advantage of package deals with the nearby country club. ⊠ *Blvd. Agua Caliente 4558, 22420,* ☎ *66/81–70–00 or 800/472–6385,* ℻ *66/81–70–16. 422 rooms with bath. Restaurant, pool, tennis courts, health club, nightclub, travel services. MC, V.*

$$ 🏨 **Lucerna.** Once one of the most charming hotels in Tijuana, the Lucerna has become run-down, and the rooms are in need of renovation. Still, the lovely gardens, large swimming pool surrounded by palms, touches of tile work, and folk art lend Mexican character to the hotel. The Lucerna's travel agency is particularly helpful with planning trips into Mexico. ⊠ *Paseo de los Héroes 10902, and Av. Rodríguez, 22320,* ☎ *66/34–20–00 or 800/582–3762,* ℻ *66/34–24–00. 170 rooms with bath, 9 suites. Restaurant, coffee shop, pool, nightclub, travel services. MC, V.*

$$ 🏨 **Otay Bugambilias.** Proximity to the Tijuana airport and the Otay Mesa manufacturing plants makes this modest hotel a great find for both business and pleasure travelers. The pink three-story Bugambilias has motel-like rooms with kitchenettes; suites have separate seating areas. Extras include a small gym, sauna, and swimming pool, and free transportation to and from the Tijuana airport. The location is inconvenient for those who just want to tour Tijuana, but it's great if you're catching an early flight to mainland Mexico. ⊠ *Blvd. Industrial at Carretera Aeropuerto, 22450,* ☎ *66/23–84–11 or 800/472–1153,* ℻ *66/23–76–00. 129 rooms. Restaurant, bar, pool, exercise room, meeting rooms. MC, V.*

$ 🏨 **Corona Plaza.** Though the exterior of this hotel resembles that of a nondescript office building, the interior is surprisingly pleasant. Rooms, furnished in handsome bleached wood, overlook an atrium lobby and restaurant. For less noise and more air, ask for a second- or third-floor room near the pool. The bullring is within walking distance;

other attractions are just a short cab ride away. ⊠ *Blvd. Agua Caliente 1426, 22450,* ☎ *66/81–81–83,* FAX *66/81–81–85. Restaurant, pool. AE, MC, V.*

$ ⛉ **La Villa de Zaragoza.** This brown stucco motel is such a success that the management keeps adding rooms—the newest have kitchenettes, and all offer air-conditioning and cable TV. The location, near the Jai Alai Palace and one block from Revolución, is ideal. The neighborhood can be noisy, however, and it's best to choose a room at the back. The guarded parking lot is a major plus, though you won't need a car if you stay here. The motel is used by tour groups, so book ahead for holidays and weekends. Discounts are available for extended stays. ⊠ *Av. Madero 1120, 22000,* ☎ *66/85–18–32,* FAX *66/85–18–37. 66 rooms. Restaurant. MC, V.*

$ ⛉ **Villas Juvenil Youth Hostel.** The hostel is set in a quiet, peaceful park and is part of a sports complex. The 20 beds are in same-sex dorms, and there is a cafeteria. ⊠ *Av. Padre Kino, 22320,* ☎ *66/84–25–23 or 66/84–75–10. No credit cards.*

Nightlife and the Arts

Tijuana has toned down its Sin City image; much of the nighttime action now takes place at the **Palacio Frontón** and the racetrack. Several hotels, especially the **Holiday Inn Pueblo Amigo** and **Gran Hotel,** feature live entertainment. **Rodeo de Media Noche** (⊠ Blvd. Paseo de los Héroes, ☎ 66/82–49–67), at the Pueblo Amigo shopping center, is a staggering concept incorporating an indoor rodeo ring, a cocktail lounge, and a disco. The midnight rodeo, with real bulls and cowboys, is presented from Thursday through Sunday nights. Dancing to recorded music is available every night, though the action doesn't begin until at least 10 PM.

The Hard Rock Café (⊠ Av. Revolución 520 between Calles 1 and 2, ☎ 66/85–02–06) has the same menu and decor as other branches of the famous London club and is popular with both families and singles. **OH! Laser Club** (⊠ Paseo de los Héroes 56, ☎ 66/84–02–67) is one of the oldest discos in town, popular with the sophisticated set. **Heaven & Hell** (⊠ Paseo de los Héroes 10501, ☎ 66/84–84–84) is less formal than most and extremely frenetic. **Baby Rock** (⊠ Calle Diego Rivera 1482, ☎ 66/88–04–40), an offshoot of a popular Acapulco disco, attracts a young, hip crowd. Tijuana's discos are elegant and sophisticated and usually have strict dress codes, with no T-shirts, jeans, or sandals allowed.

Outdoor Activities and Sports

BULLFIGHTS

Bullfights feature skilled matadors from throughout Mexico and Spain. They are held at **El Toreo de Tijuana** (⊠ Av. Agua Caliente outside downtown, ☎ 66/85–22–10) on Sunday at 4, May through September. In July and August you can also see fights at the **Plaza de Toros Monumental** (⊠ Playas Tijuana area, Ensenada Hwy., ☎ 66/85–22–10) on Sunday at 4. Admission to bullfights varies, depending on the fame of the matador and the location of your seat.

GOLF

The **Tijuana Country Club** (⊠ Blvd. Agua Caliente, east of downtown, ☎ 66/81–78–55) is open to guests of some hotels. It provides rental clubs, electric and hand carts, and caddies for the 18-hole course.

GREYHOUND RACES

At the **Hipódromo de Agua Caliente,** horse racing was phased out in 1993, but greyhounds race nightly at 7:45 and afternoons at 2 on weekends. In the Foreign Book area, gamblers can bet on races taking place in California and shown at Caliente on TV monitors. ✉ *Blvd. Agua Caliente at Salinas,* ☎ *66/81–78–11; in San Diego, CA, 619/231–1919.*

This ancient Basque sport, in some ways similar to handball but using a large, scooped-out paddle called a *frontón,* is played in the Moorish-style **Palacio Frontón,** or Jai Alai Palace. Matinee games start at noon from Monday through Wednesday; night games start at 8 PM from Thursday through Saturday. General admission is $2; box seats in the Concha Club are $20. ✉ *Av. Revolución and Calle 8,* ☎ *66/85–25–24; in San Diego, CA, 619/231–1919.*

Shopping

The Avenida Revolución shopping area spreads down Calle 1 to the pedestrian walkway leading from the border. Begin by checking out the stands along the border-crossing walkway, comparing prices as you travel toward Avenida Revolución. You may find that the best bargains are closer to the border; you can pick up your piñatas and serapes on your way out of town. The traditional shopping strip is Avenida Revolución, between Calles 1 and 8; it's lined with shops and arcades that display a wide range of crafts and curios. Bargaining is expected on the streets and in the arcades, but not in the finer shops.

The shops in **Plaza Revolución,** at the corner of Calle 1 and Avenida Revolución, stock quality crafts. **La Piel** (✉ Av. Revolución between Calle 4 and 5, ☎ 66/87–23–98) offers dependable quality in leather jackets, backpacks, and luggage. **Ralph Lauren Polo Outlet** (✉ Viva Tijuana Center, ☎ 66/88–76–98) is a licensed outlet for the designer's sportswear. **Sanborns** (✉ Av. Revolución at Calle 8, ☎ 66/88–14–62) has beautiful crafts from throughout Mexico, an excellent bakery, and chocolates from Mexico City. **Sara's** (✉ Av. Revolución at Calle 4, ☎ 66/88–29–32), one of the best department stores in Tijuana, features imported perfumes and fine clothing. The finest folk-art store, **Tolan** (✉ Av. Revolución between Calles 7 and 8, ☎ 66/88–36–37) carries everything from antique carved wooden doors to tiny ceramic miniature village scenes.

The **Mercado Hidalgo** (✉ Av. Independencia at Av. Sanchez Taboada, 2 blocks south of Paseo de los Héroes) is Tijuana's municipal market, with rows of fresh produce, grains, and herbs, some souvenirs, and the best selection of piñatas in Baja.

Mexitlán, on Avenida Ocampo, stocks high-quality folk art from throughout Mexico. **Plaza Fiesta,** on Paseo de los Héroes across from Plaza Río Tijuana, has a collection of boutiques, jewelry stores, and stained-glass shops. Next door, the **Plaza de los Zapatos** gathers together more than a dozen stores selling designer shoes imported from throughout the world. You can find great buys on fashionable clothing and shoes at **Plaza Río Tijuana** on Paseo de los Héroes. **Pueblo Amigo,** also on Paseo de los Héroes, has a few small folk-art shops and Ley, a gourmet grocery that sells salad by the pint and hard-to-find Mexican delicacies such as fresh mole sauce and pickled carrots and cauliflower.

Tecate

32 km (20 mi) east of Tijuana, 144 km (90 mi) west of Mexicali, 112 km (70 mi) northeast of Ensenada.

Tecate is a quiet community, a typical small Mexican town (population about 100,000) that happens to be on the border. So incidental is the border to local life that its gates are closed from 10 PM until 6 AM. Tecate beer, one of the most popular brands in Mexico, is brewed here. Maquiladoras and agriculture are the other main industries. Tecate's primary tourist draw is Rancho la Puerta, a fitness resort that caters to well-heeled southern Californians. A bit farther south, the valleys of Guadalupe and Calafía boast some of Mexico's lushest vineyards. Olives and grain are also grown in profusion here.

If you allocate an hour for exploring Tecate, you'll be hard put to fill your time. **Parque Hidalgo,** in the center of town, is a typical Mexican village plaza, with a small gazebo and a few wrought-iron benches. On summer evenings, dance and band concerts are held in **Parque López Mateos,** on Highway 3 south of town.

Dining and Lodging

$$ ✕ **El Passetto.** The best Italian restaurant in Tecate, El Passetto has superb garlic bread and homemade pasta. The proprietor makes his own wines, which are pretty good. There's live music on weekends. ⊠ *Callejón Libertad 200,* ☎ *665/4–1361. MC, V.*

$ ✕ **Panadería El Mejor.** Some say this is the best bakery in all of Baja, and it's open 24 hours daily. The fresh breads and pastries are legendary, and free coffee comes with your purchase. The bakery is just east of town, two blocks from the main plaza. ⊠ *Av. Juárez 331,* ☎ *665/4–00–40. No credit cards.*

$ ✕ **Plaza Jardin.** The setting is plain and the food simple Mexican fare, but the café tables outside offer a gratifying view of the plaza. ⊠ *Andador Libertad 274,* ☎ *665/4–34–54. No credit cards.*

$$$$ ▥ **Rancho la Puerta.** This peaceful, isolated health spa and resort, just west of Tecate, is nice—for those who can afford $1,600 or more a week. Spanish-style buildings with red-tiled roofs and modern glass-and-wood structures are spread throughout the sprawling ranch. Hiking trails lead off into scrub-pine hills surrounding the resort, and a large bright-blue pool is a central gathering spot. Guests stay in luxurious private cottages and usually check in for a week or more, taking advantage of the special diet and exercise regimen to lose weight and shape up. Transportation is available to and from the San Diego airport. ⊠ *Hwy. 2, 5 km (3 mi) west of Tecate, 21275,* ☎ *65/4–11–55 or 800/443–7565; in CA, 619/744–4222;* ℻ *65/4–11–08. 80 rooms. Restaurant, pool, beauty salon, massage, tennis courts, health club. AE, MC, V.*

$$ ▥ **Hacienda Santa Veronica.** Billed as an off-road and dirt-racing country club, the Hacienda is a pretty countryside resort featuring rooms furnished with Mexican colonial beds, bureaus, and fireplaces. The off-road raceway is sufficiently far away from the rooms to keep the noise of revving engines from disturbing the guests, and a number of trails for horseback riding traverse the property. ⊠ *Hwy. 2, 3 km (2 mi) east of Tecate, 21275, no tel.; reservations in the U.S.,* ☎ *619/298–4105 or 800/522–1516. 87 rooms. Restaurant, bar, pool, tennis courts, horseback riding. MC, V.*

Mexicali

136 km (85 mi) east of Tijuana.

Mexicali, with a current population estimated at 850,000, shares the Imperial Valley farmland and the border crossing with Calexico, a small California city. The capital of Baja California, Mexicali sees a great deal of government activity and a steady growth of *maquiladoras* (foreign manufacturing plants). Though water is scarce in these largely desert lands, the Mexicali area is blessed with some of the world's richest top-soil, and agriculture is a primary source of income in this section of Mexico. Mexicali is not a tourist destination but rather a place where politicians and bureaucrats meet.

Most visitors come to town on business, and the city's sights are few and far between. A tourist-oriented strip of curio shops and sleazy bars is located along Avenida Francisco Madero, one block south of the border. **The Museo del Estado** (State Museum), administered by the Autonomous University of Baja California (UABC), provides a comprehensive introduction to the natural and cultural history of Baja. ⊠ *Av. Reforma 1998 near Calle L,* ☎ *65/52–57–17.* ▦ *Free.* ☉ *Tues.–Sat. 9–6, Sun. 10–2.*

Parque Obregón at Avenida Reforma and Calle Irigoyen and **Parque Constitución** at Avenida México and Zuazua are the only two parks in downtown Mexicali. The **Mexicali Zoo** is in the City Park, **Bosque de la Ciudad,** south of town; the entrance is at the south end of Calle Victoria, between Cárdenas and Avenida Independencia.

Dining and Lodging

$$$ ✕ **La Misión Dragón.** With its eclectic landscape, this restaurant resembles a combination mission house and Chinese palace. Behind its gates are fountains, a garden, and Asian and Mexican artifacts. The locals hold large dinner celebrations here, and the Chinese food is top-notch. ⊠ *Av. Lázaro Cárdenas 555,* ☎ *65/66–43–20 or 65/66–44–51. MC, V.*

$ ✕ **Cenaduría Selecta.** This charming restaurant has been serving traditional Mexican food since 1945. Service is formal and efficient, the menus come in wooden folders, and the rows of booths always seem to be filled with locals enjoying themselves. ⊠ *Av. Arista and Calle C 1510,* ☎ *65/62–40–47. MC, V.*

$$$ ▦ **Holiday Inn.** This is the perennial favorite of those doing business in the city, with standard rooms and services and no surprises. ⊠ *Av. Benito Juárez 2220, 21270,* ☎ *65/66–38–01 reservations in the U.S., 800/465–4329;* ℻ *65/57–05–55. 158 rooms. Restaurant, bar, coffee shop, pool. AE, MC, V.*

$$ ▦ **La Lucerna.** The prettiest hotel in Mexicali, the colonial-style La Lucerna has lots of palms and fountains around the pool and carved wood furnishings in the dark, somber rooms. A newer section offers suites with separate seating areas and more modern furnishings. ⊠ *Av. Benito Juárez 2151, 21270,* ☎ *65/66–10–00 or 800/582–3762,* ℻ *65/66–47–06. 175 rooms and 28 suites. Restaurant, coffee shop, bar, pool. MC, V.*

Outdoor Activities and Sports

GOLF

You can tee off at the 18-hole **Mexicali Campestre Golf Course** (Km 11.5 on Hwy. 5 south of town, ☎ 65/61–71–30).

Rosarito Beach

29 km (18 mi) south of Tijuana.

Not so very long ago, Playas de Rosarito (Rosarito Beach) was a small seaside community with virtually no tourist trade. It was part of the municipality of Tijuana, an overlooked suburb on the way to the port city of Ensenada. But as the roads improved, and particularly after Baja's Transpeninsular Highway was completed in 1973, Rosarito Beach began to flower. In 1995 it became its own municipality, with a government separate from that of Tijuana. Rosarito's population, about 110,000, is growing steadily.

Rosarito's main street, alternately known as the Old Ensenada Highway and Boulevard Benito Juárez, reflects the unrestrained growth and speculation that have both helped and harmed the city. The street is packed with restaurants, bars, and shops in a jarring juxtaposition of architectural styles, with some of the largest developments halted midway for lack of investors.

It nevertheless remains a relaxing place to visit. Southern Californians have practically made Rosarito a weekend suburb. Surfers, swimmers, and sunbathers come here to enjoy the beach, one of the longest in northern Baja: It's an uninterrupted stretch of sand from the power plant at the far north end of town to below the Rosarito Beach Hotel, about 8 kilometers (5 miles) south. Horseback riding, jogging, and strolling are popular along this strand. Whales pass not far from shore on their winter migration; dolphins and sea lions sun on rocks jutting out from the sea. Rosarito has always attracted a varied crowd, and today's group is no exception—an assemblage of prosperous young Californians building villas in vacation developments, retired Americans and Canadians homesteading in trailer parks, and travelers of all ages from all over the world.

Hedonism and health get equal billing in Rosarito. One of the area's major draws is its seafood, especially lobster, shrimp, and abalone. The visiting Americans act as if they've been dry for months—margaritas and beer are the favored thirst quenchers. People throw off their inhibitions here, at least to the degree permitted by the local constables. A typical Rosarito day might begin with a breakfast of eggs, refried beans, and tortillas, followed by a few hours of horseback riding on the beach. Lying in the sun or strolling through the shops takes care of midday. Siestas are imperative and are usually followed by more shopping, strolling, or sunbathing before dinner, dancing, and sleep.

Rosarito Beach has few historic or cultural attractions, beaches and bars being the main draws. Sightseeing consists of strolling along the beach or down Boulevard Benito Juárez, which runs parallel to it.

An immense PEMEX gasoline installation and electric plant anchor the northern end of Boulevard Juárez, which then runs along a collection of new shopping arcades, restaurants, and motels. The eight-story **Quinta Del Mar** condo and hotel complex is the first major landmark, followed by the **Quinta Plaza** shopping center, which hosts a car wash, pharmacy, bakery, specialty shops, and restaurants, as well as the tourism office and the Centro de Convenciones, a 1,000-seat convention center. The **Festival Plaza** hotel and shopping center, with its distinctive roller coaster–like facade, sits a bit farther south on Boulevard Juárez, just before the Rosarito Beach Hotel, which marks the end of the strip.

NEED A BREAK?   The long glassed-in bar that sits on a little hill between the pool and the beach at the **Rosarito Beach Hotel** (☎ 661/2-01-44) is the best place for absorbing the local ambience. The margaritas are a potent reminder that you're in Mexico, and the nachos are pretty good.

Dining and Lodging

$$$ ✕ **Chabert's.** The original owners of the Rosarito Beach Hotel lived
★   in an adjacent European-style mansion that has since been transformed into a spa. The mansion's dining room has become the most sophisticated restaurant in town, with glistening crystal chandeliers, antique furnishings, and harpists playing during dinner. The steaks, rack of lamb, escargots, and lobster are all well prepared and served with finesse. ⊠ *Rosarito Beach Hotel, Blvd. Juárez,* ☎ *661/2–01–44. MC, V.*

$$$ ✕ **Dragon del Mar.** A miniature waterfall greets guests in the marble foyer of this elegant Chinese restaurant, which features a pianist playing relaxing music. Carved wooden partitions in the expansive dining room help create an intimate dining experience. The food is well prepared and appealing to the eye as well as the palate. ⊠ *Blvd. Juárez 283,* ☎ *661/2–06–04. MC, V.*

$$$ ✕ **El Nido.** A dark, wood-paneled restaurant with leather booths and a large central fireplace, this is one of the oldest eateries in Rosarito. Diners unimpressed with the newer, fancier establishments come here for the good mesquite-grilled steaks and for grilled quail from the owner's farm in the Baja wine country. ⊠ *Blvd. Juárez 67,* ☎ *661/2–14–30. MC, V.*

$$$ ✕ **La Casa de la Langosta.** You needn't drive to Puerto Nuevo for lobster; just visit this branch of one of that area's best restaurants. The traditional lobster dinner is the house specialty, of course, but you can also get grilled fish and shrimp. The second-story dining room and kitchen are impeccably clean and the food dependable, though not overly exciting. ⊠ *Quinta Plaza,* ☎ *661/2–09–24. MC, V.*

$$ ✕ **Azteca.** The enormous dining room at the Rosarito Beach Hotel has a view of the pool and beach area. Many visitors come here exclusively for the Sunday brunch; expect to wait in line on holiday weekends. Both Mexican and American dishes are offered, and the size of the portions makes up for the erratic quality of the food. The hotel offers a Mexican buffet and fiesta here on Friday nights. ⊠ *Rosarito Beach Hotel, Blvd. Juárez,* ☎ *661/2–01–44. MC, V.*

$$ ✕ **Calafia.** The owners of this restaurant and trailer park have added a historic element to their property by filling the public spaces with photos and artifacts from Baja's early days. But most visitors are drawn to Calafia's dining room, where tables are scattered on small terraces down the cliffside to the crashing sea. The food is standard Mexican fare, but it all tastes great when combined with the fresh salt air and sea breezes. Calafia has an outdoor dance floor at the base of the cliffs, where live bands sometimes perform. ⊠ *Km 35.5 Old Ensenada Hwy., 22710,* ☎ *661/2–15–81. MC, V.*

$$ ✕ **La Leña.** The cornerstone restaurant of the Quinta Plaza shopping
★ center, La Leña sits on a rise that enables you to see the ocean from the window tables. The dining room is spacious, with the tables spread far enough apart for privacy. Try any of the beef dishes, especially the tender *carne asada* (grilled strips of beef) with tortillas and guacamole. There's a branch of the Caliente Race Book wagering center on the premises. ⊠ *Quinta Plaza,* ☎ *661/2–08–26. MC, V.*

$$ ✕ **René's.** One of the oldest restaurants in Rosarito (1924), René's features chorizo (Mexican sausage), quail, frogs' legs, and lobster. There's an ocean view from the dining room, a lively bar, and mariachi music. ⊠ *Blvd. Juárez south of Rosarito Beach Hotel,* ☎ *661/2–10–20. MC, V.*

$$ ✕ **Ortega's Place.** Music blares from this two-story restaurant-bar where tourists flock to inexpensive buffets. The breakfast and lunch spreads include scrambled eggs, lots of beans and rice, and basic Mexican dishes. The à la carte entrées are much more expensive, and though Ortega's is known for its lobster, you'll get a better deal elsewhere. ⊠ *Blvd. Juárez 200,* ☎ *661/2–27–91. MC, V.*

$ ✕ **Juice 'n Juice.** Rosarito's Mexican health-food restaurant is a no-frills lunch counter with lots of salads, juices, yogurt, and granola. Good cheese enchiladas and other meatless Mexican dishes give vegetarians a chance to sample the local fare. Beef burgers and burritos are also served. ⊠ *Blvd. Juárez 98,* ☎ *661/2–03–38. No credit cards.*

$ ✕ **La Flor de Michoacán.** Carnitas (marinated pork roasted over an open pit) Michoacán-style, served with homemade tortillas, guacamole, and salsa, are the house specialty. The tacos, *tortas* (sandwiches), and tostadas are great. The surroundings are simple but clean. Takeout is available. ⊠ *Blvd. Juárez 291,* ☎ *661/2–18–58. No credit cards. Closed Wed.*

$ ✕ **Rosarito Village Café.** Inexpensive margaritas, mariachis, and take-out Mexican food make this restaurant a popular watering hole; it's also a good place for U.S.-style breakfasts. ⊠ *Next to Rosarito Beach Hotel, Blvd. Juárez 777,* ☎ *661/2–86–54. MC, V.*

$$$ 🏨 **Marriott Real Del Mar Residence Inn.** Golfers and escapists relish
★ their privacy at this all-suites hotel set on a cliff with far-away views of the sea. The standard accommodations have living rooms with vaulted-brick ceilings, fireplaces, kitchens, and two double beds; larger units offer one or two bedrooms. Greens fees at the on-site golf course are included in packages. The hotel, 19 kilometers (12 miles) south of the border and 6 miles north of Rosarito, is completely removed from the action. ⊠ *Km. 19.5 Ensenada Toll Road, 22710,* ☎ *661/3–34–01 or 800/331–3131,* FAX *661/3–36–77. 66 rooms and suites. Restaurant, bar, pool, 18-hole golf course. MC, V.*

$$ 🏨 **Brisas del Mar.** A modern motel (built in 1992), the Brisas del Mar is especially good for families, since the large pastel rooms comfortably accommodate four persons. A few of the suites on the second story have hot tubs and views of the ocean; all have air-conditioning and TV. The motel is located on the inland side of Boulevard Juárez, and traffic noise can be a problem. ⊠ *Blvd. Juárez 22, 22710,* ☎ FAX *661/2–25–47; reservations in the U.S., Box 1867, Chula Vista, CA 91912,* ☎ *800/697–5223. 66 rooms. Bar, coffee shop, heated pool, volleyball court. MC, V.*

$$ 🏨 **Festival Plaza.** Designed with unrestrained fun in mind, Festival Plaza is geared toward a youthful crowd. The motel-like rooms are in an eight-story building with a unique facade meant to resemble a roller coaster. The casitas (in the $$$ range) close to the beach are the quietest accommodations and have small hot tubs, separate living rooms with fold-out couches, and private garages, but no kitchen facilities. The hotel also operates a complex of 14 villas just south of Rosarito; these have full kitchens for the same price. Within the hotel complex are several bars, and the central courtyard serves as a concert stage, children's playground, and party headquarters. Noise is a definite factor; stay elsewhere unless you want to join the festivities. ⊠ *Blvd. Juárez 11, 22710,* ☎ *661/2–08–42 or 800/453–8606,* FAX *661/2–01–24. 114 rooms and suites. 2 restaurants, 3 bars, pool, dance club, playground. AE, MC, V.*

$$ 🏨 **Los Pelicanos Hotel.** One of the few hotels situated directly on the beach, the Pelicanos is a favorite with Americans and Canadians who stay for weeks on end in the winter. The best rooms have oceanfront balconies, though the others—with white walls, light wood furnishings, and large bathrooms—are nice as well. The second-story restaurant and bar, popular sunset-watching spots, tend to attract an older, more subdued clientele. ⊠ *Calle Cedros 115, 22710,* ☎ *661/2–04–45,* FAX *661/2–17–57; U.S. mailing address, Box 3871, San Ysidro, CA 92073. 39 rooms. Restaurant, bar. MC, V.*

$$ 🏨 **Rosarito Beach Hotel.** Dating from the Prohibition era, this venerable hotel continues to be Rosarito's centerpiece. It's a charmer, with huge ballrooms, tiled public rest rooms, and a glassed-in pool deck overlooking a long beach. The very plain rooms and suites in the tower facing the beach are air-conditioned; some of the units in the original building surrounding the swimming pool have fans only and are very run-down. It's a good idea to check a few rooms before choosing one, keeping in mind the noise factor when looking at those near the pools, the chil-

dren's playground, and the side lawn where live bands play on summer afternoons. Midweek reduced rates and special packages including meals are often available; ocean-view rooms are in the expensive ($$$) category. A refurbished mansion 1930s next door hosts the Casa Playa Spa, a full-service European facility with massage, beauty treatments, exercise equipment, saunas, and hot tubs. The prices for treatments are quite reasonable. ⊠ *Blvd. Juárez, south end of town, 22710,* ☎ *661/2–01–44 or 800/343–8582,* 𝖥𝖠𝖷 *661/2–11–76; reservations in the U.S., Box 430145, San Diego, CA 92143. 275 rooms and suites. 2 restaurants, bar, 2 pools, spa, tennis courts, health club, beach. MC, V.*

$ ⌘ **Cupalas del Mar.** This small hotel between Boulevard Juárez and the beach is quieter than most, with sunny, clean rooms and satellite TV. ⊠ *Calle Guadalupe Victoria 9, 22710,* ☎ *661/2–24–90. 39 rooms. Pool, hot tub. AE, MC, V.*

$ ⌘ **Motel Quinta Chica.** You don't come to this motel at the south end of town for character but for comfortable beds. Rooms in the front face the free road and enjoy ocean breezes; those in the back have the constant roar of traffic on the toll road. ⊠ *Km 26.8 Old Ensenada Hwy., 22710,* ☎ *661/2–13–00,* 𝖥𝖠𝖷 *661/2–12–15. 90 rooms. MC, V.*

Nightlife and the Arts

The many restaurants in Rosarito Beach keep customers entertained with live music, piano bars, or *folklórico* (folk music and dance) shows; the bar scene is also active. Drinking-and-driving laws are stiff—the police will fine you no matter how little you've had. If you plan to drink, take a cab or assign a designated driver.

There's a lot going on at night at the **Rosarito Beach Hotel** (⊠ Blvd. Juárez, ☎ 661/2–01–44): live music at the ocean-view Beachcomber Bar and Hugo's; a Mexican Fiesta on Friday nights; and a live band at the cavernous disco. The **Festival Plaza** (⊠ Blvd. Juárez 11, ☎ 661/2–08–42) has become party central for Rosarito's youthful crowd and presents live concerts on the hotel's courtyard stage most weekends; in the hotel complex are **El Museo Cantina Tequila,** dedicated to the art of imbibing tequila and offering more than 130 brands of the fiery drink; and **Rock & Roll Taco**—as its name suggests, a taco stand and boisterous bar all in one. **Papas and Beer** (⊠ Blvd. Juárez near Rosarito Beach Hotel, ☎ 661/2–03–43) draws a young, energetic crowd. **Calafia** (⊠ Km 35.5 Old Ensenada Hwy., ☎ 661/2–15–81) often hosts live salsa and rock bands at its outdoor stage.

Outdoor Activities and Sports
GOLF
The **Real del Mar Golf Club** (⊠ 18 km [12 mi] south of border on Ensenada toll road, ☎ 66/13–34–01) has 18 holes overlooking the ocean. Golf packages are available at some Rosarito Beach hotels.

HORSEBACK RIDING
Horses can be rented at the north and south ends of Juárez and on the beach south of the Rosarito Beach Hotel for $8 per hour. In the past, some of the animals were pathetically thin and misused. Their number is now restricted and the horses are better cared for. If you're a dedicated equestrian, ask about tours into the countryside, which can be arranged with the individual owners.

SURFING
The waves are particularly good at **Popotla,** Kilometer 33; **Calafia,** Kilometer 35.5; and **Costa Baja,** Kilometer 36, on the Old Ensenada Highway. **Tony's Surf Shop** (⊠ Blvd. Juárez 312, ☎ 661/2–11–92) offers surfing gear for sale or rent.

Shopping

Rosarito is a great place to shop for pottery and wood furniture. Curio stands and open-air artisans' markets line Boulevard Juárez both north and south of town, with the best pottery stands on the highway to the south. The major hotels have shopping arcades with restaurants, taco stands, and some decent crafts stores.

Artesanias Hacienda (⊠ Blvd. Juárez 349, ☎ 661/2–24–35) has a beautiful selection of painted tiles sold individually or in tiled wall murals or furnishings. **Casa del Arte y La Madera** (⊠ Quinta del Mar Plaza, ☎ 661/2–13–00) always features an irresistible selection of Mexican folk art with a fish and sea theme, and creatively painted furnishings. **Casa la Carreta** (⊠ Km 29 Ensenada Hwy., ☎ 661/2–05–02), one of Rosarito's best furniture shops, is worth a visit just to see the wood-carvers create elaborate desks, dining tables, and armoires. **Casa Torres** (⊠ Rosarito Beach Hotel Shopping Center, ☎ 661/2–10–08) carries a wide array of imported perfumes. **Margarita's** (⊠ Rosarito Beach Hotel Shopping Center, no tel.) has a great selection of Guatemalan textiles and clothing. **Oradia Imports** (⊠ Quinta Plaza Center, ☎ 661/2–16–37) focuses on imported perfumes and crystal. **Rangel** (⊠ Blvd. Juárez 151-A, ☎ 661/2–14–26) specializes in rattan and wood furnishings. The shelves of **Taxco Curios** (⊠ Quinta del Mar Plaza, ☎ 661/2–18–77) are filled with hand-blown glassware.

The **Calimax** grocery store on Boulevard Juárez is a good place to stock up on necessities.

Puerto Nuevo

Km 44, Old Ensenada Hwy, 12 km (7.5 mi) south of Rosarito Beach.

Not that many years ago, the only way you could tell you'd reached this fishing community at Kilometer 44 on the old highway from Rosarito Beach was by the huge painting of a 7-Up bottle on the side of a building. You'd drive down the rutted dirt road to a row of restaurants where you were served the classic Newport meal: grilled lobster, refried beans, rice, homemade tortillas, butter, salsa, and lime. The meal became a legend, and now at least 30 restaurants in the same area have the identical menu. An artisans' market sits at the entrance to the restaurant row; other stands selling pottery, serapes, and T-shirts line the nearby highway. Several hotels have opened in the area, making Puerto Nuevo a self-contained destination where diners can party all day and night and not have to drive to hotels in Rosarito or Ensenada. Several longtime favorite small inns and restaurants are also in the area.

Dining and Lodging

$$$ Don't expect there to be much variation on the food at any of the Puerto Nuevo restaurants: Diners come here for the classic lobster meal and they're not about to be disappointed. Some places have full bars; others serve only wine and beer. **Ortega's,** with four branches in Newport and two in Rosarito, is the most crowded; **Ponderosa** is smaller and quieter and is run by a gracious family; **Costa Brava** is more elegant, with tablecloths and an ocean view; and **La Casa de la Langosta** serves grilled fish along with lobster and shrimp. Lobsters in most places are priced as small, medium, and large—medium is about $15. Some of the lobster served in Newport comes from local waters during lobster season (October through March), though the supply can hardly keep up with the demand and most of the lobster is imported the rest of the year. There is some concern that the waters close to shore have become polluted, but the fishermen say they catch the lobsters a mile

or so offshore, where the waters are safe. Most places are open for lunch and dinner on a first-come, first-served basis. Some take credit cards.

$$$ ☷ **Grand Baja Resort.** A good value for families and groups, this resort offers beachfront condo rentals with daily and long-term rates; split the cost of a suite or studio between two couples and you'll be in the moderate ($$) range. The units come in a variety of sizes, from studios to two-bedroom oceanfront condos; most have kitchens. The Grand Baja is a block away from the cluster of Puerto Nuevo lobster restaurants. ⊠ *Km 44.5 Old Ensenada Hwy., 22710, ☎ 661/4–14–84, 𝖥𝖠𝖷 661/4–11–42; reservations in the U.S., 619/298–4105 or 800/225–2786; in CA, NV, AZ, 800/522–1516. 150 units. Pool, tennis courts. MC, V.*

$$$ ☷ **Hacienda Las Glorias.** Located on the grounds of the Bajamar golf resort, which lies about halfway between Rosarito and Ensenada, the Hacienda Las Glorias is one of the prettiest hotels on the coast. Designed like a Mexican hacienda surrounding a central courtyard, it features rooms with French doors leading to landscaped patios, handcarved furnishings, and tables and chairs by the windows. Staying here is peaceful except when golfers neglect to remove their shoes and clomp around the brick hallways like herds of goats. The pool, clubhouse, and restaurant are a few yards away from the hotel rooms. Private homes and condos edge the golf course and the cliffs overlooking the ocean. ⊠ *Km 77.5 Old Ensenada Hwy., Ensenada, 22800, ☎ 615/5–01–51, 𝖥𝖠𝖷 615/5–01–50; reservations in the U.S., 619/298–4105 or 800/225–2786; in CA, NV, AZ, 800/533–1516. 80 rooms. Restaurant, bar, pool, golf course, tennis courts. AE, MC, V.*

$$$ ☷ **Oasis Resort.** This full-scale resort on a long, perfect beach is incredibly popular, especially with families. The hotel section has one-bedroom, ocean-view suites with heat, air-conditioning, cable TVs, minibars, and fold-out couches; two children under the age of 12 stay free with two adults. Deluxe RVs with full kitchens, cable TV, and maid service are also available and are the most costly accommodations. Full hook-ups for those who bring their own mobile homes are the least expensive, though the rates are far higher than those in less elaborate campgrounds. Though not especially peaceful, the Oasis is a fun spot where guests quickly become friends and end up booking return visits together. ⊠ *Km 40 Old Ensenada Hwy., 22710, ☎ 661/3–32–55, 𝖥𝖠𝖷 661/3–32–52; reservations in the U.S., 800/462–7472. 100 suites, 22 RVs, 55 RV spaces. Restaurant, bar, 2 pools, wading pool, 2 hot tubs, sauna, miniature golf, tennis courts, exercise room, recreation room. MC, V.*

$$ ☷ **Las Rocas.** Though still the prettiest hotel in the area, this white hotel with blue tiled domes is beginning to show its age. The building is terraced up a hillside, giving all the rooms ocean views, but the accommodations are not otherwise equal. The least expensive ones are small, with dripping faucets and worn furnishings. The most expensive are much larger and offer fireplaces, coffeemakers, and microwaves. The pool and whirlpool seem to spill over the cliffs into the ocean. ⊠ *Km 37 Old Ensenada Hwy., 22710, ☎ 𝖥𝖠𝖷 661/2–21–40; reservations in the U.S., Box 8851, Chula Vista, CA 91912, 619/425–2682; outside CA, 800/733–6394. 74 rooms and suites. Restaurant, bar, hot tub, beach. AE, MC, V.*

$$ ☷ **Hotel New Port Baja.** The closest accommodations to the lobster restaurants are in this sand-colored complex framing a pool and ocean views. The rooms don't have air-conditioning, which can be a drawback if you've been sitting by the pool on a hot day. But they do have heaters for chilly winter nights, along with cable TV, small balconies, and simple blue-gray and white furnishings. Leave your car in the guarded lot and walk to the restaurants and pottery yards. ⊠ *Km 45 Old En-*

senada Hwy., 22710, ☎ *661/4–11–66,* FAX *661/4–11–75; reservations in the U.S., 619/298–4105 or 800/225–2786; in CA, NV, AZ, 800/533–1516. 150 rooms. Restaurant, bar, pool, tennis courts, fitness room. MC, V.*

$$ ✕▣ **La Fonda.** A longtime favorite with beachgoers, La Fonda has a
★ few well-worn rooms, decorated with carved-wood furniture and folk
art, with great views of the ocean. There are no phones or televisions,
just the sound of the surf and miles of empty beach to keep you en-
tertained. Even the hotel doesn't have a phone; reservations can only
be made by mail (allow two weeks to receive your confirmation) or in
person. At the very popular restaurant, you can sit on an outdoor patio
and sip potent margaritas served with nachos and hot salsa. Fresh lob-
ster, grilled steaks, prime rib, suckling pig, and traditional Mexican dishes
are accompanied by a delicious black-bean soup. The bar is usually
packed, and the patrons boisterous. If you plan on getting any sleep,
ask for a room as far away from it and from the restaurant as possi-
ble. ✉ *Km 59 Old Ensenada Hwy., 22710, no tel.; reservations in the
U.S., Box 268, San Ysidro, CA 92073. 18 rooms. Restaurant, bar, beach.
No credit cards.*

Outdoor Activities and Sports

GOLF

Bajamar (✉ Km 77.5 Old Ensenada Hwy., ☎ 615/5–01–51), a 1976
course revamped and reopened in late 1993, offers 18 holes of chal-
lenging championship golf. A second 18-hole course is under con-
struction, with the first 9 holes scheduled for completion by 1996.

En Route Vast vistas of pounding surf and solitary cliffs are interspersed with
one-of-a-kind hotels and restaurants along the coastline between Rosar-
ito Beach and Ensenada. The paved highway (Mexico Route 1) between
the two cities often cuts a path between low mountains and high
oceanside cliffs; exits lead to rural roads, oceanfront campgrounds, and
an ever-increasing number of resort communities. The small fishing com-
munities of **San Miguel** and **El Sauzal** sit off the highway to the north
of Ensenada, and the **Coronado Islands** can be clearly seen off the coast.

Ensenada

104 km (65 mi) south of Tijuana, 75 km (47 mi) south of Rosarito.

In 1542 Juan Rodríguez Cabrillo first discovered the seaport that Se-
bastián Vizcaino named Ensenada–Bahía de Todos Santos (All Saints'
Bay) in 1602. Since then the town has drawn a steady stream of "dis-
coverers" and developers. First ranchers made their homes on large
spreads along the coast and up into the mountains. Gold miners fol-
lowed, turning the area into a boomtown during the late 1800s. After
the mines were depleted, the area settled back into a pastoral state for
a while, but the harbor gradually grew into a major port for shipping
agricultural goods from the surrounding ranches and farms. Now,
with a population of some 300,000, it is one of Mexico's largest sea-
ports and has a thriving fishing fleet and fish-processing industry. The
smell of fish from the canneries lining the highway can be overpow-
ering at times.

There are no beaches in Ensenada proper, but beaches north and south
of town are satisfactory for swimming, sunning, surfing, and camp-
ing. On summer and holiday weekends the population swells, but the
town rarely gets overly crowded. The hotels and resorts along the coast,
especially around Rosarito Beach, attract most of the travelers seek-
ing weekend escapes, and Ensenada's hotels are languishing.

In a concerted effort to attract vacationers, conventioneers and business travelers, the waterfront area has been razed and rebuilt, with taco stands replaced by shopping centers, hotels, and the massive Plaza Marina. Several strip malls have opened in town, but many of the storefronts remain empty. Cruise ships occasionally anchor offshore, bringing daytrippers for shopping and dining.

Numbers in the margin correspond to points of interest on the Ensenada map.

Ensenada, the third largest city in Baja, hugs the harbor of Bahía de Todos Santos. As Alternate Highway 1 leads into town from the north, it becomes Boulevard Costero, running past shipyards filled with massive freighters. Between the water and the street, the massive Plaza Marina is completed but far from filled with the expected restaurants and shops.

❶ El Mirador (The Lookout) at the top of Calle 2 is a great spot to get an overview of the area. From here you can see the entire Bahía de Todos Santos, from the canneries of San Miguel south to the towns of Punta Banda and La Bufadora.

At the northernmost point at the water's edge sits an indoor-outdoor **❷ Fish Market,** where row after row of counters display piles of shrimp as well as tuna, dorado, marlin, snapper, and dozens of other species of fish caught off Baja's coasts. Outside, stands sell grilled or smoked fish, seafood cocktails, and fish tacos. Browsers can pick up some standard souvenirs, eat well for very little money, and take some great photographs. The hot-pink Plaza de Mariscos, which blocks the view of the traditional fish market from the street, is a comfortable place in which to eat.

NEED A BREAK?	You can't visit the fish market without trying at least one fish taco. Strips of fresh snapper, halibut, or other freshly caught fish are dipped in batter and deep-fried, then wrapped in fresh corn tortillas. Choose your topping—cilantro, salsa, tomatoes, onions, pickled carrots—from an array of dishes set out on the counter.

The main street along the waterfront is Boulevard Costero. Fishing **❸** and whale-watching tours depart from the **Sportfishing Pier** (✉ Blvd. Costero at Av. Alvarado).

❹ Plaza Cívica (✉ Blvd. Costero at Av. Riveroll) is a nice, small square with sculptures of Mexican heroes Benito Juárez, Miguel Hidalgo, and Venustiano Carranza. Cruise ships dock offshore from the waterfront **❺** and passengers are ferried to the pier by the **Centro Artesenal de Ensenada** shopping center, home of one of the finest folk art shops in Baja.

❻ The **Riviera del Pacífico** is a rambling, white hacienda-style mansion built in the 1920s with money raised on both sides of the border. An enormous gambling palace, hotel, restaurant and bar, the glamorous Riviera was frequented by wealthy U.S. citizens and Mexicans, particularly during Prohibition. When gambling was outlawed in Mexico and Prohibition ended in the United States, the palace lost its raison d'être. During daylight, visitors can now tour the elegant ballrooms and halls, which host occasional art shows and civic events, and stroll among the lavish gardens. Riviera del Pacífico is now officially called the Centro Social, Cívico y Cultural de Ensenada (Social, Civic and Cultural Center of Ensenada), and there are plans to include it in a major convention-center complex along the waterfront. ✉ *Blvd. Costero and Av. Riviera,* ☎ *617/6–43–10.* ⬚ *Free.* ☉ *Daily 9–5.*

Ensenada

❼ Ensenada's traditional tourist zone is centered along **Avenida López Mateos.** High-rise hotels, souvenir shops, restaurants, and bars line the avenue from its beginning at the foot of the Chapultepec Hills for eight blocks south to the dry channel of the Arroyo de Ensenada. Locals shop for furniture, clothing, and other necessities on **Avenida Juárez** in Ensenada's downtown area.

❽ Locals shop for furniture, clothing, and other necessities on **Avenida Juárez** in Ensenada's downtown area.

❾ **Las Bodegas de Santo Tomás,** Baja's oldest winery, gives tours and tastings of its downtown winery and bottling plant. The restaurant in the winery is one of Baja's finest. ✉ *Av. Miramar 666,* ☎ *617/8–33–33; in the U.S., 619/454–7166.* 🎫 *$1.* ☉ *Tours Mon.–Sat. 11 AM, 1 PM, and 3 PM; Sun. 11 AM and 1 PM.*

❿ The city's largest cathedral, **Our Lady of Guadalupe** (✉ Av. Floresta at Av. Juárez) is the center of processions and celebrations during religious holidays.

⓫ **La Bufadora** (✉ Hwy. 23, 31 km, or 20 mi, south of Ensenada) is an impressive blowhole in the coastal cliffs at Punta Banda. Water splashes up to 75 feet in the air with startling power, spraying sightseers standing nearby. The area around the blowhole was cleaned up recently, and a new viewing platform and electricity were added. Future plans include a paved parking lot, permanent buildings for restaurants and artisans' stands, and rest rooms. The road to La Bufadora is lined with stands where growers sell wonderful locally grown olives, along with homemade tamales and strands of chilis and garlic.

Beaches

Since the waterfront in Ensenada proper is taken up by fishing boats, the best swimming beaches are south of town. **Estero Beach** is long and clean, with mild waves. Surfers populate the beaches off Highway 1 north and south of Ensenada, particularly at **San Miguel, California,**

Tres Marías, and La Joya beaches; scuba divers prefer Punta Banda, by La Bufadora. Lifeguards are rare; swimmers should be cautious. The tourist office in Ensenada has a map that shows safe diving and surfing beaches.

Dining and Lodging

$$$ ✕ El Rey Sol. A family-owned French restaurant more than 40 years
★ old, El Rey Sol is in a charming building with stained-glass windows and is decorated with wrought-iron chandeliers and heavy oak tables and chairs. Specialties include French and Mexican presentations of fresh fish, poultry, and vegetables grown at the owner's farm in the Santo Tomás Valley. Appetizers come with the meal; the excellent pastries are baked on the premises. ⊠ *Av. López Mateos 1000,* ☎ *617/8– 17–33. AE, MC, V.*

$$$ ✕ La Embotelladora Vieja. The most elegant restaurant in Ensenada
★ is set in a converted wine-aging room at the Santo Tomás winery. The decor is classic country French, with wine bins stacked floor-to-ceiling under brick arches and crystal goblets glistening on candlelit tables. The so-called Baja French menu includes appetizers of smoked tuna and French pâté; among the most sublime entrées are the grilled lobster in cabernet sauvignon sauce, beef Montpellier with green peppercorns, and quail with sauvignon blanc sauce. Teetotalers, note: Nearly every dish is prepared with wine, though you can order some without alcohol-laden sauces. All of Baja's wineries are represented on the impressive wine list. The restaurant is so outstanding that southern Californians drive to Ensenada for long lunches here. ⊠ *Av. Miramar 666,* ☎ *617/4–08–07. MC, V.*

$$ ✕ Bronco's Steak House. A great find near the San Nicolas Hotel, Bronco's serves exceptional steaks and Mexican specialties. Try the Boca del Rio, a New York steak stuffed with grilled onions and fiery serrano chilies. Tripe appears frequently on the menu, satisfying the cravings of local diners gathered at many of the wood tables. Brick walls, wood plank floors, and hanging spurs and chaps give the place a Wild West feel, but the mood is subdued and relaxed. ⊠ *Av. López Mateos 1525,* ☎ *617/6–49–00. MC, V.*

$$ ✕ Casamar. A long-standing, dependable restaurant, Casamar is known for its wide variety of excellent seafood. Lobster and shrimp are prepared in several ways but seem freshest when grilled *con mojo y ajo* (with butter and garlic). When choosing a fish dish, always ask about the catch of the day; you may luck out and get a thick steak of fresh yellowfin tuna. ⊠ *Blvd. Lázaro Cárdenas 987,* ☎ *617/4–04–17. MC, V.*

$$ ✕ El Charro. You can find far less expensive rotisserie chicken, beans, rice, and tortillas at other places in downtown, but El Charro still attracts a steady stream of locals and tourists. Part of the draw is the location—not far from Hussong's Cantina (☞ Nightlife and the Arts, *below*) and other watering holes—and the food is consistently good. Hungry patrons hover over platters of chilies rellenos, enchiladas, and fresh chips and guacamole at heavy wooden picnic tables under a ceiling of charred wooden beams. Plump chickens slowly circle over a wood fire by the front window, and the aroma of grilled beef and simmering beans fills the air. ⊠ *Av. López Mateos 475,* ☎ *617/8–38– 81. MC, V.*

$$ ✕ Haliotis. It's worth the search to find this out-of-the-way seafood house. The owners are from Mazatlán and rely on recipes from back home to educate local palates. You can't miss with the *sopa de mariscos* (seafood soup) or the *parrillada* (a charcoal grill heaped with steaming lobster, shrimp, octopus, and fish). ⊠ *Calle Delante 179 at Av. Ejercito Nacional,* ☎ *617/6–37–20. MC, V.*

$ ✕ **Plaza Mexico.** You can eat in or take out your meals at this brightly lit café, where mariachis add to the festive ambience on Friday and Saturday nights. Thick grilled steaks and marinated carne asada are the best dinner bets; the tacos are good for inexpensive meals or snacks. Margaritas and beer are available. ⊠ *Av. López Mateos 2184,* ☎ *617/7–21–51. No credit cards.*

$$$ ▥ **Coral Hotel & Marina.** This ambitious project, nearing completion at press time, is the largest resort on the Baja Norte coast. A marina, long needed in Ensenada, has slips for 600 boats and facilities for clearing customs. The all-suites hotel offers 149 units decorated in burgundy and dark green, with waterfront balconies, seating areas, cable TV, and in-room international phone service (still a novelty in this area). Extensive sports facilities, including tennis courts, an exercise room, and a spa, are among the attractions. ⊠ *Mexico Hwy. 1 north of town, 22800,* ☎ *800/222–6725. 149 rooms and suites. Restaurant, 2 swimming pools, 2 hot tubs, spa, tennis courts, exercise room. MC, V.*

$$$ ▥ **Las Rosas.** This elegant pink palace just north of town is by far the
★   most upscale hotel in the area; the atrium lobby features marble floors, mint green–and–pink upholstered couches facing the sea, and a green-glass ceiling that glows at night. All rooms face the ocean and pool; some have fireplaces and hot tubs, and even the least expensive accommodations are lovely. The hotel is booked solid most weekends; make reservations far in advance. ⊠ *Mexico Hwy. 1 north of town, 22800,* ☎ *617/4–43–20,* ⅎⅅ *617/4–45–95. 32 rooms and suites. Restaurant, bar, pool, hot tub. AE, MC, V.*

$$ ▥ **Estero Beach Resort.** Families settle in for a week or more at this long-standing resort on Ensenada's best beach. The rooms and suites (some with kitchenettes) reflect years of hard wear, but no one expects anything fancy here. There are also hookups for motor homes. Guests spend their days swimming in the ocean (there's no pool), fishing, riding horses, playing volleyball, and generally hanging out with friends. Nights are spent at the casual restaurant and bar. The resort is 10 kilometers (6 miles) south of town. ⊠ *Mexico Hwy. 1 between Ensenada and Maneadero, 22810,* ☎ *617/6–62–35,* ⅎⅅ *617/6–69–25. 100 rooms. Restaurant, bar, tennis courts, playground. MC, V.*

$$ ▥ **Quintas Papagayo.** A bungalow and low-rise seaside establishment opened in 1947, Quintas Papagayo is a place where couples honeymoon and come back each year for their anniversaries. The accommodations are rustic, but you feel as if you've discovered a special hideaway where everyone remembers your name. Fireplaces, kitchens, patios, and decks are available. The small restaurant on the property is known for its great seafood. ⊠ *Mexico Hwy. 1 north of town, Box 150, 22800,* ☎ *617/4–41–55 or 617/4–45–75; in the U.S., 619/491–0682. 50 rooms. Restaurant, bar, pool, tennis courts, beach. MC, V.*

$$ ▥ **San Nicolás.** Hidden behind cement walls painted with Indian murals, this massive resort doesn't look like much from the street. The San Nicolás was built in the early 1970s, but much of it has been refurbished. The suites boast tiled hot tubs; living rooms with deep green carpeting, mauve furnishings, and beveled-glass doors; and mirrored ceilings in the bedrooms. The less extravagant rooms are comfortable and decorated with folk art. A waterfall cascades into the pool, and a good restaurant overlooks the gardens. An indoor swimming pool (the only one in an Ensenada hotel) opened in 1994, and there is a branch of Caliente Sports Book on the premises. Special rates are often available on weekdays and in the winter. ⊠ *Av. López Mateos (also called Calle 1) and Av. Guadalupe, Box 19, 22800,* ☎ *617/6–19–01,* ⅎⅅ *617/6–49–30; reservations in the U.S., Box 43706, San Diego, CA*

92143; 619/491–0682. 150 rooms and suites. 2 restaurants, bar, 2 pools, hot tub, dance club. AE, MC, V.

$$ ⊞ **Villa Fontana Days Inn Ensenada.** An architectural oddity in a town full of Spanish tiled roofs, this peak-gabled hotel has a New England look. The rooms are decorated in pastels—choose one at the back, away from street noise. There is enclosed parking—a major plus in downtown Ensenada. ⊠ *Av. López Mateos 1050, 22800,* ☎ FAX *617/8–34–34; reservations in the U.S., 800/329–7466. 60 rooms. Pool, hot tub, travel services. MC, V.*

$$ ⊞ **Villa Marina.** At 12 stories, the blue-and-white Villa Marina is the tallest hotel in town, though not necessarily the most luxurious. Rooms face either the waterfront or downtown and have small balconies, blue carpeting and walls, bathtubs with showers, and sinks outside the bathroom. The nightclub on top of the hotel has a spectacular view of the region, but noise from live bands on weekends makes rooms on the floor below less than desirable. A small shopping plaza fronts the hotel on the main shopping and dining street. ⊠ *Av. López Mateos at Balancarte, 22800,* ☎ *617/8–33–21,* FAX *617/8–33–51; reservations in the U.S., Box 727, Bonita, CA 91908. Restaurant, bar, pool, nightclub. MC, V.*

$ ⊞ **Joker Hotel.** A bizarre, brightly colored mishmash of styles makes it hard to miss this hotel, conveniently located for those traveling south of Ensenada. Spacious rooms have private balconies, satellite TV, and phones. ⊠ *Mexico Hwy. 1, Km 12.5, 22800,* ☎ FAX *617/6–72–01. 40 rooms. Pool, hot tub. MC, V.*

$$$ ✕⊞ **Punta Morro.** For seclusion and the sound of crashing surf, you
★ can't beat this all-suites hotel beside the university campus. The three-story tan building faces the north end of the bay. The lovely restaurant sits on rock pilings above the waves; you won't find a more romantic spot than at a window seat here. Enjoy eggs Benedict or French toast in the morning (breakfast is served only on weekends in winter, daily in summer), or dine early and toast the sunset with champagne while feasting on lobster, steak, or quail. All accommodations have terraces facing the ocean, kitchenettes, and seating areas; some also feature fireplaces. Stairs lead down to a rocky beach, but the surf is usually too rough for swimming. Rates are significantly lower on weekdays. ⊠ *Mexico Hwy. 1, 3 km (2 mi) north of town, Box 2891, 22800,* ☎ *617/8–35–07 or 800/526–6676,* FAX *617/4–44–90; reservations in the U.S., Box 43-4263, San Ysidro, CA 92143. 30 suites. Restaurant, bar, pool, hot tub, beach. MC, V.*

Nightlife and the Arts

Ensenada is a party town for college students, surfers, and other young tourists. **Hussong's Cantina** (⊠ Av. Ruíz 113, ☎ 617/8–32–10) has been an Ensenada landmark since 1892 and has changed little since then. A security guard stands by the front door to handle the often-rowdy crowd—a mix of locals and tourists of all ages over 18. The noise is usually deafening, pierced by mariachi and ranchera musicians and the whoops and hollers from the inebriated. **Papas and Beer** (⊠ Av. Ruíz at López Mateos, ☎ 617/8–42–31) is oriented toward the college set, who hang out the second-story windows shouting at their friends.

Outdoor Activities and Sports

FISHING

Boats leave the **Ensenada Sportfishing Pier** regularly. The best angling is from April through November, with bottom fishing good in the winter. Charter vessels and party boats are available from several outfitters along Avenida López Mateos, Boulevard Costero, and off the sportfishing pier. Trips on group boats cost about $60 per day. You can book sportfishing packages including transportation, accommodations, and fishing through **Baja California Tours** (in the U.S., ☎ 619/454–7166). Licenses are available at the tourist office or from charter companies. **Ensenada Clipper Fleet** (✉ Sportfishing pier, ☎ 617/8–21–85) has charter and group boats. **Gordo's Sportfishing** (✉ Sportfishing pier, ☎ 617/8–21–90), one of the oldest sportfishing companies in Ensenada, features charter boats, group boats, and a smokehouse. Gordo's also operates whale-watching trips from December through February.

GOLF

The **Baja Country Club** (✉ Hwy. 1 south of Ensenada at Maneadero, ☎ 617/3–03–03) has a secluded 18-hole course in a resort development.

Shopping

Most of the tourist shops are located along Avenida López Mateos beside the hotels and restaurants. There are several two-story shopping arcades, many with empty shops. Dozens of curio shops line the street, all selling similar selections of pottery, woven blankets and serapes, embroidered dresses, and onyx chess sets.

Artes de Quijote (✉ Av. López Mateos 503, ☎ 617/6–94–76) has an impressive array of carved-wood doors, huge terra-cotta pots, crafts from Oaxaca, and large brass fish and birds. **Artesanías Castillo** (✉ Av. López Mateos 656, ☎ 617/6–11–87) and **Los Castillo** (✉ Av. López Mateos 815, ☎ 617/6–11–87) both have extensive displays of silver jewelry from Taxco. **Girasoles** (✉ Av. López Mateos, no phone) features a great selection of dolls, pine-needle baskets, and pottery made by the Tarahumara Indians from the Copper Canyon. **La Mina de Salomón** (✉ Av. López Mateos 1000, ☎ 617/8–28–36) carries elaborate jewelry by artist Sergio Bustamante in a tiny gallery next to El Rey Sol restaurant. **Xuchitl** (✉ Av. López Mateos at Alvarado, ☎ 617/4–09–76) is one of the best shops in town for wooden masks, tin mirrors and frames, and hand-painted pottery.

Centro Artesenal de Ensenada, a shopping center on the waterfront, caters to cruise-ship visitors. The best shop by far is the **Galería de Pérez Meillón** (✉ Blvd. Costera 1094–39, ☎ 617/4–03–94), which carries museum-quality pottery and varied folk art by the indigenous peoples of northern Mexico.

San Felipe

198 km (124 mi) south of Mexicali, 244 km (151 mi) southeast of Ensenada.

San Felipe (population 18,000) is the quintessential dusty fishing village with one main street (two if you count the highway into town). The *malecón* (waterfront boardwalk) runs along a broad beach facing the Sea of Cortés and San Felipe Bay, with a swimming area in the middle and public changing rooms at the north end. Taco stands, bars, and restaurants line the sidewalk across the street from the beach. The only landmark in town is the shrine of the Cerro de la Virgen (Virgin of Guadalupe), at the north end of the malecón on a hill overlooking the sea.

Not until 1948, when the first paved road from the northern capital was completed, did San Felipe become a town of permanent residence. Now it is home to an impressive fishing and shrimping fleet. Bahía San Felipe has dramatic changes in its tides. The tides crest at 6 meters (20 feet), and since the beach is so shallow, the waterline can move in and out up to 1 kilometer (about ½ mile). The local fishermen are well aware of the peculiarities of this section of the Sea of Cortés. Many of them visit the shrine of Guadalupe before setting sail.

A popular getaway spot for years, San Felipe used to be a place where only hardy travelers in recreational vehicles and campers hid out for weeks on end. Now there are at least two dozen campgrounds and a dozen hotels in town and on the coastline both north and south of town, which fill up quickly during the winter and spring holidays. Dune buggies, motorcycles, and off-road vehicles abound. On holiday weekends San Felipe can be boisterous, but most of the time it's a quiet, relaxing place. The town also draws many sportfishermen, especially in the spring; launches, bait, and supplies are readily available.

Dining and Lodging

$$ ✕ **George's.** A favorite with resident Americans, George's has comfy padded red Naugahyde booths, powerful margaritas, and very good chilies rellenos, carne asada, and seafood. ✉ *Av. Mar de Cortés 336,* ☎ *657/7–10–57. MC, V.*

$ ✕ **Juan's Place.** A family-run operation two blocks east of the waterfront, Juan's offers consistently excellent home-style cooking at reasonable prices. The catch of the day and grilled meats come with boiled vegetables—ask for beans, rice, and the delicious homemade tortillas instead. ✉ *Calle de Ensenada, no phone. No credit cards.*

$ ✕ **Tony's Tacos.** The most popular of the many taco stands along the waterfront, Tony's is a simple spot with sidewalk picnic tables and a counter lined with condiments for the house specialty—cheap, delicious fish tacos. ✉ *Malecón at Av. Chetumal, no phone. No credit cards.*

$ ✕ **El Toro.** Open only for breakfast, El Toro is renowned among locals and San Felipe regulars for its chorizo, *machaca* (shredded beef), *huevos rancheros,* and American-style breakfasts. The parking lot fills with trailers hauling dune buggies and motorcycles as large groups gather to fuel up before a long day on the dunes. ✉ *Hwy. 5 north of town,* ☎ *657/7–10–32. No credit cards.*

$$$ 🏨 **San Felipe Marina Resort.** This full-scale resort will eventually include a 100-slip marina along with resort homes and hotels. At present, the low-slung terra-cotta building facing the sea has 59 units available as hotel rooms, time-share units, or private condos. Most rooms have kitchens with microwaves, coffeemakers, and refrigerators; woven rugs on white-tile floors and folk art decorations; and balconies or patios with sea views. The least expensive rooms lack kitchens and ocean views. The pool sits above the beach next to a palapa bar; a second indoor pool is a delight on cold winter days. The resort is a five-minute drive south of town and has an RV campground next door. ✉ *Km 4.5 Carretera San Felipe Aeropuerto, 21850,* ☎ *657/7–15–68 or 619/558–0295; in the U.S., 800/777–1700,* FAX *657/7–14–55. Restaurant, bar, 2 pools, tennis courts, exercise room, camping. MC, V.*

$$ 🏨 **Costa Azul.** The Costa Azul is the largest hotel right in town, at the south end of the malecón. Several three-story buildings frame a parking lot and pool area, and the restaurant and bar are in a two-story building on the beach. The rooms are far from spectacular and look like they may not hold up well, but the location can't be beat. Monday through Wednesday, room rates are almost 20% lower. ✉ *Av. Mar de Cortés at Calle Ensenada, 21850,* ☎ *657/1–15–49; reservations in the U.S., 233 Pauline Ave., 6252, Calexico, CA 92231. 140 rooms. Restaurant, bar, pool. MC, V.*

$$ 🏨 **Las Misiones.** A pretty oasis of blue pools and green palms by the beach, this resort is big with group tours. It's also a good choice for travelers who want to get away from it all—but you'll need a car or cab to get to town. A building just down the street from the hotel contains suites with kitchens. ⊠ *Av. Misión de Loreto 130, 21850,* ☎ *657/7–12–80 or 800/664–7466,* ℻ *657/7–12–83. 241 rooms, 20 suites. Restaurant, bar, 2 pools, tennis courts. MC, V.*

$ 🏨 **El Cortez.** Easily the most popular hotel in San Felipe, the El Cortez has several types of accommodations, including moderately priced bungalows and modern hotel rooms with white walls, pastel bedspreads and drapes, and white-tile floors; some have two bedrooms. The hotel's beachfront and second-story bars are both enduringly beloved, and the restaurant is the nicest water-view dining spot in town. The hotel is a five-minute walk from the malecón. ⊠ *Av. Mar de Cortez s/n, 21850,* ☎ *657/7–10–56,* ℻ *657/7–10–55; reservations in the U.S., Box 1227, Calexico, CA 92232. 102 rooms. Restaurant, bar, pool. MC, V.*

Outdoor Activities and Sports

FISHING

The Sea of Cortés offers plentiful sea bass, snapper, corbina, halibut, and other game fish. Clamming is good here as well. Several companies offer sportfishing trips; among the most established are **Alex Sportfishing** (☎ 657/7–10–52), **Pelicanos** (☎ 657/7–11–88), and **San Felipe Sportfishing** (☎ 657/7–10–55). **Del Mar Cortés Charters** (⊠ Box 9, San Felipe, 21850, ☎ 657/7–13–03) conducts fishing trips, full- and half-day trimaran tours of the Sea of Cortés, and boat charters. It can also arrange kayak and Hobie Cat rentals through the El Dorado private community north of town. **Enchanted Island Excursions** (⊠ 233 Paulin 8512, Calexico, CA 92231, ☎ 657/7–14–31) offers off-road, dune-buggy tours in addition to boat excursions.

BAJA NORTE A TO Z

Arriving and Departing

By Bus

Greyhound (☎ 619/239–1288 or 800/231–2222) serves Tijuana from San Diego several times daily; the Greyhound terminal in Tijuana is at Avenida Mexico at Madero (☎ 66/86–06–95).

Buses connect all the towns in Baja Norte and are easy to use. **Tres Estrellas de Oro, Elite,** and **Autotransportes de Baja California** cover the entire Baja route and connect in Mexicali with buses to Guadalajara and Mexico City. **Transportes del Pacífico** goes to Mexico City and other points on the mainland from Mexicali; **Transportes Norte de Sonora** frequents border towns in Baja and on mainland Mexico; and **Autotransportes de Baja California** goes to San Felipe, Tijuana, and Ensenada.

Bus stations in Baja Norte are **Ensenada** (⊠ Av. Riveroll between Calles 10 and 11, ☎ 617/8–67–70), **Mexicali** (⊠ Centro Cívico, Av. Independencia, ☎ 65/57–24–22), **Rosarito** (⊠ Av. Benito Juárez across from Rosarito Beach Hotel, no phone), **San Felipe** (⊠ Av. Mar Caribe at Av. Manzanillo, ☎ 657/7–15–16), **Tecate** (⊠ Av. Benito Juárez and Calle Abelardo Rodríguez, ☎ 665/4–12–21), and **Tijuana** (⊠ Calzada Lázaro Cárdenas and Blvd. Arroyo Alamar ☎ 66/26–17–01).

By Car

From San Diego, U.S. 5 and I–805 end at the border crossing into Tijuana at San Ysidro; Highway 905 leads from I–5 and I–805 to the Tijuana border crossing at Otay Mesa, near the Tijuana airport. U.S. 94 from San Diego connects with U.S. 188 to the border at Tecate, 57 kilometers (35 miles) east of San Diego. I–8 from San Diego connects with U.S. 111 at Calexico—203 kilometers (126 miles) east—and the border crossing to Mexicali. San Felipe lies on the coast, 200 kilometers (125 miles) south of Mexicali via Highway 5.

To head south into Baja from Tijuana, follow the signs for Ensenada Cuota, the toll road (also called Highway 1) that runs south along the coast. There are two clearly marked exits for Rosarito Beach, and one for Puerto Nuevo, Bajamar, and Ensenada. The road is excellent, though it has some hair-raising curves atop the cliffs and is best driven in daylight (the stretch from Rosarito Beach to Ensenada is one of the most scenic drives in Baja). Toll booths accept U.S. and Mexican currency; tolls are usually about $2.50. Rest rooms are available near the booths. The alternate free road—Highway 1D or Ensenada Libre—has been vastly improved, but it is difficult for the first-timer to navigate. Highway 1 continues south of Ensenada through Guerrero Negro at the border between Baja California and Baja Sur and on to the southernmost tip of Baja; it is no longer a toll road past Ensenada, however.

Mexico Highway 2 runs from Tijuana to Tecate and Mexicali. A toll road between Tijuana and Tecate opened in 1994, and another is still under construction between Tecate and Mexicali. The 134-kilometer (84-mile) journey from Tecate east to Mexicali on La Rumorosa, as the road is known, is as exciting as a roller-coaster ride, with the highway twisting and turning down steep mountain grades and over flat, barren desert.

Visitors to this area will not need tourist cards but should purchase Mexican car insurance at agencies near the border.

Many car-rental companies do not allow their cars to be driven into Mexico (☞ Car Rentals, *below*).

By Plane

Tijuana's Aeropuerto Alberado Rodriguez is located on the eastern edge of the city, near the Otay Mesa border crossing, and is served by **Mexicana** (☎ 66/83–28–50), **Aeromexico** (☎ 66/85–44–01), **Aero-California** (☎ 66/84–21–00), and **Taesa** (☎ 66/82–48–57). Mexicali's international airport is served by **Mexicana** (☎ 65/52–93–91).

By Trolley

The **San Diego Trolley** (☎ 619/233–3004) travels from the Santa Fe Depot, at Kettner Boulevard and Broadway, to within 100 feet of the border every 15 minutes from 5 AM to midnight. The 45-minute trip costs $1.75.

Getting Around

By Bus

In **Tijuana,** the downtown station for buses within the city is at Calle 1a and Avenida Madero (☎ 66/86–95–15). Most city buses at the border will take you downtown; look for the ones marked CENTRO CAMIONERA. To catch the bus back to the border from downtown, go to Calle Benito Juárez (also called Calle 2a) between Avenidas Revolución and Constitución. **Five Star Tours/Mexicoach** (☎ 619/232–5049) runs buses from the trolley depot on the U.S. side of the border to their depot on Avenida Revolución in Tijuana.

By Car

The best way to tour Baja Norte is by car, though the driving can be difficult and confusing at times. If you're just visiting Tijuana, Tecate, or Mexicali, it's easiest to park on the U.S. side of the border and walk across.

The combination of overpopulation, lack of infrastructure, and heavy winter rains makes many of **Tijuana**'s streets difficult to navigate by automobile. It's always best to stick to the main thoroughfares. There are parking lots along Avenida Revolución and at most major attractions. Most of **Rosarito Beach** proper can be explored on foot, which is a good idea on weekends, when Boulevard Juárez has bumper-to-bumper traffic. To reach **Puerto Nuevo** and other points south, continue on Boulevard Juárez (also called Old Ensenada Highway and Ensenada Libre) through town. Most of **Ensenada**'s attractions are situated within five blocks of the waterfront; it is easy to take a long walking tour of the city. A car is necessary to reach La Bufadora and most of the beaches.

By Train

Although there is no train service available through Baja, **El Tren del Pacífico** (✉ Estación de Ferrocarril, Box 3-182, Mexicali, Baja California, Mexico, ☎ 65/57–2101 or 65/57–23–86) runs from Mexicali to points south in the mainland interior. The station is located at the south end of Calle Ulises Irigoyen, a few blocks north of the intersection of Avenida López Mateos and Avenida Independencia.

Contacts and Resources

Car Rentals

Avis (☎ 800/331–1212) permits its cars to go from San Diego into Baja as far as 724 kilometers (450 miles) south of the border. Cars must be returned by the renter to San Diego, and Mexican auto insurance is mandatory. Cars leased from **Courtesy Rentals** (✉ 2975 Pacific Hwy., San Diego, 92101, ☎ 619/497–4800 or 800/252–9756) may be taken as far as Ensenada and San Felipe. **M&M Jeeps** (✉ 2200 El Cajon Blvd., San Diego, 92104, ☎ 619/297–1615 or 800/464–5724) rents two- and four-wheel-drive vehicles with packages covering tours of the entire Baja California peninsula.

ENSENADA

Ensenada Rent-a-Car (☎ 617/8–18–96) has an office on Avenida Alvarado between Lázaro Cárdenas and López Mateos.

TIJUANA

The larger U.S. rental agencies have offices at the Tijuana International Airport. Offices in town include **Avis** (✉ Av. Agua Caliente 3310, ☎ 66/86–40–04), **Budget** (✉ Paseo de los Héroes 77, ☎ 66/34–33–03), and **National** (✉ Av. Agua Caliente 5000, ☎ 66/86–21–03).

Emergencies

THROUGHOUT BAJA NORTE

Police (☎ 134), **Red Cross** (☎ 132), and **Fire** (☎ 136).

TIJUANA

U.S. Consulate (☎ 66/81–74–00). **The Attorney General for the Protection of Tourists Hot Line** (☎ 66/88–05–55) takes calls weekdays to help with tourist complaints and problems.

Guided Tours

Baja California Tours (✉ 6986 La Jolla Blvd., 204, La Jolla, CA 92037, ☎ 619/454–7166, ℻ 619/454–2703) offers comfortable, informative bus trips throughout Baja and can arrange special-interest tours, including shopping, culture, whale-watching and fishing trips and tours to the wineries and La Bufadora. **San Diego Mini-Tours** (✉ 1726 Wilson Ave., National City, CA 91950, ☎ 619/477–8687 or 800/235–5393, ℻ 619/477–0705) has frequent departures throughout the day from San Diego hotels to Avenida Revolución in Tijuana and back, and connections with a Mexican-operated trolley tour of Tijuana.

Language Classes

A great way to get to know Ensenada and simultaneously improve your Spanish is to attend weekend or weeklong classes at the **International Spanish Institute of Ensenada** (☎ 617/6−1−09; in CA, 619/472−0600).

Reservation Agencies

Several companies specialize in arranging hotel reservations in Baja Norte. Contact **Baja Information** (✉ 7860 Mission Center Ct., Suite 202, San Diego, CA 92108, ☎ 619/298−4105; in the U.S., Canada, Puerto Rico, 800/225−2786; in CA, NV, AZ, 800/522−1516; FAX 619/294−7366); **Baja California Tours** (✉ 6986 La Jolla Blvd., 204, La Jolla, CA 92037, ☎ 619/454−7166, FAX 619/454−2703); **Baja Lodging** (☎ 619/491−0682); **Mexico Resorts International** (✉ Box 120637, Chula Vista, CA 91912, ☎ 619/422−6900 or 800/336−5454, FAX 619/422−6910); and **Mexico Travel Net** (☎ 800/678−7244).

Travel Club

A monthly newsletter and discount Mexican auto insurance are available through **Discover Baja Travel Club** (✉ 3065 Clairmont Dr., San Diego, CA 92117, ☎ 619/275−4225 or 800/727−2252, FAX 619/275−1836).

Visitor Information

Regional tourist offices are usually open daily from 9 to 7, though some may close in early afternoon for lunch: **Ensenada** (✉ Blvd. Costera 1477, ☎ 617/2−30−22, FAX 617/2−30−81; Blvd. Costera at entrance to town, ☎ 617/8−24−11), **Mexicali** (✉ Convention and Tourism Bureau, Calz. López Mateos at Calle Compresora, ☎ 65/52−23−76; State Secretary of Tourism Office, Calle Calafia at Calz. Independencia, ☎ 65/56−10−72), **Rosarito Beach** (✉ Blvd. Juárez, on 2nd floor of Quinta Plaza shopping center, ☎ 661/2−03−96 or 661/2−30−78), **San Felipe** (✉ Av. Mar de Cortés, ☎ 657/7−11−55), **Tecate** (✉ 1305 Libertad Alley, ☎ 665/4−10−95), **Tijuana** Chamber of Commerce (✉ Av. Revolución and Calle 1, ☎ 66/88−16−85), and the **Tijuana Tourism & Convention Bureau** (✉ inside San Ysidro border crossing, ☎ 66/83−14−05; Av. Revolución between Calles 3 and 4, ☎ 66/83−14−05).

BAJA SUR

Baja Sur was nearly inaccessible by land until the 1,708-kilometer-long (1,059-mile-long) Transpeninsular Highway, also called Mexico Highway 1, was completed in 1973. Until then, commerce was conducted via boats from mainland Mexico, across the Sea of Cortés. After the paved, four-lane road was completed, travelers gradually found their way south, drawn by the wild terrain and the pristine beaches along the Pacific Ocean and Sea of Cortés coastlines. In 1974, Baja California Sur became Mexico's 30th state, and the population and tourism began to increase. Still, Baja Sur remains a mysterious and largely undeveloped land. Highway 1, which travels through some of the most desolate desert and mountains imaginable, could hardly be called a freeway. Most travelers still make their way here via plane.

Whale-watching draws winter visitors to Guerrero Negro and Scammon's Lagoon. History buffs enjoy Loreto, where Padre Eusebio Kino established the first mission in the Californias. La Paz, today a busy governmental center and sportsfishing city, was the Spaniard's first settlement in Baja. At the southernmost tip of the peninsula, where the Pacific Ocean and the Sea of Cortés merge, fishing aficionados and sun

Baja California (South)

Isla Angel de
la Guarda

Isla del
Tiburón

HERMOSILLO

Mazatán

Pta.
San Gabriel

San Rafael

Tecoripa

Cieneguita

El Arco

GUAYMAS

15

San Ignacio

Santa Rosalía

Mulege

Isla
Lobos

Ciudad
Obregón

Laguna
de San
Ignacio

Pta.
Concepción

Navajoa

15

Bahía
Concepción

Huatabampo

BAJA

Rosarito

Golfo de California

Loreto

La Poza

Isla
Carmen

Las Grullas Márgen
Derecha

Misión
San Javier

CALIFORNIA

Puerto
Escondido

TO LOS
MOCHIS

Insurgentes

SIERRA GIGANTA

Constitución

Isla
San José

Bahía
Magdalena

SUR

Santa
Rita

Isla
Partida

Isla Santa
Margarita

1

Bahía
de la
Paz

La Paz

Isla
Cerralvo

TO
MAZATLÁN

N

El Triunfo

Ensenada de
los Muertos

PACIFIC OCEAN

Todos
Santos

Los Barriles

SIERRA DE LA LAGUNA

Santiago

9

1

Cabo
Pulmo

KEY

San José
del Cabo

—— Rail Lines

Cabo
San Lucas

Ferry Lines

0   100 miles

0   150 km

worshippers flock to Los Cabos, one of Mexico's most popular coastal resorts.

Guerrero Negro and Scammon's Lagoon

720 km (450 mi) south of Tijuana, 771 km (479 mi) northwest of La Paz.

Humans aren't the only travelers who migrate below the border in the winter months. Every January through March, thousands of great gray whales swim 8,000 kilometers (6,000 miles) south from the Bering Strait, off Alaska, to the tip of the Baja Peninsula. For those few months, travelers come from all over the world to Guerrero Negro and a few bays and lagoons farther south. Up to 6,000 stop close to the shore at several spots along the Baja coast, including Scammon's Lagoon—at the 28th parallel, just over the state line between Baja California and Baja Sur—to give birth to their calves. Far from diminutive, the newborns weigh about one-half ton and drink nearly 50 gallons of milk each day.

If it weren't for the whales, and the Transpeninsular Highway, which runs near town, few travelers would venture to **Guerrero Negro,** a town of 10,000; the name Guerrero Negro, which means Black Warrior, was derived from a whaling ship that ran aground in nearby Scammon's Lagoon in 1858. Near the Vizcaíno desert, on the Pacific Ocean, the area is best known for its salt mines, which provide work for much of the town's population and produce one-third of the world's salt supply. Saltwater collects in more than 780 square kilometers (300 square miles) of sea-level ponds and evaporates quickly in the desert heat, leaving huge blocks of pure white salt.

Scammon's Lagoon is about 27 kilometers (17 miles) south, down a passable but rough sand road that crosses the salt flats. The lagoon got its name from U.S. explorer Charles Melville Scammon of Maine, who discovered it off the coast of Baja in the mid-1800s. The whales and calves that visited these waters were a much easier and more plentiful prey for the whalers than the great leviathans swimming in the open sea. On his first expedition to the lagoon, Scammon and his crew collected more than 700 barrels of valuable whale oil, and the whale rush was on. Within 10 years, nearly all the whales in the lagoon had been killed, and it took almost a century for the whale population to increase to what it had been before Scammon arrived. It wasn't until the 1940s that the U.S. and Mexican governments took measures to protect the whales and banned the whalers from the lagoon.

Today whale-watching boats must have permission from the Mexican government to enter Scammon's Lagoon, now a national park called Parque Natural de Ballenas Gris (Gray Whale Natural Park). Whale-watching from the shores of the lagoon can be disappointing without binoculars. But it is still an impressive sight to see the huge mammals spouting water high into the air, their 12-foot-wide tails striking the water.

Many of the whale-watching tour operators offer expeditions to Scammon's Lagoon, either by boat or motorcoach from California. The other major whale-watching spots are farther south at **Laguna San Ignacio** and **Bahía Magdalena,** both on the Pacific coast. If traveling on your own, you can reach Laguna San Ignacio from the town of San Ignacio (☞ *below*); Magdalena Bay (called "Mag Bay" by regulars) is about a four-hour drive across the peninsula from La Paz. Fishermen will take you out in their boats to get closer to the whales at both places. But for a better view, and an easier stay in this rugged country, travel with an outfitter who will arrange your travel, your accommodations, and your time on the water. The whales will come close to your boat, rising majestically from the water, and sometimes swim close enough to be petted on their backs.

Dining and Lodging

There are several hotels in Guerrero Negro, none of which is worth visiting as a destination in itself. Double-occupancy rooms cost from about $25 to $70 per day; rates tend to increase during the peak whale-watching season from January through March. None of the hotels has heat, and winter nights can be downright frigid. Credit cards are not normally accepted, but the hotels do take traveler's checks. The dining rooms in the hotels recommended below are far from haute cuisine, but they're about as good as you're going to get in this area.

$$ ✕▦ **La Pinta.** A few kilometers outside of town and looking like an oasis of palms in the desert, La Pinta is the largest hotel in town. The clean, functional rooms are dependable, the setting more attractive than that of other local lodgings, and the American-Mexican restaurant decent, but the rates are high for the area. Package deals are sometimes available for travelers using the La Pinta hotels throughout the peninsula. Whale-watching excursions can be arranged here. ✉ *La Pinta Hwy. 1 at 28th parallel, Domicilio Conocido, Guerrero Negro 23940,* ☎ *115/7–13–05,* ℻ *115/7–1306; reservations in the U.S., 800/336–5454. 26 rooms. Coffee shop. No credit cards.*

$ ✕▦ **Malarrimo.** This popular trailer park and Mexican and seafood restaurant has an eight-room motel, with private baths and TV. It fills up quickly and is one of the best deals in town. The whale-watching excursions from the hotel are also immensely popular and are run by knowledgeable local guides. ✉ *Blvd. Zapata, Guerrero Negro 23940,* ☎ *115/7–02–50. 10 rooms. Restaurant. No credit cards.*

San Ignacio

227 km (142 mi) southeast of Guerrero Negro.

This small town is set in an oasis by a lovely river. The Spanish mission on the town square is one of the best preserved on the peninsula. Some whale-watching groups use the hotels in town as a base for whale-watching trips to Laguna San Ignacio and Magdalena Bay.

Lodging

$$ ▦ **La Pinta.** If the room rates weren't so high, this small hotel would be a wonderful Baja hideaway. White arches frame the courtyard and pool, and the rooms are decorated with folk art and wood furnishings. Both the river and town are within walking distance. The hotel staff can set up whale-watching trips with local guides. ✉ *2 km (1 mi) west of Hwy. 1 on unnamed road into town, Apdo. 37, San Ignacio, 23943, no phone; reservations in the U.S., 800/336–5454. 28 rooms. Restaurant, bar, pool. No credit cards.*

Santa Rosalia

77 km (48 mi) southeast of San Ignacio.

You'll find a fascinating mix of French, Mexican, and American Old West–style architecture in the dusty mining town of Santa Rosalia. It's known for its **Iglesia Santa Barbara,** a prefabricated iron church designed by Alexandre-Gustave Eiffel, creator of the Eiffel Tower. Be sure to stop by **El Boleo** (✉ Av. Obregón at Calle 4), the best-known bakery in Baja, where fresh breads bring a lineup of eager customers weekday mornings at 10 AM.

Mulege

64 km (40 mi) south of Santa Rosalia.

Once a mission settlement and now a charming tropical town set beside a river flowing into the Sea of Cortés, Mulege has become a popular destination for travelers who are interested in exploring the nearby mountains and for kayakers drawn to Bahía Concepción, the largest protected bay in Baja. The village of some 5,000 residents swells in the winter months, when Americans and Canadians escaping the winter cold arrive in their motor homes. There are several campgrounds outside town, and a few good hotels and restaurants both in town and along the coast.

Dining and Lodging

$ 🏨 **Hacienda.** French-Canadian Jean-Pierre bought this historic Mulege hacienda in 1992 and is gradually restoring its rooms, including a large ballroom with fireplace. Guests read and lounge in rocking chairs by the pool or at stools along the bar, where snacks and meals are served throughout the day. Special festivities include paella nights, pig roasts, and trips to the nearby cave paintings in the mountains. Even when other hotels in the area are nearly empty, the Hacienda is filled with European travelers attracted by the ambience and incredibly low (by Baja standards) room rates. ⊠ *Calle Madero, 23900,* ☎ FAX *115/3–00–21. 18 rooms. Restaurant, bar, pool, travel services. No credit cards.*

$$ ✕🏨 **Serenidad.** Looking like a mountain lodge set atop an oceanfront cliff, this older hotel attracts a loyal following (it even has a private airstrip). Several brick, stone, and stucco buildings surround overgrown courtyards and the pool. The rooms have fireplaces (nights can be chilly) and vary in comfort depending on their age. The dining room serves good Mexican and American meals, and the Saturday barbecue is a Baja institution. ⊠ *Hwy. 1, 4 km (2½ mi) south of Mulege, 23900,* ☎ *115/3–01–11,* FAX *115/3–03–11. 48 rooms. Restaurant, pool. MC, V.*

Outdoor Activities and Sports

KAYAKING

Baja Tropicales (⊠ Box 60, Mulege, BCS 23900, ☎ FAX 115/3–01–90) offers rentals of kayaks, wet suits, and other gear and several types of kayaking tours, including day trips and overnighters in the area of Mulege; whale-watching trips on the Pacific coast are also available.

Loreto

134 km (84 mi) south of Mulege.

On the Sea of Cortés, Loreto's setting is truly spectacular. The gold and green hills of the Sierra Gigante seem to tumble into the cobalt sea. Rain is rare. According to the local promoters, the skies are clear 360 days of the year. There are few bugs to plague vacationers. The dry, desert climate is not one in which insects thrive.

Loreto was the site of the first California mission, founded in 1697 by Jesuit Father Juan María Salvatierra. In 1769 Father Junípero Serra, a Franciscan monk from Mallorca, Spain, set out from Loreto to establish a chain of missions from San Diego to San Francisco, in the land then known as Alta California. Four Indian tribes—the Kikiwa, Cochimi, Cucapa, and Kumyaii—inhabited the barren lands of Baja when Father Salvatierra arrived; it didn't take long for war and European diseases to nearly obliterate them.

Mexico won its independence from Spain in 1821, and the missions were gradually abandoned. The priests, who often were from Spain, were ordered to return home. Loreto had been the administrative as well as the religious center of the Californias, but with the withering of the mission and the 1829 hurricane that virtually destroyed the settlement, the capital of the Californias was moved to La Paz. A severe earthquake struck the Loreto area in 1877, further demolishing the town.

For a century the village languished. The U.S. fishermen who rediscovered Loreto were a hearty breed who flew down in their own aircraft and went after marlin and sailfish in open launches. Loreto's several small hotels were built to serve this rough-and-ready set; most of the properties were built before 1960, when no highway came down this far and there was no airport worthy of the name.

In 1976, when the coffers were filled with oil revenue, the government tapped the Loreto area for development. Streets were paved in the dusty little village, and telephone service, electricity, potable water, and sewage systems were installed in both the town and the surrounding area; even an international airport was built. A luxury hotel and championship tennis center were opened in Nopolo, about 8 kilometers (5 miles) south of town. Then the money dried up, investors could no longer be found, and everything came to a halt. A second surge of development occurred in the early 1990s, when the government invested in an 18-hole golf course at the edge of the sea in Nopolo. But the course has not drawn the anticipated crowds and is empty much of the time.

Today Loreto, with a population of 15,000, is a good place to escape the crowds, relax, and go fishing. The fears of sports enthusiasts that the town would be spoiled have thus far been largely unfounded, though the residential trailer parks are filling up and private homes are clustered in secluded enclaves. Loreto is much the way it was decades ago, except that now it is more accessible.

One could allocate 15 minutes for a tour of downtown Loreto and still have time left over. The renovated **malecón**, built in 1991, has turned the waterfront into a pleasant place for a stroll: A marina houses the panga fleet and private yachts; the adjoining beach is a popular gathering spot for locals, especially on Sunday afternoons; and the beach playground has a great assortment of play equipment for children. The small **zócalo** and town center is one block west of the waterfront, on Calle Salvatierra.

Loreto's only historic sight is La Misión de Nuestra Señora de Loreto, the first of the California missions. The carved stone walls, wood-beam ceilings, gilded altar, and primitive-style portraits of the priests who have served there are worth seeing. The Museum of Anthropology and History, also called El Museo de los Misiones (☎ 113/5–05–41), contains religious relics, tooled leather saddles used in the 19th century, and displays of Baja's history; it's next door to the mission and is open Wednesday–Friday 9–4, weekends 9–2.

Nopoló, an area being developed for luxury resorts, is about 8 kilometers (5 miles) south of town. The nine-court tennis complex and 18-hole golf course are ready for play, though there are few travelers using them. Plans for more hotels, condos, and private homes in the area are in the works but, for now, sidewalks and concrete foundation slabs run through fields of weeds and shrubs.

In **Puerto Escondido,** 16 kilometers (10 miles) down the road from Nopoló, the marina contains more than 100 boat slips. A recreational vehicle park, Tripui, has a good restaurant, a few motel rooms, a snack shop, a bar, stores, showers, a laundry, a pool, and tennis courts. A boat ramp has been completed at the marina; in order to pay the fee required to launch here, go to the port captain's offices (☎ 113/5–06–56, FAX 113/5–04–65), just south of the ramp; the offices are open weekdays 8–3. **Isla Danzante,** 5 kilometers (3 miles) southeast of Puerto Escondido, has good diving and reefs.

Picnic trips to nearby **Coronado Island,** inhabited only by sea lions, may be arranged in Loreto at Nopoló or in Puerto Escondido. The snorkeling and scuba-diving on the island are excellent.

Dining and Lodging

$$ ✕ **The Embarcadero.** This restaurant's open-air deck looking out at the marina and beach is the perfect spot for catching up on the local fishing news. Alfredo's sportfishing is next door, and anglers with their own boats in the marina often stop by for lunch. Fish tacos and grilled-fish dinners are the best choices. ✉ *Blvd. Mateos at Juárez,* ☎ *113/5–01–65. No credit cards.*

$$ ✕ **El Super Burro.** This large, palapa-covered restaurant a half-block from the waterfront is as popular with locals as tourists. Meats are grilled at the front of the dining room, where cooks juggle take-out and dine-in orders. The Mexican combination plate isn't outstanding, but it is plentiful; a better choice is the fresh fish. Those on a budget can fill up on tacos or baked potatoes stuffed with cheese and meat. ✉ *Paseo Hidalgo between Madero and malecón, no phone. No credit cards.*

$ ✕ **Café Olé.** The best taquería in town also offers good burgers, ice-cream cones, chocolate shakes, and french fries. ✉ *Calle Francisco Madero,* ☎ *113/5–04–96. No credit cards.*

$$ 🏨 **La Pinta.** Part of a chain of Baja California hotels, the La Pinta is a collection of plain brick buildings housing spacious, air-conditioned rooms with satellite TVs. ✉ *Blvd. Misión de Loreto, 23880,* ☎ *113/5–00–25; reservations in the U.S., 800/336–5454;* FAX *113/5–00–26. 48 rooms. Restaurant, bar, pool, tennis courts, fishing. MC, V.*

$$ 🏨 **Misión.** This is an old favorite, with one of the most popular swimming pools and second-story bars in town. The rooms and public spaces are in desperate need of renovation, but that doesn't deter the diehard anglers who enjoy being across the street from the marina. ✉ *Blvd. Mateos at Calle de la Playa, Box 49, 23880,* ☎ *113/5–00–48; reservations in the U.S., 800/777–2664;* FAX *113/5–06–48. 35 rooms. Restaurant, bar, pool, fishing. MC, V.*

$$ 🏨 **Oasis.** One of the original fishing camps, Oasis remains a favorite with those who want to spend as much time as possible on the water. Many of the rooms, set amid a tropical oasis of palms, have a view of the water. The hotel has its own fleet of skiffs. ✉ *Calle de la Playa at Zaragoza, Box 17, 23880,* ☎ *113/5–01–12; reservations in the U.S., 800/777–2664;* FAX *113/5–07–95. Pool, tennis courts, boating, fishing. MC, V.*

$$ 🏨 **Plaza Loreto.** Since its opening in 1992, the Plaza Loreto has gar-
★ nered a loyal following of Loreto regulars who appreciate the comfortable rooms and prime downtown location near the old mission. The two-story hotel has an upstairs bar overlooking the street. The rooms are by far the best in town, with TVs, coffeemakers, and huge showers. Construction on the swimming pool has stopped, and although breakfast is served on the terrace, there is no full restaurant yet. ✉ *Paseo Hidalgo, 23880,* ☎ FAX *113/5–08–55; reservations in the U.S., 800/777–2664. 20 rooms. Bar. MC, V.*

$$ 🏨 **Villas de Loreto.** New owners took over this long-defunct property in 1994 and created one of Loreto's nicest hideaways just south of town. There are eight large rooms with separate kitchenettes and front

porches, along with a large swimming pool and palapa bar. An RV and tent campground is located behind the hotel buildings. Bikes are available for guests' use free of charge, and horseback riding and fishing tours can be arranged. Breakfast is included in the room rate. To get here, turn right off Salvatierra onto Madero and drive across the dry riverbed to signs for the hotel. ✉ *Antonio Mijares at beach, 23880,* ☎ FAX *113/5–05–86. 8 rooms. Bar, pool, laundry. No credit cards.*

Outdoor Activities and Sports

FISHING

Fishing put Loreto on the map, especially for the American sports enthusiast. Cabrillo and snapper are caught year-round; yellowtail in the spring; and dorado, marlin, and sailfish in the summer. Visitors who plan to fish should bring tackle with them because top-notch gear can be difficult to find, though some sportfishing fleets do update their equipment regularly. All Loreto-area hotels can arrange fishing, and many own skiffs; the local fishermen congregate with their small boats on the beach at the north and south ends of town. **Alfredo's Sportfishing** (✉ Blvd. Mateos at Juárez, across from marina, ☎ 113/5–01–65, FAX 113/5–05–90) has good guides for anglers. **Arturo's Fishing Fleet** (✉ Calle Juárez and Callejón 2, 1 block from marina, ☎ 113/5–04–09 or 800/777–2664) has several types of boats and fishing packages.

GOLF

The first 9 holes of the 18-hole Loreto Campo de Golf (☎ 113/5–07–88), located along Nopoló Bay at the south side of Fonatur's resort development, opened in 1991. Several hotels in Loreto offer golf packages and reduced or free greens fees.

TENNIS

The **Loreto Tennis Center** (☎ 113/5–07–00), 8 kilometers (5 miles) south of Loreto, is open to the public.

Shopping

There are few opportunities for shopping in Loreto. Curios and T-shirts are available at shops at the hotels and downtown. **El Alacran,** which is in the small complex behind the church on Calle Salvatierra, has a remarkable selection of folk art, jewelry, and sportswear. You can also find some nice silver shops in this complex. Groceries and ice are available on Calle Salvatierra at **El Pescador,** the town's only supermarket.

La Paz

354 km (220 mi) south of Loreto.

La Paz is one of those cities that make you wish you'd been here 20 years ago. In the slowest of times, in late summer when the heat is oppressive, you can easily see how it must have been when it was a quiet place, living up to its name: "Peace." Today the city has a population of 170,000, with a large contingent of retirees from the United States and Canada. Travelers use La Paz as both a destination in itself and a stopping-off point en route to Los Cabos. Sportfishing is a major lure, though some enjoy La Paz as the most Mexican city on the peninsula, with the feel of a mainland community that has adapted to tourism while retaining its character.

Hernán Cortés and his soldiers were drawn to La Paz in 1535 by stories of the magnificent pearls and beautiful women. In 1720 the Jesuits arrived to civilize and convert the Indians. Instead, the missionaries inadvertently decimated the local populace by introducing smallpox. Within 30 years, there was no one left to convert.

While the rest of Mexico was being torn apart by revolution, a permanent settlement was established in 1811. La Paz became a refuge for those who wished to escape the mainland wars. In 1829, after then-capital Loreto was leveled by a hurricane, La Paz became the capital of the Californias. Troops from the United States occasionally invaded, but sent word to Washington that the Baja Peninsula was not worth fighting for. In 1853 a different group of invaders arrived from the United States. Led by William Walker, these southerners were intent on making La Paz a slave state but were quickly banished by the Mexicans. Peace reigned for the next century. In 1940, disease wiped out the oyster beds, and with the pearls gone, La Paz no longer attracted prospectors and was left tranquil.

La Paz officially became the capital of Baja California Sur in 1974 and is now the state's largest settlement. It is the site of the power plant for all the state, a fleet of cruise ships, the ferry to Mazatlán, the state bureaucracy, the governor's home, and the state jail. It is the stop-off for fishermen and divers headed for Cerralvo, La Partida, and Espíritu Santo islands, where parrot fish, manta rays, neons, and angels blur the clear waters by the shore, and marlin, dorado, and yellowtail leap out of the deep, dark sea.

Numbers in the margin correspond to points of interest on the La Paz map.

❶ The **malecón** (waterfront walkway) is La Paz's sea wall, tourist zone, and main drag rolled into one. As you enter town from the southwest, Paseo Alvaro Obregón turns into the malecón at a cluster of high-rise condos. Construction continues at the west entrance to town, where
❷ a marina and hotel have opened at the 500-acre **Fidepaz Marina.**

❸ A two-story white gazebo is the focus of the **Malecón Plaza,** a small cement square where musicians sometimes appear on weekend nights. The tourist information center sits beside the gazebo. Across the street, Calle 16 de Septiembre leads inland to the city center. Around the plaza and all along the malecón, a steady stream of teens cruise through town, red and yellow car lights twinkling around their license plates and the latest U.S. hits blaring on their radios.

La Paz's downtown district is the busiest in all Baja Sur, with shops crammed together on narrow crowded streets. The central plaza, or
❹ zócalo, also goes by the names **Plaza Constitución** and Jardín Velazco.
❺ **La Catedral de Nuestra Señora de La Paz** (Our Lady of La Paz Cathedral) is downtown's big attraction. It was built in 1860 near the site of La Paz's first mission, which was established in 1860 by Jesuit Jaime Bravo. You'll see it just across from the zócalo.

❻ The **Biblioteca de las Californias,** a library specializing in the history of Baja California, has reproductions of the local prehistoric cave paintings, oil paintings of the missions, and the best collection of historical documents on the peninsula. Films and lectures are sometimes presented in the evening. Check the bulletin board outside the library or ask the librarian for information. ✉ *Madero at Cinco de Mayo,* ☎ *112/2–01–62.* ⊙ *Weekdays 8–6.*

One gets an excellent sense of La Paz's culture and heritage at the **Museum of Anthropology,** constructed in 1983. Exhibits include re-creations of Comondo and Las Palmas Indian villages, photos of cave paintings found in Baja, and copies of Cortés's writings on first sighting La Paz. Many of the exhibit descriptions are written only in Spanish, but the museum's staff will help translate for you. ✉ *Altamirano*

La Paz

and Cinco de Mayo, ☎ *112/2–01–62.* ✉ *Free.* ⏲ *Weekdays 8–6, Sat. 9–2.*

South of town, Paseo Alvaro Obregón, or the malecón, becomes what is commonly known as the Pichilingue Road, which curves north along the bay about 16 kilometers (10 miles) to the terminals where the ferries from Mazatlán and Topolobampo arrive and many of the sportfishing boats depart. Just outside town the road divides, with outgoing traffic climbing up a steep cliff overlooking deserted beaches.

⑧ The **Government House,** surrounded by guards and gates, is a few kilometers south of the spot where the road divides. Home of the governor of Baja California Sur, the house has an impressive view of the curving bay and city lights. At the **Ferry Terminal,** farther south from Government Hosue, warehouses serve as waiting rooms. Roadside stands ⑨ serving oysters and grilled fish line the highway across the street.

⑩ Since the time of pirate ships and Spanish invaders, **Pichiline** was known for its preponderance of oysters bearing black pearls. 1940 an unknown disease killed off all of them, leaving the beach erted. Now Pichilingue is a pleasant place for sunbathing and watcg the sportfishing boats bring in their haul. Palapa-covered restarts on the beach serve cold beer and oysters *diablo* (raw oysters std in a fiery-hot sauce), as well as some of the freshest and least expengrilled fish in town.

Beaches

Paved roads to La Paz's most beautiful beaches were completl 1992. Off a dirt road just past Pichilingue, **Playa Tecolote** is a smystal-blue cove with a clean beach and no facilities. The larger **Coyote** has a restaurant, water-sports equipment rentals, and as for shade; the facilities are only open when tourism is high. Overnight camping is currently allowed at both beaches.

Dining and Lodging

$$$ ✕ **El Bismark.** You've got to wander a bit out of your way to reach El
★ Bismark, where locals go for good, home-style Mexican food. Specialties include the *cochinita píbil* (marinated pork chunks); carne asada served with beans, guacamole, and homemade tortillas; and enormous grilled lobsters. The seafood cocktails are huge, too, and the fish fillets are always fresh from the sea. You'll see families settle down for hours at long wood tables, while waitresses divide their attention between the patrons and the soap operas on the TV above the bar. ⊠ *Santos Degollado and Av. Altamirano,* ☎ *112/2–48–54. MC, V.*

$$$ ✕ **Restaurant Bermejo.** The most upscale, elegant restaurant in town has a faithful following of locals and tourists in search of comfortable booths, candles, and courteous waiters. The menu is primarily Italian these days. There are a few moderately priced dishes here, and the steaks are worth splurging on. Reservations are recommended. ⊠ *Paseo Obregón 498,* ☎ *112/2–27–44. AE, MC, V.*

$$ ✕ **La Paz-Lapa.** The noise level here is deafening, but this is a fun place, with a wide-screen TV in the bar and waiters so jolly you expect them to break into song. The food—your basic beef, chicken, fish, and Mexican selections—is tasty and plentiful. Also referred to as Carlos 'n' Charlie's, La Paz-Lapa is a member of the popular Carlos Anderson restaurant chain. Live bands appear on weekend evenings on the back patio. ⊠ *Paseo Obregón at Calle 16 de Septiembre,* ☎ *112/5–92–90. MC, V.*

$$ ✕ **La Terraza.** The open-air restaurant at the Hotel Perla is the best people-watching spot in town, with sidewalk-level tables facing the malecón. The menu includes everything from French toast to pasta—with decent enchiladas, *huevos rancheros,* and fresh fish. La Terraza is a good hangout for morning coffee and afternoon and evening snacks. ⊠ *Paseo Obregón,* ☎ *112/2–07–77. MC, V.*

$$ ✕ **Trattoria La Pazta.** Trendy and sleek, La Pazta is furnished with black lacquered tables and chairs set against white walls and tiled floors. Local and imported ingredients are blended with homemade pastas; try the pasta with squid in a wine-and-cream sauce, or curried chicken. Those craving an espresso or cappuccino will be more than pleased with the café's selection of coffees. ⊠ *Allende 36-B,* ☎ *112/5–11–95. No credit cards. Closed Tues.*

$ ✕ **El Quinto Sol Restaurante Vegetariano.** El Quinto's bright green exterior walls are painted with Indian snake symbols and smiling suns. The back room is a natural-foods store stocked with grains, soaps, lotions, oils, and books. The restaurant serves yogurt with bananas and wheat germ, ceviche tostadas, and a nonmeat version of *machaca* (a marinated shredded-beef dish). ⊠ *Belisario Domínguez and Independencia,* ☎ *112/2–16–92. No credit cards.*

$ ✕ **Taco Hermanos Gonzalez.** La Paz has many great taco stands, but the Gonzalez brothers still corner the market with their hunks of fresh fish wrapped in corn tortillas. Bowls of condiments line the small stand, and customers jam the sidewalk while munching on the best fast food in town. ⊠ *Mutualismo and Esquerro, no phone. No credit cards.*

$$$ ▥ **Club El Moro.** A vacation-ownership resort with suite rentals on a nightly and weekly basis, El Moro boasts a garden of lush palms and a densely landscaped pool area with one of the few hot tubs in town. You can recognize the building by its stark-white turrets and domes; rooms are Mediterranean in style and decor, with arched windows, Mexican tiles, and private balconies. Rooms vary in size; some have kitchens and can sleep up to five persons. The restaurant is excellent and elegant. ⊠ *Km 2 Carretera a Pichilingue, Box 357, 23010,* ☎ FAX *112/2–40–84 or 112/2–70–10. 17 suites. Restaurant, bar, pool, travel services. AE, MC, V.*

$$$ ⊡ **Mar y Sol.** Those planning to stay a week or more will be delighted
★   with these lovely apartments. Each is furnished with folk art, colorful serapes, leather equipale chairs, and full kitchens. Fountains and a square swimming pool are set amid palms and flowering plants. It's a two-block walk to the beach, and the owners can arrange fishing, diving and whale-watching tours. ⊠ *Calle Insurgentes at Margaritas, Box 438, 23000,* ☎ *112/5–24–67,* FAX *112/2–01–80. 10 apartments. Pool. No credit cards.*

$$ ⊡ **La Concha Beach Resort.** Come to La Concha for its clean, curving beach; modern, well-maintained rooms; and very good restaurant. Some of the rooms are currently being remodeled and turned into suites. All rooms have TVs, phones, and small refrigerators; guests who want to socialize gather around the large-screen TV in an upstairs lounging area, which also has tables for playing cards and games and a small selection of English-language novels. The on-site water-sports center specializes in scuba trips and has kayaks and other water toys for rent; its whale-watching trips are extremely popular in winter. The hotel operates a free shuttle to town twice daily. Condo units adjacent to the hotel are available on a nightly, weekly, and monthly basis. ⊠ *Km 5 Carretera a Pichilingue, 23010,* ☎ *112/1–63–44; reservations in the U.S., 800/999–2252;* FAX *112/1–62–18. 109 rooms. Restaurant, palapa and lobby bars, pool, tennis courts, gift shop. AE, MC, V.*

$$ ⊡ **La Perla.** Recent renovations have brought La Perla back to its long-standing reputation as one of the best hotels in La Paz. The rooms have pristine white walls, light wood furnishings, and cable TV; some offer king-size beds. The pool is located on a second-story sun deck away from the traffic on the main street. Noise is a factor in the oceanfront rooms; the trade-off is a wonderful view of the malecón and the sunset. ⊠ *Paseo Obregón 1570, 23010,* ☎ *112/2–07–77,* FAX *112/5–5363. 101 rooms. Restaurant, bar, pool, gift shop. MC, V.*

$$ ⊡ **La Posada de Englebert.** Long-time La Paz visitors have their favorites among this small hotel's casitas, which feature wood shutters, haphazardly tiled bathrooms, fireplaces, worn couches in the living rooms, and rocking chairs on the porches. The standard rooms are less spacious. At night, miniature lights twinkle in the palm trees and guitarists stroll among the blue umbrellas on the patio while guests dine on grilled fish and lobster. Saturday-night Mexican fiestas are held when tourism is high. The hotel is located outside town, but taxis are readily available. ⊠ *Av. Reforma and Playa Sur, Box 152, 23000,* ☎ *112/2–40–11,* FAX *112/2–06–63. 26 suites, 4 casitas. Restaurant, palapa bar, pool, beach. MC, V.*

$$ ⊡ **Los Arcos.** Many say Los Arcos is the nicest hotel in La Paz—it's certainly the only true colonial Mexican lodging in town—but that depends on the location of your room. Resist the waterfront view and request a room in the central courtyard, where the rush of water in the fountain drowns out the music from the street and the noise from the pool area. All rooms have balconies and TVs. The self-service coffee shop opens early so those headed out on fishing boats can have breakfast and pick up a box lunch; it's also a cool escape from the midday heat at lunch time. The Cabañas de Los Arcos next door offers several small brick cottages surrounded by gardens and a small hotel with a swimming pool. ⊠ *Paseo Obregón 498 between Rosales and Allende, 23000,* ☎ *112/2–27–44,* FAX *112/5–43–13; reservations in the U.S., 18552 MacArthur Blvd., Suite 205, Irvine, CA 92715, 714/476–5555 or 800/347–2252,* FAX *714/476–5560. 180 rooms at main hotel, 30* *bungalows and rooms at Cabañas. Restaurant, coffee shop, bar, 2 pools, sauna, fishing. MC, V.*

$ ⊞ **Hotel Lorimar.** A favorite with annual visitors to La Paz, the Lorimar is located up a slight hill behind the Los Arcos Hotel, within easy walking distance of the malecón. The rooms are well maintained, with double beds and tiled bathrooms. Guests congregate on the back patio or at the second-story restaurant, which has a view of the waterfront. ⊠ *Bravo 110, 23000,* ☎ *112/5–38–22,* FAX *112/5–63–87. 20 rooms. Restaurant. No credit cards.*

$ ⊞ **Hotel Mediterrane.** Situated behind Trattoria La Pazta, the Mediterrane has five cool white rooms with air-brushed blue ceilings, pale wood furnishings, and king-size beds. Two rooms are air-conditioned; large windows and fans provide sufficient breeze for the rest. A second-story terrace at the front of the building offers a view of the water. The management and maintenance are a bit haphazard, and you may need to check out more than one room before finding one to your liking. ⊠ *Allende 36-B, 23000,* ☎ FAX *112/5–11–95. 5 rooms. Restaurant. MC, V.*

$ ⊞ **Hotel Revolucion.** The former Maria Cristina Hotel, a longtime favorite of budget travelers, has new owners and a new name. The building is now a bright orange, and the rooms have been repainted and refurbished; all offer private bathrooms and TVs. There is a small economical restaurant on the property. ⊠ *Av. Revolución 86 at Degollado, 23000,* ☎ *112/5–80–22. 20 rooms. Restaurant. No credit cards.*

$ ⊞ **Pension California.** This run-down hacienda, offering clean blue-and-white rooms with baths and a courtyard with picnic tables and a TV, draws backpackers and low-budget travelers. A laid-back, friendly camaraderie prevails. ⊠ *Av. Degollado 209, 23000,* ☎ *112/2–28–96. 25 rooms. No credit cards.*

Nightlife and the Arts

El Teatro de la Ciudad (⊠ Av. Navarro 700, ☎ 112/5–00–04) is La Paz's cultural center. The theater seats 1,500 and is used for stage shows by visiting performers as well as local ensembles.

Outdoor Activities and Sports

BOATING AND FISHING

The considerable fleet of private boats in La Paz now has room for docking at three marinas: the **Fidepaz** at the north end of town, and the **Marina Palmira** and **Marina La Paz** south of town. Most hotels can arrange sportfishing trips. The **Dorado Velez Fleet** (⊠ Box 402, La Paz 23000, ☎ 112/2–27–44, ext. 608), operated by Jack Velez in the Los Arcos hotel, has cabin cruisers that can be chartered starting at about $240 per day. Fishing tournaments are held in August and November.

DIVING

Popular diving spots include the white coral banks off Isla Espíritu Santo, the sea lion colony off Isla Partida, and the seamount 14 kilometers (9 miles) farther north. **Scuba Aguilar** (⊠ Independencia 107, Box 179-B, ☎ 112/2–18–26, FAX 112/2–86–44) gives windsurfing and sailing lessons, rents equipment, and operates dives and excursion tours to Espíritu Santo and the wreck of the *Salvatierra*, a sunken ferry boat. Two-tank dive trips run about $65. Dive trips can also be set up through the Cortez Water-sports center at the hotel La Concha (☞ Lodging, *above*).

Shopping

Shops carrying a predictable assortment of sombreros, onyx chess sets, and painted plaster curios are scattered along Avenida Obregón across from the malecón. **Artesanías la Antigua California** (⊠ Av. Obregón 220, ☎ 112/5–52–30) has the nicest selection of Mexican folk art in La Paz, including wooden masks and lacquered boxes from

Guerrero, along with a good supply of English-language books on Baja. At **México Lindo** (⊠ Av. Obregón at Calle Bravo, ☎ 114/2–18–90) you'll find a good display of hand-blown glassware. **La Tiendita** (⊠ Los Arcos Hotel, Av. Obregón 498, ☎ 114/2–27–44) has embroidered guayabera shirts and dresses, tin ornaments and picture frames, and some black pottery from Oaxaca.

Los Cabos

195 km (122 mi) south of La Paz.

At the southern tip of the 1,600-kilometer (1,000-mile) Baja California peninsula, the land ends in a rocky point called El Arco (The Arch), a place of stark and mysterious beauty. The warm waters of the Sea of Cortés swirl into the Pacific Ocean's rugged surf as marlin and sailfish leap above the waves. The desert ends in sand coves, with cactus standing at their entrances like sentries under the soaring palm trees.

Pirates found the capes at the tip of the peninsula an ideal lookout for spotting Spanish galleons traveling from the Philippines to Spain's empire in central Mexico. Missionaries soon followed, seeking to save the souls of the few thousand local Indians who lived off the sea. The good fathers established the missions of San José del Cabo and Cabo San Lucas in the mid-1700s, but their colonies did not last long. The missionaries had brought syphilis and smallpox along with their preachings, and by the end of the century the indigenous population had been nearly wiped out.

A different sort of native, the massive gamefish that appeared to be trapped in the swirl of surf where the ocean meets the sea, brought the explorers back. In the 1940s and 1950s the capes became a haven for millionaires, who built lodges on rocky gray cliffs overlooking secluded coves and bays. By the 1960s, lavish resorts had begun to rise in the barren landscape.

Connected by a 32-kilometer (20-mile) stretch of highway called the Corridor, the two towns that grew around the Spanish missions, Cabo San Lucas and San José del Cabo, were distinct until the late 1970s, when the Mexican government's office of tourism development (Fonatur) targeted the southern tip of Baja as a major resort and dubbed the area Los Cabos. The destination now consists of three major areas: San José del Cabo, Cabo San Lucas, and the 32-kilometer-long (20-mile-long) Corridor separating the two towns.

The region has become one of Mexico's most popular and most expensive coastal getaways, with deluxe hotels, championship golf courses, and some of the finest sportfishing in the world. Despite all the development that has taken place there, and its steep prices, Los Cabos remains a mysteriously natural hideaway.

Numbers in the margin correspond to points of interest on the Los Cabos Coast, San José del Cabo, and Cabo San Lucas maps.

San José del Cabo

San José del Cabo is the municipal headquarters for the two Los Cabos towns, with a population of about 25,000. The hotel zone faces a long stretch of waterfront on the Sea of Cortés, and an 18-hole golf course and private residential community have been constructed south of the town center. The picturesque downtown, with colored lights in the fountains along the main street, still maintains the languid pace of a Mexican village. Despite the development, San José remains the more peaceful of the two towns and is the one that travelers seeking a quiet escape prefer.

❶ The main street in San José del Cabo is **Boulevard Mijares.** The south end of the boulevard has been designated the tourist zone, with the Los Cabos Club de Golf as its centerpiece. Fonatur owns 4,000 acres along this stretch and has built a Commercial and Cultural Center in the middle. A few reasonably priced hotels are situated along this strip, on a beautiful long beach where the surf, unfortunately, is too dangerous for swimming.

❷ The **Estero de San José,** where the freshwater Río San José flows into the sea, is located at the end of the tourist strip, on Paseo San José by the Hotel Presidente Forum. The estuary is now a natural preserve closed to boats. Wildlife is gradually reappearing; more than 200 species of birds can be spotted here. A building at the edge of the estuary has been refurbished as a cultural center with exhibits on Baja's indigenous people.

Within town, Boulevard Mijares is lined with restaurants and shops. **❸** The modest yellow **City Hall** is near Avenida Zaragoza, where Boulevard Mijares ends—a spot marked by a long fountain illuminated at night by colored lights. There is a small, shaded plaza here with a few café tables in front of small restaurants.

❹ Locals and travelers mingle at the large central **plaza,** with a white wrought-iron gazebo and green benches set in the shade. The town's **❺** church, the **Iglesia San José,** looms above the plaza. Be sure to walk up to the front and see the tile mural of a captured priest being dragged toward a fire by Indians.

BEACHES

Playa Hotelera is the stretch of beach that most of the finer hotels use. It's beautiful, but the current is dangerously rough, and swimming is not advised. At the east end of the beach, near the Hotel Presidente, there is a freshwater lagoon filled with tropical birds and plants. If you plan to spend time here, be sure to douse yourself with insect repellent. The best swimming beach near San José is **Playa Palmilla,** which is protected by a rocky point just south of town. The northern part of the beach is cluttered with boats and shacks, but if you walk south you'll reach the Hotel Palmilla beach, a long stretch of white sand and calm sea.

DINING AND LODGING

$$$ ✕ **Damiana.** For a special night out, visit this small hacienda tucked **★** beside the plaza, past the center of town. The lounge area has overstuffed couches where you can unwind before claiming your table on the patio. Fuchsia bougainvillea wraps around the tall pines shading the wrought-iron tables, and the pink adobe walls glow in the candlelight. Start with fiery oysters diablo; then move on to the tender chateaubriand, charbroiled lobster, or the restaurant's signature imperial shrimp steak, made with ground shrimp. You'll find the setting so relaxing and charming that you will want to linger well into the night. ⊠ *Blvd. Mijares 8,* ☎ *114/2–04–99. AE, MC, V. No lunch.*

$$$ ✕ **La Paloma.** This restaurant, with an upstairs patio overlooking the Hotel Palmilla's pool and gardens as well as the sea, offers both a sublime setting and unparalleled food. The Continental menu has taken a turn toward lighter, healthier fare. The Sunday brunch is still the most lavish in the area, and worth a few hours of your time, followed by a long siesta. Have at least one meal here. ⊠ *Hotel Palmilla, Hwy. 1 north of San José,* ☎ *114/2–05–82. AE, MC, V.*

$$ ✕ **Tropicana Bar and Grill.** Start the day with coffee and French toast at the sidewalk tables in front of this enduringly popular restaurant. Later, as the temperature rises, it's more comfortable to sit inside the large air-conditioned bar over an ice-cold lemonade, watching sporting events and music videos on TV. In the evening, the back patio quickly fills with a loyal clientele who enjoy the garden setting and reliable cooking. The menu has grown over the years to include U.S. cuts of beef along with fajitas, chilies rellenos, and lobster, always in demand. The nightly dinner special is usually a good deal. The service can be downright slow and inefficient, but most diners are so laid back they don't mind. ⊠ *Blvd. Mijares 30,* ☎ *114/2–09–07. MC, V.*

$ ✕ **Las Hornillas.** Chicken roasted on a spit over an open fire is the specialty at this casual eatery, more popular with locals than tourists. The half chicken with rice, beans, and tortillas is more than sufficient for a ravenous diner, and the chicken fajitas come on a platter loaded with grilled onions, green peppers, and white meat. ⊠ *Calle Manuel Doblado 610,* ☎ *114/2–23–24. No credit cards.*

$ ✕ **Pescaderia del Mar.** Seafood doesn't get any better than at this small fish market and café on the highway just outside downtown San José. A brick smoker stoked with mesquite sits in one corner of the patio restaurant, and the aroma of smoking dorado, marlin, and wahoo fills the air. Budget diners can fill up on fish tacos or chilies stuffed with smoked fish but may find themselves splurging on giant shrimp cocktails followed by grilled lobster or a whole fried fish. If you've caught a few big ones on a sportfishing trip, consider having them smoked here for a tasty souvenir. ⊠ *Blvd. Mauricio Castro 1110,* ☎ *114/2– 32–66. No credit cards.*

$ ✕ **Restaurant La Playita.** A longtime local secret, this small out-of-the-way restaurant has a new owner and chef and is beginning to draw in the tourists. The main attraction is the seafood brought in daily by fishermen who beach their boats just a few yards away. Burgers, decent fries, and grilled chicken are also served. Lunch here is a nice midday outing, especially when followed by a long walk down the largely deserted beach. ⊠ *Pueblo la Playa, 2 km (1 mi) south of San José,* ☎ *114/ 2–37–74. No credit cards.*

$$ 🏨 **Fiesta Inn.** The nicest moderately priced hotel on San José's long beach, the Fiesta has buildings that frame a garden of cactus and palms. The well-maintained rooms have two double or one king-size bed, satellite TV, carpeting (which can tend to smell musty), and oceanfront balconies. The large swimming pool gets lots of use since the ocean here is too rough for swimming. Horses are available for rides along the beach to the nearby estuary. ⊠ *Blvd. Malecón s/n 30, 23400,* ☎ *114/2–07–01; in the U.S., 800/345–5094;* ⒻⒶⓍ *114/2–04–80. 152 rooms. Restaurant, bar, pool. MC, V.*

$$ 🏨 **La Playita.** The small community of Pueblo la Playa just outside San José has long been a favorite day-trip escape for those in the know. A small hotel opened on the beach in 1995, and it's the perfect hideaway if you're not interested in shopping or bar-hopping. The rooms in the two-story building are painted stark white and have air-conditioning, tiled bathrooms, ceiling fans, but no TVs or phones. There's a palapa bar beside the lap pool; the restaurant is a two-minute walk away. A fleet of small fishing launches bobs up and down in front of the hotel. ⊠ *Pueblo la Playa, 2 km (1 mi) south of San José, 23400,* ☎ FAX *114/2–41–66; reservations in the U.S., 800/777–2664. 24 rooms. Restaurant, bar, pool, beach, fishing. No credit cards.*

$$ ⊞ **Tropicana Inn.** This small hotel is a great option for those who aren't desperate to be on a beach. The stucco buildings frame a pool and palapa bar in a quiet enclave behind San José's main boulevard. The rooms are air-conditioned, have satellite TV, and are maintained to look brand-new. ⊠ *Blvd. Mijares 30, 23400,* ☎ *114/2–09–07; in the U.S., 510/939–2725;* FAX *114/2–15–90. 40 rooms. Restaurant, bar, pool. MC, V.*

$ ⊞ **Posada Terranova.** San José's best budget hotel is a friendly place where guests return so frequently they're almost part of the family. The large rooms are painted a clean, bright white and have two double beds and tiled bathrooms. The hotel has expanded in recent years, but, what with guests congregating at the front patio tables or in the restaurant to compare their days, it still feels like a private home. Advance reservations are a must during holidays. ⊠ *Calle Degollado at Zaragoza, 23400,* ☎ *114/2–05–34,* FAX *114/2–09–02. 25 rooms. Restaurant, bar. MC, V.*

$$$$ ✕⊞ **Hotel Presidente Los Cabos Forum.** By far the nicest hotel in San José, this property sits at the end of the hotel zone, next to the estuary. It resembles a pueblo set amid beachside cactus gardens. The buildings curve around an enormous blue pool; the rooms have shaded patios, minibars, king-size beds, deep bathtubs, and couches, tables, and chairs that face the sliding glass doors. The hotel now operates on an all-inclusive basis, with all meals and some activities included in the room rate. As there are no other restaurants in the immediate vicinity, you'll save on taxis by eating here. ⊠ *Paseo San José, at end of hotel zone, 23400,* ☎ *114/2–02–11; in the U.S., 800/327–0200;* ℻ *114/2– 02–32. 244 rooms, 6 suites. 2 restaurants, bar, pool, tennis courts, horseback riding, beach, fishing. AE, MC, V.*

NIGHTLIFE AND THE ARTS

The hottest nightspot in town is **Bones Disco** at the Hotel Presidente Forum (⊠ Paseo San José, ☎ 114/2–00–38). **Iguana Bar** (⊠ Blvd. Mijares 24, ☎ 114/2–02–66) is a local hangout, with live rock 'n' roll on weekend nights during the high season.

OUTDOOR ACTIVITIES AND SPORTS

Fishing. Most hotels in San José can arrange fishing trips. As there is no marina in town, you'll have to board your boat at the marina in Cabo San Lucas. Hotels typically can set up the excursions and provide transportation to the marina and box lunches. There is a fleet of pangas (small skiffs) at Pueblo la Playa, about 1½ kilometers (1 mile) south of San José.

Golf. The public, nine-hole **Los Cabos Club de Golf** (⊠ Blvd. Mijares, ☎ 114/2–09–05) in San José was built in 1988 and for many years was the only golf course in Los Cabos. It now has plenty of competition from the lavish courses in the Corridor. The green fees are much lower here, however.

Surfing. Killer Hook Surf Shop (⊠ Av. Hidalgo, ☎ 114/2–24–30) sells and rents snorkeling gear, along with surfboards and boogie boards.

Tennis. The **Los Cabos Campo de Golf** (☞ Golf, *above*) has lighted tennis courts that are open to the public; fees are $8 per hour during the day and $12 per hour at night.

SHOPPING

Shopping opportunities in San José del Cabo occur in the few streets around the main plaza and City Hall. Across from City Hall is **Almacenes Goncanseco** (⊠ Blvd. Mijares 18, ☎ 114/2–09–12), where you can get film, postcards, groceries, and liquor. **ADD** (⊠ Av. Zaragoza at Hidalgo, ☎ 114/2–27–27), an interior design shop, sells gorgeous handpainted dishes from Guanajuato and carved-wood furniture from Michoacán. **Copal** (⊠ Zaragoza 20, ☎ 114/2–30–70) has a nice array of carved animals from Oaxaca, masks from Guerrero, and heavy wooden furnishings. For fresh produce, flowers, meat, fish, and a sampling of local life in San José, visit the **Mercado Municipal** off Calle Doblado.

The Corridor

Many of the legendary fishing lodges and exclusive resorts built before the government stepped in were located along the wild cliffs between San José del Cabo and Cabo San Lucas. Since the mid-1980s, the area has developed as a destination unto itself. It now has several private communities and large-scale resorts, and three championship golf courses. The highway along the Corridor has been widened to four lanes.

Two bays, **Bahía Chileno** and **Bahía Santa María,** offer terrific diving and snorkeling (☞ Outdoor Activities and Sports, *below*).

BEACHES

Costa Azul is the most popular surfing beach in Los Cabos. A few small campgrounds and casual restaurants line the beach facing the waves. **Playa Palmilla** is one of the Corridor's best swimming beaches.

DINING AND LODGING

$$$ ✕ **Pitahayas.** Now that the Corridor resorts are firmly established, smaller businesses are cropping up to take advantage of the upscale clientele. This elegant restaurant has found its niche in a lovely setting just above the beach at Cabo del Sol. The wide-ranging menu features Pacific Rim cuisine, blending touches of Thai, Polynesian, and Chinese cooking in unusual recipes. Lobster appears in the form of gourmet hash, duckling is served with a plum tangerine sauce, and fresh organic vegetables are lightly stir-fried and served while still crisp. Soft jazz plays in the background, and the setting is decidely romantic. ✉ *Km 10 on Hwy. 1,* ☎ *114/3–21–57. MC, V.*

$$ ✕ **Da Giorgio.** The best sunset-watching in all of Los Cabos may be enjoyed at the cliffside tables outside this restaurant. The tables, staggered along the cliffs and poised beside a small pond with a waterfall, have a great view of the arch at land's end. The menu focuses on pastas and pizza, and the salad bar has an abundance of fresh veggies. ✉ *Km 5 on Hwy. 1,* ☎ *114/3–29–88. MC, V.*

$$$$ ▦ **Palmilla.** Just outside San José, the Palmilla is a gracious, sprawl-
★ ing hacienda-style resort with a small white adobe chapel—and a private airstrip. Tiled stairways lead up from flower-lined paths to large apartments with hand-carved furniture, French doors opening onto private patios, and tiled baths. The rooms underwent some much-needed renovations in 1996. The buildings are spread along a hillside overlooking the beach, the service is delightfully personalized, and the hotel's La Paloma restaurant is excellent. Construction is under way on a large-scale resort development surrounding the hotel; a 27-hole Jack Nicklaus–designed golf course was completed in 1993. The only drawback at the hotel is its small pool; dedicated swimmers will be happier at the beach, where a small natural cove keeps the water calm. The cove also enables the Palmilla to keep its fleet of fishing boats anchored just offshore, unlike other Corridor hotels. The Palmilla's fishing and scuba-diving operations are among the best in the area. ✉ *Carretera Transpeninsular, Km 1 (about 8 km [5 mi] from San José), 23400,* ☎ *114/2–05–82,* 𝔽𝔸𝕏 *114/2–05–83; reservations in the U.S., 4343 Von Karman Ave., Newport Beach, CA 92660, 800/637–2226. 62 rooms, 7 suites, 2 villas. Restaurant, bar, pool, golf privileges, tennis courts, beach. AE, MC, V.*

$$$$ ▦ **Twin Dolphin.** Sleek and Japanese-modernistic, with an austere air, the Twin Dolphin has been a hideaway for the rich and famous since 1977. Guest rooms are in low-lying casitas along a seaside cliff and are furnished in minimalist style. The hotel is worth a visit if only for the reproductions of Baja's cave paintings on the lobby wall. ✉ *Km 12, Carretera Transpeninsular, Cabo San Lucas, 23410,* ☎ *114/3–18–03,* 𝔽𝔸𝕏 *114/3–18–04; reservations in the U.S., 1625 W. Olympic Blvd., Suite 1005, Los Angeles, CA 90015, 800/421–8925,* 𝔽𝔸𝕏 *213/380–1302. 44 rooms, 6 suites. Restaurant, bar, pool, putting green, tennis courts, beach, fishing. MC, V.*

$$$$ ▦ **Westin Regina Resort.** The Westin is architecturally astounding, if a bit intimidating in size. It's a long walk from the parking lot and lobby to the rooms and pool, set on a cliff atop a man-made beach. The luxurious rooms are among the best in Los Cabos, with satellite TV, in-room safes, hair dryers, bathtubs and separate walk-in showers, and both air-conditioning and ceiling fans—a boon to those who prefer open windows and sea breezes. Two of Los Cabos's best golf courses are nearby, and the hotel is designed to keep its guests happy without their ever having to leave the grounds. ⊠ *Km 22.5 Carretera Transpeninsular, Box 145, San José del Cabo, 23400,* ☎ *114/2–90–00 or 800/228–3000,* ℻ *114/2–90–10. 243 rooms. 3 restaurants, 3 pools, tennis courts, exercise room, beach. AE, MC, V.*

$$$ ⊡ **Hotel Cabo San Lucas.** A holdover from the days when Los Cabos was a rugged fishermen's hideaway, this hotel looks like a mountain lodge nearly buried in palms. Far from glamorous, the rooms are furnished with sturdy, dark wood pieces; the color scheme is brown and orange. Maintenance is a bit lax and some of the rooms have ancient, noisy air conditioners. Still, there is a certain breed of Baja devotee who wouldn't stay anywhere else. The hotel is located right above Chileno Beach, one of the best diving spots in Los Cabos. ⊠ *Km 14.5 Carretera Transpeninsular, Cabo San Lucas, 23410,* ☎ *114/3–34–57; in the U.S., 800/733–2226. 89 rooms. Restaurant, pool, beach, dive shop, fishing. MC, V.*

$$$ ⊡ **Meliá Cabo Real.** This Meliá is incredibly huge and opulent, spread over a hilltop with a meandering crystal-blue pool, fountains, waterfalls, white canopies shading rest areas, and a private beach created by a small jetty jutting from the rocky hillside. Maya carvings and bas reliefs adorn the walls in the rooms, which all have landscaped terraces. The Cabo Real resort development around the hotel is still ongoing, with an 18-hole golf course now open. Meliá guests can use it for a fee. The hotel operates a shuttle service to its sister property in Cabo San Lucas. ⊠ *Km 19.5 Carretera Transpeninsular, Cabo San Lucas, 23410,* ☎ *114/3–09–67,* ℻ *114/3–10–03; reservations in the U.S., 800/336–3542,* ℻ *305/854–0660. 299 rooms. 2 restaurants, café, room service, pool, tennis courts, exercise room, beach, dive shop, fishing. AE, MC, V.*

OUTDOOR ACTIVITIES AND SPORTS

Diving and Snorkeling. Bahía Chileno, an underwater preserve, teems with marine life, making it a wonderful place for snorkeling and diving. You'll need to bring your own equipment. **Bahía Santa María,** a picture-perfect white-sand cove protected by towering brown cliffs, also has superb snorkeling, with hundreds of colorful fish swarming through chunks of white coral. There is a concession stand on the beach where you can rent snorkeling gear, but its hours are erratic.

Fishing. Most Corridor hotels have excellent fishing fleets, with the boats anchored at the marina in Cabo San Lucas. Hotels typically can set up the trips and provide transportation to the marina and box lunches. **Victor's Aquatics** (☎ 114/2–10–92 or 800/521–2281, ℻ 114/2–10–93) has a fleet of pangas on the Palmilla beach.

Golf. In just the past few years, Los Cabos has become a major golf destination. The courses that have brought so much attention this way are all located in the Corridor and serve as the centerpieces for megaresort developments. Among the most spectacular is the 27-hole Jack Nicklaus–designed course at the **Palmilla Golf Club** (⊠ Palmilla Resort, ☎ 114/2–17–01, 114/2–17–08, or 800/637–2226). A second 18-hole Nicklaus course is open at **Cabo del Sol** (☎ 114/2–17–01 or 800/637–2226), a resort development in the Corridor that will eventually include three 18-hole courses. The Robert Trent Jones–designed **Cabo Real Golf Club** (⊠ Melia Cabo Real Hotel, ☎ 114/2–90–00, ext. 9205) has 18 of its 36 holes open for play.

Cabo San Lucas

Cabo San Lucas, once an unsightly fishing town with dusty streets and smelly canneries, has become the center of tourism activity for Los Cabos.

The sportfishing fleet is headquartered here, and cruise ships anchored off the marina disperse passengers into town. Trendy restaurants and bars line the streets, and massive hotels have risen on every available plot of waterfront turf; a five-story condo-hotel complex along the bay blocks the view from the town's older hotels. Cabo San Lucas has become an in spot for travelers seeking fun, rowdy nightlife, and extensive dining and shopping options.

⑥ Highway 1 leads into the center of Cabo San Lucas, ending at Kilometer 1 on the Transpeninsular Highway. The main downtown street, Avenida Lázaro Cárdenas, passes the pretty **Plaza San Lucas** with its white wrought-iron gazebo. Buildings around the plaza are gradually being refurbished to house galleries and restaurants. Most of the shops, services, and restaurants are located between Avenida Cárdenas and the waterfront.

Boulevard Marina has been transformed from a dusty main drag into a busy thoroughfare lined with hotels and cafés. Paved walkways now run from here to the hotels and beaches on the east end of town and west
⑦ to the **Handicrafts Market** at the Cabo San Lucas marina (☞ Shopping,
⑧ *below*). The sportfishing fleet is docked in the **Bahía de Cabo San Lucas,** and there are glass-bottom boats available at the water's edge.

⑨ The most spectacular sight in Cabo San Lucas is **El Arco.** The natural rock arch is visible from the marina and from some of the hotels but is more impressive from the water. **El Faro de Cabo Falso** (Lighthouse of the False Cape), built in 1890 and set amid sand dunes, is a little bit farther on from El Arco. You need a four-wheel-drive vehicle to reach the lighthouse by land. If you don't take at least a short boat ride out to the arch and Playa de Amor, the beach underneath, you haven't fully appreciated Cabo.

BEACHES

Playa de Amor consists of a secluded cove at the very end of the peninsula, with the Sea of Cortés on one side and the Pacific Ocean on the other. The contrast between the peaceful azure cove on the Sea of Cortés and the pounding white surf of the Pacific is dramatic.

Playa Hacienda, in the inner harbor by the Hacienda Hotel, has the calmest waters of any beach in town and good snorkeling around the rocky point.

Playa Médano, just north of Cabo San Lucas, is the most popular stretch in Los Cabos (and possibly in all Baja) for sunbathing and people-watching. The 3-kilometer (2-mile) span of white sand is always crowded, especially on weekends.

Playa Solmar, fringing the Solmar Hotel, is a beautiful wide beach at the base of the mountains leading into the Pacific, but it has dangerous surf with a swift undertow. Stick to sunbathing here.

DINING AND LODGING

$$$ ✕ **Casa Rafael's.** European antiques and a pair of tropical toucans in a glass-fronted cage provide the visual distractions in this intimate, elegant restaurant. The chef, a transplant from Maui, has created an exciting Pacific Rim menu featuring lamb, lobster medallions in black bean sauce, imported steaks, and smoked local dorado, all with Asian and Mexican touches. A pianist plays romantic ballads during dinner, and couples sip champagne in cozy upholstered booths that allow ample privacy. Reservations are recommended. ⊠ *On road to Hacienda Hotel,* ☎ *114/3–07–39. AE, MC, V.*

✕ **El Galeón.** Considered the most distinguished dining room in town, El Galeón is located across from the marina. The choice seats

Cabo San Lucas

Golfo de
California

Playa
de Amor

Blvd. Marina

0   500 meters
0   500 yards

PACIFIC OCEAN

are on the outside terraces facing the water; the inside is decorated with lots of heavy wood furniture. Traditional Italian, Mexican, and American dishes are prepared expertly, with an emphasis on thick, tender cuts of beef. The piano bar is a nice setting for a late-night brandy. ✉ *Across from marina by road to Finesterra Hotel,* ☎ *114/3–04–43. AE, MC, V.*

$$$ ✕ **Mi Casa.** One of Cabo's best restaurants is in an eye-catching, ★ cobalt-blue building painted with a mural of a burro, just across the street from the main plaza. Mexican cuisine reaches gourmet status here with fresh tuna and dorado served with tomatillo salsa or Yucatecan *achiote,* or with sophisticated dishes such as *chili en nogada* (a meat-stuffed pepper topped with walnut sauce and pomegranate seeds). The restaurant quickly outgrew its small dining room and has spread into a large back courtyard. It's especially nice at night, illuminated by candlelight and the moon. ✉ *Av. Cabo San Lucas,* ☎ *114/3–19–33. MC, V.*

$$$ ✕ **Peacocks.** The ubiquitous fresh-fish dinner achieves gustatory em-★ inence when prepared by chef Bernard Voll. His dorado is coated with a crust of chopped pecans, and his shrimp masterfully tossed with spinach fettuccine. This chef is known for his incredible desserts—if you miss dinner, be sure to stop by for a cappuccino and tequila mousse. The candle-lit two-level dining room has an open kitchen and is topped by an enormous palapa; you can also dine on an outdoor patio. ✉ *Paseo Pescador near Playa Médano,* ☎ *114/3–18–58. AE, MC, V.*

$$ ✕ **El Rey Sol.** This is one of the most traditionally Mexican restaurants in Cabo San Lucas. The abalone is succulent, and the seafood combination—lobster, oysters, crab, and fish—incredibly generous and outrageously good, though expensive. The spicy *7-Mares* soup—with seven varieties of seafood, from octopus to clams—is guaranteed to *levantar los muertos* (raise the dead) or, at the very least, cure tequila hangovers. This large brick restaurant is warm and cozy, and the Mexican breakfasts are popular with both townsfolk and tourists. ✉ *On road to Playa Médano,* ☎ *114/3–11–17. AE, MC, V.*

$$ ✕ **El Shrimp Bucket.** This is the calmest of the three Carlos Anderson restaurants in Cabo San Lucas. A few tables are set out on the walkway that runs along the marina in front of the Marina Fiesta Hotel, a good spot to relax and watch the boats rock on the water. The indoor dining room has the chain's typical mishmash decor with quirky adornments hanging about. The food——barbecued ribs and chicken, burgers, piles of fried shrimp——is dependable and abundant. ✉ *Blvd. Marina in Marina Fiesta complex,* ☎ *114/3–25–98. AE, MC, V.*

$ ✕ **The Fish Company.** It's easy to overlook this small seafood restaurant surrounded by flashier establishments. But the owner has perfected the art of preparing flavorful meals for reasonable prices. Nine tables covered with blue-and-white cloths sit just in from the sidewalk in the narrow dining room, and the aroma of fresh grilled fish fills the air. Breakfast specialties include a great chorizo-and-cheese omelette; among the lunch and dinner choices are shrimp with oyster sauce and fresh fish smothered in garlic. You can bring your catch here and have it prepared in a low-cost feast. ⊠ *Av. Guerrero between Blvd. Marina and Zapata*, ☎ *114/3–14–05. No credit cards.*

$ ✕ **Tacos Chidos.** Taco stands are beginning to appear all over Cabo San Lucas. Chidos has been around for a long time and serves one of the cheapest breakfasts in town: Egg dishes served with beans, rice, tortillas, and coffee run well under $5. Tostados, tamales, and torta sandwiches fill out the menu, along with the requisite fish, beef, and pork tacos. Best of all, Chidos will deliver your order to your hotel. ⊠ *Av. Zapata at Guerrero*, ☎ *114/3–05–51. No credit cards.*

$ ✕ **Taquería San Lucas.** Longtime Cabo devotees know this simple restaurant as the Broken Surfboard; by any name, it's the best budget place in town. A few rickety wooden tables and chairs sit next to the sidewalk, where there's always someone lounging about ready to share fishing tales and surfing lore. The menu sticks with such basic Mexican and American fare as tacos, burgers, and burritos. Breakfast is an especially good deal. ⊠ *Av. Hidalgo between Madero and Zapata, no tel. No credit cards.*

$$$ ▥ **Meliá San Lucas.** From the moment you enter the Meliá and spot
★ El Arco framed by the lobby's arches, you know you're at a hotel where details are important. The blue walls and linens in the rooms complement the views of the aquamarine sea; the outer adobe walls of the terraced hotel buildings glow orange and gold with the changing sunlight. The Meliá has a long beach with calm waters, a spacious hot tub under the palms, and all the equipment you could need for playing on and in the water. ⊠ *Playa Medano, 23410*, ☎ *114/3–10–00 or 114/3–10–60; in the U.S., 800/336–3542;* FAX *114/3–04–18. 161 rooms and suites. 3 restaurants, 2 pools, hot tub, beach, meeting rooms. AE, MC, V.*

$$$ ▥ **Casa Rafael's.** An intimate boutique hotel, this is the perfect spot for those seeking privacy rather than abundant diversions. The rooms are individually decorated with an eclectic collection of antiques and modern furnishings; all have air-conditioning and private baths. A lap pool on the terrace behind the house is surrounded by plants, and there's a small exercise room and hot tub. ⊠ *Carretera a Hotel Hacienda, 23410*, ☎ FAX *114/3–07–39. 12 rooms. Restaurant, pool, hot tub, exercise room. MC, V.*

$$$ ▥ **Finisterra.** One of the oldest hotels in Cabo, the Finisterra is now also one of the most modern, thanks to a new eight-story tower rising directly from the beach. A second tower should be completed by the end of 1996. A three-story-high palapa covers the restaurant and bar on the beach next to two free-form swimming pools. The rooms in the new building, with oceanfront balconies, are by far the nicest; some have king-size beds. The older section of the hotel is favored by longtime guests who like the fishing-lodge feel of the stone buildings. The restaurant is only fair, but the Whale Watcher bar atop a high cliff has the best view in town. ⊠ *Blvd. Marina, 23410*, ☎ *114/3–00–00,* FAX *114/3–05–90; reservations in the U.S., 18552 MacArthur Blvd., Suite 205, Irvine, CA 92715, 714/476–5555 or 800/347–2252,* FAX *714/476–5560. 197 rooms. 2 restaurants, bar, 3 pools, travel services. AE, MC, V.*

$$$ ▥ **Hotel Hacienda.** Set on the tip of a tree-filled point jutting into San Lucas Bay, the Hacienda resembles a Spanish colonial inn with its white arches and bell towers, stone fountains, and statues of Indian gods set

amid scarlet hibiscus and bougainvillea. The white rooms have red-tile floors, tile baths, and folk art on the walls; the bar is a veritable museum of Indian artifacts. The water sports center, located on the calmest beach in town, has kayaks, Jet Skis, snorkeling equipment, and any other gear you might need. ⊠ *Playa Medano, 23410,* ☎ *114/3-01–22; reservations in the U.S., Box 48872, Los Angeles, CA 90048, 800/733–2226. 112 rooms, suites, and beachfront cabanas. Restaurant, bar, pool, beach, dive shop. MC, V.*

$$$ 🏨 **Solmar Suites.** From afar, the Solmar looks like a space colony, set
★   against granite cliffs at the tip of Land's End, facing the wild Pacific. The rooms, decorated in Mexico–Santa Fe style, have separate sitting areas and tile baths; the best ones are set up against the rocks right over the beach. A few of the adjacent time-share units with kitchenettes and a private pool area are available on a nightly basis. The surf here is far too dangerous for swimming, but don't miss a stroll along the wide strip of beach. Most visitors hang out around the pool and swim-up bar, joining in with the ever-present musicians. The Solmar's sport-fishing fleet is first-rate. The good restaurant hosts a Saturday night Mexican fiesta and buffet dinner. ⊠ *Blvd. Marina, Box 8, 23410,* ☎ *114/3–35–35,* FAX *114/3–04–10; reservations in the U.S., Box 383, Pacific Palisades, CA 90272, 310/459–9861 or 800/344–3349,* FAX *310/454–1686. 66 rooms, 4 suites, 68 condos. Restaurant, bar, pool, tennis courts, beach, dive shop. AE, MC, V.*

$$ 🏨 **Mar de Cortés.** A favorite among die-hard fishers, this small, casual inn has a new entryway with a shopping arcade on the street. The pool is surrounded by palms and shrubs, offering a cool respite from the hectic street scene. The oldest rooms have brick ceilings, tiled floors, and colonial-style furnishings. Newer rooms are brighter but lack character. Some units have patios by the swimming pool. ⊠ *Av. Cárdenas, 23410,* ☎ *114/3–00–32,* FAX *114/3–02–32; reservations in the U.S., 17561 Vierra Canyon Rd., 99, Salinas, CA 93907, 408/663–5803 or 800/347–8821,* FAX *408/663–1904. 72 rooms. Restaurant, pool. MC, V.*

$ 🏨 **Las Villas Turismo Juvenil.** Cabo's youth hostel is about 10 blocks from the waterfront in a quiet neighborhood. Two dormitory rooms have bunk beds and shelves, and there are several private rooms with shared baths. In the courtyard, guests can use sinks and counters to wash their clothes and fix meals. Reservations are suggested, especially from November through February. ⊠ *Av. de la Juventud, 23410,* ☎ *114/3–01–48. 2 dorms, 11 private rooms. No credit cards.*

$ 🏨 **Siesta Suites.** You'll have to forgo air-conditioning to remain in the inexpensive range, but you'll get a large, immaculate room with kitchenette. The three-story hotel sits on a fairly quiet side street just two blocks from the marina, and the proprietors are the friendliest in town. Opened in 1994, the hotel quickly garnered a loyal following; reservations are a must in the winter season. ⊠ *Calle Zapata, Box 310, 23410,* ☎ FAX *114/3–27–73; reservations in the U.S.,* ☎ FAX *909/945–5940. 15 suites. Kitchenettes. No credit cards.*

NIGHTLIFE AND THE ARTS

The nightlife in Cabo San Lucas took a definite upturn when members of the rock band Van Halen opened **Cabo Wabo** (⊠ Calle Guerrero, ☎ 114/3–11–88). The latest U.S. bands play over an excellent sound system, but the real highlight is the impromptu jam sessions with appearances by Van Halen's many friends in the music business. **Squid Roe** (⊠ Av. Cárdenas, ☎ 114/3–06–55) is the rowdiest spot in town, packed with young foreigners who work in the local tourist industry and know how to party. **Giggling Marlin** (⊠ Blvd. Marina, ☎ 114/3–06–06) seems like it's been around forever as the favorite watering hole for fishermen and their girlfriends. **Río Grill** (⊠ Blvd. Marina, ☎ 114/

3–13–35) absolutely booms with rock 'n' roll and reggae, except when the live bands give way to the karaoke contingent. **El Galeón** (✉ Blvd. Marina, ☎ 114/3–04–43) is about the only refuge for the quieter crowd, who sip brandy by the piano bar.

OUTDOOR ACTIVITIES AND SPORTS

Diving. El Arco is a prime diving and snorkeling area, as are several rocky points off the coast. Most hotels offer diving trips and equipment rental. The oldest and most complete dive shop in the area is **Amigos del Mar** (✉ near sportfishing docks at harbor, ☎ 114/3–05–05 or 800/344–3349, FAX 114/3–08–87). The **Solmar V** (✉ at Solmar Hotel and marina, ☎ 114/3–00–22 or 800/344–3349, FAX 310/454–1686), a live-aboard dive and fishing boat, takes weeklong trips to the islands of Socorro, San Benedicto, and Clarion, and the coral reefs at Cabo Pulmo. It has 12 cabins with private baths (maximum: 24 passengers).

Fishing. There are more than 800 species of fish in the waters off Los Cabos. Most of the hotels will arrange fishing charters, which include a captain and mate, tackle, bait, licenses, and drinks. Prices start at $250 per day for a 25-foot cruiser. Some charters provide lunch, and most can arrange to have your catch mounted, frozen, or smoked. Most of the boats leave from the sportfishing docks in the Cabo San Lucas marina. Usually there are a fair number of pangas for rent at about $25 per hour with a five-hour minimum. Dependable companies include the **Gaviota Fleet** (✉ at marina, ☎ 114/3–04–30 or 800/521–2281), **Minerva's** (✉ at marina and on Madero between Blvd. Marina and Guerrero, ☎ 114/3–12–82, FAX 114/3–04–40), **Pisces Sportfishing Fleet** (✉ at marina, ☎ 114/3–12–88 or 800/521–2281), and **Solmar Fleet** (✉ at Solmar Hotel and Marina, ☎ 114/3–00–22 or 800/344–3349, FAX 310/454–1686).

SHOPPING

Some of the nicest shops in Cabo San Lucas are located in **Plaza Bonita** on the waterfront at the beginning of Boulevard Marina. **Cartes** (✉ Plaza Bonita, ☎ 114/2–17–70) is the best of the many interior-design stores in Los Cabos, with an irresistible array of hand-painted pottery and tableware, pewter frames, hand-blown glass and carved furniture. **Libros** (✉ Plaza Bonita, ☎ 114/3–17–70) carries a vast number of English-language novels and magazines. **Dos Lunas** (✉ Plaza Bonita, ☎ 114/3–19–69) offers a trendy selection of colorful sportswear. **Francisco's Café del Mundo** (✉ Plaza Bonita, no tel.) is the place to take a break for an espresso or cappuccino.

Boulevard Marina and the side streets between the waterfront and the main plaza are filled with an ever-changing parade of small shops. **Necri** (✉ Blvd. Marina between Madero and Ocampo, ☎ 114/3–02–83) has an excellent selection of folk art and furnishings. **Casa Mexicanas** (✉ Av. San Lucas, ☎ 114/3–19–33) handles special order furnishings and fabrics along with pottery, wall hangings, and folk art. **Galeria El Dorado** (✉ Blvd. Marina between Guerrero and Madero, ☎ 114/3–08–17) displays paintings and sculpture by local artists in the front room and various curios in the back. **Magic of the Moon** (✉ Hidalgo near Blvd. Marina, ☎ 114/3–31–61) displays handmade lingerie, dresses, and ruffled blouses. **Cuca's Blanket Factory** (✉ Cardenas at Matamoros, ☎ 114/3–19–13) sells the typical array of serapes and cotton blankets with a twist—you can design your own and have it ready the next day. **Mama Eli's** (✉ Av. San Lucas, ☎ 114/3–16–16) is a three-story gallery with fine furnishings, ceramics, appliquéd clothing, and children's toys. **Galeria Gatemelatta** (✉ on dirt road to Hotel Hacienda, ☎ 114/3–11–66) specializes in colonial furniture and antiques.

At the **Handicrafts Market** in the marina you can pose for a photo with an iguana, plan a ride in a glass-bottomed boat, or browse to your heart's content through stalls packed with blankets, sombreros, and pottery.

BAJA SUR A TO Z

Arriving and Departing

By Boat
Several cruise lines—including **Carnival** (☎ 800/327–9501), **Princess** (☎ 800/421–0522), and **Royal Caribbean** (☎ 800/327–0271)—use Cabo San Lucas as a port of call.

By Bus
Tres Estrellas de Oro bus line runs the length of the peninsula from Tijuana to Los Cabos, stopping at towns enroute; the peninsula-long trip takes 22 hours. The **Aguila** bus line runs from Santa Rosalia to Los Cabos.

GUERRERO NEGRO
Tres Estrellas de Oro (☎ 112/2–64–76) runs buses from La Paz to Guerrero Negro; the bus stops at the highway entrance to town.

LA PAZ
Tres Estrellas de Oro (☎ 112/2–64–76) and **Aguila** (☎ 112/2–70–94) operate buses along the Transpeninsular Highway to the border and to Los Cabos.

LORETO
Loreto is serviced by both Tres Estrellas de Oro and Aguila. The **bus terminal** (✉ Salvatierra and Tamaral, ☎ 113/5–07–67) sits at the entrance to town.

LOS CABOS
Tres Estrellas de Oro (☎ 114/2–02–00) travels from Tijuana to Los Cabos and between Cabo San Lucas and San José daily.

By Car
Mexico Highway 1, also known as the Transpeninsular Highway, runs the entire 1,600 kilometers (1,000 miles) from Tijuana to Cabo San Lucas. The highway's condition varies depending on the weather and intervals between road repairs. It should not be driven at high speed or at night (the road is not lit). There are exits for all the principal towns in Baja Sur.

The city of La Paz curves along the bay of La Paz and faces the sea in a northwesterly, rather than an easterly, direction. When you approach the city on Highway 1 from the north, you'll enter from the southwest.

The road between San José del Cabo and Cabo San Lucas was widened to four lanes and is in good condition, though dips and bridges become flooded in heavy rains.

By Ferry
LA PAZ
The ferry system connecting Baja to mainland Mexico has been privatized and is constantly undergoing changes in rates and schedules. Currently there are Sematur ferries from La Paz to Mazatlán and La Paz to Topolobampo. Tickets are available at the ferry office at the dock on the road to Pichilingue (☎ 112/2–94–85, FAX 112/5–65–88) and at the downtown Sematur office (✉ Av. 5 de Mayo 502, ☎ 112/5–38–33, FAX 112/5–46–66). Purchase your ticket personally in advance of your trip—and expect confusion. Travelers planning to take cars and

motor homes on the ferry to the mainland must obtain a vehicle permit before boarding the ferry. Tourism officials in La Paz strongly suggest that you obtain the permit when crossing the border into Baja; though permits are not needed in Baja, offices at the border are better equipped to handle the paperwork than those in La Paz. Everyone crossing to the mainland needs a tourist card, also available at the border.

SANTA ROSALIA

The ferry travels from Santa Rosalia to Guaymas on the mainland Pacific coast. Currently, the ferry departs for the 12-hour trip to the mainland at 8 AM on Wednesday and Sunday and arrives in Santa Rosalia on Tuesday and Friday at 3 PM. Advance tickets are available at the Santa Rosalia ferry terminal (☎ 115/2–00–14, FAX 115/2–00–13), just south of town on the Highway 1, but schedules are often erratic.

By Plane

LA PAZ

The La Paz airport, about 16 kilometers (10 miles) north of town, is served by **Aero California** (☎ 112/5–10–23) from Tijuana and Loreto and **Aeromexico** (☎ 112/2–00–91) from Los Angeles, Tucson, Tijuana, Mexico City, and other cities within Mexico.

LORETO

Aero California (☎ 113/5–00–50 or 113/5–05–66) has daily flights from Los Angeles and La Paz to Loreto's airport, which is 7 kilometers (4 miles) southwest of town.

LOS CABOS

The **Los Cabos International Airport** (☎ 114/2–03–41) is about 11 kilometers (7 miles) north of San José del Cabo and about 48 kilometers (30 miles) from Cabo San Lucas. **Aero California** (☎ 114/2–09–43) flies to Los Cabos from Los Angeles, Tijuana, and Phoenix; **Mexicana** (☎ 114/2–09–60) from Guadalajara, Mexico City, Mazatlán, Puerto Vallarta, Denver, and Los Angeles; **Alaska Airlines** (☎ 114/2–09–59) from Anchorage, Fairbanks, Portland, Phoenix, San Francisco, San Diego, Los Angeles, and Seattle. **United** (no tel. in Los Cabos) flies from New York and Chicago, connecting in Los Angeles, from December through June.

Getting Around

La Paz

A car isn't necessary if you plan to stay in town; taxis are readily available and inexpensive. It's also fairly easy to get around by bus in La Paz: City buses run along the malecón and into downtown. If you'd like to explore the remote beaches, a car is necessary (☞ Car Rentals, *below*).

Loreto

Taxis are in good supply and fares are inexpensive. There are two gas stations in Loreto; be sure to fill your tank before heading out on any long jaunts.

Los Cabos

The best way to see the sights is on foot. The downtown areas of San José and Cabo San Lucas are compact, with the plaza, church, shops, and restaurants within a few blocks of one another. There is bus service between the two towns, although buses may not stop along the Corridor.

Contacts and Resources

Car and Jeep Rentals

LA PAZ

Avis (⊠ airport, ☎ 112/2–26–51), **Budget** (⊠ Paseo Obregón at Hidalgo, ☎ 112/2–10–97), **Hertz** (⊠ airport, ☎ 112/2–09–19), and **Servitur Autorento** (⊠ 5 de Febrero at Abasolo, ☎ 112/2–14–48).

LOS CABOS

The following car-rental agencies all have desks at the airport and in one or both towns: **Amca** (☎ 114/3–25–15), **Avis** (☎ 114/2–06–80), **Budget** (☎ 114/3–02–41), **Dollar** (☎ 114/2–06–71), **Hertz** (☎ 114/3–02–11), **National** (☎ 114/3–60–00), and **Thrifty** (☎ 114/2–16–71). **M&M Jeeps** (⊠ at Hotel Presidente Forum, ☎ 114/2–11–81; in San Diego, CA, ☎ 619/297–1615 or 800/464–5724), which rents two- and four-wheel-drive vehicles, offers a package option: Travelers can rent the vehicles for a one-way trip from San Diego to Los Cabos without a drop-off fee and arrange their own accommodations or they can purchase an all-inclusive self-guided tour package.

Emergencies

LA PAZ

Police (☎ 112/2–66–10), **Fire** (☎ 112/2–00–54), and **Red Cross** (☎ 112/2–11–11).

LOS CABOS

Police: Cabo San Lucas (☎ 114/3–39–77) and San José del Cabo (☎ 114/2–03–61). **Hospital:** Cabo San Lucas (☎ 114/3–01–02) and San José del Cabo (☎ 114/2–00–13).

Guided Tours

GUERRERO NEGRO

The best way to see the whales is with a tour company that's familiar with the area. **Baja Expeditions** (⊠ 2625 Garnet Ave., San Diego, CA 92109, ☎ 619/581–3311; in the U.S. and Canada, 800/843–6967), the premier Baja adventure operator in the United States, has whale-watching trips on boats and kayaks. The company can also arrange trips to Mulege and Bahía Concepción, especially popular for paddling. **Baja Discovery** (⊠ Box 152527, San Diego, CA 92195, ☎ 619/262–0700 or 800/829–2252) operates a whale-watching camp at Laguna San Ignacio south of Guerrero Negro, with tent camping on an island in the lagoon and boat trips among the whales. **Baja California Tours** (⊠ 6986 La Jolla Blvd., 204, La Jolla, CA 92037, ☎ 619/454–7166, FAX 619/454–2703) has information and makes reservations with several companies offering whale-watching tours. **Eco-Tours Malarrimo** (⊠ Blvd. Zapata at entrance to Guerrero Negro, ☎ 115/7–02–50) conducts guided tours from Guerrero Negro to Scammon's Lagoon; two hours in a small boat watching the whales runs $40 per person.

LA PAZ

Travel agencies in the hotels and along Paseo Obregón offer tours of the city, daylong trips to Los Cabos, sportfishing, and boating excursions. **Baja Expeditions** (☞ Guerrero Negro, *above*) offers hotel and diving packages and live-aboard dive boat trips to the islands, seamount, and wrecks.

LORETO

Picnic cruises to Isla Coronado, excursions into the mountains to visit the San Javier Mission and view prehistoric rock paintings, and day trips to Mulege can be arranged through hotels. **Alfredo's Sportfishing** (⊠ on malecón, Box 39, Loreto BCS 23880, ☎ 113/5–01–65,

FAX 113/5−05−90) can arrange tours as well as fishing excursions and is a good source of general information on the area.

LOS CABOS

With the water as the main attraction, most tours involve getting into a boat and diving or fishing. It's a must to take a ride to El Arco, the natural rock arches at Land's End, and Playa de Amor (Lover's Beach), where the Sea of Cortés blends into the Pacific. Nearly all hotels have frequent boat trips there; the fare depends on how far your hotel is from the point. Tour boats dock by the arts-and-crafts market in the Cabo San Lucas marina, and the sidewalk along the water is lined with salesmen offering boat rides. Check out the boat before you pay, and make sure there are life jackets on board.

Contactours (⊠ Hotel Finisterra, ☎ 114/3−33−33, and at several other hotels) and **TourCabos** (⊠ Plaza los Cabos, Paseo San José, ☎ 114/2−09−82, FAX 114/2−20−50) offer tours of the region, boat trips, horseback riding, and information on water sports. **Baja Travel Adventures** (☎ 114/3−19−34) runs trips to Todos Santos and La Paz and individually designed tours; ask at the hotel tour desks if there's no answer when you phone.

Pez Gato (⊠ on marina near Plaza Las Glorias hotel, ☎ 114/3−37−97) has sailing and sunset cruises on a 46-foot catamaran, with live music and free drinks ($50 per person), as well as snorkeling and sailing tours ($30 per person). All trips depart from the marina in Cabo San Lucas; call or stop by the booth at the marina for further information.

Visitor Information

Cabo San Lucas (⊠ Av. Hidalgo at Guerrero, ☎ 114/3−41−80, FAX 114/3−22−110). **La Paz** (⊠ Mariano Abasolo s/n, ☎ 112/4−01−00, FAX 112/4−07−22; on malecón near Calle 16 de Septiembre, ☎ 112/2−59−39). **San José del Cabo** (⊠ Zaragoza at Mijares, no phone).

4 Sonora

Cowboys continue to ride the range in Mexican ranch country, but beef has been upstaged by beaches in this northwestern state's economy. Along with relatively unspoiled (and inexpensive) coastal towns such as Kino Bay and Guaymas, Sonora's lures include colonial Alamos, an immaculate former silver mining center, and a sprinkling of Spanish missions.

By Dan Goss Anderson

Updated by Susana Sedgwick

SONORA, MEXICO'S second-largest, second-richest state, is a vacationland with its own band of devoted followers. Many are from Arizona, for whom the beaches of Sonora, its sister state, are closer, cheaper, and more interesting than those of southern California. This stretch of the Mexican northwest is reminiscent of the old Wild West in the United States. Ranchero ballads, not unlike country-and-western songs, blare from saloons and radios. Irrigated ranchlands feed Mexico's finest beef cattle, and rivers flowing westward from the Sierra Madre are diverted by giant dams to water the once-barren land that now produces cotton, sugarcane, and vegetables. Hermosillo, Sonora's capital, bustles with agricultural commerce in the midst of the fertile lands that turn barren again toward the coast.

Mexico Highway 15 begins at the border town of Nogales, Sonora, adjacent to the U.S. town of Nogales, Arizona. It passes southward through Hermosillo and reaches the Gulf of California (also called the Sea of Cortés) at Guaymas, 418 kilometers (261 miles) from the Arizona border. The Sonoran desert dominates the landscape through northern Sonora, as it does in southern Arizona. Long stretches of flat scrub are punctuated by brown hills and mountains, towering saguaros, and organ-pipe cacti. Highway 15 continues southward after Guaymas, as the landscape gradually takes on a more tropical aspect, and finally enters the state of Sinoloa just north of the city of Los Mochis. Except in the mountains, the entire region is uncomfortably warm between May and late September, with afternoon temperatures sometimes exceeding 120°F.

In 1540 Francisco Vázquez de Coronado, governor of the provinces to the south, became the first Spanish leader to walk the plains of Sonora. More than a century later, Father Eusebio Francisco Kino led a missionary expedition to Sonora and what is now southern Arizona (an area referred to historically as the Pimeria Alta), founding several towns and missions there. Although Alamos, in the south of Sonora, boomed with silver-mining wealth in the late 17th century, no one paid much attention to the northern part of the region for the next three centuries; it was not part of the Mexican territory ceded to the American flag after the War of 1847. Sonora became a haven for Arizona outlaws, and international squabbles bloomed and faded over the next decades as officials argued over issues such as the right to pursue criminals across the border. During the last quarter of the 19th century, Porfirio Díaz, dictator of Mexico for three decades, finally moved to secure the state by settling it.

For Don Porfirio, however, developing Sonora may have been a mistake: The revolutionaries who later overthrew him came from here. In fact, Mexico was ruled by the Sonora dynasty for nearly a quarter of a century and, until the tragic 1994 assassination of Sonora native son Luis Donaldo Colosio, the ruling party candidate for president, it appeared likely that a Sonoran would soon control the destiny of the country again. The Mexican Revolution brought prosperity to the state, and it continues to thrive. Its inhabitants have adopted modern farming techniques that allow them to grow enough wheat not only for Mexico but for export as well.

Pleasures and Pastimes

Beaches

There are lively hotels and restaurants by the shores of San Carlos, Guaymas, Puerto Peñasco, and Bahía Kino, but those willing to take the time to get there and forgo facilities will also find miles and miles of more secluded beaches that run along the Sea of Cortés. All the main beaches of the state have paved access roads.

Dining

Sonoran cuisine is distinguished by the excellent quality of its steaks as well as the freshness of its fish. There are no five-star restaurants in the state, but shrimp aficionados will find plenty to like in Sonora (especially in Guaymas), as will those drawn to traditional Mexican dishes such as enchiladas, burritos, tamales, and *carne asada* (grilled meat); indeed, the style of Mexican cooking with which most Americans are familiar derives from this region. Casual dress (but not beachwear) is always acceptable, and reservations are rarely needed.

CATEGORY	COST*
$$$$	over $35
$$$	$25–$35
$$	$15–$25
$	under $15

per person, excluding drinks, service, and tax

Lodging

In Sonora you may find yourself sleeping in a converted convent in fashionable Alamos, growing a Hemingway beard in a beach bungalow at Bahía Kino, or luxuriating in a five-star resort in San Carlos. Lodging in Sonora is no longer the bargain it once was, but prices are still lower here than for comparable accommodations in the better-known vacation spots in other parts of Mexico.

CATEGORY	COST*
$$$$	over $90
$$$	$60–$90
$$	$25–$60
$	under $25

All prices are for a standard double room, excluding tax.

Missions

Nestled among the hills and river valleys of Sonora are a handful of almost forgotten missions founded by Jesuit fathers in the 17th and early-18th centuries, and completed by the Franciscans in the late-18th and 19th centuries. Some of the churches, such as San Ignacio, still service the small agricultural communities around them, whereas others, like Cocospera, are no more than a vestige of a remarkable past.

Great Itineraries

Numbers in the text correspond to numbers in the margin and on the Sonora map.

Because it is so diverse, the state of Sonora requires a visit of eight days or more to really do it justice. Those who have less time must decide whether seashore, mountains, or missions are most important.

IF YOU HAVE 3 DAYS

Take Highway 15 south from Nogales to **Magdalena** ⑤; stop off to see the church where the bones of missionary explorer Padre Kino are displayed. If you're interested in churches, you might spend the night in this area; nine missions founded by Father Kino are accessible from here by car. Then continue south on the same highway to the state capital, **Hermosillo** ⑥, where a variety of good hotels and restaurants are available. Overnight here and spend the next morning touring the city or browsing through the Centro Ecologico, of special interest to children. After lunch, drive west on Highway 16 to **Bahía Kino** ⑦, a perfect beach retreat, for a one- or two-night stay. It's about six hours from Kino Bay back to the Arizona border.

An alternative three-day itinerary would be to cross the U.S. border at Lukeville-Sonoyta, explore the lunar-like regions of the **Sierra del Pinacate** ②, and then cool off on the beaches of **Puerto Peñasco** ③ for the rest of that day and the next one. Then take Highway 2 to **Magdalena,** a drive of about 2¾ hours, where you can stop for lunch and a visit to the Kino shrine before heading north on Highway 15 to **Nogales** ① and an afternoon of shopping before crossing the U.S. border.

IF YOU HAVE 5 DAYS

Take Highway 15 from Nogales to **Guaymas** ⑨; the drive will take about six or seven hours. Exploring the town of Guaymas and the adjacent resort area of **San Carlos** ⑩ will give you plenty to do for two days and nights. Continue south and then east for 3½ hours to charming colonial **Alamos** ⑪, in the foothills of the Sierra Madre. After one or two nights in Alamos, head back north; you might overnight in Bahía Kino on your way home.

IF YOU HAVE 8 DAYS

Combine the second of the three-day itineraries with the five-day itinerary, but stop off at Hermosillo on the way down to Guaymas. Those with additional time might want to take a short side trip from Alamos to **Aduana** ⑫, where a very wealthy silver mine once thrived.

When to Tour

The temperatures in Sonora in the summer months are as high as they are in southern Arizona, so unless you are prepared to broil, plan your trip around the months between September and May.

EXPLORING

The landscape of Sonora is as vast and varied as the state itself. From the seemingly endless tracks of Sonoran desert that finally tumble into the Sea of Cortés to the mountains of the Sierra Madre and the agricultural fields and valleys that produce its livestock, Sonora is a place of dramatic contrasts.

Mexico Highway 2 enters Sonora's far northwest from Baja California, paralleling the U.S. border. There are several crossing points, but most people entering from the United States do so at Nogales, which is also a point of entry for winter fruit and vegetables exported to the United States.

Nogales

❶ *About 100 km (60 mi) south of Tucson via Highway 19, on the Arizona-Mexico border.*

Bustling Nogales can become fairly rowdy on weekend evenings, when underage Tucsonans head south of the border to drink. It has some good restaurants, however, and visitors can find fine-quality crafts and furnishings in addition to the usual border schlock. If you're just coming for the day, it's best to park on the Arizona side of the border (you'll see many guarded lots that cost about $4 for the day) and walk across. Practically all the good shopping is within easy strolling distance of the border.

The shopping area centers mainly on Avenida Obregón, which begins a few blocks west of the border entrance and runs north–south; just follow the crowds. Most of the good restaurants near the border are also on Obregón. Take Obregón as far south as you like; you'll know

Sonora

Golfo de Santa Clara

Sierra del Pinacate 2

Sonoyta

ARIZONA

Bahía del Adaír

8

Puerto Peñasco 3

Bahía de San Jorge

Río Concepción

Coborca

Nogales 1

El Desemboque

Imuris

15

Cocospera 4

Agua Prieta

2

Magdalena

Cananea

5

Santa Ana

Isla Angel de la Guarda

El Dátil

Arizpe

Nacozari de García

Bavispe

Carbo

SONORA

Moctezuma

Isla del Tiburón

15

Ures

Papigochic

Punta Chueca 8

Hermosillo 6

Sonora

Bahía Kino 7

San Rafael

BAJA CALIFORNIA NORTE

Cienaguita

Tecoripa

Golfo

San Carlos 10

Guaymas 9

Santa Rosalía

de

Yaqui

CHIHUAHUA

1

Pta. Concepción

Isla Lobos

Rosario

BAJA CALIFORNIA SUR

California

Ciudad Obregón

Rosarito

Mayo

Navojoa

Aduana 12

Huatabampo

Alamos 11

SIERRA DE LA GIGANTA

Loreto

Isla Carmen

15

KEY

Rail Lines

Ferry Lines

Río Fuerte

0   50 miles

1

N

Villa Constitución

75 km

El Fuerte

San Blas

you have entered workaday Mexico when the shops are no longer fronted by smiling, English-speaking hucksters trying to hustle you in the door ("Take a look! Good prices!").

Dining

$$$ ✕ **El Balcon de la Roca.** This elegant restaurant on the sprawling second floor of a stately old stone house has huge beamed ceilings, fireplaces, and a variety of dining rooms to choose from. The best place for a margarita is on the balcony overlooking a charming patio with magnolia trees and a gurgling fountain. Among the excellent variety of meat and seafood dishes is *carne tampiqueña,* an assortment of grilled meats that comes with a chile relleno and an enchilada. The *queso la Roca* (seasoned potato slices covered with melted cheese) makes a fine starter. ⊠ *Calle Elias 91,* ☎ *631/2–07–60, 631/2–08–91. AE, DC, MC, V.*

$$ ✕ **El Cid.** The menu here offers a wide selection—everything from sandwiches and burgers to fresh seafood. There is candlelight dining and dancing with live music on Friday and Saturday nights and mariachi music on Sunday evenings. ⊠ *Av. Obregón 124,* ☎ *631/2–64–00. AE, MC, V.*

$$ ✕ **El Greco.** As its name suggests, this place has a distinctly Mediter-
★ ranean ambience, but with a Mexican colonial twist. You can choose from excellent Greek salads, Alaskan king crab, or typical American and Mexican fare. Free margaritas come with lunch and dinner. ⊠ *Av. Obregón 152,* ☎ *631/2–42–59. AE, MC, V.*

$ ✕ **Elvira.** The free shot of tequila that comes with each meal will whet your appetite for Elvira's fine fish dishes, chicken mole, or chile rellenos. This large, friendly restaurant (divided into more intimate dining areas) is at the very end of Avenida Obregón next to the border and popular with frequent visitors to Nogales. ⊠ *Av. Obregón 1,* ☎ *631/2–47–73. Reservations not accepted. DC, MC, V.*

Shopping

Nogales is one of Sonora's best shopping areas, with a wide selection of handicrafts, furnishings, and jewelry. At the more informal shops, bargaining is not only acceptable but expected. The following shops, however, tend to have fixed prices: **El Sarape** (⊠ Av. Obregón 161, ☎ 631/2–03–09) specializes in sterling-silver jewelry from Taxco and designer clothing for women. **Mickey & CIA** (⊠ Av. Obregón 128–130, ☎ 631/2–22–99) has two floors of handcrafted Mexican treasures, *equipale* (pigskin) furniture, Talavera ceramic dishes, pottery, glassware, and liquors. **Firenze** (⊠ Av. Obregón 111, ☎ 613/2–22–52) features gifts, fine perfumes and beauty products, and crafts. East of the railroad tracks and off the beaten tourist path, **El Changarro** (⊠ Calle Elias 93, ☎ 613/2–05–45) carries high-quality furniture, antiques, pottery, and handwoven rugs.

Sierra del Pinacate

❷ *50 km (31 mi) west of Lukeville-Sonoyta.*

Midway between the Arizona border and the beach town of Puerto Peñasco is Sierra del Pinacate, a Biosphere Reserve International Park most notable for its rock formations and craters so moonlike that they were used for training the Apollo astronauts. The diversity of the lava flows makes Pinacate unique, as does the striking combination of Sonoran desert and volcanic field. Highlights of the area include Santa Clara peak, a little more than 4,000 feet high and 2.5 million years old, and El Elegante crater, 1 mile across and 750 feet deep, created by a giant steam eruption 150,000 years ago. There are no facilities of any kind at Pinacate; you'll need to bring your own water (take plenty of it), food, and extra gasoline, as well as a good map; you can get one in Arizona at Si Como No bookstore in Ajo or at Tucson's Map and Flag Center, or in Mexico at CEDO (☞ Puerto Peñasco, *below*). A high-clearance vehicle is strongly advised, and four-wheel drive is recommended. Camping is allowed with a permit obtainable from the Oficina Sierra del Pinacate in Sonoyta, a block south of the border crossing on the west side of the street. Visitors must register at the park entrance.

Summer temperatures can be blistering; the best time to visit is between November and March, when daytime temperatures hover between 60 and 90°F. Tours can be arranged through the tourism office in Puerto Peñasco; an excellent naturalist-led tour in English is also available from **Ajo Stage Lines** (✉ 1041 Solana St., Ajo, AZ 85321, ☎ 520/387–6559 or 800/942–1981). As with protected wilderness areas in the United States, no animals, plants, or archaeological artifacts may be removed.

Puerto Peñasco

❸ *104 km (65 mi) south of the Arizona border at Lukeville on Mexico Highway 8.*

Set at the northern end of the Sea of Cortés, this is a popular wintering spot for American RVers and retirees, and a favorite weekend getaway for beach-seeking Arizonans—especially college kids during school breaks. It was dubbed Rocky Point by British explorers in the 18th century, and that's the name most Americans know it by today. The Mexican immigration laws are relaxed for tourists crossing in this so-called free zone; simply drive through (but don't neglect to get Mexican auto insurance—crucial in case of an accident).

The town was established about 1927, when Mexican fishermen found abundant shrimp beds in the area and American John Stone built the first hotel; Al Capone was a frequent visitor during the Prohibition era, when he was hiding from U.S. law. Puerto Peñasco is rather faceless, but the "old town" area has a number of interesting shopping stalls, fish markets, and restaurants. The real draw, however, is the miles of sandy beaches, often punctuated by stretches of black, volcanic rock that get inundated at high tide. Rocky Point boasts one of the largest tide changes in the world—as much as 23 feet, depending on the season. At low tide the rocky stretches of coastline are great for poking among countless shallow tidal pools inhabited by such local marine life as octopus, shrimp, and starfish. This coastline will probably change very soon, however; the construction of the $150 million Marina Peñasco—a complex that will eventually include a shopping center, luxury hotel, condos and villas, a yacht club, and a 200-slip marina—is designed to attract a more upscale U.S. clientele, and other developers are waiting in the wings.

The northern Gulf area forms a desert-coast ecosystem unmatched in the Western Hemisphere, and scientists from both the United States and Mexico conduct active research programs at the **Desert and Ocean Studies Center** (known as CEDO, its acronym in Spanish), on the eastern edge of town. You can tour the facility to learn about its history and current projects, or come by to pick up a tide calendar—useful if you're planning beach activities. *Turn east at the municipal building and follow signs for Caborca Rd., where there will be signs for Las Conchas Beach and CEDO.* ☎ 638/3–54–03. *Tour hours are posted on the door.*

| NEED A BREAK? | No stay in Puerto Peñasco is complete without a visit to **Flavio's** seafood café, down by the fish markets. Stop by for some succulent fresh oysters and a quick tequila. If you have kids or a sweet tooth, try the ice cream at **Thrifty's** across from the church. |

Dining and Lodging

$$$ ✕ **Puesta del Sol.** A perfect place to see the sun set, with plenty of out-
★ door seating on a patio overlooking the beach, Puesta del Sol offers
many seafood dishes and soups, with appetizers for the American
palate. The fish mornay (with a creamy cheese sauce) is good, as is the
grilled lobster—and the margaritas are to die for. ⊠ *Hotel Playa
Bonita, Paseo Balboa,* ☎ *638/3–25–86. MC, V.*

$$–$$$ ✕ **Costa Brava.** This small, split-level restaurant has excellent service
and a great view overlooking the Gulf. For four, try the excellent
marinera de la casa, a seafood combination featuring octopus, shrimp,
sea snails, and clams. The Shrimp Carlos V—broiled fish and shrimp
stuffed with cheese and wrapped in bacon—is also very tasty. Hun-
dreds of business cards on the wall testify to this place's popularity with
Americans. ⊠ *Blvd. Kino and 1° de Junio,* ☎ *638/3–31–30. MC, V.*

$$ ✕ **The Friendly Dolphin.** You'll recognize this charming downtown
spot by the bright blue dolphins decorating its doorway. Inside, the place
feels like a wealthy Mexican family's home, with ornately stuccoed ceilings, wood-paneled windows, and exquisite hand-painted tiles; interesting old photographs, including some of Emiliano Zapata and Pancho
Villa, line the hallways. Gaston, the owner, can often be found on the
premises singing in an operatic baritone as rich and robust as the food
he serves. Unique family recipes include foil-wrapped shrimp or fish
prepared *estilo delfin*—steamed in orange juice, herbs, and spices. An
upstairs porch overlooks the harbor. ⊠ *Av. Alcantar 44,* ☎ *638/3–
26–08. AE, DC, MC, V.*

$$ ✕ **La Curva.** This friendly family restaurant, featuring great Mexican
food, is easy to spot if you look for the mermaid on the sign. Turn east
where the railroad tracks cross the main road into town. ⊠ *Blvd. Kino
and Comonfort,* ☎ *638/3–34–70. Reservations advised for dinner in
winter and on holiday weekends. MC, V.*

$$ ✕ **La Casa del Capitan.** Perched atop Rocky Point's tallest "rock," this
restaurant has the best views over the bay and the town below. There's
inside dining, but the long outdoor porch overlooking the sea is the
place to be. A wide-ranging menu includes everything from nachos and
quesadillas to flaming brandied jumbo shrimp. ⊠ *Follow Blvd. Benito Juárez to* LA CASA DEL CAPITAN *sign and head up the steep hill,*
☎ *683/3–60–27. Reservations not accepted. No credit cards.*

$$$–$$$$ ▥ **Plaza Las Glorias.** One of a chain of hotels in Mexico, Plaza Las
Glorias is the first lodging of its kind to arrive on the horizon at Puerto
Peñasco. Changing the face of the town, this soaring monument to Mex-
ico's desire to promote tourism at any cost sits like a sand-colored fortress
overlooking the beach. The open, marble-floored lobby with its tow-
ering quadrangular ceiling and bamboo-covered skylights draws gasps
of admiration from the busloads of tourists who have started to flock
to the hotel after its inauguration in 1995. Rooms are well appointed,
many of them with kitchenettes; all offer ocean views. The hotel sells
condominiums and time shares and is in the process of putting in a
marina and shopping center. ⊠ *Paseo Las Glorias, Las Explanadas
83550,* ☎ *638/3–60–10, 638/3–60–27, or 800/544–4686. 210
rooms. Restaurant, pool. AE, MC, V.*

$$$ ▥ **Playa Bonita.** One of the first three hotels in Rocky Point, Playa Bonita
offers clean, comfortable rooms; ask for one facing the hotel's broad,
sandy beach. This place is very popular with Americans, who also enjoy
the Puesta del Sol restaurant (☞ Dining, *above*). An RV park offers
200 hookups at $16 a day. ⊠ *Paseo Balboa 100, 83550,* ☎ *638/3–
25–86; 520/994–4475 or 800/569–1797 in the U.S. 76 rooms,
2 suites. Restaurant, bar, beach. MC, V.*

$$ 🏨 **Costa Brava.** All the rooms in this small, clean, and economical down-
town hotel overlook the Gulf. Right down the street are the fish mar-
kets, popular with those who like to bring the catch of the day back
across the border. ⊠ *Malecón Kino and 1° de Julio, 83550,* ☎ *638/3–
41–00 or 638/3–41–01,* 🗵 *638/3–36–21. 25 rooms. Bar. MC, V.*

Nightlife and the Arts

Nightlife tends to be spontaneous and informal in Puerto Peñasco, al-
though the Playa Bonita hotel offers live music that attracts an older
crowd. A younger group tends to congregate along the beaches near
Manny's Beach Club (☞ Watersports, *below*), where recorded music
is always blaring. Manny's is the place for those who don't want to
put too much distance between the water's edge and their next mar-
garita; it's right on the beach, with signs like NO SHOES, NO SHIRT, NO
PROBLEM. The food is nothing special, but as the quintessential beach
hangout for all ages, Manny's is not to be missed.

Outdoor Activities and Sports

WATERSPORTS

Manny's Beach Club (⊠ Av. Coahuila and Blvd. Matamoros, ☎ 638/3–
36–05) offers an all-day fishing trip in the Gulf for $40, as well as day
and sunset cruises. At **China Sea Sailing and Diving** (⊠ Paseo Victor
Estrella, ☎ 638/3–54–50 or 520/566–7614 in Arizona) you can rent
diving equipment or receive snorkeling and scuba instruction.

Cocospera

4 *About 104 km (65 mi) southeast of Nogales, between Imuris and
Cananea.*

Cocospera is one of the two dozen churches established in the state of
Sonora and Arizona by Father Eusebio Francisco Kino between 1687
and 1711; the crumbling adobe mission sits on a bluff above an oak
forest and farmlands in a mountain pass in the Sierra Madre Occidental.
To get here, take Highway 15 Libre to Highway 2.

Magdalena

5 *25 km (13 mi) south of Imuris, 96 km (60 mi) from Nogales.*

The grave of Father Eusebio Francisco Kino was discovered in Mag-
dalena in 1966. His remains are in a mausoleum across the plaza from
Santa Maria Magdalena de Buquivaba, one of the missions he founded.
A $1 million monument to the memory of this pioneer priest also stands
here. A number of shops surround the plaza, selling curios, blankets,
and religious artifacts; stop in at the bakery for some excellent sweet
rolls and bread. Magdalena is now also known as the final resting place
of its beloved native son, slain presidential candidate Luis Donaldo Colo-
sio, whose statue also presides over the plaza.

If you're really interested in Spanish missions and in rural Mexican
life as it has been lived for centuries, drive just a few kilometers north
of Magdalena on a clearly marked dirt road to **San Ignacio,** another
of Father Kino's churches, still in use in a tiny Mexican farming
village.

Hermosillo

6 *185 km (115 mi) south of Magdalena on Highway 15.*

Hermosillo (population about 600,000) is the capital of Sonora, a sta-
tus it has held on and off since 1831. It is the seat of the state univer-
sity and benefits from that institution's cultural activities. Although those

who know a bit of Spanish might think the city's name means "little beauty," it actually honors José Mariá González Hermosillo, one of the leaders in Mexico's War of Independence. Settled in 1742 by Captain Augustín de Vildosola and a contingent of 50 soldiers, Hermosillo was originally called Pitic, the Pima Indian name for "the place where two rivers meet." The city's most prestigious neighborhood—home to the governor and U.S. consul, among other prominent citizens—still bears the name Pitic. Located immediately north of the highway into town and just behind the Hotel Bugambilia, the area is worth an hour's stroll to view the creative handling of concrete, tile, and other materials in the homes of Hermosillo's more affluent residents.

A business center for the state of Sonora, Hermosillo is largely modern, but some lovely plazas and parks hark back to a more graceful postcolonial past. Although Hermosillo is usually just considered a jumping-off point for Bahía Kino or Guaymas, it has a number of attractions in its own right, as well as the best accommodations and restaurants until you reach Guaymas. The city's main boulevard is lined with monuments to Sonora's famous sons: Adolfo de la Huerta, Alvaro Obregón, Plutarco Elías Calles, and Abelardo Rodríguez (after whom the boulevard is named), all presidents of the country after the revolution (Rodríguez also served as governor of Sonora). At the center of town, the **Plaza Zaragoza** boasts the impressive **Catedral de San Agustín** (1878), recently regilded at great expense. Across from the cathedral is the **Palacio de Gobierno del Estado,** its graceful courtyard surrounded by somewhat disjunctive modern murals depicting Sonoran history, and between the two buildings sits an ornate Victorian gazebo. On the south edge of town, the **Plaza de los Tres Pueblos** marks the original settlement.

Two museums are worth a visit. Overlooking the city, on the Cerro la Campana (Hill of Bells), the **Museo de Sonora,** a former penitentiary, now hosts a variety of regional history displays; you can also tour the tiny, dark prison cells. The **Museo de la Universidad de Sonora** (on Blvds. Luis Encinas and Rosales) has interesting exhibits of pre-Columbian artifacts. On the highway south of town, stop at the **Centro Ecologico,** a zoo modeled after the Arizona-Sonora Desert Museum in Tucson. (It's best visited November through March because of summer heat.) If you don't feel like walking through the entire zoo, which is rather spread out, consider arranging for a golf cart by calling the office of tourism. ☉ *Museums and Centro Ecologico Wed.–Sun. 9–3.*

Dining and Lodging

$$$ ✕ **Xochimilco.** This large and friendly place, which offers indoor and outdoor dining, is deeply shaded by large fiddle-leaf figs and yucateca trees on a narrow side street in the southern part of town (from Rosales, follow the sign near the Oxxo store). Popular with locals and regulars from across the border, Xochimilco serves well-prepared typical Sonoran dishes. ✉ *Av. Obregón 5,* ☎ *62/50–40–89. AE, MC, V.*

$$ ✕ **El Chalet de la Guitarra.** This small, immaculate restaurant specializes in pastas and other Italian dishes, served in ample portions. There's live music nightly. ✉ *Just off Blvd. Kino, at Villareal, across from B.F. Goodrich,* ☎ *62/14–91–41. MC, V.*

$$ ✕ **Hotel Bugambilia Restaurant.** A small dining room with beamed ceilings and red-checked tablecloths and curtains, this cheerful place serves excellent tortilla soup and Mexican-style veal cutlets. For breakfast, try the *chilaquiles con huevos* (chopped tortillas, cooked in a red chile sauce, topped with scrambled or fried eggs), a specialty of the house. ✉ *Blvd. Kino 712,* ☎ *62/14–50–50. Reservations not accepted. AE, MC, V.*

$$ ✕ **La Siesta.** This family-run inn, located in the Siesta Motel, is best known for its fine cuts of Sonoran beef. ⊠ *Blvd. Kino Norte and 1° de Mayo,* ☎ *62/14–39–89. Reservations not accepted. MC, V.*

$$$ ▥ **Fiesta Americana.** This full-service property is the largest in town and popular among business travelers. The decor is predictable, but some rooms have excellent views, and the beds are large and firm. ⊠ *369 Blvd. Kino, 83010,* ☎ *62/15–18–20; for U.S. reservations, 800/FIESTA–1;* FAX *62/15–37–31 or 62/15–14–90. 222 rooms. Restaurant, cafeteria, lobby bar, pool, hot tub, tennis courts, dance club, travel services. AE, MC, V.*

$$$ ▥ **Holiday Inn Hermosillo.** Two-thirds of the attractive rooms in this contemporary Spanish-style hotel look out on extensive, well-kept gardens and a good-size pool. The staff is geared toward accommodating the many Mexican business travelers who stay here. ⊠ *Blvd. Kino and Ramon Corral, 83010,* ☎ *62/14–45–70. 144 rooms with shower. Restaurant, bar, pool, nightclub, travel services. AE, MC, V.*

$$ ▥ **Hotel Gandara.** One of the old traditional spots in Hermosillo, this hotel, with its palm trees, gardens, and colonnades, has the charm of Old Spain still clinging to it. You can stay in bungalows or in conventional-style hotel rooms; all offer cable TV and coffeemakers. ⊠ *Blvd. E. Kino 1000,* ☎ *62/14–44–14 or 62/14–42–40,* FAX *62/14–99–26. 154 rooms. Restaurant, coffee shop, cocktail lounge, pool. AE, MC, DC, V.*

Nightlife and the Arts

Hermosillo is home to several lively night spots: **Bar Ali Baba** at the Plaza Pitic (⊠ Blvds. Kino and Roman Yocupicio, ☎ 62/14–43–87) and, for the younger set, **Blocky'O Disco** (⊠ Blvd. Rodríguez at Aguascalientes, no phone).

Outdoor Activities and Sports

HUNTING

Hunting for birds (duck, dove, and pigeon) and deer draws an increasing number of Americans to Sonora every winter. The bird season is October through March, and deer season is during November and December. Hunting is not permitted without a Mexican guide; a reliable one in Hermosillo is Alberto Noriega at **Sonora Outfitters** (⊠ Aguascalientes 132, ☎ 62/14–10–01, 62/16–47–01, or 62/14–82–52). In Guaymas, contact **Solimar Hunting Adventures** (☎ 622/4–00–15).

Shopping

In the downtown markets of Hermosillo, particularly along Avenidas Serdán and Monterrey, you can buy anything from blankets and candles to wedding attire, as well as a variety of *charro* (Mexican cowboy) items; the variety of goods concentrated in this area equals what you'll find in Nogales, and the prices are better.

En Route　Drive from Hermosillo through flat agricultural land and dusty vineyards to where the desert finally meets the sea and the monochrome landscape gives way to a refreshing palette of colors.

Bahía Kino

❼ *104 km (65 mi) west of Hermosillo on Highway 16.*

On the shore of the Sea of Cortés lies Bahía Kino (Kino Bay), home to the prettiest beaches in northwest Mexico. For many years, Bahía Kino was undiscovered except by RV owners and other aficionados of the unspoiled; but a great change has taken place in the last decade as Arizonans have begun to build condos here. Bahía Kino itself is divided into

Kino Viejo (Old Kino), the Mexican village, and Kino Nuevo (New Kino), where the condos, RV sites, and other typical tourist facilities are.

Consider taking a run across the narrow channel to **Isla del Tiburón** (Shark Island), which is being developed into one of the finest wildlife and game refuges in North America. Permission to visit Tiburón may be obtained from the Port Captain, at the end of the main street in Kino Viejo. Ask at any of the area hotels or RV parks where to find a reliable guide. Only the Seri Indians, for whom Isla del Tiburón is a traditional fishing ground, need no permit. You might see some of these Indians at Bahía Kino selling their fine ironwood carvings of animals (☞ Punta Chueca, *below*). Turtle hunting used to be an integral part of the Seri culture, and the capture of a turtle was once the subject of a ritual observance, but these creatures are now protected by law. (Note: The Seris are sensitive about having their picture taken. The polite thing to do is to ask their permission before snapping.)

Dining and Lodging

$$$ ✕ **El Pargo Rojo.** The best-known restaurant in town has fish and fishnets decorating its two rooms (with a small bandstand for musicians). The catch of the day varies, but you can depend on excellent dishes, including such classics as a brimming shrimp cocktail for starters and fresh lobster any way you want it. ☒ *Kino Nuevo, Blvd. Mar de Cortés 1426,* ☎ *624/2–02–05. MC, V.*

$ ✕ **Restaurant Kino Bay.** Owned by an American, this clean, comfortable family restaurant overlooks the bay. One of the few places serving breakfast, lunch, and dinner, it's a perfect spot for coffee, morning pancakes, and pelican viewing. ☒ *Blvd. Mar de Cortés, Kino Nuevo,* ☎ *624/20–04–9. Reservations not accepted. No credit cards.*

$ ✕ **Restaurant Marlin.** This restaurant in Kino Viejo is only hard to find the first time; after that, you will return frequently, drawn by the clean, unpretentious atmosphere and congenial service—not to mention margaritas as big as fishbowls. After serving you superb seafood dishes such as *sopa de siete mares* (soup of the seven seas) or *jaiba a la diabla* (deviled crab), your waiter might produce a guitar and serenade you free of charge. ☒ *Calle Tastiota and Calle Guaymas,* ☎ *624/2–01–11. Reservations not accepted. No credit cards.*

$$$ ▢ **Posada Santa Gemma.** On a beautiful strip of beach, these eclectically furnished two-story bungalows with kitchenettes, fireplaces, and spectacular views of the sea are ideal for families. Each has two bedrooms and sleeps four or five comfortably. Bring your own cooking utensils and settle in. ☒ *Blvd. Mar de Cortés, 83340,* ☎ *624/2–00–26. 14 bungalows. Beach. MC, V.*

$$ ▢ **Posada del Mar.** Across the street from the beach, set back from a rambling garden with a small swimming pool and winding walkways hewn from rock, this mission-style hotel was one of the first in Kino Nuevo. Antiques and Mexican art lend the place an Old World charm. ☒ *Blvd. Mar de Cortés and Creta, Box 132, 83340,* ☎ *624/2–01–55;* ☎ *62/18–12–17 in Hermosillo. 42 rooms, 2 suites, 4 bungalows. Restaurant, bar, pool. MC, V.*

$ ▢ **Kino Bay RV Park and Motel.** This small, friendly motel offers rooms with two double beds, microwaves, refrigerators, and sinks; in addition are 180 RV spaces with full hookups ($14). A barbecue area sits under a huge rubber tree. ☒ *At the end of the main road (reservations: Box 857, Hermosillo, 83000),* ☎ *624/2–02–16,* FAX *624/531–97. 8 rooms. MC, V.*

Punta Chueca

❽   *27 km (15 mi) north of Bahía Kino.*

This rustic Seri fishing village is well worth driving the bumpy, winding dirt road from Bahía Kino that leads to it: You'll pass exquisite vistas of the bay, empty beaches, and rolling mountains. The inhabitants of this community eke a meager living from sea and desert, much the way they have for hundred of years.

With fewer than one thousand Seris left in existence, this tribe represents an ancient culture on the verge of extinction. The Seris' love for their natural surroundings is evident in the necklaces that they have traditionally worn and now create to sell. Pretty little shells are wound into the shape of flowers and strung with wild desert seeds and tiny bleached snake vertebrae to result in delicate lei-like necklaces.

As you get out of your car and head toward the only "store" in town for a soda, be prepared to encounter a growing entourage of Seri women, dressed in colorful ankle-length skirts, their heads covered with scarves and their eager outstretched arms laden with necklaces for sale. As well as making necklaces, the Seri also carve figures from ironwood that represent the animal world around them, including dolphins, turtles, and pelicans. (Note: In recent years, many Mexican merchants have taken to machine-making large figures out of ironwood for the tourist trade, thereby seriously depleting the supply of the unique tree that grows only in the Sonoran desert. Make sure the ones you want to buy are made by the Seris.)

Guaymas

❾   *128 km (83 mi) south of Hermosillo.*

Long considered a quiet fishing town that drew only the most hardy, adventuresome travelers, in the past 20 years Guaymas has begun to emerge as a major commercial port and tourist destination. In many parts of Mexico, it can be said that the mountains come down to meet the sea; but at Guaymas, both the mountains and the desert abut the water. The clear air and the sun shining on the mountains provide panoramas of striking, ever-changing beauty.

The Spanish arrived in this "port of ports" as early as the mid-16th century. In 1701, two Jesuit priests, Father Francisco Eusebio Kino and his colleague Juan María Salvatierra, erected a mission base here intended to convert the native Guaimas, Seri, and Yaqui Indians.

Guaymas was officially declared a port in 1814 and became an important center of trade with Europe as well as within Mexico. In 1847, during the Mexican War, the town was attacked by naval forces from the United States and occupied for a year. In 1866, during Maximilian's brief reign, the harbor was taken over by the French. The waters of Guaymas Bay have been raided by pirates and plumbed by the once-legendary pearl divers.

Downtown, take a walk on the **malecón,** and look out over the bay at fishing boats loaded down with heavy black nets and the giant shrimp Guaymas is famous for. Fishing boats are only allowed to go out to sea between September and May so that the shrimp have time to replenish themselves. A small plaza along the port has a handsome bronze statue commemorating the local fishermen. After pushing your way through the throngs at the *mercado,* a daily municipal market, the 19th-century **Cathedral of San Fernando** offers a quiet respite. Or you might relax in the typical Mexican park across the street from the church, **Plaza 13 de Julio,** with its white, Moorish-style, lacy wrought-iron bandstand and time-worn, tree-shaded benches. Within walking distance is the **Plaza de los Tres Presidentes,** where, in front of the 1899 Palacio Municipal (City Hall), loom imposing statues of the three presidents of Mexico born in Sonora: Plutarco Elías Calles, Adolfo de la Huerta, and Abelardo Rodríguez.

The original **mission of San José de Guaymas** no longer stands, but another church was erected in its place at the end of the last century. During the past decade, it has been somewhat remodeled by a group of American Franciscan monks. The small church is located about 16 kilometers (10 miles) north of the center of the city, near a field of giant saguaro cactus (some measuring taller than 40 feet).

After you get too much history and downtown dust in your head, the only thing left is to soak up some sea at the various beaches in the area. Guaymas has not one but two bays: Bacochibampo (more commonly known as Guaymas Bay) and San Carlos (☞ *below*).

Dining and Lodging

$$ ✕ **Del Mar.** On the main street of town, this place does surf-and-turf Guaymas-style. A series of small dining rooms with beamed ceilings and tiled floors are separated by bricked arches, from which hang fishing nets and assorted flotsam and jetsam. The fish Santo Domingo (broiled local bass with mushrooms, green peppers, and melted cheese) is popular, as is the mixed seafood grill. ⊠ *Av. Serdán and Calle 17,* ☎ *622/4–02–25. AE, MC, V.*

$$ ✕ **Los Barcos.** Across the street from the harbor, Los Barcos offers a predictable seafood-and-steak menu. The main room is large and pseudo–beach casual, with picnic tables and overhead palm fronds and nets; there are also two smaller, more traditional dining rooms. Especially good is the house special seafood plate, which includes calamari, octopus, and shrimp in a white wine sauce. ⊠ *Malecón Malpica between Calles 21 and 22,* ☎ *622/2–76–50. Reservations not accepted. MC, V.*

$ ✕ **Los Delfines.** Overlooking the harbor in Guaymas, this spacious restaurant is a winner for the variety of no-frills fresh seafood it offers and for its postcard-perfect view of the water. Popular with the locals, who enjoy the *ambiente familiar* (family atmosphere), Los Delfines has a festive air, enhanced by strolling musicians; on weekends, a band starts playing in the afternoon. ⊠ *At the end of Blvd. Sanchez Taboada,* ☎ *622-2-92-30. Reservations not accepted. No credit cards.*

$$-$$$ 🏨 **Hotel Armida.** Close to the shops and restaurants of downtown Guaymas, this sand-colored hotel features a large, well-kept pool; a good coffee shop where locals gather for power breakfasts; and an excellent steak house, El Oeste. Rooms in the hotel's old section are dark, with ill-matched furnishings. The larger, brighter accommodations in the newest section, done in light wood, are worth the higher rates; many have balconies overlooking the pool. ⊠ *Carretera Internacional, Box 296, Guaymas 85420,* ☎ *622/4–30–35; for U.S. reservations 800/732–0780; ℻ 622/2–04–48. 80 rooms, 45 suites. 2 restaurants, coffee shop, bar, room service, pool, dance club, laundry service, car rental, airport shuttle. AE, MC, V.*

$$ 🏨 **Las Playitas.** The best deal in town, this combination trailer park–motel
★ on Guaymas Bay has plain but appealing rooms—with tinwork mirrors and beamed ceilings—opening out onto a cobblestoned, bougainvillea-lined path. Even if you don't sleep here, come for the lively, eclectically decorated restaurant and bar. The food is good and inexpensive, but if you'd rather eat what you caught that day, you can get it cooked up,

with trimmings added, for a small price. ⌧ *Carretera al Varadero Nacional, Guaymas 85420,* ☏ *622/1–52–27 or 622/1–51–96. 29 bungalows with shower, 93 RV spaces. Restaurant, bar, pool. MC, V.*

Nightlife and the Arts

Gathering spots in the area include the disco **Xanadu** (⌧ Malecón Malpica, ☏ 622/2–83–88) and, for the younger set, **Charles Baby** (⌧ Av. Serdán and Malecón, no phone).

Shopping

Plaza el Vigía, a huge shopping center on the main road from the north into Guaymas, has everything from groceries, film, toiletries, and clothes to household wares. In Guaymas itself, visit the **Casa de las Conchas** (⌧ Calle 23 and Av. Serdán, across from Plaza de los Tres Presidentes, ☏ 622/2–01–99) and sample beautiful handicrafts, as well as 400 to 500 types of seashells; right next door is a great little ice cream parlor.

San Carlos

⑩ *32 km (20 mi) northwest of Guaymas.*

Long considered an extension of Guaymas, this resort town—on the other side of the rocky peninsula that separates Bacochibampo Bay from San Carlos Bay—has a personality of its own. Whitewashed, red tile–roofed houses snuggle together along the water where countless yachts and motorboats are docked. The town is a laid-back favorite among professional anglers, North American tourists, and the time-share crowd, as well as wealthy Mexican families from Guaymas. There is a growing assortment of hotels, motels, and condominiums, as well as a country club with 18-hole golf course.

The overlapping of desert and tropical flora and fauna has created a fascinating diversity of species along this coast, particularly astonishing among marine life. More than 650 species of fish exist here; among those commonly caught are red snapper, marlin, corbina, yellowtail, sea bass, and flounder. Whales have been spotted in San Carlos Bay and there is an abundance of dolphins and pelicans. The water is calm and warm enough through October to enjoy excellent swimming for the whole family. Scuba, snorkeling, fishing, and boat excursions are very popular, too.

The quiet 5-kilometer (3-mile) stretch of sandy beach at **Los Algodones,** where the Howard Johnson's and Club Med are now, was in the 1960s a location site for the film *Catch 22.* Mexico's first man-made marina lies in the shadow of the jagged twin-peaked **Tetakawi mountain,** once a sacred site where Indian warriors gathered to gain spiritual strength. An interesting day trip can be made by boat out to the pristine **San Pedro Island,** where sea lions frolic on the rocks.

To reach San Carlos, take the road north of Guaymas for about 8 kilometers (5 miles), past the signs to your left for the turnoff to Bocachibampo Bay and the residential area of Miramar. Continue along for 24 kilometers (15 miles) on the four-lane Corredor Escenico (Scenic Corridor), completed in 1995 to replace an infamously bumpy road.

Dining and Lodging

$$ ✕ **Bananas.** American food (BLTs, burgers, fries) and Mexican fare—try the fish tacos—are served in a single large room with a peaked ceiling lined with palm fronds; there are a few seats in the entrance patio as well. A copy of Charlie Chaplin's 1924 carriage license hangs on the wall by the rest rooms. ⌧ *On the main road through San Carlos, no phone. Reservations not accepted. MC, V.*

$–$$ ✕ **Rosa's Cantina.** Picnic tables fill two large dining rooms where diners feast on ample breakfasts of *huevos rancheros* or eggs with chorizo. The tortilla soup is great for lunch or dinner. ✉ *Carretera San Carlos,* ☎ *622/6–03–07. Reservations not accepted. MC, V.*

$ ✕ **Jax Snax.** Located on the one main thoroughfare of San Carlos, this little place, which could be missed in the blink of an eye, tastes better than it looks. Open for breakfast, lunch, and dinner, it offers something quick and easy for all appetites. From pizza any way you request it (even cheeseless with veggies—vegan style), grilled shrimp with garlic, hamburgers, guacamole, and pancakes to hot coffee or cold Tecate, this is Mexican-American fast food for the taste buds. ✉ *Carretera San Carlos,* ☎ *622–6–02–70. Reservations not accepted. MC, V.*

$$$$ 🏨 **Club Med Sonora Bay.** Although San Carlos is expanding rapidly in its direction, this Club Med is still secluded from the main tourist area, its verdant 42-acre complex spread behind a large gate fronted by saguaro cactus. Accommodations are characteristically charming but plain, and the range of available activities is as great as one would expect from the chain. All meals, drinks, and tips—and many sports, such as sailing and scuba diving—are included. It's worth paying extra for the dawn horseback ride to the foothills of the nearby Sierra Madre. ✉ *Playa de los Algodones, San Carlos 85400,* ☎ *622/6–01–66, for U.S. reservations 800/CLUB–MED,* ℻ *622/6–00–70. 375 rooms. Restaurant, bar, pool, 2 saunas, beach, windsurfing, boating, golf course, horseback riding, 31 tennis courts. AE, MC, V. Closed Oct. 27–Mar. 12.*

$$$$ 🏨 **Howard Johnson's.** Forget the familiar orange roofs: This huge structure, rising from San Carlos Bay en route to Club Med, is thoroughly, strikingly, pink. Opened in 1992 by a wealthy Mexican family, this is the most luxurious hotel in Sonora, with an impressive marble-floor atrium lobby that opens out onto a large pool and beach. Rooms are done in an attractive contemporary style. All have safes and minibars, and rooms on the first two floors have balconies overlooking the sea. Children love the swimming-pool slide and horseback riding on the beautiful beach. ✉ *Mar Barmejo, 4, Los Algodones, Box 441, San Carlos 85506,* ☎ *622/6–07–94, for U.S. reservations 800/654–2000,* ℻ *622/6–07–77. 148 rooms, 25 suites. 2 restaurants, snack bar, 2 bars, 2 pools, hot tub, exercise room, 2 tennis courts, volleyball, horseback riding, car rental, travel services, beach. AE, MC, V.*

$$$ 🏨 **Playas de Cortés.** This fine, older hotel, built in the colonial style, is set amid lush gardens that lead down to the sea. The rooms are furnished with hand-carved antiques and many have fireplaces; unfortunately, accommodations are not as well maintained as they might be. To reach this hotel from the highway, take the turnoff for Colonia Miramar. ✉ *Bahía Bacochibampo, San Carlos 85506,* ☎ *622/1–12–24 or 622/1–10–48,* ℻ *622/1–01–35. 120 rooms. Restaurant, bar, pool, beach, tennis. AE, DC, MC, V.*

$$$ 🏨 **Plaza Las Glorias.** This condo-hotel complex, opened in 1994, overlooks the San Carlos marina. It's smaller than the Howard Johnson's, but nearly as impressive, and also caters to American tastes. Subtle pastels set a tasteful tone in the comfortable modern rooms. Most accommodations offer a tiny kitchenette; a few feature private hot tubs. ✉ *Plaza Comercial San Carlos 10, Planta Baja, San Carlos 85006,* ☎ *622/6–10–21 through 6–10–34,* ℻ *622/6–10–35. 87 rooms, 18 suites. Restaurant, snack bar, 3 pools, golf, baby-sitting, travel services, car rental. AE, MC, V.*

$$ \quad \boxdot \textbf{ Fiesta San Carlos.} This small hotel on the bay has mismatched furnishings but is clean and comfortable. Accommodations with kitchens are available. Breakfast is included in the room rate. ⊠ *San Carlos Bay, San Carlos 85006,* ☎ *622/6–02–29,* FAX *622/6–37–33. 33 rooms. Restaurant, bar, pool. MC, V.*

Nightlife and the Arts

Gathering spots in the area include **Bar El Yate** (⊠ Carretera San Carlos, ☎ 622/6–05–50), a sports bar at the Marina San Carlos; **Pappas Tappas** (⊠ Sector Creston, Lot 37, ☎ 622/6–07–07), a bar and grill; and **Ranas Ranas** (⊠ Carretera San Carlos, Km 9.5, ☎ 622/6–07–27), from which you can enjoy a view of the beach.

Outdoor Activities and Sports

DIVING

San Carlos Diving Center (⊠ main street of San Carlos, Apdo. 655, ☎ 622/6–00–49) runs diving excursions in the Sea of Cortés.

FISHING

Cortez Explorers (⊠ Carreterra Bahía, across from Marina San Carlos, ☎ 622/6–08–08, or 520/577–4982 in Tucson; Howard Johnson's, ☎ 622/6–07–94) runs deep-sea fishing trips as well as sunset cruises and diving charters. The company also rents Jet Skis and ski boats. Other smaller outfitters have boats for rent in the bay.

GOLF

Most hotels in the Guaymas–San Carlos area can arrange for temporary membership at the **San Carlos Country Club,** which has an 18-hole golf course.

HORSEBACK RIDING

Inquire at the Howard Johnson's about the few small *ranchitos* next door that have horses for hire.

Shopping

Lourdes Gift Shop (⊠ Plaza Comercial San Carlos 16, ☎ 622/6–00–22), next to the Plaza Las Glorias Hotel, offers an extensive selection of folk art, glassware, and clothing. **Sagitario's Gift Shop** (⊠ Carretera San Carlos 132, ☎ 622/6–00–90), across from the entrance to the San Carlos Country Club, features clothing and a variety of crafts, including wood carvings, baskets, and Talavera tile. **Kiamy's Gift Shop** (⊠ Carretera San Carlos, Km 10, ☎ 622/6–04–00) is like a bazaar, with something for everyone, at a reasonable price; silver jewelry, earrings, leather bags, Yaqui Indian masks, T-shirts, and caps, as well as a variety of ceramics can be found here.

Alamos

⑪ *53 km (32 mi) east of Navojoa, 257 km (160 mi) southeast of Guaymas.*

A Mexican national monument, Alamos is the most authentic colonial-style town in Sonora. It's set at the spot where the lower Sonoran desert meets the dry tropical forest in the foothills of the Sierra Madre Occidental, an area marked by rivers, cottonwoods (for which the town of Alamos is named), and evergreens.

Coronado camped here in 1540, and a Jesuit mission was established in 1630, but the town really boomed when silver was discovered in the area during the 1680s. Wealth from the mines financed Spanish expeditions to the north—as far as Los Angeles and San Francisco during the 1770s and 1780s—and the town became the capital of the state of Occidente, which combined the provinces of Sinaloa and Sonora, from 1827 to 1832. A government mint was established here in 1864. The mines closed by the end of the 19th century, and the town went into decline; but today, Alamos, with many houses beautifully restored by Americans who have settled here, serves as a showcase of its glorious past. A British visitor to the town in the early 19th century remarked on its cleanliness, and Alamos remains spotless today, with streets swept by local residents early every morning.

Points of interest include the imposing **cathedral** in the central Plaza las Armas, begun in 1787 on the site of a 17th-century Jesuit adobe church and completed in 1894. It is fronted by an ornate Moorish-style wrought-iron gazebo, brought from Mazatlán in 1904. To the west of the square, on Guadalupe Hill, is the Alamos **jail,** built around the turn of the century; visitors may tour the structure on certain days, and the shop by the prison entrance sells items such as bolo ties, belts, and key chains made by the inmates. Tours of the many beautiful **restored colonial homes** in town are also offered; the tourist office and all the local hotels have listings of the times and rates.

Not to be missed, the **Museo Costumbrista de Sonora** gives an excellent overview of the cultural history of the entire state of Sonora. The numerous well-marked (but only in Spanish) displays include artifacts from the nearby silver mines and coins from the mints of Alamos and Hermosillo, as well as typical examples of the clothing and furnishings of prominent local families. *Calle Guadalupe Victoria 1 (on Plaza las Armas),* ☎ *642/8–00–53.* ✉ *Free; donation suggested.* ☉ *Wed.–Sat. 9–1 and 3–6, Sun. 9–6.*

Dining and Lodging

$$$ ✕ **La Mansion Restaurant.** Opened in 1995, this restaurant dazzles with haute Spanish cuisine. Typical Iberian dishes like paella can be savored along with more unusual ones such as *pollo chilindron* (grilled chicken breast in a Serrano ham sauce). A varied vegetarian plate is also available, as are desserts for all palates. ✉ *Hotel Mansion, Calle Obregón 2,* ☎ *642/8–02–21. Reservations not accepted. No credit cards.*

$ ✕ **Asadero Los Sabinos.** This small, unpretentious café, with indoor and outdoor seating, offers house specials of beef tips and ranch-style shrimp, along with several types of tacos and hamburgers. It's two blocks west of the Hotel Casa de los Tesoros, across the arroyo. ✉ *2 de Abríl No. 5, no phone. Reservations not accepted. No credit cards.*

$ ✕ **Casa de Café.** In the morning, expatriots gather at this American-run coffeehouse in the Mansión de la Condesa Magdalena for good cappuccino, café latte, pastries, and scones. Bring a newspaper and sit for a while in the lushly landscaped courtyard of a 1685 mansion. ✉ *Calle Obregón 2,* ☎ *642/8–02–21. Reservations not accepted. No credit cards.* ☉ *7 AM–noon.*

$$$ ▦ **Hacienda del Perico.** Formerly called La Posada, this refurbished adobe building sits on a hill overlooking the trees and cathedral domes of Alamos; it's the latest acquisition of the American couple who own Hotel la Mansion and the Casa Encantada (☞ *below*). The ruins of a 19th-century hospital have been left as part of the hotel's dramatic backdrop, lending it a theatrical touch. A van will take you from La Mansion or Casa Encantada for the five-minute ride through the barrio to the Hacienda, where Sonoran-style barbecues and folkloric dancing are often on the evening's agenda. Rates include breakfast. ✉ *45, Barrio el Perico, 85760,* ☎ *642/8–00–45. 8 rooms. Kitchenettes. No credit cards.*

$$$ ▦ **Hotel la Mansion.** With its stately rooms centered on a flowering courtyard, this pretty 17th-century mansion and well-run hotel holds the honor of having hosted several of Mexico's presidents. There is an

excellent restaurant (☞ La Mansion, *above*), a European style coffee-house, and a tapas bar. ⊠ *Calle Obregón 2, 85760,* ☎ *642–8–02–21. 12 rooms. Restaurant, tapas bar. No credit cards.*

$$$ ⊞ **Casa de los Tesoros.** This hotel, the House of Treasures, is a picturesque and romantic converted 18th-century convent. Recently renovated and redecorated, the rooms are former nuns' cells and have fireplaces, tiled baths, antique furnishings, and high-quality handicrafts on the walls. Room rates include breakfast. ⊠ *Av. Obregón 10, Box 12, 85760,* ☎ *642/8–00–10,* 𝖥𝖠𝖷 *642/8–04–00. 14 rooms. Restaurant, bar, pool. MC, V.*

$$$ ⊞ **Casa Encantada.** Set just off the main square, this lovely bed-and-breakfast owned by a California couple is the converted 250-year-old mansion of one of Alamos's former Spanish mine owners. Rooms retain a colonial character, with high-beamed ceilings, fireplaces, and carved-wood furnishings, but all have tiled private baths and good lighting. The copious breakfast, served on a plant-filled patio overlooking a small pool, might include frittatas, fresh fruit, and homebaked breads. ⊠ *Calle Juárez 20, 85760,* ☎ *642/8–04–82 or 800/422–5485,* 𝖥𝖠𝖷 *011–52–642/8–02–21. 9 rooms. Pool, bicycles, meeting room. MC, V.*

$$$ ⊞ **Casa Obregón Dieciocho.** It would be hard to find more charming
★ accommodations at a better price ($48 a night) than those in this 275-year-old mansion owned by artist and chef Roberto Bloor. Each of the inn's three suites has a bedroom, sitting room, fireplace, coffeemaker, bath, and private patio. Guests can sit out in a lovely, lush garden; colorful crafts and paintings abound throughout the house. Write away for reservations or (at a slightly extra expense) book through Fraser & Pratt Real Estate in Alamos (☎ 642/8–07–90 or 642/8–01–18). ⊠ *Av. Obregón 18, 85760, no phone. 3 suites. No credit cards.*

Shopping

It's worth a peek into three small rooms of **El Nicho Curios** (⊠ Calle Commercio 4, no phone), filled with treasures from Mexican *retablos* (religious paintings) to old jewelry and regional pottery. In addition, small stores lining the Alameda (northwest of the central plaza) sell Mexican sweets, fabrics, belts, and hats, among other items.

Aduana

🄬 *8 km (5 mi) west of Alamos.*

Aduana was formerly the site of one of the richest mines in the district. There's not much to see here now except the **church of Nuestra Señora de Balvanere.** A cactus that grows out from one of its walls is said to mark the spot where the Virgin appeared to the Yaqui Indians in the late 17th century, an event that is celebrated by a procession every November 21.

SONORA A TO Z

Arriving and Departing

By Bus

In Mexico, **Elite** runs a deluxe air-conditioned coach from Nogales to Hermosillo for around $12. Frequent buses travel to Hermosillo and Guaymas from Nogales, Tijuana, and Mexicali via **Tres Estrellas de Oro** and **Transportes de Sonora.** Try the new, comfortable **TUFESA** buses, which travel all the way to Ciudads Obregón and Navajoa.

By Car

Many visitors to Sonora travel by car from Tucson via I–19 to the border in Nogales, Arizona, and then pick up Mexico 15, which begins in Nogales, Sonora. Highway 15 is now a divided four-lane highway, making the ride much quicker and easier than it used to be. This convenience, however, doesn't come cheap: Drivers heading down to Alamos can expect to pay approximately $30 in fees. The alternative "Libre" (Free) routes are much slower and often poorly maintained.

There are two points of entry into Nogales. Most drivers take U.S. I–19 all the way to the end and then follow the signs to the border crossing. This route, however, will take you through the busiest streets of Nogales. It's better to take the Mariposa exit west from I–19, which leads to the international truck crossing and joins a small periphery highway that connects with Highway 15 after skirting the worst of Nogales traffic.

The official checkpoint for entering Mexico is 21 kilometers (13 miles) south of Nogales. It is here that you have to buy insurance and complete the paperwork to bring in your car if you haven't already done so in Tucson at either **Sanborn's Mexico Insurance** (⊠ 2900 E. Broadway, ☎ 520/327–1255) or the **Arizona Automobile Association** (⊠ 8204 E. Broadway, ☎ 520/296–7461; or 6950 N. Oracle Rd., ☎ 520/885–0694). *See* Driving *under* Smart Travel Tips *in* Important Contacts A to Z regarding the requirements for driving into Mexico.

As a result of a new **Sonora Only** program, started in September 1995, if you are not planning to go farther into Mexico, you no longer have to leave a credit-card imprint or pay a $10 deposit (though insurance is still required). Stop at the "Sonora Only" booth at the kilometer 21 checkpoint.

By Ferry
Ferries run from Guaymas to Santa Rosalia on the Baja coast; the crossing takes about 12 hours. At press time, the management of the ferry was changing and schedules were erratic. Check with the Guaymas tourist office (☞ Visitor Information, *below*) for the latest information and schedules. Cars can be shipped on the ferry; reserve at least three days in advance.

By Plane
AeroCalifornia offers a daily nonstop jet service from Los Angeles and Tucson to Hermosillo (☎ 62/60–25–55). **Aeromexico** has daily flights to Hermosillo (☎ 62/16–82–06) and Guaymas (☎ 622/1–11–22) from Tucson and flights from Los Angeles to Hermosillo via Tijuana. **Arizona Airways** flies from Tucson and Phoenix to Hermosillo (☎ 62/62–02–27; three flights a day), Guaymas (☎ 622/1–22–66; one flight a day), and Ciudad Obregón (☎ 64/13–08–28; three flights a day). Aeromexico has direct flights to Hermosillo from many cities in Mexico—including Mexico City, Chihuahua, and Guadalajara—and from La Paz and Mexico City to Guaymas; connections to other U.S. cities can be made from these points.

By Train
As we went to press, Mexican first-class train service from the U.S. border into Sonora was nonexistent. For the most current information, contact **Mexico by Train** (☎ FAX 210/725–3659 or 800/321–1699).

Getting Around
By far the easiest way to get around is by automobile; Guaymas and San Carlos are particularly spread out. Most hotels have car-rental agencies. Buses between towns are frequent and inexpensive.

Contacts and Resources

Car Rental Agencies
In **Guaymas,** the agencies to contact are **Budget** (☎ 622/2–14–50) and **Hertz** (☎ 622/2–10–00), both on the main highway.

Rental agencies in **Hermosillo** include **Hertz** (✉ Blvds. Rodríguez and Tamaulipas, ☎ 62/14–81–00) and, across the street, **Budget** (☎ 62/14–08–85).

Consulate
There is a U.S. consulate in Hermosillo (✉ Calle Monterrey, in back of the Hotel Calinda near downtown, ☎ 62/17–26–13; for emergencies, ☎ 62/17–23–75).

Emergencies
Guaymas: Police (☎ 622/2–00–30), **Red Cross** (☎ 622/2–08–79), **hospital** (☎ 622/2–01–22).

Hermosillo: Police (☎ 62/16–15–64), **Red Cross** (☎ 62/14–07–69), **hospital** (☎ 62/12–18–70). **The Green Angels,** a very helpful state-run road service for travelers, can be reached at 62/14–63–04.

Kino Bay: Rescue One (☎ 624/2–03–21), a volunteer search-and-rescue unit, can help with both land and sea emergencies. Notify the group if you're planning a trip over water or into isolated desert regions; if you're very late in returning, Rescue One will go looking for you.

Guided Tours
Arizona Coach Tours (✉ 5865 E. 2nd St., Tucson, AZ 85711, ☎ 520/748–0369) runs mostly senior citizen package tours to Alamos, San Carlos, and Puerto Peñasco. **Mexico Tours** (✉ 2780 N. Campbell, Tucson, AZ 85719, ☎ 520/323–6054) offers package tours to San Carlos and Puerto Peñasco.

Visitor Information
Note: In addition to the tourism offices listed below—which are better to visit than to try to reach by phone—the Sonora Department of Tourism has an excellent Travel Fax line that operates out of Arizona. If you dial 602/930–4815 from a fax phone, a recorded menu will allow you to receive information about Puerto Peñasco, Hermosillo, Guaymas, or Kino Bay. Those who don't have a fax can phone 602/930–4871 to receive an information packet by mail.

Alamos: *Main Plaza, Calle Juárez 6,* ☎ 642/8–04–50.

Guaymas: *Av. Serdán 441, between Calles 12 and 13, 2nd floor,* ☎ 622/2–56–67 or 622/4–29–32.

Hermosillo: *Palacio Administrativo, Calles Tehuántapec and Comonfort,* ☎ 62/14–63–04, FAX 62/17–00–60; *from the U.S., 800/4–SONORA.*

Puerto Peñasco: *Blvds. Juárez and V. Estrella,* ☎ 638/3–41–29 or 638/3–25–55.

5 The Copper Canyon: From Los Mochis to Chihuahua City

The Copper Canyon is actually a series of gorges, some of them deeper than the United States' Grand Canyon; they are home to the Tarahumara Indians, renowned for their running ability. A train trip through this magnificent, largely uncharted region usually begins or ends in Chihuahua, a lively midsize city with a museum devoted to Pancho Villa.

By Edie Jarolim

Updated by
Susana
Sedgwick

THE MAGNIFICENT series of gorges known collectively as the Copper Canyon (in Spanish, *Barranca del Cobre*) is the real hidden treasure of the Sierra Madre. Inaccessible to the casual visitor until the early 1960s and still largely uncharted, the canyons may now be explored by taking one of the most breathtaking rides in North America: The *Chihuahua al Pacífico* railroad whistles down 661 kilometers (410 miles) of track, passing through 87 tunnels and crossing 35 bridges through rugged country as rich in history and culture as in physical beauty.

The *barrancas* (canyons) of the Sierra Tarahumara, as this portion of the Sierra Madre Occidental is known, are on the western edge of the Pacific "Ring of Fire." Formed by seismic and volcanic activity, which at the same time hurled a good quantity of the earth's buried mineral wealth to the surface, the canyons were carved throughout the millennia by the Urique, Serpentrión, Batopilas, and Chínipas rivers and further defined by wind erosion. Totaling more than 1,452 kilometers (900 miles) in length and capable of enveloping four of the Arizona Grand Canyons, the gorges are nearly a mile deep and wide in places; the average height of the peaks is 8,000 feet, and some rise to more than 12,000 feet. Four of the major barrancas—Copper, Urique, Sinforosa, and Batopilas—descend deeper than the Grand Canyon, Urique by nearly 1,500 feet.

The idea of building a rail line to cross this region was first conceived in 1872 by Albert C. Owen, an idealistic American socialist. Owen met with some success initially. More than 1,500 people came from the states to join him in Topolobampo, his utopian colony on the Mexican west coast, and in 1881 he obtained a concession from Mexican president General Manuel Gonzáles to build the railroad. Construction on the flat stretches near Los Mochis and Chihuahua presented no difficulties, but eventually the huge Sierra Madre mountains got in the way of Owen's dream, along with the scourge of typhoid and disillusionment within the community.

After Owen abandoned the project in 1893, it was taken up in 1900 by American railroad magnate and spiritualist Edward Arthur Stilwell. One of Stilwell's contractors in western Chihuahua was Pancho Villa, who ended up tearing up his own work during the Mexican Revolution in order to impede the movement of government troops. By 1910, when the Mexican Revolution started, the Mexican government had taken charge of building the railroad line; but progress was very slow until 1940, when surveying of the difficult Sierra Madre stretch finally began in earnest. Some 90 years and more than $100 million after it started, the Ferrocarril Chihuahua al Pacífico was dedicated on November 23, 1961.

The rail line no longer starts at Topolobambo but at nearby Los Mochis. Chihuahua City, at the other end of the line, was established in 1709. Today Chihuahua, the capital of the state of that name and a prosperous economic center, derives its wealth from mining—the Spanish discovered silver in the region as early as 1649—as well as from ranching, agriculture, and lumber.

The Tarahumara Indians, who once occupied the entire state of Chihuahua, were not unaffected by the foreign activity in the area: They were forced to serve in the mines by the Spanish and on the railroad by the Mexicans and the Americans. The threat of slavery and the series of wars that began in the 1600s and continued until the 20th century forced them to retreat deeper and deeper into the canyons, where they are still subject to having their lands taken over by loggers or drug lords. Semi-nomadic, many roam the high plateaus of the Sierra Madre in summer and move down to the canyon floor in winter to live in stone cliff dwellings or hidden wooden houses. The Tarahumara population, ravaged by disease and poverty, is now estimated at approximately 50,000.

Pleasures and Pastimes

Dining

Along the Copper Canyon trail you'll encounter rustic areas where there are few eateries besides those connected with lodges. In Los Mochis and Topolobampo your best bet is seafood. Restaurants tend to be inexpensive. At the hotels in Cerocahui, Divisadero, and Posada Barrancas, food is included in the price of the room. Don't even think about dieting here: You'll get three freshly cooked, hearty meals a day, often with meat courses and dessert at both lunch and dinner. There are a few more dining options in Creel, where, in addition to the hotel dining rooms, you'll find a number of inns along the town's main street, Avenida López Mateos.

You'll have the most choice of restaurants in Chihuahua City. The state is a large producer of beef, so upscale steakhouses and places serving *carne asada* (charbroiled strips of marinated beef) abound, but a variety of Mexican specialties and seafood flown in from the coast is also available. Many of Chihuahua's well-appointed international restaurants are located in the Zona Dorada, on Calle Juárez starting from its intersection with Calle Colón.

Dress is casual everywhere except at a few of the more upscale restaurants in Chihuahua. Unless otherwise indicated, reservations are not necessary.

CATEGORY	COST*
$$$$	over $20
$$$	$15–$20
$$	$8–$15
$	under $8

per person, excluding drinks, service, and sales tax (10%)

Hiking

Hiking in the Copper Canyon can be an unforgettable experience, if the proper precautions are taken; *Mexico's Copper Canyon Country,* by M. John Fayhee, is a good source of information. But even the most experienced trekkers should enlist the help of local guides, who can be contacted through all the hotels in the area or through travel agents in Los Mochis and Chihuahua. Few adequate maps are available for even the so-called marked trails, and many of the better-worn routes into the canyon are made by the Tarahumara, whose prime concern is getting from one habitable area to the next rather than getting to the bottom.

Urique Canyon is most easily reached from Cerocahui (Bahuichivo stop). The Copper Canyon is most accessible from Divisadero; trails range from easy rim walks to a 27-kilometer (17-mile) descent to the bottom, which takes seven or eight hours. If you're in Creel, a gentle and rewarding hike is the 5-kilometer (3-mile) walk from the Copper Canyon Lodge to the Cusárare Falls. More difficult but equally scenic are the treks down to Recohauta Hot Springs and to the base of Basaseachic Falls; both are about three hours round-trip. The descent into Batopilas Canyon from Creel requires an overnight stay.

Horseback Riding

All hotels in the canyon area can arrange for local guides with gentle horses. Most trips are not for couch potatoes, however. The trails into the canyon are badly defined and can be rocky as well as slippery if the weather is icy or wet; at rough spots you might be asked to dismount and walk part of the way. A fairly easy and inexpensive ride is to Wicochic Falls at Cerocahui, about two hours round-trip, including a half-hour hike at the end, where the trail is too narrow for the horses. From Divisadero, the trip to Bacajipare, a Tarahumara village in the Copper Canyon, affords stunning vistas; it's an exciting four-hour ride round-trip, but it's not for the faint of heart.

Lodging

Accommodations in this area tend to fall into two categories: comfortable but characterless in the large cities, and charming but to varying degrees rustic in the small ones. In Cerocahui, Divisadero–Posada Barrancas, and Creel, all the hotels send buses or cars to meet the train; if you don't have a reservation, you'll have to make a quick decision and then hop on a vehicle sent out by the hotel of your choice. During the summer and around Christmas and Easter, it's important to book in advance. Where indicated, rates for hotels include meals.

CATEGORY	COST*
$$$$	over $90
$$$	$60–$90
$$	$25–$60
$	under $25

*All prices are for a standard double room, excluding 10% tax.

Nightlife

Sitting around and chatting with fellow guests in your lodge is about the extent of nighttime activity in the heart of Sierra Madre country, though occasionally one of the hotels in Divisadero or Posada Barrancas will have performances in the evening by Tarahumara dancers. Things are a bit more lively in Los Mochis and Creel, and Chihuahua is a typical late-night Mexico city.

Shopping

Tarahumara crafts, which provide the Indians with their only cash income, include lovely handwoven baskets made from *sotol* (a claw-like plant) and pine bark; carved wooden dolls; crude pottery; brightly colored belts and sashes woven using backstrap looms; and wooden fiddles, sometimes with mask faces, from which the men produce haunting music. The Tarahumara, who are generally shy about talking with tourists, sell their wares throughout the Copper Canyon area; their prices are fair, so bargaining is unnecessary (as well as inappropriate). Baskets run from $1 for the smallest to about $15 for the largest. Tarahumara wares are sold at the market outside the train station at Divisadero and at a number of shops in Creel, the best one of which is Artesanías Misión (where proceeds benefit the Tarahumara hospital), right off the central plaza.

Great Itineraries

Numbers in the text correspond to numbers in the margin and on the Copper Canyon map.

You'll see some beautiful scenery if you just ride the railroad, including a panoramic look at Copper Canyon during a 15-minute stop at Divisadero, but you'll experience only a fraction of what the canyons have to offer if you don't get off the train. If possible, plan on a night in Cerocahui (Bahuichivo stop), one at Posado Barrancas or Divisadero (the train stations are five minutes apart), and one or two at Creel.

About 60% of the people who visit the Copper Canyon come via Los Mochis, which is the easiest route if you're traveling from California or Arizona. It's also by far the most desirable route if you come in winter, because some of the best scenery is to be seen at the western end of the ride and you're likely to miss it if you approach Los Mochis in the evening. Your choice of route matters less in the extended daylight hours of summer.

Even if you drive down to either Los Mochis or Chihuahua, your itinerary will be largely dependent on the schedule of the *Chihuahua al Pacífico* train: It runs in each direction only once a day, so you must plan the time spent in each stop accordingly. The following itineraries assume you will add on a day's train ride to return to your starting point.

IF YOU HAVE 3 DAYS

Departing from **Los Mochis** ①, take the 6 AM Chihuahua al Pacífico train and get off at Bahuichivo, where you can explore the mission at **Cerocahui** ③ and the overlook into Urique Canyon. The next day, continue on to **Divisadero** ④, where it's practically impossible not to get a room with a view. Spend your last day exploring **Creel** ⑤ and taking a short hike to the falls near Cusárare. Those starting out from **Chihuahua City** ⑧ should make Cerocahui their final stop.

IF YOU HAVE 5 DAYS

Starting out in the west, consider spending a day in the old colonial town of **El Fuerte** ② and then catching the train through the canyons at 7:30 the next morning. Follow the three-day itinerary, *above,* and then for your last day and night, extend your time in **Creel** ⑤ with a visit to the Tarahumara community of San Ignacio or a drive to Basaseachic Falls. Those departing from the east might take the extra day to explore Chihuahua City; be sure to stop in at Pancho Villa's home, now a museum.

IF YOU HAVE 8 OR MORE DAYS

Pull out (or rather, pull into) all the stops: Spend a day each in El Fuerte, Cerocahui, and Divisadero, and then extend your stay in Creel to include a trip down to the former silver mining town of **Batopilas** ⑥; it's an eight-hour excursion each way, so you'll want to spend at least two nights. You'll be ready for the modern world after that, so plan to enjoy the restaurants and museums of Chihuahua City for an additional day; another option (and another excursion into the past) might be a day trip from Chihuahua to the Mennonite community in **Cuauhtémoc** ⑦.

When to Tour

Unless you are planning to head down deep into the barrancas, winter—December through February—is not the best time to come; many of the hotels in the region are inadequately prepared for the cold, and the minor rainy season in January renders some of the roads for side excursions impassable. The warm months are May through September; the rainy season, June through September, brings precipitation for a short period every day, but this shouldn't interfere with your enjoyment in any way. It's temperate in the highlands during the summer; if you're planning to hike down into the canyons, however, remember that the deeper you go, the hotter it will get. The best months to visit are October and November, when the weather is still warm and rains have brought out all the colors in the Sierra Tarahumara.

Many people visit during Christmas and Easter, specifically to see the Tarahumara celebrations of those holidays. Closely related to the Pima Indians of southern Arizona, the Tarahumara are renowned for their running ability. (*Tarahumara* is a Spanish corruption of *Rarámuri,* which means "running people" in their language; it is said that in earlier times they survived as hunters by chasing deer to the point of collapse.) Around Christmas, Easter, and other religious feast days, the Tarahumara compete in races that can last up to three days. The men run in small groups, kicking a wooden ball for a distance of 161 kilometers (100 miles) or more. On these and other feast days, tribal elders consume peyote or *tesguino,* a sacred fermented corn liquor.

EXPLORING THE COPPER CANYON

Imagine visiting the Grand Canyon in the days before it was tamed by tourist facilities, and you'll have some sense of what a trip through the Copper Canyon will be like—for better and for worse. That is, with the opportunity to encounter a relatively untouched natural site come some of the attendant discomforts of the rustic experience. But if you are careful in your choice of time to visit and are properly prepared, the trip's myriad rewards should far outstrip any temporary inconveniences.

Los Mochis

1 *763 km (474 mi) south of Nogales on the Arizona-Mexico border.*

The first stop on the western end of the rail line, Los Mochis (population about 300,000) is an agricultural boomtown; its location near the harbor at Topolobampo and the railroad makes it the export center of the state of Sinaloa, which produces many of Mexico's basic crops. Visitors can tour Benjamin Johnston's sugar refinery, the Ingenio Azucarero, around which the town grew. Near Johnston's estate you can still see the American colony—the group of brick bungalows that housed his associates—as well as a workers' hostel and the country club. The **Museo Regional del Valle del Fuerte** has rotating exhibits of paintings and crafts by local artists, and the public library next door displays pictures of the early days of the city. Labels are in Spanish only. ⊠ *Calles Obregón and Mina,* ☎ *681/2–46–92.* ▧ *$1.60.* ☉ *Tues.–Sun. 10–1 and 4–7.*

Cottonwood trees and bougainvillea line the highway from Los Mochis to Topolobampo; on both sides of the road are fields planted with crops ranging from sugarcane to marigolds and mangos (36 varieties are produced here). Once the site of Albert Owen's utopian colony and the center of the railroad-building activity in the area, **Topolobampo** is now considered a suburb of Los Mochis, 15 minutes away. A huge tuna-packing factory sits at the entrance to the bay, and local fisherman—90% of the population—ply the harbor in small shrimp boats; they compete for their catch with the many dolphins that cavort in the bay. **Isla El Farallón,** just off the coast, is a breeding ground for the sea lions that gave the town its name: In the language of the Mayo Indians who once dominated the area, Topolobampo means "watering place of the sea lions."

Dining and Lodging

$$ ✕ **El Farallón.** With its nautical decor and murals, the dining room of this simple restaurant sets the tone for the excellent fish served here. ⊠ *Obregón 593, corner Angel Flores,* ☎ *681/2–14–28. Reservations not accepted. MC, V.*

$$ ✕ **Restaurante España.** This slightly upscale restaurant in downtown Los Mochis is popular with the local business crowd. Good seafood and Spanish dishes are served around an intriguing-looking indoor fountain. ⊠ *Obregón 526,* ☎ *681/2–22–21 or 681/2–23–35. AE, MC, V.*

Copper Canyon

$ ✕ **El Taquito.** Located in the very center of Los Mochis, this diner-style restaurant offers well-prepared and reasonably priced Mexican standards 24 hours a day, every day. For a hearty meal try the *Tampiqueña*—a tasty steak with enchiladas, guacamole, and *frijoles* (beans) on the side. ⊠ *Calle Leyva between Hidalgo and Independencia,* ☎ 681/2–81–19. *Reservations not accepted. MC, V.*

$$ 🏨 **El Dorado.** On the main street of town and, as a result, noisy as well as convenient to restaurants and shops, this modest but clean motel-hotel is a good value. Rooms are light-filled and have TVs; a small pool is set among palm trees in the back. ⊠ *525 N. Leyva, corner Valdez, 82000,* ☎ 681/5–11–11, 𝖥𝖠𝖷 681/2–01–79. *93 rooms with bath. Coffee shop, bar, pool, travel services. AE, MC, V.*

$$$ ✕🏨 **Hotel Santa Anita.** The central reservations link of the Balderrama chain, this downtown hotel is also an informal information center for what's happening along the *Chihuahua al Pacífico* route, as well as the place to book tours. The restaurant is one of the best in town, too. Built in 1959, the property has been renovated continually; rooms are large and tastefully furnished in muted pastels, with comfortable modern furniture. All have cable TV, and many have hair dryers—unusual for this part of the country. ⊠ *Leyva and Hidalgo, Apdo. 159, 82000,* ☎ 681/8–70–46, 𝖥𝖠𝖷 681/2–00–46. *133 rooms with bath. Restaurant, bar, travel services. AE, DC, MC, V.*

Nightlife

Locals kick up their heels at **Fantasy** (⊠ Hotel Plaza Inn, Leyva and Cardenas, ☎ 681/5–80–20) and **Morocco** (⊠ Leyva and Rendon, ☎ 681/2–13–88), two downtown discos.

El Fuerte

❷ *80 km (50 mi) northeast of Los Mochis.*

The small colonial town of El Fuerte was named after the 17th-century fort built by the Spaniards to protect against attacks by the local Mayo, Sinaloa, Zuaque, and Tehueco Indians. Originally called San Juan de Carapoa, it was founded in 1564 by Spanish conquistador Don Francisco de Ibarra and a small group of soldiers. Located on the central El Camino Real route, El Fuerte was at one time the frontier outpost from which the Spanish set out to explore and settle New Mexico and California. For three centuries, it was also a major trading post for gold and silver miners from the nearby Sierras and the most important commercial and farming center of the area; it was chosen as Sinaloa's capital in 1824 and remained so for several years. There are intact colonial mansions in what is now a rather sleepy town of 25,000; one of the best is the Hotel Posada Hidalgo (☞ Dining and Lodging, *below*). Most of El Fuerte's historic houses are set off the cobblestoned streets leading from the central plaza; a number of them have been converted into government offices.

Dining and Lodging

$$$ ✕▥ **Hotel Posada Hidalgo.** You'll be transported back to a more gra-
★ cious era at this lovely restored hacienda, with its lush tropical gardens and cobblestoned paths. Designated a Historic Landmark in 1913, it was built in 1895 by Rafael Almada, a rancher and the richest man in nearby Alamos; he had furniture shipped from as far as San Francisco for his lavish home, where he entertained the local elite. It's difficult to choose between the larger rooms with balconies, set off of a lobby filled with period artifacts, and the ones that open out onto the gardens; all are decorated with rough-hewn handcrafted furniture in Spanish colonial style. *Langostino* (crayfish) is a specialty of the hotel dining room. ✉ *Hidalgo 101,* ☎ *689/3–0242; for reservations, Hotel Santa Anita, Box 159, Los Mochis, Sin.,* ☎ *681/8–70–46,* FAX *681/2–00–46. 40 rooms with bath. Dining room–bar, pool, dance club. AE, MC, V.*

En Route   As the train ascends almost 5,906 feet into the mountains from El Fuerte to Bahuichivo, it passes through 87 tunnels and over 24 bridges, including the longest and highest ones of the rail system. The scenery shifts from Sinaloan thorn forest, with cactus and scrublike vegetation, to the pools, cascades, and tropical trees of the Río Serpentrión canyon, to the oak and pine forest that begins to take over past Temoris, where a plaque marks the dedication of the railroad by President López Mateos in 1961.

Cerocahui

❸ *160 km (100 mi) northeast of El Fuerte.*

From the train station at Bahuichivo, two hotels have buses that make the 45-minute ride up the bumpy, unpaved road to the quiet mountain village of Cerocahui. This is a good place to get a sense of how people live in the canyon area. Next door to the Hotel Misión is a **Jesuit mission,** established around 1690 by Juan María de Salvatierra, who proselytized widely in the region; it is said that because the Tarahumara were the most difficult Indians to convert, he considered this mission his favorite among the many he founded. Nearby, the church operates a boarding school for Tarahumara children. Visitors can hike or ride horses to two nearby **waterfalls** and to a **silver mine** (closed since 1988), but the prime reason to come to Cerocahui is its accessibility to Urique Canyon. It's a kidney-crunching ride to the **Cerro del Gallego lookout point,** where amid mountains spread against the horizon, you can make out the Urique River and the town of Urique, a slim thread and a dot on the distant canyon bottom. On the way up you'll pass a Tarahumara cave where Indian women sell baskets; nearby, a shrine to the Virgin is strikingly set against a spring in the mountainside surrounded by tropical foliage. From Cerro del Gallego the road continues down the canyon into the old mining town of **Urique,** which has a few basic hotels and restaurants. A public bus makes the trip from Cerocahui a few times a week, but many visitors opt for the round-trip, full-day tours offered by the local hotels (☞ Lodging, *below*).

Dining and Lodging

$$$$ ✕▦ **Hotel Misión.** Part of the Balderrama chain—the Copper Canyon's equivalent of the Grand Canyon's Fred Harvey hotel empire—this is the only tourist accommodation in Cerocahui itself. The main house, which looks like a combination ski lodge and hacienda, contains the hotel's office, small shops, dining room, bar, and lounge. In winter guests huddle for warmth around two large fireplaces, the prime sources of heat and light: Cerocahui isn't wired for electricity, and the hotel uses its generator for only a few hours, generally from 7 to 9 in the morning and 7 to 11 in the evening. The plain but characterful rooms, with beamed ceilings and Spanish colonial–style furnishings, are a pyromaniac's dream: They're equipped with fuel and matches for guests to light the wood-burning stove and a kerosene lamp for light. ✉ *Cerocahui; mailing address: Santa Anita Hotel, Box 159, Los Mochis, Sin.,* ☎ *681/ 8–70–46, ext. 432,* ℻ *681/2–00–46. 30 rooms with bath. Restaurant, bar. AE, MC, V.*

$$$$ ✕▦ **Paraiso del Oso Lodge.** This lodge near Cerocahui offers plain rooms with simple wooden furniture handmade by locals. Guests must stoke the stove for heat at night, since there is no electricity here. A huge window-filled lobby affords excellent views of the cliffs above the lodge, and a gift shop carries local crafts as well as wares from other parts of Mexico. ✉ *5 km (3 mi) outside of Cerocahui; for reservations: Columbus Travel, 900 Ridge Creek La., Bulverde, TX 78163,* ☎ *210/885– 2000 or 800/843–1060. 16 rooms with bath. Dining room. MC, V in U.S.; cash or personal checks only on premises.*

Divisadero

❹ *80 km (50 mi) northeast of Cerocahui.*

There's little to do in Divisadero, a postage stamp of a place on the Continental Divide, but it's impossible to remain unastounded by the vistas of the Copper Canyon, said to have derived its name both from the copper that used to be mined in the area and the color the canyon turns at sunset. You can also glimpse a bit of the distant Urique and Tararechua canyons from here. A popular excursion that takes about four hours round-trip, whether you're traveling on two feet or on horseback, is a visit to Bacajipare, a Tarahumara village. Divisadero and Posada Barrancas, the train stop five minutes away, offer the most comfort in the most spectacular setting on the route.

Dining and Lodging

$$$$ ✕▦ **Hotel Divisadero-Barrancas.** This property sits right on the edge of the Copper Canyon; the dining room and rooms 1 through 10 in the old section and 35 through 52 in the new section all enjoy panoramic views. The old rooms, with dark furnishings, have decks; the new ones, lighter in decor and somewhat farther from the dining room, have balconies. Food and service get mixed reviews from the international visitors who sign the guest log, but you're not likely to notice what you're

eating when you look out of the dining-room window. ⊠ *Divisadero; reservations: Av. Mirador 4516, Box 31238, Colonia Residencial Campestre, Chihuahua, Chih.,* ☎ *14/10–33–30,* FAX *14/15–65–75. 52 rooms with shower. Restaurant, bar. AE, MC, V.*

$$$ ╳▥ **Hotel Mansion Tarahumara.** It's a bit disconcerting to come across a red-turreted, medieval-style castle out here in barranca country, but somehow this whimsical property works. All the rooms (15 of them, in separate cabins) have light-pine furniture beautifully designed in Spanish contemporary style, as well as fireplaces and individual heaters. The newest units have pine-log walls; the older rooms feature gray cobblestoned walls that match the castle's exterior. The large dining room with its high-vaulted ceiling is hard to keep warm in winter but has wonderful views of the Sierra Madre. ⊠ *Posada Barrancas; reservations: Av. Juárez 1602, 1-A, Colonia Centro, Chihuahua, Chih., 31000,* ☎ FAX *14/16–54–44. 46 rooms with bath. Restaurant, bar, dance club. AE, MC, V.*

$$$$ ╳▥ **Hotel Posada Barrancas El Rancho.** This is a good base from which to explore the Barranca del Cobre. The rooms in the newer section, done in light wood, are your best bet; the older accommodations have undistinguished dark, contemporary-style furnishings, pseudo-stucco walls, and linoleum-tile floors. From the vertical beams in the main lodge–dining room hang strings of butterfly cocoons used in Tarahumara ceremonial dances, which are sometimes performed at the hotel in the evening. ⊠ *Posada Barrancas; reservations: Hotel Santa Anita, Box 159, Los Mochis, Sin.,* ☎ *681/8–70–46,* FAX *681/2–00–46. 78 rooms with bath. Restaurant, bar, exercise room. AE, DC, MC, V.*

$$$$ ╳▥ **Hotel Posada Barrancas Mirador.** This beautiful pink hotel—the
★   latest link in the Balderrama chain—is perched on the edge of the Copper Canyon. The dining room and all the guest rooms have spectacular views; balconies seem to hang right over the abyss. Accommodations are light and bright, with custom-made furniture and individually controlled air-conditioning and heat, and meals are copious and tasty. ⊠ *Posada Barrancas; reservations: Hotel Santa Anita, Box 159, Los Mochis, Sin.,* ☎ *681/8–70–46,* FAX *681/2–00–46. 36 rooms. Restaurant, bar, meeting room. AE, DC, MC, V.*

Creel

❺ *60 km (37 mi) northeast of Divisadero.*

Nestled in pine-covered mountains, Creel is a rugged mining and logging town that grew up around the railroad station. The largest settlement in the area, it's a gathering place for Tarahumara Indians seeking supplies and markets for their crafts. It's easy to imagine American frontier towns at the turn of the century looking like Creel—without, of course, the backpacking contingent that makes this town its base. A cluster of small hotels here offer tours to the many points of interest in the area.

It's 19 kilometers (12 miles) from Creel to **Cusárare**, an Indian village that hosts a 300-year-old mission built by the Jesuits for the Tarahumara. En route you'll pass limpid-blue Lake Arareco and the Valley of the Mushrooms, with its strange volcanic-rock formations. An impressive waterfall can be reached by an easy 4-kilometer (2½-mile) hike from Cusárare through a lovely piñon forest.

If the unpaved roads are passable, consider taking the longer trips to the **Recohuata Hot Springs,** a fairly strenuous hike down from the rim of the Tararecua Canyon, and to **El Tejaban,** a spectacular overlook at the Copper Canyon. Among several worthwhile day trips along the way to the colonial city of Batopilas (☞ *below*) are **Basihuare,** where huge vertical outcroppings of rock are crossed with wide horizontal bands of color; the **Urique Canyon overlook,** affording a perspective of that barranca that differs from the one at Cerocahui; and **La Bufa,** site of a former Spanish silver mine. Seventy-three kilometers (45 miles) northeast of Creel but reached via an unpaved, winding road, the 806-foot **Basaseachic Falls** are among the highest cascades in Mexico and a most impressive sight.

Dining and Lodging

$$ ✕ **La Estufa.** The restaurant of the Hotel Cascada, this is a fun place to have dinner; taped music and a good bar draw both locals and tourists in the evening. As the name suggests, steak is the focus of the menu, but there are tasty seafood dishes, all reasonably priced, as well. ⊠ *Av. López Mateos 49,* ☎ *145/6–01–51. Reservations not accepted. AE, MC, V.*

$ ✕ **Veronica's.** This clean, unpretentious little eatery on the main street is popular with locals and tourists alike, and it's easy to see why: a wide selection of Mexican standards prepared simply but with care and at very reasonable prices. *Comida corridas*—set meals with soup, main course, and dessert—are available, or you can order à la carte off the menu. Try the excellent *sopa de verduras* (vegetable soup). ⊠ *Av. López Mateos, no phone. Reservations not accepted. No credit cards.*

$$ ☷ **Parador de la Montaña Motel.** Built in the 1970s, the Parador is considered the fanciest hotel in Creel, but it's showing its age. The furniture is dark, as is the lighting. Recently remodeled rooms still have the same cheerless decorating scheme, but the hotel is used by many tour operators and is frequently booked up, so its bar and restaurant are often lively in the evening. ⊠ *Av. López Mateos 44,* ☎ *145/6–00–75,* FAX *145/6–00–85. Reservations: Allende 114, Chihuahua, Chih.,* ☎ *14/10–45–80,* FAX *14/15–34–68. 50 rooms with shower. Restaurant, bar. AE, MC, V.*

$–$$ ☷ **La Posada de Creel.** This hotel, the oldest in Creel, was recently renovated and offers 10 private rooms and 11 rooms that sleep four. Right off the train tracks and two blocks from the station, the inn provides simple but clean accommodations. Breakfast is included in the room rate. ⊠ *Apdo. 7, Creel,* ☎ *145/6–01–42; reservations in the U.S.: Box 3, Cleburne, TX 76033,* ☎ *817/558–9979 or 817/641–9979,* FAX *817/641–9979. 21 rooms. Restaurant. No credit cards.*

$$ ☷ **Margarita's Plaza Mexicana.** This pretty hotel with two floors of rooms wrapped around a private courtyard was built to accommodate the demand for more of the hospitality, solid meals, and low prices found at Margarita's (☞ *below*). The rooms, with private baths, individual heat, and plenty of hot water, are tastefully decorated with pine furniture made in the area and charming murals depicting Tarahumara activities. Room prices include breakfast and dinner. ⊠ *Calle E. Batista Caro, two blocks from the church on the left off Lopez Mateos,* ☎ FAX *145/6–02–45. 25 rooms. Restaurant, bar. No credit cards.*

$ ☷ **Margarita's.** If a small boy at the train station offers to take you to
★ Margarita's, go with him. Otherwise you might miss one of the best deals in town: There's no sign on the door, and even if you follow directions (right off the main town plaza, between the two churches perpendicular to each other), you're likely to think you're walking into a private kitchen when you open the door. At this gathering spot for backpackers, you can get anything from a bunk bed in the dorm ($5) to a double room with two beds (around $8 per person); all prices include a tasty home-cooked breakfast and dinner. The rooms—with wrought-iron lamps, light-wood furnishings, and clean, modern baths—are as pleasant as anything you'll find for twice or three times the price. ⊠ *Av. López Mateos y Parroquia 11,* ☎ *145/6–00–45 or 145/6–02–45*

(new hotel). 21 rooms, most with private bath. Restaurant. No credit cards.

$$$$ ✕🏨 **Copper Canyon Lodge.** About 24 kilometers (15 miles) from the
★ train station, near Cusárare Falls and overlooking a piñon forest, this
rustic hotel couldn't have a nicer setting. The pine-walled rooms, with
their light-wood, Spanish-style furnishings and tiled modern baths, are
very attractive, and the lodge where hearty meals are served family style
is cozy and appealing. The only catch is that there's no electricity. The
kerosene lamps are fine for light year-round. ✉ *Creel, Chihuahua, no
phone; reservations in the U.S.: Copper Canyon Lodges, 2741 Paldan,
Auburn Hills, MI 48326,* ☎ *810/340–7230 or 800/776–3942. 23
rooms. Restaurant, bar.*

Nightlife
When the sun goes down in Creel, head to the **Steak House** or the
Parador de La Montaña Motel (☞ Dining and Lodging, *above*) for an
after-dinner drink; there's often a sports match on TV at **El Caballo Bayo**
(✉ Av. Lopez Mateos, at the west end of town, no phone).

Batopilas

❻ *110 km (80 mi) southeast of Creel.*

A remote village of about 600 people, Batopilas was once one of the
wealthiest towns in Mexico because of the nearby veins of silver mined
on and off from the time of the conquistadores; at one time it was the
only place in the country besides Mexico City that had electricity. The
80-kilometer (48-mile) ride down dusty, unpaved roads to the now-
sleepy town at the bottom of Batopilas Canyon takes about 6½ hours
by car from Creel (closer to eight hours on the local bus, which runs
about three times a week). Sights in this lush, flower-filled oasis include
the ruined **hacienda of Alexander Shepherd,** built in the late 1800s by
one of the town's wealthiest mine owners; the original **aqueduct,** which
still services the town (it's set along the Camino Real); and a triple-
domed 17th-century **cathedral,** mysteriously isolated in the Satevo
Valley and reached via a scenic 6.4-kilometer (4-mile) hike from town.
You'll need to stay overnight at one of Batopilas's modest posadas or
at the Riverside Lodge (☞ Dining and Lodging, *below*).

Dining and Lodging
$$$$ ✕🏨 **Riverside Lodge.** A restored late-19th-century hacienda, this lodging is quirkily charming. Each of the high-ceilinged rooms is individually decorated—for example, one with a prayer niche, another with vintage
Elizabeth Taylor posters—but all have spacious private baths and huge,
soft feather duvets. Only partially wired for electricity, the accommodations have an odd mix of kerosene reading lamps and electrical outlets for hair dryers. The home-cooked meals are excellent, and guests
are free to raid the refrigerator and liquor cabinet (just sign the book;
you'll be billed later). ✉ *Batopilas; for reservations in the U.S.: Copper Canyon Lodges, 2741 Paldan, Auburn Hills, MI 48326,* ☎ *810/340–
7230 or 800/776–3942. 15 rooms. Library, hiking. MC, V.*

Cuauhtémoc

❼ *128 km (94 mi) northeast of Creel, 105 km (65 mi) southwest of
Chihuahua.*

A rather anomalous experience in Mexico is a visit to the large **Mennonite community** (Campos Menonitas) in the town of Cuauhtémoc.
Approximately 20,000 Mennonites came to the San Antonio Valley in
1922 at the invitation of President Alvaro Obregón, who gave them

the right to live freely and autonomously in return for farming the 247,000 acres of land they purchased. Tours can be arranged either in Chihuahua (☞ Guided Tours *in* The Copper Canyon and Chihuahua City A to Z, *below*) or at the Tarahumara Inn in Cuauhtémoc.

Chihuahua City

8 *375 km (233 mi) south of the El Paso–Ciudad Juárez border, 1,440 km (895 mi) northwest of Mexico City.*

If you're arriving from the peaceful Copper Canyon, the sprawling city of Chihuahua, with nearly 1 million inhabitants, may come as a bit of a jolt. But, then, the city is known for its jolting nature: Two of the most famous figures in Mexico's revolutionary wars are closely tied to Chihuahua. Father Miguel Hidalgo, the father of Mexican independence, and his co-conspirators were executed by the Spanish here in 1811. And Chihuahua was home to General Pancho Villa, whose revolutionary army, the División del Norte (Army of the North), was decisive in overthrowing dictator Porfirio Díaz in 1910 and securing victory in the ensuing civil war. In addition, Benito Juárez, known as the Abraham Lincoln of Mexico, made Chihuahua his base in 1865 during the French invasion of the country.

Whatever you do, don't miss a visit to the Museo Histórico de la Revolución en el Estado de Chihuahua, better known as **Pancho Villa's House.** Villa lived in this home, completed in 1909, with his second wife, Luz Corral (he had three wives, none of whom he divorced). She stayed here until her death on June 6, 1981, willing the residence to the government, which restored it as a national museum. The 50 small rooms that used to board Villa's bodyguards have been converted into exhibition rooms displaying artifacts of Chihuahua's cultural and revolutionary history. Parked outside in the museum's courtyard is the bullet-ridden 1919 Dodge in which Villa was assassinated in 1923 at the age of 45. ⊠ *Calle Décima 3014,* ☎ *14/16–29–58.* ▩ *Less than $1.* ⊘ *Daily 9–1 and 3–7.*

Another must-see is the **Catedral,** on the town's central square. Construction on this beautiful Baroque structure was started by the Jesuits in 1726 but not completed until 1825 because of Indian uprisings in the area. The exterior is made of the pinkish limestone quarried in this region; inside, the opulent church has altars made of Carrara marble, a 24-karat solid-gold ceiling, a beautiful cedar-and-brass carved depiction of Saint Peter and Saint Paul, and a huge German-made organ. In the back of the cathedral, the Museum of Sacred Art displays the work of seven local artists of the 18th-century Mexican Baroque tradition, as well as commemorations of the 1990 visit of Pope John Paul II. ⊠ *Plaza de la Constitución, no phone.* ▩ *50¢.* ⊘ *Weekdays 10–2 and 4–6.*

The **Palacio del Gobierno** (State Capitol) was built by the Jesuits as a convent in 1882. Converted into government offices in 1891, it was destroyed by a fire in the early 1940s and rebuilt in 1947. Murals around the patio by artist Pino Mora depict famous episodes from the history of the state of Chihuahua; a plaque commemorates the spot where Father Hidalgo was executed on the morning of July 30, 1811. ⊠ *Plaza Hidalgo,* ☎ *14/10–63–24.* ⊘ *Daily 8–11 AM.*

The **Palacio Federal** (Federal Building) houses the city's main post office and telegraph office, as well as the dungeon where Hidalgo was imprisoned before he was executed by the Spanish; his pistols, traveler's trunk, crucifix, and reproductions of his letters are on display here. ⊠ *Calle Libertad, around the corner from Plaza Hidalgo,* ☎ *14/15–14–17 or 14/10–35–95.* ⊘ *Daily 9–7.*

The **Iglesia de San Francisco** (San Francisco Church) is the oldest (1721) church built in Chihuahua that is still standing. Father Hidalgo's decapitated body was interred in the chapel of this simple church from 1811 to 1827, when it was sent to Mexico City; his head was publicly displayed for 10 years by Spanish Royalists in Guanajuato on the Alhóndiga de Granaditas (☞ Guanajuato *in* Chapter 8). ⊠ *Av. Libertad at Calle 15, no phone.* ☉ *Daily 7–7.*

Slightly outside the center of town but well worth a visit is the Cultural Museum of the University of Chihuahua, known as **Quinta Gameros.** This Art Nouveau mansion—with beautiful stained-glass windows, ornate carved wooden staircases, and Italian blown-glass chandeliers—was built in 1910 by Julio Corredor, a Columbian architect, for Manuel Gameros, a wealthy mining engineer. An eclectic collection includes European art from the 18th and 19th centuries, pottery of the local Paquime Indians, and artifacts of the nearby Mennonite community. Concerts, lectures, and exhibitions of local artists are also held here. ⊠ *Calle Bolívar 401,* ☎ *14/16–66–84.* ☒ *$2.* ☉ *Tues.–Sun. 10–2 and 4–7.*

A restoration project has made the site of the town's original settlement, **Santa Eulalia,** particularly appealing. The 20-minute drive southeast of town is compensated by the colonial architecture and cobblestoned streets of this small town; the religious artwork in the 18th-century cathedral is noteworthy, and the Mesón de Santa Eulalia Restaurant has a lovely location.

Dining and Lodging

$$$ ✕ **La Mansión del Gourmet.** If you dine at this stately 1950s mansion, just across the canal from downtown, you'll feel as though you're at a private party; the effect is enhanced by the piano in the center of the dining room, played each afternoon and evening. A variety of international fare is available, including a large selection of steaks, the house specialty. For visual as well as culinary excitement, try a sizzling *platillo flameado* with either beef or shrimp. ⊠ *Av. Universidad,* ☎ *14/14–38–78. AE, DC, MC, V.*

$$ ✕ **Club de Los Parados.** Almost four decades of Chihuahua's history
★   have passed through the doors of this landmark restaurant, set in an adobe-style house that would seem more at home in New Mexico. It was started by Tony Vega, a wealthy cattle rancher who died in 1991, as a place for him to come with his fellow ranchers. The story goes that when they went out drinking, the one who sat (or fell) down first had to pick up the tab; Los Parados means "the standing ones." Excellently grilled steaks and chicken as well as tasty Mexican specialties are served in a large room, decorated in muted southwestern colors, with a wood-burning kiva fireplace; the *carne asada* (charbroiled strips of marinated beef) with guacamole is particularly good. A private dining room is lined with photographs of Tony Vega and all the important people in town, including native Chihuahuan Anthony Quinn. ⊠ *Av. Juárez 3901,* ☎ *14/15–35–09 or 14/10–53–35. AE, MC, V.*

$$ ✕ **La Calesa.** A large, dimly lit room with wood paneling and red tablecloths and curtains, this looks like the classic steakhouse it is. The onion soup and chilies with *aserdo* (a local cheese) make good appetizers. The filet mignon and rib-eye steaks from the area are particularly recommended as entrées; try the former cooked in garlic with shrimp and mushrooms. The clubby bar has a good selection of wines and liquors. ⊠ *Av. Juárez 3300,* ☎ *14/10–10–38 or 14/16–02–22. AE, MC, V.*

$ ✕ **El Taquito.** Three blocks south of the Palacio del Gobierno, this modest restaurant specializes in tacos and other typical Mexican dishes, although the dining room, with vines and black-and-white etchings of local scenes on the wall, looks somewhat Mediterranean. The chilies rellenos, enchiladas suizas, and chicken burritos with mole sauce are all good choices; you can get a bottle of sangria to accompany your meal for about $6. ✉ *Venustiano Carranza 1818,* ☎ *14/10–21–44. Reservations not accepted. No credit cards.*

$ ✕ **La Parilla.** A good place to take a break from downtown sightseeing, this fast-food eatery across the street from the Hotel San Francisco will delight dedicated carnivores. After the waiter hands you an order form–menu on which you mark your choice, he'll come over with a tray bearing the cuts of meat being offered that day. A strolling guitarist makes the rounds of this plain, white-walled room with plastic tables and chairs and an open grill in the back. The *menu turístico* includes steak with mashed potatoes, soup, and salad for about $6.50; you'll get your own grill if you order the house special, *parillados*—a sirloin platter served with guacamole and chili sauces as well as potatoes. ✉ *Victoria 420,* ☎ *14/15–58–56. Reservations not accepted. AE, MC, V.*

$$$$ ▦ **Villa Suites.** This appealing property combines comfort, style, and
★ convenience: Ten minutes from the downtown sights but set off in a quiet area, it is the first all-suites hotel in Chihuahua. Tastefully decorated in contemporary style with a green or blue and beige color scheme, each of the rooms has a kitchenette with stove, dishwasher, and coffeemaker, as well as a VCR and an exercycle. A complimentary Continental breakfast buffet is served at the Clubhouse, which also houses the hotel's indoor pool, hot tub, and exercise equipment. Eager to accommodate the many American business travelers who stay here, the English-speaking staff is friendly and helpful. ✉ *Escudero 702, 31000,* ☎ *14/14–33–50,* FAX *14/14–33–13. 72 suites. Restaurant, room service, indoor and outdoor pools, spa, health club, basketball, Ping-Pong. AE, DC, MC, V.*

$$$ ▦ **Hotel San Francisco.** A favorite of Mexican business travelers, this modern four-story hotel has a prime location right next to the Catedral and Plaza de Armas. Its clean and comfortable if somewhat bland rooms are equipped with color televisions and telephones. The lobby, somewhat gloomy during the day, is lively at night. ✉ *Victoria 409, 31000,* ☎ *14/16–75–50, or toll-free in Mexico, 91–800/1–41–07, or in the U.S., 800/847–2546;* FAX *14/15–35–38. 111 rooms, 20 suites. Restaurant-bar, travel services. AE, MC, V.*

$$ ▦ **Posada Tierra Blanca.** Across the street from the Palacio del Sol but considerably less expensive, this modern motel-style property is convenient to the downtown sights. Rooms, decorated in red and black with pseudo-antique furnishings, are large and well heated in winter; all have TVs. The striking *Stages of Man* mural in the lobby was painted by Pina Mora, the same artist who decorated the courtyard of the Palacio del Gobierno. ✉ *Niños Heroes 100,* ☎ *14/15–00–00. 103 rooms with bath. Restaurant, piano bar, pool. AE, MC, V.*

Nightlife and the Arts

Chihuahua has the most nightlife options in the Copper Canyon area. **La Reggae** (✉ Blvd. Ortiz Mena and Bosque de la Reina, ☎ 14/15–47–55) draws a crowd with dancing feet for its rock 'n' roll bands. At **Chihuahua Charlie** (✉ Av. Juárez 3329, ☎ 14/17–70–65), DJs spin discs nightly; come early for dinner—the food is as good as the music. The popular **La Puerta de Alcalá** disco (✉ Av. Revolución 1608, ☎ 14/15–83–93) sometimes has live music. The bar at the **Hotel San Francisco** (☞ Dining and Lodging, *above*) features a good lounge singer. The **Hotel Sicomoro** (✉ Blvd. Ortiz Mena 411, ☎ 14/13–54–45) has live entertainment nightly in its lobby bar.

Shopping

Mercado de Artesanías (✉ Calle Victoria 506, across from the cathedral, ☎ 14/16–27–16) sells everything from jewelry, candy, and T-shirts to crafts from all over the region. The small **gift shop at the Museo de Arte Popular** (✉ Calle Reforma 5, no phone) has a good selection of items from all over Mexico, including many that are made by the Tarahumara. In addition to selling gems and geodes from the area, the **Rock Shop** (✉ Calle Décima, directly across from Pancho Villa's home, ☎ 14/15–28–82) offers a wide variety of crafts.

THE COPPER CANYON AND CHIHUAHUA CITY A TO Z

Arriving and Departing

By Boat

The Baja Express catamaran from La Paz to Topolobampo is no longer running; the only service provided for passengers is via **car ferry,** which takes eight to nine hours and is not always available. In Los Mochis, contact Viajes Paotan (✉ Serapio Rendon 517 Pte., ☎ 681/5–19–14) for information and reservations; in Topolobampo, contact Grupo Sematur de California (☎ 681/2–01–04 or 800/6–96–96, 🖷 681/2–00–34).

By Bus

CHIHUAHUA

The **Transportes de Norte** (☎ 14/29–02–42 or 14/29–02–40), **Chihuahuenses** (☎ 14/29–02–42 or 14/29–02–40), and **Omnibus de México** (☎ 14/10–30–90) lines run clean, air-conditioned buses from Ciudad Juárez to Chihuahua; these leave approximately every 15 minutes from 7 AM to 8 PM. The cost of the trip, which takes about 4½ hours, is approximately $17 for first class, $22 for the new Ejectivo luxury coaches. Buses shuttle between El Paso and Ciudad Juárez every two hours; the price is $5.

LOS MOCHIS

The **Elite** (☎ 631/3–54–01), **Transportes del Pacífico** (☎ 631/3–16–06), **Transport Norte de Sonora** (☎ 631/2–54–54), and **TUFESA** (☎ 631/3–38–62) bus lines all leave every hour from Nogales, Sonora, to Los Mochis; with luck, the trip should take about 12 hours. The cost is approximately $30.

By Car

Most U.S. visitors drive to **Chihuahua** via Mexico Highway 45 from the El Paso–Ciudad Juárez border, a distance of 375 kilometers (233 miles), or up from Mexico City, 1,440 kilometers (895 miles). The drive down to **Los Mochis** from Nogales on the Arizona border via Mexico Highway 15, four lanes much of the way, is a distance of 763 kilometers (474 miles).

Paved roads now connect Chihuahua to **Creel**: Take Mexico Highway 16 west to San Pedro, then State Highway 127 south to Creel. The 300-kilometer (186-mile) trip takes 3½ to 4 hours if the weather is good. This drive, through the pine forests of the Sierra Madre foothills, is more scenic than the railroad route via the plains area. Driving is a good option if you have a four-wheel-drive vehicle, because there are many worthwhile, if difficult, excursions into the canyons from Creel. A road from Chihuahua to **Bahuichivo** via **Divisadero** has recently been finished, but it is not recommended: It's full of potholes and especially dangerous during rain or snow, even with a four-wheel-drive vehicle. A route to Urique Canyon is also planned.

By Plane

CHIHUAHUA

Aeromexico (☎ 14/15–63–03 in Chihuahua) has a daily direct flight to Chihuahua from Los Angeles, as well as daily flights from Tucson (with a plane change at Hermosillo) and from San Antonio (with a connection in Monterrey). Within Mexico, the airline has four daily flights to Chihuahua from Mexico City, two from Monterrey, one from Guadalajara, and one from Tijuana.

LOS MOCHIS

AeroCalifornia (☎ 681/8–16–16 in Los Mochis) has daily flights from Los Angeles and Tucson to Los Mochis and also flies from Tijuana, Mexico City, and Guadalajara daily. On **Aeromexico** (☎ 681/5–29–50 in Los Mochis) you can get to Los Mochis from Tucson, Mexico City, and La Paz every day.

By Train

At present, there is no first-class service from any U.S. border city to either Los Mochis or Chihuahua. For the most current information, contact **Mexico by Train** (☎ FAX 210/725–3659 or 800/321–1699). Some luxury trains go directly from the U.S. to the Copper Canyon, (☞ Train Tours *in* Guided Tours, *below*).

Getting Around

By Taxi

In **Chihuahua,** taxis are easy to find; they can be engaged at your hotel or hailed on the street. They're also readily available in **Los Mochis,** but not very cheap for long distances. It costs about $17 to get to the airport from downtown Los Mochis. Since fares are negotiable, always agree on a price before entering the cab. You'll usually pay less if you speak some Spanish.

By Train

The Ferrocarril Chihuahua al Pacífico line (or Che'Pa', as it is affectionately called by locals) runs a first-class and a second-class train daily in each direction from Chihuahua and Los Mochis through the Copper Canyon.

The first-class train departs from Los Mochis at 6 AM (be sure to sit on the right side of the train for the best views) and arrives in Chihuahua 12 hours later; westbound, it departs from Chihuahua at 7 AM and arrives in Los Mochis around 7 PM (most of the time, but problems with the weather or other difficulties may cause long or short delays). Tickets can be purchased through almost any hotel in Los Mochis or Chihuahua or directly at the train station. The price is about $40 each way, but there's a 15% charge for any stopovers en route. These should be arranged at the time of ticket purchase. Reservations (☎ 14/15–77–56 in Chihuahua, ☎ 681/5–77–75 in Los Mochis) should be made at least a week in advance during the busy months of July and August and around Christmas and Easter. It's best to book through a hotel, tour company, or travel agency, as the phones in the local train stations are rarely answered. Note: Once the pride of the Mexican rail system, the first-class train, called *El Tren Estella,* has become run-down in recent years. It's the scenery, not the vehicle, that continues to draw passengers. We've also had reports of tourist robberies on the Chihuahua al Pacífico train. Exercise caution by carrying passports and cash in a money belt and leaving your jewelry at home.

The second-class train, referred to as *El Pollero*, leaves an hour later from each terminus but makes many stops and is scheduled to arrive 3½ hours later in both directions than the first-class train. Though it is less comfortable, this train is a good way to meet the locals. No reservations are needed; prices are approximately $12 each way. There are no dining cars on either train; it's best to bring your own food and water. Soda, beer, snacks, and ham-and-cheese sandwiches are available on the first-class train.

It's possible to ship your car on the train, but it's not worth the expense or the bother. If you're driving down to Los Mochis, you're better off leaving your car there and taking the train round-trip. If you're coming via Chihuahua, however, you should consider driving to Creel and doing a round-trip from there (☞ Arriving and Departing by Car, *above*).

Contacts and Resources

Car Rentals

CHIHUAHUA

Avis (⊠ Av. Universidad 1703, ☎ 14/14–19–99), **Hertz** (⊠ Av. Revolución 514, ☎ 14/16–64–73), and **Dollar** (⊠ Hotel Sicomoro, Ortiz Mena 405, ☎ 14/14–21–71) all have offices at the airport also.

LOS MOCHIS

Car companies in town include **Budget** (⊠ Leyva and Angel Flores, behind the Santa Anita Hotel, ☎ 681/5–83–00, FAX 681/5–84–00); **National** (⊠ Leyva 127 Nte., ☎ 681/2–65–52); and **Aga** (⊠ Leyva and Callejón Municipal, ☎ 681/2–53–60).

Emergencies

CHIHUAHUA

Police (☎ 14/81–19–00), **Cruz Roja** (Red Cross; ☎ 14/11–14–84 or 14/11–22–11), and **Bomberos** (Fire Department; ☎ 14/10–07–70). Two facilities for handling the injured or sick are **Clínica del Parque** (⊠ Calle de la Llave and Leal Rodriguez, ☎ 14/15–74–11 or 14/15–90–87) and **Hospital del Centro del Estado** (⊠ Calle 33 and Rosales, ☎ 14/15–47–20).

LOS MOCHIS

Police (☎ 681/2–00–33); **Cruz Roja** (⊠ Guillermo Prieto and Tenochtitlan, ☎ 681/5–08–08).

Guided Tours

Almost all of the large hotels in Los Mochis and Chihuahua have in-house travel agencies that can arrange both city tours and tours of the Copper Canyon area, as well as hiking, hunting, and fishing expeditions. In Los Mochis, the Santa Anita and La Colinas hotels (☞ Dining and Lodging, *above*) offer city tours for about $17 per person; these take approximately 3½ to 4 hours and include a boat trip around Topolobampo Bay. In Chihuahua, independent travel agents include **Quezada Tours** (⊠ Calle Aldama 316–3, ☎ 14/15–75–13 or 14/15–70–19, FAX 14/15–75–44), the American Express agent **Rojo y Casavantes** (⊠ Calle Vincent Guerrero 1207, ☎ 14/15–58–58 or 14/15–74–70, FAX 14/15–53–80), and, particularly recommended, **Turismo Al Mar** (⊠ Av. Reforma 400, ☎ 14/16–65–89 or 14/16–59–50, FAX 14/16–65–89). Half-day city tours for a minimum of two people average $16 per person; full-day van trips into Mennonite country run about $40 per person, with a minimum of four needed.

From the United States, the oldest operator in the area is **Pan American Tours** (⊠ Box 9401, El Paso, TX 79984, ☎ 915/778–5395 or

800/876–3942). Prices for mostly tailor-made, independent tours between Los Mochis and Chihuahua—based on double occupancy and including train but not airfare—range from about $200 to $500 per person, depending on length of stay and number of stops made; some meals and all transfers are covered. **Synergy Tours** (✉ 7336 E. Shoeman Lane, Suite E114, Scottsdale, AZ 85251, ☎ 800/369–1797, 🆁🅰🆇 602/994–4439) features packages to the Copper Canyon via Chihuahua City about eight to 10 times a year. The company also acts as a travel agent for those who want to get off the beaten path. **Columbus Travel** (✉ 900 Ridge Creek Lane, Bulverde, TX 78163, ☎ 210/885–2000 or 800/843–1060, 🆁🅰🆇 210/885–2010) offers daily departures to the Copper Canyon from Presidio or El Paso, Texas, as well as from Tucson and Los Angeles. Trips range from $680 for five nights to $2,000 for a 12-day excursion including a stay in Batopilas. The company has agents in Divisadero, Cerocahui, and Alamos who arrange day hikes. Five to 10% of their profits go to benefit the Tarahumara. **California Native** (✉ 6701 W. 87th Pl., Los Angeles, CA 90045, ☎ 800/926–1140) runs a seven-day escorted trip through the Copper Canyon every month for $1,500, which includes round-trip airfare from Los Angeles, Tucson, or El Paso, as well as ground transportation, lodging, meals, and tips. It also offers a nine-day backpacking trip into the area for about $450. This rate includes train fare from Los Mochis or Chihuahua into the canyons, three nights' lodgings, a guide for the hike, much of the food for the hike, and burros to carry food and cooking supplies. Hikers carry their own packs.

TRAIN TOURS

Sierra Madre Express of Tucson (✉ Box 26381, Tucson, AZ 85726, ☎ 520/747–0346 or 800/666–0346) runs its own deluxe trains (with dome car, dining car, and Pullman) to the Copper Canyon from Tucson, offering eight-day, seven-night trips approximately four times a year; its trips combine the charm of sleeping on the train with first-class accommodations. Two other tour operators, **Tauck Tours** (✉ Box 5027, Westport, CT 06881, ☎ 800/468–2825) and **RFD Travel** (✉ 5201 Johnson Dr., Mission, KS 66205, ☎ 800/365–5389), charter the trains and their personnel for similar excursions the rest of the time. Excursions into the area are also offered by **DRC Rail Tours** (✉ 16800 Greenspoint Park Dr., Suite 245 N, Houston, TX 77060, ☎ 800/659–7602); they depart from El Paso. Prices start from $1,300 (per person, based on double occupancy) for a five-day trip and can run as high as $4,300 for an eight-day trip, though DRC offers a nine-day excursion for $2,400.

Late-Night Pharmacies

CHIHUAHUA

Chihuahua has an abundance of pharmacies in the center of the city that provide late-night service. **Farmacia Mendoza** (✉ Calle Aldama 1901, ☎ 14/16–44–14 or 14/10–27–96) is open 24 hours.

LOS MOCHIS

Farmacia San Jorge (✉ Av. Independencia and Angel Flores, ☎ 681/5–74–74) in Los Mochis is open 24 hours a day.

Money Exchange

Be sure to change money before you get into real barranca country: There are no banks in Cerocahui, Divisadero, or Posada Barrancas, and no guarantee that the hotels in those places will have enough cash to accommodate you. A bank in the main plaza at Creel transacts foreign exchanges only from 10:30 to noon. Even in Los Mochis, banking hours are, for the most part, limited to weekdays between 9 and 1; some banks reopen at 3 and a few are open on Saturday morning. In Chihuahua banks are open weekdays from 9 to 1:30 and from 3:30

to 7:30, and Saturday from 9 to 1:30; the **Casa de Cambio Rachasa** (✉ Av. Ocampo and Niños Heroes, ☎ 14/10–03–33; ⊘ Mon.–Sat. 9–9, Sun. 9–2) and **Rubarza** (✉ Aldamá 202A, ☎ 14/16–60–44; ⊘ weekdays 9–7, Sat. 10–1) both offer good exchange rates and quick service. In general, you're best off getting your pesos at the hotels in Los Mochis and Chihuahua; the exchange rate is slightly lower, but no commission is charged, and you won't have to spend a confusing half hour or more switching lines at the bank.

Visitor Information

CHIHUAHUA

Government Tourist Office: ✉ *Av. Libertad and Calle 13, 1st Floor,* ☎ *14/16–21–06 or 14/15–91–24, ext. 4511 or 4512.* ⊘ *Weekdays 8– 1:30 and 3:30–6.* **Oficina de Información:** ✉ *Central patio of the Palacio del Gobierno in Plaza Hidalgo,* ☎ *14/15–91–24, ext. 4515.* ⊘ *Mon.–Sat. 9–7 and Sun. 9–4.*

LOS MOCHIS

Oficina de Turismo: ✉ *Allende and Ordoñez, inside the Unidad Administrativa del Gobierno del Estado building, on the first floor in the back,* ☎ *681/2–66–40 or 681/2–76–10, ext. 131.*

6 Pacific Coast Resorts

Hollywood introduced us to two of the Mexican Riviera's most popular towns: Liz Taylor and Richard Burton's sleepy, steamy Puerta Vallarta in The Night of the Iguana *and the sparkling Manzanillo coast that served as the backdrop to Bo Derek in* 10. *These days both places are prime cruise ship destinations, as is Mazatlán, a bustling port that attracts sportsfishing enthusiasts and surfers. Ixtapa/ Zihuatanejo is a twofer attraction, a laid-back fishing village adjoining a glitzy resort.*

Updated by
Wendy Luft

ACROSS THE GULF OF CALIFORNIA from the Baja California Peninsula lies Mazatlán, Mexico's largest Pacific port and the major Mexican resort closest to the United States, some 1,200 kilometers (750 miles) south of the Arizona border. This is the beginning of what cruise-ship operators now call the Mexican Riviera, or the Gold Coast. The coastline for the next 1,400 kilometers (900 miles) is Mexico's tropical paradise. The Gulf of California, or the Sea of Cortés, as it is also called, ends just below the Tropic of Cancer, leaving the Pacific coastline open to fresh sea breezes. The Mexican Riviera resorts—Mazatlán, Puerto Vallarta, Manzanillo, Ixtapa, Zihuatanejo, and Acapulco—are therefore less muggy than gulf towns to the north. The temperature of the water is a bit lower, however, and waves can get very rough.

The Pacific coast doesn't have the rich cultural heritage of Mexico's inland colonial villages and silver cities, and the history is sketchy at best. This is not an area for touring ruins, museums, and cathedrals but rather a gathering spot for sun worshipers, sportfishing enthusiasts, surfers, and swimmers. Not far from the resort regions are jungle streams and ocean coves, but the majority of visitors never venture to these isolated sites, preferring instead to immerse themselves in the simultaneously bustling and restful resort lifestyle, where great dining, shopping, and sunbathing are the major draws.

Mazatlán is first and foremost a busy commercial center, thanks to an excellent port and the fertility of the surrounding countryside. More than 600,000 acres of farmland near Mazatlán produce tomatoes, melons, cantaloupes, wheat, and cotton, much of which is shipped to the United States. And nearly all the 150,000 tons of shrimp that are hauled in annually are processed and frozen for the American and Japanese markets.

Sportfishing accounts for Mazatlán's resort status. The port sits at the juncture of the Pacific and the Sea of Cortés, forming what has been called the world's greatest natural fish trap. But fishing is not the only attraction. Hunters are drawn to the quail, duck, and dove that thrive in the hillsides, and surfers find great waves on nearby beaches. Another draw is the relatively low price of accommodations—about half the going rate of accommodations in Cancún.

Tepic, capital of the state of Nayarit, lies between Mazatlán and Puerto Vallarta. It's the jumping-off point to these destinations for train travelers, who can catch public buses to the coast. Budget travelers and those who eschew the bustle of the megaresorts often head straight for San Blas, a small seaside village some 37 kilometers (23 miles) northwest of Tepic through the jungle.

Some 323 kilometers (200 miles) south of Mazatlán is Puerto Vallarta, by far the best-known resort on the upper Pacific coast. The late film director (and sometime resident) John Huston put the town on the map when he filmed Tennessee Williams's *The Night of the Iguana* on the outskirts of the village in 1964. The gossip about stars Richard Burton and Elizabeth Taylor—both married at the time, but not to each other—brought this quaint Mexican fishing village with its cobblestoned lanes and whitewashed, tile-roofed houses to the public's attention. Before long, travel agents were deluged with queries about Puerto Vallarta, a place many had never heard of before.

More than 250,000 people live in Puerto Vallarta today, and upwards of 700,000 foreign tourists arrive each year. The fabled cobblestoned

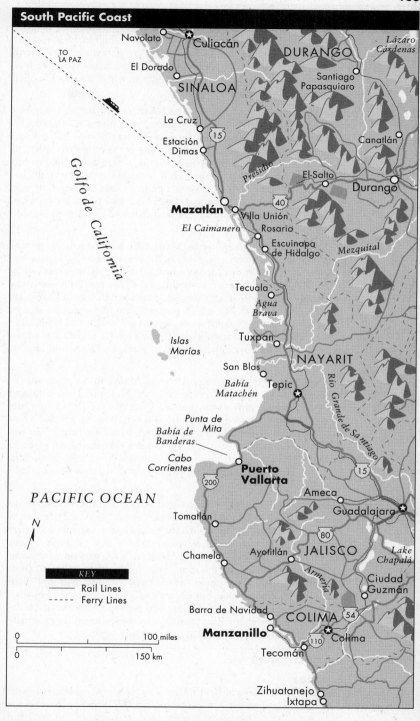

Navolato
Culiacán
DURANGO
Lázaro Cárdenas
TO LA PAZ
El Dorado
SINALOA
Santiago Papasquiaro
La Cruz
15
Canatlán
Estación Dimas
Presidio
El-Salto
Durango
40
Golfo de California
Mazatlán
Villa Unión
El Caimanero
Rosario
Escuinapa de Hidalgo
Mezquital
Tecuala
Agua Brava
Islas Marías
Tuxpan
NAYARIT
San Blas
Tepic
Bahía Matachén
Río Grande de Santiago
Punta de Mita
Bahía de Banderas
Cabo Corrientes
Puerto Vallarta
200
15
Ameca
Guadalajara
PACIFIC OCEAN
Tomatlán
N
80
Lake Chapalá
Chamela
Ayotitlán
JALISCO
Armería
Ciudad Guzmán
KEY
Rail Lines
Ferry Lines
Barra de Navidad
COLIMA
54
Manzanillo
110
Colima
Tecomán
0 ——— 100 miles
0 ——— 150 km
Zihuatanejo
Ixtapa

streets are clogged with bumper-to-bumper traffic during the holiday season, and the sounds of construction often drown out the pounding surf. Elizabeth Taylor's and Richard Burton's adjoining homes are now a bed-and-breakfast. Despite its resort status, parts of Puerto Vallarta are still picturesque. For a sense of the Eden that once was, travel out of town to the lush green mountains where the Río Tomatlán tumbles over boulders into the sea.

Manzanillo, marking the southern end of the central Pacific coast, had more of a storybook start than did Puerto Vallarta. Conquistador Hernán Cortés envisioned the area as a gateway to the Orient: From these shores, Spanish galleons would bring in the riches of Cathay to be trekked across the continent to Veracruz, where they would be off-loaded to vessels headed for Spain. But Acapulco, not Manzanillo, became the port of call for the Manila galleons that arrived each year with riches from beyond the seas. Pirates are said to have staked out Manzanillo during the colonial era, and chests of loot are rumored to be buried beneath the sands.

With the coming of the railroads, Manzanillo became a major port of entry, albeit not a pretty one. Forty or 50 years ago, a few seaside hotels opened up on the outskirts of town, which vacationers reached by train. The jet age, however, seemed to doom the port as a sunny vacation spot. Then Bolivian tin magnate Antenor Patiño built Las Hadas (The Fairies), a lavish Moorish-style resort complex, inaugurated in 1974. It attracted the beautiful people, and for a while Las Hadas was better known than Manzanillo itself. The film *10* made a star of the resort as well as household names of its stars, Bo Derek and Dudley Moore.

In recent years, there's been a push to turn Manzanillo and coastal villages to the north, such as Barra de Navidad, Melaque, Tenacatita, and Costa de Careyes, into a tourist zone. A four-lane toll road now cuts the driving time between Manzanillo and Guadalajara, Mexico's second-largest city, to three hours. Older hotels have been spruced up and all-inclusive resorts constructed. On the drawing board are plans to build a $50 million marina complex in downtown Manzanillo, with 240 slips, hotels, restaurants, shops, and a pedestrian walkway along the shore.

The southernmost of the Pacific Coast resorts and the newest kid on the scene—like Cancún, it was developed by the Mexican government in the early 1970s—Ixtapa/Zihuatanejo lies in the northwestern part of the State of Guerrero coastline, some 500 kilometers (300 miles) south of Manzanillo. It's unique among Mexican beach getaways in that it comprises two distinct destinations only 7 kilometers (4 miles) from each other. Ixtapa is the glitzier of the two, with international chain hotels lining its hotel zone, but it's far smaller and more low key than older resorts like Puerto Vallarta and new ones such as Cancún. Its development put neighbor Zihuatanejo, a sleepy fishing village virtually unknown even among Mexicans, on the tourist map.

Pleasures and Pastimes

Beaches

This area boasts some of North America's most inviting beaches, with deliciously warm waters and spectacular sunsets. There are beaches for every taste: long stretches of creamy sand, crescents of soft gold and black volcanic grains, secluded coves, and pristine shores accessible only by boat.

Dining

The emphasis in **Mazatlán** is on casual, bountiful dining, and the prices are reasonable. Shrimp and fresh fish are the highlights; be sure to have a seafood cocktail along the beach. **Puerto Vallarta** has the widest array of restaurants, some with spectacular views, others hidden in the small, romantic patios of former homes, and still others—especially those on the malecón—as popular for people-watching as they are for their great seafood. Several **Manzanillo** dining spots offer scenic views of the jungle and water that compensate for their lack of culinary excitement. In **Ixtapa/Zihuatanejo,** restaurants range from simple beach eateries to deluxe establishments with international chefs. Even the most glamorous restaurants here cost considerably less than those in other resorts such as Acapulco or Puerto Vallarta.

Dress in all the resorts is usually casual but not sloppy (no bathing suits or bare feet); chic resortwear is appropriate in the more expensive spots. Reservations are almost never necessary, but we have indicated those places that require them. Be aware that some restaurants, particularly in the hotels, add a 10%–15% service charge to your tab, as well as 10% tax.

CATEGORY	COST*
$$$$	over $35
$$$	$25–$35
$$	$15–$25
$	under $15

per person, excluding drinks, service, and sales tax (10%)

Fishing

Mazatlán is considered to be the top billfish port on the Mexican Pacific. The sailfish run from May to November and the marlin from November to May, and there is also plenty of swordfish, tuna, shark, bonito, and red snapper, year-round. Nine fishing fleets operate some 80 cruisers. Light tackle fishing in the lagoons is also popular.

Sportfishing is good off **Puerto Vallarta** most of the year, particularly for billfish, roosterfish, dorado, yellowtail, and bonito. The marlin season begins in November.

Manzanillo claims to be the sailfishing capital of the world; the season runs from mid-October through March, with an international sailfish tournament held every November. Blue marlin and dorado are also abundant.

Ixtapa/Zihuatanejo is just being discovered as Mexico's new sportfishing destination. Anglers revel in the profusion of sailfish, black and blue marlin (the record is over 1,000 pounds), as well as yellowfin tuna and dorado. Aeromexico Vacations (☎ 800/245–8585), the airline's in-house tour program, offers comprehensive sportfishing packages including air, hotel and sportfishing on specialized cruisers with expert bilingual skippers.

Horseback Riding

In most of the Pacific Coast resorts, horseback riding along the shore is popular and horses can be rented by the hour at major beaches. In **Puerto Vallarta,** several stables offer three-hour trips into the mountains, sunset rides, and longer excursions to charming colonial villages in the Sierra Madre.

Lodging

Although not known for its upscale resorts, **Mazatlán** now offers travelers a fair dose of luxury properties, along with comfortable beachfront hotels; it also has one of the highest concentrations of trailer parks in the country. In **Puerto Vallarta,** accommodations range from tiny inns to luxury waterfront hotels and spectacular resorts tucked away on hidden coves. Even today, **Manzanillo** is still best known for Las Hadas, the spectacular hotel built in 1974 by Bolivian tin magnate Antenor Patiño. **Ixtapa/Zihuatanejo** runs the lodging gamut—big beachfront properties are the norm in Ixtapa, whereas Zihuatanejo offers downtown budget hotels along with two of the most exclusive small hotels in Mexico.

Most hotels raise their rates for the November–April high season; rates are lowest in the summer, during the rainy season. Price categories are based on high-season rates—expect to pay 25% less during the off-season.

CATEGORY	COST*
$$$$	over $160
$$$	$90–$160
$$	$40–$90
$	under $40

All prices are for a standard double room, excluding 10% tax.

Shopping

You can spend as much time shopping in **Puerto Vallarta** as you can lazing in the sun; shops selling excellent crafts from around the country vie with upscale art galleries and clothing boutiques for buyers' attention, especially in the downtown area. **Zihuatanejo** has some extremely colorful crafts markets; the unique ceramics and masks from the state of Guerrero, where the little fishing town is located, are especially plentiful.

Water Sports

Parasailing, swimming, windsurfing, sailing, and waterskiing are all popular activities in the warm waters of the Pacific Coast resorts. Manzanillo and Mazatlán offer some of the finest surfing in Mexico, while the best diving spots in this area are found off Puerto Vallarta. In November, there are international fishing tournaments in Manzanillo and Puerto Vallarta.

Exploring the Pacific Coast Resorts

When to Tour the Pacific Coast Resorts

The winter season (December through April) is when the Pacific Coast resorts are at their best, with temperatures generally in the 70s and 80s (they're a bit higher in Ixtapa/Zihuatanejo, which is the farthest south). The off-season brings humidity and mosquitos along with temperatures in the 80s and 90s (here northernmost Mazatlán is the cooler exception), but at this time of year you'll also enjoy emptier beaches, warmer water (well into the 70s) and less-crowded streets—as well as a 25% to 35% reduction in room rates and the opportunity to do a little bargaining on rental car costs. Toward the end of the rainy season (June through September), which generally involves only brief daily showers, the countryside and the mountainous backdrop of the Sierra Madre del Sur turn brilliantly green with multicolored blossoms of trees and flowers.

Mazatlán holds an especially colorful Carnival during the week preceding Ash Wednesday, featuring parades, charreadas (Mexican-style rodeos), floats, fancy dress balls, and lots of eating and dancing. During the entire month of May, Puerto Vallarta celebrates the incorporation of its city with various festive activities, including bullfights and fireworks.

...ATLÁN

Mazatlán is the Aztec word for "place of the deer," and long ago its islands and shores sheltered far more deer than humans. Today it is a city of some 400,000 residents and draws more than 1 million tourists a year. Sunning, surfing, and sailing have caught on here, and in the winter months visitors from inland Mexico, the United States, and Canada flock to Mazatlán for a break in the sun. Hotel and restaurant prices are lower than elsewhere on the coast, and the ambience is more that of a fishing town than a tourist haven.

Upscale resorts and ritzy restaurants are not part of Mazatlán's repertoire, though there is a fair dose of luxury at El Cid, Royal Villas, and Pueblo Bonito resorts. Work is under way on two adjacent marinas on the estuary that stretches north from the El Cid golf course. The El Cid Resort complex is being expanded, and one of Mexico's leading development companies, Grupo Situr, is building a residential resort community that calls for an 18-hole golf course, a large marina, villas, condos, and a Bel-Air hotel.

Hunting and fishing were the original draw for visitors. At one time duck, quail, pheasant, and other wildfowl fed in the lagoons; jaguars, mountain lions, rabbits, and coyotes roamed the surrounding hills. Hunters have to search a little harder and farther for their these days, but there's still plenty of wildlife near Mazatlán. The is the base for Mexico's largest sportfishing fleet; fishermen ha biggest catches (in size and number) on the coast. The average a haul is 10,000 sailfish and 5,000 marlin; a record 973-pound and 203-pound sailfish were pulled from these waters.

The Spaniards settled in the Mazatlán region in 1531 and use digenous people as a labor force to create the port and village. ter of Mazatlán gradually moved north, so that the original s 32 kilometers (20 miles) southeast of the harbor.

The port has a history of blockades. In 1847 during the Me U.S. forces marched down from the border through northe and closed the port. In 1864, the French bombarded the ci controlled it for several years. Mexico's own internal warr took over from time to time. And after the Civil War in the a group of southerners tried to turn Mazatlán into a sla

Today Mazatlán has the largest shrimping fleet in Mexic of Mexico's richest states, uses Mazatlán's port to shi products.

Exploring Mazatlán

Mazatlán's highlights are spread far and wide, an section of town to the other can take hours. The via pulmonías, so you can sunbathe and take p along, although you won't be able to roll up ar yourself from automobile fumes. If you choose you can tour at your own pace. There are no t except near the market in downtown, where pa problem. Downtown is virtually the only a be walked; many visitors never see it, but it' ing here.

A Good Tour
Numbers in the text correspond to numb Mazatlán map.

Most visitors set out to tour the city from the **Zona D**
Mazatlán's tourist region, which begins at Punta Camaró
travel north from here along the coast on Avenida Sábalo, yo
some of the city's most luxurious and priciest hotels; oppos
beach are many of the better low-cost motels. This route affords a
view of Mazatlán's three Pacific islands—**Isla de los Pájaros, Isl**
los Venados, and **Isla de los Chivos.** Just past the Camino Real rese
Avenida Camarón Sábalo becomes Avenida Sábalo Cerritos and cross
over the **Estero del Sábalo,** a long lagoon popular with bird-watchers
The area north of here will someday be an exclusive touring and resort area; towering condos are already being built.

South of the Zona Dorado, the main road changes names frequently.
The 16-kilometer (10-mile) **malecón,** Mazatlán's version of a main highway and beachfront boardwalk, begins at Punta Camarón and is here
called Avenida del Mar. In a few blocks, you'll come to the city's
aquarium, **Acuario Mazatlán** ②, down Avenida de los Deportes. Avenida
del Mar continues past beaches popular with the locals and travelers
staying at the budget hotels across the street. You're sure to notice the
avenue's main landmark, the **Monumento al Pescador**: An enormous,
voluptuous, nude woman reclines on an anchor, her hand extended toward a nude fisherman dragging his nets.

Calle Juárez and Calle Cinco de Mayo intersect with Avenida del Mar
and lead to Mazatlán's real downtown, where the streets are filled with
uses and locals rushing to and from work and the market. The heart
the city is the **Plaza Revolución** ③ or the zócalo; just across the street
'll see the spires of the **Mazatlán Catedral** ④. On the streets facing
ócalo are the City Hall, banks, post office, and telegraph office.
t three blocks southeast of the zócalo, the **Teatro Angela Peralta,**
1860 and now beautifully restored, was declared a historic mon-
1990. Three blocks to the east is the **Museo Arqueológico** ⑤.

g the waterfront, Avenida del Mar turns into Paseo Claussen
south. Some of Mazatlán's best surfing beaches are along
cluding Playa los Piños. If you continue along the malecón,
Fuerte Carranza, an old Spanish fort built to defend the
e French; **Casa del Marino,** a shelter for sailors; **High-**
here young men climb to a white platform and plunge
ectacular at night, when the divers leap carrying flam-
de la Neveria, so named because wealthy landown-
ported ice from San Francisco in the late 1800s and
und tunnels here; and **La Mazatleca,** a bronze nymph
wave. Across the street is a small bronze deer,
Paseo Claussen leads into **Olas Altas,** site of Old
for tourism in the 1940s. Olas Altas (which
at a small traffic circle. A plaque at the circle
inaloa. Above Olas Altas is **Cerro de Vigía** ⑥.

road becomes Paseo del Centenario and
peninsula. Here you'll come to **Cerro**
he second-highest lighthouse in the
f 36 nautical miles. It takes about
se, but you get a great view of
sula is devoted to boats, and
d military installations is
t is anchored at the base
sed by cruise ships and
dra leave from a small dock

Mazatlán

0 1000 meters
0 1000 yards

N

Playa los Cerritos
Playa Sábalo

Estero del Sábalo

Av. Camarón Sábalo

Isla de los Pájaros

ZONA DORADA

El Cid Resort ❶

Isla de los Venados

Isla de los Chivos

Playa las Gaviotas

Playa Isla de los Venados

Punta Camarón

Av. Loaiza

■ Bullring
Boulevard Rafael Buelna

15

Teodoro Mariscal Baseball Stadium

Av. del Mar

Av. Reforma

TO AIRPORT, COPALA AND CONCORDIA

Av. Insurgentes

Estero del Infiernillo

Bahía del Puerto Viejo

❷
Los Deportes
Bus Station
Río Tamazula
Playa Norte

Av. Juan Carrasco

Punta de Tiburón

Playa los Pinos

Playa Olas Altas

Cerro de la Nevería

Bahía Olas Altas

5 de Mayo
Juárez
Zaragoza
Paseo Claussen
Ocampo
❹ M. Escobedo
❸
❺
Av. M. Aleman

Gutierrez Najera

Av. Gabriel Leyva

Av. del Puerto

Canal de Navegación

Paseo del Centenario

❻

Av. Carnaval

Isla de la Piedra

Cerro del Creston

Sights to See

❷ Acuario Mazatlán. A perfect child-pleaser, Mazatlán's aquarium features tanks of sharks, sea horses, eels, lobsters, and multicolored salt- and freshwater fish. A fanciful bronze fountain and sculpture of two boys feeding a dolphin marks the aquarium's entrance, and an aviary sits amid the trees in the adjacent botanical garden. ⊠ *Av. de los Deportes 111,* ☎ *69/81–78–15.* ☒ *About $3.50.* ☉ *Daily 9:30–6:30.*

❻ Cerro de Vigía (Lookout Hill). The view from this windy hill above Olas Altas is fantastic: You can see both sides of Mazatlán, the harbor, and the Pacific. It's a steep climb up, better done by taxi than on foot. At the top of the hill you'll see a weather station, along with a rusty canon and the **Centenario Pérgola,** used by the Spaniards as a place to watch for pirates.

❹ Mazatlán Catedral. The blue-and-gold spires of the downtown cathedral are a city landmark. Built in 1890 and made a basilica in 1935, this church has a gilded and ornate triple altar, with murals of angels overhead and many small altars along the sides. A sign at the entrance requests that visitors be appropriately attired (no shorts or tank tops inside). ⊠ *Calles Juárez and Plazuela República.*

❺ Museo Arqueológico. The town's archaeological musuem houses a small but fairly interesting collection of artifacts from the region. ⊠ *Sixto Osuna 76, off Paseo Olas Altas,* ☎ *69/85–35–02.* ☒ *About $1, free Sun.* ☉ *Tues.–Sun. 10–1 and 4–7.*

❸ Plaza Revolución. This city square at the center of downtown hosts one of the most fascinating gazebos in Mexico—what looks like a '50s diner inside the lower level and a wrought-iron bandstand on top. The green-and-orange tile on the walls, ancient jukebox, and soda fountain serving shakes, burgers, and hot dogs couldn't make a more surprising sight. ⊠ *Bounded by 21 de Marzo to the north, Flores to the south, Benito Juaréz to the east, and Nelson to the west.*

❶ Zona Dorada. Marking the beginning of Mazatlán's tourist zone is **Punta Camarón (Shrimp Point),** the rocky outcropping on which Valentino's Disco sits, resembling a Moorish palace perched above the sea. To the north, Avenida Camarón Sábalo forms the eastern border of the zone, while Avenida Loaiza runs closer to the beach. In this four-block pocket are most of the hotels, shops, and restaurants, and the majority of nonresidents intent on having a good time sunning, shopping, and partying. This is the place to souvenir-shop, hit the discos, and check out the hotel bars.

NEED A
BREAK?
No Name Café (⊠ Av. Loaiza 417, ☎ 69/13–20–31), in the Mazatlán Arts and Crafts Center, is a good spot for a beer or *agua mineral* (mineral water) and lime. Mexico's version of Baskin-Robbins, **Helados Bing** (⊠ Av. Camarón Sábalo and Av. Gaviotas, no phone) has good hot-fudge sundaes and ice cream cones. At the **Panadería Panamá** (⊠ Camerón Sábalo across from Las Palmas hotel, ☎ 69/13–69–77), you can sit at a table and enjoy fragrant cinnamon-flavored coffee with fresh-baked pastries.

Beaches

Playa Isla de la Piedra

On weekends, local families bearing toys, rafts, and picnic lunches ride over to the island on *pangas* (small, open boats) from the dock near the train tracks. Sixteen kilometers (10 miles) of unspoiled beaches here allow enough room for all visitors to spread out and claim their own space. On Sundays, the island looks like a small village, with lots of music and fun. Many of the small *palapas* (beach shacks) set up along the sportfishing docks serve a tasty smoked marlin. The palapas near the launches to Isla de la Piedra sell sugarcane sticks, which look like bamboo and are good for quenching your thirst.

Playa Isla de los Venados

Boats make frequent departures from the Zona Dorada hotels for this beach on Deer Island. It's only a 10-minute ride, but the difference in ambience is striking; the beach is pretty, uncluttered, and clean, and you can hike around the southern point of the island to small, secluded coves covered with shells.

Playa Los Cerritos

The northernmost beach on the outskirts of town, which runs from Camino Real Resort to Punta Cerritos, is also the cleanest and least populated. The waves can be too rough for swimming, but they're great for surfing.

Playa Norte

This strand begins at Punta Camarón (Valentino's is a landmark) along Avenida del Mar and the malecón and runs to the Fisherman's Monument. The dark brown sand is dirty and rocky at some points, but clean at others, and is popular with those staying at hotels without beach access. Palapas selling cold drinks, tacos, and fresh fish line the beach; be sure to try the fresh coconut milk.

Playa Olas Altas

This beach, whose name means "high waves," was the first tourist beach in Mazatlán, running south along the malecón from the Fisherman's Monument. Surfers congregate here during the summer months, when the waves are at their highest.

Playa Sábalo and Playa las Gaviotas

Mazatlán's two most popular beaches are along the Zona Dorada. There are as many vendors selling blankets, pottery, lace tablecloths, and silver jewelry as there are sunbathers. Boats, Windsurfers, and parasailers line the shores. The beach is protected from heavy surf by the three islands—Venados, Pájaros, and Chivas. You can safely stroll these beaches until midnight and eavesdrop on the social action in the hotels while enjoying a few solitary, romantic moments sans vendors and crowds.

Dining

$$$ ✗ **Angelo's.** With its fresh flowers, cream-and-beige decor, and soft can-
★ dlelight, this is by far the most attractive restaurant in Mazatlán. The Italian and Continental cuisine is outstanding—try the veal scaloppini with mushrooms or shrimp marinara on pasta—and the service impeccable. ✉ *Pueblo Bonito hotel, Av. Camarón Sábalo 2121,* ☎ *69/ 14–37–00. AE, DC, MC, V. No lunch.*

$$$ ✗ **La Concha.** One of the prettiest waterside dining spots, La Concha
★ is a large enclosed palapa with three levels of seating, including a spacious dance floor decked with twinkling lights and outdoor tables by the sand. Adventurous types might attempt the stingray with black butter or calamari in its ink, while the more conservative can try a thick filet mignon cooked to perfection. During the winter season, a singer croons Las Vegas–style ballads as couples dance. La Concha is also open for breakfast. ✉ *El Cid Resort, Av. Camarón Sábalo,* ☎ *69/13–33– 33. AE, DC, MC, V.*

$$$ ✕ **Sr. Peppers.** Elegant yet unpretentious, with ceiling fans, lush foliage, and candlelit tables, Sr. Peppers serves choice steaks and lobsters cooked over a mesquite grill. Enjoy the dance floor and live music. ⊠ *Av. Camarón Sábalo across from Camino Real hotel,* ☎ *69/14–01– 20. AE, MC, V. No lunch.*

$$ ✕ **Casa Loma.** An out-of-the-way, elegant restaurant in a converted villa, Casa Loma serves international specialties such as chateaubriand, duck à l'orange, and osso buco. Lunch on the patio is less formal. Have a martini made by an expert, and save room for the fine pastries. ⊠ *Av. Gaviotas 104,* ☎ *69/13–53–98. MC, V. Closed late May–Sept.*

$$ ✕ **El Paraíso Tres Islas.** A wonderful palapa on the beach, across from
★ Sea Shell City (☞ Shopping, *below*), Tres Islas is a favorite with families who spend all Sunday afternoon feasting on fresh fish. Try smoked marlin, oysters diablo, octopus, or the seafood platter. The setting is the nicest in town, close to the water with a good view of the three islands. The waiters are friendly and eager to help. ⊠ *Av. Rodolfo T. Loaiza 404,* ☎ *69/14–28–12. MC, V.*

$$ ✕ **El Shrimp Bucket.** In Old Mazatlán, under forest-green awnings, is an establishment that was the original Carlos 'n Charlie's. The garden patio restaurant is much quieter than its successors—some would call it respectable. Best bets are fried shrimp served in clay buckets and barbecued ribs. Portions are plentiful. Early breakfast (from 6 AM) is also served. It's the place to see where all the action of the wildly popular Carlos Anderson chain began. ⊠ *Olas Altas 11-126,* ☎ *69/81–63– 50. AE, MC, V.*

$$ ✕ **Señor Frog.** Another member of the Carlos Anderson chain, Señor Frog is as noisy and entertaining as the rest. Bandidos carry tequila bottles and shot glasses in their bandoliers, leather belts that held ammunition in the old westerns. Barbecued ribs and chicken, served with corn on the cob, and heaping portions of standard Mexican dishes are the specialty, and the drinking, dancing, and carousing go on well into the night. The tortilla soup is excellent. ⊠ *Av. del Mar 225,* ☎ *69/82– 19–25. AE, MC, V.*

$$ ✕ **The Shrimp Factory.** This plain, open-sided restaurant, with white
★ plastic tables and chairs, offers no soups, desserts, or views, just top-quality shrimp and lobster, by the kilo (boiled) or the plate (virtually any style), accompanied with salad or rice and guacamole. ⊠ *Av. de las Garzas 14 and Rodolfo T. Loaiza, across from Playa Mazatlán hotel,* ☎ *69/16–53–18. MC, V.*

$ ✕ **Club Natural.** Inviting fresh fruit cocktails, with or without yogurt or cream, granola and honey, as well as fruit and vegetable drinks, hearty breakfasts, and tasty sandwiches make this a popular spot for breakfast or a late-night snack. ⊠ *Av. Camarón Sábalo 204–1,* ☎ *69/16– 51–09. No credit cards.*

$ ✕ **Doney.** This big downtown hacienda has been serving great Mexi-
★ can meals since 1959. The large dining room has old photos of Mazatlán, a high brick ceiling, and embroidered tablecloths, all of which give you the feeling that you're sitting in someone's home. The Doney is named after a restaurant in Rome, though there is nothing Italian about the menu. Try the chilaquiles (casserole of tortillas and chile sauce), mole, or fried chicken. The meringue and fruit pies are excellent. ⊠ *Mariano Escobedo at Calle Cinco de Mayo,* ☎ *69/81–26–51. AE, MC, V.*

$ ✕ **Karnes en Su Jugo.** A small family-run café on the malecón, with
★ a few outdoor tables and a large indoor restaurant, this establishment specializes in *karnes en su jugo,* literally, "beef in its juice," a Mexican stew with chopped beef, onions, beans, and bacon. It's a satisfy-

ing meal, especially when eaten with a basket of homemade tortillas. ⊠ *Av. del Mar 550,* ☎ *69/82–13–22. MC, V.*

$ ✕ **Mucho Taco.** This bright blue taco stand in the heart of the Zona Dorada is open 24 hours—a blessing for those who stay out at the discos until the wee hours. The tacos are fresh and tasty, and you can eat at the small sidewalk tables or take your feast back to your room. ⊠ *Av. Camarón Sábalo, no tel. No credit cards.*

Lodging

Most of Mazatlán's hotels are in the Zona Dorada, along the beaches. Less expensive places are in Old Mazatlán, the original tourist zone along the malecón on the south side of downtown.

$$$$ 🏨 **Rancho Las Moras.** Ideal for riders and nonriders alike, this aban-
★ doned 19th-century tequila ranch, tucked away at the foot of the Sierra Madre mountains about 30 minutes away from Mazatlán, has been renovated with the finest authentic Mexican furnishings and art. There are more than 3,000 acres to explore either by horseback, wagon, or foot. Exotic animals roam the grounds, along with horses. Accommodations are in six villa-suites or in five individual casitas. There are no televisions, clocks, or even telephones. Communication is by radio with the ranch office in Mazatlán. The rate includes three meals and transportation to and from the airport. ⊠ *Mailing address: Av. Camarón Sábalo 204-6, Mazatlán, 82110, Sin.,* ☎ *69/16–50–44,* FAX *69/16–50–45. 12 units. Restaurant, bar, pool, tennis, horseback riding.*

$$$ 🏨 **Pueblo Bonito.** By far the most beautiful property in Mazatlán, this
★ all-suite hotel and time-share resort has an enormous lobby with chandeliers, beveled glass doors, and gleaming red-and-white tiled floors. The pink terra-cotta rooms have domed ceilings. An arched doorway leads from the tiled kitchen into the elegant seating area, which is furnished with pale pink and beige couches and glass tables. Pink flamingos stroll on the manicured lawns, golden koi swim in small ponds, and bronzed sunbathers repose on padded white lounge chairs by the crystal-blue pool. Angelo's (☞ Dining, *above*) is a dining must. This is as elegant as Mazatlán gets. ⊠ *Av. Camarón Sábalo 2121, 82110,* ☎ *69/14–37–00; in the U.S., 800/442–5300;* FAX *69/14–13–76. 250 suites. 3 restaurants, bar, 2 pools, beach. AE, MC, V.*

$$$ 🏨 **Camino Real.** Location is the big plus at this property, which is far from the frenzy of the Golden Zone, past a rocky point at the northernmost edge of town. The beach is a bit of a hike from the hotel rooms, through the densely landscaped grounds and down a small hill. The hotel, one of the first in Mazatlán, is still comfortable, if a bit worn. A pink color scheme now prevails. If you're more interested in relaxing in peace than in carousing, this is one of your best bets. ⊠ *Av. Camarón Sábalo, 82110,* ☎ *69/13–11–11; in the U.S., 800/722–6466;* FAX *69/14–03–11. 169 rooms. 2 restaurants, bar, pool, beach, 2 tennis courts. AE, DC, MC, V.*

$$$ 🏨 **Royal Villas Resort.** This startling 12-story structure, shaped like a
★ pyramid, is decidedly more attractive on the inside. Panoramic elevators transport guests from the cool marble atrium lobby to the upper floors. The large guest rooms with tile floors are decorated in cool colors; all feature remote-control TV, balcony, and kitchenette. Access to the inviting pool is by a bridge that crosses over a tropical fish-filled pond. ⊠ *Av. Camarón Sábalo 500, 82110,* ☎ *69/16–61–61; in the U.S., 800/888–4498;* FAX *69/14–07–77. 130 rooms. 2 restaurants, bar, pool, hot tub, beach, health club. AE, MC, V.*

$$ ⊞ **El Cid.** The largest resort in Mazatlán, and perhaps in Mexico, El
★ Cid has 1,100 rooms spread over 900 acres. A 100-slip marina began
operating in 1994, and the Marina El Cid and Yacht Club, with 210
suites, opened in 1995. A mega-travel service, with its own deep-sea
fishing fleet, sightseeing and cultural tours, sailing, snorkeling, sunset
cruises, bass fishing, and hunting, is also planned, as is an additional
18-hole golf course. The spacious hotel rooms overlook the pool and
beach (one of the longest and cleanest in the area), and the hotel is pop-
ular with convention groups as well as individual travelers. The glass-
enclosed arcade has nice boutiques, and La Concha (☞ Dining, *above*)
is one of the most romantic spots on the beach. ✉ *Av. Camarón
Sábalo, 82110,* ☎ *69/13–33–33; in the U.S., 800/525–1925;*
FAX *69/14–13–11. 1,100 rooms, suites, and villas. 5 restaurants, 4 bars,
6 pools, 18-hole golf course, 17 tennis courts, shops, dance club. AE,
DC, MC, V.*

$$ ⊞ **El Quijote Inn.** On the beach, in the midst of the hotel zone, the five-
story El Quijote Inn is a tranquil alternative to some of the more fren-
zied facilities. Accommodations include studios and one- or two-bedroom
suites (the suites have full kitchens); all the units offer tile floors, rattan furnishings, and patios or balconies. ✉ *Av. Camarón Sábalo and
Tiburón, 82110,* ☎ *69/14–11–34,* FAX *69/14–33–44. 67 suites. Restaurant, bar, pool. AE, MC, V.*

$$ ⊞ **Fiesta Inn.** One of Mazatlán's newest hotels, the Fiesta Inn is oper-
ated by Posadas, a large Mexican hotel chain. The two sleek nine-story
towers are situated on the beach between the Holiday Inn and the Cara-
velle hotels. All the guest rooms are nicely decorated with tile floors,
light wood furniture, and pleasing pastels. ✉ *Av. Camarón Sábalo 1927,
82110,* ☎ *69/89–01–00; in the U.S., 800/343–7821;* FAX *69/89–01–
00. 117 air-conditioned rooms. 2 restaurants, bar, exercise room, pool.
AE, DC, MC, V.*

$$ ⊞ **Holiday Inn Sunspree Resort.** A consistently good hotel, the Holiday Inn has been much improved by a drastic renovation in 1994. It's
a long walk from here to the Zona Dorada, and little traffic runs by.
Tour and convention groups fill the rooms and keep the party mood
going by the pool and on the beach. Children have a small play area
with swings and a wading pool, and there is live, upbeat music in the
lobby. All of the rooms are done in whites and pastels, with large sliding doors that open to pretty views of the islands. Standard amenities
now include remote-control cable TV, hair dryer, refrigerator, safe, and
coffeemaker. ✉ *Av. Camarón Sábalo 696, 82110,* ☎ *69/13–22–22.
183 rooms. 2 restaurants, 2 bars, air-conditioning, pool, exercise room,
beach, tennis court, volley ball, minimart. AE, MC, V.*

$$ ⊞ **Los Sábalos.** A white high-rise in the center of the Zona Dorada, Los
Sábalos has a great location, a long clean beach, and lots of action. You
feel as though you're a part of things, amid the flight attendants who
lay over here, and it's only a short walk to Valentino's, the best disco
in town. ✉ *Av. Loaiza 100, 82110,* ☎ *69/83–53–33; in the U.S.,
800/528–8760;* FAX *69/83–81–56. 185 rooms. 2 restaurants, 3 bars,
pool, health club, beach, 2 tennis courts. AE, DC, MC, V.*

$$ ⊞ **Playa Mazatlán.** Palapas are set up on the patios by the rooms in
★ this casual hotel, which is popular with Mexican families and laid-back
singles more concerned with comfort than style. The bright, sunny rooms
have tiled headboards over the beds and tiled tables by the windows.
There's a volleyball net on the beach, and two small stands sell good,
inexpensive snacks. ✉ *Av. Loaiza 202, 82110,* ☎ *69/13–44–44,*
FAX *69/13–44–44. 425 rooms. Restaurant, bar, air-conditioning, 4
pools, beach. AE, MC, V.*

$ 🏨 **Azteca Inn.** This hotel across the street from El Sábalo beach is a great find for budget travelers who like to be in the center of things. The pleasant pink-and-white exterior color scheme isn't carried over into the rooms, which are decorated in reds and yellows, but most of the accommodations have two double beds, and all have cable TV. The staff couldn't be friendlier. ⊠ *Av. Loaiza 307, 82110,* ☎ *69/13–44–77 or 69/13–44–25,* FAX *69/13–74–76. 74 rooms. Restaurant, bar, pool, hot tub. AE, DC, MC, V.*

$ 🏨 **Casa Contenta.** A small surprise on the beach between Las Flores and
★ Playa Mazatlán, this property offers seven one-bedroom apartments in a colonial-style building as well as a large beachfront house with three bedrooms, 4½ baths, living and dining room, and even servants' quarters that can accommodate eight people. Casa Contenta has many longtime repeat clients who book years in advance. ⊠ *Av. Rodolfo T. Loaiza, 82110,* ☎ *69/13–49–76,* FAX *69/13–99–86. 8 units. Pool. MC, V.*

$ 🏨 **Plaza Gaviotas.** Most of the salmon-colored rooms in this clean, colonial-style budget hotel, located across the street from Playa Mazatlán, have balconies and all have showers. ⊠ *Av. Loaiza, 82110,* ☎ *69/13–43–22,* FAX *69/13–60–85. 66 rooms. Restaurant, bar, pool. MC, V.*

Nightlife

Caracol Tango Palace (☎ 69/13–33–33) at El Cid is Mazatlán's premier nightspot. **Fandango's** (☎ 69/812–58–00), in the Las Palmas shopping center, is also popular. **Valentino's** (☎ 69/86–49–49), its stark white towers rising on Punta Camarón at the beginning of the Zona Dorada, still draws a glitzy crowd. Enjoy easy listening or romantic music here, or opt for rock around the clock on the dance floor. Also at the Valentino's complex is **Bora Bora** (☎ 69/13–62–12), a casual palapa bar on the beach that stays alive with music and dancing from 8 PM to 4 AM. **Sheik** (☎ 69/86–28–48), a restaurant extravaganza, is also located here, but it needs a lot of improvement in the food and service departments. Still, don't miss it—stop in during early evening for a drink at least.

One of the **Mexican fiestas** at the Playa Mazatlán is also a good entertainment bet; the fiesta held Tuesday, Thursday, and Saturday at 7 PM at the Plaza Maya offers a buffet and a two-hour show that includes a performance of the Flying Indians of Papantla. Almost all hotel travel desks can provide you with information on days and times.

Outdoor Activities and Sports

Participant Sports

FISHING

More than a dozen sportfishing fleets operate from the docks south of the lighthouse. Hotels can arrange charters, or you can contact the companies directly. Charters include a full day of fishing, bait, and tackle. Prices range from $60 per person on a party boat to $300 to charter an entire boat. Charter companies to contact include **Bill Heimpel's Star Fleet** (☎ 69/82–26–65), **Flota Faro** (☎ 69/81–28–24), **Estrella** (☎ 69/82–38–78), **Flota Bibi** (☎ 69/81–36–40), and **De Oro** (☎ 69/82–31–30).

GOLF

The spectacular 18-hole course at **El Cid** (☎ 69/13–33–33), designed by Robert Trent Jones, is reserved for members of the resort, hotel guests, and their guests, so you'll need to make friends with someone who's staying there if you want to play. Another 18-hole course, next door at **Marina Mazatlán** (☎ 69/16–46–72), should be playable by 1997.

HORSEBACK RIDING
You don't have to stay at Rancho Las Moras (☞ Lodging, *above*) to mount one of their steeds; day-trippers are welcome at this huge, converted tequila ranch.

HUNTING
Several species of duck and white-wing doves, mourning doves, and quail abound in the Mazatlán area. The season runs from September through March. **Aviles Brothers** (⊠ Box 221, 82000, ☎ 69/81–37–28) is the most experienced outfitter, arranging licenses and the rental of firearms. The cost of a six-hour hunt is $175, including transportation, retriever, and English-speaking guide. Nonhunters can go along for $50.

TENNIS
Many of the hotels have courts, some of which are open to the public, and there are a few public courts not connected to the hotels. Call in advance for reservations at **El Cid Resort** (☎ 69/13–33–33), 17 courts; the **Racket Club** (☎ 69/13–59–39), 6 courts; **Costa de Oro** (☎ 69/13–53–44), 3 courts; and **Camino Real** (☎ 69/13–11–11), 2 courts.

WATER SPORTS
Jet Skis, Hobie Cats, and Windsurfers are available for rent at most hotels, and parasailing is very popular along the Zona Dorada. Scuba diving and snorkeling are catching on, but there are no really great diving spots. The best is around Isla de los Venados. For rentals and trips, contact the following operators: **Caravelle Beach Club** (⊠ Av. Camarón Sábalo, ☎ 69/13–02–00), **El Cid Resort Aqua Sport Center** (⊠ Av. Camarón Sábalo, ☎ 69/13–33–33), **Los Sábalos** (⊠ Av. Camarón Sábalo, ☎ 69/83–53–33), and **Ocean Sports Center** (⊠ Punta de Sábalo, ☎ 69/13–11–11).

Parque Acuático Mazaguas (⊠ Av. Sábalo Cerritos and Entronque Autopista Costera, ☎ 69/88–00–41) has water slides, wading pools, and a pool with man-made waves—a total of 20 water activities on 4 acres.

Spectator Sports
BASEBALL
The people of Mazatlán loyally support their team, Los Venados, a Pacific League Triple A team. Games are played at the Teodoro Mariscal Stadium (⊠ Av. Deportes) from October through April.

BULLFIGHTS AND CHARREADAS
Bullfights are held most Sunday afternoons between December and Easter at the bullring on Calzada Rafael Buelna. *Charreadas* (Mexican-style rodeos) take place year-round. Tickets are available at the bullring, through most hotels, and from Valentino's (☎ 69/84–17–77).

Shopping

Zona Dorada
In the Zona Dorada, particularly along Avenida Camarón Sábalo and Avenida Rodolfo T. Loaiza, you can buy everything from piñatas to designer clothing. Leather shops are clustered along the southern end of the Zona Dorada.

CLOTHING
For sportswear, visit **Aca Joe** (⊠ Av. Camarón Sábalo and Av. Gaviotas, ☎ 69/13–33–00), whose line of well-designed casual clothes for men is popular throughout Mexico and the United States.

Designer's Bazaar (⊠ Av. Rodolfo T. Loaiza 217, ☎ 69/83–60–39), a two-story shop near Los Sábalos Hotel, has a nice selection of folk art, leather wallets and belts, hand-embroidered clothing, and a good sampling of fashionable swimsuits.

Señor Frog's Official Store (⊠ Av. Rodolfo T. Loaiza 4B, ☎ 69/82–19–25) carries its own fun line of souvenirs, sports, and beachwear.

CRAFTS

The best place for browsing is the **Mazatlán Arts and Crafts Center** (⊠ Av. Rodolfo T. Loaiza 417, ☎ 69/13–50–22), originally designed as a place to view artisans at work and buy their wares. Now the center is filled with shops and boutiques, and the only craft you see is the fine art of bartering. The center offers a good sampling of the city's souvenir selection—onyx chess sets, straw sombreros, leather jackets, and Mickey Mouse piñatas. The shops are open 9–6.

Madonna (⊠ Las Garzas, ☎ 69/14–23–89) displays an extensive collection of silver and gold jewelry as well as masks and handicrafts.

Dealers Ron and Teresa Tammekand represent a number of top artists at **Mazatlán Art Gallery** (⊠ Plaza Balboa on Av. Camarón Sábalo, ☎ 69/14–36–12) and hold one-person shows during the winter season.

La Carreta (⊠ Playa Mazatlán, ☎ 69/13–44–44) has the finest selection of high-quality Mexican folk art in town.

Decorative Maya reproductions, as well as an excellent selection of crafts and leather goods, are found at **Casa Maya** (⊠ Rodolfo T. Loiaza 411, no phone).

Sea Shell City (⊠ Av. Rodolfo T. Loaiza 407, ☎ 69/13–13–01) is a must-see; it has two floors packed with shells from around the world that have been glued, strung, and molded into every imaginable shape from lamps to necklaces. Check out the enormous fountain upstairs, covered with thousands of shells.

Downtown

The **Mercado Central,** between Calle Juárez and Serdán, is a gigantic place filled with produce, meat, fish, and handicrafts that are sold at the lowest prices in town. It takes more searching to find good-quality handicrafts, but that's part of the fun. Browse through the stalls along the street outside the market for the best crafts.

Side Trips

Concordia

48 km (29 miles) northeast of Mazatlán.

Concordia is known for its furniture makers (a huge wood chair marks the entrance to the small town), its 18th-century church, and its brown clay pottery. The trip, over a spectacular road, makes a nice change of pace from Mazatlán.

Copala

25 km (15 miles) east of Concordia.

A scenic colonial mining town at the foot of the Sierra Madre Occidental, Copala features a charming zócalo, cobblestoned streets, colorful facades, and beautiful ironwork balconies and windows.

San Blas

211 km (127 miles) southeast of Mazatlán.

Known as the "budget travelers resort," San Blas is neither pretty nor especially interesting, but it's worth a trip here for the boat ride that takes you upriver through mangrove jungle for a swim in a small spring-fed pond.

MAZATLÁN A TO Z

Arriving and Departing

By Bus

Transportes Norte de Sonora (☎ 69/81–36–84) has service to Mazatlán from Nogales, Sonora. Other companies, including **Tres Estrellas de Oro** (☎ 69/81–53–08), connect the coast with inland Mexico. The bus terminal is on Carretera Internacional 1203 (☎ 69/81–70–20).

By Car

Mazatlán is 1,212 kilometers (751 miles) from the border city of Nogales, Arizona, via Mexico Route 15, either on the excellent, but quite expensive, toll road or on the federal highway. An overnight stop is recommended, as driving at night in Mexico can be hazardous.

By Ferry

Ferry service between La Paz and Mazatlán was privatized a few years back and the service is now fairly reliable. The ferry departs daily from Mazatlán's Playa Sur terminal at 3 PM and takes about 18 hours to reach La Paz. The fare is $15 for regular passage and $38 per person for a private cabin for two with bed and bath (☎ 69/81–70–20).

By Plane

Airport and Airlines. Mazatlán's Rafael Buelna International Airport (☎ 69/82–56–66) is serviced by several airlines. **Aeromexico** (☎ 69/14–11–11) has flights from Tucson and several cities in Mexico. **Alaska Airlines** (☎ 69/85–27–30) flies in from San Francisco and Los Angeles. **Delta** (☎ 69/14–41–56) and **Aerocalifornia** (☎ 69/13–20–42) have flights from Los Angeles, and **Mexicana** (☎ 69/82–72–92) flies in from Denver, Los Angeles, and several Mexican cities.

Between the Airport and Hotels. The airport is a good 40-minute drive from town. **Autotransportes Aeropuerto** (☎ 69/82–70–08) provides shuttles using Volkswagen vans. The price is charge $4 per person for *colectivo* service, $13 for a private car.

By Ship

The Enchanted Isle, Dawn Princess, Son of America, and **Jubilee,** among other cruise ships, include Mazatlán on their winter itineraries.

By Train

The Mexican train system is in a state of flux, with schedules changing constantly. Contact **Mexico by Train** (☎ FAX 210/725–3659 or 800/321–1699) for the most current information about trains to Mazatlán. The train depot is located south of town. Tickets may be purchased at the train station in the neighborhood of Col. Esperanza (☎ 69/84–66–04).

Getting Around

By Bus

There are several bus lines, which run frequently along all major avenues. Routes are clearly marked. Fares start at about 14¢ and increase slightly depending on the destination.

By Car

A car is not necessary in town since public transportation is good, but you might want one for a self-guided tour of the area. Rentals usually include free mileage. A Volkswagen Beetle costs about $65 per day with insurance; a sedan with air-conditioning and automatic transmission is about $117 per day.

By Taxi and Jitney

Most tourist hotels are located in the Zona Dorada, about 3 kilometers (5 miles) north of downtown, but taxis cruise the strip regularly. Fares start at $1.50. A fun way to get around is on the *pulmonías* (open-air jitneys, literally "pneumonias"). The fare, for up to three passengers, starts at about $1 and increases according to the length of the trip. Complaints have been registered, however, about one's susceptibility to fumes from other vehicles.

Contacts and Resources

Car Rentals

The following rental firms have desks at the airport: **Hertz** (⊠ Av. Camarón Sábalo 314, ☎ 69/13–60–60), **Budget** (⊠ Av. Camarón Sábalo 402, ☎ 69/13–20–00), and **National** (⊠ Av. Camarón Sábalo in Plaza el Camarón, ☎ 69/13–60–00).

Embassies and Consulates

United States (⊠ Av. Rodolfo T. Loaiza 202, ☎ 69/16–58–89), **Canada** (⊠ Albatros 705, ☎ 69/13–73–20).

Emergencies

The **Public Tourism Ministry** (☎ 69/14–32–22) is an agency of the police department instituted specifically for tourists. **Red Cross** (☎ 69/81–36–90); **IMSS Hospital** (☎ 69/84–22–44).

Guided Tours

Marlin Tours and **Viajes el Sábalo** (☞ Travel Agencies, *below*) offer a full range of tours with pickup service. Note: Formerly ubiquitous sidewalk stands staffed by persuasive individuals offering free tours of the area along with free drinks and meals—whose true goal is to sell time-shares and condos—have been limited to areas in front of these properties.

The three-hour **city tour,** which should cost around $10, is a good way to get the lay of the land, particularly downtown, which can be a bit confusing.

Cruises aboard the *Yate Fiesta* (☎ 69/85–22–37) cost about $9 and navigate the bay and the harbor, past the islands and sportfishing fleet; these and other harbor cruises generally last about three hours and feature music and dancing. Viajes El Sábalo runs a five-hour tour to see the seals at Isla de la Piedra (Stone Island), with time for lunch and a swim. The cost is about $20.

Also available are all-day **country tours,** which go to Concordia and Copala (⊠ About $25). Marlin Tours runs a trip to Teacapan, an ecological reserve. The eight-hour excursion costs $35 and includes Continental breakfast served on the bus, a stop at Rosario, and a seafood lunch at the almost deserted La Tambora beach. **Jungle tours** take you to San Blas and the Río Tovara (in the state of Nayarit). The tour companies also offer **individual guided tours** and **sportfishing outings.**

Travel Agencies

American Express (⊠ Plaza Balboa, Locale 4/16, ☎ 69/13–04–66), **Marlin Tours** (⊠ Calle Laguna 300, ☎ 69/13–53–01), **Viajes el Sábalo**

(✉ Los Sábalos hotel, ☎ 69/14–30–09, with branch at Camino Real hotel; ☞ Lodging, *above*). Agencies are open weekdays 10–2 and 4–7, Saturday 10–2.

Visitor Information
City Tourism Bureau (✉ Paseo Olas Altas 1300, Bank of Mexico Building, ☎ 69/85–12–21). The office is open weekdays 8:30–2 and 5–7.

PUERTO VALLARTA

On the edge of the Sierra Madre range sits one of the most popular vacation spots in Mexico. When Puerto Vallarta first entered the public's consciousness, with John Huston's 1964 movie, *The Night of the Iguana,* it seemed an almost mythical tropical paradise. Indeed, at the time it was a quiet fishing and farming community in an exquisite setting.

Puerto Vallarta's Bahía de Banderas (Bay of Flags) attracted pirates and explorers as early as the 1500s; it was used as a stopover on long sailings, as a place for the crew to relax (or maybe plunder and pillage). Sir Francis Drake apparently stopped here. In the mid-1850s, Don Guadalupe Sánchez Carrillo developed the bay as a port for the silver mines by the Río Cuale. Then it was known as Puerto de Peñas and had about 1,500 inhabitants. It remained a village until 1918, when it was made a municipality by the state of Jalisco and named after Ignacio L. Vallarta, a governor of Jalisco.

In the 1950s, Puerto Vallarta was essentially a pretty hideaway for those in the know—the wealthy and some hardy escapists. After the publicity brought on by *The Night of the Iguana,* tourism began to boom. PV—as the former fishing village is called these days—is now a city with more than 250,000 residents. Airports, hotels, and highways have supplanted palm groves and fishing shacks. About 1½ million tourists visit each year, and from November through April cobblestoned streets are clogged with pedestrians and cars. There are now more than 9,000 hotel rooms in Puerto Vallarta.

Despite the transformation, every attempt has been made to keep the town's character and image intact. Even the parking lot at the local Gigante supermarket is cobblestoned, and by law any house built in town must be painted white. Visitors still see houses with red-tile roofs on palm-covered hills overlooking glistening blue water. Pack mules clomp down the steep cobblestone streets. Within 16 kilometers (10 miles) of town are peaceful coves, rivers rushing to the sea, and steep mountain roads that curve and twist through jungles of pines and palms.

Exploring Puerto Vallarta

Central Puerto Vallarta has three major parts: the northern hotel and resort region, the downtown area (also called Old Town), and the Río Cuale and Playa de los Muertos. A rental car or cab is necessary to explore the hotel zone, which is basically a long stretch of shopping centers, restaurants, and hotels, but you don't want to have a car downtown and in the Río Cuale area. Most of the interesting sights can be covered on foot—just be sure you wear comfortable shoes for the cobblestone streets.

A Good Walk
Numbers in the text correspond to numbers in the margin and on the Puerto Vallarta map.

When you start seeing cobblestoned streets, you're in the downtown area also known as Old Town. This is the heart of PV, a vestige of old

Puerto Vallarta

TO AIRPORT, PLAYA NORTE,
MARINA VALLARTA,
NUEVO VALLARTA,
PUNTA MITA, SAN BLAS

Bahía de Banderas

Díaz Ordaz
Allende
Pipila
Morelos
Vicario
Aldama
Miramar
Corona
Galeana
Iturbide

Plaza de
Armas

Juárez
Libertad
Rodríguez
Encino

Río Cuale

Aquiles
Madero
Serdán
Ignacio Vallarta
Lázaro
Venustiano
Av. Insurgentes
Cárdenas
Carranza
Aguacate

Olas Altas
Frac.
Rodríguez

Playa de
los Muertos

El
Pulpito

Pulpito

Cafeto

Amapas

TO SAN SEBASTIAN
DEL OESTE

Av. Insurgentes

Amapas

Av. Insurgentes

N

Las Arcos
Underwater Preserve

Playa
Mismaloya

TO LAS ANIMAS,
MANZANILLO, YELAPA

0   500 meters
0   500 yards

Puerto Vallarta. The **malecón** ① (seaside walkway) begins at Díaz Ordáz. Two and a half blocks south of Díaz Ordáz, which merges with Morelos at Zargoza, is the town's main zócalo, **Plaza de Armas.** On the north side of the plaza you'll see the **City Hall** ②. Dominating the square from a block east is **La Iglesia de Nuestra Señora de Guadalupe** ③. Head south a few blocks and you'll come to the **Mercado Municipal** (☞ Shopping, *below*); it's at the foot of the upper bridge over the Río Cuale, which runs into the bay just past Plaza Serdán. In the middle of the river lies **Río Cuale Island** ⑤, reachable via steps leading under the two bridges. The steep hillside above the island's upper end, dotted with charming villas, is called **Gringo Gulch** ④.

Sights to See

❷ **City Hall.** This building is home to a colorful mural, painted in 1981 by Puerto Vallarta's most famous artist, Mañuel Lepe. The mural (above the stairs on the second floor) depicts Puerto Vallarta as a fanciful seaside fishing and farming village. The tourism office is on the first floor. ✉ *Av. Juárez by zócalo.*

❹ **Gringo Gulch.** Named after the thousands of expatriates from the United States who settled here in the 1950s, this neighborhood's most famous attraction is Elizabeth Taylor's home, **Casa Kimberly.** The house was sold in 1990 and has been converted into a bed-and-breakfast (☞ Lodging, *below*), but non-guests need not despair. Tours include the new Liz and Dick museum (tours run daily 9–6 in theory, although you can't be sure there'll be anyone on the premises to take you around if it's not high season). ✉ *Calle Zaragoza 445,* ☎ ☏ *322/2–13–36.*

❸ **La Iglesia de Nuestra Señora de Guadalupe** (Church of Our Lady of Guadalupe). The town's main church is topped by an ornate crown that replicates the one worn by Carlota, the empress of Mexico in the late 1860s. The crown toppled during the earthquake that shook this area of the Pacific Coast in October 1995, and was quickly replaced with a fiberglass version in time for the celebration of the Feast of the Virgin of Guadalupe (December 12). Most of the townsfolk are up in arms about the new crown, claiming that it is distorted and that the choice of material is not sufficiently dignified for their beloved church. Signs posted at the entrances to the church ask that you not visit wearing shorts or sleeveless T-shirts. ✉ *Calle Hidalgo, one block east of the zócalo.*

❶ **Malecón.** The malecón is downtown's main drag, a nice place to rest on a white wrought-iron bench. A seawall and sidewalk run along the bay, and restaurants, cafés, and shops are across the street. There are some interesting sculptures along the walkway, including the bronze sea horse that has become Puerto Vallarta's trademark. ✉ *The malecón runs parallel to Díaz Ordáz approximately 16 blocks, extending from the Río Cuale northeast to 31 de Octubre.*

NEED A BREAK?
Dining and drinking are the malecón's big attractions, from early morning till just before dawn. For a quick picker-upper, sample great fresh squeezed juices at **Tutifruti** (✉ Morelos 552 and Corona, ☎ 322/2–10–68); choose your desired combination of mango, papaya, melon, and pineapple. Filling *tortas* (sandwiches) cost about $1.50.

❺ **Río Cuale Island.** The island has an outdoor marketplace with boutiques, souvenir stands, trendy restaurants, and inexpensive cafés; a bronze statue of film director John Huston dominates the main square. The **Museo Arqueológico** (western tip of the island, no phone) hosts a nice collection of pre-Columbian figures and Indian artifacts. The museum director lectures in English Tuesdays at 1 PM. The museum is open daily 10–2 and 4–6. ✉ *To reach Río Cuale Island from the north end of town, go to Encino and Juárez to cross at the Lower Bridge, or Libertad and Miramar to cross at the Upper Bridge. If you're coming from the south, the approach to the Lower Bridge is at Ignacio Vallarta and Aquiles Serdán, to the Upper Bridge at Insurgentes and Aquiles Serdán. Steps leading under both bridges give pedestrians access to the island.*

Beaches

Puerto Vallarta's stellar attraction is its amazing beaches: crescents of golden sand, fringed with palms, along the hotel zone; endless stretches of gloriously unpopulated beaches to the north; and soft creamy beaches on craggy coves to the south.

North of Puerto Vallarta on the coast of Nayarit are a whole string of beautiful unpopulated beach areas. **Lo de Marcos,** about 40 kilometers (25 miles) away, is one of the most attractive. **Sayulita,** about 30 minutes from Puerto Vallarta, with a great beach, excellent surfing, and some good eating spots, has been described as Puerto Vallarta 40 years ago.

Playa de los Muertos

Playa de los Muertos, the beach on the south side of the Río Cuale, has long been the budget traveler's domain, though it has some of the more expensive restaurants and shops; it's by far the most popular and most crowded beach in Puerto Vallarta. Long ago, the beach was the site of a battle between pirates and Indians. The town's boosters tried for years to change the name Playa de los Muertos (Beach of the Dead) to Playa del Sol (Beach of the Sun), but they weren't successful; if you see an address for the latter, head for the former. Vendors selling lace tablecloths, wooden statues, kites, and jewelry stroll the beach, almost as abundant as sunbathers. Beach toys for rent include everything from rubber inner tubes to Windsurfers. Plaza Lázaro Cárdenas is a pretty spot at the north end of the beach; to the south, Playa de los Muertos ends at a rocky point called El Púlpito.

NEED A BREAK?

Eating grilled fish on a stick at Playa de los Muertos is like having a hot dog at Coney Island: it's what you *do.* Buy it from one of the stands at the south end of the beach, then stroll along and watch the show. For a sit-down break, try the dorado-style fish, broiled with a thick layer of melted cheese at **El Dorado** (✉ Amapas and Púlpito, ☎ 322/2-15-11), on the north end of the beach.

Playa Las Animas and Yelapa

Playa las Animas and Yelapa are secluded fishing villages accessible only by boat; the former is about 25 minutes from Puerto Vallarta, the latter approximately an hour away. Both villages have small communities of hardy isolationists; of late, Yelapa has attracted more and more foreigners who settle in for good. At Yelapa, take a 20-minute hike from the beach into the jungle to see the waterfalls. Tour groups visit the beaches daily and motor launches leave from Boca de Tomatlán (☞ *below*) for Las Animas, Quimixto—another beautiful beach with calm clear waters to the south of Mismaloya—and Yelapa; the cost is from $3 to $6 per person, per hour.

Playa Mismaloya and Boca de Tomatlán

A visit to Puerto Vallarta without a side trip to Playa Mismaloya is nearly unthinkable, since this is where "the movie" was made. The 13-kilometer (8-mile) drive south from the center of town on Route 200 passes by spectacular houses, some of PV's oldest and quietest resorts, and a slew of condo and time-sharing developments. A pretty cove, somewhat spoiled by La Jolla de Mismaloya, a huge hotel complex built on its shores, Mismaloya is backed by rugged, rocky hills and affords a good view of Los Arcos, a rock formation in the water.

Boca de Tomatlán is a small village at the mouth of the Tomatlán River, about 4 km (2½ miles) south of Mismaloya and 15 km (9½ miles) south of Puerto Vallarta. It's a beautiful spot where you can wade in fresh-water pools. Just before you reach the dirt road to the beach, there are several large palapa restaurants. Chee Chee's, a massive restaurant, shopping, and swimming-pool complex, spreads down a steep hillside like a small village. Farther along the main road, through Boca, is Chico's Paradise (☞ Dining, *above*). Tour boats leave from here to Los Arcos and the more secluded beaches of Playa Las Animas and Yalapa (☞ *above*).

Punta Mita

Twelve kilometers (7 miles) north of Nuevo Vallarta, on yet another beautiful beach, is the town of Bucerias. From there, you follow the bend of Banderas Bay past several small and pristine beaches—including Cruz de Huanacaxtle and Anclote—to Punta Mita, on the northern tip of the Bahía de Banderas. Punta Mita features blue bay water that's perfect for swimming and, around the bend, waves for surfing. Here, the views of the bay and of the Sierra Madre mountains are fantastic, and this is definitely a prime spot to view a sunset and, during the winter months, the whales that come here to mate in the warm waters of the Mexican Pacific. Scuba divers like the fairly clear waters around the Isla Marietas, offshore.

Playa Norte

Also known as Playa de Oro, this is Puerto Vallarta's northernmost beach, stretching from the marina and cruise-ship terminal to downtown. The beach changes a bit with the character of each hotel it fronts; it is particularly nice by the Fiesta Americana and the Krystal hotels.

Dining

$$$$ ✕ **La Perla.** This restaurant and its chef are famous for their sublime
★ Mexican haute cuisine, service, and ambience. The best dish by far is the veal stuffed with squash flowers, though the chicken in red wine and the beef fillet with stuffed chili, rice, and beans is also superb. The chef really shows his worth with the pastries, which are renowned throughout PV—and by all means try the flaming crepes prepared here. There is a separate lounge in the restaurant for after-dinner drinks, coffee, and dessert. The dining room is lovely, with neoclassical columns, an arched ceiling, and stained-glass murals. ✉ *Hotel Camino Real, Playa Las Estacas,* ☎ *322/3–01–23. AE, DC, MC, V. No lunch.*

$$$ ✕ **Bombo's.** This place is elegant and romantic, with a serene orchid and white decor, flickering candles, and a sweeping view of Vallarta. An exceptionally creative international menu includes red pepper mousse, kiwi margaritas, and cream of artichoke soup with pistachio nuts. ✉ *Corona 327 and Matamoros,* ☎ *322/2–51–64. MC, V. No lunch.*

$$$ ✕ **Chef Roger.** The cozy patio of a typical Puerto Vallarta house is the
★ unpretentious setting for one of the best restaurants in town. Roger Dreier, the Swiss owner and chef, combines his European training with Mexican ingredients, and the results are superb. Don't leave town without trying the red snapper fillet with banana and almonds and, for dessert, the fried apples with vanilla sauce. ✉ *Augustín Rodríguez 267,* ☎ *322/2–59–00. Reservations essential. AE, DC, MC, V. No lunch.*

$$$ ✕ **Le Bistro.** This may be the chicest restaurant in town, with its art
★ deco–style black-and-white tiled bar and marble-topped bistro tables
set off by colorful folk art furniture. A jazz pianist tickles the ivories
on the weekends. The food is excellent, too. Try the brochette Brubeck,
made of grilled giant shrimp and generous hunks of tenderloin. The
mango and lemon pie is a must, as is a cup of Republic coffee, spiked
with chocolate, rum, and amaretto and topped with whipped cream.
⊠ *Río Cuale Island,* ☎ *322/2–02–83. Reservations not accepted. AE,
MC, V. Closed Sun.*

$$$ ✕ **Señor Chico's.** On the Alta Vista hill overlooking all of Puerto Val-
larta, Señor Chico's is a magnificent spot from sunset into nighttime.
The Caesar salad is good, as is any seafood choice, but it's the view
that really makes the place. Enjoy live music from 7:30 to 10:30 PM.
⊠ *Púlpito 377,* ☎ *322/2–35–70. MC, V. No lunch.*

$$ ✕ **Andale.** A Playa de los Muertos hangout and a good spot for an af-
ternoon beer with the locals, this restaurant serves good fettuccine with
scallops, great garlic bread, and an unusual chicken *mestizo* with white
wine, pineapple juice, and jalapeño peppers. ⊠ *Paseo de Velasco 425,*
☎ *322/2–10–54. AE, D, MC, V.*

$$ ✕ **Don Pedro's.** Everything is a treat at this giant beachfront palapa
★ in Sayulita, half an hour north of the airport, where European-trained
chef and co-owner Nicholas Parrillo offers an array of the freshest fish,
seafood, and poultry sprinkled with herbs and grilled over mesquite.
Everything is fresh and made on the premises, from the crusty herbed
breads and pizzas baked in wood burning ovens and the tapenada dip
of olives, anchovies, garlic, and spices to the rich mango ice cream.
⊠ *Midway on Sayulita town beach, 35 km (22 mi) north of Puerto
Vallarta airport,* ☎ *327/5–02–29. MC, V.*

$$ ✕ **La Fuente del Puente.** Located just across from the market, above
the riverbank, this outdoor café is popular with budget travelers. The
bright pink-and-blue neon along the ceiling is an unusual touch for PV.
The prices are low, the food good, and the crowd amiable. ⊠ *Av. Mi-
ramar at old bridge,* ☎ *322/2–11–41. MC, V.*

$$ ✕ **Las Palomas.** Breakfast at this malecón café is a daily ritual for many
and a place for the reunion of Puerto Vallarta regulars upon their re-
turn to town. Have *jugo de lima* (similar to lemonade but made with
the region's tart limes). Homesick? Go for hot oatmeal with cinnamon
and sugar; otherwise, stick with the *huevos con chorizo* (eggs with spicy
sausage) and coffee spiced with cinnamon. The people in the mural on
one of the walls are all well-known characters in Puerto Vallarta. Stick
around town long enough and you'll probably run into a few of them.
⊠ *Díaz Ordáz at Aldama,* ☎ *322/2–36–75. Reservations not accepted.
AE, MC, V.*

$$ ✕ **Red Cabbage Café.** Lola Bravo, who used to be in charge of the kitchen
at the Chez Elena restaurant at Los Cuatro Vientos hotel, chose a tran-
quil street on the Río Cuale for her new venture. The decor of this cozy
place is eclectic, the ambience Mexican chic, the food top quality, and
the prices exceptionally reasonable. Photos of artists, writers, singers,
actors, and musicians cover the walls, and each of the nine tables is
covered with collages. The thoughtfully conceived menu includes light
soups, salads, and sandwiches as well as more substantial entrées like
chiles en nogada (stuffed chilies in a sauce prepared with nuts and cream)
and shrimp cooked in tequila. Special reservations-only dinners fea-
ture menus from *Frida and Diego's Fiestas* and *Like Water for Choco-
late.* There's a piano player on the weekends. ⊠ *Rivera Del Río 204-A,*
☎ *322/3–04–11. No credit cards.*

$–$$ ✕ **Chico's Paradise.** You can practically plan your day around a visit
★ to this delightful restaurant, about 20 minutes south of town. It's easy
to while away hours under the huge palapa, looking out at the wa-

terfall rushing down from the Cuale Mountains; when the river is calm, you can descend down a series of stone steps and take a dip. Watching pineapple and watermelon being cut and fresh tortillas being made is also enjoyable, and two parrots will keep you occupied with their antics. Seafood, including fresh jumbo shrimp or stuffed crab, is a specialty, but chile rellenos and chicken burritos are also popular. If you think you might want to go for some of the huge tropical drinks—say, the clay pot filled with vodka, pineapple juice, and cream of coconut— take the bus here (they run about every half hour or so). ⊠ *Carretera a Manzanillo Km 20, no phone. No credit cards.*

$ ✗ **The Pancake House.** This is the town's most popular spot for breakfast, serving 12 varieties of pancakes, waffles, eggs, French toast, and great coffee. ⊠ *Basilio Badillo 289,* ☎ *322/2–62–72. No credit cards.*

$ ✗ **Rito Baci's.** This popular deli and pizza parlor delivers to homes and hotels. All the pastas are made on the premises. The crispy-crusted pizza is excellent, and the sausage is spicy and flavorful. Try the sausage sandwich as well. ⊠ *Calle Ortiz de Domínguez 181,* ☎ *322/2–64–48. MC, V.*

Lodging

Most of PV's deluxe resorts are located to the north of downtown. Many are concentrated in the Marina Vallarta complex, practically a town unto itself with a marina, hundreds of condominiums, shopping centers, an 18-hole golf course, and the Royal Pacific Yacht Club. Farther north is Nuevo Vallarta, just over the Jalisco state line in Nayarit, at the mouth of the Río Ameca. This beautiful new community with beachfront houses and condos on canals with direct access to the bay is home to several all-inclusive resorts, including Jack Tar Village, the Plaza Sierra Radisson, and the Diamond Resort Puerta Vallarta. South of downtown and the Río Cuale, in the Playa de los Muertos and Olas Altas areas, the rates are lower. If you head farther south still, the prices go up again: Some spectacular properties are tucked away on hidden coves on the road to Manzanillo.

Budget hotels maintain the same rates year-round, but rates at the pricier places usually go down 25% to 30% just after Easter week through December 15. Reservations are a must at Christmas, New Year's, and Easter.

$$$$ ▥ **Fiesta Americana.** A seven-story palapa covers the lobby and a large round bar. The dramatically designed terra-cotta building rises above a deep blue pool that flows under bridges, palm oases, and palapa restaurants set on platforms over the water. The rooms have a modern pink and terra-cotta color scheme; each has white marble floors, tiled bath with powerful shower, and balcony. The beach bustles with activity—parasailing, windsurfing, boat touring, snorkeling, and, of course, sunbathing. The restaurants are excellent, especially the breakfast buffet by the pool. ⊠ *Carretera Aeropuerto, 48300,* ☎ *322/4–20–10 or 800/343–7821,* FAX *322/4–21–08. 291 rooms with bath. 4 restaurants, 3 bars, karaoke bar, pool, hair salon, beach, travel services. AE, DC, MC, V.*

$$$$ ▥ **La Jolla de Mismaloya.** Despite the fact that the overpowering de-
★ sign of this hotel has ruined the view of beautiful Mismaloya Bay, the lucky guests here literally have half of the bay (this is where the movie *The Night of the Iguana* was filmed) to themselves, as well as a fabulous view of Puerto Vallarta's famous arches (rock formations jutting out of the sea). The southern half of the bay is crowded with beachfront restaurants and motor launches that go to even more remote beaches. The hotel's huge one- and two-bedroom suites have kitchenettes

as well as terraces; this fact, together with the many on-site activities for kids, makes it an ideal family getaway. This hotel consistently gets high marks from its guests. ⊠ *Off Hwy. 200 at Mismaloya Bay, 48300,* ☎ *322/8–06–60; in the U.S., 800/322–2344;* FAX *322/8–05–00. 303 suites. Restaurant, bar, 3 pools, exercise room, beach, tennis courts. AE, DC, MC, V.*

$$$$ 🏨 **Marriott Casa Magna.** Located in Marina Vallarta, with El Salado beach to the front and the Marina's 18-hole, Joe Finger–designed golf course to the rear, the Marriott Casa Magna is one of Vallarta's newest, largest, and most glamorous hotels. The vast, plant-filled, marble lobbies that open onto the huge pool area are hung with chandeliers. The rooms are decorated with light woods and soft colors. All have at least a partial view of the bay. And if the water sports, tennis, restaurants, night clubs, and other amenities of the hotel aren't enough, guests have access to the facilities of the Marina Vallarta complex, including a huge shopping center, a yacht club, and yet more restaurants. Rates include a gigantic buffet breakfast. ⊠ *Marina Vallarta, 48300,* ☎ *322/1–00–04 or 800/223–6388,* FAX *322/1–07–60. 433 rooms and suites with bath. 3 restaurants, bars, pool, beach, tennis, dance club. AE, DC, MC, V.*

$$$$ 🏨 **Royal Maeva Puerto Vallarta.** On the beach in Marina Vallarta, this
★ former Meliá hotel is now being operated as a top-of-the-line all-inclusive resort. The exterior is an off-putting institutional style, but the lobby is a delicious blend of textures and colors, with marble and tile floors contrasting with colorful Mexican crafts and cozy wicker furniture. The large rooms are decorated in soft natural tones of cream and sand, with colorful accents. Amenities include hair dryers, servibars, and safes in the rooms, one of the largest pools in all Puerto Vallarta, a miniclub for children, and an outdoor theater. Two children under the age of seven can stay free of charge (including meals and activities) if they share a room with their parents. ⊠ *Paseo de la Marina Sur, 48300,* ☎ *322/1–02–00 or 800/466–2382,* FAX *322/1–02–20. 370 rooms with bath. 3 restaurants, 5 bars, pool, beach, tennis courts. AE, DC, MC, V.*

$$$$ 🏨 **Sierra Hotel Nuevo Vallarta.** Situated on a long, wide expanse of creamy sand beach in Nuevo Vallarta, the Sierra is another deluxe all-inclusive property. The rooms are light and airy, with tile floors, light wood and wicker furniture, and the ubiquitous pastel bedspreads. Activities are nonstop: There are cookouts, beach parties and Mexican fiestas, disco blasts, theme nights, musicals, karaoke, restaurants, and bars. Daytime activities include aerobics, beach and pool volleyball, tennis, minigolf, windsurfing, kayaking, water biking, and hot air ballooning, as well as jungle and city tours. A golf course is minutes away. ⊠ *Paseo de los Cocoteros 19, Nuevo Vallarta, 63732,* ☎ *329/7–13–00,* FAX *329/7–08–00. 350 rooms and suites. 3 restaurants, 3 bars, pool, beach, tennis courts, water sports, dance club. AE, DC, MC, V.*

$$$ 🏨 **Bel-Air.** Reminiscent of a grand hacienda, this pale pink mansion with white columns is simply but elegantly decorated. Fresh flowers and plants, antiques, and folk art furnishings grace the rooms and corridors of this spacious property. There are 50 suites in the main building and free-standing villas. This property's location between the 1st and 18th holes of the Marina Vallarta Golf Course makes it ideal for golfers. Transportation is provided to and from the airport and within the Marina complex. The pool is lovely and the amenities are many, but the fact that the hotel is not directly on the beach is a drawback. ⊠ *Marina Vallarta, Pelicanos 311, 48300,* ☎ *322/1–08–00 or 800/457–7676. 50 suites and 25 1- to 3-bedroom villas. Restaurant, bar, room service, pool, spa, golf course. AE, MC, V.*

$$$ ⊡ **Camino Real.** One of PV's first hotels, this property sits on a lovely
★   small bay south of town. The rooms have cool marble floors with white furniture and bright pink, yellow, and purple highlights against stark white walls. The hotel has all the five-star touches—from plush robes in the rooms and the feel of an established, comfortable resort to the palapas on the beach and the fragrant white jasmine blooming along the natural waterfall. The La Perla restaurant (☞ Dining, *above*) is one of the best in town. A newer 11-story tower houses the Royal Beach Club, which also has a convention-banquet center. ⊠ *Playa Las Estacas, 48300,* ☎ *322/1–50–00; in the U.S., 800/722–6466. 337 rooms. 5 restaurants and bars, 2 pools, wading pool, beach, 2 tennis courts. AE, DC, MC, V.*

$$$ ⊡ **Continental Plaza Puerto Vallarta.** Ideal for tennis buffs, this Mediterranean-style complex features a tennis club with eight courts and daily tennis clinics. The resort has a shopping plaza, several restaurants and bars, a large swimming pool, and a nice beach. ⊠ *Carretera Aeropuerto, 48300,* ☎ *322/4–01–23; in the U.S., 800/882–6684. 424 rooms with bath. Restaurants, bars, pool, beach, 8 tennis courts. AE, DC, MC, V.*

$$$ ⊡ **Costa Azul Adventure Resort.** This environment-friendly resort, some 48 kilometers (30 miles) north of Puerto Vallarta, was designed by a group of southern California surfers, so you know water sports are going to be big here. But horseback riding and mountain biking through an ecological preserve are also featured. Rooms in this intimate, friendly place are simply but attractively decorated, and the adventure package, including all meals and activities, is very reasonably priced. There is a minimum two-night stay. ⊠ *San Francisco, Nayarit; for reservations contact DFW Tours,* ☎ *800/527–2589, ext. 171. 28 units. Restaurant, bar, boating, snorkeling, surfing, horseback riding. MC, V.*

$$$ ⊡ **Krystal Vallarta.** A full-service resort that sprawls over acreage
★   equivalent to that of a small town, the Krystal offers hotel rooms and villas with private pools. Many of the accommodations have lots of Mexican character, with tiled floors and Spanish colonial–style furnishings. There are five restaurants, including Tango, which serves Argentine *churrasco* (barbecue); Kamakura, which serves Japanese food; and Bogart's, the signature restaurant of the Krystal chain, with a Casablanca theme. Not all rooms are by the ocean, but the secluded beach can accommodate all sunseekers. Christine's disco has a knock-'em-dead light show, and the hotel complex even has a miniature bull-ring for fiesta performances. ⊠ *Carretera Aeropuerto, 48300,* ☎ *322/4–02–02 or 800/231–9860,* 🖷 *322/4–02–22. 421 rooms with bath, 33 villas. 5 restaurants, bars, pools, beach, 2 tennis courts, dance club, travel services. AE, DC, MC, V.*

$$$ ⊡ **Qualton Club & Spa.** The Qualton hotel is a spa, with a fitness center and state-of-the-art machines, a jogging trail running through the hotel grounds, beauty treatments from hydromassage to herbal wraps, nutritional analysis, and computerized exercise and diet regimes. You don't have to be a fitness freak to stay here, though. The rooms in the two wings and main 14-story tower are done in peaceful mauves and blues; deluxe rooms have ocean-view balconies. Meals, drinks, and most sports activities and spa services are included in the room rate, and a "dine-around" program allows guests to sample restaurants in other areas. ⊠ *Carretera Aeropuerto, 48300,* ☎ *322/4–44–46; in the U.S., 800/446–2727;* 🖷 *322/4–44–47. 219 rooms. 3 restaurants, bar, pool, hot tub, spa, beach. AE, DC, MC, V.*

$$ ⊡ **Buenaventura.** This hotel's location is ideal, on the edge of down-
★   town, within walking distance (10 blocks or so) of the Río Cuale and, in the opposite direction, of the shops, hotels, and restaurants on the airport highway. From the street it looks rather austere, but just inside

the door is an enormous five-story open lobby and bar. The bright, cheerful rooms, decorated in white and green, have beamed ceilings and pale wood furnishings. ✉ *Av. México 1301, 48300,* ☎ *322/2–37–37; in the U.S., 800/223–6764;* FAX *322/4–64–00. 206 rooms with bath, 4 suites. 2 restaurants, 2 bars, pool, beach. AE, DC, MC, V.*

$$ 🏨 **Casa Kimberly.** The former homes of Elizabeth Taylor and Richard Burton, located on opposite sides of the street but joined by a footbridge (in a part of town now called Gringo Gulch), have been converted into a bed-and-breakfast. Both houses are surprisingly unpretentious; only Liz's had a pool. The current owner, naturally enough, exploits the Liz and Dick legend and has added on a museum devoted to them. Lavender (supposedly Elizabeth's favorite color, at least during her Puerto Vallarta days) prevails, and tables and walls are adorned with photos of the famous lovers. The rate includes a full breakfast. ✉ *Calle Zaragoza 445, 48300,* ☎ FAX *322/2–13–36. 8 suites. Pool. No credit cards.*

$$ 🏨 **Hacienda Buenaventura.** This consistently good, Mexican colonial–style hotel isn't on the beach, but there is a huge pool with a swim-up bar, and guests have access to the beach at the neighboring Krystal. The comfortable rooms are decorated in soft pastels, with marble floors. ✉ *Paseo de la Marina, 48300,* ☎ *322/4–66–67,* FAX *322/4–64–00. 155 rooms. 2 restaurants, 2 bars, pool. AE, DC, MC, V.*

$$ 🏨 **Las Palmas.** The palapa entrance to Las Palmas is unique—four bam-
★ boo bridges suspended from the ceiling and parrots screeching under the palms. The rooms have balconies and brown spreads and drapes. The accommodations are first-rate for this price category. ✉ *Cerrada las Palmas 50, 48300,* ☎ *322/4–06–50,* FAX *322/4–05–43. 114 rooms with bath. Restaurant, bar, pool. AE, DC, MC, V.*

$$ 🏨 **Los Cuatro Vientos.** The most charming small hotel in PV, Cuatro Vientos (meaning Four Winds) is located up a steep hill behind town, tucked among the red-tile-roofed cottages. Its 16 rooms are often booked a year in advance by repeat guests. The simple rooms with arched brick ceilings have colorful flowers stenciled on the walls and folk-art knickknacks. There's a pleasant rooftop bar open in high season. ✉ *Matamoros 520, 48300,* ☎ *322/2–01–61. 16 rooms with bath. Restaurant, bar. MC, V.*

$$ 🏨 **Mar Elena.** These one- and two-bedroom suites on the north side of town are a good bargain for travelers who want a kitchen and living-room setup. The building is rather plain, but the kitchens and bathrooms are beautifully tiled and some of the rooms have TV. The pool is on the roof; the beach is a block away. ✉ *Carretera Aeropuerto Km 2, 48300,* ☎ FAX *322/4–44–25. 30 suites. Pool. MC, V.*

$$ 🏨 **Molino de Agua.** This hotel's bungalows are spread out along the riverbed amid lush trees and flowers. Stone pathways wind under willows, past caged parrots and monkeys, and lead to cottages with wood shutters and redbrick walls. However, the din emanating from the bar area after 5 PM can be disturbing, and none of the cottages have telephones or TVs. ✉ *Vallarta 130, 48300,* ☎ *322/2–19–07. 62 rooms with bath. Restaurant, snack bar, 2 pools, hot tub, beach. AE, MC, V.*

$$ 🏨 **Playa Los Arcos.** By far the most popular hotel on the beach by the Río Cuale, Los Arcos has a pretty central courtyard and pool and a friendly air. A glass elevator rises by the pool to the rooms, which have been redone in light wood and pastel furnishings and offer small balconies. ✉ *Olas Altas 380, 48300,* ☎ *322/2–05–83. 140 rooms with bath. Restaurant, bar, pool, beach. AE, DC, MC, V.*

$ 🏨 **Posada de Roger.** One of the least expensive hotels, the Posada de
★ Roger is in many ways the most enjoyable, if you like the company of Europeans and Canadians who are savvy about budget traveling. The showers are hot, the beds comfortable, and the pool an international

meeting spot. You can have your mail held there, and the desk clerks are knowledgeable about other budget hotels and restaurants. ⊠ *Basilio Badillo 237, 48300,* ☎ *322/2–08–36,* FAX *322/3–04–82. 50 rooms with bath. Restaurant, bar, pool. AE, MC, V.*

$ ☰ **Posada Río Cuale.** This small, friendly inn on the south side of Río
★ Cuale has one of the best gourmet restaurants in town (aptly named Le Gourmet) and a nice sense of serenity. The beds are big and comfortable; flowers are placed on each nightstand; and with only 21 rooms, the place rarely becomes noisy. ⊠ *Calle Aquiles Serdán 242, 48300,* ☎ *322/2–04–50,* FAX *322/2–09–14. 21 rooms with bath. Restaurant, bar, pool. AE, MC, V.*

En Route to Manzanillo

The coastline south of Puerto Vallarta is sprinkled with some of the Mexican Riviera's most exclusive and secluded one-of-a-kind resorts. But you'll never see them from the highway when you take 200 south— a rugged, twisting road through a tropical forest of pines and palms. Most of the resorts are reached by unpaved roads (though the coast is only a short distance from Highway 200). Guests usually fly to Puerto Vallarta or Manzanillo (one hour south) and take a taxi or hotel van to the resort. Once there, they stay put for a week or more, leaving only for the requisite shopping spree in PV. As you travel south, the best resorts are in Quemaro, Tecuán, Careyes, and Tenacatita.

$$$$ ☰ **Blue Bay Village Los Angeles Locos.** Canadians come here by the charter-jet load, drawn to the amiable surroundings, the all-inclusive drinks and meals, and the chance to relax with friends. The hotel's design is similar to that of other Fiesta Americana properties, with the large, comfortable rooms clustered in a horseshoe-shaped terra-cotta building around the bay. Tours to Puerto Vallarta and Manzanillo are available through the Tlaloc Travel Agency on the premises. ⊠ *Hwy. 200, Km 20 in Tenacatita, 48989,* ☎ *335/1–50–05,* FAX *322/1–50– 50. 201 rooms and suites. Restaurant, bar, pool, beach, horseback riding, dance club, travel services. AE, DC, MC, V.*

$$$$ ☰ **Las Alamandas.** One of Mexico's most exclusive—and expen-
★ sive—resorts, Las Alamandas is low key rather than glitzy. Surrounded by a natural preserve that hosts abundant wildlife, the property's villas and casitas are decorated with folk art and traditional Mexican furnishings (some offer TVs and VCRs). Among the various outdoor activities are horseback riding, fishing, hot air balloon rides, and boat rides along the San Nicolas River. Many guests fly into the hotel's private helipad; others take the hotel's air-conditioned limo from either the Puerto Vallarta (1¾ hours) or Manzanillo (1½ hours) airport. There's a two-night-stay minimum; meal packages are available. ⊠ *Apdo. Postal 201, San Patricio Melaque, Jalisco 48980,* ☎ *328/5– 55–00,* FAX *328/5–50–27. Reservations in the U.S.: 3525 Sage Rd., Houston, TX 77056,* ☎ *713/961–3117 or 800/223–6510,* FAX *713/961–3411. Casita, 4 villas. Restaurant, in-room VCRs, pool, Ping-Pong, croquet, exercise room, volleyball, beach, mountain bikes, tennis court. AE, MC, V.*

$$$ ☰ **Playa Blanca.** This Club Med has all the services the pioneer all-inclusive chain is known for—diving, fishing, pool bars, horseback riding, and even a trapeze and circus school. The food, usually served buffet style, is ample and good, and there are two restaurants where you can be served by waiters. The guests tend to be young and frenetic, and the resort is far from having a feeling of isolation: With 300 rooms, a disco, and aerobic classes, the ambience is more celebratory than somnolent. ⊠ *Off Hwy. 200, next to Bel-Air hotel, 48970,* ☎ *335/1–00–01; in*

the U.S., 800/258–2633. 300 rooms. 2 restaurants, bar, dining rooms, pool, beach, horseback riding, tennis court. AE, DC, MC, V.

$$ 🖭 **El Tecuán.** Small and economical, this beachfront hotel has all the facilities of larger resorts, including its own lagoon and two tennis courts. ⊠ *Km 33.5 Carretera Barra de Navidad–Puerto Vallarta, 48989,* ☎ *335/1–50–18. 40 rooms. Restaurant, bar, pool, beach, tennis courts. AE, MC, V.*

Outdoor Activities and Sports

Swimming, sailing, windsurfing, and parasailing are popular sports at the beachfront hotels. The hotels have stands on the beach offering boat trips and equipment, and you need not be a guest to buy these services.

Biking

Bike Mexico (⊠ Guerrero 361, ☎ 335/3–16–80) provides the gear (21-speed mountain bikes, helmets, lunch, and refreshments) for four-to six-hour bike tours that are tailored to each rider's experience and fitness level.

Fishing

The Progreso Fishermen's Cooperative has a shack on the north end of the malecón and offers a variety of options for fishing trips; most hotels can arrange your reservations. Large group boats cost about $60 per person for a day's fishing; other cruisers may be chartered for prices ranging from $150 to $350 a day, depending on the size of the boat and the length of the trip. Charters include a skipper, license, bait, and tackle; some also include lunch.

Golf

There is a Joe Finger–designed, 18-hole course at the **Marina Vallarta** complex (☎ 322/1–01–71). The 18-hole course at **Los Flamingos Country Club** (⊠ 12 km [8 mi] north of airport, ☎ 329/8–02–80) was designed by Percy Clifford. Reservations should be made through your hotel a day in advance.

Horseback Riding

Horseback riding along the shore is popular, and horses can be rented by the hour at major beaches. Several stables, including **Rancho Charro** (⊠ Francisco Villa 895, ☎ 322/4–01–14) and **Rancho El Ojo de Agua** (⊠ Francisco Villa s/n, ☎ 322/4–82–40), offer three-hour trips into the mountains, sunset rides, and longer excursions to charming colonial villages in the Sierra Madre; time is alloted for lunch and a swim in a mountain stream or lake.

Tennis

Most of the larger hotels have tennis courts. Nonmembers may also play at the **Continental Plaza Tennis Club** (☎ 322/4–01–23), **Los Tules** (☎ 322/4–45–60), and **Los Flamingos Country Club** (☎ 329/8–02–80).

Water Sports

Snorkeling and diving are best at Los Arcos, a natural underwater pre-serve on the way to Mismaloya. Punta Mita, about 80 kilometers (50 miles) north of Puerto Vallarta, has some good diving spots, as does Quimixto Bay, about 32 kilometers (20 miles) south and accessible only by boat. Experienced divers prefer Las Marietas, a group of three is-lands off the coast.

Some of the hotels have snorkeling and diving equipment for rent and offer short courses on diving at their pools. For dive trips and rentals, contact **Chico's Dive Shop** (⊠ Díaz Ordáz 772, ☎ 322/2–18–95) or **Silent World Diving Center** (⊠ Hotel Las Palmas, ☎ 322/4–06–64, ext. 626).

Nightlife and the Arts

Puerto Vallarta is a party town, where the discos open at 10 PM and stay open until 3 or 4 AM. A minimum $10 cover charge is common in the popular discos, many of which are at the hotels. The Krystal has **Christine's,** which features a spectacular light show set to music from disco to classic rock nightly at 11:30. **Sixties,** at the Marriott, features music for almost all ages, and **Friday López,** at the Fiesta Americana, has karaoke and dancing. **Ta'izz** (✉ Marina Vallarta, ☎ 322/1–09–97) attracts a young crowd. Tables start to disappear from the lower level of the **Hard Rock Café** (✉ Díaz Ordáz 652 at Absolo, ☎ 322/2–55–32), downtown on the malecón, at about 10:30 PM, and by 11 PM the live music starts and there is dancing everywhere. **La Pachanga** (✉ Av. México 918, ☎ 322/3–10–95) is a popular place with live entertainment, mariachis, and a folk ballet. **El Panorama** (✉ Hotel La Siesta, Josefa O. de Domínguez and Miramar, ☎ 322/2–18–18) is a real nightclub with a floor show and live music during the high season. Everything its name implies and more, **Collage** (☎ 322/1–05–05), on the highway at the Marina Vallarta complex, hosts several restaurants, a bowling alley, a large-screen video golf game, billiards, two bars, shuffleboard, a video arcade, and a disco. If a quiet drink and a stupendous view are what you crave, **El Faro** (✉ Royal Pacific Yacht Club, Marina Vallarta, ☎ 322/1–02–33) is the place to go.

Mexican fiestas are popular at the hotels and can be lavish affairs with buffet dinners, folk dances, and fireworks. Reservations may be made with the hotels or travel agencies. Some of the more spectacular shows are at La Iguana Tourist Center, the Krystal, the Sheraton, and the Westin Regina.

Shopping

Puerto Vallarta has been described as being one huge shopping mall interspersed with hotels and beaches. This is undoubtedly an exaggeration, but Puerto Vallarta can definitely get into a shopper's blood. There are dozens of excellent shops stocked with some of the best crafts from all around Mexico, as well as several fine art galleries. Prices in the shops are fixed, and American dollars and credit cards are accepted. Bargaining is expected in the markets and by the vendors on the beach, who also freely accept American money. Most stores are open 10–8. A few close for siesta at 1 or 2, then reopen at 4.

Art

The late Mañuel Lepe is perhaps Puerto Vallarta's most famous artist. His primitive style can be seen in the prints and posters that are still available at several of the galleries and shops around town. Sergio Bustamante, the creator of life-size brass, copper, and papier-mâché animals, has his own galleries: **Sergio Bustamente** (✉ Av. Juárez 275, ☎ 322/2–11–29; Paseo Díaz Ordaz 700 A, ☎ 322/3–14–07; and Paseo Díaz Ordaz 542, ☎ 322/2–54–80). **Galería Uno** (✉ Morelos 561, ☎ 322/2–09–08) specializes in art from all over Mexico, but owner Jan Lavender is especially enthusiastic about promoting local talent. Contemporary art and sculpture are displayed in one of Mexico's finest galleries, **Galería Pacífico** (✉ Insurgentes 109, ☎ 322/2–19–82). On the promenade in Marina Vallarta, **Arte de las Américas** (✉ Marina las Palmas 11-16, ☎ 322/1–19–85) features celebrated and emerging contemporary artists.

Clothing

Most of the brand-name sportswear shops are located along the malecón and down its side streets. Many of these stores also have branches in the shopping centers or along Carretera Aeropuerto. **Aca Joe** (✉ Díaz Ordáz 588, ☎ 322/3–04–24) offers excellent quality pants, T-shirts, shorts, jackets, and sweats in smashing colors, all neatly displayed. **Express–Guess** (✉ Paseo Díaz Ordaz 660, ☎ 322/2–64–70) carries its own line of well-designed quality sportswear. As the store's name suggests, the attractive sports and casual wear sold at **Nautica** (✉ Plaza Marina 46A, ☎ 322/1–02–01) have a nautical influence.

More elegant, dressier clothes, made of soft flowing fabrics in tropical prints, can be found at **Sucesos Boutique** (✉ Libertad and Hidalgo, ☎ 322/2–10–02), which features handpainted fabrics and fashionable gauze resortwear that is sold in exclusive boutiques throughout Mexico. Just behind the John Huston statue on Río Cuale island is **Tabu Artwear** (✉ Río Cuale-28, ☎ 322/2–35–28), displaying handpainted clothing created by owner Patti Callardo, accessories for the home, metal sculptures, and wall hangings. **Valenciana** (✉ Corona 160, ☎ 322/3–04–18) offers hand-painted straw hats; cotton fashions for women by Tipicano, Opus I, and Dunas; and some imaginative accessories. **Maria de Guadalajara** (✉ in Puesta del Sol condominiums in Marina Vallarta, ☎ 322/1–02–62, ext. 1015; Morelos 550, ☎ 322/2–23–87; Plaza Malecón and Paseo Díaz Ordaz, ☎ 322/2–47–35) carries easy-to-wear clothing for women in gauzy cotton fabrics dyed in luscious colors.

Folk Art

Few cities in Mexico have a collection of the country's fine folk art that is as representative as the one in Puerto Vallarta. Masks, pottery, lacquerware, clothing, mirrors, glass dishes, windows and lamps, carved-wood animals and doors, antiques and modern art, hand-dyed woven rugs, and embroidered clothing are all available in the markets and from vendors. **Alfarería Tlaquepaque** (✉ Av. México 1100, ☎ 322/3–21–21) stocks a varied selection of baked earthenware suns, carved wood figures, blown glass, baskets, ceramics, and painted animals from all over Mexico. **Attica** (✉ Plaza Marina 38-A, ☎ 322/1–01–20) carries interior design and gift items, including hand-woven materials, quilted bedspreads, custom-made hand-painted furniture, pewter, and baskets. **Mundo de Azulejos** (✉ Carranza 374, ☎ 322/2–26–75) offers a line of Talavera tiles and will create tile replicas of your favorite scene or work of art in 24 to 48 hours. **Olinalá** (✉ Lázaro Cárdenas 274, ☎ 322/2–49–95) is a two-story gallery and shop filled with masks from all over Mexico, as well as lacquered boxes and trays from Michoacán. Original hand-loomed rugs, fabrics, and hand-painted furniture are on display at **Tamacani** (✉ Plaza Marina D-2, ☎ 322/1–09–82). **La Rosa de Cristal** (✉ Insurgentes 272, ☎ 322/2–56–98) features a full line of blown-glass items made in its Tlaquepaque workshop.

Jewelry

There is a good selection of Mexican silver in Puerto Vallarta, but watch out for fake silver made with alloys. Real silver carries the 925 silver stamp required by the government. It is best to visit a reputable jeweler, such as **Ric Taxco** (✉ Pueblo Viejo shopping center, ☎ 322/3–01–43; Villa Vallarta shopping center, ☎ 322/4–45–98), where much of the sterling silver and gold jewelry was inspired by pre-Hispanic designs. **Joyas Finas Suneson** (✉ Morelos 593, ☎ 322/2–57–15) specializes in fine silver jewelry and objets d'art by some of Mexico's finest designers.

Markets

The **Mercado Municipal,** at Avenida Miramar and Libertad, is a typical market plopped down in the busiest part of town. Flowers, piñatas, produce, and plastics are all shoved together in indoor and outdoor stands that cover a full city block. The strip of **shops along Río Cuale Island** is an outdoor market of sorts, with souvenir stands and exclusive boutiques interspersed with restaurants and cafés. Bargaining at the stalls in the market and on the island is expected.

Shopping Centers

The highway on the north side of town is lined with small arcades and large shopping centers that are occupied by handicrafts and sportswear shops. The best selections are at **Plaza Malecón,** at the beginning of Díaz Ordáz; **Plaza Marina,** on the highway at Marina Vallarta; the **Gigante Plaza,** by the Fiesta Americana hotel; and **Villa Vallarta,** by the Plaza las Glorias hotel.

PUERTO VALLARTA A TO Z

Arriving and Departing

By Bus

There is no central bus station in Puerto Vallarta, but most of the carriers are located on Avenida Insurgentes between the Río Cuale and Calle Serdán: **Transportes del Pacífico** (⊠ Av. Insurgentes 282, ☎ 322/2–10–15) and **Elite** (⊠ Basilio Badillo 11, ☎ 322/3–11–17), which incorporates three lines (Estrella Blanca, Tres Estrellas de Oro, and Norte de Sonora). Elite offers excellent first-class service (reclining seats, air-conditioning, refreshment service, functioning bathroom) to Guadalajara, Aguascalientes, and Mexico City.

By Car

Puerto Vallarta is about 1,900 kilometers (1,200 miles) from Nogales, Arizona, at the United States–Mexico border, 354 kilometers (220 miles) from Guadalajara, and 167 kilometers (104 miles) from Tepic. Driving to Puerto Vallarta is not difficult, but driving in the city can be horrid. From December through April—peak tourist season—traffic clogs the small cobblestoned streets; during the rainy season, from July through October, the streets become flooded and the hills are muddy and slippery.

By Plane

Airport and Airlines. Puerto Vallarta's **Gustavo Díaz Ordáz International Airport** (☎ 322/1–19–94) is 6½ kilometers (4 miles) north of town, not far from the major resorts. The Mexican airlines have daily flights from Mexico City, Guadalajara, Monterrey, Manzanillo, Tampico and Tepic. **Mexicana** (☎ 322/4–89–00) has service from Chicago, Los Angeles, and Denver; **Aeromexico** (☎ 322/4–27–77) flies from Los Angeles, New York, Dallas, and San Diego. Several American carriers also serve Puerto Vallarta, including **Alaska Airlines** (☎ 322/1–13–53), **American** (☎ 322/1–17–99), **Continental** (☎ 322/1–10–25), and **Delta** (☎ 322/1–19–86). **America West** (☎ 800/235–9292) flies in from Phoenix.

Between the Airport and Hotels. Volkswagen vans provide economical transportation from the airport to hotels, and all the car-rental agencies have desks in the airport.

By Ship

Several cruise lines, including Carnival, Bermuda Star, Princess, Royal Caribbean, Holland-America, Norwegian, and Seaborn, sail to Puerto Vallarta from Los Angeles during the winter months.

By Train

Trains run daily from Mexicali, Nogales, and Guadalajara to Tepic; from Tepic, it is a three-hour bus ride to Puerto Vallarta. The train is unreliable, crowded, and slow and is best left to those with plenty of time and patience.

Getting Around

By Bus

City buses and *combis* (Volkswagen vans) serve downtown, the northern hotel zone, and the southern beaches. Bus stops—marked by a blue-and-white sign with a drawing of a bus—are located every two or three blocks along the highway (Carretera Aeropuerto) and in town. To take a combi to Mismaloya or other points south, go to the Combi Terminal on Calle Piño Suárez or the bus stop at Plaza Lázaro Cárdenas just south of Los Arcos Hotel.

By Rental Car

There are several agencies in Puerto Vallarta that rent Jeeps, open-air Volkswagen Beetles, and automatic-transmission sedans (☞ Car Rental Agencies, *below*). During the high season, rentals start at $60 per day, including insurance and mileage; off-season, they start at $45 per day. Be certain to ask about special promotions, even during the high season. All the car-rental agencies below have desks at the airport; some have offices along the highway, but they are spread out, so compare prices at the airport or call from your hotel.

By Taxi

Many hotels post fares to common destinations; be sure to agree on a fare before the cab takes off. The ride from the northside hotels to downtown costs about $2.50, plus 50¢ to cross the bridge.

Contacts and Resources

Car Rentals

Agencies to contact include **Avis** (✉ Carretera Aeropuerto Km 2.5, ☎ 322/1–11–12), **Budget** (✉ Carretera Aeropuerto Km 5, ☎ 322/1–18–88), **Hertz** (✉ Lucerna 109 A, ☎ 322/2–00–24), **National** (✉ Carretera Aeropuerto Km 1.5, ☎ 322/2–11–07), and **Dollar** (✉ Paseo de las Palmas 1728, ☎ 322/3–13–54).

Consulates

U.S. Consul (✉ Parian del Puente 12A, ☎ 322/2–00–69), **Canadian Consul** (✉ Av. Hidalgo 226, ☎ 322/2–53–98).

Emergencies

Police (✉ City Hall on Av. Juárez, ☎ 322/2–01–23), **Red Cross** (✉ Río de la Plata and Río Balsas, ☎ 322/2–15–33), **Hospital** (✉ Basilio Badillo 365, ☎ 322/2–35–72).

Guided Tours

The three-hour **city tour** is a good way to get the lay of the land, from Gringo Gulch and the Río Cuale to Mismaloya Beach. Almost everyone goes on at least one daytime or sunset cruise around the bay, sighting pretty isolated coves and barren beaches from the deck of a sailboat or yacht. A full-day excursion to Yelapa or Las Animas, seaside communities that can be reached only by boat, gives you a feeling of what life is like in a secluded tropical paradise.

Tropical tours visit mango and banana plantations in Nayarit and include stops in Nayarit's capital, Tepic, and the small seaside town of San Blas for a boat ride on the Río Tovara, through jungle thick with tropical plants and birds, with a stop for a refreshing swim in a natural spring. Other trips head south to Boca de Tomatlán, the mouth of the river that flows from the mountains into the sea.

Charter **airline tours** fly to San Sebastián del Oeste, an interesting old mining town in the Sierra Madre, 62 kilometers (37 miles) from Puerto Vallarta.

Tours may be arranged through your hotel or one of the many tour operators with offices at hotels and in town. City tours run about $13; tours to Yelapa run about $25; and tours to Las Animas and Quimixto cost from $30 to $35. It's worth the few extra dollars to go on a private tour (small groups) in a van rather than with a large group on a tour bus.

Travel Agencies
American Express (✉ Morelos 660, ☎ 322/3–29–55) and **Intermar Vallarta** (✉ Paseo de la Marina s/n, Condominio via Golf, ☎ 322/1–07–34).

Visitor Information
State Tourism Office (✉ City Hall on Av. Juárez by zócalo, ☎ 322/2–02–42). The office is open weekdays 9–9, Saturday 9–1.

MANZANILLO

Nature is undoubtedly Manzanillo's best attraction. Its twin *bahías* (bays), Manzanillo and Santiago, where crystal blue waters lap the black and gold volcanic sand, have caught outsiders' eyes since Cortés conquered Mexico. In the July–September rainy season, rivers and lagoons swell, forming waterfalls and ponds. White herons and pink flamingos flock to the fertile waters, and white butterflies flutter above the flowers in the chamomile fields (*manzanillo* is Spanish for chamomile).

Santiago Peninsula, which divides Bahía Santiago and Bahía Manzanillo, is the site of Las Hadas (The Fairies) resort. From the water or points above the beach, the resort seems a mirage, a sea of white domes and peaks that radiate in the midday heat. When Bolivian tin magnate Antenor Patiño conceived of this white palace in the early 1960s, Manzanillo was easier to reach by sea than land, a rugged, primitive port that attracted the hardy who didn't mind creating their own tropical paradise. In 1974, when Señor Patiño's retreat was complete, the international social set began to visit Manzanillo, thus putting the city in magazines and on television screens around the world. Even then, Manzanillo remained essentially a port city with only a few tourist attractions.

The October 1995 earthquake did considerable damage to the area. It leveled one of the hotels as well as the headquarters of the state attorney general and caused a great deal of damage to the golf courses. With typical Mexican resilience in the face of adversity, however, most everything was back in shape by the start of the winter season.

Manzanillo is still relatively undeveloped, a sleeper compared with other Pacific Coast resorts. Investors have plenty of land to divvy up for their financially rewarding havens, and existing resorts are spread out. The latest of these, Isla Navidad, is going up on 1,230 acres on a peninsula about 20 minutes north of the Manzanillo airport. Aside from a 27-hole golf course, the project calls for villas, a tennis club, and a 158-room hotel. Many shops and hotel desks close for afternoon siesta, and on Sunday most businesses are shut (including restaurants) and everyone heads for the beach.

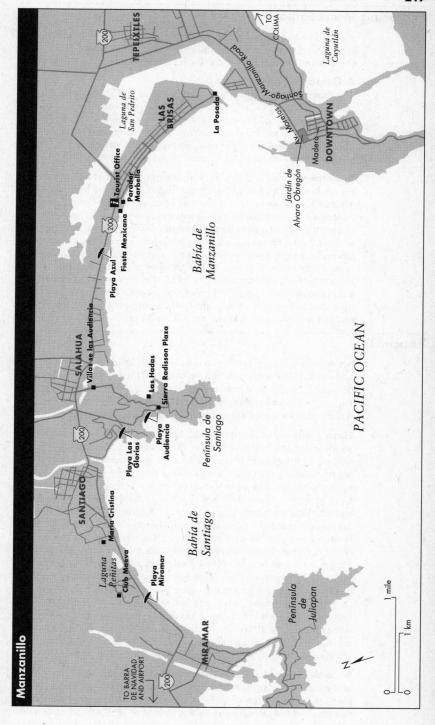

Manzanillo

Exploring Manzanillo

A vacation in Manzanillo is not spent shopping and sightseeing. You stay put, relax on the beach, and maybe take a few hours' break from the sun and sand to survey the local scene casually.

A Good Tour

The **Santiago** area, on Santiago Bay between the Santiago and Juluapan peninsulas, is tourist-oriented, with clusters of shops and restaurants by the beach. The next area to the east, **Salahua,** is residential, with a baseball field and restaurants. Farther southeast, past the traffic circle and Avenida Morelos, you'll see **Las Brisas** beach, where some of the more reasonably priced hotels are located.

Downtown is busy and jam-packed, but of little tourist interest, except for the bustling seaport. At the beginning of the harbor, Route 200 jogs around downtown and intersects with Highway 110 to Colima. Avenida Morelos leads past the shipyards and into town. Just before you reach the port, stop at **Laguna de San Pedrito,** where graceful white herons and vivid pink flamingos assemble at sunset. The **zócalo,** or **Jardín de Obregón,** is right on the main road by the waterfront. It's a small square, quite lively in the evening. Although work still hasn't started on the marina project, announced in late 1992, which calls for public and private developers to invest $50 million to create a downtown pier complex that will have a cruise-ship dock, a shopping center, a heliport, and gardens, local authorities are still sanguine.

Beaches

Manzanillo's biggest attraction is its beaches. Every day is a beach day, and Sundays are downright festive, with half the town gathered to play onshore. The volcanic sand is a mix of black, white, and brown, with the southernmost beaches the blackest. Most beaches post warning flags if the conditions are dangerous or jellyfish have been sighted.

Playa Miramar, at the north end of Santiago Bay, is populated by windsurfers and boogie-boarders. The beach in front of Club Santiago, once the favored hangout for locals, is now accessible only by walking north along the beach from the highway or by passing the guards at the club gates. The main stretch of beach is across the highway from Club Maeva. Manzanillo's best beach is probably **Playa Audiencia,** in a cove along the north side of Santiago Peninsula. The local Indians supposedly granted Cortés an audience here—thus the name. Located between two rock outcroppings, it's a good spot for snorkeling. The Sierra Radisson Plaza hotel is located in the middle of the beach, making public access limited. **Playa Azul,** also called Playa Santiago, is a long strand that runs from Santiago along Manzanillo Bay to Playa Las Brisas. The surf gets rough along the north end; swimming is better toward Las Brisas. South of town is **Playa Cuyutlán,** a black-sand beach on the open sea. Legend has it that the great *ola verde* (green wave) rises some 30 feet each spring during the full moon. In reality, the surf is high in spring but not quite as big as the original ola verde, which took the tiny town of Cuyutlán by surprise in 1959.

Barra de Navidad and **San Patricio Melaque,** to the north, have popular beaches that are good for surfing in the fall months. Palapa restaurants along the beach serve fresh fish. In Barra there are panga trips to a small island just offshore, where unbroken seashells are abundant. When the tide is low, it is possible to walk along the beach from Barra to Melaque, a distance of about 6 kilometers (almost 4 miles).

Dining

$$$$ ✕ **Legazpi.** Manzanillo's only gourmet restaurant is at Las Hadas, and
★ it is beautiful. The service is white-gloved perfection, but friendly
rather than pretentious, and the food is decidedly elegant. The emphasis
is on caviar and smoked salmon, consommés and bisques, seafood and
steaks with French sauces, and wonderful pastries. ⊠ *Las Hadas,*
☎ *333/4–00–00. AE, DC, MC, V. Closed Wed., Fri., Sun. No lunch.*

$$$ ✕ **El Vaquero.** *Vaquero* means "cowboy," so it's no surprise to find a
setting reminiscent of a ranchers' saloon and a menu emphasizing beef,
either marinated and seasoned as *carne asada* or grilled as good old Amer-
ican steaks. Some steaks are served and priced by weight to satisfy the
healthiest appetite. ⊠ *Crucero Las Brisas,* ☎ *333/3–16–54. MC, V.*

$$$ ✕ **Los Tibores.** One of Manzanillo's special occasion spots, this place
★ is popular with locals and visitors alike. The menu doesn't try to be in-
ventive, offering standard international and Mexican fare. The food is
well-prepared and beautifully presented, and the seafood dishes are truly
outstanding, especially the parrillada de mariscos (seafood grill), which
contains an amazing variety of tasty shellfish. ⊠ *Sierra Radisson Plaza,*
Av. de la Audiencia 1, ☎ *333/3–20–00. AE, DC, MC, V. No lunch.*

$$$ ✕ **Willy's.** Some people have been known to dine at Willy's every
★ night of their stay in Manzanillo. The food is that good, and the owner,
Jean François, is that personable and gracious. Michelle, Jean's wife,
prepares delicious onion soup, a sublime bordelaise sauce, and deca-
dent desserts. A guitarist enlivens the informal beachfront setting of
wooden chairs and tables under a wooden roof. ⊠ *Crucero Las Brisas,*
☎ *333/3–17–94. MC, V. No lunch.*

$$ ✕ **Carlos 'n Charlie's.** Can any Mexican beach destination survive
without at least one member of the Anderson chain? Obviously not.
And this is one of the best. The decor, as usual, is frenetic, as are the
waiters, the service, and most of the clientele. The menu offers the standard selection of tasty ribs, steaks, and salads. There's a great view of
the sunset and a DJ who selects music to suit the clientele. ⊠ *Santiago–Manzanillo Rd., Km 6.5,* ☎ *333/3–11–50. AE, DC, MC, V.*

$$ ✕ **Osteria Bugatti.** The most popular dinner spot near downtown,
Bugatti's has a loyal following of locals and tourists who crave seafood
prepared in the Italian manner and oysters Rockefeller. ⊠ *Santi-
ago–Manzanillo Rd. near Las Brisas,* ☎ *333/3–29–99. DC, MC, V.
Closed Sun. No lunch.*

$ ✕ **Juanito's.** This gringo hangout is owned by an American who mar-
ried a local girl and settled in Manzanillo. It specializes in great burg-
ers, malts, and fries, American breakfasts, barbecued ribs, and fried
chicken. ⊠ *Blvd. Costero M. de la Madrid, Km 14,* ☎ *333/3–13–88.
Reservations not accepted. AE, MC, V.*

$ ✕ **La Posada.** Breakfast here is an integral part of any Manzanillo ex-
perience. Pancakes, French toast, fried eggs, and bacon are made to
order and served in the large *sala* (living room) facing the sea. The mood
is casual. Sandwiches and drinks are offered in the afternoon, but
breakfast is your best bet. ⊠ *La Posada, Las Brisas,* ☎ *333/3–18–
99. Reservations not accepted. MC, V.*

$ ✕ **Pancho's.** A popular spot packed with seashells, caged parrots, and
beer-drinking merrymakers, Pancho's serves fresh fish that pulls peo-
ple in and keeps them coming back. ⊠ *Av. Miguel López de Legazpi,
53,* ☎ *333/7–01–76. MC, V.*

$ ✕ **Rosalba's.** Tasty *huevos rancheros,* American-style breakfasts,
seafood, steaks, and tacos served under a palapa have made this place
popular with locals and tourists alike. ⊠ *Blvd. Miguel de la Madrid,
Km 13, next to gas station in Santiago,* ☎ *333/3–04–88. MC, V. No
dinner.*

Lodging

Lodging in Manzanillo was at one time a bargain, and although the $10 room is a thing of the past, there are still several decent places where you can lay your head for less than $40. Travelers on a tighter budget usually head to the towns of Barra de Navidad and Melaque. As with the rest of the Pacific Coast, Manzanillo is undergoing a building boom, mainly condominiums, to accommodate the growing number of people from Guadalajara buying vacation homes here. The resorts are spread out along the Santiago–Manzanillo Road.

$$$$ ⊞ **Club Maeva.** Families love the playgrounds and children's pools, small theater, tennis courts, and disco at this all-inclusive resort. The blue-and-white bungalows are spread over a high hillside across the highway from the beach; a bridge crosses over the road to the water. ✉ *Santiago–Manzanillo Rd. at Playa Miramar, 28200, ☎ 333/5–05–93 or 800/466–2382, FAX 333/3–03–95. 514 rooms with bath. 4 restaurants, 2 pools, beach, water slide, 12 tennis courts, disco. AE, MC, V.*

$$$$ ⊞ **Las Hadas.** Though its creator, Antenor Patiño, is long gone, Las
★ Hadas is still something to marvel at. A member of the Leading Hotels of the World, Las Hadas was for many years Manzanillo's premier resort, the kind of place where vacationers were content to check in and stay put. The setting and grounds are still beautiful, but some of the rooms and furnishings and—even more important—the once impeccable service have been somewhat neglected lately. Even so, a stay at Las Hadas is a very special experience. ✉ *Santiago Peninsula off Santiago–Manzanillo Rd., 28200, ☎ 333/4–00–00 or 800/228–3000, FAX 333/4–13–70. 220 rooms with bath, 41 suites. 4 restaurants, 5 bars, pools, hair salon, massage, beach, golf course, 10 tennis courts. AE, DC, MC, V.*

$$$$ ⊞ **Sierra Radisson Plaza.** This 19-story white stucco giant is popular with families (two children under 18 years of age stay free in their parents' room) and conventioneers. Most of the 350 inviting rooms and suites have private balconies and a view of the bay. A large free-form pool, four tennis courts, and several bars and restaurants round out the property. Light wood and pastel colors dominate the pleasant decor. Three buffet meals, domestic drinks, and tennis are included in the price. ✉ *Av. de la Audiencia 1, 28200, ☎ 333/3–20–00 or 800/333–3333. 350 rooms and suites. 3 restaurants, 4 bars, pool, beach, 4 tennis courts. AE, DC, MC, V.*

$$ ⊞ **Fiesta Mexicana.** This bright white five-story hotel stands out on
★ the highway. It has a lovely central courtyard with a large swimming pool. The rooms have pretty wood-frame windows and comfortable bentwood lounges; those on the ocean side are the most quiet. ✉ *Santiago–Manzanillo Rd., Playa Azul, 28200, ☎ 333/3–21–80, FAX 333/3–21–80. 186 rooms with bath. Restaurant, bar, piano bar, dance club, travel services. AE, MC, V.*

$$ ⊞ **La Posada.** This "passionate pink" hotel has been a hangout for North
★ Americans since 1957. With only 24 rooms, most guests get to know each other well, mingling in the *sala,* a large living-dining room with a communal coffee pot. Rooms are comfortable and simple; old iron keys work the antique locks. The room rate includes a complete breakfast. ✉ *Las Brisas, 28200, ☎ 333/3–18–99, FAX 333/3–18–99. 24 rooms with bath. Bar, snack bar, pool, beach. MC, V.*

$ ⊞ **María Cristina.** This superclean two-story motel is located in the Santiago area, just a couple of blocks from the beach. All the rooms have TVs, but only two of them—they call them "suites"—are air-conditioned; they're well worth the small difference in price. ✉ *Calle 28 de*

Agosto 36, 28200, ☎ 333/3–09–66, FAX *333/4–14–30. 21 rooms with bath. Pool. AE, MC, V.*

$ 🖫 **Parador Marbella.** This hotel is one of the few reasonably priced places on the beach. The best rooms are on the ocean; each has a tiny balcony under the palms. The accommodations are now color-coordinated and offer air-conditioning and TV. ⊠ *Santiago–Manzanillo Rd., Km 9.5, 28200, ☎ 333/3–11–03,* FAX *333/3–11–03. 94 rooms with bath. Restaurant, bar, pool. MC, V.*

$ 🖫 **Villas la Audiencia.** Well located—it's a block from the Las Hadas turnoff and about four blocks from the beach—this small white-and-red hotel and villa complex overlooks the Mantarraya golf course. Everything is spotless and the rooms and villas are pleasantly decorated and quite comfortable. ⊠ *Av. de la Audiencia off Santiago–Manzanillo Rd., 28200, ☎ 333/3–08–61,* FAX *333/3–26–53. 46 rooms with bath. Restaurant, pool. AE, MC, V.*

Nightlife and the Arts

During the high season, there is nightlife at **Paradise** (☎ 333/3–21–80) at the Fiesta Mexicana. For a rowdy drinking and dancing scene, head for **Carlos 'n' Charlie's** (☎ 333/3–11–50). **VOG** (⊠ Km 9.2 on the Santiago–Manzanillo Rd., ☎ 333/3–18–75) is another popular place to boogie. The **Legazpi** (☎ 333/4–00–00) piano bar at Las Hadas is relaxing, romantic spot for a nightcap.

Outdoor Activities and Sports

Fishing

Sportfishing charters ($130–$500) are available at the major hotels and tour agencies.

Golf

La Mantarraya (☎ 333/4–00–00), the 18-hole golf course at Las Hadas, designed by Roy Dye, has been rated among the world's 100 best courses by *Golf Digest*. **Club Santiago** (☎ 333/5–04–10) has a 9-hole course designed by Larry Hughes. Robert von Hagge created the 27-hole course at **Isla Navidad** (☎ 333/5–51–70).

Water Sports

Windsurfing has become quite popular on Manzanillo's beaches, and Jet Skis roar about, but there isn't much in the way of parasailing. The rocky points off Manzanillo's peninsulas and coves make good spots for snorkeling and scuba diving. Small boats called *pangas* can be rented on some beaches so you can reach the better spots.

Shopping

Most of the hotels offer a small selection of folk art and beachwear, but, in general, shops selling items that might interest tourists don't fare well in Manzanillo, probably because most visitors are more interested in activities involving the sun and sea. There are some fairly uninteresting shops around Manzanillo's main square, hardly worth the trip downtown. Most of the shops are closed from 2 to 4; many are open Sunday from 10 to 2.

Centro Artesenal Las Primaveras (⊠ Juárez 40 in Santiago, ☎ 333/3–16–99) is about the best bet for handcrafted folk art. **Arte y Diseño** (⊠ Las Hadas shopping center, ☎ 333/3–18–64), an interior design shop, offers an interesting selection of handcrafted decorative objects in ceramic and wood, as well as Huichol Indian yarn paintings and bead work.

Side Trip

Colima
311 km (192 mi) northeast of Manzanillo.

Colima, the state capital, is less than two hours from Manzanillo via an excellent toll road that continues on to Guadalajara. An easygoing provincial city, with well-maintained colonial buildings, Colima is most famous for the pre-Hispanic "Colima Dog" figurines, which originated in this state and which are on display, along with other archaeological pieces, at the **Museo de las Culturas del Occidente** (Museum of Western Cultures) (⊠ Casa de la Cultura, Calzada Glaván and Av. Ejército Nacional, ☎ 331/2–31–55). The **Museo Nacional de la Máscara, la Danza y el Arte Popular del Occidente** (Museum of Masks, Dance and Popular Arts of the West) (⊠ Calle 27 de Septiembre and Manuel Gallardo, ☎ 331/2–68–69) displays a large collection of pre-Hispanic and contemporary Indian costumes, masks, instruments, and other artifacts. The town of **Comala,** a 15-minute ride north of Colima, is noted for hand-painted colonial furniture and ironwork. The imposing twin peaks of Colima's volcanoes rise up from the **Volcán de Colima National Park,** about 30 kilometers (18 miles) farther north on the road to Comala.

MANZANILLO A TO Z

Arriving and Departing

By Bus
Tres Estrellas de Oro and **Estrella Blanca** (☎ 333/2–01–35 for both) have first-class service (lavatory, TV, and air-conditioning) to Guadalajara, Tijuana, Acapulco, and Mexico City. Service is also available to the coastal towns. Many of the area's resorts are located 1 to 2 kilometers (½ to 1 mile) from the bus stop on the highway.

By Car
The trip south from the Arizona border to Manzanillo is about 2,419 kilometers (1,500 miles); from Guadalajara, it is 332 kilometers (200 miles); from Puerto Vallarta, 242 kilometers (150 miles). Highway 200 runs along the coast from Tepic, Nayarit, to Manzanillo. The road is quite narrow but well maintained. However, drivers should constantly be on the alert for an unexpected cow, burro, dog—or drunk—on the road. Detours are frequent, especially during the raining season.

By Plane
Airport and Airlines. Manzanillo's **Aeropuerto Internacional Playa de Oro** (☎ 333/2–25–25) is 32 kilometers (20 miles) north of town, on the way to Barra de Navidad. **Aeromexico** (☎ 333/2–08–25) flies in direct from Los Angeles. Both Aeromexico and **Mexicana** (☎ 333/3–23–23) have connecting service to most major cities via Guadalajara and Mexico and Mexico City. **America West** (☎ 800/235–9292, no local phone) flies in from Phoenix with a stop in Puerto Vallarta.

From the Airport. Volkswagen vans transport passengers from the airport to the major resorts; these shuttle services are less expensive than taxis.

By Train
Second-class trains run to Manzanillo from Guadalajara—an adventure for some, but for most a tedious trip, lasting a minimum of eight hours and ending at the ship and freight yards outside town.

Getting Around

A car is almost essential for exploring the area on your own. The highway from Santiago to Manzanillo is commonly called Carretera Santiago–Manzanillo, Manzanillo–Aeropuerto, Salahua–Santiago, or any number of things depending on the closest landmark. It's called the Santiago–Manzanillo Road throughout this chapter to lessen confusion. Route 200 runs north along the coast past Manzanillo and Santiago bays to Barra de Navidad and Melaque; Route 110 goes east to Colima.

Avenida Morelos, the main drag in town, runs from Manzanillo Bay past the port and shipyards to the plaza. If you plan to explore the downtown, park along the waterfront across from the plaza and walk—all the shops and hotels are within a few blocks. Rates vary depending on where you rent your car, but rentals are generally costly ($45, with standard shift and no air-conditioning, to $110 per day, including insurance). Most offer 300 kilometers (186 miles) free, which should give you enough roaming for one day.

Street addresses are not often used in Manzanillo; instead, locations are designated by neighborhood—the Las Brisas area, Santiago Peninsula (also known as the Las Hadas Road), and so on. Maps with actual street names are rare (or inaccurate).

Contacts and Resources

Car Rentals

Avis (☎ 333/3–01–90), **Budget** (☎ 333/3–14–45), and **National** (☎ 333/3–06–11) have offices in the airport, and most big hotels have at least one company represented.

Emergencies

Police (☎ 333/2–10–04), **Hospital** (☎ 333/2–00–29).

Guided Tours

Manzanillo is so spread out that if you want to get the lay of the land, it's best to go on a guided tour. More appealing, though, than the city tours are the sportfishing trips, sunset cruises, horseback outings, and excursions to Colima, Comala, and the volcanoes that can be arranged through a travel agency.

Travel Agencies

Most hotels offer at least one agency's services. Agencies include **Bahías Gemelas Agencia de Viajes** (✉ Sierra Radisson Plaza hotel, ☎ 333/3–20–00), **Aeroviajes Manzanillo** (✉ Av. México 69, ☎ 333/2–25–65), and **Agencia de Viajes Tecnológico** (✉ Manzanillo–Santiago Rd., Km 11.5, ☎ 333/3–29–99).

Visitor Information

State Tourism Office (✉ Blvd. Costero Miguel de la Madrid, Km 9.5, ☎ 333/3–22–77). The office is open weekdays 9–3 and 5–7.

IXTAPA/ZIHUATANEJO

One of the most appealing of the Pacific Coast destinations, Ixtapa/Zihuatanejo offers visitors a taste of both Mexico present and past. Ixtapa (pronounced eeks-*tah*-pa), where most Americans stay—probably because they can't pronounce Zihuatanejo (see-wha-tah-*nay*-ho)—is young and glitzy. Exclusively a vacation resort, it was created in the early 1970s by Fonatur, Mexico's National Fund for Tourism Development, which also brought us Cancún. World-class hotels cluster in the Hotel Zone around Palmar Bay, where conditions are ideal for swimming and water sports; across the road are clusters of shopping plazas. The hotels are well spaced; there's always plenty of room on the beach, which is lighted for strolling at night; and the pace is leisurely.

Zihuatanejo, only 7 kilometers (4 miles) down the coast (southeast) from Ixtapa, is an old fishing village on a picturesque sheltered bay. Until the advent of Ixtapa, it was hardly known even among Mexicans. But long before Columbus sailed to America, Zihuatanejo was a sanctuary for indigenous nobility. Figurines, ceramics, stone carvings, and stelae still being found in the area verify the presence of civilizations dating as far back as the Olmecs (3,000 BC). The original name, Cihuatlán, means "place of women" in the Náhuatl language. Weaving was likely the dominant industry in this matriarchal society, as evidenced by pre-Hispanic figurines, bobbins, and other related artifacts found in the area.

In 1527, Spanish conquistadors launched a trade route from Zihuatanejo Bay to the Orient. Galleons returned with silks, spices, and, according to some historians, the first coconut palms to arrive in America, brought from the Philippines. But the Spaniards did little colonizing here. A scout sent by Hernán Cortés reported back to the conquistador that the place was nothing great, tagging the name Cihuatlán with the demeaning Spanish suffix "nejo"—hence "Zihuatanejo."

With the advent of Ixtapa, Zihuatanejo began to grow and the little dirt streets were paved with decorative brick. The place has managed to retain its charm, but it's also the area's municipal center, and its *malecón* (waterfront) and narrow streets are lined with hotels, restaurants, and boutiques.

Exploring Ixtapa/Zihuatanejo

Ixtapa and Zihuatanejo have few sights per se, but they're both pleasant places to stroll—the former especially if you enjoy a modern beach ambience and shops, the latter if you like local color.

A Good Tour

The entire **hotel zone** in **Ixtapa** extends along a 3-kilometer (2-mile) strip of wide sandy beach called Playa del Palmar, on the open Pacific. It's fun to walk along the beach to check out the various hotel scenes and watersports activities. Alternatively, you can stroll the length of the zone on **Boulevard Ixtapa,** a nicely landscaped and immaculate thoroughfare; a series of Mexican village–style shopping malls line the boulevard across the street from the hotels. At one end of the hotel zone (when you enter from Zihuatanejo) is the 18-hole Ixtapa Golf Club, while on the other (generally described as being "up the coast," but actually lying to the northwest) you'll come to the Marina Ixtapa development, which includes a 600-slip yacht marina, a promenade with restaurants and shops, and the new 18-hole Marina Golf Course. If you want to venture out of this compact resort area, take a taxi 15 minutes up the coast to **Playa Linda;** it's a 10-minute boat ride from here to **Ixtapa Island** (☞ Beaches, *below,* for both), where you can spend the day eating, sunning, and swimming.

Zihuatanejo flanks a charming enclosed bay with calm beaches. A simple way to tour the town is to take a taxi to the **municipal pier** (*muelle*), from which skiffs continually depart for the 10-minute ride to **Las Gatas**(☞ Beaches, *below*), accessible only by water. The sportsfishing boats depart from this pier, too, and it's the beginning of the **Paseo del Pescador** (Fisherman's Walk) or **malecón,** which runs along the municipal beach, the most picturesque part of town. The brick-paved seaside path, only a quarter of a mile long, is lined with small restaurants and overflowing shops; you'll pass a basketball court that doubles as the town square. The malecón ends at the **Museo Arquélogico** (✉ east end of Paseo del Pescador, ☎ 753/3–25–52), where close to a thousand pre-Hispanic pieces as well as murals and maps are on permanent display; it's open Tuesday–Sunday 10–6. If you continue beyond the museum, you can take a footpath cut into the rocks to **Playa la Madera** (☞ Beaches, *below*).

Beaches

Ixtapa

IXTAPA ISLAND

The most popular beach on Ixtapa Island is **Playa Cuachalalate,** named for a local tree whose bark has been used as a remedy for kidney ailments since ancient times. This beach is lined with good seafood eateries. A short walk across to the other side of the island takes you to the gorgeous sandy **Varadero beach,** a wonderful spot for sunset viewing. It is also lined with small restaurants, and there are water-sports facilities. Just behind the restaurants is **Playa Coral,** with crystal-clear water that's ideal for snorkeling. **Playa Carey,** toward the south end of the island, is small and isolated. The pangas run between the boat landings at both Cuachalalate and Varadero beaches and Playa Linda on the mainland.

PLAYA DEL PALMAR

Ixtapa's main beach, this 3-kilometer-long (2-mile-long) broad sandy stretch runs along the Hotel Zone. Water-sports facilities are available all along the shore. Since this is essentially open sea, the surf can be quite strong.

PLAYA LINDA

About 10 minutes beyond the Ixtapa Hotel Zone, the long, pristine Playa Linda has a handicraft mart at its edge, as well as a rock jetty from which covered pangas take passengers on a 10-minute ride to Ixtapa Island (☞ *below*). The boats run continuously from early morning until 5 PM. A round-trip costs about $2 (hold on to your ticket stub for the return).

Zihuatanejo

PLAYA LA MADERA

Across Zihuatanejo Bay from Playa Principal, Playa la Madera may be reached via a seaside footpath cut into the rocks. Also accessible by car, this pancake-flat beach has a sprinkling of small hotels and restaurants. It was named madera, or "wood," beach because it was a Spanish port for shipping oak, pine, cedar and mahogany cut from the nearby Sierra Madre Sur.

PLAYA LA ROPA

On the other side of a rocky point, Playa la Ropa is the most beautiful beach in the area; it's a five-minute taxi ride from town. Along this 1-kilometer (½-mile) stretch of soft sand are water-sports facilities, open-air restaurants, and a few hotels. It got its name ("clothes beach") when a Spanish galleon returning from the Orient ran aground here, strewing its cargo of silks and clothing.

PLAYA LAS GATAS

Named for the *gatas* (docile nurse sharks) that used to linger here, this beach has a mysterious long row of hewn rocks just offshore that serves as a breakwater. Legend has it that a Tarascan king built it to shelter his royal daughter's private beach. It is now lined with simple seafood eateries that also have lounge chairs for sunning. Las Gatas is accessible only by boat, and small pangas (motor-powered skiffs) run continuously to and from the municipal pier until 5 pm. Purchase your round-trip ticket (about $2) at the Cooperativa office at the beginning of the pier. Keep the ticket stub for your return trip.

PLAYA PRINCIPAL

At the edge of town, the town's picturesque main beach is rimmed by the Paseo del Pescador (fisherman's walk). Here local fishermen keep their skiffs and gear, used for nightly fishing journeys out to sea. They return here in the morning to sell their catch to the local townspeople and to restaurateurs.

Dining

Ixtapa

$$$$ ✕ **Bogart's.** Play it again: The setting is strikingly Moroccan, à la the film *Casablanca,* and anyone who's been to any of the links in the Krystal hotel chain is familiar with this exotic (and expensive) eatery. A Moorish fountain and piano music add to the movie-theme atmosphere. The largely Continental menu includes Suprema Casablanca, breaded chicken breasts stuffed with lobster. ⊠ *Hotel Krystal, Blvd. Ixtapa.* ☎ *755/3-03-03. Reservations essential. AE, DC, MC, V.*

$$$$ ✕ **Villa de la Selva.** The multilevel clifftop terraces offer romantic views of the sunset, the stars, and the night-lit surf breaking on the rocks below. Excellent international dishes include grilled steaks, seafood, and Mexican specialties. ⊠ *Beyond Westin Brisas on Paseo la Roca,* ☎ *755/3-03-62. AE, DC, MC, V. No lunch.*

$$$ ✕ **Beccofino.** Part of the promenade along Marina Ixtapa, this restaurant offers excellent northern Italian cuisine in a serene Mediterranean-style atmosphere. There's alfresco seating on a canopied deck that sits on the water. ⊠ *Plaza Marina Ixtapa,* ☎ *755/3-17-70. AE, DC, MC, V.*

$$$ ✕ **El Galeón.** Seafood lovers and people-watchers like to settle in at Marina Ixtapa's nautical-decor bar and outdoor terrace; there's additional seating on a simulated galleon right on the water. The fresh tuna steak is outstanding, and upscale Mexican fare is also available. ⊠ *Plaza Marina Ixtapa,* ☎ *755/3-21-50. AE, DC, MC, V.*

$$ ✕ **El Infierno y la Gloria.** "Hell and Glory" is a very typical Mexican cantina-bar and restaurant, serving an array of typical dishes. The food is good and you'll enjoy looking at the walls, hand-painted with Mexican scenes and allegories. ⊠ *La Puerta Shopping Center,* ☎ *755/3-02-72. AE, DC, MC, V.*

$$ ✕ **El Marlin.** This a great place to settle in at tables or beach lounges for some lunch, swimming, and sun. Simple, wholesome, and delicious seafood dishes include (naturally) marlin: Try it steamed with vegetables in aluminum foil. El Marlin closes at 5 PM, when the last boats leave for the mainland. ⊠ *Varadero Beach, Ixtapa Island, no phone. No credit cards.*

$$ ✕ **Señor Frog's.** You can tell this is part of the Anderson chain of zany restaurants by the entrance signs that read, SORRY, WE'RE OPEN and MEMBERS AND NON-MEMBERS ONLY. As usual the atmosphere is raucous and the food—tapas, burgers, and Mexican dishes—plentiful and good. ⊠ *La Puerta Shopping Center,* ☎ *755/3-06-92. Reservations not accepted. AE, DC, MC, V. No lunch.*

$ ✕ **Marina Café.** Located at the base of the Lighthouse Tower on the Marina promenade, this upscale seaside stand serves everything from pizza to sushi, tacos, and cocktails. Seating is outdoors on plastic chairs. ⊠ *Marina Ixtapa,* ☎ *755/3-22-88. Reservations not accepted. No credit cards.*

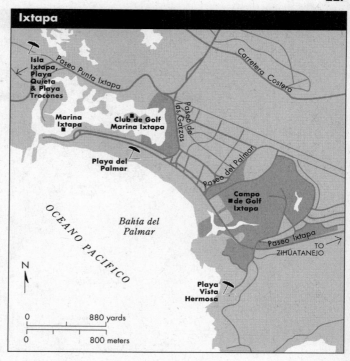

Ixtapa

Isla Ixtapa, Playa Quieta & Playa Trocones

Paseo Punta Ixtapa

Carretera Costera

Marina Ixtapa

Club de Golf Marina Ixtapa

Paseo de las Garzas

Playa del Palmar

Paseo del Palmar

Campo de Golf Ixtapa

OCEANO PACIFICO

Bahía del Palmar

Paseo Ixtapa

TO ZIHUATANEJO

N

Playa Vista Hermosa

0   880 yards

0   800 meters

$ ✕ **Nueva Zelanda.** From breakfast through dinner everybody drops in to this sparkling little coffee shop–style eatery, which serves *tortas* (Mexican sandwiches on baguettes) and an array of fresh tropical fruit juices and fruit salads. ⊠ *Los Patios Shopping Center, behind band-stand, Ixtapa,* ☎ *755/3–08–38; Calle Cuauhtémoc 23, Zihuatanejo,* ☎ *755/4–23–40. Reservations not accepted. No credit cards.*

$ ✕ **Pizzeria Mamma Norma.** You can dine indoors or al fresco at this casual Italian eatery, which offers the best pizzas in town as well as wholesome salads. ⊠ *La Puerta Shopping Center,* ☎ *755/3–02–74. Reservations not accepted. MC, V. No lunch.*

Zihuatanejo

$$$ ✕ **Kau-Kan.** Opened at the end of 1995, this restaurant immediately became a local favorite. Owner-chef Ricardo Rodriguez, previously the chef at the nearby Casa que Canta and, before then, at Mexico City's Champs Elysées restaurant, serves imaginative, exquisitely prepared seafood, from fillet of sea bass to delicate manta ray in butter sauce. Although the restaurant is right on Madera beach, the service and setting are elegant. ⊠ *Playa Madera,* ☎ *755/4–21–42. MC, V.*

$$ ✕ **Casa Elvira.** Opened in 1956, this Zihuatanejo institution has a pleasant dining room and serves a wide variety of seafood and Mexican dishes. It gets crowded during high season. ⊠ *Paseo del Pescador 16,* ☎ *755/4–20–61. MC, V.*

$$ ✕ **El Patio.** Seafood and authentic Mexican dishes are served in a delightful hacienda-style garden. There's live music during high season. ⊠ *5 de Mayo 3,* ☎ *755/4–30–19. AE, MC, V.*

$$ ✕ **Paul's.** Swiss chef-owner Paul Karrer prepares every entrée, including escargots, sashimi, duck breast, fresh quail, and shrimp in dill sauce, with loving attention to detail. The setting is far more casual than the menu. ⊠ *5 de Mayo across from handicraft market,* ☎ *755/4–80–63. Reservations not accepted. No credit cards.*

Zihuatanejo

TO IXTAPA

TO AIRPORT

Cam. Viejo a Zihuatanejo

Paseo de la Boquita

D O W N T O W N

Paseo Zihuatanejo

Paseo del Ocotal

5 de Mayo

Av. Gral. Juan N. Alvarez

N

Playa la Madera

Camino Escénico a Playa la Ropa

Bahía de Zihuatanejo

Playa la Ropa

Playa Las Gatas

0   1100 yards

0   1000 meters

$$ ✗ **La Perla.** Eat indoors if you want video sports-bar action, or outdoors on La Ropa beach. Among the seafood specialties, *filete de huachinango al vino blanco* (fillet of red snapper in white wine) is a favorite. ⊠ *Playa la Ropa,* ☎ *755/4–27–00. MC, V.*

$$ ✗ **Rossy.** A local favorite for dining on the roof terrace or right on the beach, Rossy's offers an array of seafood dishes, including a tempting shrimp-and-pineapple brochette. Musicians usually serenade diners on the weekends. ⊠ *South end of Playa la Ropa,* ☎ *755/4–40–04. Reservations not accepted. MC, V.*

$$ ✗ **La Sirena Gorda.** Oil paintings and a bronze statue depict the namesake "fat mermaid," and a small boutique sells logo T-shirts and memorabilia. Specialties at this friendly restaurant near the pier include seafood tacos and octopus kebab. The setting is casual, with an outdoor patio. ⊠ *Paseo del Pescador 20,* ☎ *755/4–26–87. Reservations not accepted. MC, V. Closed Wed.*

$$ ✗ **Tamales y Atoles Any.** Jos Ramón Muñoz and his wife, Any, have created this Zihuatanejo favorite, famed for its authentic and wholesome Mexican fare. The vast menu includes moles, a wide selection of tamales, and green or white *pozole* (hominy stew), a Guerrero specialty—it's usually served only on Thursdays, but it's served daily here by popular demand. The fresh fruit drinks are excellent, too. ⊠ *Ejido and Vicente Guerrero,* ☎ *755/4–73–73. Reservations not accepted. AE, MC, V.*

$$ ✗ **Ziwok.** A play on the town's nickname, "Zihua," this small restaurant serves "wok-art" stir-fry dishes using fresh vegetables and seafood. ⊠ *Juan N. Alvarez behind La Sirena Gorda,* ☎ *755/4–31–36. MC, V. Closed Wed. No lunch.*

$ ✗ **Casa Puntarenas.** Talk about homey restaurants: Casa Puntarenas is not only family-owned and -operated, but it's run out of the family residence. You'll select from a menu of seafood specialties and write your order on a piece of paper, which later becomes your check. To get here, cross the footbridge over the lagoon at the west end of the town near the pier (or take a taxi). ✉ *Noria 12,* ☎ *755/4–21–09. Reservations not accepted. No credit cards. Closed in low season.*

$ ✕ **Garrobos.** Seafood specialties at this casual restaurant include *tiritas de pescado* (marinated strips of raw fish, typical of Zihuatanejo), and a house version of paella. Service is attentive. ✉ *Juan N. Alvarez 52,* ☎ *755/4–29–77. Reservations not accepted. MC, V. No lunch.*

$ ✕ **La Mordida.** Join the throngs at this simple, very popular eatery for pizza and tasty charcoal-broiled burgers. ✉ *Paseo de la Boquita 20,* ☎ *755/4–82–16. Reservations not accepted. No credit cards. No lunch.*

Dining and Lodging

Troncones

$$ ✕⌂ **El Burro Borracho.** For out-of-the-way seclusion, you can venture some 30 minutes northwest up the coast to the pristine 5-kilometer-long (3-mile-long) beach of Troncones, near the tiny village of the same name. Six comfortable stone cottages and a congenial restaurant-bar sit right on the beach. The menu ranges from cheeseburgers to fresh lobster; for breakfast, try the grilled pork chops with three eggs. Then lie in a hammock or go beachcombing, boogie boarding, hiking, or cave exploring. Owners Dewey and Carolyn are also known for their Casa de la Tortuga bed-and-breakfast, just up the beach. ✉ *Troncones Beach, Apdo. 277, Zihuatanejo, Guerrero 40880,* ☎ FAX *755/4–32–96. 6 bungalows. Restaurant. No credit cards.*

Zihuatanejo

$$$$ ✕⌂ **La Casa Que Canta.** Resembling a thatched-roof pueblo village, "The
★ House That Sings" is perched on a cliffside high above Zihuatanejo Bay. The multilevel palapa-topped lobby is adorned with folk-art furnishings, including hand-painted chairs with Frida Kahlo motifs. The individually designed rooms, named for Mexican songs, also feature beautiful handcrafted pieces and offer modern amenities such as air-conditioning and hair dryers. Because of the stepped architecture, the main swimming pool seems to be airborne. Below, overlooking the sea, a saltwater pool features a therapeutic whirlpool. Seven extraspacious suites—five of them in a wing completed in early 1996—have their own pools. The multilevel restaurant offers fine Continental and Mexican fare as well as stupendous views (reservations required). Children under 16 are not accepted at either the restaurant or the hotel. ✉ *Camino Escénico a Playa la Ropa, 40880,* ☎ *755/4–27–22 or 800/525–4800,* FAX *755/4–20–06. 23 suites. Restaurant, 2 pools, exercise room. AE, DC, MC, V.*

$$$$ ✕⌂ **Villa del Sol.** This is the ultimate in luxurious beach living. One-
★ and two-story suites in a series of casitas nestle amid coconut palms, lush tropical gardens, fountains, and meandering paths leading to Playa la Ropa, one of the loveliest beaches on the Pacific Coast. Guest rooms and baths are artistically designed, with canopied king-size beds, colorful folk-art furnishings, and terraces or balconies with hammocks; all offer air-conditioning, satellite TV, minibars, and hair dryers, and some boast private outdoor hot tubs. You can sit under a palapa on the beach and order snacks, lunch, or drinks from a casual menu. In the evening, the European and Mexican chefs prepare fine international and local dishes, using the freshest of ingredients. Even if you're not staying here, don't miss the elaborate "Mexican Fiesta" buffet on Friday nights. Children under 14 are not accepted during high season. ✉ *Playa la Ropa, Box 84, 40880,* ☎ *755/4–22–39 or 800/223–6510,* FAX *755/4–40–66. 36 1- and 2-bedroom suites. Restaurant, 2 pools, 2 tennis courts, beach. AE, DC, MC, V.*

Lodging

There is a wide range of hotel accommodations in Ixtapa and in Zihuatanejo. High-priced Ixtapa has almost exclusively deluxe, beachfront properties, and almost all are located along the Zona Hoteleria, a 3-kilometer (2-mile) stretch of Palmar Beach; they do not always match the other members of international chains whose names they bear in quality, however. Most of the budget accommodations are in Zihuatanejo, where the best hotels are on or overlooking La Madera or La Ropa beach, and the least expensive are downtown.

JOB Representations (⊠ Villas del Pacifico Edifio C, Dept. 1, 40880 Zihuatanejo, Guerrero, ☎ ᖴAX 755/4–43–74) specializes in apartment, home, and villa rentals.

Ixtapa

$$$$ ⍟ **Westin Brisas Ixtapa.** This immense, pyramid-shaped architectural
★ wonder slopes down a hillside to its own secluded cove and beach, Playa Vista Hermosa. The grounds are luxuriant with jungle vegetation; fresh flowers on the bed welcome you to your room. Every vibrantly colorful unit has a private balcony with a hammock, ocean view, and a table for room-service dining; spacious junior suites offer larger balconies with hot tubs. Guests and non-guests enjoy the hotel's excellent Portofino and El Mexicano restaurants. ⊠ *Playa Vista Hermosa, Box 97, 40880,* ☎ *755/3–21–21 or 800/228–3000,* ᖴAX *755/3–07–51. 428 rooms and suites. 3 restaurants, 2 bars, 3 pools, wading pool, 4 tennis courts. AE, DC, MC, V.*

$$$$ ⍟ **Krystal Ixtapa.** This beachfront hotel, shaped like a boat with its bow pointing to the sea, is part of a Mexican chain. Rooms are standard contemporary style. The Club Krystalito provides recreational activities for children, and because of its meeting facititilies, the hotel is often filled with conventioneers. The Krystal is home to Christine, Ixtapa's most popular disco, and Bogart's (☞ *Dining, above*). ⊠ *Blvd. Ixtapa, 40880,* ☎ *755/3–03–33 or 800/231–9860,* ᖴAX *755/3–02–16. 254 rooms and suites. 2 restaurants, coffee shop, pool, 2 tennis courts, dance club. AE, DC, MC, V.*

$$$ ⍟ **Dorado Pacifico.** This privately owned beachfront hotel is known for its good service and fine food. The furnishings are fairly nondescript, but the ocean-view rooms have private balconies. Glass elevators look out on the dramatic atrium lobby and fountains. The hotel's recently installed health and fitness club is the most complete in Ixtapa. Try the beachside Cebolla Roja restaurant for lunch and dinner. ⊠ *Blvd. Ixtapa, 40880,* ☎ *755/3–20–25 or 800/448–8355,* ᖴAX *755/3–01–26. 285 rooms and suites. 3 restaurants, bar, pool, 2 tennis courts. AE, DC, MC, V.*

$$$ ⍟ **DoubleTree.** Formerly the Omni, this beachfront hotel is located at the north end of the Hotel Zone, within easy walking distance of Marina Ixtapa. The Mexican colonial decor, with its bright pastel colors, is cheerful, and the new management has generally improved the place. La Gran Tapa Spanish-style restaurant features good paella and bullfight videos. ⊠ *Blvd. Ixtapa, 40880,* ☎ *755/3–00–03 or 800/222–8733, fax 755/3–15–55. 300 rooms and suites. 4 restaurants, 2 bars, pool, 2 tennis courts. AE, DC, MC, V.*

$$$ ⍟ **Presidente Forum Resort.** A member of the Inter-Continental Hotel chain, this is the only all-inclusive property in the hotel zone: Room rates include all meals, beverages, and extensive recreational activities. If you want tranquillity, request a room near the east pool, away from where the action is. ⊠ *Blvd. Ixtapa, 40880,* ☎ *755/3–00–18 or 800/327–0200,* ᖴAX *755/3–23–12. 400 rooms and suites. 3 restaurants, bar, 2 pools, wading pool, 2 tennis courts. AE, DC, MC, V.*

$$$ ⊞ **Villa del Lago.** This bed-and-breakfast in a modern colonial-style house is the only listed Ixtapa property that is not on the beach. It is, however, a golfer's dream, facing the sixth hole of the Campo de Golf Ixtapa (by Robert Trent Jones Jr.). The two-level master suite, terrace, and swimming pool offer views of the lush green course and the mountains beyond. Golf packages are available. ⊠ *Retorno Alondras 244, 40880,* ☎ *755/3–14–82; in the U.S., 619/575–1766;* ℻ *755/3–14–22. 6 suites. Library-lounge. AE, DC, MC, V.*

$$ ⊞ **Posada Real.** Smaller and more intimate than most of the other Ixtapa hotels, this member of the Best Western chain sits on Palmar Beach, has lots of charm, and offers good value. ⊠ *Blvd. Ixtapa, 40880,* ☎ *755/3–16–85 or 800/528–1234,* ℻ *755/3–18–05. 110 rooms. 3 restaurants, 2 bars, pool, wading pool, dance club. AE, DC, MC, V.*

Zihuatanejo

$$$$ ⊞ **Puerto Mío.** Just inside the mouth of Zihuatanejo Bay, this small hotel has a seaside level with a pool, terrace bar, dining room, guest rooms, and a marina where the Zihuatanejo Scuba Center is based. A hilltop "mansion" level features another pool and additional suites with sweeping bay views. Locals as well as guests enjoy the seafood, Continental cuisine, and romantic setting of the hotel's restaurant. ⊠ *Playa del Almacen, 40880,* ☎ *755/4–27–48,* ℻ *755/4–36–24. 31 rooms and suites. Restaurant, bar, 2 pools, yacht slips, scuba diving. AE, DC, MC, V.*

$$$ ⊞ **Irma.** One of Zihuatanejo's originals, this simple and clean colonial-style hotel sits on a bluff overlooking Madera Beach (accessible by a stairway). ⊠ *Playa la Madera, Box 4, 40880,* ☎ *755/4–21–05 or 800/336–5454,* ℻ *755/4–37–38. 73 rooms. Restaurant, bar, pool. AE, DC, MC, V.*

$$ ⊞ **Avila.** In the center of town facing the beachside Paseo del Pescador, the Avila has large clean rooms (all are air-conditioned), TVs, and ceiling fans. ⊠ *Calle Juan N. Alvarez 8, 40880,* ☎ *755/4–20–10,* ℻ *755/4–32–99. 27 rooms with bath. AE, MC, V.*

$$ ⊞ **Bungalows Pacíficos.** Terraced down a cliffside above Madera Beach, each of the spacious bungalows has its own large veranda with a sweeping view of Zihuatanejo Bay as well as a fully equipped kitchen. The owner speaks Spanish, English, and German. ⊠ *Cerro de la Madera, Box 12, 40880,* ☎ ℻ *755/4–21–12. 6 units. No credit cards.*

$$ ⊞ **Catalina-Sotavento.** Really two hotels in one, this multilevel oldie-but-goodie sits on a cliff overlooking the bay. Below, accessible by extensive stairs, is Playa la Ropa and the hotel's beach bar and lounge chairs. Rooms are large and well maintained, with ceiling fans and ample terraces. ⊠ *Playa la Ropa, Box 2, 40880,* ☎ *755/4–20–32,* ℻ *755/4–29–75. 120 units. 2 restaurants, 2 bars. AE, DC, MC, V.*

$$ ⊞ **Las Urracas.** Each of the casita-style units has a porch in a shaded garden, a kitchen, and a stove. Located on La Ropa Beach, it is a great bargain—which lots of people know about, so reserve far in advance. ⊠ *Playa la Ropa, Box 141, 40880,* ☎ *755/4–20–53. 16 bungalows. No credit cards.*

$$ ⊞ **Villas Miramar.** This pleasant colonial-style hotel is in two sections (divided by a small street). The front section overlooks and has access to Madera Beach. Rooms, some with balconies, are nicely decorated and have tiled showers, air-conditioning, and ceiling fans. ⊠ *Playa la Madera, Box 211, 40880,* ☎ *755/4–21–06,* ℻ *755/4–21–49. 17 rooms, 1 suite. Restaurant, bar. AE, MC, V.*

$ ⊞ **Solimar Inn.** Near the town center, this comfortable hotel features large, air-conditioned rooms with kitchenettes, ceiling fans, and satellite TVs. Guests tend to stay for weeks or more. ⊠ *Plazas los Faroles, 40880,* ☎ ℻ *755/4–36–92. 12 rooms. Bar, pool. MC, V.*

Nightlife

A good way to start an evening is a happy hour at one of Ixtapa's hotels. Sunset is an important daily event, and plans should be made accordingly. Tops for sunset viewing (with live music) is the lobby bar at the **Westin Brisas.** To follow sunset viewing by dancing to tropical music until about 2 AM, take the elevator up to the **Faro Bar** nightclub atop the 85-foot-high faux-lighthouse tower in Marina Ixtapa (☎ 755/3–20–90). **Christine,** at the Krystal in Ixtapa, is the town's liveliest high-tech disco, and a spectacular runner-up is **Euforia** alongside the Posada Real Hotel. **Carlos 'n' Charlie's** (⊠ Blvd. Ixtapa, next to the Hotel Camino Real, ☎ 755/3–10–85) has a party atmosphere, with late-night dancing on a raised platform by the beach.

A number of hotels feature **Mexican Fiesta Nights** with a buffet, handicraft bazaars, and live folkloric music and dance performances. At the Sheraton, these take place every Wednesday, year-around. During high season, you'll find Fiesta Nights on Mondays at the Krystal and on Tuesdays at the Dorado Pacifico.

Outdoor Activities and Sports

Fishing
Bookings and information about sportsfishing can be obtained through **Ixtapa Sportfishing Charters** (⊠ 33 Olde Mill Run, Stroudsburg, PA 18360, ☎ 717/424–8323, FAX 717/424–1016) or in Zihuatanejo (☎ 755/4–44–26 or 755/4–41–62).

Golf
There are two 18-hole championship courses in Ixtapa. The **Campo de Golf Ixtapa** (☎ 755/3–10–62), designed by Robert Trent Jones Jr., is on a wildlife preserve that runs from a coconut plantation to the beach. Part of the Marina Ixtapa complex, the highly challenging **Club de Golf Marina Ixtapa** (☎ 755/3–14–10) layout was designed by Robert von Hagge. Each has its own clubhouse with a restaurant as well as tennis courts. Green fees run approximately $55; caddies or carts cost about $20.

Horseback Riding
You can rent horses at Playa Linda just up the coast from Ixtapa, or at La Manzanillo Ranch, near Playa la Ropa in Zihuatanejo.

Scuba Diving
Some 30 dive sites in the area range from deep canyons to shallow reefs. The waters here are teeming with sea life and visibility is excellent. At the north end of Playa Cuachalalate on Ixtapa Island, **Nacho's Dive Shop** (no phone) provides rental equipment, instruction, and guided dives. The **Zihuatanejo Scuba Center** (⊠ Calle Cuauhtémoc 3, ☎ FAX 755/4–21–47; also at marina of Hotel Puerto Mío), owned and operated by master diver and marine biologist Juan Barnard, offers one- and two-tank dives as well as an intensive five-day certification course. Divers can have their underwater adventures videotaped for an additional fee. This authorized NAUI (National Association of Underwater Instructors) Pro Facility has an enthusiastic and knowledgeable staff, including some expatriate Americans.

Tennis
All major Ixtapa hotels have night-lit tennis courts as do the **Campo de Golf Ixtapa** (☎ 755/3–10–62) and the **Club de Golf Marina Ixtapa** (☎ 755/3–14–10).

Water Sports

You'll find a variety of water sports along Playa del Palmar in Ixtapa. Parasailing costs about $20 for about a 10-minute ride; water skiing and wave runners run about $30 per half hour; banana boat rides are about $5 for a 20-minute trip. On La Ropa Beach, in front of Hotel Villa del Sol, Hobie Cats rent for $20 per hour and classes cost $30 per half hour. Windsurfers rent for $10 per hour; classes, which include six hours over four days, cost $40.

Shopping

Ixtapa

As you enter Ixtapa from the airport or from Zihuatanejo, you'll see a large handicrafts market, **Mercado de Artesanía Turístico,** on the right side of Boulevard Ixtapa. The result of a state law that banned vendors from the beach, this markets hosts some 150 stands, selling handicrafts, T-shirts, folk apparel, and souvenirs.

Farther down on the right, across the street from the Hotel Zone, the shopping area is loosely divided into *centros comerciales,* or malls. These clusters of pleasant colonial-style buildings feature patios containing boutiques, restaurants, cafés, and grocery mini-markets. The first one you'll come to is **Los Patios,** where **Tanga Boutique** (☎ 755/3–05–98) offers a nice selection of Mexican and imported beachwear, and **La Fuente** (☎ 755/3–17–33) sells native-designed clothes, art, crafts, and home furnishings. Behind Los Patios, in a terra-cotta-colored building, is **Plaza Ixpamar,** host to **El Amanecer** (☎ 755/3–19–02) and its nice array of folk art. Then comes **Las Fuentes,** where you'll find **Polo Ralph Lauren** (☎ 755/3–12–72); **Bye-Bye** (☎ 755/3–09–79) beach and casual wear; the ubiquitous sportswear emporium **Aca Joe** (☎ 755/3–03–02); and the handy **Supermercado Scruples** (☎ 755/3–21–28). The last mall on this strip is **La Puerta,** which includes **Ferrioni Collection** (☎ 755/3–23–43) with colorful Scottish terrier–logo casual wear, and **Mic-Mac** (☎ 755/3–22–66) for crafts and Mexican regional art and clothing.

Zihuatanejo

Downtown Zihuatanejo has a colorful **municipal market** with a labyrinth of small stands on the east side of the town center, on Calle Benito Juárez at Antonio Nava. On the west edge of town, along Calle 5 de Mayo, is the **Mercado de Artesanía Turístico,** similar to the craft and souvenir market in Ixtapa, but larger, with 255 stands. Good purchases include local hand-painted Guerrero wooden masks and ceramics, huaraches, and silver jewelry.

Near the mercado, across from the Aeromexico office and facing the waterfront, **Casa Marina** (⊠ Paseo del Pescador 9, ☎ 755/4–23–73) is a two-story building containing several boutiques, all belonging to the same family. **El Embarcadero** has an extensive selection of folk art from all over Mexico; **Manos** sells handicrafts; **La Zapoteca** features hammocks and hand-loomed rugs; and **El Jumil** has an array of Guerrero ceremonial masks. You might want to poke around here first to check prices, and then head for the market, where you'll often pay less for the same wares if you have a good eye and are willing to bargain.

There are a number of interesting shops in the tiny three-block nucleus of central Zihuatanejo. **Galeria Maya** (⊠ Calle Nicolás Bravo 31, ☎ 755/4–46–06) is very browsable for its folk art and leather goods. **Nando's** (⊠ Juan N. Alvarez 5, ☎ 755/4–22–38) features a selection of colorful handmade tropical-chic women's apparel from Oaxaca and Chiapas. **Alberto's** (⊠ Calle Cuauhtémoc 12 and 15, ☎ 755/4–21–61) is one of the best places to find authentic Taxco silver jewelry. **Coco Cabaña** (⊠ Agustín Ramírez 1, ☎ 755/4–25–18) is a fascinating folk-art shop. Over at Playa la Ropa, **Gala Art** (⊠ Hotel Villa del Sol, ☎ 755/4–22–39) exhibits and sells paintings and sculptures by prominent local artists.

IXTAPA/ZIHUATANEJO A TO Z

Arriving and Departing

By Bus
Estrella Blanca (☎ 755/4–34–77) and **Estrella de Oro** (☎ 755–4–21–75) offer deluxe service (with air-conditioning, video, bathrooms, and soft drinks) between Acapulco and Zihuatanejo. The trip takes less than four hours and costs about $15.

By Car
The trip from Acapulco is a 3½-hour drive over a good two-lane road that passes through small towns and coconut groves and has some spectacular ocean views for the last third of the way.

By Plane
Mexicana (☎ 755/4–22-27) offers direct daily flights from Los Angeles and Chicago, while **Aeromexico** (☎ 755/4-22–37) flies direct every day from New York/JFK, Houston, Miami, and Dallas/Ft. Worth. Both airlines operate several daily nonstops (35 minutes) between Mexico City and Zihuatanejo. **Continental** (☎ 755/4–25–79) flies nonstop from Houston. Seasonally, **TWA** (☎ 755/4–52–20) has service from its St. Louis hub, and **Northwest** (☎ 91–800/9–07–47) departs from Minneapolis/St. Paul.

Getting Around

Unless you plan to travel great distances or visit remote beaches, taxis and buses are by far the best way to get around. Taxis are plentiful, clean, and reliable, and fares are reasonable and fixed. The fare from the Ixtapa Hotel Zone to Zihuatanejo is under $4. Taxis are usually lined up in front hotels. Two radio taxi companies are **APAAZ** (☎ 755/4–36–80) and **UTAAZ** (☎ 755/4–33–11). Mini-buses run frequently between the Ixtapa hotels and between the Ixtapa Hotel Zone and downtown Zihuatanejo; fare is about 30¢.

Rental cars, from Jeeps to sedans with automatic transmission and air-conditioning, are available from major car rental agencies (☞ *below*). You can also rent an electric-powered golf cart in Ixtapa from **Tropical Transportation** (⊠ Las Fuentes Shopping Center, ☎ 755/3–24–88). They're for local transportation only, however—don't consider taking one to Zihuatanejo—and cost from about $12 for one hour to $55 for 24 hours.

Contacts and Resources

Car Rentals
Hertz, Avis, National, and **Dollar** have locations at the airport and in Ixtapa and/or Zihuatanejo. A good local agency is **Quick Rent-A-Car** (⊠ Westin Las Brisas, ☎ 755/3–18–30).

Emergencies
Police (☎ 755/4–38–37), **Public Safety** (Seguridad Publica; ☎ 755/4–71–71), **Red Cross** (☎ 755/4–20–09).

Guided Tours

Most major hotels have lobby tour desks or travel agencies that offer a selection of sightseeing tours of Ixtapa, Zihuatanejo, and surrounding areas. Another option is a six-hour cruise on the 12-passenger trimaran *Tri-Star,* which sets sail from the Puerto Mío hotel marina in Zihuatanejo. For $60, you'll get an open bar (domestic drinks), live music, dancing, and a fresh-fish lunch at Ixtapa Island. You can also book a two-hour sunset cruise of Zihuatanejo Bay or a four-hour cruise to Playa Manzanillo, just outside the mouth of the bay, for great snorkeling and swimming. For details about all of these cruises, contact **Yates del Sol** (☎ 755/4–35–89).

Travel Agency

American Express (✉ arcade of Krystal Hotel, Ixtapa, ☎ 755/3–08–53, 𝔽𝔸𝕏 755/3–12–06).

Visitor Information

Municipal Tourism Office (✉ Zihuatanejo City Hall, ☎ 755/4–20–01), **Guerrero State Tourism Office** (✉ La Puerta Shopping Center, Ixtapa, ☎ 755/3–19–68).

7 Guadalajara

The colonial architecture that dates to Guadalajara's heyday as a regional commercial center for the Spanish is among the lures of Mexico's second-largest city; Guadalajara also introduced the world to mariachis and tequila. Some of the best arts and crafts in the country can be found at Tlaquepaque, on the outskirts of town, and Tonalá, about 10 minutes farther away.

TRADITIONS ARE preserved and customs perpetuated in Guadalajara; it's a place where the siesta is an institution and the fiesta an art form. The city is the birthplace of *el jarabe tapatío* (the Mexican hat dance), *charreadas* (rodeos), mariachis, and tequila.

Updated by
Trudy Balch

Mexico's second-largest city, and capital of the state of Jalisco, Guadalajara is engaged in a struggle to retain its provincial ambience and colonial charm as its population approaches 6 million. Emigrés from Mexico City after the devastating 1985 earthquake and staggering numbers of the rural poor seeking employment have created a population explosion that strains the capacity of public services and the city's often outdated infrastructure. Visitors to the city can enjoy the tree-lined boulevards, parks, plazas, and stately Churrigueresque architecture, but recent years have brought traffic jams and occasional heavy pollution, coming from the industrial zone in the southern part of the city to the downtown area.

Guadalajara has always been one of the most socially traditional and politically conservative cities in Mexico. It has also been the seat of Christian fundamentalism and was one of the strategic areas of the *Cristeros,* a movement of right-wing Catholic zealots in western Mexico in the 1920s. *Tapatíos,* as the city's residents are called (the name comes from *tlapatiotl,* three units or purses of cacao or other commodities used as currency by the Indians of the area), even seem to take a certain amount of pride in their straight and narrow outlook.

Still, Tapatíos are historically accustomed to challenge and change. Within 10 years of its founding in 1531, the location of the city changed three times. In 1542 the City Council followed the advice of Doña Beatriz Hernández to build the city in the center of the Atemajac Valley, where it could expand. Thus Guadalajara was placed on a mile-high plain of the Sierra Madre, bounded on three sides by rugged cliffs and on the fourth by the spectacular Barranca de Oblatos (Oblatos Canyon). A near-perfect semitropical climate and proximity to the Pacific Ocean (240 kilometers, or 150 miles, away) ensure warm, sunny days with just a hint of humidity and cool, clear nights.

Geographically remote from the rest of the republic during the nearly 300 years of Spanish rule, the city cultivated and maintained a political and cultural autonomy. By the end of the 16th century, money was flowing into Guadalajara from the rich farms and silver mines in the region, creating the first millionaires of what was then known as New Galicia. Under orders from Spain, much of the wealth was lavished on magnificent churches, residences, and monuments. Many of these reminders of the golden era still stand in a series of contiguous plazas in downtown Guadalajara.

The suburbs of San Pedro Tlaquepaque (Tla-kay-*pah*-kay) and Tonalá (Toe-na-*la*) produce some of Mexico's finest and most popular traditional crafts and folk art. Lake Chapala and the nearby towns of Chapala and Ajijic have attracted retired former residents of the United States and Canada, who enjoy most of the amenities and services they were accustomed to north of the border.

Pleasures and Pastimes

Arts and Architecture

All manner of Mexican and international arts can be found in Guadalajara. You'll find everything in the performing arts from the traditional

Ballet Folklórico at the Teatro Degollado to Bob Dylan at the Instituto Cultural Cabañas. Galleries and museums around town also offer the best of modern and traditional creations. Numerous 16th-century colonial buildings fill the downtown area, connected by a series of large, Spanish-style plazas.

Churches

Guadalajara seems to have a church every block or two—there are 15 in the downtown area alone, all dating to the colonial era. Some have elaborately carved facades, and others conceal ornate Baroque altars and priceless colonial oil paintings behind sober stone exteriors.

Dining

Guadalajara offers an impressive variety of restaurants, with choices ranging from classic Mexican dishes to continental delicacies, Argentine-style steaks, and fresh seafood. Savory regional specialties—often served in simpler establishments—include *birria,* a spicy stew prepared with goat, lamb, or pork in a light tomato broth; *pozole,* a thick pork and hominy soup; and *carne en su jugo,* consisting of steak bits in a clear spicy broth with bacon and beans, usually served with a side of tiny, grilled whole onions.

Lodging

Hotel choices run the gamut from older establishments in the downtown historic district—including one lovingly restored building that has been a hotel since 1610—to representatives of the large chains, most of which are on or near Avenida López Mateos Sur, a 10-mile strip extending from the Minerva Fountain to the Plaza del Sol shopping center. In the mid-1990s several hotels have also gone up close to Expo-Guadalajara (one of Latin America's largest convention centers), which opened in 1987.

Shopping

Traditional to the area are blown glass, delicately painted pottery, hand-carved wood furniture, and fine leatherwork. Guadalajara is also home to a thriving shoe industry. At sprawling markets you can bargain for anything from embroidered shirts to huaraches, and sleek shopping malls offer full-service department stores and trendy boutiques.

Sports

Highly stylized *charreadas,* or traditional Mexican rodeos, are presented here weekly, and there are bullfights in October and November. From late August through April, enthusiastic soccer fans crowd Jalisco Stadium.

EXPLORING GUADALAJARA

Metropolitan Guadalajara consists of the historic city center and the nearby urban districts, as well as the neighboring towns of Tlaquepaque and Tonalá and the tranquil villages on the shores of Lake Chapala.

Great Itineraries

It's not surprising that Guadalajara has been described as *señorial y moderna* (lordly and modern). Here, you can experience the graciousness of colonial Mexico, accompanied by however much you want of the 20th century. The nearby pueblos offer an eye into traditional rural life. Ten days would allow you to fully explore the city and surrounding villages, as well as take an excursion or two to points farther afield. With five days to spend here, you'll have time to tour many city highlights and get to know Tlaquepaque, Tonalá, and the Lake Chapala area. In three days, you can take in the historic city center and make day trips to Tlaquepaque, Tonalá, and Lake Chapala.

IF YOU HAVE 3 DAYS

Spend your first day in the historic city center (*el centro*), making sure you see the cathedral, the Iglesia de Nuestra Señora de Aranzazú, the Iglesia de San Agustín, the Instituto Cultural Cabañas, the Mercado Libertad, the Museo Region de Guadalajara, the Palacio de Gobierno, and the Teatro Degollado. The next day, spend the morning in Tlaquepaque, have lunch there, and visit Tonalá in the afternoon. On your third day, head for the Lake Chapala area; stroll and shop, perhaps take a boat trip on the lake, and enjoy lunch or dinner in one of the area's fine restaurants.

IF YOU HAVE 5 DAYS

See the city center on your first day. Then consider your interests. If traditional crafts lure you, devote a day to Tlaquepaque and the following day to Tonalá. Or you can explore the two towns in one day, leaving you a day—or two—for the Lake Chapala area. During your final one or two days, you can spend part or all of a day visiting other historical or art museums in, around, and outside the city center, such as the Casa-Museo López Portillo, the Museo de la Ciudad de Guadalajara, Museo de Arqueología del Ocidente de México, Museo de Cera, Museo de las Artes de la Universidad de Guadalajara, and Museo del Periodismo y las Artes Gráficas. You might take in some additional churches, including the Zapopan basilica, for which you'll need several hours; and visit the Guadalajara zoo and planetarium. If you decide to stop by the village of Tequila, allow at least half a day. If your taste runs more to naturist activities, allow a day to see the zoo and hike in the nearby Barranca de Oblatos.

IF YOU HAVE 10 DAYS

You will be able to cover all of *el centro* plus the other city sights, and Tlaquepaque, Tonalá, and the Lake Chapala area. Fill in the gaps with a visit to Tequila and a stay in the soothing thermal waters of San Juan Cosalá or Rancho Río Caliente. For an excursion to the Sierra de Manantlán, allow two to three days.

Guadalajara

Beginning around 1960, 20th-century architecture started to threaten the historical integrity of this provincial state capital. In the early 1980s the city declared a 30-square-block area in the heart of downtown a cultural sanctuary. The 16th-century buildings here are connected by a series of large Spanish-style plazas where today's inhabitants enjoy life: Young children chase gaily colored balloons, young lovers cuddle on tree-shaded park benches, and grandparents stroll hand in hand past vendors and marble fountains. At nearby Plaza de los Mariachis, the nostalgic songs and music of sombrero-topped troubadours can be heard.

In addition to *el centro* downtown, most tourist sights and large hotels are located in three other areas: near Avenida Chapultepec; near the Minerva Fountain and Los Arcos monument; and in the Plaza del Sol shopping area (several miles southwest of downtown).

A Good Walk

Numbers in the text correspond to numbers in the margin and on the Downtown Guadalajara map.

Begin a tour of downtown at the 17th-century **catedral** ① on Avenida Alcalde between Avenida Hidalgo and Calle Morelos. Go out through the main doors and cross Avenida Alcalde to **Plaza Guadalajara,** dotted with benches beneath square-cut laurel trees. To your right (with your back toward the cathedral) across Avenida Hidalgo is the **Pala-**

cio Municipal, or City Hall, a clever colonial-style fake: It was built in 1952 with an arched facade and interior patio so it would fit in with neighboring buildings. Inside is a colorful mural depicting the founding of Guadalajara. For a brief detour into the history of journalism and print, head east (left) around the corner from the Palacio to the new **Museo del Periodismo y las Artes Gráficas** at Avenida Alcalde 225, just north of Calle San Felipe; it's located in a building long known as Casa de los Perros because of the two wrought-iron dogs (*perros*) guarding the roof.

Return to Avenidas Alcalde and Hidalgo and proceed one block east to Calle Liceo, where you'll see the **Museo Regional de Guadalajara** ②. You'll pass the **Rotonda de Hombres Ilustres de Jalisco,** a tree-shaded square whose central colonnaded rotunda covers a mausoleum containing the remains of 17 of the state of Jalisco's favorite sons. Surrounding the square are brass sculptures representing those buried inside.

When you exit back onto Calle Liceo, you have two alternatives: Three blocks to your right is the **Casa-Museo López Portillo** ③. Around the corner to the left, on Avenida Hidalgo, are the **Palacio Legislativo,** a former customs house, tobacco warehouse, and inn that today houses Jalisco's state legislature, followed by the **Palacio de Justicia,** built in 1588 as part of Guadalajara's first convent and now the state courthouse. Across Avenida Hidalgo on your right sprawls the **Plaza de la Liberación,** at the east end of which rises the spectacular **Teatro Degollado** ④. Behind it begins the **Plaza Tapatía,** a five-block-long pedestrian mall lined with shops, trees, and whimsical sculptures and frequented by mimes and street musicians. At the end of Plaza Tapatía, visit the **Instituto Cultural Cabañas** ⑤; then proceed back west through Plaza Tapatía to the modernistic **Quetzalcóatl Fountain** in the center. Turn left and walk down the stairs to the three-story **Mercado Libertad** (☞ Shopping, *below*). Turn left again when you leave the market and cross the pedestrian bridge over Avenida Javier Mina to the **Plaza de los Mariachis** ⑥.

Return to Plaza Tapatía by heading right to the intersection of Calzada Independencia Sur and Avenida Javier Mina, in front of the Iglesia de San Juan de Dios. Continue two blocks past the church and go back up the stairs. Turn left and walk west four blocks (giving you the opportunity to see the stores on this side of the plaza) to the **Iglesia de San Agustín** ⑦.

As you leave the church, turn left down Calle Morelos to Avenida Corona. Turn left again and walk a half-block to the main entrance of the **Palacio de Gobierno** ⑧. Exit the Palacio de Gobierno back onto Avenida Corona (the way you came in) and cross the street to the **Plaza de Armas,** where you can rest on a wrought-iron bench, or imagine yourself a gracious *don* or *doña* as you stroll amid the trees and flower beds surrounding an ornately sculpted kiosk, a gift from France in 1910. You have now come full circle, with the cathedral to your right, on the north side of the plaza.

TIMING

You can take in most of downtown Guadalajara in a day. The other groups of sights can easily take one-half or one full day each. Most museums, the zoo, and the planetarium are closed on Monday. During October, the city puts on the Fiestas de Octubre, a monthlong cultural festival that's sprinkled with top-flight international entertainment.

Sights to See

Basílica de la Virgen de Zapopan. This vast church, with an ornate Plateresque facade and *mudejar* tiled dome, was consecrated in 1730.

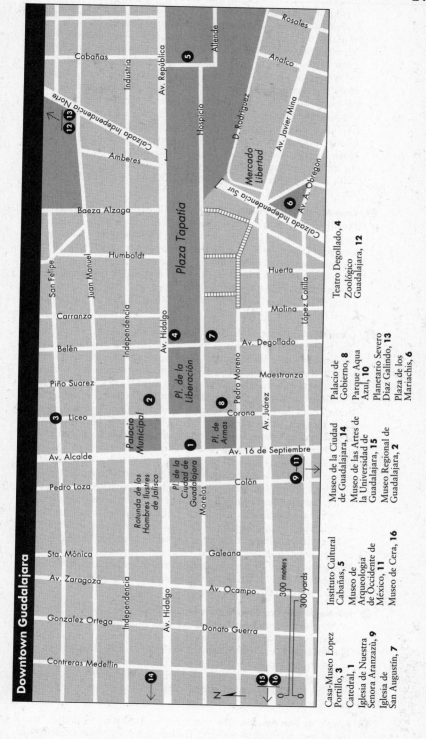

Downtown Guadalajara

Casa-Museo Lopez Portillo, **3**
Catedral, **1**
Iglesia de Nuestra Senora Aranzazú, **9**
Iglesia de San Augustín, **7**

Instituto Cultural Cabañas, **5**
Museo de Arqueología de Occidente de México, **11**
Museo de Cera, **16**

Museo de la Ciudad de Guadalajara, **14**
Museo de las Artes de la Universidad de Guadalajara, **15**
Museo Regional de Guadalajara, **2**

Palacio de Gobierno, **8**
Parque Aqua Azul, **10**
Planetario Severo Diaz Galindo, **13**
Plaza de los Mariachis, **6**

Teatro Degollado, **4**
Zoológico Guadalajara, **12**

It is known throughout Mexico as the home of La Zapopanita, Our Lady of Zapopan. The 10-inch-high statue is venerated as the source of many miracles in and around Guadalajara. Every year on October 12, more than 1 million people crowd the streets leading to Zapopan as the Virgin is returned to the basilica after a five-month absence, during which she visits every parish church in the state. In the right side of the basilica is the **Museo Huichol,** a small gallery and shop featuring exquisite beadwork and other handicrafts by the Huichol Indians of northern Jalisco and neighboring states Zacatecas and Nayarit. The basilica is 7 kilometers (4½ miles) east-northeast of downtown. Additional information is available from the municipal tourist office, a block behind the basilica. ⊠ *Museo Huichol: Av. Avila Camacho and Av. de las Américas.* ☉ *Weekdays 10–1:30 and 4–7, weekends 10–1:30. Tourist office: Vicente Guerrero 233,* ☏ *3/633–0571.* ☉ *Weekdays 8–8, Sat. 9–1.*

❸ Casa-Museo López Portillo. Members of Guadalajara's illustrious López Portillo family included prominent writers and politicians, such as an early-20th-century Jalisco governor and his Mexico City–born grandson, José López Portillo, president of Mexico from 1976 to 1982. As is typical of many homes built by Mexico's 19th-century upper class, the plain stucco exterior belies the polished, richly furnished interior, where French Baroque–style rooms ring a spacious interior patio. ⊠ *Liceo 177, at San Felipe,* ☏ *3/613–2411.* ▧ *Free.* ☉ *Weekdays 9 AM–8:30 PM, Sat. 9–1.*

★ ❶ Catedral. Consecrated in 1618, this is the focal point of downtown. The building is an intriguing mélange of Baroque, Churrigueresque, neoclassical and other architectural styles, the result of design and structural modifications during its 57 years of construction. Its emblematic twin towers replaced the original, much shorter ones, which were toppled in the devastating earthquake of 1818. The interior contains fine examples of 16th- to 18th-century Spanish art and decor. Ten of the silver-and-gilt altars were gifts of King Fernando VII (in appreciation of Guadalajara's financial support of Spain during the Napoleonic Wars); the 11th, of sculpted white marble, was carved in Italy in 1863. The altar and statue dedicated to Our Lady of the Rose are exquisite. The statue, carved from a single piece of balsa wood, was a gift from King Charles V in the 16th century. The image and remains of Saint Innocence, brought here from the catacombs of Rome, are on the left side of the main altar. On the walls of the cathedral hang some of the world's most beautiful *retablos* (altarpieces); above the sacristy is the priceless 17th-century painting of Bartolomé Esteban Murillo, *The Assumption of the Virgin.* In a loft high above the main entrance is a magnificent late-19th-century French organ, featured in an organ festival usually held every May. ⊠ *Av. Alcalde between Av. Hidalgo and Morelos.* ☉ *Daily 7 AM–8 PM.*

❾ Iglesia de Nuestra Señora de Aranzazú. Don't be fooled by Our Lady of Aranzazú's drab brown stone exterior: Inside is a glorious baroque *retablo* (altarpiece) whose 14 niches contain life-size statues of saints. The walls and ceilings are painted in bright shades of turquoise, rose, and rust, with intricate floral detail. The church sits at the west side of Parque San Francisco, a small green oasis that draws food vendors, families, and sedate senior citizens. ⊠ *Av. 16 de Septiembre and Prisciliano Sánchez.*

❼ Iglesia de San Agustín. The venerable St. Augustine Church is one of the oldest churches in the city. Though it has been remodeled many times since its consecration in 1574, the sacristy has been preserved in its original form. The building to the left of the church, originally a cloister of the Augustinian monks, is now the **Escuela de Música,** or School of Music, of the University of Guadalajara. Free recitals and concerts are held on the school's patio. ⊠ *Morelos at Av. Degollado.*

★ ❺ **Instituto Cultural Cabañas.** A Guadalajara landmark and major cultural center, this sprawling building topped by a stately, pillared dome was originally an orphanage founded by Bishop Juan Cruz Ruíz de Cabañas y Crespo in the early 19th century. It was home for 400 orphans and indigent children until the 1970s, when the orphanage moved to a new location. The rooms, which surround 23 flower-filled patios, contain permanent and revolving art exhibits. The central dome and walls of the main chapel display a series of murals painted by José Clemente Orozco in 1938–39. *The Man of Fire,* which depicts a man enveloped in flames who is ascending toward infinity and yet not consumed by the fire, represents the spirit of humankind. It is generally considered to be his finest work. There is a permanent exhibit of Orozco's paintings, cartoons, and drawings in Room 33. Ask the attendant at the front desk for an English-speaking guide. ⊠ *Calle Cabañas 8, at Plaza Tapatía,* ☎ *3/617–4322 or 3/617–4440.* ☞ *About $1.35; free on Sun.* ◷ *Tues.–Sat. 10:15–6, Sun. 10:15–3.*

⓫ **Museo de Arqueología de Occidente de México.** The Archaeological Museum of Western Mexico houses pottery and other artifacts used by ancient peoples of what are now the states of Colima, Jalisco, and Nayarit. It's across from the entrance to Parque Agua Azul. ⊠ *Calzada Independencia Sur and Calzada del Campesino, no phone.* ☞ *20¢.* ◷ *Tues.–Sun. 10–2 and 4–7.*

☞ ⓰ **Museo de Cera.** Guadalajara's 120-figure wax museum is in an elegantly restored turn-of-the-century house. Go eye-to-eye with Madonna, Mahatma Gandhi, and beloved Mexican comic Cantinflas, as well as a host of other Mexican and international political and artistic luminaries. Finish with the dungeonlike chamber of horrors in the basement. The museum is located three blocks south of Avenida Chapultepec, behind the U.S. Consulate. ⊠ *Libertad 1872,* ☎ *3/825–8956.* ☞ *About $2.50 adults, $1.70 children.* ◷ *Daily 10–7.*

⓮ **Museo de la Ciudad de Guadalajara.** In a series of rooms surrounding a tranquil interior patio, you'll find artwork, artifacts, and reproductions of documents that provide extensive information about the city's development. Originally a large private home, the building was converted into a museum in 1992 to commemorate the 450th anniversary of the founding of the city. ⊠ *Av. Independencia 684, between Contreras Medellín and Mariano Bárcenas,* ☎ *3/658–2531 or 658–3706.* ☞ *50¢ adults, 20¢ under 18; free on Sun.* ◷ *Wed.–Sun. 10–5.*

⓯ **Museo de las Artes de la Universidad de Guadalajara.** This impressive contemporary art museum, housed in an exquisite early-20th-century building belonging to the University of Guadalajara, has a permanent collection of early-20th-century drawings, as well as revolving exhibits of modern Latin American, U.S., and European works. Also in the building are the first murals painted by Orozco after he returned to Guadalajara at age 53, as well as a charming café and small gift shop. Behind the museum, you'll see the **Templo Expiatorio,** a striking Gothic-style church built at the turn of the century and modeled after the Cathedral of Orvieto in Italy. ⊠ *Av. Juárez at Av. Enrique Díaz de León,* ☎ *3/826-6032 or 3/825-7553.* ☞ *Free.* ◷ *Tues.–Sat. 10–8, Sun. noon–8.*

★ ❷ **Museo Regional de Guadalajara.** Constructed as a seminary in the late 17th century, this distinguished building has been home to the Regional Museum (also known as the State Museum) since 1918. The first-floor galleries, which surround a courtyard of Roman arches and tropical gardens, contain artifacts and memorabilia that trace the history of western Mexico from prehistoric times through the Spanish conquest. On the second-floor balcony are five antique carriages from the 19th century; the second-floor galleries feature an impressive collection of paintings by European and Mexican artists, including Bartolomé Esteban Murillo, and displays about the history of Jalisco. ☒ *Liceo 60.* ☎ *3/614–9957.* ☒ *About $2.35 adults; free Sun.* ☉ *Tues.–Sat. 9–3:45, Sun. 9–3.*

❽ Palacio de Gobierno. Built in 1643, this Churrigueresque and neoclassical structure houses Jalisco's state government offices and two of José Clemente Orozco's most imaginative and passionate murals. You'll see the first one in the stairwell to the right after you enter: a gigantic Father Miguel Hidalgo looming amid shadowy figures representing oppression and slavery. The second, in the former state legislature quarters on the upper level, depicts Juárez and other figures of the 1850s Reform era. ☒ *Av. Corona between Morelos and Pedro Moreno.* ☉ *Daily 9–9.*

🐾 ❿ Parque Agua Azul. Amid acres of trees and flowers, this popular park has carnival rides, tropical birds in cages, an orchid house, a geodesic dome covering a tropical garden, and benches surrounding a pleasant artificial lake. Next to the park entrance, the small **Teatro Experimental** (☎ /619–3770) presents many Spanish-language children's plays, including English-language classics in translation. Dramas and chamber music are also performed here. The displays at the lively **Museo Infantil** (no phone), on the southeast side of the park, focus on geography, space, and natural history. ☒ *Calzada Independencia Sur and Calzada del Campesino.* ☒ *Park 70¢; museum about $1.50.* ☉ *Park Tues.–Sun. 10–6; museum Tues.–Sun. 9–1 and 3–7.*

🐾 ⓭ Planetario Severo Díaz Galindo. A modern facility with astronomy shows and aeronautical displays, the planetarium also features exhibits that allow children to test the forces and laws of nature. It's 6 kilometers (nearly 4 miles) northeast of downtown. *Calzada Ricardo Flores Magón 599,* ☎ *3/674–4106 or 3/674–3978.* ☒ *Museum 20¢; astronomy show and movie 45¢.* ☉ *Tues.–Sun. 9–7.*

❻ Plaza de los Mariachis. Experience the most Mexican of music in this picturesque little plaza where strolling mariachi groups perform. Although the action and ambience are best during the evening, you might enjoy a break from sightseeing in one of the cafés. The plaza is next to the **Iglesia de San Juan de Dios,** or San Juan de Dios Church; use the pedestrian overpass from the Mercado Libertad to avoid the heavy traffic. ☒ *Calzada Independencia Sur between Av. Javier Mina and Alvaro Obregón. A mariachi serenade is about $5 a song.*

★ ❹ Teatro Degollado. Inaugurated in 1866, this magnificent theater was modeled after Milan's La Scala. Above the Corinthian columns gracing the entranceway is a relief depicting Apollo and the nine Muses. Inside, red and gold balconies ascend to a multitiered dome adorned with Gerardo Suárez's depiction of Dante's *Divine Comedy.* The theater is the permanent home for the Jalisco Philharmonic and the Ballet Folklórico of the University of Guadalajara and also hosts visiting orchestras, plays and numerous other performances. According to tradition, Guadalajara was founded on the site of what is now the **Plaza de los Fundadores,** which flanks the east side of the theater. A sculpted frieze on the rear wall of the Teatro Degollado depicts the historic event. ☒ *Calle Belén, between Av. Hidalgo and Morelos.* ☎ *3/614–4773.* ☉ *Daily 10–1 and 4–7 and during performances.*

A signature pink-and-white color scheme heralds the city's most popular ice-cream chain. A stop at **Helados Bing** (on the north side of Plaza Tapatío Fountain) provides a welcome respite from an afternoon of sight-seeing. Choose from more than 20 flavors of pasteurized ice cream and ices, and find a shaded bench where you can take in the activity.

⑫ Zoológico Guadalajara. Located on the edge of the jagged Barranca Huentitán, or Huentitán Canyon, the Guadalajara Zoo has more than 1,500 animals representing some 300 species. For 50¢ a train provides guided tours. The adjacent **Selva Mágica,** or Magic Jungle amusement park, has carnival rides and attractions for about $3.35. The complex is 6 kilometers (nearly 4 miles) northeast of downtown, near the Planetarium. ✉ *Paseo del Zoológico 600,* ☎ *3/674–1034.* ✈ *About $1.65 adults, $1 children 3–10.* ☉ *Tues.–Sun. 10–6 (Selva Mágica until 7).*

Barranca de Oblatos. A spectacular 2,000-foot-deep gorge, Oblatos Canyon also has hiking trails and the narrow **Cola de Caballo** waterfall, named for its horsetail shape. For the best view, go to the lookout area, or Parque Mirador, at the top. ✉ *10 km (6 mi) northeast of downtown Guadalajara via Calzada Independencia Norte.*

DINING

Most Guadadalajara restaurants are open throughout the evening, though seafood establishments often close earlier. A number of restaurants listed below have branches elsewhere in the city; our choices are either the most colorful, original locations or those most convenient to the hotel areas. Generally, you will feel comfortable wearing casual-chic clothes at establishments in the $$ and $ categories, but Guadalajara is a big, business-oriented city, which means diners tend to dress up a bit. Still, Maximino's is the only restaurant where men are likely to feel out of place without a jacket. Some restaurants close on national holidays; call ahead to be sure.

CATEGORY	COST*
$$$$	over $35
$$$	$25–$35
$$	$15–$25
$	under $15

per person, excluding drinks, service, and sales tax (10%)

$$$ ✕ **Maximino's.** A favorite with the upper crust of Guadalajara, Maximino's is located in a beautiful two-story mansion in a quiet neighborhood near the U.S. Consulate. The elegantly decorated interior is dominated by a sweeping staircase, and tables are set up on both floors as well as—in season—on the back patio. The international menu has strong French influences, offering such delicacies as quail stuffed with pâté suffused in sherry; the seafood choices are extensive, including Dutch sole and a variety of shrimp dishes. Soft strains of a jazz trio play during most meals. ✉ *Lerdo de Tejada 2043,* ☎ *3/615–3424, 3/615–3435, or 3/825–0076. AE, MC, V.*

$$$ ✕ **Maxim's de Paris.** In 1996 Mexico acquired its second branch of
★ the legendary Paris restaurant (the other one is in Mexico City). It's as elegant as one might expect. The formal dining room features a patterned leaded-glass ceiling and an Art Nouveau–style fresco of dancers as in the original Maxim's. Modern Mexican and classical French specialties include salmon fillet in white wine and butter sauce, lamb chops in fine herbs, and snails in cilantro butter. A chamber music trio plays during dinner. ✉ *Av. Vallarta 2452, at corner of Francisco de Quevedo,* ☎ *3/615–1476 and 3/615–1477. AE, MC, V. Closed Sun.*

$$$ ✕ **Picasso.** Replicas of the namesake artist's masterpieces crowd the walls here, as polished hardwood floors and mirrored columns lend a touch of 1980s-style glitz. Eclectic offerings range from spicy chicken-based *sopa azteca* to pan-fried yellowtail snapper, egg rolls, and steak in red wine sauce with tequila butter. The back page of the menu gives a one-page summary of Picasso's stylistic periods. The restaurant is across the street from the Plaza Patria mall. ⊠ *Av. de las Américas 1939,* ☎ *3/636-6141. Reservations essential. AE, MC, V.*

$$ ✕ **Copenhagen.** The decorative tilework of Tonalá artisan Jorge Wilmot
★ covers the walls of this restaurant, which bills itself as the Paella Place. Since 1952 the Copenhagen has featured the famous dish of Valencia, Spain. The secret of a great paella lies in the texture of the rice: loose and dry but still tender. The menu also features beef and seafood entrées, pastas and Spanish-style tortillas, which—unlike the Mexican variety— are large omelets stuffed with potato and onion. Copenhagen is also the unofficial headquarters for Guadalajara's jazz aficionados; it showcases some of the city's best jazz musicians, who entertain each evening after 8. ⊠ *Marcos Castellanos 140-Z,* ☎ *3/825–2803. AE, MC, V.*

$$ ✕ **El Farallón de Tepic.** Set back from the street underneath a bright
★ blue awning, this open-air establishment is reminiscent of beach restaurants in Tepic, a popular seaside town in the nearby state of Nayarit. Order your fresh *pescado*—usually red snapper or an equally mild fish— grilled with garlic or butter, in classic tomato sauce, breaded, or stuffed with seafood and cheese. *Pescado zarandeado* is grilled to order over a wood fire and worth every second of the 30-minute wait. Try the homemade flan for dessert. ⊠ *Av. Niño Obrero 560,* ☎ *3/121–2616 or 3/121–9616. MC, V.*

$$ ✕ **Guadalajara Grill.** Fun and revelry share top billing with the food at this Carlos 'n Charlie's affiliate. The large, trilevel room is decorated with Mexican knickknacks and antique street lamps; turn-of-the-century photographs of Guadalajara are displayed in the foyer and on the back wall. The tender barbecued baby ribs are by far the favorite of both natives and tourists. Shrimp lovers will be happy to find the crustaceans grilled, baked, boiled, or served in a casserole. There is live entertainment every evening. ⊠ *Av. López Mateos Sur 3771,* ☎ *3/631–5622. AE, MC, V.*

$$ ✕ **La Copa de Leche.** This family-owned and -operated restaurant—a Guadalajara institution—moved in 1996 from downtown to a sleek white stucco-and-stone house near the Los Arcos monument. Sit indoors in a pastel split-level dining room, or outside on the rear patio facing a spacious lawn. Though the menu features the Mexican *sopa azteca,* most specialties here have a more Continental twist, such as *filete de pescado en salsa de tamarindo* (fish grilled with a sweet-and-sour tamarind sauce), *pechuga de pollo parmesana* (chicken Parmesan), and filet mignon. ⊠ *Av. Luis Pérez Verdía 38, between Av. Hidalgo and Morelos,* ☎ *3/615–2300. AE, DC, MC, V. Closed Mon.*

$$ ✕ **La Pianola.** The entrance—through what looks like an open-air kitchen where costumed women are making tortillas—may be misleading to first-timers: In back is an expansive restaurant and garden with hundreds of items on a huge menu. Specialties include *pozole,* a thick pork and hominy soup; *chiles en nogada,* spicy stuffed chili peppers in a walnut cream sauce; and *menudo,* a spicy tripe soup. The signature player-piano music accompanies your meal. ⊠ *Av. México 3220,* ☎ *3/813– 1385 or 3/813–2412. AE, MC, V.*

$$ ✕ **Parilla Argentina.** Animal hides and posters of Argentina adorn the walls of this restaurant where—as throughout Argentina—tender grilled meat reigns supreme. Choose from T-bones, ribs, flank steaks, sausages and Argentine-style *parillada* (a mixed grill of beef, sausages, and selected organ meats). Grilled chicken is also on the menu. Sprin-

kle your meat with lightly spiced *chimichurri* sauce, also an Argentine standard. ⊠ *Fernando Celada 176,* ☎ *3/615–7361. AE, MC, V.*

$ ✕ **Café Madrid.** White-jacketed waiters with black bow ties offer a sharp contrast to the Formica-topped tables and bright orange booths. This downtown institution offers daily lunch specials, as well as hamburgers, sandwiches, traditional Mexican dishes, and absolutely delicious coffee. ⊠ *Av. Juárez 264,* ☎ *3/614–9504. No credit cards.*

$ ✕ **Dainzu.** Named after the centuries-old Mixtec ruin just outside of
★ Oaxaca City, this 12-table restaurant is painted bright blue on the outside; inside, you'll find a red-tiled ceiling and regional posters. Generous portions are brought to you on hefty white ceramic plates. The tasty Oaxacan specialties include tender beef, pork, and chicken dishes prepared in a tangy green or black mole sauce. Complete the Oaxacan experience with a mug of *chocolate caliente* (hot chocolate) and sweet *pan de Oaxaca.* ⊠ *Av. Diamante 2598A,* ☎ *3/647–5086. Reservations not accepted. No credit cards. Closed Mon.*

$ ✕ **La Chata.** Dark-toned beams and brick archways are offset by brightly striped table coverings in this popular eatery. An outstanding selection is *caldo Tlalpeño,* a thick stew of chicken, avocado, rice, and cheese. Or try one of the spicy roasted meat dishes, such as *carne tampiqueña,* served with rice, beans, and enchiladas. Complement your meal with a cool, sweet *horchata,* a drink made from rice and brown sugar simmered in milk and then chilled. ⊠ *Av. López Mateos Sur, across from Holiday Inn,* ☎ *3/632–4532. Reservations not accepted. AE, MC, V.*

$ ✕ **Los Itacates.** Excellently prepared traditional Mexican dishes at
★ more than reasonable prices are what draw diners here. Most entrée items can also be ordered in tacos, so you can try unfamiliar food in small portions. Even the ambience is solidly traditional, featuring carved wooden chairs and brightly painted pottery. ⊠ *Av. Chapultepec Norte 110, between Av. México and Justo Sierra,* ☎ *3/825–1106. MC, V.*

$ ✕ **Restaurant Vegetariano Zanahoria.** The name of this casual dining spot means "carrot," but that's far from the only vegetable on the all-vegetarian menu. Choose from fresh fruit juices, fruit and vegetable salads, soups, and "fish" dishes made from cheese, potatoes, and soy. ⊠ *Av. de las Américas 538,* ☎ *3/616–6161. AE, MC, V.*

$ ✕ **Saint Michel.** The front dining room mimics the stone walls and arches of a French castle, but the room to the rear has a contemporary Mexican flair, with beige walls, beamed ceilings, and a pleasant view of the patio and gardens. Saint Michel serves more than 50 varieties of crepes, half of which are desserts. Crepe specialties include *Azteca* (with chicken and cheese); beef Stroganoff; *Scissy* (with strawberries, cheese, and cream); and *Gran Amirante* (with shrimp in a thick white-wine sauce). Meals include a trip to the salad bar. ⊠ *Av. Vallarta 1700,* ☎ *3/630–1820. AE, MC, V.*

LODGING

Guadalajara offers a fine variety of hotels in all price ranges. Call ahead if you're apprehensive about noise levels outside your hotel room. Many hotels are located on busy intersections, and you'd be well advised to consult the reservation clerk on the matter of a room away from the hubbub.

The rates given are based on the year-round or peak-season price; off-peak (summer) rates may be slightly lower. You can expect hotels in the $$$ and $$$$ categories to have purified-water systems and English-language TV channels.

CATEGORY	COST*
$$$$	over $160
$$$	$90–$160
$$	$40–$90
$	under $40

All prices are for a standard double room, excluding 15% tax.

$$$$ ★ 🏨 **Quinta Real.** Stone and brick walls, colonial arches, and objets d'art highlight the classical Mexican architecture in all public areas of this luxury hotel on the city's west side. Suites are plush and intimate, with select neocolonial furnishings, including glass-topped writing tables with carved-stone pedestals, fireplaces with marble mantelpieces, and original art. Tiled baths feature marble sinks and bronze fixtures; some suites have sunken tubs with hot tubs. Deluxe accommodations, located in the recently completed tower, are more lavish, though removed from the lush gardens below. ⊠ *Av. México 2727, at corner of López Mateos Sur, 44680,* ☎ *3/615–0000 or 800/445–4565 in the U.S., 800/3–62–15 in Mexico;* 𝖥𝖠𝖷 *3/630–1797. 78 suites. Restaurant, piano bar, pool. AE, DC, MC, V.*

$$$ 🏨 **Camino Real.** A 15-minute cab ride from downtown will bring you to this sprawling resort located 3 kilometers (2 miles) west of the Minerva Fountain. By day, you can relax in the shade of rubber and jacaranda trees; by night, you can enjoy the turn-of-the-century Aquellos Tiempos restaurant or live entertainment in La Diligencia lounge. The rooms are in two-story wings surrounding manicured lawns and tropical gardens. They are large and have placid pastel color schemes, matching bedspreads and curtains, and modern furniture. Those in the rear wing face busy, noisy Avenida Vallarta. ⊠ *Av. Vallarta 5005, 45050,* ☎ *3/121–8000 or 800/772–6466 in the U.S., 800/9–01–23 in Mexico;* 𝖥𝖠𝖷 */121–8060. 205 rooms. 2 restaurants, bar, coffee shop, 5 pools, tennis court, health club, baby-sitting, playground. AE, DC, MC, V.*

$$$ 🏨 **Carlton.** This modern 20-story tower hotel on the edge of downtown Guadalajara offers oversize rooms with light beige walls and ceilings and matching pale turquoise curtains and bedspreads. Public areas are well maintained but sparsely decorated; the rear gardens and fountain are surrounded by ivy-draped walls. Though the hotel is convenient for tourists, it caters to the business traveler. The upper floors offer a spectacular view of the city and a retreat from the horrendous street noise. ⊠ *Av. Niños Héroes 105, at corner of Av. 16 de Septiembre, 44100,* ☎ *3/614–7272 or 800/3–62–44 in Mexico,* 𝖥𝖠𝖷 *3/613–5539. 195 rooms, 5 suites. Restaurant, 2 bars, pool, health club, dance club. AE, MC, V.*

$$$ ★ 🏨 **Fiesta Americana.** The dramatic glass facade of this luxury highrise faces the Minerva Fountain. The location, warm contemporary Mexican ambience, and excellent service make this hotel a popular choice for both business travelers and tourists. Four glass-enclosed elevators ascend above the 11-story atrium lobby and adjoining Lobby Bar, one of Guadalajara's most popular nightspots. The ample rooms have a pastel color scheme, modern furnishings, and panoramic city views. The best rooms are on the upper floors, well away from the revelers down in the bar. ⊠ *Aurelio Aceves 225, 44110,* ☎ *3/825–3434, or 800/323–7821 in the U.S., 800/5–04–50 in Mexico;* 𝖥𝖠𝖷 *3/630–3725. 391 rooms, 38 suites. Restaurant, coffee shop, 2 bars, pool, exercise room, 2 tennis courts. AE, DC, MC, V.*

$$$ 🏨 **Holiday Inn.** Those who come to Guadalajara for its eternally springlike climate will enjoy the Holiday Inn. There are expansive, welltended gardens; shade-giving jacaranda, tulip, and rubber trees; and a large pool and sunbathing area. Indoors, everything is just as well tended,

and the staff is efficient and bilingual. The rooms feature marble baths, upholstered furniture, carpeting, and lots of natural light. Choose a room in the tower for a view of the mountains or one adjacent to the courtyard and its parklike greenery. ✉ *Av. López Mateos Sur 2500, 45050,* ☎ *3/634–1034, 800/465–4329 in the U.S., 800/3–65–55 in Mexico;* FAX *3/631–9393. 291 rooms, 4 suites. Restaurant, coffee shop, bar, pool, health club, 2 tennis courts, playground, car rental. AE, DC, MC, V.*

$$$ ▦ **Hyatt Regency.** This imposing pyramidal structure dominates the López Mateos Sur hotel strip. Opened in 1983, the Hyatt is popular with vacation charter groups and business travelers seeking the comfortable uniformity the hotel chain affords. Street-level escalators lift you past cascading waterfalls to the plush 12-story atrium lobby; two glass-enclosed elevators whisk you up to your floor. Spacious rooms feature hypoallergenic carpets and queen- or king-size orthopedic mattresses. The Hyatt succeeds in integrating varied restaurant, club, and common areas and in providing all with consistently good service by an attentive staff. For the best city view, request a room on an upper floor facing the bustling Plaza del Sol shopping center. ✉ *Av. López Mateos Sur and Moctezuma, 45050,* ☎ *3/678–1234, 800/228–9000 in the U.S., 800/0–05–00 in Mexico;* FAX *3/678–1222. 420 rooms, 42 suites. Restaurant, coffee shop, bar, pool, health club. AE, DC, MC, V.*

$$$ ▦ **Plaza Del Sol.** Location and price make families and young adults head for this hotel's two towers rising over the south end of the Plaza del Sol shopping center. The intimate Solaris Restaurant and the Bar Sol provide enjoyable and romantic evenings. Public areas and rooms feature glossy white walls trimmed in aquamarine or beige. The accommodations have modern furniture and wall-to-wall carpeting. Rooms in the newer tower are a bit larger and have a view of the shopping center below. ✉ *Av. López Mateos and Av. Mariano Otero, 45050,* ☎ *3/647–8790,* FAX *3/122–9685. 341 rooms with bath, 14 suites. Restaurant, coffee shop, bar, pool, nightclub. AE, DC, MC, V.*

$$ ▦ **De Mendoza.** Mature travelers and tour groups from the United States and Canada often choose this downtown hotel because of its convenient location—on a quiet side street just one block from the Teatro Degollado—and charming postcolonial architecture and ambience. Beamed ceilings, hand-sculpted wood furniture and doors, and wrought-iron railings decorate public areas and rooms. The staff is bilingual and will be glad to direct you on a tour of nearby historical sites. ✉ *Venustiano Carranza 16, 44100,* ☎ *3/613–4646 or 800/876–5278 in the U.S.,* FAX *3/613–7310. 93 rooms, 17 suites. Restaurant, pool. AE, DC, MC, V.*

$$ ▦ **Diana.** Mexican and European tourists favor this six-story hotel, located two blocks from the Minerva Fountain. The white-stucco lobby adjoins a small lounge and busy restaurant. Standard-size rooms have white-on-white walls and ceilings with brightly patterned curtains and bedspreads. The best rooms are on the upper floors in the rear, away from the activity and traffic on Yáñez; suites have private saunas. ✉ *Circunvalación Agustín Yáñez 2760, 44100,* ☎ *3/615–5510 or 800/3–67–89 in Mexico,* FAX *3/630–3685. 136 rooms, 19 suites. Restaurant, coffee shop, bar, pool. AE, DC, MC, V.*

$$ ▦ **Fénix.** This mid-rise hotel, part of the Best Western chain, is located just off a principal downtown intersection and caters to business travelers and national tourists. The lobby is bustling and the staff efficient. Comfortable standard-size rooms have simple appointments and furnishings. The Co-Co & Co-Co Disco is one of Guadalajara's livelier venues, and guests are allowed free admission. ✉ *Av. Corona 160, at corner of López Cotilla, 44100,* ☎ *3/614–5714, 800/528–1234 in the U.S., 800/3–61–11 in Mexico;* FAX *3/613–4005. 240 rooms, 19 suites. Restaurant, bar, dance club. AE, DC, MC, V.*

$$ ★ 🏨 **Francés.** The brothers Oliveros carefully renovated Guadalajara's oldest hotel (1610), preserving and restoring its original architecture and charm. During reopening ceremonies in 1981, the four-story downtown hotel was designated a national monument. The venerable Francés has a three-story enclosed atrium lobby with stone columns and colonial arches surrounding a polished marble fountain and cut-crystal and gilt chandelier. Though room sizes vary, all share a colonial ambience, with beige stucco walls, polished wood floors, and high-beamed ceilings. For the best city views, ask for a room facing Calle Maestranza. The Francés is ideal for travelers willing to exchange the amenities of a modern hotel for the hospitality of Guadalajara's grande dame. ⊠ *Maestranza 35, 44100,* ☎ *3/613–1190 or 613–0917,* ℻ *3/658–2831. 52 rooms, 8 suites. 2 restaurants, bar, dance club. AE, DC, MC, V.*

$$ 🏨 **Posada Guadalajara.** Rooms in this colonial-style hotel's four contiguous towers open onto airy, wrought-iron railed hallways overlooking the small patio and circular pool. The unassuming accommodations are clean and comfortable, with traditional appointments. In addition to a loyal cadre of international patrons, the Posada welcomes visiting sports teams. Depending on your disposition (and the age and inclinations of your fellow guests), you will find the evenings here to be either festive or raucous. The hotel is just south of Calzada Lázaro Cárdenas (arterial access to downtown). ⊠ *Av. López Mateos Sur 1280, 45040,* ☎ *3/121–2022,* ℻ *3/121–1834. 152 rooms, 18 suites. Restaurant, pool, bar, beauty salon. AE, DC, MC, V.*

$$ 🏨 **Santiago de Compostela.** Opened in 1996, this cozy and quiet downtown hotel in a converted older building is across from the Parque San Francisco. Rooms overlooking the park—where you can watch worshippers file into the two colonial churches—have traditional tall, narrow windows with metal grillwork in front; inside, all rooms open onto an atrium painted in turquoise and lavender. The Rio Bajas restaurant adjoining the lobby serves Mexican specialties, steaks, and fish, and there is a small lobby bar. ⊠ *Colón 272, 44100,* ☎ *3/613–8880 or 800/3–65–53 in Mexico,* ℻ *3/658–1925. 102 rooms, 3 suites. Restaurant, bar, pool. AE, DC, MC, V.*

SPA

$$ 🏨 **Rancho Río Caliente.** Many activities at this health resort and vegetarian, alcohol-free spa are literally in hot water—therapeutic hot mineral water. You can steam away your mental tensions and body toxins in front of the 20-foot-high wall of volcanic rock and then dip into one of the mineral-water–filled swimming pools. The resort offers sparse but comfortable accommodations, facials and massages, t'ai chi instruction, hiking, horseback riding, and classes in yoga and body awareness. Rates include three meals a day; activities are extra. The spa is off Highway 15, 30 kilometers (19 miles) northeast of the Minerva Fountain; bookings must be prepaid to the U.S. office via personal or traveler's check. ⊠ *Apdo. 5-67, Zapopan, Jal. 43042,* ☎ *3/615–7800 (answering service in Guadalajara); U.S. reservations: Box 897, Millbrae, CA 94030,* ☎ *415/615–9543,* ℻ *415/615–0601. 50 rooms. Restaurant, spa, tour desk. No credit cards.*

NIGHTLIFE AND THE ARTS

Guadalajara is an active cultural and performing arts center, offering excellent local talent and well-known artists and entertainers from abroad. In addition, the active U.S. and Canadian communities have developed a schedule of English-language cultural events. You can attend a performance, an exhibition, or a recital almost any day of the year.

The Arts

Dance

Ballet Folklórico of the University of Guadalajara. The university's nationally acclaimed troupe offers traditional Mexican folkloric dances and music in the Teatro Degollado every Sunday at 10 AM. ☎ *3/614–4773 or 826–9283.*

Performance Venues

Centro Cultural Roxy. Come to this converted theater to satisfy your craving for live, up-to-the-minute rock music. It's about two blocks west of the Museo de la Ciudad de Guadalajara. ⊠ *Mezquitán 80,* ☎ *3/658–0053.*

Cine Cinematógrafo. Founded by two Guadalajara-area movie buffs, this theater often features English-language films with Spanish subtitles. It's two blocks west of the Museo de las Artes de la Universidad de Guadalajara. ⊠ *Av. Vallarta 1102,* ☎ *3/825–0514.*

Instituto Cultural Cabañas. Large-scale theater, dance, and musical performances take place on a patio within the institute. The Tolsá Chapel hosts more intimate events, and a movie theater often features subtitled English-language films. ⊠ *Calle Cabañas 8, at Plaza Tapatía,* ☎ *3/617–4322 or 3/617–4440.*

Plaza de Armas. The State Band of Jalisco plays here every Thursday and Sunday evening at 6:30. On Tuesday evening, the **Municipal Band of Guadalajara** performs at 6:30. ⊠ *Av. Corona between Morelos and Pedro Moreno, across from the Palacio de Gobierno.*

Teatro Degollado. Nationally and internationally famous artists perform here throughout the year. The refurbished velvet seats are comfortable, the acoustics are excellent, and the central air-conditioning is a treat. ⊠ *Av. Degollado and Belén,* ☎ *3/614–4773.*

Symphony

Orquesta Filarmónica de Jalisco. Conducted by Maestro José Guadalupe Flores, the state symphony orchestra performs Sundays and Fridays at the Teatro Degollado (☞ *above*). ☎ *3/658–3812.*

Nightlife

Guadalajara is not known for its nightlife. The nightclubs in major hotels provide good local entertainment and, occasionally, internationally known recording artists. The best hotel clubs are the Fiesta Americana's sleek **Lobby Bar,** dotted with small tables and offering pop and mariachi-style music; **La Diligencia,** a tranquil and romantic dance club featuring tropical music in the Camino Real; and the Holiday Inn's **Jaguar,** a sort of jungle theme park (including waiters in pith helmets and hunters garb), with game room, large-screen TV, and Latin and mariachi music for dancing.

As in the coffeehouses of the 1960s, patrons sit around a small stage at **Peña Cuicacalli** (⊠ Av. Niños Héroes 1988, on the traffic circle, ☎ 3/825–4690) and listen to jazz, blues, and folk, or Latin American music; performances are Tuesday through Saturday at 8 PM, and Sunday at 2 PM. **La Peñita** (⊠ Av. Vallarta 1110, ☎ 3/825–5853) features similar music Tuesday through Sunday at 9 PM in an airy patio setting.

Dance Clubs and Discos

You can dance all night to live Latin music at the multilevel **Tropigala** (⊠ Av. López Mateos Sur and Iztaccíhuatl, across from the Plaza del Sol shopping center, ☎ 3/122–5553 or 3/122–7903). Downtown, the spare **Salón Veracruz** (✉ Manzano 486, ☎ 3/613–4422) offers top-quality live music for serious Latin-style dancers; it's open Wednesday through Saturday, 10 PM–4 AM.

A good downtown disco is **Maxim's** in the Hotel Francés; it's decorated in red with colonial-style arched doorways. Other decent hotel discos include the **Factory**; there's one in the Hotel Plaza del Sol and another in the Hotel Aranzazú (✉ Av. Revolución 110, ☎ 3/613–3232).

OUTDOOR ACTIVITIES AND SPORTS

Spectator Sports

Bullfights

Corridas begin at 4:30 PM at **Plaza Nuevo Progreso**; they're usually held on Sundays in October and November. You can buy tickets for either the *sol* (sunny) or *sombra* (shady) side of the bullring. Since the action begins in the late afternoon, opt for the cheaper seats on the sunny side. You can buy tickets at the bullring or at the Plaza del Sol, Plaza México, and Plaza Revolución shopping centers. ✉ *Calzada Independencia Norte across from the Estadio Jalisco,* ☎ 3/637–9982 *or* 3/651–8506. 🎫 *About $6–$32.*

Charreadas

Traditional Mexican rodeos take place at the **Lienzo Charros de Jalisco** every Sunday at noon. The *charros* (cowboys) compete in 10 events; mariachis perform during breaks in the action. ✉ *Campo Charro Jalisco, Av. Dr. R. Michel 577, next to Parque Agua Azul,* ☎ 3/619–3232. 🎫 *$3.50.*

Soccer

You can see professional soccer matches on Saturday at 8:45 PM and Sunday at noon at **Estadio Jalisco.** ✉ *Calzada Independencia Norte, across from the bullring,* ☎ 3/637–0563. 🎫 *$1–$17, depending on the team.*

Participant Sports

Fitness Clubs

The **Hyatt** (☎ 3/678–1234) and **Holiday Inn** (☎ 3/634–1034) fitness clubs are open to nonguests for a fee. At **Nuevo Gold's Gym** (✉ Xóchitl 4203, near the Plaza del Sol shopping center, ☎ 3/647–0420) guest passes are available for about $4.50 per day.

Golf

Golf clubs that admit foreign travelers who belong to U.S. golf clubs include **Atlas Golf Club** (✉ Carretera Guadalajara-Chapala, across from Montenegro Park, ☎ 3/689–0006 and 3/689–0009), **Las Cañadas Country Club** (✉ Carretera a Saltillo, Km 14.5, ☎ 3/685–0512, 3/685–0285 or 3/685–0412), the **Chula Vista Country Club** (✉ near Lake Chapala, ☎ 376/5–22–81), and the **Club de Golf Santa Anita** (✉ Carretera a Morelia, Km 6.5, ☎ 3/686–0361 and 3/686–0386).

Ice-Skating

The **Iceland Pista de Hielo** (✉ Av. México 2582, ☎ 3/615–4438) offers one-hour public ice-skating sessions, as well as classes. There's also a restaurant and ice cream parlor.

Tennis

The **Holiday Inn** (☎ 3/634–1034) allows nonguests to use its courts for a fee. The municipal courts at **Parque Avila Camacho** (✉ Av. Avila

Camacho, near the Plaza Patria shopping mall, no phone) can be used for a nominal entrance fee.

SHOPPING

Shoppers in Guadalajara can choose from a broad variety of high-quality merchandise at low prices. Of course, you will also find low-quality products at high prices, so *caveat emptor.* Store hours are generally Monday–Saturday 9–8, Sunday 10–2; stores in shopping malls do not generally close for the afternoon lunch period. Street markets, or *tianguis,* are set up every day throughout the Guadalajara area; you never know what you'll find. The local newspaper *Siglo 21* lists locations daily.

The major areas for shopping in the city are outlined below; those interested in traditional arts and crafts should visit Tlaquepaque and Tonalá (☞ Side Trips, *below*).

Malls

In Guadalajara, as in all other major cities, shopping malls are springing up everywhere; the metropolitan area now has more than 30 of them.

La Gran Plaza. A sleek new three-story glass-and-steel exterior houses 334 stores and a 14-plex movie theater. It's just east of the Guadalajara Chamber of Commerce and the Camino Real hotel, on the city's far west side. ☒ *Av. Vallarta 3959,* ☎ *3/122-3004.* ☉ *Daily 8–10.*

Plaza del Sol. The city's largest mall sprawls like a park, with 270 commercial spaces, outdoor patios, trees and garden areas, and parking for 2,100 cars. It's across from the Hyatt Regency hotel. ☒ *Av. López Mateos Sur and Av. Mariano Otero,* ☎ *3/121–5950.* ☉ *Weekdays 10– 8, Sat. 10–9, Sun. 10–7.*

Plaza Galería del Calzado. The 60 stores in this west-side complex all sell shoes. Guadalajara is one of Mexico's leading shoe centers, and high-quality footwear and accessories are available here, many at lower prices than in the States. ☒ *Av. México and Juan Palomar y Arias (formerly Yáquis),* ☎ *3/647–6422.* ☉ *Mon.–Sat. 10–8:30, Sun. 11–8.*

Plaza México. There is room for 120 commercial establishments in the city's second most popular shopping mall, seven blocks west of the Plaza Galería del Calzado. ☒ *Av. México 3300,* ☎ *3/647–0098.* ☉ *Weekdays 9–8, weekends 10–8.*

Markets and Handicrafts

El Baratillo. This is one of the world's largest flea markets. Thirty city blocks are lined with stalls, tents, and blankets piled high with new, used, and antique merchandise. ☒ *On and around Calle Juan Zavala, east of Mercado Libertad.* ☉ *Sun. 7–3.*

Casa de las Artesanías de Jalisco. The state government runs this store, which has a wide selection of the exquisite blown glass and hand-painted pottery typical of Jalisco artisans. There is also a small selection of fine crafts from other parts of Mexico. Everything here is sold at fixed prices. ☒ *Calzadas Independencia Sur and González Gallo, next to Parque Agua Azul.* ☎ *3/614–4664.* ☉ *Weekdays 10–6, Sat. 11–5, Sun. 11–3.*

Mercado Libertad. Also known as the Mercado San Juan de Dios, the Liberty Market is one of Latin America's largest enclosed markets. Within a three-square-block area you can browse through more than 1,000 privately owned stalls selling everything from clothing to crafts to live animals and gold watches. ✉ *Calzada Independencia Sur between Dionisio Rodríguez and Av. Javier Mina.* ⊙ *Daily 10–8.*

SIDE TRIPS

Tequila

56 km (35 mi) northwest of Guadalajara.

If you want to get a close look at how Mexico's most famous liquor is made from the spiny blue agave cacti that grow in the fields alongside the highway, spend part or all of a day here. Centuries ago the Tiquilas, a small Nahuatl-speaking tribe, were said to have discovered that the heart of the agave produced a juice that could be fermented to produce various intoxicating drinks. When distilled (an innovation introduced after the arrival of the Spanish in the 16th century), the fermented liquid turns into the heady liquor for which Mexico is now well known. You can tour the famous Sauza Distillery or one of the other modern tequila distilleries here. Follow the signs, and plan to arrive between 10 AM and 1 PM. Frequent bus service is available from Guadalajara's old bus station, and various Guadalajara tour companies offer guided excursions (☞ Guadalajara A to Z, *below*).

Around Lake Chapala

Perhaps it is the Mexican arts and culture, or perhaps the favorable exchange rate, or perhaps the springlike climate; whatever the reason, more than 25,000 U.S. and Canadian citizens have retired in the Guadalajara area. The majority reside along the shores of Lake Chapala, Mexico's largest inland lake.

The jagged mountains that ring the lake that make its 45-kilometer (28-mile) distance from Guadalajara seem three times that great. The tranquillity of the area offers a welcome contrast to bustling Guadalajara. Sunsets are spectacular, and there's just enough humidity to keep the abundant bougainvillea blooming and ensure no drastic temperature fluctuations. Unfortunately, the lake is polluted, and fighting an ongoing battle with *lirio* (water hyacinth), a succulent plant that threatens to cover much of the water surface. Water levels are shrinking to alarming lows, while demand from Guadalajara, which the lake supplies with water, remains high.

Spanish settlement in the area dates to 1538, when Franciscan friar Miguel de Bolonio arrived and began to convert the Taltica Indians to Christianity. Their chief was named Chapalah, from which the name Chapala is said to have originated.

The town of Chapala is the area's largest settlement; 8 kilometers (5 miles) to the west, the village of Ajijic has been home to expatriate artists and writers since the 1920s. Though Chapala is more bustling, Ajijic has a larger selections of hotels and restaurants, making it a better base for a longer stay.

Numbers in the text correspond to points of interest on the Lake Chapala Area map.

Chapala
45 km (28 mi) south of Guadalajara.

With Chapala's proximity to rapidly growing Guadalajara, as well as its comfortable climate, it is surprising that tourists did not frequent the area until the late 19th century. Then-president Porfirio Díaz heard that aristocrats had discovered the ideal place for weekend getaways.

The president began spending holidays here in 1904. Soon summer homes were built, and in 1910 the Chapala Yacht Club opened. Word of the town, with its lavish lawn parties and magnificent estates, spread quickly to the United States and Europe.

Nowadays the town of Chapala has a population of some 35,000 and attracts a less influential but equally fun-loving assortment of visitors. On weekends the streets are filled with Mexican families. Throughout the week American and Canadian retirees stroll along the lakeside promenade, play golf, and relax on the verandas of downtown restaurants.

Avenida Madero, lined with pleasant restaurants, shops and cafés, is the town's main drag. On Madero two blocks north of the lake, the **❶ Iglesia de San Francisco** is easy to spot by the blue neon crosses on its twin steeples. The church was built in 1528 and reconstructed in 1580. **❷** Also on Avenida Madero, between Galeana and Moreles, the **plaza** is a relaxing spot for townspeople and tourists to sit and read the paper. **❸** On weekends, the tranquil lakeside **Parque la Cristianíais,** on the south side of the malecón, fills with *tapatíos* taking a respite from the city. Street vendors cluster in booths, and there are a number of open-air cafés featuring *pescado blanco,* the white fish native to the lake. Because of pollution, we do not recommend that you partake of this regional delicacy, though other food is fine. At the end of the park is a small handicrafts market.

❹ A visit to **Isla de los Alacranes** (Scorpion Island) is a popular excursion from the Chapala pier, which sits on the lake at the end of Avenida Madero. The view of the shore area is enchanting. From the same pier, **❺** you can also take a trip to **Isla de Mezcala,** about 12 kilometers (7½ miles) northeast of Isla de los Alcranes, and explore the ruins of a fortress that housed a band of rebels during the early-19th-century war of independence with Spain. Depending on the duration of the trip, the price ranges from about $10 to $50 for a launch with a capacity of eight adults.

DINING AND LODGING

$$ ✕ **Beer Garden.** Enjoy the expansive lake view while you eat one of the tasty seafood, chicken, or beef specialties. ⊠ *Paseo Ramón Corona, at corner of Av. Madero, at the lake,* ☎ *376/5–22–37. MC, V.*

$$ ✕ **Restaurant Cazadores.** This grandly turreted building was once the summer home of the Braniff family, owners of the now-defunct airline. Enjoy a cool liquid refreshment here, and maybe some guacamole, and watch the action along the *malecón.* (You can skip the main courses, which focus on steak.) ⊠ *Av. Madero and Paseo Ramón Corona,* ☎ *376/5–21–62. Closed Mon.*

$$$ 🏨 **Quinta Quetzalcóatl.** Behind 12-foot stone walls, the "QQ" is lo-
★ cated on the grounds of the villa where D.H. Lawrence wrote *The Plumed Serpent* in the 1920s. Owners Dick and Barbi Henderson have restored and enlarged it to include eight luxurious individual suites furnished with colorful antiques; guests also enjoy a living-dining room and lush tropical gardens. Barbi cooks breakfast daily and offers two gourmet dinners and one barbecue weekly (in high season, these are included in the room rates). There's a three-night minimum and prepaid reservations are required by check, preferably through the U.S. office. ⊠ *Zaragoza 307, 45900* ☎ 📠 *376/5–36–53; in the U.S., 800/577–2555;* 📠 *206/840–6747; c/o Sulik, 8606 63rd Ave. East, Puyallup, WA 98371. 8 suites. Bar, pool, hot tub, library. No credit cards.*

$$ 🏨 **Hotel Villa Montecarlo.** Look out on spacious lawns, complete with strolling peacocks, high on a hill above the lake. The comfortable (but TV-less) rooms, in two-story contiguous units, are all furnished in

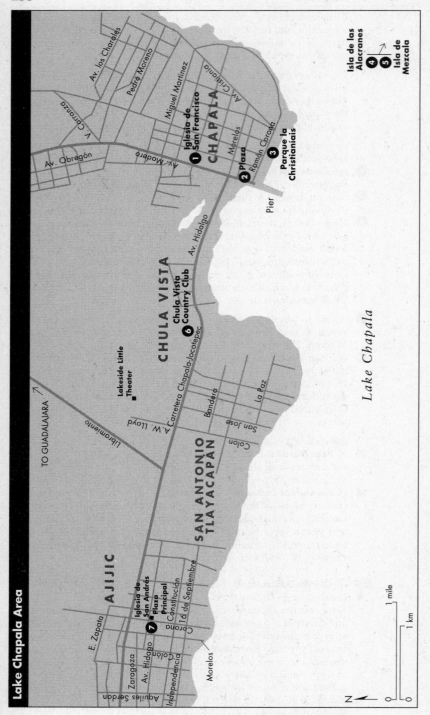

Lake Chapala Area

AJIJIC

E. Zapata

Iglesia de San Andrés
7 Plaza Principal
Zaragoza
Av. Hidalgo
Colón
Independencia
Constitución
16 de Septiembre
Corona
Morelos

SAN ANTONIO TLAYACAPAN

TO GUADALAJARA

Libramiento

Lakeside Little Theater

CHULA VISTA

Chula Vista Country Club 6

Carretera Chapala-Jocotepec

A.W. Lloyd

Colón
San José
Bandera
La Paz

Av. Hidalgo

Av. los Chárales

Av. Carranza

Pedro Moreno

Av. Madero

Av. Obregón

Miguel Martínez

Av. Cristiania

CHAPALA

Iglesia de San Francisco 1

Morelos

2 Plaza

Ramón Corona

3 Parque la Christianiais

Pier

Lake Chapala

Isla de las Alacranes 4
5 Isla de Mexcala

N

0 1 mile
0 1 km

blue and beige. The two swimming pools are filled with natural thermal water. ✉ *Hidalgo 296, about 1km (½ mi) west of Av. Madero, 45900* ☎ *376/5–22–16, 376/5–21–20, or 376/5–20–24,* ✉ *376/5–33–66. 46 rooms, 1 suite. Restaurant. MC, V.*

$ 🏨 **Hotel Nido.** The oldest hotel on the lake was built in the early 1900s to accommodate President Porfírio Díaz and his entourage during their frequent visits. In the 1940s Mexican film star María Félix spent the first of her numerous honeymoons here, and the dark high-ceilinged lobby still feels like the scene of a melodrama waiting to happen. There are pictures of turn-of-the-century Chapala on the walls and a picturesque patio and garden in the rear. However, the rooms are strictly functional, and only the ones in the front have TVs. ✉ *Av. Madero 202, 45900,* ☎ ✉ *376/5–21–16. 30 rooms. Restaurant, bar, pool. MC, V.*

Chula Vista
3 km (2 mi) west of Chapala.

The community of Chula Vista, the most American colony in Mexico, lies between Chapala and Ajijic. On the hillside north of the road, there
❻ are dozens of condos. Among them is the **Chula Vista Country Club** (✉ Paseo de Golfo No. 1, ☎ 376/5–22–81), a favorite of the local *norteamericano* community. The "billygoat" golf course here—open to travelers with home golf club credentials—affords great vistas of the lake as well as a workout, since the rugged terrain cannot be negotiated by golf cart.

DINING
$ ✕ **Chicken Little.** As its name suggests, this place serves infinite varieties of chicken (chicken lasagna, anyone?) as well as American-style pies and cakes. You know the birds are fresh—you're right next door to Puritan Poultry. ✉ *Carretera Chapala-Ajijic 101, in the Riberas del Pilar subdivision,* ☎ *376/5–43–99. No credit cards. Closed Sun.*

NIGHTLIFE AND THE ARTS
Just west of Chula Vista, above the PAL Trailer Park and next to the Oak Hill High School, is the 112-seat **Lakeside Little Theater** (☎ 376/6–09–54), which stages English-language musicals and plays throughout the year. Box office hours are 10 AM to 1 PM starting three days before performances and during the run of any show.

Ajijic
8 km (5 mi) west of Chapala.

The village of Ajijic has been home to expatriate artists and writers since the 1920s. Despite blocks of galleries and crafts shops, its small-town ambience is still defined by its narrow cobblestoned streets, whitewashed buildings, and a gentle pace. Still, the foreign influence is unmistakeable: English is spoken almost as widely here as Spanish, and license plates run the gamut from Alaska to Texas.

❼ Most visitors park their cars near the **Plaza Principal** (also called the Plaza de Armas or Jardín), the tree- and flower-filled central square where weekly events and festivities take place. The **Iglesia de San Andrés** (Church of St. Andrew) sits on the Jardín's north side. In late November the plaza fills for the saint's nine-day fiesta, including fireworks, parades, music, and dancing.

If you walk down Calle Morelos (the continuation of Avenida Colón) toward the lake, along the way you can stop in at the many stores and boutiques that sell everything from designer fashions to traditional arts and crafts.

DINING AND LODGING

In addition to the hotels listed below, there are also several bed-and-breakfasts in the area. Consult the tourist office in Chapala, the *Ojo del Lago* newspaper, or the *Guadalajara Colony Reporter*.

$$ ✕ **Los Telares.** Walk up several stairs to the elegant candlelit dining room,
★ where tables are arranged around a tranquil patio with a bubbling stone fountain. Some of the best food in town is served here, including curried and lemon shrimp, filet mignon in mushroom sauce, Asian vegetables, and various pasta dishes. ⊠ *Morelos 4,* ☎ *376/6–04–28. MC, V. Closed Tues.*

$ ✕ **Rose Café.** This cheery breakfast and lunch spot specializes in vegetarian dishes and ice cream. There's also a charity bazaar on the premises. ⊠ *Carretera a Jocotepec 26, on the lakeward side of the road,* ☎ *376/6–15–99. No credit cards. Closed Mon.*

$ ✕ **Yves Restaurant.** Take your meal in the intimate dining room or out on the patio, where there's also an observation tower that offers an excellent view of the lake. Chef Yves de Choulot Pugibet's varied menu includes chicken mesquite, lamb ribs in mint sauce, and chicken and crab crepes. There's also a salad bar. ⊠ *Galeana 22-A,* ☎ *376/6–12–50. MC, V.*

$$ 🛏 **Real de Chapala.** Suites here have small individual swimming pools and cable TV. The restaurant is popular with weekend visitors from Guadalajara. ⊠ *Paseo del Prado 20, 45920,* ☎ *376/6–00–28, 376/6–00–25, or 376/6–00–42;* 🖷 *376/6–00–25; reservations in Guadalajara at the Hoteles Real (⊠ La Villita 78, Colonia Chapalita,* ☎ *3/121–8878,* 🖷 *3/122–1936). Restaurant, bar, pool, tennis court, game room. AE, MC, V.*

$$ ✕🛏 **La Nueva Posada.** Luxuriant gardens framed in bougainvillea over-
★ look the lake at this charming inn, run by a gracious Canadian family. The spacious, airy, and well-lit rooms have colonial furniture and original watercolors. Chef Lorraine Rousseau's eclectic menu is delicious, and there is fine entertainment most evenings, typically an American jazz trio or tropical music. ⊠ *Donato Guerra 9, Apdo. 30, 45920,* ☎ *376/6–14–44,* ☎ 🖷 *376/6–13–44. 17 suites. Restaurant, bar, pool. MC, V.*

NIGHTLIFE AND THE ARTS

The rambling, hacienda-style **Posada Ajijic** (⊠ Calle Morelos, across from the lake, ☎ 376/6–07–44 or 376/6–04–30) is a restaurant, bar, and popular weekend dance place with a spectacular view of the water. **Estampida** (⊠ Plaza Maskaras, on Carretera a Jocotepec, ☎ 376/5–45–40), a spacious hall that hosts dance classes during the day, offers live or taped country and ballroom music to kick up your heels by at night.

SHOPPING

Though Ajijic does not have as many boutiques and crafts shops as inhabitants, it sometimes seems that way. **Casa de la Tortuga** (⊠ Marcos Castellanos 4, no phone) features high-end crafts, beadwork, and lovely watercolors by local artists. **Casa de las Artesanías Ajijik** (⊠ Km 6.5, Carretera a Jocotepec, ☎ 376/6–05–48) is a branch of the state-run Casa de las Artesanías de Jalisco crafts shop (☞ Guadalajara Shopping, *above*). Inside the bright yellow building of **La Colección Bárbara** (⊠ Av. Colón 30, ☎ 376/6–01–65) are traditional crafts, antiques, and fine furniture. **La Colección Moon** (⊠ Río Zula 44, at the corner of Ocampo, ☎ 376/6–10–00) features a selection of owner Billy Moon's lamps, wrought-iron furniture, and other decorative items. The factory, finishing workshop, and gallery are all open to the public. **Mi**

México (✉ Morelos 8, ☎ 376/6–01–33) boutique sells pottery, blown glass, batik caftans, and other crafts and gifts.

San Juan Cosalá

10 km (6½ mi) west of Chapala.

The village of San Juan Cosalá is known for its natural thermal-water spas located on the shores of Lake Chapala, with the mountains rising to the north. The **Hotel Balneario San Juan Cosalá** (☎ 376/3–03–02) welcomes both daytrippers and overnight guests to its three large swimming pools and three wading pools. The **Villas Bonaventura Cosalá** (☎ 376/1–03–03) only accepts overnight guests. Facilities here include one- and two-bedroom furnished suites, with kitchenettes, TVs, and thermal-water bathtubs; there are also thermal hot tubs and swimming pools. Both hotels share the same reservations address: Apdo. Postal 181, Chapala, Jalisco 45900.

Lake Chapala A to Z

ARRIVING AND DEPARTING

By Bus. There is frequent bus service to Chapala, Ajijic, and other lakeside towns from Antigua Central Camionera and Chapala bus station in Guadalajara.

By Car. From downtown Guadalajara take Avenida Federalismo south to Calzada Lázaro Cárdenas, turn left, and continue southeast. Follow the signs as Lázaro Cárdenas converges with the Carretera a Chapala, which becomes Highway 44 to Mexico City; the trip takes 50 minutes.

ENGLISH-LANGUAGE PUBLICATIONS

The *Ojo del Lago* monthly newspaper is available free of charge throughout town. The *Guadalajara Colony Reporter* weekly newspaper (☞ Guadalajara A to Z, *below*) devotes a section to lakeside news and events. **Libros de Chapala,** across from the plaza at Avenidas Madero and Galeana, has an extensive range of English-language magazines, with some newspapers and books as well.

VISITOR INFORMATION

The **Jalisco state tourism office** has a Lake Chapala area branch in Chapala. ✉ *Aquiles Serdan 26,* ☎ *376/5–31–41.* ☉ *Weekdays 9–3, Sat. 9–1.*

In Ajijic, the nonprofit **Lake Chapala Society** provides information about the lakeside area. ✉ *16 de Septiembre No. 16A, no phone.* ☉ *Mon.–Sat. 10–1.*

Sierra de Manantlán Biosphere Reserve

144 km (90 mi) southwest of Guadalara.

Consider this trip if you are a confirmed nature lover. The 345,000-acre Sierra de Manantlán Biosphere Reserve is a vast nature preserve high in the Sierra Madre del Sur, near the town of Autlán de Navarro. Oak and pine forests abound, with hiking paths lined by bright-colored wildflowers. Stand at a mountain lookout and on a clear day you can see all the way to the beach resort of Manzanillo, on the Pacific Ocean. The area was incorporated into the United Nations worldwide chain of biosphere reserves in 1987 and is administered by the University of Guadalajara, which runs a research outpost here.

Accommodations here are rustic and the food simple but filling. You must reserve space in advance, preferably with a group; unaccompanied, unannounced guests are not permitted. Guadalajara-area writer and guide Tony Burton (✉ Apdo. Postal 79, Jocotepec, Jalisco 45800, ☎ FAX 376/3–04–92) arranges and leads excellent group tours. (The university staff, which also runs tours, tends to be occupied with research and other duties.) The reserve may only be visited during the dry season, from late October through early May; at other times, the roads are impassable. The trip to Autlán de Navarro takes several hours, after which it takes another two to three hours—in a four-wheel-drive vehicle—to get to the preserve. Plan to spend at least one night in the preserve and maybe another in Autlán.

Tlaquepaque and Tonalá

For inveterate shoppers, a combined visit to the crafts meccas of Tlaquepaque and Tonalá makes a perfect day trip from Guadalajara. There's at least one bed-and-breakfast in Tlaquepaque if you really want to shop until you drop, but it's easy enough to return to the better selection of lodgings in Guadalajara.

Tlaquepaque

7 km (4½ mi) southeast of downtown Guadalajara.

Tlaquepaque is known throughout Mexico as an arts-and-crafts center; among its specialties are intricate blown-glass miniatures; exquisite hand-painted pottery; jewelry, silver and copperware; leather and hand-carved wood furniture; and handwoven clothing. More than 300 shops line pedestrian malls and plazas in this charming town, which is also said to be the birthplace of mariachi music.

Distinctive hand-painted pottery, sold in stores throughout the town, was first fashioned by nearby Tonaltecan Indians in the mid-16th century. The small village remained virtually isolated until June 13, 1821, when Mexico's Treaty of Independence with Spain was signed here. Soon after, the wealthy residents of Guadalajara, who had used the village as a weekend retreat, began to build palatial mansions in which to spend the summers. Many of these magnificent buildings have been restored, and today they house shops and restaurants.

During this period, according to one legend, a growing French colony living in the area was (inadvertently) responsible for naming one of Mexico's most renowned musical institutions. French aristocrats hired groups of street singers and musicians to entertain at weddings. The French word *mariage* was soon transformed into *mariachi.*

In 1870 the art of glass-blowing was introduced from Europe. As people started coming to purchase the pottery and intricate glass creations, more artisans—weavers, jewelers, and wood-carvers—arrived and built workshops. A new tradition was born.

In 1973 downtown Tlaquepaque underwent a major renovation, the highlight of which was the creation of a wide pedestrian mall, Calzada Independencia. Twentieth-century commercialism had arrived. Typical store hours here are Monday through Saturday 10–2 and 4–7, and Sunday 10–2; unless otherwise indicated, the stores listed here keep roughly these hours.

The following are some of the highlights you'll come across if you start walking from the west end of Calzada Independencia.

Numbers in the margin correspond to numbers on the Tlaquepaque map.

★ ❶ Housed in a colonial mansion, **Museo Regional de la Cerámica,** the Regional Museum of Ceramics, features exhibits that trace the evolution of ceramics in the Atemajac Valley during the past century. There is also an exhibit of Indian folk art from the area and prizewinning entries from the national ceramics competition. ⊠ *Independencia 237,* ☎ *3/635–5404.* 🖼 *Free.* ☉ *Tues.–Sat. 10–6, Sun. 10–3.*

❷ Color seems to explode in the more than 10 rooms of **La Casa Canela,** exquisitely decorated with vivid papier-mâché flowers and delicately painted pottery. All surround a patio blooming with tropical plants. Another patio in the rear hosts a display of decorative garden statues. ⊠ *Independencia 258,* ☎ *3/635–3717 or 3/657–1343.*

❸ High-quality carved wood furniture is the specialty in **Antigua de México,** a restored mansion with each room carefully arranged as a sitting room, dining room, or bedroom. ⊠ *Independencia 255,* ☎ *3/ 639–2997 or 3/635–3402.*

❹ Sergio Bustamante's work is found in galleries throughout the world, but you can purchase one of his whimsical sculptures for considerably less at **Galería Sergio Bustamante.** Silver- and gold-plated jewelry and bronze sculptures are on display in this modern gallery; the flamingos under the waterfall in the rear are real. ⊠ *Independencia 236,* ☎ *3/ 657–8354.* ☉ *Closed Sun.*

❺ The store in Tlaquepaque's oldest blown-glass factory, **La Rosa de Cristal,** contains a large variety of hand-blown glass objects and figures; the intricate miniatures are surprisingly inexpensive. Plan to arrive before lunch so you can go into the factory and watch the glassmakers shove long tubes into a white-hot fire, retrieve a bubbling glob, and in a few minutes create one of the pieces you saw in front. ⊠ *Independencia 232,* ☎ *3/639–7180.* ☉ *Store weekdays 9–7, weekends 9–6; factory weekdays 10:30–1:30, Sat. 10–noon.*

❻ Wander through the 12-room hacienda of **Bazar Hecht,** filled with hand-carved furniture, antiques, and designer fashions, and wonder what it would have been like to grow up in the colonial-style ambience of 19th-century Tlaquepaque. The Hecht family is known throughout Mexico for its high-quality, ornately sculpted tables and chairs. ✉ *Independencia 158,* ☎ *3/635–2241 or 3/635–0316.*

❼ Franciscan friars founded the **Templo Parroquial de San Pedro** during the Spanish conquest, naming the parish church in honor of San Pedro de Analco. In keeping with the custom that says a town is to be named after its principal church, in 1915 the town's name was officially changed to San Pedro Tlaquepaque. The altars of Our Lady of Guadalupe and the Sacred Heart of Jesus are intricately carved in silver and gilt. ✉ *In the square at the corner of Calles Guillermo Prieto and Morelos.* ⊗ *Daily 7 AM–9 PM.*

In 1959 craftsman Ken Edwards developed a technique to transform the fragile Tonalá pottery into a lustrous, hardened, lead-free glazed
❽ stoneware. His store, **Cerámica de Ken Edwards,** is filled with brightly colored, hand-painted plates, cups, and vases. Prices are much lower than you would pay outside Mexico; ask to see the seconds, some real bargains. ✉ *Francisco Madero 70,* ☎ *3/635–2426.* ⊗ *Mon.–Sat. 10:30–7, Sun. 11–6.*

When you're ready to have lunch, take Francisco Madero one block
❾ south of Independencia to reach **El Parián,** a square ringed by outdoor cafés and frequented by mariachis eager to perform. Named after the Chinese section of Manila, with which the conquistadors traded, El Parián is the heart of Tlaquepaque. The atmosphere is festive, if not boisterous, on weekends. The shops in the arcades around El Parián should be used only to compare prices; do your shopping in the galleries and boutiques on Calle Independencia or another main street.

DINING

$ ✕ **Casa Fuerte.** Dine on such gourmet Mexican dishes as chilies stuffed with zucchini flowers and cheese, topped with walnut sauce, and shrimp in tamarind sauce. For dessert, try some homemade ice cream. There are tables in the lush patio garden or on the sidewalk in front. ✉ *Independencia 224,* ☎ *3/639–6481. MC, V. Closed Mon.*

✕ **Restaurant sin Nombre.** Enjoy eating either indoors or on the patio of this 17th-century colonial mansion. High adobe walls surround the building and the extensive gardens, which are filled with orchids and exotic birds. The "Restaurant with No Name" serves Spanish nouvelle cuisine, a combination of pre-Hispanic and modern recipes. Daily entertainment includes *suave* jazz and traditional Mexican music. ✉ *Francisco Madero 80,* ☎ *3/635–4520 or 3/635–9677. AE, MC, V.*

Tonalá
8 km (5 mi) east of Tlaquepaque.

Tonalá is 10 minutes away but centuries removed from its commercial neighbor, Tlaquepaque. One of Mexico's oldest pueblos, Tonalá is a quiet village with dusty, cobblestoned streets and adobe houses. Here, craftspeople—primarily ceramicists—welcome tourists into their homes and workshops.

Tonalá was both the pre-Hispanic capital of the Indians of the Atemajac Valley and the capital of New Spain when Captain Juan de Oñate moved the city of Guadalajara here in 1532. Within three years, however, unfriendly Indians and a lack of water had forced the Spaniards to abandon the location.

Over the past 450 years, the village has existed in contented seclusion. The simple adobe houses and dusty streets belie the artistic refinement of Tonalá's residents. It is in this small pueblo that most of the ceramics and pottery sold in Tlaquepaque (and in many other parts of the world) are made; municipal officials say more than 6,000 artisans live and work here. In small home studios, families create the lovely ceramics, cobalt-blue glassware, and playful animals with the same materials and techniques their ancestors used centuries ago. It's possible to visit many home studios (☞ Casa de Artesanos, *below*), but it's a good idea to call first. If you don't speak Spanish, ask someone who does to call for you.

On Thursdays and Sundays, much Tonalá merchandise is sold at bargain prices at one of the best *tianguis* (street markets) in all of Mexico. Most stores in Tonalá are open Monday through Saturday 10–2 and 4–7, Sunday 10–2.

When you arrive in Tonalá, proceed due north on Avenida de los Tonaltecas, a main north–south thoroughfare. There are numerous cafés and restaurants along this street, as well as in the area around the **main plaza,** at Calles Juárez and Hidalgo. Also in the main plaza is the **Santuario,** a parish church with simple plaster walls and spare wooden pews. It's next door to the **Palacio Municipal,** or City Hall.

The showroom of the **Casa de Artesanos** displays an excellent selection of works—mainly ceramics—by Tonalá artisans. Of the more than 20 ceramic techniques used in the village, two of the most common are *barro bruñido,* in which the pieces are hand-burnished to a soft sheen, and *petatillo,* featuring finely painted cross-hatched patterns on red-glazed clay. The staff here has also prepared a comprehensive directory of local artisans. ⊠ *Av. de los Tonaltecas 140,* ☏ *3/683–0590.* ☉ *Daily 9–7.*

The Bernabe family has made exquisite, colorful *petatillo* pieces for generations, as well as more simple stoneware. The sprawling workship in back of the **Galería José Bernabe** is also open to visitors. ⊠ *Hidalgo 83, between Zapata and Constitución,* ☏ *3/683–0040.* ☉ *Weekdays 9–2 and 4–7, weekends 9–3. Workshop closed Sun.*

Exhibits at the **Museo Nacional de la Cerámica** (National Ceramics Museum) include ceramics and pottery of several Mexican states dating from pre-Columbian times to the present. There is also a workshop and a small store. ⊠ *Constitución 104,* ☏ *3/683–0494.* ☞ *Free.* ☉ *Tues.–Sun. 10–5.*

The **Taller (Factory) de Jorge Wilmot** produces intricately designed, hand-painted stoneware ceramic plates, cups, and figurines that are sold throughout the world. ⊠ *Morelos 88,* ☏ *3/683–0058.* ☉ *Weekdays 7–10 AM, 11–2:30, 3:30–5.*

At the **Cerámica de Ken Edwards,** meet the man who revolutionized centuries-old ceramics techniques by developing lead-free stoneware. Either Edwards or his wife, Jackie, is usually on hand to show visitors the facilities. ⊠ *Morelos 184,* ☏ *3/683–0313.* ☉ *Weekdays 10–5, Sat. 10–3, Sun. 10–2.*

In a small patio behind his home, **Salvador Vásquez Carmona** molds enormous ceramic pots, which he then paints with intricate and fanciful designs. Numerous awards certificates hang over his living-room sofa. ⊠ *Av. de los Maestros 328, west of Av. de los Tonaltecas.* ☏ *3/683–2896.* ☉ *Weekdays; call first.*

Tonalá native J. Cruz Coldívar, who signs his work **El 7,** makes striking hand-painted masks, as well as decorative plates and other wall hangings. He has exhibited throughout Mexico, as well as in the United States, Canada, Europe, and South America. ⊠ *Privado Obregón 28, north of the town center,* ☏ *3/683–0873.* ☉ *Weekdays 9–6, Sat. 9–1.*

Tlaquepaque and Tonalá A to Z

By Bus. There is frequent public bus service from downtown Guadalajara and the Plaza del Sol shopping center to Tlaquepaque and Tonalá. The trips take around 30 minutes and 45 minutes, respectively.

By Car. From Guadalajara, take Avenida Revolución southeast; at the Plaza de la Bandera, jog to your right onto Boulevard General Marcelino García Barragán, which becomes Boulevard Tlaquepaque as it leads into town. When you reach the *glorieta* (traffic circle), follow the circle around to Avenida Niños Héroes. The first intersection is Calle Independencia, the pedestrian mall, where you'll begin your tour on foot. The entire trip takes around 20 minutes.

To get from Tlaquepaque to Tonalá, take Avenida Revolución to the Carretera a Zapotlanejo and then the Carretera a Tonalá, which leads into town.

By Taxi. The fare from downtown Guadalajara to Tlaquepaque is about $4; from downtown Guadalajara, the cab ride to Tonalá costs about $7. A cab from Tlaquepaque to Tonalá runs approximately $4.25.

The **Tlaquepaque municipal tourist office** is in the Centro Cultural el Refugio. ✉ *Donato Guerra 160,* ☎ *3/635–0238.* ☉ *Weekdays 9–3.*

Tonalá's municipal tourist office is next to the Casa de los Artesanos. ✉ *Av. de los Tonaltecas 140 Sur,* ☎ *3/683–1740.* ☉ *Weekdays 9–3, Sat. 9–1.*

GUADALAJARA A TO Z

Arriving and Departing

By Bus

First-class, air-conditioned buses with rest rooms provide daily service to Guadalajara from most major cities on the border. **Greyhound** (☎ 800/231–2222) has schedule and fare information for service from the United States into Mexico, though you will have to change to a Mexican carrier at the border. Guadalajara's **Nueva Central Camionera** (New Bus Station) is located 10 kilometers (6 miles) southeast of downtown Guadalajara on the highway to Zapotlanejo. First-class bus companies that serve Guadalajara from within Mexico include **Elite** (☎ 3/600–0843 or 3/600–0715); **ETN** (☎ 3/600–0477 or 3/600–0858); **Primera Plus** (☎ 3/600–0398 or 3/600–0014); and **Omnibus de México** (☎ 3/600–0469).

Buses to and from such nearby destinations as Chapala, Ajijic, and Tequila depart from the Antigua Central Camionera (Old Bus Station), located just north of the Parque Agua Azul on Avenida Dr. R. Michel between Calles Los Angeles and 5 de Febrero.

By Car

Major routes include Highway 54, which leads south to Colima (220 kilometers, or 136 miles) and north to Zacatecas (320 kilometers, or 198 miles). Highway 15 goes southeast to Morelia (367 kilometers, or 228 miles), continuing to Mexico City (309 kilometers, or 192 miles). If you have a choice between a free or toll road, remember that the latter tend to be quite expensive but are usually in far better condition than their free counterparts.

By Plane

The **Libertador Miguel Hidalgo International Airport** (☎ 3/688–5248 or 3/688–5127) is 16.6 kilometers (11 miles) south of Guadalajara. A new international terminal is planned in the next decade to help meet the demands of the increased air service to the area.

Aeromexico (☎ 3/669–0202 or 800/3–62–02) has nonstop service to Guadalajara from Los Angeles and San Diego; **Mexicana** (☎ 3/112–0101 or 800/5–02–20) offers direct flights from Los Angeles; **Taesa** (☎ 3/615–9761 or 800/9–04–63) flies direct from Chicago and Oakland. Through Dallas, **American Airlines** (☎ 3/616–4090 or 800/3–62–70) provides service to Guadalajara from all cities in its system. **Continental Airlines** (☎ 3/647–4446 or 800/9–00–50) provides the same service through Houston. **Delta Airlines** (☎ 3/630–3530 or 800/9–02–21) flies direct from Los Angeles.

FROM THE AIRPORT

By Car. The Chapala Highway 44—a well-paved four-lane thoroughfare—stretches north from the airport to the city. The 30-minute trip can be delayed by slow-moving caravans of trucks and weekend recreational traffic.

By Limousine. Royal Limousines (✉ Hotel Quinta Real, Av. Mexico 2727, ☎ 3/615–0000, ext. 121, or Miguel de Cervantes 382, ☎ 3/616–3932) has chauffeur-driven stretch limousines to downtown Guadalajara for $30. Reserve at least three hours in advance.

By Taxi. Taxis charge between $12 and $15 to city hotels. (Fares from hotels to the airport are often slightly cheaper.)

By Van. Autotransportes Terrestres de l'Aeropuerto (☎ 3/688–5890 or 3/688–54–31) is a *combi* (VW minibus) and taxi service to and from city hotels and other destinations in the Guadalajara area. Fares, based on distance from the airport, are between $10 and $15 for up to three people going to the same destination. At the airport, buy a ticket from the booth outside the terminal exit.

By Train

The Mexican train system has been in a state of flux. At press time, the only first-class rail service to Guadalajara from near the U.S. border was via *La Estrella,* which departs from Mexicali (across from Calexico, CA) at 8 AM daily and arrives in about 36 hours; trains from Guadalajara to Mexicali depart at 9:30 AM. The *Tapatío,* departing from Mexico City at 8:30 PM, arrives at Guadalajara at 8:30 AM; it departs Guadalajara at 9 PM, arriving in Mexico City at 9 AM. The round-trip fare to Mexicali (no meals, only snacks available) is approximately $45 (first-class coach); to Mexico City, $12 first-class coach, $32 Pullman. Information about current schedules and fares can be obtained from **Mexico by Train** (☎ 800/321–1699, FAX 210/725–3659). The Estación de Ferrocarriles (train station; ☎ 3/650–0826 or 3/650–1082) is at the south end of Avenida 16 de Septiembre, just past Parque Agua Azul.

Getting Around

Guadalajara's major attractions are best seen on foot. For points outside the city center, Guadalajara has an inexpensive, well-organized public transportation system.

By Bus

This is without a doubt the most economical and efficient but sometimes least comfortable means of traversing the city. Buses run every few minutes between 6 AM and 10 PM from the center of the city to all

local attractions, including Tlaquepaque, Tonalá, and Zapopan. The
15¢–25¢ fares (depending on the type of vehicle) make buses the preferred mode of transportation for Guadalajara natives, so expect to
stand during daylight hours. The new Tur III buses—which run on some
of the main routes through the city, including out to Tlaquepaque and
Tonalá—cost 50¢ and are much less crowded than the smaller, older
buses.

By Car
Beware of heavy traffic and *topes* (speed bumps). *Glorietas* (traffic circles) are common at many busy intersections. Parking in the city center can be scarce, so take a taxi or public bus if you're not staying nearby;
otherwise, try the underground lots across from the Palacio Municipal (✉ Av. Hidalgo and Calle Pedro Loza) and below the Plaza de la
Liberación (✉ Av. Hidalgo and Calle Belén, in front of the Teatro Degollado). If you park illegally, the police may remove your license
plates (*placas*), and you'll have to go to the municipal transit office to
pay a fine and retrieve them.

By Subway
Guadalajara's underground *tren ligero* (light train) system is clean, safe,
and efficient. Line 1 runs along Avenida Federalismo from the Periférico
(city beltway) Sur to Periférico Norte, near the Benito Juárez Auditorium. Line 2 runs east–west along Avenida Javier Mina (which becomes
Avenida Juárez at the Calzada Independencia) from Tetlán in eastern
Guadalajara to Avenida Federalismo. Trains run about every 15 minutes from 6 AM to 11 AM; a token for one trip costs about 25¢.

By Taxi
Taxis are readily available and reasonably economical. Tell the driver
where you are going and agree on a fare *before* you enter the cab. Also,
fare schedules, listing prices to downtown and all major attractions,
are posted in the lobby of all hotels. *Sitios* (cab stands) are near all hotels and attractions.

Contacts and Resources

Car Rentals
Car-rental agencies with offices at the Guadalajara airport include
Avis (☎ 3/688–5528), **Budget** (☎ 3/689–0859; also ✉ Av. Niños Héroes
934, at the corner of Av. 16 de Septiembre, ☎ 3/613–0027), **Dollar**
(☎ 3/615–3623; also ✉ Av. Federalismo Sur 540A, ☎ 3/616–5023),
Hertz (☎ 3/688–5633; also ✉ Av. 16 de Septiembre 738B, ☎ 3/614–
6162), and **National** (☎ 3/688–5021; also ✉ Av. Niños Héroes 961C,
☎ 3/614–7994).

Consulates
United States: ✉ Progreso 175, between López Cotilla and Libertad,
☎ 3/825–2700 or 3/825–2998; after-hours emergency ☎ 3/826–
5553, FAX 3/826–6549. ☉ Weekdays 8–4:30.

Canada: ✉ Fiesta Americana hotel, Aurelio Aceves 225, ☎ 3/625–
3434, ext. 3005, or 3/616–5642). ☉ Weekdays 9:30–1:30.

For information about other consulates, including **Great Britain,** call
Guadalajara's consular association. ☎ 3/616–0629. ☉ Weekdays 9–3
and 5–8.

Emergencies
City police (☎ 3/617–6060); **state police** (☎ 3/617–5838 or 3/617–
5538); **highway patrol** (☎ 06); **fire department** (☎ 3/619–5241 and
3/623–0833); **Cruz Roja** (Red Cross; ☎ 3/613–1550, 3/614–5600, and

3/614–2707), and **Cruz Verde** (municipal emergency medical service; ☎ 3/613–5389).

DOCTORS AND DENTISTS

The U.S. Consulate (☞ Consulates, *above*) maintains a list of English-speaking doctors and dentists. All major hotels have the names of doctors who are on 24-hour call.

HOSPITALS

Hospital del Carmen (Tarascos 3435, near the Plaza México mall, ☎ 3/813–0025 or 3/813–0042), **Hospital México-Americano** (Colomos 2110, ☎ 3/641–3141 or 3/641–3319), and **Hospital Santa María Chapalita** (Av. del Niño Obrero 1666, in the Chapalita neighborhood, ☎ 3/678–1400).

English-Language Bookstores and Publications

Sandi Bookstore (✉ Av. Tepeyac 718 in the Chapalita neighborhood, ☎ 3/121–0863) features a variety of newspapers, magazines, and books.

The weekly *Guadalajara Colony Reporter* newspaper, sold for 70¢ at newsstands and hotels, is the best of a mixed lot of English-language periodicals. Its stories and community and cultural listings provide a great deal of information otherwise unavailable. An excellent source of information on the Lake Chapala area and other excursions in the states of Jalisco, Colima, Nayarit, and Michoacán is Tony Burton's *Western Mexico: A Traveller's Treasury* (University of New Mexico Press).

Guided Tours

Most of the tour operators in the city offer guided city tours and excursions to Tequila, Lake Chapala, Tlaquepaque, and Tonalá.

CALANDRIAS

You can hire a horse-drawn carriage in front of the Museo Regional, the Mercado Libertad, or Parque San Francisco. The charge is about $8.50 for a half-hour tour and about $13.50 for a full hour, for up to four passengers. Few drivers speak English.

PERSONAL GUIDES

The **Sindicato de Guías de Turistas** (Roberto Arellano Deyran, secretary; ☎ 3/657–8376) maintains a list of licensed bilingual guides, though you may have trouble getting an answer if you phone. These guides charge about $13.50 per hour for orientation or special-interest tours in their own automobiles and $8.50 per hour for tours on foot. Most hotels have a list of guides available on short notice.

TOUR OPERATORS

Copenhagen Tours (✉ Blvd. J. Manuel Clouthier 152, in Colonia Prados Vallarta, ☎ 3/629–7957 or 3/629–4758). **Panoramex** (✉ Calzada Federalismo Sur 944, ☎ 3/610–5109 or 3/610–5005).

Money Exchange

The most convenient places to change dollars are *casas de cambio,* generally open weekdays from 9 until 6 (though they may close between 2 and 4) and Saturday mornings. There are many such establishments on Calle López Cotilla downtown and in the Plaza del Sol area. Banks tend to have more limited hours and longer waits.

Pharmacies

Farmacias Guadalajara (✉ Av. Las Americas 2, ☎ 3/615–8516; ✉ Av. Javier Mina 221, ☎ 3/617–8555; Av. Tepeyac 646, in the Chapalita neighborhood, ☎ 3/121–2580; Plaza México, ☎ 3/813–2698) has several branches that are open 24 hours.

Travel Agencies

Many of the city's more than 100 travel agencies are in the two hotel zones, *el centro* (downtown) and on Avenida López Mateos Sur, on the city's southwest side. **American Express** (⊠ Av. Vallarta 2440, near the Los Arcos monument, ☎ 3/615–8712 or 3/615–8910).

Visitor Information

The **Jalisco state tourist office** downtown can also provide information about other parts of Mexico. ⊠ *Calle Morelos 102, in the Plaza Tapatía,* ☎ *3/65–8–2222.* ☉ *Weekdays 9–8, weekends and holidays 9–1.*

The city of Guadalajara has **tourist information booths** downtown in the Plaza Guadalajara and in front of the Instituto Cultural Cabañas, and a **tourist information office** on the ground level of the Los Arcos monument. *Av. Vallarta just east of the Minerva Fountain,* ☎ *3/616–3332, 3/616–3333, or 3/616–3335.* ☉ *Weekdays 9–7.*

8 The Heartland of Mexico

Rich with the history of Mexico's revolution, the heartland is a treasure of colonial towns—Zacatecas, Guanajuato, Querétaro, Morelia, and Pátzcuaro—whose residents now lead quiet, largely traditional lives. Even in San Miguel de Allende, an American art colony and home to a well-known language institute, women wash their clothes and gossip at the local lavandaría *as they have for hundreds of years.*

Updated by
Chris
Humphrey

MEXICO'S HEARTLAND, so named for its central location, has neither the beaches of the west coast nor the ruins of Yucatán. Rather, this fertile farmland along with the surrounding mountains is known for its leading role in Mexican history, particularly during the War of Independence, and for its especially well preserved examples of colonial architecture. The Bajío (ba-*hee*-o), as it is also called, corresponds roughly to the states of Guanajuato and parts of Querétaro and Michoacán. In the hills surrounding the cities of Guanajuato, Zacatecas, Querétaro, and San Miguel de Allende, the Spaniards found silver in the 1500s, leading them to colonize the area heavily.

Three centuries later, wealthy Creoles (Mexicans of Spanish descent) in Querétaro and San Miguel took the first audacious steps toward independence from Spain. When their clandestine efforts were discovered, two of the early insurgents, Ignacio Allende and Father Miguel Hidalgo, began in earnest the 12-year War of Independence. One of the bloodiest skirmishes was fought in the Alhóndiga de Granaditas, a mammoth grain-storage facility in Guanajuato that is now a state museum.

When Allende and Hidalgo were executed in 1811, another native son, José María Morelos, picked up the independence banner. This mestizo (mixed race) priest turned soldier, with his army of 9,000, came close to gaining control of the land before he was killed in 1815. Thirteen years later, the city of Valladolid was renamed Morelia in his honor.

Long after the War of Independence ended in 1821, the cities of the Bajío continued to play a prominent role in Mexico's history. Three major events took place in Querétaro alone: In 1848 the Mexican-American War ended with the signing of the Treaty of Guadalupe Hidalgo; in 1867 Austrian Maximilian of Hapsburg, crowned emperor of Mexico by Napoléon III of France, was executed in the hills north of town; 50 years later the Mexican Constitution was signed here.

The heartland honors the events and people that helped to shape modern Mexico. In ornate cathedrals or bucolic plazas, down narrow alleyways or high atop hillsides, the traveler will discover monuments—and remnants—of a heroic past. During numerous fiestas, the visitor can savor the region's historic spirit. On a night filled with fireworks, off-key music, and tireless celebrants, it's hard not to be caught up in the vital expression of national pride.

Tourism is welcomed in the heartland, especially in these hard economic times, and tourists are treated naturally by residents, who go about their lives in an ordinary fashion. Families visit parks for Sunday picnics, youngsters tussle in school courtyards, old men chat in shaded plazas, and Tarascan women in traditional garb sell their wares in crowded *mercados* (markets). Though a tour operator or vendor may attempt to persuade foreign passersby to part with their money, rarely is the overture less than good-natured. Unlike areas where attractions have been specifically designed for tourism, the Bajío relies on its historic ties and the architectural integrity of its cities to appeal to the traveler.

Note: This is an interesting area to tour by car, but there is also frequent inexpensive bus service from one city to the next throughout the Bahío.

In case you want to see the world.

At American Express, we're here to make your journey a smooth one. So we have over 1,700 travel service locations in over 120 countries ready to help. What else would you expect from the world's largest travel agency?

do more.®

http://www.americanexpress.com/travel

Travel

In case you want to be welcomed there.

We're here to see that you're always welcomed at establishments everywhere. That's why millions of people carry the American Express® Card – for peace of mind, confidence, and security, around the world or just around the corner.

do more

Cards

In case you're running low.

We're here to help with more than 118,000 Express Cash locations around the world. In order to enroll, just call American Express before you start your vacation.

do more

AMERICAN
EXPRESS

Express Cash

And just in case.

We're here with American Express® Travelers Cheques and Cheques *for Two*.® They're the safest way to carry money on your vacation and the surest way to get a refund, practically anywhere, anytime.

Another way we help you...

do more ®

Travelers Cheques

©1996 American Express Travel Related Services Company, Inc.

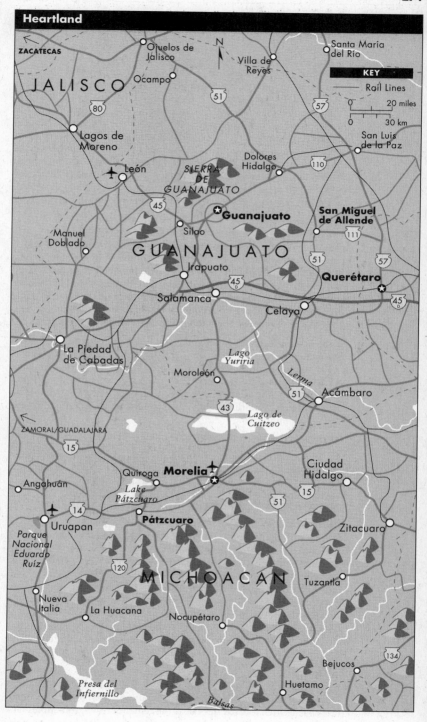

Heartland

ZACATECAS

JALISCO

Ojuelos de
Jalisco

Santa María
del Río

Villa de
Reyes

Ocampo

KEY

Rail Lines

0   20 miles
0   30 km

San Luis
de la Paz

Lagos de
Moreno

León

SIERRA
DE
GUANAJUATO

Dolores
Hidalgo

110

Guanajuato

San Miguel
de Allende

Manuel
Doblado

Silao

GUANAJUATO

111

Irapuato

51

57

Querétaro

Salamanca

45
D

Celaya

45
D

La Piedad
de Cabadas

Lago
Yuriria

Moroleón

Lerma

ZAMORA/GUADALAJARA

43

Lago de
Cuitzeo

51

Acámbaro

15

Quiroga

Morelia

Ciudad
Hidalgo

Angahuán

Lake
Pátzcuaro

51

15

14

Uruapan

Pátzcuaro

Zitacuaro

Parque
Nacional
Eduardo
Ruíz

120

MICHOACAN

Tuzantla

Nueva
Italia

La Huacana

Nocupétaro

134

Presa del
Infiernillo

Bejucos

Huetamo

Balsas

Pleasures and Pastimes

Architecture

Paid for in large part by the region's fabulously wealthy silver mines, the cities of the heartland are architectural masterpieces. From the stately, almost European grandeur of Morelia to the steep, labyrinthine allure of Guanajuato and the sandstone pink splendor of Zacatecas, no two towns are alike. La Parroquia, the Gothic-style parish church of San Miguel de Allende, designed by an Indian mason, puts a Gallic touch on an otherwise very Mexican skyline. Guanajuato boasts a 17th-century Baroque centerpiece, the Basílica Colegiata de Nuestra Señora. Zacatecas, a national monument city, has the best example in Mexico of a Baroque cathedral. The 200-foot Baroque towers of the central cathedral in Morelia are among the tallest in Mexico; and in Pátzcuaro and Querétaro, the ornate 16th-century colonial mansions surrounding the city squares have been converted into hotels and government offices.

Dining

It's no surprise that culinary tastes vary widely in the heartland, which spans a huge area across central Mexico. In the southern state of Michoacán, Tarascan Indian influences predominate. The tomato-based *sopa tarasca* (a soup with cheese, cream, and tortillas) is one of the best-known regional specialties, served in many restaurants in Pátzcuaro and Morelia. Because of the numerous lakes and rivers in the state, several types of freshwater fish are often featured in Michoacán restaurants.

At the other end of the heartland, in northern Zacatecas, the hearty, meat-eating tastes of the norteños rule the dinner table. While beef is the favored dish, other specialties include *pipián ranchero,* a chicken and pumpkin seed concoction. The region is also known for its fine wines. Although it doesn't have a particular specialty, San Miguel de Allende offers a wealth of fine dining opportunities because of its expatriate community.

CATEGORY	COST*
$$$$	over $20
$$$	$15–$20
$$	$8–$15
$	under $8

per person, excluding drinks and service

Hiking and Walking

With its rolling farmland, lofty volcanoes, lakes, and Indian villages, Michoacán is a perfect area in which to take day hikes. Trails near Pátzcuaro wind up to the top of nearby hilltops for great views across town and the surrounding countryside, while in the mountains farther south near Uruapan, one can walk along a lush, raging river valley. And of course no tour of the heartland could possibly be complete without a few days of leisurely strolling the avenues and back streets of the colonial cities and towns—admiring the architecture, lingering in the museums, or resting with a cup of coffee on the plaza, watching the world go by.

Lodging

In many of the heartland's colonial cities, the best lodgings are to be found in the restored haciendas of the fabulously rich residents of centuries past. Often located right near the center of town, sometimes facing directly onto the plaza, some of these beautiful mansions date from the 16th century. There are also deluxe modern high-rises and functional, low-cost hotels for those with different tastes or budgets.

CATEGORY	COST*
$$$$	over $90
$$$	$60–$90
$$	$25–$60
$	under $25

All prices are for a standard double room, excluding 10% tax.

Exploring the Heartland

Many travelers barrel past the heartland to points north or west of Mexico City. But there are many reasons others make it their destination. Some stop for a few days to browse in the shops of San Miguel or Guanajuato for bargains in silver and other local crafts. Others venture to the state of Michoacán, renowned for its folklore and folk crafts, especially ceramics and lacquerware. Those who stay longer and tour the region can linger over the wealth of architectural styles that each of the colonial cities has to offer.

Great Itineraries

Those with only a couple of days to spare can visit any of several colonial cities to catch a taste for life in the Mexican heartland, but each one has its own particular flavor. Visitors who fall under the spell of this peaceful, friendly region will want to spend a week to 10 days to allow themselves the time to sit back and drink in the atmosphere of two or three of the heartland cities.

IF YOU HAVE 3 DAYS

Head to Guanajuato (432 kilometers, or 268 miles, from Mexico City), the most architecturally dramatic of the heartland cities. Make a day trip from here to the sleepy town of San Miguel de Allende, just 90 minutes away by car or bus, to shop for arts and crafts.

Another option would be to go from Mexico City to the Michoacán capital of Morelia (about four hours by car) and spend a day enjoying its stately architecture and café-lined plaza. The next day, drive 56 kilometers (34 miles) through Quiroga to Pátzcuaro, set among volcanoes in the center of Tarascan Indian country. Spend the morning walking through the bustling market or strolling the surrounding countryside before returning to Mexico City in the late afternoon.

IF YOU HAVE 5 DAYS

Make Guanajuato your base, and then devote an extra day to its churches and museums—even the gruesome Mummy Museum. Stop off at the town of Dolores Hidalgo, home of Mexican independence, on your way to a day of shopping in San Miguel. Overnight in San Miguel and the next morning head for Querétaro, 63 kilometers (38 miles) away; this quiet colonial city is considered the capital of the Bajío. Take a soothing thermal bath at nearby Tequisquiapan. After a night in one of Querétaro's many downtown hotels, drive the three hours to Mexico City or the 2½ to Guanajuato airport in León.

Visitors choosing to spend several days in Michoacán will easily fill their time exploring the state's colonial towns and enjoying the lush, mountainous countryside. After three days in Morelia and Pátzcuaro, take a day trip to explore the crater on an extinct volcano in San Juan Parangaricútiro or the ruins of an ancient Tarascan Indian capital, Tzintzuntzán (both are less than an hour from Pátzcuaro) before returning on the final day to Morelia and Mexico City.

IF YOU HAVE 7 DAYS

From your base in Guanajuato, consider adding to the first of the five-day itineraries a round-trip flight from Guanajuato airport to Zacatecas; that would give you a day and a half to explore this northern colonial mining city. Because it lies off the main tourist track, Zacatecas has a refreshingly unselfconscious feel to it. Another possibility for a weeklong heartland tour would be to make a loop from Mexico City that includes both Morelia and Guanajuato; you'd have time for leisurely side trips to Pátzcuaro and San Miguel and a stop-off in Querétaro. When in Pátzcuaro, be sure to take a boat out to the island town of Janítzio on nearby Lake Pátzcuaro, home of Mexico's most famous November 2 Day of the Dead festival.

When to Tour the Heartland

One of the most pleasing aspects of the heartland is its superb climate—it rarely gets overly hot, even in the middle of summer, and although February days can get nippy, especially in the northern city of Zacatecas, winters are generally temperate. Average temperatures in the southern city of Morelia range from 20°C (68°F) in May to just under 10°C (49°F) in January. Zacatecas is more extreme, with winter temperatures as low as 0°C (32°F) and snow flurries every several years, and summer highs of 28°C–30°C (81°F–85°F). Nights are cool all year in most of the region's cities, with the exception of Querétaro and León, which are in the plains. The rainy season all across the heartland hits between April and September and is generally strongest in July and August.

Another compelling reason to check your calendar when planning a trip to the heartland is two renowned annual events. The International Cervantes Festival, a two-week-long celebration of the arts, attracts actors, musicians, painters, and thousands of people to Guanajuato every year in October. And on the island of Janítzio, local Tarascan Indians hold a spectacular November 2 festival in honor of their dead ancestors during Mexico's version of Halloween, the Day of the Dead.

SAN MIGUEL DE ALLENDE

San Miguel de Allende first began luring foreigners in the late 1930s when Stirling Dickinson, an American, and prominent locals founded an art school in this mountainous settlement. The school, now called the Instituto Allende, has grown in stature over the years—as has the city's reputation as a writers' and artists' colony. Walk down any cobblestoned street and you're likely to see residents of a variety of national origins. Some come to study at the Instituto Allende or the Academia Hispano-Americana, some to escape the harsh northern winters, and still others to retire.

Cultural offerings in this town of about 110,000 reflect its large American community. There are literary readings, art shows, a lending library, and aerobics classes. Nevertheless, San Miguel, declared a national monument in 1926, retains its Mexican characteristics. Wandering down streets lined with 18th-century mansions, you'll also discover fountains, monuments, and churches—all reminders of the city's illustrious, and sometimes notorious, past. The onetime headquarters of the Spanish Inquisition in New Spain, for example, is located at the corner of Calles Hernández Macías and Pila Seca; the former Inquisition jail stands across the way.

Exploring San Miguel de Allende

Most of San Miguel's sights are clustered in the downtown area and can be seen in a couple of hours.

A Good Walk

Numbers in the text correspond to numbers in the margin and on the San Miguel de Allende map.

Begin at the main plaza, otherwise known as **El Jardín** ①; after you get a feel for the square, stop into **La Parroquia** ②, the sandstone church on its south side. Three blocks northeast of La Parroquia (take Calle San Francisco, on the north side of El Jardín, to Calle Juárez) is the **Iglesia de San Francisco** ③, with its fine Churrigueresque facade. Take a few steps north on Calle Juárez to Calle Mesones, where the colorful **Mercado Ignacio Ramírez** (☞ Shopping, *below*) occupies a small plaza. The dome of the **Oratorio de San Felipe Neri** ④ is visible just beyond the market.

Go a block west from the church on Calle de los Insurgentes to reach **La Biblioteca Pública** ⑤, a great place to catch up on town events and rest your feet. From the library, continue west for two blocks to Calle Hernández Macías and then head south to the **Bellas Artes Cultural Center** ⑥ at No. 75 and the **Iglesia de la Concepción** ⑦ right behind it. Take Hernández Macías south for a block and turn left on Umarán to reach the **Casa de Ignacio Allende** ⑧, birthplace of the Mexican national hero. You've circled back to the west side of the Jardín.

After exploring the center of town, you might want to take a leisurely stroll to sights a bit farther afield. From the south side of the plaza (where La Parroquia sits), head west four blocks on Calle de Umarán until you reach **Calle Zacateros.** Turn south on this narrow cobblestoned street to reach some of the town's most interesting crafts shops—stocked with everything from silver jewelry to Mexican ceremonial masks.

Past the shops, Calle Zacateros becomes Ancha de San Antonio. On your left at No. 20 is the renowned **Instituto Allende** ⑨, where many of San Miguel's foreign visitors come to study. From the institute, continue south on Ancha de San Antonio until you reach Callejón del Cardo on your left. Continue past **St. Paul's Episcopal Church,** where many Americans worship, until you arrive at the cobblestoned Calle Aldama on your left. Head downhill and walk briefly through a neighborhood of whitewashed houses before reaching the north entrance to the 5-acre **Parque Benito Juárez,** the largest park in town and an oasis of evergreens, palm trees, and gardens.

From the north edge of the park, follow Calle Diezmo Viejo until the imposing terra cotta–colored mansion known as **La Huerta Santa Elena** is in front of you. From here turn left and walk one block uphill to the **Lavandería** ⑩, San Miguel's outdoor laundry and a favorite gathering spot for local women. Calle de Recreo, above the Lavandería, heads north back toward the plaza: Follow Recreo until reaching Calle Correo, turn left, and walk three blocks to return to El Jardín.

Sights to See

⑥ **Bellas Artes Cultural Center.** Across the street from the building that houses the U.S. Consulate is this impressive cloister, once the Royal Convent of the Conception and now an institute for the study of music, dance, and the visual arts. Several murals, including one by the famed Mexican painter David Siqueiros, are on exhibit. There's also a cafeteria inside. ⊠ *Calle Hernández Macías 75,* ☎ *415/2–08–89.* ☉ *Daily 10–2:30 and 5–7:30.*

⑧ **Casa de Ignacio Allende.** Now housing a museum and gallery, this is the birthplace of Ignacio Allende, one of Mexico's great independence heroes. Allende was a Creole aristocrat who, along with Father Miguel

San Miguel de Allende

Hidalgo, plotted in the early 1800s to overthrow the Spanish regime. At clandestine meetings held in San Miguel and nearby Querétaro, the two discussed strategies, organized an army, gathered weapons, and enlisted the support of clerics for the struggle ahead.

Spanish Royalists learned of their plot and began arresting conspirators in Querétaro on September 13, 1810. Allende and Hidalgo received word of these actions and hastened their plans. At dawn on September 16, they rang out the cry for independence, and the fighting began. Allende was the military leader of the insurrection and was captured and executed by the Royalists the following year. As a tribute to his brave efforts, San Miguel El Grande became San Miguel de Allende in the 20th century. ✉ *Calle Cuna de Allende 1,* ☎ *415/2–24–99.* 🔲 *Free.* ☉ *Tues.–Sun. 10–4.*

NEED A BREAK?	On the southwest corner of the main plaza is **Café del Jardín** (✉ Portal Allende 2, ☎ 415/2–06–50). This unassuming little café has excellent coffee, cappuccino, hot chocolate, and snack food; breakfasts are tasty and inexpensive. There's friendly service and best of all—it's that American influence—two cups of coffee for the price of one!

❶ El Jardín. The heart of San Miguel is the plaza commonly known as El Jardín (the Garden). Seated on one of its gray wrought-iron benches, you'll quickly get a feel for the town: Old men with canes exchange tales, youngsters in school uniforms bustle by, fruit vendors hawk their wares, and bells from the nearby La Parroquia pierce the thin mountain air at each quarter hour. ✉ *Bounded by Calle Correo on the south, Calle San Francisco on the north, Portal Allende on the west, and Portal Guadalupe on the east.*

⑪ El Mirador. For great views, consider a climb to El Mirador (the Lookout), which offers a panorama of the city, mountains, and reservoir below. The vista is most commanding at sunset, and chances are you won't be alone; locals and tourists like to join Ignacio Allende, whose bronze image commands this spot. ⊠ *1 block before town, turn right off Calle Recreo onto Calle Hospicio. Follow Hospicio 3 blocks to Calle Pedro Vargas. Turn right and head uphill to the overlook.*

❼ Iglesia de la Concepción. Located just behind the Bellas Artes cultural center, this church touts one of the largest domes in Mexico. Its two-story roof, completed in 1891, boasts both elegant Corinthian columns and ornamental pilasters and is said to have been inspired by the dome of Les Invalides in Paris. Ceferino Gutiérrez (of La Parroquia fame) is credited with its design. ⊠ *Calle Canal between Hernández Macías and Zacateros.*

❸ Iglesia de San Francisco. José Churriguera, a 17th-century Spanish architect, was noted for his extravagantly decorative Baroque style; the San Francisco Church has one of the finest Churrigueresque facades in the state of Guanajuato. Built in the late 18th century, it was financed by donations from wealthy patrons and by revenue from bullfights. Topping the elaborately carved exterior is the image of Saint Francis of Assisi; below are sculptures of Saint John and Our Lady of Sorrows, as well as a crucifix. ⊠ *Calle Juárez between San Francisco and Mesones.*

❾ Instituto Allende. The school is set in the former hacienda of the Count of Canal. Since its founding in 1951, thousands of students from around the world have come to learn Spanish and to take classes in social studies and the arts. Courses last from a couple of weeks to a month or longer. Lush with bougainvillea, rose bushes, and ivy vines, the grounds provide a quiet refuge for students and visitors alike. ⊠ *Ancha de San Antonio 20,* ☎ *415/2–01–90,* FAX *415/2–45–38.* ⊙ *Building daily 9–7, office hours weekdays 9–1 and 3–6, Sat. 9–1.*

❺ La Biblioteca Pública. Posted on the bulletin board in the entranceway to the library are many notices (mostly in English) about events such as literary readings or yoga and aerobics classes. Inside are the offices of the bilingual newspaper, *Atención San Miguel,* as well as a reading room with back issues of popular publications and English books. It's a great place to take a breather from sightseeing. On Sundays the library offers a two-hour house-and-garden tour of San Miguel that departs at noon. Tickets cost about $10, with all proceeds going to the library. ⊠ *Calle de los Insurgentes 25,* ☎ *415/2–02–93 or 415/2–37–70.* ⊙ *Weekdays 10–2 and 4–7, Sat. 10–2.*

❷ La Parroquia. This imposing pink Gothic-style parish church, made of local *cantera* sandstone, was designed in the late 19th century by self-trained Indian mason Ceferino Gutiérrez, who sketched his designs in the sand with a stick. Gutiérrez was purportedly inspired by postcards of European Gothic cathedrals. Since the postcards gave no hint of what the back of those cathedrals looked like, the posterior of La Parroquia was done in quintessential Mexican style.

La Parroquia still functions as a house of worship, though its interior has been changed over the years. Gilded wood altars, for example, were replaced with neoclassical stone altars. The original bell, cast in 1732, still calls parishioners to Mass several times daily. ⊠ *South side of El Jardín on Calle Correo.*

❿ Lavandería. At this outdoor public laundry—a collection of cement tubs set above Juárez Park—local women gather daily to wash clothes and gossip as their predecessors have done for centuries. Though some women claim to have more efficient washing facilities at home, the lure of the spring-fed troughs—not to mention the chance to catch up on the news— brings them daily to this shaded courtyard. ⊠ *Calle Jesús.*

❹ Oratorio de San Felipe Neri. Built by local Indians in 1712, the original chapel can still be glimpsed in the eastern facade, made of pink stone and adorned with a figure of Our Lady of Solitude; the newer, southern front was built in an ornate Baroque style. In 1734 the wealthy Count of Canal paid for an addition to the Oratorio. His **Templo de Santa Casa de Loreto,** dedicated to the Virgin of Loreto, is just behind the Oratorio; its main entrance, now blocked by a grille, is on the Oratorio's left rear side. Peer through the grille to see the heavily gilded altars and effigies of the count and his wife, under which they are buried. ⊠ *Calle de los Insurgentes and Calle Loreto.*

Dining

For its size, San Miguel has a surprising number of international restaurants (about 170 at last count). The recent influx of Americans has given rise to new Tex-Mex and health-food establishments; a European influence has contributed to nearly authentic French, Italian, and Spanish cuisines. Regional Mexican food is available in a variety of price ranges. Much of this fare is made from pork, chicken, or ground beef and is often broiled, fried, or covered with a bread-crumb batter. Dishes are prepared with onions or garlic and served with a red or green chili sauce. Unless otherwise indicated, dress is casual.

$$$ ✕ **La Antigua Restaurant y Tapa Bar.** A cheerful room with fewer than a dozen tables (each with a baby-blue tablecloth and a vase of orange carnations) and a polished wood bar that can seat up to 15 people, La Antigua puts its clientele in the mood for a large variety of tapas with its European café furniture and Spanish bolero music. Among its specialties are *queso antiguo* (baked cheese with chilies), *chisterra* (a sliced and fried Spanish-style sausage), *camarones con tocineta* (jumbo shrimp fried with bacon), and *pulpo antiguo* (squid sautéed in garlic and herbs). All dishes are served with bread or tortillas. ⊠ *Calle Canal 9,* ☎ *415/2–25–86. AE, MC, V.*

$$$ ✕ **La Princesa.** More upscale restaurants have opened in San Miguel recently, but La Princesa is still *the* place to go for intimate dining. The romantic ambience is enhanced by cloth-covered tables, dark wood paneling, lazily turning ceiling fans, a large wine selection, and musicians who entertain from 7 PM to 3 AM. The Executive Menu, served daily 1–8 PM, includes soup, one of eight entrées (ranging from fillet of red snapper to Mexican-style stuffed peppers), dessert, coffee or tea, and a complimentary margarita. After 8 PM the menu features steak dishes, including chateaubriand for two, and the prices climb. ⊠ *Calle de Recreo 5,* ☎ *415/2–14–03. AE, MC, V.*

$$ ✕ **Fonda Meson de San José.** On a tree-shaded cobblestoned patio in-
★ side a complex of small shops, this well-established restaurant offers German as well as Mexican cuisines. Owner-chef Angela Merkel is enthusiastic about her roulade, potato pancakes, and German chocolate cake and once a month invites other local chefs to display their talents. The German buffet, originally offered for Oktoberfest, is in great demand. ⊠ *Mesones 38,* ☎ *415/2–38–48. MC, V.*

$$ ✕ **Mamá Mía.** Those who want a change from Mexican food will enjoy Mamá Mía's satisfying assortment of pastas and pizzas, as well as a decent fettuccine Bolognese and spaghetti Parmesana. House specials include fettuccine Alex (with white wine, ham, cream, and mushrooms) and fettuccine à la Mexicana (with ground sausage, peppers, onions, and tomatoes). Folk musicians entertain on the lush outdoor patio come dusk. ⊠ *Calle de Umarán 8,* ☎ *415/2–20–63. MC, V.*

$$ ✕ **Rincon Español.** The soft pink walls of this pleasant Spanish restaurant are covered with reproductions of the works of famous Spanish artists—Joan Miró, Picasso, and Salvador Dalí—and its nickname, La Casa de la Paella, reveals the dining room's specialty. Not a little of the charm of this place derives from the evening guitar music and flamenco dancing, pleasing adjuncts to dessert. ⊠ *Correo 29,* ☎ *415/2– 29–84. MC, V.*

Lodging

San Miguel has a wide selection of hotels ranging from cozy bed-and-breakfasts to elegant all-suite properties. Rooms fill up quickly during summer and winter seasons, when northern tourists migrate here in droves. Make reservations several months in advance if you plan to visit at these times.

$$$ 🏨 **Villa Jacaranda.** An all-suites hotel located near the Parque Benito Juárez, the Villa Jacaranda boasts a full range of amenities. Rooms, though unimaginatively decorated, have space heaters and cable TVs (with channels from the United States). The hotel's Cine/Bar shows American movies Tuesday–Saturday at 7:30 PM and live sports events on a giant screen. The price of admission—roughly $3—includes a drink. ⊠ *Calle Aldama 53, 37700,* ☎ *415/2–10–15 or 415/2–08–11,* FAX *415/2–08–83. 15 suites. Restaurant, pool, hot tub. AE, MC, V.*

$$–$$$ 🏨 **Casa Carmen.** Run by a very friendly longtime San Miguel family, this pension is an oasis of peace in the center of town. Set in a 200-year-old hacienda just two blocks from the Plaza, it features large, immaculate rooms tastefully decorated with antiques and other wooden furnishings. Two of the double rooms in the front have an upstairs loft for the bed, and the two small patios are ideal places to relax with a good book after walking around San Miguel. Reservations are strongly recommended. ⊠ *Correo 31, 37700,* ☎ *415/2–08–44. 12 rooms. Breakfast and lunch included in room rate. No credit cards.*

$$ 🏨 **La Mansión del Bosque.** Located on a quiet side street across from
★ the Parque Benito Juárez, this renovated hacienda opened as a guest house and restaurant in 1968. Its American owners, George and Ruth Hyba, cater to long-term guests in the winter and more transient visitors in the off-season. The hotel, which operates on a Modified American Plan that includes breakfast and dinner, has guest rooms with such homey touches as handwoven cotton spreads, locally made throw rugs and artifacts, and bookshelves. Many rooms feature working fireplaces as well as private, plant-filled terraces. The lounge off the foyer has books and magazines, a telephone for long-distance calls, and a house cat that watches over the premises. ⊠ *Calle Aldama 65, 37700,* ☎ *415/2–02–77. 23 rooms with bath. Restaurant, bar. No credit cards.*

$$ 🏨 **Posada de las Monjas.** This 19th-century structure has been operating as a hotel for more than 50 years. It caters to long-term visitors, mainly students from the Instituto Allende or Academia Hispano-Americana but welcomes guests for shorter stays. Rooms are furnished in a colonial style, with some furniture in the old wing looking worn enough to be authentically 17th century. The rooftop public terrace has tables and lounge chairs and offers commanding views of mountains and city. Some rooms have fireplaces, and there's a communal television in the lobby. ⊠ *Calle de Canal 37, 37700,* ☎ *415/2–01–71,* FAX *415/2–62–27. 65 rooms with bath. Restaurant, bar, laundry service. AE, MC, V.*

$$ ▣ **Posada de San Francisco.** This colonial-style property, located on the main plaza downtown, resembles an old Spanish monastery—a crucifix hangs in the lobby beneath a stone archway, and some rooms have crosses over the beds. Rooms on the plaza will appeal to people-watchers, but on weekends and during the busy season these quarters can be rather noisy. For a quieter setting, request a room on the second or third floor (some overlook nearby mountains and churches) or one inside, facing the bougainvillea-draped courtyard. ⊠ *Plaza Principal 2, 37700,* ☎ FAX *415/2–14–66, 415/2–00–72, or 415/2–05–39. 46 rooms, suites, and junior suites. Restaurant, bar. AE, MC, V.*

$$ ▣ **Villa Mirasol.** Each of this lodging's seven rooms is decorated with original prints, oil paintings, pastels, and small sculptures; most of the rooms are flooded with sunlight during the day. All have either a private or shared terrace; the ones facing Calle Pila Seca have beautiful vistas of the surrounding hills. Located on a quiet and secluded street no more than a 10-minute walk from the principal plaza, Villa Mirasol includes in its price a rich breakfast—such as *chilaquiles* (baked tortillas with cheese and chicken) or Mexican-style scrambled eggs with chilies, tomatoes, and onions—as well as coffee and pastries in the afternoon. The hotel was a private house until 1983, and today its cozy and intimate atmosphere affords visitors a welcome distinction from the larger, less personal hotels in the area. It also offers its guests who stay more than a week use of the Club de Golf free of charge. ⊠ *Pila Seca 35, 37700,* ☎ *415/2–15–64. 7 rooms with bath. MC, V.*

$$$$ ✕▣ **Casa de Sierra Nevada.** Once the home of the archbishop of
★   Guanajuato and the marquise of Sierra Nevada, this elegant country-style inn (built in 1580) hosted George Bush in 1981 and continues to attract ambassadors, diplomats, heads of state, film stars, and bullfighters. Its complex of four colonial buildings, on either side of a cobblestoned street a few blocks from La Parroquia, contains 18 individually decorated suites and five standard rooms. Lace curtains, handwoven rugs, chandeliers, and prints by artist Diego Rivera adorn some rooms; fireplaces, cozy private terraces, and skylights enhance others. From the terrace of room No. 1, there's an excellent view of La Parroquia. The Continental cuisine at the hotel's restaurant is delicately prepared and beautifully presented. ⊠ *Calle Hospicio 35, 37700,* ☎ *415/2–04–15 or 415/2–18–95; in the U.S., 800/525–4800;* FAX *415/2–23–37. 24 rooms with bath. Restaurant, bar, pool, spa. AE, MC, V.*

Nightlife and the Arts

The Arts

San Miguel, long known as an artists' colony, continues to nurture that image today. Galleries, museums, and art shops line the streets near El Jardín, and two government-run salons—at **Bellas Artes** and **Instituto Allende** (☞ Exploring San Miguel de Allende, *above,* for both)—showcase the work of a variety of Mexican artists. For a sampling of regional talent, visit the **Galería San Miguel** (⊠ Plaza Principal 14, ☎ 415/2–04–54), **Galería Atenea** (⊠ Calle Cuna de Allende 15, ☎ 415/2–07–85), and the **Kligerman Gallery** (⊠ San Francisco 11, ☎ 415/2–09–51 or 415/2–15–14). If a rather large painting or photograph strikes your fancy, don't despair: Some gallery owners will ship your newfound treasure back to the States for you.

Nightlife

On most evenings in San Miguel you can readily satisfy a whim for a literary reading, an American movie, a theatrical production, or a turn on a disco dance floor. The most up-to-date listings of events can be found in the bilingual paper *Atención San Miguel,* published every Friday. The bulletin board at the public library (⊠ Calle de los Insurgentes 25) is also a good source of current events.

La Taberna del Rey (⊠ Hidalgo 3, ☎ 415/2–08–15) features dance music from 9 PM until 2 AM Thursday through Sunday, with dinner theater on Wednesday at 9:30 PM. Live music can be heard at **Pancho and Lefty's** (⊠ Calle Mesones 99, ☎ 415/2–19–58) from rock, jazz, or blues bands, depending on the night. **La Fragua** (⊠ Calle Cuna de Allende 3, ☎ 415/2–11–44), located just a couple of doors off the Plaza, often has traditional Mexican bands. At **Mamá Mía** (⊠ Calle de Umarán 8, ☎ 415/2–20–63) you can hear everything from Peruvian folk music, classical guitar, and flamenco to salsa and rock. **El Jardín** (⊠ San Francisco 4, ☎ 415/2–17–06), though more of a restaurant than a club, has a piano bar. **Laberintos Disco** (⊠ Calle Ancha de San Antonio 7, ☎ 415/2–03–62), across from the Instituto Allende outside the center of town, is often hopping until the early morning hours. **El Ring Disco Club** (⊠ Calle de Hidalgo 25, ☎ 415/2–19–98) invariably attracts a good crowd on the weekends.

Outdoor Activities and Sports

Participant Sports

Travelers who enjoy the sporting life will find good facilities for swimming, tennis, horseback riding, and golf at deluxe and first-class hotels situated near the Instituto Allende or on the outskirts of town. (The San Miguel tourist office can provide a list of these properties.) The **Hotel Hacienda Taboada** (⊠ Km 8 on Dolores Hidalgo Hwy., ☎ 415/2–08–88, ℻ 415/2–17–98) has simmering thermal pools that are open to the public for a nominal fee. The **Club de Golf Malanquin** (⊠ Km 3 on Celaya Hwy., ☎ 415/2–05–16) features a heated pool, steam baths, tennis courts, and nine holes of golf, all of which are open to the public.

Spectator Sports

Visitors who want to witness the pageantry of a traditional Mexican bullfight can do so at the **Plaza de Toros Oriente** (⊠ off Calle de Recreo) several times a year. The most important contest takes place during the last week of September when the town's patron saint, San Miguel, (known in English as Saint Michael the Archangel) is commemorated. Posters announcing fights are set up in El Jardín in the center of town and at the Fonda La Mesa del Matador restaurant at Calle Hernández Macías 76.

Shopping

For centuries San Miguel's artisans have been creating a wide variety of crafts ranging from straw products to metalwork. Though some boutiques in town may be a bit pricey, you can find good buys on silver, brass, tin, woven-cotton goods, and folk art; locally crafted metal objects—such as plates and trays, chests, mirrors, and decorative animals and birds—are popular souvenirs. Opening and closing hours are erratic; a number of stores open at 9 AM, but many others don't start conducting business until 11; some shut their doors for traditional afternoon siesta (2 through 4 or 5). Closing hour tends to be around 7 or 8 PM, and most (but not all) shops are closed on Sunday. Most San Miguel shops accept MasterCard and Visa.

Market

Occupying the small plaza directly in front of the Oratorio de San Felipe Negri, the **Mercado Ignacio Ramírez** spills over onto the surrounding streets (for about six blocks). It is particularly active on

Sundays, when country folk come to town with pigs, chickens, and other livestock, along with succulent produce. During the week, rows of fresh fruits and vegetables are supplemented by racks of cheaply made clothing, inexpensive American toys, and blaring Mexican-made tapes and records.

Specialty Shops

BRASS AND TINWARE

Casa Cohen (⊠ Reloj 12, ☎ 415/2–14–34) carries furniture and metalware in all shapes and sizes. **Casa Canal** (⊠ Calle de Canal 3, ☎ 415/2–04–79), set in a beautiful old hacienda, sells new furniture, though much of it is made in traditional styles.

DESIGNER CLOTHING

Sidell (⊠ Quebrada 117, ☎ 415/2–04–86) markets one-of-a-kind clothing (mostly for women) designed and made by the owners. The pieces are all hand-dyed and silk-screened. Among the smart shops that have emerged on Calle Jesus, a block from the Jardín, is **Char** (⊠ Calle Jesus 5, ☎ 415/2–08–37), which has a sister store in Santa Fe and features suede fashions.

FOLK ART

Artes de México (⊠ Aurora 47 at Dolores Hidalgo exit, ☎ 415/2–07–64) has been producing and selling traditional crafts, including furniture, metalwork, and ceramics, for more than 40 years. **Casa Maxwell** (⊠ Calle de Canal 14, ☎ 415/2–02–47) is ideal for one-stop shoppers: This seemingly endless building offers folk art, ceramics, jewelry, furniture, glassware, metalware, modern clothing, and a lot more. **El Pegaso** (⊠ Corregidora 6, ☎ 415/2–13–51), a combined art shop and restaurant, sells traditional art from Mexico and Guatemala, including some rare pieces on the second floor. **La Calaca** (⊠ Mesones 93, no phone) also focuses on folk art from the Americas, mainly Mexico, Guatemala, and Peru. **Tonatiu Metzli** (⊠ Las Flores 27, ☎ 415/2–08–69) features a colorful selection of work from Mexico, China, Africa, and elsewhere. **Veryka** (⊠ Zacateros 6-A, ☎ 415/2–21–14), whose emphasis is on Latin American folk art, has a particularly fine selection of *muertos* (skeleton figurines for the Day of the Dead) from Puebla.

JEWELRY

Established in 1963, **Joyería David** (⊠ Calle Zacateros 53, ☎ 415/2–00–56) has an extensive selection of gold, silver, copper, and brass jewelry, all made on the premises. A number of pieces contain Mexican opals, amethysts, topaz, malachite, and turquoise. The extremely reputable **Beckmann Joyería** (⊠ Calle Hernández Macías 115, ☎ 415/2–16–13) designs its own gold and silver pieces. **Platería Cerro Blanco** (⊠ Calle de Canal 17, ☎ 415/2–05–02) also creates and crafts its own silver and gold jewelry and will arrange a visit to its *taller* (workshop) on request. **Platería y Joyería Julio** (⊠ Calle del Correo 8, ☎ 415/2–02–48) sells silver pieces made by San Miguel artists and carries a large selection of religious jewelry—crucifixes, medallions of the Virgin, and the like.

Side Trip

Dolores Hidalgo

50 km (30 mi) north of San Miguel via Route 51.

Dolores Hidalgo played an important role in the fight for independence. It was here, before dawn on September 16, 1810, that Father Miguel Hidalgo—the local priest—gave an impassioned sermon to his clergy that ended with the *grito* (cry), "Viva Ferdinand VII [king of Spain at the time]! Death to bad government!" At 11 PM on September 15, politicians throughout the land repeat a revised version of the *grito*—"Viva Mexico! Viva Mexico! Viva Mexico!"—signaling the start of Independence Day celebrations. On September 16 (and only on this day), the bell in Hidalgo's parish church is rung.

Casa Hidalgo, the house where the patriot lived, is now a museum. It contains copies of important letters Hidalgo sent or received, and other independence memorabilia. ⊠ *Calle Morelos 1,* ☎ *468/2–01–71.* 🖾 *About $3.* ☉ *Tues.–Sun. 10–5:45.*

The town is also known for its output of hand-painted ceramics, most notably tiles and tableware. Dolores Hidalgo can be reached easily by bus from San Miguel de Allende. Buses depart frequently from the Central de Autobuses; travel time is about one hour.

San Miguel de Allende A to Z

Arriving and Departing

BY BUS
Direct bus service is available daily between the Central del Norte (North Bus Station) in Mexico City and the Central de Autobuses in San Miguel. Several major lines—including **Flecha Amarilla, Herradura de Plata, Primera Plus,** and **Tres Estrellas de Oro**—offer frequent service. Travel time is about four hours.

BY CAR
Driving time from Mexico City to San Miguel is roughly four hours via Route 57 (to Querétaro) and Route 111 (Querétaro to San Miguel). Traveling on Route 45 from Mexico City, drivers can take a road connecting to Route 57, bypassing Querétero and saving a half hour.

BY PLANE
International airlines that fly into Guanajuato International Airport, which is about two hours from San Miguel, include **Aeromexico** (☎ 47/14–05–74), from Los Angeles; **American** (☎ 47/16–05–02), from Dallas–Fort Worth; **Continental** (☎ 47/14–71–10), from Houston; **Mexicana** (☎ 47/13–45–50), from Chicago; and **Taesa** (☎ 47/16–98–31), from Oakland, CA.

Taxis from the airport to downtown cost about $25.

BY TRAIN
The *Aztec* leaves Mexico City for San Miguel de Allende at 9 AM, arriving in San Miguel at 2 PM; it departs San Miguel at 2 PM and arrives in Mexico City at 7 PM. The first-class round-trip fare is $11. The train from Monterrey to Mexico City also stops at San Miguel. For current schedules and fares, contact **Mexico by Train** (☎ FAX 210/725–3659 or 800/321–1699).

The **San Miguel train station** (☎ 415/2–00–07) is located on La Calzada de Estación (Station Highway).

Getting Around
San Miguel de Allende is best negotiated on foot, keeping in mind two pieces of advice. The city is more than a mile above sea level, so visitors not accustomed to high altitudes may tire quickly during their first few days there. Streets are paved with rugged cobblestone, and some of them do not have sidewalks. Sturdy footwear, such as athletic or other rubber-soled shoes, is therefore highly recommended.

BY TAXI
Taxis can easily be hailed on the street or found at taxi stands such as **Sitio Allende** in the main plaza (☎ 415/2–05–50 or 415/2–01–92),

Sitio San Francisco on Calle Mesones (no phone), or **Sitio San Felipe** on Calle Juárez (no phone). Flat rates to the bus terminal, train station, and other parts of the city apply. It's best to bring change if possible.

Contacts and Resources

BUSINESS SERVICES
La Conexion (✉ Aldama 1, ☎ FAX 415/2–16–87 or 415/2–15–99) offers 24-hour answering and fax service, a Mexico address for receiving mail, lockboxes, a Macintosh computer center, and other services.

CAR RENTAL AGENCY
Renta de Autos Gama (✉ Calle de Hidalgo 3, ☎ 415/2–08–15) has a limited selection of standard-shift compacts available.

CONSULATE
The U.S. Consular agent is Colonel Phil Maher. ✉ *Calle Hernández Macías 72; during office hours,* ☎ *415/2–23–57; emergencies,* ☎ *415/ 2–00–68 or 415/2–00–99.* ☉ *Mon. and Wed. 9–1 and 4–7, Tues. and Thurs. 4–7.*

EMERGENCIES
Police (☎ 415/2–00–23). **Ambulance–Red Cross** (☎ 415/4–82–92 or 415/4–82–96). **Fire Department** (415/2–08–77 or 415/2–01–64).

Hospital. The staff at **Hospital de la Fe** (✉ Carretera a Dolores Hidalgo s/n, ☎ 415/2–22–33 or 415/2–17–61) can refer you to an English-speaking doctor.

Pharmacies. San Miguel has many pharmacies, but American residents recommend **Botica Agundis** (✉ Calle de Canal 26, ☎ 415/2–11–98), where English speakers are often on hand. ☉ *Daily 10–midnight.*

ENGLISH-LANGUAGE BOOKSTORES
El Colibri (Sollano 30, ☎ FAX 415/2–07–51) has a good selection of novels, magazines, and a few art supplies. Mostly magazines are available at **Lagundi** (✉ Umarán 17, ☎ 415/2–08–30).

MONEY EXCHANGE
A better bet for money exchange than the slow-moving bank lines is **Deal Casa de Cambio.** ✉ *San Francisco 4,* ☎ *415/2–29–32.* ☉ *Weekdays 9–2 and 4–6, Sat. 9–2.*

TRAVEL AGENCIES
Major agencies are **Viajes Vértiz** (American Express representative at Calle de Hidalgo 1A, ☎ 415/2–18–56 or 415/2–16–95, FAX 415/2–04–99) and **Viajes San Miguel** (✉ Sollano 4, ☎ 415/2–25–37 or 415/2–28–32, FAX 415/2–25–38).

VISITOR INFORMATION
Delegación de Turismo. ✉ *Southeast corner of Plaza Principal,* ☎ *415/2–17–47.* ☉ *Mon.–Sat. 10–4, Sun. 10–2.*

GUANAJUATO

Once Mexico's most prominent silver-mining city, Guanajuato is a colonial gem, tucked into the mountains at 6,700 feet. This provincial state capital is distinguished by twisting cobblestoned alleyways, pastel-walled houses, 15 shaded plazas, and a vast subterranean roadway (where a rushing river once flowed). In the center of town is Alhóndiga de Granaditas—an 18th-century grain-storage facility that was the site of the first battle in Mexico's War of Independence from Spain.

The city comes alive in mid-October with the International Cervantes Festival, a two-week-long celebration of the arts. Day-to-day affairs, however, continue as usual. Students still rush to class with books tucked under their arms, women eye fresh produce at the Mercado Hidalgo, and old men utter greetings from behind white-washed doorways. On weekend nights, *estudiantinas* (student minstrels dressed as medieval troubadours) serenade the public in the city squares.

At first Guanajuato's underground roadways and poorly marked streets may seem daunting. Armed with a good map and a sense of adventure, however, you can enjoy exploring the city's hidden passages. If you do get lost, just remember that the top of the Alhóndiga (which can be seen from many spots in town) points north, and the spires of the Basílica Colegiata Nuestra Señora de Guanajuato, at the Plaza de la Paz, point south.

Exploring Guanajuato

Although many of Guanajuato's major attractions are within walking distance of one another, the fact that the downtown is shaped like an oblong loop makes this a confusing city to get around. The map that you'll pick up at the tourist office probably won't make things too much clearer. It's difficult to notate on maps the frequent changes of street names—or the fact that many of the streets don't have signs.

A Good Walk

Numbers in the text correspond to numbers in the margin and on the Guanajuato map.

The tourist office, at Plaza de la Paz 14, is still a good place to begin a walking tour. Turn right and walk up Avenida Juárez to reach **Jardín Unión** ①, Guanajuato's central square. The ornate **Teatro Juárez** ② is just past the Jardín to your right on Calle Sopeña. The hardy might want to make a detour to **El Pípila** ③, a monument looming over the center of the city and a steep hour's climb. Those interested should bear right on Calle Sopeña just past the Teatro Juárez; a sign marked El Pípila will direct you onto Callejón de Calvario, which eventually leads up to the hillside memorial.

Head back into town via Calle Cantarranas, a main street that winds down the hill and around the Jardín Unión. Just before Calle Cantarranas changes its name to Calle Pocitos, you'll see the **University of Guanajuato** ④. A short way down from where Calle Cantarranas becomes Calle Pocitos is **El Museo Casa Diego Rivera** ⑤, birthplace of Mexico's famous muralist. Calle Pocitos weaves past more residences and eventually becomes Calle 28 de Septiembre. On the left, just past the junction with Mendizabal, looms the **Alhóndiga de Granaditas** ⑥, a former fortress since converted into a state museum. Head one block south to return to Avenida Juárez and the enclosed **Mercado Hidalgo** ⑦.

Turn right on Juárez as you leave the market and continue on until the road splits near the Jardín Reforma. Bear to the left and cut down Calle Reforma, a short alleyway lined with shops. Keep right at the end of the street and you'll come to two pleasant courtyards: Plaza San Roque, which hosts outdoor performances during the Cervantes Festival, and Plaza San Fernando, a shady square where many book fairs are held. This short detour will return you to Avenida Juárez, where it's a slight climb up to Plaza de la Paz, a square built from 1895 to 1898 and surrounded by some of the city's finest colonial buildings, including the 18th-century **Mansion del Conde de Rul** ⑧. Dominating the plaza is the imposing **Basílica Colegiata de Nuestra Señora de Guanajuato** ⑨, a bright yellow 17th-century Baroque church. If you continue up Avenida

Juárez about half a block past the plaza, you'll pass the tourist office again and arrive back at the Jardín Unión.

Sights to See

❻ Alhóndiga de Granaditas. A massive stone structure with horizontal slit windows, this 18th-century grain-storage facility served as a fortress during the War of Independence and the site of the courageous act of ☞ **El Pípila.** It is now a state museum with exhibits on local history, archaeology, and crafts. The hooks on which the Spanish Royalists impaled the heads of Father Hidalgo, Ignacio Allende, and two other independence leaders still hang on the exterior. ⊠ *Calle 28 de Septiembre 6,* ☎ *473/2–11–12.* ⊡ *About $4; free Sun.* ☉ *Tues.–Sat. 10–2 and 4–6, Sun. 10–3.*

❾ Basílica Colegiata de Nuestra Señora de Guanajuato. A 17th-century Baroque church painted a striking yellow, the Basílica dominates the Plaza de la Paz. Inside is the oldest Christian statue in Mexico, a bejeweled 8th-century statue of the Virgin. The highly venerated figure was a gift from King Philip II of Spain in 1557. On the Friday preceding Good Friday, miners, accompanied by floats and mariachi bands, parade to the basilica to pay homage to the Lady of Guanajuato. ⊠ *Between Calle Aguilar and Calle Obregón.*

❺ El Museo Casa Diego Rivera. This small museum is the birthplace of Mexico's best-known muralist, Diego Rivera. On view are 97 works by the master, among them his studies for the controversial mural commissioned for New York City's Rockefeller Center. Completed in 1933, the painting contained a portrait of Russian revolutionary Vladimir Lenin, which caused it to be removed immediately after it was displayed. The museum also contains family portraits, as well as the bed in which Rivera slept as a child and other family furniture. ⊠ *Calle Pocitos 47,* ☎ *473/2–11–97.* ☉ *Tues.–Sat. 10–2 and 4–6, Sun. 10–3.*

❸ El Pípila. An hour's walk from downtown is the monument to Juan José de los Ríos Martínez, a young soldier of the War of Independence of 1810. Nicknamed El Pípila, De los Ríos was a young miner who crept into the **Alhóndiga de Granaditas,** where Spanish Royalists were hiding. With a stone shield strapped to his back, he set the front door ablaze. He died, but the Spanish troops were captured by Father Hidalgo's army in this early battle, giving the independence forces their first major military victory. There's a splendid panoramic view of the city from the monument. It's easiest to take a taxi or a bus (marked Pípila) from the Jardín. ⊠ *Carretera Panorámica, on bluff above south side of Jardín Unión.*

❶ Jardín Unión. This tree-lined, wedge-shaped plaza is Guanajuato's central square. Two sides of the wedge are unnamed pedestrian walkways; the third is Avenida Juárez. On Thursday and Sunday evenings, musical performances take place in the bandshell here; at other times, groups of musicians break into impromptu song along the plaza's shaded tile walkways.

NEED A BREAK?   For alfresco dining at the Jardín, try the terrace at the **Hotel Museo Posada Santa Fe** (⊠ Jardín Unión 12, ☎ 473/2-00–84). The menu includes such pricey specialties as broiled trout and chicken with mole, but you can just order a cappuccino and a slice of cake. **El Agora** (⊠ El Agora del Baratillo, ☎ 473/2-33–00), an outdoor café located down an alley off the plaza's southeast corner, has less expensive offerings. A four-course lunch—including soup, rice, entrée, and dessert—runs about $4.

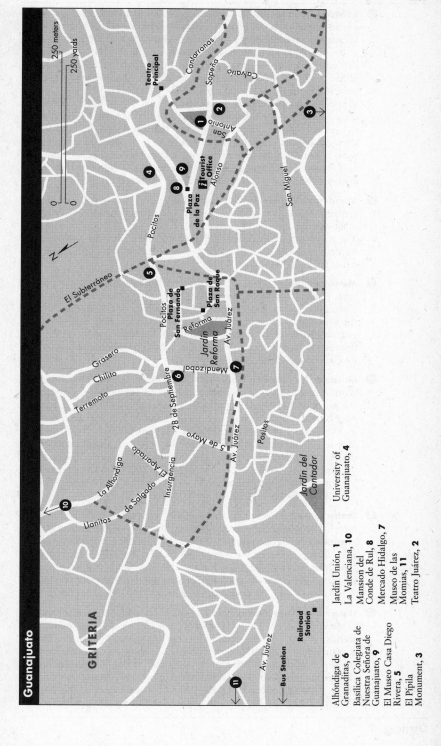

Guanajuato

GRITERIA

Teatro Principal

Cantarranas

Sopeña

Calvario

San Antonio

Tourist Office

Alonso

San Miguel

Plaza de la Paz

Pocitos

El Subterráneo

Pocitos

Plaza de San Fernando

Plaza de San Roque

Reforma

Av. Juárez

Jardín Reforma

Grasero

Chilito

Terremoto

Mendizábal

28 de Septiembre

La Alhóndiga

de Salgado

El Apartado

Insurgencia

5 de Mayo

Av. Juárez

Pósitos

Jardín del Cantador

University of Guanajuato, **4**

Llanitos

Av. Juárez

Railroad Station

Bus Station

250 meters

250 yards

Alhóndiga de Granaditas, **6**
Basílica Colegiata de Nuestra Señora de Guanajuato, **9**
El Museo Casa Diego Rivera, **5**
El Pípila Monument, **3**

Jardín Unión, **1**
La Valenciana, **10**
Mansion del Conde de Rul, **8**
Mercado Hidalgo, **7**
Museo de las Momias, **11**
Teatro Juárez, **2**

⑩ La Valenciana. Officially called La Iglesia de San Cayetano, this is one of the best-known colonial churches in all of Mexico. The pink stone facade, constructed over 20 years in the latter part of the 18th century, is brilliantly, baroquely ornate. Inside are three altars, each hand-carved in wood and covered in gilt, in separate styles: Plateresque, Chiaroscuro, and Baroque. There are also fine examples of religious painting from the viceregal period. The silver mine near the church, also called La Valenciana, is said to have produced one-fourth of all the silver in the world from the mid-1500s to the early 1800s. It's still in operation today. Although you can't descend into the 1,650-foot-deep mine shaft, if the caretaker is around he'll usually let you take a peek down. La Valenciana is included in any guided tour of the city, and there are also frequent buses (marked LA VALENCIANA) from the center. ⊠ *Carretera a Dolores Hidalgo, Km 2.*

⑧ Mansion del Conde de Rul. This 18th-century residence, now a government office, housed the count of Rul and Valenciana, who owned what was then the country's richest silver mine (☞ La Valenciana, *above*). The two-story structure was designed by famed Mexican architect Eduardo Tresguerras. ⊠ *Plaza de la Paz at Av. Juárez and Callejón del Estudiante.* ⊙ *Weekdays 8–3.*

⑦ Mercado Hidalgo. You can't miss this 1910 cast-iron-and-glass structure, reminiscent of Victorian England's train stations and markets. Though the balcony stalls are filled with T-shirts and cheap plastic toys, the lower level offers authentic local wares, including fresh produce, peanuts, honey-drenched nut candies, and colorful basketry. Vendors line the sidewalk in front of the market, hawking flowers and local crafts. ⊠ *Calle Juárez near Mendizabal.*

⑪ Museo de las Momias. For a macabre thrill, check out this unique museum located at the municipal cemetery off Calzada del Panteón, at the north end of town. In the museum, mummified human corpses—once buried in the cemetery—are on display. Until the law was amended in 1858, if a gravesite had not yet been paid for after five years, the corpse was removed to make room for new arrivals. Because of the mineral properties of the local soil, these cadavers (the oldest is about 100 years old) were in astonishingly good condition upon exhumation. The most gruesome are exhibited in glass cases. ⊠ *Panteón Municipal,* ☎ *473/2–06–39.* ▦ *About $1.50.* ⊙ *Daily 9–6.*

❷ Teatro Juárez. Adorned with bronze lion sculptures and a line of large Greek muses looming over the Jardín from the roof, the theater was inaugurated by Mexican dictator Porfirio Díaz in 1903 with a performance of *Aïda*. It now serves as the principal venue of the annual International Cervantes Festival (☞ Nightlife and the Arts, *below*). A brief tour of the Art Deco interior is available for a nominal fee. ⊠ *Calle de Sopeña,* ☎ *473/2–01–83.* ⊙ *Tues.–Sat. 9–2 and 5:15–7:45, Sun. 10–2.*

❹ University of Guanajuato. Founded in 1732, the university was formerly a Jesuit seminary. The original Baroque church, La Compañia, still stands next door. The current university building, built in the 1950s, was designed to blend in with the town's architecture, but the modern interior is at odds with the colonial facade. If you do wander inside, check out the bulletin boards for notices of cultural events in town. (Also check bulletin boards along the pedestrian walkways of the Jardín.) ⊠ *Calle Pocitos, 1 block north of Plaza de la Paz,* ☎ *473/2–00–06.*

Dining

Guanajuato's better restaurants are located in hotels near the Jardín la Unión and on the highway to Dolores Hidalgo. For simpler fare, private establishments around town offer a good variety of Mexican and international dishes. Dress tends to be casual in this provincial university town.

$$$ ✕ **El Comedor Real.** Continental cuisine served in a medieval environment
★ defines El Comedor Real. The bright whitewashed and brick-domed restaurant in the Hotel Castillo Santa Cecilia serves such specialties as *filete pimiente* (steak with peppercorns), breaded trout with tartar sauce, and fish soup with vegetables. Troubadours perform every Friday and Saturday at 10:30 PM at La Cava, the bar next door. ⊠ *Carretera a la Valenciana s/n,* ☎ *473/2–04–85. AE, MC, V.*

$$ ✕ **El Retiro.** This traditional Mexican restaurant up the street from the Teatro Juárez lives up to its name, the Retreat. Though it is often crowded for the main midday meal, at other times you can relax with a steaming cappuccino and listen to classical music. A full *comida corrida* runs about $4; for more substantial fare, try the mole poblano with chicken, broiled steak with mushroom sauce, or a Spanish omelet. ⊠ *Calle de Sopeña 12,* ☎ *473/2–06–22. Reservations not accepted. MC, V.*

$$ ✕ **Tasca de los Santos.** This cozy restaurant, located across the street
★ from the Basílica, specializes in Spanish and international cuisines. Recommended dishes include the *sopa de mariscos* (shellfish soup with shrimp, clams, and crabs) and *filete parrilla* (grilled beef with baked potatoes and spinach). *Huevos Reina* is a delicious light dish consisting of eggs and mushrooms baked in a cheese and wine sauce. Dine indoors or outside under white umbrellas on the plaza, with a view of the fountain. A variety of music, ranging from French to Russian, enhances the cosmopolitan mood. ⊠ *Plaza de la Paz 28,* ☎ *473/2–23–20. MC, V.*

$ ✕ **El Pingüis Cafeteria.** Cheap and plentiful food attracts the university crowd to this spartan eatery decorated with Mexican art posters. A midday meal consisting of soup, Mexican rice, a chicken or beef dish, dessert, and coffee costs about $3. The *café americano* is excellent, as is the *consume de verduras* (vegetable soup). The service can be slow, but vibrant music and a lively crowd will keep you entertained. ⊠ *Jardín la Unión at Allende 3,* ☎ *473/2–14–14. Reservations not accepted. No credit cards.*

$ ✕ **El Unicorno Azul.** Those growing weary of heavy meat dishes might want to stop by this food counter just behind Jardín la Unión: It offers fruit drinks, yogurt, and vegetarian hamburgers and sandwiches. Next door is a health-food store under the same ownership. ⊠ *Agora del Baratillo,* ☎ *473/2–07–00. No credit cards.*

$ ✕ **Restaurant Valadez.** Dark wood-paneled walls give way to large windows overlooking the Teatro Juárez at this downtown restaurant. House dishes include *filete à la Tampiqueña* (beefsteak served with guacamole, cheese enchiladas, and beans), hamburger Valadez (topped with cheese and bacon), and crepes with tequila and blackberries. The bar serves Campari, Dubonnet, and tequila drinks for less than $2. ⊠ *Jardín la Unión 3,* ☎ *473/2–11–57. MC, V.*

Lodging

Guanajuato's less expensive hotels are located along Avenida Juárez and Calle de la Alhóndiga. Moderately priced and upscale properties are near the Jardín la Unión and on the outskirts of town. It's best to secure reservations at least six months in advance if you plan to attend the Cervantes Festival, which usually runs from mid- to late October.

$$$ ⊡ **Hotel Museo Posada Santa Fe.** This colonial-style property, located at the Jardín la Unión, has been in operation since 1862. Large historic paintings by local artist Don Manuel Leal hang in the wood-paneled lobby; a sweeping carpeted stairway leads to second-floor quarters. Each room—decorated in warm, autumnal colors—has a wood minibar, color TV, and telephone. Rooms facing the plaza can be noisy; quieter rooms face narrow alleyways. ⊠ *Plaza Principal at Jardín la Unión 12, 36000,* ☎ *473/2–00–84 or 473/2–02–07,* FAX *473/2–46–53. 47 rooms with bath. Restaurant, bar, outdoor hot tub. AE, MC, V.*

$$–$$$ 🏨 **Parador San Javier.** This immaculately restored hacienda was con-
   ★   verted into a hotel in 1971. In fact, a safe from the Hacienda San Javier and old wood trunks still decorate the large, plant-laden lobby. The rooms are clean and have attractive appointments: lace curtains, crisp coverlets, and blue-and-white–tiled baths. There are 16 rooms that feature some rugged colonial detail, reached via a stone archway. A word of caution: Large convention groups sometimes crowd the facility. ⊠ *Plaza Aldama 92, 36000,* ☎ *473/2–06–26,* FAX *473/2–31–14. 115 rooms with bath. 2 restaurants, bar, café, outdoor pool, dance club. AE, MC, V.*

$$ 🏨 **Hostería del Frayle.** Just a half block off Jardín la Unión, this quiet four-story lodging was once the Casa de Moneda, where ore was taken to be refined after it was brought out of the mines. Built in 1673 and turned into a hotel in the mid-1960s, it features whitewashed plaster and wood-beamed rooms arranged around a small maze of stairways, landings, and courtyards; all have TVs and telephones, and some afford excellent views of the Pípila, Teatro Juárez, and Jardín la Unión. The staff is extremely friendly and helpful. ⊠ *Calle Sopeña 3,* ☎ *473/2–11–79,* FAX *473/2–11–79, ext. 138. 37 rooms with bath. Restaurant-bar. MC, V.*

$ 🏨 **Hotel Socavón.** One of Guanajuato's newer hotels, this modest five-story property was built in 1981. Don't be put off by the gloomy, tunnel-like entrance: Open-air walkways, with views of surrounding mountains, lead to guest quarters. Each room—simply furnished with a bed, desk, and television—has a wood-beamed ceiling and a modern bath. Fourth-floor corner rooms offer some good views. ⊠ *Calle de la Alhóndiga 41A, 36000,* ☎ *473/2–48–85 or 473/2–66–66. 37 rooms with bath. Restaurant. AE, MC, V.*

Nightlife and the Arts

Guanajuato, on most nights a somnolent provincial capital, awakens each fall for the **International Cervantes Festival.** During two weeks in October world-renowned actors, musicians, and dance troupes (which have included the Bolshoi Ballet) perform nightly at the Teatro Juárez and at other venues in town. The Plaza San Roque, a small square near the Jardín Reforma, hosts a series of *Entremeses Cervantinos*—swashbuckling one-act farces by classical Spanish writers. Grandstand seats require advance tickets, but crowds often gather by the edge of the plaza for free. If you plan to be in Guanajuato for the festival, contact the Festival Internacional Cervantino office in Mexico City (⊠ Alvaro Obregón 273, piso 3, Colonia Roma, 06700, ☎ 5/533–4122) or Ticketmaster (☎ 5/325–9000) at least six months in advance for top-billed events.

At other times of the year, nightlife in Guanajuato is mostly relegated to dramatic, dance, and musical performances at the **Teatro Juárez** (⊠ Calle de Sopeña, ☎ 473/2–01–83) and the **Teatro Principal** (⊠ Calle Hidalgo, ☎ 473/2–15–23), which has begun showing American movies several times a week. Some hotels, including the Parador San Javier and the Castillo Santa Cecilia, provide evening musical entertainment. There are also several nightclubs located in or near the downtown area, including **Discoteque El Pequeño Juan** (⊠ Panorámica Al Pípila at Callejón de Guadalupe, ☎ 473/2–23–08), whose panoramic view of the city at night is stunning, and the small but lively **Discoteque La Fragua** (⊠ Calle Tepetapa 45, ☎ 473/2–27–15).

Side Trip

León

56 km (35 mi) northwest of Guanajuato.

Best known as the shoemaking capital of Mexico, León is also an important center for industry and commerce. With more than 1 million people, it is the state's most populous urban area.

If you know footwear and have the time (and patience) to browse through the downtown shops, you may find some good buys in León. First try the **Plaza de Zapatos,** a mall with 70 stores located on Boulevard Adolfo López Mateos, roughly one block from the bus station. From here take a taxi west (about a 10-minute ride) to the **Zona Peatonal,** a pedestrian zone with several shoe stores. On **Calle Praxedis Guerrero** there are various artisans' stands selling leather goods.

Flecha Amarilla buses leave Guanajuato's Central Camionera every 15 minutes for León; the ride takes about 45 minutes and costs less than $1. Pick up a map of León at the tourist office in Guanajuato.

Guanajuato A to Z

Arriving and Departing

BY BUS

Direct bus service is available between the Central del Norte (North Bus Station) in Mexico City and Guanajuato's Central Camionera (☎ 473/3–13–33); taxis to downtown from the Camionera cost $3 to $4. Several lines—including **Flecha Amarilla** and **Estrella Blanca**—offer hourly service; travel time is about five hours.

BY CAR

Guanajuato is 432 kilometers (268 miles) northwest of Mexico City via Route 57 (to Querétaro) and Route 45 (through Celaya and Irapuato), approximately a five-hour drive.

BY PLANE

Guanajuato International Airport is 56 kilometers (35 miles) north of Guanajuato. *See* Arriving and Departing by Plane *in* San Miguel A to Z, *above,* for international carriers that service this airport. The one-hour taxi ride from the airport to town costs about $25.

Getting Around

Don't bother with a car in Guanajuato. Many of the attractions are within strolling distance of one another and located between Avenida Juárez and Calle Pocitos, the city's two major north–south arteries. The twisting subterranean roadway—El Subterráneo—also has a primarily north–south orientation.

BY TAXI

Nonmetered taxis can be hailed on the street or found at *sitios* (taxi stands) near the Jardín la Unión, Plaza de la Paz, and Mercado Hidalgo.

Contacts and Resources

EMERGENCIES

Police (☎ 473/2–02–66). **Ambulance–Red Cross** (☎ 473/2–04–87). **Hospital General** (☎ 473/3–15–77 or 473/3–15–76). Note: Few people in Guanajuato have a good command of English, so in an emergency it's best to contact your hotel manager or the tourist office.

GUIDED TOURS

Transporte Exclusivo de Turismo (⊠ Av. Juárez and Calle 5 de Mayo, ☎ 473/2−59−68) is a kiosk that offers several tours of Guanajuato and its environs. A 3½-hour tour, with an English-speaking guide, of the Museum of Mummies, the church and mines of Valenciana, the monument to Pípila, the Panoramic Highway, subterranean streets, and residential neighborhoods costs $18 per person, minimum six people. A five-hour evening tour of the Pípila monument and one or two nightclubs, including one drink, is about $20 per person, minimum six people. *Estudiantinas* perform during the weekend tours.

PHARMACY

A recommended pharmacy is **El Fenix** (⊠ Juárez 104, ☎ 473/2−61−40). It is open Monday–Saturday 7:45 AM–9:45 PM, Sunday 8:45 AM–9 PM.

TRAVEL AGENCIES

Viajes Georama, the American Express representative (⊠ Plaza de la Paz 34, ☎ 473/2−59−09, 473/2−19−54, or 473/2−51−01; FAX 473/2−35−97); **Viajes Mandel** (⊠ Plaza de la Paz 62, ☎ 473/2−60−37 or 473/2−71−95, FAX 473/2−60−89).

VISITOR INFORMATION

The **Guanajuato tourist office** is at the back of a courtyard. ⊠ *Plaza de la Paz 14,* ☎ *473/2−15−74, 473/2−00−86, or 473/2−19−82;* FAX *473/2−42−51.* ⊘ *Weekdays 8:30−7:30, weekends 10−2.*

There is also a **tourist information kiosk** at the Central Camionera bus station.

ZACATECAS

In colonial days Zacatecas was the largest silver-producing city in the world and sent great treasures of the precious metal to the king of Spain. Still a large silver-mining center, with factories producing silver jewelry and trade schools training apprentices in the fine art of handmade silver craft, Zacatecas is a relatively undiscovered jewel for tourists. Although it is a state capital with a population of some 300,000, it has the feel of a much smaller place; the town is kept spotlessly clean by Zacatecan pride, under a mandate by the governor of the state of Zacatecas. This destination is also famous for its historical role as the scene of one of Pancho Villa's most spectacular battles and for its 18th-century colonial architecture.

One of the town's unique charms is the *tambora,* a musical walk up and down the streets and alleyways led by a *tamborazo,* a typical local band that shatters the evening quiet with merriment. Also known as a *callejóneada* (*callejón* means "alley"), the tambora is a popular free-for-all, in which everyone along the way either joins in the procession or leans from balconies and doorways to cheer the group on. During the December *feria* (festival), the tamborazos play night and day as they serenade the Virgin of Zacatecas.

Exploring Zacatecas

Most of Zacatecas's colonial sights are located near the center of the city, making it an easy place to explore on foot. There is rarely much traffic in town, an added bonus. By walking or taking a taxi up to the mine, a visitor can then take an elevator to a nearby hilltop and take the cable car across the city to the opposite side and take a taxi or bus down, making a convenient loop tour.

A Good Walk

Numbers in the text correspond to numbers in the margin and on the Zacatecas map.

Start your tour at the Plaza de Armas, in the center of the city. Here you'll find the **Catedral de Zacatecas** ① and the **Palacio del Gobierno** ②. Across the street from the plaza are two beautiful colonial buildings worth exploring; one is known as the **Palacio de la Mala Noche** ③ because of a local legend. Go to the Plaza Santo Domingo, two blocks west of the cathedral, to see the **Pedro Coronel Museum** ④ and the 17th-century **Templo de Santo Domingo** ⑤ right next door. To visit the museum of the other Coronel brother—both were equally fanatical art collectors—return to the cathedral, turn left on Avenida Hidalgo, and walk about a kilometer (half a mile) north of the plaza to the **Rafael Coronel Museum** ⑥.

For a longer walk, head south on Avenida Hidalgo until you come to Juárez, then go right (roughly west) up the hill, passing the several-block-long Alameda park and the Social Security Hospital to arrive at the **Eden Mine** ⑦. Following a tour of the mine, visitors can take an elevator up to Cerro del Grillo (Cricket Hill) and catch the **Teleferico** ⑧ cable car across the city to **Cerro de la Bufa** ⑨, site of Pancho Villa's famous battle.

Sights to See

❶ **Catedral de Zacatecas.** The ornate cathedral is considered one of the best examples of Mexican Baroque style in the country. Each of the facades tells a different legend; according to one of them, an anticlerical governor of the state used the cathedral's silver cross and baptismal font to mint Zacatecas's first silver coins. ⊠ *South side of Plaza de Armas on Av. Hidalgo.*

NEED A BREAK?	The **Café y Neveria Acropolis** (⊠ Av. Hidalgo at Plazuela Candelario Huizar, ☏ 492/2-12-84), alongside the cathedral, is an ice cream parlor in the daytime and a coffeehouse at night. Come here for Turkish coffee (under $1), ice cream, and other desserts. Breakfast is served from 8 to 12:30.

❾ **Cerro de la Bufa.** The city trademark, this rugged hill is the site of Pancho Villa's definitive battle against dictator Victoriano Huerta in June 1914. The spacious **Plaza de la Revolución,** paved with the three shades of pink Zacatecan stone, is crowned with three huge equestrian statues of Villa and two other heroes, Felipe Angeles and Panfilo Natera. Also on the site are the **Sanctuary of the Virgin of Patrocinio,** a chapel dedicated to the patron of the city, and the **Museo de la Toma de Zacatecas,** which has nine rooms filled with historic objects such as guns, newspapers, furniture, and clothing from the days of Pancho Villa. On the very tip-top of the hill there's a meteorological observatory; you'll need to get special permission from the Zacatecas tourist office to visit. ⊠ *If driving, follow Av. Hidalgo north from town to Av. Juan de Tolosa; turn right and continue until you come to a fountain; take first immediate right off retorno onto Calle Mexicapan, which leads to Carretera Panorámica. Turn right to signposted Carretera La Bufa, which leads to top of hill. Museum,* ☏ 492/2-80-66. ☞ *$1.* ☉ *Tues.–Sun. 10–5.*

❼ **Eden Mine.** Now a tourist attraction, El Mina Eden supplied most of Zacatecas's silver from 1586 until 1960. An open mine train runs down into the underground tunnels; there is a small gift shop at the entrance. The tour (for a nominal fee) is in Spanish, but you'll have no trouble imagining what the life of the miners was like. Be sure to wear sturdy shoes. Remember that mines are pretty dark, and this one is no exception; through much of the tour, your only light may be the guide's flashlight. Farther down the train track there is another stop at, of all places, a discotheque (☞ Nightlife and the Arts, *below*). ⊠ *Entrance on Antonio Dovali off Av. Torreon beyond Alameda García de la Cadena,* ☎ *492/2–30–02.* ☟ *$2.* ⊙ *Daily 10–6.*

❸ Palacio de la Mala Noche. The Palace of the Bad Night is one of two beautiful 18th-century colonial buildings, both declared national monuments, right across from the downtown plaza. They are built from native pink stone and have lacy ironwork balconies. One of them now houses the Radisson Paraiso Zacatecas Hotel (☞ Lodging, *below*), and the other is presently a municipal building known as La Palacio de la Mala Noche. Legend has it that this was the home of a silver-mine owner who was called upon so often to help the needy that he built a hidden door from which he could enter and leave the palace undisturbed. One night a terrible storm was raging, yet a worker had the temerity to pound on the front door. He finally gained entrance with his good news: Silver had been found in a mine considered exhausted. Up the hill along the side of the palace, you will find the so-called hidden door. ⊠ *Av. Hidalgo 639.* ⊙ *Weekdays 10–2 and 4–7.*

❷ Palacio del Gobierno. The Governor's Palace is an 18th-century mansion containing flower-filled courtyards and, on the main staircase, a powerful mural depicting the history of Zacatecas. ⊠ *East side of Plaza de Armas.*

❹ Pedro Coronel Museum. Originally a Jesuit monastery, this building was used as a jail in the 18th century. The museum is one of a kind in Mexico and Latin America, housing the work of Zacatecan artist and sculptor Pedro Coronel and his extensive collection of the works of Picasso, Dali, Miró, Braque, and Chagall among others, as well as an abundance of art from Africa, China, Japan, India, Greece, and Egypt. ⊠ *Av. Fernando Villalpando at Plaza Santo Domingo,* ☎ *492/2–80– 21.* 🎫 *Mon.–Sat. about $1.50; free Sun.* ⊙ *Mon.–Wed., Fri., and Sat. 10–2 and 4–7; Sun. 10–5.*

❻ Rafael Coronel Museum. The museum is in the Ex-Convento de San Francisco, northeast of the town center toward Lomas del Calvario. Its 18th-century facade of mellowed pink tones conceals a rambling structure of open-arched corridors, all leading through garden patios to rooms that contain an amazing collection of some 3,700 *máscaras* (masks)—including saints and devils, wise men and fools, animals and humans—used in regional festivals all over Mexico. There is also an outstanding display of puppets. ⊠ *Off Vergel Nuevo between Chaveño and Garcia Salinas,* ☎ *492/2–81–16.* 🎫 *About $1.50; free Sun.* ⊙ *Mon., Tues., and Thurs.–Sat. 10–2 and 4–7; Sun. 10–5.*

❽ Teleferico. The only cable car in the world that crosses an entire city, the Teleferico takes passengers from Cerro del Grillo (Cricket Hill) above the Eden Mine to Cerro de la Bufa and runs from 10 to 7 daily. True, it crosses at the narrowest point, but it presents a magnificent panoramic view of the city and its many Baroque church domes and spires. It's also well worth the cost (about a dollar) to get the ride up to Cerro de la Bufa, which is quite a climb up otherwise. The price is the same whether you ride both ways or walk one. ⊠ *Cerro del Grillo station of Teleferico is just off Paseo Díaz Ordaz, a steep walk from plaza, no phone.* ⊙ *Daily noon–7:30.*

❺ Templo de Santo Domingo. Built by the Jesuits in the 18th century, this church has an ornate Baroque facade and an elaborate interior, including gold-leaf religious paintings. The sacristy also contains a collection of religious art. ⊠ *Av. Fernando Villalpando at Plaza Santo Domingo.*

Dining

Several of Zacatecas's better restaurants are located in hotels; another is right in El Mercado, the boutique area on Calle Hidalgo near the cathedral. Other popular restaurants can be found on Avenida Juárez, which intersects Hidalgo. Unless otherwise indicated, dress is casual.

$$$$ ✕ Quinta Real. In the Quinta Real hotel, this elaborate, formal restaurant with white tablecloths and flowers on the tables serves fine Continental cuisine, with such specialties as medallion of beef in a tangy port sauce and desserts flambéed at the table. There is also a bar. ⊠ *Gonzáles Ortega at aqueduct,* ☎ *492/2–91–04 or 492/2–91–05. AE, MC, V.*

$$$ ✕ Candiles. This popular downtown meeting place is situated in the Radisson Paraiso Zacatecas hotel, a great spot to observe the local business crowd as well as the interesting assortment of hotel guests. Candiles has cream-and-vermilion walls, arches, and soft lighting. Black lacquer slatted chairs contrast with white tablecloths and crystal. The impressive menu includes both Continental and regional dishes. Try the veal marsala or the *filete pimienta* (steak with peppercorns). ⊠ *Radisson Paraiso Zacatecas hotel, Av. Hidalgo 703,* ☎ *492/2–61–83. Reservations not accepted. AE, MC, V.*

$$$ ✕ La Cuija. Zacatecas specialties such as an appetizer basket filled with four sweet varieties of cactus flower, peeled and juicy, are the rule here. Also try the *pollo adobada* (chicken in a rich chili sauce) or *carne à la Mexicana* (beef grilled with tomatoes, onion, and salsa). The decor approximates a wine cellar, and in addition to fine food, the restaurant serves wine from the owner's Cachola Vineyards (☞ Side Trips, *below*).

A traditional Mexican trio plays Thursday–Sunday evenings. ✉ *Centro Commercial El Mercado,* ☎ *492/2–82–75. MC, V.*

$ ✗ **Cenaduria Los Dorados.** Enchilada lovers should be sure not to miss this quiet little restaurant, a local favorite just a few blocks northeast of the cathedral. Among the 12 different varieties available here are the excellent *enchiladas Villistas*—tortillas stacked like pancakes filled with chicken or cheese. A side order of guacamole and chips is huge and very tasty. ✉ *Plazuela de García 1314,* ☎ *492/2–57–22. No credit cards.*

$ ✗ **Rancho Viejo.** This informal ranch-style restaurant serves dishes with a Zacatecan flavor, including *huchepos* (tamales with sour cream) and enchiladas covered with vegetables and a rich red chili sauce. ✉ *Av. Universidad 101,* ☎ *492/2–67–47. AE, MC, V.*

Lodging

Many of Zacatecas's best lodgings are in the city's treasured historic buildings, which have been preserved in all their 18th- and 19th-century beauty. Others are situated in the surrounding mountains and have wonderful views of the picturesque city as well as the silver-mined hills.

$$$$ ▦ **Mesón de Jobito.** Built in the early half of the 19th century, this build-
★ ing has been a hotel for well over a hundred years but only came to its current owners in 1992. It combines the amenities of a luxury hotel with the pleasant, relaxed ambience of a hacienda: The reception area is a tastefully decorated *sala* where the guests sit down on antique chairs to sign in. Two levels of guest rooms, painted in rich colors and decorated in a modern but tasteful style, surround a narrow courtyard. The staff is extremely friendly and helpful. The pervasively restful atmosphere is enhanced by the Mesón's perfect location on a blissfully quiet little plaza just a few blocks from the cathedral. ✉ *Jardín Juárez 143, 98000,* ☎ FAX *492/4–17–22. 31 rooms with bath. Restaurant, bar. AE, MC, V.*

$$$$ ▦ **Quinta Real.** This hotel must be one of the most unusual in Mexico—or any country: It is built around Mexico's oldest bullring, the second one constructed in the Western Hemisphere. Although spirited bullfight music plays softly in the background, matadors no longer face the snorting beasts here. Instead, the terrazzo-paved ring provides a unique view for the 49 guest rooms, each with a balcony overlooking the *plaza de toro.* Large and bright, the rooms are decorated in pastel fabrics that complement the dark traditional furniture. The bar occupies some of the former bull pens, and an outdoor café with bright-yellow umbrellaed tables occupies two levels of the spectator area. ✉ *Gonzáles Ortega at aqueduct, 98000,* ☎ *492/2–91–04, 492/2–91–05, 492/2–91–06, 492/2–91–07, or 800/426–0494;* FAX *492/2–84–40. Restaurant, bar, café. AE, MC, V.*

$$$$ ▦ **Radisson Paraiso Zacatecas.** Facing the Plaza de Armas and the cathedral in the heart of the city, the Radisson is in one of Zacatecas's beautiful old colonial buildings, which has been declared a national monument. The pink-stone facade dates from the 18th century, and the more recent additions match perfectly. Rooms are decorated in cream, blue, and fuschia and furnished with copies of Spanish antiques as well as modern pieces. Those facing the plaza are susceptible to late-night and early morning tamborazo music during festivals; on the other hand, from your small balcony you'll get a great view of the goings-on. The rooms facing the interior courtyard are quieter. ✉ *Av. Hidalgo 703, Colonia Centro, 98000,* ☎ *492/2–61–83, 492/2–61–84, 492/2–61–85, 492/2–61–86, or 492/2–61–87; in the U.S., 800/333–3333;*

FAX *492/2–65–45. 115 rooms with bath. Restaurant, bar, convention center. AE, MC, V.*

$$$ ▦ **Holiday Inn.** One of the most modern hotels in Zacatecas, this pleasant property is located only three blocks from the historic town center. From the bay windows of its front rooms you can see over the rooftops of the whitewashed dome of the beautiful Baroque-style Templo San José. Rooms—all with satellite TV, individual climate control, and marble baths—are done in cool blue, green, and white; furnishings include Mexican chests painted white and lacy white ironwork headboards. The staff is extremely friendly and helpful. ✉ *Blvd. López Matéos y Callejón del Barro, 98000,* ☎ *492/2–33–11; in the U.S., 800/465–4329;* FAX *492/2–34–15. 131 rooms with bath, 4 suites. Restaurant, bar, coffee shop, indoor pool, sauna, 2 squash courts, nightclub, meeting rooms. AE, MC, V.*

$$ ▦ **Motel del Bosque.** *Bosque* means "forest" or "woods" in Spanish, and this clean and quiet motel near the greenbelt offers a superb view of Zacatecas. Close to the Teleferico station at Cerro del Grillo high above the city, yet not terribly far from the center, the motel has clean, carpeted bungalows spread along the hillside in rows and divided by cobblestoned parking areas. ✉ *Paseo Díaz Ordaz, 98000,* ☎ *492/2–07–45, 492/2–07–46, or 492/2–07–47. 70 rooms with bath. Restaurant. AE, MC, V.*

Nightlife and the Arts

If only for its uniqueness, a must-visit is **El Malacate** (☎ 492/2–30–02), the discotheque in the El Mina Eden, a stop on the Eden Mine train and more than 1,000 feet underground. It's best to make reservations at this popular place, which is both crowded and noisy. There is a $5 cover charge. Atop a mountain outside Zacatecas is **El Elefante Blanco** (✉ Mina La Gallega 15, ☎ 492/2–71–04), a discotheque with a panoramic view of the city. For some surprisingly good local blues and jazz, head to **Arcano** (✉ Hidalgo 111, downstairs, ☎ 492/2–05–38), a small lounge-bar favored by the Zacatecas art and intellectual crowd. The band plays Thursday through Saturday until 1 AM. There's live music in the lobby bar of the **Radisson Paraiso Zacatecas,** and the **Holiday Inn** has a nightclub with live entertainment (☞ Lodging, *above,* for both).

Shopping

Crafts

Opposite the east end of the Plaza de Armas is **La Cazzorra** (✉ Hidalgo 713, ☎ 492/4–04–84), a collectibles shop with authentic antiques, books about Zacatecas, wood furniture, Huichol art, and ceramics. The owners—husband and wife—are a good source of information about the city.

Silver

Since this is a silver town, you won't want to miss a visit to the **Centro Platero Zacatecas** (✉ Colonia Bernardez, ☎ 492/3–10–07), a school and factory for fine handmade silver jewelry and other items; it's housed in the 18th-century mansion of Don Ignacio de Bernardez. It's fascinating to watch student silversmiths master this fine tradition. The factory's shop is located downtown in **Centro Commercial El Mercado** (✉ Calle Hidalgo, next to cathedral), a group of boutiques in what was once a covered market.

Side Trips

Guadalupe
7 km (4 mi) southeast of Zacatecas.

Those interested in colonial art and architecture should not miss seeing this small town. Its centerpiece is the **Ex-Convento de Guadalupe,** founded by Franciscan monks in 1707. It currently houses the **Museo de Arte Virreinal** (*virreinal* means "viceregal," or colonial), run by the Instituto Nacional de Antropología y Historia. The convent is itself a work of art, with its Baroque-style Templo de Guadalupe and the Capilla de Nápoles, but even more impressive is the stunning collection of art under its roof. Works by Miguel Cabrera, Nicolás Rodriguez Juárez, Cristóbal de Villalpando, and Andrés López are included, among others. ✉ *Jardín Juárez s/n,* ☎ *492/3–23–86.* 🎫 *$2.50; free Sun.* 🕐 *Tues.–Sun. 10–5.*

Cachola Vins
27 km (16 mi) east of Zacatecas.

A visit to this award-winning vineyard in Valle de las Arsinas is a worthwhile side trip. The cold winters, mild springtimes, and temperate summers in the valley produced a silver medal for the vineyard's 1986 Cachola French Columbard at the VINEXPO 1991 in France. Tours of the vineyard are best arranged beforehand, especially if you would like a tasting. ✉ *Cruce de Carretera Panamericana, Km 634, Las Arsinas, Guadalupe,* ☎ *492/2–72–56.*

Zona Arqueológica La Quemada
50 km (30 mi) southwest of Zacatecas.

This ancient city was already a ruin before the Spaniards arrived in the 16th century. Seven different Indian cultures built one community atop the other, and the present site rises high above the plain. The spot is totally undeveloped as a tourist attraction, making the climb quite rugged, but once you reach the top, the whole area spreads out below you. The edifices—what remain of them—appear to be constructed of thin slabs of stone wedged into place. The principal draw is a group of rose-colored ruins containing 11 large, round columns built entirely of the same small slabs of rock seen in the rest of the ruins. 🎫 *$3; free Sun.* 🕐 *Tues.–Sun. 10–5.*

Zacatecas A to Z

Arriving and Departing

BY BUS
Omnibus de México operates several first- and second-class buses daily from Mexico City to Zacatecas.

BY CAR
Zacatecas is 603 kilometers (375 miles) northwest of Mexico City via Route 57 (to Querétaro and San Luis Potosi) and Route 49, approximately a 7½- to 8-hour drive.

BY PLANE
Mexicana (☎ 492/2–74–29, 492/2–74–70, or 492/2–32–48) has direct service to Zacatecas from Chicago, Denver, and Los Angeles. In Zacatecas, the Mexicana Airlines office is located on Hidalgo. The airport is 29 kilometers (18 miles) north of town; **Aerotransportes** (☎ 492/2–59–46) provides transportation. A taxi ride to town will cost about $25.

Getting Around

You can reach most of the town-center attractions by foot, although you will need to rent a car or hire a taxi if you want to tour a mine or take a ride on the Teleferico (cable car) to the top of Cerro de la Bufa. The city has an excellent and inexpensive bus system.

Contacts and Resources

EMERGENCIES

Police (☎ 492/2–01–80). **Red Cross** (☎ 492/2–30–05). **Hospital** (☎ 492/3–30–04). **Emergency Service** (☎ 06). English is not generally spoken in Zacatecas, so it's best to contact your hotel manager or the tourist office in case of an emergency.

GUIDED TOURS

Viajes Mazzoco (✉ Enlace 115, ☎ 492/2–08–59 or 492/2–51–59, ☎ FAX 492/2–55–59), a well-established travel agency and the local American Express representative, can arrange tours of the city center, the Eden Mine, the Teleferico, and La Bufa for about $25 per person.

PHARMACY

Farmacia Isstezac (✉ Dr. Ignacio Hierro 522, ☎ 492/2–80–89) is open 24 hours a day.

VISITOR INFORMATION

The **tourist information** booth (Módulo de Información Turistica) is located near the town cathedral. ✉ *Av. Hidalgo 629, no phone.* �) *Weekdays 9–8, Sat. 9–7, Sun. 9–5.*

The state **Dirección Estatal de Turismo** is across from the train station. ✉ *Prolongación Gonzalez s/n,* ☎ *492/4–05–52 or 492/4–03–93,* FAX *492/2–93–29.*

QUERÉTARO

A state capital and industrial center of nearly 800,000 people, Querétaro, like other Bajío cities, has played a significant role in Mexican history. In 1810, in the home of Josefa Ortiz de Domínguez—a heroine of the independence movement known as La Corregidora—the first plans for independence were hatched. In 1848 the Mexican-American War was concluded in this city with the signing of the Treaty of Guadalupe Hidalgo. Emperor Maximilian made his last stand here in 1867 and was executed by firing squad in the Cerro de las Campañas (Hill of the Church Bells), north of town. A small memorial chapel, built by the Austrian government, marks the spot. A gigantic statue of Benito Juárez crowns a park on the crest of the hill just above it. In 1917 the Mexican Constitution, which still governs the land, was signed in this city.

Throughout Querétaro are markers, museums, churches, and monuments that commemorate the city's heroes and historic moments. A prevailing sense of civic pride is evident in the impeccably renovated mansions, the flower-draped cobblestoned pedestrian walkways, and the hospitable plazas, which are softly lit at night. The people are among the most congenial in central Mexico and are quick to share their favorite sites and tales with travelers.

Querétaro is also renowned for opals—red, green, honey, and fire stones, as opposed to the blue Australian kind. However, visitors should beware of street vendors, who may sell opals so full of water that they crumble shortly after purchase; depend upon reputable dealers (☞ Shopping, *below*).

Exploring Querétaro

Though Querétaro's boundaries extend for some distance, the historic district is in the heart of town. A day or two can easily be spent here, visiting museums, admiring the architecture, and learning the local history.

A Good Walk

Numbers in the text correspond to numbers in the margin and on the Querétaro map.

Most of the city's sights are near the **Plaza Independencia** ①. The **Palacio del Gobierno del Estado** ② is on the plaza's northwest corner; if you walk around the square counterclockwise, you'll come to the **Palacio de Justicia,** originally built as a mansion for the wealthy Domingo Iglesia and, beside it, the **Casa de Ecala** ③. Just past the Casa de Ecala is Avenida Libertad Oriente, one of the city's bougainvillea-draped pedestrian walkways. Turn west here and walk two blocks to reach Calle Corregidora. Bear right again, and in the middle of a long block you'll find the entrance to the **Museo Regional de Querétaro** ④. Cross the street to Avenida Madero, another "pedway," this one lined with shops. The city's main square, **Jardín Obregón,** will be on your right.

One block past Avenida Juárez on the corner of Allende Sur, you'll see the former **Casa de la Marquesa,** an old hacienda recently converted into a hotel (☞ Lodging, *below*). Across Allende, next to the Church of Santa Clara, is the neoclassical **Fountain of Neptune** ⑤. From the fountain, make a left on Calle Allende and walk almost a block to a fine example of Baroque architecture, the **State Museum of Art** ⑥. Retrace your steps back to Calle Corregidora. Make a left and walk one block to Calle 16 de Septiembre. Across the street is the **Jardín de la Corregidora** ⑦.

Sights to See

❸ Casa de Ecala. Currently housing the offices of DIF, a family services organization, this Baroque palace retains its original facade. As the story goes, its 18th-century owner adorned his home elaborately in order to outdo his neighbor. When the neighbor complained, city hall stepped in and halted construction. Visitors are welcome to walk around the courtyard when the offices are open. ⊠ *Plaza Independencia 4.* ☺ *Weekdays 7 AM–9 PM, Sat. 9–3.*

❺ Fountain of Neptune. Built in 1797 by Eduardo Tresguerras, the renowned Mexican architect and a native of the Bajío, the fountain originally stood in the orchard of the Monastery of San Antonio. When the monks faced serious economic problems, they sold part of their land and the fountain along with it. It now stands next to the Church of Santa Clara. ⊠ *Calle Allende Madero.*

❼ Jardín de la Corregidora. This plaza is prominently marked by a statue of the War of Independence heroine after whom it is named. Behind the monument stands the **Arbol de la Amistad** (Tree of Friendship). Planted in 1977 in a mixture of soils from around the world, the tree symbolizes Querétaro's hospitality to all travelers. You may want to find a bench in the Jardín and sit for a while: This is the calmest square in town, with many choices for outdoor eating. ⊠ *Calle Corregidora and Av. 16 de Septiembre.*

❹ Museo Regional de Querétaro. This bright yellow, 17th-century Franciscan monastery displays the works of colonial and European artists in addition to historic memorabilia, including early copies of the Mexican Constitution and the table on which the Treaty of Guadalupe Hidalgo was signed. ⊠ *Calle Corregidora Sur 3,* ☎ *42/12–20–31.* ▣ *About $2.50.* ⊙ *Tues.–Sun. 10:30–4:30.*

❷ Palacio del Gobierno del Estado. Also known as La Casa de la Corregidora, the Palacio houses municipal government offices, but in 1810 it was the home of Querétaro's mayor-magistrate (El Corregidor) and his wife, Josefa Ortiz de Domínguez (La Corregidora). On many evenings conspirators—including Ignacio Allende and Father Miguel Hidalgo—came here under the guise of participating in La Corregidora's literary salon. When the mayor-magistrate learned that they were actually plotting the course for independence, he imprisoned his wife in her room. La Corregidora managed to whisper a warning to a co-conspirator, who notified Allende and Hidalgo. A few days later, on September 16, Father Hidalgo tolled the bell of his church to signal the beginning of the fight for freedom. A replica of the bell can be seen atop the building. ⊠ *Northwest corner of Plaza Independencia.* ⊙ *Weekdays 9–9, weekends 9–6.*

❶ Plaza Independencia. Bordered by carefully restored colonial mansions, this immaculate square, also known as Plaza de Armas, is especially lovely at night, when the central fountain is lit. Built in 1824, the fountain is dedicated to the Marquis de la Villa del Villar, who constructed Querétaro's elegant aqueduct and provided the city with drinking water. The old stone aqueduct with its 74 towering arches still stands at the east end of town, though it no longer brings water into the city. ⊠ *Bounded by Av. 5 de Mayo on the north, Av. Libertad on the south, Luis Pasteur on the east, and Vergara Sur on the west.*

❻ State Museum of Art. A fine example of Baroque architecture, the museum is housed in an 18th-century Augustinian monastery. Its collection focuses on European and Mexican paintings from the 17th through

20th centuries. ⊠ *Calle Allende 14,* ☎ *42/12–23–57.* ☎ *About $1.50.*
☺ *Tues.–Sun. 11–7.*

Dining

Many of Querétaro's dining spots are located near the main plaza
(Jardín Obregón), along Calle Corregidora, near the Teatro de la
República, and particularly in the Jardín de la Corregidora. There are
more upscale restaurants in hotels on the Plaza Independencia or off
Route 57, north of the city. In early evenings women set up stoves in a
square near the Plaza Independencia and tempt passersby with cheap
and hearty fare—but for health reasons, food cooked on the street
should be avoided throughout Mexico. Unless otherwise indicated,
dress is casual.

$$$ ✕ **Fonda del Refugio.** Situated in the Jardín de la Corregidora, this restau-
rant offers intimate indoor and outdoor dining. Inside, fresh flowers
adorn white-clothed tables; outside, comfortable leather chairs face the
surrounding gardens. Seafood and beef fillets are a specialty; order the
fillet of beef cooked in red wine, lemon, mustard, and peppers, or the
scallops prepared in marsala. Cocktails are served on the terrace at night.
⊠ *Jardín de la Corregidora 26,* ☎ *42/12–07–55. AE, MC, V.*

$$$ ✕ **Restaurante Josecho.** Bullfight aficionados and other sports fans fre-
★   quent this highway road stop next to the bullring at the southwest end
of town as much for the lively atmosphere as for the food. Wood-paneled walls are hung with hunting trophies, including geese, elk, bears,
and leopards; waiters celebrate patrons' birthdays by banging on
pewter plates and blasting a red siren. Though the place can be raucous, it does quiet down at night, when a classical guitarist or pianist
performs. House specialties include *filete Josecho* (steak with cheese
and mushrooms), *filete Chemita* (steak sautéed in butter with onions),
and shrimp crepes smothered in a cheese-and-tomato sauce. ⊠ *Dalia
1 next to Plaza de Toros Santa María,* ☎ *42/16–02–29 or 42/16–02–
01. AE, DC, MC, V.*

$$ ✕ **El Cortijo de Don Juan.** At lunchtime businessmen and families favor
this garden location, making it the busiest spot in the shaded Jardín.
Vendors stroll by with a variety of wares, from homemade cheeses to
large, inflatable crayons; and children sing songs for a small donation.
Free snacks are served with drinks in the afternoon, or you can order
from a menu that includes *pollo adobado* (chicken in a rich chili
sauce), *jamón serrano* (a prosciutto-type ham), and—on Saturdays
only—*paella Valenciana* (rice casserole with chicken, sausage, and
seafood). The inside rooms are filled with photos of famous matadors;
a bull's head is mounted prominently on the wall. A guitarist plays Thurs-
day, Friday, and Saturday nights. ⊠ *Jardín de la Corregidora 14,*
☎ *42/14–30–37. AE, MC, V.*

$ ✕ **Comedor Vegetariano Natura.** This natural-foods kitchen, one of a
chain of four in Querétaro, will be of interest to the vegetarian trav-
eler. (A second one, not far away, is located at Juárez 47, off Plaza
Obregón.) Traditional vegetarian fare, such as soy burgers with cheese,
is on the menu, as are Mexican-influenced dishes such as guayaba- or
papaya-flavored yogurt and enchiladas stuffed with soy and cheese.
⊠ *Vergara Sur 7,* ☎ *42/14–10–88. Reservations not accepted. No credit
cards. Closed Sun.*

$ ✕ **La Mariposa.** Celebrating more than 50 years in business, La Mari-
posa is easily recognized by a wrought-iron butterfly (*mariposa*) over
the entrance. This is the place for light Mexican lunches—enchiladas,
tacos, tamales, and *tortas* (sandwiches). ⊠ *Angela Peralta 7,* ☎ *42/12–*

It helps to be pushy in airports.

Stable 4-wheel design.

Introducing the revolutionary new TransPorter™ from American Tourister® It's the first suitcase you can push around without a fight. TransPorter's™ exclusive four-wheel design lets you push it in front of you with almost no effort–the wheels take the weight. Or pull it on two wheels if you choose. You can even stack on other bags and use it like a luggage cart.

TransPorter™ is designed like a dresser, with built-in shelves to organize your belongings. Or collapse the shelves and pack it like a traditional suitcase. Inside, there's a suiter feature to help keep suits and dresses from wrinkling. When push comes to shove, you can't beat a TransPorter™ For more information on how you can be this pushy, call 1-800-542-1300.

Shelves collapse on command.

Making travel less primitive®

©1996 American Tourister®

©MCI Telecommunications Corporation, 1996. All rights reserved.

Your passport around the world.

- Worldwide access
- Operators who speak your language
- Monthly itemized billing

MCI Calling Card

415 555 1234 2244
J.D. SMITH

Use your MCI Card® and these access numbers for an easy way to call when traveling worldwide.

American Samoa	633-2MCI (633-2624)
Antigua †	#2
(Available from public card phones only)	
Aruba ÷	800-888-8
Argentina ★†	001-800-333-1111
Bahamas (CC)†	1-800-888-8000
Barbados	1-800-888-8000
Belize	815 from pay phones
	557 from hotels
Bermuda ÷ †	1-800-888-8000
Bolivia ♦	0-800-2222
Brazil (CC) †	000-8012
British Virgin Islands ÷	1-800-888-8000
Cayman Islands†	1-800-888-8000
Chile (CC)†	
To call using CTC ■	800-207-300
To call using ENTEL ■	123-00316
Colombia (CC) ♦†	980-16-0001
Costa Rica ♦†	0800-012-2222
Dominica	1-800-888-8000
Dominican Republic (CC)	1-800-888-8000
Ecuador (CC) ÷ †	999-170
El Salvador ♦	800-1767
Grenada ÷	1-800-888-8000

Guatemala ♦	189
Guyana	177
Haiti (CC) ÷	001-800-444-1234
Honduras ÷	122
Jamaica	1-800-888-8000
(From Special Hotels only)	873
Mexico ▲†	95-800-674-7000
Netherlands Antilles (CC) ÷ †	
	001-800-950-1022
Nicaragua (CC)	166
(Outside of Managua, dial 02 first)	
Panama†	108
Military Bases	2810-108
Paraguay ÷	008-11-800
Peru	170
Puerto Rico (CC)†	1-800-888-8000
St. Lucia ÷	1-800-888-8000
Trinidad & Tobago ÷	1-800-888-8000
Turks & Caicos ÷	1-800-888-8000
Uruguay	00-412
U.S. Virgin Islands (CC)†	1-800-888-8000
Venezuela ÷♦	800-1114-0

To sign up for the MCI Card, dial the access number of the country you are in and ask to speak with a customer service representative.

http://www.mci.com

† Automation available from most locations. ÷ Limited availability. ★ Not available from public pay phones. (CC) Country-to-country calling available.
May not be available to/from all international locations. (Canada, Puerto Rico, and U.S. Virgin Islands are considered Domestic Access locations.)
♦ Public phones may require deposit of coin or phone card for dial tone. ■ International communications carrier.
▲ When calling from public phones use phones marked LADATEL.

11–66, 42/12–48–49, or 42/12–18–71. Reservations not accepted. No credit cards.

Lodging

Several new properties in various price ranges have opened in Querétaro in the past 10 years. Lower-priced hotels are located near the main plaza and thus tend to be noisy; newer high-rises are near the bus station but are quiet inside; and deluxe properties, including a Holiday Inn, are on the outskirts of town.

$$$$ ⊞ **La Casa de la Marquesa.** A beautifully restored 18th-century hacienda, La Casa was built by Marques Juan Antonio de Urrutia, reputedly to house his mistress, Doña Josefa Paula Guerrero. The Marques did not live to see the completion of the building (1756), and its first resident was his widow, the Marquesa de la Villa del Villar, who had a penchant for things Arabic: Notice the studios on the second floor, one of which is covered with Middle Eastern tiles. The central courtyard leads to rooms decorated with antique furniture but that boast all the modern amenities: air-conditioning and heat, cable TV, and telephones. La Casa is popular with the increasing flood of Mexican and foreign business travelers visiting Querétaro. ⊠ *Madero 41, 76000,* ☎ *42/12–00–92,* ℻ *42/12–00–98. 25 rooms. Restaurant, bar. AE, MC, V.*

$$$$ ⊞ **Mesón de Santa Rosa.** Located on the quiet Plaza Independencia, ★ this elegant all-suite property occupies a restored hacienda. Rooms are clustered around a quiet courtyard. Each has a lace-hung glass door and a decor that includes warm autumn colors and wood-beamed ceilings. ⊠ *Pasteur Sur 17, 76000,* ☎ *42/24–29–07 or 42/24–29–05,* ℻ *42/12–55–22. 21 suites. Restaurant, bar, pool. AE, MC, V.*

$$$ ⊞ **Hotel Mirabel.** A favorite among business travelers and conventioneers, this modern high-rise hums with activity. Its carpeted rooms, however, are insulated and quiet and feature color TVs, telephones, wood desks, and air-conditioning. Some double rooms have views of the Alameda Hidalgo park; some single rooms overlook a soccer stadium. ⊠ *Av. Constituyentes Oriente 2, 76000,* ☎ *42/14–30–99 or 42/14–34–44,* ℻ *42/14–35–85. 171 rooms with bath. Restaurant, bar, convention center. AE, MC, V.*

$$ ⊞ **Hotel Señorial.** Built in 1981, this sprawling four-story property has clean, modern rooms with telephones and TVs. Beds are covered with printed spreads that clash with the floral drapes. Rooms in front face a narrow, busy street, but traffic slows in the evening. There are purified-water dispensers in the hallways. ⊠ *Guerrero Norte 10-A, 76000,* ☎ *42/14–37–00,* ℻ *42/14–19–45. 45 rooms with bath. Restaurant. MC, V.*

$ ⊞ **Hotel Plaza.** This modest property, located on the main plaza, offers clean accommodations and lots of hot water. Rooms facing the principal square are extremely noisy—even at night. Inside rooms, particularly those on the second floor, are much quieter but dark. All rooms have telephones and most have TVs, but for those that do not, there is a small color TV above the soda machine in the tiled lobby. ⊠ *Av. Juárez Norte 23, 76000,* ☎ *42/12–11–38 or 42/12–65–62. 29 rooms with bath. MC, V.*

Nightlife

Band concerts are held in the Jardín Obregón, Querétaro's main square, every Sunday evening at 6.

Shopping

A number of stores around town sell opals (not blue, like Australian opals, but beautiful nonetheless) and other locally mined gems. If you're in the market for loose stones or opal jewelry, do some comparison shopping, as you're apt to find better prices here than in the United States. Just off Plaza Principal, **El Rubí** (✉ Av. Madero 3 Pte., ☎ 42/12–09–84) is a reputable dealer. The owner, Señora Villalon, provides information on the mining, care, and value of opals. The store is open weekdays 10–2 and 4–5, Saturday 10–2.

Side Trips

San Juan del Río and Tequisquiapan

San Juan del Río and Tequisquiapan, both within an hour's drive of Querétaro, have long been frequented by harried Mexican urbanites who come to shop for semiprecious gems and to soak in the area's thermal waters. It's best, however, to avoid Tequisquiapan, home to more than 20 volcanic spas, on weekends, when locals book up most of the hotels. The tourist office in Querétaro can supply you with brochures.

The simplest way to reach these towns is by car. Buses service both towns from Querétaro, but the trip is longer. You'll probably want to do your shopping first in San Juan del Río (a center of commerce), then head to Tequisquiapan to relax at its lush resort spas.

SAN JUAN DEL RÍO
51 km (32 mi) southeast of Querétaro via Route 57.

Most of San Juan's gem shops are located near the main plaza downtown. **Lapidaria Guerrero** (✉ Av. Juárez Poniente 4, ☎ 472/2–14–81) specializes in opal, amethyst, turquoise, and topaz jewelry. **La Guadalupana** (✉ Calle 16 de Septiembre 16, ☎ 472/2–09–13)—a cluster of shops in a large courtyard—sells opal, amethyst, topaz, and onyx jewelry; hand-embroidered blouses; brassware; and wood carvings.

TEQUISQUIAPAN
19 km (12 mi) east of San Juan, off Route 120.

Your first stop in Tequisquiapan should be the tourist office. The staff has a list of the spas in town and can tell you which hotels rent out facilities for the afternoon. There is no phone, but during the week the office of municipal government (☎ 472/3–02–95) may be able to answer questions. ✉ *Av. Morelos 7.* ☉ *Weekdays 9–2 and 5–8, weekends 10–1.*

After visiting the spas, stop by the verdant main plaza for a beverage or snack; then head to the shops or to the Mercado de Artesanías, where woven goods, jewelry, and locally made furniture are sold. Each summer the city hosts a weeklong wine and cheese festival that includes bullfights and mariachi bands.

Querétero A to Z

Arriving and Departing

BY BUS
Direct bus service is available daily between the Central del Norte (North Bus Station) in Mexico City and Querétaro's Central de Autobuses. Major lines—including **Flecha Amarilla, Omnibus de México, Tres Estrellas de Oro,** and **Transportes del Norte**—offer frequent service; travel time is about three hours.

BY CAR

Querétaro is 220 kilometers (136 miles) northwest of Mexico City, a three-hour drive via Route 57.

BY TRAIN

The *Constitucionalista* departs from Mexico City at 7 AM and arrives in Querétaro at 10 AM; the return trip leaves Querétaro at 2:40 PM and arrives in Mexico City at 6:30 PM. Tickets should be purchased one day in advance; the round-trip fare is $13. For current schedule and rate information, contact **Mexico by Train** (☎ FAX 210/725–3659 or 800/321–1699) or call the local station (☎ 42/12–17–03 or 42/12–17–89).

Getting Around

Many of Querétaro's historic sites are within walking distance of one another in the downtown district and can be reached by a series of walkways that are closed to automobile traffic most of the day. If you want to venture farther afield, you will find that buses and taxis run frequently along the main streets and are inexpensive.

Contacts and Resources

CAR RENTAL AGENCIES

Budget (✉ Av. Constituyentes Oriente 73, ☎ 42/13–44–98, FAX 42/13–44–38). **Auto Rent** (✉ Av. Constituyentes Oriente 24-B, ☎ 42/15–02–79 or 42/14–50–96). **National** (✉ Calle 13 de Septiembre 34, ☎ FAX 42/16–52–40 or 42/16–35–44).

EMERGENCIES

Police (☎ 42/12–30–03 or 42/12–02–06). **Ambulance–Red Cross** (☎ 42/29–05–05 or 42/29–06–63). **Fire Department** (☎ 42/12–06–27 or 42/12–39–39). **Protectur** (☎ 42/14–04–28) offers legal assistance with robberies, fraud, and detention or arrest.

Hospital. Sanatorio Alcocer Pozo (✉ Calle Reforma 23, ☎ 42/12–01–49 or 42/12–17–87).

GUIDED TOURS

On request, the tourist office conducts a free 90-minute English-language walking tour of the city's historic landmarks. To arrange a city tour, call the office (☞ Visitor Information, *below*) one day in advance.

MONEY EXCHANGE

Casa de Cambio Acueducto (✉ Av. Juárez Sur 58, ☎ 42/12–93–04 or 42/14–31–89) is open weekdays 9–2 and 4–6, Saturday 9–1.

TRAVEL AGENCIES

Wagons-Lits Viajes (✉ Av. Tecnologia N-2, interior 209, ☎ 42/14–30–20 or 42/14–33–44).

VISITOR INFORMATION

Dirección de Turismo del Estado (✉ Plaza de la Independencia at Pasteur 4 Norte, ☎ 42/12–12–87 or 42/12–09–07, FAX 42/12–10–94). ☺ Daily 9–3 and 6–8.

MORELIA

With its long, wide boulevards and earth-tone colonial mansions, Morelia is the gracious capital of the state of Michoacán. Founded in 1541 as Valladolid (after the Spanish city), it changed its name in 1828 to honor José María Morelos, the town's most famous son. The legendary mule skinner turned priest took up the battle for independence after its early leaders were executed in 1811.

Morelos began with an ill-equipped army of 25 but soon organized a contingent of 9,000 that nearly gained control of the country. Though he was defeated and executed in 1815, he left behind a long-standing reformist legacy that called for universal suffrage, racial equality, and the demise of the hacienda system.

The city today still pays tribute to Morelos: His former home has been turned into a museum, and his birthplace is now a library. Although Morelia's colonial heritage is preserved by its status as a national monument, the city is also forward-thinking. It's the site of a politically liberal university that often holds rallies supporting social and political causes. Look closely along Avenida Madero, and you'll see political fliers posted on buildings.

In addition, Morelia has the delicious distinction of being the candy capital of Mexico. So strong, in fact, is the sweet-eating tradition that the city offers a *Mercado de Dulces,* or sweets market. Morelia is also the home of writers, artists, philosophers, and poets, as well as American retirees.

Exploring Morelia

To explore Morelia and its surrounding hillside neighborhoods thoroughly would take some time. However, if you stroll through the historic plazas and frequent the cafés (as many locals do), you will begin to feel the city's vitality. Although the vehicle and sidewalk traffic can get a little heavy at times, Morelia is a pedestrian-friendly city.

A Good Walk
Numbers in the text correspond to numbers in the margin and on the Morelia map.

Begin your walk in Morelia's tree-lined downtown **Plaza de Armas** ①, on the east side of which is the city's famed **Catedral** ②. As you leave the cathedral, cross Avenida Madero to the **Palacio de Gobierno** ③, a former seminary. From the palace it's four blocks east along Avenida Madero to Calle de Belisario Domínguez. Make a right and walk one block south to the Church of San Francisco. To the rear of the church, in the former convent of San Francisco, is the entrance to the **Casa de las Artesanías del Estado de Michoacán** ④, a virtual cornucopia of crafts from around the state.

Walk two blocks south on Calle Vasco de Quiroga, a street lined with vendors, until you come to Soto Saldaña. Head west another two blocks to Avenida Morelos Sur; the corner building on your right is the **Casa Museo de Morelos** ⑤, featuring memorabilia of the independence leader. It's one block north from the museum to Calle Corregidora and then one block west to Calle García Obeso. On this corner stands the **Casa Natal** ⑥, Morelos's birthplace. Continue west on Calle Corregidora until you reach Calle Abasolo; on Calle Allende, one block to the north, you'll find the **Museo Michoacana** ⑦.

After leaving the museum, take Calle Abasolo back to the plaza; a block and a half to the north, you'll see the **Museo del Estado** ⑧ on the right side of the street (which changes its name to Calle Guillermo Prieto at Avenida Madero). Return to Avenida Madero, and then go two blocks to the right to the corner of the Valentín Gómez Farías, where the **Mercado de Dulces** ⑨ is located.

Those seeking a longer stroll might take Avenida Madero east a dozen blocks or so to where it forks. Stay to the right; you'll see the **Fountain of the Tarascans** on a square to your left. Just past the square, Morelia's mile-long **aqueduct** begins. This structure, which consists of 253 arches, was built in 1785 and was once the city's main source of drinking water. It's particularly beautiful at night when its arches—some rising to 30 feet—are lit. Two blocks farther along (Madero is now called Avenida Acueducto) is the entrance to **Bosque Cuauhtémoc,** Morelia's largest park. If you happen by during the week, you may encounter university students studying (or lounging) beneath the palms and evergreens; on weekends, especially Sunday, families on outings take over. Two blocks past the park entrance, you'll see the **Museo de Arte Contemporáneo** ⑩, also on the right side of the street.

Sights to See

❹ **Casa de las Artesanías del Estado de Michoacán.** In the 16th century, Vasco de Quiroga, the bishop of Michoacán, helped the Tarascan Indians develop artistic specialties so they could be self-supporting. At this two-story museum and store, you can see the work the Tarascans still produce: copper goods from Santa Clara del Cobre, lacquerware from Uruapan, straw items and pottery from Pátzcuaro, guitars from Paracho, macabre ceramic figures from Ocumicho. At the **Museo Michoacana de las Artesanías** in the two main floors around the courtyard (the entrance is directly in front when you come in), some of these items are showcased behind glass while artists demonstrate how they are made. The **store** is located in several rooms to the right of the museum entrance. ⊠ *Calle Fray Juan de San Miguel 129; museum,* ☎ *43/12–24–86; store, 43/12–12–48.* ⊙ *Daily 9–8.*

❺ **Casa Museo de Morelos.** What is now a two-story museum was acquired in 1801 by the Mexican independence leader and served as home to generations of the Morelos family until 1934. Owned by the Mexican government, it contains family portraits (including one of Morelos's mother, who, he said, "gave him constant spirit and strength"), a copy of Morelos's birth certificate, various artifacts from the independence movement (such as a camp bed used by Ignacio Allende), and the blindfold Morelos wore for his execution. The excellent free tour is in Spanish only. ⊠ *Av. Morelos Sur 323,* ☎ *43/13–26–51.* 🎟 *Small fee.* ⊙ *Daily 9–7.*

❻ **Casa Natal.** Morelos's birthplace is now a library and national monument housing mostly history and literature books (as well as two murals by Alfredo Zalce). Be sure to visit the courtyard in back: It's a tranquil square, adjacent to the Church of San Agustín, with rosebushes, evergreens, and wild poinsettias; a marker and an eternal flame honor the fallen hero. ⊠ *Calle Corregidora 113,* ☎ *43/12–27–93.* 🎟 *Free.* ⊙ *Weekdays 9–2 and 4–8, Sat. 9:30–2, Sun. 9–2.*

❷ **Catedral.** Morelia's famed cathedral is a majestic structure built between 1640 and 1744. It is known throughout Mexico for its 200-foot Baroque towers, among the tallest in the land, and for its 4,600-pipe organ, one of the finest in the world. The organ is on the balcony at the back of the cathedral. An international organ festival is held here each May. ⊠ *Av. Madero between Plaza de Armas and Av. Morelos.*

❾ **Mercado de Dulces.** Those with a sweet tooth won't want to miss Morelia's famous candy market, just behind the tourist office. All sorts of local sweets are for sale, such as *ate* (a candied fruit) and various confections made from evaporated milk. ⊠ *Av. Madero Poniente and Valentín Gómez Farías.* ⊙ *Daily 9–9.*

⑩ **Museo de Arte Contemporáneo.** The works of contemporary Mexican and international artists are on view at this museum near the Bosque Cuauhtémoc. ⊠ *Av. Acueducto 18,* ☎ *43/12–54–04.* 🎟 *Free.* ⊙ *Tues.–Sun. 10–1:45 and 4–7:45.*

Morelia

---

⑧ Museo del Estado. Just across from a small plaza with statues of Don Quiroga de Vasco and Miguel de Cervantes, this history museum is located in a stately mansion that was once the home of Augustín de Iturbide, Mexico's only native-born emperor. ⊠ *Guillermo Prieto 176,* ☎ *43/13–06–29.* ⊡ *Free.* ☉ *Weekdays 9–2, Sat. and holidays 9–7:30.*

⑦ Museo Michoacana. An 18th-century former palace, the museum traces the history of Mexico from its pre-Hispanic days through the Cardenista period, which ended in 1940. President Lázaro Cárdenas, a native of Michoacán, was one of Mexico's most popular leaders because of his nationalization of the oil industry and his support of other populist reforms. The ground floor contains an art gallery, plus archaeological exhibits from Michoacán and other parts of Mexico. Upstairs is an assortment of colonial objects, including furniture, weapons, and religious paintings. ⊠ *Calle Allende 305,* ☎ *43/12–04–07.* ⊡ *About $4.* ☉ *Tues.–Sat. 9–7.*

....

NEED A BREAK? When you've finished your tour of the Museo Michoacana, walk across the street to the *portales.* A number of popular sidewalk cafés are set among these colonial stone arcades. For a sandwich or a fruit cocktail, or a good selection of juices, coffees, and teas, try **Café Catedral** (⊠ Portal Hidalgo 213, ☎ 43/12–32–89). No one will mind if you linger over a book or newspaper for the better part of an hour sipping an excellent *café americano* (and, in fact, you might have to wait that long just to get the bill).

....

❸ Palacio de Gobierno. This former Tridentine seminary, built in 1770, has had such notable graduates as independence hero José María Morelos, social reformer Melchor Ocampo, and the first emperor of Mexico, Agustín de Iturbide. Striking murals decorate the stairway and second floor. Painted by local artist Alfredo Zalce in the early 1960s, they depict dramatic, often bloody scenes from Mexico's history. From the second floor you can catch a glimpse of the cathedral's spires across the way. ⌧ *Av. Madero 63,* ☎ *43/12–78–72.* ☉ *Daily 7 AM–10 PM.*

❶ **Plaza de Armas.** During the War of Independence, several rebel priests were brutally murdered on this site, and the plaza, known as Plaza de los Mártires, is named after them. Today, however, the square belies its violent past: Sweethearts stroll along the tree-lined walks, vendors sell mounds of peanuts, placards announce cultural events, and lively recorded music blasts from a silver-domed bandshell. ⌧ *Bounded on the north by Av. Madero, on the south by Calle Allende, on the west by Calle Abasolo, and on the east by cathedral.*

Dining

Some of Michoacán's tastiest dishes—Lake Pátzcuaro white fish, tomato-based Tarascan soup, corn products such as *huchepos* and *corundas,* and game (rabbit and quail)—are featured at Morelia restaurants. Traditional chicken and beef fare are also available, as well as international dishes. As a rule, more upscale restaurants are located in hotels near the plaza and on the outskirts of town. Unless otherwise indicated, dress is casual.

$$ ✕ **Boca del Rio.** Large picture windows opening onto a busy intersec-
★ tion provide lots of light for this cheerful restaurant, which claims to have fresh fish and seafood trucked in daily from Sinaloa and Veracruz. Located between the bus station and the Mercado de Dulces, it provides light snacks, such as *cocktel de camarones* (shrimp cocktail) or *sopa de mariscos* (a rich broth filled with clams, mussels, shrimp, and crab), and heartier fare, such as *pescadillos* (tostadas stuffed with lightly cooked, marinated fish and served with a salad) or *jaiba rellena* (crabs stuffed with mushrooms and cheese and liberally seasoned with garlic). ⌧ *Valentín Gómez Farías 185,* ☎ *43/12–99–74. AE, MC, V.*

$$ ✕ **El Rey Tacamba.** Brightly colored decorations mark this pleasant restaurant, located on the north side of the Plaza de Armas. Among its specialties are *mixiote de carnero,* a piquant (although not spicy) mutton dish, first stewed and then steamed in banana leaves; *pollo moreliano,* chicken roasted in a rich red chili sauce and served with enchiladas covered in vegetables; and *carne Tampiqueña,* a grilled flank steak accompanied by guacamole, refried beans, and tostadas. Once completely reliable, both food and service have gotten mixed reports lately. ⌧ *Portal Galeana 157,* ☎ *43/12–20–44. Reservations not accepted. No credit cards.*

$$ ✕ **Los Comensales.** This garden restaurant, a downtown favorite
★ among the bullfight crowd, is set in an old colonial house north of the main plaza. Tables are spaced casually around a plant-filled courtyard where caged birds sing energetically. Regional dishes include *pollo de plaza* (chicken with enchiladas, carrots, potatoes, and cheese) and *huchepos* (tamales and sour cream). For breakfast, try *calabaza con leche* (baked squash with brown sugar and milk). ⌧ *Calle Zaragoza 148,* ☎ *43/12–93–61. No credit cards.*

$ ✕ **Café del Bosque.** During the week, university students frequent this 1960s-style restaurant. It's tacky—floral carpet and bright green booths—but the food is good and fairly cheap. Most students can afford sandwiches or burgers; if you feel like spending a bit more, order *pollo moreliano* (chicken with enchiladas, vegetables, and french fries) or *carne à la Mexicana* (grilled beef cooked with onions, tomatoes, lemon juice, and salsa). There's a small but pleasant terrace for outdoor dining. ⌧ *Plaza Rebullones, Local C-7,* ☎ *43/13–28–13. Reservations not accepted. No credit cards.*

$ ✕ **El Paraíso.** To jump-start your day, have a cup of the strong, rich cappuccino at El Paraíso. Breakfasts—the recommended meal at this downtown eatery—run the gamut from eggs and pancakes to fresh fruit, granola, and exotic juices (watermelon, mango, pineapple, and guayaba). The specialty is *jamón Paraíso* (fried eggs, ham, and grated cheese). The plain surroundings—Formica tables and blue-tiled walls—don't deter locals. ✉ *Portal Galeana 103,* ☎ *43/12–03–74. Reservations not accepted. No credit cards.*

Lodging

Morelia offers a number of pleasant colonial-style properties both in the downtown and outlying areas. Generally, the cheapest hotels are located near the bus station, moderately priced selections are clustered around the plaza (or on nearby side streets), and deluxe resort properties are in or near the Santa María hills.

$$$$ ⊡ **Villa Montana.** This deluxe property, owned by French count Philippe
★   de Reiset, has all the markings of a wealthy Mexican estate. Set high above Morelia in the Santa María hills, its five impeccably groomed acres are dotted with a pool, tennis court, and fanciful stone sculptures. Each individually decorated unit has at least one piece of antique furniture and often a fireplace and private patio. A renowned restaurant offers North American, French, and Mexican food. Guests have a choice of either CP (Continental Plan with breakfast) or MAP (Modified American Plan with breakfast and lunch or dinner). ✉ *Calle Patzimba s/n, 58000,* ☎ *43/14–02–31 or 43/14–01–79; in the U.S., 800/525–4800;* ⅀ *43/15–14–23. 55 rooms with bath. Restaurant, piano bar, pool, tennis court, recreation room, laundry service, convention hall. AE, MC, V.*

$$–$$$ ⊡ **Hotel Posada de la Soledad.** Set in a restored private mansion built
★   in the late 17th century, the Posada de la Soledad is conveniently located one block from the Plaza de Armas. The rooms in the front of the hotel, the oldest section, are surrounded by an elegant patio with a large fountain and bougainvillea, as well as vintage carriages from the colonial era. Rooms located here have sturdy wood furnishings, elegantly hand-carved by Michoacán craftsmen. The rooms facing north on Calle Melchor Ocampo, however, should be avoided due to heavy traffic on that street. Rooms in a newer (1960s) section at the back of the hotel are smaller and less elaborately furnished but stay quiet and are comfortably appointed with earth-tone carpeting and bedspreads. In the off-season, they can be had for a discount. The Posada also has an elegant restaurant and a darkly lit bar where a guitar trio plays plaintive, romantic music. ✉ *Ignacio Zaragoza 90, 58000,* ☎ *43/12–18–88,* ⅀ *43/12–21–11. 58 rooms with bath. Restaurant, bar. AE, DC, MC, V.*

$$ ⊡ **Hotel Catedral.** Located in a restored colonial mansion, this three-story property began operating as a hotel some 30 years ago. Its modern rooms are clustered around a skylit courtyard; some overlook the main plaza and cathedral on Avenida Madero. Interior quarters have less dramatic views but are less noisy. All rooms have dark wood furnishings, telephones, and color TVs. ✉ *Calle Zaragoza 37, 58000,* ☎ *43/13–04–06 or 43/13–04–67,* ⅀ *43/13–07–83. 44 rooms with bath. Restaurant, bar, dry cleaning. AE, MC, V.*

$$ ⊡ **Hotel Mansion Acueducto.** An elaborate wood and wrought-iron staircase leads from the elegant lobby to more modest quarters upstairs. Rooms have dark, colonial-style furniture, telephones, and black-and-white TVs. Older rooms overlook the aqueduct and nearby park; rooms in the motel-like wing have views of the garden, pool, and surrounding mountains. Student groups at times book the entire property.

✉ *Av. Acueducto 25, 58000,* ☎ *43/12–33–01 or 43/12–20–20. 36 rooms with bath. Restaurant, bar, pool. AE, MC, V.*

$ ⊞ **Hotel Concordia.** Rooms are simply furnished at this hotel (some spreads are slightly worn), but sheets are clean and showers have hot water throughout the day. On weekends Mexican families with young children frequent this spot and tend to rise (and wake others) early. ✉ *Valentín Gómez Farías 328, 58000,* ☎ *43/12–30–53. 51 rooms with bath. MC, V.*

Morelia A to Z

Arriving and Departing

BY BUS
Direct bus service is available daily between the Terminal Poniente (West Terminal) in Mexico City and Morelia's **Central de Autobuses** (☎ 43/12–56–04). Several bus lines offer frequent service; the most direct trip (cost $19) takes five hours and is on Herradura de Plata (via Corta). Buses leave every hour or two around the clock.

BY CAR
The drive from Mexico City to Morelia (302 kilometers, or 187 miles) on the toll road through Toluca, Atlacamulco, Contepec, and Maravatio takes about 3 hours and 45 minutes.

BY PLANE
There are daily flights between Francisco Mujica International Airport, 24 kilometers (15 miles) north of Morelia, and Mexico City's International Airport on **Aeromexico** (☎ 43/13–58–33). Flights are subject to cancellation, and flight times change often and must be confirmed one day in advance. The 25-minute taxi ride from the airport to Morelia costs about $10.

BY TRAIN
The *Purepecha* leaves Mexico City at 10 PM, arriving in Morelia at 6:30 AM; the return train leaves Morelia at 11 PM and arrives in Mexico City at 7:30 AM. The round-trip fare costs $15 first-class. Train schedules are subject to change without notice. For current schedules and rates, contact **Mexico by Train** (☎ FAX 210/725–3659 or 800/321–1699) or the local train station (☎ 43/16–16–97).

Getting Around
As in many of the heartland cities, Morelia's principal sights are near the center of town and you can reach them on foot. Street names in Morelia change frequently, especially on either side of Avenida Madero, the city's main east–west artery. Taxis in Morelia can be hailed on the street or found near the main plaza. Buses run the length of Avenida Madero.

Contacts and Resources

CAR RENTAL AGENCY
Budget has an office at Francisco Mujica International Airport (☎ 43/13–33–99).

EMERGENCIES
Police (☎ 43/12–22–22). **Ambulance–Red Cross** (Cruz Rojo; ☎ 43/14–51–51 or 43/14–50–25). **Consumer Protection Office** (☎ 43/12–40–49). **Fire Department** (☎ 43/12–12–35). **Hospital Memorial** (☎ 43/15–10–47 or 43/15–10–99).

GUIDED TOURS
The following operators conduct tours of Morelia: **Autoturismo Morelia** (✉ Calle Colima 406, ☎ 43/14–08–26), **Michoacán Tour Guides and Conductors Association** (✉ Calle Nigromante 79, ☎ 43/13–26–

54), **Tours Lindo Michoacán** (✉ Colima 502, ☎ 43/14–99–43), **Turís-tica Juriata** (✉ Manuela Medina 157, ☎ 43/16–06–22).

MONEY EXCHANGE
Casa Cambio Valladolid (✉ Portal Matamoros 86, ☎ 43/12–85–86) is open weekdays 9–6, Saturday 9–1:30.

TRAVEL AGENCIES
Viajes Lopsa, the American Express representative (✉ Service Las Américas, Local 27, Artilleros del 47, ☎ 43/14–19–50, FAX 43/14–77–16). **Servicios Establecidos Para el Turismo** (✉ Portal Hidalgo 229, ☎ 43/12–36–64).

VISITOR INFORMATION
Secretaría Estatal de Turismo. ✉ *Palacio Clavijero, Calle Nigromante 79,* ☎ *43/13–26–54 or 43/12–80–81,* FAX *43/12–98–16 or 43/12–04–15.* ✆ *Weekdays 9–9, weekends 9–4.*

PÁTZCUARO

Pátzcuaro, the 16th-century capital of Michoacán, exists in a time warp. A bit more than an hour by car from Morelia, this beautiful lakeside community set at 7,250 feet in the Sierra Madre is home to the Taras-can Indians, who fish, farm, and ply their crafts as they have for centuries. Women wrapped tightly in their striped wool *rebozos* (shawls) hurry to market in the chill, smoky morning air. Men in traditional straw hats wheel overburdened carts down crooked, dusty back streets.

The architecture, too, has remained largely unchanged throughout the years. In the 16th century, under kindly Bishop Vasco de Quiroga, Pátzcuaro underwent a building boom of sorts. After he died in 1565, the state capital was moved to Morelia, and the town became a cultural (and architectural) backwater for hundreds of years. Modern visitors will see 16th-century mansions surrounding the downtown plazas; one-story whitewashed houses with sloping tile roofs line the side streets and hills.

Despite the altitude, the weather in Pátzcuaro is temperate year-round. (Autumn and winter nights, however, are cold; sweaters and jackets are a must.) On November 1—the night preceding the Mexican Day of the Dead—the town is inundated with tourists en route to Janitzio, an island in Lake Pátzcuaro, where one of the most elaborate graveyard ceremonies in all of Mexico takes place.

Exploring Pátzcuaro

Most of Pátzcuaro's sights can be seen in a few hours, but the town deserves to be explored at a leisurely pace. There can be some traffic in the Plaza Bocanegra and on the main road coming into town, but elsewhere is blissfully quiet.

A Good Walk
Numbers in the text correspond to numbers in the margin and on the Pátzcuaro map.

Start your stroll at the **tourist office** (Ibarra 2), where you can pick up maps and brochures. Directly across the street is the large **Plaza Vasco de Quiroga** ①. Go to the east side of the square and turn right on Calle Dr. José María Coss; in less than a block you'll see a long cobblestone walkway leading to **La Casa de los 11 Patios** ②, a former old convent now housing a number of shops. As you leave the complex, continue up a stone walkway to Calle Lerín. A block to the north (past Calle Portugal) is the **Templo de la Compañía** ③, the state's first cathedral.

After visiting the church, continue another half-block along Calle Lerín to the **Museo de Artes Populares** ④ on your right.

Directly down Calle Lerín and across a cobblestoned courtyard is **La Basílica de Nuestro Señora de la Salud** ⑤. Walk downhill from the basilica (take Buenavista to Libertad and turn left) to reach the **Biblioteca Pública Gertrudis Bocanegra** ⑥. For a nice detour from the library, continue for a half-block to the large outdoor **mercado** sprawled along Calle Libertad and its side streets. At times the road is so crowded with people and their wares—fruit, vegetables, beans, rice, herbs, and sponges—that it is difficult to walk. On Friday, market day, the street is particularly packed. If you press on for about a block, you'll see an indoor market to your left, filled with more produce, large hanging slabs of meat, hot food, and a variety of cheap trinkets. When you're done with your market tour, retrace your steps down Calle Libertad. Across the street from the library, you can rest at **Plaza Bocanegra** ⑦, just one block north of your starting point, Plaza Vasco de Quiroga.

Sights to See

⑥ **Biblioteca Pública Gertrudis Bocanegra.** In the back of this library, a vast mural painted by Juan O'Gorman in 1942 depicts in great detail the history of the region and of the Tarascan people. If you look closely at the bottom, you may be able to make out the image of Gertrudis Bocanegra, a local heroine who was shot in 1814 for refusing to divulge the revolutionaries' secrets to the Spaniards. ⊠ *North side of Plaza Bocanegra.* ☉ *Weekdays 9–7.*

⑤ **La Basílica de Nuestra Señora de la Salud.** The church was begun in 1554 by Vasco de Quiroga but was never completed. Throughout the centuries others—undaunted by earthquakes and fires—took up the cause and constructed a church in honor of the Virgin of Health. Near the main altar is a statue made of cornstalk paste and orchid "juice." Several masses are still held here daily; the earliest begins shortly after dawn. Out front, Tarascan women sell hot tortillas, herbal mixtures for teas, and religious objects. You can glimpse Lake Pátzcuaro in the distance from here. ⊠ *Calle Lerin s/n near Calle Cerrato.*

② **La Casa de los 11 Patios.** An 18th-century convent, La Casa houses a number of high-quality shops featuring Tarascan handiwork. As you meander through the gardens and courtyards, you'll encounter weavers producing large bolts of cloth, artists trimming black lacquerware with gold, and seamstresses embroidering blouses. Children may approach you and ask if you'd like to hear the history of the Casa. In return they expect a small donation. If you plan to shop in Pátzcuaro, this is a good place to start. You can view the selection of regional goods and begin to compare prices. ⊠ *Calle Madrigal de los Altos 2.* ☉ *Daily 10–2 and 4–8.*

④ **Museo de Artes Populares.** Home to the Colegio de San Nicolás Obispo in the 16th century, the building today houses displays of colonial and contemporary crafts, such as ceramics, masks, lacquerware, paintings, and ex-votos in its many rooms. Behind this building is a *troje* (traditional Tarascan wood house) braced atop a stone platform. ☎ *434/2-10–29.* 🎫 *About $2.* ☉ *Tues.–Sat. 9–7, Sun. 9–3.*

⑦ **Plaza Bocanegra.** While Bocanegra is the smaller of the two squares in the city, it is the center of Pátzcuaro's commercial life. Bootblacks, pushcart vendors, and bus and taxi stands to Lake Pátzcuaro are all found in this plaza, marked by a statue of the local heroine. ⊠ *Bounded by Av. Libertad on the north, Portal Regules on the south, Dr. Benito Mendoza on the west, and Calle Zaragoza on the east.*

Pátzcuaro

NEED A
BREAK?

Before heading to the lake, sit in the shady square for a moment and enjoy a rich Michoacán ice-cream or fruit bar. Then grab a taxi or the San Bartolo–Lago bus to the *embarcadero* (wharf).

① **Plaza Vasco de Quiroga.** A tranquil courtyard surrounded by ash trees and 16th-century mansions (since converted into hotels and shops), the larger of the two downtown plazas commemorates the bishop who restored dignity to the Tarascan people. During the Spanish conquest, Nuño de Guzmán, a lieutenant in Hernán Cortés's army, committed atrocities on the local population in his efforts to conquer western Mexico. He was eventually arrested by the Spanish authorities, and in 1537 Vasco de Quiroga was appointed bishop of Michoacán. Attempting to regain the trust of the indigenous people, he established a number of model villages in the area and promoted the development of commerce among the Tarascans. Quiroga died in 1565, and his remains were consecrated in the ☞ **Basílica de Nuestra Señora de la Salud.** ⊠ *Bounded by Calle Quiroga on the north, Av. Ponce de León on the south, Portal Hidalgo on the west, and Dr. José María Coss on the east.*

③ **Templo de la Compañia.** Michoacán's first cathedral was begun in 1540 by order of Vasco de Quiroga and completed in 1546. When the state capital was moved to Morelia some 20 years later, the church was taken over by the Jesuits. Today it remains much as it was in the 16th century. Moss has grown over the crumbling stone steps outside; the dank interior is planked with thick wood floors and lined with bare wood benches. ⊠ *Calle Lerin s/n near Calle Alcantaría.*

OFF THE
BEATEN PATH

Lake Pátzcuaro – Just a 10-minute taxi ride from downtown are the tranquil shores of Lake Pátzcuaro. There are a few lakeside restaurants here that serve fresh whitefish and other local catches. Amble along the dock or peek into the waterfront crafts shops. If you have time, a boat trip to **Janitzio** (the largest of Lake Pátzcuaro's five islands) is highly recommended.

Wooden launches, with room for 25 people, depart for Janitzio daily from 9 to 6. Purchase round-trip tickets for $3 at a dockside office (where prices are controlled by the tourist department). The ride to Janitzio takes about 30 minutes and is particularly beautiful in late afternoon, when the sun is low in the sky. Once you're out on the lake, fishermen with butterfly nets may approach your boat. The nets are no longer used for fishing, but for a small donation these locals will let you take their picture.

On most days (November 2 being the exception), Janitzio is a quiet island inhabited by Tarascan Indians. It is crowned by a huge statue of independence hero José María Morelos, which is accessible by a cobblestoned stairway. Though the road twists past many souvenir stands as it ascends, don't be discouraged. The view from the summit—of the lake, the town, and the surrounding hills—is well worth the climb. Inside the statue are some remarkable murals that spiral up from the base to the tip of the monument.

Dining

Most restaurants in Pátzcuaro specialize in seafood. In addition to whitefish (which is featured on most menus), look for *trucha* (trout) and *charales* and *boquerones* (two small, locally caught fish served as appetizers). Tarascan specialties, such as a tomato-based soup with cheese, cream, and tortillas (called *sopa tarasca*) are also common. As a rule, restaurants are located around the two plazas and in hotels. Since the large meal is served at midday, many dining establishments are shuttered by 9. Unless otherwise indicated, dress is casual.

$$ ✕ **La Casona.** This unpretentious restaurant on Plaza Vasco de Quiroga, with whitewashed walls and white ceiling *vigas* (beams), is brightened by orange tablecloths. The house specialties include *caldo de pesca* (fish soup) and *pescado blanca* (whitefish), among other local dishes. ✉ *Plaza Vasco de Quiroga 65,* ☎ *434/2–11–79. AE, MC, V.*

$ ✕ **El Patio.** Though this low-key restaurant features mouthwatering white-
★ fish platters (including salsa, vegetables, and french fries), it's possible to duck in at midday for just a strong cappuccino or glass of local wine. (There are several varieties of wine; waiters can help you choose among them.) For a late-afternoon snack, a plate of quesadillas with a side order of guacamole is highly recommended, and the *sopa tarasca* is superb. ✉ *Plaza Vasco de Quiroga 19,* ☎ *434/2–04–84. DC, MC, V.*

$ ✕ **Restaurante Gran Hotel.** Though this one-room restaurant is connected to the Gran Hotel, it is independently owned and attracts a mix of locals and tourists to its midday meal. The furnishings are simple: tables covered with amber-colored cloths and set beneath wood chandeliers. The food is good and wholesome. Specialties include lightly breaded whitefish, chicken with mole sauce, and Tarascan soup. ✉ *Portal Regules 6,* ☎ *434/2–04–43. Reservations not accepted. V.*

$ ✕ **Restaurante Hotel Posada La Basílica.** From a corner table in this
★ glass-enclosed restaurant, patrons have views of the mountains, the lake, and tile-roofed homes. Open for breakfast and lunch (8–4), this dining spot offers such regional specialties as broiled trout with garlic and tamales with cheese and cream. Mexican-style eggs and a fresh-fruit platter are recommended morning fare. ✉ *Calle Arciga 6,* ☎ *434/2–11–08. Reservations not accepted. AE, MC, V.*

$ ✕ Restaurante Los Escudos. This colonial-style restaurant, located on the Plaza Vasco de Quiroga, is frequented by foreigners who stay in the adjoining hotel. The varied menu ranges from club sandwiches to multicourse midday meals. Two particularly tempting treats are the Tarascan soup and *pollo especial Los Escudos* (chicken sautéed in tomato sauce and vegetables). Checked tablecloths and yellow chimney lamps create a cozy atmosphere. ✉ *Portal Hidalgo 74,* ☎ *434/2–01–38 or 434/2–12–90. Reservations not accepted. MC, V.*

Lodging

Though Pátzcuaro has no deluxe properties, there are an ample number of clean, moderately priced hotels. Most are located on or within a few blocks of the Plaza Vasco de Quiroga. Several more expensive properties are situated on Avenida Lázaro Cárdenas, the road to Lake Pátzcuaro. If you're planning to be in town on or near November 2, the Mexican Day of the Dead, make hotel reservations at least six months in advance.

$$$ ⊞ Hotel Posada de Don Vasco. Located several minutes out of town on the road to Lake Pátzcuaro, this sprawling resort hotel offers a wide range of indoor and outdoor amenities. Its 30 newer rooms are thickly carpeted and have either balconies or patios; the older quarters, decorated in a colonial style, are smaller and open onto a courtyard. The manicured grounds are relatively quiet despite the occasional rumbling of a passing bus or truck. ✉ *Av. Las Americas 450, 61500,* ☎ *434/2–39–71 or 434/2–24–90,* FAX *434/2–02–62. 99 rooms with bath, 4 suites. Restaurant, pool, tennis courts, badminton, bowling, billiards. AE, MC, V.*

$$ ⊞ Hotel Posada La Basílica. This colonial-style inn, housed in a 17th-century building, faces the Basilica of the Virgin of Health. On some mornings strains from a postdawn Mass filter softly into the hotel; in the evenings, when there's a fair across the way, louder, more resonant music is audible. Though noisy, the property deserves a positive mention for its comfortable, individually decorated rooms. Thick wood shutters cover floor-to-ceiling windows, walls are trimmed in hand-painted colonial designs, and the rugs are handwoven. Some rooms have fireplaces, but check with management before attempting to use them, as not all of them are functional. ✉ *Calle Arciga 6, 61600,* ☎ *434/2–11–08 or 434/2–11–81; reservations, 434/2–06–59. 11 rooms with bath. Restaurant. AE, MC, V.*

$$ ⊞ Los Escudos. The 16th-century home of the Count de la Lama and the Marquis of Villahermosa de Alfaro on the Plaza Vasco de Quiroga is today a cozy hotel. Its courtyards bloom with potted plants, and some guest rooms contain small murals of Tarascan Indian scenes. Ten rooms situated in back and shielded from street noise open onto an outdoor patio. All rooms have color TVs and telephones; five rooms offer fireplaces. ✉ *Portal Hidalgo 73, 61600,* ☎ FAX *434/2–01–38 or 434/2–12–90. 30 rooms with bath. Restaurant. MC, V.*

$$ ⊞ Mansión Iturbe. This hotel, housed in a 17th-century mansion, still
★ retains much of its colonial charm. Plant-filled courtyards are ringed by stone archways. Rooms, featuring large wood-and-glass doors, are partially carpeted and decorated with red-and-black–checked spreads and drapes. The tranquil second-floor courtyard has a good view of the neighborhood. ✉ *Portal Morelos 59, 61600,* ☎ *434/2–03–68. 12 rooms with bath. Restaurant, bicycles. MC, V.*

$$ ⊞ Mesón del Gallo. Located on a fairly quiet side street near the Casa de los 11 Patios, this two-story property offers modern rooms in a garden setting; the beds have wood-and-tile headboards and magenta spreads and drapes. Suites, complete with minibars, are furnished in more subdued hues. The patio is encircled by bougainvillea, fruit trees, and a rock garden. ✉ *Calle Dr. José María Coss 20, 61600,* ☎ *434/2–14–74,* FAX *434/2–15–11. 20 rooms with bath, 5 suites. Restaurant, bar. AE, MC, V.*

Nightlife and the Arts

The **Dance of Los Viejitos** (Old Men), a widely known Mexican native dance, is performed on Wednesday and Saturday evenings at the Hotel Posada de Don Vasco (✉ Av. Las Americas 450, ☎ 434/2–39–71). A buffet dinner with entertainment costs approximately $12.

Side Trips

Tzintzuntzán
17 km (10½ mi) northeast of Pátzcuaro.

When the Spanish came to colonize the region in the 16th century, some 40,000 Tarascans lived and worshipped in this lakeshore village, which they called "place of the hummingbirds." The ruins of the pyramid-shape temples, or *yacatas,* found in the ancient capital of the Tarascan kingdom still stand today and are open to the public for a small admission charge. Visitors can also find vestiges of a 16th-century Franciscan monastery where Spanish friars attempted to convert the Indians to Christianity. Though Tzintzuntzán lost some prominence when Bishop Vasco de Quiroga moved the seat of his diocese to Pátzcuaro in 1540, the village is still well known for the straw and ceramic handicrafts made by the Tarascan Indians and sold in numerous shops along the main street of town. To reach Tzintzuntzán, take the bus marked Quiroga from Pátzcuaro's Central Camionera; travel time is about 30 minutes.

Uruapan
64 km (40 mi) west of Pátzcuaro.

The subtropical town of Uruapan is distinctly different from its lakeside neighbor: Some 2,000 feet lower than Pátzcuaro, though still at an elevation of 5,300 feet, it is a populous, commercial center with a warm climate and lush vegetation. The town's name is derived from the Tarascan word *urupan,* meaning "where the flowers bloom."

Uruapan can be reached from Pátzcuaro by either car or bus. Route 14 is the most direct route between the two cities. There is also frequent bus service on the Flecha Amarilla and other major lines; travel time is about 70 minutes.

You can see several points of interest within a few hours. The first, **La Huatápera,** is located off Uruapan's Plaza Principal. This 16th-century hospital has been converted into the **Museo Regional de Arte Popular.** It houses a collection of crafts from the state of Michoacán, including an excellent display of lacquerware made in Uruapan. ☎ *452/4–34–34.* ✍ *Free.* ☉ *Tues.–Sun. 10–6.*

The **Mercado de Antojitos,** an immense, sprawling market, begins directly in back of the museum and extends quite a distance north along Calle Constitución. Along the road, Tarascan Indians sell large mounds of produce, fresh fish, beans, homemade cheese, and a variety of cheap manufactured goods. If you travel south along Calle Constitución, you'll come to a courtyard where vendors sell hot food.

At the **Parque Nacional Eduardo Ruiz,** located about a kilometer (½ mile) from the Plaza Principal off Calle Independencia, you can stroll through the verdant acreage to the source of the River Cupatitzio and abundant fountains, waterfalls, and springs.

Eleven kilometers (7 miles) south along the river is the magnificent waterfall at **Tzaráracua.** At this point the Cupatitzio plunges 150 feet off a sheer rock cliff into a riverbed below; a rainbow seems to hang perpetually over the site. Buses marked Tzaráracua leave sporadically from the Plaza Principal in Uruapan. You can also take a taxi or drive there via Avenida Lázaro Cárdenas.

Farther afield, about 32 kilometers (20 miles) north of Uruapan, lies the dormant **Paricutín volcano.** Its initial burst of lava and ashes wiped out the nearby village of San Juan Parangaricutiro in 1943. Today travelers can visit this buried site by hiring gentle mountain ponies and a Tarascan guide in the town of Angahuan. To reach Angahuan, take the Los Reyes bus from Uruapan's Central Camionera or go by car via the Uruapan–Carapan highway.

DINING

For good *carne asada* (charbroiled beef served with grilled scallions, avocado, and *frijoles charro*—beans in broth), try **Parilla Tarasca** (⊠ Calle Alvaro Obregón 4, no phone), a two-level restaurant specializing in grilled meat.

Pátzcuaro A to Z

Arriving and Departing

BY BUS

Direct bus service is available daily between the Terminal Poniente (West Terminal) in Mexico City and Pátzcuaro's Central Camionera. Several bus lines offer frequent service; the most direct trip, which takes six hours, is on **Herradura de Plata** (⊠ via Corta).

BY CAR

Driving time from Mexico City to Pátzcuaro is about seven hours. From Morelia, two roads lead to Pátzcuaro: The newer passes through Tiripetio; the older passes through Quiroga and Tzintzuntzán. Cars can be rented at locations in Mexico City or Morelia; there are no rental outlets in Pátzcuaro.

BY TRAIN

Train service between Mexico City and Pátzcuaro is available daily on the Mexican National Railways. The *Purepecha* departs Mexico City at 10 PM and arrives in Pátzcuaro at 7:30 AM; the return trip leaves Pátzcuaro at 10 PM and arrives in Mexico City at 7:30 AM. The round-trip fare is $24. There are no sleeping cars, but train seats do recline. Train schedules are subject to change without notice. For current schedules and rates, contact **Mexico by Train** (☎ FAX 210/725–3659 or 800/321–1699) or the local train station (☎ 434/2–08–03).

Getting Around

Many of Pátzcuaro's principal sights are located near the Plaza Vasco de Quiroga and Plaza Bocanegra in the center of town. Taxis and buses to the lake can also be found at these main squares. If you want to visit surrounding villages, taxi drivers will drive you for a reasonable rate. Be sure to agree on a fee before setting out.

Contacts and Resources

EMERGENCIES

Police (☎ 434/2–05–65 or 434/2–00–04).

Clinics. Centro Médico Quirúrgico (⊠ Portal Hidalgo 76, ☎ 434/2–19–98). **Hospital Civil** (☎ 434/2–02–85).

Pharmacy. Farmacia La Paz (⊠ La Paz and Bocanegra in Plaza Bocanegra, ☎ 434/2–08–10).

MONEY EXCHANGE

Banca Promex (✉ Portal Regules 9, ☎ 434/2–24–66). **Banamex** (✉ Portal Juárez 32, ☎ 434/2–15–50 or 434/2–10–31). **Bancomer** (✉ Zaragoza 23, ☎ 434/2–03–34). A **Banamex Caja Permanente ATM** is located on Dr. Benito Mendoza, between the two plazas. Note: Many Pátzcuaro restaurants and hotels do not accept traveler's checks, though some will take major credit cards.

VISITOR INFORMATION

Delegación de Turismo. ✉ *Ibarra 2, Interior 4, off Plaza Vasco de Quiroga,* ☎ *434/2–12–14.* ⊙ *Mon.–Sat. 9–2 and 4–7, Sun. 9–2.*

9 Acapulco

If Acapulco no longer tops the glitterati top-ten list, it remains both a sentimental favorite and a party-hearty resort town, boasting miles of beaches and some of the glitziest discos this side of the Pacific. A delightful three-hour drive from Acapulco is Taxco, a colonial treasure, where the Baroque towers of Santa Prisca church poke up among cobblestoned streets lined with silversmiths.

Updated by
Wendy Luft

FOR SUN LOVERS, beach bums, and other hedonists, Acapulco is the ideal holiday resort. Don't expect high culture, historic monuments, or haute cuisine. Anyone who ventures to this Pacific resort 433 kilometers (260 miles) south of Mexico City does so to relax. Translate that as swimming, shopping, and enjoying the nightlife. Everything takes place against a staggeringly beautiful natural backdrop. Acapulco Bay is one of the world's best natural harbors, and it is the city's centerpiece. By day the water looks temptingly deep blue; at night it flashes and sparkles with the city lights.

The weather is Acapulco's major draw—warm waters, almost constant sunshine, and year-round temperatures in the 80s. It comes as no surprise, then, that most people plan their day around laying their towel on some part of Acapulco's many miles of beach. Both tame and wild water sports are available—everything from waterskiing to snorkeling, diving, and parasailing. Less strenuous possibilities are motorboat rides and fishing trips. Championship golf courses, tennis courts, and the food and crafts markets also occasionally lure some visitors away from the beach, but not out of the sun.

Most people rouse themselves from their hammocks, deck chairs, or towels only when it is feeding time. Eating is one of Acapulco's great pleasures. In addition to the glitzy places, there are many good no-frills, down-home Mexican restaurants. Eating at one of these spots gives you a glimpse into the real Mexico: office workers breaking for lunch, groups of men socializing over a cup of coffee.

At night Acapulco is transformed as the city rouses itself from the day's torpor and prepares for the long hours ahead. Even though Acapulco's heyday is past, its nightlife is legendary. This is true despite the fact that many of the discos along the main drag still look as if they were designed in the early '70s by an architect who bought mirrors and strobe lights wholesale. Perpetually crowded, the discos are grouped in twos and threes, so most people go to several places in one night.

Acapulco was originally an important port for the Spanish, who used it to trade with countries in the Far East. The Spanish built Fuerte de San Diego (Fort San Diego) to protect the city from pirates, and today the fort houses a historical museum. The name of the late Teddy Stauffer, an entrepreneurial Swiss, is practically synonymous with that of modern Acapulco. He hired the first cliff divers at La Quebrada in Old Acapulco and founded the Boom Boom Room, the town's first dance hall, and Tequila A Go-Go, its first discotheque. The Hotel Mirador at La Quebrada and the area stretching from Caleta to Hornos beaches, near today's Old Acapulco, were the center of activity in the 1950s, when Acapulco was a town of 20,000 with an economy based largely on fishing.

Former president Miguel Alemán Valdés bought up miles of the coast just before the road and the airport were built. Avenida Costera Miguel Alemán bears his name today. Since the late 1940s, Acapulco has expanded eastward so that today it is one of Mexico's largest cities, with a population of approximately 2 million. Currently under development is a 3,000-acre expanse known as Acapulco Diamante, which encompasses the areas known as Punta Diamante and Playa Diamante and some of Acapulco's glitziest hotels and residential developments.

Pleasures and Pastimes

Beaches

The lure of sun and sand in Acapulco is legendary. Every sport is available, and you can eat in a beach restaurant, dance, and sleep in a *hamaca* (hammock) without leaving the water's edge. If you want to avoid the crowds, there are also plenty of quiet and even isolated beaches within reach.

Dining

Dining in Acapulco is more than just eating out—it is the most popular leisure activity in town. Every night the restaurants fill up, and every night the adventurous diner can sample a different cuisine: Italian, Belgian, Japanese, American, Tex-Mex, and, of course, plain old Mex. The variety of styles matches the range of cuisines: from greasy spoons that serve regional specialties to gourmet restaurants with gorgeous views of Acapulco Bay. Most restaurants fall somewhere in the middle, and on the Costera are dozens of beachside restaurants, roofed with palapa (palm frond), as well as wildly decorated rib and hamburger joints popular with visitors under 30—not necessarily in age, but definitely in spirit.

Another plus for Acapulco dining is that the food is garden fresh. Each morning the Mercado Municipal is abuzz with restaurant managers and locals buying up the fish, poultry, and vegetables that will appear on plates that evening. Although some top-quality beef is now being produced in the states of Sonora and Chihuahua, many of the more expensive restaurants claim that they import their beef from the States. Whether or not they're telling the truth, the beef is excellent in most places. Establishments that cater to tourists purify their drinking water and use it to cook vegetables.

Lodging

Accommodations in Acapulco run the gamut from sprawling, big-name complexes with nonstop amenities to small, family-run inns where hot water is a luxury. Wherever you stay, however, prices will be reasonable compared with those in the United States, and service is generally good, since Acapulqueños have been catering to tourists for more than 40 years.

Nightlife

Acapulco has always been famous for its nightlife, and justifiably so. For many visitors the discos and restaurants are just as important as the sun and the sand. The minute the sun slips over the horizon, the Costera comes alive with people milling around window-shopping, deciding where to dine, and generally biding their time till the disco hour. The legendary Acapulco discos are open 365 days a year from about 10:30 PM until they empty out, often not until 4 or 5 AM. Obviously you aren't going to find great culture here; theater efforts are few and far between and there is no classical music. But disco-hopping is a high art in Acapulco, and for those who care to watch, there are live shows and folk-dance performances.

Shopping

The abundance of air-conditioned shopping malls and boutiques makes picking up gifts and souvenirs one of the highlights of a visit to Acapulco. The malls are filled with clothing shops, and many others are strung along the Costera. There are also a few high-fashion boutiques that carry custom-designed clothes. Malls in Acapulco range from the shopping arcades at several of the more lavish hotels to the huge completely enclosed and air-conditioned Plaza Bahía.

The Mercado Municipal, whose rows are piled high with fruits, vegetables, poultry, fish, and meats, is also is a good source of local handicrafts. Flea markets abound, carrying what seems to be an inexhaustible supply of inexpensive collectibles and souvenirs.

Silver is a real bargain in Mexico. Taxco, three hours away, is one of the silver capitals of the world.

Sports and the Outdoors

Acapulco has lots for sports lovers to enjoy. Most hotels have pools, and many have several private tennis clubs as well as courts. The fitness craze has caught on, and many of the hotels have gyms, too. Acapulco's waters are teeming with sailfish, marlin, shark, and mahimahi, and although the waters aren't as clear as in the Caribbean, scuba diving is popular, as are waterskiing, windsurfing, kayaking, and bronco riding (an activity done in one-person motorboats). Parasailing is an Acapulco highlight. It looks terrifying and can be dangerous, but most people who do it love the view and go back again and again. Golfers can tee off at the 9-hole municipal course, in town, or at one of the five 18-hole championship courses (three are open to the public) in the Acapulco Diamante area.

EXPLORING ACAPULCO

It's possible to get a feel for Acapulco during a short stay if you take in some downtown sights along with your beach activities. Those who have a longer time to spend can really soak up the ambience of the place and can enjoy excursions to some isolated beaches as well as to Taxco.

Great Itineraries

Numbers in the text correspond to numbers in the margin and on the Acapulco map.

IF YOU HAVE 3 DAYS

Spend the first day enjoying your favorite beach activity, be it parasailing, waterskiing, or simply sunning. That evening, to get the lay of the land, take a sunset cruise that includes a ringside view of Acapulco's daredevil *clavadistas* (divers) at **La Quebrada.** The following day, experience Acapulco at its most authentic, paying an early visit to the **Mercado Municipal,** the **waterfront,** and the **zocálo** (town square). After some late afternoon shopping in the boutiques and handicrafts markets along the Costera Miguel Alemán, "shake off the dust" (as they say in Mexico) at one of the city's glitzy discos. The next day you'll want to try to land a sailfish, take in the Mexican Fiesta at the **Acapulco International Center** (drinks and show only), and bid farewell to Acapulco with a late candlelit dinner at one of the city's romantic dining spots.

IF YOU HAVE 5 DAYS

Add on to the three-day itinerary a visit to **El Fuerte de San Diego,** built in the 18th century to protect Acapulco from pirates, and today home of the Anthropology Museum. For a taste of the 1950s Acapulco of John Wayne and Johnny Weissmuller, get a taxi to take you up into the hills above Caleta and Caletilla. Head out to Pie de la Cuesta for a late lunch and boat ride or waterskiing on Coyuca Lagoon, and then cross the road and park your body under a palm-frond umbrella for a spectacular sunset on the beach. Especially if you're traveling with kids, devote a day to **Mágico Mundo Marino** and the glass-bottom boat trip to Roqueta Island.

IF YOU HAVE 7 DAYS

For a complete change of pace, you'll want to rent a car or arrange for a tour to **Taxco,** a glorious treasure of twisting cobblestone streets and some 1,000 silver shops, about a three-hour drive from Acapulco; plan to spend the night. For a change from shopping for silver, visit the Santa Prisca church, Taxco's most important landmark, on Plaza Borda, and the Casa Humboldt, which now houses a museum of viceregal art. Try to get a front-row seat at one of the bars or restaurants on the square and spend about an hour watching the constant activity: weddings, communions, funerals and baptisms, and vendors selling baskets and painted animals. The following day, before the return trip to Acapulco, tour the **Caves of Cacahuamilpa,** an amazing expanse of subterranean chambers.

Exploring Acapulco

Acapulco is a city that is easily understood, easily explored. During the day the focus for most visitors is the beach and the myriad activities that happen on and off it. At night the attention shifts to the restaurants and discos. The Costera Miguel Alemán, the wide boulevard that hugs Acapulco Bay from the Scenic Highway to Caleta Beach (about 8 kilometers, or 5 miles), is central to both day and night diversions. All the major beaches, shopping malls, and big hotels—minus the more exclusive Acapulco Diamante properties—are off the Costera. Hence most of the shopping, dining, and clubbing takes place within a few blocks of this main drag, and many an address is listed only as "Costera Miguel Alemán." Although the Costera runs completely across Acapulco, most of the action is between the naval base, La Base, next to the Hyatt (which anchors the eastern terminus of the Costera) and Papagayo Park. Because street addresses are not often used and streets have no logical pattern, directions are usually given from a major landmark, such as CiCi (a theme park) or the zócalo.

Old Acapulco, the colonial part of town and the only area of Acapulco that can easily be visited on foot, is where the Mexicans go to run their errands: mail letters at the post office, buy supplies at the Mercado Municipal, and pay their taxes. Also known as El Centro, it's where you'll find the zócalo, the church, and Fort San Diego. Just up the hill from Old Acapulco is La Quebrada.

The peninsula south of Old Acapulco contains remnants of the first version of Acapulco. This primarily residential area was prey to dilapidation and abandonment for many years, but efforts were made to revitalize it—such as reopening the Caleta Hotel and opening the aquarium on Caleta Beach and the zoo on Roqueta Island. Although its prime is definitely past, it is now a popular area for budget travelers, especially Mexican and European. The Plaza de Toros, where bullfights are held on Sundays from Christmas to Easter, is in the center of the peninsula.

If you arrived by plane, you've already had a royal introduction to Acapulco Bay. Acapulco Diamante is the area stretching east of Acapulco proper from Las Brisas to Barra Vieja beach. You'll need a car or a taxi to explore this area, where you'll find most of Acapulco's poshest hotels—Las Brisas, the Acapulco Sheraton, Camino Real, the Princess and Pierre Marqués, and Vidafel—and residential developments, as well as several exclusive private clubs, pounding surf, and beautiful beaches.

A Good Tour

If you want to get the lay of the land, you might take a drive or taxi ride along the Costera Miguel Alemán, starting on its eastern edge at **La Base,** the Mexican naval base south of Playa Icacos. When you come to Playa Icacos, you'll see the **Casa de la Cultura** ① cultural complex on the beach side (just past the Hyatt Regency hotel); a little farther down is **CiCi** ②, a children's amusement park. About a kilometer (half mile) past CiCi, on the right side of the Costera, lies the **Acapulco International Center** (often called the Convention Center); you might return here in the evening to attend a Mexican fiesta. Continue along through the commercial heart of the Costera until you reach **Papagayo Park** ③, one of the top municipal parks in the country. When you arrive at the intersection of the Costera with Pro. D. H. de Mendoza, detour a few blocks inland to find Old Acapulco and the sprawling **Mercado Municipal** ④. You'll want to park your car nearby or have your taxi drop you off; it's best to navigate this area by foot. A few blocks west and closer to the water, **El Fuerte de San Diego** ⑤ sits on the hill overlooking the harbor next to the army barracks. You'll next see the **waterfront** ⑥ (locally known as the *malecón*) with its series of docks and, adjoining it, the **zócalo** ⑦, the center of Old Acapulco. A 15-minute walk up the hill from the zócalo brings you to **La Quebrada** ⑧, where the famous cliff divers do their daredevil stunt daily.

Sights to See

❶ Casa de la Cultura. This cultural complex includes a small archaeological museum, an exhibit of crafts from the entire state of Guerrero, and the Ixcateopan art gallery, with changing exhibits. ⊠ *Costera Miguel Alemán 4834,* ☎ *74/84–38–14.* ▭ *Free.* ⊙ *Weekdays 9–2 and 5–8, Sat. 9–2.*

❷ CiCi (Centro Internacional para Convivencia Infantil). A water-oriented theme park for children, CiCi features dolphin and seal shows, a freshwater pool with wave-making apparatus, a water slide, mini-aquarium, and other attractions. ⊠ *Costera Miguel Alemán, across from the Hard Rock Café,* ☎ *74/84–82–10.* ▭ *$5.* ⊙ *Daily 10–6.*

❺ El Fuerte de San Diego. An 18th-century fortress, El Fuerte de San Diego was designed to protect the city from pirates. (The original fort, destroyed in an earthquake, was built in 1616.) The fort now houses the **Museo Historico de Acapulco,** under the auspices of Mexico's National Institute of Anthropology and History. The exhibits portray the city from prehistoric times through Mexico's independence from Spain in 1821. Especially noteworthy are the displays touching on the Christian missionaries sent from Mexico to the Far East and the cultural interchange that resulted. ⊠ *Calle Hornitos and Morelos,* ☎ *74/82–38–28.* ▭ *$2; free Sun.* ⊙ *Tues.–Sun. 10:30–4:40.*

❽ La Quebrada. High on a hill above downtown Acapulco, La Quebrada is home to the Mirador Hotel, *the* place for tourists in the 1940s; it still retains some sheen from its glory days. But these days most visitors eventually make the trip here because this is where the famous cliff divers jump from a height of 130 feet daily at 1 PM and evenings at 7:30, 8:30, 9:30, and 10:30. The dives are thrilling, so be sure to arrive early. Before they take the plunge, the brave divers say a prayer at a small shrine near the jumping-off point. Sometimes they dive in pairs; often they carry torches. There's an admission fee (about $1), paid at a booth outside the hotel before you enter the viewing area; when you exit, some of the divers may also be waiting to greet you— and to ask for tips. (For information about viewing the divers on sunset cruises, *see* Guided Tours *in* Acapulco A to Z, *below*.)

❾ Mágico Mundo Marino. In addition to an aquarium, the Magic Marine World features a sea lion show, swimming pools, a toboggan, scuba diving, and (for rent) Jet Skis, inner tubes, bananas (inflatable rubber

Av. Rancho Acapulco

Paseo del Farallon

Av. Almirante Magallanes

Acapulco International Center

Golf Course

Almirante Cristobal Colón

Horacio Nelson

Lobo Solitario

Costera Miguel Alemán

Av. Cuauhtemoc

Diana Glorieta

Costera Miguel Alemán

Av. W. Massieu

Playa Icacos

Playa Condesa

❷

❶

Playa Hornitos

Punta Guitarrón

Escénica

A C A P U L C O

Carretera

D I A M A N T E

TO AIRPORT ⟶

ozo del Rey

Bahía de Acapulco

Tropical

❾ **Playa Caleta**

Playa Roqueta

Punta Bruja

Bahía de Puerto Marqués

TO PUNTA DIAMANTE ⟶
AND BARRA VIEJA

N

| 0 | 880 yards |
| 0 | 800 meters |

tubes pulled along the beach by motorboats), and kayaks—not to mention clean rest rooms. From Mágico Mundo Marino, you can take the glass-bottom boat to **Roqueta Island** (about 10-minutes each way) for a visit to the small zoo. Palao's restaurant on Roqueta Island has a sandy cove for swimming, a pony, and a cage of monkeys that entertain youngsters. ⊠ *Caleta Beach, no phone.* ☜ *Aquarium $3; round-trip ferry service to Roqueta Island, including zoo, $2.50.* ☉ *Mágico Mundo daily 9–7; zoo daily 9–5.*

❹ **Mercado Municipal.** It's not for everyone, but the sprawling municipal market is Acapulco as the locals experience it. They come to purchase their everyday needs, from fresh vegetables and candles to plastic buckets and love potions. The stalls within the mercado are densely packed together but are awning-covered, so things stay relatively cool despite the lack of air-conditioning.

There are hundreds of souvenirs to choose from here: woven blankets, puppets, colorful wooden toys and plates, leather goods, baskets, hammocks, and handmade wooden furniture, including child-size chairs. There is even a stand offering charms, amulets and talismans, bones, herbs, fish eyes, sharks' teeth, lotions, candles, and soaps said to help one find or keep a mate, increase virility or fertility, bring peace to the home, or ward off the evil eye. Kitschy gems abound: Acapulco ashtrays and boxes covered with tiny shells or enormous framed pictures of the Virgin of Guadalupe. There are also silver jewelry vendors, but unless you really have a good eye for quality, it's best to buy silver only from a reputable dealer (☞ Shopping, *below*).

It's best to come as early as possible to avoid the crowds. Ask to be dropped off near the *flores* (flower stand) closest to the souvenir and crafts section; from the flower stall, as you face the ceramic stand, turn right and head into the market. If you've driven to the mercado, locals may volunteer to watch your car; be sure to lock your trunk and tip about 35¢. ⊠ *Viaducto Aguas Blancas and Constituyentes, a few blocks west of the Costera.*

👆 ❸ **Papagayo Park.** Named for the hotel that formerly occupied the grounds, Papagayo Park sits on 52 acres of prime real estate on the Costera, just after the underpass that begins at Hornos beach. Youngsters enjoy the life-size model of a Spanish galleon, made to look like the ones that once sailed into Acapulco when it was Mexico's capital of trade with the Orient. There is an aviary, a roller-skating rink, a racetrack with mite-size race cars, a replica of the space shuttle *Columbia*, bumper boats in a lagoon, and other rides. ⊠ *Costera Miguel Alemán,* ☎ *74/85–96–23.* ☜ *No entrance fee; rides cost about 50¢ to $2.* ☉ *Daily 10–8.*

❻ **Waterfront.** A stroll by the docks will remind you that Acapulco is still a lively commercial port and fishing center. The cruise ships anchor here, and at night Mexican parents bring their children to play on the small treelined promenade. Farther west, by the zócalo, are the docks for the sightseeing yachts and smaller fishing boats. It's a good spot to join the Mexicans in people-watching. ⊠ *Costera Miguel Alemán, between Calle Escudero on the west and the San Diego Fort on the east.*

❼ **Zócalo.** You'll find the hub of downtown and Old Acapulco at this shaded plaza, overgrown with dense trees. All day it's filled with vendors, shoeshine men, and people lining up to use the pay phones. After siesta, they drift here to meet and greet. On Sunday evenings there's often music in the bandstand. There are several cafés and news agents selling the English-language *Mexico City News,* so tourists lodging in the area are drawn here, too. The flea market, inexpensive tailor shops, and Woolworth's (☞ Shopping, *below*) are nearby. The zócalo fronts **Nuestra Señora de la Soledad,** the town's modern but unusual church, with its stark-white exterior and bulb-shaped blue and yellow spires. ✉ *Bounded by Calle Felipe Valle on the north, Calle J. Carranza on the south, Calle J. Azueta on the west, and Calle J. Carranza on the east.*

NEED A BREAK?	Just off the zócalo, **Sanborns** attracts locals and tourists alike; many linger for hours over the newspaper and a cup of coffee. The unnamed **café** at 45 Cinco de Mayo serves *churros* every afternoon beginning at 4. This Spanish treat of fried dough dusted with sugar and dipped in hot chocolate is popular at *merienda,* which means "snack time."

BEACHES

Some beaches, such as Revolcadero and Pie de la Cuesta, have very strong undertows and surfs, so swimming is not advised. Despite an enticing appearance and claims that officials are cleaning up the bay, it remains polluted. In addition, although vending on the beach has been officially outlawed, you'll still find yourself approached by souvenir hawkers. If these things bother you, we suggest that you follow the lead of the Mexican cognoscenti and enjoy the waters at your hotel pool.

Beaches in Mexico are public, even those that seem to belong to a big hotel.

Barra Vieja

About 27 kilometers (16 miles) east of Acapulco, between Laguna de Tres Palos and the Pacific, this magnificent beach is even more inviting than Pie de la Cuesta (☞ *below*) because the drive out is much more pleasant.

Caleta and Caletilla

On the peninsula in Old Acapulco, these two beaches once rivaled La Quebrada as the main tourist area in Acapulco's heyday. Now they attract families. Motorboats to Roqueta Island (☞ Mágico Mundo Marino *in* Exploring, *above*) leave from here.

Condesa

Facing the middle of Acapulco Bay, this stretch of sand has more than its share of tourists, especially singles, and the beachside restaurants are convenient for bites between parasailing flights.

Hornos and Hornitos

Running from the Plaza las Glorias Paraíso to Las Hamacas hotel, these beaches are packed shoulder to shoulder on the weekends with locals and Mexican tourists who know a good thing: Graceful palms shade the sand, and there are scads of casual eateries within walking distance.

Icacos

Stretching from the naval base to El Presidente hotel, this beach is less populated than others on the Costera, and the morning waves are especially calm.

Pie de la Cuesta

You'll need a car or cab to reach this relatively unpopulated spot, about a 25-minute drive west of Acapulco, through one of the least picturesque parts of town. A string of rustic restaurants border the wide beach, and straw palapas provide shade. What attracts people to Pie de la Cuesta, besides the long expanse of beach and spectacular sunsets, is beautiful **Coyuca Lagoon,** a favorite spot for waterskiing, freshwater fishing, and boat rides.

Puerto Marqués

Tucked below the airport highway, this strand is popular with Mexican tourists, so it tends to get crowded on weekends.

Revolcadero

A wide, sprawling beach next to the Vidafel, Pierre Marqués and Princess hotels, its water is shallow and its waves are fairly rough. People come here to surf and ride horses.

DINING

The top restaurants in Acapulco can be fun for a splurge and provide very good value. Even at the best places in town, dinner rarely exceeds $50 per person, and the atmosphere and views are fantastic. Ties and jackets are out of place, but so are shorts or jeans. Unless stated otherwise, all restaurants are open daily from 6:30 or 7 PM until the last diner leaves. Several restaurants have two seatings: 6:30 for the *gringos* and 9 for the Mexican crowd, who wisely head directly to the discos after dinner to dance off the calories.

Note: Loud music blares from many restaurants along the Costera, and proprietors will aggressively try to hustle you inside with offers of drink specials. If you're looking for a hassle-free evening, it's best either to avoid this area or decide in advance precisely where you want to dine.

CATEGORY	COST*
$$$$	over $35
$$$	$25–$35
$$	$15–$25
$	under $15

per person, excluding drinks, service, and sales tax (10%)

American

$$ ✕ **Carlos 'n' Charlie's.** This is without a doubt the most popular restaurant in town; a line forms well before the 6:30 PM opening. Part of the Anderson group (with restaurants in the United States and Spain as well as Mexico), Carlos 'n' Charlie's cultivates an atmosphere of controlled craziness. Prankster waiters, a jokester menu, and eclectic decor—everything from antique bullfight photos to a tool chest of painted gadgets hanging from the ceiling—add to the chaos. The crowd is mostly young and relaxed, which is what you need to be to put up with the rush-hour traffic noise that filters up to the covered balcony where people dine. The menu straddles the border, with ribs, stuffed shrimp, and oysters among the best offerings. ✉ *Costera Miguel Alemán 112,* ☎ *74/84–12–85 or 84–00–39. Reservations not accepted. AE, DC, MC, V.*

$$ ✕ **Hard Rock Café.** This link in the international Hard Rock chain is one of the most popular spots in Acapulco, and with good reason. The southern-style food—fried chicken, ribs, hamburgers—is very well

prepared and the portions are more than ample. The taped rock music begins at noon, and a live group starts playing at 11 PM (except Tuesday). There's always a line at the small boutique on the premises, where you can buy sports clothes and accessories bearing the Hard Rock label. ⊠ *Costera Miguel Alemán 37,* ☎ *74/84–66–80. Reservations not accepted. AE, MC, V.*

Belgian

$$ ✕ **La Petite Belgique.** Mexican-born Yolanda Brassart, who spent
★ years in Europe studying the culinary arts, reigns in the kitchen of this small bistro. Guillermo, her Belgian husband, obviously adores his wife—and her cooking—and makes certain that the customers are happy. Diners are greeted by the enticing aromas of goose-liver pâté, home-baked breads, and apple strudel, all displayed temptingly at the entrance. The menu changes every four months but usually includes boned duck stuffed with almonds and mushrooms and served with a white wine and mushroom sauce. ⊠ *Plaza Marbella,* ☎ *74/84–77–25. AE, DC, MC, V.*

Continental

$$$ ✕ **Bella Vista.** This alfresco restaurant in the exclusive Las Brisas area has fantastic sunset views of Acapulco. Its large menu offers a wide variety of dishes that range from Asian appetizers to Italian and seafood entrées. Try the delicious (and spicy!) Thai shrimp, sautéed in sesame oil, ginger, Thai chili, and hoisin sauce; or the red snapper étouffée, cooked in chardonnay, tomato, herbs, basil, and oyster sauce. ⊠ *Carretera Escéncia 5255,* ☎ *74/84–15–80, ext. 500. Reservations essential. AE, DC, MC, V.*

$$$$ ✕ **Coyuca 22.** This is possibly the most expensive restaurant in Aca-
★ pulco; it is certainly one of the most beautiful. Diners eat on terraces that overlook the bay from the west, on a hilltop in Old Acapulco. The understated decor consists of Doric pillars, sculptures, and large onyx flower stands near the entrance. Diners gaze down on an enormous illuminated obelisk and a small pool. The effect is that of eating in a partially restored Greek ruin sans dust. Diners can choose from two fixed menus or order à la carte. Seafood and prime ribs are house specialties. ⊠ *Av. Coyuca 22 (a 10-minute taxi ride from the zócalo),* ☎ *74/82–34–68 or 74/83–50–30. Reservations essential. AE, DC, MC, V. ☉ Closed Apr. 30–Nov. 1.*

$$$ ✕ **Madeiras.** One of Acapulco's favorite dining spots, Madeiras is
★ very difficult to get into, especially on weekends and during the Christmas and Easter holidays; many people make reservations by letter before they arrive. The bar-reception area features Art Nouveau–style chairs and startling coffee tables made of glass resting on wooden animals; the dishes and flatware were created by silversmiths in nearby Taxco; and all the tables have a view of Acapulco glittering at night. Dinner is served from a four-course, prix-fixe menu and costs about $25 without wine. Entrées include the delicious Spanish dish of red snapper in sea salt, tasty chilled soups, stuffed red snapper, and a choice of steaks and other seafood, as well as the *crepas de huitlacoche (huitlacoche,* or *cuitlacoche,* is a corn fungus that was a delicacy to the Aztecs). Desserts are competently prepared but have no special flair. There are seatings every 30 minutes from 7 to 10:30 PM. ⊠ *Scenic Hwy. 33-B, just past La Vista shopping center,* ☎ *74/84–69–21. Reservations essential. No children under 8. AE, DC, MC, V.*

332

Acapulco Dining and Lodging

Dining
Bella Vista, **34**
Beto's, **18**
Blackbeard's, **17**
Carlos 'n'
Charlie's, **20**
Casa Nova, **35**
Coyuca 22, **6**
El Cabrito, **27**
El Olvido, **28**
Hard Rock Cafe, **25**
La Casa de Tere, **9**
La Petite Belgique, **28**

La Vela, **36**
Los Rancheros, **31**
Madeiras, **33**
100% Natural, **13**
Paradise, **16**
Pipo's, **26**
Sirocco, **10**
Suntory, **29**
Villa Fiore, **23**
Zapata,
Villa y Cia, **29**
Zorrito's, **12**

Lodging
Acapulco Plaza, **15**
Acapulco Princess, **38**
Boca Chica, **4**
Camino Real
Acapulco
Diamante, **36**
Fiesta Americana
Condesa
Acapulco, **21**
Hotel Acapulco
Tortuga, **19**
Hotel Misión, **7**

Howard Johnson
Moralisa, **14**
Hyatt Regency
Acapulco, **30**
Majestic, **5**
Parador del Sol, **1**
Pierre Marqués, **37**
Plaza las Glorias
El Mirador, **8**
Plaza las Glorias
Paraíso, **11**
Royal El Cano, **24**
Sheraton
Acapulco, **32**

Bahía de Acapulco

N

| 0 | 880 yards |
| 0 | 800 meters |

Paseo del Farallón

Diana Glorieta

Villa Fiore

Golf Course

Lobo Solitario

Centro International

Av. Almirante Horacio Nelson

Magallanes

Almirante Cristóbal Colón

Costera Miguel Alemán

El Olvida

Playa Icacos

La Base

Punta Guitarrón

Escénica

Carretera

TO AIRPORT →

French

$$$ ✕ **El Olvido.** The view, the foliage, the Mediterranean decor, and the flickering candles combine to make this one of Acapulco's most romantic dining spots. A terraced dining area and huge windows provide all diners with a panoramic vista of the bay. French chef Daniel Janny blends the techniques of his native land with Mexican ingredients, which results in creations such as salmon roll with mango vinaigrette and quail in a honey, pineapple, and *pasilla* chili sauce. ⊠ *Plaza Marbella,* ☏ *74/81–02–14. AE, DC, MC, V.*

Health Food

$ ✕ **100% Natural.** Six family-operated restaurants specialize in light, healthful food—yogurt shakes, fruit salads, and sandwiches made with whole-wheat bread. The service is quick and the food is a refreshing alternative to tacos, particularly on a hot day. Look for the green signs with white lettering. ⊠ *Costera Miguel Alemán 200, near the Acapulco Plaza,* ☏ *74/85–39–82. Another branch across from Oceanic 2000,* ☏ *74/84–84–40. No credit cards.*

Italian

$$$ ✕ **Casa Nova.** Another ultraromantic spot created by Arturo Cordova,
★ the man behind Coyuca 22 (☞ *above*), Casa Nova is carved out of a cliff that rises up from Acapulco Bay. The views, both from the terrace and the air-conditioned interior dining room, are spectacular, the service impeccable, and the Italian cuisine divine. The menu includes antipasto, fresh pastas, a delightful *cotolette de vittello* (veal chops with mushrooms), lobster tail, and *linguini alle vongole* (linguini with clams, tomato, and garlic). ⊠ *Scenic Hwy., just past Madeiras,* ☏ *74/84–68–19. Reservations essential. AE, DC, MC, V.*

$$ ✕ **Villa Fiore.** Here, the owners of Madeiras (☞ *above*) bring you fine Italian dining in the candlelit garden of what looks like an 18th-century Venetian villa. Diners can choose from two fixed menus that include appetizer, soup, main course (chicken, fish, meat, or pasta), dessert, and coffee. Opt for the *calamari fritti* (fried squid in marinara sauce) as a starter, and fillet of stuffed sea bass with crab or ravioli for an entrée. Service is excellent. ⊠ *Av. del Prado 6,* ☏ *74/84–20–40. AE, DC, MC, V. Closed Wed.*

Japanese

$$$ ✕ **Suntory.** At this traditional Japanese restaurant you can dine either in a blessedly air-conditioned interior room or in the delightful Asian-style garden. It's one of the few Japanese restaurants in Acapulco and also one of the only deluxe restaurants that are open for lunch. Specialties are the sushi and the teppan-yaki, prepared at your table by skilled chefs. ⊠ *Costera Miguel Alemán 36, across from the La Palapa hotel,* ☏ *74/84–80–88. AE, DC, MC, V.*

Mexican

$$ ✕ **Los Rancheros.** With a view of the water in the posh East Bay, here's dining at about half what you'd pay at some of the big-name places. The decor is colorful, folksy Mexican with paper streamers, checked tablecloths, and lopsided mannequins in local dress. Specials include *carne tampiqueña* (fillet of beef broiled with lemon juice), chicken enchiladas, and *queso fundido* (melted cheese served as a side dish with chips). Mariachis entertain at lunch and dinner, Thursdays through Sundays. ⊠ *Scenic Hwy. just before Extasis disco (on left as you head toward airport)*, ☎ *74/84–19–08. AE, MC, V. Closed Tues.*

$$ ✕ **Zapata, Villa y Cia.** This is a Mexican version of the Hard Rock Café, where the music and food (excellent) are strictly Mexican and the memorabilia is Mexican Revolution, with guns, hats, and photographs of Pancho Villa. The definite highlight of an evening here is a visit from a sombrero-wearing baby burro, so be sure to bring your camera. ⊠ *Hyatt Regency, Costera Miguel Alemán 1*, ☎ *74/84–28–88. AE, DC, MC, V.*

$$ ✕ **Zorrito's.** When Julio Iglesias is in town, this is where he heads in the wee hours of the morning, after the discos close. He's been known to sing along with the band that's on hand to play every evening, from 6 PM on. The menu features a host of steak and beef dishes, and the special, *filete tampiqueña*, comes with tacos, enchiladas, guacamole, and frijoles. ⊠ *Costera Miguel Alemán and Anton de Alaminos, next to Banamex*, ☎ *74/85–37–35. Reservations not accepted. AE, MC, V.* ☾ *Closed 6 AM–9 AM and Tues.*

$ ✕ **El Cabrito.** This is a local favorite for true Mexican cuisine and ambience. The name of the restaurant—"The Goat"—is also its specialty. In addition, you can choose among mole; jerky with egg, fish, and seafood; and other Mexican dishes. ⊠ *Costera Miguel Alemán, between Nina's and the Hard Rock*, ☎ *74/84–77–11. Reservations not accepted. MC, V.*

$
★ ✕ **La Casa de Tere.** Hidden in a commercial district downtown (signs point the way), La Casa de Tere offers little in the way of upscale atmosphere—beer-hall tables and chairs, colorful Mexican decorations, and photos of Acapulco of yore—and even less of a view, but its tasty food and low prices make it a favorite with savvy *acapulqueños*. Doña Teresa Cabrera de Saab, who keeps a sharp eye on her spotlessly clean, open-air establishment, offers diners a small but varied menu that includes an outstanding *sopa de tortilla* (tortilla soup), chicken in mole sauce, and corn custard. The *comida corrida*—which includes soup, a main dish, and dessert—is an exceptionally good buy. Powerful overhead fans make up for the lack of air-conditioning. ⊠ *Alfonso Martín 1721, two blocks from Costera Miguel Alemán*, ☎ *74/85–77–35. Reservations not accepted. No credit cards.* ☾ *Closed Mon.*

Seafood

$$$ ✕ **Blackbeard's.** Dark, with a pirate-ship motif, Blackbeard's has maps covering the tables in the cozy booths, and the walls are adorned with wooden figureheads. Every movie star, from Bing Crosby to Liz Taylor, who ever set foot here has his or her photo posted in the lounge. Jumbo portions of shrimp, steak, and lobster keep customers satisfied. A disco on the premises starts throbbing at 10:30 PM. ⊠ *Costera Miguel Alemán, on Condesa Beach near the Fiesta Americana Condesa*, ☎ *74/84–25–49. AE, MC, V.*

$$$
★ ✕ **La Vela.** Set on a wharf that juts out into Pichilingue Bay, this open-air dining spot is protected by a dramatic roof that simulates a huge white sail. It's very atmospheric after dark, when a stillness hangs over the bay and the lights of Puerto Marqués flicker in the distance. The menu features a variety of fish and shellfish dishes, but the specialty of the house is the red snapper *à la talla* (basted with chili and other spices and broiled over hot coals). There are no overhead fans, and although there is usually a delightful breeze, the atmosphere can get quite uncomfortable on steamy summer nights. ⊠ *Camino Real Acapulco Diamante, Carretera Escénica Km 14*, ☎ *74/66–10–10. AE, DC, MC, V.*

$$ ✕ **Beto's.** By day you can eat right on the beach and enjoy live music; by night this palapa-roofed restaurant is transformed into a dim and romantic dining area lighted by candles and paper lanterns. Whole red snapper, lobster, and ceviche are recommended. There is a second branch next door and a third at Barra Vieja Beach—where the specialty is *pescado à la talla* (fish spread with chili and other spices and then grilled over hot coals). Beto's Safari turns into a disco on Fridays and Saturdays after 10. ⊠ *Beto's, Costera Miguel Alemán at Condesa Beach,* ☎ *74/84–04–73. Beto's Safari, Costera Miguel Alemán, next to Beto's,* ☎ *74/84–47–62. Beto's Barra Vieja, Barra Vieja Beach, no phone. AE, MC, V.*

$$ ✕ **Paradise.** This is the leading beach-party restaurant. T-shirted waiters drop leis over your head as you arrive, hand roses to the ladies, teach dance steps, and sing tropical songs. The menu (primarily seafood) has the same number of dishes as drinks, a pretty good indicator of what this place is like. Paradise has one of the biggest dance floors in Acapulco and live music day and night. Chaos reigns at lunchtime (from 2 to 5), and the mood picks up again from 8:30 to 10:30. Expect a young crowd. ⊠ *Costera Miguel Alemán 107, next to Mimi's Chili Saloon,* ☎ *74/84–59–88. Reservations not accepted. AE, DC, MC, V.*

$$ ✕ **Pipo's.** Situated on a rather quiet part of the Costera, this family-★ run seafood restaurant doesn't have an especially interesting view, but diners come here for the fresh fish, good service, and reasonable prices. *Huachinango veracruzano* (red snapper prepared with tomatoes, peppers, onion, and olives) and fillet of fish in *mojo de ajo* (garlic butter) are about as sophisticated as the food preparation gets. The ceviche is an Acapulco tradition, as is *vuelve à la vida,* an immense seafood cocktail that, as the name implies, is guaranteed to bring you "back to life." ⊠ *Costera Miguel Alemán and Nao Victoria, across from the Acapulco International Center,* ☎ *74/84–01–65; also downtown at Almirante Bretón 3,* ☎ *74/82–22–37. Reservations not accepted. AE, MC, V.*

Spanish

$$ ✕ **Sirocco.** This beachside eatery is numero uno for those who crave Spanish food in Acapulco. The tiled floors and heavy wooden furniture give it a Mediterranean feel. Specialties include *pulpo en su tinta* (octopus in its own ink) and other types of seafood. Order paella (there are 10 varieties) when you arrive at the beach—it takes a half hour to prepare. ⊠ *Costera Miguel Alemán, across from Aurrerá,* ☎ *74/85–23–86 or 74/85–94–90. AE, MC, V.* ◷ *1:30–11 PM.*

LODGING

Although Acapulco has been an important port since colonial times, it lacks the converted monasteries and old mansions found in Mexico City. But the Costera is chockablock with new luxury high-rises and local franchises of such major U.S. hotel chains as Hyatt and Howard Johnson. Since these hotels tend to be characterless, your choice will depend on location and what facilities are available. All major hotels can make water-sports arrangements.

In Acapulco geography is price, so where you stay determines what you pay. The most exclusive area is the Acapulco Diamante, home to some of the most expensive hotels in Mexico—so lush and well equipped that most guests don't budge from the minute they arrive. The minuses: Revolcadero Beach is too rough for swimming (though great for surfing), and this area is a 15- to 25-minute (expensive) taxi ride from the heart of Acapulco. The atmosphere of Acapulco Diamante is refined and revolves around a game of golf or tennis, dining at some of Acapulco's better restaurants, and dancing at the glamorous Extravaganzza, Palladium, and Fantasy discos.

There is much more activity on Costera Miguel Alemán, where the majority of large hotels, discos, American-style restaurants, and airline offices may be found, along with Acapulco's most popular beaches. All the Costera hotels have freshwater pools and sun decks, and most have restaurants and/or bars overlooking the beach, if not on the sand itself. Hotels across the street are almost always less expensive than those directly on the beach; because there are no private beaches in Acapulco, all you have to do is cross the road to enjoy the sand.

Moving west along the Costera leads you to downtown Acapulco. The beaches and restaurants here are popular with Mexican vacationers, and the dozens of hotels attract Canadian and European bargain hunters.

You can assume that accommodations that cost above $90 (double) will be air-conditioned (though you can find air-conditioned hotels for less) and will include a minibar, TV, and a view of the bay. There is usually a range of in-house restaurants and bars, as well as a pool. Exceptions exist, such as Las Brisas, which, in the name of peace and quiet, has banned TVs from all rooms. So if such extras are important to you, be sure to ask ahead. If you can't afford air-conditioning, don't panic. Even the cheapest hotels have cooling ceiling fans.

Note: Most hotels are booked solid Christmas and Easter week, so if you plan to visit then, it's wise to make reservations months in advance.

CATEGORY	COST*
$$$$	over $160
$$$	$90–$160
$$	$40–$90
$	under $40

All prices are for a standard double room, excluding 10% sales (called IVA) tax.

Acapulco Diamante

$$$$
★ 🏨 **Acapulco Princess.** This is the first hotel you'll see as you leave the airport. A pyramid-shaped building flanked by two towers, the Princess has the largest capacity of any hotel in Acapulco. The hotel's fact sheet makes fascinating reading: 50 chocolate cakes are consumed daily and 2,500 staff meals are served. The Princess is one of those megahotels that are always holding at least three conventions, with an ever-present horde in the lobby checking in and greeting their fellow dentists or club members. But more rooms equals more facilities. The Princess has seven restaurants, seven bars (several of which close during the low season—April through October), a disco, tennis, golf, and shopping in a cool arcade. The pool near the reception desk is sensational—fantastic tropical ponds with little waterfalls and a slatted bridge leading into a swimming-sunning area. Rooms are light and airy, with cane furniture and rugs and curtains in colorful tropical prints. Guests can also use the facilities of the hotel's smaller sibling, the Pierre Marqués; a free shuttle bus provides transport. Accommodations include breakfast and dinner (in high season). ⊠ *Box 1351, Playa Revolcadero, 39300,* ☎ *74/69–10–00 or 800/223–1818,* 🖷 *74/69–10–16. 1,019 balconied rooms with bath. 7 restaurants, 7 bars, 5 pools, 2 18-hole golf courses, 11 tennis courts, exercise room, 2 basketball courts, dance club. AE, DC, MC, V.*

$$$$ ⊞ **Pierre Marqués.** This hotel is doubly blessed: It is closer to the
★ beach than any of the other East Bay hotels, and guests have access to
all the Princess's facilities without the crowds. In addition, it has three
pools and five tennis courts illuminated for nighttime play. Rooms are
furnished identically to those at the Princess (no TVs here, however),
but villas and duplex bungalows with private patios are available.
Many people stay here to relax, then hit the Princess's restaurants and
discos at night—the shuttle bus runs about every 10 minutes 24 hours
a day. Accommodations include mandatory breakfast (breakfast and
dinner during Christmas week). ⊠ *Box 1351, Playa Revolcadero,
39907,* ☎ *74/66–10–00 or 800/223–1818,* ℻ *74/66–10–46. 344
rooms with bath. 2 restaurants, bar, 3 pools, 2 18-hole golf courses,
5 tennis courts.* ☉ *Winter season only. AE, DC, MC, V.*

$$$$ ⊞ **Vidafel Mayan Palace.** This all-suites resort will knock your socks
off. Guests are welcomed in a 100,000-square-foot lobby that's sheltered under 75-foot palm-roofed palapas, with full-scale Maya-in-
spired statues surrounded by reflecting pools. The rooms, on the other
hand, are surprisingly subdued. Airy and spacious, they are beautifully
appointed with marble floors, light-wood furniture, sand-colored walls,
original paintings, and luxurious baths; they range from a studio with
hot tub (Crown Suite) to a one-bedroom with kitchenette and sitting
areas (Acapulco Suite). Guests may ride a canoe or a paddleboat
around the man-made, fish-filled canal that winds through the 200-
acre property or swim in the 850-yard pool. ⊠ *Playa Revolcadero,
39300,* ☎ *74/69–02–01 or 800/VIDAFEL,* ℻ *62–00–08. 350 suites
with bath. Restaurant, bar, 18-hole golf course, 12 lighted tennis
courts, game room. AE, DC, MC, V.*

$$$$ ⊞ **Westin Las Brisas.** Set high on a hillside and across the bay from most
★ of the other main hotels, the Las Brisas hotel remains distinct in Acapulco for the secluded haven it provides its guests. This self-contained
luxury complex covers 110 acres and has accommodations that range
from one-bedroom units to deluxe private casitas, complete with private
pools that are small yet swimmable. All have beautiful bay views. Most
of the facilities are open only to guests, though outsiders with a reservation may dine at the Bella Vista restaurant. Attention to detail is Las
Brisas's claim to fame: Fresh hibiscus blossoms are set afloat in the pools
each day, and registration takes place in a comfortable lounge, where
guests are given tropical mixed drinks to sip. There are almost three em-
ployees per guest during the winter season. Transportation is by white-
and-pink Jeep. You can rent one for $50 a day, including tax, gas, and
insurance; or, if you don't mind a wait, the staff will do the driving. And
transport is necessary—it is a good 15-minute walk to the beach restaurant, and all the facilities are far from the rooms. There is an art gallery
and a few other stores. Tipping is not allowed, but a service charge of
$16 a day is added to the bill. The rate includes Continental breakfast
and temporary membership in the La Concha Beach Club. ⊠ *Carretera
Escénica 5255, 39868,* ☎ *74/84–15–80 or 800/228–3000,* ℻ *74/84–
22–69. 300 rooms with bath. 3 restaurants, 2 bars, 3 pools (2 saltwater), hot tub, sauna, 5 tennis courts, beach. AE, DC, MC, V.*

$$$ ⊞ **Camino Real Acapulco Diamante.** Opened in 1993, Acapulco's
★ newest hotel is set at the foot of a lush tropical hillside on exclusive
Pichilingue Beach, far from the madding crowd. All rooms are done
in luscious pastels, with tiled floors, balcony or terrace, luxurious
baths, ceiling fans, and air-conditioning. Each has a view of peaceful
Puerto Marqués bay. Rates include a buffet breakfast. ⊠ *Carretera
Escénica Km 14, Calle Baja Catita, 39867,* ☎ *74/66–10–10 or 800/
7–CAMINO,* ℻ *74/66–11–11. 156 rooms. 2 restaurants, 2 bars,
3 pools, 1 tennis court, exercise room. AE, DC, MC, V.*

$$$ 🏨 **Sheraton Acapulco.** Perfect for those who want to enjoy the sun and the sand but don't have to be in the center of everything, this Sheraton is isolated from all the hubbub of the Costera and is rather small in comparison with the chain's other properties in Mexico. The spacious, attractively decorated rooms and suites—all with private balconies, and many with sweeping views of the entire bay—are distributed among 13 villas that are set on a hillside on secluded Guitarrón Beach, 10 kilometers (6 miles) east of Acapulco proper. In order to reach your room, however, it's necessary to wait for a staff-operated funicular—a slow, sometimes frustrating procedure. The hotel's romantic fine-dining room, La Bahía, serves excellent Continental cuisine. ✉ *Costera Guitarrón 110, 39359,* ☎ *74/81–22–22 or 800/325–3535,* FAX *74/84–37–60. 197 rooms with bath, 15 suites. 3 restaurants, 3 bars, 2 pools. AE, DC, MC, V.*

The Costera

$$$$ 🏨 **Hyatt Regency Acapulco.** Another megahotel that you never have to leave, this property is popular with business travelers and conventioneers. The entire hotel was totally refurbished in 1995, and soft pastels have been replaced with strong Caribbean colors. Tennis courts, five eateries (including a beachside seafood place, a popular Mexican dining spot, and a kosher restaurant), four bars, and a lavish shopping area are among the reasons for guests to stay put. The Hyatt is a little out of the way, a plus for those who seek quiet. To avoid the noise of the maneuvers at the neighboring naval base, ask for a room on the west side of the hotel. ✉ *Costera Miguel Alemán 1, 39869,* ☎ *74/69–12–34 or 800/223–1234,* FAX *74/84–30–87. 690 rooms with bath. 4 restaurants, 4 bars, snack bar, 2 pools, massage, sauna, 5 tennis courts, parking (fee). AE, DC, MC, V.*

$$$$ 🏨 **Royal El Cano.** One of Acapulco's traditional favorites has been com-
★ pletely remodeled, while still (thankfully) maintaining its '50s flavor. The interior decorators get an A+: The rooms are snappily done in white and navy blue, with white tiled floors and beautiful modern bathrooms. The only exception is the lobby, which is excruciatingly blue. There's a delightful outdoor restaurant, a more elegant indoor one, and a gorgeous pool that seems to float above the bay, with whirlpools built into its corners. Maintenance is excellent throughout the hotel. ✉ *Costera Miguel Alemán 75, 39690,* ☎ *74/84–19–50 or 800/222–7692,* FAX *74/84–86–37. 180 rooms with bath. 2 restaurants, bar, pool. AE, DC, MC, V.*

$$$ 🏨 **Acapulco Plaza.** Although the Plaza is once again a single pyramid-shaped tower (the other two towers are now under separate management), this Fiesta Americana resort still has more facilities than many Mexican towns: four bars and an equal number of restaurants, tennis courts, a sauna, three pools, and a location next door to the Plaza Bahía, Acapulco's largest shopping mall. The lobby bar is most extraordinary—a wooden hut, suspended by a cable from the roof, reached by a gangplank from the second floor of the lobby and overlooking a garden full of flamingos and other exotic birds. Guest rooms tell the same old story—pastels and blond wood replacing passé dark greens and browns—but guests continue to be content with the facilities and service. ✉ *Costera Miguel Alemán 123, 39670,* ☎ *74/85–90–50 or 800/FIESTA–1,* FAX *74/85–54–93. 506 rooms with bath. 4 restaurants, 4 bars, 3 pools, sauna, 4 tennis courts, health club. AE, DC, MC, V.*

$$$ 🏨 **Fiesta Americana Condesa Acapulco.** Right in the thick of the main shopping-restaurant district, the Condesa, as everyone calls it, is ever popular with tour operators. The rooms and baths, which were totally redecorated in 1994, have a nice fresh look. The bathrooms have new fixtures and raspberry shower curtains; bedrooms feature hot-pink lamps,

pastel bedspreads, and deep blue curtains. ⊠ *Costera Miguel Alemán 1220, 39690,* ☎ *74/84–28–28 or 800/FIESTA–1,* FAX *74/84–18–28. 500 rooms with bath. 2 restaurants, bar, 2 pools. AE, DC, MC, V.*

$$ 🔛 **Hotel Acapulco Tortuga.** A helpful staff and prime location make the "Turtle Hotel" an appealing choice. It is also one of the few non-beach hotels to have a garden (handkerchief-size), a beach club (in Puerto Marqués), and a pool where most of the guests hang out. At night the activity shifts to the piano bar. The downside of this merriment is the noise factor. The best bet is a room facing west on an upper floor. All rooms have blue-green pile rugs and small tables. Breakfast is served in the lobby café; lunch and dinner can be taken in the more formal restaurant. ⊠ *Costera Miguel Alemán 132, 39300,* ☎ *74/84–88–89 or 800/832–7491,* FAX *74/84–73–85. 252 rooms with bath. 2 restaurants, coffee shop, piano bar, pool. AE, DC, MC, V.*

$$ 🔛 **Howard Johnson Maralisa.** Formerly the sister hotel of the Villa Vera
★ (☞ *below*), this hotel, located on the beach side of the Costera, is now a part of the Howard Johnson chain. The sun deck surrounding two small pools—palm trees and ceramic tiles—is unusual and picturesque. The rooms are light, decorated in whites and pastels. This is a small, friendly place; all rooms have TVs and balconies, and the price is right. ⊠ *Box 721, Calle Alemania, 39670,* ☎ *74/85–66–77 or 800/IGO–HOJO,* FAX *74/85–92–28. 90 rooms with bath. Restaurant, bar, 2 pools, beach. AE, DC, MC, V.*

$$ 🔛 **Plaza Las Glorias Paraíso.** The last of the big Costera hotels is a favorite of tour groups, so the lobby is forever busy. The rooms look brighter and roomier since the management replaced the heavy Spanish-style furniture with light woods and pastels. Guests lounge by the pool or at the beachside restaurant by day. The pool area is rather small and the beach can get crowded, but the restaurants are exceptionally good and the staff couldn't be nicer. Book early for high season, which is prime time for the tour groups. ⊠ *Costera Miguel Alemán 163, 39670,* ☎ *74/85–55–96 or 800/342–AMIGO,* FAX *74/82–45–64. 422 rooms with bath. 2 restaurants, bar, coffee shop, pool, sauna. AE, DC, MC, V.*

$$ 🔛 **Villa Vera.** A five-minute drive north of the Costera leads to what was once one of Acapulco's most exclusive hotels. Some of the villas, which were once private homes, have their own pools. Standard rooms, in pastels and white, are not especially large. No matter. No one spends much time in the rooms. The main pool, with its swim-up bar, is the hotel's hub. By night guests dine at the terraced restaurant, with its stunning view of the bay. There's an exercise facility, and two championship tennis courts host the Celebrity and Veterans tennis tournaments. ⊠ *Box 560, Lomas del Mar 35, 39690,* ☎ *74/84–03–33,* FAX *74/84–74–79. 74 rooms with bath. Restaurant, piano bar, pools, beauty salon, massage, sauna, 2 tennis courts. AE, MC, V.*

Old Acapulco

$$$ 🔛 **Boca Chica.** This small hotel is in a secluded area on a small penin-
★ sula, and its terraced rooms overlook the bay and Roqueta Island. It's a low-key place that's a favorite of Mexico City residents in the know. There's a private beach club with a natural saltwater pool for guests and a seafood, sushi, and oyster bar. Accommodations include mandatory breakfast and dinner in high season. ⊠ *Caletilla Beach, 39390,* ☎ *74/83–67–41,* FAX *74/83–95–13. 40 rooms. Restaurant, seafood bar, 2 pools. AE, DC, MC, V.*

$$ 🔛 **Plaza las Glorias El Mirador.** The old El Mirador has been taken over by the Plaza las Glorias chain, which is part of the Sidek conglomerate responsible for marina and golf developments all over Mexico. Very Mexican in style—white with red tiles—the Plaza las Glorias is set high on a hill with a spectacular view of Acapulco and of the cliff divers performing at La Quebrada. ⊠ *Quebrada 74, 39300,* ☎ *74/83–11–55 or 800/342–AMIGO,* ℻ *74/82–45–64. 143 rooms with bath. 2 restaurants, 3 pools. AE, DC, MC, V.*

$$ 🏨 **Suites Alba.** Situated on a quiet hillside in "Acapulco Tradicional," the Alba is a resort-style hotel that offers bargain prices. All suites are air-conditioned and have a kitchenette, private bath, and terrace. There is no extra charge for up to two children under 12 sharing a room with relatives, which makes it especially popular with families. Caleta and Caletilla beaches are within walking distance, and the hotel has a beach club at Caleta with a 330-foot toboggan. ⊠ *Grand Via Tropical 35, 39390,* ☎ *74/83–00–73,* ℻ *74/83–83–78. 283 rooms. 3 restaurants, bar, grocery, 3 pools, tennis court, beach. AE, DC, MC, V.*

$ 🏨 **Majestic.** This dowager hotel was totally renovated in 1995. The
★ electric-blue postmodern exterior is somewhat shocking, but the stunning decor of the spacious rooms—tile floors, cool colors, and good lighting—is completely unexpected in a hotel in this price category. Entrance is through the seventh-floor lobby, and the rest of the hotel is terraced down a rocky cliff (in fact, seen from the Costera Miguel Alemán, the Majestic has often been described as looking like a typewriter). The rooms in the main building each have air-conditioning, cable TV, private terrace, a double bed, and two studio couches; the villa rooms are smaller. There is no beach at the hotel, but free transportation is provided to the hotel's beach club, which is located next to the Club de Yates. An all-inclusive plan is also available. ⊠ *Av. Pozo del Rey 74, 39390,* ☎ *74/83–227–13,* ℻ *74/82–16–14. 200 rooms. 2 restaurants, 2 bars, disco, 2 pools, tennis court, beach club, parking. AE, DC, MC, V.*

$ 🏨 **Hotel Misión.** Two minutes from the zócalo, this attractive budget hotel is the only colonial-style hotel in Acapulco. The English-speaking family that runs the Misión lives in a traditional house built in the 19th century. A newer structure housing the guest rooms was added in the 1950s. It surrounds a greenery-rich courtyard with an outdoor dining area. The rooms are small and by no means fancy, with bare cement floors and painted brick walls. But every room has a shower, and there is even hot water. The Misión appears in several European guidebooks, so expect a Continental clientele. The best rooms are on the second and third floors; the top-floor room is large but hot in the daytime. ⊠ *Calle Felipe Valle 12, 39300,* ☎ *74/82–36–43. 27 rooms, showers only. No credit cards.*

Pie de la Cuesta

$$$ 🏨 **Parador del Sol.** Traversing both the lagoon and the Pacific Ocean
★ sides of the Pie de la Cuesta road, this all-inclusive property gives the impression that it was designed as a luxury resort. The 150 rooms are distributed among pink villas that are scattered over some 1,100 square feet of gardens. Spacious, with tile floors and baths, each room is air-conditioned and equipped with color TV, phone, and a fan-cooled terrace complete with hammocks. The rate includes all meals and refreshments, domestic drinks, tennis, and nonmotorized water sports. ⊠ *Km 5 Carretera Pie de la Cuesta–Barra de Coyuca, Box 1070, 39300,* ☎ *74/60–20–03,* ℻ *74/60–16–49. 150 rooms with bath. Restaurant, 2 bars, 2 pools, 4 tennis courts, miniature golf, health club, dance club. AE, DC, MC, V.*

$ 🏨 **Ukae Kim.** A cluster of 10 junior suites that is especially popular with Europeans and Canadians, Ukae Kim is set among towering palms on Acapulco's famous "sunset" beach, just across the road from the tranquil Coyuca Lagoon. The charming rooms are fitted with canopied beds, sitting areas, and Mexican tiled baths, and although the furnishings are a bit worn, a fresh coat of bright pink paint gives the place a festive air. The rooms on the beach aren't air-conditioned, but there is generally enough of a breeze to make them comfortable. ⊠ *Av. Pie de la Cuesta 358,* ☎ *74/60–21–87,* FAX *74/60–21–88. 10 rooms with bath. Restaurant, pool. No credit cards.*

NIGHTLIFE AND THE ARTS

The companies listed in the Orientation Tours section of Acapulco A to Z (☞ *below*) can organize evening jaunts to most of the dance and music places listed below. And don't forget the nightly entertainment at most hotels. The big resorts have live music to accompany the early evening happy hour, and some feature big-name bands from the United States for less than you would pay at home. Many hotels sponsor theme parties—Italian Night, Beach Party Night, and similar festivities.

Cultural Shows

The Acapulco International Center (⊠ Costera Miguel Aleman, ☎ 74/ 84–70–50), also known as the Convention Center, has a Mexican fiesta Wednesday and Friday; it features mariachi bands, singers, and the "Flying Indians" from Papantla. The show with dinner and drinks costs about $20, entrance to the show alone is $10, and the performance with open bar is $12. The buffet dinner starts at 7:15, the performance at 8. On Friday, Cantina Night at El Mexicano restaurant in **Las Brisas** hotel, the fiesta starts off with a *tianguis* (marketplace) of handicrafts and ends with a spectacular display of fireworks.

Dance

Nina's (⊠ Costera Miguel Alemán 2909, ☎ 74/84–24–00) is a combination dance hall and disco where the bands play salsa and other Latin rhythms. There's a live show—mostly impersonations of famous entertainers—at 12:45.

Discos

Reservations are advisable for a big group, and late afternoon or after 9 PM are the best times to call. New Year's Eve requires advance planning.

Except for Pyramid Club, Palladium, Fantasy, and Extravaganzza, all the discos are clustered on the Costera.

Baby O, an old favorite, packs them in even in the middle of the week. Eschewing the glitz and mirrors of most discos in Acapulco, Baby O resembles a cave in a tropical jungle. The crowd is 18–30 and mostly tourists, although many Mexicans come here, too. In fact, this is one of Acapulco's legendary pickup spots, so feel free to ask someone to dance. When the pandemonium gets to you, retreat to the little hamburger restaurant. ⊠ *Costera Miguel Alemán 22,* ☎ *74/84–74–74.*

Discobeach is Acapulco's only alfresco disco and its most informal one. The under-30 crowd sometimes even turns up in shorts. The waiters are young and friendly—some people find them overly so. One night they're all in togas carrying bunches of grapes; the next they're in pajamas. Every Wednesday, ladies' night, all the women receive flowers. "Sex on the Beach"—rum, vodka, Cointreau, fruit juice, and grenadine (don't say you weren't warned!)—is the house specialty, in all senses of the word. This is a very popular place. ⊠ *On Condesa Beach,* ☎ *74/84–70–64.*

Extravaganzza vies with Palladium for first place as Acapulco's most splendiferous disco, boasting the ultimate in light and sound. It accommodates 700 at a central bar and in comfortable booths, and a glass wall provides an unbelievably breathtaking view of Acapulco Bay. No food is served, but Los Rancheros is just a few steps away. The music (which is for all ages) starts at 10:30. ⊠ *On the Scenic Hwy. to Las Brisas,* ☎ *74/84–71–64.*

Fantasy is one of the most exclusive of all the discos in Acapulco. If there are any celebrities in town, they'll be here, rubbing elbows with or bumping into local fashion designers and artists—since Fantasy is quite snug, to put it nicely. This is one of the only discos where people really dress up, with the men in well-cut pants and shirts and the women in racy outfits and cocktail dresses. The crowd is 25–50 and mainly in couples. Singles gravitate toward the two bars in the back. A line sometimes forms, so people come here earlier than they do to other places. By midnight the dance floor is so packed that people dance on the wide windowsills that look out over the bay. At 2 AM there is a fireworks display. A glassed-in elevator provides an interesting overview of the scene and leads upstairs to a little shop that stocks T-shirts and lingerie. ⊠ *On the Scenic Hwy., next to Las Brisas,* ☎ *74/84–67–27.*

Hard Rock Café, filled with rock memorabilia, is part bar, part restaurant, part dance hall, and part boutique (☞ Dining, *above*).

News is enormous, with seating for 1,200 people in love seats and booths. The most popular nights are Wednesday and Friday, when everyone is bathed in foam, with a kind of wet-T-shirt effect. From 10:30 (opening time) to 11:30, the music is slow and romantic; then the disco music and the light show begin, and they go on till dawn. ⊠ *Costera Miguel Alemán 3308, across from the Hyatt Regency,* ☎ *74/84–59–02.*

Palladium, inaugurated at the end of 1993, proves that Acapulco remains the disco capital of the world. Extravaganzza creator Tony Rullán has produced another spectacle: a waterfall that cascades down the hill from the dance-floor level and makes this place hard to miss. As at Extravaganzza, the dance floor is nearly surrounded by 50-foot-high windows, giving dancers a spectacular view of all Acapulco. ⊠ *On the Scenic Hwy. to Las Brisas,* ☎ *74/81–03–30.*

Pyramid Club, a combination disco and video bar designed to look like a 21st-century Aztec pyramid and equipped with the last word in sound systems, has replaced Tiffany, the posh disco at the Princess Hotel. ⊠ *Princess Hotel,* ☎ *74/69–10–00.*

OUTDOOR ACTIVITIES AND SPORTS

Participant Sports

Fishing

Fishing trips can be arranged through your hotel, downtown at the Pesca Deportiva near the *muelle* (dock) across from the zócalo, or through travel agents. At the docks near the zócalo you can hire a boat for $30 a day (two lines). It is safer to stick with one of the reliable companies whose boats and equipment are in good condition. Boats accommodating 4 to 10 people cost $180–$500 a day, $45–$60 by chair. Excursions usually leave about 7 AM and return at 1 or 2 PM. You are required to get a fishing license ($7) from the Secretaría de Pesca;

you'll find their representative at the dock. Don't show up during siesta, between 2 and 4 in the afternoon.

For deep-sea fishing, **Divers de México** (☞ Scuba Diving, *below*) has well-maintained boats for 4 to 10 passengers for $200 to $500. It also offers private yacht charters. Small boats for freshwater fishing can be rented at **Cadena's** and **Tres Marías** at Coyuca Lagoon.

Fitness and Swimming
Most of the time, Acapulco weather is like August in the warmest parts of the United States. This means that you should cut back on your workouts and maintain proper hydration by drinking plenty of water.

Acapulco Princess Hotel offers the best hotel fitness facilities, including a gym with stationary bikes, Universal machines, and free weights. Because the Princess is about 15 kilometers (9 miles) from the city center and the pollution of Acapulco, you can even swim in the ocean here if you beware of the strong undertow.

Westin Las Brisas is where you should stay if you like to swim but don't like company or competition. Individual casitas come with private, or semiprivate, pools; the beach club has two saltwater pools (☞ Lodging, *above*, for both). Most of the major hotels in town along the Costera Miguel Alemán also have pools.

Villa Vera Spa and Fitness Center (⊠ Lomas del Mar 35, ☎ 74/84–03–33) has a modern spa and fitness center and is equipped with exercise machines (including step machines), free weights, and benches. Masseuses and cosmetologists give facials and massages inside or by the pool, as you wish. Both the beauty center and the gym are open to nonguests.

Golf
Two 18-hole championship golf courses are shared by the **Princess** and **Pierre Marqués** hotels. Reservations should be made in advance (☎ 74/84–31–00). Greens fees are $60 for guests and $80 for nonguests. A round at the 18-hole **Vidafel** (☎ 74/69–02–01) course is $70 for nonguests. There is also a public golf course at the **Club de Golf** (☎ 74/84–07–81) on the Costera across from the Acapulco Malibú hotel. Greens fees are $16 for 9 holes, $25 for 18 holes. The links at Tres Vidas and Diamante Country Club are reserved for members and their guests.

Horseback Riding
A gallop on Revolcadero Beach can be arranged through the **Charro Association** (⊠ Costera Miguel Alemán 137, ☎ 74/85–64–67). Round-trip transportation to Revolcadero, a guide, and an hour on a sturdy mount should run you about $30.

Jogging
If you don't like beach jogging, the only real venue for running in the downtown area is along the sidewalk next to the Costera Miguel Alemán at the seafront, but you'll have to go very early, before traffic fumes set in. Away from the city center, the best area for running is out at the Acapulco Princess Hotel, on the airport road. A 2-kilometer (1-mile) loop is laid out along a lightly traveled road, and in the early morning you can also run along the asphalt trails on the golf course.

Scuba Diving
Divers de México (⊠ downtown near the Fiesta and Bonanza yachts, ☎ 74/82–13–98), owned by a helpful and efficient American woman, provides English-speaking captains and comfortable American-built yachts. A three- to four-hour scuba-diving excursion—including equip-

ment, lessons in a pool for beginners, and drinks—costs about $55 per person. If you are a certified diver, the excursion is $45.

Arnold Brothers (⊠ Costera Miguel Alemán 205, ☎ 74/82–18–77) also runs daily scuba-diving excursions and snorkeling trips. The scuba trips cost $25 and last for 2 to 2½ hours.

Tennis

Court fees range from about $3 to $20 an hour during the day and are 15% more in the evening. At the hotel courts, nonguests pay about $5 more per hour. Lessons with English-speaking instructors start at about $10 an hour; ball boys get a $2 tip.

Places in town to play tennis include **Acapulco Plaza** (☎ 74/85–90–50), four hard-surface courts, two lighted; **Acapulco Princess** (☎ 74/69–10–00), two indoor courts, nine outdoor; **Club de Tennis and Golf** (⊠ Costera Miguel Alemán, across from Hotel Malibu, (☎ 74/84–07–81); **Hyatt Regency** (☎ 74/69–12–34), five lighted courts; **Pierre Marqués** (☎ 74/66–10–00), five courts; **Tiffany's Racquet Club** (⊠ Av. Villa Vera 120, ☎ 74/84–79–49), five courts; and **Villa Vera Hotel** (☎ 74/84–03–33), two outdoor lighted clay courts.

Water Sports

Waterskiing, broncos (one-person motorboats), and parasailing can all be arranged on the beach. Parasailing is an Acapulco highlight and looks terrifying until you actually try it. Most people who do it love the view and go back again and again. An eight-minute trip costs $12. Waterskiing is about $30 an hour; broncos cost $20 an hour. Windsurfing can be arranged at Caleta and most of the beaches along the Costera but is especially good at Puerto Marqués. At Coyuca Lagoon, you can try your hand (or feet) at barefoot waterskiing. The main surfing beach is Revolcadero.

Spectator Sports

Bullfights

The season runs from Christmas to Easter, and *corridas* are held on Sunday at 5:30. Tickets are available through your hotel or at the **Plaza de Toros** ticket window (⊠ Av. Circunvalación, across from Caleta Beach, ☎ 74/82–11–81) Monday–Saturday 10–2 and Sunday 10:30–5. Tickets cost $12, and a $14 seat in the first five rows—in the shade (*sombra*)—is worth the extra cost. Preceding the fight are performances of Spanish dances and music by the Chili Frito band.

Jai Alai

The **Jai Alai Acapulco Race & Sports Book** (⊠ Costera Miguel Alemán 498, ☎ 74/81–16–50) has a capacity for 1,500 spectators. The fast-paced games take place Tuesday through Sunday at 9 PM, December through September. Entrance is $7, but $4 is reimbursed with your first bet. In addition to bets on jai alai, bets are taken on all major sports events—basketball, football, baseball, boxing, horse and greyhound racing—that are transmitted directly via satellite.

SHOPPING

The main shopping strip is on Costera Miguel Alemán from the Acapulco Plaza to the El Presidente Hotel. Here you can find Guess, Peer, Aca Joe, Amarras, Polo Ralph Lauren, and other fashionable sportswear boutiques. Downtown (Old) Acapulco doesn't have many name shops, but this is where you'll find the inexpensive tailors patronized by the Mexicans, lots of little souvenir shops, and a vast flea market with crafts.

Also downtown are Woolworth's and Sanborns. Most shops are open from 10 to 7 Monday through Saturday and close on Sunday.

Department Stores and Supermarkets

Except for the waitresses' uniforms, the food, and a good handicrafts selection, **Sanborns** is very un-Mexican. Still, it is an institution throughout Mexico. It sells English-language newspapers, magazines, and books, as well as a line of high-priced souvenirs. This is a useful place to come for postcards, cosmetics, and medicines. Sanborns' restaurants are popular for their *enchiladas suizas* (prepared with lots of cream and cheese), *molletes* (toasted rolls spread with refried beans and cheese), their seven-fruit drink, and their slow service. The Estrella del Mar branch (⊠ Costera Miguel Alemán 1226, ☎ 74/84–44–13) and the downtown branch (⊠ Costera Miguel Alemán 209, ☎ 74/82–61–67) are both open from 7 AM to midnight during the high season and from 7 AM to 11 PM during the low season.

Branches of **Aurrerá, Gigante, Price Club, Sam's,** and Acapulco's original supermarket, fittingly called **Super-Super,** are all on the Costera and sell everything from light bulbs and newspapers to bottles of tequila and postcards. If you are missing anything at all, you should be able to pick it up at these stores or at the **Comercial Mexicana,** which has three branches (⊠ *Av. Farallón 216, near the Diana; Costera Miguel Alemán 243, downtown; and Av. Ruiz Cortines 13*).

Woolworth's (⊠ Escudero 250 in Old Acapulco) is much like the five-and-dime stores found all over the United States, but with a Mexican feel.

Malls

Malls in Acapulco range from the delightful air-conditioned shopping arcade at the Princess hotel to rather gloomy collections of shops that sell cheap jewelry and embroidered dresses. Malls are listed below from east to west.

On the Costera, across from the Fiesta Americana Condesa hotel, is the **Plaza Condesa,** which offers a cold-drink stand, an Italian restaurant, a gym and weight-training center, and a greater concentration of silver shops than you'll find anywhere else in Acapulco. The multilevel **Marbella Mall,** at the Diana Glorieta, features Martí, a well-stocked sporting-goods store, and Bing's Ice Cream, as well as several restaurants. **Aca Mall,** which is next door, is all white and marble; here you'll find Polo Ralph Lauren, Ferrioni, Aca Joe, and another Martí.

Plaza Bahía, next to the Acapulco Plaza hotel, is a place for serious shopping. It is a huge, completely enclosed and air-conditioned mall where you could easily spend an entire day. Stores include Dockers, Benetton, Nautica, and Ferrioni, for chic casual wear for men and women; Ragazza, which carries an exquisite line of fine lingerie; Aspasia, which offers locally designed, glitzy evening dresses and chunky diamanté jewelry; Bally for shoes; restaurants and snack bars; and a video-game arcade.

Markets

The **Mercado Municipal,** a good place to shop for crafts, is described in Exploring (☞ *above*).

El Mercado de Artesanías, a conglomeration of every souvenir in town, is a 20-minute walk from the zócalo. You'll find fake ceremonial masks, the ever-present onyx chessboards, $15 hand-embroidered dresses, imitation silver, hammocks, ceramics, even skin cream made from turtles (don't buy it, because turtles are endangered and you won't get it through U.S. Customs). The market is open daily 9–9. ✉ *To get to the market from the zócalo, turn left as you leave Woolworth's and continue to the Multibanco Comermex. Turn right, go one block, and then turn left; when you reach the Banamex, you'll see the market on your right.*

In an effort to get the itinerant vendors off the beaches and streets, the local government set up a series of **flea markets** along the Costera, mostly uninviting dark tunnels of stalls that carry what seems to be an inexhaustible supply of inexpensive collectibles and souvenirs, including serapes, ceramics, straw hats, shell sculptures, carved walking canes, and wooden toys. The selections of archaeological-artifact replicas, bamboo wind chimes, painted wooden birds (from $5 to $30 each), shell earrings, and embroidered clothes begin to look identical. Prices at the flea markets are often quite low, but it's a good idea to compare prices of items you're interested in with prices in the shops, and bargaining is essential. It's best to buy articles described as being made from semiprecious stones or silver in reputable establishments. If you don't, you may find that the beautiful jade or lapis lazuli that was such a bargain was really cleverly painted paste, or that the silver was simply a facsimile called *alpaca*.

Specialty Shops

Art
Edith Matison's Art Gallery (✉ Costera Miguel Alemán 2010, across from the Club de Golf, ☎ 74/84–30–84) shows the works of renowned international and Mexican artists, including Calder, Dalí, Siquieros and Tamayo. **Galería Rudic** (✉ Yañez Pinzón 9, across from the Continental Plaza, ☎ 74/84–48–44) is one of the best galleries in town, with a good collection of top contemporary Mexican artists, including Armando Amaya, Leonardo Nierman, Norma Goldberg, Trinidad Osorio, and Casiano García. **Pal Kepenyes** (✉ Guitarrón 140, ☎ 74/84–37–38) continues to receive good press for his sculpture and jewelry, on display in his workshop. The whimsical painted papier-mâché and giant ceramic sculptures of **Sergio Bustamente** (✉ Costera Miguel Alemán 120-9, across from the Fiesta American Condesa hotel (☎ 74/84–49–92), can be seen at his gallery.

Boutiques
KOS (✉ Costera Miguel Alemán, outside entrance to the Fiesta Americana Condesa del Mar hotel, ☎ 74/81–24–34; Acapulco Plaza Hotel, ☎ 74/85–25–15) carries a sensational line of swimsuits for equally sensational bodies. **Nautica** (✉ Plaza Bahía, ☎ 74/85–75–11; smaller shop at Las Brisas hotel, ☎ 74/84–16–50) is a boutique stocked with stylish casual clothing for men. **Pasarela** (✉ Galerís Acapulco Plaza, at the entrance to Acapulco Plaza hotel, ☎ 74/85–00–17) carries its own line of gauzy dresses with a Mexican flavor, as well as some interesting accessories. **Pit** (✉ Princess arcade, ☎ 74/69–10–00) offers a smashing line of beach cover-ups and hand-painted straw hats, as well as bathing suits and light dresses.

Custom-Designed Clothes
Esteban's (✉ Costera Miguel Alemán 2010, across from the Club de Golf, ☎ 74/84–30–84) is the most glamorous shop in Acapulco, boasting a clientele of international celebrities and many of the important local families. Estaban's made-to-order clothes are formal and fashionable; his opulent evening dresses range from $200 to $3,000, though daytime dresses average $100. The real bargains are on the second floor,

where some items are marked down as much as 80%. If you scour the racks, you can find something for $10 to $15. Esteban has a back room filled with designer clothes.

Benny (⊠ Costera Miguel Alemán 114, across from the Torres Gemelas Condominium, ☎ 74/84–15–47; downtown at Ignacio de la Llave 2, local 10, ☎ 74/82–22–28), known for years for his custom-designed resort wear for men, now caters to women as well.

Handicrafts

AFA (⊠ Horacio Nelson and James Cook, near the Hyatt Regency, ☎ 74/84–80–39) is a huge shop offering a vast selection of jewelry, handicrafts, clothing, and leather goods from all over Mexico. **La Placita** (⊠ Plaza Bahía, no phone) comprises two shops designed to look like flea-market stalls. Top-quality merchandise is on display, including papier-mâché fruits and vegetables, Christmas ornaments, wind chimes, and brightly painted wooden animals from Oaxaca.

Silver and Jewelry

Antoinette (⊠ Acapulco Princess shopping arcade, ☎ 74/69–10–00) has gold jewelry of impeccable design, set with precious and semiprecious stones, that you wouldn't be surprised to find on Fifth Avenue. Also on display is Emilia Castillo's line of brightly colored porcelain ware, inlaid with silver fish, stars, and birds. It's worth going to window-shop, even if you know you won't buy anything.

Suzette's (⊠ Hyatt Regency hotel, ☎ 74/69–12–34), a tony shop that's been around for years, has a very laudable selection of gold jewelry.

Tane (⊠ Hyatt Regency hotel, ☎ 74/84–63–48; Las Brisas hotel, ☎ 74/81–08–16) carries small selections of the exquisite flatware, jewelry, and objets d'art created by one of Mexico's most prestigious (and expensive) silversmiths.

SIDE TRIP

Taxco, the Silver City

275 km (165 mi) north of Acapulco.

It's a picture-postcard look—Mexico in its Sunday best: white stucco buildings nuzzling cobblestoned streets, red-tiled roofs, and geranium-filled window boxes bright in the sun. Taxco (pronounced *tahss*-co), a colonial treasure that the Mexican government declared a national monument in 1928, tumbles onto the hills of the Sierra Madre in the state of Guerrero. Its silver mines drew foreign mining companies here for centuries. Now its charm, mild temperatures, sunshine, flowers, and silversmiths make Taxco a popular tourist destination.

Hernán Cortés discovered Taxco's mines in 1522. The silver rush lasted until the next century, when excitement tapered off. Then in the 1700s a Frenchman, who Mexicanized his name to José de la Borda, discovered a rich lode that revitalized the town's silver industry and made him exceedingly wealthy. After Borda, however, Taxco's importance faded, until the 1930s and the arrival of William G. Spratling, a writer-architect from New Orleans. Enchanted by Taxco and convinced of its potential as a silver center, Spratling set up an apprentice shop, where his artistic talent and his fascination with pre-Columbian design combined to produce silver jewelry and other artifacts that soon earned Taxco its worldwide reputation as the Silver City. Spratling's inspiration lives on in his students and their descendants, many of whom are the city's current silversmiths.

Numbers in the margin correspond to points of interest on the Taxco Exploring map.

❶ The **Church of San Sebastián and Santa Prisca** has dominated Plaza Borda—one of the busiest and most colorful town squares in all of Mexico—since the 18th century. Usually just called Santa Prisca, it was built by French silver magnate José de la Borda in thanks to the Almighty for his having literally stumbled upon a rich silver vein. The style of the church—sort of Spanish Baroque meets Rococo—is known as Churrigueresque, and its pink exterior is a stunning surprise. This is one of Mexico's most beautiful colonial churches and Taxco's most important landmark. ⊠ *Southwest side of Plaza Borda.*

NEED A
BREAK? Around Plaza Borda are several *neverías* where you can treat yourself to an ice cream in exotic flavors such as tequila, corn, avocado, or coconut. **Bar Paco's,** directly across the street from Santa Prisca, is a Taxco institution; its terrace is the perfect vantage point for watching the comings and goings on the zócalo while sipping a margarita or a beer.

❷ The former home of William G. Spratling houses the **Spratling Museum.** This small gallery explains the working of colonial mines and displays Spratling's collection of pre-Columbian artifacts. ⊠ *Porfírio Delgado and El Arco,* ☎ *762/2–16–60.* ☞ *Small entrance fee.* ☉ *Tues.–Sat. 10–5, Sun. 10–3.*

❸ **Casa Humboldt** was named for the German adventurer Alexander von Humboldt, who stayed here in 1803. The Moorish-style 18th-century house has a finely detailed facade. It now houses a wonderful little museum of colonial art. ⊠ *Calle Juan Ruíz Alarcón 6,* ☎ *762/2–55–01.* ☞ *Small entrance fee.* ☉ *Tues.–Sat. 10–5, Sun. 10–3.*

❹ If you want to experience a typical Mexican market, with everything from peanuts to electrical appliances, the **Municipal Market** is worth a visit. On Saturday and Sunday mornings, when locals from surrounding towns come with their produce and crafts, the market spills out onto the surrounding streets. You'll find it directly down the hill from Santa Prisca.

The largest caverns in Mexico, the **Caves of Cacahuamilpa** (Grutas de Cacahuamilpa) are about 15 minutes northeast of Taxco. These 15 large chambers comprise 12 kilometers (8 miles) of geological formation. Only some caves are illuminated. Plans to turn the caves into a dinosaur park have, thankfully, been laid to rest. A guide can be hired at the entrance.

Dining and Lodging

Gastronomes can find everything from tagliatelle to iguana in Taxco restaurants, and meals are much less expensive than in Acapulco. Dress is casual, but less so than at the resorts. There are several categories of hotel to choose from within Taxco's two types: the small inns nestled on the hills skirting the zócalo and the larger, more modern hotels on the outskirts of town.

$$ ✕ **La Ventana de Taxco.** The Italian recipes of manager Mario Cavagna, coupled with Mexican specialties and a fantastic view, still draw an enthusiastic crowd to this restaurant, in spite of its location in what has become an unattractive neighborhood. ⊠ *Hacienda del Solar Hotel, Hwy. 95, south of town,* ☎ *762/2–05–87. Reservations essential on weekends. AE, MC, V.*

$$ ✕ **Pagaduría del Rey.** This restaurant has a long-standing reputation
★ for Continental fare served in comfortable surroundings. ⊠ *Calle H.*

Taxco Exploring

Colegio Militar 8 (Colonia Cerro de la Bermeja, south of town),
☎ *762/2–34–67. MC, V.*

$$ ✕ **Toni's.** Prime rib and lobster are the specialties. There's also a great
view and a romantic setting. ⊠ *Monte Taxco Hotel,* ☎ *762/2–13–
00. AE, DC, MC, V.*

$ ✕ **Cielito Lindo.** This charming restaurant features a Mexican-inter-
national menu. Give the Mexican specialties a try—for example, *pollo
en pipian verde,* a chicken simmered in a mild, pumpkin-seed–based
sauce. ⊠ *Plaza Borda 14,* ☎ *762/2–06–03. Reservations not ac-
cepted. MC, V.*

$ ✕ **Hosterí El Adobe.** The lack of view (there are only two window ta-
★ bles) is more than made up for by the original decor—for example, hang-
ing lamps made of a cluster of masks—and the excellent food. Favorites
include the garlic-and-egg soup and the *queso adobe* (fried cheese
served on a bed of potato skins and covered with a green tomatillo sauce).
⊠ *Plazuela de San Juan 13,* ☎ *762/2–14–16. MC, V.*

$ ✕ **Santa Fe.** Mexican family-type cooking at its best is served in this sim-
ple place. Puebla-style mole, Cornish hen in garlic butter, and enchiladas
in green or red chili sauce are among the tasty offerings. ⊠ *Hidalgo 2,*
☎ *762/2–11–70. Reservations not accepted. AE, MC, V.*

$ ✕ **Señor Costilla.** That's right. This translates as Mr. Ribs, and the whim-
sical name says it all. The Taxco outpost of the zany Anderson chain
serves barbecued ribs and chops in a restaurant with great balcony seat-
ing. ⊠ *Plaza Borda 1,* ☎ *762/2–32–15. Reservations not accepted.
MC, V.*

$ ✕ **Pizza Pazza.** All nine varieties of pizza served here are tasty, but for
★ a real treat order the *pozole norteño,* a spicy pork and hominy soup
that comes with pork cracklings, chopped onion, lemon, and avo-
cado. This cozy place, with scotch-plaid tablecloths and flowering

plants, overlooks Plaza Borda. ⊠ *Calle del Arco 1,* ☎ *762/2–55–00. Reservations not accepted. MC, V.*

$ 🏨 **Agua Escondida.** Popular with some regular visitors to Taxco, this small hotel has simple rooms decorated with Mexican-style furnishings. ⊠ *Guillermo Spratling 4, 40200,* ☎ *762/2–07–26,* FAX *762/2– 13–06. 50 rooms with bath. Restaurant, café-bar, pool. MC, V.*

$ 🏨 **De la Borda.** Long a Taxco favorite, De la Borda is a bit worn, but the rooms are large and comfortable and the staff couldn't be more hospitable. Ask for a room overlooking town. There's a restaurant with occasional entertainment, and many bus tours en route from Mexico City to Acapulco stay here overnight. ⊠ *Box 6, Cerro del Pedregal 2, 40200,* ☎ *762/2–00–25,* FAX *762/2–06–17. 95 rooms with bath. Restaurant, pool. AE, MC, V.*

$$ 🏨 **Hacienda del Solar.** This small resort (off Highway 95 south of town) was once the best in town. The rooms, grounds and restaurant are still beautiful, but the surrounding neighborhood has seen better days. Its restaurant, La Ventana de Taxco (☞ *above*), maintains many loyal patrons. ⊠ *Box 96, 40200,* ☎ *762/2–03–23,* FAX *762/2–03–23. 22 rooms with bath. Restaurant, pool, tennis court. MC, V.*

$ 🏨 **Los Arcos.** For those seeking lodgings in central Taxco, Los Arcos offers basic accommodations around a pleasant patio. ⊠ *Calle Juan Ruíz de Alarcón 12, 40200,* ☎ *762/2–18–36,* FAX *762/2–32–11. 25 rooms with bath. MC, V.*

$$ 🏨 **Monte Taxco.** A colonial style predominates at this hotel, which has a knockout view, a funicular, three restaurants, a disco, and nightly entertainment. ⊠ *Box 84, Lomas de Taxco, 40200,* ☎ *762/2–13–00,* FAX *762/2–14–28. 156 rooms, suites, and villas with bath. 3 restaurants, 9-hole golf course, 3 tennis courts, horseback riding, dance club. AE, DC, MC, V.*

$$ 🏨 **Posada de la Misión.** Laid out like a village, this hotel is close to town.
★ The pool area is adorned with murals by the noted Mexican artist Juan O'Gorman. ⊠ *Box 88, Cerro de la Misión 32, 40230,* ☎ *762/2–00– 63,* FAX *762/2–21–98. 150 rooms with bath. Pool. AE, DC, MC, V.*

$ 🏨 **Posada de los Castillo.** This in-town inn is straightforward, clean, and good for the price. The Emilia Castillo silver shop is off the lobby. ⊠ *Juan Ruíz de Alarcón 7, 40200,* ☎ *762/2–13–96,* FAX *762/2–34– 71. 15 rooms with bath. DC, MC, V.*

$ 🏨 **Posada de San Javier.** This sprawling, very private establishment
★ is set somewhat haphazardly around a charming garden with a pool and wishing well. In addition to the rooms, there are seven one-bedroom apartments with living rooms and kitchenettes (generally monopolized by wholesale silver buyers). ⊠ *Estacas 1 or Exrastro 4, 40200* ☎ *762/2–31–77,* FAX *762/2–00–80. 25 rooms with bath. MC, V.*

$ 🏨 **Rancho Taxco-Victoria.** This in-town hotel, in two buildings connected by a bridge over the road, is under the same management as the De la Borda (☞ *below*). Like the De la Borda, it is past its prime but exudes a certain charm. The rooms have been freshly painted, and the Mexican decor is simple but attractive. There's also the requisite splendid view. ⊠ *Box 83, Carlos J. Nibbi 5, 40200,* ☎ *762/2–02–10,* FAX *762/2– 00–10. 64 rooms with bath. Restaurant, bar, pool. AE, MC, V.*

$ 🏨 **Santa Prisca.** The patio with fountains is a plus at this colonial-style hotel. ⊠ *Cena Obscuras 1, 40200,* ☎ FAX *762/2–00–80. 40 rooms. Restaurant, bar. AE, MC, V.*

Nightlife and the Arts

FESTIVALS

Except for the Jornadas Alarconas—which honors one of Mexico's greatest dramatists with theater, dance and concerts (dates change every year)—Taxco has no abundance of cultural events. But it *is* noted for its festivals, an integral part of the town's character. These fiestas provide an opportunity to honor almost every saint in heaven with music, dancing, marvelous fireworks (Taxco is Mexico's fireworks capital), and lots of fun. The people of Taxco demonstrate their pyrotechnical skills with set pieces—wondrous blazing "castles" made of bamboo. (Note: Expect high occupancy at local hotels and inns during fiestas.)

January 18, the feast of Santa Prisca and San Sebastián, the town's patron saints, is celebrated with music and fireworks.

Holy Week, from Palm Sunday to Easter Sunday, brings processions and events that blend Christian and Indian traditions; the dramas involve hundreds of participants, images of Christ, and, for one particular procession, black-hooded penitents. Most events are centered on Plaza Borda and the Santa Prisca Church.

September 29, Saint Michael's Day (Dia de San Miguel), is celebrated with regional dances and pilgrimages to the Chapel of Saint Michael the Archangel.

In **early November,** on the Monday following the Day of the Dead celebrations on November 1 and 2, the entire town takes off to a nearby hill for the Fiesta de los Jumiles. The *jumil* is a crawling insect that is said to taste strongly of iodine and is considered a great delicacy. Purists eat them alive, but others prefer them stewed, fried, or combined with chili in a hot sauce.

In **late November or early December,** the National Silver Fair (Feria Nacional de la Plata) draws hundreds of artisans from around the world for a variety of displays, concerts, exhibitions, and contests held around the city.

NIGHTLIFE

Travelers should satisfy their appetite for fun after dark in Acapulco. Taxco has a few discos (open only on weekends), a couple of piano bars, and some entertainment, but the range is limited.

Still, you might enjoy spending an evening perched on a chair on a balcony or in one of the cafés surrounding the Plaza Borda. Two traditional favorites are the **Bar Paco** (⊠ Plaza Borda 12, ☎ 762/2–00–63) and **Bertha's** (⊠ Plaza Borda 9, ☎ 762/2–01–72), where a tequila, lime, and club-soda concoction called a Bertha is the house specialty. In addition, some of the town's best restaurants have music on weekends.

Or immerse yourself in the thick of things, especially on Sunday evening, by settling in on a wrought-iron bench on the zócalo to watch children, lovers, and fellow people-watchers.

Most of Taxco's nighttime activity is at the Monte Taxco hotel, either at the **Bongolé** discotheque or at **Tony's Bar,** where the Papantla fliers ($6) perform nightly, except Sunday. On Saturday nights, the hotel offers a buffet, a terrific fireworks display, and a show put on by the hotel's employees.

Outdoors Activities and Sports

You can play golf or tennis, swim, and ride horses at a few hotels around Taxco. Call to see if the facilities are open to nonguests. Bullfights are occasionally held in the small town of Acmixtla, 6 kilometers (4 miles) from Taxco. Ask at your hotel about the schedule.

Shopping
CRAFTS

Lacquered gourds and boxes from the town of Olinalá, masks, bowls, straw baskets, bark paintings, and many other handcrafted items native to the state of Guerrero are available from strolling vendors and are displayed on the cobblestones at "sidewalk boutiques."

Arnoldo (⊠ Palma 1, ☎ 762/2–12–72) has an interesting collection of ceremonial masks; originals come with a certificate of authenticity as well as a written description of origin and use.

Elsa Ruíz de Figueroa (⊠ Plazuela de San Juan 13, ☎ 2–16–83) offers a selection of native-inspired clothing for women, and a wide and well-chosen selection of arts and handicrafts.

Sunday is market day, which means that artisans from surrounding villages descend on the town, as do visitors from Mexico City. It can get crowded, but if you find a seat on a bench in Plaza Borda, you're set to watch the show and peruse the merchandise that will inevitably be brought to you.

SILVER

Most of the people who visit Taxco come with silver in mind. Many of the more than 1,000 silver shops carry almost identical merchandise, although a few are noted for their creativity. Three types are available: sterling, which is always stamped .925 (925 parts in 1,000) and is the most expensive (and desirable); plated silver; and the inexpensive *alpaca*, which is also known as German silver or nickel silver. Sterling pieces are usually priced by weight according to world silver prices; of course, fine workmanship will add to the cost. Work is also done with semiprecious stones; you'll find garnets, topazes, amethysts, and opals.

Bangles start at $3 and bracelets range from $10 to $250. Miguel Pineda, Tane and Los Castillo are some of the more famous design names. Designs range from traditional bulky necklaces (often inlaid with turquoise) to streamlined bangles and chunky earrings.

When comparison shopping in the more than 1,000 silver shops in Taxco, you will see that many carry almost identical merchandise, although a few are noted for their creativity.

Alvaro Cuevas (⊠ Plaza Borda 1, ☎ 762/2–18–78) has fine workmanship to match its fine designs.

The stunning pieces at **Galería de Arte en Plata Andrés** (⊠ Av. John F. Kennedy 28, ☎ 762/2–37–78) are created by the talented Andrés Mejía.

Emilia Castillo (⊠ Juan Ruíz de Alarcón 7, ☎ 762/2–34–71) is the most famous and decidedly one of the most exciting silver shops; it's known for innovative design and for combining silver with porcelain and other metals such as copper and brass. The artisans are disciples of Spratling.

Joyería San Agustín (⊠ Cuauhtemoc 4, ☎ 762/2–34–16) carries a large collection of well-crafted silver jewelery and serving pieces. There's a branch at Talleres de los Ballesteros (⊠ Florida 14, ☎ 762/2–10–76).

Spratling Ranch (⊠ south of town on Highway 95, ☎ 62/2–61–08) is where the heirs of William Spratling turn out designs using his original molds.

Taxco A to Z

ARRIVING AND DEPARTING

By Car. There are several ways to travel to Taxco from Acapulco, and all involve ground transport. It takes about three hours to make the drive, using the new—and expensive—toll road. It is common practice to take an overnight tour. Check with your hotel for references and prices.

By Bus. First-class **Estrella de Oro** buses leave Acapulco several times a day from the Terminal Central de Autobuses de Primera Clase (⊠ Av. Cuauhtémoc 158, ☎ 74/85–87–05). The cost for the approximately 5½-hour ride is about $10 one way for deluxe service. The Taxco terminal is at Avenida John F. Kennedy 126 (☎ 762/2–06–48). First-class **Flecha Roja** buses depart Acapulco several times a day from the Terminal de Autobuses (⊠ Ejido 47, ☎ 74/69–20–29). The one-way ticket is about $8 for first-class service. The Taxco terminal for this line is at Avenida John F. Kennedy 104 (☎ 762/2–01–31).

GETTING AROUND

Unless you're used to byways, alleys, and tiny streets, maneuvering anything bigger than your two feet through Taxco will be difficult. Fortunately, almost everything of interest is within walking distance of the zócalo. Minibuses travel along preset routes and charge only a few cents, and Volkswagen "bugs" provide inexpensive (average $1) taxi transportation. Remember that Taxco's altitude is 5,800 feet. Wear sensible shoes for negotiating the hilly streets, and if you have come from sea level, take it easy on your first day.

CONTACTS AND RESOURCES

Visitor Information. Tourism Office: ⊠ *Av. de los Plateros 1,* ☎ *762/2–22–74.* ⊗ *Weekdays 9–2 and 4–7.*

ACAPULCO A TO Z

Arriving and Departing

By Bus

Bus service from Mexico City to Acapulco is excellent. First-class buses, which leave every hour on the hour from the Tasqueña station, are comfortable and in good condition. The trip takes 5½ hours, and a one-way ticket costs about $13. There is also deluxe service, called *Servicio Diamante,* with airplanelike reclining seats, refreshments, rest rooms, air-conditioning, movies, and hostess service. The deluxe buses leave four times a day, also from the Tasqueña station, and cost about $21. *Futura* service (regular reclining seats, air-conditioning, and a rest room) costs $15.

By Car

The trip to Acapulco from Mexico City on the old road takes about six hours. A new, privately built and run four-lane toll road connecting Mexico City with Acapulco is expensive (about $28 one-way) but well maintained, and it cuts driving time between the two cities from six hours to 3½ hours. Many people opt for going via Taxco, which can be reached from either road.

By Plane

The **Juan N. Alvarez International Airport** (☎ 74/66–94–34) is located about 20 minutes east of the city. From the United States, **American** (☎ 74/85–16–00) has nonstop flights from Dallas, with connecting service from Chicago and New York. **Continental** (☎ 91–800–9–00–50) offers nonstop service from Houston. **Delta's** (☎ 74/66–90–32) direct flights are from Los Angeles. **Mexicana** (☎ 74/84–12–15) has nonstops from Chicago, and connecting service from Los Angeles, Miami, New York, San Antonio, and San Jose, California. **Aeromexico's** (☎ 74/85–16–00) flight from New York to Acapulco stops in Mexico City. The carrier also offers one-stop or connecting service from Atlanta, Chicago, Houston, Los Angeles, Miami, and Orlando.

From New York via Dallas, flying time is 4½ hours; from Chicago, 4¼ hours; from Los Angeles, 3½ hours.

BETWEEN THE AIRPORT AND CITY CENTER

Private taxis are not permitted to carry passengers from the airport to town, so most people rely on **Transportes Aeropuerto** (☎ 73/66–99–88), a special airport taxi service. The system looks confusing, but there are dozens of helpful English-speaking staff to help you figure out which taxi to take.

Look for the name of your hotel and the number of its zone on the overhead sign on the walkway in front of the terminal. Then go to the desk designated with that zone number and buy a ticket for an airport taxi. The ride from the airport to the hotel zone on the trip costs about $3.50 per person for the *colectivo* and starts at $17 for a nonshared cab, depending on your destination. The drivers are usually helpful and will often take you to hotels that aren't on their list. Tips are optional. The journey into town takes 20 to 30 minutes.

By Ship

Many cruises include Acapulco as part of their itinerary. Most originate from Los Angeles. Cruise operators include **Cunard Line** (☎ 800/5–CU-NARD), **Holland America Lines** (☎ 800/628–4855), **Krystal Cruises** (☎ 800/446–6645), **Princess Cruises** (☎ 800/421–0522), **Royal Caribbean Cruise Line** (☎ 800/327–6700), **Royal Cruise Line** (☎ 800/227–4534), **Regency Cruise Line** (☎ 213/785–9300), and **Crystal P & O**(☎ 212/972–4499). Bookings are generally handled through a travel agent.

By Train

There is no train service to Acapulco from anywhere in the United States or Canada, nor is there service from Mexico City.

Getting Around

Getting around in Acapulco is quite simple. You can walk to many places, and the bus costs less than 15¢. Taxis cost less than they do in the United States, so most tourists quickly become avid taxi takers.

By Bus

The buses tourists use the most are those that go from Puerto Marqués to Caleta and stop at the fairly conspicuous metal bus stops along the way. If you want to go from the zócalo to the Costera, catch the bus that says "La Base" (the naval base near the Hyatt Regency). This bus detours through Old Acapulco and returns to the Costera just east of the Ritz Hotel. If you want to follow the Costera for the entire route, take the bus marked "Hornos." Buses to Pie de la Cuesta or Puerto Marqués say so on the front. The Puerto Marqués bus runs about every half hour and is always crowded. If you are headed anywhere along the Costera Miguel Alemán, it's best to go by the Aca Tur bus. For 30¢ you can ride in deluxe, air-conditioned vehicles that travel up and down the main drag from the Hyatt to the Caleta hotels every 10 minutes.

By Car

If you plan to visit some of the more remote beaches or decide to visit Taxco on your own, renting a car is convenient but fairly expensive. Prices start at about $50 a day for a Volkswagen sedan without air-conditioning. Don't expect a full tank; your car will have just about enough gas to get you to the nearest Pemex station.

By Horse and Carriage

Buggy rides up and down the Costera are available evenings. There are two routes: from Papagayo Park to the zócalo and from Condesa Beach to the Naval base. Each costs about $5.

By Taxi

How much you pay depends on what type of taxi you get. The most expensive are hotel taxis. A price list that all drivers adhere to is posted in hotel lobbies. Fares in town are usually about $1.50 to $3; to go from downtown to the Princess Hotel or Caleta Beach is about $6 to $12. Hotel taxis are by far the plushest and are kept in the best condition.

Cabs that cruise with their roof light off occasionally carry a price list but usually charge by zone. There is a minimum charge of $1.50; the fare should still be less than it would be at a hotel. Some taxis that cruise have hotel or restaurant names stenciled on the side but are not affiliated with an establishment. Before you go anywhere by cab, find out what the price should be and agree with the driver on a price.

The cheapest taxis are the little Volkswagens. Officially there is a $1.50 minimum charge, but some cab drivers don't stick to it. A normal—i.e., Mexican-priced—fare is about $1.50 to go from the zócalo to the International Center. Rates are about 50% higher at night, and though tipping is not expected, Mexicans usually leave small change.

You can also hire a taxi by the hour or the day. Prices vary from about $12 an hour for a hotel taxi to $8 an hour for a street taxi. Never let a taxi driver decide where you should eat or shop, since many get kickbacks from some of the smaller stores and restaurants.

Contacts and Resources

Car Rentals

Local car rental agencies include **Hertz** (☎ 74/85–89–47), **Avis** (☎ 74/62–00-85), **Quick** (☎ 74/86–34–20), and **Saad** (☎ 74/84–34–45). All have offices at the airport.

Consulates

United States (✉ Club del Sol Hotel, ☎ 74/85–72–07); **Canada** (✉ Club del Sol Hotel, ☎ 74/85–66–21).

Doctors and Dentists

Your hotel can locate an English-speaking doctor, but they don't come cheap—house calls are about $100. The U.S. consular representative has a list of doctors and dentists, but it's against their policy to recommend anyone in particular.

Emergencies

Police (☎ 74/85–06–50). **Red Cross** (☎ 74/85–41–22). Two reliable hospitals are **Hospital Privado Magallanes** (✉ Wilfrido Massiue 2, ☎ 74/85–65–44) and **Hospital Centro Médico** (✉ J. Arevalo 620, ☎ 74/82–46–92).

English-Language Bookstores

English-language books and periodicals can be found at **Sanborns,** a reputable American-style department-store chain, and at the newsstands in some of the larger hotels. Many small newsstands and the Super-Super carry the *Mexico City News* and the *Mexico City Times,* English-language daily newspapers that are flown in from Mexico

City. *Acapulco Heat,* also in English, is a good source of information about local events and gossip.

Guided Tours

ORIENTATION TOURS

There are organized tours everywhere in Acapulco, from the red-light district to the lagoon. Tours to Mexican fiestas in the evenings or the markets in the daytime are easy to arrange. Tour operators have offices around town and desks in many of the large hotels. If your hotel can't arrange a tour, contact **Consejeros de Viajes** at the Torre de Acapulco (⊠ Costera Miguel Alemán 1252, ☎ 74/84–74–00) or **Turismo Caleta** (⊠ Andrea Doria 2, in Costa Azul, ☎ 74/84–65–70).

SUNSET CRUISES

The famous cliff divers at La Quebrada (☞ Exploring, *above*) give one performance in the afternoon and four performances every night. For about $27, **Divers de México** organizes sunset champagne cruises that provide a fantastic view of the spectacle from the water. For reservations, call 74/82–13–98 or stop by the office downtown near the *Fiesta* and *Bonanza* yachts. The *Fiesta* (☎ 74/83–18–03) runs cruises at 7:30 PM on Tuesday, Thursday, and Saturday for about $24. The *Bonanza*'s (☎ 74/83–18–03) sunset cruise, with open bar (domestic drinks) and live and disco music, costs about $10. All boats leave from downtown near the zócalo. Many hotels and shops sell tickets, as do the ticket sellers on the waterfront.

Travel Agencies

American Express (⊠ La Gran Plaza shopping center, Costera Miguel Alemán 1628, locals 7, 8, and 9, ☎ 74/69–11–00 to 09); **Viajes Wagon-Lits** (⊠ Las Brisas Hotel, Scenic Hwy. 5255, ☎ 74/84–16–50, ext. 392).

Visitor Information

State of Guerrero Department of Tourism (SEFOTUR). ⊠ *Costera Miguel Alemán 187, across from Bodegas Aurrerá,* ☎ *74/86–91–64 or 74/86–91–71.* ☽ *Mon.–Sat. 9–2 and 4–7.*

10 Oaxaca

The geographic, ethnic, and culinary diversity of Oaxaca has made the state a favorite of Mexico aficionados. Descendants of the Mixtec and Zapotec Indians, who built the Monte Albán and Mitla complexes near Oaxaca City, compose the majority of residents; their handicrafts and festivals are extremely colorful. Although less exotic, the state's coastal developments of Puerto Escondido and Bahías de Huatulco are beloved by surfers and beach bums.

Updated by
Patricia Alisau

THE CITY OF OAXACA (Wah-*hah*-kah), one of Mexico's colonial treasures, sits on the vast, fertile, mile-high plateau of the Oaxaca Valley, encircled by the majestic Sierra Madre del Sur mountain range. It is located in the geographic center of the state of Oaxaca, of which it is the capital.

The state, Mexico's fifth largest, is situated in the country's southernmost section, bordered by the states of Chiapas to the east, Veracruz and Puebla to the north, and Guerrero (whose touristic claims to fame are Acapulco and Ixtapa) to the west. The south of Oaxaca State spans 509 kilometers (316 miles) of lush tropical Pacific coastline with magnificent beaches. Until recently, these beaches had been relatively unknown and unexploited, except for the long-established small fishing town and seaside hideaway of Puerto Escondido and the even smaller town of Puerto Angel. But now Huatulco, 125 kilometers (75 miles) west of Puerto Escondido, is beginning to appear on maps as the government works to turn it into a world-class resort.

Oaxaca is endowed with a vast geographic and ethnic diversity. Together with neighboring Chiapas, Oaxaca has the largest Indian population of the region, which explains its richness and variety in handicrafts, folklore, culture, and gastronomy. Most are descendants of the Mixtec or Zapotec Indians, whose villages dot the valleys, mountainsides, and coastal lowlands. Today two out of every three Oaxaqueños are Indians and come from one of 16 distinct groups within the Mixtecs and Zapotecs. They speak 52 dialects and, for the most part, can barely understand one another. If they speak Spanish, it is a second language to them.

The Zapotecs and Mixtecs flourished in the area thousands of years ago. The archaeological ruins of Monte Albán, Mitla, and Yagul are among the vivid reminders of their splendid legacies. Located within a 40-kilometer (25-mile) radius of the city of Oaxaca, the ruins bear witness to highly religious, creative, advanced civilizations that were knowledgeable in geometry.

Their civilizations were conquered by the Aztecs, who in the 15th century gave Oaxaca its name: *Huaxyaca*. In the Náhuatl language it probably means "by the acacia grove," referring to the location of the Aztec military base. Then came the Spanish conquest in 1528. The Spanish monarch Charles V gave Cortés the title of Marqués del Valle de Oaxaca as a reward for his conquest of Mexico. Cortés preferred to live elsewhere, so an estate was never built on the lands conferred with the title, but Cortés's descendants kept the property until Mexico's bloody 1910 Revolution.

Oaxaca's legacy to Mexican politics was two presidents: Benito Juárez, the first full-blooded Indian to become chief of state, and Porfirio Díaz, a military dictator who declared himself President-for-Life. Juárez, a Zapotec, was a sheepherder from San Pablo Gelatao, a settlement about 64 kilometers (40 miles) north of Oaxaca. As a child he spoke only his native Zapotec tongue. Often referred to as Mexico's Abraham Lincoln, Juárez was trained for the clergy but later studied law and entered politics. He was elected governor of the state (1847), chief justice of the Supreme Court of Mexico (1857), and then president (1858–1872), defeating efforts to convert the country into a monarchy under Maximilian. Porfirio Díaz, one of Juárez's generals, seized the presidency by coup in 1877 and held office until overthrown by the Mexican Revolution in 1911.

Pleasures and Pastimes

Dining

Though you can dine on overpriced Continental food, one of the highlights of visiting Oaxaca is the opportunity to enjoy its traditional cuisine, one of the finest and most elaborate in all Mexico. Oaxaca is known as "the land of seven moles" because of its seven distinct kinds of multispiced mole sauces. Only one of them is made with chocolate and rivals that of Puebla (mole poblano) in thickness and flavor because of the outstanding quality of the local chocolate. Tamales stuffed with chicken or pork are another treat. The home- and factory-produced mezcal, made from a cactus, differs in flavor with its maker and can be as high as 80 proof, so be careful when you imbibe. One variety, slightly sweeter, is flavored with oranges or lime; others are sold is festive ceramic jugs.

Unfortunately, Oaxacan cuisine—the cheeses, mole sauces, and meats that make dining in the capital memorable—is in short supply along the coast. Seafood is your best bet. Huatulco's restaurants are getting better, and some of the places in Puerto Escondido are very good. With a few exceptions, the cooking in Puerto Angel is mediocre; the palapa restaurants along the Playa Panteón are distinguished mainly for their high prices, bad service, and aggressive young sidewalk hawkers. Dress is casual at all restaurants except where noted, and reservations are not necessary unless noted. Prices tend to be slightly cheaper in the coastal dining establishments except Huatulco.

CATEGORY	COST*
$$$	over $25
$$	$15–$25
$	under $15

per person, excluding drinks and tip

Lodging

Oaxaca City has no luxury resorts, but it does have some magnificently restored properties including a 16th-century convent and dozens of smaller, moderately priced accommodations, most in downtown locations. These smaller hotels are very popular around December and January and require six months to a year advance booking. The Day of the Dead (November 1 and 2 nationwide) and Holy Week are also times of high occupancy for locals so make plans accordingly.

Hotel rates vary considerably in the coastal area. In Puerto Escondido and Puerto Angel, accommodations tend toward the mosquito-net-over-the-bed variety, falling into $$ or $ price range. Those in Huatulco, where you'll find luxury compounds, are considerably pricier, with the Omni Zaashila topping the scale. The high season along the coast runs from mid-December through Holy Week; rates increase by 20% during this time. Budget accommodations are scarce in Huatulco, although more moderately priced rooms are becoming available.

CATEGORY	COST*
$$$$	over $160
$$$	$90–$160
$$	$40–$90
$	under $40

All prices are for a standard double room, excluding 15% tax.

Shopping

Oaxaca City was and remains the focus of Indian life, mostly that of Zapotecs and Mixtecs who live in the valley and nearby mountains. They come to town to buy and sell, especially on Saturdays. Although the market is no longer as colorful as it was in D. H. Lawrence's day (read his *Mornings in Mexico*), it remains an authentic exotic spectacle. This is the largest Indian market in all of Mexico, and only Michoacán and Chiapas can rival Oaxaca in the variety and quality of crafts. Expect hectic activity and bright colors. (It might come as a surprise not to hear much Spanish spoken at the markets but rather the singsong Zapotec and Mixtec languages, in which changes in the pitch of the voice change the meaning of the word.) In town, stark-white galleries exhibit the pottery, textiles, and fanciful wooden animals, called *alebrijes,* that have drawn international attention to Oaxaca's artisans.

Surfing

Oaxaca's Puerto Escondido is a household name for serious surfers who migrate to this sunny port for top-of-the-line surfing championships each year. These challenging waves have been attracting surfers from all parts of the globe since the 1960s, when the word first got out.

Exploring Oaxaca

Oaxaca has two main regions favored by tourists—Oaxaca City, the state capital, spread over a valley in the Sierra Madre mountains, and the coastal area on the rim of the Pacific Ocean due south of the capital.

Great Itineraries

The rugged mountain terrain of Oaxaca makes traveling to these two areas rather lengthy by car or bus, but the trip takes only a half hour by plane. If you only have three days to spend in the state, choose between Oaxaca City and the coast. Outdoor buffs seeking unspoiled beaches and wildlife should gravitate toward Puerto Escondido or Puerto Angel, while those looking for a chic, upscale ambience will like the million-dollar resort hotels of Huatulco. Oaxaca City is food for the soul for history and folk-art aficionados, with its magnificent colonial buildings, world-famous handicrafts, and the shimmering temples from ancient times just outside the city. If you want a culture-beach combination, a minimum of seven days is advisable—both Oaxaca City and the coastal resorts deserve at least three days apiece.

IF YOU HAVE 3 DAYS IN OAXACA CITY

Explore downtown to see the stunning colonial monuments that have been declared World Heritage structures by the United Nations. The first day, take in the Cathedral, Museum of Contemporary Art, the Santa Domingo church, and the adjoining Regional Museum of Oaxaca. Day 2, start with a visit to the 16th-century Catalina convent, now the Camino Real hotel, and view the pretty patio garden with the stone tub where the nuns washed clothes; then catch a tour or bus for the ruins at Monte Alban. Day 3, visit the colonial Rufino Tamayo Museum and then head to the Benito Juárez market for regional arts and crafts.

IF YOU HAVE 5 DAYS IN OAXACA CITY

Follow the three-day itinerary and, on Day 4, add a visit to the Mixtec ruins at Mitla; then spend the rest of the afternoon back in Oaxaca City people-watching and dining at the zócalo. Day 5, take a trip to at least three Indian villages near Oaxaca City, where beautiful handicrafts are made before your eyes. Back again in Oaxaca City, visit the Soledad Basilica and the boutiques full of high-quality crafts on Calle Macedonia Acalá.

IF YOU HAVE 3 DAYS IN THE COASTAL BEACH RESORTS

Using Bahías de Huatulco as your base, take a boat tour of the bays on the first day, followed by a spell at the beach for a blazing sunset finale. Day 2, tour the small beaches and hidden bays of picturesque Puerto Angel and Puerto Escondido. On Day 3, laze on the beach and, in late afternoon, taxi to Crucecita for some strolling, followed by dining at one of the small restaurants on the main square.

IF YOU HAVE 5 DAYS IN THE COASTAL BEACH RESORTS
Sign up for bird-watching with an ornithologist on the Manialtepec Lagoon on Day 4. Day 5, book the Museum of the Sea Turtle tour.

IF YOU HAVE 7 DAYS OR MORE
You can immerse yourself in the cultural treasures of Oaxaca City and then kick back with some sea and sun. Day 1 to 4 should be spent in Oaxaca City visiting the sights outlined in the first four days of the itinerary. On Day 5, fly to Huatulco and, on arrival, sign up for a boat tour of the bays. Days 6 and 7 can follow the program laid out for Day 2 and 3 in the coastal resorts agenda. Those staying longer should not miss the Museum of the Sea Turtle tour.

When to Tour Oaxaca

Oaxaca celebrates Mexican holidays and its own state's fiestas with an intensity of color, tradition, and talent that attracts visitors in hordes. *El día de Muertos* (Day of the Dead) begins with graveyard celebrations in the nearby villages of Xoxo and Atzompa on October 31 and ends in the cemeteries on November 2, when families partake of the favorite food of the dead; in between, the city, and especially the zócalo, are abuzz with activity. On December 23, the *Noche de Rabanos* (Night of the Radishes), the zócalo is packed with growers and artists displaying their hybrid radishes carved and arranged in tableaux that depict everything from Nativity scenes to space travel. Prizes are awarded for the biggest and the best, and the competition is fierce. Other arrangements are made with *flores immortales* (small dried flowers) or *totomoxtl* (corn husks). Bring plenty of film.

Oaxaca's other major celebration is the *Guelaguetza* (Zapotec for "offering" or "gift"), held on the last two Mondays in July. Dancers from all the various mountain and coastal communities converge on the city bearing tropical fruits, baskets, weavings, and pottery. They perform elaborate dances in authentic costumes from early morning until late at night at the Guelaguetza Auditorium, an open-air amphitheater often shown on maps as *Lunes del Cerro* (Monday of the Hill). Various hotels in town offer mini-Guelaguetzas at night; the best is at the Hotel Camino Real Oaxaca on Wednesday and/or Friday.

Keep in mind, of course, that if you plan to come for these celebrations, you'll need to book far in advance; don't expect to come to town and find a hotel room.

Saturday is the best day for markets in Oaxaca City and the surrounding villages.

OAXACA CITY AND ENVIRONS

Oaxaca City—officially, Oaxaca de Juárez—is still the state's major attraction, with a population of about 180,000 and more than 2 million visitors a year. The city is traditionally Indian, but cosmopolitan touches are everywhere. Women and children sell woven bracelets, and men offer shoe shines around the city's many parks and squares while painters and weavers display their wares on grassy lawns.

A trip to the colonial city of Oaxaca sees its natural complement in an exploration of the area's more ancient past. The dramatic settings of the Zapotec ruins of Monte Albán, Mitla, and Yagul enhance the interest of these ruins. Similarly, it's fascinating to see the wares sold in the Oaxaca City market being produced in nearby villages that have changed little over the centuries. None of the visits will take more than an hour and all the destinations are easily reached by public transportation or tour. At a minimum, visit Monte Albán and one Indian village.

Oaxaca City

Numbers in the margin correspond to points of interest on the Oaxaca City map.

The colonial heart of Oaxaca is laid out in a simple grid, with all major attractions within walking distance of one another. Most explorations of the town begin at the shady **zócalo,** the heart of the city and its pedestrian-only main square. During the day, locals and visitors are drawn to its shaded walks, commodious park benches, and ornate bandstand. At night, mariachi and marimba bands play under colonial archways, filling the air with music and song.

If you head up the pedestrian mall from the northeast corner of the zócalo on **Calle Macedonio Alcalá,** you'll see pastel restored colonial mansions and some of Oaxaca's best galleries, shops, and restaurants. It is also lively and well lit at night, and there are frequent outdoor arts-and-crafts exhibits.

1 The splendid **Palacio de Gobierno** (State Capitol building), constructed in the 19th century in neoclassical style, sits on the south side of the zócalo. The fascinating murals inside depict the history and cultures of Oaxaca. ☉ *Weekdays 8–8, weekends 8–3.*

2 Begun in 1544, the **Catedral Metropolitana de Oaxaca** was destroyed by earthquakes and not finished until 1733. The facade is Baroque, with a wood-cogged clock presented to the city by the king of Spain. It's on the zócalo's northwest corner. ⊠ *Av. Independencia 50,* ☎ *951/6–55–80.* ☉ *Daily 7 AM–9 PM.*

3 The **Museo de Oaxaca,** also known as the Museo de Arte Contemporaneo de Oaxaca, is housed in a former colonial residence that's often erroneously called the Casa de Cortés—in fact, the conqueror never built a home for himself in Oaxaca. Inside are exhibits featuring the crafts and artworks of local artists in a variety of media. Be sure to check out what remains of the frescoes in the second-floor gallery at the front of the building. ⊠ *Calle Macedonio Alcalá 202,* ☎ *951/6–84–99.* ▨ *Donations appreciated.* ☉ *Wed.–Mon. 10:30–8.*

4 In a city renowned for its many churches, the **Iglesia y Ex-Convento de Santo Domingo** (Church and Ex-Monastery of Santo Domingo) is one of the most brilliantly decorated. The 16th-century monastery has an ornate carved facade between two high bell towers. The interior is a profusion of white and gold—yes, that's real gold leaf—typical of the energy with which Mexico seized on the Baroque style and made of it something unique. ⊠ *Calle Macedonio Alcalá and A. Gurrión,* ☎ *951/6–3720.* ☉ *Daily 7–1 and 4–8.*

5 Part of the Iglesia y Ex-Convento de Santo Domingo, the **Museo Regional de Oaxaca** (Oaxaca State Museum) is laid out in a series of galleries around the cloister. The centerpiece of this ethnological collection, which focuses on the various Indian groups within Oaxaca, is the treasure taken from the tombs at Monte Albán (☞ *below*), just outside the city; the stunning gold jewelry from Tomb 7 was one of the greatest archaeological finds of all times. There is also a large collection of ceremonial masks and costumes from the different tribes of the valley; some of the Indian women who come into town for the market still wear traditional costumes, and with a bit of study here at the

museum, you will be able to identify their home villages. The other part
of the old convent next to the church, a military barracks until January 1994, is being converted into a Museum of Colonial Art and already has some pieces on display. As you leave the church and enter
the wide Santo Domingo Plaza, you are likely to be accosted by Indian boys selling rough sketches on bark (they make an easy-to-carry
gift) and a variety of other crafts. ☎ *951/6–29–91.* 🎫 *Both museums $2; free on Sun. and national holidays.* ⊙ *Tues.–Fri. 10–6, week-
ends 10–5.*

⑥ Memorabilia of the Mexican hero is displayed at the **Museo Casa de
Benito Juárez** (the Juárez House Museum), located in the 19th-century
colonial house where he was a servant during his youth. ⊠ *Calle García Vigil 609,* ☎ *951/6–18–60.* 🎫 *No entrance fee but donations appreciated.* ⊙ *Tues.–Sun. 9–7.*

An old, carefully restored colonial mansion with an interior courtyard
now hosts **Museo de Arte Prehispánico "Rufino Tamayo"** (Tamayo Mu-
⑦ seum of Pre-Hispanic Art), featuring a small but excellent collection
of pre-Hispanic pottery and sculpture. It was originally the private collection of the late painter-muralist Rufino Tamayo, who presented it
to his hometown in 1979. There are exhibits from all over the country, arranged geographically and chronologically. Perhaps the most delightful item is the model of a ball court for sacred Indian games with
figurines representing the participants and spectators. ⊠ *Av. Morelos
503,* ☎ *951/6–47–50.* 🎫 *$1.* ⊙ *Mon. and Wed.–Sat. 10–2 and 4–
7, Sun. 10–3.*

⑧ The Baroque **Basílica de Nuestra Señora de la Soledad** (Basilica of Our
Lady of Solitude) houses the statue of this Virgin, who is Oaxaca's patron saint. She now stands in a gilded shrine and wears a magnificent
robe of jewel-studded black velvet, but she was found in the pack of

a stray mule that had died. This event was construed by the faithful as a miracle, and the church was built in 1682 to commemorate it. Believed to have supernatural healing powers, the statue remains the object of fervent piety for the devout populace. ⊠ *Av. Independencia 107 at Galeana,* ☎ *951/6–7566.* ⊙ *Daily 6 AM–8 PM.*

Dining and Lodging

The open-air cafés surrounding the zócalo are good for drinks, snacks, and people-watching, with the scene changing from peaceful serenity over early-morning coffee to pulsating frenzy in late evening. If you want to join the crowds at these restaurants, the *comida corrida* (set menu served at midday) makes an economical choice. But you won't be very much out of pocket wherever you choose to dine: The devaluation of the peso has put even the highest-quality restaurants into the $$ price range.

$$ ✕ **El Refectorio.** The dining room at the Hotel Camino Real does not disappoint. It's open for breakfast, lunch, and dinner, but the best meal is the Saturday-night buffet accompanied by mariachi music, served from 7 to 10. The regular menu offers high-end versions of local dishes such as chicken in mole, Oaxacan (mole-filled) tamales, and fish fillet baked in banana leaf. Choose a table overlooking the garden courtyard, and linger over your meal in this 16th-century convent. ⊠ *Hotel Camino Real Oaxaca, Cinco de Mayo 300,* ☎ *951/6–06–11.* AE, DC, MC, V.

$$ ✕ **El Tule.** On a hill above town, the Hotel Victoria's prime location is enhanced by this veranda dining room, which serves international fare in addition to such Oaxacan specialties as chicken in mole and *queso asadero,* Oaxacan cheese baked to a crisp crust on the outside and creamy on the inside. The restaurant overlooks the hotel gardens and the valley below. ⊠ *Hotel Victoria, Km 545 of Rte. 190,* ☎ *951/5–26–33.* AE, MC, V.

$ ✕ **Catedral.** This local favorite calls itself the House of Fillets. It offers six meat fillet entrées, as well as regional dishes, hamburgers, sandwiches, and a variety of soups. The most pleasant place to dine is by the fountain in the courtyard. ⊠ *1 block north of the Catedral, at the corner of Calle García Vigil and Av. Morelos,* ☎ *951/6–32–85.* MC, V.

$ ✕ **Del Jardín.** Everybody seems to wind up at this place, the happening café on the zócalo from 8 till late. The Oaxacan tamales (with chicken and mole) and piquant chile rellenos are good, as are many of the sandwiches, soups, tacos, and more substantial pork and seafood dishes on the menu. ⊠ *Portal de Flores 10 (west side of zócalo),* ☎ *951/6–26–29.* AE, MC, V.

$ ✕ **El Asador Vasco.** Basque (*vasco*) cuisine is featured here along with
★ an outstanding Oaxacan version of mole sauce—steamy, black, and marvelous on chicken or turkey—and a sumptuous gratiné of oysters in chipotle sauce. The tables overlooking the zócalo are in great demand. Live serenading by the *tuna* student minstrels evokes medieval Spain (Thurs.–Sat. evenings starting at 8:30). ⊠ *On the west side of the zócalo, upstairs, Portal de Flores 10-A,* ☎ *951/4–73–14.* AE, DC, MC, V.

$ ✕ **El Biche Pobre "2."** This place is a bit of a hike from the city center, but your bill for the fine *botana surtida* (sampler plate)—with tamales, *sopas* (soups), chile rellenos, croquettes, and other treats—will be astonishingly low. You can walk the meal off afterward in nearby Juárez Park. ⊠ *Calzada de la República 600 at Calle Hidalgo,* ☎ *951/3–46–36.* AE, MC, V. ⊙ *Daily 1–6.*

$ ✕ **El Mesón.** The spanking-clean dining room and open-air kitchen in
★ this restaurant right off the zócalo make it a favorite for locals and visitors, who stop by for a snack or full meal from the long paper menu,

where you check off your items of choice. Try the *cebollitas* (grilled whole green onions) as a side dish with your *cecina enchilada* (grilled strips of pork covered with chili powder) and fresh corn tortillas made at the tortilleria at the entrance. For an intense sugar fix, have a cup of rich Oaxacan chocolate and a slice of nut or cheese pie. ✉ *Av. Hidalgo 805, at Valdivieso,* ☎ *951/6–27–29. MC, V.* ☉ *Daily 8 AM–midnight.*

$ ✕ **El Mirador.** The view is spectacular at this 25-table cliffside restaurant,which adorns the Cerro de Fortin, where the annual Guelaguetza (☞ Nightlife and the Arts, *below*) is staged. Locals head here for the house special, *parillada,* a heaping plate of jerked beef, chilied beef, and plain beef grilled tableside with large scallions and cheese (it serves two or three). Top this off with a *yarda* of beer served in tall glasses British pub–style and homemade flan or fried bananas in cream for dessert. Romantic souls favor dining on the terrace at night. ✉ *Calle 21 de Mayo 101,* ☎ *951/6–58–20. MC, V.*

$ ✕ **La Casita.** Many in the know consider this the best place to enjoy the cuisine of Oaxaca. The actual dishes are displayed on a counter by the door, so you can see what your food will look like before you order. This eatery is especially famous for *chapulines* (grasshoppers, in season in the fall months), but there are also more conventional dishes, such as enchiladas with chicken and spicy mole sauce. Try to get a table by the second-floor window so you can watch the activity in the park below while you dine. ✉ *Av. Hidalgo 612 (south side of Alameda de León),* ☎ *951/6–29–17. AE, MC, V.* ☉ *Daily noon–7.*

$ ✕ **La Morsa.** The name means "walrus," the informal palapa setting is tastefully tropical amid gardens and fountains, and superfresh seafood is the specialty. Try the *platón de mariscos* (shellfish platter) with oysters, shrimp, squid, and octopus; or fish fillet *a la veracruzana* (with tomato sauce), *a la mexicana* (with green chili sauce), or with a creamy chipotle sauce. The oyster dishes are a bargain. Come early for dinner; the place closes at 8. ✉ *Calzada (not Calle) Porfirio Díaz 240, Col. Reforma,* ☎ *951/5–22–13. AE, MC, V. Closed Mon.*

$ ✕ **Nuu-Luu.** The name in Mixtec, "picturesque place," couldn't be more ★ appropriate. Located in a pretty suburb in the northern part of town (just eight minutes from the zócalo), this delightful open-air restaurant overlooks a large country garden lush with exotic fruit trees. Renowned chef-owner Guadalupe Salinas prepares a changing array of Oaxacan specialties, including a spectacular mole made with seven kinds of chilies; it's served with turkey, chicken, or pork. The cost of a meal that allows you to sample nearly everything on the menu is extremely reasonable. Private transportation is provided from and to your hotel. ✉ *Iturbide 100, San Felipe del Agua,* ☎ *951/5–31–87. AE, MC, V.* ☉ *Daily 8–6.*

$$$ 🏨 **Hotel Camino Real Oaxaca.** A monastic air lingers in the breezy pa-★ tios and small enclosed gardens of this beautifully restored former convent (1576), designated a National Monument; it became part of the Camino Real hotel chain in late 1994. One of the hotel's three courtyards, the one with the large stone basin in the center, is still called La Lavandería (the laundry); it is where the nuns of the convent used to wash their clothes. The rooms, of course, are far from austere; all have deluxe conveniences and are undergoing a million-dollar remodeling for further soundproofing (it should be finished by 1997). Stop in for a meal (☞ El Refractorio, *above*) or a drink and look around even if you don't stay here. ✉ *Cinco de Mayo 300, 68000 Oaxaca, Oax.,* ☎ *951/6–06–11 or 800/7–CAMINO,* 📠 *951/6–07–32. 91 rooms. Restaurant, 2 bars, pool, travel services. AE, DC, MC, V.*

$$ 🏨 **Mesón de Angel.** This large hotel near the markets is a favorite with Mexican families, groups, and traveling salesmen. There is a big pool

in the hotel garden and attractive newly remodeled rooms with terraces, orthopedic mattresses, desk fans, and TVs (channels in Spanish only). Tourist buses to Monte Albán and Mitla leave from here. ⊠ *F. J. Mina 518, 68000 Oaxaca, Oax.,* ☎ *951/6–66–66,* FAX *951/4–54–05. 50 rooms. Restaurant, pool, travel services. No credit cards.*

$$ ☷ **Misión de los Angeles.** Though this resort-style hotel is a long way from the zócalo, its peaceful gardens and relaxed ambience make it a good choice. The hotel is near Plaza Juárez, a central park and plaza frequented more by locals than by tourists, and the commodious dining room is popular with tour groups. ⊠ *Calzada Porfirio Díaz 102, 68000 Oaxaca, Oax.,* ☎ *951/5–15–00,* FAX *951/5–16–80. 173 rooms. 2 restaurants, 2 bars, pool, tennis court, jogging, recreation room, dance club. AE, MC, V.*

$$ ☷ **Victoria.** Surrounded by terraced grounds and well-kept gardens, ★ this sprawling salmon-color complex is perched on a hill overlooking the city. Draw back your curtains at dawn and catch your breath at the view: Oaxaca awakening under the Sierra Madre. The hotel has a good restaurant, tennis court, and heated pool, and the property is strewn with picture-perfect bougainvillea. Rooms, bungalows, and suites are available; be sure to request one with a view. ⊠ *Lomas del Fortín 1, 68070, Oaxaca, Oax.,* ☎ *951/5–26–33,* FAX *951/5–24–11. 149 units. Restaurant, bar, pool, tennis court. AE, MC, V.*

$ ☷ **Fortin Plaza.** This modern six-story hotel, with beautifully landscaped gardens overlooking town and the surrounding mountains, is just downhill from the Victoria. Its rather modest exterior is offset by an exquisitely designed interior that makes lavish use of marble, wood, glass, and stone. Front balconied rooms offer the best views, but if you're looking for a good night's sleep, choose the quieter rear rooms. The hotel has a pool, but it's small and is sandwiched between the highway and the building. ⊠ *Av. Venus 118, 68000 Oaxaca, Oax.,* ☎ *951/5–77–77,* FAX *951/5–13–28. 93 rooms. Restaurant, bar, pool. AE, DC, MC, V.*

$ ☷ **Las Rosas.** This small second-floor hotel half a block off the zócalo offers clean, basic rooms—no phones or TVs—around a central courtyard at a price that's hard to beat. The owners are pleasant, and there are pretty mountain views from the little roof garden. ⊠ *Trujano 112, 68000 Oaxaca, Oax.,* ☎ *951/4–22–17. 19 rooms. MC, V.*

$ ☷ **Marqués del Valle.** Right on the zócalo and in the middle of things, the property's restaurant serves a good breakfast, from bananas and cream to hotcakes. Rooms with colonial-style furnishings have been newly carpeted and painted, and new sinks are being installed in all the bathrooms. Amenities include color TVs (Spanish only) and telephones. The hallways can act like echo chambers for the cathedral bells from next door. ⊠ *Portal de Clavería s/n, 68000 Oaxaca, Oax.,* ☎ *951/6–32–95,* FAX *951/6–99–61. 95 rooms. Restaurant, travel services. AE, DC, MC, V.*

$ ☷ **Principal.** This popular budget hotel—one of the best of the group— fills up quickly, but the owners can refer you to other hotels in the area as well as provide insider touring tips. Rooms in this colonial house face a bare central courtyard ringed by potted geranium plants. Each room has small folk-art touches, and the whole place has a friendly, homey feeling. Reservations for dates from December to mid-January must be made at least six months in advance; the hotel fills up fast during this period. ⊠ *Cinco de Mayo 208, 68000 Oaxaca, Oax.,* ☎ FAX *951/6–25–35. 16 rooms. No credit cards.*

$ ☷ **Villa María.** Popular with Americans, Europeans, and Japanese, this compound is sprinkled with one-, two-, and three-bedroom furnished apartments overlooking a spacious patio. Friendly, bilingual hostess María García makes her guests feel as though they're part of a family.

Linens and dishes come with the units (which have suitable touches of Mexican decor), but phones, cable TV, and maid service are extra. It's a small hike to the main square from here, but taxis and buses run frequently. Rentals are by the week or month, with rates starting at $400 a month for a one-bedroom unit; advance reservations and deposits—up to a year prior to arrival depending on the season—are required. ✉ *Arteaga 410, 68000 Oaxaca, Oax.,* ☎ *951/6–50–56,* 𝕱𝕬𝕏 *951/4–25–62. 14 apartments. No credit cards.*

Shopping

Prospective folk-art buyers in Oaxaca City and surrounding villages should heed one major caveat, or risk being saddled with more than they expected. It is not too difficult to ship your purchases home from many of the city's shops and shipping services, provided you have a receipt showing that you paid the 15% sales tax on all items purchased. Many of the artisans have begun giving out official government tax receipts, but if you buy from one who does not, you may have a hard time finding someone to ship your wares for you, and when you do, it will be very expensive. Ask for receipts and for referrals to shipping agents. Also, check out the displays at the shops in town and learn about quality and design before you start spending lots of pesos.

MARKETS

The Saturday market is held at the **Central de Abastos** (Supply Center) on the southern edge of the town center. Late Friday and early Saturday, Indians stream to this site, spreading their wares over blocks and blocks of empty lots and through an enormous central warehouse. By noon on Saturday, the market is swarming with thousands of sellers and shoppers, and the experience can be quite overwhelming. Don't burden yourself with a lot of camera equipment or purses and bags; you'll have a hard enough time keeping track of companions in the jostling, bumping crowd. If you see something you really want, purchase it on the spot—you'll never find your way back. The market is active during the rest of the week, too; if you go then, you can check out the mounds of multicolored chilies and herbs, the piles of tropical fruit, and the aisles of baskets, rugs, and jewelry. Some sections are filled with plastic household products, others with automotive and electronic gadgets. But it's on Saturday that you see the best handicrafts: *huipiles* (embroidered blouses) that vary with the village of origin; *rebozos* (shawls) of cotton and silk; pottery shaped without a wheel; colorful woven baskets; wooden and tin toys; machetes with leather sheaths. Bargaining is expected.

The several market areas in Oaxaca are active daily, though Saturday is the busiest day. **Mercado Benito Juárez** and **Mercado 20 de Noviembre** are two blocks south of the zócalo on Calle 20 de Noviembre between Calle las Cases and Calle Mina. This two-block area has some crafts, but most tempting are the food stalls, which serve simple meals for locals and budget travelers alike. Two blocks farther south is **Mercado de Artesanías,** at the corner of Calles José P. García and Ignacio Zaragoza, which features mostly textiles. While they tend their stands, Trique Indian women and children weave wall hangings with simple backstrap looms.

For information on the colorful markets in the Indian villages outside Oaxaca, *see* Excursions, *below.*

SHOPS

Besides having a mother lode of markets, Oaxaca also has some spectacular shops and galleries, most near the zócalo. The huge, sprawling **Fonart** store (✉ Manuel M. Bravo 116 at García Vigil, ☎ 951/6–57–

64) has a representative selection of arts and crafts, not only from Oaxaca but also from other regions of the country. Several gallery-style shops feature the true masters of the folk arts. The prices can be quite high, but as your eye becomes adjusted to the differences in quality and technique, you can appreciate the talent involved. **Artesanías "Chimalli"** (✉ García Vigil 513–A, ☎ 951/4–21–01) has shelves and shelves of *alebrijes*—bright pink, orange, and purple carved copal-wood cats, dogs, tigers, rabbits, and snakes with comical expressions and fantasy shapes. The shop's inventory also includes decorative tin picture frames and wooden chairs painted with a likeness of Pancho Villa. **La Mano Mágica** (✉ Macedonio Alcalá 203, ☎ 951/6–42–75) is a large gallery inside a hacienda, with rotating shows from Oaxaca's premier artists, working on-site in either pottery, textiles, wood or paint. Such folk art as life-size papier-mâché skeletons and devils add a macabre touch to the scene, while vats of boiling dye steam in the open patio. Prices tend to be a little high here. **Yalalag** (✉ Macedonio Alcalá 104, ☎ 951/6–21–08) has delicately woven huipiles and a courtyard filled with tons of black Oaxacan pottery plus miniature ceramic chapels and Spanish dolls. **Artesanías de Oaxaca** (✉ A. Gurrión, corner of Macedonia Alcalá, ☎ 951/4–32–01) has a more eccentric selection than most of its neighbors; the Mestas family is happy to guide you through their treasure of masks, traditional costumes, antique hobby horses, and other unusual wood crafts. **Oro de Monte Albán** (✉ Macedonia Alcalá 307, ☎ 951/6–18–12) is one of several branches of the store selling gold and silver reproductions of pre-Columbian jewelry found in the tombs of royalty at the Monte Albán archaeological site. Ten different pieces, including Xipe, the god of Spring, are beautifully reproduced. Leading local artists exhibit and sell their paintings and sculptures at **Galería Arte de Oaxaca** (✉ Trujano 102, ☎ 951/4–09–10).

Several shops specialize in gold and silver jewelry designed in the style of the jewels found at Monte Albán. You'll find a number of them along Calle Macedonia Alcalá and A. Gurrión. Most shops close from 2 to 4 in the afternoon; many are closed Sunday.

Monte Albán

9 km (5½ mi) southwest of Oaxaca.

The onetime holy city of more than 40,000 Zapotecs, Monte Albán is among the most interesting and well-preserved archaeological ruins in the country. Experts estimate that a mere 10% of the site is uncovered; excavations are constantly taking place to unearth more knowledge about the fascinating Zapotec culture.

Monte Albán overlooks the Oaxaca Valley from a flattened mountaintop 1,300 feet high. The Zapotecs leveled the area in about 600 BC. They arranged the buildings along a perfect north–south axis, with the exception of one structure thought to have been an observatory that is more closely aligned with the stars than with the earth's poles. The oldest of the four temples is the **Temple of the Dancers,** so named because of the remains of elaborately carved stone figures that once covered the building. The figures are nude and, because of their distorted positions, have since come to be thought of not as dancers but as prisoners of war on their way to be sacrificed.

Another major point of interest is the **ball court,** site of a complicated game—part basketball, part soccer. The players' objective was to navigate the ball into a lowered area in the opponents' court with only their hips and elbows. There is some speculation that the captain of the losing team was sacrificed, but this is dubious.

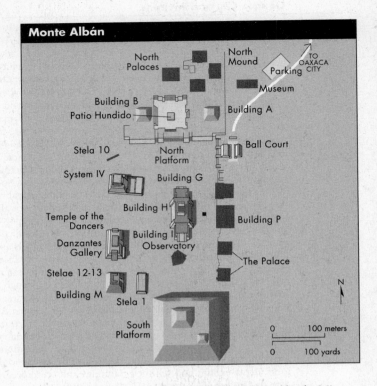

About 1,000 years ago, the Zapotecs were conquered by the Mixtecs. The Mixtecs never lived in Monte Albán but used it as a city of the dead, a massive cemetery of lavish tombs. More than 160 have been discovered, and in 1932 Tomb 7 yielded a treasure unequaled in North America. Inside were more than 500 priceless Mixtec objects, including gold breastplates; jade, pearl, ivory, and gold jewelry; and fans, masks, and belt buckles of precious stones and metals. All are now on view at the Museo Regional de Oaxaca.

There are special tourist buses to Monte Albán from the Mesón del Angel hotel running every hour or so from 8:30 to 3:30; the last bus back is at 5:30. The fare is about $1 round-trip. A taxi from the zócalo should run $4 or $5. ☎ $2.50; free Sun. and holidays. ☉ Daily 8–5.

Mitla

40 km (25 mi) southeast of Oaxaca.

Mitla, like Monte Albán, is a complex of ceremonial structures started by the Zapotecs but taken over and heavily influenced by the Mixtecs. However, the architecture here is totally different from that of any of the other ruins in the area. The stone walls are inlaid with smaller stones cut into geometric patterns, forming a mosaic that is sometimes almost Grecian in appearance. Unlike other ancient buildings in North America, there are no human figures or mythological events represented— only abstract designs. The name, from the Aztec word *mictlan*, means "place of the dead." A trip here can be nicely combined with a stop at the Tule Tree (☞ *below*); the colonial church of Mitla, built against the walls of other Mixtec ruins; and the large open-air crafts market by the ruins. ☎ $2; free Sun. and holidays. ☉ Archaeological zone daily 8:30–6.

Yagul

30 km (19 mi) southeast of Oaxaca.

The ruins at Yagul are as elaborate as those at Monte Albán and are set in a lovely spot on top of a hill. Yagul is certainly beautiful and interesting enough to make it worth the trip. This city is predominantly a fortress that is set slightly above a group of palaces and temples; it includes a ball court and more than 30 uncovered underground tombs. ▨ *$1; free Sun. and holidays.* ☉ *Archaeological zone daily 8–6.*

Indian Villages

Many of the dozen or more villages surrounding the Oaxaca City are known for the skills of their artisans, who use both ancient and modern techniques to create their folk-art pieces; they often live among generations of families who have their own special designs for pottery, woven rugs, and wood carvings.

A west-to-south counterclockwise route from the city takes in **Atzompa,** where the descendants of Teodora Blanca create fanciful *muñecas* (dolls) from clay and other potters make the region's traditional green-glazed plates, bowls, and cups—all in array on Tuesday market day. In **Arrazola,** artists carve *alebrijes,* grand dragons and snakes from copal wood, then paint them with surrealistic designs in vivid colors. On Thursdays, **Zaachila** has the most authentic livestock and food market in the area, while **Etla's** Wednesday market is famous for its cheeses, mole, and chocolate. The southern route goes to **San Bartolo Coyotepec,** the center for glossy black pottery sold in people's yards and from a multistalled building on the side of the road. In **Santo Tomás Jalietza,** women work on small, backstrap looms in the center of town, weaving elaborate belts and table runners from pastel cotton. Friday's market in **Ocotlán** is known for its handicrafts, especially woven baskets, and for its handcrafted machetes and knives, famous throughout Mexico. Some of the machetes are inscribed with colorful local sayings.

An eastward route includes **Teotitlán del Valle,** where giant rug looms sit in front of many houses, and the new Museo Comunitario on the main square focuses on the anthropology, crafts, and culture of the area; **Santa Ana del Valle,** where Lucio Aquino is famous for his rugs; and **Tlacolula,** where the Sunday market spreads for blocks around a Baroque 16th-century chapel. On Sundays it seems that all of Oaxaca takes this route, starting at the Tule Tree (☞ *below*), moving to the ruins of Mitla, and then on to the crafts centers and market. The markets on other routes are held on special days throughout the week, and you can easily fill a week with tours and never see the same sight twice. If you have to budget your time, use tour guides for these trips so you don't miss out on the fascinating details.

The Tule Tree

14 km (8 mi) east of Oaxaca.

In the town of Santa María del Tule stands a huge ahuehuete cypress estimated to be more than 2,000 years old. One of the largest in the world, it is some 140 feet high, with roots buried more than 60 feet in the earth; it takes 35 adults with their arms outstretched to embrace it. The tree is the traditional center of the town of Santa María and is larger than the church behind it.

OAXACA CITY AND ENVIRONS A TO Z

Arriving and Departing

By Bus

There are nonstop deluxe bus trips from Mexico City to Oaxaca. The rest have innumerable stops in between. The first-class bus terminal is at Calzada Niños Héroes de Chapultepec at Emilio Carranza (☎ 951/6–22–70). **ADO** (☎ 951/5–17–03) and **Cristóbal Colon** (☎ 951/5–12–14) both provide first-class service; Cristóbal Colon also offers deluxe-class service. The second-class bus station is on the Periférico at Las Casas (☎ 951/4–57–00 or 951/6–22–70). Several other bus lines serve the surrounding states and have desks at one or both terminals.

By Car

From Mexico City, you can take Mexico 190 (Pan American Highway) south and east through Puebla and Izúcar de Matamoros to Oaxaca City—a distance of 546 kilometers (338 miles) along a rather curvy road. This route takes about six hours. Better is the new toll road (in operation since December 1994), which connects Mexico City to Oaxaca City via Tehuacan; it cuts down on curves and on driving time by about an hour and a half.

By Plane

Mexicana (☎ 951/6–57–97) offers service from Chicago to Oaxaca City with a stop in Mexico City to pick up more passengers. Otherwise, flights from the United States require travelers to change planes in Mexico City for either an **Aeromexico** (☎ 951/6–10–66) or **Mexicana** nonstop to Oaxaca City's **Benito Juárez Airport,** about 8 kilometers (5 miles) south of town. There is also service for triangle flight itineraries, including the Oaxacan coastal resorts of Huatulco or Puerto Escondido. Local domestic airlines serving Oaxaca are **Aviacsa** (☎ 951/3–18–09) from Tuxtla Gutiérrez; **Aero Vega** (☎ 951/6–27–77), which operates as a chartered air taxi from Puerto Escondido; and **Aeromorelos** (☎ 951/1–51–00) from Puerto Escondido and Huatulco. **Aerocaribe** (☎ 951/6–02–66) started service in December 1995 between Oaxaca City, Acapulco, Puerto Escondido, and Huatulco.

Getting Around

By Car

It's not necessary to have a car in Oaxaca City, which is very compact; most visitors opt to take taxis or tours to the outlying sights.

By Taxi

Taxis are clearly marked, plentiful, and reasonably priced; you can usually find them at any hour of the day cruising in front of your hotel or on any downtown street. It's a good idea to check with your hotel for going rates to sights you want to visit.

Contacts and Resources

Car Rental

Cars are for rent at the airport, in town, and through travel agencies at various hotels. **Hertz** (✉ Labastida 115, 4 blocks from zócalo, ☎ 951/6–24–34).

Consulate

The **U.S. Consulate** is at Macedonio Alcalá 201, int. 204 (☎ FAX 951/4–30–54). ☉ *Weekdays 9–2.*

Emergencies

Dial 06 locally for all emergencies, including police and hospital. **Police** (☎ 951/6–95–34 or 951/6–04–55). **Hospital–Red Cross** (☎ 951/6–48–09 or 951/6–78–28).

Guided Tours

Unless you're on a strict budget, take advantage of the many tour companies that offer guided trips to the archaeological sites, colonial churches and monasteries, outlying towns (some of which have weekly market days), and folk-art centers; prices start at $10. Licensed guides are available as well through the tourism office and travel agencies for up to $5 per hour for a minimum of three persons. **Turismo El Convento de Oaxaca** (⊠ Calle Cinco de Mayo 300, in the Hotel Camino Real Oaxaca, ☎ 951/6–28–48), **Viajes Turísticos Mitla** (⊠ F. J. Mina 518, in the Hotel Mesón de Angel, ☎ 951/6–53–27 or 951/4–31–61), and **Agencia Marqués del Valle** (⊠ Portal de Clavería s/n, ☎ 951/4–69–70, 951/4–69–62, or 951/6–62–94) are among the most established agencies.

Visitor Information

Tourist office. ⊠ *Cinco de Mayo 200, corner of Morelos,* ☎ *951/6–48–28.* ☉ *Daily 8–8.*

There is also a small branch at Independencia and García Vigil (no phone). ☉ *Daily 9–3 and 4–8.*

THE OAXACA COAST

Oaxaca's 520-kilometer (322-mile) coastline is mainland Mexico's last Pacific frontier. Huatulco is the newest project of Fonatur, the Mexican government's tourism developers, although it was launched more than 10 years ago. The Bahías de Huatulco, as the entire area is being called, covers 51,900 acres of mountain lowlands and coastal stretches, the vast majority of which have never been developed. The focal point of the master-planned development is a string of nine sheltered bays (bahías) swathed in golden sand beaches that stretch across 23 miles of the Pacific coastline.

Today Huatulco's beauty can best be seen from a boat (☞ Guided Tours *in* Oaxaca Coast A to Z, *below*), even though six of the bays are accessible by road now. Tangolunda Bay is the site of the area's major hotels. The towns of Santa Cruz de Huatulco and La Crucecita are being developed as well. (The town of Santa María Huatulco, for which the tourism destination is named, is 18 kilometers, or 11 miles, from the bays and is largely ignored by developers.)

Puerto Escondido has long been prime territory for international surfers. The town has the coast's first airport (not international) and is in many ways better developed for travelers than Huatulco. It also has the largest resident community of Americans and Canadians along the coast who couldn't resist its laid-back allure and stayed to put up some of the town's most popular hotels, restaurants, and bars. Puerto Angel, midway between the two airports, is the budget traveler's destination, with a ragtag selection of hotels and bungalows spread into the hills overlooking the bay and, incongruously, a military installation smack in its center.

Numbers in the margin correspond to points of interest on the Oaxaca Coast map.

Puerto Escondido

❶ *414 km (260 mi) from Oaxaca City.*

A coffee shipping port in the 1920s, Puerto Escondido is the first coastal town in Oaxaca south of Acapulco on Highway 200. The airport is on the northern edge of town, as are the hotels favored by charter groups. **Playa Bacocho,** just south of the airport, is an upscale housing-and-hotel development, and some inviting bars, discos, and restaurants have opened in this area.

The main intersection in Puerto Escondido is at Highway 200 and Avenida Alfonso Pérez Gasga, which travels south into the tourist zone. On the north side of the highway this street is called Avenida Oaxaca. Traveling down a steep hill, Avenue Gasga passes many of the tourist hotels; at the bottom, traffic is prohibited and the street becomes a four-block-long pedestrian mall lined with shops, restaurants, and lodgings that spread to the sands of the main beach. The town market, **Mercado Benito Juárez,** is a long walk from most of the tourist hotels, but it's more vibrant and entertaining than anything along the tourist strip. The panga fleet is at the north end of the main beach, where the water is calm albeit polluted. **Laguna Agua Dulce** is at the south end of the tourist strip, followed by **Marinero Beach,** then a sharp outcropping of rocks, and, finally, the most famous beach of all, **Zicatela** (☞ Beaches, *below*).

Beaches

One of the top 10 surfing beaches in the world, **Zicatela** is a long stretch of cream-color sand battered by the Mexican Pipeline, as this stretch of mighty surf is called. In August and November international surfing championships are held here, and the town fills with sun-bleached blonds of both sexes intent on serious surfing and hard partying. Do not swim in these waters unless you can withstand deadly undertows and rip currents. Instead, watch the surfers at sunset from the palapa restaurant at the Hotel Santa Fe.

The safest swimming and snorkeling beaches in Puerto Escondido are **Puerto Angelito** and **Carrizalillo;** both are complicated to reach by foot, but they're 10 minutes by boat from the town beach. Transportation is available from the many fishermen who park their *pangas* (small boats) on the sand near town and use them as water taxis. The ride should cost a few dollars.

Dining and Lodging

$$ ✕ **Santa Fe.** By all means treat yourself to at least one meal here. The menu is divided between seafood, vegetarian, and traditional Mexican dishes. The fruit salad is a pyramid of papaya, pineapple, and melon; the avocado cocktail is perfectly spiced; and if you like flan, the coconut version here is heaven. The tables overlooking the surf are wonderful at dawn and sunset, and in the noonday heat it's nice to relax in the shade under a whirring fan. ⊠ *Hotel Santa Fe, Calle del Morro s/n,* ☎ *958/2–01–70. MC, V.*

$ ✕ **Art 'n' Harry's.** This surfer hangout overlooking the Pipeline is the place to relax with a drink and watch videos or zone out on heavy-metal CDs. The menu offers all types of stir-fries, salad, spaghetti dishes, and seafood. ⊠ *South end of Zicatela Beach, no phone. No credit cards.*

$ ✕ **Bananas.** This happening place under a palapa roof features seafood and fish platters along with hamburgers and nachos. Whenever football, baseball, and other U.S. sports events are on TV, Bananas fills up fast. ⊠ *Av. Gasga,* ☎ *958/2–00–05. MC, V.*

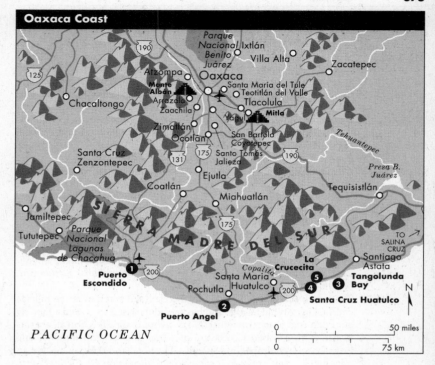

Oaxaca Coast

PACIFIC OCEAN

$ ✕ **Cafeteria Cappuccino.** In this small restaurant and coffeehouse, locals play backgammon in the shade at tiny wrought-iron tables. The menu is pretty much the same as everywhere else. Try the lime mousse or *crepas con cajeta* (crepes with caramel sauce) for dessert, or some yogurt and fruit for breakfast. ⊠ *Av. Gasga,* ☎ *958/2–03–34. No credit cards.*

$ ✕ **La Gota de Vida.** This small vegetarian café and health-food store on the bottom of the Gasga hill has all sorts of salads made from vegetables washed in purified water; *licuados* (milk shakes) made with yogurt, papaya, and mango; vegetable soups; and fresh carrot juice—all for under $5. ⊠ *Av. Gasga, no phone. No credit cards.*

$ ✕ **La Patisserie** (a.k.a. **Carmen's Bakery**). This little place, on a small nameless road that connects the main highway with Playa Marinero, sells great breads, croissants, and sandwiches; it's also good for a breakfast of fruit salad with yogurt and granola. *No phone. No credit cards.*

$ ✕ **La Perla.** Because it's in the "real" town uphill from the tourist zone, this excellent seafood restaurant has some of the best prices in town. *Pulpo* (octopus) is wonderfully tender; the excellent ceviche comes in a spicy cocktail sauce. It's a bit of a walk but a short, cheap cab ride. ⊠ *Av. Rafael Ortega Velarde s/n,* ☎ *958/2–04–61. MC, V.* ☺ *Daily 10–10. No credit cards.*

$ ✕ **Mario's Pizzaland.** The proprietor is a courtly, generous Italian who produces pizzas with all sorts of exotic toppings, including seafood. Even better are the gigantic green salads made with vegetables washed in purified water—a precaution one cannot rely on at most other restaurants. ⊠ *Av. Gasga just past the tourist zone,* ☎ *958/2–05–70. No credit cards.*

$ ✕ **Perla Flameante.** The fresh dorado, shark, tuna, and pompano come with teriyaki, Cajun, or garlic seasonings at this second-story bamboo restaurant overlooking the beach. The deep-fried onion rings and zucchini are terrific. The restaurant is open for breakfast. ⊠ *Av. Gasga, near end of tourist strip,* ☎ *958/2–01–67. No credit cards.*

$$–$$$ 🖬 **Fiesta Mexicana.** This hotel at the Playa Bacocho hotel zone a few miles from the airport is decorated with bold, sunny colors, thatch, and nautical designs. It has a warm ambience and a helpful staff. Rooms are large and simply furnished with two double beds, mosquito nets, air-conditioning, and color TV (in Spanish). Twenty-two more rooms were added in 1995. ⊠ *Blvd. Benito Juárez, 71980 Puerto Escondido, Oax.,* ☎ *958/2–01–50,* 𝔽𝔸𝕏 *958/2–01–15. 86 rooms. 2 restaurants, bar, pool, tennis, dance club, travel services. AE, MC, V.*

$$–$$$ 🖬 **Hotel Santa Fe.** This is the prettiest hotel in town. Your room here
★   will have colonial furnishings, a tiled bath, drapes and spreads of heavy woven Mexican cloth in soothing lavenders and blues, a telephone, air-conditioning and a ceiling fan, and maybe a balcony overlooking the pool. Six rooms were recently added to the property. The hotel also manages the eight one-bedroom **Bungalows Santa Cruz** next door, which are also decorated in Mexican style. ⊠ *Calle del Morro by Zicatela Beach, Apdo. 96, 71980 Puerto Escondido, Oax.,* ☎ *958/ 2–01–70,* 𝔽𝔸𝕏 *958/2–02–60. 51 rooms, 8 bungalows. Restaurant, bar, pool, travel services. AE, MC, V.*

$$ 🖬 **Paraíso Escondido.** This colonial-style hotel perches on the hillside overlooking Avenida Gasga and has splendid coastal vistas and a friendly aura that encourages mingling. No two rooms are alike, and all are furnished with a folkloric mixture of wood dressers, tin mirrors, and brightly colored drapes and spreads. The hotel and the grounds are an ongoing, lovingly crafted art project. ⊠ *Calle Union 10, 71980 Puerto Escondido, Oax.,* ☎ *958/2–04–44. 20 rooms. Restaurant, bar, pool. No credit cards.*

$$ 🖬 **Studios El Tabichin.** The former manager of the hotel Santa Fe (☞ *above*) opened up his own place adjacent to his old employer. But the two properties maintain a most friendly relationship: All the facilities of the Santa Fe are available to the El Tabichin guests. Six splendidly furnished apartments offer kitchens, satellite TVs, and monthly rates—if you're lucky enough to be staying that long. The owner also manages a small country inn called **Posada Nopala** about two hours north of town, which operates from October 31 to April 30. It sits in the pine forests of the Oaxaca mountains, amid coffee plantations and crystal-clear rivers. ⊠ *Calle de Morro by Zicatela Beach, Apdo. 210, 71890, Puerto Escondido, Oax.,* ☎ 𝔽𝔸𝕏 *958/2–11–79. 6 apartments. AE, MC, V.*

$ 🖬 **Casas de Playa Acali.** You can choose from six sizes and styles of accommodations at this cluster of cabanas and bungalows by the main beach. The least expensive rooms are in small cabanas without air-conditioning; the most expensive, though still a bargain, are five new bungalows offering terraces, kitchens, air-conditioning and a dining area. This is a good choice for groups of four or six surfers who want to share expenses and prepare their own meals. ⊠ *Calle del Morro s/n, 71980 Puerto Escondido, Oax.,* ☎ *958/2–07–54. 9 cabanas and 5 bungalows. Kitchens, pool. No credit cards.*

$ 🖬 **Castillo del Reyes.** Manager Don Fernando runs an amiable show in his small, immaculately clean establishment. It has no pool or restaurant, so clients tend to congregate around the front desk, drinking their own sodas and beer. The simple rooms have clean white walls and powerful showers with plenty of hot water. ⊠ *Av. Gasga 105, 71980 Puerto Escondido, Oax.,* ☎ 𝔽𝔸𝕏 *958/2–04–32. 26 rooms. Restaurant, bar, pool. MC, V.*

$ ⊞ **Villas Los Delfines.** An enterprising couple from the capital have cre-
★ ated this solitary paradise atop a hill overlooking the coast, with eight
first-class cabanas spread along the hillside. The cabanas have full
kitchens, separate bedrooms, and hammocks hanging outside. The
husband is an architect with a fine eye for classical Mexican design.
The cool blue pool sits in the middle of the compound, beside a palapa
restaurant. ✉ *Carretera Costera del Pacífico Km 71, about 3 km (2
mi) from Puerto Escondido, Apdo. 150, 71980 Puerto Escondido, Oax.,*
☎ *958/2–04–67,* FAX *958/2–07–85. 8 cabanas. Restaurant, bar, pool.
MC, V.*

Puerto Angel

② *81 km (50 mi) southeast of Puerto Escondido.*

The leading seaport of the state 100 years ago, Puerto Angel today is
a dusty village on a beautiful bay that, sadly, shows signs of pollution.
The central town beach has been taken over by the navy, and the most
popular swimming-and-sunning territory is at **Playa Panteón,** just past
the oceanfront cemetery (*panteón* means "cemetery"). Other good
(and less populated) swimming and snorkeling beaches are nearby. Six
kilometers (about 4 miles) west of town is **Zipolite,** a bay known for
its nude sunbathing; it's a favorite with surfers, aging hippies, and travelers who are content with a hammock on the beach and little else in
the way of creature comforts. The undertow is extremely dangerous
here—*zipolite* means killer, and several dozen foolish swimmers die in
these waters every year.

The recently opened **Museum of the Sea Turtle** in Mazunte makes an
interesting side trip from Puerto Angel. The popularity of turtle hunting once put the sea creatures, who come to this coastal area to lay
eggs each year, in danger of extinction; Mazunte even had its own slaugh-
ter house for their meat. The carnage stopped with the 1990 government ban on turtle hunting, and now Mazunte is devoted to protecting
the species. A dozen aquariums are filled with turtle specimens that
once again flourish in the nearby ocean. To get here from Puerto Angel,
take Highway 200 toward San Pedro Pochutla; about 15 kilometers
(9 miles) past the town, follow the turnoff marked SAN AGUSTÍN. A few
miles down the road, you'll come to a sign for PLAYA MAZUNTE; ask for
directions to the "museo," which is on the beach. *Playa Mazunte, no
phone.* ✉ *$1.25.* ☉ *Tues.–Sun. 9–4.*

Dining and Lodging

$ ✕ **Posada Rancho Cerro Largo.** Feeling adventurous? Take a cab from
town, or a bus to Zipolite and a cab from there, to this simple inn with
a spectacular view. You can take the path down to the beach, or just
relax in a hammock while the proprietor, Mario Corella, whips up an
excellent lunch of local fish or, if you're vegetarian, produce. If you *really* want to get away from it all, you can rent one of his four pretty
palapa cabins overlooking the water (no plumbing, but jugs of clean,
fresh water) and let him cook three meals a day for you. ✉ *Above Playa
Aragon, off the hwy. west of Zipolite and before San Agustínillo and
Mazunte,* ☎ *958/4–30–55 (leave message). No credit cards.*

$ ⊞ **La Buena Vista.** This pretty hotel, which added five rooms in 1995,
offers clean, simple accommodations—some with balconies, some
with hammocks just outside, but none with hot water—and a third-
floor restaurant that has a superb view (hence the name) and one of
the most dependable kitchens in town. Don't be put off by the approach,
which is up a narrow alley off a dirt road just west of the bridge and
before the 20 de Noviembre supermarket on Avenida Principal, the

town's main road. ⊠ *Apdo. 48, 70902 Puerto Angel, Oax.,* ☎ ⓕⓐⓧ
958/4–31–04. 18 rooms. No credit cards.

$ ⓣ La Cabaña de Puerto Angel. Just across from Playa Panteón, this is
the best-located hotel in town. The accommodating proprietors keep
a big pot of coffee at the front desk for early risers, along with a library of paperback novels and maps of Mexico. The rooms have lou-
vered windows with screens and ceiling fans; some have small balconies.
⊠ *Across from Playa Panteón at Calle Pedro Sainz de Barranda s/n,
70902 Puerto Angel, Oax.,* ☎ *958/4–31–05 or 958/4–00–26. 23
rooms. No credit cards.*

$ ⓣ Posada Cañon Devata. California comes to Puerto Angel in this eco-
logical hideaway carved into a forested hillside. The greenness of the
place in winter, when the rest of the coastal landscape dries to brown,
attests to the owners' ingenuity. The simple bungalows on the hill
offer private quarters; at the top is El Cielo (Heaven), where guests gather
to take in the sunset. The restaurant below, open to nonguests (you
must reserve in the morning for dinner), is a find for vegetarians. Like
the town itself, this is a comfortable place for single women. The
posada offers boat trips and occasional hatha yoga retreats. ⊠ *Past
the cemetery, off Blvd. Virgilio Uribe, Apdo. 10, 70902 Puerto Angel,
Oax.,* ☎ ⓕⓐⓧ *958/4–30–48. 10 inn rooms, 6 bungalows. Restaurant.
No credit cards. Closed May–June.*

Bahías de Huatulco

*291 km (180 mi) from Oaxaca City, 111 km (70 mi) from Puerto Es-
condido and 48 km (30 mi) from Puerto Angel.*

Bahías de Huatulco, the Fonatur development, is still suffering growing pains. The vast majority of Huatulco's tourists rarely leave the bars,
restaurants, and beaches of their respective resorts. But there are a total
of 36 beaches contained by Huatulco's pristine bays. If you have a car
at your disposal, you can drive to several bays that, so far, have not
been subject to any development and play Robinson Crusoe to your
heart's content.

Another popular option is to tour the bays by boat. The venture takes
four to eight hours (depending on how many you visit) with stops at
Bahía San Agustín or El Maguey (where fishermen grill their catch over
open fires) and at one of several secluded beaches for swimming and
snorkeling. Bay cruises are available at the Sheraton Hotel beach and
cost about $10–$20 a person. You can also catch one at the marina at
Santa Cruz, where the local cooperative charges a couple of dollars less.

❸ The Huatulco of the future is most evident at **Tangolunda Bay,** where
the major hotels are in full swing, and parasailers glide over fleets of
sightseeing boats. The site was chosen by developers because of its five
beautiful beaches. A small shopping-restaurant center is located across
from the entrance to the Sheraton, but most of the shopping and dining take place in the towns of Santa Cruz and La Crucecita, each
about 10 minutes from the hotels by taxi.

❹ **Santa Cruz** is located on the bay of the same name, where glass-bottom boats and sightseeing tours are available. The waterfront is lined
with bright blue, pink, and orange stalls offering a disappointing selection of crafts and souvenirs for sale. A central zócalo with a wrought-
iron gazebo has been built nearby, and tourists and locals alike mingle
in the grassy plaza.

❺ **La Crucecita,** just off Highway 200, is more developed, with a few condominium complexes and a central park. Modern buildings with arches
and balconies are going up along the streets by the park, and this is

becoming the place for hanging out at sidewalk cafés and shopping in boutiques. The bus station, tourism office, Bing's ice cream shop, and long-distance telephone office are here, along with a smattering of budget rooms.

Dining and Lodging

$$$ ✕ **Casa Real.** Your only choice for glamorous dining thus far is in the Sheraton Hotel. The menu emphasizes northern Italian dishes—any of the pastas is a good choice—and the ambience is decidedly upscale, with heavy polished tables and chairs, stained-glass doors, and elaborate floral arrangements. It's very romantic at night when flickering candles grace the tables. Try the hotel's Mexican restaurant as well. ✉ *Sheraton Hotel, Blvd. Benito Juárez, Tangolunda Bay,* ☎ *958/1-00-55. AE, MC, V. No lunch.*

$$ ✕ **½ Carlos 'n' Charlie's.** The odd name refers to the size of this closet-like addition to the Carlos 'n' Charlie's chain, with all the trappings of the famous franchise packed in meager space. ½ has dependable food—barbecued ribs, tortilla soup, burgers, fries, and platters of fresh oysters—and fun for those who like downing shots of tequila and beer. ✉ *Ave. Flamboyan and Calle Carrizal, Crucecita,* ☎ *958/7-00-05.* ◷ *4 AM–1 AM. AE, MC, V.*

$ ✕ **Restaurante María Sabina.** Oddly named for a Oaxaca medicine woman who was responsible for starting the "magic" (hallucenogenic) mushroom craze in the 1960s, this is a great place for sitting at a sidewalk table and watching the locals and tourists mingle in Crucecita's pretty plaza. No mystery exists here about how your food is prepared, since the grill is on the sidewalk, and the cook will chat with you as he chars your steak or fish. ✉ *West side of plaza, Crucecita,* ☎ *958/7-10-39. MC, V.*

$$$$ ⌂ **Omni Zaashila.** Huatulco's most recently built showpiece is a con-★ temporary stucco Mexican-cum-Mediterranean palace overlooking a secluded lagoon with its own private beach. The resort has been landscaped with 27 acres of gardens, fountains, and waterfalls; a third of the rooms have their own private pools. The rates are high, and unlike those at most of the other high-end properties here, they aren't all-inclusive. ✉ *Playa Rincón Sabroso s/n, Tangolunda Bay, 70989 Bahías de Huatulco, Oax.,* ☎ *958/1-04-60; 800/843-6664 in the U.S.;* ℻ *958/1-04-61. 128 rooms, 32 1-bedroom suites, 32 2-bedroom suites. 3 restaurants, bar, pool, tennis court. AE, MC, V.*

$$$$ ⌂ **Royal Maeva.** This all-inclusive resort caters to charter groups and Mexican families as well as lone travelers. The emphasis is on fun, fun, fun—and if you're not a fan of loud music, stay in a room that's away from the pool area. The rooms are spacious, colorful, and adorned with heavy blue-and-peach fabric and light-wood furniture. There are plenty of activities, from talent shows to sports demonstrations. ✉ *Tangolunda Bay, Blvd. Benito Juárez 227, 70989 Bahías de Huatulco, Oax.,* ☎ *958/1-00-00; 800/431-2822 in the U.S.;* ℻ *958/1-02-20. 300 rooms. 3 restaurants, 5 bars, pool, 5 tennis courts, exercise room, beach. AE, MC, V.*

$$$–$$$$ ⌂ **Club Med.** The club's biggest compound in Mexico sprawls over a sloping hillside overlooking Tangolunda Bay. The 500 rooms are spread out in lavender-and-blue clusters with giant color-coded towers on top to help guests find their way home. There are three beaches, and the list of amenities is endless. The idea is to keep the guests so absorbed in Club Med's goings-on that they never leave the grounds. Weeklong fitness programs are particularly popular. Packages with airfare included are usually available. Advance booking is mandatory. ✉ *Tangolunda Bay, 70989; reservations: 40 W. 57th St., New York, NY 10019,* ☎

958/1–00–33; reservations: 800/CLUB–MED; FAX 958/1–01–01. 500 rooms. 5 restaurants, 3 pools, 12 tennis courts, exercise room, 3 beaches. AE, MC, V.

$$$–$$$$ 🏨 **Holiday Inn Crowne Plaza.** This all-suites hotel consists of 10 buildings built in a series of tiers separated by banks of steps. It is set on 2½ acres of landscaped gardens. Rooms are large, with private terraces, and have regional furnishings complemented by bright Mexican color schemes. All rooms have minibars, and the 32 master suites offer whirlpool baths. Although the hotel is not on the water, it offers free transportation to its beach club next to the Sheraton. You can opt for either all-inclusive or standard room rates. ⊠ *Tangolunda Bay, Blvd. Benito Juárez 8, 70989 Bahías de Huatulco, Oax.,* ☎ *958/1–00–44; 800/HOLIDAY in the U.S.;* FAX *958/1–02–21. 135 suites. 3 restaurants, 3 bars, 2 pools, steam room, 18-hole golf course, tennis court, exercise room, beach. AE, DC, MC, V.*

$$$–$$$$ 🏨 **Sheraton.** Now offering all-inclusive as well as standard room tariffs, the Sheraton is the most user-friendly of the upscale hotels on Tangolunda Bay, with boutiques, a travel agency, and a selection of restaurants. The rooms are done in soft peaches and pinks, with blessedly powerful air-conditioning, heavy drapes to block the sun, and bathtubs—a real luxury in these parts. ⊠ *Tangolunda Bay, Blvd. Benito Juárez, 70989 Bahías de Huatulco, Oax.;* ☎ *958/1–00–55, reservations in the U.S., 800/325–3535;* FAX *958/1–01–13. 347 rooms. 3 restaurants, 3 bars, 2 pools, 4 tennis courts, exercise room, beach, shops. AE, DC, MC, V.*

$$ 🏨 **Hotel Castillo Huatulco.** The closest accommodations to the plaza and Santa Cruz Bay are the well-maintained rooms at the Castillo, which overlook the Santa Cruz Marina. This hotel resembles a motel from the front but looks like a quasi-resort inside. It's a good choice if you want to be near rental boats, close to the luxury hotels, and away from the business bustle of Crucecita. There's free transportation to the hotel's beach club on Chahue Bay. ⊠ *Blvd. Bahía Santa Cruz, Crucecita, 70989 Bahías de Huatulco, Oax.,* ☎ *958/7–00–51,* FAX *958/7–01–31. 107 rooms. Restaurant, bar, pool, beach. AE, D, MC, V.*

$$ 🏨 **Posada Binniguenda.** The first hotel in Santa Cruz, the Binniguenda is not on the beach but stands close to the marina, in the center of the town's developing hotel-restaurant-shopping scene. The dusty-pink building with a red-tile-roof forms a "U" around the courtyard and pool. The rooms have heavy colonial furnishings, commodious showers, satellite color TV, and wood-and-glass French doors leading to small wrought-iron balconies. ⊠ *Blvd. Benito Juárez 5, 70989 Santa Cruz, Bahías de Huatulco, Oax.,* ☎ *958/7–00–77; 800/262–2656 in the U.S.;* FAX *958/7–02–84. 74 rooms. 2 restaurants, bar, pool, car rental. AE, MC, V.*

$ 🏨 **Hotel Griffer.** This is the least expensive place to stay in Huatulco and thus fills up quickly. Located on a busy in-town corner, the hotel offers simple, serviceable rooms and no frills. The restaurant is operated separately from the hotel and is a good spot for down-home breakfasts and lunch with the locals. ⊠ *Av. Guamuchil at Carrizal, Crucecita, 70989 Bahías de Huatulco, Oax.,* ☎ FAX *958/7–00–48. 18 rooms. Restaurant, bar. No credit cards.*

OAXACA COAST A TO Z

Arriving and Departing

By Bus

Estrella del Valle (☎ *951/4–57–00* or *951/6–65–29*) has deluxe Marco Polo bus service from Oaxaca City to Puerto Escondido and

Huatulco. The trip to the coast, which is supposed to take seven hours, leaves from the bus station on the Periférico at Las Casas.

Don't attempt to take the second-class bus from Oaxaca City to Puerto Escondido or Huatulco unless you have an iron-clad stomach and lots of time. The twisting, jarring ride through the mountains takes about 10 hours. The 370-kilometer (230-mile) trip from Acapulco is less strenuous—about 7 hours—and buses run hourly. The bus station in Puerto Escondido is on Avenida Oaxaca (☎ 958/2-04-27). Huatulco's bus station is in La Crucecita, on Avenida Gardenias at Calle Ocotillo (☎ 958/7-02-61).

By Car

The drive from Oaxaca City to the coast on Highway 175 or 190 is rough, and although the scenery through the mountains is superb, all your attention will be focused on the twisting, roughly paved road. Do not attempt this drive at night. Plan on taking 10 hours or so, and leave early enough to be at your destination before dark. Once at the coast, Highway 200 links Huatulco, Puerto Angel, and Puerto Escondido, in that order from east to west. If you want to tool around the various beaches, a car is useful here.

Note: We received one report of a violent abduction of two tourists on Highway 200 between Salina Cruz and Puerto Angel at noon, so be careful even in daylight.

By Plane

Puerto Escondido has a national airport with daily service from Oaxaca on **Aeromorelos** (☎ 958/2-06-53) and air charter service on tiny Cessnas run by **Aero Vega** (☎ 958/2-01-51). **Mexicana** (at the airport, ☎ 958/2-03-00) flies to Puerto Escondido daily from Mexico City and also from Los Angeles (via Mexico City).

Mexicana (☎ 958/1-02-28) flies to Huatulco from Mexico City, Guadalajara, Monterrey, and several other Mexican and U.S. gateways. **Aeromorelos** and private charters connect Huatulco with Oaxaca City and other destinations. In December 1995, **Continental** (☎ 958/1-90-28) started service from Houston to Huatulco three times weekly during the high winter season. A regional air carrier, **Aerocaribe** (☎ 958/7-12-20), inaugurated Mexico City–Acapulco–Huatulco flights during the same time period.

Aeropuerto Bahías de Huatulco is about 16 kilometers (10 miles) from town on Highway 200.

Getting Around

By Bus

There are direct buses stringing together Puerto Escondido, Puerto Angel, and Huatulco, but you must stop at Pochutla, just off the highway near Puerto Angel, where buses leave off and pick up passengers. If you are going to Huatulco, be sure to specify that your final destination is the bus terminal in La Crucecita, which is closest to the bays.

By Car

The drive on Highway 200 from Puerto Escondido to Huatulco should be relatively hassle-free (but see Note in By Car, above), and having a car allows you to turn off the main road onto unmarked dirt roads leading to secluded beaches.

Contacts and Resources

Car Rentals

Cars can be rented at the Huatulco airport, in Puerto Escondido, and in the Huatulco Bays area. International firms include **Budget** (☎ 958/7–00–34 in Huatulco and 958/2–03–12 in Puerto Escondido) and **Dollar** (☎ 958/1–00–55 in Huatulco). Rental cars are expensive, starting at $40 per day for a Volkswagen Beetle, for example, and there is an additional drop-off fee if you don't return the car where you picked it up. Nonaffiliated local firms often quote lower rates, but their vehicles may be in questionable condition.

Emergencies

For all emergencies including police and hospital, dial 06 locally.

Guided Tours

In **Puerto Escondido** the most exciting tours are run by ornithologist Michael Malone, who offers dawn and sunset excursions (Dec.–Apr.) into the Manialtepec Lagoon, a prime bird-watching area. Tours are $38 per person and can be arranged through your hotel or through **Turismo Rodimar** (✉ Av. Gasga 905, ☎ 958/2–07–34 or 958/2–07–37), the most reliable and comprehensive agency in town. The agency also has a day tour to Puerto Angel, which includes the Museum of the Sea Turtle.

Bahías Plus, with offices in the Royal Maeva hotel (☎ 958/1–00–00) and in Santa Cruz at the Posada Binniguenda (☎ 958/7–09–32, FAX 958/7–02–16), is one of the most comprehensive travel agencies in **Huatulco** and has suburban van or bus tours to Puerto Angel and Puerto Escondido (van tours start at $20 per person in a group of six), as well as plane tours to Oaxaca ($337 per person). Most of the major hotels also have travel agencies.

In the U.S., **Zapotec Tours** (✉ 500 N. Michigan Ave., Suite 1920, Chicago, IL 60611, ☎ 800/44–OAXACA) are specialists in the state of Oaxaca, offering Oaxaca City–coast resorts packages.

Visitor Information

Puerto Escondido tourism office. ✉ *Blvd. Benito Juárez, about a block from the Aldea del Bazar Hotel at the Playa Bacocho development, ☎ 958/2–01–75. ☉ Weekdays 9–1 and 5–8, Sat. 9–2. There's also a small information desk (no phone) at the local airport.*

Huatulco municipal tourist office. ✉ *Crucecita, Blvd. Chahue near the post office building, ☎ 958/7–00–95 or 958/7–01–96. ☉ Weekdays 9–3 and 6–9, Sat. 9–3.*

11 Chiapas and Tabasco

The state of Chiapas has always been an off-the-beaten-path destination, best known for the colonial town of San Cristóbal and for the jungle-covered ruins of Palenque, considered by many to be the most fascinating in Mexico. But many who plan just to pass through here on the way to Guatemala find themselves lingering on.

Updated by
Patricia Alisau

KNOWN TO MOST foreigners only as gateways to Guatemala and home to the ruins of Palenque and the colonial town of San Cristóbal de Las Casas, Chiapas and Tabasco were never prime destinations for first-time visitors to Mexico. World attention was drawn to Chiapas in early 1994 as the site of a native uprising, but as peace negotiations progress, it's been almost forgotten again. For those looking for an outstanding travel experience, a well-planned trip to this area can be very satisfying, particularly if you arrange for your visit to coincide with a local festival. Unlike beach resorts such as Cancún and Acapulco, this area is not one that visitors can jet to in a few hours from major U.S. gateways. Substantial ground transportation, either by bus or car, is absolutely necessary. People working in the tourist industry often don't speak English but are becoming more professional in dealing with tourists. Tourist information can be more difficult to obtain in Tabasco than in Chiapas.

The less touristic nature of these states has its own appeal. In Chiapas, at least, the locals are less self-conscious, less sophisticated, and they seem less out to make a quick buck. And though gringos are hardly a novelty, it can be refreshing to be noticed as an outsider rather than ignored as one more anonymous face in an ongoing "invasion."

The Indians' wariness of strangers has a historic basis. A bloody past of exploitation by and fierce confrontation with outsiders remains vividly present, as already impoverished indigenous communities in Chiapas are forced to compete for their lands with developers and new settlers. Most of eastern Chiapas borders on Guatemala, and during the past 20 years it has been overrun, first by the landless poor relocated from other parts of Mexico, and then by tens of thousands of Guatemalan refugees (most of whom have been repatriated to their native country through an amnesty program that went into effect in 1993). Because of its isolation, Chiapas has been at the margin of the nation's development. It is one of the poorest states in Mexico, with appallingly high rates of alcoholism, violence, illiteracy, and death due to unhygienic conditions. Land distribution, too, is skewed: 1% of the landowners hold 15% of the territory, keeping the colonial system nearly intact, and repression is rampant. It was the indifference of the Mexican government to their plight that helped bring the anger of the indigenous people to a boil in early 1994, leading to an armed uprising by a group calling themselves the Zapatista National Liberation Army. The willingness of the government to negotiate with the rebels—and international interest in their plight—bodes well for the possibility of change in the region. The pipe-smoking Zapatista spokesman, Subcomandante Marcos, has become a cult figure in Mexico, his ski-masked image appearing on everything from magazine covers to children's toys, and he puts his poetic communiqués on the Internet for worldwide consumption.

Although it was nominally made rich half a century ago with the discovery of oil in the Gulf of Mexico on its northern border, Tabasco also has a bloody past. During the 1920s and 1930s, Tomás Garrido Canabal, a vehemently anticlerical governor, outlawed priests and had all the churches either torn down or converted to other uses. Riots, deportations, and property confiscations were common. When British writer Graham Greene visited Tabasco in 1938, he called it "the Godless state"; his novel *The Power and the Glory* grew out of his experience. No wonder he found people voicing "the rather wild dream . . .

of a rising which will separate Chiapas, Tabasco, Yucatán, and Quintana Roo from the rest of Mexico and of an alliance with Catholic Guatemala!" Yet to the visitor, Tabasco's turbulent past is barely evident today; a wholly different spirit prevails here than in Chiapas.

Although the Mexican economic crisis will delay some plans for building more tourism infrastructure, Chiapas is getting an extra boost from a new government promotion program. It is an important segment of the Mundo Maya travel circuit created by the Mexican government in the early 1990s to showcase its splendid Maya ruins and colonial cities in the name of regional development and preservation. Development in the past has been a two-edged sword. The Lacandon jungle is already disappearing, its Maya inhabitants being driven to live in a smaller portion of their ancestral lands. Massive erosion and deforestation are taking their toll as the new settlers burn the forest and exhaust the soil by raising cattle.

For the present, however, travelers threading their way along tortuous mountain roads—full of dramatic hairpin turns along the edges of desolate ravines—will come upon remote clusters of huts and cornfields planted on near-vertical hillsides. They will pass Indian women wrapped in deep blue shawls and coarsely woven wool skirts, and Indian children selling fruit and flowers by the roadside. Chiapas has nine separate Indian groups, primarily the highland-dwelling Maya Tzeltals and Tzotzils, many of whom do not speak Spanish.

Tabasco is of interest primarily as a gateway to the Maya ruins at Palenque in Chiapas and to "green" tourists, lured by lakes, lagoons, and caves and by the wild rivers surging through the jungle. Travelers will find Villahermosa's museum of pre-Columbian archaeology at the CICOM complex and the collection of Olmec heads at Parque Museo La Venta a good introduction to the Indian heritage of Tabasco, so evident also in Chiapas. (And no, Tabasco sauce does not come from here or from anywhere else in Mexico; it originated in Louisiana.)

Note: As of spring 1996, travel to Chiapas was considered safe. If you are in doubt, however, contact the Mexican Government Tourist Office in New York City for any change in status, or the U.S. State Department for any traveler's advisories at the time you are planning to visit.

Pleasures and Pastimes

Archaeological Sites
Ruins of Maya cities in mysterious, overgrown jungle are a big draw in this area. Unparalleled Palenque attracts the most visitors, but inveterate archaeology buffs are also attracted to more obscure sites such as Bonampak and Yaxchilán.

Dining
Chiapas has regional specialties but borrows heavily from Yucatán and Oaxaca. Adventurous palates should try *atole* (cornmeal drink), tamales, locally smoked ham, candied fruit, and any dishes that contain the tasty herbs *chipilin* and *yerba santa* (or *mumu*, as the locals call it). San Cristóbal's restaurants offer an ample choice of Mexican and international cuisines and can be rated the best in the state, although they're not outstanding compared to those in other regions of Mexico. Prices, however, are quite reasonable: A filling dinner (helped out by tortillas in one of their myriad forms) with beer rarely costs more than $10 per person. There is no dress code to speak of in this part of Mexico, and no reservations are necessary. San Cristóbal closes down

early, so unlike in other parts of Mexico, it is a fairly common practice to eat dinner before 8.

Tabasco saves some of its export beef for the Villahermosa restaurants, which also serve lots of fresh fish from the Gulf coast. Local specialities, or oddities, if you wish, include *pejelagarto,* a fish that resembles a small, ugly alligator but that, nonetheless, is succulent. Fried plantain chips, dried bananas, banana liquor, chocolate, and a special white cheese are some local food products you can enjoy.

Generally speaking, the food served in Palenque town is modest in both quality and price. On the other hand, most of the restaurants are open-air, which is where you want to be in this humid, hot part of Mexico (except when it rains, and then the thatched roofs are welcome).

CATEGORY	COST*
$$	$8–$15
$	under $8

per person, excluding drinks, service, and sales tax (15%)

Lodging

Almost all the hotels in **San Cristóbal** are within walking distance of the major attractions. Most of those listed are colonial, either historically or architecturally, in keeping with the rest of town. All rooms, unless otherwise stated, have showers; air-conditioning is not necessary at this high altitude and, in fact, fireplaces are welcome.

Tuxtla Gutiérrez lodgings tend to be more functional than frilly and more matter-of-fact than pretty because the town is the no-nonsense business and transportation hub of the state. An exception to the rule is the Camino Real, opened in 1994 and resembling a small palace perched on a hilltop.

Villahermosa hotels are relatively expensive, especially when compared with those in San Cristóbal. New, American-style hotels tend to be away from the city center, near Tabasco 2000 and Parque La Venta, while the older and more modest hotels are downtown.

Palenque is no longer the jungle outpost that it used to be, fit only for souls who considered rustic amenities colorful or liked "going native." Instead, it's metamorphosized into a pretty little tropical town with modern, comfortable hotels. The best and newest are strung along the highway that goes to the Palenque ruins just outside town. Geared for groups as well as individuals, these hotels have lush gardens, inviting pools and air-conditioning and/or ceiling fans, and private baths. There's a clutch of simple, older remodeled hostels downtown.

CATEGORY	COST*
$$$$	over $90
$$$	$60–$90
$$	$25–$60
$	under $25

All prices are for a standard double room, excluding 15% tax.

Shopping

The artisans of San Cristóbal and Chiapas produce some of the most striking indigenous folk art of Mexico. Best are the blouses, tunics, bedspreads, and tablecloths finely embroidered with native designs; brightly colored *fajas* (sashes); and leather goods, such as belts and purses. Lacandon bows and arrows, and the beribboned hats worn by local men, also make good souvenirs. Chiapas is also one of the few spots in the world that, along with Russia, have amber mines, so finely crafted jewelry made from this prehistoric resin is easy to find in San Cristóbal. San Cristóbal is also known for its quality wrought-iron crosses.

Tuxtla Gutiérrez and Palenque, although not known for handicrafts, have a few shops selling quality crafts from other parts of the state.

Exploring Chiapas and Tabasco

Tabasco is lush, green, and flat, the abode of the ancient Olmecs, the mother culture of Mexico, whereas Chiapas is sinuous, mountainous, and filled with Maya ruins and villages where time stands still. The colonial city of San Cristóbal de las Casas once dominated both regions when the Spanish conquistadors held sway over the country. Modern Villahermosa now is the dominant economic force in the two regions due to the petroleum industry. Each will be described in detail below.

The highlights of a trip to Chiapas or Tabasco are still the ruins of Palenque and the colonial town of San Cristóbal de las Casas. These and all other major attractions are accessible by road from either Tuxtla Gutiérrez or Villahermosa, the only two cities with international airports. Charter service to the ruins on bush planes is also available from here as well as from San Cristóbal, and there's bus service to the ruins from the major towns. If you're a first-time visitor, and especially if you don't speak Spanish, it's faster, more efficient, and more comfortable to take tours to the area's major attractions. But if you prefer to rent a car, road directions are included in the listing of the sights.

Great Itineraries

Numbers in the text correspond to numbers in the margin and on the Chiapas and Tabasco map.

The farther you wander into the region, the more you'll be fascinated with its natural diversity and its remnants of Maya and Spanish colonial cultures. A three-day trip gives only a fairly superficial glance at what the region has to offer, but it will afford you the opportunity to visit Palenque and San Cristóbal de las Casas, two of Mexico's outstanding attractions. Stays of 5, 8, or 10 days will allow you to cover greater distances in an area where the major cities are at least two hours by road from one another.

IF YOU HAVE 3 DAYS
Spend the first day and night at the Maya ruins at **Palenque** ㉓, with a side visit to the lovely jungle waterfalls at **Misol-Há** ㉒ and **Agua Azul** ㉑. The next day drive south to colonial **San Cristóbal de las Casas** ①–⑨, the oldest city in Chiapas; spend at least two hours on a walking tour of town, starting at the centuries-old zócalo. Overnight at San Cristóbal and, on the third day, visit the Indian villages of **San Juan Chamula** ⑪, known for its Christian church with pre-Hispanic rituals, and **Zinacantán** ⑫, famous for its hand-woven tunics and pink shawls. Return to San Cristóbal to visit the market and shop for Indian handicrafts, and overnight there again.

IF YOU HAVE 5 DAYS
Spend the first day and night in **Villahermosa** ㉗, exploring the giant Olmec heads, the river walkway, and the anthropology museum. Day 2, visit Palenque, Misol-Há, and Agua Azul, and overnight in Palenque. Day 3, drive to San Cristóbal de Las Casas, stopping off at the small Maya site of **Toniná** ⑳ along the way; overnight in San Cristóbal. Day 4, see San Juan Chamula and Zinacantán in the morning and then return to San Cristóbal to shop for native crafts and spend the night. On

Chiapas and Tabasco

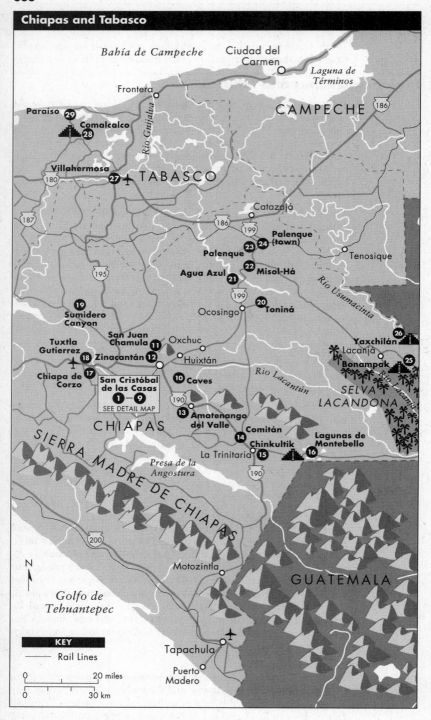

Bahía de Campeche

Ciudad del Carmen

Laguna de Términos

CAMPECHE

Frontera

Río Grijalva

186

Paraíso **29**

Comalcalco **28**

Villahermosa **27**

TABASCO

180

187

Catazajá

186

199

Palenque (town) **24** **23**

Palenque

Tenosique

Agua Azul **21** **22** Misol-Há

195

199

20 Toniná

Río Usumacinta

Sumidero Canyon **19**

Ocosingo

Tuxtla Gutíerrez

San Juan Chamula **11** Oxchuc

Zinacantán **12**

Huixtán

Yaxchilán **26**

Lacanjá

Bonampak **25**

18

Chiapa de Corzo **17**

10 Caves

Río Lacantún

SELVA LACANDONA

San Cristóbal de las Casas

1 — 9

SEE DETAIL MAP

13 Amatenango del Valle

CHIAPAS

14 Comitán

Chinkultik

Lagunas de Montebello **16**

La Trinitaria **15**

190

Presa de la Angostura

190

SIERRA MADRE DE CHIAPAS

200

N

Golfo de Tehuantepec

Motozintla

GUATEMALA

KEY

— Rail Lines

0   20 miles

0   30 km

Tapachula

Puerto Madero

Day 5, start early for the drive south on Highway 190 to the **Lagunas de Montebello** ⑯; en route, visit **Amatenango del Valle** ⑬ and the small Maya ruins at **Chincultik** ⑮.

IF YOU HAVE 8 DAYS

Spend the first day and night in Villahermosa. Next day, drive north of the city to visit the unusual Maya temples at **Comalcalco** ㉘; return to Villahermosa for a dinner cruise on the *Capítan Buelo* along the Grijalva River and overnight here again. Spend the next four days as you would were you following the five-day itinerary, above. On Day 7, drive to **Tuxtla Gutiérrez** ⑱, stopping off at colonial **Chiapa de Corzo** ⑰ along the way; overnight in Tuxtla. On Day 8, tour the impressive **Sumidero Canyon** ⑲ by boat, and then head for Tuxtla's zoo; overnight in Tuxtla again.

IF YOU HAVE 10 DAYS

Add an excursion to the Maya ruins of **Bonampak** ㉕ on one day and **Yaxchilán** ㉖ on another; although they look close to each other on the map, there's impenenetrable jungle between them, so they must be visited separately. You can fly to each from Palenque, San Cristóbal, or Tuxtla Gutiérrez. Extend your exploration of the Montebello Lakes with an overnight stay in **Comitán** ⑭.

Timing

It is worthwhile to try to schedule your visit to coincide with one of the local festivals. Major festival dates in the area (check with the tourist office for a broader sampling) are January 20–22, San Sebastian festival in Zinacantán; Carnival and Easter Week in San Juan Chamula, Zinacantán, and other villages; every Friday during Lent in Zinacantán; June 22–24, San Juan festival in Chamula; July 24–25, festival of the patron saint of San Cristóbal; August 9–10, celebration of San Lorenzo in Zinacantán; December 12, feast of the Virgin of Guadalupe (celebrated for a week in Tuxtla Gutiérrez); and December 31 in several indigenous highland villages, celebrations to install the new civil officials.

SAN CRISTÓBAL DE LAS CASAS AND LAGUNAS DE MONTEBELLO

San Cristóbal, the chief city of the Chiapas highlands, is a pretty town of about 120,000 situated in a valley of pine forests and orchards. Native Indian women are as common a sight as young and aging backpackers, who come because the place is inexpensive and relatively unfettered by tourism. More Europeans than Americans visit San Cristóbal. Small enough to be seen on foot in the course of a day, the town is also captivating enough to invite a stay of three days, a week, or even a month. In addition to viewing the monuments from the colonial era, visitors usually plan an early morning visit to see the Indians gather at the *mercado* (market), browse for local handicrafts, or explore one of the indigenous villages in the vicinity. Just soaking up the ambience in one of San Cristóbal's little cafés or unpretentious restaurants is a pleasure.

East of San Cristóbal lies one of the least explored and most exotic regions of Chiapas: the Selva Lacandona. Incursions of developers, land-hungry settlers, and refugees from neighboring Guatemala are transforming Mexico's last frontier, which for centuries has been the homeland of the Lacandons, a small tribe descended from the ancient Maya who still live in huts, wear long tunics, and maintain their ancient customs. However, their custom of not marrying outside the tribe is causing serious problems and their numbers have been reduced to a mere 350. The beautiful Lakes of Montebello are within this region.

San Cristóbal de las Casas

85 km (53 mi) southeast of Tuxtla Gutiérrez, 177 km (110 mi) southwest of Palenque and 294 km (180 mi) south of Villahermosa.

San Cristóbal is among the finest colonial towns in Mexico: It has churches, red-tile roofs, elegant Spanish mansions, and cobblestoned streets. The haunting atmosphere of the place is intensified by the remarkable quality of the early morning and late-afternoon light.

In 1524, the Spaniards under Diego de Mazariegos decisively defeated the Chiapan Indians at a battle outside town. Mazariegos founded the city, which was called Villareal de Chiapa de los Españoles, in 1528. For most of the viceroyalty, or colonial era, Chiapas, with its capital at San Cristóbal, was a province of Guatemala. It was of greater strategic than economic importance to the Spaniards, lacking the gold and silver of the north. Instead, the state's agricultural resources became entrenched in the *encomienda* system, tantamount to slavery. "In this life all men suffer," lamented a Spanish friar in 1691, "but the Indians suffer most of all."

The situation improved only slightly through the efforts of Bartolomé de las Casas, the eponymous bishop of San Cristóbal who in the mid-1500s protested the colonials' torture and massacre of the Indians. The Indians protested in another way, murdering priests and other *ladinos* (whites) in infamous uprisings. (Chiapans still refer to whites as either ladinos or *Españoles*—Spaniards—whether they are "pure-blooded" or mestizo.)

Mexico, Guatemala, and the rest of New Spain declared independence in 1821. For a brief two years, Chiapas remained part of Guatemala, electing by plebescite to join Mexico on September 14, 1824, the *día de la mexicanidad* of Chiapas (the day is still celebrated in San Cristóbal and all over Chiapas). In 1892, because of San Cristóbal's allegiance to the Royalists during the War of Independence, the capital was moved to Tuxtla Gutiérrez; with it went all hope that the town would keep pace with the rest of Mexico. It was not until the 1950s that the roads into town were paved and the first automobiles arrived. Modern times came late to San Cristóbal, for which most visitors are thankful.

San Cristóbal is laid out in a grid pattern and centered on the zócalo, with street names changing on either side of the square. For example, Francisco Madero to the east of the square becomes Calle Diego de Mazariegos to the west.

The town is divided into several **barrios** (neighborhoods) that are within easy walking range. The barrios originated in colonial times, when the Indian allies of the triumphant Spaniards were moved onto lands on the outskirts of the nascent city. Each barrio was dedicated to a different occupation. There were Mexican weavers, Tlaxcala fireworks manufacturers, and pig butchers from Cuxtitali. Although these divisions no longer exist, other customs have been kept alive. For example, each Saturday certain houses downtown will put out red lamps, to indicate that fresh homemade tamales are for sale. The San Cristóbal tourist office can provide more details and arrange trips to the barrios.

Numbers in the margin correspond to points of interest on the San Cristóbal de las Casas map.

1 The **zócalo** around which the colonial city is built has in its center the gazebo used by musicians on festive occasions. Surrounding the square are a number of 16th-century buildings, many former mansions of the conquistadores. Tile roofs and wood-beamed ceilings adorn corridors flanking central patios, which are surrounded by arched columns and filled with huge potted plants. (Don't be afraid to go into buildings whose doors are open.) ⊠ *Between Gral. Utrillo, Diego de Mazariegos, 16 de Septiembre, and Guadalupe Victoria.*

2 Perhaps the most famous mansion in San Cristóbal is the **Casa de Diego de Mazariegos.** One of the most exquisite specimens of colonial architecture in Mexico, the Casa is now the Hotel Santa Clara. The stone mermaid and lions outside it are typical of the period's Plateresque style, as ornate and busy as the work of a silversmith. ⊠ *Insurgentes 14.*

3 **Palacio Municipal,** with its wide colonial arches and tiled patio, was the seat of the state government until 1892, when Tuxtla Gutiérrez became the capital. ⊠ *Av. Hidalgo between Diego de Mazariegos and Guadalupe Victoria.*

4 **La Catedral** was built in 1528, then demolished and rebuilt in 1693, with subsequent additions during the 18th and 19th centuries. Noteworthy attractions in the cathedral include the painting *Our Lady of Sorrows,* to the left of the altar; the gold-plated *retablo de los Reyes* (altarpiece); the Chapel of Guadalupe; and the gold-encrusted pulpit. ⊠ *On Guadalupe Victoria between 20 de Noviembre and Av. General Utrilla.* ⊙ *Daily 10:30–8.*

NEED A
BREAK?
The cozy and relaxing **Los Amorosos** (The Lovers) **Cafe** (⊠ Calle Dr. José Flores 12A, corner of Av. Belisario Domínguez, ☎ 967/8-49-28), in the Jaime Sabines cultural center, is the favorite haunt of local intellectuals and poets who dine on Mexican specialties or drink their way through seven different kinds of cappuccino until midnight.

5 The **Museo del Ambar** (Amber Museum) is a must for those intrigued by this prehistoric resin, which produces some of the most beautiful ornamental jewelry around. José Luis Coria and his wife, Guadalupe, are the proud owners of this immense collection of pieces carved by local artisans. Many items contain fossilized insects and plant life and others are shaped into pre-Hispanic figures, which are absolutely fascinating. ⊠ *Av. General Utrilla 10,* ☎ *967/8-35-07.* ☜ *Free.* ⊙ *Sun.–Fri. 10–8.*

6 Those interested in regional ethnic apparel might consider a visit to the **Museo Sergio Castro.** It's a private gallery run by the anthropologist-agronomist for whom the museum is named. Sergio Castro has spent more than 20 years working with the Indians; many of the ceremonial costumes are collector's items. You must call ahead for an appointment. ⊠ *Calle Guadalupe Victoria 47,* ☎ *967/8-42-89.* ☜ *$3.*

7 The **Templo de Santo Domingo,** a three-block-long complex, houses a church, former convent, regional history museum, and Templo de la Caridad. A two-headed eagle—emblem of the Hapsburg dynasty that once ruled Spain and its American dominions—broods over the pediment of the church, which dates from 1547 to 1569. The pink stone facade, carved in an intensely ornamental style known as Baroque Solomonic, was clearly influenced by the church of Antigua, Guatemala: Saints' figures, angels, and grooved columns overlaid with vegetation motifs abound. The interior is dominated by lavish altarpieces; an exquisitely fashioned pulpit; a sculpture of the Holy Trinity; and wall panels of carved cedar, one of the precious woods of Chiapas that cen-

San Cristobal de las Casas

turies later lured the woodsmen of Tabasco to the obscure highlands surrounding San Cristóbal.

At the southeast corner of the church park lies the tiny Templo de la Caridad, built in 1711 to venerate the Immaculate Conception. Its highlight is the finely carved altarpiece. The Ex-Convento de Santo Domingo, immediately adjacent to the Santo Domingo church, now houses San Jolobil, an Indian cooperative selling rather expensive local weavings and a good selection of colorful postcards. The Templo is open daily 9–2 and 4–7; the small regional history museum, also part of the complex, is open Tuesday–Sunday 9–6. ⊠ *Calzada Lazaro Cardenas 42.*

8 The municipal **mercado,** or market, occupies an eight-block area. Best visited early in the morning—especially on the busiest day, Saturday— the market is the social and commercial center for the Indians from surrounding villages. Stalls overflow with local produce, such as turkeys, medicinal herbs, flowers, firewood, and wool, as well as *huaraches,* grinding stones, and candied fruit. The market is open daily, but it is most colorful on Saturdays. Be very discreet about taking photographs. ⊠ *Between Gral. Utrilla, Nicaragua, Honduras and Belisario Domínguez.*

Visitors who are interested in the culture and history of the Indians, particularly the Lacandons, should set aside an afternoon to tour the **9** **Centro de Estudios Científicos Na-Bolom,** a handsome former colonial building built in 1891 on the outskirts of town. Na-Bolom (House of the Jaguar) began as the residence of Franz and Gertrude "Trudi" Blom, who purchased the 22-room house in 1950. Trudi was a social activist born in the Swiss Alps and Franz was a Danish archaeologist. Together they founded an institute dedicated to ethnological and ecological research on the region. The property is blissfully isolated from the rest of San Cristóbal, notably because of its extensive garden of firs, fruit trees, vegetables, and flowers.

Na-Bolom features the Bloms' collection of religious treasures that had been hoarded in attics during the anticlerical 1920s and 1930s. A museum houses Franz Blom's findings from the classic Maya site of Moxviquil (mosh-vee-*keel*), found in the outskirts of San Cristóbal, and his personal effects, like his Remington typewriter, eye glasses, and bottle of mezcal liquor. Trudi's bedroom, which is like a minimuseum, has just been opened to the public and contains a case full of ethnic silver jewelry, along with her shawls, canes, collection of indigenous handicrafts, and wondrous wardrobe of 95 embroidered dresses. Also on the premises is a room full of objects from the daily life of the Lacandons, a tribe descended from the ancient Maya; the Bloms documented their traditions and helped ensure their survival. A library holds more than 18,000 volumes on Chiapas and the Maya. Na-Bolom is also a guest house, and revenues from guests, tours, and the bookshop go to support the work of the institute (*see* Lodging, *below*). Arrange for a meal at Na-Bolom at the very least, even if you are not staying there.

Na-Bolom is dedicated to reforestation of the surrounding area, planting 35,000 trees each year. Trudi Blom, who was born in 1901, received the United Nations' 500 Global Roll of Honor award in 1991 for her lifelong work on the preservation of the environment. She died in 1993, but the nonprofit, private institute is being run by a carefully selected board of directors. ⊠ *Av. Vicente Guerrero 31 between Comitán and Chiapa de Corzo,* ☎ *967/8–14–18.* ⊠ *$1, including library.* ⊙ *Daily 7AM–7PM; tours given Tues.–Sun. at 11:30 and 4:30 (about $2).*

NEED A BREAK?	Drop into **Na-Bolom** in the late afternoon (4 to 6) for high tea (or coffee) served with flaky pastries—baked according to instructions gleaned from the recipe box of the late Trudi Blom—in an intimate tree-shaded patio. Also new on the institute's agenda is a Sunday Mexican buffet (1:30–4 PM), sometimes accompanied by folk dances or a piano concert.

Surrounding San Cristóbal are many small and seldom-visited Indian villages that are celebrated for the exquisite colors and embroidery work of their inhabitants' costumes. Huixtán (Hwees-*tan*) and Oxchuc (Os-*chuc*) are about 28 and 43 kilometers (17 and 26 miles), respectively, on the road to Ocosingo; Chenalhó lies 32 kilometers (20 miles) along the paved road beyond Chamula. The Sunday market and weaver's cooperative in Tenejapa (27 kilometers, or 17 miles, northeast of San Cristóbal) are worth seeing. Tenejapa has a small pension.

Dining and Lodging

$ ✕ **Casa del Pan Cantante.** Organically grown fruits, vegetables, and coffee get top billing at this hip vegetarian restaurant, which even has meat-lovers changing their eating habits. Owner "Kippy" Crocker Blake from Denver put together menu offerings such as *tamales Chiapanecos* with local spices in a cheese filling, hot bean soup, curried vegetable *empanadas* (turnovers), and vegetable pizza served on a flaky strudel crust. Chocolate brownies (not to be found elsewhere in Chiapas) and cheese-fruit pie are house favorites for dessert. The four-course special of the day, which includes other variations on traditional Mexican cooking, really shines. A small bakery sells homemade breads, chocolate chip and oatmeal cookies, and fruit preserves—as well as Celtic flute music cassettes. Musical groups with repertoires from jazz to pop perform 8–11 PM weekends. ⊠ *Av. Belisario Domínguez and Dr. Navarro,* ☎ *967/8–04–68. MC, V.*

\$ ✕ **Fogón de Jovel.** Owned by A.T.C., one of the largest travel agencies in town, this restaurant has a crafts shop, a marimba band, and costumed waiters. A cover charge is in effect when folkloric dances are performed. The menu leans toward southeast Mexican cooking and the variety is impressive. Warning: Fogón de Jovel caters mainly to tourists. ⊠ *Av. 16 de Septiembre 11,* ☎ *967/8–11–53 or 967/8–25–57,* 𝖥𝖠𝖷 *967/8–31–45. MC, V.*

\$ ✕ **La Langosta.** This simply furnished restaurant with bright tablecloths is San Cristóbal's best-kept secret for authentic colonial cuisine. Some samples? Try *chalupa coleta,* a deep-fried tortilla covered with refried beans, chopped vegetables, cheese, pork chunks, and salsa Mexicana; tamales stuffed with either pork or chicken, chopped prunes, almonds, mole, and bits of *chile morron; tascalate,* a cold corn-meal drink made with sugar and mild *achiote* spice; and several dishes using smoked and pressed ham made in San Cristóbal. Although La Langosta means lobster, only one lobster dish is served here. ⊠ *Madero 9,* ☎ *967/8–22–38. MC, V.*

\$ ✕ **La Parilla.** A meat eaters' enclave, La Parilla has a menu chock-full of charcoal-grilled steak, sausage, ribs, brochettes, plus smoked chicken prepared *à la Mexicana,* with beans and piping hot tortillas on the side. Wooden beams, beribboned hats hanging from the ceiling, and bright Mexican colors add a cheerful touch to this otherwise somber-looking eatery. ⊠ *Av. Belisario Domínguez 32 A,* ☎ *967/8–22–20. MC, V.*

\$ ✕ **Restaurante el Teatro.** Decorated with both European and local artwork, this popular French-Italian restaurant across from the Hotel Flamboyant Español specializes in chateaubriand, crepes, fresh pasta dishes, and chocolate mousse. The French owner keeps the atmosphere relaxed and unhurried. ⊠ *Av. 1 de Marzo 8,* ☎ *967/8–31–49. AE, MC, V.*

\$\$ 🏨 **La Catedral.** Reconstructed from a colonial inn and movie house, this luxury hotel, opened in December 1995, uses church nomenclature for its public areas: The bar is called El Confesionario (the confessional), the pool is El Pila (baptismal fount), and the travel agency is El Peregrino (the pilgrim). Beamed ceilings, terrazo floors, and replicas of hand-made wood furniture from the 16th and 17th centuries add to the colonial atmosphere, but the hotel also boasts a San Cristóbal first—solar energy for heating the bath water and the swimming pool. The guest rooms surround a three-story atrium topped with a stained-glass image of San Cristóbal's cathedral. All have tiled baths with phones, piped-in music, and color satellite TV; 20 rooms offer hot tubs, and those that face the street have blackout curtains. ⊠ *Guadalupe Victoria 21, in the Historic Center, 29200,* ☎ *967/8–05–56 or 976/8–01–92,* 𝖥𝖠𝖷 *967/8–29–40 or 967/8–13–63. 104 rooms, including 20 suites. Restaurant, bar, heated pool, room service, business center, secretarial services, children's activities, meeting rooms, free parking, travel agency, car rental. AE, MC, V.*

\$\$ 🏨 **Flamboyant Español.** Opened in 1907, the hotel is a sister to the Flamboyant in Tuxtla Gutiérrez. The colonial charm of the former Hotel Español, with its fireplaces and bougainvillea-filled courtyard, blue-tiled seats, and fountain, has been retained. The older section, a restored colonial house, has rooms with fireplaces. We have received reports, however, of room reservations not being honored and deposits not being returned. ⊠ *1 de Marzo 15, 29200,* ☎ *967/8–00–45 or 967/8–06–23,* 𝖥𝖠𝖷 *967/8–05–14. 52 rooms. Restaurant, bar, meeting room, travel services. AE, MC, V.*

\$\$ 🏨 **Hotel Casa Mexicana.** This beautifully designed hotel in a restored
★   colonial mansion is colorful, clean, bright, and friendly. Large rooms, good beds, beamed ceilings, a lovely garden, attractive artwork, and

a Swiss chef in the hotel restaurant all help make this an outstanding hostelry. All the accommodations have telephones and TV, and the two junior suites offer hot tubs. ✉ *28 de Agosto 1, 29200,* ☎ *967/8–06–98, 967/8–06–83, or 967/8–13–41;* FAX *967/8–26–27. 23 rooms, 2 junior suites, 3 villas. Restaurant, bar, room service, sauna, massage, tennis, baby-sitting, travel services. AE, DC, MC, V.*

$$ ★ 🏨 **Hotel Casavieja.** Three blocks east of the zócalo and close to many of the town's attractions, this spectacular hotel is built around a centuries-old house and replicates the colonial architecture of that structure. Each spacious, comfortable room has large windows looking out onto one of the three charming interior courtyards; in addition to the telephones and TVs found in all the accommodations, the suites boast hot tubs. The Espinosa family, who run and own the hotel, are extremely warm and knowledgeable hosts. ✉ *Ma. Adelina Flores 27, 29230,* ☎ *967/8–03–85,* FAX *967/8–52–23. 38 rooms, 2 suites. Restaurant, bar, parking. MC, V.*

$$ 🏨 **Posada Diego de Mazariegos.** This hotel is in two sections that face each other across the street. Rooms on the second floor of the older and quieter half, a 200-year-old mansion that also houses the restaurant, have wrought-iron window frames, oak balustrades, red-tile floors, and wood-beamed ceilings; some rooms offer fireplaces. The newer section is covered with a giant fiberglass dome that keeps out rain but seals in noise. Many consider this to be San Cristóbal's most elegant property, but others feel that it has become tacky and pretentious. ✉ *5 de Febrero 1, 29200,* ☎ *967/8–06–21 or 967/8–07–28,* FAX *967/8–08–27. 77 rooms. Restaurant-bar, cafeteria, travel services, car rental. AE, DC, V.*

$ 🏨 **Hotel Posada El Paraíso de Eden.** One of San Cristóbal's newer inns (opened 1993), this charming colonial home has 13 guest rooms with beamed ceilings; some have lofts and carpeting, but there are no TVs or phones. Comfortable leatherback chairs in the guest lounge overlook a sunny patio. The bar-restaurant offers piped-in classical music and the personal attention of owners Daniel and Teresa Suter, who met in Switzerland—thus the presence of Swiss dishes such as raclette (melted cheese and potatoes) on the otherwise Mexican menu. Choose a room away from the street and lounge for more solitude. ✉ *Av. 5 de Febrero 19, 29200,* ☎ FAX *967/8–00–85. 13 rooms. Restaurant-bar. MC, V.*

$ 🏨 **Hotel Santa Clara.** In the historic Casa de Diego Mazariegos on the zócalo, this clean, quiet, and appealing hotel is convenient to all town-center attractions. During daylight hours, two brilliantly colored guacamaya birds entertain guests in the lovely indoor patio. ✉ *Insurgentes 1, 29200,* ☎ *967/8–08–71 or 967/8–11–40,* FAX *967/8–10–41. 53 rooms. Restaurant, bar, cafeteria, pool, travel services. AE, DC, MC, V.*

$ 🏨 **Mansión del Valle.** A few blocks from the zócalo, this 19th-century property has been converted into a hotel with tasteful Spanish colonial design details, such as wrought-iron banisters, terrazzo floors, and a large inner atrium filled with greenery. Rooms are spacious; seven have patios overlooking a park. ✉ *Calle Diego de Mazariegos 39, 29240,* ☎ *967/8–25–82 or 967/8–25–83,* FAX *967/8–25–81. 45 rooms. Restaurant-bar, cafeteria. AE, MC, V.*

$ ★ 🏨 **Na-Bolom.** Each of the rustic but cozy rooms available at this center for the study and preservation of the Lacandon Indians and the rain forest is decorated with the accoutrements of a specific indigenous community—crafts, photographs, and books—and contains what might be the only bathtubs in San Cristóbal hostelries. Guests staying at Na-Bolom receive a free tour of the house, free entrance to a documentary presentation, access to the library, and information about the area. Book well in advance; ask for a garden view. Guests share the dining room with staff and volunteers at a separate charge. ⊠ *Av. Vicente Guerrero 33, 29200,* ☎ *967/8–14–18. 15 rooms. Restaurant. No credit cards.*

$ 🏨 **Posada Jovel.** Students as well as professionals on a budget choose this converted three-story home, four blocks from the main square, for its simple but clean rooms and free breakfasts. Nine rooms have private baths and nine share baths. ⊠ *Flavio A. Paniagua 28, 29240,* ☎ *967/8–17–34. 18 rooms. No credit cards.*

$ 🏨 **Rincón del Arco.** Near Na-Bolom, this hotel has charming touches, especially each room's fireplace (some are shaped like bulls or jaguars) and bedspreads. The best room is number 11. The dining room features two fireplaces, wrought-iron wagon-wheel chandeliers, and other regional touches. Service can be slow. ⊠ *Calle Ejército Nacional 66, 29200,* ☎ *967/8–13–13,* 🅵🅰🆇 *967/8–15–68. 36 rooms. Restaurant, bar. AE, MC, V.*

Outdoor Activities and Sports

A horseback ride into the neighboring indigenous villages can exercise the mind as well as the body. Most hotels can arrange for rentals of horses. Guides working through the tourist office and travel agencies can also hire horses and will accompany tourists. Allow a minimum of six hours for a satisfying trip.

Nightlife and the Arts

San Cristóbal has only a modest offering of cultural events. Inquire at the tourist office and bookshops about upcoming lectures on regional ethnography and the Selva Lacandona. **Na-Bolom** occasionally sponsors talks and audiovisual presentations. **La Galeria** (☞ Shopping, *below*) and **La Puente** (⊠ Real de Guadalupe 55, ☎ 967/8–37–23) have art expositions and movie nights.

Although San Cristóbal has one disco—frequented mostly by young locals—nightlife is not one of the city's main draws. While a few of the restaurants and hotels that cater to tourists provide lively marimba music, the best diversion can be found in front of a fireplace. Bring along one of B. Traven's jungle novels.

Shopping

There are no department stores in San Cristóbal. The market, while picturesque, sells more produce than handicrafts. The side streets leading to the market are flooded with goods from Guatemala and not always those of the highest quality. Always ask if an item comes from Guatemala. If the answer is yes—you'll be lucky to encounter such honesty—bargain fiercely: Guatemalan goods are priced several times higher in San Cristóbal than they would be if purchased in Guatemala. Guatemalan cloth is easily recognizable: Most of it is rough, dark blue cotton with multicolor cotton needlepoint or trim.

Shops in town are generally open 9–2 and 4–8. Indian women and children often accost visitors on the streets with their wares, mostly textiles, but their selections are not as varied as those in the shops, and prices will not necessarily be any better. You can be assured, though, that the proceeds go directly to the craftspersons themselves.

Among its excellent selection of wares, **San Jolobil** (⊠ Ex-Convento de Santo Domingo, 20 de Noviembre, ☎ 967/8–26–46), the regional crafts cooperative, sells hand-dyed woolen sweaters and men's tunics, embroided pillow covers, and pre-Hispanic design wall hangings. The plaza in front of the Ex-Convento is filled with handicrafts laid out on the ground by Indian women who bring them in from neighboring villages. Although prices may be cheaper than those in the cooperative, the quality of the work is inferior. At a workshop across the street, you can watch Indian weavers working on the traditional backstrap loom.

La Galería (✉ Hidalgo 3, ☎ 967/8–15–47) offers exclusive designs by Kiki Oberstenfeld, who imbues her dolls, posters, woodcuts, and children's books with primitive and folk-art motifs. The store also carries hand-painted tiles and winsome weavings from Teneapa and appealing items from other regions of Mexico. Among the smart shops clustered along Real de Guadalupe is **El Arbor de la Vida** (formerly Citlali) (✉ Real de Guadalupe 27, ☎ 967/8–40–85), which specializes in attractive designer amber jewelry mixed with silver and gold. Although the prices are higher than those in other shops, the designs are more sophisticated. The government-run **Casa de las Artesanías** (✉ Calle Niños Héroes and Av. Hidalgo, ☎ 967/8–1–80) has wooden toys, ceramic jugs, embroidered blouses, bags and handwoven textiles for sale by the yard, and a tiny ethnographic museum with indigenous costumes in back. **Arte Sandía** (✉ Calle 28 de Agosto, No. 2-C, in front of the Casa Mexicana Hotel, ☎ 967/8–42–40), which means "Watermelon Art" is a whimsical little boutique with handicrafts sporting—you guessed it—watermelon motifs; in addition to the coffee mugs, swizzle sticks, rugs, and T-shirts there are non-watermelon articles, such as embroidered designer dresses and hard-to-find gold filigree jewelry. **Textiles Soriano** (✉ Rincón del Arco Hotel, Calle Ejercito Nacional 66, ☎ 967/8–13–13) specializes in hand-woven bedspreads.

An unusual shop in an old colonial home, **Taller Leñateros** (✉ Flavio A. Paniagua 54, ☎ 967/8–51–74) carries handmade books, boxes, postcards, and writing paper fashioned on the premises out of recycled flower petals, plants, and bark. Owner Amber Past from Minneapolis conducts tours of the workshop (50¢), which employs about two dozen Maya.

The Caves of San Cristóbal

10 *11 km (7 mi) southeast of San Cristobal off Route 190*

The spectacular limestone stalactites and stalagmites are illuminated for 1 entire kilometer (more than half a mile) inside these labyrinthine caves, which were discovered in 1960 and were fully explored only a few years ago. The park surrounding the caves has a picnic area. A Spanish-speaking guide is usually available for a small fee. Horses can be rented on weekends. The caves are located in the San Cristóbal Recreational Park, in the midst of a pine forest. *No phone. ⌨ 25¢ ☉ Check with the San Cristóbal tourist office to see if caves are open; they have an erratic schedule. When caves are open, hours are 10–5.*

San Juan Chamula

11 *12 km (7½ mi) northwest of San Cristóbal de las Casas.*

The spiritual and administrative center of the Chamula Indians is justly celebrated, as much for its rich past as for its turbulent present. The Chamula are a Tzotzil-speaking Maya group of nearly 52,000 individuals (out of a total of 300,000 Tzotzils) who live in hamlets scattered throughout the highlands; there are several thousand of them in San Juan Chamula.

The Chamula are fiercely religious, a trait that has played an important role in their history. The Chamula uprising of 1869 started when some tribesmen were imprisoned for crucifying a boy in the belief that they should have their own Christ. Some 13,000 Chamula then rose up to demand their leaders' release and massacred scores of *ladino* villagers in the process. More recently, the infiltration of Protestant evangelists into the community led to the expulsion of the Indian converts by Chamula authorities. In the last 20 years, more than 30,000 have been forced to abandon their ancestral lands and now live on the outskirts of San Cristóbal de las Casas, dressing in conventional clothing and usually found selling handicrafts in San Cristóbal's street markets. The Human Rights Commission is trying to mediate their return to the Chamula community.

Physically and spiritually, life in San Juan Chamula revolves around the church, a white-stucco building with red, blue, and yellow trim. To get permission to enter the church, go first to the tourist office on the main square. Admission to the church is about 40¢. Extreme care must be exercised once you are inside. A "guardian" inside, dressed in a wool tunic and carrying a big club, will tell you that taking photographs is absolutely prohibited.

There are no pews in the church, the floor of which is strewn with fragrant pine needles. The Indians sit chanting while facing colorfully attired saints' statues that are so highly polished they resemble porcelain dolls. For the most part, worshipers appear oblivious to intruders, continuing with their rituals: They burn candles of various colors, drink Coca-Cola, and may have a live chicken or eggs with them for healing the sick. They "pass" the illness to the chicken or egg, which then gets disposed of outside the church. The church is named after Saint John the Baptist, the main god of the universe, according to Chamulan belief—which also relegates Jesus Christ to the position of a minor saint.

Outside the church there is no taboo against photography, but adults prefer not to be photographed. Flocks of children will pester you to buy small trinkets from them and will allow you to photograph them in exchange for a small fee (about 30¢ a shot). The best time to visit San Juan Chamula is on Sunday, when the market is in full swing and more formal religious rites are performed. Some male market vendors can act surly at times, so be prepared.

To get to San Juan Chamula from San Cristóbal, head west on Guadalupe Victoria, which forks to the right onto Ramón Larrainzar. Continue 4 kilometers (2½ miles) until you reach the entrance to the village. Most of these roads are paved, and they are far more interesting than the alternate route, which is to take the main road to Tuxtla 8 kilometers (5 miles) and then turn right when you see signs.

Zinacantán

⑫ *4 km (2½ mi) west of San Juan Chamula.*

The village of Zinacantán (Place of the Bats) is even smaller than San Juan Chamula (☞ *above*) and is reached by taking a paved road west just outside San Juan Chamula (from San Cristóbal, take the Tuxtla road about 8 kilometers (5 miles) and look for the signed turnoff on your right). Here photography is totally forbidden, except for the row of village weavers on view along the main street. It is the scenery en route to Zinacantán—terraced hillsides with cornfields and orchards—that draws visitors. There isn't much to see in the village except on Sundays, when people gather from the surrounding parishes, or during religious festivals. The men wear bright pink tunics; the women cover themselves with bright pink *rebozos* (shawls). Watch for the plethora of crosses around the springs and mountains on the way to Zinacantán: They mark a Chamula cemetery of Christian origin.

The **Museo Ik'al Ojov,** which shows off Zinacatlan costumes down through the ages, has recently added two exhibit rooms. ⊠ *Main street, no phone.* 🎫 *Free.* ☉ *Tues.–Sun. 8–5.*

Amatenango del Valle

13 *35 km (22 mi) south of San Cristóbal.*

Amatenango del Valle is a small village known for its handsome, primitive pottery. By the side of the road, women sell ocher, black, and brown clay flowerpots and animal figurines that have been fired on open kilns.

En Route The rugged foothills and pine groves surrounding San Cristóbal subside into a low plain along the next stretch of the road; the mountains appear to have been sliced in two, revealing their rust-red innards, sad artifacts of the devastating erosion caused by the clearing of the forests.

Comitan

14 *50 km (31 mi) southeast of Amatenango del Valle.*

Comitán is at the halfway point between San Cristóbal and the Lagunas de Montebello, and though the city has few attractions, it is one of the few places on the way to Guatemala that offer lodgings and restaurants.

Many of the Mexicans who work at the few remaining Guatemalan refugee camps in Chiapas live in Comitán. Beginning in 1981, some 46,000 Guatemalan peasants fled a wave of political repression by crossing the border into ramshackle camps, only to be hunted down by the Guatemalan army. Mexico eventually moved more than half of the refugees to safer, more distant camps, but many Guatemalans preferred to remain in Chiapas, and there are still camps near Comitán at Las Margaritas and La Trinitaria. However, most of these refugees have headed home under an amnesty program put into effect in 1993. Comitán, whose original Maya name was Balún-Canán, or "Nine Stars," flourished early on as a major center linking the lowland temperate plains to the edge of the Maya empire on the Pacific. Even today, it serves as the principal trading point for the Tzeltal Indians and such Guatemalan goods as sugarcane liquor and orchids. The present city was built by the Spaniards, but few traces of the colonial era remain. Notable exceptions are two churches, Santo Domingo de Guzmán and San Sebastián, in which part of Chiapas's struggle for independence from Spain took place. From the zócalo there are fine views of the hills.

The **Casa-Museo Dr. Belisario Domínguez,** former home of a martyr of the revolution, opened as a museum in 1985 and re-creates that turbulent era with an array of documents and photographs. ⊠ *Av. Dr. Belisario Domínguez Sur 17.* 🎫 *About 25¢.* ☉ *Tues.–Sat. 10–6:45, Sun. 9–12:45.*

On the outskirts of town, small Maya sites that were newly uncovered include **Tenan Puente** and **Junchavin,** ceremonial centers built around the same time as Chincultik (☞ *below*). Restoration work has begun on Tenan Puente; both sites are open to the public.

Chincultik

15 *49 km (30 mi) southeast of Comitán.*

The small, late-classic Maya site of Chincultik will interest only hardcore archaeology buffs, although it has a lovely forest location, a view of the Montebello Lakes, and a large *cenote* (sacred well). The ruins, which are only partially restored, include a ball court, pyramid, cenote, and stelae. 🖭 *About $1.50.* 🕒 *Daily 8–4.*

To get to Chincultik from Comitán, continue south 15 kilometers (9 miles) on Route 190 until you see a very small turnoff for the lakes (marked only by a green-and-white sign depicting a tree) outside of La Tinitaria; after 39 kilometers (24 miles), there is a dirt road on the left that leads to the ruins, which are another 5 kilometers (3 miles) off the highway; a 10-minute hike is then required.

Dining and Lodging
$ ✕🖭 **Museo Parador Santa Maria.** Built around the remains of an old hacienda, this modest lodging offers seven rooms and a restaurant. These are adequate, inexpensive accommodations. ✉ *22 km (13½ mi) from Chincultik,* ☎ *963/2–40–47 for reservations through Helen's, a local restaurant.*

Lagunas de Montebello

16 *9 km (5 mi) east of Chincultik, 155 km (96 mi) southeast of San Cristóbal.*

The 60-odd lakes and surrounding selva of Lagunas de Montebello (Montebello Lakes) constitute a 2,437-acre national park, which is shared with Guatemala. A different color permeates each lake, whose waters glow with vivid emerald, turquoise, amethyst, azure, and steel-gray tints, caused by various oxides. The setting is serene and majestic, with clusters of oak, pine, and sweet gum. Practically the only denizens of the more accessible part of the forest are the clamorous goldfinch, mockingbirds, and the rare quetzal bird. To the east, wild animals roam: pumas and jaguars, deer and bears.

At the park entrance, the road forks. The left leads to the Lagunas Coloradas (Colored Lakes). At **Laguna Bosque Azul,** the last lake along that road, there are picnic tables, rest rooms, and, at the end of the road, a shabby but serviceable café. The right fork at the park entrance continues along dirt roads for 14 kilometers (9 miles) before dwindling into a footpath. If you walk down the right fork, you will see some of the more beautiful lakes. The largest, **Tziscao,** forms the border between Mexico and Guatemala and is the site of the Tziscao Lodge and the Hospedaje La Orquidia hostelries, both of which are dirt-cheap and very basic (no hot water) but offer food service, horses, boats, and excellent fishing. Buses leave infrequently from Comitán (✉ *2 Av. Poniente Sur 17–B,* ☎ *963/2–08–75)* to Laguna Bosque Azul and Tziscao.

NORTH AND WEST OF SAN CRISTÓBAL

The small colonial town of Chiapa de Corzo will be the first major town you come to when you drive west from San Cristóbal along Route 190. Tuxtla Gutiérrez, the modern state capital, is a short distance away. From Tuxtla, the Sumidero Canyon can be easily reached.

Chiapa de Corzo

17 *70 km (44 mi) northwest of San Cristóbal.*

Chiapa de Corzo was founded in 1528 by Diego de Mazariegos, who one month later fled the mosquitoes and transported all the settlers to San Cristóbal (then called Chiapa de los Españoles, to distinguish it from Chiapa de los Indios, as Chiapa de Corzo was originally known). The mosquitos are still here.

Life in this small, dusty town on the banks of the Grijalva revolves, inevitably, around the **zócalo,** lorded over by a bizarre 16th-century

Mozarabic fountain modeled after Isabella's crown. The interior is decorated with stories of the Indians. Several handicraft shops line the square, selling huaraches, ceramics, lacquerware, the famous Parachico masks, and regional costumes.

Chiapa's **lacquerware museum,** facing the plaza, contains a modest collection of delicately carved and painted *jícaras* (gourds). ("The sky is no more than an immense blue jícara, the beloved firmament in the form of a cosmic jícara," explains the *Popul Vuh,* a 16th-century chronicle of the Quiché Maya.) The lacquerware on display is both local and imported, coming from Michoacán, Guerrero, Chiapas, and Asia. A workshop behind the museum is open during the week and generally keeps the same hours as the museum. *No phone.* ✆ *Free.* ⊘ *Tues.–Sat. 9–2 and 4–6, Sun. 9–1.*

Just outside of town, behind the Nestlé plant, are some nearly unnoticeable **Maya-Olmec** ruins dating from 1450 BC.

Dining

On the opposite side of the square from the museum, the **Jardines de Chiapa** (Portal Oriente s/n) serves an excellent and inexpensive variety of regional cuisines in a lovely patio setting. Try the *tasajo* (sundried beef served with pumpkin-seed sauce) and the *chipilín con bolita* soup, made with balls of ground corn paste cooked in a creamy herbal sauce and topped with Chiapas's famous cheese.

Tuxtla Gutiérrez

18 *289 km (180 mi) southwest of Villahermosa, 15 km (9 mi) northwest of Chiapa de Corzo, 85 km (54 mi) northwest of San Cristóbal.*

Tuxtla Gutiérrez is the thriving capital city of the state of Chiapas. In 1939 Graham Greene characterized it as "not a place for foreigners—the new ugly capital of Chiapas, without attractions . . . It is like an unnecessary postscript to Chiapas, which should be all wild mountain and old churches and swallowed ruins and the Indians plodding by." That bleak description is slowly changing, as new luxury buildings like the Camino Real Hotel (opened in 1994) add sparkle to the city. Nonetheless, Tuxtla Gutiérrez is a city through which most visitors to Chiapas will pass, and it is of vital economic and political importance. It is the state's transportation hub, and it has what is probably the most exciting zoo in Latin America, along with a comprehensive archaeology museum. It is also convenient for its proximity to Chiapa de Corzo and the Sumidero Canyon, which have little in the way of accommodations.

Tuxtla's first name derives from the Nahuatl word *tochtlan,* meaning "abundance of rabbits." Its second name, Gutiérrez, honors Joaquín Miguel Gutiérrez, who fought for the state's independence and incorporation into Mexico.

The highway into town is endless. Tuxtla (population 525,000), the state capital since 1892, does not have many conveniences for tourists, but you can get your bearings best by staying on the main drag, which will run you smack into the zócalo, known locally as the **parque central,** which is fronted by huge government buildings.

Only the most obstinate animal-hater would fail to be captivated by the free-roaming inmates of the **Tuxtla Zoomat,** all native Chiapans. The 100-plus species on display include black widows, jaguars, marsupials, iguanas, quetzal birds, boa constrictors, tapirs, eagles, and monkeys. ⊠ *Southeast of town off Libramiento Sur.* ✆ *Free but donation appreciated.* ⊘ *Tues.–Sun. 8:30–5.*

Amateur archaeologists and botanists should head for Parque Madero, which includes the **Botanical Garden**, the **Orchid House**, and the **Regional Museum of Chiapas**. One of the largest collections of Maya artifacts worldwide is on the ground floor of the museum, an innovative structure of glass, brick, and marble. On the upper floor are displays of colonial pieces and regional handicrafts and costumes. ⊠ *Northeast of downtown, between 5a Av. Norte and 11a Calle Oriente.* ☎ *Free.* ☉ *Garden Tues.–Sun. 8–6, Orchid House Tues.–Sun. 10–1, museum Tues.–Sun. 9–4.*

A fine small museum of indigenous Indian cultures throughout Chiapas opened in 1993 at the government-run **Casa de Las Artesanías**, which also has a good selection of regional handicrafts. Amber from Chiapas fashioned into necklaces, earrings, and pendants, as well as hand-embroidered and brocaded table mats and leather bags, gold filigree jewelry, and lacquerware, are among the local specialties. ⊠ *Blvd. Dr. Belisario Domínguez Km 1083,* ☎ *961/2–22–75.* ☎ *Free.* ☉ *Daily 9–2 and 5–8.*

As its name suggests, **Parque de Las Marimbas** (⊠ Centro and 8 Pte.) hosts marimba bands, which play old-fashioned dancing music—you can grab a partner and join in—Thursday through Sunday at 7 PM.

Dining and Lodging

$$$ ✕ **Montebello.** Lobster and prime rib headline the menu at this classy specialty restaurant at the Camino Real Hotel. This intimate (only 16 tables) place is most romantic at night, when the city lights shimmer into view. The elegance of the earth-tone decor is set off by an unusual white mural of the Sumidero cliffs sculpted into a wall. The chef at the chain's Oaxaca City resort hotel is now heading the kitchen. ⊠ *Blvd. Dr. Belisario Domínguez 1195,* ☎ *961/7–77–77. AE, MC, V. Closed Sun.*

$$ ✕ **La Selva.** Specialties from Chiapas such as a mixed *Chiapaneco* platter with mole, rice, beans, and grilled beef top a menu that satisfies multiple tastes with a broad sampling of international dishes. A tropical atmosphere sizzles with marimba music. It's open from 8 AM to midnight. ⊠ *Blvd. Dr. Belisario Domínguez 1360,* ☎ *961/5–07–18. MC, V.*

$ ✕ **Las Pichanchas.** This restaurant, open for breakfast, lunch, and din-
★ ner, features an outstanding variety of regional dishes, as well as live marimba music and nightly folkloric dances. ⊠ *Central Oriente 837,* ☎ *961/2–53–51. AE, MC, V.*

$$$ 🏨 **Camino Real.** A new star appeared on the hotel horizon in 1994 with
★ the opening of this hilltop oasis of luxury and comfort. It has already been dubbed "the Chiapanecan Dream" by locals who have never seen anything so fairy-tale beautiful in the state capital. Rooms surround a huge open-air pool and bar area with exotic vegetation; the sounds of jazz emanate at night. A concierge floor, business center with computer rentals, and meeting facilities draw many business travelers, who entertain clients in the Azulejos restaurant, enclosed in a sky-blue glass dome (there's a champagne brunch on Sundays), or at the upscale Montebello (☞ Dining, *above*). All rooms have a view of the mountains, remote-control satellite color TV, room safes, minibars, phones, and full bathroom amenities. ⊠ *Blvd. Dr. Belisario Domínguez 1195, 29060,* ☎ *961/7–77–77 or 800/7–CAMINO,* 📠 *961/7–77–71. 210 rooms and suites. 2 restaurants, bar, pool, health club, tennis courts, travel agency, car rental. AE, MC, V.*

$$$ 🏨 **Hotel Flamboyant.** If you want something with Moorish touches and a restful atmosphere, try one of the guest rooms in this luxury hotel.

Accommodations are set off long hallways with wide archways; all are air-conditioned and have TVs. Twenty-four rooms face the large garden, while a dozen are located off a smaller and extremely tranquil inner garden. Capacious is the byword: The pool is huge, and so are the public areas. The restaurant is light and airy, but the bar is dark and tacky. A disadvantage is the location—a 10-minute drive west of town—but there's a pretty shopping mall next door. ⊠ *Blvd. Dr. Belisario Domínguez Km 1081, 29000,* ☎ *961/5–08–88 or 961/5–09–99,* ℻ *961/5–00–87. 118 rooms. Restaurant, bar, dance club, travel agency, car rental. AE, MC, V.*

$$ ⊡ **Bonampak.** A hotel that has recently been completely and tastefully redone, Bonampak has small rooms and a pool set in lush gardens, which have been whittled down to make way for a shopping mall next door. The cafeteria and restaurant have a well-deserved reputation for good regional cooking, steaks, and soups. ⊠ *Blvd. Dr. Belisario Domínguez 180, 29030,* ☎ *961/3–20–50,* ℻ *961/2–77–37. 70 rooms. Restaurant, cafeteria, bar, pool, tennis, travel agency, car rental. AE, MC, V.*

$ ⊡ **Gran Hotel Humberto.** Close to the main square, this hotel has small, functional but air-conditioned rooms, all with TVs (local stations only). The elevators in this eight-story property are old and the hallways are dismal, but proximity to downtown is an advantage. ⊠ *Central Poniente 180, 29030,* ☎ *961/2–20–80 or 961/2–20–44,* ℻ *961/2–97–71. 112 rooms. Restaurant. AE, MC, V.*

Sumidero Canyon

⑲ *18 km (11 mi) northeast of Tuxtla.*

The gaping, almost vertical walls of Sumidero Canyon descend 4,000 feet for some 15 kilometers (9 miles). The gorge lends itself to comparison with the Grand Canyon; it was formed about 12 million years ago, and the Grijalva River slices through it, erupting in waterfalls and coursing through caves. Ducks, pelicans, herons, raccoons, iguanas, and butterflies live at the base, which can be viewed from five lookout points off the highway; the two-hour trip via colectivo costs $4 per person for a minimum of 12 persons. As you visit the canyon, think about the fate of the Chiapa Indians, who jumped into it rather than face slavery at the hands of the Spaniards. Boat trips to the hydroelectric dam in Chicoasen and back depart daily between 7 AM and 4 PM from the tiny island of Cahuaré and the dock at Chiapa de Corzo; they take approximately two hours and cost about $6 per person (there's a four-person minimum). You can rent your own boat for about $40.

THE ROAD TO PALENQUE AND BEYOND

The road from San Cristóbal to Palenque veers slightly east on Highway 199 upon leaving town, then links up to Highway 190, which heads north to Palenque. You'll pass Ococingo and the turnoff to Toniná along the first half of the journey, then Agua Azul and Misol-Há before reaching the ruins. It's hilly sierra country most of the way, and the climate will get progressively hot the closer you get to Palenque. The vegetation will also change from mountain pine to thick, green tropical foilage. To get to Villahermosa from Palenque, head north for a short stretch on Highway 190, and then turn left onto Highway 186 at Catazajá for a leisurely drive on a fairly straight road.

Toniná

㉚ *98 km (60 mi) northeast of San Cristóbal.*

Between San Cristóbal and Palenque, on a dirt road running along the Jatate River in the midst of the steamy jungle, is the archaeological site of Toniná. Currently under exploration, this site is closely linked to Palenque. Recent excavations indicate that the vanquished rulers of Palenque and Yaxchilán were brought here as prisoners for execution. To date, several ball courts and the main pyramid platform, taller than those of Tikal and Teotihuacán, have been uncovered, and an on-site museum was scheduled to open by 1997. As one of the last major ceremonial centers to flourish before the Maya decline in this area, Toniná, with its monumental architecture and noteworthy sculptures, is rapidly adding to our knowledge of Maya civilization. Toniná can be reached by following the dirt road from Ocosingo, off Route 199.

Agua Azul

㉑ *68 km (42 mi) northwest of Toniná.*

The series of waterfalls at Agua Azul are breathtaking to behold as they surge and foam in and out of small gorges slowly descending to earth. Unfortunately, since a road to the falls was cleared in the 1980s, the place has been littered with food shacks; the government is currently working on cleaning it up. Swimming is permitted. The cataracts are surrounded by giant palm fronds and tropical flowers; monkeys and toucans frolic in the vicinity.

Misol-Há

㉒ *42 km (26 mi) northeast of Agua Azul, 18 km (11 mi) southwest of Palenque.*

Smaller than the falls at Agua Azul (☞ *above*), the cascades at Misol-Há are also less littered with vendors and trash. Swimming is permitted in the pool formed by the 100-foot cascade, surrounded by oversize tropical vegetation. Rustic rest rooms, restaurants, and camping grounds are available here.

Palenque

㉓ *177 km (110 mi) northeast of San Cristóbal de las Casas, 150 km (95 mi) southeast of Villahermosa.*

The ruins of Palenque are to many people the most beautiful in all Mexico. Chichén Itzá may be more expansive, and Teotihuácan more monumental, but Palenque possesses a mesmerizing quality, perhaps because of its intimacy. It is, after all, just a cluster of ocher buildings intermingled with grassy mounds and tall palm groves set in a rain forest. But in the early morning or late afternoon, sunlight illuminates the structures in a hazy, iridescent glow; there are the eerie shrill calls of birds, and the local Indians, descendants of the Maya, wander about collecting banana leaves, oranges, and avocados. Whether or not visitors are archaeology fans, they cannot fail to be moved by the sanctity of Palenque.

Antonio de Solis, a Spanish priest, accidently dug into a buried wall of Palenque in 1740 while he was trying to plant crops; in 1805 a royal Spanish expedition made its way to Palenque to follow up on the discovery. In 1832 an eccentric German count, Jean-Frederic Maximilien de Waldeck, set up house with his mistress for a year in a building known today as the Templo del Conde (Temple of the Count). American explorers John Lloyd Stephens and Frederick Catherwood lived briefly

Palenque

Northern Group · Museum of Ruins · Temple of the Count · Ball Court · Pyramid · East Court of Palace · Entrance · Palace · Tower · Temple 13 · Temple of the Inscriptions · Temple of the Cross · Rio Otolum Aqueduct · Temple of the Bas Relief · Temple of the Foliated Cross · Temple of the Sun · N · 0 100 yards · 0 100 meters

in the palace during their 1840 expedition. In 1923 serious excavations began under the direction of Franz Blom, cofounder of Na-Bolom in San Cristóbal. Work continued intermittently until 1952, when Alberto Ruz Lhuillier, a Mexican archaeologist, uncovered the tomb of the 7th-century ruler Pacal beneath the Temple of the Inscriptions.

Seeing Palenque, one can understand why archaeologist Sylvanus Morley honored the Maya as the "Greeks of the New World." The most important buildings of the site date from the mid- to late-classic period (6th–9th centuries), although it was inhabited as early as 1500 BC. Palenque was a contemporary of Yaxchilan and Toniná in Mexico and Seibal and Tikal in Guatemala and dominated the greater part of Tabasco and Chiapas at its zenith. It is now hypothesized that Palenque reached its peak during a period of transition for Maya civilization, when the rulers—Pacal in particular—were bent on expanding the city-state's power over rival city-states. The site was abandoned around AD 800 for reasons still hotly disputed, making it one of the earliest Maya sites to be deserted in a west-to-east extinction pattern.

Palenque marks the architectural apogee of the western Maya empire, with its mastery of the ability to model stucco, ceramic, and stone into ornate but ethereal-looking designs. The rulers of Palenque had no interest in free-standing sculpture, so you will find no stelae here. Artificial terraces were built to support the temples, which surrounded plazas, a ball court, altars, and burial grounds. The temples themselves had a complex array of corridors, narrow subterranean stairways, and galleries; they served as fortresses in time of war.

Since the early 1970s, groundbreaking work has been done on the Maya by archaeologists, linguists, and astronomers. The ruling priest-kings communicated life at Palenque in elaborate glyphs and reliefs on the temples; writing was the daughter of memory, they believed, and worthy of being prominently displayed. The deciphering of a good portion of Palenque's hieroglyphics in 1988 has revolutionized scholars' understanding of both the Maya and the bloody history of Palenque. Only 800 out of thousands of glyphs have been deciphered so far, but they have already revealed the complex history of the Palenque dynasties and shown how prevalent self-mutilation was.

Apparently the Palenque lords saw themselves as "True Man" or "Halach Uinic" of the universe. "Palenque," in fact, was never the name of the site, just a name tacked on to it by the Spaniards. Palenque's real name may have been Na-Chan or Gho-Chan—"place [or head] of the snake." Pacal, Palenque's most famous ruler, means "Sun Shield" or "White Macaw" in Maya. A lord such as Pacal, after leading his troops in battle, would usually be immortalized in stone afterward wearing a protective vest, a shield, and sandals trimmed in jaguar skin.

Death according to the Palenque Maya was just a transition to another world. They believed that the ruler-priests retained their power even after leaving their bodies. Tombs of these man-gods always contained engraved bones or shells, needles, jaguar teeth, or manta ray spines. Their concept of the world was spelled out in symbols: A lizard represented the surface of the earth; heaven was a two-headed snake (four silk cotton trees, representing the four cardinal points, supported the celestial dome); a jaguar represented the cold sun of the underworld; an eagle or owl meant death; and a serpent was spiritual power.

In its heyday, Palenque encompassed more than 50 square miles; only about 25 percent of the site has been excavated. Since late 1994, a huge portion of the ruins around the Temple of the Inscriptions have been reconstructed and can now be visited. In addition, explanations in Spanish, English, and Tzotzil have newly been placed at all major buildings.

The first temple you see on your right as you enter the site is the newly reconstructed **Temple of the Skull,** which was once painted red and blue. A skull-shaped stucco relief, presumed to be that of a rabbit, was found at the small entrance to the temple and can be reached by climbing the stairway.

At the left of this temple, past Temple 13, is a 75-foot pyramid, the **Temple of the Inscriptions.** Reaching the tomb inside involves a relatively easy, if slow, climb. The pyramid is dedicated to Pacal, the "Mesoamerican Charlemagne," who took Palenque to its most glorious heights during his 70-year reign, which ended circa AD 692.

Once at the summit, take a good, long look around you, particularly at the imposing palace to your right, which fills the field of vision. This is the best view of Palenque, and it provides an excellent orientation to the other buildings. Atop this temple and the smaller surrounding temples are vestiges of roof combs—delicate vertical extensions that resemble ornamental hair combs worn by Spanish women—one of the most distinctive architectural features of the southern Mayas. Then descend 80 feet down a steep, damp flight of stairs into the tomb, one of the first crypts ever found inside a Mexican pyramid. (This is not for claustrophobes, particularly on very warm days and when the site is crowded.) Pacal's diadem and majestic jade, shell, and obsidian mask are in Mexico City's Museum of Anthropology. The intricately carved sarcophagus lid, weighing some 5 tons and measuring 10 by 7 feet, however, remains. A "psychoduct," or hollow stone tube in the shape of a snake through which Pacal's soul was thought to have passed to the netherworld, leads up to the temple. It can be difficult to make out the carvings on the slab, but they depict Pacal, prostrate beneath a sacred ceiba tree. The lords of the nine underworlds are carved into stucco reliefs on the walls around him; his more earthly companions were several youths, whose remains were uncovered in an antechamber of the sepulcher. ☉ *Tomb daily 10:30–4.*

In 1994, the small and unassuming **Temple 13** attached to the Temple of the Inscriptions revealed a royal tomb hidden in its depths. The tomb, which probably belonged to Pacal's mother or grandmother, is under investigation at this writing, but since there are no inscriptions spelling out the name of the personage buried there, it may take some time. The tomb is being studied on site and will return to public view in the future.

Built at different times, the **Palace** is a complex of patios, galleries, and other buildings set on a 30-foot-high platform. Stucco work adorns the pillars of the galleries and the inner courtyards. There are numerous friezes and masks inside, most of them depicting Pacal and his dynasty. Remarkably well preserved, their style is sinuous and linear, stylized but restrained. Steam baths in the Southwestern Patio suggest that priests once dwelled in the adjoining cellars and that the galleries were probably used for religious ceremonies. One building called the Tower was built on three levels, representing the three levels of the universe as well as the movement of the stars.

To the right of the Palace you'll cross the tiny Otulum River, which in ancient times was roofed over to form a 9-foot-high vaulted causeway, or aqueduct. It leads to the reconstructed **Plaza of the Cross**, which contains the Temple of the Exfoliated Cross, Temple of the Sun, Temple 14, and the Temple of the Cross, the largest of the group where tombs were discovered. Inside Temple 14, associated with the death of Pacal, there's an underworld scene in stucco relief, done 260 days after he died. The most exquisite roof combs are found on these buildings, which are now, thankfully, open to the public.

To reach the cluster called the **Northern Group,** walk north along the river, passing the palace and then the unexcavated ball court on your left. This group includes five buildings in varying states of disrepair, of which the largest and best preserved is the Temple of the Count.

A short hike northwest of the Northern Group lies **Grupo C,** a recently opened area containing remains of the homes of Maya nobles and a few small temples completely shrouded in jungle. In order to maintain the natural setting in which the ruins were found, minimal restoration is being done. Human burials, funeral offerings of Jaina figurines, ceramics, and kitchen utensils have been found here as well as in **Grupo B,** located near a small waterfall called El Baño de la Reina (The Queen's Bath). Early explorers like John L. Stephens cut pathways through the area, which can still be followed down through two meandering creeks with footbridges today.

A **museum,** which opened in 1994, has a remarkable collection of finely preserved heads of Maya deities in elaborate zoomorphic headdresses, discovered in front of the Temple of the Foliated Cross; the group includes 13 different figures of the sun god, Kinich Ahau. Also noteworthy are the handsome stucco faces of Maya men; their realistic style can be compared to that of ancient Greece sculpture. There are also maps of the Maya zone and of Palenque itself. The displays are labeled in English, Spanish, and Tzotzil. In addition, there's a snack bar and a very good handicrafts store. Sponsored by the Mexican Family Institute (DIF), it features merchandise such as weavings, hand-embroidered fabrics, leather, ceramics, amber jewelry, hand-painted wooden crosses, and children's toys. The museum, about a kilometer (half-mile) before the parking lot entrance to the ruins along the highway, is open

Tuesday–Sunday 9–4:15. You can visit before entering the ruins or get there by walking through the newly opened Grupo C and B sections of the ruins, which end at the highway. The museum is about 100 yards away. Entrance is free when you show your purchased ticket to the ruins area; otherwise it's around $2.

The ruins are open daily 9–5, and there is an admission charge of about $2. You can hire one of Palenque's multilingual guides at the ticket booth; if you want a guidebook, you'll have to buy one in town.

Palenque Town

㉔ *8 km (5 mi) east of the ruins.*

Whereas cool highlander San Cristóbal presents a polite but reserved exterior to the visitor, by comparison, tropical Palenque town is all hugs and kisses. Still, its days as a sleepy little cattle town are far behind it, as more tourists interested in visiting Palenque discover it. In only the last few years, it has turned into a sparkling little tourist center with upgraded services like cellular phones, new signage identifying major attractions in town, public long distance telephone booths, satellite color TV in hotel rooms, and, on the highway to Palenque, its first ATM machine. Shops on the main street look less tacky than before and are selling higher-quality regional crafts.

The principal landmark in Palenque town is the "cabeza Maya," a giant sculpture of the head of a Maya chieftain that graces Palenque's one traffic circle.

Dining and Lodging

$$ ✕ **La Selva.** This spacious palapa-roof restaurant wrapped in jungle gardens serves good local cuisine. ⊠ *Carr. Ruinas Km 5,* ☎ *934/5–03–63. No credit cards.*

$ ✕ **The Maya.** The most famous restaurant in Palenque, the Maya is a
★ plain-looking eatery where service can be slow. The place exudes such local ambience, however, that it's always packed. Try *huevos chiapanecos* (eggs scrambled in fried tortilla chips) for breakfast, or the *pollo Palenque* (chicken cooked in beer) for lunch or dinner. ⊠ *Corner of Hidalgo and Independencia, in front of the town park,* ☎ *934/5–00–42. No credit cards.*

$$$ 🏨 **Misión Palenque.** A lovely resort property, surrounded by several
★ acres of tropical gardens and resembling a private estate from the outside, Misión Palenque is the only luxury hotel in town. The lobby is a sweeping affair set off with elegant dark wood paneling, and the terraced restaurant glows with candlelight at night. Located on the north side of town off Route 199, it offers a free shuttle bus to the ruins. All rooms are air-conditioned and have a terrace, minibar, and phone. ⊠ *Rancho San Martín de Porres, 29960,* ☎ *934/5–00–66 or 934/5–04–44; in the U.S., 800/221–6509;* 𝔽𝔸𝕏 *934/5–03–00. 144 rooms. Restaurant-bar, pool, tennis court, travel services. AE, DC, MC, V.*

$$ 🏨 **Chan Kah.** Four kilometers (2½ miles) from the ruins in a paradisi-
★ acal jungle setting, Chan Kah has a stone-lined, lagoon-style pool, a resident spider monkey, aromatic jasmine bushes, and a stream flowing around the back. The restaurant is overpriced, and meals are accompanied by Muzak and movie sound tracks, but the 14 bungalows feature mahogany furnishings and have ceiling fans (surprisingly adequate, despite the humidity); bungalows 6 through 10 offer views of both the pool and the stream. ⊠ *Carr. Ruinas Km 3.5, 29960,* ☎ *934/5–11–00, 934/5–07–62, 934/5–08–26, or 934/5–09–74;* 𝔽𝔸𝕏 *934/5–08–20. 38 units. Restaurant-bar, pool. MC, V.*

$$ ⚿ **Nututún Calinda Viva Palenque.** This property, belonging to the Calinda chain, has light-filled air-conditioned rooms with color satellite TV, phones, and simple wooden furnishings. The real draw is the natural pool, which forms from a river running through the grounds. The restaurant is worth trying, even if you're not staying here. ⊠ *Apdo. 74, Carr. Ruinas Km 3.5, 29960,* ☎ *934/5−01−00 or 934/5−01−61; in the U.S., 800/221−2222;* FAX *934/5−06−33. 60 rooms. Restaurant-bar, pool. AE, DC, MC, V.*

$$ ⚿ **Plaza Palenque Best Western.** This pleasant, low-slung hotel, opened in 1992 on the outskirts of town, was custom-built for tropical Palenque: A large, airy marble lobby leads to an inviting pool for cooling off in the heat of the day, and the place is decorated in equally cool pastels. Rooms were repainted in 1995–96, a gymnasium was added, and a palapa snack bar, angled to catch the sunset, was opened. Turn-of-the-century *National Geographic* photos of the ruins of Palenque are hung in the restaurant, adding a touch of the Maya past. Guest rooms, which open onto the garden, all offer air-conditioning, color TV, and two double beds; two suites have minibars. ⊠ *Carr. Ruinas Km 27, 29960,* ☎ *934/5− 05−55 or 800/334−7234 in the U.S.,* FAX *934/5−03−95. 100 rooms. Restaurant, bar, pool, meeting rooms, gift shop. AE, MC, V.*

$ ⚿ **Tulija.** You can't beat the price or location of this cheerful little hotel, about a 10-minute walk from downtown. Part of the Days Inn chain since late 1995, it has a fresh open-air lobby, a warm, efficient staff, and the basics for a comfortable stay: Color satellite TV, air-conditioning, and phones in the smallish rooms, some of which face the garden. ⊠ *Carr. Ruinas Km 27.5, Apdo. 57, 29960,* ☎ *934/5−01−04 or 934/5−01−65; in the U.S., 800/325−2525;* FAX *934/5−01−63 or 934/5− 10−33. 48 rooms. Restaurant-bar, pool, tours. MC, V.*

Bonampak

㉕ *183 km (114 mi) southeast of Palenque.*

Because access is difficult, only the most devoted fans of the Maya will attempt the trip to the ruins of Bonampak and Yaxchilán (☞ *below*). Both sites can be reached by making arrangements for a small chartered plane in Palenque, Tuxtla Gutiérrez, or San Cristóbal. A road that will connect Bonampak with Yaxchilán is scheduled for completion at the end of 1996. Whether you go on a tour or travel independently, wear sturdy shoes, carry insect repellent, good sunglasses, and a hat to protect yourself from mosquitoes, ticks, sandflies, undergrowth, and the jungle sun.

Bonampak is renowned for its vivid murals of ancient Maya life, though some segments of them are sadly deteriorated; they are under constant restoration because the high humidity in the area eats away at the colors and thick white deposits of calcium from dripping water have covered some of them over completely. In 1984, Mexican experts devised a technique for cleaning and restoring the murals, and with the recent help of the National Geographic Society, using digital amplification with computers, remarkable details and color have come to light. (Still, the reproductions at the archaeological museums in Mexico City and Villahermosa are better than the on-site specimens.)

Bonampak was built on the banks of the Lacanjá River during the 7th and 8th centuries and remained undiscovered until 1946. Explorer Jacques Soustelle called it "a pictorial encyclopedia of a Mayan city." Indeed, the scenes portrayed in the three rooms of the Templo de las Pinturas graphically recall subjects such as life at court and the prelude and aftermath of battle with unusual realism.

Yaxchilán

 50 km (32 mi) northeast of Bonampak.

Recent excavations at Yaxchilán (Ya-she-*lan*), bordering the Usumicinta River, have uncovered captivating temples and carvings in a superb jungle setting. Yaxchilán, which means "place of green stones," is a contemporary of Bonampak. It is dominated by two acropolises containing a palace, temples with finely carved lintels, and great staircases. Until very recently, the Lacandon, who live in the vicinity, made pilgrimages to this site in the heart of the jungle, leaving behind "god pots" (incense-filled ceramic bowls) in honor of ancient deities. They were particularly awed by the headless sculpture of Xachtun (Washa-*tun*) at the entrance to the temple (called structure 33) and believe that the world will end when its head is replaced on its torso.

Yaxchilán was situated on the trade route between Palenque and Tikal, and the existence of a 600-foot bridge crossing the Usumacinta River to connect Yaxchilán to Guatemalan territory was recently discovered. The engineering know-how of the people of Yaxchilán is still being deciphered by modern-day engineers. The site has been threatened with destruction by plans for a huge dam to be built by Mexico and Guatemala. The plans have been put on hold due to lack of funds, though they may yet come to fruition.

VILLAHERMOSA AND TABASCO

Graham Greene's succinct summation of Tabasco as a "tropical state of river and swamp and banana grove" captures its essence. Though the state played an important role in the early history of Mexico, its past is rarely on view; instead, it is Tabasco's modern-day status as a supplier of oil that defines it. Set on a humid coastal plain and crisscrossed by 1,200 miles of rivers, low hills, and unexplored jungles, the landscape is still rich in banana and cacao plantations but occasionally marred by shantytowns and refineries reeking of sulfur. The capital city of Villahermosa epitomizes the mercurial development of Tabasco (the airplane was here before the automobile). Thanks to oil and urban renewal, the cramped and ugly neighborhoods in the mosquito-ridden town of the 1970s have been replaced by spacious boulevards, lush green parks, cultural centers, and beautiful buildings.

This is not to say that the rest of Tabasco has nothing to offer the visitor. There are beaches, lagoons, caves, and nature reserves, but the tourist infrastructure is minimal. The fired-brick Maya ruins of Comalcalco attest to the influence of Palenque. Probably the most interesting region is the one to the south and east of Villahermosa, where rivers and canyons are home to jaguars, deer, and alligators; this was where the English pirate Sir Francis Drake hid from the Spaniards.

Tabasco—specifically the mouth of the River Grijalva—lay along the route of the Spanish explorations of Mexico in 1518–19. At that time, the state's rivers and waterways, along which the Olmecs and the Maya lived, served as a trade route between the peoples of the north and those of the south. When the Spaniards came to Tabasco, they had to bridge 50 rivers and contend with swarms of mosquitoes, beetles, and ants, as well as with almost unbearable heat, but the region was so lush that one early chronicler termed it a Garden of Eden.

The Spanish conquest was facilitated by the state of almost constant tribal warfare between the Tabascans and their Aztec overlords. Among the 20 slave women turned over to the victors was a Chiapan named

Malintzín, or Malinche, who was singled out by the Spaniards for her ability to speak both the Maya and the Nahuatl languages. Called Marina by the Spaniards, she learned Spanish and became not only Cortés's mistress and the mother of his illegitimate son but also the willing interpreter of Indian customs. Marina's cooperation helped the conquistador trounce both Moctezuma and Cuauhtémoc, the last Aztec rulers.

Until the early 20th century Tabasco slumbered; it did not become a state until 1924. After the American Civil War, traders from the southern United States began operating in the region and on its rivers, hauling the precious mahogany trees upstream from Chiapas and shipping them north from the small Tabascan port of Frontera. This was Tabasco's most prosperous era until the discovery of oil 50 years ago and the oil boom of the 1980s. Although PEMEX (the government-run oil monopoly) was plagued with workers' strikes throughout 1995 in Villahermosa, the oil company plans to relocate its research offices there.

Villahermosa

㉗ *821 km (503 mi) southeast of Mexico City, 632 km (398 mi) southwest of Mérida.*

There are a good many ways to spend your time in Tabasco's capital. Downtown Villahermosa contains a pedestrian street with beautifully restored colonial buildings, a museum of popular culture, and a folkart shop, but the **Carlos Pellicer Camera Museo de Antropologia** (Museum of Anthropology) should be seen first. Named after the man who donated many of the artifacts and to whom the locals refer as the "poet laureate of Latin America," the museum is located on the right bank of the Grijalva and is part of the huge CICOM cultural complex dedicated to research on the Olmec and Maya (which is what the Spanish acronym CICOM stands for). It provides one of the last tranquil vistas of Villahermosa as it might have looked 50 years ago. Although all of the explanations are in Spanish, that should not detract from the visual pleasure of the displays.

The entire ground floor is devoted to Tabasco and the Olmec, or "inhabitants of the land of rubber," who flourished in Tabasco as early as 1800 BC and disappeared about 1,600 years later. The Olmecs have long been honored as the mother culture of Mesoamerica and as inventors of the numerical and calendrical systems that spread throughout the region; the pyramid is also attributed to them. Some of the most interesting artifacts of the Olmec, other than the giant stone heads on view at Parque Museo La Venta (☞ *below*), are the remnants of their jaguar cult displayed here. The jaguar symbolized the earth fertilized by rain, and many Olmec sculptures portray werejaguars (half-human, half-jaguar, similar to a werewolf) or jaguar babies. Other sculptures portray human heads emerging from the mouth of a jaguar, bat gods, bird-headed humans, and female fertility figurines. The collection of burial urns, found in the Tapijulapa caves west of Palenque, is outstanding.

All of Mexico's ancient cultures are represented on the upper two floors, from the red-clay dogs of Colima and the nose rings of the Huichol Indians of Nayarit to the huge burial urns of the Chontal Maya, who built Comalcalco. The CICOM building complex also houses a theater, restaurant, and handicrafts shop. ✉ *Carlos Pellicer 511, an extension of the malecón,* ☎ *93/12–95–21.* 🎟 *About 30¢.* ◷ *Daily 9–8.*

....

NEED A
BREAK?

Stop off for a beer and a plate of fresh shrimp at the **Capitán Beulo** (✉ Paseo Malecón Madrazo and Zaragoza, ☎ 93/12-92-17 or 93/12-9209), a small riverboat restaurant that also runs 90-minute cruises along the Grijalva. There's no admission charge for the cruise, but passengers must order food (no minimum). The cruise departs at 1:30, and 9 PM every day except Monday.

The giant stone heads carved by the Olmec and salvaged from the oil fields of La Venta, on the western edge of Tabasco near the state of Veracruz, are on display in **Parque Museo La Venta,** situated west of CICOM in a tropical garden on the beautiful Lago de las Ilusiones (Lake of Illusions). These 6-foot-tall, African-featured heads, wearing helmets and weighing upwards of 20 tons, have sparked endless scholarly debate. It has been theorized that they depict ancient Phoenician slaves who wound up on the coasts of Mexico, that they were meant to represent space invaders, and that because of the obesity and short limbs of the figures, they are proof of endocrine deficiencies among the ancient Olmec. More likely, they simply celebrate the earth's fecundity. La Venta contains 30 sculptures, not all of them heads. There are also jaguars, priests, monsters, stelae, and stone altars oddly reminiscent of ancient Mesopotamian art. The park also has a tiny zoo with creatures such as Tabascan river crocodiles, deer, coatimundi, monkeys, and wild parrots.

A small natural history museum, the Museo del Historia Natural, is located just outside the entrance to the park, to the left of the admission booths. It's filled with attractive displays of Tabasco's native plants and animal species, which are now under the protection of the government's new conservation policies. ⊠ *Blvd. Ruíz Cortines near Paseo Tabasco,* ☎ *93/5–22–28.* ⊡ *Museum, zoo, and park about $1.50; park only 90¢.* ☉ *Tues.–Sun. 9–5, Mon. 8–4.*

Dining and Lodging

$$ ✕ **El Mesón del Duende.** This restaurant, which translates as the House of the Elf, adds a regional accent to standard meat and fish dishes. Try the house favorites of *filete en salsa de espinaca y queso* (beef filet in a cheese and spinach sauce) and *la posta de robalo* (snook grilled in butter). The modest decor is in keeping with the family-style atmosphere. ⊠ *Gregorio Méndez 1703,* ☎ *93/15–13–24. AE, MC, V.* ☉ *Thur.–Tues. until 1 AM.*

$$ ✕ **Los Tulipanes.** Next door to the CICOM Museum, the spacious Los
★   Tulipanes specializes in steaks and seafood and has a tranquil view of the river. Try the stuffed crab, shrimp, or the Tabasco specialty, *pejelagarto,* a fish that resembles a small, ugly alligator but is a succulent treat. ⊠ *Carlos Pellicer 511,* ☎ *93/12–92–09 or 93/12–92–17. AE, MC, V.*

$ ✕ **Leo.** This popular spot for tasty beef and pork tacos, with a large menu and a spacious dining area, is frequented by local artists and students. ⊠ *Paseo Tabasco 429,* ☎ *93/12–44–63. MC, V.* ☉ *Daily until 1 AM.*

$$$ ▥ **Holiday Inn.** Situated across from La Choca Park, this inviting nine-story resort property offers air-conditioned rooms with cable TV, minibars, and room service. The rambling lobby, with attractive niches and corners and rattan furniture, eventually leads to the Tabasco 2000 shopping mall, which has the largest number of upscale stores in Villahermosa. A restaurant below the hotel lobby has floor-to-ceiling windows shaded by bamboo curtains and a lovely garden view. There's live entertainment in the Jaguar Lounge nightly except Sunday. ⊠ *Paseo Tabasco 1407, 86030,* ☎ *93/16–44–00 or 800/HOLIDAY,* 𝐅𝐀𝐗 *93/16–45–69. 190 rooms. Restaurant, bar, pool, exercise room, travel services, car rental. AE, DC, MC, V.*

$$$ ☰ **Hyatt Regency Villahermosa.** This American-style luxury hotel built in 1983 offers the amenities of the worldwide Hyatt chain: air-conditioned rooms with cable TV, voice mail, and minibars, plus two executive floors with concierge service. The coffee shop has been recently remodeled with pleasing tropical decor, and the popular El Plataforma video bar in the lobby is decked out like the inside of an offshore oil platform with photos of oilmen at work. The lobby bar has live music nightly at 9:30. ✉ *Av. Juárez 106, Zona Hotelera, 86050,* ☏ *93/13– 44–44, 93/15–12–34 or 800/228–9000;* 𝙁𝘼𝙓 *93/15–58–08 or 93/15– 12–35. 206 rooms. 2 restaurants, 3 bars, pool, 2 tennis courts, travel services, car rental. AE, DC, MC, V.*

$$ ☰ **Calinda Viva Villahermosa.** This hotel has an attractive white-washed exterior reminiscent of a hacienda and a spacious lobby decorated in earth tones that has an Old Mexico feeling about it. The hotel's restaurant, in fact, is named La Hacienda and features many regional dishes, like tamales with *chipílin* herb and cream of *cha-ya* (a spinach-like plant) soup. The staff is friendly and very helpful. All of the rooms have air-conditioning, FM stereos, color TVs, and phones; many have balconies. ✉ *Paseo Tabasco 1201, 86050,* ☏ *93/15–00–00,* 𝙁𝘼𝙓 *93/15– 30–73. 241 rooms. Restaurant, 2 bars, coffee shop, pool, dance club. AE, DC, MC, V.*

$$ ☰ **Cencali.** This colonial-style hotel in the new hotel zone is situated in a park and surrounded by lakes and lush greenery; it definitely has the best view in town. All the cheerfully decorated rooms have lots of light and vistas of either the lakes or the lagoon; 30 of the best also have balconies looking out over coconut palm, guava, and almond trees. All the accommodations are air-conditioned. ✉ *Av. Juárez and Paseo Tabasco, 86040,* ☏ *93/15–19–94 through 93/15–19–99,* 𝙁𝘼𝙓 *93/15– 66–00. 116 rooms, 3 suites. Restaurant, bar, pool. AE, DC, MC, V.*

$$ ☰ **Maya Tabasco Best Western.** The Maya Tabasco offers rooms with air-conditioning, TVs, and phones; a rather plain lobby; a gift shop; and a staff that acts as if it would rather be out fishing. This is the best hotel in the neighborhood near the crowded downtown area and will do if all other hotels listed are full (which happens quite often). ✉ *Ruíz Cortines 907, 86000,* ☏ *93/14–44–66, 93/14–03–60 or 800/528– 1234;* 𝙁𝘼𝙓 *93/12–10–97. 156 rooms. 2 restaurants, bar, pool, dance club (open Thurs.–Sat.) MC, V.*

$ ☰ **Don Carlos.** Formerly the Manzur, this downtown hotel has always been popular for its unpretentious atmosphere and good service. TVs and phones are available in every room, and all the suites have new minibars. ✉ *Av. Madero 422, 86000,* ☏ *93/12–24–99,* 𝙁𝘼𝙓 *93/12– 46–22. 80 rooms, 14 suites. Restaurant, bar, lounge. AE, MC, V.*

Comalcalco

㉘ *60 km (37 mi) northwest of Villahermosa off Route 187.*

Comalcalco is the most important Maya site in Tabasco. The abundant cacao trees in the region provided food and livelihood for a booming population during the late classic period (AD 600–900), when Comalcalco was built; the site marks the westernmost reach of the Maya. Descendants of the Chontal Maya, who constructed Comalcalco, still live in the vicinity. This site is unique among Maya cities for its use of fired brick (made of sand, sea shells, and clay), as the Tabasco swamp-lands lacked the stone for building that was found elsewhere in the Maya empire. The bricks were apparently inscribed and painted with enigmatic "anonymous messages" before being covered with stucco. The major pyramid, Temple IV, on the Great Eastern Acropolis, is decorated with large stucco masks of the sun god, Kinich Ahau, and carvings, and the museum houses many of the artifacts that were uncovered there. ▣ *About $1.50.* ☉ *Daily 9–4:30.*

Paraíso

㉙ *19 km (12 mi) north of Comacalco.*

If not seeing the Gulf of Mexico will leave you feeling deprived, you can continue on from Comalco (☞ *above*) to the coast and Paraíso. Bear in mind, however, that Tabasco is not known for its beaches: For the most part, they are dirty and almost totally lacking in tourist infrastructure. There are several small hotels on the beach and others in the town of Paraíso, a few kilometers inland.

CHIAPAS AND TABASCO A TO Z

Arriving and Departing

By Bus

PALENQUE

First- and second-class service is available from Villahermosa (2½ hours), San Cristóbal (5 hours), Mexico City (14 hours), Mérida (8 hours), Campeche (6 hours), and Tuxtla Gutiérrez (9 hours). In Palenque, the **ADO** and **Cristóbal Colón** buses leave from the new terminal at Cinco de Mayo and Juárez (☎ 934/5–00–00).

SAN CRISTÓBAL

The **Cristóbal Colón** terminal in San Cristóbal is at Avenida Insurgentes and Pan American Highway (Highway 190). Second-class service on **Transportes Tuxtla Express Plus** to Tuxtla, Palenque, and Guatemala departs from the terminal at Allende and Pan American Highway.

TUXTLA GUTIÉRREZ

Omnibus Cristóbal Colón (✉ Av. 2 Norte Pte., ☎ 961/2–16–39 or 961/2–26–24) offers deluxe and first- and second-class bus service between Tuxtla and Oaxaca, Palenque, Villahermosa, Tapachula, Mérida, Mexico City, and San Cristóbal.

VILLAHERMOSA

There is frequent second-class service to Campeche, Chetumal, Mérida, Mexico City, Palenque, San Cristóbal, Tapachula, Tuxtla Gutiérrez, Veracruz, and elsewhere. Buses arrive and depart from **Central Camionera de 2nd Clase** (✉ Av. Ruíz Cortines s/n, ☎ 93/12–4184, 93/12–1689). Deluxe and first-class service is available to the above cities at the **ADO** bus terminal (✉ Calle F.J. Mina 297), which is serviced by **ADO** (☎ 93/12–7627 and 93/12–14–46), **UNO** (☎ 93/14–58–18), **G.L.** (☎ 93/12–76–27), and **Cristóbal Colón** (☎ 93/12–89–00).

By Car

From Tuxtla Gutiérrez, Highway 190 goes east through Chiapa de Corzo to San Cristóbal before continuing southeast to Comitán and the Guatemalan border. Highway 199 to Highway 186 (the turnoff is at Catazajá) is the preferred route from San Cristóbal to Villahermosa; it'll take you via Toniná, Agua Azul, and Palenque. The drive from San Cristóbal to Palenque takes about four hours, and it's another 90 minutes from Palenque to Villahermosa; most of the way the roads are straight and paved. On the map, Highway 195 may look like the most direct way to travel between San Cristóbal and Villahermosa, but it entails hours upon hours of hairpin curves; it's only for the stalwart and absolutely not to be traveled at night because of seasonal fog as well as a lack of reflectors, illumination, and other cars to help in case of emergency. To get to Villahermosa from Coatzacoalcos and Veracruz, take Highway 180. In all cases, exercise caution during the rainy season (June through October), when the roads are slick. Though expensive, car rentals are available at the Tuxtla and Villahermosa airports as well as in San Cristóbal (☞ Car Rental Agencies, *below*).

By Plane

BONAMPAK AND YAXCHILÁN

For charter flights to the ruins of Bonampak and Yaxchilán, contact **Montes Azules** (☎ 961/3–22–56 or 961/3–22–93), an air charter company in Tuxtla Gutiérrez, or **Servicios Aereos Cristóbal** (☎ 967/8–42–23), a new air charter company in Comitán near San Cristóbal de las Casas.

PALENQUE

Chartered flights are available through travel agencies in Tuxtla Gutiérrez, San Cristóbal, and Villahermosa.

SAN CRISTÓBAL

The closest major airport is in Tuxtla Gutiérrez (☞ *below*), 85 kilometers (53 miles) to the west. San Cristóbal's intended airport has been indefinitely postponed. The easiest way to get from Tuxtla to San Cristóbal is by taxi. The two-hour ride costs about $13 for one to four persons. Many travel agencies in both cities provide private taxi service. By car, follow Route 190. First-class bus service on Cristóbal Colon costs under $4. You can also catch a *colectivo* (shared taxi service in a van or minibus) to San Cristóbal at either of the two airports in Tuxtla Gutiérrez: From the Mexicana airport, it costs about $5 per person; from the Aviasca airport, $3 per person.

TUXTLA GUTIÉRREZ

Mexicana (✉ Belisario Domínguez 1934, ☎ 961/2–00–20 or 961/1–14–90, ☎ 961/2–20–53; at the airport, ☎ 961/3–49–21) flies nonstop from Mexico City to the Tuxtla airport, which is in the town of Ocozocoautla, 22 kilometers (14 miles) west. **Aviacsa** (in Tuxtla, ☎ 961/2–80–81, ☎ 961/3–50–29; at the airport, ☎ ☎ 961/5–10–11) also operates daily flights from Mexico City. Note: Mexicana uses the Tuxtla airport, which is frequently fogged in; Aviacsa flies into Aeropuerto Fco. Sarabia, which is not. In 1994, Mexicana got permission to use Aviacsa's airport in foggy weather.

VILLAHERMOSA

Aeromexico (93/12–69–11 or 93/12–95–54) has daily nonstop service from Mexico City. **Mexicana** (93/16–31–32 or 93/16–31–33) has three daily nonstop flights from Mexico City, and both airlines offer connecting flights to other Mexican cities.

By Train

PALENQUE

Daily trains from Mexico City take at least 24 hours and are very uncomfortable. First-class service from Mérida takes 11 hours; second-class service makes more stops and takes 16 hours. The train station is 10 kilometers (6 miles) from town.

Getting Around

Palenque

Visitors with a car or those taking a tour through a local travel agency will have the easiest time reaching both Palenque and its surrounding attractions; inexpensive *colectivo* service to the ruins is also available from town at the corner of Hidalgo and Allende. The local *sitio* (taxi stand) is at the town park (☎ 934/5–01–12). The town itself is small enough to traverse on foot.

San Cristóbal

As with many other colonial towns, the most enjoyable and thorough way to explore San Cristóbal is on foot. Trying to maneuver a car on its narrow, cobblestoned streets filled with pedestrians is a needless test of patience. If you do come to town with a car, leave it in the hotel garage until you're ready to take an excursions outside San Cristóbal. Taxis cruise the streets and can also be found at the *sitio* next to the cathedral (☎ 967/8–03–96); there is *colectivo* service to outlying villages, departing from and returning to the market.

Villahermosa

Villahermosa is surrounded by three rivers but oriented toward the River Grijalva to the east, which is bordered by the *malecón* (boardwalk). The city is huge, and driving can be tricky. The main road through town is almost a highway; exit ramps are about 1 kilometer (½ mile) apart, and tourist destinations are not clearly marked. Most taxi service is collective and runs along fixed routes, but if an empty one comes along, the driver will gladly take you to where you want to go. Hotels can also call a private cab. Information about city buses can be difficult to find.

Contacts and Resources

Car Rental Agencies

SAN CRISTÓBAL
Budget (✉ Calle Diego de Mazariegos 36, ☎ 967/8–18–71 or 967/8–31–00).

TUXTLA GUTIÉRREZ
Budget (☎ 961/5–13–82 or 961/5–76–72) and **Dollar** (☎ 961/2–52–61 or 961/2–89–32) are both represented at the Tuxtla airport.

VILLAHERMOSA
Avis, Budget, Hertz, and **National** have offices in town and at the airport. Reliable local companies include **Tabasco Auto Rent** (✉ Blvd. Ruíz Cortines 1201, ☎ 93/2–80–03 or 93/12–34–69) and **Rentauto Usumacinta** (✉ Hotel Cencali, ☎ 93/15–18–21 or 93/12–7756; also at the airport).

Emergencies

Throughout the region, dial **06** for fire, theft, and medical emergencies.

PALENQUE
Contact the office of the local **tourism delegate** (✉ Jiménez and Cinco de Mayo, ☎ 934/5–03–56), open 9–3 and 6–9 weekdays; for missing persons or cars, call **LOCATEL** (☎ 934/5–01–46 or 934/5–02–39), available 24 hours.

SAN CRISTÓBAL
Municipal police (☎ 967/8–05–54); **Federal Highway Police** (☎ 967/8–64–66); **Cruz Roja (Red Cross;** ✉ Prolongación Ignacio Allende, ☎ 967/8–07–72); **Hospital Regional** (✉ Insurgentes 26, ☎ 967/8–07–70); **Social Security Clinic** (✉ Calle Tabasco and Diagonal Centenario, outside of town, ☎ 967/8–07–68).

TUXTLA GUTIÉRREZ
Fire (☎ 961/2–11–15); **Police** (☎ 961/2–16–76); **Red Cross Hospital** (☎ 961/2–00–96). **24-Hour Pharmacy: Farmacia del Ahorra** (✉ Calle Central and 8 Poniente, ☎ 961/2–26–54; 9 Sur and 2 Poniente, no phone).

Cruz Roja (⊠ Paseo Usumacinta and Ayuntamiento ☎ 93/13–35–93 or 93/13–34–39); **Fire and Police Department** (⊠ Av. 16 de Septiembre and the Periférico ☎ 93/13–91–42).

English-Language Bookstores
In San Cristóbal, **Soluna** (⊠ Calle Real de Guadalupe 13B) has a good selection of archaeology and travel books in English.

Guided Tours
PALENQUE
From the town of Palenque you can book day trips to the ruins of Palenque, Tonina, and waterfalls at Misol-Há and Agua Azul. Longer trips to San Cristóbal and the Sumidero Canyon are also available. Contact **Viajes Shivalva** (⊠ Calle Merle Green 1A or Apdo. 237, ☎ 934/5–04–11, FAX 934/5–03–92) or **Viajes Yax-Ha** (⊠ Av. Juárez 123, ☎ 934/5–07–67) for trips to Bonampak and Yaxchilán; these take five hours and cost about $300. Some trips add the Lacandon village of Lacanjá. **Ceiba Adventures** (⊠ Box 2274, Flagstaff, AZ 86003, ☎ 602/527–0171, FAX 602/527–8127) offers guided adventure tours from Palenque to Bonampak and Yaxchilán, including cave explorations plus river rafting along several Chiapan waterways sunk deep in the jungle.

SAN CRISTÓBAL
Orientation Tours. Full-day city bus tours also cover the village of San Juan Chamula and the San Cristóbal Caves. Five-hour horseback tours to the caves or San Juan Chamula can also be arranged.

Personal Guides. Check with the head of the municipal tourist office (☞ Visitor Information, *below*) for names of licensed, bilingual guides who lead tours to San Juan Chamula, Zinacantán, and area ruins.

Regional Tours. A.T.C. (⊠ Av. 5 de Febrero 15; ☎ 967/8–25–50, 967/8–25–57, 967/8–18–75, or 967/8–25–88), **Viajes Pakal** (⊠ Calle Cuauhtémoc, No. 6A, ☎ 967/8–28–18 or 967/8–42–93, FAX 967/8–28–19), **Lacantún** (⊠ Calle Madero 18–21, ☎ 967/8–25–87 or 967/8–25–88), and **Viajes Pedrero** (⊠ Calle Insurgentes Sur, N1 on the main square, ☎ 967/8–11–40) all organize tours to Bonampak, Yaxchilán, Palenque, Agua Azul, Lagunas de Montebello, Amatenango, Chincultik, Comitán, Sumidero Canyon, and Tuxtla Gutiérrez; trips to Guatemala, the Yucatán, and Belize are also offered by the first three. The six-hour round-trip tour to Bonampak and Yaxchilán costs about $300 (possibly less, with a minimum of four people) and includes lunch. Special-interest tours and treks—Lacandon Indians, bird-watching, flora and fauna, river trips, rain-forest excursions—are also available through **Pronatura** (⊠ Av. Juárez 9, ☎ 967/8–50–00); 10% of the profits go to Chiapas conservation programs. Most tour operators transport passengers in minibuses and can arrange hotel pickup.

TUXTLA GUTIÉRREZ
Viajes Miramar (⊠ 1A Oriente Norte 310, ☎ 961/2–39–83 or 961/2–39–30; or Hotel Camino Real, local 2, ☎ 961/7–77–77, ext. 7230, FAX 961/5–59–25), run by the Fernandez sisters, offers city tours of Tuxtla Gutiérrez, plus excursions to Chiapa de Corzo and Sumidero Canyon.

VILLAHERMOSA
Agencia de Viajes Tabasco (Madero 718, ☎ 93/12–53–18 or 93/12–50–96, FAX 93/14–27–80; or Galeria Tabasco 2000, ☎ 93/16–40–88, FAX 93/16–43–37) and **Turismo Grijalva** (Zaragoza 911, ☎ 93/14–42–04 or 93/14–42–05, FAX 93/12–25–96) both offer city tours as well as trips to Comalcalco, Palenque, and San Cristóbal.

Visitor Information

The state of Chiapas has a toll-free tourist information number, which can be dialed from anywhere in Mexico: ☎ 91–800/2–80–35.

COMITÁN

Tourist office (☎ 963/2–23–03 through 963/2–23–07, ext. 138 or 139, on the ground floor of the Municipal Palace, facing the zócalo). ☉ *Mon.–Sat. 9–8:30, Sun. 9–2.*

PALENQUE

Tourist information (✉ Av. Juárez and Abasolo at the Plaza de las Artesanias, ☎ 934/5–03–56). ☉ *Mon.–Sat. 8:30–8:30, Sun. 9–1.*

SAN CRISTÓBAL

Municipal tourist office (✉ Palacio Municipal [City Hall], ground floor, on the zócalo, ☎ 967/8–06–65 or 967/8–01–35). **State tourist office** (✉ Miguel Hidalgo s/n, a half-block from the zócalo, ☎ 967/8–65–70, FAX 967/8–08–65). The latter office was scheduled to move in 1996; check at the old office for the new address. ☉ *Mon.–Sat. 8–8, Sun. 8–2 for both.*

TUXTLA GUTIÉRREZ

Tourist office (✉ Edificio Plaza de las Instituciones, ground floor, Blvd. Dr. Belisario Domínguez 950, ☎ 961/2–55–09 or 961/2–45–35). ☉ *Weekdays 9–3 and 6–9.*

VILLAHERMOSA

Tourist Office (✉ Paseo Tabasco 1504, Tabasco 2000 complex, ☎ 93/16–2890 or 93/16–28–89). ☉ *Weekdays 9–3 and 6–8.* Auxiliary office at Parque Museo La Venta. ☉ *Daily 9–4.*

12 Northeastern Mexico and Veracruz

Many winter Texans get their first taste of Mexico in the northeastern border towns of Nuevo Laredo, Reynosa, and Matamoros; those who venture farther down to Monterrey are rewarded with the far more sophisticated dining, shopping, and cultural attractions of the country's third-largest city. The little-explored pyramids of El Tajín and the raffish charm of Veracruz, the first European city established on the North American mainland, are among the many reasons to continue south.

IF THE NORTHEASTERNMOST Mexican states of Nuevo Leon and Tamalipaus are not, for the most part, the Mexico touted in glossy color brochures and full-page magazine ads, they are by no means bereft of attractions. A hybrid of Mexican and U.S. culture, the three border cities of Nuevo Laredo, Reynosa, and Matamoros are good places to pick up handicrafts and sample authentic Mexican dishes at relatively low prices. Improved roads have also led more people to take advantage of the opportunity to visit Monterrey, Mexico's third-largest city and the region's highlight, offering cultural attractions, five-star hotels and restaurants, and, of course, shops. In Monterrey, you can arrange horseback rides, mountain biking excursions, and treks into the pine forests of the nearby Sierra Madre mountains. And just north of the border between the states of Veracruz and Tamaulipas, the port of Tampico prides itself on its fine river fishing.

Updated by
Patricia Alisau

Those who venture down into the state of Veracruz will be well rewarded for their efforts. The area is rich in culture and history: Visitors can explore El Tajín, one of Mexico's most fascinating and least visited archaeological sites; wander the venerable port of Veracruz, where the Spanish first landed in 1519; witness the fascinating ritual of the *voladores* of Papantla; and enjoy an archaeological museum second only to the one in Mexico City. They can also stroll the plazas of quaint mountain villages, laze on sandy beaches, and dine on some of the best seafood in Mexico, prepared in the famous Veracruz style.

Pleasures and Pastimes

Dining

Although northeastern Mexico isn't especially renowned for its cuisine, a nice variety of dishes from around the country is available here. Among the regional specialties are *cabrito* (roast kid), *huachinango* (red snapper), and *café de olla,* a delicious blend of coffee, cinnamon, and brown sugar brewed in a clay pot. With the exception of Monterrey's Residence, where a jacket and tie are necessary, restaurants are generally casual.

The state of Veracruz is famous for its signature dish, known as *pescado a la veracruzana,* red snapper covered in tomatoes, onions, olives, and herbs. Leaving Veracruz without sampling this would be both a shame and a bit of a feat, as every chef has his own special version, which he will insist you try.

In **Veracruz,** as befits a hot, breezy port town, the emphasis is on simple, fresh food, mostly *pescado* (fish) and *mariscos* (shellfish). Whether at night or during the day, a stop at one of the town's cafés is de rigueur; the 18th-century Café de la Portal is known internationally for its atmosphere and its fantastic coffee. **Jalapa** probably has the best restaurants in the state; the cookery is just as creative as the town's arts and music scene. It's not uncommon to hear the pat-pat of tortillas being hand-formed as you eat, and beans, rice and cheese and occasionally chiles (this is, after all, the hometown of the jalapeño) are cleverly integrated into main dishes of meat and river fish such as trout. You can eat cheaply and heartily in **Papantla,** but with little variation. Just as **Tuxpán**'s best attractions are its pretty river and nearby beaches, some of the best places to eat here are the small, family-run seafood palapas lining the beach as well as the river as it makes its way to the Gulf at Playa Tuxpán. If you ask for the *platillo del día* (daily dish), most likely you'll be treated to a cold shrimp, calamari, or crab cocktail, or a plate of fried fish or shrimp with Mexican rice and tortillas.

Very little in the state of Veracruz is truly formal. Even in the city of Veracruz, reservations are almost never necessary, and a jacket and tie would look out of place almost anywhere (except perhaps at La Mansión in Veracruz City). In a town like Papantla, to say that dress is casual would be an understatement: Shorts and a T-shirt won't get you a second glance even in the town's fanciest dining room.

CATEGORY	COST*
$$$$	over $20
$$$	$15–20
$$	$8–$15
$	under $8

*per person, excluding drinks, service, and tax

Fishing

Northeastern Mexico is a popular place for American anglers. **Lake Vicente Guerrero,** near Ciudad Victoria, has some of the best bass fishing in Mexico. As its name (meaning "the fish") suggests, you're likely to hook something at **La Pesca,** on the Tamaulipas coast between Matamoros and Tampico east of Ciudad Victoria and Soto La Marina.

Lodging

Catering mostly to business travelers and short-term tourists, the hotels in the **border towns** are what you'd expect—not luxurious but reasonably priced and mostly well kept. **Monterrey** affords more choices in all price ranges, from luxury to bottom of the line.

Veracruz's tourist industry is less well developed than one might expect. The state is just starting to get world-class hotels like the superdeluxe Fiesta Americana, which opened in the **port of Veracruz** at the beginning of 1996. The port city also offers a number of inexpensive hotels with plenty of atmosphere, and the moderately priced and more expensive places offer good value for your money, especially in comparison with their counterparts in areas that see more foreign tourism.

Although there are plenty of clean, comfortable, and inexpensive options in downtown **Jalapa,** more upscale options are limited. The two nicest hotels, the Fiesta Inn and Posada de Coatepec, are located a bit out of town, which can be inconvenient if you don't have a car, because local bus service is infrequent and Jalapa's many cultural offerings are concentrated in the *zona centro.* Many people choose to see Tajín as a day trip from the more developed city of Tuxpán, only briefly passing through Papantla. If you decide to spend a night or two here, your options are limited. **Papantla** has few hotels, and none are exceptional, though the Premier is well equipped. Fortunately, they are concentrated in a five-block radius and almost never fill up, so you can simply walk around town once you arrive and decide which suits you best. **Tuxpán** opened its first five-star hotel, a fancy (for Tuxpán) establishment called Hotel May Palace, in 1995 on Parque Reforma. Otherwise, there are plenty of safe and comfortable budget rooms in town. The town sees very little foreign tourism, and aside from during Semana Santa (Easter week) and July and August, when middle-class Mexicans head en masse for the beach, its hotels are usually empty.

CATEGORY	COST*
$$$$	over $110
$$$	$70–$110
$$	$40–$70
$	under $40

*All prices are for a standard double room, excluding tax.

Exploring Northeastern Mexico and Veracruz

This area has two basic regions, the first comprising a string of border towns next to the U.S. as well as the city of Monterrey and some surrounding natural attractions. The second takes in the adjoining lush coastal state of Veracruz and its lively port, of vital importance in the history of the Spanish conquest of Mexico. Each of the regions will be described in detail below under its own heading.

Great Itineraries

Although the border towns are worth a visit to sample Mexican cuisine and buy handicrafts at cheaper prices than in the U.S., their charm is limited. You might want to linger longer in Monterrey, a major city with some worthwhile restaurants and attractions. The real prize in this part of Mexico, however, is Veracruz, a region rich in archaeological ruins, colonial history, and newly established adventure tourism routes.

IF YOU HAVE 3 DAYS

If you are driving down from Texas and have limited time, you could simply explore the area around **Monterrey,** the cultural and industrial giant of northeastern Mexico, to get a flavor of Mexico. Spend the first day walking around the Gran Plaza area, where the modern art and history museums are outstanding, and then drive to the Cuauhtémoc brewery, on the outskirts of town. Devote the next two days to enjoying some of the region's natural attractions, including the **Barranca de Huasteca,** an impressive gorge; the ancient **Grutas García** (García Caves); and the **Parque Nacional Cumbres de Monterrey,** with its spectacular waterfall. For some colonial color, visit the town of **Saltillo,** where the best-known Mexican tiles are made; if you get hooked on its charm, spend one night here instead of driving back to Monterrey.

If you are flying, head straight for the port of **Veracruz,** the most Caribbean of the Gulf of Mexico cities. You'll have no problem occupying two days here: In addition to the excellent aquarium or the museums exploring the city's colonial past, the city offers some of the best cafés, music, and seafood restaurants in the country. The last day, take a day trip to the state capital, **Jalapa,** and its magnificent Museum of Anthropology; stop on the way at **Antigua,** where the ruins of the house of Cortés stand, and at the archaeological site of **Cempoala,** a major Totonac religious and military city.

IF YOU HAVE 5 DAYS

If you leave early enough, you can make the drive down from the border town of Matamoros to **Tampico,** on the Gulf of Mexico, by nightfall. After spending the first night in Tampico, head south to the splendid **El Tajín** archaeological ruins and overnight in the nearby town of **Papantla de Olarte.** Leave early in the morning on Day 3 and continue south to the port of **Veracruz,** stopping on the way at **Antigua** and **Cempoala.** Day 4, tour the attractions in the city of Veracruz, and on the last day visit the renowned Museum of Anthropology in the city of **Jalapa.**

If you fly into Veracruz, add the visit to El Tajín and a side trip to the cool hill towns of Sierra de **Los Tuxtlas,** where you can consult a *curandero* (healer) for whatever ails you.

IF YOU HAVE 7 DAYS

Follow the five-day itinerary above, but extend the trip to **Jalapa** by overnighting in the picturesque colonial town of Coatepec, only about 10 kilometers (6 miles) away. The next day, go river rafting on the Río Pescados southeast of Jalapa. Drivers can add on the visit to **Los Tuxtlas,** whereas those who flew to Veracruz might want to spend a leisurely extra day enjoying the beaches and seafood restaurants of **Boca del Río,** a small fishing village that is quickly turning into a suburb of Veracruz.

When to Tour Northeastern Mexico and Veracruz

The hottest months in northeastern Mexico are April through June. The cooling rains arrive in July and last through August. There are never any crowds at the border towns nor in Monterrey except during major U.S. holidays, when Americans head south for a day or weekend.

In Veracruz, the weather is balmy between November and April. The famous *nortes*—gusty, chilly winds that blow in off the Gulf of Mexico unannounced—usually appear between October and February, and especially in December. Pack a sweater and light coat or jacket if you plan to travel during these months. In summer, both the temperature and humidity soar, but the frequent rains afford a nice respite from the heat.

The best time for many to visit Veracruz is the week before Ash Wednesday when *Carnaval,* Mexico's version of Mardi Gras, takes place. It's wild and merry but has a small-town ambience that makes it saner and safer than the better-known celebrations in Rio or New Orleans. The biggest problem at such times is finding a room, but the local tourist office can usually come up with acceptable accommodations. The same is true during Christmas and Easter week, when all of Mexico goes on vacation and heads for the beach.

NORTHEASTERN MEXICO

Few travelers go out of their way to visit northeastern Mexico, an arid area that's becoming increasingly industrial as more and more multinational companies establish *maquiladoras* (foreign-owned factories in duty-free zones) along the border accompanied by more and more air pollution. But day- and weekend-trippers from Texas enjoy the foreign color and cuisine of border towns like Nuevo Laredo, Matamoros, and Reynosa. And only about three hours from the border is Monterrey, a fast-paced city that's home to Mexico's major brewery, some good museums, and one of Latin America's finest universities.

Nature lovers can enjoy the Parque Nacional Cumbres de Monterrey, northwest of the city, with its impressive Cola de Caballo (Horsetail Falls). Also near Monterrey are the dramatic Barranca de Huasteca (Huasteca Canyon) and Grutas García, caves with an underground lake and a stalactite and stalagmite forest. Many sports enthusiasts are lured farther down into the area by the magnificent hunting and fishing at Lake Vincente Guerrero, not far from Ciudad Victoria. Those seeking saltwater attractions will find plenty by the sea near Tampico, which also boasts many interesting architectural sights.

Numbers in the margin correspond to points of interest on the Northeastern Mexico map.

Nuevo Laredo

❶ *1.6 km (1 mi) south of Laredo, TX.*

Of all the eastern border towns, Nuevo Laredo receives the largest onslaught of American souvenir-seekers. Shopping is the primary pursuit here, and you'll find a warren of stalls and shops concentrated on Avenida Guerrero in a seven-block stretch that extends from the International Bridge to the main plaza. In addition to the standard border town schlock, Nuevo Laredo shops stock a good selection of high-quality handicrafts

Northeastern Mexico

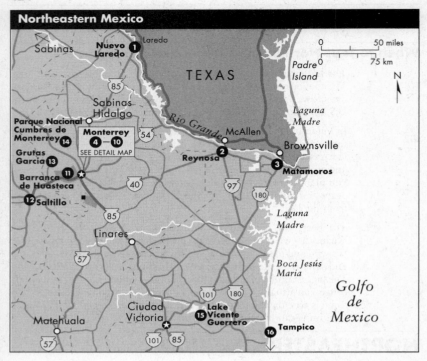

from all over Mexico, at somewhat inflated prices. Wander a few blocks off the main drag in any direction for better prices and smaller crowds. There's also a large crafts market on the east side of Avenida Guerrero, just north of the plaza.

Nuevo Laredo was founded after the Treaty of Guadalupe Hidalgo in 1848, which ended the Mexican-American War. The treaty established the Río Bravo (or Rio Grande) as the border between the two countries and forced Mexico to give up a substantial amount of territory. Many of Laredo's Mexican residents, who suddenly found themselves living in the United States, crossed the river and founded Nuevo Laredo on what had been the outskirts of town. Today, Nuevo Laredo's economy depends greatly on gringos who head south for a few days of drunken revelry, returning home with a bottle of tequila, suitcases full of souvenirs, and a mean hangover.

Dining and Lodging

$$$$ ✕ **Winery (La Vinteria).** This Mexican version of a Continental wine
★ bar serves such regional specialties as *tampiqueña* steak and *queso fundido* (melted cheese), often served in a bowl with chorizo (spicy sausage) to be spread on tortillas. It has the best selection of Mexican wines in town. ⊠ *Matamoros 308 at Victoria,* ☎ *87/12–08–95. Reservations not accepted. AE, DC, MC, V.*

$$$ ✕ **El Dorado.** Dating from the Prohibition era, this spot is a favorite with the Texas crowd—a hangout better known for its atmosphere than for its cuisine. Try the combination plate of grilled meat, which includes goat, quail, or frogs' legs. ⊠ *Ocampo at Belden,* ☎ *87/12–00–15. Reservations not accepted. AE, MC, V.*

$$$ ✕ **Mexico Tipico.** This establishment offers both indoor and outdoor patio dining, with mariachis coming in from the street to entertain patrons. The patio, partially covered, features a waterfall. Specialties are *carne asada* (grilled meat) and cabrito. True to its name, Mexico Tipico serves the typical Mexican plate of beef or chicken enchiladas with rice and refried beans. ⊠ *Guerrero 934,* ☎ *87/12–15–25. Reservations not accepted. MC, V.*

$ ⊡ **El Río.** A modern white structure spread out on large landscaped grounds, this motel has a spacious lobby and large guest rooms. Nearly 50 rooms in Section 200 have been redecorated; other rooms still have dark Spanish colonial furniture. All units include shower, satellite color TV, and telephone. ⊠ *5 km (3 mi) south on Hwy. 85, Nuevo Laredo, Tamps. 88000,* ☎ *87/14–36–66. 149 rooms. Restaurant, bar, 2 pools, free parking. AE, MC, V.*

$ ⊡ **Hotel Posada Mina.** This is a good bet for those who are seeking budget accommodations, not luxury. A remodeled old yellow brick building about six blocks west of the new bridge, the Mina has very small rooms, but they are clean with good beds, individual air-conditioning and heat, color TVs, and private baths. ⊠ *Mina 35, Nuevo Laredo, Tamps. 88000,* ☎ *87/13–14–73. 5 rooms. Coffee shop. MC, V.*

$ ⊡ **Hotel Reforma.** An older hotel just a half block south of Plaza Hidalgo, Reforma has a restaurant that you can enter either from the lobby or from the street and secure parking in back a block away. Rooms in the older section, although somewhat small and rather nondescript, are comfortable; junior suites in the newer section are spacious and have fresh carpets and curtains. All units come with shower, TV, and telephone. ⊠ *Guerrero 822, Nuevo Laredo, Tamps. 88000,* ☎ *87/12–62–50,* ℻ *87/12–67–14. 38 rooms. Restaurant, bar. MC, V.*

Nightlife and the Arts

Victoria's, three blocks from Bridge 1, is a noisy favorite; the **Winery** and **El Dorado** are somewhat more sedate; and **Quintana Rock** is the local disco.

Shopping

On the stretch where International Bridge 1 leads into Avenida Guerrero you'll find most of Nuevo Laredo's shops—classy and junky alike. **Granada** (⊠ Guerrero 504, ☎ 87/12–86–44) has better-quality items than many of the other vendors, including lead crystal and serapes. In addition, a number of artisan shops are located in the **Nuevo Mercado de la Reforma** mall, three blocks south of the bridge. The **Ma Cristina** mall, one-half block north of the square, houses about three dozen curio outlets. Most stores remain open until 8 PM.

Reynosa

❷ *16 km (10 mi) south of McAllen, TX.*

Because of its manageable size and mellow attitude, Reynosa is one of the most pleasant points of entry into Mexico and a convenient starting point if you're bound for Mexico City, Monterrey, or Veracruz. That said, Reynosa is still an industrial border town of limited charm, driven economically by the petrochemical industry, agriculture, and the ever-present tourist trade. As you enter town, you'll see the Zona Rosa (Pink Zone) tourist district, with a few curio shops and a couple of bars and restaurants. The heart of the city, around Plaza Principal, is about five blocks from the International Bridge and is one of the nicest parts of town. The rest is a jumble of tacky border-town urban sprawl.

Plaza Principal is in many ways a typical Mexican town center, but its original colonial church has been joined like a Siamese twin to an ultramodern newer addition with arches and stained-glass windows. Hidalgo Street, a colorful pedestrian mall of shops and street vendors, leads off from the plaza. Many Texans save money by having their teeth fixed south of the Rio Grande—which explains the many dental offices you'll see in this area.

Dining and Lodging

$$$ ✕ **Sam's.** Wild game like quail and dove served in season (November–January) and seafood are the specialties here. Desserts, however, are limited to flan (caramel custard) and cheese cake. In winter, Sam's is frequented by Americans from the Rio Grande Valley and snowbirds from Minnesota. ⊠ *Allende 990, Reynosa,* ☎ *89/22–00–34 or 89/22–34–34. Reservations not accepted. MC, V.*

$ ✕ **La Majada.** Like all good cabrito restaurants, this is one is simple and to the point: Roast kid, guacamole, and quesadillas are pretty much what you'll find. Don't come for the atmosphere but for the local specialty at its best. ⊠ *Av. Miguel Aleman (½ block from bridge), no phone. Reservations not accepted. MC, V.*

$ ▦ **Astromundo.** Downtown and handy to the market and the few good local restaurants, this popular hotel gets a lot of traffic from weekending winter Texans. ⊠ *Juárez at Guerrero, Reynosa, Tamps. 88500,* ☎ FAX *89/22–56–25. 94 rooms. Restaurant, bar. AE, MC, V.*

$ ✕ **Hotel Virrey.** On the Monterrey highway, 10 kilometers (6 miles) from town, this quiet modern lodging is a good bet for those who got a late start driving to Monterrey or want to avoid the congestion of downtown. Rooms have two queen-size beds with floral-print spreads, a small work table, air-conditioning, and satellite TV. The good service, outdoor pool, and plentiful parking inside a huge garden area all help draw repeat customers. ⊠ *Blvd. Hidalgo (Hwy. 40) at Praxedis Balboa, Reynosa, Tamps. 88500,* ☎ *89/23–10–50,* FAX *89/23–88–67. 160 rooms. Restaurant, pool, bar, free parking. MC, V.*

$ ▦ **San Carlos.** This five-story hotel on the square has air-conditioned rooms with colonial-style furniture and satellite TV. Business travelers and tourists appreciate its central location, close to the square and shopping center, and the friendly staff, which aims to please. ⊠ *Hidalgo 970, Reynosa, Tamps. 88500,* ☎ *89/22–12–80,* FAX *89/22–26–20. 65 rooms. Restaurant. AE, MC, V.*

Nightlife and the Arts

The **Imperial** offers quiet, slow-dance music with a combo or strolling trio, depending on the night; the older clientele is well dressed. The Zona Rosa has several discos and **Trevino's,** with a piano bar.

Shopping

Trevino's (⊠ Av. Los Virreyes 1075, ☎ 89/22–14–44) has a good selection of Mexican arts and crafts, sculpture, papier-mâché, perfumes, liquors, and clothing, with a cocktail lounge in the rear.

Matamoros

❸ *1 km (about ½ mi) south of Brownsville, TX.*

Matamoros, across from Brownsville, Texas (the southernmost point in the continental United States), is the most historic of the border towns, dating from the 18th century. It is named H. Matamoros, or Heroic Matamoros, for one of the many rebellious priests who were executed by the Spaniards during the War of Independence (1810–1821). The first major battle of the Mexican-American War was fought here when guns in Matamoros began shelling Fort Brown on the north side of the Rio Grande. Shortly afterward, troops of Zachary Taylor occupied Matamoros and began their march south. During the U.S. Civil War, nearby Bagdad became a major port for Confederate blockade runners. A wild and wicked place, Bagdad was destroyed by a hurricane a century ago; treasure hunters often discover bits and pieces of it among the dunes on the beach.

Today Matamoros is the commercial center of a rich agricultural area and a manufacturing center for Mexico's in-bond industry. Some 20 years ago, Avenida Alvaro Obregón, which leads from the main bridge, was spruced up to "dignify" the Mexican side of the border, and today it's the prettiest entryway into Mexico of the three border towns. This is where you'll find some of the best shops, restaurants, and accommodations. Also of interest is the **Casa Mata Museum** in the remains of Fort Mata, built in 1845 to defend the city against American invasion. The fortress wasn't completed in time, and Zachary Taylor's troops were able to capture Matamoros easily. Casa Mata now displays photos and artifacts, mostly from the Mexican Revolution. ⊠ *Guatemala and Santos Degollado,* ☎ *88/13–59–29.* ◩ *Free.* ☉ *Tues.–Sun. 9:30–5:30.*

Beach

About 30 kilometers (18 miles) from downtown Matamoros is **Playa Bagdad,** the site of the Confederacy's only open harbor during the U.S. Civil War. Freighters skirting the Union naval blockade unloaded their war supplies and loaded up with Confederate cotton destined for Europe. Today, there's an air of decrepit charm about the place: About 100 palapas are lined up in neat rows along the gritty shore waiting for visitors, accompanied by a couple of seafood restaurants that seem to be barely surviving. On the weekends, hordes of Mexican middle-class families pour into the place. The entrance fee is $1.25 per vehicle, but half of that is returned to you upon departing if you turn in a plastic bag (given to you on entering) full of your trash. This green program seems to be working—the beach is spotless.

Dining and Lodging

$$$ ✕ **The Drive Inn.** In spite of the name, this is a formal restaurant with crystal chandeliers, linen tablecloths, and a dance floor. Expect a romantic evening, and stick with steak and seafood specialties. ⊠ *Av. Hidalgo at Calle 6a,* ☎ *88/12–00–22. Reservations not accepted. MC, V.*

$$$ ✕ **Garcia's.** Rebuilt and redecorated over its own parking garage, this
★ is a romantic place for dancing and dining on lobster or steak and your choice of a dozen fine tequilas. An elevator from the garage leads up to a gift shop with wares from all over Mexico as well as to the restaurant and a bar. ⊠ *Calle Alvaro Obregón,* ☎ *88/12–39–29 or 88/13–18–33. Reservations not accepted. AE, DC, MC, V.*

$ ✕ **Los Nortenos.** A goat slow-roasting over hot coals in the window is the not-so-subtle advertisement for the best cabrito in town. A dozen plain tables with plastic tablecloths are the setting for an equally spare menu—goat, guacamole, and quesadillas. ⊠ *Calle 9a and Abosolo across from market, no phone. Reservations not accepted. No credit cards.*

$$ ▦ **Gran Hotel Residencial.** The best hotel in the city, this pleasant low
★ rise built along Spanish colonial lines is the center of activity for much of Matamoros. All rooms were remodeled in 1995 and have a terrace, two queen-size beds, air-conditioning, heat, and color cable TV. There's also a large pool and a play area for children in the lush garden. ⊠ *Alvaro Obregón at Amapolas, 6 blocks from new bridge, Matamoros, Tamps. 87330,* ☎ *88/3–94–40. 120 rooms. Restaurant, bar, pool. AE, MC, V.*

Nightlife and the Arts

Garcia's and the **Gran Hotel Residencial** are where the action is in Matamoros.

Shopping

The most appealing shops are on Calle Alvaro Obregón, the street that leads from the border bridge to the center of town. The salmon-colored building that hosts **Garcia's** restaurant (☞ Dining and Lodging, *above*) also contains a huge gift shop, where you can buy everything from tacky souvenirs and big sombreros to quality tequila, silver, Oaxaca wedding dresses, and leather jackets. Across from Garcia's, the shack-like **Bob's Azteca Gift Shop** (✉ 77 Alvaro Obregón, ☎ 88/12–88–19) offers run-of-the-mill woolen rugs and crafts at discount prices. **Barbara** (✉ Obregón 37, ☎ 891/6–54–56) has an attractive assortment of quality handicrafts, carved wood, home furnishings, and even good costume jewelry and imported cosmetics. **Matamoros Market,** a block-long covered affair downtown, is the place to haggle for bargains; you get what you pay for.

Monterrey

235 km (146 mi) southwest of Nuevo Laredo, 225 km (140 mi) west of Reynosa, 325 km (200 mi) west of Matamoros.

Mexico's third-largest city and the capital of the state of Nuevo León, Monterrey is an industrial center, a brewer of beer and forger of steel, with nothing in the way of a laid-back lifestyle. This is where some of the country's most powerful captains of industry hold sway—a fact that earned the city its nickname, the Sultan of the North. Still, it is a favorite with weekenders and "winter Texans" from the Rio Grande valley who find Monterrey so near—a three-hour drive from the border or a short flight from Dallas, Houston, or San Antonio—and yet so foreign. The top hotels are clustered close together downtown in an area called the Zona Rosa (Pink Zone) or Barrio Antiguo (Old Quarter), and several streets, including Avenida Morelos—the main drag—are now pedestrian malls.

Numbers in the margin correspond to points of interest on the Monterrey map.

The impressive **Gran Plaza**—at 100 acres one of the world's largest squares—was completed in 1985 as part of an urban renewal project that will eventually include a San Antonio–style riverwalk with cafés and shops; it's within walking distance of the downtown hotels. Better known as Macroplaza, it extends from the new and modernistic Palacio Municipal (City Hall) several blocks past the cathedral, the old City Hall, and the Legislative Palace to the Palacio de Gobierno (State House).

❹ Towering above the neoclassical **Palacio de Gobierno** is a concrete slab topped by the Lighthouse of Commerce, a laser beam that flashes from 8 to 11 nightly. It was designed by Luis Barragán to commemorate the 100th anniversary of the founding of the city's Chamber of Commerce. Handsome Saddle Mountain and the craggy Sierra Madre provide a majestic backdrop to this austere postmodern monument. ✉ *Between Av. Constitución, Av. Cuauhtemoc, Calz. Francisco Madero, and Av. Felix Gomez.*

❺ The opulent **Museo de Arte Contemporaneo (MARCO)** (Museum of Contemporary Art), which opened in the early 1990s, is the crown jewel of the Gran Plaza. Designed in the style of a Moorish palace by renowned Mexican architect Ricardo Legorretta, it features 14 galleries that display the cutting-edge art of Mexico and Latin America and, at times, of other parts of the world. You can listen to live music on a beautiful water-filled marble patio on Wednesday and Sunday afternoons (5:30–7:30) and watch the candlelit tables fill up with arts

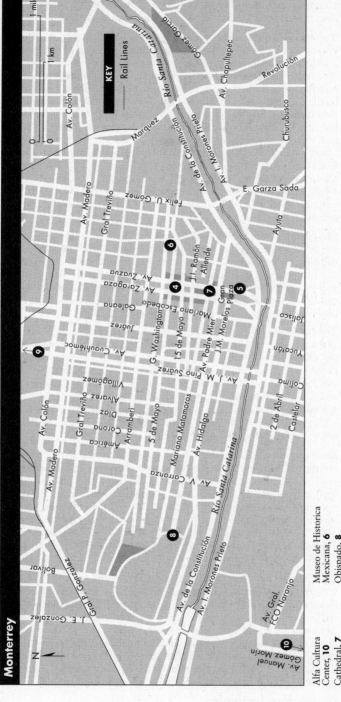

Monterrey

Alfa Cultura
Center, **10**
Cathedral, **7**
Cuauhtémoc
Brewery, **9**
Museo de Arte
Contemporaneo, **5**

Museo de Historica
Mexicana, **6**
Obispado, **8**
Palacio de
Gobierno, **4**

KEY
— Rail Lines

types, sipping coffee and nibbling on pieces of pie. ⊠ *Gran Plaza at Zuazua and Ocampo,* ☎ *8/342–4820.* ⊡ *About $1.50; free Wed. and Sat.* ⊘ *Tues. and Thurs.–Sat. 11–6, Wed. and Sun. 11–9.*

❻ The **Museo de Historia Mexicana** (Mexican History Museum) is the newest star on the Gran Plaza's cultural horizon. Opened in 1995, this two-story building boasts the most complete history of the 1910 Revolution in the country. Battles, marches, and political protagonists come to life in the newsreels of the period, part of a sophisticated multimedia show held inside a railroad car that served as a troop carrier for the insurgents. Life-size plaster-of-Paris casts of the "Villistas" (soldiers under the command of Pancho Villa) sit shotgun on the roof of a car that we are led to believe has just been "liberated" from the Mexican army. Other exhibits include the first bottle-capping machine used by Coca Cola; a depiction of café society in Mexico circa 1910; and a collection of Huastec pre-Hispanic artifacts. ⊠ *Dr. Coss 445 Sur,* ☎ *8/345–9898.* ⊡ *Free; small donation welcome.* ⊘ *Mon.–Thurs. 11–6:30, Fri.–Sun. 11–7:30. Guided tours in English available for 90¢ per person.*

❼ Monterrey dates from 1596, although for the first couple of centuries it was little more than an outpost. Construction of the **cathedral** began in 1600 but took some 250 years to finish. Distinct architectural styles can thus be seen: A Baroque facade is set off by neoclassical columns and two huge ornate Plateresque medallions on the main door. Murals by local artists adorn the area framing the main altar. ⊠ *Gran Plaza and Ocampo and Dr. Coss.*

❽ The **Obispado** (Bishop's House) is the only landmark to be completed in the colonial era (1788). Built on a hilltop as a home for retired prelates, the Obispado was used as a fort during the Mexican-American War (1847), the French Intervention (1862), and again during the Mexican Revolution (1915). Today it houses the **Obispado Regional Museum**, with exhibits that focus on the history of the entire area. The museum's major appeal, however, is its splendid view of Monterrey. ⊠ *Far west end of Av. Padre Mier at Rafael José Berger,* ☎ *8/346–0404.* ⊡ *Small fee.* ⊘ *Tues.–Sun. 10–5.*

❾ In recent years, Mexican beer has taken the world by storm. Monterrey started the trend when the **Cuauhtémoc Brewery** opened a century ago. Named after a famous Aztec chief, the brewery is the heart of an industrial empire producing Carta Blanca and Tecate beer. Today the brewery complex includes the Mexican Baseball Hall of Fame, a sports museum, an art gallery, and a beer garden with free beer (the biggest draw). ⊠ *Av. Alfonso Reyes 2202,* ☎ *8/328–5746.* ⊡ *Free.* ⊘ *Tues.–Sun. 10–6. Brewery tours weekdays 9–1 and 3–6, but call (*☎ *8/375–2200) to confirm.*

❿ The Cuauhtémoc Brewery spawned a glass factory for bottles, a steel mill for caps, a carton factory, and, eventually, several industrial conglomerates. One of the last, Alfa, gave Monterrey the **Alfa Cultural Center,** probably the best museum of science and technology in the country. The museum has many hands-on exhibits and an IMAX theater. Free buses to the museum run from the downtown *alameda* (main square) every hour from 3 to 8 weekdays and from noon to 8 on weekends. ⊠ *Av. Gómez Morín at Roberto Garza Sada,* ☎ *8/356–5696.* ⊡ *About $1.75.* ⊘ *Tues.–Fri. 3–9, weekends noon–9.*

Dining and Lodging

$$$ ✕ **Luisiana.** Perhaps the most elegant dining room downtown, this is
★ a taste of how New Orleans is imagined in Mexico. There are no Cajun specialties on the menu, but the deepwater crawfish are divine. Won-

derfully prepared steak and seafood dishes make this one of the best restaurants in the country. The waiters wear tuxedos, and there's always soft piano music playing at dinnertime. ⊠ *Hidalgo Ote. 530,* ☎ *8/340–2185 or 8/343–1561. AE, DC, MC, V.*

$$$ ✕ **Residence.** A clubby meeting place for Monterrey's high-power in-
★ dustrialists and executives, Residence has a menu featuring both Mexican specialties and Continental dishes like prime rib cooked slowly in its juice. ⊠ *Degollado and Matamoros,* ☎ *8/345–5418, 8/345–5040, or 8/345–5478. Jacket and tie. AE, DC, MC, V.*

$$ ✕ **El Rey de Cabrito.** The restaurant's name ("King of Cabrito") is no lie: This is *the* place to try the regional specialty dish, probably the best roast kid you'll ever eat. The owner keeps his own goat herds and has become so well known that he's constantly filling out-of-town orders. Steaks and ribs can be ordered as well as the famous cabrito. ⊠ *817 Constitución,* ☎ *8/345–33–52 or 8/344–15–00. Reservations not accepted. MC, V.*

$ ✕ **Sanborns.** Part of a national chain that is a Mexican institution, this is the place for hamburgers and malts as well as tacos and enchiladas. ⊠ *Escobedo 920 off Plaza Hidalgo,* ☎ *8/343–1834. Reservations not accepted. AE, MC, V.*

$$$$ ▥ **Ancira Radisson Plaza Hotel Monterrey.** Built in 1912, this hotel is
★ reminiscent of the grand hotels of Europe: An elegant spiral staircase dominates an expansive Art Deco lobby accented by a black-and-white tile floor and crystal chandeliers. Legend has it that Pancho Villa, taken with the place, settled in and stabled his horse in the lobby. One of the most popular spots in town is the Ancira's Bar 1900, a classy cantina with stained-glass windows and wooden booths. Rooms are conservatively decorated with tasteful pastel walls and matching furnishings; all offer minibars, satellite TVs, and large marble baths. The Plaza Club business-floor suites offer exercise bicycles and impeccable concierge service. ⊠ *Hidalgo at Escobedo, 64000,* ☎ *8/345–7575 or 800/333–3333,* ℻ *8/344–5226. 240 rooms and suites. Restaurant, coffee bar, 2 bars, pool, business center, free and valet parking. AE, DC, MC, V.*

$$$$ ▥ **Chipinque.** This hilltop resort overlooking the city on 700 acres of
★ forest land is an ideal choice if you have a car. The view from the restaurant is extraordinary, especially at night. All rooms were remodeled in 1995 and offer fireplaces, matrimonial beds, cable TVs, and phones. There's also a small zoo on the premises. ⊠ *Meseta de Chipinque, Monterrey, NL 66297,* ☎ *8/378–1100,* ℻ *8/378–1338. 43 rooms. Restaurant-bar, pool, tennis court. AE, MC, V.*

$$$ ▥ **Ambassador.** One of the best hotels in this part of Mexico, this down-
★ town landmark was restored several years ago and is now operated by the Camino Real chain. It offers spacious rooms and an executive floor with concierge service. A health club, a French restaurant, and a piano bar with an old-fashioned stained-glass ceiling are among the Ambassador's many amenities. ⊠ *Hidalgo at Emilio Carranza, 64000,* ☎ *8/340–6390 or 8/342–2040; in the U.S., 800/722–6466;* ℻ *8/342–1904. 241 rooms and suites. 2 restaurants, 3 lounges, pool, racquetball, 2 tennis courts, travel services, free parking. AE, DC, MC, V.*

$$$ ▥ **Howard Johnson Hotel Plaza Suites.** In the center of the Zona Rosa is a spiffy-looking pink sandstone building with a striking atrium lobby. Opened in 1994, it's been abuzz with business travelers ever since. The units (all of them two-room suites) include an office with a hookup for a personal computer and fax; they're tastefully decorated in light colors and have lots of light. The high-ceiling restaurant offers a big picture window facing a garden. ⊠ *Av. Corrigidora Ote. 519, Zona Rosa, 64000,*

☎ *8/319–0900 or 91–800/5–0549; in the U.S., 800/654–2000;* FAX *8/319–0909. 155 suites. Restaurant, 2 bars, pool, exercise room, business center, meeting rooms, free parking. AE, DC, MC, V.*

$$ ☷ **Colonial.** This no-frills hotel—the oldest in Monterrey—is ideal because of its central downtown location and budget-price rooms. The small lobby, furnished in colonial style, features one of the last remaining manually operated elevators in the city (it's more than 100 years old). Rooms have been remodeled, and new color TVs, bathroom tiles, carpeting, and air-conditioning units have been installed. There's no restaurant or bar and the noisy disco next door is going out of business, so guests can get a peaceful night's rest. ⊠ *Hidalgo 475, 64000,* ☎ *8/343–6791,* ☎ FAX *8/342–1169. 100 rooms. MC, V.*

$$ ☷ **Motel Dorado.** A good buy, this motel is quiet and offers a pool as well as clean, air-conditioned rooms. The staff is friendly and helpful. ⊠ *Carretera Laredo No. 901 Nte., 64000,* ☎ *8/352–4050,* ☎ FAX *8/352–4058, ext. 119. 65 rooms. Restaurant. MC, V.*

$$ ☷ **Royalty.** You get your money's worth at this downtown hotel, where prices are lower than usual for this expensive city. In 1995, the Royalty got new doors, cable TVs, air-conditioning units, bathroom fixtures, and thicker windows for cutting down on street noise. The interior, including the lobby and terrace restaurant, is dominated by a cheerful pink and white color scheme. Extras include a tiny outdoor pool, video bar, massage services, happy hour every afternoon between 4 and 6, and a complimentary American-style breakfast Monday–Saturday. ⊠ *Hidalgo Oriente 402, 64000,* ☎ *8/340–2800,* FAX *8/340–5812. 66 rooms. Restaurant, bar, pool, gym. MC, V.*

Nightlife and the Arts

Fashionable folk, residents, and visitors alike flock to the downtown hotels for after-dark action. The **Crowne Plaza Lobby Bar** is loud enough to dismay guests who turn in early, but it delights the young-at-heart crowd. At the **Ambassador,** the pianist is more reserved. **El Cid,** in the Hotel Monterrey, packs them into a new off-track betting parlor, and **Bar 1900** (⊠ Gran Ancira Radisson Plaza), a classic but upscale Mexican cantina, has flamenco dancers every Thursday night. **Baccarat** (⊠ Río Grijalva and Mississippi) is a top disco, reachable by taxi.

Shopping

Top-quality shops center on Plaza Hidalgo, near the major hotels, with leather and cowboy boots as the local specialties. Owner Porfirio Sosa has handpicked every item he sells at the upscale **Carapan** (⊠ Hidalgo 305, Monterrey Ote., ☎ 8/345–4422) and loves to tell you about them. His array of Mexican antiques, hand-loomed rugs, shawls, clay figures from Michoacán, metal sculptures, and hand-blown glassware rivals that of stores anywhere in the country. **Sanborns** (⊠ Escobedo 920 off Plaza Hidalgo, ☎ 8/342–1441 or 8/343–1824) offers a standard selection of silver, onyx, and other Mexican craft items. Take a taxi from your hotel to seek out the superb lead crystal made by **Krystaluxus** (⊠ José María Vigil 200, ☎ 8/354–6396 or 8/351–9100, ext. 112); there are showrooms in town, but their prices are higher. Guided tours of the factory are given Monday through Saturday at 10:30 AM. The **Mercado Indio** (⊠ Bolivar Nte. 1150), a typical Mexican market with dozens of stalls, is a favorite with souvenir hunters, although the selections are a litle monotonous.

Sports

GOLF

Hotels can arrange temporary memberships in one of **Monterrey**'s three golf courses.

Numbers in the margin correspond to points of interest on the Northeastern Mexico map.

Barranca de Huasteca

🐾 ⑪   *43 km (27 mi) southeast of Monterrey.*

The Barranca de Huasteca (Huasteca Canyon), with its 1,000-foot-deep gorge, is spectacular for the striated grooves etched into its walls, making it resemble a giant piece of Lalique glassware. A play area for children includes a miniature train ride, two pools, and restrooms. ⊠ *From Monterrey, 20 km (12 mi) east on Hwy. 40 to Santa Catarina, then 3 km (2 mi) south marked road to canyon.* 🎫 *Free.*

Saltillo

⑫   *40 km (25 mi) southwest of Monterrey.*

Saltillo is perhaps best known these days for the unglazed terra-cotta tiles it produces; knockoffs of these plain but attractive tiles line patios and floors throughout Mexico and the southwest United States. But the city, founded in 1577 by Spanish captain Alberto de Canto, was a crucial colonial outpost in its heyday because it occupied a strategic position along the Camino Real, the main artery from Mexico City north into what is now Texas. In fact, it served as the capital of the Texas territory from 1835 to 1847, when Mexico lost it to the U.S. Although Saltillo is a prosperous city with a great deal of industrial sprawl, the city fathers have preserved the historical **main plaza,** which is surrounded by buildings dating back to the colonial period. Although much smaller than Monterrey, Saltillo has its own convention center and some outstanding hotels and restaurants.

Grutas García

⑬   *49 km (30 mi) southwest of Monterrey.*

The Grutas García (Garcia Caves) are an estimated 50 to 60 million years old and at one time were submerged by an ocean; petrified sea animals can be seen in some of its walls. A swaying funicular can take you to the caves, where guides lead the way through a mile of underground grottoes through 16 caverns. This site is far less commercialized than are similar attractions north of the border. ⊠ *From Monterrey, Hwy. 40 west for 40 km (25 mi) to Saltillo, then 9 km (6 mi) on marked road to caves.* 🎫 *$3.50.* ◷ *Daily 9–5.*

Parque Nacional Cumbres de Monterrey

⑭   *90 km (56 mi) northwest of Monterrey.*

One of the highlights of a trip to the Parque Nacional Cumbres de Monterrey, tucked into the Sierra Madre mountains, is a view of **La Cascada Cola de Caballo** (Horsetail Falls), a dramatic 75-foot-high waterfall that tumbles down from the pine-forested heights. The waterfall is about half a mile from the park's entrance, up a cobblestone road; you can rent a docile horse for about $1.50 from the local kids who hang out by the ticket booth, or hop on a horse-pulled carriage for 90¢. ⊠ *From Monterrey, Hwy. 85 145 km (90 mi) northwest to falls, no phone.* 🎫 *$1.50.* ◷ *Daily 8–7.*

Lake Vicente Guerrero

⑮   *316 km (192 mi) southwest of Matamoros, 304 km (191 miles) southeast of Monterrey.*

The man-made Lake Vicente Guerrero is a favorite with American bass fishermen year-round and, during the winter months, an excellent place to hunt duck and white-wing dove. Several camps in the area, such as El Tejon and El Sargento lodges, cater to American sports enthusiasts. For information on the most popular sports in the area, contact **Sunbelt Hunting and Fishing** (⊠ Box 3009, Brownsville, TX 78520, ☎ 210/546–9101 or 800/876–4868, ℻ 210/544–4731). ⊠ *From Monterrey, south on Hwy. 85 288 km (181 mi) to Ciudad Victoria, then 16 km (10 mi) northeast on Hwy. 101 to lake.*

Tampico

16   *504 km (320 mi) south of Matamoros, 583 km (330 mi) southeast of Monterrey.*

Tampico is a picturesque port adjoining Ciudad Madero, an oil-refining center. Usually a low-profile kind of place, Tampico made big news in 1995 when it was discovered to be the hometown of the elusive subcomandante Marcos, spokesman of the Zapatista rebels in Chiapas.

Shortly after the Spanish conquest, the Franciscans established a mission in the area near a Huastec fishing village, but the settlement was constantly battered by hurricanes and pirate attacks. In 1828 the Spaniards attempted to reconquer then-independent Mexico by landing troops at Tampico, but they were soundly defeated. With later invasions by the Americans and then the French, the port languished until oil was discovered in the region at the turn of the 20th century. The British and Americans developed the industry until a strike in 1938 led to its nationalization. Petroleum helped Tampico prosper but didn't do much to enhance tourism in the area. Río Pánuco is so polluted that it no longer attracts tarpon fishermen, although the big ocean freighters are an impressive sight.

Still, because of its relative proximity to the border, Tampico gets a smattering of U.S. visitors and is a fascinating place in which to wander around for a spell; the old part has a bit of the feel of a run-down New Orleans French Quarter. **Plaza Libertad,** near the harbor, is shaggy and unkempt—very much the tropical waterfront. A block away is the regal **Plaza de Armas,** with its majestic City Hall guarded by towering palms. The **cathedral** here, started in 1823, was completed with funds donated by Edward L. Doheny, an oil magnate implicated in the Teapot Dome scandal of the 1920s.

Beaches

Playa Miramar, about 5 kilometers (3 miles) from town, is a favorite with locals. Lounge chairs, towels, and showers are available for rent from the hotels and restaurants along the beach. Public transportation is available from Tampico for about 35¢.

Dining and Lodging

$$ ✕ **Diligencias.** Stuffed crabs are the specialty at this well-known seafood café. It's easy to find: The facade is covered with a colorful mural depicting denizens of the deep. ⊠ *Ayuntamiento 2702,* ☎ *12/13–76–42. AE, MC, V.*

$ ✕ **Café y Nevería Elite.** This is a popular gathering spot for breakfast, coffee, and ice-cream treats as well as other short-order meals. Don't be put off by the noise and the rather worn Formica tables; it's all part of the local color. ⊠ *Av. Díaz Mirón 211 Ote.,* ☎ *12/12–03–64. No credit cards.*

$$$$ 🏨 **Camino Real.** Attractively decorated, this low-rise property 20 minutes from the city center is a resort hotel and the best you'll find in Tampico (in spite of the name, it's not part of the Camino Real chain). Its rooms and bungalows surround a huge garden filled to overflowing with tropical trees and flowers. Rooms have been newly redecorated and contain Chippendale-style furniture, minibars, satellite color TV, and direct-dial telephones; the front desk provides in-room courtesy movies to guests. Fishing excursions can be booked through the hotel's travel agency. ✉ *Hidalgo 2000, Tampico, Tamps. 89140,* ☎ *12/13–88–11 or 800/57–0040,* FAX *12/13–92–26. 102 rooms. Restaurant, bar, pool, tennis, golf, car rental agency, travel service. AE, DC, MC, V.*

$ 🏨 **Hotel Colonial.** This hotel, touting a new image with added services, also has a fresh look. White walls make the rather small rooms seem larger, and deep red drapes complement the dark-toned furniture. ✉ *Madera 210 Ote., Tampico, Tamps. 89000,* ☎ *12/12–76–76. 138 rooms. Restaurant, bar, travel services. AE, MC, V.*

$ 🏨 **Hotel Plaza.** This centrally located budget hotel is clean and comfortable, if a little drab. Rooms are small but air-conditioned, and all have phones and TVs. ✉ *Madero 204, Tampico, Tamps. 89000,* ☎ *12/14–16–78 or 12/14–17–84. 40 rooms. Restaurant. MC, V.*

Nightlife and the Arts

Eclipse (✉ Universidad 2004, ☎ 12/13–14–95) has dancing on Thursday only; the rest of the week, it's a video bar. **Byblos** (✉ Byblos 1, ☎ 12/13–08–27) is another popular disco. The bar at the **Camino Real Hotel** (✉ Hidalgo 2000, ☎ 12/13–88–11) offers music and dancing in the evening.

Outdoor Activities and Sports

FISHING

Although the river is polluted, tarpon and snapper fishing is still popular at **Chairel Lagoon,** with boats and equipment available for rent (just don't plan to eat what you hook). You can also arrange for a boat, guide, and equipment through the Camino Real Hotel in Tampico.

GOLF

Lagunas de Miralta Country Club (☎ 12/23–87–27) sells day passes at Centro Commercial Tres Arcos on Hidalgo for its golf course at Km 26.1 on the Carretera Tampico–Altamira. Ask at your hotel about passes or special discounts at other local clubs.

NORTHEASTERN MEXICO A TO Z

Arriving and Departing

By Car

With unleaded gasoline now more widely available, an increasing number of American motorists are exploring Mexican highways. A car trip is not without its red tape, however.

For details about driving into Mexico, *see* Driving *in* Smart Travel Tips A to Z. **Sanborn's Mexican Insurance** (✉ 2009 S. 10th St., McAllen, TX, ☎ 800/222–0158, FAX 210/686–0732) can help you complete the paperwork in advance—for free if you buy insurance there, otherwise for a fee.

Distances are deceiving in this part of Mexico because of mountainous driving in the Sierra Madre Oriente. It generally takes three hours to drive from the border to Monterrey; from Monterrey to Ciudad Victoria, it's another four hours.

Downtown Nuevo Laredo is reached by two bridges: International Bridge 1 in town, and the Columbia–Laredo Bridge (42 kilometers, or 26 miles, northwest of Laredo). Both have facilities for clearing people and vehicles for travel to the interior of Mexico. The New Bridge is the best route from downtown Brownsville to downtown Matamoros. U.S. 281 leads down to Hidalgo, Texas, and the bridge crossing into Reynosa. For brief excursions across the border, consider leaving your car in Texas and walking over. This eliminates the long wait—often a half hour or more—to bring a car back into the United States.

From Matamoros, Mexico 180 runs down the Gulf coast to Tampico, Veracruz, and beyond. A turnoff on Mexico 101 leads to the hunting and fishing camps at Lake Vicente Guerrero. Mexico 97 leads from Reynosa into Mexico 101/180, which meet up for a bit. From Reynosa, you can drive the free routes Mexico 40 to Mexico 35 to Linares; here Mexico 58 will lead you across to San Roberto (and Mexico 57) via a spectacular road with a most unusual mural by Frederico Cantu chiseled out of the side of a mountain.

From Laredo, the old Pan-American Highway, Mexico 85 Libre (free), and the four-lane Mexico 85 Cuota (toll) both lead to Monterrey, some 242 kilometers (150 miles) south; the latter road, which ends in Monterrey, is a much better one, although the toll is expensive (about $12). It's exactly the same price to take the toll road Mexico 40 to Monterrey from Reynosa; although the Laredo route is more scenic, traversing some nice mountains, Laredo itself is more congested to get through than Reynosa. The Reynosa road, although flat and dull, is more convenient to downtown Monterrey.

The port is roughly a seven-hour drive from Matamoros on Mexico 180, or eight hours from Monterrey via Mexico 85, which connects with Mexico 80.

By Plane

From Mexico City, **Aeromexico** has service to Matamoros (☎ 89/7–79–45) and Reynosa (☎ 89/22–1115); **Mexicana** flies to Nuevo Laredo (☎ 87/12–20–52).

Mexicana (☎ 8/343–0551) has flights from Chicago and San Antonio to Monterrey. **Aeromexico** (☎ 8/343–5560) offers service from Houston, New York, and Los Angeles via Mexico City. **Continental** (☎ 8/333–2622) flies from Chicago, Las Vegas, Los Angeles, Miami, and New York, via Houston. **American** (☎ 8/340–3031) has five flights a day to Monterrey from Dallas. **Aerolitoral** (reservations through Aeromexico, ☎ 8/343–5560) has service from McAllen and San Antonio, Texas. **Taesa** (☎ 8/343–3077) flies from Mexico City.

Monterrey's **Aeropuerto Internacional Mariano Escobedo** (☎ 8/345–4432), equipped with luggage storage ($4 per day) and a money exchange booth, is 6 kilometers (4 miles) northeast of downtown. The only way to get here is by taxi, which will cost about $9.

Aerolitoral (☎ 12/28–08–57) has nonstop flights to Tampico from Mexico City. Both **Aeromexico** (☎ 12/17–08–88) and **Mexicana** ☎ 12/28–21–95) offer flights between Tampico and Mexico City.

By Train

Currently, there is no first-class train service from the border to Monterrey or Tampico, although the first-class *El Regiomontano,* with seats and sleeping berths, runs from Monterrey to Saltillo and Mexico City. For the most up-to-date information about schedules and prices, contact **Mexico by Train** in Laredo (☎ FAX 210/725–3659 or 800/321–1699).

Getting Around

By Bus

Northeastern Mexico is well connected by buses, which are becoming downright luxurious while fares remain low. Information on Mexican bus service is available from terminals in Laredo (Valley Transit, ☎ 210/723–4324), McAllen (Valley Transit, ☎ 210/686–5479), and Brownsville (Valley Transit, ☎ 210/546–7171). **Transportes del Norte** (☎ 8/318–3745), in conjunction with **Greyhound,** goes from San Antonio, Dallas, and Houston to Monterrey.

By Subway

The Monterrey metro, which runs along elevated tracks across the city, is modern and efficient. There are only two lines, but a third is in the works. Magnetic cards are used to enter the station; buy them from station vending machines in units of one, three, or five rides; each ride costs less than 25¢. The metro runs every day from 6 AM to midnight.

By Taxi

Taxis are pretty scarce in border towns but plentiful in Monterrey and Veracruz. They usually cruise the streets on a 24-hour basis.

Contacts and Resources

Consulates

MATAMOROS
United States (⊠ Calle 1, 2002 and Azaleas, ☎ 88/12–44–02).

MONTERREY
Canada (⊠ Edificio Kalos, Calle Mariano Escobedo and Av. Constitución, Suite 108, ☎ 8/344–3200). **United States** (⊠ Av. Constitución 411 Poniente, ☎ 8/343–0650 or 8/345–2120).

Emergencies

MATAMOROS
Police (⊠ González and Calle Venteuno, ☎ 88/17–88–83). **Cruz Roja (Red Cross) Hospital** (⊠ García and L. Caballero, ☎ 88/12–00–44).

MONTERREY
Police (⊠ Gonzalitos and Lincoln, ☎ 8/343–2576). **Cruz Roja (Red Cross) Hospital** (⊠ Universidad and Camelo, ☎ 8/375–1212).

NUEVO LAREDO
Police (⊠ Maclovio Herréra and Ocampo, ☎ 87/12–21–46 or 87/12–30–25). **Cruz Roja** (⊠ Independencia 1619 and San Antonio, ☎ 87/12–09–49 or 87/12–09–89).

REYNOSA
Police (⊠ Morales between Veracruz and Nayarit, ☎ 89/22–00–08 or 89/22–09–02). **Hospital Santander** (⊠ Alvaro Obregón 101, ☎ 89/22–96–22).

TAMPICO
Police (⊠ Sor Juana Ines de la Cruz and Tamaulipas, ☎ 12/12–10–32. **Cruz Roja Hospital** (⊠ Tamaulipas and Colegio Militar, Zona Centro, ☎ 12/12–13–33).

English-Language Bookstore
In Monterrey, the **American Bookstore** (✉ Garza Sada 2404-A near Pemex station, ☎ 8/387–0838) has a great selection of books in English.

Guided Tours
Several U.S. tour operators, including **Sanborn's Viva Tours** (✉ 2015 S. 10th St., McAllen, TX, ☎ 210/682–9872 or 800/395–8482), run shopping and sightseeing tours to the border towns and coach excursions into the interior. **Viva** has also inaugurated a four-day tour to El Tajín (☞ Veracruz, *below*). **Osetur Tours** (☎ 8/347–1533, 8/347–1599, or 8/347–1614) in Monterrey provides sightseeing excursions in the areas.

Visitor Information
The best information about this part of Mexico is found in Texas border towns, especially at places that sell the (mandatory) Mexican automobile insurance. These include **Sanborn's Viva Tours** (✉ 2015 S. 10th St., McAllen, ☎ 210/682–9872 or 800/395–8482), **Sanborn's Mexican Insurance** (✉ 2009 S. 10th St., McAllen, ☎ 800/222–0158, FAX 210/686–0732), **Bravo Insurance** (✉ 2212 Santa Ursula, Laredo, ☎ 210/723–3657, FAX 210/723–0000), and **Johnny Ginn's Travel** (✉ 1845 Expressway 77, Brownsville, ☎ 210/542–5457, FAX 210/504–2919). The **Brownsville Chamber of Commerce** (✉ 1600 E. Elizabeth, 1 block from International Bridge into Matamoros, ☎ 210/542–4341) is open daily 9–5.

Matamoros Tours-Transport (✉ Tamaulipas and Alvaro Obregón, a few blocks from International Bridge, ☎ 88/12–21–18) is open daily 8–6. **Nuevo Laredo** (✉ Guerrero near Puente Internacional, ☎ 87/12–01–04) is open daily 8:30–8. **Reynosa** (✉ Puente Internacional, ☎ 89/2–11–89 or 89/2–24–49) is open weekdays 7:30 AM–8 PM. **Monterrey Infotour** (✉ Zaragoza at Matamoros at Gran Plaza building, ☎ 8/345–0870, 8/345–0902, or 91–800/83–222; in the U.S., 800/235–2438) is open daily 10–5. **Tampico** (✉ Olmos 101 at Carranza, ☎ 12/12–26–78) is open weekdays 9–7.

THE STATE OF VERACRUZ

A long, skinny crescent of land bordering the Gulf of Mexico, the state of Veracruz is often ignored by travelers, many of whom do no more than glimpse the state through the window of a bus barreling toward the Yucatán Peninsula. But while Veracruz's ruins and beaches can't compare with those on the Yucatán, the state is popular with vacationing Mexicans, drawn to the cool hill towns of the Sierra de Los Tuxtlas and the liveliness of Veracruz city.

Descending from the volcanic Sierra, the Veracruz coast consists of flat lowlands characterized by terrible heat and swamps and pockmarked by noisome oil refineries. As you head inland a ways—Veracruz is only 140 kilometers (87 miles) across at its widest point—the land rises to meet the Sierra Madre Oriental range, with its 5,610-meter Pico de Orizaba (also called Citlaltépetl), Mexico's highest mountain. In the foothills of this range, you'll find the university town and state capital of Jalapa, where students share the colonial streets with local farmers who have come to town to market their crops. The state does have some good beaches along the coast, particularly around the northern city of Tuxpán, but the real reasons to come are the atmosphere, the history, and the people. All of these are to be found at their best in the city of Veracruz, a working port with so many marimba bands in the *zócalo* (main square) on weekend evenings that they must compete to be heard.

Olmec civilization thrived in Veracruz long before the rise of the Maya. The state's best-preserved ruins, at El Tajín near Papantla, are thought to have been the work of yet another civilization, which had its heyday later, between AD 550 and AD 1100. By the time Hernán Cortés landed in Veracruz in 1519, the Aztecs held sway, but within a very short time the Indian population was decimated by disease and war.

The state of Veracruz played a pivotal role in Cortés's march to Tenochchitlan. Foreign tourism is expected to be boosted through a new travel circuit sponsored by the Mexican government called the *Ruta de Cortés* (Route of Cortés), which traces the Spanish conquistador's footsteps, beginning with his Veracruz landing through to his arrival in Mexico City, where he defeated the Aztec rulers. It's a mélange of soft adventure excursions like river rafting combined with visits to colonial cities, old haciendas, and archaeological zones that were instrumental in the Spanish Conquest.

In modern times, the discovery of oil in Veracruz caused a population explosion that saw the number of Veracruzanos go from about 1 million at the beginning of the century to more than 7 million today. For most foreign travelers, the occasional sulfurous stench of a coastal oil refinery is an unpleasant intrusion on their tropical reverie, but for many of the state's residents, it's their lifeblood.

Numbers in the margin correspond to points of interest on the Veracruz and East Central Mexico map.

Veracruz

502 km (320 mi) south of Tampico, 345 km (211 mi) west of Mexico City

Veracruz was Mexico's premier seaside resort and the port of entry for most foreign visitors until a few decades ago; travelers arrived by ship, then boarded a train to Mexico City, often looking wistfully back. Today relatively few foreigners find their way to Veracruz's beaches, but domestic vacationers are lured into the fun-loving but not particularly sophisticated town by prices that are far lower than those found in Acapulco, Puerto Vallarta, or Cancún.

Veracruz was the first European city to be established on the North American mainland and the major gateway for Spanish settlement of Mexico, although the spot where Cortés landed in 1519 lies about 50 kilometers (30 miles) to the northwest in a tiny slip of a place called Antigua (☞ *below*). The city, in keeping with its prominent position in history, was decorated four times for heroism: in 1826 when the last of the Spanish colonial rulers was kicked out of the San Juan Ulúa fortress in the country's bid for independence from Spain; in 1838, when French troops invaded Veracruz during the French Pastry War; and in 1846–1847 and again in 1914 when the U.S. Army invaded the city. It was during the Pastry War—an account of which would fit nicely into a Gilbert and Sullivan operetta—that the infamous General Santa Anna, a native son of Veracruz, got his leg shot off by a French canon. His conceit later prompted him to bury the leg with full military honors.

To meet their labor needs, the Spanish brought a large number of Africans to Veracruz as slaves. Later, the port was flooded with Cuban immigrants. The presence of both groups has had a strong effect on the character of the place. For one thing, the port has more offshoots of Judeo-Christian religion than anywhere else in Mexico, some of them quite bizarre. This mix has also created an open-minded city, where tourists of all cultural extractions are generously welcomed.

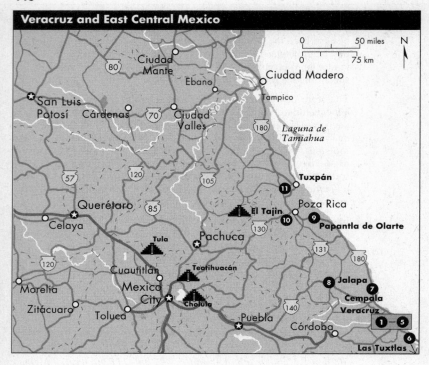

Veracruz and East Central Mexico

But perhaps the most profound influence of Veracruz's mixed population can be seen in its music and dance. Veracruz is the hometown of La Bamba, a song that dates back to the 17th century. It recounts how the Countess of Malibrán defended her hacienda against an attack by the infamous pirate Lorenzillo, who was pillaging the coast of Veracruz. She led the women of the hacienda onto the beach to cheer on the efforts of her small army of workers, who had taken up arms to defend the estate. The pirate chief bypassed her hacienda—its forlorn ruins along the Río Jamapa can still be seen today—and went on to plunder the port. In addition to its most famous song, the city has a special brand of music, played by lively trios outfitted in white and slapping away at tiny guitars and portable harps. In the evening, mariachis entertain outside the sidewalk cafés around the main plaza. Whether at night or during the day, a stop at one of these coffeehouses is de rigueur (☞ Dining and Lodging, *below*, for details on some of the best-known ones).

The danzón was introduced to the city by penniless refugees fleeing Cuba in 1879 following its War of Independence. Most ended up living outside the city walls (only Veracruz aristocrats were allowed to live inside), but the sons of the elite, who sneaked into the poor neighborhoods at night, eventually introduced the danzón to high society. Sensuous compared to the stiff and formal dance that had been the norm until this time, the danzón was at first considered scandalous, but it soon won the hearts of even its detractors and became the most popular dance in the city. It has since spread throughout the country.

Numbers in the margin correspond to points of interest on the Veracruz map.

If this is your first visit to the port of Veracruz, a good place to get oriented is the **Museo de la Ciudad.** The region's history is narrated via artifacts and displays, and scale models of the city help you get the lay

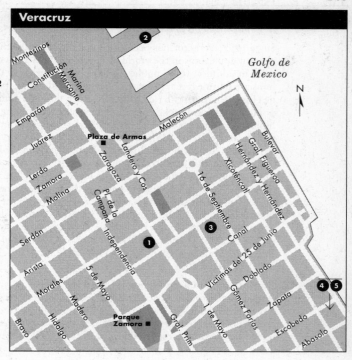

Veracruz

*Golfo de
Mexico*

N

Montesinos · Constitución · Marina Mercante · Emparán · Juárez · Lerdo · Zomora · Molina · Serdán · Arista · Morales · Bravo · Hidalgo · Madero · 5 de Mayo · Zaragoza · Landero y Cos · Pl. de la Campana · Independencia · Gral. Prim · 1 de Mayo · 16 de Septiembre · Canal · Víctimas del 25 de Junio · Gómez Farías · Doblado · Zapata · Escobedo · Abasolo · Grai. Figueroa · Hernández y Hernández · Xicoténcatl · Malecón · Bulevar

Plaza de Armas

**Parque
Zamora**

❷ · ❶ · ❸ · ❹ ❺

of the land. Also exhibited are copies of pre-Columbian statues and
contemporary indigenous art. A $1 donation pays for a guided tour
by a bilingual student. ✉ *Zaragoza at Morelos, no phone.* 🎫 *$3.*
🕐 *Mon.–Sat. 9–4.*

During the Viceregal era, Veracruz was the only east-coast port permitted to operate in New Spain. As a result, it was frequently attacked
❷ by pirates. The great **Fort of San Juan de Uluá,** built shortly after the
conquest and the last territory in Mexico to be held by the Spanish Royalists, is a monument to that swashbuckling era. A miniature city in
itself, the island fort is a maze of moats, ramparts, and drawbridges
smack in the middle of the busy port area (it's now connected to the
mainland by a causeway). Fortification of the island began in 1535 under
the direction of Antonio de Mendoza, the first viceroy of New Spain.
Ground coral, sand, and oyster shells were used for the original walls.
A few centuries later, the fort was used as a prison, housing such figures as Benito Juárez, who was held prisoner here by conservative dictator Santa Anna before being exiled to Louisiana in 1853. After
Independence, it was used in unsuccessful attempts to fight off first the
invading French, the Americans, then the French again and, in 1914,
the Americans. ✉ *Reached via causeway from downtown Veracruz,
no phone.* 🎫 *$3; free Sun. and holidays.* 🕐 *Tues.–Sun. 9–4.*

❸ The **Baluarte de Santiago,** a fortress and museum, is all that's left of
the old city walls; like the Fort of San Juan de Uluá, the colonial bul-
wark was built as a defense against pirates (but some 100 years later,
in 1635). The structure is impressively solid from the outside and ro-
mantically lit at night. Inside is a small museum that has an exquisite
permanent exhibit of beautiful gold pre-Columbian jewelry—definitely Spanish plunder—which was accidently discovered by a fisher-

man 25 years ago and has been on display since 1991. ⊠ *Canal at 16 de Septiembre, no phone.* 🖼 *$2; free Sun.* ☉ *Tues.–Sun. 10–4:30.*

❹ Since 1993, Veracruz has been the home of one of the three most important aquariums in the world, the state-of-the-art **Acuario de Veracruz.** In addition to its public displays, this impressive complex also houses a marine research center. Located in a shopping plaza on Playa de Hornos, a quick cab ride from the center, the aquarium is extremely popular with locals, who flock here on weekends. Among the main exhibits are a tank containing 3,000 different species of marine life native to the Gulf of Mexico, including nurse sharks, manta rays, barracudas, sea turtles, and the pre-Hispanic *pejelagartos,* which look like a combination of crocodile and fish. Smaller display cases host swimming sea horses and the lethal but beautiful scorpion fish, with its long, porcupine-like quills. Shark movies, of the make-you-never-want-to-set-foot-in-the-ocean-again variety, are shown near the exit. If that doesn't do the trick, check out the 18-foot-long outline on the far wall, above the caption "This is the actual size of a great white shark caught off the coast of Tuxpán, Veracruz." ⊠ *Plaza Acuario in Malecón del Puerto de Veracruz,* ☎ *29/34–79–84.* 🖼 *$2.* ☉ *Mon.–Thurs. 10–7, Fri.–Sun. 10–7:30.*

❺ Don't miss the **Casita Blanca** (White House), the museum-home of Agustín Lara, one of Mexico's most beloved songwriters and singers. Lara's occupations included playing the piano in a house of ill repute and being a bullfighter; he is also famous for marrying seven women, including Mexican screen goddess Maria Félix. He died in 1970 at the age of 73 after spending the last years of his life writing and recording music at La Casita Blanca, his name for his home overlooking the sea in his adopted city of Veracruz. Among his most famous songs, piped in via cassette, are "Maria Bonita," which he dedicated to Félix, and "Granada." Newspaper clippings, caricatures, photos of Lara with Hollywood stars, and a replica of the radio station where Lara went on the air nightly with "La Hora Azul" (The Blue Hour) help plunge you into a life that was constantly in the public eye. ⊠ *Blvd. Adolfo Ruíz Cortines s/n, Boca del Río, no phone.* 🖼 *$1.25.* ☉ *Tues.–Sun. 10–2 and 4–8.*

OFF THE BEATEN PATH	**Antigua –** This town, which was given its name by the Spaniards after they abandoned it, was the site of the first European landing in the New World and the conquistadors' capital for 75 years. Cortés's home, which once had 22 rooms surrounding a huge courtyard, lies abandoned on the northern edge of the village; it's worth seeing if only for its crumbling, roofless masonry, taken over by clinging vines and massive tree roots. Antigua also hosts the first church of New Spain, a little white stucco structure in remarkably good condition. Here, where Cortés and his soldiers prayed and the first converted Indian was baptized, masses are still said today.

Beaches

Veracruz City's beaches are much less inviting than you might expect: Most are somewhat dirty, and the water is fairly polluted. The beach begins on the southern edge of the city at **Villa del Mar** but is at its best down toward **Mocambo,** about 7 kilometers (4 miles) from downtown Veracruz. Better beaches are farther from town: About 4 kilometers (2½ miles) south of Playa Mocambo is **Boca del Río,** a small fishing village at the mouth of the Río Jamapa that is quickly getting sucked into Veracruz.

Dining and Lodging

In addition to the restaurants in Veracruz, you'll want to try one in the fishing village of Boca del Río, where the little Jamapa river meets the sea about 10 kilometers (6 miles) south of downtown. Many of them—they seem to turn up between every other house—are modest but serve some of the finest seafood in Mexico. (Boca del Río holds a spot in *The Guinness Book of Records* for the largest fish fillet stuffed with shellfish.) Similarly, the area fronting the water south of downtown toward Boca del Río, and especially along Playa Mocambo, is showing signs of turning into a mini *zona hotelera* (hotel zone). It is here that you will find the better beaches, as well as most of the fancier hotels and resorts. In all cases you might want to avoid hotels with no air-conditioning, since the air is hot and muggy most of the year.

$$$ ✕ **La Mansion.** This elegant restaurant is part of a nationwide chain specializing in grilled meats. The Veracruz branch, on the boulevard east of downtown in Boca del Río, features attractive southwestern decor in subdued greens and peach, as well as brisk and efficient service. A few soups and salads are served, but the menu is dominated by thick cuts of steak. The extensive wine selection consists almost exclusively of domestic, Spanish, and French reds. ✉ *Blvd. Adolpho Ruíz Cortines s/n next to Agustín Lara Museum, Boca del Río,* ☎ *29/37–13–38. AE, MC, V. Closed Mon.*

$$$ ✕ **Mariscos Villa Rica.** This casual, seafront palapa restaurant is worth
★ the small effort to find it. Hidden on a small street that runs parallel to Playa Mocambo, the Villa Rica is a favorite with locals in the know but sees almost no casual tourists. The menu consists entirely of seafood. Specialties include sea bass, snapper, prawns, and lobster, prepared as you wish. There is a small, reasonably priced wine list, but the beverage of choice among loyal patrons is cold Corona with lime. Live music is featured daily from 2:30 PM on. ✉ *Calle Mocambo s/n, Boca del Río,* ☎ *29/37–76–80. MC, V.*

$$ ✕ **La Fragata.** Those who are not staying in the old-fashioned Hotel Mocambo can visit its restaurant for an evening meal and see the place at its best—when the breezes off the water blow at night and the terraced gardens are illuminated. For the full effect, request an outdoor table. Dinner offerings range from filt mignon to huachinango stuffed with shrimp and calamari, but there's nothing in the way of lighter fare beyond a few disappointing salads. The restaurant is rarely crowded, and service is casual and very friendly. ✉ *Ruíz Cortines s/n on Playa Mocambo, Boca del Río,* ☎ *29/22–05–05. AE, MC, V.*

$$ ✕ **Pardiño's.** This modest eatery is a star among Boca del Río's many
★ seafood restaurants and a favorite of the port's residents. Plain tables in a storefront on the village's main square belie the elegant preparation of such dishes as crabs *salpicón* (finely chopped with cilantro, onion, and lime), grilled sea bass, and, of course, *huachinango à la veracruzana,* here served with sweet *plátanos fritos* (fried plantains). Also delicious are the simple, fresh appetizers, such as shrimp cocktail with generous chunks of ripe avocado. Pardiño's has another, much smaller location in downtown Veracruz in a restored colonial building. ✉ *Zamora 40, Boca del Río,* ☎ *29/86–01–35; Landero y Coss 146 at malecón, Veracruz,* ☎ *29/31–48–81. MC, V.*

$$ ✕ **Restaurant Albatros.** This unlikely establishment, tucked away in a residential neighborhood a few blocks from the waterfront, has the feel of a semi-exclusive men's club. It's furnished in dark woods, and waiters in bow ties scurry about to the sound of live piano music. The menu includes some unusual dishes, such as *filete de res Azteca* (steak in corn fungus sauce) and the slightly oversalted *crema de flor de calabaza* (cream of squash-flower soup). The real attraction, however, is the fresh seafood, which the accommodating chief will prepare to your specifications. ✉ *16 de Septiembre 1480 at Azueta,* ☎ *29/31–25–85. MC, V.*

$ ✕ **La Bamba.** This casual eatery sits just off the malecón, suspended on stilts above the water. Seats on the terrace enjoy a cooling sea breeze, and Mexican ballads play over the sound system. The management prides itself in its innovative seafood dishes; these include *pámpano Bamba* (the house special sea bass), which comes smothered in shrimp, calamari, and shellfish, all sautéed in garlic. The menu also features not-too-expensive lobster, as well as a number of beef and poultry dishes. A modest selection of wines, most of them Mexican, and cocktails complement the food. ✉ *Avila Camacho at Zapata,* ☎ *29/32–53–55. MC, V. Closed Mon.*

$ ✕ **Gran Café de la Parroquia.** Don't be confused if someone tells you this is the wrong Gran Café de la Parroquia: The coffeehouse that long held that name is now called Gran Café del Portal (☞ *above*); while this malecón eatery is run by a black-sheep faction of the Fernandez family, kicked out of Del Portal in 1995 after the settlement of a 20-year lawsuit. The story makes for good soap opera. The menu and music are practically the same at both places and both tend to draw lots of local families. ✉ *Insurgentes Veracruzanos 340,* ☎ *29/32–25–84. No credit cards.*

$ ✕ **Gran Café del Portal.** Opened by a Spanish immigrant in 1835 in a former monastery, this most famous of Veracruz's sidewalk cafés eventually grew to cover an entire city block. For a long time it was called the Gran Café de la Parroquia, but following a family feud that ousted the cousins who had been running the place, it resumed its original name, Gran Café del Portal. An indispensable stop for a *café lechero* (coffee with hot milk)—every Mexican president since Benito Juárez has been here—it's lively at all times of the day: Crowds of guayabera-clad functionaries from the nearby civil offices tap their glasses with spoons to call a refill-bearing waiter. (The tradition dates back to the 1930s: As tribute to a trolley-car driver who stopped in for coffee each morning, patrons clinked their glasses as his casket passed by in imitation of his trolley bell.) Marimba music puts a lively sheen on dining here; only veteran musicians are allowed to play inside. The menu features a wide selection of egg dishes, as well as soups, sandwiches, a traditional version of *huachinango à la veracruzana,* and hearty steak and chicken entrées, but the coffee—the formula for which is a well-guarded family secret—is the real draw. ✉ *Independencia 105 across from cathedral,* ☎ *29/31–27–59. No credit cards.*

$ ✕ **Tortas Koy Koy.** This unpretentious sandwich joint, set right on the verdant Parque Zamora, is a favorite date spot for young *jarochos* (as natives of Veracruz are known). It specializes in excellent sandwiches of house-roasted chicken, pork, or beef served with beans, cheese, tomato, and avocado and accompanied by a plate of spicy pickled vegetables. Burgers and fries are also on the menu, along with traditional Mexican offerings such as tacos and *tamales.* ✉ *Manuel Doblado s/n,* ☎ *329/1–50–49. No credit cards.*

$$$ 🏨 **Continental Plaza Veracruz.** Opened in early 1994 between Veracruz and Boca del Río, this Mexican chain hotel was built atop a 3,000-capacity convention facility. It features a complete business center staffed by bilingual secretaries. The amply furnished rooms, decorated in a bright, tropical motif, have climate control, satellite TVs, minibars, and taps spouting potable water. One- or two-bedroom suites, some with hot tubs, are also available, and accommodations on an executive floor entitle guests to exclusive concierge service and complimentary Continental breakfast. ✉ *Av. Adolpho Ruíz Cortines 3501, Boca del*

Río, 94260, ☎ *29/85–05–05 or 91/800/9–02–29; in the U.S., 800/882–6684;* FAX *29/85–05–01. 212 rooms, 23 suites. Restaurant, bar, indoor pool, exercise room, baby-sitting. AE, MC, V.*

$$$ 🏨 **Fiesta Americana.** This splashy new hotel on Playa Costa de Oro, inaugurated by the Mexican president in January 1996, touts the ultimate in luxury and business facilities in the state of Veracruz. It has six floors and miles of marble corridors, all of which seem to lead to the giant serpentine pool and lush gardens facing the ocean. There are three hot tubs, one with a waterfall. Rooms are done in soft creams and beiges; amenities include terraces, voice mail, closet safes, and hair dryers. The swank Fiesta Club floors offer a business center, concierge service, and bilingual staff. Guests have access to a nine-hole golf course, 20 minutes away. No-smoking rooms and disabled-accessible units are available. ✉ *Blvd. Manuel Avila Camacho at Bacalao, Fraccionamiento Costa de Oro, Veracruz 94299,* ☎ *29/22–22—28 or 29/22–22–30; in the U.S., 800/343–7821. 233 rooms and suites. 2 restaurants, 3 bars, room service, 2 pools, 3 hot tubs, exercise room, beauty salon, barber shop, business center, babysitting, travel agency, car rental. AE, DC, MC, V.*

$$$ 🏨 **Torremar.** This deluxe high-rise resort on Playa Mocambo underwent a complete refurbishing in 1994, and 50 new rooms and a pool were added. The accommodations, somewhat excessively decorated in pastels, contain all the amenities, including minibars. Suites feature small balconies with fantastic views of the Gulf of Mexico. An executive floor, with special concierge service and complimentary breakfast, is also available. Kids will like the cascading poolside fountain and the organized activities in the children's play area. ✉ *Av. Adolpho Ruíz Cortines 4300, Boca del Río, 94260,* ☎ *29/21–34–35, 29/21–34–43, 29/21–34–75, or 91–800/29–900,* FAX *29/21–02–91. 232 rooms. 2 restaurants, 2 bars, 2 pools, beauty salon, exercise room, business center, travel agency, car rental, children's activities. AE, MC, V.*

$$ 🏨 **Emporio.** This large, business-oriented hotel, well situated on the
★ malecón, has been turned into an elegant-looking hostelry following a top-to-bottom makeover in 1995. The lobby is a dramatic sweep of marble and rattan furniture and the guest rooms are bright and cheery. Some have sea views, and all boast marbled bathrooms with bathtubs (those in the suites are hot tubs), satellite color TV, and air-conditioning. Dine in the popular restaurant, redecorated in neoclassic French style, or in the shade of an umbrella at any of the hotel's three pools (one is equipped with a waterfall, slides, and a miniature ship for children). Business travelers have a small business center and meeting rooms at their disposal. ✉ *Insurgentes Veracruzanos 210, Veracruz 91700,* ☎ *29/32–00–20 or 91/800/2–95–20,* FAX *29/31–22–61. 202 rooms, 40 suites. Restaurant, coffee shop, bar, 3 pools, exercise room, game room, children's activities, business center, travel agency, free parking. AE, MC, V.*

$$ 🏨 **Hotel Mocambo.** When the Mocambo was built in 1934, it was Mexico's only Gulf Coast resort. However, what used to be the loveliest and most romantic hotel in the Veracruz area is becoming a bit threadbare. The spacious guest rooms are the freshest looking and offer cable TV, direct-dial telephones, and air-conditioning. The hotel's sprawling, terraced gardens lead down toward the palm-lined Playa Mocambo, but it's a long trek down to the beach and pools. Dark wood fixtures, art-deco touches (such as a set of flowerlike pillars around the indoor pool and stained-glass windows in the lobby) all add to the feeling that the Mocambo belongs in another, more decorous age. ✉ *Av. Adolpho Ruíz Cortines s/n on Playa Mocambo, Boca del Río, 94260,* ☎ *29/22–02–05 or 91–800/2–90–01,* FAX *29/22–02–12. 123* *rooms. Restaurant, bar, coffee shop, 2 pools, exercise room, free parking. AE, MC, V.*

$$ 🏨 **Villa del Mar.** This unassuming hotel, just across from one of the nicer sections of downtown beach, is an ideal place to bring kids. The standard, motel-style rooms are spacious and comfortable and surround a large, pretty garden with a tennis court, pool, and small playground. All the accommodations have color TVs, telephones, and air-conditioning. The staff is very helpful, and some English is spoken at the reception desk. A number of bungalows (accommodating up to five people) are also available: These are a bit gloomy and lack air-conditioning, but some have kitchenettes. ⊠ *Avila Camacho s/n at Bartolomé de las Casas, Veracruz 91700,* ☎ *29/31–15–90 or 29/31–33–66,* 𝐅𝐀𝐗 *29/32–71–35. 90 rooms, 15 bungalows. Restaurant, bar, pool, hot tub, tennis court, playground, free parking. AE, MC, V.*

$–$$ 🏨 **Hotel Imperial.** This hotel, built in 1750, is not only a National Monument but also the best place to sleep on the zócalo. Emperor Maximilian and President Alvaro Obregón are said to have stayed here. Reopened in 1994 after a massive renovation, the hotel has a dazzling lobby with a stained-glass ceiling, cage elevator, grand staircase, and antique furniture. However, most of the rooms are nondescript. At present they offer air-conditioning but no phones or TVs (although these are promised for 1997), and are reached by way of an unattractive cement staircase off a carpeted corridor. If you can afford it, stay in one of the split-level junior suites, which feature attractive colonial furnishings and clawfoot tubs. ⊠ *Miguel Lerdo 153, Veracruz 91700,* ☎ *29/31–17–41, 29/31–18–66, or 29/31–65–65. 76 rooms, 16 suites. Restaurant, bar. MC, V.*

$ 🏨 **Hotel Concha Dorada.** The basically characterless Concha Dorada has the cheapest rooms on the zócalo. Accommodations are cramped but clean, and some have color TVs (local stations only), telephones, and air-conditioning. The downstairs restaurant–sidewalk café serves simple fare and is especially popular (noisy) at lunchtime and on weekend nights. ⊠ *Miguel Lerdo 77 near Zaragoza, Veracruz 91700,* ☎ *29/31–29–96,* 𝐅𝐀𝐗 *29/31–31–21. 36 rooms. MC, V.*

$ 🏨 **Hotel Hawaii.** This little jewel of a hotel with a prime location on
★ the malecón is one of the best deals in town, offering comfort, class, and personalized service at a reasonable price. All of the impeccably maintained rooms come with a pair of queen-size beds, air-conditioning, phone, color cable TV, purified water, and a neat marble bathroom. The staff is eager to please, and there's always a bowl of fresh flowers at the check-in desk. Guests can have all the free coffee they want at the snug ground-floor coffee shop, and free maps are available for the asking. The management also sees to it that each guest gets a bag of fine Veracruz coffee to take home. ⊠ *Insurgentes Veracruzanos 458, Veracruz 91700,* ☎ *29/38–00–00 or 29/31–04–27,* 𝐅𝐀𝐗 *29/32–55–24. 32 rooms. Coffee shop, room service, laundry service, free parking. MC, V.*

$ 🏨 **Hotel Ruiz Milan.** This multistory waterfront hotel is a good value for the price. Guest rooms, though on the small side, are clean, comfortable, and modern. All have color cable-TVs, telephones, balconies, ample closet space, and sizable bathrooms; you have to request air-conditioning. The pleasantly cool pink-and-marble lobby is always crowded with Mexican businesspeople, and the hotel itself has all the amenities of a much more expensive establishment, including an indoor pool with a bar, a lobby bar, a comfortable restaurant, and free covered parking. ⊠ *Paseo del Malecón 432, Veracruz 91700,* ☎ *29/32–27–72,* ☎𝐅𝐀𝐗 *29/32–37–77, ext. 106. 88 rooms. Restaurant, 2 bars, pool, room service. MC, V.*

$ 🏨 **Hotel Villa Florencia.** This comfortable, quiet hotel is tucked away on an affluent residential street paralleling one of the prettier stretches of Playa Mocambo. Large, standard motel-style rooms are brightened by splashes of tilework; all have two beds, televisions, and sliding-glass doors that open onto patios overlooking the attractive pool area. None of the rooms, however, has a phone. ✉ *Calzada Mocambo 207, Boca del Río, 94260,* ☎ *29/21–02–44. 27 rooms. Free parking. MC, V.*

Nightlife and the Arts

Every Saturday night after 8, at the **Plaza de Armas** (zócalo), a local troupe dressed in white performs danzón on stage and then goes into the street to join the townsfolk in this traditional Veracruz dance, accompanied by live marimba music. Sunday nights, the dancing is to salsa and moves to **Parque Zamora.** The **Instituto Veracruzo de Cultura** (Veracruz Cultural Institute) (✉ Calles Rayon and Gomez Farias, ☎ 29/22–45–03) offers danzón classes for a minimal fee three times a week.

For a larger dose of authentic Cuban music, head for the unpretentious **El Rincón de la Trova** (✉ Callejon de Lagunilla 59, no phone), where people of all ages gather to dance to a famous tropical band until the wee hours; the floors are cement and the ambience is fun and strictly local.

Discos and video bars are plentiful along the malecón. Both **Ocean** (✉ Av. Adolpho Ruíz Cortines 8 at Ávila Camacho, ☎ 29/37–63–27), a flashy, modern discotheque, and **Blue Ocean** (✉ Ávila Camacho 9, ☎ 29/22–03–66), a video bar with a light show, are packed on Friday and Saturday nights with a young, largely local crowd.

Outdoor Activities and Sports

Deep-sea fishing is popular in Veracruz, and you'll find places to windsurf in the coastal areas a few miles beyond Boca del Río.

Shopping

Stands lining the **malecón** sell a variety of ocean-related items: seashells and beauty creams and powders derived from them; black coral jewelry; ships-in-a-bottle; key rings with miniature sea-life inside; and more. You'll also find flasks of the famous vanilla from Papantla, T-shirts, and tacky stuffed frogs, iguanas, and armadillos. The **Playa Artesania** market on the malecón purveys higher-quality goods, including leather and jewelry, with higher prices to match. You can bargain at the waterfront stands but not at the Playa.

One of the most unusual shops in town is in the aquarium: **Fiora** (✉ Plaza Aquario, ☎ 29/31–90–29) sells unique and beautiful jewelry designed from miniature flowers grown in Veracruz.

Numbers in the margin correspond to points of interest on the Veracruz and East Central Mexico map.

Los Tuxtlas

❻ *140 km (84 mi) south of Veracruz.*

A small volcanic mountain range, the Sierra de Los Tuxtlas, meets the sea at Las Tuxtlas; this area has lakes, waterfalls, rivers, mineral springs, and access to beaches, making it a popular stopover for travelers heading east from Mexico City to the Yucatán. The region's three principal towns—**Santiago Tuxtla, San Andrés Tuxtla,** and **Catemaco**—are carved into the mountainsides more than 200 meters above sea level, lending them a coolness even in summer that's the envy of the perspiring masses on the coastal plain. The Tuxtlas gain an air of mystery from the cool, gray fog that slips over the mountains and lakes and the whisperings among the townspeople about the *brujos* (witches), also called *curanderos* (healers), who read tarot cards, prescribe herbal remedies, and cast spells here. Today, the economic life of Los Tuxtlas depends on cigar manufacturing (the town of San Andrés Tuxtla is famous for its hand-rolled variety, which comes in several sizes) and tourism.

Although much of the architecture here is of the 1960s school of looming cement, all three towns are laid out in the colonial style around a main plaza and a church, and all have a certain amount of charm; Santiago Tuxtla has managed to retain more of its colonial character than the other two Tuxtla towns. The region was also a center of Olmec culture, and Olmec artifacts and small ruins abound. A huge stone Olmec head dominates the zócalo at Santiago Tuxtla, and 21 kilometers (13 miles) east are the ruins of **Tres Zapotes,** now decidedly unspectacular but once an important Olmec ceremonial center believed to have been occupied as early as AD 100. The town also has an informative museum, where you can learn about the region's indigenous heritage and contemporary local cultures.

The largest of the three towns is San Andrés, which is also the local transport hub. With plenty of hotels, it serves as a good base from which to explore the entire region. **Lake Catemaco** is popular among Mexicans as a summer and Christmas resort and is also the place to go for a *consulta* (consulation) with a brujo or curandero, should you have any problems or questions that require some spiritual clarity or supernatural intervention.

Cempoala

❼ *42 km (26 mi) north of Veracruz.*

Cempoala (often spelled Zempoala) was the capital of the Totonac nation, whose influence spread throughout Veracruz in pre-Hispanic times; the name means "Place of 20 Waters" after the sophisticated irrigation system employed by the Totonacs. The site gains its role in history as the place where, in 1519, conquistador Hernán Cortés formed his first alliance with a native chief; at the time, the population of Cempoala was estimated at around 20,000. The alliance with the Totonacs enlarged Cortés's paltry army of 200 men and encouraged the Spaniard to push on to Mexico City and fight the Aztecs. In his turn, the leader of the Totonacs—dubbed "Fat Chief" by his own people because of his enormous girth—was an avowed enemy of the powerful Aztecs, who forced his people to perform human sacrifices to their war god and put military garrisons on Totonac land.

Cempoala was discovered by Francisco del Paso y Troncoso in 1891. Seven out of the 60 to 90 structures at Cempoala have been excavated and can be visited; all are built of river stones, shells, sand, and "glue" made from the whites of turtle and bird eggs. As the story goes, when Cortés first sighted Cempoala at night, the buildings glowed white under a full moon and the avaricious Spaniard thought he had discovered a city of silver.

Upon entering the ruins, one comes upon **Circulo de los Gladiadores,** a small circle of waist-high walls to the right of center. This was the site of contests between captured prisoners of war, who were required to fight two armed Totonac warriors. One such prisoner, the son of a king from Tlaxcala, won the unfair match and became a national hero. His statue stands in a place of honor in Tlaxcala (☞ *below*). Another small structure to the left of the circle marks the spot where an eternal flame was kept lit during the sacred 52-year cycle of the Totonacs.

The **Templo Mayor**, the main pyramid, is the largest structure on the site; follow the dirt path that lies straight when you enter. Cortés, after gaining the allegiance of the Fat Chief, placed a Christian cross atop this temple—the first gesture of this sort in New Spain—and had Mass said by a Spanish priest in his company.

At the smaller **Templo de la Luna** (Temple of the Moon), to the far left of Templo Mayor, outstanding warriors were honored with the title "Eagle Knight" or "Tiger Knight" and awarded an obsidian nose ring to wear as a mark of their status. Just to the left of the Moon Temple is the **Templo del Sol** (Temple of the Sun), where the hearts and blood of sacrificial victims were placed.

Back toward the dirt road and across from it is the **Templo de la Diosa de la Muerte** (Temple of the Goddess of Death), where a statue of the pre-Hispanic deity was found along with 1,700 small idols.

A small on-site museum is being remodeled and should have opened by 1997. The flyers (voladores) of Papantla usually give a performance on weekends. Well-trained guides are available but tours are mainly in Spanish. *No phone.* ✉ *$1.25; free Sun.* ☉ *Daily 10–5.*

Jalapa

8 *104 km (66 mi) northwest of the port of Veracruz.*

Jalapa, which was a Totonac ceremonial center when Cortés arrived, is perched on the side of a mountain, between the coastal lowlands of Veracruz and the high central plateau. A little more than 1,400 meters above sea level, the city has a bizarre climate—sun, rain, and fog are all likely to show themselves in the course of a day. However, for perspiration-soaked escapees from the coast, its an enviable change. The capital and cultural hub of the state of Veracruz, Jalapa is a univerity town and boasts a diverse population; you are as likely to see long-haired young people sitting around in cafés as you are wizened campesinos walking to work. The town is also home to a symphony orchestra, ballet company, and a state theater that attracts big-name performers. Jalapa is filled with pretty parks and lakes, and since the grit has been removed from their surfaces, the government buildings downtown are showing off their stateliness once more. The hills here pose intriguing engineering problems—in some places you'll find the twisting, cobblestone streets bordered by six-foot-high sidewalks built to compensate for sudden, sharp inclines. (Note: You'll often see the name of the city spelled Xalapa; Jalapa is the Hispanicized version of the latter, a Nahuatl word.)

The town's prime cultural attraction is the **Museo de Antropología de Jalapa.** With 3,000 out of 29,000 pieces on display, it is second only to Mexico City's archaeological museum and is a treasure trove of artifacts from the three main pre-Hispanic cultures of Veracruz: Huastec, Totonac, and, most important, Olmec. Its three sections are filled with magnificent stone Olmec heads; carved stelae and offering bowls; terra-cotta jaguars and cross-eyed gods; cremation urns in the forms of bats and monkeys; lovely Totonac murals; and, most touching of all, life-size sculptures of women who died in childbirth (the ancients elevated them to the status of goddesses). At a burial site, you can see ancient bones, ritually deformed skulls, and ceremonial figurines. Guided tours by English-speaking students are available Tuesday–Sunday 11 AM–4 PM, but you may want to call in advance and make an appointment, as the tour schedule is unpredictable. ✉ *Av. Jalapa s/n,* ☎ *28/15-49-52.* ✉ *$1.25.* ☉ *Daily 10–5.*

Dining and Lodging

$$ ✕ **La Casa de Mama.** This extremely popular restaurant is on a busy
★ thoroughfare just east of the center of town. The dark, antique furnishings
and lazy ceiling fan almost succeed in giving this place the feel of a north-
ern Mexican hacienda, but the incessant street noise reminds you that
you're in a busy capital city. Never mind; you'll be focussing on the gen-
erous portions of charcoal-broiled steaks and the succulent shrimp and
fish dishes, served with *charro* beans (black beans cooked in a spicy sauce)
or Mexican rice. The place is especially well known for its desserts, which
include smooth lemon tarts, bananas flambéed in brandy, and vanilla
ice cream topped with Kahlua. ⊠ *Ávila Camacho 113,* ☎ *28/17–31–
44 or 28/17–62–32. AE, MC, V. No dinner Mon.*

$$ ✕ **La Estancia de los Tecajetes.** For fine regional dishes with a dash of
★ creativity, try this rustic, lodge-like restaurant overlooking beautiful
Juárez Park. It's cozy and relaxing, always buzzing with diners feasting on *cecina* (paper-thin filet of beef) with enchiladas, beans, and avocado; *pollo à la Ribera* (deboned chicken breast, grilled and bathed
in a salsa mushrooms); or *crepa consentida* (crepes filled with chicken
and smothered in poblano chiles and local cheese). Corn tortillas are
made on the premises, and the walls are filled with charming sepia-
tone photos of Jalapa past. ⊠ *Avila Camacho 90–12, Plaza Tecajetes,*
☎ *28/18–07–32. AE, MC, V.*

$$ ✕ **La Pérgola.** Designed in the early 1960s by Enrique Murillo, the at-
tractive Pérgola is a relaxing place for an afternoon or evening meal.
The menu concentrates on steaks and shrimp, painstakingly prepared
and imaginatively presented. For dessert, try the *plátanos flameados
con brandy* (bananas flambéed in brandy) or an order of crepes suzette.
Umbrella-shaded tables on the patio offer a view of the leafy entrance
to the Universidad Veracruzana and its enormous sports stadium. ⊠
Av. Universidad at Calle Pérgola, Lomas del Estadio, ☎ *28/17–47–
14. AE, MC, V. No dinner Sun.*

$ ✕ **El Balcón de la Agora.** This small café, part of the Agora de la Ciu-
dad cultural center in Parque Juárez, is popular with students who come
to study over a strong cup of coffee or an inexpensive sandwich. Open-
air balcony seating provides an excellent view of the green city below
and, in the distance, the Pico de Orizaba mountain. Order at the cash
register as you enter, and then present your receipt at the counter as
you repeat your order. ⊠ *Bajos del Parque Juárez,* ☎ *28/18–57–30.
No credit cards.*

$ ✕ **La Fonda.** The entrance to this charming, traditional restaurant is hid-
den on a small pedestrian walkway off the busy Calle Enríquez, a block
from Parque Juárez. Brightly colored streamers, baskets, flowers, and
murals adorn the walls and ceiling, and the warm corn tortillas served
with every meal are made before your eyes. The food is well prepared,
hearty northern Veracruzan fare: Beef or chicken and beans, *nopales*
(cactus strips), and/or chile are essential elements of almost every dish.
⊠ *Antonio M. de Rivera 1 (also known as Callejon del Diamante) at
Enríquez,* ☎ *28/18–45–20. AE, MC, V. Closed Sun.*

$ ✕ **La Sopa.** Modest as it may look, this 20-table restaurant draws food
connoisseurs from all ranks of society—local politicians, students, and
blue-collar workers—who make a beeline for the bargain *comida cor-
rida* (fixed price) lunch. One of the best-kept secrets in town, La Sopa's
four-course attraction might include carrot-and-potato soup, chicken
with rice accompanied by fresh corn tortillas, and vanilla pudding served
with coffee or tea. The menu features light Mexican *antojitos* (appe-
tizers) in the evening, including chile rellenos, enchiladas and tamales.
Live salsa music fills the air every Wednesday night. ⊠ *Antonio M. de*

Rivera 3-A (also known as Callejon del Diamante), ☎ *28/17–80–69. No credit cards. Closed Sun.*

$ ✕ **1–2–3.** This midsize restaurant, located on a busy thoroughfare in the northern part of the city, looks unpromising from the street, but the interior is a pleasant surprise. Painted in muted, contrasting shades of green and purple, the dining-room walls are lined with the work of local artists, and modern sculpture is scattered about the room. The food, a combination of Mexican and international dishes, is more than reasonably priced. Mexican entrées include sirloin tips with chipotle chiles and *crepas de huitlacoche* (crepes filled with a delicacy corn fungus and bathed in cream sauce). International choices such as Waldorf salad, curried chicken, and steak tartare are knowledgeably prepared. Adjoining the dining rooms is a quiet, casual bar that opens onto the restaurant's simple courtyard. ✉ *Av. Adolpho Ruíz Cortines 857,* ☎ *28/14–71–22. AE, MC, V. No dinner Sun.*

$$$ 🏨 **Posada Coatepec.** When actor Harrison Ford was filming *Clear*
★ *and Present Danger* in this area, he stayed at this member of the prestigious Small Grand Hotels of Mexico group, a 15-minute drive from Jalapa. Specializing in fine food (but slow service) and catering to French and German travel groups, the Posada is the former villa of a coffee baron. It now comprises beautifully decorated one- and two-room suites, each with color satellite TV and minibar; some units have heaters for Coatepec's chilly, rainy winters. Ask for one away from the murmur of street noise. The lobby and inner courtyard are splendidly decorated with a fine collection of antiques; a new bar framed by lead crystal windows is cozy and clubby. The hotel offers tours to nearby coffee plantations. ✉ *Hidalgo 9, Coatepec, 91501,* ☎ *28/16–05–44,* 📠 *28/16–00–40. 24 suites. Restaurant, bar, pool. AE, MC, V.*

$$ 🏨 **Fiesta Inn Xalapa.** This pretty chain hotel, which opened in 1993, has the fresh look of a beach property in tropical climes—perhaps to offset the rather gloomy weather typical of Jalapa. Although it's a bit out of the way—in a primarily residential neighborhood, some 10 minutes by car from the center of town—it's a good bet for those who have wheels and are looking for a comfortable, quiet, secure, and well-equipped base. The modern guest rooms in the two-story, colonial-style structure are decorated in cool blues and grays and have color TVs (local stations only), telephones, air-conditioning, bathtubs, and plenty of morning sunlight. Airport transfers from the port of Veracruz are available at an extra charge. ✉ *Km 2.5 Carretera Xalapa–Veracruz, Fracc. Las Animas, 91000,* ☎ *28/12–79–20 or 800/343–7821,* 📠 *28/12–79–46. 116 rooms, 4 suites. Restaurant, bar, pool, business services, free parking. AE, MC, V.*

$ 🏨 **Hotel Xalapa.** The Hotel Xalapa is the best-equipped downtown hotel, with all the amenities of a much more expensive establishment: a bar, restaurant, and gift shop; air-conditioning, telephones, color TV (with local stations), bathtubs, and minibars in every room; and free, covered parking for guests. The building itself—another 1960s-style institutional behemoth—is not particularly attractive, but the rooms are large, sunny, and very quiet. ✉ *Esq. Victoria y Bustamante, Zona Centro, 91000,* ☎ *28/18–22–22 or 28/17–70–64,* 📠 *28/18–94–24. 170 rooms, 30 suites. AE, MC, V.*

$ 🏨 **Hotel Salmones.** Once a high-class establishment, the Hotel Salmones has clearly seen better days. Still, vestiges of its lost glory remain—the high ceilings, sweeping staircases, dark-wood fixtures, and big, beautiful windows are untouched by time. The very clean rooms lack air-conditioning (hardly necessary in this cloudy city) but are tastefully and simply decorated. All have televisions (local stations only) and telephones;

some offer small balconies. ⊠ *Zaragoza 24, 91000,* ☎ *28/17–54–31.*
60 rooms. Restaurant, bar. MC, V.

Nightlife and the Arts

The **Ágora** (⊠ Parque Juárez, ☎ 28/18–57–30) cultural center stages
art exhibits and the occasional folk-music performance and shows classic and avant-garde films in its cinema club. Stop by during the day to
see what's planned. The **Teatro del Estado** (⊠ Ignacio de la Llave s/n,
☎ 28/17–41–77, ext. 38) is the big, modern, state theater of Veracruz.
The Orquesta Sinfónica de Jalapa performs here, often giving free
concerts during the off-season (early June–mid-August). Check *El
Diario de Jalapa* (the Jalapa city newspaper, available at newsstands)
for dates and times of performances, or stop by the Ágora.

Such other nightlife as there is in this student town is generally youth
oriented. **Video Bar Terraza,** above the restaurant-bar Terraza Jardín,
is a crowded lounge popular with students and young professionals.
The upscale **Café El Escorial** purveys beer, coffee, and live music to a
well-heeled crowd. **La 7a Estación** (⊠ 20 de Noviembre near Central
Camionera) is packed with salsa dancers on Wednesday nights; Thursday–Saturday, rock and alternative music are featured. The **Bar Lovento**
(⊠ 20 de Noviembre Ote. 641) heats up with a salsa beat for dancing
Wednesday–Saturday nights.

Outdoor Activities and Sports

RIVER RAFTING

River rafting along the Río Pescados is gaining in popularity. Most of
the operators who run these trips are trained in Canada and are very
professional. Base camps with tents, rafting equipment, and dining facilities are located near the river at Jalcomulco, 42 kilometers (26
miles) southeast of Jalapa. *See also* Guided Tours *in* Veracruz A to Z,
below, for additional information.

Shopping

Mexico's finest export coffee is grown in this region, specifically in the
highlands around the picturesque colonial towns of Coatepec and
Xico, less than 10 kilometers (6 miles) from Jalapa. Shops selling the
prized *café de altura* abound in the main squares of both places, and
you can get the beans ground to your specifications.

Papantla de Olarte

❾ *250 km (150 mi) northwest of Veracruz.*

Papantla de Olarte sits amid tropical hills, the center of a vanilla-pro-
ducing region. A distinctive mix of Spanish colonial and indigenous
influence can be seen here: Totonac men in flowing white pants lead
their donkeys through the crowded streets, and palm trees shade the
traditional, tiled zócalo. The town is best known for its *voladores* (fliers),
who twirl off a 25-meter pole next to Papantla's ornate cathedral. This
ritual was originally performed as a tribute to the god of sun and rain—
the tree or pole used in the ceremony was meant to bring the participants closer to the heavens. The four fliers begin the dance on a
platform at the top of the ceremonial pole, each facing one of the cardinal directions. They begin their descent from the side of the platform
facing east—where the sun rises and the world awakes—twisting left
for 13 full rotations each. Between them, the four fliers circle the pole
52 times, representing the sacred 52-year cycle of the Totonacs. A fifth
man, the prayer giver, sits atop the pole, playing a small flute while
keeping rhythm on a drum as the fliers descend. Originally, the ceremony was held on the vernal equinox, but now the voladores fly for

the crowds every Saturday and Sunday at 12:45 PM and give special performances during Corpus Christi.

El Tajín

10 *13 km (8 mi) west of Papantla.*

The extensive ruins of El Tajín (a Totonac word meaning "thunder") express the highest degree of artistry of any ancient city in the coastal area. The city remained hidden until 1785, when it was discovered by a Spanish engineer. Early theories attributed the complex—believed to be a religious center—to a settlement of Maya-related Huastecs, one of the most important cultures of the Veracruz area. Because of its immense size and unique architecture, however, scholars now believe it may have been built by a distinct El Tajín cultural group related to the Maya. Although much of the site has been restored, many structures are still hidden under thick jungle growth; some archaeologists speculate that hundreds of buildings remain to be excavated.

El Tajín is thought to have reached its peak from about AD 600 to 1200. During this time, hundreds of structures of native sandstone were built here, including temples, double-storied palaces, ball courts, large retaining walls, and hundreds of houses. But El Tajín was already an important religious and administrative center during the first three centuries AD. Its influence is in part attributed to the fact that it had large reserves of cacao beans, used as money in pre-Hispanic times.

Evidence suggests that the southern half of the uncovered ruins—the area around the lower plaza—was reserved for ceremonial purposes. Its centerpiece is the 60-foot-high **Pyramid of the Niches,** an impressive seven-level structure with 365 indentations—one for each day of the ancient solar year. The reliefs on the pyramid depict the ruler, 13-Rabbit—all the rulers' names were associated with sacred animals—and allude also to El Tajín's main god, the benign Quetzalcóatl. One panel on the pyramid tells the tale of heroic human sacrifice and of the soul's imminent descent to the underworld, where it is rewarded with the gift of sacred *pulque* from the gods.

Just south of the pyramid, a series of 10 I-shaped **ball courts** were the site of a sacred ball game; the cross-like glyphs on the facades are related to the planet Venus. This game, played throughout Mesoamerica, is similar in some ways to soccer—players used a hard rubber ball that could not be touched with the hands, and suited up in knee pads and body protectors—but far more deadly: Intricate carvings at this and other complexes indicate that the games ended with human sacrifice. It's still a subject of debate whether the sacrificial victim was the winner or loser of the match. It is surmised that the players may have even been high-standing members of the priest or warrior classes.

El Tajín Chico, to the north, is thought to have been the secular part of the city, administrative and residential; it was likely the location of the elite's living quarters. Floors and roofing were made out of a pre-Colombian cement of volcanic rock and limestone. The most important structure here is the Complejo de los Columnos (Complex of the Columns). The columns once held up the cement ceilings, but early settlers in Papantla removed the ceiling stones to construct the first houses in the town.

Guided tours of the El Tajín are not available: The plaque at the entrance tells some of what little is known about the site in Spanish, English, and French, but the rest is up to your imagination. The entrance is lined with fondas that sell inexpensive meals and mountains of tacky souvenirs, and there's a large, cafeteria-style restaurant at the site. If the "killer beast" exhibit in the museum at the entrance doesn't dissuade you, and you're prepared to work your way through the thick jungle, you can see some more recent finds along the dirt paths that lead over the nearby ridges. 🖾 *$2.50; free Sun.* 𐰀 *Tues.–Sun. 9–6.*

Note: In early 1994, the most important archaeological find in the Veracruz area in more than 200 years ago was announced. Another ancient site was discovered some 64 kilometers (40 miles) from El Tajín, near the coastal village of El Pital. Covered by jungle, this seaport, which likely thrived between AD 100 and 600, extended more than 40 square miles and was occupied by thousands of people. Research is still at very preliminary stages and excavation has barely begun, but it is believed that El Pital may shed much light on the history of pre-Hispanic culture and perhaps even provide a missing link between the Olmec and Maya civilizations.

Dining and Lodging

$ ✕ **Restaurante Sorrento.** The Sorrento is the most popular restaurant
★ in Papantla, crowded at mealtimes with locals who come to enjoy the cheap regional seafood and to catch a few minutes of the *telenovela* (soap opera) on the corner set. The dining room is painted entirely lavender and lined with colorful tilework. 🖾 *Enríquez 104, no phone. No credit cards.*

$ ✕ **Restaurant Tajín.** The Hotel Tajín's sunny restaurant is comparatively elegant and hardly more expensive than the storefont eateries near the second-class bus station. House specialties include a fillet of fish stuffed with shellfish, *jaibas rellenas* (stuffed crab), rabbit marinated in chile, and Yucatecan *pollo píbil* (chicken in an *achiote* sauce). Don't be alarmed by the misleading bilingual menu—the *tasajo cerdo* is not, in fact, "steak porpoise" but marinated pork. 🖾 *Hotel Tajín, Nuñez y Domínguez 104,* ☎ *784/2–17–34. MC, V.*

$ 🎬 **Hotel Premier.** Right on Papantla's pretty, lively zócalo, the Premier is the town's swankiest hotel. The lobby is lined with mirrors and furnished with small, purple chairs that were once dedicated to the no-longer-functional bar. The rooms themselves are spotless and good-size and have tiny balconies overlooking the square. Amenities include tiled bathrooms, air-conditioning, telephones, and color satellite TVs. However, if you want to dine or drink, you'll have to frequent one of the restaurants or bars around the square. 🖾 *Enríquez 103, 93400,* ☎ *784/2–00–80,* FAX *784/2–10–72. 20 rooms. MC, V.*

$ 🎬 **Hotel Tajín.** Under the same management as the Hotel Premier, the Tajín is less expensive than its slightly more central cousin and has more amenities. Some of the televisions are black and white, some rooms have ceiling fans instead of air-conditioning, and the telephones don't always work, but all in all, the Tajín isn't a bad deal. Its hillside perch makes for nice views, and the rooms, while fairly small, are spotless and comfortable. Hotel services are located in an annex adjoining the main building; there's usually an English-speaking staff member at the reception desk. With two weeks' notice, the hotel can arrange horseback-riding tours to the ruins at El Tajín. 🖾 *Nuñez y Domínguez 104, 93400,* ☎ *784/2–06–44 or 784/2–16–23,* FAX *784/2–01–21 or 784/2–01–62. 59 rooms. Restaurant, bar, beauty salon, pharmacy, free parking. MC, V.*

$ 🎬 **Hotel Totonacapan.** This slightly gloomy hotel is located a few blocks from the center, near the second-class bus station. It's acceptable but should be an option only if you don't want to pay for the Premier and the Tajín is full. The rooms are big and bare, with large windows that don't quite dispel a sense of claustrophobia. Still, the staff is extremely friendly and the rooms have air-conditioning, color TVs (local stations only), and telephones. Coolers in the hall dispense purified water, and a diner-style restaurant downstairs serves standard breakfast. ✉ *20 de Noviembre at Olivo, 93400,* ☎ *784/2–12–16. 36 rooms and suites. No credit cards.*

Tuxpán

⑪ *193 km (125 mi) south of Tampico, 309 km (192 mi) north of Veracruz, 133 km (84 mi) northeast of Papantla.*

Tuxpán is a peaceful riverside town—the Río Tuxpán is even clean enough to swim in—with graceful winding streets. **Juárez,** the main street, running parallel to the river, is lined with diners, hotels, and shops. The **Parque Reforma** is the center of social activity in town, with more than a hundred tables set around a hub of cafés and fruit stands. It hosts a memorial to Fausto Vega Santander, a member of the 201st squadron of the Mexican Air Force and the first Mexican to be killed in combat during World War II. *Lanchas* (flat-bottom boats) shuttle passengers across the river to the **Casa de Fidel Castro,** where Castro lived for a time while planning the overthrow of Fulgencio Batista. A replica of the *Granma,* the ship that carried Fidel's men from Tuxpán to Cuba, moulders outside. Inside, the casa is bare save some black-and-white photos of Fidel and Mexican president Lázaro Cárdenas.

Beaches

Tuxpán's main draw is the untouristed miles of beaches that begin just 7 kilometers (4 miles) the east of town. The first, and most accessible, is **Playa Tuxpán.** The surf here isn't huge, but there's enough action to warrant breaking out your surf- or boogieboard. Of the palapas on Playa Tuxpán, the most established is Restaurant Miramar, which has an extensive menu and also provides umbrellaed beach chairs for customers. Farther down, try El Tigre Costeño, run by a friendly family whose male members moonlight weaving palm-frond hats to sell on the beach.

Dining and Lodging

$$ ✕ **Antonio's.** Next to the Hotel Reforma on Juárez and serving as its restaurant, Antonio's is a quiet, comparatively elegant eatery with a varied menu. The *cazuela de mariscos* (shellfish stew) is excellent, as are the prawns, served grilled or in garlic sauce. A number of beef dishes and sandwiches are also available, as well as cocktails from the full bar. ✉ *Av. Juárez s/n at Garizurieta,* ☎ *783/4–16–02. MC, V.*

$$ ✕ **Charlôt.** For anything other than seafood or tacos, the best place in Tuxpán is undoubtedly Charlôt. This French and international restaurant is a favorite of local businesspeople, and it's not uncommon to find an entire corner of the restaurant taken over by an expansive lunch meeting. The pretty dining room is decorated with ceramics and other artesanía. The house specialty is medallions of beef in mushroom sauce, but simple steaks as well as some fish dishes and pizzas are also featured. Service is good and there's a full bar. ✉ *Reyes Heroles 35 at Zozimo Pérez,* ☎ *783/4–40–28. MC, V. Closed Mon.*

$$ ✕ **El Volador.** The restaurant in the Hotel Tajín, across the river from central Tuxpán, is bright and airy, with a semicircular wall of windows overlooking the Río Tuxpán. Corn chips and fresh salsa with plenty of cilantro arrive at your table as soon as you order. Dishes run the gamut from local favorites such as *camarones al mojo de ajo* (shrimp in garlic sauce) and *pescado à la veracruzana* to American-style offerings such as T-bone steaks and hamburgers. It's nothing to make a special trip for, but come if you happen to be on this side of the river visiting the Casa de Fidel Castro (still a taxi ride away from here, however) or

just want an excuse to make the pleasant skiff crossing. ⊠ *Hotel Tajín, Km 2.5 Carretera a Cobos,* ☎ *783/4–22–60. MC, V.*

$ ⊞ **Hotel May Palace.** The most luxurious lodgings in Tuxpán can be secured at this five-star hotel in the center of town. Opened in early 1995, the modern five-story property is geared to a business clientele. The rooms are swathed in pastels and set off by cool-looking rattan furniture custom designed for the hotel; all the units offer phones, satellite-reception TVs, and air-conditioning. Guest services include a small video bar, a restaurant specializing in seafood and regional dishes, a rooftop pool, and meeting salons. ⊠ *Av. Juárez 44 facing Parque Reforma, 92800,* ☎ FAX *783/4–88–82 or 783/4–44–61. 70 rooms. Restaurant, bar, room service, free parking. MC, V.*

$ ⊞ **Hotel Reforma.** The Reforma is a lovely building located a block from the waterfront in the heart of downtown. It lacks a lobby but has a central courtyard with a number of skylights, a fountain, and a few wrought-iron tables where guests often congregate in the afternoon. The hotel was remodeled in 1995, and rooms have been spruced up with new air-conditioning units, beds, bureaus, carpets, and a coat of paint; there are phones, color satellite-TVs and good-size bathrooms in all of them. Street noise can be a problem on the first floor. ⊠ *Av. Juárez 25, 92801,* ☎ *783/4–02–10 or 783/4–04–60,* FAX *783/4–06–25. 98 rooms. Restaurant-bar, room service, free parking. MC, V.*

$ ⊞ **Hotel Tajín.** This place looks like a first-class resort from the outside, but once you enter, you'll be reminded of nothing so much as a college dorm: Long beige hallways with faded blue carpets lead past scores of identical, bland rooms with almost no decorative touches. However, the Tajín's location on the banks of the river, a bit east of and across from the center, means that almost every room overlooks the water and the green city of Tuxpán. It also means that the traffic noise of downtown is replaced by the sounds of river birds at night. The hotel is easy to reach by car (just cross the bridge and drive east for about 5 minutes), but there is no bus service. Pedestrians must take either a longish taxi ride from the center or catch a beach-bound bus to the Paso de Esquifes La Peñita, where a small motorboat shuttles passengers across the river. From the skiff landing, the hotel is a three-minute (if often muddy) walk away. ⊠ *Km 2.5 Carretera a Cobos, 92801,* ☎ *783/4–22–60 or 783/4–25–72,* FAX *783/4–51–84. 140 rooms. Restaurant, bar, pool, water sports, dock, dance club. AE, MC, V.*

$ ⊞ **Hotel Florida.** Don't be deceived by the dark lobby or the cramped
★   elevator: The Hotel Florida is the best hotel deal in downtown Tuxpán. The rooms are decorated in bright pastels and offer ample light and space, as well as large, immaculate bathrooms. Basic rooms have telephones and vigorous ceiling fans; slightly more expensive rooms add TVs (local stations only) and air-conditioning. Terraces on each floor enjoy views of the cathedral and waterfront. ⊠ *Av. Juárez 23 across from cathedral, 92801,* ☎ *783/4–02–22 or 783/4–06–02. 78 rooms. Restaurant-bar, coffee shop. MC, V.*

Outdoor Activities and Sports

WATER SPORTS

There are some nice places to submerge in the Tuxpán area. For scuba diving, head to **Tamiaula,** a small village just north of Tuxpán, where you can hire a fishing boat for the 45-minute journey to the prime diving around **Isla Lobos** (Wolf Island), a protected eco reserve that shares its space with a military outpost and a lighthouse. In the shallow water offshore you'll find a few shipwrecks and colorful reefs that are home to a large variety of sealife, including pufferfish, parrotfish, damselfish, and barracuda. **Aquasport** (☎ 783/7–02–59), just before Playa Tuxpán, arranges scuba-diving trips to Isla Lobos and also offers deep-sea fishing excursions. Other outfits run trips to the island that include permits, scuba gear, lunch, and transportation.

VERACRUZ A TO Z

Arriving and Departing

By Car

The city of Veracruz can be reached within about eight hours by traveling south from Tampico via Mexico 180, or within six hours from Mexico City via Mexico 150. The roads throughout the state, paved and kept up with oil money, are generally very good.

By Plane

Both **Mexicana** (☎ 29/32–22–42 or 29/32–86–99) and **Aeromexico** (☎ 29/34–70–76 or 29/34–34–28) provide nonstop service from Mexico City to the port of Veracruz. **Aerocaribe** (☎ 29/37–02–60 or 29/35–05–68), a regional airline, has flights from Cancún to Veracruz. No city bus serves the airport, and a cab to the city center costs $7. An air-conditioned minivan ($9) runs between the airport and the downtown office of **Transportación Terrestre Aeropuerto** (✉ Hidalgo 826 between Canal and Morales, ☎ 29/32–32–50).

Getting Around

By Bus

Veracruz's main bus terminal (✉ Díaz Mirón 1698, ☎ 29/37–57–44) is about 4 kilometers (2½ miles) south of the zócalo. The main bus company is **Autobuses del Oriente (ADO)** (☎ 29/37–57–88), with daily service to Jalapa every 20 minutes from 6 AM to midnight and round-the-clock departures for Mexico City. ADO also offers first- and second-class service to Reynosa, on the Texas border. For those headed north and east, the deluxe bus line **UNO** (☎ 29/35–03–17) goes to Jalapa, Puebla, and Mexico City; **Cuenca** (☎ 29/35–54–05) goes south to Oaxaca and Chiapas. **Cristóbal Colón** (☎ 29/37–57–44) operates from another station on the same block and offers frequent first- and second-class service to Los Tuxtlas.

Contacts and Resources

Car Rentals

JALAPA

Viajes Herlu (✉ Av. Orizaba 125, ☎ 28/15–51–81, FAX 28/15–45–53) can arrange car rentals.

VERACRUZ

Avis (✉ airport, ☎ 29/31–15–80), **Dollar** (✉ Víctimas del 5 y 6 de Julio 883, ☎ 28/35–52–31), **Hertz** (✉ Aquiles Serdan 14, downtown, ☎ 29/32–40–21), **National** (✉ Díaz Mirón 1036, ☎ 28/31–75–56).

Consulate

VERACRUZ

United States Consulate (✉ Víctimas del 25 del Julio 384 between Gómez Farias and 16 de Septiembre, ☎ 29/31–58–21).

Currency Exchange

JALAPA

One block from Parque Juárez, **Casa de Cambio Jalapa** (✉ Zamora 36, ☎ 28/18–68–60) offers good rates; it's open 9–1:30 and 4–6 weekdays. You can also change money in the mornings at several banks on Parque Juárez.

Banamex (✉ Enríquez 102 past Andy's Cadillac Bar) changes both cash and traveler's checks weekdays 9–noon and has an ATM that accepts Cirrus, Plus, Visa, and MasterCard.

Bancomer (✉ Av. Juárez at Escuela Médico Militar, ☎ 783/4–00–09) changes cash and traveler's checks weekdays 8:30–1:30.

The best rates in town are available at **Bancomer** (✉ Av. Juárez at Independencia), but money-changing hours are limited (weekdays 9 AM–11:30 AM), so you'll have to arrive early to make it through the lines. For later hours, try **Casa de Cambio Puebla** (✉ Av. Juárez 112, ☎ 29/31–24–50), open weekdays 9–6, or use the ATM at **Banamex** (✉ Av. Juárez at Independencia).

Emergencies

Police (☎ 28/17–63–10); for an ambulance, call the **Cruz Roja** (Red Cross) (☎ 28/14–45–00).

Police (☎ 784/2–01–93), **Cruz Roja** (☎ 784/2–01–01).

Police (☎ 783/4–02–52), **Cruz Roja** (☎ 783/4–01–58).

Dial **06** for medical, fire, and theft emergencies. **Oficinas Para La Seguridad del Turista** (☎ 91/800/9–03–92) operates a 24-hour toll-free hot line to provide legal and medical help for tourists in Veracruz. **Police** (✉ Playa Linda 222, ☎ 29/38–06–64 or 29/38–06–93); **Hospital Regional de Veracruz** (✉ 20 de Noviembre s/n, ☎ 29/32–27–05 or 29/32–36–90); **Cruz Roja** (☎ 29/37–55–00).

Pharmacies

Calle Enríquez is lined with pharmacies. For 24-hour service, the **Farmacia Plus** (✉ Revolución 171 at Sagayo, ☎ 28/18–09–35) is your best option.

Farmacia Médico (✉ Gutierrez Zamora 3, ☎ 784/2–19–41), open daily 7:30 AM–10 PM, is the largest pharmacy in town.

Benavides (✉ Independencia 1291 at Serdán ☎ 29/31–89–29) is a big, convenient drugstore downtown, but it closes at 10 PM daily. For 24-hour service, try **Farmacia Mercado Bravo** (✉ Independencia 1197, ☎ 29/31–08–83).

Guided Tours

Expediciones Mexico Verde (✉ José M. Vigil 2406, Colonia Italia Providencia, Guadalajara, Jal. 44610, ☎ 3/641–09–93, 641–55–98, or 91–800/36–288) offers river rafting for individuals or groups along the Río Pescados near Jalapa; one-day or overnight excursions are available. All equipment, including life jackets, helmets, and oars, is provided. English is spoken.

VERACRUZ

A new ecotourism outfit called **Campamento Jamapa** (✉ Cotaxtla Sur 16, Colonia Petrolero, Boca del Río, ☎ FAX 29/21–15–50), with an all-female staff, offers river rafting, diving, kayaking, sportsfishing, windsurfing, and mountain-biking excursions in the state of Veracruz. The company's private camp along the Jamapa River, 11 kilometers (7 miles) from Boca del Río, provides large tents, a dining room, bar, and hammocks. Night dives, diving instruction, and rental equipment are also available at the camp. Most of the staff speaks English.

Boat tours of the bay depart from the malecón daily 7–7. Boats leave whenever they're full, and the $2.50 half-hour ride includes a (Spanish-language) talk on Veracruz history. Longer trips to nearby **Isla Verde** (Green Island) and **Isla de Enmedio** (Middle Island) leave daily from the shack marked PASEO EN LANCHITA near the Plaza Acuario. Again, boats wait until they're full to set off, so it's best to be in a group. The cost should be about $3–$5 per person, but feel free to bargain.

Operadora Terrestre de Veracruz (✉ Pedro de Alvarado 223, Fracc. Reforma, ☎ 29/37–66–19 or 29/37–06–61) offers city tours as well as tours of Tajín and Papantla, Los Tuxtlas, and Jalapa. Diving and fishing trips are available, too. There are also travel desks at the Torremar, Emporio, Continental Plaza, and Fiesta Americana hotels.

Intercontinental Adventures (✉ Georgia 120, Suite 9A, Colonia Napoles, Mexico, D.F. 03810, ☎ 5/536–3700 or FAX 5/69–0086; in the U.S., 800/382–3249) is the exclusive operator for the new 7- or 10-day Cortes Route tour, which includes Veracruz City, Antigua, Cempoala, Jalapa, and Coatepec in the state of Veracruz and continues on to conquistador-related sites in the states of Tlaxcala, Puebla, and Mexico. The company also runs river-rafting excursions to the Río Pescados near Jalapa.

Visitor Information

The **Jalapa tourist office** (✉ Blvd. Cristóbal Colón 5, Jardines de las Animas on main square, ☎ 28/12–85–00, ext. 126 or 127) is open weekdays 9–9.

The **Papantla tourist office** (✉ Palacio Municipal on zócalo, ☎ 784/2–01–77) is open weekdays 9–3, Saturday 9–1.

The **Tuxpán tourist office** (✉ Av. Juárez 65, ☎ 783/4–01–77) is open daily 10–3 and 5–7.

The **Veracruz Dirección Municipal de Turismo** (✉ Palacio Municipal on zócalo, ☎ 29/32–19–99) is open Monday–Saturday 9–9, Sunday 3–9.

13 The Yucatán Peninsula

Mexico's most visited region, the Yucatán has something for everyone: the high-profile sparkle of Cancún; the spectacular snorkeling of Cozumel; the laid-back beachcombing of Isla Mujeres; the fascinating Spanish-Maya mix of Mérida; and the evocative Maya ruins of Tulum, Chichén Itzá, and Uxmal. The region is an ecotourist's dream, too, from the huge Sian Ka'an Biosphere Reserve on the Caribbean Coast to Río Lagartos National Park on the Gulf of Mexico, migration ground for thousands of flamingos and other birds.

WHEN ASKED what attracts them to Mexico, most visitors will mention beaches and ruins—and some of the best of each are found on the Yucatán Peninsula.

Yucatán comprises Mexico's most popular tourist destination, Cancún, and some of the country's most celebrated ruins, the pre-Columbian cities of the Maya. Although much of the peninsula is vast, scrubby desert—"one living rock," as an early Spanish priest put it—with a smattering of jungles and hills, its eastern coastline on the clear, turquoise waters of the Caribbean has superb natural endowments. In addition to a semitropical climate, the Caribbean coast offers unbroken stretches of beach and the world's fifth-longest barrier reef, which lies just off the island of Cozumel. Also part of the Yucatán is the diminutive Isla Mujeres (Isle of Women) and, on the west side of the peninsula, Mérida, a city that deserves more tourists than it gets. Mérida was one of the first cities built by the Spaniards, and it retains its colonial ambience and charm.

The peninsula's spectrum of attractions is matched by an equal range of accommodations, from the never-leave-the-site resorts of Cancún to more modest properties near the ruins and humble but adequate beach shacks. Yucatán therefore appeals to travelers of all budgets and inclinations, from package tour–takers to backpackers and travelers who prefer to rent a car. It offers bird-watching, water sports, archaeology, handicrafts, and the savory Yucatecan cuisine. Above all, however, there are the *Yucatecos* themselves: Veteran travelers to Mexico often remark on the openness and friendliness of these people, who, like their Maya ancestors, are short and swarthy, with prominent cheekbones and aquiline noses.

The peninsula encompasses the states of Yucatán, Campeche, Quintana Roo (until 1974 a Mexican territory), Belize, and a part of Guatemala and covers 113,000 square kilometers (43,630 square miles). International airports at Cancún and Cozumel provide nonstop service from several North American cities; the Mérida airport handles primarily domestic flights. Cruise ships call at Cozumel and Playa del Carmen, and other harbor facilities are being developed at Progreso on the north coast off the Gulf of Mexico.

PLEASURES AND PASTIMES

Beaches

Cancún and the rest of Yucatán offer a wonderful variety of beaches: Those who thrive on the resort atmosphere will probably enjoy Playa Chac Mool and Playa Tortugas on the bay side of Cancún, which is calmer, if less beautiful than, the windward side. On the north end of Isla Mujeres, Playa Cocoteros and Playa Norte offer handsome sunset vistas. Beaches on the relatively sheltered leeward side of Cozumel are wide and sandy. The Caribbean Coast abounds with hidden and not-so-hidden beaches (at Xcaret, Paamul, Chemuyil, Xcacel, Punta Bete, south of Tulum, and along the Boca Paila peninsula). There are also long stretches of white sand, usually filled with sunbathers, at Puerto Morelos, Playa del Carmen, and especially Akumal. Travelers to Campeche and Progreso will find the waters of the Gulf of Mexico deep green, shallow, and tranquil.

Bird-Watching

The Yucatán Peninsula is one of the finest areas for birding in Mexico. Habitats range from wildlife and bird sanctuaries to unmarked lagoons, estuaries, and mangrove swamps. Frigates, tanagers, warblers, and macaws inhabit Isla Contoy (off Isla Mujeres) and the Laguna Colombia on Cozumel; an even greater variety of species are to be found in the Sian Ka'an Biosphere Reserve on the Boca Paila peninsula south of Tulum. Along the north and west coasts of Yucatán—at Río Lagartos, Laguna Rosada, and Celestún—flamingos, herons, ibis, cormorants, pelicans, and peregrine falcons thrive.

Dining

The mystique of Yucatecan cooking has a lot to do with the generous doses of local spices and herbs, although generally the food tends not to be too spicy. Among the specialties are *cochinita píbil* and *pollo píbil* (succulent pork or chicken baked in banana leaves with a spicy, pumpkin-seed-and-chile sauce); *poc chuc* (Yucatecan pork marinated in the same sour-orange sauce with pickled onions); *tikinchic* (fried fish prepared with sour orange); *panuchos* (fried tortillas filled with black beans and topped with turkey, chicken, or pork, pickled onions, and avocado); *papadzules* (tortillas piled high with hard-boiled eggs and drenched in a sauce of pumpkin seed and fried tomato); and *codzitos* (rolled tortillas in pumpkin-seed sauce). *Achiote* (annatto), cilantro (coriander), and the fiery *chile habanero* are heavily favored condiments.

The following price categories apply everywhere outside of Cancún and Cozumel, which are more expensive than the rest of the destinations in the Yucatán and for which we have included separate price charts.

CATEGORY	COST*
$$$$	over $20
$$$	$15–$20
$$	$8–$15
$	under $8

per person, excluding drinks and service

Fishing

Sport fishing is popular in Cozumel and throughout the Caribbean Coast. The rich waters of the Caribbean and the Gulf of Mexico support hundreds of species of tropical fish, making the Yucatán coastline and the outlying islands a paradise for deep-sea fishing, fly-fishing, and bonefishing. Particularly between the months of April and July, the waters off Cancún, Cozumel, and Isla Mujeres teem with sailfish, marlin, red snapper, tuna, barracuda, and wahoo, among other denizens of the deep. Bill fishing is so rich around Cozumel and Puerto Aventuras that each holds an annual tournament.

Farther south, along the Boca Paila peninsula, banana fish, bonefish, mojarra, shad, permit, and sea bass provide great sport for flat fishing and fly-fishing, while oysters, shrimp, and conch lie on the bottom of the Gulf of Mexico near Campeche and Isla del Carmen. At Progreso, on the north coast, sport fishing for grouper, dogfish, and pompano is quite popular.

Lodging

Accommodations in the Yucatán range from the ultraglitzy megaresorts of Cancún to the charming colonial mansions in Mérida and the rustic but characterful lodgings near the ruins. The following price categories apply everywhere outside of Cancún and Cozumel, which are more expensive than the rest of the destinations in the Yucatán and for which we have included separate price charts.

The best places to travel may be the best places to get hepatitis A.

You can pick up hepatitis A when traveling to high-risk areas outside of the United States. From raw shellfish or water you don't think is contaminated. Or from uncooked foods — like salad — prepared by people who don't know they're infected. At even the best places.

Symptoms of hepatitis A include jaundice, abdominal pain, fever, vomiting and diarrhea. And can cause discomfort, time away from work and memories you'd like to forget.

The U.S. Centers for Disease Control and Prevention (CDC) recommends immunization for travelers to high-risk areas. *Havrix*, available in over 45 countries, can protect you from hepatitis A. *Havrix* may cause some soreness in your arm or a slight headache.

Ask your physician about vaccination with *Havrix* at your next visit or at least 2 weeks before you travel. And have a great trip.

Please see important patient information adjacent to this ad.

Havrix®
Hepatitis A Vaccine, Inactivated

The world's first hepatitis A vaccine

For more information on how to protect yourself against hepatitis A, call

1-800-HEP-A-VAX (1-800-437-2829)

Manufactured by
SmithKline Beecham Biologicals
Rixensart, Belgium

Distributed by
SmithKline Beecham Pharmaceuticals
Philadelphia, PA 19101

HA8590   © SmithKline Beecham, 1996

Havrix is a registered trademark of SmithKline Beecham.

Hepatitis A Vaccine, Inactivated
Havrix®

See complete prescribing information in SmithKline Beecham Pharmaceuticals literature. The following is a brief summary.

INDICATIONS AND USAGE: *Havrix* is indicated for active immunization of persons ≥ 2 years of age against disease caused by hepatitis A virus (HAV).

CONTRAINDICATIONS: *Havrix* is contraindicated in people with known hypersensitivity to any component of the vaccine.

WARNINGS: Do not give additional injections to patients experiencing hypersensitivity reactions after a *Havrix* injection. (See CONTRAINDICATIONS.)

Hepatitis A has a relatively long incubation period. Hepatitis A vaccine may not prevent hepatitis A infection in those who have an unrecognized hepatitis A infection at the time of vaccination. Additionally, it may not prevent infection in those who do not achieve protective antibody titers (although the lowest titer needed to confer protection has not been determined).

PRECAUTIONS: As with any parenteral vaccine (1) keep epinephrine available for use in case of anaphylaxis or anaphylactoid reaction; (2) delay administration, if possible, in people with any febrile illness or active infection, except when the physican believes withholding vaccine entails the greater risk; (3) take all known precautions to prevent adverse reactions, including reviewing patients' history for hypersensitivity to this or similar vaccines.

Administer with caution to people with thrombocytopenia or a bleeding disorder, or people taking anticoagulants. Do not inject into a blood vessel. Use a separate, sterile needle or prefilled syringe for every patient. When giving concomitantly with other vaccines or IG, use separate needles and different injection sites.

As with any vaccine, if administered to immunosuppressed persons or persons receiving immunosuppressive therapy, the expected immune response may not be obtained.

Carcinogenesis, Mutagenesis, Impairment of Fertility: *Havrix* has not been evaluated for its carcinogenic potential, mutagenic potential or potential for impairment of fertility.

Pregnancy Category C: Animal reproduction studies have not been conducted with *Havrix*. It is also not known whether *Havrix* can cause fetal harm when administered to a pregnant woman or can affect reproduction capacity. Give *Havrix* to a pregnant woman only if clearly needed. It is not known whether *Havrix* is excreted in human milk. Because many drugs are excreted in human milk, use caution when administering *Havrix* to a nursing woman.

Havrix is well tolerated and highly immunogenic and effective in children.

Fully inform patients, parents or guardians of the benefits and risks of immunization with *Havrix*. For persons traveling to endemic or epidemic areas, consult current CDC advisories regarding specific locales. Travelers should take all necessary precautions to avoid contact with, or ingestion of, contaminated food or water. Duration of immunity following a complete vaccination schedule has not been established.

ADVERSE REACTIONS: *Havrix* has been generally well tolerated. As with all pharmaceuticals, however, it is possible that expanded commercial use of the vaccine could reveal rare adverse events.

The most frequently reported by volunteers in clinical trials was injection-site soreness (56% of adults; 21% of children); headache (14% of adults; less than 9% of children). Other solicited and unsolicited events are listed below:

Incidence 1% to 10% of Injections: Induration, redness, swelling; fatigue, fever (>37.5°C), malaise; anorexia, nausea.

Incidence <1% of Injections: Hematoma; pruritus, rash, urticaria; pharyngitis, other upper respiratory tract infections; abdominal pain, diarrhea, dysgeusia, vomiting; arthralgia, elevation of creatine phosphokinase, myalgia; lymphadenopathy; hypertonic episode, insomnia, photophobia, vertigo.

Additional safety data
Safety data were obtained from two additional sources in which large populations were vaccinated. In an outbreak setting in which 4,930 individuals were immunized with a single dose of either 720 EL.U. or 1440 EL.U. of *Havrix*, the vaccine was well-tolerated and no serious adverse events due to vaccination were reported. Overall, less than 10% of vaccinees reported solicited general adverse events following the vaccine. The most common solicited local adverse event was pain at the injection site, reported in 22.3% of subjects at 24 hours and decreasing to 2.4% by 72 hours.

In a field efficacy trial, 19,037 children received the 360 EL.U. dose of *Havrix*. The most commonly reported adverse events were injection-site pain (9.5%) and tenderness (8.1%), reported following first doses of *Havrix*. Other adverse events were infrequent and comparable to the control vaccine Engerix-B® (Hepatitis B Vaccine, Recombinant).

Postmarketing Reports: Rare voluntary reports of adverse events in people receiving *Havrix* since market introduction include the following: localized edema; anaphylaxis/anaphylactoid reactions, somnolence; syncope; jaundice, hepatitis; erythema multiforme, hyperhydrosis, angioedema; dyspnea; lymphadenopathy; convulsions, encephalopathy, dizziness, neuropathy, myelitis, paresthesia, Guillain-Barré syndrome, multiple sclerosis; congenital abnormality.

The U.S. Department of Health and Human Services has established the Vaccine Adverse Events Reporting System (VAERS) to accept reports of suspected adverse events after the administration of any vaccine, including, but not limited to, the reporting of events required by the National Childhood Vaccine Injury Act of 1986. The toll-free number for VAERS forms and information is 1-800-822-7967.

HOW SUPPLIED: 360 EL.U./0.5 mL: NDC 58160-836-01 Package of 1 single-dose vial.

720 EL.U./0.5 mL: NDC 58160-837-01 Package of 1 single-dose vial; NDC 58160-837-02 Package of 1 prefilled syringe.

1440 EL.U./mL: NDC 58160-835-01 Package of 1 single-dose vial; NDC 58160-835-02 Package of 1 prefilled syringe.

Manufactured by **SmithKline Beecham Biologicals**
Rixensart, Belgium
Distributed by **SmithKline Beecham Pharmaceuticals**
Philadelphia, PA 19101
BRS–HA:L5A

Havrix is a registered trademark of SmithKline Beecham.

CATEGORY	COST*
$$$$	over $90
$$$	$60–$90
$$	$25–$60
$	under $25

All prices are for a standard double room in the high season, excluding service charges and tax.

Ruins

Amateur archaeologists will find heaven in the Yucatán, where the ancient Maya most abundantly left their mark. Pick your period and your preference, whether for well-excavated sites or overgrown, out-of-the-way ruins barely touched by a scholar's shovel. The major Maya sites are Cobá and Tulum on the Caribbean Coast and Chichén Itzá and Uxmal in the state of Yucatán, but smaller ruins scattered throughout the peninsula are often equally fascinating.

Scuba Diving and Snorkeling

Underwater enthusiasts come to Cozumel, Akumal, Xcalak, Xel-Ha, and other parts of Mexico's Caribbean Coast for the clear turquoise waters, the colorful and assorted tropical fish, and the exquisite coral formations along the Belize reef system. Currents allow for drift diving, and both reefs and offshore wrecks lend themselves to dives, many of which are safe enough for neophytes. The peninsula's cenotes, or natural sinkholes, provide an unusual dive experience.

Water Sports

All manner of water sports—jet skiing, catamaran sailing, sailboarding, waterskiing, sailing, and parasailing—are practiced in Cancún, Cozumel, and along the Caribbean Coast, where you'll find well-equipped water-sports centers.

When to Tour the Yucatán Peninsula

Thousands of visitors swarm to Chichén Itzá for the vernal equinox (the first day of spring) to witness the astronomical phenomenon that makes a shadow resembling a snake—which represented the plumed serpent god Kukulcán—appear on the side of the main pyramid. The phenomenon also occurs on the first day of fall, but the rainy weather typical at that time of year tends to discourage visitors. Both the capital and outlying villages of Campeche state, with their predominantly Maya population, celebrate the Day of the Dead (November 1 and 2) with special fervor because it corresponds to a similar observance in ancient Maya tradition.

High season in the states of Yucatan and Campeche generally corresponds to high season in the rest of Mexico: the Christmas period, Easter week, and the month of August. Rainfall is heaviest between May and October, bringing with it an uncomfortable humidity. On the Caribbean Coast, including Cancún, Cozumel, and Isla Mujeres, the peak tourist times are mid-December–late March. In the less visited towns, levels of service differ drastically between the high and low seasons (when staff and activities may be cut back), so you should be prepared for a trade-off.

Great Itineraries

Most people who travel to the major beach-resort destinations of Cancún and Cozumel tend to settle in for their entire stay, perhaps taking side trips to the ruins of Tulum or Chichén Itzá and to Xcaret, a man-made theme park that re-creates the Yucatecan landscape. Those who want to try two distinct types of beach experiences might divide their time between the higher-profile (and more expensive) Cancún and laid-back Isla Mujeres. The following itineraries are designed for those who want to keep on the move and have based themselves either in one of the Caribbean Coast towns or in Mérida. The former is ideal for the watersports oriented, the latter for lovers of the ancient Maya civilization.

IF YOU HAVE 3 DAYS

If you want to base yourself on the Caribbean Coast, get a room in Playa del Carmen and start out by visiting **Tulum** to view the cliffside Castillo temple; afterward, climb down to the small beach alongside it for a dip in the ocean. Day 2, head out to the cenote at **Xel-Ha**, where you can snorkel, swim, or sunbathe. Follow this with a visit to the CEDAM museum at **Puerto Aventuras,** full of displays salvaged from old shipwrecks. Day 3, head for **Akumal** for a diving or deep-sea fishing excursion, snorkeling or swimming; later in the day visit the tiny lagoons of **Xpuhá** and **Yalkú,** which were around during the time of the Maya traders.

An alternative is to spend two days in Mérida, savoring the city's unique character as you make your way among the historic churches and mansions and enjoy the parks and restaurants. You can easily devote a full day to exploring the heart of downtown, including the **Parque Principal** and its surrounding buildings, the **Casa de Montejo, Palacio Municipal,** and the **Catedral.** Take a second, more leisurely day to visit the Museum of Anthropology and History in the **Palacio Cantón** and, perhaps, the **Museo de Arte Popular** or the **El Centenario Zoo.** On the third day, drive or take a tour to one of Yucatán's most famous Maya ruins—either **Chichén Itzá** or **Uxmal.** Each is within about two hours of Mérida, making for an ideal day trip.

IF YOU HAVE 7 DAYS

Again basing yourself in Playa del Carmen, visit Tulum on the first day, and then spend Day 2 touring **Xcaret,** an ecological theme park where you can swim with dolphins, snorkel in a cenote, and take in a Mexican rodeo show. Day 3, start the morning at the archaeological ruins of **Cobá** and spend the afternoon at **Xel-Ha** cooling off in the water. Day 4, head for Akumal and its water sports. Day 5, sign up for a tour of the **Sian Ka'an biosphere.** On Day 6, drive to the enormous **Bacalar Lagoon** to marvel at its transparent layers of turquoise, green, and blue waters (it should take about three hours if you drive straight through); visit the colonial San Felipe Fortress in the village of **Bacalar** and overnight in **Chetumal.** On Day 7, head out early for **Kohunlich,** which has a huge stucco mask of the Maya sun god surrounded by jungle ruins. Then head back up the coast to Playa del Carmen, stopping at the **Cenote Azul,** the largest sinkhole in Mexico; at the town of **Felipe Carrillo Puerto,** where you can get a taste of old Maya culture; and finally at **Chunyaxché,** with its pretty Maya temple.

Those with a week in the Mérida area should first explore the sights of the city and then take two separate overnight excursions. Spend the night at one of the archaeological hotels near **Uxmal,** and the next day explore the Ruta Puuc, the series of lost cities south of Uxmal that includes **Kaba, Sayil,** and **Labná,** as well as the fascinating **Loltún Cave.** On the second excursion, to **Chichén Itzá,** allow as much as a full day en route to explore some of the present-day Maya villages along the way, especially **Izamal.** After visiting Chichén Itzá, you may wish to beat the afternoon heat by exploring the **Cave of Balankinché** or swimming in one of the cool subterranean cenotes nearby; you might also head north from **Valladolid** to see to see the flamingo nesting grounds at **Río Lagartos National Park.**

IF YOU HAVE 10 DAYS

Those who have a longer time to spend in this area might want to continue on from Mérida to **Campeche City.** After spending a day exploring the city's sights—almost all those of interest to visitors are located within the compact historical district—head inland the next morning to visit **Edzná,** a magnificently restored ceremonial center an hour's drive from the city. Return to your Campeche City hotel—accommodations are crude or nonexistent in the area—and set out the next day to the **Hopelchén** region, beyond Edzná, where you can explore the little-known Maya temples at **Hochob** and **Dzibilnocac,** as well as **Bolonchén de Rejón,** one of the large cave systems on the peninsula.

CANCÚN

Updated by
Gloria
McDarrah

The jewel of Mexico's Caribbean Coast, Cancún is for those who want dazzle for their dollar: The hotel zone is lined with high-rise lodgings, glitzy discos, air-conditioned malls, and gorgeous beaches. For a glimpse of the real Mexico, go downtown, where Yucatecan specialties are served at casual eateries.

Flying into Cancún, Mexico's most popular destination, all you see are green treetops for miles. It's clear from the air that this resort was carved out of the jungle. When development began here in 1974, the beaches were deserted except for their iguana inhabitants. Now, luxury hotels line the oceanfront, and nearly 2 million visitors a year come for the white sand beaches and crystalline Caribbean waters. They also come for the sizzling nightlife and, in some cases, for proximity to the Yucatán ruins. Although the resort is too glitzy and tourist-oriented for many, it draws thousands of repeat visitors.

Cancún City is on the mainland, but the hotel zone is on a 22½-kilometer (14-mile) barrier island off the Yucatán peninsula. The resort is designed to please American tastes; most people speak English, and devotees of cable TV and Pizza Hut will not be disappointed. Beach lovers can bask in Cancún's year-round tropical warmth and sunny skies. The sun shines an average of 240 days a year, reputedly more than at almost any other Caribbean spot. Temperatures linger appealingly at about 80°F. You can sample Yucatecan foods and watch folkloric dance demonstrations as well as knock back tequila slammers at the myriad nightspots.

But there can be more to the resort than plopping down under a *palapa* (pre-Hispanic thatched roof). For divers and snorkelers, the reefs off Cancún, nearby Cozumel, and Isla Mujeres are among the best in the world. Cancún also provides a relaxing home base for visiting the stupendous ruins of Chichén Itzá, Tulum, and Cobá on the mainland—remnants of the area's rich Maya heritage—as well as the Yucatán coast and its lagoons.

Cancún has gone through the life cycle typical of any tourist destination. At its inception, the resort drew the jet set; lately, it has attracted increasing numbers of less affluent tourists, primarily package-tour takers and college students, particularly during spring break, when hordes of flawless, tanned young bodies people the beaches and restaurants.

As for the island's history, not much was written about it before its birth as a resort. The island does not appear on the early navigators' maps and little is known about the Maya who lived here; apparently Cancún's marshy terrain discouraged development. It is recorded that Maya settled the area during the pre-classical era, in about AD 200, and remained until about the 14th or 15th century. In the mid-19th century minor Maya ruins were sighted; however, they were not studied by archaeologists until the 1950s and mid-1970s. In 1970 then-President Luis Echeverría first visited the site that had been chosen to retrieve the state of Quintana Roo from obscurity and abject poverty.

Exploring

Cancún is divided into two zones: the hotel zone, which is shaped roughly like the numeral 7, and Cancún City or downtown Cancún, known as *el centro*, 4 kilometers (2½ miles) west of the hotel zone on the mainland.

Paseo Kukulcán is the main drag in the hotel zone, and because most of the 7 is less than a kilometer wide, both the Caribbean and the lagoons can be seen from either side of it. The hotel zone consists entirely of hotels, restaurants and shopping complexes, marinas, and time-share condominiums; there are no residential areas as such. The lagoon side of the boulevard consists of scrubby stretches of land, many of them covered with construction cranes, alternating with marinas, shopping centers, and restaurants.

A Good Tour
Numbers in the text correspond to numbers in the margin and on the Cancun map.

Cancún's scenery consists mostly of its beautiful beaches and crystal-clear waters, but there are also a few intriguing historical sites tucked away among the modern hotels. In addition to the attractions listed below, two modest vestiges of the ancient Maya civilization are worth a visit only for dedicated archaeology buffs. Neither is identified by name. On the 12th hole of Pok-Ta-Pok golf course (⊠ Paseo Kukulkán, between Km 6 and Km 7), whose Maya name means "ball game," stands a ruin consisting of two platforms and the remains of other buildings. And the ruin of a tiny Maya shrine is cleverly incorporated into the architecture of the Hotel Camino Real (on the beach at Punta Cancún).

You don't need a car in Cancún, but if you've rented one to make extended trips, it might be worth starting in the southern hotel zone at **Ruinas del Rey** ① and **San Miguelito** ②, driving north to **Yamil Lu'um** ③ and then stopping in at the **convention center** ④ before heading west to **downtown** ⑤.

Sights to See

④ Cancún Convention Center. This strikingly modern venue for cultural events is the jumping-off point for a ½-mile-long string of shopping malls that extend west to the Hotel Presidente. In the convention center complex itself, **Inter Plaza** contains 15 restaurants, 21 boutiques, a bank, and several airline offices. ⊠ *Paseo Kukulcán Km 9,* ☎ *98/830199.*

The **National Institute of Anthropology and History,** the small museum on the ground floor of the convention center, traces Maya culture by showcasing a fascinating collection of 1,000- to 1,500-year-old artifacts collected throughout Quintana Roo. ☎ *98/830305.* ⊠ *About $3; free Sun.* ☉ *Tues.–Sun. 9 AM–7 PM. Guided tours available in English, French, German, and Spanish.*

⑤ Downtown Cancún. The main thoroughfare is Avenida Tulum, which begins at the spot where Paseo Kukulcán turns into Avenida Cobá. Many restaurants and shops are located along here, as is Ki Huic, the largest crafts market in Cancún. Life-size reproductions of ancient Mexican art, including the Aztec calendar stone, a giant Olmec head, the Atlantids of Tula, and the Maya chac mool (reclining rain god), line the grassy strip dividing Tulum's northbound and southbound lanes. Vis-

Cancún

itors looking for shopping bargains, however, generally find better prices if they stick to the parallel Avenida Yaxchilán.

❶ Ruinas del Rey. Located on the lagoon side at Cancún Island, roughly opposite El Pueblito and Playa de Oro, these small ruins have been incorporated into the Caesar Park Resort complex; large signs point out the site. Del Rey may not be particularly impressive when compared to major archaeological sites such as Tulum or Chichén Itzá, but it is the largest ruin in Cancún and definitely worth a look. Skeletons found buried both at the apex and at the base indicate that the site may have been a royal burial ground. ⌧ *Paseo Kukulkán Km 17. No phone.* ⌧ *About $3; free Sun.* ☯ *Daily 8 AM–5 PM.*

❷ San Miguelito. On the east side of Paseo Kukulcán is a very small stone building (about the size of a shack) with a number of columns about 4 feet high. At press time, this modest Maya site was fenced off and not accessible to the public, but this may change after archaeologists have fully examined the ruins. ⊠ *Paseo Kukulkán Km 16.5. No phone.*

❸ Yamil Lu'um. A small sign at the Sheraton will direct you to the dirt path leading to this site, which stands on the highest point of Cancún adjoining the hotel—the words "Yamil Lu'um" mean hilly land. Although it comprises two structures—one probably a temple, the other probably a lighthouse—this is the smallest of Cancún's ruins. Discovered in 1842 by John Lloyd Stephens, the remains date from the late-13th or early-14th century. ⊠ *Paseo Kukulkán Km 12. No phone.*

Dining

At last count, there were more than 1,200 restaurants in Cancún, but—according to one profiting restaurateur—only about 100 are worth their salt, so to speak. Finding the right restaurant in Cancún is not easy. The downtown restaurants that line the noisy Avenida Tulum often have tables spilling onto pedestrian-laden sidewalks; however, gas fumes and gawking tourists tend to detract from the romantic outdoor-café ambience. Many of the hotel-zone restaurants, on the other hand, cater to what they assume is a tourist preference for bland, not-too-foreign-tasting food.

One key to good dining in Cancún is to find the haunts—mostly in the downtown area—where locals go for Yucatán-style food prepared by the experts. A cheap and filling trend in Cancún's dining scene is the sumptuous buffet breakfasts offered by an increasing number of restaurants and hotels on the island. Another hint: Many $$$$ and $$$ restaurants feature floor shows during peak months (mid-December–late March). Usually there are two seatings nightly, each including entertainment and dinner; reservations are advised, since the shows draw crowds.

Generally speaking, dress is casual here, but many restaurants will not admit diners with bare feet, short shorts, or no shirts.

CATEGORY	COST*
$$$$	over $35
$$$	$25–$35
$$	$15–$25
$	under $15

per person, excluding drinks and service

Hotel Zone

Hotel-zone restaurants are located on the Cancún Hotel Zone Dining and Lodging map.

$$$$ ✕ Bogart's. Whether you consider it amusingly elaborate or merely pretentious, it's hard to be neutral about Bogart's, probably the most expensive and talked-about restaurant in town. Taking off from the film *Casablanca*, the place is decorated with Persian rugs, fans, velvet-cushioned banquettes, and fountains. A menu as eclectic as the patrons of Rick's Cafe features many seafood and Mediterranean dishes. The food is okay, but don't expect large portions; servings are nouvelle style. ⊠ *Paseo Kukulcán, Hotel Krystal,* ☎ *98/831133. Reservations essential; seatings at 6:30 and 9:30. AE, DC, MC, V. No lunch.*

$$$$ ✕ Club Grill. Another prime choice for that romantic, special-occasion ★ dinner, the Ritz-Carlton's fine dining room is divided into intimate chambers; one of them has a dance floor and a small stage for live music in the evening. Tall windows look out onto a bubbling courtyard fountain and the Caribbean beyond. European grill is the house specialty; rich sauces and decorative touches give a distinctly Mexican spin to

Dining

Bogart's, **9**
Captain's Cove, **2, 17**
Carlos 'n Charlie's, **3**
Casa Rolandi, **6**
Club Grill, **13**
Hacienda El
Mortero, **9**
La Dolce Vita, **15**
Lorenzilbs, **10**
100% Natural, **5, 11**
Splash, **11**

Lodging

Caesar Park Beach &
Golf Resort, **18**
Calinda Viva
Cancún, **4**
Casa Turquesa, **12**
Club Las Velas, **1**
El Pueblito Beach
Hotel, **19**
Fiesta Americana Coral
Beach Cancún, **7**
Hyatt Regency
Cancún, **8**
Marriott Casa
Magna, **14**
Meliá Cancún, **16**
Ritz-Carlton
Cancún, **13**
Westin Regina Resort
Cancún, **20**

Cancún Hotel Zone Dining and Lodging

the grilled chops, steaks, chicken, and seafood. Service is attentive and discreet. ✉ *Paseo Kukulcán (Retorno del Rey 36),* ☎ *98/850808. AE, DC, MC, V.*

$$$ ✕ **Hacienda El Mortero.** Pampering waiters, strolling mariachis, lush hanging plants, fig trees, and candlelight make this reproduction plantation home a very popular spot to dine. The menu offers a selection of country cooking, and the chicken fajitas and rib steaks are first class. ✉ *Paseo Kukulcán, Hotel Krystal,* ☎ *98/831133. Reservations essential for 6:30 and 9:30 seatings. AE, DC, MC, V. No lunch.*

$$$ ✕ **La Dolce Vita.** Over the past decade, this appealing restaurant de-
★ veloped a strong and well-deserved local following at its original downtown location on Avenida Cobá. In its new (1996) incarnation in the hotel zone, across from the Marriott CasaMagna and overlooking Laguna Nichupté, La Dolce Vita has maintained its romantic atmosphere, while almost doubling its space. Favorites from the excellent Northern Italian and Continental menu include seafood antipasto, boquinete dolce vita (a local white fish stuffed with shrimp and mushrooms and baked in puff pastry), and creamy tiramisù. ✉ *Paseo Kukulkán, Km 14.5,* ☎ *98/850150 or 850161. AE, MC, V. No weekend lunch.*

$$ ✕ **Captain's Cove.** Both waterfront locations feature popular breakfast buffets served under palapa roofs. The decor is decidedly nautical, with rigging draped on the walls and chandeliers in the shape of ships' steering wheels. The restaurant near the Casa Maya Hotel overlooks the Caribbean Sea toward Isla Mujeres; the other is situated beside the Nichupté Lagoon. Both present lunch and dinner menus filled with seafood dishes and charbroiled steak and chicken. Parents appreciate the lower-priced children's menu, an unusual feature in Cancún. ✉ *Paseo Kukulcán, Km 16.5, lagoon-side across from Royal Mayan Hotel,* ☎ *98/850016; beach-side next to Casa Maya Hotel,* ☎ *98/830669. Reservations not accepted. AE, MC, V.*

$$ ✕ **Carlos 'n Charlie's.** A lively atmosphere, a terrific view of the lagoon, and good food make this restaurant—part of the popular Anderson chain—Cancún's best-known hot spot. You'll never run out of bric-a-brac to look at: Sombreros, bird cages, and wooden birds and animals hang from the ceilings. Try the barbecued ribs sizzling on the open grill, or one of the steak or seafood specials. After your meal, dance off the calories under the stars at the Pier Dance Club. ✉ *Paseo Kukulcán, Km 5.5,* ☎ *98/830846. Reservations not accepted. AE, MC, V.*

$$ ✕ **Casa Rolandi.** Authentic northern Italian and Swiss dishes are skill-
★ fully prepared by the Italian owner-chef, who grew up near the Swiss border. If it's on the menu, start with the lobster-stuffed black ravioli, and go on to grilled seafood garnished with a zesty olive oil. Alternatively, try the homemade lasagna, baked in the large stucco oven; accompanied by a lavish antipasto bar, it makes for a satisfying dinner. Service is friendly and efficient, and prices surprisingly reasonable for this level of quality cuisine. The decor is appropriately Mediterranean and the back room offers a view of the beach. ✉ *Plaza Caracol,* ☎ *98/831817. AE, MC, V.*

$$ ✕ **Lorenzillos.** Perched on its own peninsula in the lagoon, this nautical spot provides a pleasant place to watch the sun set, sip a drink on the outdoor patio, or sample excellent seafood. Specialties include grilled or broiled lobster (you can pick your own) and whole fish Veracruz-style. The seafaring theme extends to the names of both the dishes (like Jean Lafitte beef) and the restaurant itself (Lorenzillo was a 17th-century pirate). ✉ *Paseo Kukulcán, Km 10.5,* ☎ *98/831254. AE, MC, V.*

$$ ✕ **Splash.** Good-quality Art Deco furnishings, lots of purple and aqua,
★ and neon lights add to the sleek atmosphere of this restaurant. During high season, the outside terrace with its peek-a-boo view of the la-

goon is usually full. Never mind—the inside bar area and dining room are cooler. The downstairs area offers the most intimate dining experience. You can't go wrong with any of the homemade pastas or the charcoal-grilled grouper Bora Bora–style (in a rich sauce of peaches and clarified butter). Splash has great happy-hour specials and all-you-can-eat breakfast, lunch, and dinner deals. ⊠ *Paseo Kukulcán at Kukulcán Plaza,* ☎ 98/853011. *Reservations not accepted. MC, V.*

$ ✕ **100% Natural.** Looking for something light? Head to one of the three locations of this cheery open-air eatery. Identical menus at all of them appeal to vegetarians, with a broad array of soups, salads, and fresh fruit drinks. Egg dishes, sandwiches, grilled chicken and fish, and Mexican and Italian fare are available as well. ⊠ *Paseo Kukulcán at Kukulcán Plaza,* ☎ 98/852904; *Plaza Terramar,* ☎ 98/831180; *Av. Sunyaxche 62,* ☎ 98/843617. *Reservations not accepted. AE, MC, V.*

Downtown

Downtown restaurants are located on the Downtown Cancún Dining and Lodging map.

$$$ ✕ **Bucanero.** Quiet dining in a candlelit marine atmosphere is the drawing card for this seafood restaurant, built to resemble the interior of a Spanish galleon, and the seafood—particularly the lobster specialties—is tops. Heaping servings are enough to feed two (which puts this in the $$ price range if you don't mind sharing your meal). Piano music played throughout the evening and waiters dressed as pirates add character to the place. ⊠ *Av. Cobá 88,* ☎ 98/842280. *AE, MC, V. No lunch.*

$$$ ✕ **La Habichuela.** This charmer—once an elegant home—is perfect for hand-holding romantics or anyone looking for a relaxed, private atmosphere. The candlelit garden, with white, wrought-iron chairs, pebbled ground, and thick, tropical greenery, exudes peacefulness. Try the *cocobichuela*—lobster and shrimp in a light Indian sauce served on a bed of rice inside a coconut—a specialty of the house. ⊠ *Margaritas 25,* ☎ 98/843158. *AE, MC, V. No lunch during low season.*

$$ ✕ **El Pescador.** It's first-come, first-served, with long lines, especially during high season. But people still flood into this rustic Mexican-style restaurant with nautical touches; the open-air patio is particularly popular. Heavy hitters on the menu include red snapper broiled with garlic and freshly caught lobster specials. La Mesa Del Pescador, a newer offshoot in Plaza Kukulcán (☎ 98/850505), is not usually as crowded as this place. ⊠ *Tulipanes 28,* ☎ 98/842673. *Reservations not accepted. AE, MC, V.*

$$ ✕ **La Parrilla.** If you're looking for the place where local Mexicans—young and old—hang out, you've found it in this popular downtown spot, an old classic by Cancún standards (it opened in 1975). Everything from the food to the bougainvillea and palapa roof is authentic. Popular dishes include the grilled beef with garlic sauce and the *tacos al pastor* (tacos with pork, pineapple, coriander, onion, and salsa). ✕ *Av. Yaxchilán 51,* ☎ 98/845398. *Reservations not accepted. AE, MC, V. No lunch. Closed Dec. 25.*

$$ ✕ **Perico's.** Find the antique car perched atop the palapa roof and you've found this zany, eclectic restaurant and bar. Saddles top bar stools, and caricature busts of political figures from Castro to Queen Elizabeth line the walls. The Mexican menu, including Pancho Villa (grilled beef with Mexican side dishes), is reliable, but the real reason to come here is the party atmosphere that begins nightly at 7 when the mariachi and marimba bands play. ⊠ *Av. Yaxchilán 61,* ☎ 98/843152. *Reservations essential for 8 or more. AE, MC, V.*

$$ ✕ **Rosa Mexicano.** One of Cancún's prettiest Mexican colonial–style restaurants presents waiters dressed as *charros* (Mexican cowboys), embroidered wall hangings, and floor tiles with floral designs. For extra

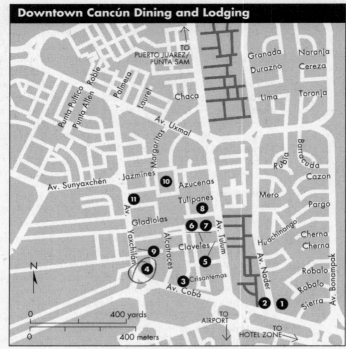

Downtown Cancún Dining and Lodging

romance, make a reservation for the candlelit patio. Specialties include *filete Rosa* (beef and onions in a tequila-orange sauce) and *camarones al ajillo* (shrimp sautéed in olive oil and garlic, with chili peppers). ⊠ *Calle Claveles 4,* ☎ *98/846313. AE, MC, V. No lunch.*

$ ✕ **El Tacolote.** A lively neighborhood *taquería*, El Tacolote has successfully expanded on its original tacos offerings and now serves fajitas, grilled kebabs, and other traditional Mexican favorites. ⊠ *Av. Cobá 19,* ☎ *98/873045. Reservations not accepted. MC, V.*

Lodging

Cancún has a bewildering variety of hotels to choose from. For the most part, those in the downtown area don't offer anything near the luxury or amenities of the hotel-zone properties. They do, however, afford visitors the opportunity to stay in a popular resort without paying resort prices, and many offer free shuttle service to the beach. Expect minibars, satellite TV, laundry and room service, private safes, and bathroom hair dryers in hotels in the $$$$ category; in addition, almost every major hotel has suites, rooms for people with disabilities, and no-smoking rooms, an in-house travel agency and/or a car-rental concession, guest parking, water-sports facilities, and a daily schedule of planned games and activities for guests. Unless otherwise noted, all hotels have air-conditioning and private baths. All Cancún hotels are within the 77500 postal code.

CATEGORY	COST*
$$$$	over $175
$$$	$120–$175
$$	$50–$120
$	under $50

All prices are for a standard double room, excluding the 10% tax.

Hotel Zone

Hotel-zone properties are located on the Cancún Hotel Zone Dining and Lodging map.

$$$$ ▦ **Caesar Park Beach & Golf Resort.** Liberal use of Mérida marble, Mexican tile murals, and colorful oil paintings give this appealing Westin property, one of Cancún's newest luxury resorts, a distinctly Mexican flavor. Rooms, too, carry out the theme, with terra-cotta tile floors, rattan furniture, woven fiber headboards, and local artwork; some have a private balcony with a view of the ocean, and a few let you see the resort's championship 18-hole golf course across Paseo Kukulcán. Lavish interconnecting pools (*seven* of them) and streams wind through palm-dotted lawns; a terraced fountain in the cavernous central atrium brings the dancing water into the hotel's interior. ⊠ *Paseo Kukulcán, Km 17 (Box 1810),* ☎ *98/818000 or 800/228–3000,* ℻ *98/818080. 428 rooms. 3 restaurants, 3 bars, lobby lounge, 7 pools, beauty salon, 2 hot tubs, 2 saunas, 18-hole golf course, 2 tennis courts, aerobics, exercise room, shops, children's programs. AE, DC, MC, V.*

$$$$
★ ▦ **Casa Turquesa.** The tranquil atmosphere of this small, elegant retreat belies its central location next to the bustling Plaza Kukulkán. The public rooms are palatial, with high ceilings, stone bas-reliefs, and marble floors. The 31 spacious suites are decorated individually in pastel tones, with modern furnishings; all have ocean-view private balconies with hot tubs. The privacy and discreet service afforded at this intimate retreat have made it the choice for celebrities such as Ivana Trump and the Planet Hollywood crew. They also enjoy frequenting the aptly named Celebrity restaurant, a subtly lit, romantic spot with a wonderfully creative menu that highlights local seafood. ⊠ *Paseo Kukulkán, Km 13.5,* ☎ *98/852924 or 800/634–4644,* ℻ *98/852922. 31 suites. 2 restaurants, 2 bars, pool, beauty salon, sauna, tennis court, exercise room. AE, MC, V.*

$$$$ ▦ **Fiesta Americana Coral Beach Cancún.** The newest of the Cancún Fiesta properties, this all-suite hotel lies just in front of the convention center and shopping malls. All rooms in the large salmon-colored structure are ample in size, with oceanfront balconies and marble floors; slate-blue, lavender, and beige tones create a soothing, pleasant mood. The hotel's La Joya restaurant, serving nouvelle-style Mexican fare, is a fine spot for dinner. As for outdoor activities, choose between the 1,000-foot beach and the 660-foot pool. This is Cancún's largest convention hotel; expect the clientele and occasional slow service to match. ⊠ *Paseo Kukulcán, Lote 6 (Box 14),* ☎ *98/832900 or 800/FIESTA–1,* ℻ *98/833173. 602 suites. 3 restaurants, 3 bars, pool, 3 tennis courts, health club, shops. AE, DC, MC, V.*

$$$$ ▦ **Marriott CasaMagna.** The six-story Marriott is rather eclectically designed: In the lobby modern furnishings are set in an atrium with Mediterranean-style arches, crystal chandeliers, and hanging vines. The rooms, decorated in contemporary Mexican style, have tile floors and ceiling fans and follow a soft rose, mauve, and earth-tone color scheme. You can learn to prepare Mexican dishes if you attend cooking lessons (one of many guest activities), or you can sit back and watch the chef do the work at Mikado, the hotel's fine Japanese steak house. ⊠ *Paseo Kukulcán (Retorno Chac L-41),* ☎ *98/852000 or 800/228–9290,* ℻ *98/851385. 450 rooms, including 36 suites. 3 restaurants, bar, beauty salon, 2 hot tubs, sauna, health club, 2 tennis courts, shops, nightclub. AE, DC, MC, V.*

$$$$ ▦ **Meliá Cancún.** The Meliá Cancún is a boldly modern version of a Maya temple, fronted by a sheer black marble wall and a sleek waterfall. Public spaces exude elegance; the boutiques could not be more chic. Ivory, dusty-pink, and light-blue hues softly brighten rooms (all with private balcony or terrace); ivory-lacquered furniture and wall-to-wall carpeting create a luxurious ambience. An upscale spa, with modern equipment and an array of body treatments, was added in 1995. The Meliá Turquesa, a 408-room sister property across the street from Flamingo Plaza, is not as glitzy but has a more intimate, friendlier atmosphere. ⊠ *Paseo Kukulcán, Km 16,* ☎ *98/851160 or 800/336–3542,* ℻ *98/851263. 450 rooms. 5 restaurants, 3 bars, 2 pools, spa, 18-hole golf course, 3 tennis courts, health club, 2 paddle tennis courts, shops. AE, DC, MC, V.*

$$$$ ⊞ **Ritz-Carlton Cancún.** This ultraposh, peach-colored property set
★   new standards for luxury and service in Cancún when it opened in 1993. The air-conditioned lobby and public areas are richly appointed with fine European and American antiques, thick carpets, and marble floors. Stylish rooms, done in comfortable shades of blue, beige, and peach, offer all the amenities—wall-to-wall carpeting, travertine marble bathrooms with telephones, separate tub and shower, plush terry robes, and large balconies overlooking the Caribbean. The hotel's elegant restaurants, especially the Club Grill (☞ Dining, *above*) and the newer Fantino (serving northern Italian dinner fare), are standouts. ⊠ *Paseo Kukulcán, Retorno del Rey 36,* ☎ *98/850808 or 800/241–3333,* ℻ *98/851015. 370 rooms, including suites. 3 restaurants, 2 bars, 3 pools, beauty salon, hot tub, men's and women's spas with sauna and steam rooms, 3 tennis courts, health club, pro shop, shops. AE, DC, MC, V.*

$$$$ ⊞ **Westin Regina Resort Cancún.** This luxury property at the southern end of the island, on Punta Nizuc, is one of the few hotels with direct access to both a 1,600-foot beach and Laguna Nichupté. The low-rise, postmodern-style hotel was designed and decorated by one of Latin America's leading architects. From the lobby, you can look down on a stylish restaurant with stunning ocean views. In the spacious guest rooms, handsome rustic furnishings and colorful Mexican folk art stand out against white walls and pale marble floors. Concierge tower rooms are available. ⊠ *Paseo Kukulcán, Km 20 (Box 1808),* ☎ *98/850086, 98/850537, or 800/228–3000;* ℻ *98/850074. 391 rooms. 4 restaurants, 3 bars, 5 pools, hot tub, 5 outdoor hot tubs, 2 tennis courts, exercise room, children's programs. AE, DC, MC, V.*

$$$ ⊞ **Club Las Velas.** Once you go past the wrought-iron gates of this all-
★   inclusive property, you'll be in a delightfully private enclave. The complex is a replica of a Mexican village, complete with central plaza and lush gardens. Nonmotorized water sports, children's programs, and a water taxi to a nearby ocean beach are part of the package. Rooms are light and airy, with white stucco walls, tropical print bedspreads, and rattan furniture, and the duplex villas are especially suited to families. The food—served buffet style at breakfast, and buffet style or à la carte at dinner—is plentiful and good. Nightly theme parties with live entertainment fill the plaza after dinner. ⊠ *Paseo Kukulkán y Galeon,* ☎ *98/832222 or 800/223–9815,* ℻ *98/832118. 285 rooms, including 59 villas. 2 restaurants, snack bar, 2 bars, 2 pools, 2 tennis courts, aerobics, exercise room, children's programs, shops. AE, MC, V.*

$$$ ⊞ **Hyatt Regency Cancún.** A cylindrical 14-story tower with the Hyatt trademark atrium affords a 360° view of the sea and the lagoon. Soothing blue, green, and beige tones prevail in the rooms, which also feature contemporary Mexican furniture and striking green or rose-colored marble vanities. This hotel, much larger and livelier than its sister property, boasts an enormous two-level pool with a waterfall. Cilantro, the hotel's pretty waterfront dining room, has a good breakfast buffet. The hotel is convenient to the convention center and several shopping malls. ⊠ *Paseo Kukulcán (Box 1201),* ☎ *98/830966, 98/831234, or 800/233–1234;* ℻ *98/831349. 300 rooms. 2 restaurants, 3 bars, pool, health club, recreation room. AE, DC, MC, V.*

$$ ⊞ **Calinda Viva Cancún.** This beige stucco eight-story building—part of the Quality hotel chain—is not one of the most attractive in town, but it makes a reliable standby and is in a good location, on the north beach near many malls. The functional, moderate-size rooms have marble floors and contemporary pastel decor; half have private balconies and ocean views. The property also features a small garden, a beach, and a Mexican restaurant. ⊠ *Paseo Kukulcán, Km 8.5 (Box 673),* ☎ *98/830800 or 800/344–5049. 216 rooms. Restaurant, bar, pool, 2 tennis courts, marina, water sports, shop. AE, DC, MC, V.*

$$ ⊞ **El Pueblito Beach Hotel.** El Pueblito, meaning "little town," is an
★ apt name for this property, which consists of clusters of guest rooms in tri-level units that invoke Old Mexico. Interconnecting pathways lined with tropical foliage lead to terrace pools with waterfalls and stone archways; there's even a long water slide for kids. Rooms, which are large for the price, feature marble floors and simple rattan furnishings; a few have kitchenettes. ⊠ *Paseo Kukulcán, Km 17.5,* ☎ *98/850672,* FAX *98/850731. 239 rooms. 3 restaurants, bar, 5 pools, tennis court, shop, travel services. AE, MC, V.*

Downtown

Downtown properties are located on the Downtown Cancún Dining and Lodging map.

$$$ ⊞ **Holiday Inn Centro Cancún.** The place to stay if you want to be down-
★ town and have all the amenities, the upscale Holiday Inn is less expensive than similar properties in the hotel zone and provides free transportation to the beach of the Crown Princess Club. The attractive pink four-story structure, with a Spanish tile roof, affords easy access to restaurants and shops. Although rooms are somewhat generic motel modern, with mauve and blue color schemes, they have appealing Mexican touches. ⊠ *Av. Nader 1, SM 2,* ☎ *98/84455 or 800/HOLIDAY,* FAX *98/847954. 246 rooms. 2 restaurants, 2 bars, pool, beauty salon, tennis court, exercise room, nightclub, coin laundry, travel services, car rental. AE, DC, MC, V.*

$$ ⊞ **Antillano.** This old but prettily appointed property features wood
★ furnishings, a cozy little lobby bar, and a tiny pool. Extras such as tiled bathroom sinks and air-conditioning in the halls and rooms make this hotel stand out a bit from the others in its league. ⊠ *Av. Tulum at Calle Claveles,* ☎ *98/841532 or 98/841132,* FAX *98/841878. 48 rooms. Bar, pool, shop. AE, DC, MC, V.*

$$ ⊞ **Plaza Carrillo's.** One of the first hotels to be built in Cancún City,
★ this one is conveniently located in the heart of the downtown area next to the Plaza Carrillo shopping arcade and Carrillo's restaurant, which are under the same ownership. The hotel corridors are exceptionally clean and well maintained. Rooms are bright, with simple functional decor. ⊠ *Calle Claveles 35,* ☎ *98/841227,* FAX *98/842371. 43 rooms. Restaurant, pool. AE, MC, V.*

$$ ⊞ **Plaza del Sol.** This three-story Spanish colonial–style hotel, a block south of the Margarita Cancún, reopened in 1995 after a floor-to-ceiling renovation. Long popular with students, Europeans, and Canadians, its rooms are done in tasteful tones of brown. A pretty courtyard entrance leads to the reception desk. ⊠ *Av. Yaxchilán 31,* ☎ *98/843888 or 800/446–4656,* FAX *98/849209. 87 rooms. Restaurant, bar, pool. AE, DC, MC, V.*

Nightlife and the Arts

The multistory **Party Center** (⊠ Paseo Kukulcán, Km 9, ☎ 98/830351), next to the convention center, is an entertainment complex that hosts several clubs, a sports bar, and two discos (Tequila Rock and Baja Beach

Club), as well as numerous restaurants, specialty boutiques, and a money exchange. Live folkloric bands perform nightly in the central courtyard, which provides access to the clubs, bars, discos, and restaurants.

Dinner Cruises

A dinner cruise on board the 62-foot vessel *Columbus* (☎ 98/831488 or 98/833268) includes a full lobster or steak spread, open bar, and dancing for $70. The *Cancún Queen* (☎ 98/852288), a paddle wheeler departing from the AquaWorld Marina (✉ Paseo Kukulcán, Km 15.2), runs a similar excursion for $65. **Aqua Tours Adventures** (✉ Paseo Kukulcán, Km 6.25, ☎ 98/830400) offers a pleasantly romantic lobster dinner and sunset cruise to Isla Mujeres that includes dancing under the stars and an open bar.

Discos

Cancún wouldn't be Cancún without its glittering discos, which generally start jumping about 10:30. **Azucar** (✉ Camino Real Hotel, ☎ 98/830100) sizzles to a salsa beat nightly; the beautiful people don't turn up here until *really* late. **Dady'O** (✉ Paseo Kukulcán, Km 9.5, ☎ 98/833333) has been around for a while but is still a very "in" place, especially with the younger set. The **Dady Rock** (✉ Paseo Kukulcán, Km 9.5, ☎ 98/831626) bar and grill, next door to Dady'O, opens at 6 PM and draws a high-energy clientele with live music, a giant screen, contests, and food specials. **Christine** (✉ Krystal Cancún hotel, ☎ 98/831133) attracts a slightly older, elegantly attired crowd and features an incredible light show. **La Boom** (✉ Paseo Kukulcán, Km 3.5, ☎ 98/830404) includes a video bar with a light show and is not always crowded, although it can squeeze in 1,200 people.

Festivals

Cancún's **Jazz Festival** premiered in 1991 and featured Wynton Marsalis and Gato Barbieri. It's an annual event that takes place in late May; at press time, the 1997 schedule was not yet available. The Cancún Hotel Association (✉ Av. Ign. García de la Torre, SM 1, Lote 6, Cancún, QR 77500, ☎ 98/842853) can provide information about this popular gathering.

Music

Batacha (✉ Hotel Miramar Misión, ☎ 98/831755), a small Caribbean nightclub, is a low-key spot to enjoy some Latin sounds. Visit the **Hard Rock Cafe** (✉ Plaza Lagunas, Paseo Kukulcán, ☎ 98/832024) for live rock bands (generally six nights a week) and molto music nostalgia. You can hear Caribbean-beat dance music (marimba, mariachi, reggae, etc.) at **Jalapeños** (✉ Paseo Kukulcán, Km 7, ☎ 98/8328960) nightly from 8. The place to go for hot live reggae is **Mango Tango** (✉ Paseo Kukulcán, Km 14.2, ☎ 98/850303), which sits lagoonside across the street from the Ritz-Carlton. **Planet Hollywood** (✉ Flamingo Plaza, Paseo Kukulcán, Km 11.5, ☎ 98/850723) is currently the top ticket in town; crowds push their way in for the Hollywood memorabilia— and hope to catch a glimpse of such stars as Demi Moore and Arnold Schwarzenegger, who occasionally check in on their investment.

Performances

The most elaborate ballet folklórico dinner show is held at the **Hotel Continental Villas Plaza** (✉ Paseo Kukulcán, Km 11, ☎ 98/831095); it consists of stylized performances of regional Mexican dances including the hat dance and *la bamba*. The **Convention Center** hosts another popular ballet folklórico dinner show nightly (✉ Paseo Kukulcán, Km 9, ☎ 98/830199). **El Mexicano** (✉ La Mansión-Costa Blanca Shopping Center, ☎ 98/832220 or 98/832220), one of Cancún's largest restaurants, seats 300 for a folkloric dinner show every evening. Mexican fiesta dinner shows are held once a week at the **Westin Regina** (☎ 98/850086, ext. 193/194) and the **Meliá Turquesa** (☎ 98/832544). For all of the above, expect large buffet spreads and at least one drink to be included in the admission charge; call ahead for dates, prices, and reservations.

A Mexican *charreada,* or rodeo show (⊠ El Corral de JF, Km 6, Prolongación Av. Lopez Portillo, no phone), is performed Monday–Saturday at 7 PM. In addition to the show you get dinner and domestic drinks. You can book reservations through your hotel.

Outdoor Activities and Sports

Bullfighting

The Cancún **bullring,** a block south of the Pemex station, hosts year-round bullfights. A matador, *charros* (Mexican cowboys), a mariachi band, and flamenco dancers entertain during the hour preceding the bullfight (2:30 PM). ⊠ *Paseo Kukulcán at Av. Bonampak,* ☎ *98/845465 or 98/848248.* ▣ *About $40.* ◯ *Fights Wed. at 3:30.*

Golf

The main course is at **Pok-Ta-Pok** (⊠ Paseo Kukulcán between Km 6 and Km 7, ☎ 98/830871), a club with fine views of both sea and lagoon, whose 18 holes were designed by Robert Trent Jones, Sr. There is a new 18-hole championship golf course at the **Caesar Park Cancún** (⊠ Paseo Kukulcán, Km 17, ☎ 98/818000). The 18-hole executive course (par 53) at the **Hotel Melia Cancún** (⊠ Paseo Kukulcán, Km 12, ☎ 98/851160) forms a semicircle around the property and shares its beautiful ocean views.

Water Sports

There are myriad ways you can get your adrenalin going while getting wet in Cancún. The most popular ones are detailed below. In addition, you'll also be able to find places to go parasailing (about $35 for eight minutes); waterskiing ($70 per hour); or jet skiing ($70 per hour, or $60 for Wave Runners, double-seated Jet Skis). Paddle boats, kayaks, catamarans, and banana boats are also readily available. **Aqua Tours** (⊠ Paseo Kukulcán, Km 6.25, ☎ 98/830400, FAX 98/830403) and **Aqua-World** (⊠ Paseo Kukulcán, Km 15.2, ☎ 98/852288, FAX 98/852299) maintain large fleets of water toys.

FISHING

Some 500 species of tropical fish, including sailfish, bluefin, marlin, barracuda, and red snapper, live in the waters adjacent to Cancún. Deep-sea fishing boats and other gear may be chartered from outfitters for about $350 for four hours, $450 for six hours, and $550 for eight hours. Charters generally include a captain, a first mate, gear, bait, and beverages. **Aqua Tours, AquaWorld,** and the **Royal Yacht Club** (⊠ Paseo Kukulcán, Km 16.5, ☎ 98/852930) are just a few of the companies that operate large fishing fleets.

SAILBOARDING

Although some people sailboard on the ocean side in the summer, activity is limited primarily to the bay between Cancún and Isla Mujeres. If you visit the island in July, don't miss the National Windsurfing Tournament (☎ 98/843212), in which athletes test their mettle. The **International Windsurfer Sailing School** (☎ 98/842023), at Playa Tortugas, rents equipment and gives lessons; the **Windsurf Association of Quintana Roo** (☎ 98/871771) can provide information about the tournament. Sailboards are available for about $50 an hour; classes go for about $35 an hour.

SNORKELING AND SCUBA DIVING

Snorkeling is best at Punta Nizuc, Punta Cancún, and Playa Tortugas, although you should be especially careful of the strong currents at the latter; gear can be rented for $10 per day. Some charter-fishing companies offer a two-tank scuba dive for about $100. As the name implies, **Scuba Cancún** (☎ 98/831011) specializes in diving trips and offers NAUI, CMAS, and PADI instruction. **Aqua Tours Adventures** (☎ 98/830400 or 98/830227) offers scuba tours and a resort course, as well as snorkeling trips. **AquaWorld Adventures** (☎ 98/852288) runs 2½-hour daily jungle tours through dense mangroves. A guide leads the way as you drive your own Aqua Ray on Laguna Nichupté. The $40 price includes snorkeling and light refreshments. If you've brought your own snorkeling gear and want to save money, just take a city bus down to Club Med and walk along the resort's beach for about a mile until you get to Punta Nizuc.

Carla says this is nice

Shopping

Resort wear and handicrafts are the most popular purchases in Cancún, but the prices are high and the selection standard; if you're traveling elsewhere in Mexico, it's best to postpone your shopping spree until you reach another town. Bargaining is expected in Cancún, but mostly in the market. If you can do without plastic, you may get the 10% sales tax lopped off at shops that don't want to pay high commissions to credit card companies.

Shopping hours are generally weekdays 10–1 and 4–7, although more and more stores are staying open throughout the day rather than closing for siesta between 1 and 4 PM. Many shops keep Saturday morning hours, and some are now open on Sunday until 1 PM. Shops in the malls tend to be open weekdays from 9 or 10 AM to 8 or 10 PM.

Downtown

The wide variety of shops downtown along Avenida Tulum (⊠ between Av. Cobá and Uxmal) includes **Fama** (⊠ Av. Tulum 105, ☎ 98/846586), a department store offering clothing, English reading matter, sports gear, toiletries, liquor, and *latería* (crafts made of tin). Also on Tulum is the oldest and largest of Cancún's crafts markets, **Ki Huic** (⊠ Av. Tulum 17, between Bancomer and Banco Atlantico, ☎ 98/843347), which is open daily from 9 AM to 10 PM and houses about 100 vendors.

Hotel Zone

Fully air-conditioned malls (known as *centros comerciales*), as streamlined and well kept as any in the United States or Canada, sell everything from fashion clothing, beachwear, and sportswear to jewelry, household items, video games, and leather goods.

The newest mall on the scene is **Kukulcán Plaza** (⊠ Paseo Kukulcán, Km 13), with around 130 shops (including Izod, Benetton, and Harley Davidson boutiques), 12 restaurants, a bar, a liquor store, a bank, a cinema, bowling lanes, and a video arcade.

Flamingo Plaza (⊠ Paseo Kukulcán, Km 11.5, across from the Hotel Flamingo) includes an exchange booth, some designer emporiums and duty-free stores, several sportswear shops, two boutiques selling Guatemalan imports, a drug store, and a Planet Hollywood boutique. At the food court, in addition to the usual McDonald's and fried chicken concessions, you'll find Checandole, offering what might be the only fast-food molé enchiladas around.

Just across from the convention center site, **Plaza Caracol** (⊠ Paseo Kukulcán, Km 8.5) is the largest and most contemporary mall in Cancún, with about 200 shops and boutiques, including two pharmacies, art galleries, a currency exchange, and folk art and jewelry shops, as well as cafés and restaurants. Fashion boutiques include Benetton, Bally, Gucci, and Ralph Lauren; in all these stores, prices are lower than in their U.S. counterparts.

To the back of—and virtually indistinguishable from—Plaza Caracol are two outdoor shopping complexes. The pink stucco **La Mansíon–Costa Blanca** specializes in designer clothing and has several restaurants, art galleries, a bank, and a liquor store. **Plaza Lagunas** is the home of the Hard Rock Cafe; some fast food places (KFC, Subway, Dunkin' Donuts); sportswear shops, such as Ellesse; and a number of souvenir stands. Also near Plaza Caracol, **Plaza Terramar** (opposite the Hotel Fiesta Americana) sells beachwear, souvenirs, and folk art and has a restaurant and a pharmacy.

Plaza Nautilus (⊠ Paseo Kukulcán, Km 3.5, lagoon side), the mall closest to downtown, has lost most of its pizzazz and shops, with just a small restaurant, a Super Deli and liquor shop, and a car rental office among the few survivors.

Specialty Shops

Orbe (⊠ Plaza Caracol, ☎ 98/831571) specializes in sculptures and paintings by contemporary Mexican artists. **Mordo's** (⊠ La Mansíon–Costa Blanca mall, ☎ 98/830838) is the local outlet for a small Mexico City chain that sells handcrafted leather jackets, belts, and boots, and can customize your purchase with decorative patches, needlework, or metallic trim. **Mayart** (⊠ La Mansíon–Costa Blanca mall, ☎ 98/841272 or 98/841569) displays replicas of Maya art, temple rubbings, and contemporary painting and sculpture. Those interested in contemporary art should stop by the **Xamanek Gallery** (⊠ Plaza Caracol, no phone) to see the work of Sergio Bustamante, one of the most popular Mexican artists today.

CANCÚN A TO Z

Arriving and Departing

By Bus

The bus terminal (⊠ Av. Tulum and Av. Uxmal, ☎ 98/841378 or 98/843948) downtown serves first-class buses making the trip from Mexico City and first- and second-class buses arriving in Cancún from Puerto Morelos, Playa del Carmen, Tulum, Chetumal, Cobá, Valladolid, Chichén Itzá, and Mérida. Public buses (Rte. 8) make the trip out to Puerto Juárez and Punta Sam for the ferries to Isla Mujeres.

By Car

Cancún is at the end of Route 180, which goes from Matamoros on the Texas border to Campeche, Mérida, and Valladolid. The road trip from Texas to Cancún can take up to three days. Cancún can also be reached from the south via Route 307, which passes through Chetumal and Belize. There are few gas stations on these roads, so try to keep your tank filled.

By Plane

Cancún International Airport is 16 kilometers (9 miles) southwest of the heart of Cancún City, 10 kilometers (6 miles) from the southernmost point of the hotel zone. **Aeromexico** (☎ 98/841097 or 98/843571) flies nonstop from Houston, Miami, and New York. **American** (☎ 98/860086) has nonstop service from Dallas and Miami. **Continental** (☎ 98/860040) offers daily direct service from Houston. **Mexicana** (☎ 98/874444 or

98/860120) nonstops depart from Los Angeles, Miami, and New York. In Cancún, Mexicana subsidiaries **Aerocaribe** (☎ 98/842000 downtown, 98/860083 airport) and **Aerocozumel** (☎ 98/842000 downtown, 98/860162 airport) offer flights to Cozumel, the ruins at Chichén Itzá, Mérida, and other Mexican destinations.

BETWEEN THE AIRPORT AND HOTELS

A counter at the airport exit sells tickets for buses (called *colectivos*) and for taxis; prices for the latter range from $15 to $25, depending on the exact destination. Buses, which cost about $8, are air-conditioned and sell soft drinks and beer on board but may be slow if they're carrying a lot of passengers and need to stop at many hotels.

Getting Around

Motorized transportation of some sort is necessary, since the island is somewhat spread out. Public bus service is good, and taxis are relatively inexpensive.

By Bus

Public buses operate between the hotel zone and downtown from 6 AM to midnight; the cost is about 50¢. There are designated bus stops, but drivers can also be flagged down along Paseo Kukulcán. The service is a bit erratic, but buses run frequently and can save you considerable money on taxis, especially if you're staying at the southern end of the hotel zone.

By Car and Moped

Renting a car for your stay in Cancún is probably an unnecessary expense, entailing tips for valet parking, as well as gasoline and rather costly rental rates (on a par with those in any major resort area around the world). What's more, driving here can be harrowing when you don't know your way around. Downtown streets, being cobblestoned to give the area an "Old Mexico" look, are frequently clogged with traffic. However, if you plan to do some exploring, using Cancún as a base, the roads are excellent within a 100-kilometer (62-mile) radius.

By Ship

Boats leave Puerto Juárez and Punta Sam—both north of Cancún City—for Isla Mujeres every half hour or so (☞ Isla Mujeres A to Z, *below*, for details).

By Taxi

Taxis to the ferries at Punta Sam or Puerto Juárez cost $15–$20 or more; between the hotel zone and downtown, $8 and up; and within the hotel zone, $5–$7. All prices depend on the distance, your negotiating skills, and whether you pick up the taxi in front of the hotel or go onto the avenue to hail a green city cab (the latter will be cheaper). Most hotels list rates at the door; confirm the price with your driver before you set out. If you lose something in a taxi or have questions or a complaint, call the **Sindicato de Taxistas** (☎ 98/831840 or 98/886990).

Contacts and Resources

Car and Moped Rentals

Rental cars are available at the airport or from any of a dozen agencies in town, and most are standard-shift subcompacts and Jeeps; air-conditioned cars with automatic transmissions should be reserved in advance. Rental agencies include **Avis** (☎ Airport, 98/860222; Hotel Calinda Viva, 98/830800; Mayfair Plaza, 98/830803); **Budget** (8 locations, ☎ Airport 98/860026; Av. Tulum 231, ☎ 98/840204); **Econo-**

Rent (☎ Airport, 98/876487; Av. Bonampak, 98/860171); **National** (☎ Airport, 98/860153); and **Hertz** (9 locations, ☎ Airport, 98/860150; Reno 35, 98/876644). The **Car Rental Association** (☎ 98/842039) can help you arrange a rental as well. Rates average around $45 per day.

Mopeds and scooters are also available throughout the island. While fun, they are risky, and there is no insurance available for the driver or the vehicle. The accident rate is high, especially downtown, which is considered too congested for novice moped users. Rates start at around $25 per day.

Consulates

U.S. Consulate (✉ Av. Nader 40, SM 2A, Edificio Marruecos 31, ☎ 98/842411) is open daily 9–2 and 3–6.

Canadian Consulate (✉ Plaza Mexico Local 312, upper floor, ☎ 98/846716) is open daily 11 AM–1 PM. For emergencies outside office hours, call the Canadian Embassy in Mexico City (☎ 5/254–3288).

Doctors and Dentists

Hospital Americano (✉ Calle Viento 15, ☎ 98/846133) and **Total Assist** (✉ Claveles 5, ☎ 98/841092 or 98/848116), both with English-speakers on staff, provide emergency medical care.

Emergencies

Police (☎ 98/841913). **Red Cross** (✉ Av. Xcaret and Labná, SM 21, ☎ 98/841616). **Highway Patrol** (☎ 98/841107).

Guided Tours

AIR TOURS

Trans Caribe (☎ 98/871599 or 98/871692) sea planes offer panoramic tours of Cancún that depart daily from Laguna Nichupté. Prices vary according to the length of the ride, starting at about $35 for 20 minutes. Trans Caribe also will take you island-hopping to Isla Mujeres or Cozumel for diving, and sightseeing to the archaeological sites at Tulum and Chichén Itzá.

Aeroquetzal (✉ Plaza México, Av. Tulum 200, ☎ 98/871353 or 98/843938), a small Guatemalan carrier, flies between Cancún and Guatemala City, continuing on to Flores and the ruins at Tikal, for $290 round-trip.

DAY CRUISES

Day cruises to Isla Mujeres are popular; they include snorkeling in El Garrafón, time for shopping downtown, as well as Continental breakfast, open-bar buffet lunch, and music. **Aqua Tours Adventures** (✉ Paseo Kukulkán, Km 6.25, ☎ 98/830400) books the "Isla Mujeres Adventure," which is particularly popular with locals; it departs at 10 AM from the pier in front of Fat Tuesday's, returns at 5 PM, and costs about $55. The **Tropical Cruiser** (✉ Playa Langosta, ☎ 98/831488) runs an excursion cruise to Isla Mujeres Monday through Saturday, departing from Playa Langosta.

SUBMARINE CRUISES

Nautibus (☎ 98/833552 or 98/832119), or the "floating submarine," has a 1½-hour Caribbean-reef cruise that departs the Playa Linda marina four times daily. The $30 price includes music and drinks. Tours aboard one of the **Sub See Explorer** (☎ 98/852288) "yellow submarines" depart from AquaWorld in the central hotel zone and can be combined with snorkeling for a full day's outing; the cost with snorkeling is about $40, $35 without. Latest to join the underwater ranks is **Atlantis** (☎ 98/833021), Cancún's first true submarine (the others float on the surface and have window seats below). Tours, available every hour from 10 to 3, include an hour-long cruise from Playa Linda to and from the submarine site, and 50 minutes dive time in the sub. The basic price is $80 (half that for children 4–12); add $10 and more time if you want to include lunch (not advised if you're prone to motion sickness).

Late-Night Pharmacies

Farmacia Turística (⊠ Plaza Caracol, ☎ 98/831894) and **Farmacia Extra** (⊠ Plaza Caracol, ☎ 98/832827) deliver to hotels 9 AM–10 PM, and **Farmacia Paris** (⊠ Av. Yaxchilán, in the Marrufo Bldg., ☎ 98/840164) also fills prescriptions.

Travel Agencies and Tour Operators

American Express (⊠ Av. Tulum at Agua, ☎ 98/841999); **Intermar Caribe** (⊠ Av. Bonampak at Calle Careza, ☎ 98/844266); **Turismo Aviomar** (⊠ Calle Venado 30, ☎ 98/846433).

Visitor Information

State tourist office (⊠ Av. Tulum 26, next to Multibanco Comerex, ☎ 98/848073), open daily 9–9.

ISLA MUJERES

Updated by
Gloria
McDarrah

A tiny fish-shape island 8 kilometers (5 miles) off Cancún, Isla Mujeres (*ees*-lah moo-*hair*-ayce) is a tranquil alternative to its bustling western neighbor. Only about 8 kilometers (5 miles) long by a kilometer (½ mile) wide, Isla has flat sandy beaches on its northern end and steep rocky bluffs to the south. Because of its proximity to Cancún, it has turned into a small-scale tourist destination, but it is still a peaceful island retreat with a rich history and culture centered on the sea.

Part of that history is blessed by the presence of Isla's first known inhabitants, the ancient Maya. Their legacy lies in the names, features, and language of their descendants here, but not, unfortunately, in the observatory they built on the southern tip—Hurricane Gilbert obliterated the well-preserved ruin in 1988 (restoration efforts are ongoing). The Spanish conquistadors followed: After setting sail from Cuba in 1517, Hernández de Córdoba's ship blew here accidentally in a storm. Credited with "discovering" the island, he and his crew dubbed their find Isle of Women. One explanation of the name's origins is that Córdoba and company came upon wooden idols of Maya goddesses. Another theory claims the Spaniards found only women when they arrived—the men were out fishing.

For the next several centuries, Isla, like many Caribbean islands, became a haven for pirates and smugglers, then settled into life as a quiet fishing village. In this century, it started out as a vacation destination for Mexicans; the '60s witnessed a hippie influx; and since the late '70s, day-trippers from Cancún increasingly disembark here, sending Isla's hotel, restaurant, and shop owners more business than ever.

Exploring

For orientation purposes, think of Isla Mujeres as an elongated fish: The southern tip is the head and the northern prong the tail. The island's only town, known simply as *el pueblo,* extends the full width of Isla's northern tail. The village is sandwiched between sand and sea to the north, south, and east; no high-rises block the view.

A Good Tour

Numbers in the text correspond to numbers in the margin and on the Isla Mujeres map.

Start out in the island's little town and walk north on Avenida López Mateos to reach Isla's historical **cemetery** ③. To explore the rest of the island, you'll need to take a moped or taxi south along Avenida Rueda Medina, which leads out of town. The first landmark you'll pass after the piers is the Mexican naval base. It's off-limits to tourists, but from the road you can see the modest flag-raising and -lowering ceremonies at sunrise and sunset (no photo-taking permitted). Continue south and you'll see the **Laguna Makax** ⑦ on your right.

At the end of the lagoon, a dirt road to the left leads to the remains of the **Hacienda Mundaca** ⑧. About a block southeast of the hacienda, turn right off the main road at the sign that says PESCA to a smaller, unmarked side road, which loops back north. Approximately ½ kilometer (¼ mile) farther on the left is the entrance to the **Tortuga Marina Turtle Farm** ⑨. When you return to the main Avenida Rueda Medina and go south past Playa Lancheros, you'll soon see **El Garrafón National Park** ⑫. Slightly more than a kilometer (½ mile) along the same road, on the windward side of the tip of Isla Mujeres, is a small **Maya ruin** ⑬. You've now come to one of the island's most scenic patches of coastline. Follow the paved perimeter road north into town; it's a beautiful drive, with a few rocky pull-off areas along the way, perfect for a secluded picnic, since this road sees little traffic.

Sights to See

③ **Cemetery.** You'll find Isla's unnamed cemetery, with its hundred-year-old gravestones, on López Mateos, the road parallel to Playa Norte. Among the lovingly decorated tombs, many in memory of children, is that of Fermín Mundaca (☞ Hacienda Mundaca, *below*). A notorious 19th-century slave trader (often billed more glamorously as a pirate), Mundaca is said to have carved his own tombstone with a skull and crossbones. The monument is not easy to find—ask a local to point out the unidentified marker.

⑫ **El Garrafón National Park.** Garrafón—which lies at the bottom of a bluff—was once almost magical in its beauty. Now, as a result of the hands and fins of eager divers, Hurricane Gilbert, and anchors cast from the fleets of tourist boats continually arriving from Cancún, the coral reef here is virtually dead. Still, nearly 25,000 visitors each year are impressed by the scenery—parrotfish, angelfish, and the rich blue-green water. Arrive early if you want to avoid the crowds, which start to form about 10 AM. There are food stands and souvenir shops galore, as well as palapas, lockers, equipment rental, rest rooms, and a small aquarium. Garrafón is located near the southern end of the main road, Avenida Rueda Medina, about 2½ kilometers (1½ miles) past Playa Lancheros. *No phone.* 🖃 *Less than $2.* ⊘ *Daily 9–4.*

⑧ **Hacienda Mundaca.** A dirt drive and stone archway mark the entrance to the remains of the mansion built by Fermín Mundaca de Marechaja, the 19th-century slave trader–cum–pirate. When the British navy began cracking down on slavers, he settled on the island and built an ambitious estate with resplendent tropical gardens. The story goes that he constructed it to woo a certain island maiden who, in the end, chose another man. What little remained of the hacienda has mysteriously vanished, except for a sorry excuse of a guardhouse, an arch, a pediment, and a well. If you push your way through the jungle—the mosquitoes are fierce—you'll eventually come to the ruined stone archway and triangular pediment. To get here, continue south from town along the main road until you come to the "S" curve at the end of Laguna Makax (☞ *below*). You'll see the dirt road to your left. *No phone.* 🖃 *Free.*

Isla Mujeres

TO ISLA
CONTOY

*Punta
Norte*

Playa Norte

Cemetery
Playa Cocoteros

Piers

Mexican Naval Base

Main Square

TO
PUNTA SAM

TO
PUERTO JUAREZ

Guerrero

Hidalgo

Bravo

Airport

Av. Rueda Medina

Caribbean Sea

Laguna
Makax

Salina Grande

Bahía de Mujeres

Tortuga Marina
Turtle Farm

Hacienda
Mundaca

Playa Paraíso

Playa
Lancheros

N

KEY
Ferry

0   1 mile

0   1 km

El Garrafón
National Park

Maya Ruin

Punta Sur

❼ Laguna Makax. Heading south from town along Avenida Ruida Malina, you'll pass a Mexican naval base and see some *salinas* (salt marshes) on your left; across the road is this lagoon, where pirates are said to have anchored their ships as they lay in wait for the hapless vessels plying Spanish Main (the geographical area in which Spanish treasure ships trafficked).

⓭ Maya Ruin. The sad vestiges of a temple once dedicated to Ixchel, the goddess of fertility, are about 1 kilometer (½ mile) below El Garrafón National Park, at the southern tip of Isla. The adjacent **lighthouse** still stands, and the keeper sometimes allows visitors to go up. The island's most scenic patches of coastline lie along the perimeter road between the lighthouse and town.

❾ Tortuga Marina Turtle Farm. Run by an outfit called Eco Caribe, this facility is devoted to the study and preservation of sea turtles. During working hours, visitors can examine tanks that contain hundreds of hatchlings and young turtles of various species. To get here, follow the main road until, about a block southeast of Hacienda Mundaca, it forks. Follow the right-hand fork, the smaller road that loops back north. About ½ kilometer (¼ mile) to the left you'll see the entrance to the turtle farm. *No phone.* 🖂 *$2.* 🕙 *Daily 9–5.*

NEED A BREAK?	Walk north from the Turtle Farm along the lovely beach past the Cristalmar Hotel to reach **Hacienda Gomar** (☎ 987/70541), a good Mexican restaurant featuring a buffet lunch and marimba music. If you'd rather not put your shoes back on, try the excellent barbecued grouper, snapper, or barracuda at **Blacky's** (no phone) open grill on the beach. Also in the area you'll find handicraft and souvenir shops, a beach bar, and small palapas for shade.

Beaches

The island's finest and most popular beach is on the northwest part of the island: Follow any of the north–south streets in town to **Playa Norte** (sometimes called Playa Cocoteros, or Cocos). You can sit at congenial palapa bars for drinks and snacks; recommended is **Rutilio's y Chimbo's**, twin palapa restaurant-bars right on the beach. There are lots of stands on the beach where you can rent snorkel gear, Jet Skis, floats, sailboards, and sometimes parasails. At the northernmost end of Playa Norte, you'll find **Punta Norte** and come upon an abandoned hotel on its own private islet. The other building you'll see jutting out on a rocky point is a private home.

On the western side of Isla Mujeres lie **Playa Paraíso** and **Playa Lancheros,** tranquil spots where you can have lunch or shop for handicrafts, souvenirs, and T-shirts at the small stands. Also housed at Playa Lancheros, in a sea pen, are some pet sea turtles and harmless *tiburón gato* (nurse sharks). On the ocean side live the carnivorous *tintorera* (female sharks), which have seven rows of teeth and weigh as much as 500 kilograms (1,100 pounds).

Dining

$$$ ✕ Maria's Kan Kin. Near El Garrafón, at the southern end of the island, this appealing beach restaurant has a choice location and attractive decor. Choose a live lobster or try one of the specialties, which tend to be prepared with a French twist, like lobster bisque and coconut mousse. It's the perfect spot for a long lunch that extends to sunset. ✉ *On main road to Garrafón,* ☎ *987/70015. AE, MC, V.*

$$$ ✕ **Zazil-Ha.** This fine restaurant, on the grounds of the Na-Balam
★ hotel (☞ Lodging, *below*) at Playa Norte, offers well-prepared regional
specialties as well as interesting vegetarian dishes. The service is friendly
and the setting is relaxing; you can eat indoors in the cozy palapa din-
ing room or outdoors on a shady terrace. Try the shrimp ceviche for
the first course, followed by the seafood special of the day. ⊠ *Na-Balam
hotel,* ☎ 987/70279. *AE, MC, V.*

$$ ✕ **Bucanero.** With a prime location, near the *parque* on one of the main
pedestrian drags, this appealing restaurant has attractive wood tables
with blue-and-white inset tiles and terra-cotta floors. The hearty breakfasts are very reasonably priced. Lunch and dinner specialties include
avocado stuffed with shrimp and *mar y cielo* (fish fillet and chicken
breast with french fries and onions). ⊠ *Av. Hidalgo 11,* ☎ 987/70210.
Reservations not accepted. MC, V.

$$ ✕ **Pizza Rolandi.** Red tables, yellow director's chairs, and green walls
★ and window trim set an upbeat tone at this very "in" chain restaurant.
Select from a broad variety of Italian food: lobster pizzas, calzones,
and pastas. Grilled fresh fish and shrimp are highly recommended, and
salads are excellent. Or just stop in for a drink at one of the outside
tables; the margaritas, cappuccino, and espresso are the best in town.
⊠ *Av. Hidalgo (between Avs. Madero and Abasolo),* ☎ 987/70430.
Reservations not accepted. AE, MC, V.

$ ✕ **Lonchería La Lomita.** With a bright aqua interior and plastic table-
★ cloths, this simple, homestyle diner isn't much to look at, but you'll
find hearty servings of chicken, steak, and seafood cooked to order
(grilled, fried, or sautéed) here. Amazingly low-priced lunch and din-
ner set menus include beans, rice, and tortillas or bread; breakfast is
also available. On Avenida Juárez between Avenidas Madero and
Morelos is La Lomita II, like its sister establishment a no-frills eatery
that offers daily specials featuring generous servings and good value.
⊠ *Av. Juárez 25-B (past Av. Allende), no phone. Reservations not ac-
cepted. No credit cards.*

$ ✕ **Mirtita's** and **Villa del Mar.** Next to each other on Avenida Rueda
Medina across from the ferry dock, these are favorite local hangouts.
Both serve fresh seafood and Yucatecan specialties. ⊠ *Av. Rueda Med-
ina, no phone. No credit cards.*

Lodging

The approximately 25 hotels (about 600 rooms) on Isla Mujeres gen-
erally fall into one of two categories: The older, more modest places
are situated right in town, and the newer, more costly properties tend
to have beachfront locations around Punta Norte and, increasingly, on
the peninsula near the lagoon. Most hotels have ceiling fans; some have
air-conditioning, but few offer TVs or phones. Luxurious, self-contained
time-share condominiums are another option, which you can learn more
about from the tourist office (☎ 987/70316). All hotels share the
77400 postal code.

$$$ ⌂ **Na-Balam.** This intimate, informal hostelry set on Playa Norte will
★ fulfill all your tropical-paradise fantasies. Three corner suites with
balconies affording outstanding views of sea and sand are well worth
$85. The simple, attractive rooms have turquoise-tiled floors, carved
wood furniture, dining areas, and patios facing the beach. Breakfast
at the hotel's Zazil-Ha restaurant (☞ Dining, *above*) is a delightful way
to kick off the day. ⊠ *Calle Zazil Ha 118,* ☎ 987/70279, ℻ 987/70446.
26 rooms. Restaurant, bar, air-conditioning, pool, beach. AE, MC, V.

$$ ⌂ **Belmar.** Right in the heart of town, above Pizza Rolandi, this small
hotel shares a charming plant-filled inner courtyard with the restau-
rant, which means it can occasionally be noisy here until 11 PM. Stan-

dard rooms are pretty, with tiled baths and light-wood furniture. One enormous suite features a private hot tub on a patio, a tiled kitchenette, and a sitting area. All rooms have phones, satellite TV, and air-conditioning. ⊠ *Av. Hidalgo 110 (between Avs. Madero and Abasolo),* ☎ *987/70430,* FAX *987/70429. 11 rooms. AE, MC, V.*

$$
★ **⊡ Cabañas María del Mar.** A rather mind-boggling assortment of rooms is available in this friendly beachfront hotel, but all have a great deal of Mexican character. Some of the rooms are rather spare, but those in the slightly more expensive "castle" section have hand-carved wood furnishings by local artisans in a combination of Spanish and Maya styles. The hotel has a prime location on Playa Norte, next to Na-Balam, and its reasonable room rates include Continental breakfast. ⊠ *Av. Carlos Lazos 1,* ☎ *987/70179,* FAX *987/70213. 55 rooms, including 14 cabanas. Restaurant-bar, air-conditioning, pool, moped rental, travel services. MC, V.*

$$ **⊡ Perla del Caribe.** On the eastern edge of town facing the new sea wall and promenade, the three-story Perla has rooms that look out either on the open sea or town, priced accordingly. All rooms have balconies and are comfortable and functional but not palatial. You can listen to music in the restaurant-bar most evenings. ⊠ *Av. Madero 2,* ☎ *987/70444 or 800/258–6454,* FAX *987/70011. 91 rooms. Restaurant-bar, air-conditioning, pool. AE, MC, V.*

$$ **⊡ Posada del Mar.** This hotel's assets include its prime location between town and Playa Norte and its reasonable prices. Rooms have balconies overlooking a main road and beyond to the waterfront. The simple wood furnishings appear somewhat worse for wear, although baths are clean, with cheerful colored tiles. Private bungalows in the $ price category are also available. A recently added bar next to the pool is as popular as the street-front palapa-roof restaurant. ⊠ *Av. Rueda Medina 15A,* ☎ *987/70300 or 987/70044,* FAX *987/70266. 40 rooms. Restaurant, bar, pool. AE, MC, V.*

Nightlife and the Arts

Nightlife

Most restaurant bars feature a happy hour from 5 to 7; the palapa bars at Playa Norte are an excellent place to watch the sun set. The current hot spot is **Ya Ya's** (⊠ Av. Rueda Medina 42 near the lighthouse and Playa Norte, no phone), run by some good ol' boys from Dallas who serve up huge Texas steaks, chili dogs, and shrimp etouffée along with live jazz, rock, and reggae jam sessions until 2 or 3 AM. The bar at the **Posada del Mar** (⊠ Av. Rueda Medina 15, ☎ 987/70300) can be subdued or hopping, depending on what's going on in town. **Buho's,** the bar-restaurant at Cabañas María del Mar (⊠ Av. Carlos Lazo 1, ☎ 987/70179), serves food and is a good choice for a relaxing drink at sunset or later at night. **Restaurante La Peña** (⊠ Av. Guerrero 5, ☎ 987/70309) has music and dancing on its open-air terrace overlooking the sea.

The Arts

Festivals and cultural events are held on many weekends, with live entertainment on the outdoor stage in the main square. The whole island celebrates the spring regattas and the Caribbean music festivals. **Casa de la Cultura,** near the youth hostel, offers folkloric dance classes year-round. The center also operates a small public library and book exchange. ⊠ *Av. Guerrero,* ☎ *987/70639.* ◷ *Mon.–Sat. 9–1 and 4–8.*

For English-language films visit **Cine Blanquita** (⊠ Av. Morelos, between Avs. Guerrero and Hidalgo, no phone).

Outdoor Activities and Sports

For any water sport, beaches on the north and west sides are the calmest.

Fishing

Bahía Dive Shop (⊠ Av. Rueda Medina 166, across from pier, ☎ FAX 987/70340) charges $250 for a day of deep-sea fishing, $200 a day for cast fishing (tarpon, snook, and bonefish), and $20 an hour for off-shore fishing (barracuda, snapper, and smaller fish).

Snorkeling and Scuba Diving

Bahía Dive Shop (☞ Fishing, *above*) rents snorkeling and scuba equipment and runs three-hour boat and dive trips to the reefs and the Cave of the Sleeping Sharks. Snorkel gear goes for $5 a day; tanks, $45–$60, depending on the length of the dive. **Mexico Divers** (⊠ Av. Rueda Medina and Av. Medaro, 1 block from ferry, ☎ 987/70131), also called **Buzos de México,** runs three-hour snorkeling tours for $15; two-tank scuba trips start at $55 for a reef dive and $75 for the shark cave dive. Rental gear is available. Dive master Carlos Gutiérrez also gives a resort course for $80 and open-water PADI certification for $350 (his prices are generally negotiable).

Shopping

Casa del Arte Mexica (⊠ Av. Hidalgo 6, ☎ 987/70459) has a good choice of clay reproductions, silver jewelry, batiks, rubbings, wood carvings, leather, and hammocks. **La Loma** (⊠ Av. Guerrero 6, 2nd floor, east side of main square, ☎ 987/70223) carries exquisite crafts from all over Mexico and Guatemala, including amber, silver, black jade, leather jewelry, masks, pottery, and textile bags. Although the shop is not inexpensive, La Loma offers the biggest and best collection on the island. **Rachat & Romero** (⊠ Av. Rueda Medina, ☎ 987/70331), housed in the pink building by the dock, sells gold, silver, and gemstones. In 1991, the owners of Rachat & Romero opened **Van Cleef & Arpels** (⊠ Avs. Juárez and Morelos, ☎ 987/70299), with an impressive jewelry selection in a large corner shop. **Tienda Paulita** (⊠ Avs. Morelos and Hidalgo, ☎ 987/70014) features a standard selection of folk art and handmade clothing in a fairly large space.

ISLA MUJERES A TO Z

Arriving and Departing

By Boat

TO ISLA MUJERES

The **Caribbean Express** and the **Caribbean Miss** (☎ 987/70254 or 987/70253), both air-conditioned cruisers with bar service, make several 30-minute crossings daily. They leave Puerto Juárez on the mainland for the main ferry dock in Isla Mujeres from 7:30 AM to 7:30 PM at approximately 30-minute intervals; the fare is under $4 per person.

There are three slower **passenger ferries**; the schedule varies depending on the season, so check the times posted at the dock. The one-way fare is only about $1.50 and the trip takes 45 minutes, but delays and crowding are frequent.

It's possible to hire a **private lancha,** or motorboat, which makes the crossing from Punta Sam, 5 kilometers (3 miles) north of Punta Juárez, in about 18 minutes. The fare is usually about $4 per person but varies: Water taxis charge a flat fee, about $20, divided by the number of passengers; a full load keeps the price low. A convenient, more expensive service, the **Shuttle** (Cancún, ☎ 98/83448), runs directly from the Playa Tortugas dock in Cancún's hotel zone at least four times a day and costs about $15 round-trip. Cars are unnecessary on Isla, but **municipal ferries** that accommodate vehicles as well as passengers leave from Punta Sam and take about 45 minutes. Check departure times posted at the pier, but you can count on the schedule running from about 7 AM to 9 PM. The fare is under $2 per person and $10 per vehicle.

FROM ISLA MUJERES

The **Caribbean Express** and the **Caribbean Miss** (☎ 987/70254 or 987/70253) make the trip from Isla Mujeres to Puerto Juárez between 8 AM and 8 PM at approximately 30-minute intervals; the fare is under $4 per person. The slower **passenger ferry** departs from the main dock at Isla Mujeres to Puerto Juárez. The first **car ferry** from Isla Mujeres to Punta Sam leaves at about 6 AM and the last departs at about 7:15 PM. Again, schedules vary, so you should call ahead or check the boat schedule posted at the pier.

Getting Around

By Bicycle

Bicycles are available for hardy cyclists, but don't underestimate the hot sun and the tricky road conditions. Watch for the many speed bumps, which can give you an unexpected jolt, and avoid riding at night; some roads have no street lights. **Rent Me Sport Bike** (✉ Avs. Juárez and Morelos, 1 block from main pier, no phone) offers five-speed cycles starting at less than $2 for an hour; a full day costs about $5.

By Car

There is little reason for tourists to bring cars to Isla Mujeres, because there are plenty of other forms of transportation that cost far less than renting and transporting a private vehicle. Moreover, though the main road is paved, speed bumps abound and some areas are poorly lighted.

By Golf Cart

The newest way for tourists to explore Isla is by golf cart. **Ppe's Rentadora** (✉ Av. Hidalgo 19, ☎ 987/70019) and almost all of the moped rental shops listed below, as well as some hotels, rent them for about $10 an hour.

By Moped

The island is full of moped rental shops. **Motorent Kankin** (✉ Av. Abasolo 15, no phone) will provide a two-seater, three-speed Honda for about $5 per hour or $20 per day ($40 for 24 hours); a $20 deposit—or a credit card or passport left behind—is required. **Ppe's Rentadora** (✉ Av. Hidalgo 19, ☎ 987/70019) offers two-seater, fully automatic Honda Aeros, starting at $5 per hour, for a minimum of two hours; it's under $35 for 24 hours. **Ciro's Motorent** (✉ Av. Guerrero N 11 at Av. Matamoros, ☎ 987/70578) has two-seater Honda Tact 50 mopeds.

By Taxi

If your time is limited you can hire a **taxi** (✉ Av. Rueda Medina, ☎ 987/70066) for a private island tour at about $15 an hour. Fares run $1–$2 from the ferry or downtown to the hotels on the north end, at Playa Norte. Taxis line up right by the ferry dock around the clock.

Contacts and Resources

Emergencies

Medical Service (☎ 987/70195 or 987/70607). **Hospital** (☎ 987/70001). **Police** (☎ 987/70082). **Red Cross** (☎ 987/70085).

Guided Tours

BOAT TOURS

Cooperativa Lanchera (waterfront, near the dock, no phone) offers four-hour launch trips to the Virgin, the lighthouse, the turtles at Playa Lancheros, the coral reefs at Los Manchones, and El Garrafón, for about $45. **Cooperativa Isla Mujeres** (⊠ Av. Rueda Medina, ☎ 987/70274), next to Mexico Divers, rents out boats at $120 for a maximum of four hours and six people, and $15 per person for an island tour with lunch (minimum six people). At least two of Isla Mujeres's boating co-operatives sell day tours to Isla Contoy, a national wildlife park and bird sanctuary. **Sociedad Cooperativa "Isla Mujeres"** (pier ☎ 987/70274) and **La Isleña** (⊠ half a block from the pier, corner of Avs. Morelos and Juárez, ☎ 987/70036) launch boats daily at 8:30 AM; they return at 4 PM. The trip takes about 45 minutes, depending on the size of the boat, and runs about $35 to $40.

Late-Night Pharmacies

Farmacia Isla Mujeres (⊠ Av. Juárez, next to the Caribbean Tropic Boutique, ☎ 987/70178) and **Farmacia Lily** (⊠ Avs. Madero and Hidalgo, ☎ 987/70164) are open Monday–Saturday 8:30 AM–9:30 PM and Sunday 8:30 AM–3 PM.

Visitor Information

Tourist office (⊠ Av. Hidalgo 6, main square behind the basketball court, ☎ 987/70316) is open weekdays 9–2 and 7–9.

COZUMEL

Updated by
Gloria
McDarrah

Cozumel provides a balance between Cancún and Isla Mujeres: Though attuned to North American tourism, the island has managed to keep development to a minimum. Its expansive beaches, superb coral reefs, and copious wildlife—in the sea, on the land, and in the air—attract an active, athletic crowd. Rated one of the top destinations in the world among underwater enthusiasts, Cozumel is encircled by a garland of reefs entrancing divers and snorkelers alike. Despite the inevitable effects of docking cruise ships (shops and restaurants actively recruit customers on an increasingly populous main drag), the island's earthy charm and tranquillity remain intact. The relaxing atmosphere here is typically Mexican—friendly and unpretentious. Cozumel's rich Maya heritage is reflected in the faces of 60,000 or so isleños; you'll see people who look like ancient statues come to life, and occasionally hear the Maya language spoken.

A 490-square-kilometer (189-square-mile) island 19 kilometers (12 miles) to the east of Yucatán, Cozumel is mostly flat, its interior covered by parched scrub, dense jungle, and marshy lagoons. White sandy beaches with calm waters line the island's leeward (western) side, which is fringed by a spectacular reef system, while the powerful surf and rocky strands on the windward (eastern) side, facing the Caribbean, are broken up here and there by calm bays and hidden coves. Most of Cozumel is undeveloped, with a good deal of the land and the shores set aside as national parks; a few Maya ruins provide what limited sightseeing there is aside from the island's glorious natural attractions. San Miguel is the only established town.

Exploring

Cozumel is about 53 kilometers (33 miles) long and 15 kilometers (9 miles) wide, but only a small percentage of its roads—primarily those in the southern half—are paved. Dirt roads can be explored, with care, in a four-wheel-drive vehicle. Aside from the 3% of the island that has been developed, Cozumel is made up of expanses of sandy or rocky beaches, quiet little coves, palm groves, scrubby jungles, lagoons and swamps, and a few low hills (the maximum elevation is 45 feet).

A Good Tour

Numbers in the text correspond to numbers in the margin and on the Cozumel map.

It's worth renting a Jeep to explore Cozumel, which has more sights than either Cancún or Isla Mujeres. If you go south from Cozumel's principal town, **San Miguel** ①, in about 10 minutes you'll come to **Chankanaab Nature Park** ②. Continue past Chankanaab and past Playa Corona, Playa San Francisco, and Playa del Sol; at Km 17.5 a turnoff leads about 3 kilometers (2 miles) inland to the village and ruins of **El Cedral** ③ (take this detour only if you have a four-wheel-drive vehicle). Backtrack to the coast and go south past Playa de Palancar (the famous reef lies offshore) to the island's southern tip, where you'll find a dirt trail to **Laguna Colombia** ④.

If you head east on the paved road, you'll come to the eastern Caribbean coast. Make a right turn onto a dirt road and follow it for 4 kilometers (3 miles) south to get to the **Punta Celerain Lighthouse** ⑤. When you return to the paved road and head north, you will first pass the Tumba del Caracol, another Maya ruin that may have served as a lighthouse; a bit farther on are the minuscule ruins of El Mirador and the Throne. Beyond Punta Chiqueros, Playa Bonita, Playa Chen Río, and Punta Morena you'll see Playa Oriente, where the cross-island road meets the east coast; you can take the cross-island road west toward town or continue north. If you choose the latter route, you'll need a four-wheel-drive vehicle to travel on a rough dirt road that dead-ends past Punta Molas; eventually you'll have to turn around. A sign at this junction warns that drivers proceed at their own risk. This pothole-ridden road is the preferred sunbathing spot of boa constrictors, crocodiles, and other jungle denizens.

If you're going toward town, it's worth making a detour inland to view the ruins of **San Gervasio** ⑥; take the cross-island road west to the army airfield and turn right; follow this road north for 7 kilometers (4 miles). The road to the ruins is a good one, but a nearly unmaneuverable dirt road leads northeast of San Gervasio back to the unpaved coast road. At the junction is a marvelously deserted beach where you can camp. Heading north along this beach, you'll come to **Castillo Real** ⑦, another Maya site. A number of other minor ruins are spread across the northern tip of Cozumel, which terminates at the **Punta Molas Lighthouse** ⑧.

Sights to See

❼ Castillo Real. A Maya site on the eastern coast, near the northern tip of the island, the castillo (castle) comprises a lookout tower, the base of a pyramid, and a temple with two chambers capped by a false arch. The waters here harbor several shipwrecks, remnants from the days when buccaneers lay in wait for richly cargoed galleons en route to Europe. It's a fine spot for snorkeling because there are few visitors to disturb the fish.

❷ Chankanaab Nature Park. Chankanaab (the name means "small sea"), a 10-minute drive south of San Miguel, is a lovely saltwater lagoon that the government has made into a wildlife sanctuary, botanical garden, and archaeological park. Underwater caves, offshore reefs, a protected bay—which hides crusty old cannons and anchors as well as statues of Jesus Christ and Chac Mool—and a sunken ship attract droves of snorkelers and scuba divers. An interactive educational museum, four

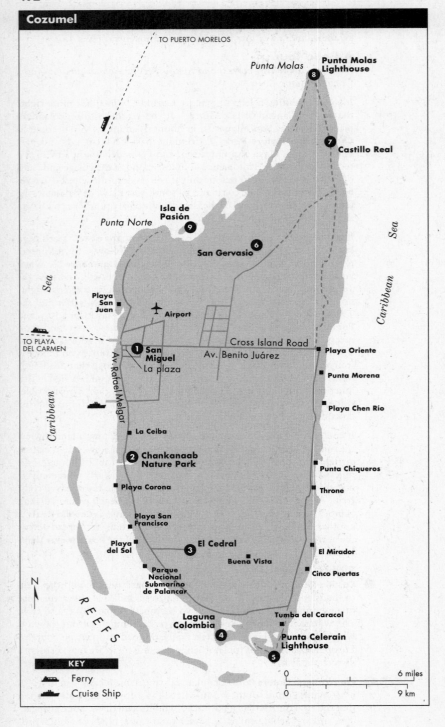

Cozumel

TO PUERTO MORELOS

Punta Molas

Punta Molas Lighthouse

8

7 **Castillo Real**

Isla de Pasión

Punta Norte

9

6

San Gervasio

Caribbean Sea

Sea

TO PLAYA DEL CARMEN

Playa San Juan

✈ **Airport**

Cross Island Road

Av. Benito Juárez

1 **San Miguel**

La plaza

Playa Oriente

Punta Morena

Playa Chen Río

Av. Rafael Melgar

La Ceiba

2 **Chankanaab Nature Park**

Playa Corona

Punta Chiqueros

Throne

Playa San Francisco

Playa del Sol

3 **El Cedral**

Buena Vista

El Mirador

Cinco Puertas

Parque Nacional Submarino de Palancar

Caribbean

N

R E E F S

Laguna Colombia

Tumba del Caracol

4

5 **Punta Celerain Lighthouse**

KEY

🛳 Ferry

🚢 Cruise Ship

0 ⊢─────────────⊣ 6 miles

0 ⊢─────────────⊣ 9 km

dive shops, a restaurant, four gift shops, a snack stand, and a dressing room with lockers and showers are on the premises. ⊠ *Carretera Sur, Km 9, no phone.* ☎ *$5.* ☉ *Daily 6–5:30.*

❸ El Cedral. Once the tiny village and ruins composed the largest Maya site on Cozumel; this was the temple sighted by the original Spanish explorers in 1518, and the first Mass in Mexico was reportedly celebrated here. These days, there's little archaeological evidence of El Cedral's past glory. All that remains is a small structure capped by jungle growth; its Maya arch, best viewed from inside, is covered by faint traces of paint and stucco. After exploring the ruins, you can take a rest nearby in a small green-and-white cinder-block church, typical of rural Mexico. ⊠ *Turnoff at Km 17.5 of main island road, then 3 km (2 mi) inland to site, no phone.*

❾ Isla de Pasión. Beyond Punta Norte, in the middle of Abrigo Bay, this tiny island is now part of a state reserve. Fishing is permitted and the beaches are secluded, but there are no facilities on the island, and since so few people go, there are no scheduled tours. You'll have to bargain with a local boat owner for transportation if you want to visit.

❹ Laguna Colombia. A prime site for jungle aficionados, this lagoon lies at the island's southern tip and is most commonly reached by boat, although there is a trail. Fish migrate here to lay their eggs, and barracuda, baby fish, and birds show up in great numbers in season. Popular diving and snorkeling spots can be found offshore in the reefs of Tunich, Colombia, and Maracaibo.

❺ Punta Celerain Lighthouse. Located on the southernmost tip of the island, the lighthouse is surrounded by sand dunes at the narrowest point of land. Alligators were once hunted nearby; nowadays you may spot a soldier or two from the adjacent army post catching an iguana. The point comes to life at midday when the lighthouse keeper serves fried fish and beer and locals and tourists gather to chat; Sundays are particularly popular. The lighthouse is at the end of a 4-kilometer-long (2½-mile-long) dirt road—a four-wheel-drive vehicle is strongly recommended if you plan to visit.

❽ Punta Molas. If you are going to attempt to reach the northernmost tip of the island, be sure you have plenty of time and a reliable four-wheel-drive vehicle: The pothole-ridden road is the preferred sunbathing spot of boa constrictors, crocodiles, and other jungle denizens. **Punta Molas Lighthouse** is an excellent spot for sunbathing, birding, and camping. Although this entire area is accessible only by four-wheel-drive vehicles or by boat, the jagged shoreline and the open sea offer magnificent views, making it well worth the trip.

❻ San Gervasio. The largest existing Maya and Toltec site on Cozumel, San Gervasio was once the island's capital and probably its ceremonial center, dedicated to the fertility goddess Ixchel. The classical- and postclassical-style site was continuously occupied from AD 300 to AD 1500. Typical architectural features from the era include limestone plazas and masonry superstructures atop stepped platforms, as well as stelae, bas-reliefs, and frescoes. What remains today are several small mounds scattered around a plaza and several broken columns and lintels that were once part of the main building or observatory. There are a snack bar and some gift shops at the entrance. To get here, take the cross-island road (Av. Juárez) to the San Gervasio access road; follow this road north for 7 kilometers (4 miles). ☎ *$1 access to road, $3.50 access to ruins.* ☉ *Daily 8–5.*

❶ **San Miguel.** Cozumel's only town retains the laid-back tenor of a Mexican village, although its streets are dotted with an interesting variety of shops and restaurants. Avenida Rafael Melgar, San Miguel's waterfront boulevard, has a wide cement walkway, called the *malecón,* separating Avenida Melgar from the town's narrow sandy beach. As in most Mexican towns, the main square, here called the **Plaza del Sol,** is where townspeople and visitors hang out, particularly on Sunday nights, when mariachi bands join the nightly assortment of food and souvenir vendors.

🍂 **Museo de la Isla de Cozumel** is housed on two floors of what was once the island's first luxury hotel. Four permanent exhibit halls of dioramas, sculptures, and charts explain the island's history and ecosystem. Well laid out and labeled displays cover pre-Hispanic, colonial, and modern times and detail the local geology, flora, and fauna. A charming reproduction of a Maya house is a highlight. The museum also presents temporary exhibits, guided tours, and workshops. ⊠ *Av. Rafael Melgar between Calles 4 and 6 N,* ☎ *987/21475.* ⌷ *$3.* ☉ *Daily 10–6.*

🍂 Three thousand years of pre-Hispanic Mexican culture and art are showcased in the **Cozumel Archaeological Park,** 10 minutes by cab from the pier and plaza area. Mesoamerican history is traced through full-size replicas of Toltec, Mexicas, and Maya statues and stone carvings surrounded by jungle foliage. A guided walking tour, included in the admission price, takes about an hour. Clean-up of the extensive damage caused in 1995 by Hurricane Roxanne was proceeding slowly at press time; call to verify the site's reopening before visiting. ⊠ *Av. 65 S,* ☎ *987/20914.* ⌷ *$3.* ☉ *Daily 8–6.*

NEED A BREAK?	On the terrace off the second floor of the museum, the **Restaurante del Museo** (☎ 987/20838) offers breakfast, drinks, or a full meal of fajitas or grilled red snapper, all enhanced by a great waterfront view.

Beaches

Cozumel's beaches vary from long, treeless, sandy stretches to isolated coves and rocky shores. Virtually all development remains on the leeward (western) side, where the coast is relatively sheltered by the proximity of the mainland 19 kilometers (12 miles) to the west. Reaching beaches on the windward (eastern) side is more difficult and requires transportation, but you'll be rewarded if you are looking for solitude.

Dining

Dining options on Cozumel reflect the nature of the place as a whole, with some harmless pretension at times but mainly the insouciant, natural style of the tropical island. More than 80 restaurants in the downtown area alone offer a broad choice, from air-conditioned fast-food outlets and Americanized places serving Continental fare and seafood in semiformal "nautical" settings to simple outdoor eateries that specialize in fish. Resort hotels offering buffet breakfasts and dinners are good values for bottomless appetites.

CATEGORY	COST*
$$$	$25–$35
$$	$15–25
$	under $15

*per person, excluding drinks and service

$$$ ✕ ★ **Arrecife.** A well-trained staff and impeccably prepared seafood and Mediterranean fare put this hotel restaurant in a class by itself. Tall windows and excellent views of the sea complement the stylish decor—potted palms, white wicker furniture, pink walls—while musicians, who play regularly, further enhance the romantic mood. However, you have to have good timing to dine here; you might find Arrecife's doors unlocked on the weekends if the hotel is hopping during high season, but the restaurant is supposed to be open on a regular basis from November through Labor Day weekend. ⊠ *Hotel Presidente Inter-Continental Cozumel,* ☎ *987/20322. AE, DC, MC, V. Closed Sept.–Oct.*

$$$ ✕ **La Cabaña del Pescador.** To get to this rustic palapa-covered hut, you've got to cross a gangplank, but it's worth it if you're looking for well-prepared fresh lobster. The tails are sold by weight, and the rest—including a delicious eggnog-type drink served at the end of the meal—is on the house. Seashells and nets hang from the walls of this small, dimly lit room; geese stroll outside. ⊠ *Carretera San Juan, Km 4, across from Playa Azul Hotel north of town, no phone. No credit cards. No lunch.*

$$ ✕ **El Capi Navegante.** Locals say you'll find the best seafood in town here: The captain's motto is: "The fish we serve today slept in the sea last night." Specialties like whole red snapper and stuffed squid are skillfully prepared and sometimes flambéed at your table. Highly recommended dishes include conch ceviche and deep-fried whole snapper. Nautical blue-and-white decor, accented by the life preservers on the walls, adds personality to this place. ⊠ *Av. 10a S 312 at Calle 3,* ☎ *987/21730. MC, V.*

$$ ✕ ★ **La Choza.** Home-cooked Mexican food—primarily from the capital and among the best in town—is the order of the day at this family-run establishment. Dona Elisa Espinosa's specialties include chicken mole, red snapper in sweet mustard sauce, and grilled lobster. For dessert, try the refreshing frozen avocado pie. The informal palapa-covered patio is furnished with simple wood tables and chairs and hand-painted pottery dishes. ⊠ *Calle Rosada Salas 198 at Av. 10a S,* ☎ *987/20958. AE, MC, V.*

$$ ✕ ★ **Pancho's Backyard.** A jungle of greenery, trickling fountains, ceiling fans, and leather chairs set the tone at this inviting restaurant, located on the cool patio of Los Cincos Soles shopping center. The menu highlights local standards such as black bean soup, *camarones al carbon* (grilled prawns), and fajitas. Round out your meal with coconut ice cream in Kahlua. ⊠ *Av. Rafael Melgar N 27 at Calle 8 N,* ☎ *987/22141. AE, MC, V. No lunch Sat., closed Sun.*

$$ ✕ **Tony Rome's.** Finger-licking, Texas-style barbecued ribs and Las Vegas–style crooning (courtesy of owner Tony Rome) are the drawing cards of this open-air eatery wrapped around a palapa-covered dance floor. In addition to the ribs and the live entertainment, you'll find chicken, lobster, Kansas City steaks, and great happy-hour specials. ⊠ *Av. 5 S 21 between Av. Rosado Salas and Calle 3 S,* ☎ *987/20131. AE, MC, V.*

$ ✕ **Diamond Café.** This airy retreat in the back of the elegant Diamond Creations is artfully decorated like a typical Mexican patio, with a central fountain and terraced seating at wrought-iron tables. The café specializes in home-baked pastries to accompany the espresso and cappuccino brewed on the premises and served all day long. ⊠ *Av. Rafael Melgar 131,* ☎ *987/23869. AE, MC, V. Closed Sun.*

$ ✕ **El Foco.** A *taquería* serving soft tacos stuffed with pork, chorizo (spicy Mexican sausage), and cheese, this eatery also does ribs and steak. Graffitied walls and plain wood tables make it a casual, fun spot to grab a bite and a *cerveza*. ⊠ *Av. 5 S 13-B, between Calle Rosado Salas and Calle 3, no phone. No credit cards.*

$ ✕ **El Moro.** This family-run restaurant on the eastern edge of town specializes in low-priced local cuisine—seafood, chicken, and meat. Inside, the decor follows the regional theme, beginning with Yucatecan baskets hanging on the walls. Divers flock to this place, so you know portions are hearty and the food is delicious. Take a taxi; El Moro is too far to walk to, and difficult to find. ⊠ *Calle 75 N between Calles 2 and 4,* ☎ *987/23029. MC, V. Closed Thurs.*

$ ✕ **Prima Pasta & Prima Deli.** You'll find hearty, inexpensive pizzas, calzones, sandwiches, and pastas at this northern Italian diner just off the plaza. The breezy dining area on the second-floor terrace above the kitchen has a charming Mediterranean mural painted on two walls. Business has been so good that the owner branched out in 1994, opening Prima Deli, a tiny sandwich shop, just a few doors down (at Calle Rosado Salas 113). ⊠ *Calle Rosado Salas 109,* ☎ *987/24242. MC, V.*

Lodging

Cozumel's hotels are located in three main areas, all on the island's western, or leeward, side: in town, and north and south of town. Because of the proximity of the reefs, divers and snorkelers tend to congregate at the southern properties. Sailors and anglers, on the other hand, prefer the hotels to the north, where the beaches are better. Most budget hotels are in town. All hotels have air-conditioning unless otherwise noted, and all share the 77600 postal code.

CATEGORY	COST*
$$$$	over $160
$$$	$90–$160
$$	$40–$90
$	under $40

All prices are for a standard double room in the high season, excluding service charges and tax.

$$$$ ▥ **Meliá Mayan Peradisus.** Lush tropical foliage and spectacular sunsets over the beach combine with modern architecture and amenities to make this property north of town a memorable place to stay. Standard rooms, some with small patios opening out onto the lawn, are attractively decorated with colorful tropical print bedspreads and light-wood furniture; superior rooms are larger and have balconies overlooking the water. This resort turned all-inclusive in late 1994, bringing on an international staff of entertainers and activity coordinators to keep guests busy. ⊠ *Box 9, Carretera a Sta. Pilar 6,* ☎ *987/20411 or 800/336–3542,* 𝔽𝔸𝕏 *987/21599. 200 rooms. 3 restaurants, 3 bars, 2 pools, hot tub, miniature golf, 2 tennis courts, horseback riding, dive shop, water sports, bicycles, children's program, playground, shops. AE, DC, MC, V.*

$$$$ ▥ **Presidente Inter-Continental Cozumel.** This hotel exudes luxury,
★ from the courteous, prompt, and efficient service to the tastefully decorated interior. The Presidente is famed not only for possessing one of the best restaurants on the island, Arrecife (☞ *Dining, above*), but also for its professional water-sports center. Located on its own broad, white beach south of the town of San Miguel, the property ranks among the best on the island for snorkeling. All rooms are done in bright, contemporary colors with white cedar furnishings; deluxe rooms, with their own private terraces fronting the beach or gardens, are huge. ⊠ *Carretera a Chankanaab, Km 6.5,* ☎ *987/20322, 987/21520, or 800/327–0200,* 𝔽𝔸𝕏 *987/21360. 253 rooms. 2 restaurants, coffee shop,*

3 bars, pool, hot tub, 2 tennis courts, water sports, dive shop, motorbikes, children's program, shops, car rental. AE, DC, MC, V.

$$$ ⊞ **Fiesta Americana Cozumel Reef.** Reasonable prices and a good location have made the Fiesta Americana one of the most popular hotels on the island. The hotel's beach—reachable via a walkway from the property—offers easy access to spectacular underwater scenery. Standard rooms are large, with sea-green headboards and well-made lightwood furnishings; all have balconies looking out on the ocean, as well as hair dryers and direct-dial phones. Fifty-six rooms were recently added in a semicircular cluster of villas facing the hotel's main entrance. ⊠ *Carretera a Chankanaab, Km 7.5,* ☎ *987/22622 or 800/FIESTA–1,* FAX *987/22666. 172 rooms. 3 restaurants, 3 bars, 2 pools, 2 tennis courts, dive shop, nonmotorized water sports, motorbikes, car rentals, travel services. AE, MC, V.*

$$$ ⊞ **Galápago Inn.** This pretty white stucco hotel just south of town primarily accommodates divers; the simply furnished, brightly tiled rooms are not sold by the night but exclusively as part of dive packages—booked in Houston—that take full advantage of the hotel's expert diving staff and advanced certification diving school. The central garden, with tiled benches and a small fountain, contributes to the inn's Mediterranean feel. The staff here are cheerful and accommodating. ⊠ *Carretera a Chankanaab, Km 1.5,* ☎ *987/20663 or 800/847–5708. 58 rooms. 2 restaurants, bar, pool. AE, MC, V.*

$$ ⊞ **Casa del Mar.** Located south of town near several boutiques, sports
★ shops, and restaurants, this three-story hotel is frequented by divers. An unpretentious but tasteful lobby overlooks a small garden. Cheerful rooms feature yellow-tiled headboards, nightstands, and sinks; Mexican artwork; and small balconies with views of the pool just outside or the sea across the road. The bilevel cabanas, which sleep three or four, are a very good buy at $115. ⊠ *Box 129, Carretera a Chankanaab, Km 4,* ☎ *987/21944 or 800/877–4383,* FAX *987/21855. 98 rooms, 8 cabanas. 2 restaurants, 2 bars, pool, hot tub, dive shop, travel services, car rental. AE, MC, V.*

$$ ⊞ **Villas Las Anclas.** Conveniently located parallel to the malecón, these
★ villas are actually furnished apartments for rent by the day, week, or month. The duplexes include a downstairs sitting room, dining area, and kitchenette; a spiral staircase leads up to a small bedroom with a large desk (but no phone or TV). Rooms are extremely attractive, with tastefully bright patterns set off against white walls; they all overlook a quiet courtyard garden. Each apartment is stocked with fresh coffee and a coffeemaker. ⊠ *Box 25, Av. 5a S 325, between Calles 3 and 5 S,* ☎ *987/21955,* ☎ FAX *987/25476. 7 units. Kitchenettes. No credit cards.*

$ ⊞ **Bazar Colonial.** This attractive, modern three-story hotel, located over a small cluster of shops, has pretty red tile floors and bougainvillea, which add splashes of color. Natural wood furniture, TVs (a recent addition), kitchenettes, bookshelves, sofa beds, and an elevator make up for the lack of other amenities, such as a restaurant and a pool. ⊠ *Av. 5a S 9 near Calle 3 S,* ☎ *987/20506,* FAX *987/20542 or 987/20211. 28 rooms. Kitchenettes, shops. AE, MC, V.*

$ ⊞ **Bed & Breakfast Caribo.** This recent (1994) Cozumel arrival was formerly a doctor's residence, renovated by a family from Michigan. The nine air-conditioned rooms are spacious and well furnished, featuring white wicker, blue floral upholstered chairs, and matching serape bedspreads. There's cable TV for guests in the first-floor sitting room. A full (meatless) breakfast buffet is included in the price. Weekly and monthly rates are available. Ask for a room in the back, away from busy Avenida Juárez. ⊠ *Av. Juárez 799,* ☎ *987/23195 or 800/830–5558. 9 rooms with bath, including 2 kitchenette apartments. MC, V.*

$ ⊡ **Mesón San Miguel.** Situated right on the square, this hotel sees a lot
★ of action because of the accessibility of its large public bar and outdoor
café, which are often filled with locals. The remodeled rooms are clean
and functional, with air-conditioning, satellite TV, phones, and balconies overlooking the plaza—amenities unusual in a budget hotel, making this a good bet for your money. ⊠ *Av. Juárez 2 Bis,* ☎ *987/20323
or 987/20233,* FAX *987/21820. 60 rooms. Bar, café, pool, recreation
room. AE, MC, V.*

Nightlife and the Arts

Fiesta Mexicana nights are offered at the **Fiesta Americana Hotel** (☎
987/22622) Thursday and Sunday from 6–9 PM during high season;
they feature folkloric dancers, mariachis, a cock fight, an open-bar buffet dinner, and tequila shots; the cost is about $70.

Bars

For a quiet drink and good people-watching, try **Video Bar Aladino** at
the Mesón San Miguel, at the northern end of the plaza. Serious bar-
hoppers like **Carlos 'n' Charlie's** (⊠ Av. Rafael Melgar 11, between Calles
2 and 4 N, ☎ 987/20191) for hang-off-the-rafters, raucous fun; don't
come here if you're the retiring type. Folks are always spilling out over
the outdoor patio (sometimes literally) at **Chilly's** (⊠ Av. Rafael Melgar near Av. Benito Juárez, ☎ 987/21832), where a papier-mâché
Marilyn Monroe in a *Some Like It Hot* pose surveys a rowdy crowd.
The **Hard Rock Cafe** (⊠ Av. Rafael Melgar 2A near Av. Benito Juárez,
☎ 987/25271) includes all the nostalgic music memorabilia that char-
acterizes the international chain. You and your friends provide the entertainment at the sing-along **Laser-Karaoke Bar** (⊠ Fiesta Inn, ☎
987/22811). Jock types can play video games or check football scores
at the **Sports Page Video Bar and Restaurant** (⊠ Corner 5 Av. N and
Calle 2 N, ☎ 987/21199).

LIVE MUSIC
Sunday evenings bring locals to the **zócalo** to hear mariachis and island musicians playing tropical tunes. The piano bar in **La Gaviota** (⊠
Sol Caribe Cozumel Hotel, ☎ 987/20700, ext. 251) is well attended,
and trios and mariachis perform nightly in the lobby bar from 5 to 11
during high season. For romantic piano or guitar serenades, try the dining room of **Arrecife** (⊠ Hotel Presidente Inter-Continental Cozumel,
☎ 987/20322; high season only). If Frank Sinatra–style entertainment
turns you on, check out **Tony Rome's** (⊠ Av. 5 S 21, between Av. Rosado
Salas and Calle 3 S, ☎ 987/20131), where the owner holds forth at
the microphone. In addition to tasty lobster dishes, **Joe's Lobster House**
(⊠ Av. 10 S 229, between Calle Rosada Salas and Calle 3 S, ☎
987/23275) serves up lively reggae and salsa every night at 10:30; this
is *the* hot spot for live entertainment.

Outdoor Activities and Sports

Most people come to Cozumel to take advantage of the island's water-
related sports—scuba diving, snorkeling, and fishing are particularly
big, but jet skiing, sailboarding, waterskiing, and sailing remain popular as well. You will find services and rentals throughout the island,
especially through major hotels and water-sports centers such as **Del
Mar Aquatics** (⊠ Carretera a Chankanaab, Km 4, ☎ 987/21665 or
800/877–4383, FAX 987/21833) and **Aqua Safari** (⊠ Av. Rafael Melgar 429, between Calles 5 and 10 S, ☎ 987/20101).

Fishing

For the past 22 years, the annual **International Billfish Tournament,** held the last week in April or the first week in May, has drawn anglers from around the world to Cozumel; for more information, contact the International Billfish Tournament (⊠ Box 442, Cozumel 77600; ☎ 800/253–2701, FAX 987/20999).

High-speed fishing boats can be chartered for $300 for a half day or $350 for a full day, for a maximum of six people, from the **Club Naútico de Cozumel** (⊠ Puerto de Abrigo, Av. Rafael Melgar, Box 341, ☎ 987/20118 or 800/253–2701, FAX 987/21135), the island's headquarters for game fishing. Daily charters are easily arranged from the dock or at your hotel, but you might also try **Aquarius Fishing and Tours** (⊠ Calle 3 S, ☎ 987/21092) or **Yucab Reef Diving & Fishing** (⊠ Av. Rosado Salas 85 between Av. Rafael Melgar and Av. 5 S, ☎ 987/24110, ☎ FAX 987/21842) All rates vary with the season.

Scuba Diving

With more than 30 charted reefs whose average depths range from 50 to 80 feet and a water temperature that hits about 75°F–80°F during peak diving season (June–August, when the hotel rates are coincidentally at their lowest), Cozumel is far and away Mexico's number one diving destination. The diversity of options for divers in Cozumel includes deep dives, drift dives, shore dives, wall dives, and night dives, as well as theme dives focusing on ecology, archaeology, sunken ships, and photography. Make sure your instructor has PADI certification (or FMAS, the Mexican equivalent) and is affiliated with the **SSS recompression chamber** (⊠ Calle 5 S 21B, between Av. Rafael Melgar and Av. 5a S, next to Discover Cozumel, ☎ 987/22387 or 987/21848) or the recompression chamber at the **Hospital Civil** (⊠ Av. 11 S, between Calles 10 and 15, ☎ 987/20140 or 987/20525).

DIVE SHOPS AND TOUR OPERATORS

You can choose from a variety of two-tank boat trips and specialty dives ranging from $45 to $60; two-hour resort courses cost about $50–$60, and 1½-hour night dives $30–$35. Basic certification courses, such as PADI's Discover Scuba or Naui's introductory course, are available for about $350, while advanced certification courses cost as much as $700. Equipment rental is relatively inexpensive, ranging from $6 for tanks or a lamp to about $8–$10 for a regulator and B.C. vest; underwater camera rentals can cost as much as $35, video camera rentals run about $75, and professionally shot and edited videos of your own dive are priced at about $160.

In addition to the dive shops in town, many hotels have their own operations and offer dive and hotel packages starting at about $350 for three nights, double occupancy, and two days of diving. You can also pick up a copy of the *Chart of the Reefs of Cozumel* in any dive shop. Before choosing a shop, check credentials, look over the boats and equipment, and consult experienced divers who are familiar with the operators here. Here's a list to get you started on your search: **Aqua Safari** (⊠ Av. Rafael Melgar 429, between Calles 5 and 10 S, ☎ 987/20101); **Blue Angel** (⊠ Av. Rafael Melgar, next to Hotel Villablanca, ☎ 987/21631), for PADI certification; **Blue Bubble** (⊠ Av. 5a S at Calle 3 S, ☎ 987/21865), for PADI instruction; **Dive Paradise** (⊠ Av. Rafael Melgar 601, ☎ FAX 987/21007; **Fantasia Divers** (⊠ Av. 25 at Calle Adolfo Rosado Salas, ☎ 987/22840 or 800/336–3483, FAX 987/21210); **Michelle's Dive Shop** (⊠ Av. 5 S 201 at Calle Adolfo Rosado Salas, ☎ 987/20947); **Ramone Zapata Divers** (⊠ Chankanaab Nature Park, ☎ 987/20502); **Scuba Du** (⊠ Hotel Presidente Inter-Continental Cozumel, ☎ 987/20322 or 987/21379, FAX 987/24130); **Studio Blue** (⊠ Calle Rosado Salas 121, between Calles 5 and 10, ☎ FAX 987/24330); **Tico's Dive Center** (✉ Av. 5 N 121, between Calles 2 and 4, ☎ FAX 987/20276); **Yucab Reef** (✉ Av. Rosado Salas 85, between Av. Rafael Melgar and Av. 5 S, ☎ 987/ 24110, ☎ FAX 987/21842).

Snorkeling

Snorkeling equipment is available at the Hotel Presidente Inter-Continental, La Ceiba, Chankanaab Bay, Playa San Francisco, Club Cozumel Caribe, and directly off the beach near the Fiesta Americana Cozumel Reef and Playa Corona for less than $10 a day.

Snorkeling tours run from $25 to $50, depending on the length, and take in the shallow reefs off Palancar, Colombia, and Yucab. Contact **Snorkozumel** (✉ Av. Rafael E. Melgar 471, ☎ 987/24166 or 987/20246) or **Caribe Tours** for information and reservations. **Fiesta Cozumel** (✉ Calle 11 S 598, between Avs. 25 and 30, ☎ 987/20725, FAX 987/21389) runs snorkeling tours from the 45-foot catamaran *El Zorro*. The *Zorro* and the 60-foot catamaran *Fury* are also used for sunset cruises, both of which can be booked through Caribe Tours.

Shopping

Cozumel has three main shopping areas: **downtown** along the waterfront, on Avenida Rafael Melgar, and on some of the side streets around the plaza (there are more than 150 shops in this area alone); at the **crafts market** (✉ Calle 1 S, behind the plaza) in town, which sells a respectable assortment of Mexican wares; and at the cruise-ship **passenger terminal** south of town, near the Casa Del Mar, La Ceiba, and Sol Caribe hotels. There are also small clusters of shops at **Plaza del Sol** (on the east side of the main plaza), **Villa Mar** (on the north side of the main plaza), the **Plaza Confetti** (on the south side of the main plaza), and **Plaza Maya** (across from the Sol Caribe). As a general rule, the newer, trendier shops line the waterfront, while the area around Avenida 5a houses the better crafts shops. The **town market** (✉ Calle Rosada Salas, between Avs. 20a and 25a) sells fresh produce and other essentials.

Department Stores

Relatively small and more like U.S. variety stores than department stores, the following nevertheless carry a relatively wide array of goods, from the useful to the frivolous. **Chachy Plaza** (✉ Av. Benito Juárez 5, near church at the back of plaza, ☎ 987/20130) sells everything from liquor and perfume to snorkeling gear and snack food. **Duty Free Mexico** (✉ Av. Rafael Melgar at Calle 3 S, ☎ 987/20796) puts a strong emphasis on top-line fragrances. **Pama** (✉ Av. Rafael Melgar S 9, ☎ 987/20090), near the pier, features imported food, luggage, snorkeling gear, jewelry, and crystal. **Prococo** (✉ Av. Rafael Melgar N 99, ☎ 987/21875 or 987/21964) offers a good selection of liquor, jewelry, and gift items.

Specialty Stores

CLOTHING

Several trendy sportswear stores line Avenida Rafael Melgar (✉ between Calles 2 and 6). Try **Aca Joe** (✉ Av. Rafael Melgar 101, ☎ 987/ 23677), a Mexican-based chain, for casual resortwear in the latest styles. **Explora** (✉ Av. Rafael Melgar 49, ☎ 987/20316) offers a casual line of modish cotton sports clothing. **La Fiesta Cozumel** (✉ Av. Rafael Melgar N 164-B, ☎ 987/22032), a large store catering to the cruise ships, sells a variety of T-shirts as well as souvenirs.

JEWELRY

Jewelry on Cozumel is pricey, but it tends to be of higher quality than the jewelry you'll find in many of the other Yucatán towns. **Casablanca**

(⊠ Av. Rafael Melgar N 33, ☎ 987/21177) specializes in gold, silver, and gemstones, as well as expensive crafts. The elegant **Diamond Creations** (⊠ Av. Rafael Melgar Sur 131, ☎ 987/25330 or 800/322–6476, FAX 987/25334) lets you custom design a piece of jewelry from an extensive collection of loose diamonds—or emeralds, rubies, sapphires, or tanzanite. Nothing but fine silver, gold, and coral jewelry—particularly silver bracelets and earrings—is sold at **Joyería Palancar** (⊠ Av. Rafael Melgar N 15, ☎ 987/21468). Quality gemstones and striking designs are the strong point at **Rachat & Romero** (⊠ Av. Rafael Melgar 101, ☎ 987/20571). The toney **Van Cleef & Arpels** (⊠ Av. Rafael Melgar N 54, ☎ 987/21143) offers a superlative collection of high-end silver and gold jewelry.

MEXICAN CRAFTS

Los Cinco Soles (⊠ Av. Rafael Melgar N 27, ☎ 987/20132 or 987/22040) is your best bet for one-stop shopping. The nearly block-long store features an excellent variety of well-priced, well-displayed items, including blue-rim glassware, brass and tin animals from Jalisco, and silver jewelry. **Talavera** (⊠ Av. 5a S 349, ☎ 987/20171) carries beautiful ceramics from all over Mexico—including tiles from the Yucatán—as well as masks from Guerrero, brightly painted wooden animals from Oaxaca, and carved chests from Guadalajara.

COZUMEL A TO Z

Arriving and Departing

By Cruise Ship

At least a dozen cruise lines call at Cozumel and/or Playa del Carmen, including, from Fort Lauderdale, **Chandris/Celebrity** (☎ 800/437-3111), **Cunard/Crown** (☎ 800/221–4770), and **Princess** (☎ 800/568–3262); from Miami, **Carnival** (☎ 800/327–9501), **Costa** (☎ 800/327–2537), **Dolphin/Majesty** (☎ 800/222–1003), **Norwegian** (☎ 800/327–7030), and **Royal Caribbean** (☎ 800/327–6700); from New Orleans, **Commodore** (☎ 800/327–5617); and from Tampa, **Holland America** (☎ 800/426–0327).

By Ferry

Passenger-only ferries depart from the dock at **Playa del Carmen** (no phone; ☞ Chapter 5) for the 40-minute trip to the main pier in Cozumel. They leave approximately every hour between 5:15 AM and 8:45 PM and cost about $7 one way, $10 round-trip. Return service to Playa operates from roughly 4 AM to 7:45 PM. Verify the regularly changing schedule. The car ferry from **Puerto Morelos** (☎ 987/21722), on the mainland to the north of Playa del Carmen, is not recommended unless you *must* bring your car.

By Jetfoil

A waterjet catamaran and two large speed boats make the trip between Cozumel (downtown pier, at the zócalo) and Playa del Carmen. This service, operated by **Aviomar** (Av. 5a, between Calles 2 and 4, ☎ 987/20588 or 987/20477), costs the same as the ferry and takes almost as much time, but the vessel is considerably more comfortable and offers on-board videos and refreshments. The boats make at least 10 crossings a day, leaving Playa del Carmen approximately every one to two hours between 5:15 AM and 8:45 PM and returning from Cozumel between 4 AM and 8 PM. Tickets are sold at the piers in both ports one hour before departure; call to confirm the schedule.

By Plane

The **Cozumel Airport** (☎ 987/20928) is 3 kilometers (2 miles) north of town. **Continental** (☎ 987/20487) provides nonstop service from Houston. **Mexicana** (☎ 987/20157) flies nonstop from Miami and San Francisco; **Aerocaribe** (☎ 987/20928) and **Aerocozumel** (☎ 987/20877), both Mexicana subsidiaries, fly to Cancún and other destinations in Mexico, including Chichén Itzá, Mérida, and Playa del Carmen.

BETWEEN THE AIRPORT AND HOTELS

Because of an agreement between the taxi drivers' and the bus drivers' unions, there is no taxi service from the airport; taxi service is available *to* the airport, however. Arriving passengers reach their hotels via the *colectivo,* a van with a maximum capacity of eight. Buy a ticket at the airport exit: the charge is $5 per passenger to the hotel zones, a little under $3 into town. If you want to get to your hotel without waiting for the van to fill and for other passengers to be dropped off, you can hire an *especial*—an individual van costing a little under $20 to the hotel zones, about $8 to the city. Taxis to the airport cost about $8 from the hotel zones and approximately $5 from downtown. Most car rental agencies (☞ Contacts and Resources, *below*) maintain offices in the terminal.

Getting Around

By Bicycle, Moped, and Motorcycle

Mopeds and motorcycles are very popular here but also extremely dangerous because of heavy traffic, potholes, and hidden stop signs; accidents happen all too frequently. Mexican law now requires all passengers to wear helmets; it's a $25 fine if you don't. For mopeds, go to **Auto Rent** (✉ Carretera Costera S, ☎ 987/20844, ext. 712), **Rentadora Caribe** (✉ Calle Rosada Salas 3, ☎ 987/20955 or 987/20961), **Rentadora Chac** (✉ Calle 1 S 101, between Avs. 10 and 15, ☎ 987/23325), or **Rentadora Cozumel** (✉ Calle Rosada Salas 3 B, ☎ 987/21429; Av. 10a S at Calle 1, ☎ 987/21120). Mopeds go for about $25 per day; insurance is included. Auto Rent and Rentadora Chac also rent bicycles for approximately $5–$8 per day.

By Bus

Local bus service runs mainly within the town of San Miguel, although there is a route from town to the airport. Service is irregular but inexpensive (under 20¢).

By Car

Open-air Jeeps and other rental cars, especially those with four-wheel drive, are a good way of getting down dirt roads leading to secluded beaches and small Maya ruins (although the rental insurance policy may not always cover these jaunts). The only gas station on Cozumel, at the corner of Avenida Juárez and Avenida 30a, is open daily 7 AM–midnight.

By Taxi

Taxi service is available 24 hours a day, with a 25% surcharge between midnight and 6 AM, at the main location (✉ Calle 2 N, ☎ 987/20041 or 987/20236) or at the *malecón,* as the oceanside walkway is called, at the main pier in town. You can also hail taxis on the street, and there are taxis waiting at all the major hotels. Fixed rates of about $3 are charged to go between town and either hotel zone, about $8 from most hotels to the airport, and about $6–$12 from the northern hotels or town to Chankanaab park or San Francisco beach.

Contacts and Resources

Car Rentals

Following is a list of rental firms that handle two- and four-wheel-drive vehicles (all the major hotels have rental offices): **Budget** (✉ Av. 5a at Calle 2 N, ☎ 987/20903; cruise-ship terminal, 987/21732; airport, 987/21742), **Hertz** (airport, ☎ 987/23888), **National Interrent** (✉ Av. Juárez, Lote 10, near Calle 10, ☎ 987/23263 or 987/24101), and **Rentadora Aguilla** (✉ Av. Rafael Melgar 685, ☎ 987/20729). Rental rates start at $50 a day.

Doctors and Dentists

The **Centro de Salud clinic** (✉ Av. 20 at Calle 11, ☎ 987/20140) provides 24-hour emergency care, and the **Medical Specialties Center** (✉ Av. 20 N 425, ☎ 987/21419 or 987/22919) offers 24-hour air ambulance service and a 24-hour pharmacy. **Cozumel Chiropractic** (✉ Av. 5 Sur 24-A, between Calles 3 and 5, ☎ 987/25099) offers bargain-priced therapeutic massage.

Emergencies

Police (✉ Anexo del Palacio Municipal, ☎ 987/20092). **Red Cross** (✉ Av. Rosada Salas at Av. 20a S, ☎ 987/21058). **Air Ambulance** (☎ 987/20912). **Recompression Chamber** (✉ Calle 5 S 21-B, between Av. Rafael Melgar and Av. 5a S, ☎ 987/21430).

Guided Tours

See Tour Operators, *below,* for addresses and telephone numbers of the companies mentioned here.

Air Tours

Caribe Tours offers a plane trip to **Chichén Itzá**; the price of $145 includes the flight, transfers to the ruins, buffet lunch, and a guide. The company also flies to the **Sian Ka'an Ecological Biosphere**; in addition to lunch, this $160 plane trip includes a boat ride through the biosphere's mangroves for a closer look at the flora and fauna of the region.

Horseback Tours

Rancho Buenavista (☎ 987/21537) runs four-hour guided horseback tours that visit three Maya ruins tucked away in Cozumel's tropical forest. The tour departs from Restaurant Acuario (✉ Av. Rafael Melgar at Calle 11), weekdays at noon and Saturday at 11.

Orientation

Tours of the island's sights cost about $35 and can be arranged through a travel agency such as Fiesta Cozumel. Caribe Tours focuses on the botanical gardens, archaeological replicas, and reef snorkeling at Chankanaab; the cost is about $40 and includes an open-bar lunch. Private taxi tours range from $30 to $50 per day depending on which parts of the island you wish to visit.

Specialty Tours

Glass-bottom-boat trips are provided by Turismo Aviomar. The air-conditioned semi-submarine *Mermaid* glides over a number of reefs that host a dazzling array of fish; the daily tour, which costs about $30, lasts 1 hour and 45 minutes and includes soft drinks. A similar trip aboard the *Nautilus IV* is available through Fiesta Cozumel.

Off-island tours to **Tulum and Xel-Há,** run by Aviomar and Caribe Tours, cost about $75 and include the 30-minute ferry trip to Playa del Carmen, the 45-minute bus ride to Tulum, 1½–2 hours at the ruins, entrance fees, guides, lunch, and a stop for snorkeling at Xel-Há lagoon.

Day trips to the eco-archaeological theme park of **Xcaret,** about halfway between Playa del Carmen and Tulum, are offered by Fiesta Cozumel. The $50 price includes round-trip ferry to Playa del Carmen, entrance to the park, and a bilingual guide.

Late-Night Pharmacy

Farmacia Joaquín (Main Plaza, north side, ☎ 987/22520) is open Monday–Saturday 8 AM–10 PM and Sunday 9–1 and 5–9.

Travel Agencies and Tour Operators

Caribe Tours (✉ Av. Rafael Melgar at Calle 5 S, ☎ FAX 987/23100 or 987/23154); **Fiesta Cozumel Holidays/American Express** (in all major hotel lobbies; Calle 11 S 598, between Avs. 25 and 30, ☎ 987/20725); **Turismo Aviomar** (in several hotel lobbies, including El Presidente; Av. 5 N 8, between Calles 2 and 4, ☎ 987/20588).

Visitor Information

State tourism office (✉ upstairs in the Plaza del Sol mall, at the east end of the main square, ☎ 987/20972) is open weekdays 9–2:30. A good source of information on lodgings (and many other things) is the **Cozumel Island Hotel Association** (✉ Calle 2 N at 15a, ☎ 987/23132, FAX 987/22809), open weekdays 8–2 and 4–7.

THE NORTH CARIBBEAN COAST

Updated by
Patricia Alisau

Above all else, beaches are what define the eastern coast of the Yucatán peninsula. White, sandy strands with offshore coral reefs, oversize tropical foliage and jungle, Maya ruins, and abundant wildlife make the coastline a marvelous destination for lovers of the outdoors. The scrubby limestone terrain is mostly flat and dry, punctuated only by sinkholes, while the shores are broken up by freshwater lagoons, underwater caves, and cliffs.

The various destinations on the coast cater to different preferences. The once laid-back town of Playa del Carmen is now host to resorts as glitzy as those found in Cancún and Cozumel, though still not quite as expensive, while the lazy fishing village of Puerto Morelos so far has been only slightly altered to accommodate foreign tourists. Rustic fishing and scuba diving lodges on the even more secluded Boca Paila peninsula are gaining a well-deserved reputation for bone fishing and superb diving on virgin reefs. The beaches, from Punta Bete to Sian Ka'an, south of Tulum, are beloved of scuba divers, snorkelers, birders, and beachcombers and offer accommodations to suit every budget, from campsites and bungalows to condos and luxury hotels. Ecotourism is on the rise, with special programs designed to involve visitors in preserving the threatened sea-turtle population. Then, too, there are the Maya ruins at Tulum, superbly situated on a bluff overlooking the Caribbean, and, a short distance inland, at Cobá, whose towering jungle-shrouded pyramids evoke its importance as a leading center of commerce in the Maya world. The waters up and down the coast, littered with shipwrecks and relics from the heyday of piracy, are dotted with mangrove swamps and minuscule islands where only the birds hold sway.

Exploring

The coast is basically divided into two areas: Puerto Morelos to Tulum, which has the most sites and places to lodge; and Tulum to Chetumal, where civilization thins out quite a bit. In the following, we detail only the first part of the coast. If you want to venture farther, you'll be rewarded by alluringly beautiful but remote beaches, coves, inlets, lagoons, and tropical landscapes. The southern Caribbean area includes Xcalak, a fishing village near the tip of the Xcalak peninsula which divides Chetumal Bay from the Caribbean Sea and attracts devoted divers; the spectacularly vast and beautiful Laguna de Bacalar, the second largest lake in Mexico, also frequented by scuba divers and other lovers of water sports; and Chetumal, the last Mexican town on the southern Caribbean. Chetumal feels more Central American than Mexican—not surprising, given its proximity to Belize. Run-down (but often charming) clapboard houses interspersed with low-lying ramshackle commercial establishments line the quiet streets. The mixed population includes many black Caribbeans, and the arts reflect this eclectic combination—the music includes reggae, salsa, and calypso (but little mariachi). The many Middle Eastern inhabitants have influenced the cuisine, which represents an exotic blend of Yucatecan, Mexican, and Lebanese.

Puerto Morelos

❶ *36 km (22 mi) south of Cancún.*

Puerto Morelos has been left remarkably free of the large-scale development so common farther south, though each year more and more tourists stop here to take in its easygoing pace, cheap accommodations, and convenient seaside location near a superb offshore coral reef. The reef at Morelos—about 1,800 feet offshore—has claimed many ships over the centuries, and nowadays divers visit the sunken wrecks. The caves of the sleeping sharks of documentary movie fame are also 8 kilometers (5 miles) east of the town.

Once a point of departure for Maya women making pilgrimages by canoe to Cozumel, the sacred isle of the fertility goddess, Ixchel, Morelos today is not very different from many small towns in the Spanish-speaking Caribbean. There is not much to it beyond a gas station, a central square, and auto repair shops. Nature endowed Puerto Morelos with a fine deep-sea port (the principal port for the area until the road to Puerto Juárez was built), so today ferries and freight ships call regularly. Most of the action is centered on the long pier south of the square, where vehicles line up for hours waiting for the ferry to depart. Three lighthouses from different eras break up the long stretch of beach, and boats to take out to the surrounding reefs can be rented on the beach.

Dining and Lodging

$ ✕ **Los Pelícanos.** If you're looking for good fresh fish, stop by this thatched-roof restaurant on the beach, where you can spend hours feasting on the catch of the day and watching the boats go by. ⊠ *On oceanfront near main plaza,* ☎ *987/10014. MC, V.*

$$ ▦ **Cabañas Playa Ojo de Agua.** This dive-oriented hotel is on a lovely beach just north of town. Most of the guest rooms have kitchenettes, ceiling fans, and views of the sea or the courtyard gardens. There is a freshwater pool on the premises, but the restaurant stays open only during December–April. ⊠ *1 block north of town,* ☎ *987/10027. For reservations: Calle 12, No. 96, Mérida Yucatán, 97050,* ☎ *99/250292. 16 rooms. Pool, dive shop. No credit cards.*

$$$$ ✕▦ **Caribbean Reef Club at Villa Marina.** This rather functional-look-
★ ing white condo complex is one of the newest hideaways along the coast. The colonial-style suites have marble floors, air-conditioning, ceiling fans, blue-tile kitchenettes, floral pastel linens, and arched windows. Sliding glass doors lead to balconies outside, where you can slip in an

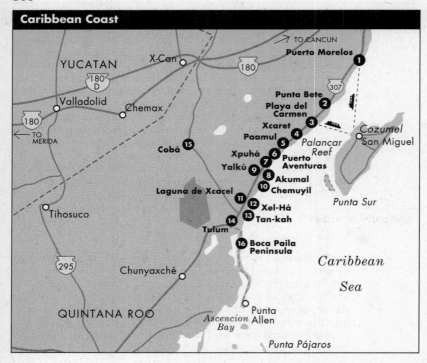

Caribbean Coast

afternoon nap on your own private hammock. The adjacent restaurant is easily the most picturesque in town, with a balcony overlooking the sea, hand-painted tile tables, and candlelight at night. A Jamaican chef prepares superb coconut shrimp, seafood gumbo, jerk chicken, and other Caribbean specialties. ⊠ *South of ferry dock. For reservations: Box 1526, Cancún, Quintana Roo, 77500, ☎ 987/10191 or 800/3–CANCÚN, ᶠᴬˣ 987/10190. 21 suites. Restaurant, bar, pool, water sports. MC, V.*

Outdoor Activities and Sports

Snorkeling gear, fishing tackle, and boats can be rented from the **Aqua Deportes** (no phone) dive shop on the town's main beach, by the plaza. The **Posada Amor** hotel can also fix you up with deep-sea fishing excursions.

Punta Bete

❷ *22 km (16½ mi) south of Puerto Morelos.*

Punta Bete is a 6½-kilometer (4-mile) white sand beach between rocky lagoons. This point is the setting for several bungalow-style hotels that have almost become cult places for travelers who love being in or on the water. All the properties are set off from Route 307 at the end of a 2⅓-kilometer (1½-mile) paved road; many of them are still recovering from the damage that Hurricane Roxanne caused in late 1995.

Lodging

$$$$ ⊞ **Posada del Capitán Lafitte.** Set on an invitingly long stretch of
★ beach just 10 kilometers (6 miles) north of Playa del Carmen at Punta Bete, this lodging is known for its genuinely chummy, unpretentious atmosphere. It's a simple cluster of two-unit cabanas, each with its own private bath and ceiling fan. A duplex at the south end of the prop-

erty has four two-bedroom, two-bath units, ideal for families. Breakfast, dinner, tax, and tips are included in the room rate. Group activities include snorkeling trips, scuba certification and dives, fishing, and birding. All reservations must be prepaid. ⊠ *On a dirt road (follow the signs), about 3 km (2 mi) off Rte. 307,* ☎ *987/3–0214,* FAX *987/4–5226. For reservations: Turquoise Reef Group, Box 2664, Evergreen, CO 80439,* ☎ *303/674–9615 or 800/538–6802,* FAX *303/674–8735. 45 rooms. Restaurant ($$), bar, beach, pool, dive shop, car rental. AE, MC, V.*

Outdoor Activities and Sports

Posada de Capitan Lafitte (☎ 800/538–6802 and 987/3–0214), on Highway 307 just north of Playa del Carmen, has an excellent, full-service dive shop called Buccaneer's Landing. Services include diving and snorkeling excursions, scuba resort courses, and horseback riding.

Playa del Carmen

❸ *10 km (6 mi) south of Punta Bete and 68 km (41 mi) south of Cancún.*

Only a few decades ago, Playa del Carmen was a deserted beach where Indian families raised coconut palms to produce copra. Nowadays its alabaster-white beach and small offshore reefs attract swimmers, snorkelers, and turtle-watchers, and the town has become the preferred destination of travelers who want easy access to gorgeous beaches and the archaeological sites of Yucatán.

The busiest parts of Playa are down by the **ferry pier,** around the **main plaza,** and along the pedestrian walkway. Take a stroll north from the pier along the beach and you'll see the essence of the town: simple restaurants roofed with palm fronds, where people sit around drinking beer for hours; a few campgrounds; and lots of hammocks. On the south side of the pier is Playacar, a first-class, lavish hotel that brought a sense of luxury and style to Playa del Carmen in 1991. If you walk away from the beach, you'll come upon the affluent section: several condominium projects and well-tended gardens and lawns that can be seen from the street. From here, only the sandy streets, the small vestiges of Maya structures, and the stunning turquoise sea on the horizon suggest you're in the tropics. The streets at both ends of town peter out into the jungle.

Dining and Lodging

$$ ✕ **La Parrilla.** The far end of the pedestrian walkway gained a social center when La Parrilla opened in 1994 at the Rincón del Sol plaza. A branch of an enduringly popular Cancún chain, the open-air restaurant sits a few feet above the street, and it's hard to resist stopping in for a beer, a platter of chicken fajitas, or the best lobster in Playa. ⊠ *Av. 5 at Calle 8, no phone. MC, V.*

$$ ✕ **Limones.** Probably the most romantic place in town, this restaurant
★ offers dining by candlelight, either alfresco in a courtyard or under the shelter of a palapa indoors. House favorites include copious entrées such as fettuccine, lasagna, and lemon-sautéed beef scaloppine. Appetizers might be home-baked pizza bread or salads. The daily dinner special is the best bargain in town. ⊠ *Av. 5 at Calle 6, no phone. MC, V.*

$$ ✕ **Máscaras.** The wood-burning brick oven here produces exception-
★ ally good thin-crusted pizzas and breads; the homemade pastas are also excellent.Be sure to try the calamari in garlic and oil. Masks from throughout the world cover the walls; live music including salsa bands starts nightly at 7. Máscaras is a central gathering spot with a view of the goings-on at the zócalo. ⊠ *Av. Juárez across from plaza,* ☎ *987/30194. MC, V.*

$ ✕ **El Tacolote.** Opened in 1992, this fanciful, colorful restaurant continues expanding, overtaking less popular eateries. Mariachis play on most evenings in front of the sidewalk tables, where diners feast on platters of grilled meats, fajitas, or tacos with all sorts of fillings. You can eat cheaply or splurge on a multi-course feast while watching the action on the plaza from an outdoor table. ✉ *Av. Juárez across from plaza,* ☎ *987/30066. MC, V.*

$$$ ⌂ **Las Palapas.** At this ideal get-away-from-it-all destination resort,
★   white cabanas are cheerfully blue trimmed, and duplexes feature balconies or porches, palapas, and hammocks. The beach and pool are complemented by a shuffleboard area, clubhouse, beach bar, palapa bar, and attractive palapa restaurant (the buffets can be elaborate, but we've had reports that the food was disappointing in low season). Room rates include breakfast and dinner. Reserve early; a three-night minimum stay is required. ✉ *Km 292 on Rte. 307, Box 116, Playa del Carmen, Quintana Roo, 77710,* ☎ *987/3–0582 or 800/433–0885,* ℻ *987/3–0458. 55 cabanas. Restaurant, 2 bars, in-room safes, pool, beach. MC, V.*

$$ ⌂ **Albatros Royale.** One of the nicest complexes right on the beach,
★   the Royale opened in 1991 but still looks brand-new. Two-story palapa-covered buildings face each other along a pathway to the sand. Sea breezes and ceiling fans cool the large rooms, simply decorated with white walls and tile floors. Complimentary coffee and sweet rolls are set out by the front desk each morning. The Royale fills up quickly; advance reservations are advised. ✉ *Calle 8 between beach and Av. 5,* ☎ *987/30001,* ℻ *987/30002. For reservations: Turquoise Reef Group, Box 2664, Evergreen, CO 80439,* ☎ *303/674–9615 or 800/538–6802,* ℻ *303/674–8735. 31 rooms. Restaurant (at Cabañas Albatros), dive shop. MC, V.*

$$ ⌂ **Alejari.** This two-story complex set amid lush gardens is one of the most pleasant accommodations on Playa's north beach. Some rooms have kitchenettes and fans or air-conditioning. A small market and a long-distance phone booth sit on the premises. ✉ *Calle 6N. For reservations: Box 166, Playa del Carmen, Quintana Roo, 77710,* ☎ *987/30374,* ℻ *987/30005. 18 rooms. Kitchenettes, grocery. MC, V.*

$ ⌂ **Maya-Bric.** Larger than most other beachfront hotels in Playa, the Maya-Bric has a pretty landscaped courtyard and pool area. The rooms have either air-conditioning or fans and are comfortable and basic, with few frills. The on-site dive shop runs snorkeling, diving, and sightseeing trips to the nearby reefs. ✉ *5a Av. Norte between Calles 8 and 10, Playa del Carmen, Quintana Roo, 77710,* ☎ ℻ *987/30011. 29 rooms. Restaurant, pool, dive shop. No credit cards.*

$ ⌂ **Posada Rosa Mirador.** This small posada less than a block from the beach has the nicest rooms in its price range, spare but clean, with one or two double beds and private baths. A dorm-type room on the top floor sleeps six. ✉ *Calle 12 at Av. 5, Playa del Carmen, Quintana Roo, 77710, no phone. No credit cards.*

$$$$ ✕⌂ **Continental Plaza Playacar.** The centerpiece of an 880-acre master-planned resort, this pastel, blush-colored palace faces the sea on the south side of the ferry pier. The tropical-style rooms have ocean views and balconies or patios. The beach is one of the nicest in Playa del Carmen and far less crowded than those to the north. The breakfast buffet is excellent. A shopping-dining-banking complex links the hotel with downtown Playa del Carmen via a pleasant pedestrian mall. There's a full-scale scuba and water-sports facility and an 18-hole championship golf course; ask about golf packages. ✉ *Fraccionamiento Playacar, Playa del Carmen, Quintana Roo, 77710,* ☎ *987/3–0100*

or 800/882–6684. 188 rooms, 16 suites. 2 restaurants, bar, pool, 18-hole golf course, dive shop, shop, travel services. AE, MC, V.

$$$$ ✕⊞ **Diamond Resort.** Part of the Playacar development, Diamond is an all-inclusive resort that sprawls down a sloping hill to the sea. The guest rooms are spread out in thatched-roof villas along winding paths. Unlike that of many other all-inclusive resorts, Diamond's design allows peace and privacy. One pool is used for games and activities, while another is reserved for quiet lounging. Guests get a bit rowdy at the karaoke bar and outdoor stage, but the noise does not reach the guest rooms. Buffet-style meals are plentiful and imaginatively prepared. ✉ *In Playacar development,* ☎ *987/3–0039,* FAX *987/3–0346. For reservations: 901 Ponce de Leon Blvd., Suite 400, Coral Gables, FL 33134,* ☎ *800/858–2258,* FAX *305/444–4848. 296 rooms. Dining room, bar, 2 pools, 4 tennis courts, dive shop, shop, car rental.*

Outdoor Activities and Sports

The oldest dive shop in town, **Tank Ha** (✉ Maya-Bric hotel, ☎ FAX 987/30011) arranges diving and snorkeling trips to the reefs. **Wet Dreams** (✉ Albatros Royale hotel, no phone) has certified, bilingual instructors. Other shops are at the Costa del Mar hotel, Cabañas Albatros, and Playacar.

Shopping

Xop (✉ Rincón del Sol, Av. 5 at Calle 8, no phone) is one of the best places on the coast for handcrafted wooden masks and statues and silver jewelry set with local semiprecious stones and amber. **El Vuelo de los Niños Pajaros** (✉ Rincón del Sol, Av. 5 at Calle 8, ☎ 987/30445) has a great selection of regional music on CD and tape, along with handcrafted paper, cards, incense, and beaded baskets.

Xcaret

❹ *6 km (4 mi) south of Playa del Carmen, 72 km (50 mi) south of Cancún.*

This sacred Maya city and port has been developed into a 250-acre ecological theme park on a gorgeous stretch of coastline. Maya ruins are scattered over the lushly landscaped property. Attractions include an underground river ride through a series of caves and the opportunity to swim with dolphins ($60); only 36 people are allowed in the water with them each day, so arrive early to sign up for your slot. An artificially created beach, breakwater, and lagoons are perfect for snorkeling and swimming; instruction and water-sports equipment rentals are available. Xcaret also includes a botanical garden, a museum with reproductions of the Yucatán peninsula's main archaeological sites, a tropical aquarium, a wild bird sanctuary, stables with riding demonstrations, a dive shop, and several restaurants. A new nighttime attraction is a dinner show and walk through a candlelit Maya village. The highlight is an exhibition by the famed Flying Indians of Papantla. The show is presented Tuesday and Thursday at 9 PM; tickets can be purchased in advance from travel agencies and major hotels at Playa del Carmen or Cancún. ☎ *98/830632 or 98/830765.* ⊟ *$25; dinner show $59.* ⊘ *Oct.–Mar., daily 8:30–5; Apr.–Sept., daily 8:30–6.*

Dining

$ ✕ **Restaurant Xcaret.** This small palapa restaurant, its walls lined with photos from diving expeditions, serves conch ceviche, lobster, poc chuc, and french fries at prices far lower than those inside the Xcaret theme park. ✉ *Hwy. 307 at the Xcaret turnoff, no phone. No credit cards.*

Paamul

❺ *10 km (6 mi) south of Xcaret.*

Beachcombers and snorkelers are fond of Paamul, a crescent-shaped lagoon with clear, placid waters sheltered by the coral reef at the lagoon's mouth. Shells, sand dollars, and even glass beads—some from the sunken pirate ship at Akumal—wash onto the sandy parts of the beach. Trailer camps, cabanas, and tent camps are scattered along the shore; a restaurant sells cold beer and fresh fish; and in the summer visitors may view one of Paamul's chief attractions: sea turtle hatchlings on the beach. A jungle path to the north leads to a lagoon four times the size of the first and even more private.

Dining and Lodging

$$ ✕🏨 **Cabañas Paamul.** This small hostelry on a perfect white sand beach combines seclusion and comfort. The seven white sea-facing bungalows all have two double beds and ceiling fans; hot-water showers and air-conditioning are gradually being added. The hotel turns Mexican holidays into fiestas for the guests, and there are activities galore. The property includes 170 camping sites for motor homes and tents, and a full-service dive shop. ✉ *Km 85, Hwy. 307. For reservations: Box 83, Playa del Carmen, Quintana Roo 77710,* ☎ *99/259422. 7 rooms. Restaurant, dive shop. No credit cards.*

Puerto Aventuras

❻ *12 km (7 mi) south of Paamul.*

Puerto Aventuras is a 900-acre self-contained resort, which will eventually include a 250-slip marina, tennis club, beach club, 18-hole golf course, shopping mall, movie theater, and five deluxe hotels with a total of 2,000 rooms. At press time, facilities in operation included several restaurants and shops, nine holes of the golf course, an excellent dive shop, and a 95-slip marina. In addition, the **CEDAM underwater archaeology museum,** founded by Mexican diver-businessman Pablo Bush Romero, displays models of old ships as well as coins, canons, sewing needles, and nautical devices recovered from Mexican waters by CEDAM members; it's open daily 10–1 and 2–6. Also in operation are three hotels and several condo and time-share units. Currently, the entire complex is losing money, and some of the services are not up to par.

Dining and Lodging

$$ ✕ **Carlos 'n' Charlie's.** Having a branch of this popular restaurant chain in town is a sign of true resort status. Carlos Anderson's restaurants are known for being wacky, wild, and rowdy and for serving ample portions of well-prepared barbecued ribs and chicken, enchiladas, carne asada, and other Mexican dishes, and powerful tequila drinks. ✉ *In commercial center, no phone. MC, V.*

$$$$ 🏨 **Club de Playa.** This 30-room hotel underwent extensive renovations in 1995 and has become part of the Colony Resorts chain. The spacious rooms have stunning views of the Caribbean, and the swimming pool seems to flow right into the sea. One of the coast's best dive shops is on the property. Guests can also enjoy the facilities (including nine holes of golf) and restaurants at the all-inclusive Club Oasis hotel on the other side of the marina. ✉ *On beach near marina. For reservations:* ☎ 🖷 *987/35100. 30 rooms. Restaurant, pool, exercise room, dive shop, marina. AE, MC, V.*

$$$$ 🏨 **Continental Plaza Puerto Aventuras.** Situated on the marina a short distance from the beach, the Continental Plaza has a variety of rooms, many with kitchenettes. Most guest quarters are decorated in soft shades of blue and peach and feature French doors opening onto balconies overlooking the pool. The hotel has a shuttle service to the beach; restaurants, shops, and water-sports services are within walking distance. ✉ *At marina, Puerto Aventuras, Quintana Roo, 77710,* ☎ *987/35133 or 800/882–6684,* FAX *987/35134. 60 rooms, 40 with kitchenettes. Restaurant, bar, pool, bicycles, car rental. AE, MC, V.*

Outdoor Activities and Sports
Mike Madden's CEDAM Dive Centers (✉ Club de Playa Hotel, ☎ 987/22233 or 987/35129, FAX 987/41339) is a full-service dive shop with certification courses; cave and cenote diving is a specialty.

Akumal

❽ *37 km (22 mi) south of Playa del Carmen, 102 km (59 mi) south of Cancún.*

The name Akumal, meaning "Place of the Turtle," recalls ancient Maya times, when the beach was the nesting ground for thousands of turtles. The place first attracted international attention in 1926, when explorers discovered the *Mantanceros,* a Spanish galleon that sank in 1741. Three decades later, Akumal became headquarters for the Mexican Underwater Explorers Club (CEDAM). Akumal continues to be famous for its diving. Area dive shops sponsor resort courses and certification courses, and luxury hotels and condominiums offer year-round packages comprising airfare, accommodations, and diving. Deep-sea fishing for giant marlin, bonito, and sailfish is also popular.

Akumal consists of three distinct areas. Half Moon Bay to the north is lined with private homes and condominiums and has some of the prettiest beaches and best snorkeling in the area. Akumal proper consists of a large resort and small Maya community with a market, laundry facilities, and pharmacy. More condos and homes and an all-inclusive resort are at Akumal Aventuras to the south. People come here to walk on the deliciously long beaches filled with shells, crabs, and migrant birds.

❾ Devoted snorkelers may want to walk to **Yalkú,** a practically unvisited lagoon just north of Akumal along an unmarked dirt road. Wending its way out to the sea, Yalkú hosts throngs of parrot fish in superbly clear water with visibility to 160 feet, but it has no facilities.

Dining and Lodging
$$ ✕ **La Lunita.** Locals and enterprising tourists congregate at the indoor and patio tables of this converted one-bedroom condo at Half Moon Bay for good conversation and innovative cuisine. Regulars swear by the fresh fish served with a lime and cilantro sauce or smothered in tomatoes and onions. You'll need a car, a cab, or strong legs to reach this place, but it's worth it. ✉ *Go through entranceway at Club Akumal Caribe, and then turn left at dirt road heading north to Half Moon Bay to the Hacienda de la Tortuga; condo office,* ☎ *987/22421. No credit cards.*

$$$$ ✕▣ **Club Oasis Akumal.** An all-inclusive luxury hotel, this sprawling property started as the private preserve of millionaire Pablo Bush Romero, a friend of Jacques Cousteau. Today the beautiful beach—protected by an offshore reef—and the pier are used as the starting point for canoeing, snorkeling, diving, fishing, and windsurfing jaunts. The U-shaped building, with nautical decor, features handsome mahogany furniture and sunken blue-tile showers between Moorish arches (no doors!). All rooms have balconies (you can choose a sea view or a garden view) and air-conditioning or ceiling fans (same price). The clientele consists primarily of Americans and Canadians on package deals, though non-group guests are also welcome. ⊠ *For reservations: 3520 Piedmont Rd. NE, Suite 325, Atlanta, GA 30305,* ☎ *987/22828 or 800/446–2747,* FAX *987/35051 or 404/240–5500. 120 rooms. Restaurant, 2 bars, 2 pools, tennis court, beach, dive shop, shops, recreation room, travel services, car rental. AE, MC, V.*

$$$ ✕▣ **Club Akumal Caribe & Villas Maya.** Accommodations at this resort, situated on the edge of a cove overlooking a small harbor, range from rustic but comfortable bungalows with red tile roofs and garden views (Villas Maya) to beachfront rooms in a modern three-story hotel building. All have air-conditioning, ceiling fans, and refrigerators. Also available are the more secluded one-, two-, and three-bedroom condominiums called the Villas Flamingo, on Half Moon Bay and a kilometer (½ mile) from the beach. The bungalows and hotel rooms are cheerfully furnished in rattan and dark wood, with attractive tile floors; the high-domed, Mediterranean-style condominium units have kitchens and balconies or terraces overlooking the pool and beach. A vast array of diving options are available, as are other water sports. The best of the three restaurants is Lol Ha: The grilled steak and seafood dinner entrées are bountiful. An optional meal plan includes breakfast and dinner. ⊠ *Km 104, Hwy. 307,* ☎ *987/2–2532. For reservations: Akutrame, Box 13326, El Paso, TX 79913,* ☎ *915/584–3552 or 800/351–1622; in Canada, 800/343–1440. 40 bungalows, 21 rooms, 4 villas, 5 condos. 3 restaurants ($$–$$$), bar, grocery, ice cream parlor, pizzeria, snack bar, pool, beach, 2 dive shops, shop. AE, MC, V.*

Outdoor Activities and Sports

Akumal Dive Center rents equipment, runs dive trips, and has certification programs. For dive packages, including accommodations, contact Akutrame Inc. (⊠ Box 13326, El Paso, TX 79913, ☎ 915/584–3552 or 800/351–1622; in Canada, 800/343–1440). There is a **Mike Madden dive shop** at the Aventuras Akumal (☎ 987/22828).

Xpuhá

❼ *9 km (5½ mi) south of Paamul.*

The little fishing village of Xpuhá, where residents weave hammocks and harvest coconuts, can be found along a dirt path. Some small, overgrown pre-Hispanic ruins in the area still bear traces of paint on the inside walls. A cluster of pastel-colored hotel buildings sit on the beach; inexpensive rooms are available on a first-come, first-served basis, although the smaller properties close for September and October.

Chemuyil

❿ *7 km (4½ mi) south of Akumal.*

You can stop for lunch and a swim at the little cove at Chemuyil. The crescent-shaped beach, which has been declared an official sea turtle reserve, is popular with tour groups and campers who pitch their tents under the few remaining palms (most were destroyed by disease and have not been replaced).

Laguna de Xcacel

⓫ *7½ km (5 mi) south of Chemuyil.*

The Laguna de Xcacel sits on a sandy ridge overlooking yet another long white beach. The calm waters provide excellent swimming, snorkeling, diving, and fishing; birders and beachcombers like to stroll in the early morning. Camping is permitted, and there's a restaurant (closed Sunday) on the site. Tour buses full of cruise-ship passengers stop here for lunch, and the showers and dressing rooms get crowded at dusk.

Xel-Há

⑫ *2 km (about 1 mi) south of Laguna de Xcacel.*

A natural aquarium cut out of the limestone shoreline, Xel-Há (pronounced zhel-*hah*) national park consists of several interconnected lagoons where countless species of tropical fish breed; the rocky coastline curves into bays and coves in which enormous parrot fish cluster around an underwater Maya shrine. In places you can swim fairly far out, or you can explore one of the underwater caves or the cenotes deep in the jungle. Glass-bottom boats travel to the far side of the lagoon, where stingrays and nurse sharks may be hovering beneath the surface. Lockers and dressing rooms are available, and you can rent snorkel gear ($10) and underwater cameras (the $18 fee includes a roll of film). Other park attractions include several small Maya ruins, a huge but overpriced souvenir shop, food stands, and a small museum. Plan to arrive in the early morning before all the tour-bus traffic hits. The restaurant serves reasonably good ceviche, fresh fish, and drinks. *No phone.* 🖼 *$5.* ☉ *Daily 8–5.*

Tan-Kah

⑬ *9½ km (6 mi) south of Xel-Há.*

In the depths of the jungle stands a small grouping of pre-Hispanic structures that cover 10 square kilometers (4 square miles) and once composed a satellite city of Tulum. They have not yet been fully explored. In the 1930s an airstrip was built here; Charles Lindbergh, who was making an aerial survey of the coast, was one of the first to land on it.

Tulum

⑭ *2 km (about 1 mi) south of Tan-kah, 130 km (80 mi) south of Cancún.*

One of the Caribbean coast's biggest attractions, and the Yucatán peninsula's most visited Maya ruin, Tulum is the largest Maya city built on the coast and the only Maya city known to have been inhabited when the conquistadores arrived. The spectacle of those gray limestone temples against the blue-green Caribbean waters is nothing less than riveting. Visitors are no longer allowed to climb or enter Tulum's most impressive buildings (only three, described below, really merit close inspection), so you can see the ruins in two hours. You may, however, wish to allow extra time for a swim or a stroll on the beach, where it's likely that the ancient Maya beached their canoes.

The first significant structure you'll see is the two-story **Temple of the Frescoes,** to the left of the entryway. The temple's vaulted roof and corbeled arch are examples of classical Maya architecture. Faint traces of blue-green frescoes outlined in black on the inner and outer walls refer to ancient Maya beliefs.

The largest and most famous building, the **Castillo** (castle), looms at the edge of a 40-foot limestone cliff just past the Temple of the Frescoes. Atop the castle, at the end of a broad stairway, sits a temple with stucco ornamentation on the outside and traces of fine frescoes inside the two chambers. The regal structure overlooks the rest of Tulum and an expanse of dense jungle to the west; the blue Caribbean blocks ac-

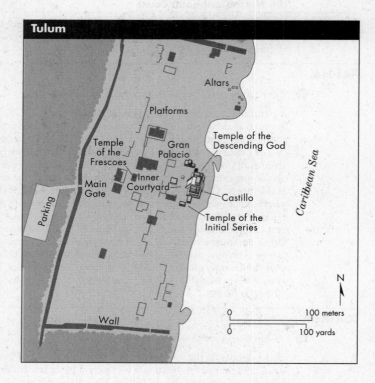

Tulum

Altars

Platforms

Temple of the Descending God

Temple of the Frescoes

Gran Palacio

Main Gate

Inner Courtyard

Castillo

Temple of the Initial Series

Caribbean Sea

Parking

N

Wall

| 0 | | 100 meters |
| 0 | | 100 yards |

cess from the east. Researchers think the Castillo may have functioned as a watchtower to monitor enemy approaches by sea. To the left of the Castillo is the **Temple of the Descending God**—so called for the carving of a winged god plummeting to earth over the doorway.

Tourist services are clustered at the old turnoff from Route 307 to the ruins, marked by restaurants and two hotels. The new road is a few yards farther south and is clearly marked with overhead signs. Still farther south is the turnoff for the Boca Paila Peninsula, the Sian Ka'an preserve, and several small waterfront hotels. The fourth turnoff you'll come to, about 4 kilometers (2½ miles) south of the ruins, is for the present-day village of Tulum. This small community is becoming rather unsightly and congested as its prosperity increases: Markets, auto-repair shops, and other businesses continue to spring up along the road, which has been widened to four lanes.

Dining and Lodging

$$ ✕ **Casa Cenote.** Don't miss this outstanding restaurant beside a large
★ cenote—this one's a mini-pool of fresh- and saltwater full of tropical fish, perfect for a pre-meal swim. The restaurant's beef, chicken, and cheese are imported from the United States, and the burgers, chicken fajitas, and nachos are superb. On Sunday afternoon the expats living along the coast gather at Casa Cenote for a lavish barbecue featuring ribs, chicken, beef brisket, or lobster kebabs. The restaurant operates without electricity or a generator (perishables are packed in ice coolers) and closes at dark. ✉ *On a dirt road off Rte. 307, between Xel-Há and Tulum, no phone. Reservations not accepted. No credit cards.*

$ ▥ **Cabañas Tulum.** This property, idyllically situated in a coconut grove on a beach, is 7 kilometers (4 miles) south of the Tulum ruins on the dirt road leading to Boca Paila. Eighteen palapa bungalows with private bathrooms (but without fans) and an indoor-outdoor restaurant, bar, and game room make a good package. ⊠ *Box 10, Tulum, Quintana Roo, 77780,* ☎ *98/258295. 18 cabanas. Restaurant, bar, recreation room. No credit cards.*

$$ ✕⛭ **Cabañas Ana y José.** Several two-story buildings face the beach
★ at this small, well-loved hotel south of the ruins. All rooms have fans, tiled floors, hot water showers, and hammock hooks; those on the second floor are cooler, thanks to the sea breezes. A new suite was added to this floor in 1995. The restaurant ($) is one of the best along this road, and management is more than helpful. Mountain bikes are available for rent, making it easy for those without cars to visit the ruins and secluded beaches in the area. ⊠ *On dirt road off Rte. 307 between ruins entrance and Tulum pueblo, 6½ km (4 mi) south of ruins; Box 15, Tulum, Quintana Roo, 77780,* ☎ *98/806022,* 𝔽𝔸𝕏 *98/806021. 16 rooms. Restaurant. AE.*

Shopping
The **Mercado de los Artesanías** at the Tulum ruins contains at least 50 stalls displaying woven rugs, clay reproductions of Maya gods and a wide array of tacky souvenirs.

Cobá

⑮ *37 km (22½ mi) northwest of Tulum, 167 km (109 mi) southwest of Cancún.*

Beautiful but barely explored, Cobá was once one of the most important city-states in the entire Maya domain. It now stands in solitude; the spell this remoteness casts is intensified by the silence at the ruins, broken occasionally by the shriek of a spider monkey or the call of a bird. Archaeologists estimate the presence of some 6,500 structures in the Cobá area, but only 5% have been uncovered, and it will take decades before the work is completed. The site is not inaccessible, however. Cobá is a 35-minute drive northwest of Tulum down a well-marked and well-paved road that leads straight through the jungle. Two tiny pueblos, Macario Gómez and Balché, with their clusters of thatched-roof white huts, are the only signs of habitation en route.

The city flourished from AD 400 to 1100, probably boasting a population of as many as 40,000 inhabitants. Situated on five lakes between coastal watchtowers and inland cities, its temple-pyramids towered over a vast jungle plain; one of them is 138 feet tall, the largest and highest in northern Yucatán. Cobá (meaning "ruffled waters") exercised economic control over the region through a network of at least 16 *sacbeob* (roads), one of which, measuring 100 kilometers (62 miles), is the longest in the Maya world. Cobá's massive, soaring structures and sheer size—the city once covered 210 square kilometers (81 square miles)—made it a noteworthy sister nation to Tikal in northern Guatemala, to which it apparently had close cultural and commercial ties.

The first major grouping, off a path to your right as you enter the ruins, is the **Cobá Group,** whose pyramids are built around a sunken patio. At the near end of the group, facing a large plaza, you'll see the 79-foot-high Iglesia (church), where some Indians still place offerings and light candles in hopes of improving their harvests. Farther along the main path to your left is the **Chumuc Mul Group,** little of which has been excavated. The principal pyramid here is covered with the stucco remains of vibrantly painted motifs (*chumuc mul* means "stucco pyramid"). A kilometer (½ mile) past this site is the **Nohoch Mul** (Large

Hill) **Group,** the highlight of which is the pyramid of the same name, the tallest at Cobá. The pyramid, which has 120 steps—equivalent to 12 stories—shares a plaza with Temple 10. The Descending God (also seen at Tulum) is depicted on a facade of the temple atop Nohoch Mul, from which the view is excellent. The unrestored **Crossroad Pyramid** opposite Nohoch Mul was the meeting point for three sacbeob.

Beyond the Nohoch Mul Group is the **Castillo** (castle); its nine chambers are reached by a stairway. To the south are the remains of a ball court, including the stone ring through which the ball was hurled. From the main route follow the sign to **Las Pinturas Group,** named for the still discernible polychromatic friezes on the inner and outer walls of its large, patioed pyramid. Take the minor path for a kilometer (½ mile) to the **Macanxoc Group,** not far from the lake of the same name. The main pyramid at Macanxoc is accessible by a stairway. Many of the stelae here are intricately carved with dates and other symbols of the history of Cobá.

Cobá can be comfortably visited in a half-day, but if you want to spend the night, opt for the Villa Arqueólogica Cobá (☞ Dining and Lodging, *below*), operated by Club Med and only a 10-minute walk from the site along the shores of Lake Cobá. Spending the night is highly advised—the nighttime jungle sounds will lull you to sleep, and you'll be able to visit the ruins in solitude when they open at 8 AM. Even on a day trip, consider taking time out for lunch and a swim at the Villa—an oasis of French civilization—after the intense heat and mosquito-ridden humidity of the ruins. *Buses depart Cobá for Playa del Carmen and Valladolid twice daily. Check with your hotel and clerk at the ruins for times, which may not be exact.* ☒ *$6.50; free Sun.* ☉ *Daily 8–5.*

Dining and Lodging

$$ ✕▥ **Villa Arqueólogica Cobá.** This Club Med property overlooks one
★ of the region's vast lakes, where turtles swim to the hotel's dock for a breakfast of bread and rolls. Tastefully done in white stucco, with museum pieces throughout the property, the hotel has a clean, airy feel. The air-conditioned rooms are small but they feel cozy, not claustrophobic. A handsome library features a large VCR and a pool table. Dining choices near the isolated Cobá ruins are quite limited, so the good restaurant here is an attractive option (food is not included in the room rates as at most other Club Med properties). *For reservations:* ☎ *800/CLUB–MED,* ☎ ℻ *987/42087 in Cobá. 40 rooms. Restaurant ($$), bar, pool, tennis court, shop. AE, MC, V.*

$ ✕▥ **El Bocadito.** Though nowhere near as lavish as the Villa, El Bocadito is a friendly, satisfactory budget alternative and only a five-minute walk from the ruins. The simple, tiled rooms fill up quickly—if you're thinking of spending the night, stop here first before visiting the ruins. There is no hot water, and only fans to combat the heat, but the camaraderie of the clientele and staff makes up for the discomforts. The restaurant is decent, clean, and popular with tour groups. ☒ *On road to ruins, Apdo. 56, Valladolid, Yucatán, Mexico 97780, no phone. 8 rooms. No credit cards.*

Shopping

Lolche, a tourist rest area en route to Cobá, has a large artisans' market packed with pottery and hammocks. Check out the carved wooden jaguars, Cobá's signature souvenir. Cold drinks and snacks are sold at a small stand, and there are clean rest rooms.

Sian Ka'an and the Boca Paila Peninsula

⑯ *15 km (9½ mi) south of Tulum to Boca Paila turnoff, located within Sian Ka'an; 137 km (84 mi) south of Cancún.*

Sian Ka'an, meaning "where the sky is born," was first settled by the Xiu tribe from Central America in the 5th century. In 1986, the Mexican government established the 1.3-million-acre Sian Ka'an Biosphere Reserve as one of UNESCO's internationally protected areas. The reserve constitutes 10% of the land in Quintana Roo and covers 100 kilometers (62 miles) of coast; its approximately 20 sites of ruins scattered about are linked by a canal system—the only one of its kind in the Maya world in Mexico

Many species of the once-flourishing wildlife have fallen into the endangered category, but the waters here still teem with rooster fish, bonefish, mojarra, snapper, shad, permit, sea bass, and alligator. Flyfishing and fishing the flats for bonefish are especially popular, and the peninsula's few lodges run deep-sea fishing trips as far away as Ascensión Bay, two hours south of the lodges by boat. Birders take launches out to Cajo Colibrí (Hummingbird Cay) or to Isla de Pájaros to view the pelicans, frigate birds, woodpeckers, sparrow hawks, and some 350 other species of birds that roost on the mangrove roots or circle overhead. The more adventuresome travelers can explore some of the waterways' myriad caves or trek out to the tiny ruins of Chunyaxché (☞ *below*).

The narrow, rough dirt road down the peninsula is dotted with campgrounds, fishing lodges, and deserted palapas and copra farms. It ends at **Punta Allen,** a fishing village whose main catch is the spiny lobster; it hosts a small guest house. The road is filled with potholes; in the rainy season it may be completely impassable. Most fishing lodges along the way close for the rainy season in August and September, and accommodations are hard to come by. If you haven't booked ahead, start out early in the morning so you can get back to civilization before dark.

Dining and Lodging

$$$$ ✕🏨 **Caphé-Ha.** Built as a private home by an American architect, this small guest house—between a lagoon and the ocean—is a perfect place to stay if you're interested in bonefishing or bird-watching. A two-bedroom house with a kitchen, bath, and living room, and a two-unit bungalow (with shared baths) are your choices; though neither has fans or electricity, all the windows have screens and catch the ocean breeze. A caretaker-chef from Mérida cooks meals that are served in the solar-powered community palapa. The room rates include breakfast and dinner; advance reservations must be accompanied by a 50% deposit, and a three-day or longer stay is required during high season. ✉ *30 km (19 mi) south of Tulum, on road to Sian Ka'an, 5 km (3 mi) past the bridge at Boca Paila and around the next rocky point. No phone; for reservations* ☎ *212/219–2198. 1 villa, 1 bungalow. Fishing. No credit cards.*

$$$$ ✕🏨 **Casa Blanca Lodge.** Punta Pájaros, to which this remote fishing resort provides unique access, is reputed to be one of the best places in the world for light-tackle saltwater fishing. The American-managed, all-inclusive lodge—just 100 feet from the ocean—is set on a rocky outcrop covered with palm trees. The lodge's nine large, modern guest rooms provide a pleasant tropical respite at dusk. The lodge is closed September through December but will open during that time for groups of four or more. Prepayment is required. To get here, you must take a charter flight from Cancún to the Punta Pájaros airstrip, or rent a car in Cancún and drive to Punta Allen (3 hours). From there, it's a one-hour boat trip across the bay. ⊠ *For reservations: Frontiers, Box 959, Wexford, PA 15090,* ☎ *412/935–1577 or 800/245–1950,* FAX *412/935–5388. 9 rooms. Restaurant-bar, fishing. No credit cards.*

CARIBBEAN COAST A TO Z

Arriving and Departing

By Bus

There is first-class service on the **ADO** line (⊠ Av. Juárez at Av. 5, ☎ 987/30109) between Playa del Carmen and Cancún, Valladolid, Chichén Itzá, Chetumal, Tulum, Xel-Há, Mexico City, and Mérida daily. **Autotransportes del Caribe** (⊠ Av. Juárez, no phone) runs second-class buses to the above destinations, and deluxe express buses to Chetumal. **Autotransportes Oriente** (⊠ Av. Juárez, no phone) has express service to Mérida eight times daily, and one bus daily to Cobá. **Playa Express** (⊠ Av. Juárez at Av. 5, no phone) has express minibus service to Cancún every hour 6 AM–9 PM and to Tulum four times daily; there's no space for luggage on the buses. **InterCaribe** (⊠ Av. Juárez at Av. 5, no phone) offers deluxe service to Cancún, Chetumal, and Mérida and frequent service to the ruins at Tulum.

By Ferry

Ferries and jet foils—which can be picked up at the dock—run between Playa del Carmen and Cozumel about every two hours (more frequently in the early morning and evening); trips on the old ferry take about 40 minutes, those on the two enclosed hydrofoils 30 minutes. The fee varies depending on which boat you choose, but the one-way trip costs approximately between $4 and $6.

By Plane

Almost everyone who arrives by air into this region flies into Cancún (☞ *above*).

Getting Around

By Car

The entire coast, from Punta Sam near Cancún to the main border crossing to Belize at Chetumal, is traversable on Route 307. This straight road is entirely paved and is gradually being widened to four lanes from Cancún south (but be careful—many motorists see the road's straightness as an opportunity to speed). Gas stations are becoming more prevalent, but it's still a good idea to fill the tank whenever you can; there are gas stations in Cancún, Puerto Juárez, Puerto Morelos, Playa del Carmen, Tulum, Felipe Carrillo Puerto, and Chetumal.

By Plane

In **Chetumal,** the airport is on the southwestern edge of town, along Avenida Alvaro Obregón where it turns into Route 186. **Bonanza** (☎ 983/28306) has daily flights from Chetumal to Cancún.

Contacts and Resources

Car Rental

In **Playa del Carmen,** car rental agencies include **National** (⊠ Hotel Molcas, ☎ 987/30070; reservations, ☎ 98/864490), **Hertz** (⊠ Hotel Diamond, ☎ 987/30340; Hotel Playacar, ☎ 987/30566), and **APSA** (⊠ Av. 5 between Av. Juárez and Playacar, ☎ 987/30033). If you want air-conditioning, reserve your car in advance. Some car rental operations in Cancún will deliver cars to Playa.

Emergencies

Throughout the region, dial 06 in any area with a telephone.

Police (✉ Av. Juárez, between Avs. 15a and 20a, next to post office, ☎ 987/30021). **Red Cross** (✉ Av. Héroes de Chapultepec at Independencia, ☎ 987/30045).

Guided Tours

Mayaland Tours (✉ Hotel America, Av. Tulum at Calle Brisa, ☎ 98/872450 or 800/235–4079, FAX 98/872438), one of Cancún's leading tour companies, is now running tours to Chichén Itzá from hotels around Punta Bete, Playa del Carmen, and Akumal. Guided tours of Sian Ka'an Reserve can be arranged through the private, nonprofit **Amigos de Sian Ka'an** (✉ Plaza América, Av. Cobá, No. 5, Suites 48–50, Cancún, QR 77500, ☎ 98/849583, FAX 98/873080).

Medical Clinics

Playa del Carmen: Centro de Salud (✉ Av. Juárez at Av. 15a, ☎ 987/21230, ext. 147).

Travel Agencies

First-class hotels in Playa del Carmen and Puerto Aventuras can arrange day tours to Tulum, Chichén Itzá, and Cobá.

Visitor Information

Both the **tourist office** (✉ Palacio del Gobierno, 2nd floor, ☎ 983/20266, FAX 983/20855) and **tourist information booth** (✉ Av. Héroes, opposite Av. Efraín Aguilar, ☎ 983/23663) in **Chetumal** are open weekdays 9–2:30 and 4–7.

The **tourist information booth** (✉ 1 block from the beach on Av. 5, no phone) in Playa del Carmen has very sporadic hours. In the United States, call 800/GO–PLAYA.

THE STATE OF CAMPECHE

Updated by
Richard Harris

Campeche, the least-visited part of the Yucatán, is not for everybody, but the adventuresome visitor will discover both charm and mystery here. Three-hundred-year-old cannons point across the Gulf of Mexico from fortress battlements, recalling pirate days and lending an air of romance to the walled capital city of Campeche. Beyond the city, ancient pyramids and ornate temple facades from the area's Maya past lie hidden deep in tropical forests.

Most of the State of Campeche is flat—never higher than 1,000 feet above sea level—but more than 60% of its territory is covered by jungle, where precious mahogany and cedar abound. Campeche's economy is based on agriculture, fishing, logging, salt, tourism, and—since the 1970s—hydrocarbons, of which it is the largest producer in Mexico. But most of the oil industry is concentrated at the southern end of the state, near Ciudad del Carmen.

Campeche City and Route 261 toward Mérida

This is by far the longer—and more interesting—way to reach the Yucatán capital. The highway takes you through green hills covered by low scrub with occasional stands of tall, dark forest. In the valleys, cornfields and citrus orchards surround the occasional thatched-roof hut.

Campeche City

Numbers in the margin correspond to points of interest on the Campeche City map.

The city of Campeche has a run-down but lovely feel to it: no self-conscious, ultramodern tourist glitz here, just an isolated, friendly city (population 270,000) content to rest on its staid old laurels. That good-humored, lackadaisical attitude is enshrined in the Spanish adjective *campechano,* meaning easygoing, hearty, genial, cheerful.

Because it has been walled since 1686, most of historic Campeche is neatly contained in an area measuring just five blocks by nine blocks. On eight corners in the old city, or Viejo Campeche, stand *baluartes* (bastions) in various stages of disrepair or reconstruction. These were once connected by a 3-kilometer (2-mile) wall in a hexagonal fortification that was built to safeguard the city against the pirates who kept ransacking it. However, it was not until 1771, when Fuerte San Miguel was built on a hilltop on the outskirts of town, that pirates finally ceased their attacks. Only short stretches of the wall exist, and two stone archways—one facing the sea, the other the land—are all that remain of the four gates that provided the only means of access to Campeche.

❶ Avenida Ruíz Cortines is Campeche's waterfront boulevard with a broad pedestrian walkway called the **malecón.** The sidewalk runs the length of the waterfront, from the Ramada Inn south to the outskirts of town, and is popular with joggers and strollers enjoying the cool sea breezes and view at sunset.

❷ A modernistic building resembling a flying saucer houses the **Congreso del Estado,** the State Congress building, where government activities take place. One block inland from the malecón, on Avenida 16 de Septiembre, the Congreo del Estado shares a broad plaza with the
❸ much taller **Palacio de Gobierno,** dubbed El Tocadiscos (The Jukebox) by locals because of its outlandish facade.

❹ The **Baluarte San Carlos,** the bastion where Avenida 16 de Septiembre curves around and becomes Circuito Baluartes, houses the Sala de las Fortificaciones (Chamber of the Fortifications), containing scale models of the original defense system and the Museo de la Ciudad, or City Museum, with photographs of the city as it developed. At press time, the facility was closed due to a municipal funding shortage. If it has reopened by the time you get there, don't miss the dungeon inside the bastion, where captured pirates were jailed.

❺ The **Ex-Templo de San José,** built by the Jesuits in 1756, occupies the full city block between Calles 10 and 12 and Calles 63 and 65. Its immense portal is completely covered with blue Talavera tiles and crowned by seven narrow, stone finials that resemble the roof combs on many Maya temples. Campeche's first lighthouse, built in 1864, sits atop a brick pillar next to the church. ☉ *Tues.–Fri. 9–2 and 5–10.*

❻ The **Iglesia de San Román** sits just outside the intramural boundary in the barrio of the same name at Calle 10 and Calle Bravo. The church became central to the lives of the Indians when an ebony image of Christ, the "Black Christ," was brought in about 1565. The legend goes that a ship that refused to carry the statue was wrecked, whereas the ship that did take it on board reached Campeche in record time. To this day, the Feast of San Román—when the icon is carried through the streets as part of a procession—is the biggest such celebration in Campeche.

Campeche City

⑦ On **Calle 59,** between Calles 8 and 18, once stood some of Campeche's finest homes. Geometric motifs decorate the cornices, and the windows are gaily adorned with iron latticework. The richest inhabitants built as close to the sea as possible, in case escape became necessary. Just east of Calle 12, the architecture and ambience of the tiny **Iglesia de San Francisquito** do justice to historic Calle 59's old-fashioned beauty.

⑧ Old Campeche ends at the **Puerta de Tierra,** the only one of the four city gates that still stands with its basic structure intact. ⊠ *Calle 18 at Calle 59.*

⑩ To take in the heart of a true Mexican inner city, stroll through the **Mercado Municipal,** where locals congregate en masse to shop for seafood, produce, and housewares. The market is open daily from dawn to dusk.

⑪ The centerpiece of the old city is **Parque Principal** or **Plaza de la Independencia,** the southern side of which—Calle 57—is lined with several agreeable cafés and hotels. Concerts are held here on Sunday evenings. ⊠ *Bounded by Calle 10 on the east, Calle 8 on the west, and Calle 55 on the north.*

⑫ On the south side of Parque Principal, the **Baluarte de la Soledad** houses the **Museo de los Estela Dr. Roman Pina Chan** in a separate section. The largest of the bastions, this one has comparatively complete parapets and embrasures that offer a sweeping view of the cathedral, the municipal buildings, and the Gulf of Mexico. Artifacts housed inside the museum include 20 beautiful and well-proportioned Maya stelae and other pieces from various periods. This museum is not to be missed. ⊠ *Calle 8 at Calle 57, no phone.* ☎ *50¢.* ☉ *Tues.–Sat. 8–8, Sun. 8–1.*

⑬ An exception to the generally somber architecture rule of colonial Campeche, the **catedral** took two centuries (from 1650 to 1850) to build and incorporates neoclassical and Renaissance elements. The present cathedral occupies the site of Montejo's original church, which was built in 1540 on what is now Calle 55, between Calles 8 and 10. Inside, the pièce de résistance is the magnificent ebony Holy Sepulcher.

⑭ Built in the early 20th century by one of the wealthiest plantation owners in Yucatán, the opulent, eclectic **Mansión Carvajal** did time as the Hotel Señorial before arriving at its present role as a government office center and headquarters for the state governor's wife and her staff. ⊠ *Calle 10 s/n, between Calles 53 and 55, no phone.* ☜ *Free.* ☺ *Mon.–Sat. 8–2:30 and 5–8:30.*

⑮ The **Baluarte Santiago,** the last of the bastions to be built (1704), has been transformed into a botanical garden. The original bastion was demolished at the turn of the century, but it was rebuilt in the 1950s. ⊠ *Calle 8 at Calle 49,* ☎ *981/66829.* ☜ *Free.* ☺ *Tues.–Sat. 9–1 and 4:30–8, Sun. 9–1.*

⑯ Away from the city center, in a residential neighborhood, stands the beautifully restored **Iglesia de San Francisco** (1546), the oldest church site in Campeche. Some contend it marks the spot where the first Mass on the North American continent was said, in 1517 (the same claim has been made for Veracruz and Cozumel). One of Cortés's grandsons was baptized here, and the baptismal font still stands. ⊠ *Av. Gustavo Díaz Ordaz at Av. Francisco I. Madero.*

⑰ A well-marked scenic drive turns off Avenida Ruíz Cortines near the south end of the city and winds its way to a hilltop, where the **Fuerte de San Miguel** commands one of the grandest views in the Yucatán, overlooking the city and the Gulf of Mexico. Built in 1771, the fort was positioned to bombard enemy ships with cannonballs before they could get close enough to attack Campeche; as soon as it was completed, pirates stopped attacking the city without a fight. The fort now houses the excellent **Museo Regional;** allow at least two hours for the archaeological collection, devoted primarily to the Maya. English-speaking guides are available for a gratuity. ⊠ *Carretera Escenica, no phone.* ☜ *$1.* ☺ *Tues.–Sat. 8–8, Sun. 8–1.*

Dining and Lodging

$$ ✕ **La Pigua.** A favorite with local professionals lingering over long
★ lunches, La Pigua is perhaps the best seafood restaurant in town, with the most pleasant ambience. The long, glass-walled dining room is surrounded by trees and plants. ⊠ *Av. Miguel Alemán 197-A,* ☎ *981/ 13365. MC, V. No dinner.*

$ ✕ **La Ceiba.** This huge place (seating 400 under two tropically inspired thatched-roof salons) specializes in lobster and shrimp plates. It's a little removed from the downtown area but definitely non-touristy; lots of local businessmen and university students congregate here for a late breakfast or early lunch. ⊠ *Av. Resurgimiento 393, near the Carretera Campeche-Lerma,* ☎ *981/13809. MC, V.* ☺ *Daily 10–7.*

$ ✕ **Marganzo.** This rustically furnished restaurant, a half block south
★ of the plaza, is a popular tourist spot—which is not to its detriment. It's impeccably clean, with a colorful decor, and the seafood dishes served at lunch and dinner are very characteristic of the cuisine for which this region is known. ⊠ *Calle 8, No. 267,* ☎ *981/13898. AE, MC, V.*

$ ✕ **Miramar.** This restaurant across from Hotel Castelmar offers fabulous *huevos motuleños* (fried eggs smothered in refried beans and garnished with peas, chopped ham, shredded cheese, and tomato sauce), red snapper, shellfish, soups, and meat dishes. The heavy wooden tables and chairs and the paintings of coats-of-arms give Miramar a colonial feel. ⊠ *Calle 8, No. 293 A,* ☎ *981/62883. MC, V.*

$$$ ☷ **Ramada Inn.** At the luxurious Ramada, fairly large rooms, with all
★ the necessary amenities, are decorated in shades of blue and have rattan furnishings; balconies overlook the pool or the bay. The lobby restaurant, El Poquito, is extremely popular with locals at breakfast and at night before the disco Atlantis opens. ⊠ *Av. Ruíz Cortines 51, along the waterfront,* ☎ *981/62233 or 800/228–9898,* ℻ *981/11618. 149 rooms. Restaurant, coffee shop, pool, exercise room, shop, dance club, travel services. AE, MC, V.*

$$ ☷ **Alhambra.** A great choice away from the bustle of the city, the Alhambra is a modern hotel facing the waterfront near the university. A wide-screen TV plays softly in the lobby; TVs in the rooms get U.S. stations, sometimes including CNN. Rooms are carpeted and clean, with king- and double-size beds. ⊠ *Av. Resurgimiento 85, between Av. Universidad and Av. Augusto Melgar,* ☎ *981/66822,* ℻ *981/66132. 98 rooms. Restaurant, bar, pool, tennis court. MC, V.*

$ ☷ **Debliz.** Those traveling by car may wish to stay outside town at this modern hotel in a residential area north of the city. Room amenities at the four-story, elevator-equipped property, renovated in 1994, include color TV, reading lamps, and double beds. The Debliz can seem deserted and lonely—until the tour buses that frequent the place pull into the parking lot. ⊠ *Av. Las Palmas 55, off Av. Pedro Sainz de Baranda, near the baseball stadium,* ☎ *981/52222,* ℻ *981/52277. 120 rooms. Restaurant, bar, cafeteria, pool. AE, MC, V.*

$ ☷ **Del Paseo.** Located in the quiet San Román neighborhood, a block from the ocean, this new hotel is cheerful and well lit. Rooms, painted in a soft rose with tasteful rattan furniture, have balconies, cable TV, and air-conditioning. A glass-roofed atrium next to the lobby is lovely, with park benches and plants. ⊠ *Calle 8, No. 215,* ☎ *981/10084 or 981/10100,* ℻ *981/10097. 40 rooms. Restaurant, bar, shop. MC, V.*

$ ☷ **Lopez.** Cheerful pink, yellow, and white walls and an open, airy ambience make this little two-story hotel a pleasant place to stay. Standard rooms include colonial-style desks and armoires, and easy chairs. The restaurant, which serves basic Continental fare, is a convenient place for meals. ⊠ *Calle 12, No. 189, between Calles 61 and 63,* ☎ *981/63021. 39 rooms. Restaurant (closed Sun.). AE, MC, V.*

Nightlife and the Arts

If you're in the mood to dance, try Campeche's two discos, **Atlantis** (⊠ Ramada Inn, ☎ 981/62233), the only chic club in town, where politicians go to party, or the more student-oriented **El Dragon** (⊠ Sajuge complex on Av. Resurgimiento, half a block from the Alhambra Hotel, ☎ 981/11810 or 981/64289). Both places are open Thursday through Saturday nights only. Two of Campeche's most conveniently located movie theaters, **Cine Estelar** (⊠ Av. Miguel Alemán and Calle 49-B) and **Cine Colón** (⊠ Calle 12 and Calle 59), show films made in the United States, with Spanish subtitles; they're only open on weekend nights.

Outdoor Activities and Sports

Hunting, fishing, and birding are popular throughout the State of Campeche. Contact Don José Sansores at his office in the Hotel Castelmar (⊠ Calle 61, No. 2, ☎ 981/62356, ℻ 981/10624) in Campeche, or his office at the Snook Inn hotel in Champotón (☎ 982/80018, ℻ 981/10624) for bookings and for information regarding the regulations and best areas for each sport.

Shopping

Folk art in Campeche is typical of the rest of Yucatán's handicrafts: basketry, leather goods, embroidered cloth, and clay trinkets. With a few exceptions, listed below, most of the shops sell cheap-looking trinkets.

Visit the **municipal market** (⊠ Circuito Baluartes at Calle 53), at the eastern end of the city, for crafts and food. The **Artesanía Boutique** (⊠ Ah-Kin-Pech shopping center, ☎ 981/12446), owned by craftsman David Pérez, stocks his miniature ships and jewelry fashioned from sanded and polished bull's horns.

Edzná

62 km (38 mi) southeast of Campeche City

Archaeologists consider Edzná one of the peninsula's most important ruins because of the crucial transitional role it played among several architectural styles. Occupied from 300 BC to AD 900, the site was not discovered until 1927 and has little funding for restoration. The 6-square-kilometer (2-square-mile) expanse of savanna is situated in a broad valley prone to flooding. Surrounding the site are vast networks of irrigation canals, the remnants of a highly sophisticated hydraulic system that channeled rainwater and water from the Champotón River into human-made *chultunes,* or wells. Commanding center stage in the **Gran Acrópolis,** or Great Acropolis complex, is the **Pirámide de los Cinco Pisos** (Five-Story Pyramid), which rises 102 feet. The temple was so constructed that, during certain dates of the year, the setting sun would illuminate the mask of the sun god, Itzamná, located inside one of the pyramid's rooms. Carved into Building 414 of the Great Acropolis are some grotesque masks of the sun god with huge and sinister protruding eye sockets. Local lore holds that Edzná, which means the House of the Gestures, or Grimaces, may have been named for these images.

If you're not driving, consider taking one of the day trips offered by most travel agencies in Campeche; this is far easier than trying to get to Edzná by bus. If you do go by bus, be forewarned that you must walk about 1 kilometer (½ mile) from the main road to the ruins. Check and double check with the driver about return buses—they are few and far between. ⊠ *From Campeche City, take Rte. 261 east for 44 km (27 mi) to Cayal, then Rte. 188 southeast for 18 km (11 mi).* ⊡ *$3.* ☉ *Daily 8–5.*

Hopelchén

41 km (25 mi) north of the Edzná turnoff on Route 261.

Hopelchén—the name means Place of the Five Wells—is a traditional Maya town noted for the lovely Franciscan church built in honor of St. Francis of Padua in 1667. Corn, beans, tobacco, fruit, and henequen are cultivated in this rich agricultural center.

Bolonchén de Rejón

34 km (21 mi) north of Hopelchén

Just short of the state line, Bolonchén de Rejón is named for the adjacent Cave of the Nine Wells, where legend says a distressed Maya girl took refuge from the vagaries of love. In ancient times, cenotes deep in the extensive cave system provided an emergency water source during droughts. Visitors can admire the delicate limestone formations in the upper part of the cave on an easy two-hour guided tour. ⊡ *$3.* ☉ *Daily 8–5.*

Hochob

41 km (25 mi) south of Hopelchén

The small Maya ruin of Hochob is an excellent example of the Chenes architectural style, which flowered in the classical period from about AD 200 to 900. Found throughout central and southern Campeche, Chenes-style temples are easily recognized by their elaborate stucco facades forming giant masks of jaguars, birds, or other creatures, with doorways representing the beasts' open jaws. Since work began at Hochob in the early 1980s, eight temples and palaces have been excavated at the site, including two that have been restored to their original grandeur. ⊠ *South of Hopelchén on the Dzibalchén–Chenko road, no phone.* ≊ *$1.35.* ⊙ *Daily 8–5.*

Dzilibnocac

25 km (16 mi) east of Hochob.

Dzilibnocac, reached by a good but unpaved road, was a fair-size ceremonial center between AD 250 and 900. Although at least seven temple pyramids have been located here, the only one that has been excavated is the Palacio Principal, an unusual rounded pyramid resembling a smaller version of the one at Uxmal and combining elements of the Puuc and Chenes architectural styles. ⊠ *East of Hochob on the Iturbide road, no phone.* ≊ *$1.35.* ⊙ *Daily 8–5.*

CAMPECHE A TO Z

Arriving and Departing

By Car

Campeche can be reached from Mérida in about 1½ hours along the 160-kilometer (99-mile) *via corta* (short way, Route 180). The alternative route, the 250-kilometer (155-mile) *via larga* (long way, Route 261), takes at least three hours but crosses the major Maya ruins of Uxmal, Kabah, and Sayil.

By Bus

ADO (⊠ Av. Gobernadores 289 at Calle 45, along Rte. 261 to Mérida, ☎ 981/62802), a first-class line, runs buses to Campeche from Ciudad del Carmen and Mérida every half hour. The deluxe **Expreso del Caribe** (☎ 981/13973) travels between Campeche, Mérida, Villahermosa, and Cancún. Buses depart from the Plaza Ah-Kim-Pech on Avenida Pedro Sainz de Baranda, No. 120. There is less desirable second-class service on **Autobuses del Sur** (☎ 981/63445) from Chetumal, Ciudad del Carmen, Escárcega, Mérida, Palenque, Tuxtla Gutiérrez, Villahermosa, and intermediate points throughout the Yucatán Peninsula. The second-class line **Camioneros de Campeche** (☎ 981/62322) has five buses daily to Uxmal and two to Edzná.

By Plane

Aeromexico (☎ 981/65678) has one flight daily from Mexico City to Campeche City.

Getting Around

By Bus

The municipal bus system covers all of Campeche City, but you can easily visit the major sights on foot. Public buses run along Avenida Ruíz Cortines and cost under $1.

By Taxi

Taxis can be hailed on the street in Campeche City, or—more reliably—commissioned from the main taxi stand (✉ Calle 8, between Calles 55 and 53, ☎ 981/62366 or 981/65230) or at stands by the bus stations and market. Because of the scarcity of taxis, it's quite common to share them with other people headed in the same direction as you. Don't be surprised to see one already occupied slow down to where you are standing if the cab driver thinks he can pick up another fare.

Contacts and Resources

Car Rental

There is a **Hertz** representative at the Hotel Baluartes in Campeche City (✉ Av. Ruíz Cortines s/n, ☎ 981/11884).

Emergencies

Throughout the state, call **06** locally in case of emergency.

Campeche City: Police (✉ Av. Resurgimiento s/n, a half block from Hotel Alhambra, ☎ 981/62329); **Red Cross** (✉ Av. Resurgimiento s/n, ☎ 981/52411).

Medical Clinics

In Campeche City, **Hospital General** (✉ Av. Central at Circuito Baluartes, ☎ 981/60920 or 981/64233) and **Social Security Clinic** (✉ Av. Lopez Mateos s/n, ☎ 981/65202) are both open 24 hours for emergencies.

Travel Agencies and Tour Operators

Campeche City: **American Express/VIPs** (✉ Prolongación Calle 59, Edificio Belmar, Depto. 5, ☎ 981/11010 or 981/11000, FAX 981/68333); **Agencia de Viajes Campeche** (✉ Calle 10, No. 339, ☎ 981/65233, FAX 981/62844).

Visitor Information

Campeche City's state and city tourist offices have been closed indefinitely due to lack of funds. The most reliable source of brochures and other travel information is the travel agency in the Ramada Inn.

THE STATE OF YUCATÁN

Updated by
Richard Harris

There is a marvelous eccentricity about Mérida. Fully urban, with maddeningly slow-moving traffic, it has a self-sufficient, self-contented air that would suggest a small town more than a state capital of some 600,000 inhabitants (locals say there are about 1 million). Gaily pretentious turn-of-the-century buildings have an Iberian-Moorish flair for the ornate, but most of the architecture is low-lying, and although the city sprawls, it is not imposing. Grandiose colonial facades adorned with iron grillwork, carved wooden doors, and archways conceal marble tiles and lush gardens; horse-drawn carriages hark back to the city's heyday as the wealthiest capital in Mexico.

Mérida is a city of subtle contrasts, from its opulent yet faded facades to its residents, very European yet very Maya. The Indian presence is unmistakable: People are short and dark-skinned, with sculpted bones and almond eyes; women pad about in *hipiles* (hand-embroidered, sacklike white dresses), and craftsmen and vendors from the outlying villages come to town in their huaraches. So many centuries after the conquest, Yucatán remains one of the last great strongholds of Mexico's indigenous population. To this day, in fact, many Maya do not even speak Spanish, primarily because of the peninsula's geographic and, hence, cultural isolation from the rest of the country.

Physically, too, Yucatán differs from the rest of the country. Its geography and wildlife have more in common with Florida and Cuba—with which it was probably once connected—than with the central Mexican plateau and mountains. A mostly flat limestone slab possessing almost no bodies of water, it is rife with underground cenotes, caves with stalactites, small hills, and intense jungle.

It is, of course, the celebrated Maya ruins, Chichén Itzá and Uxmal especially, that bring most tourists to Mérida, but small towns such as Vallidolid, while bereft of star-quality sightseeing, charm visitors with their very unpretentiousness.

Mérida and the Scenic Route to Chichén Itza

Although it's possible to reach Chichén Itzá (120 kilometers, or 75 miles, east of Mérida) along the shorter Route 180, it's far more scenic to follow Route 80 until it ends at Tekantó, then head south to Citilcúm, east to Dzitas, and south again to Pisté. These roads have no signs but are the only paved roads going in these directions. Ask directions frequently.

Mérida

Numbers in the margin correspond to points of interest on the Mérida map.

Mérida is the cultural and intellectual center of the peninsula, with museums, schools, and attractions that greatly enhance the traveler's insights into the history and character of Yucatán. Consider making it one of the first stops in your travels, and make sure your visit includes a Sunday, when traffic is light and the city seems to revert to a more gracious era.

❶ The **main square,** which the Méridanos are beginning to call the **zócalo** along with its traditional names, the **Plaza Principal** and Plaza de la Independencia, was laid out in 1542 on the ruins of T'hó, the Maya city demolished to make way for Mérida, and is still the focal point around which the most important public buildings cluster. The plaza is bordered to the east and west by Calles 60 and 62 and to the north and south by Calles 61 and 63.

❷ The **Casa de Montejo** sits on the south side of the plaza, on Calle 63. Montejo—father and son—conquered the peninsula and founded Mérida in 1542; they built this stately palace 10 years later. The property remained with the family until the late 1970s, when it was restored and converted into a bank. Built in the French style during Mérida's heyday as the world's henequen capital, it now represents the city's finest—and oldest—example of colonial Plateresque architecture, which typically features elaborate ornamentation. Step into the building weekdays between 9 and 5 to glimpse the lushly foliated inner patio.

❸ The west side of the main square is occupied by the 17th-century **Palacio Municipal** (✉ Calle 62 between Calles 61 and 63)—the city hall—which is painted yellow and trimmed with white arcades, balustrades, and the national coat of arms.

❹ Occupying the northeast corner of the main square is the **Palacio del Gobierno,** or Governor's Palace (✉ Calle 61 between Calles 60 and 62), built in 1885 on the site of the Casa Real (Royal House). The upper floor of the Governor's Palace contains Fernando Castro Pacheco's murals of the history of Yucatán, painted in 1978.

Mérida

NEED A BREAK?   Just two doors to the left of the Palacio Municipal is **Pan Montejo,** one of the best bakeries in town.

5 The oldest **catedral** on the North American mainland stands cater-corner from the Palacio del Gobierno. Begun in 1561, it took several hundred Maya laborers, working with stones from the pyramids of the ravaged Maya city, 36 years to complete. Its somber Renaissance-style facade is stark and unadorned. Inside, the black **Cristo de las Ampollas** (Christ of the Blisters), next to the altar, is a replica of the original, which was destroyed during the Revolution. According to legend, the Christ figure was carved from a tree that had burned all night yet appeared the next morning unscathed.

6 At the **Mercado de Artesanías "García Rejón"** (⊠ Calle 60 and Calle 65) you'll find local handicrafts and souvenirs. Shops selling dry goods, straw hats, and hammocks occupy both sides of Calle 65.

7 On Calle 65, between Calles 56 and 58, stand two picturesque 19th-century edifices housing the main post office and telegraph buildings. Behind them sprawls the pungent, labyrinthine **Mercado Municipal,** where almost every patch of ground is occupied by Indian women selling chilies, herbs, and fruit. On the second floor of the main building is the **Bazar de Artesanías Municipales,** the principal handicrafts market, where you can buy jewelry, pottery, embroidered clothes, hammocks, and straw bags.

8 History lovers should stop in at the small but informative **Museo de la Ciudad.** Once a hospital chapel for the only convent in the entire bishopric, it now houses prints, drawings, photographs, and other displays that recount the history of Mérida. ⊠ *Calle 61 at Calle 58, no phone.* ☎ *Free.* ☺ *Tues.–Sun. 8–8.*

❾ Only half a block north of the main plaza is the small, cozy **Parque Hidalgo,** or Cepeda Peraza, as it is officially known. Renovated mansions turned hotels and sidewalk cafés stand at two corners of the park, which comes alive at night with marimba bands and street vendors. Opposite, you'll find the **Restaurante Express,** a gathering place that attracts both local men and international travelers.

The **Iglesia de Jesús,** facing Parque Hidalgo on the north side, is one of Mérida's oldest buildings. The church was built in 1618 of limestone from a Maya temple that had previously stood on the site. The former convent rooms in the rear of the building now host a pair of small art museums—the **Juan Gamboa Guzmán Painting Museum** and the adjoining **Gottdeiner Museum.** You might pass on the former, which contains oil paintings of past governors and other public figures but rarely identifies them. The latter, on the other hand, displays striking bronze sculptures of the Yucatán's indigenous people by its most celebrated 20th-century sculptor, Enrique Gottdiener. ⊠ *Calle 59 between Calles 60 and 58. No phone.* ☎ *Free.* ⊙ *Tues.–Sun. 8–8.*

❿ The Italianate **Teatro Peón Contreras,** north of Parque Hidalgo on Calle 60, was designed in 1908 along the lines of the grand European turn-of-the-century theaters and opera houses. Today, in addition to performing arts, the theater also houses temporary art exhibits and the main **Centro de Información Turistica** (☎ 99/249122), which is to the right of the lobby. A café spills out to a patio from inside the theater to the right of the information center.

⓫ The arabesque **Universidad Autonoma de Yucatán** plays a major role in the city's cultural and intellectual life. The folkloric ballet performs on the patio of the main building. The building, dating from 1711, features Moorish-style crownlike upper reaches and uncloistered archways. It's on Calle 60 just opposite the Teatro Peón Contreras.

⓬ The rather plain **Parque Santa Lucía,** at Calle 60 and Calle 55, draws crowds to its Thursday-night serenades, performed by local musicians and folk dancers. The small church opposite the park dates from 1575 and was built as a place of worship for the African and Caribbean slaves who lived here; the churchyard functioned as the cemetery until 1821.

⓭ North of downtown, the 10-block-long street known as the **Paseo de Montejo** exemplifies the Parisian airs the city took on in the late 19th century, when wealthy plantation owners were building opulent, impressive mansions. The broad boulevard, lined with tamarinds and laurels, is sometimes wistfully referred to as Mérida's Champs-Elysées. Although the once-stunning mansions fell into disrepair from which few have recovered, their stateliness is still evident under the dowdiness.

⓮ The most compelling of the mansions on Paseo de Montejo, the pale peach **Palacio Cantón** presently houses the **Museum of Anthropology and History,** dedicated to the culture and history of the Maya; it's one of the finest of its type in the country. Although bilingual legends accompany the displays, lengthier explanations are in Spanish only; private guides are available for hire. There's also an excellent bookstore. ⊠ *Calle 43 at Paseo de Montejo,* ☎ *99/230557.* ☎ *$3.* ⊙ *Tues.–Sat. 9–8, Sun. 8–2; bookstore weekdays 9–3.*

⓯ Several blocks east of the main plaza is the **Museo de Arte Popular,** housed in a fine old mansion. The ground floor is devoted to Yucatecan arts and crafts, while the second floor focuses on the popular arts of the rest of Mexico. ⊠ *Calle 59 at Calle 52, no phone.* ☎ *Free.* ⊙ *Tues.–Sat. 8–8.*

At the far south of the city, about nine blocks south of the square at
⑯ Calles 66 and 77, stands the **Ermita de Santa Isabel** (circa 1748), part
of a Jesuit monastery also known as the Hermitage of the Good Trip.
A resting place in colonial days for travelers heading to Campeche, the
restored chapel is an enchanting spot to visit at sunset.

☾ **El Centenario Zoological Park,** Mérida's great children's attraction,
is a large, somewhat tacky amusement complex consisting of playgrounds; rides (including ponies and a small train); a roller skating rink;
snack bars; and cages with more than 300 marvelous native monkeys,
birds, reptiles, and other animals. There are also pleasant wooded
paths and a small lake where you can rent rowboats, as well as picnic
areas. ⊠ *Av. Itzaes, between Calles 59 and 65 (entrances on Calles 59
and 65).* ☎ *Free.* ☾ *Daily 9–6.*

Dining and Lodging

$$ ✕ **Alberto's Continental Patio.** The setting—an early-18th-century
★ building adorned with mosaic floors from Cuba—is romantic; an inner
patio surrounded by rubber trees is ideal for starlit dining. Most of the
guests are tourists, but that need not detract from the surroundings or
the excellent cuisine. If you order Lebanese food, your plate will be
heaped with servings of shish kebab, fried kibi, cabbage rolls, hum-
mus, eggplant, and tabbouleh. Black bean soup, enchiladas, fried ba-
nanas, and caramel custard make up the Mexican dinner; there are also
a Yucatecan dinner, an Italian dinner, and à la carte appetizers and en-
trées. ⊠ *Calle 64, No. 482, at Calle 57,* ☎ *99/285367. AE, MC, V.*

$$ ✕ **Amaro.** Amaro is no longer strictly vegetarian, but its menu is heavy
on health drinks, made mostly with local vegetables, fruit, and herbs
(all washed with purified water). Recommended dishes include eggplant curry and soup made with *chaya,* a local vegetable that looks
like spinach. The terrace of this old historic home provides a quiet dining atmosphere beneath a big tree. ⊠ *Calle 59, No. 507, between Calles
60 and 62,* ☎ *99/282451. No credit cards. Closed Sun.*

★ ✕ **La Bella Epoca.** For a truly special dinner, nothing matches the elegance and style of this second-story dining room, the former ballroom
of an old mansion that has been restored well beyond its original
grandeur. An ambitious menu includes French, Mexican, Middle Eastern, Yucatecan, vegetarian, and unusual Maya dishes—try the succulent *pollo píbil* (chicken baked in banana leaves). Arrive for dinner before
8 PM to claim one of the small balcony tables overlooking Parque Hidalgo. ⊠ *Hotel del Parque, Calle 60 between Calles 57 and 59,* ☎ *99/
281928. AE, MC, V.*

$$ ✕ **La Casona.** This pretty mansion turned restaurant near Parque Santa
Ana has an inner patio, arcade, and swirling ceiling fans; a bar features
live romantic music nightly. The accent is Yucatecan, with *poc chuc* (slices
of pork marinated in sour orange juice and spices), pollo pibil, and *huachi-
nango* (sea bass baked in banana leaf) among the recommended dishes.
Some Italian offerings include homemade pasta. ⊠ *Calle 60, No. 434,
between Calles 47 and 49,* ☎ *99/239996. AE, MC, V.*

$$ ✕ **Los Almendros.** A Mérida classic, this restaurant credits itself with
the invention of poc chuc. The restaurant provides a good introduc-
tion to the variety of Yucatecan cuisine, including *papadzules* (corn tortillas with pumpkin-seed sauce) and *pollo ticuleño* (boneless, breaded
chicken in tomato sauce filled with fried beans, peas, red peppers, ham,
and cheese). All dishes are described in English with pictures on the
paper menus. ⊠ *Calle 50-A, No. 493, between Calles 57 and 59,* ☎
99/238135 or 99/285459. AE, DC, MC, V.

$$ ✕ **Pórtico del Peregrino.** A red tile floor, iron grillwork, and lots of
★ plants set the tone in both the indoor and outdoor patio sections of
this colonial-style restaurant with only 12 tables. The menu features

lime soup, baked eggplant with chicken, mole enchiladas, and seafood stew. For dessert, try the coconut ice cream with Kahlúa. ⊠ *Calle 57, No. 501, between Calles 60 and 62,* ☎ *99/286163. MC, V.*

$ ✗ **Nicte-Ha.** Located under an arcade on the main square, this modest eatery is a fine place for people-watching. A good selection of Yucatecan fare is offered at budget prices. Afterward, stop in at the *sorbetería* next door for a sherbet. ⊠ *Calle 61, No. 500, at Calle 60,* ☎ *99/230784. No credit cards.*

$ ✗ **Santa Lucía.** Locals crowd this small dining room, a few steps below
★ the sidewalk, at lunch time, when the bountiful *comida corrida* is served. The bargain three-course lunch usually includes such Yucatecan specialties as *sopa de lima* (lime soup) and pollo pibil. Service is friendly and efficient. There's a live band Thursday through Sunday nights. ⊠ *Calle 60, No. 481, next to Parque Santa Lucía,* ☎ *99/285957. MC, V.*

$$$$ 🏨 **Casa del Balam.** This very pleasant hotel on well-heeled Calle 60 has
★ a lovely, peaceful courtyard ornamented with a fountain, arcades, ironwork, and a black-and-white tile floor; cocktails and light meals are served here. The rooms are capacious and well maintained, featuring painted sinks, wrought-iron accessories, and minibars. The suites are especially agreeable, with large bathrooms and tiny balconies. ⊠ *Calle 60, No. 488, Box 988,* ☎ *99/248844, 99/242150, or 800/223–4084;* ℻ *99/245011. 54 rooms. Restaurant, 2 bars, minibars, pool, sundeck, travel agency, car rental, gift shop. AE, MC, V.*

$$$$ 🏨 **Fiesta Americana Mérida.** Opened in early 1995, this is the town's
★ newest posh hotel, catering to business travelers, groups, and conventions but also attracting the locals who come to see and be seen. Its lovely pink facade mirrors the architecture of Paseo de Montejo mansions on an epic scale. Rich floral prints, dark wood furnishings, and slightly larger-than-life proportions maintain the theme of bygone elegance in the guest rooms, but the units feature all the modern conveniences, including modems. ⊠ *Paseo de Montejo and Av. Colón,* ☎ *99/202194 or 800/FIESTA–1,* ℻ *99/202198. 350 rooms and suites. Restaurant, bar, health club, shop, business services, meeting rooms, travel services. AE, DC, MC, V.*

$$$$ 🏨 **Hyatt Regency Mérida.** The first of the deluxe hotels to open on Paseo de Montejo (in 1994), the Hyatt brought a new level of hotel service to Mérida; at 17 stories, it's also the tallest building in the city. All rooms have satellite TV, direct-dial long-distance phone service, and minibars; Club floor rooms also feature personal safes. Amenities not commonly found in Mérida include 24-hour room service and a state-of-the-art business center. ⊠ *Calle 60, No. 344, at Av. Colón,* ☎ *99/420202 or 800/228–9000,* ℻ *99/257002. 299 rooms. 2 restaurants, bar, pool, shop, dance club, travel services, car rental. AE, MC, V.*

$$$ 🏨 **Mérida Misión Park Inn Plaza.** Part of the city's landscape for decades (in its earlier incarnation it was the Hotel Mérida), the Misión has two major assets: an excellent location in the heart of downtown and a genuine colonial ambience, with chandeliers, wood beams, archways, patios, and fountains in public areas, along with a pool and a bar with romantic music nightly. A recent modern addition offers fine views from the upper floors. ⊠ *Calle 60, No. 491,* ☎ *99/237665 or 800/221–6509,* ℻ *99/239500. 145 rooms. Restaurant, bar, snack bar, pool, shop, travel services, car rental. AE, DC, MC, V.*

$$ 🏨 **Caribe.** An old Mérida standard, the Caribe is done in typical colonial style, including tile floors, dark wood furniture, and a large inner courtyard with arcades. It is on Parque Hidalgo, but most of its rooms (38 of them with air-conditioning) overlook the inner courtyard and restaurant, as do the open balconies, which are lined with comfort-

able chairs. The rooftop sun deck and swimming pool have a great view of the plaza and downtown. The hotel's outdoor café, El Mesón, is one of the better restaurants in Parque Hidalgo. ⊠ *Calle 60, No. 500,* ☎ *99/249022 or 800/826–6842,* FAX *99/248733. 56 rooms. Restaurant, outdoor café, pool, travel services, free parking. AE, DC, MC, V.*

$$ ☷ **Casa Mexilio.** This choice bed-and-breakfast has a wonderfully eclectic decor, including Middle Eastern wall hangings, French tapestries, colorful tile floors, tile sinks, and folk-art furniture. Casa Mexilio lacks the amenities of the larger hotels (only one room has air-conditioning), but if you enjoy a casual ambience and the feeling of staying in a private home, you'll be happy here. Reservations are required between December 15 and the end of April. ⊠ *Calle 68, No. 495, between Calles 59 and 57,* ☎ FAX *99/282505; reservations 303/674–9615 or 800/538–6802,* FAX *303/674–8735. 8 rooms. Pool. AE, MC, V.*

$$ ☷ **Gran Hotel.** Cozily situated on Parque Hidalgo, this legendary 1901
★ hotel is the oldest in the city. The three-story neoclassical building exudes charm; its centerpiece is an art nouveau courtyard. High-ceiling room are drenched in cedar antique furniture. Thirteen units have balconies—request one of these; most of the others have no windows at all—and 24 have air-conditioning. Porfirio Díaz and Fidel Castro stayed in sumptuous room 17 (not together). ⊠ *Calle 60, No. 496,* ☎ *99/236963 or 99/247632,* FAX *99/247622. 31 rooms. Restaurant. MC, V.*

$ ✕ **Hotel Mucuy.** The Mucuy is one of the best bargains around. The delightful owners make you feel like part of the family and are eager to share information about the city. The rooms, which are always immaculate, have good screens on the windows and face the patio. The owners live at the front of the hotel, so there's always someone around to keep things secure. ⊠ *Calle 57, No. 481, between Calles 56 and 58,* ☎ *99/285193,* FAX *99/237801. 22 rooms. No credit cards.*

Outdoor Activities and Sports

BULLFIGHTS

Bullfights are most often held from November through January, or during other holiday periods at the **bullring** (⊠ Paseo de la Reforma), near Avenida Colón. Contact the travel desk at your hotel or one of the tourist information centers.

GOLF

There is an 18-hole championship golf course (and restaurant, bar, and clubhouse) at **Club de Golf de Yucatán** (⊠ Carr. Mérida-Progreso, Km 14.5, ☎ 99/220053 or 220071), 16 kilometers (10 miles) north of Mérida on the road to Progreso.

Nightlife and the Arts

Mérida enjoys an unusually active and diverse cultural life, including free government-sponsored music and dance performances nightly in local parks. For information on these and other performances, consult the tourist office, the local newspapers, or the billboards and posters at the Teatro Peón Contreras (⊠ Calle 60 at Calle 57) or Café Pop (⊠ Calle 57 between Calles 60 and 62).

The **Hotel Calinda Panamericana** (⊠ Calle 59, No. 455, ☎ 99/239111 or 99/239444) stages folkloric dances Friday and Saturday by the pool. **Tulipanes** (⊠ Calle 46, No. 462-A, ☎ 99/272009), a restaurant and nightclub built over a cenote, stages a folkloric ballet and "Maya ritual" performance that ends with a "sacrifice" nightly at 8. Among a variety of performances presented at the **Teatro Peón Contreras** is "The Roots of Today's Yucatán," a combination of music, dance, and theater presented by the Folkloric Ballet of the University of Yucatán on

Tuesday at 9 PM. Another theater that regularly hosts cultural events is the **Teatro Daniel Ayala** (⊠ Calle 60 between Calles 59 and 61).

A number of restaurants feature live music and dancing, including **El Tucho** (⊠ Calle 60, No. 482, between Calles 55 and 57, ☎ 99/242323), **Xtabay** (⊠ Above El Tucho, ☎ 99/280961), and **Pancho's** (⊠ Calle 59 between Calles 60 and 62, ☎ 99/230942).

There are discos that appeal to both locals and tourists at the **Holiday Inn** (⊠ Av. Colón, No. 498, at Calle 60) and, on weekends, at the **Hotel Calinda Panamericana** (⊠ Calle 59, No. 455). Pop music mixes with salsa at **Saudaje** (⊠ Prolongación Montejo, No. 477, ☎ 99/264330 or 99/292310).

Shopping

On the second floor of the **central municipal market** (⊠ Between Calles 65 and 56 and Calles 54 and 59) you'll find crafts, food, flowers, and live birds, among other items. If you're interested solely in handicrafts, visit the **Bazar García Rejón** (⊠ Corner of Calles 65 and 62), which has neat rows of indoor stalls with leather items, palm hats, and handmade guitars, among other things. On Sunday in Mérida, you will find an array of wares at the **Handicraft Bazaar** (⊠ In front of the Municipal Palace across from the main square), filled with huipiles, hats and costume jewelry, and the **Popular Art Bazaar** (⊠ Parque Santa Lucía, corner of Calles 60 and 55), a flea market offering paintings, engravings, and woodcuts by local artists.

SPECIALTY STORES

Clothing. Tastefully designed batik dresses and pillow covers with Maya motifs, along with a nice selection of silver jewelry, can be found at **El Paso** (⊠ Calle 60, No. 501, corner of Calle 61, ☎ 99/285452). You might not wear a guayabera to a business meeting as some men in Mexico do, but the shirts are cool, comfortable, and attractive; for a good selection, try **Camisería Canul** (⊠ Calle 62, No. 484, between Calles 57 and 59, ☎ 99/230158). Pick up jipi at **Tejidos Y Cordeles Nacionales** (⊠ Calle 56, No. 516-B, ☎ 99/285561), a hat emporium with styles for men and ladies in casual as well as dressy designs.

Crafts. The best place for hammocks is **Hamacas El Aguacate** (⊠ Calle 58, No. 604, at Calle 73, ☎ 99/286429), a family-run establishment selling a wide variety of sizes and designs. **Casa de Artesanías** (⊠ Calle 63, No. 503, between Calles 64 and 66, ☎ 99/235392) purveys folk art from throughout Mexico, such as hand-painted, wooden mythical animals from Oaxaca and hand-embroidered vests and place mats from Chiapas. The streets north of the main square, especially **Calle 60,** are lined with crafts and jewelry stores.

Galleries. The **Teatro Daniel Ayala** (⊠ Calle 60, between Calles 59 and 61, ☎ 99/214391) showcases contemporary paintings and photography. **Galería Manolo Rivero** (⊠ Hotel Galerí Trinidad, Calle 60 at Calle 61, ☎ 99/232463) features exotic, and occasionally erotic, paintings and sculptures by avant-garde artists.

Jewelry. Las Palomas (⊠ Calle 60, No. 476, between Calles 53 and 55, near Santa Lucia Park, ☎ 99/245263) has case after case of silver jewelry, plus a full selection of tacky and tasteful souvenirs. **La Perla Maya** (⊠ Calle 60, Nos. 485–487, between Calles 50 and 61, ☎ 99/285886) is one of the few jewelry shops selling difficult-to-find old-fashioned Yucatecan filigree earrings and bracelets—in silver dipped in gold. The store also stocks lots of quality silver jewelry in modern designs.

Numbers in the margin correspond to numbers on the State of Yucatán map.

Izamal

⑰ *68 km (42 mi) southeast of Mérida.*

Izamal is nicknamed Ciudad Amarillo (Yellow City) because its buildings are painted earth-tone yellow. In the center of town stands an enormous 16th-century **monastery** perched on—and built from—the remains of a Maya pyramid; it's one of the largest and oldest religious structures in Mexico. Another pyramid, called **Kinich Kakmó,** is all that remains of a royal Maya city that flourished here hundreds of years ago.

Chichén Itzá

⑱ *116 km (72 mi) from Mérida.*

Probably the best-known Maya ruin, Chichén Itzá was the most important city in Yucatán from the 10th to the 12th century. An architectural mélange, Chichén was altered by each successive wave of inhabitants. The site is believed to have been first settled in AD 432, abandoned for an unknown period of time, then rediscovered in 964 by the Maya-speaking Itzás, believed to have come from the Petén rain forest around Tikal, in what is now northern Guatemala; *Chichén Itzá* means "the mouth of the well of the Itzás." The Itzás also abandoned the site, and later in the 10th century it was rediscovered by the central-Mexican Toltecs, who abandoned the site forever in 1224.

The majesty and enormity of this site are unforgettable. Chichén Itzá encompasses approximately 6 square kilometers (2 square miles), though only 20 to 30 buildings of the several hundred at the site have been fully explored. It's divided into two parts, called Old and New, although architectural motifs from the classical period are found in both sections. A more convenient distinction is topographical, since there are two major complexes of buildings separated by a dirt path.

The martial, imperial architecture of the Toltecs and the more cerebral architectural genius and astronomical expertise of the Maya are married in the 98-foot-tall pyramid called **El Castillo** (the castle), which dominates the site. Atop the castle is a temple dedicated to Kukulcán (the Maya name for Quetzalcóatl), the legendary leader turned deity from Tula in the Valley of Mexico who was incarnated by the plumed serpent. An excellent sound-and-light show in the evening highlights the architectural details in the Castillo and other buildings with a clarity the eye doesn't see in daylight. A more ancient temple inside the Castillo is open to the public for only a few hours in the morning and again in the afternoon. Claustrophobes should think twice before entering: The stairs are narrow, dark, and winding.

The temple rests on a massive trapezoidal square, on the west side of which is Chichén Itzá's largest **ball court,** one of seven on the site. The game played here was something like soccer (no hands were used), but it had religious as well as recreational significance. Bas-relief carvings at the court depict a player being decapitated, the blood spurting from his severed neck fertilizing the earth.

Between the ball court and El Castillo stands a **Tzompantli,** or stone platform, carved with rows of human skulls. In ancient times it was actually covered with stakes on which the heads of enemies were impaled. In the **Sacred Well,** a cenote 65 yards in diameter that sits 1 kilometer (½ mile) north of El Castillo at the end of a 900-foot-long sacbe, skeletons of about 50 people were found. Thousands of artifacts made

State of Yucatán

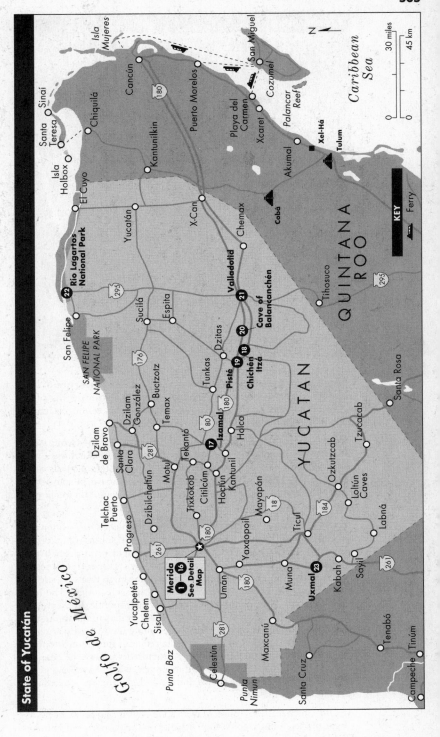

Golfo de México

Punta Baz

Santa Teresa
Sinaí
Santa Teresa
Isla Holbox
Chiquilá
El Cuyo
Kantunilkin

Concun
Isla Mujeres
Puerto Morelos
Santa Teresa
San Miguel

Caribbean Sea

30 miles
45 km

N

Cozumel
Playa del Carmen
Xcaret
Palancar Reef
Akumal
Xel-Há
Tulum

KEY
Ferry

Yucatán
X-Can
Chemax

Río Lagartos
National Park
22
295

San Felipe
SAN FELIPE NATIONAL PARK
Sucilá
Espita
Dzitas
20
18
19
Pisté
Chichén Itzá
Valladolid
21
Cave of Balancanchén

QUINTANA ROO
Tihosuco
295
Santa Rosa

176
Buctzotz
Tunkas
Holca
80
Izamal
17
180

Dzilam González
Temax
Tekantó
Citilcúm
Hoctún
Kantunil
YUCATAN

Dzilam de Bravo
Santa Clara
Motul
Tixkokob
Mayapán
18
Ticul
Ozkutzcab
Izucacab
Loltún Caves
Labná

Telchac Puerto
Dzibilchaltún
Yaxcopoil
184
Sayil
261

Progreso
261
180
Umán
Muna
Kabah
Tenabó
Campeche
Tinúm

Yucalpetén
Chelem
Sisal
Maxcanú
Uxmal
23

Punta Nimun
Celestún
281
Santa Cruz

★ **Mérida**
1—16
See Detail Map

180

Chichén Itzá

*Map labels:*
Cenote (Sacred Well)
N
Ball Court
TO MERIDA
Tzompantli
Temple of the Jaguar
Main Plaza
Venus Platform
Temple of the Warriors
Tourist Office
Platform of the Eagle and Jaguars
El Castillo
Ball Court
West Colonnade Group of the Thousand Columns
Ball Court
Tomb of the High Priests
Ball Court
Steam Bath
House of the Deer
House of the Corn Grinders
Xtoloc Cenote
The Market
El Caracol Observatory
180
Casa de las Monjas (Nunnery)
Temple of the Wall Panels
TO OLD CHICHEN ITZA
0   200 yards
0   200 meters

of gold, jade, and other precious materials, most of them not of local provenance, have been recovered from the brackish depths of the cenote. The well's excavation launched the field of underwater archaeology, later honed by Jacques Cousteau.

Returning to the causeway, you will see on your left the **Group of the Thousand Columns** with the famous **Temple of the Warriors,** a masterful example of the Toltec influence at Chichén Itzá. Murals of everyday village life and scenes of war can be viewed here, and an artistic representation of the defeat of the Maya can be found on the interior murals of the adjacent **Temple of the Jaguar.**

To get to the less visited cluster of structures at Chichén Itzá—often confused with Old Chichén Itzá—take the main road south from the Temple of the Jaguar past El Castillo and turn right onto a small path opposite the ball court on your left. Archaeologists are currently restoring several buildings, including the **Tomb of the High Priest,** where several tombs with skeletons and jade offerings were found. The most impressive structure within this area is the astronomical observatory, called **El Caracol.** The name, meaning "snail," refers to the spiral staircase at the building's core. Although definitely used for observing the heavens, it also appears to have served a religious function. After leaving El Caracol, continue south several hundred yards to the beautiful **Casa de las Monjas** (Nunnery) and its annex, which have long panels carved with flowers and animals, latticework, hieroglyph-covered lintels, and Chaac masks.

At Old Chichén Itzá, "pure Maya" style—with playful latticework, Chaac masks, and gargoyle-like serpents on the cornices—dominates. Highlights include the **Date Group** (so named because of the complete series of hieroglyphic date inscriptions), the **House of the Phalli,** and the **Temple of the Three Lintels.** Maya guides will lead you down the path by an old narrow-gauge railroad track to even more ruins, barely unearthed, if you ask. A fairly good restaurant and great ice-cream stand are in the entrance building, and there are refreshment stands by the cenote and on the pathway near El Caracol. ⌦ *Site and museum $3, free Sun. and holidays; sound-and-light show $1 in Spanish, $4 in English; parking $1; use of video camera $7.* ☉ *Daily 8–5. Sound-and-light show (Spanish) at 7 PM and (English) at 9 PM.*

Lodging

$$$ 🏨 **Mayaland.** This charming 1920s lodging, on a 100-acre site, is the
★ hotel closest to the ruins. Colonial-style rooms in the main building feature decorative tiles, ceiling fans, air-conditioning (except for five rooms), and TV; 13 bungalows set in a large garden also have TV and air-conditioning. Charm has its drawbacks: The hot water often runs cold. Tour buses fill the road in front of the hotel, so choose a room at the back. Light meals served poolside and at tables overlooking the garden are a far better choice than the fixed-price meals served in the dining room. ⌧ *Carretera Mérida–Cancún, Km 120,* ☏ *985/10129. For reservations: Mayaland Tours, Av. Colón 502, Mérida,* ☏ *99/462331 or 800/235–4079,* 🖷 *99/642335. 65 rooms. Restaurant ($$$), bar, pool. MC, V.*

$$ 🏨 **Hacienda Chichén.** A converted 17th-century hacienda, this hotel
★ once served as the home of archaeologist Edward S. Thompson and later as the headquarters for the Carnegie expedition. The rustic cottages have been modernized, and all rooms, which are simply furnished in colonial Yucatecan style, have private baths, verandas, and air-conditioning. There's a color satellite TV in the lobby area. An enormous old pool sits in the midst of the landscaped gardens. Fairly good meals are served at set hours on the patio overlooking the grounds; stick with the Yucatecan specialties. ⌧ *Carretera Mérida–Cancún, Km 120,* ☏ *985/10045, 99/248844, 99/242150, or 800/223–4084;* 🖷 *99/245011. 18 rooms. Restaurant ($$$), bar, pool. MC, V.*

Pisté

⑲ *About 1 km (½ mi) west of Chichén Itzá on Route 180.*

The town of Pisté serves mainly as a base camp for travelers to Chichén Itzá. Hotels, campgrounds, restaurants, and handicrafts shops tend to be cheaper here than south of the ruins. At the west end of town are a Pemex station and a bank. On the outskirts of Pisté, a short walk from the ruins, **Pueblo Maya,** a pseudo Maya village, provides a shopping and dining center for tour groups. The restaurant serves a bountiful buffet at lunch ($10).

Lodging

$ 🏨 **Dolores Alba.** The best low-budget choice near the ruins is this family-run hotel, a long-time favorite in the country south of Pisté. The rooms are simple, clean, and comfortable; some have air-conditioning. Hammocks hang by the small pool, and breakfast and dinner are served family-style in the main building. Free transportation to the ruins is provided. ⌧ *Carretera Pisté-Cancún, 2½ km (1½ mi) south of Chichén Itzá. For reservations: Calle 63, No. 464, Mérida,* ☏ *99/285650,* 🖷 *99/283163. 28 rooms. Dining room, pool. MC, V.*

$ 🏨 **Pirámide Inn Resort and RV Park.** This slightly tacky, American-owned two-story motel in Pisté features rooms with white walls, white tile floors, and modern furniture. The garden contains a small Maya pyramid, a swimming pool, and a tennis court, and the restaurant is one of the best in Pisté. The RV park has been closed. ⌧ *For reservations: Box 433, Mérida, Yucatán,* ☏ *985/62462. 44 rooms. Restaurant ($$), pool, tennis court, travel services. MC, V.*

Cave of Balancanché

20 *4½ km (3 mi) northeast of Chichén Itzá.*

The Cave of Balancanché, a shrine whose Maya name translates as "hidden throne," remained virtually undisturbed from the time of the Conquest until its discovery in 1959. Inside is a large collection of artifacts—mostly vases, jars, and incense burners once filled with offerings. An underground lake is filled with blindfish (small fish with functionless eyes), and an altar to the rain god rises above it. In order to explore the shrine you must take one of the guided tours, which depart almost hourly, but it's necessary to be in fairly good shape, because some crawling is required; claustrophobes should skip it, and those who go should wear comfortable shoes. Also offered at the site is a sound-and-light show that fancifully recounts Maya history. You can catch a bus or taxi to the caves from Chichén Itzá. ✉ *Caves (including tour) $6, free Sun.; show $2.50.* ☉ *Daily 9–4. Tours in English at 11 AM, 1 and 3 PM; in Spanish at 9 AM and noon; in French at 10 AM.*

Valladolid

21 *44½ km (23 mi) east of Chichén Itzá.*

The second-largest city in the State of Yucatán, Valladolid is enjoying growing popularity among travelers en route to or from Chichén Itzá or Río Lagartos who are harried by more touristy places. Montejo founded Valladolid in 1543 on the site of the Maya town of Zací. The city suffered during the Caste War, when virtually the entire Spanish population was killed by the rebellious Maya, and again during the Mexican Revolution.

Today, however, placidity reigns in this agricultural market town (population 70,000). The center is mostly colonial, although it has many 19th-century structures. The main sights are the colonial churches, principally the large **cathedral** on the central square and the 16th-century **San Bernardino Church and Convent** three blocks southwest. The latter were pillaged during the insurrection. A briny, muddy **cenote** in the center of town draws only the most resolute swimmers; instead, visit the adjacent **ethnographic museum**. Outside town, you can swim in **Cenote Dzitnup,** located in a cave lit by a small natural skylight ($3).

Valladolid is renowned for its cuisine, particularly its sausages; try one of the restaurants within a block of the square. You can find good buys on sandals, baskets, and the local liqueur, Xtabentún, flavored with honey and anise.

Lodging

$$ 🏨 **El Mesón del Marqués.** This building, on the north side of the main square, is a well-preserved, very old hacienda built around a lovely courtyard. Rooms in the modern addition at the back of the hotel have air-conditioning and are attractively furnished with rustic and colonial touches; rooms in the older section have ceiling fans. Unusually large bathrooms boast bathtubs—a rarity in Mexican hotels. El Mesón also features a pool, a crafts shop, and a restaurant that serves local specialties. ✉ *Plaza Principal, Calle 39, No. 203, 97780,* ☎ *985/62073,* FAX *985/62280. 26 rooms, 12 suites. Restaurant ($$), bar, pool, shop. MC, V.*

$ 🏨 **María del Luz.** Another choice by the main plaza, this hotel is built around a small swimming pool and courtyard. The rooms have been renovated with new floors, fresh paint, and tiled bathrooms; air-conditioning and televisions are being added to all of them. The attractive street-side restaurant offers predictable and inexpensive Mexican dishes. ✉ *Calle 2, No. 195, 97780,* ☎ *985/62071. 33 rooms. Restaurant ($), bar, pool. MC, V.*

Río Lagartos National Park

㉒ *101 km (63 mi) north of Valladolid.*

If you're a flamingo fan (flamingo season runs from April through May), don't miss Río Lagartos National Park. Actually encompassing a long estuary, not a river, the park was developed with ecotourism in mind, though the alligators for which it and the village were named have long since been hunted into extinction. In addition to sighting flamingos, birders can spot egrets, herons, ibis, cormorants, pelicans, and even peregrine falcons flying over these murky waters; fishing is good, too, and hawksbill and green turtles lay their eggs on the beach at night. Hotel Nefertiti, one of five hotels in town, offers boat tours, or you can hire a boat from the docks near the hotel.

Uxmal and the Puuc Route

As soon as they pass through the large Maya town of Uman on Mérida's southern outskirts, travelers find themselves in one of the least populated areas of the Yucatán. The highway to Uxmal and Kabah is a fairly traffic-free route through uncultivated woodlands. The forest seems to become more dense beyond Uxmal, which was connected to a number of smaller ceremonial centers in ancient times. Several of these satellite sites, including **Kabah, Sayil,** and **Labná,** are open to the public along a side road known as the Ruta Puuc, which winds its way eastward and eventually joins busy Route 184, a major highway. Along this route you'll also find the **Loltún Caves,** the largest known cave system in the Yucatán, containing wall paintings and stone artifacts from Maya and pre-Maya times. In the little town of **Ticul,** which produces much of the pottery you'll see around the peninsula, is Los Almendros, considered by many the best regional restaurant in the Yucatán.

Uxmal

㉓ *78 km (48 mi) south of Mérida on Route 261.*

If Chichén Itzá is the most impressive Maya ruin in Yucatán, Uxmal is arguably the most beautiful. Where the former has a Toltec grandeur, the latter seems more understated and elegant—pure Maya. The architecture reflects the late classical renaissance of the 7th to 9th centuries and is contemporary with that of Palenque and Tikal, among other great Maya metropolises of the southern highlands.

The site is considered the finest and largest example of Puuc architecture, which embraces such details as ornate stone mosaics and friezes on the upper walls, intricate cornices with curled noses, rows of columns, and soaring vaulted arches. Lines are clean and uncluttered, with the horizontal—especially the parallelogram—preferred to the vertical.

Although most of Uxmal remains unrestored, three buildings in particular merit attention. The most prominent, the **Pyramid of the Magician,** is, at 125 feet high, the tallest structure at the site. Unlike most other Maya pyramids, which are stepped and angular, it has a strangely elliptical design. Built five times, each time over the previous structure, the pyramid has a stairway on its western side that leads through a giant mask of Chaac with its mouth wide open to two temples at the summit.

West of the pyramid lies the **Nunnery,** or Quadrangle of the Nuns, considered by some to be the architectural jewel of Uxmal. You may enter the four buildings; each comprises a series of low, gracefully repetitive

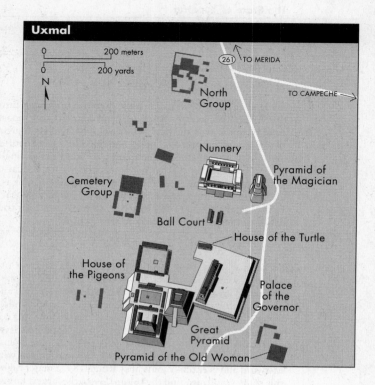

Uxmal

North Group

Nunnery

Pyramid of the Magician

Cemetery Group

Ball Court

House of the Turtle

House of the Pigeons

Palace of the Governor

Great Pyramid

Pyramid of the Old Woman

TO MERIDA

TO CAMPECHE

chambers that look onto a central patio. Elaborate decoration blankets the upper facades.

Continue walking south; you'll pass the ball court before reaching the **Palace of the Governor,** which archaeologist Victor von Hagen considered the most magnificent building ever erected in the Americas. Interestingly, the palace faces east while the rest of Uxmal faces west. Archaeologists believe this is because the palace was used to sight the planet Venus. Covering 5 acres and rising over an immense acropolis, the palace lies at the heart of what must have been Uxmal's administrative center. Decorating the uppermost section of the facade are intricate friezes that required more than 20,000 individually cut stones.

First excavated in 1929 by the Danish explorer Franz Blom, the site served in 1841 as home to John Lloyd Stephens. Today a sound-and-light show recounts Maya legends, including the kidnapping of an Uxmal princess by a king of Chichén Itzá, and focuses on the people's dependence on rain—thus the cult of Chaac. The show is performed nightly in English and is one of the better such productions. ☞ *Site and museum $3, free Sun. and holidays; sound-and-light show in Spanish $1.50, in English $4; parking $1; use of video camera $7.* ☉ *Daily 8–5; sound-and-light show (Spanish) at 7 PM, (English) at 9 PM.*

Dining and Lodging

$$ ✕ **Nicte-Ha.** This café beside the Hacienda Uxmal hotel is the least expensive dining option by the ruins, serving pizzas, sandwiches, and Mexican snacks. Diners are welcome to use the swimming pool by the restaurant. ✉ *Hacienda Uxmal, on Hwy. 261,* ☎ 𝔽𝔸𝕏 *9099/494754. MC, V.*

$ ✕ **Las Palapas.** A great alternative to the hotel dining rooms at Uxmal, this family-run restaurant specializes in delicious Yucatecan dishes served with homemade tortillas. When tour groups request it in advance, the owners prepare a traditional feast, roasting the chicken or pork pibil style in a pit in the ground. If you see a tour bus in the parking lot, stop in—you may chance upon a memorable fiesta. ⊠ *Hwy. 261, 5 km (3 mi) north of ruins, no phone. No credit cards.*

$$$ ▦ **Hacienda Uxmal.** The oldest hotel at the Maya site, built in 1955 and still owned and operated by the Barbachano family, this pleasant colonial-style building has lovely floor tiles, ceramics, and iron grillwork. The rooms—all with ceiling fans and air-conditioning—are tiled and decorated with worn but comfortable furniture. Ask about packages that include free or low-cost car rentals for the nights you spend at Uxmal and at the Mayaland hotel in Chichén Itzá. ⊠ *Within walking distance of ruins,* ☎ ℻ 9099/494754; *Mayaland Tours, Av. Colón 502, Mérida,* ☎ *99/462331 or 800/235–4079,* ℻ *99/462335. 80 rooms. Restaurant, bar, pool, shop. AE, DC, MC, V.*

$$ ▦ **Villa Arqueológica Uxmal.** The hotel closest to the ruins is this two-story Club Med property built around a large Mediterranean-style pool. The functional rooms have cozy niches for the beds, tiled bathrooms, and powerful air conditioners. Maya women in traditional dress serve well-prepared French cuisine in the restaurant. For a fee, day-trippers can use the pool, then dine in the restaurant. ⊠ *Within walking distance of ruins,* ☎ *99/247053; reservations in U.S., 800/CLUB–MED. 44 rooms. Restaurant, bar, pool, tennis court, shop. AE, MC, V.*

THE STATE OF YUCATÁN A TO Z

Arriving and Departing

By Bus
The **main bus station** (⊠ Calle 69, No. 544, between Calles 68 and 70, ☎ 99/247868) in Mérida offers frequent first- and second-class service to Akumal, Cancún, Chichén Itzá, Playa del Carmen, Tulum, Uxmal, Valladolid, and Xel-Há. The **ADO bus terminal,** nearby at Calle 70, between Calles 69 and 71, can also be reached by phone (☎ 99/247868). Several lines, such as Expreso del Oriente and Expreso del Caribe, now offer deluxe service with air-conditioning, refreshments, and movies shown en route. **Autotransportes del Sureste** (☎ 99/281595) has the best coverage for out-of-the-way destinations, with daily service to the Guatemalan border, Palenque, and San Cristóbal de las Casas, and four buses daily to Uxmal.

By Car
Route 180, the main road along the Gulf coast from the Texas border to Cancún, runs into Mérida. Mexico City lies 1,550 kilometers (960 miles) to the west; Cancún, 320 kilometers (200 miles) due east. The *autopista,* an eight-lane toll highway between Cancún and Mérida, runs somewhat parallel to Route 180 and cuts driving time between Cancún and Mérida—formerly around 4½ hours—by about one hour.

By Plane
The Mérida airport is 7 kilometers (4 miles) west of the city's central square, about a 20-minute ride. The following airlines serve Mérida: **Aeromexico** (☎ 99/279000) flies direct from Miami with a stop (but no plane change) in Cancún; **Mexicana** (☎ 99/246633, 99/246754) has a connecting flight from Newark via Cancún, and a number of connecting flights from the United States via Mexico City; **Aerocaribe** (☎ 99/249500 or 99/286786), a subsidiary of Mexicana, has flights from Cancún, Chetumal, Cozumel, Oaxaca, Tuxtla Gutiérrez, and Villahermosa; **Aviateca** (☎ 99/46196 or 99/461312), a Guatemalan car-

rier, flies from Houston and Guatemala City; and **Taesa** (☎ 99/286950) flies from Mexico City.

A private taxi costs about $6; collective service (usually a Volkswagen minibus), about $3. For both, pay the taxi-ticket vendor at the airport, not the driver. The inexpensive but irregular No. 79 bus goes from the airport to downtown.

By Train
See Rail Travel *in* Smart Travel Tips A to Z.

Getting Around

By Bus
Mérida's municipal buses run daily from 5 AM to midnight, but service is somewhat confusing until you master the system. In the downtown area, buses go east on Calle 59 and west on Calle 61, north on Calle 60 and south on Calle 62. You can catch a bus heading north to Progreso on Calle 56. Unfortunately, there is no bus service from the hotels around the plaza to the long-distance bus station.

By Car
Driving in Mérida can be frustrating because of the one-way streets (many of which end up being one-lane because of the parked cars) and because traffic is dense. But having your own wheels is the best way to take excursions from the city. Prices are sometimes lower if you arrange your rental in advance through one of the large international companies.

By Carriage
Horse-drawn *calesas* (carriages) that drive along the streets of Mérida can be hailed along Calle 60. A ride to the Paseo de Montejo and back will cost about $6.

By Taxi
Taxis don't cruise the streets for passengers; instead, they are available at 12 taxi stands around the city, or from the main taxi office (☎ 99/285324); taxis wait in front of the larger hotels, but they're often more expensive. Individual cabs cost $2 and $3; collective service, less than $1.

Contacts and Resources

Car Rentals
There are almost 20 car-rental agencies in town, including **Avis** (✉ Paseo de Montejo, No. 500, ☎ 99/283152 or 99/282828; airport, 99/842134 or 99/842135), **Budget** (✉ Paseo Montejo, No. 497, ☎ 99/245569 or 99/233637; airport, 99/462255 or 99/461380), **Dollar** (✉ Hotel Mérida Misión, ☎ 99/286759 or 99/231855; airport, 99/461323), **Executive** (✉ Calle 60, No. 446, ☎ 99/233732 or 99/280756; airport, 99/461387), and **Hertz** (✉ Calle 55, No. 479, ☎ 99/242834 or 99/248766; airport, 99/249187).

Consulates
United States (✉ Paseo de Montejo 453, ☎ 99/255011, 99/258677, or 99/255409). **United Kingdom** (✉ Calle 58, No. 450, at Calle 53, ☎ 99/286152).

Emergencies
In Mérida: **Police** (☎ 99/253634); **Red Cross** (Calle 68, No. 583, at Calle 65, ☎ 99/249813); **Fire** (☎ 99/249242); **general emergency** (☎ 06).

HOSPITAL
Hospital O'Horan (✉ Av. Internacional and Av. Itzaes, ☎ 99/244111, 99/242911, or 99/244800).

Guided Tours

There are more than 50 tour operators in Mérida, and they generally offer the same destinations. What differs is how you go—in a private car, a van, or a bus—and whether the vehicle is air-conditioned. A two-to three-hour city tour will cost between $7 and $20; or you can pick up an open-air sightseeing bus at Parque Santa Lucía. A day trip to Chichén Itzá, with guide, entrance fee, and lunch, runs approximately $40. For about the same price you can see the ruins of Uxmal and Kabah in the Puuc region, and for a few more dollars you can add on the neighboring sites of Sayil, Labná, and the Loltún Caves. Afternoon departures to Uxmal allow you to take in the sound-and-light show at the ruins and return by 11 PM, for $40–$50 (including dinner). There is also the option of a tour of Chichén Itzá followed by a drop-off in Cancún for about $50. Most tour operators take credit cards.

SPECIAL-INTEREST TOURS
Several of the tour operators in Mérida run overnight excursions to archaeological sites farther afield, notably Cobá, Tulum, Edzná, and Palenque. Tours of the Ruta Maya including sites in Mexico, Guatemala, and Belize are offered by **VN Travel** (✉ Calle 58, No. 488, ☎ 99/239061 or 99/245996) and **Mayaland Tours** (✉ Holiday Inn, Av. Colón, No. 502, ☎ 99/462331 or 800/235–4079, FAX 99/462335), which also offers self-guided tours with economical rental car rates. **Ecoturismo Yucatán** (✉ Calle 3, No. 235, at Col. Pensiones, ☎ 99/252187, FAX 99/259047) specializes in nature tours, including bird-watching, natural history, anthropology, and the Mundo Maya.

Travel Agencies and Tour Operators

Mérida's local agencies and operators include **American Express** (✉ Calle 56-A, No. 494, ☎ 99/284222, FAX 99/284373), **Buvisa** (✉ Paseo de Montejo, No. 475, ☎ 99/277933, FAX 99/277414), **Ceiba Tours** (✉ Calle 60, No. 495, ☎ 99/244477 or 99/244499, FAX 99/244588), **Intermar Caribe** (✉ Prolongación Paseo de Montejo 74 at Calle 30, ☎ 99/445249 or 99/445222, FAX 99/445259), **Mayaland Tours** (✉ Av. Colón, No. 502, ☎ 99/462331 or 800/235–4079, FAX 99/462335; Casa del Balam hotel, Calle 60, No. 488, ☎ 99/244919), **Turismo Aviomar** (✉ Calle 58A, 500-C, ☎ 99/200444 or 99/200443, FAX 99/246887), **Viajes Novedosos** (✉ Calle 58, No. 488, ☎ 99/245996, FAX 99/239061), and **Yucatán Trails** (✉ Calle 62, No. 482, ☎ 99/241928 or 99/282582, FAX 99/244919 or 99/285913).

24-Hour Pharmacies

Farmacia Yza Aviación (✉ Calle 71 at Av. Aviación, ☎ 99/238116), **Farmacia Yza Tanlum** (✉ Glorieta Tanlum, ☎ 99/251646), and **Farmacia Canto** (✉ Calle 60, No. 514, at Calle 63, ☎ 99/248265).

Visitor Information

Mérida: Tourist Information Center (✉ Teatro Peón Contreras, Calle 59 between Calles 62 and 64, ☎ 99/249127), open daily 8–8. **Information kiosks:** airport (☎ 99/246764), open daily 8–8; next to the Palacio Municipal on Calle 62 (no phone), open weekdays 8–2.

INDEX

NOTES

What's hot, where it's hot!

Condé Nast Traveler CARIBBEAN RESORT AND CRUISE SHIP FINDER

"It's not often you can call on the opinions of 12,000 vacationers when you need a little travel advice. But if your destination is the Caribbean, you're in luck." —*Hartford Courant*

$14.50 ($19.95 Canada)

AFFORDABLE FLORIDA
AFFORDABLE CARIBBEAN

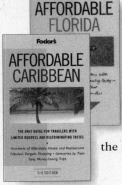

"Concentrates on life's basics...without skimping on literary luxuries."
—*New York Daily News*

"Extremely useful books, even if you forget their promise to help you find ways to save money while you travel."
—*Houston Post*

"Travelers with champagne tastes and beer budgets will welcome this series from Fodor's." —*Hartford Courant*

"Budget travelers tired of roughing it get all the maps and sightseeing ideas of Fodor's established Gold Guides with a bonus— shortcuts to savings." —*USA Today*

Priced from $16.00 ($21.95 Canada)

CARIBBEAN PORTS OF CALL

Here is a compact, fact-filled guide designed especially for Caribbean cruisers looking for all their ports have to offer, from dining and shopping to sightseeing.

$9.00 ($12.50 Canada)

CRUISES AND PORTS OF CALL

"A gold mine of information." —*New York Post*

"The most detailed of any of the standard cruise guidebooks...superb." —*Cruise Travel*

$18.50 ($25.50 Canada)

At bookstores, or call **1-800-533-6478**

Fodor's
The name that means smart travel.™

Escape to ancient cities and

journey to *exotic islands with*

CNN Travel Guide, a wealth of valuable advice. Host

Valerie Voss will take you to

all of your favorite destinations,

including those off the beaten

path. Tune-in to your passport to the world.

CNN TRAVEL GUIDE
SATURDAY 12:30 PMET   SUNDAY 4:30 PMET

CNN

WHEREVER YOU TRAVEL, *H*ELP IS NEVER FAR AWAY.

From planning your trip to providing travel assistance along the way, American Express® Travel Service Offices are always there to help.

Mexico

American Express Travel Service
Av. Tulum 208 Esq Agua
Supermanzana, Cancun
98/84-19-99

American Express Travel Service
Centro Comercial – La Gran Plaza
Costera Miguel Aleman 1628, Acapulco
74/69-11-33

American Express Travel Service
Plaza Los Arcos Local 1A
Ave. Vallarta 2440, Guadalajara
3/630-0200

American Express Travel Service
Hotel Krystal
Boulevard Ixtapa S/N, Ixtapa
753/3-08-53

American Express Travel Service
Hotel Camino Real
Mariano Escobedo 700, Mexico City
5/203-2355

American Express Travel Service
Lobby Hotel Camino Real
Playa Las Estacas, S/N, Puerto Vallarta
322/1-50-00

Viajes Carrousel, S.A. De C.V. (R)
S. Taboada, Y Jose C. Orozco
Edif Husa Zona Del Rio, Tijuana
66/84-05-56

Viajes Mazzocco, S.A. (R)
Enlace 313 Col. Sierra
De Alica, Zacatecas
492/2-08-59

Travel

http://www.americanexpress.com/travel

American Express Travel Service Offices are found in central locations throughout Mexico.

Listings are valid as of May 1996. (R) = Representative Office. Not all services available at all locations. © 1996 American Express Travel Related Services Company, Inc.